D1105820

Handbook of Special Education Technology Research and Practice

Handbook of Special Education Technology Research and Practice

Dave Edyburn
Kyle Higgins
Randall Boone
EDITORS

KNOWLEDGE
by Design, Inc.

Knowledge by Design, Inc.
Whitefish Bay, Wisconsin

Knowledge by Design, Inc.
5907 N. Kent Avenue
Whitefish Bay, WI 53217
www.knowledge-by-design.com

Handbook of Special Education Technology Research and Practice
Copyright © 2005 by Knowledge by Design, Inc.

Printed in the United States of America.
First edition.

Publisher's Cataloging-in-Publication Data
Handbook of Special Education Technology Research and Practice / edited by Dave Edyburn, Kyle Higgins, and Randall Boone.
     p. cm.
Includes bibliographic references and index.
ISBN 0-9708429-6-1 (hard)
   1. Students with disabilities – Handbooks, manuals, etc.   2. Educational technology – Handbooks, manuals, etc. I. Edyburn, Dave, 1957-   II. Higgins, Kyle. III. Boone, Randall.
LC4024 .H36 2005
371.9

Names such as companies, trade names, font names, service names, and product names appearing in this book may be registered or unregistered trademarks, service marks, whether or not identified as such. All such names and all registered and unregistered trademarks, service marks, and logos appearing in this book are used for identification purposes only and are the property of their respective owners. Acknowledgment is made to the following sources for permission to reprint selections from copyrighted materials: **p. 63**, Figure 1, Reprinted by permission of Wisconsin Assistive Technology Initiative. **pp. 90-92**, Tables 1 & 2, Copyright by H.P. Parette, reprinted with permission. **pp. 93, 95-96**, Figures 2-4, Copyright by A. VanBiervliet, reprinted with permission. **pp. 127-128**, quote, Reprinted by the permission of the publisher from *Oversold and Underused: Computers in the Classroom* by Larry Cuban, pp. 37-39, Harvard University Press, Copyright 2001 by the President and Fellows of Harvard College. **p. 284**, Figure 2, Reprinted with permission of the World Health Organization, all rights reserved. **pp. 347-349**, Figures 3-4, Copyright The Curators of the University of Missouri, a public corporation, all rights reserved. **p. 587**, Table 2, Copyright by Scott Marfilius and Kelly Fonner, reprinted with permission. **p. 588**, Table 3, Copyright 1999 by The Council for Exceptional Children, reprinted with permission. **p. 653**, Figure 2, Virtual High School Website, reprinted with permission. **p. 655**, Figure 3, Screen shot from Froguts Website, reprinted with permission. **p. 695**, Tables 4, Copyright 2000 by The Council for Exceptional Children, adapted with permission. **p. 703**, Tables 9, Copyright 1998 by The Council for Exceptional Children, adapted with permission. **p. 706**, Table 11, Repurposed with permission from *Learning and Leading with Technology*, 26(1), copyright 1998, International Society for Technology in Education. **pp. 732-742**, Appendix B, Copyright by Elizabeth A. Lahm, reprinted with permission. **p. 852**, Figure 1, Courtesy of Exact Dynamics, the Netherlands. **p. 857**, Figure 2, Reproduced with permission of Cynthia Breazeal. **p. 859**, Figure 3, Courtesy of David Hanson.

CONTENTS

Section 7 Professional Development

Section 8 Trends and Issues

Foreword

John Langone

Many of us who have been working for over 30 years with individuals who have disabilities remember the days when technology in the classroom meant being excited about using an IBM Selectric typewriter. I remember when one of my colleagues got the idea of trying to design a device to fit over the typewriter so that one of our students with physical disabilities, in spite of her spastic movements, could type messages. Her plan was to have the students in the metal shop class construct a device we now know as a key guard. I also remember the first students we taught to communicate using photographs/drawings, and how excited we were when they could express single messages.

At that time we did not realize that we were working with "assistive technology," or what assistive technology meant as an educational concept. Yet, all over the world as more and more individuals with disabilities were entering the mainstream of society and leaving the restricted environments where they had been near forgotten, parents and professionals began looking for ways to help them become more independent.

A good deal has changed since those days. We now have access to technology solutions that are proven to make a difference in the lives of people with disabilities. Many of these technologies are "exotic," that is, they wow us when we see them in action. Robotic arms for individuals with physical challenges and powerful electronic communication boards for those who face communication barriers are more commonplace in present times. Yet, the technologies that may be having the greatest impact are the ones that potentially will improve the lives of individuals with high-incidence disabilities. For example, screen reader software that helps struggling readers keep up with their work in content-area subjects by reading difficult material to them and word prediction software that can provide learners who have significant spelling problems with choices of words to help them express their thoughts represent a class of technology that is often overlooked by the general public.

Then there are the often unsung heroes of assistive technology. The "low-tech" devices, such as adaptive spoons and plate guards that improve independent eating and single switches that allow for a measure of environmental control, have made tremendous differences in the lives of many people. So, as we move closer to being halfway through the first decade of the 21st century, why is there still cause for pessimism regarding the true impact of assistive technology on the lives of persons with disabilities?

Many of us who spend a good deal time in schools and working with service agencies that support adults with disabilities have stories about the lack of use or misuse of assistive technology. Situations still occur where students with severe disabilities have no consistent access to augmentative/alternative communication (AAC) devices or those who have access are taught to use their devices as part of age-inappropriate activities. Schools enact policies that minimize the access that students with disabilities have to computer labs and teachers ignore the advances in technology that can help students with mild disabilities have access to the general education curriculum. I once read a theory that it takes 25 years for an instructional strategy or technique that has been researched and proven to work to become commonplace in education practice. This possibility disturbs me, as it does many other professionals and parents, because people with disabilities cannot wait for us to provide them access to the technology that will help them live better lives.

In part, this is the reason I agreed to write the foreword to this book. I am always looking for ways to minimize the "lag time" that makes it take so long in getting effective tools and strategies into the hands of those that can use them the most. One effective way that I have found is for professionals and parents to have access to the latest information about cutting edge advancements relative to the important tools and strategies that can help people with disabilities improve their access to all natural environments. This book, *Handbook of Special Education Technology Research and Practice* by Edyburn, Higgins, and Boone, has the potential to reduce the lag time between compiling what is considered cutting-edge work in the area of assistive technology and getting this information into the hands for those for who it will do the most good.

This book contains an impressive collection of works that include information by some of the top professionals in the field. It is unique for a variety of reasons, but most prominently because is addresses important topics not otherwise found in one impressively indexed document. For example, one section (five chapters) addresses technology access by diverse groups of individuals who have disabilities. The knowledge base presented in these chapters is critical for both professionals and parents if we are to do a better job in ensuring that all barriers to effective technology use are eliminated for all persons with disabilities, including those from typically underrepresented groups. Similarly, whole sections are devoted to disability-specific assistive technology, research and practice in special education technology and

applications of high-quality instructional design to technology interventions.

I have always believed that before we can move ahead in any professional endeavor, we must know from where came. The first chapter of this book written by Ed Blackhurst establishes this premise nicely, especially because he is one of the eminent scholars in the field and has been the driving force behind assistive technology becoming a viable discipline. His presentation of important historical events, as well as the information in subsequent chapters that targets legal and legislative mandates that have improved the access to technology by persons with disabilities, is important, particularly in these perilous financial times when government bodies are showing a tendency to cut back services. Understanding the history of the discipline and the legal mandates surrounding it will help us forge new strategies to protect the rights of all individuals with disabilities.

The high-quality chapters in this book may be used by scholars and instructors in many different ways. For example, the chapters that provide information on technology solutions for individuals with a variety of disabilities are extremely valuable for those of us who teach professionals who go on to be classroom teachers, speech pathologists, assistive technologists and administrators. And for researchers, this volume provides a wealth of up-to-date information regarding research-related projects both in the United States and around the world. There is considerably more information presented in this book, more than one can do justice to in a small space.

I urge all who are looking for a definitive resource on assistive technology applications and issues to adopt this book. Drs. Edyburn, Higgins and Boone have provided all of us an academic gem, and I for one, am thankful. This book will fulfill my professional needs for some time, and I hope these scholars are already planning the second edition.

John Langone, Ph.D.
Athens, Georgia
March 2004

Preface

Dave L. Edyburn, Kyle Higgins, and Randall Boono

Throughout history, the innovative application of technology for persons with disabilities has focused on access to opportunity, independence, and empowerment. This sentiment has been captured in a quote attributed to Judy Heumann, Assistant Secretary, U.S. Department of Education, Office of Special Education Programs: "For most of us, technology makes things easier. For a person with a disability, it makes things possible."

One of the first public policy documents to draw attention to the potential of technology was *Technology and Handicapped People* (U.S. Congress, Office of Technology Assessment, 1982). This report introduced readers to specialized technology tools, how they served a specific individual, and the impact the devices had on the person's life. These real-life stories provided powerful illustrations of the potential of technology for individuals with disabilities. As a result of these early success stories, and others that would be collected and shared in subsequent years, the argument was advanced that public investment in research and development in the area of technology and disability could reap significant dividends for individuals, in the form of improved communication skills, expanded mobility and independence, and for society, in the number of individuals gainfully employed and contributing to the tax base.

The argument that the benefits of technology for individuals with disabilities was so persuasive that federal laws would subsequently be enacted to provide mechanisms for capturing the potential of technology on an ever-increasing scale. The significance of the 1982 OTA report is that the argument was made for the unrealized potential of technology for individuals with disabilities. That is, from the benefits demonstrated in single cases we extrapolated the benefits for entire disability populations. We've been trying to scale up to capture the potential ever since. As a reader of the Handbook, perhaps you have witnessed the power and potential of special education technology first-hand. Or, perhaps you are looking for information on how to capture the potential technology holds for individuals with disabilities.

Purpose

As an early observer of the special education technology knowledge base, Hannaford (1993) seems to offer a cautionary tale: "Much of what is presented as being known about the use of computers with exceptional persons is actually what is believed, felt, or hoped. While there is an increasing amount of research and evaluation support associated with various uses of the technology, there is still relatively little empirical support for many statements found in the popular literature" (p. 12). However, the current educational climate, with its emphasis on accountability and the identification of specific instructional interventions which demonstrate gains in student achievement, clearly suggests the times are different. As a result, we perceive an urgent need for a compendium such as the one found in this Handbook.

The genesis of the project is easy to describe. As journal editors, we perceived the need for an authoritative work compiling the knowledge base of the discipline of special education technology. Lest anyone question our motivation, let us be perfectly clear: Selfishly, we wanted this book on our desktop. We longed for a comprehensive single-volume book that would facilitate our work as scholars. In addition, we wanted a means to share the immense knowledge base with the teachers, students, technology specialists, therapists, administrators, researchers, policy makers, and colleagues we work with. We felt that the efforts involved in compiling and synthesizing the literature would demonstrate the maturation of the discipline and illustrate the significance of the emerging knowledge base. A comprehensive and authoritative work would foster a shared understanding among the interdisciplinary communities that focus on technology applications in special education. And, we knew that the Handbook could enhance the quality of current research and stimulate much needed new research.

The Handbook you hold in your hands represents the collective work of many individuals over a three-year period. Over 90 renowned experts contributed chapters to the Handbook. We are deeply indebted to our colleagues and friends who responded enthusiastically to our invitations and shared our vision of what we could individually and collectively achieve.

Design Features

In recognition of the many stakeholders that could be consumers of this work, several unique design considerations were involved in the development of the Handbook. These include:

- Hardcover binding to sustain frequent use as a ready-reference resource.
- Each contribution has been prepared by noted authorities on the topic. The analysis and synthesis of the research and practice literature represents the most concise but comprehensive treatment of each topic currently available for non-specialists.

- In addition to summarizing the research and practice knowledge base on their topic, each author was asked to address the question, What do we need to know? We anticipate this information will be cited in grant writing and used to facilitate individual and collaborative research agendas in order to address gaps in the knowledge base.

How Is the HSETRP Organized?

The Handbook is comprised of 41 chapters organized into eight sections.

Section 1 focuses on the historical, policy, and legal foundations of the field of special education technology. In as much as our discipline has a shared knowledge base, we believe it focuses on the tenets presented in this section which describe the historical, legislative, policy, and legal foundations. We suspect the four chapters in this section will be essential reading for new professionals seeking to understand the context of current practice.

Section 2 reviews an array of issues involved in the accessibility of technology by diverse populations. Five chapters in this section highlight the commitment of the profession to understand and remove barriers. Readers will be introduced to how geography, race, culture, language, and design impact the creation of equitable technology systems for individuals with disabilities.

Section 3 provides four chapters on various issues associated with the use of assistive technology in schools. This section addresses topics that have been associated with the core knowledge of our discipline: assistive technology service delivery systems, the role of teams in assessing the need for assistive technology and delivering services, assistive technology in the inclusive classroom, assistive technology and high incidence disabilities, and efforts devoted to measuring quality and outcomes of assistive technology.

Section 4 offers a review of disability-specific applications of technology. Collectively, these nine chapters offer a comprehensive portrait of what is known about the research and practice of special education technology in preschool and K-college children and youth. The chapters in this section offer readers a powerful lens for viewing technology applications in the context of a specific disability. Each chapter has multiple applications for preservice and inservice personnel preparation programs.

Section 5 examines the knowledge base associated with the instructional design considerations applied in various technology applications. The four chapters in this section highlight what is known about the design and development of products and materials for children and youth with disabilities. Clearly, much more work is needed in this area to understand the similarities with instructional design for the general population and when new insight and development will be needed to respond to learning problems that are resilient to intervention.

Section 6 explores the application of technology in specific instructional contexts. Eight chapters provide in-depth analysis about technology initiatives that have been designed to enhanced the educational performance of students with disabilities. The wealth of information in this section speaks to the many contributions the special education technology base has to the general problem of low academic performance.

Section 7 reviews the knowledge base associated with professional development. Considering the extensive commitment to training in the field of special education technology, it is important to examine what is known about the methods and approaches used to train teachers, administrators, and related service personnel to use technology.

Section 8 offers insight on emerging trends and issues and their implications for the discipline of special education technology. Among the topics addressed are technology accommodations in testing, data mining, and robotic devices. Clearly, this section offers a provocative glimpse into the future.

What Have We Learned?

The opportunity to read each chapter has provided us with a unique chance to understand what the discipline knows and needs to know. In response to this vantage point, we offer several observations about what we have learned from reading the Handbook.

First, the discipline of special education technology has matured considerably in recent years. The Handbook compiles and synthesizes the explosion of diverse efforts that have been devoted to developing new products, conducting research about the efficacy of products and interventions, and improving practice. Although we like to consider ourselves well informed, we are humbled by the size, depth, and diversity of the special education technology knowledge base. We believe the profession will benefit greatly from this timely and accessible compilation of the literature. However, we challenge the discipline to go beyond a cursory review of the work presented here and engage in the necessary effort to analyze, synthesize, and integrate the extensive information base into knowledge that informs and transforms professional practice.

Second, a close reading of the Handbook will reveal that the field has been slow to develop models and frameworks which provide conceptual foundations for the work being conducted. As a result, research and development is fragmented with narrow, rather than broad, implications. We challenge the discipline to think deeply about the theoretical foundations of our work.

Third, while the research base for our profession is emerging, there is an urgent need for additional research using an array of robust methodologies. Much remains to be learned about the design, development, and implementation of effective products and services in the field of special education technology. We challenge the discipline to commit to increasing the quality and quantity of special education technology research.

Finally, the knowledge base documented in the Handbook provides ample evidence about the value and benefits of technology for individuals with disabilities. However, it is less clear that all students who could benefit from special education technology have access to appropriate devices and services. As a result, it appears that there is a significant population of individuals who are underserved or unserved and have yet to reap the benefits that technology can offer. We challenge the discipline to address the scaling-up problem by committing to expand and improve personnel preparation programs and by developing new tools for implementing the mandate to consider assistive technology.

Who will find the HSETRP useful?

We believe the Handbook will be useful for anyone interested in special education technology. In particular, we believe the Handbook will be essential reading for special education teachers, administrators, teacher educators, graduate students, technology specialists, researchers, and policy makers.

Forthcoming HSETRP Supplements

We are pleased to announce the subsequent release of the HSETRP Digital Companion. This CDROM product will provide full text access and hypermedia links to the complete content of the Handbook. The purpose of this product is to demonstrate state-of-the-art accessibility features within a digital environment that provides users with unparallel access to media, concepts, source documents, etc. that enhance understanding and application of the information presented in the Handbook. Building on our previous work on digital scholarship (Boone & Higgins, 1998; Boone, Higgins, & Edyburn, 2003; Edyburn, 1999), we believe this product will demonstrate next-generation tools for scholars and novices interested in interactive exploration of the knowledge base and the boundaries of what is known and yet to be discovered.

The Handbook represents the first product of a family of products designed to make the special education technology knowledge base accessible. In the months following publication of the Handbook, watch for announcements (www.knowledge-by-design.com) about the release of additional HSETRP supplemental products.

Feedback

Despite our best intentions, we recognize that there will be a variety of ways in which this work can be improved. Therefore, readers are invited to share their reactions, questions, and feedback with the Editors (editor@knowledge-by-design.com)

D.E., K.H., R.B.
March 2004

References

Boone, R., & Higgins, K. (1998). Digital publishing. *Teaching Exceptional Children, 30*(5), 4-5.

Boone, R., Higgins, K., & Edyburn, D.L. (2003). Digital LDQ. *Learning Disabilities Quarterly, 26*(1), 2-4.

Edyburn, D.L. (1999). *The electronic scholar: Enhancing research productivity with technology.* Upper Saddle River, NJ: Merrill/ Prentice-Hall.

Hannaford, A.E. (1993). Computers and exceptional individuals. In J.D. Lindsey (Ed)., *Computers and exceptional individuals* (pp. 3-26). Austin, TX: Pro-Ed.

Office of Technology Assessment. (1982). *Technology and handicapped people.* Washington, D.C.: U.S. Government Printing Office.

Contributors

Bob Algozzine, Ph.D., Professor, Department of Educational Leadership, University of North Carolina at Charlotte, Charlotte, North Carolina. Dr. Algozzine's research and teaching interests focus on effective instruction for all students and behavior instruction in the total school. He is the Co-Director of the Behavior and Reading Improvement Center at the University of North Carolina at Charlotte, former Co-Editor of *Exceptional Children*, and current Co-Editor of *Teacher Education and Special Education* and *Career Development for Exceptional Individuals*.

James M. Allan, Ph.D., Webmaster, Texas School for the Blind and Visually Impaired, Austin, Texas. Dr. Allan's professional endeavors focus on information access and use by people with disabilities, including electronic textbooks, courseware, and Web sites. He is the chair of Research & Development Committee of the Textbooks and Instructional Materials Solutions Forum and serves on the World Wide Web Consortium's User Agent Accessibility Working Group.

David H. Allsopp, Ph.D., Associate Professor, Department of Special Education, University of South Florida, Tampa, FL. Dr. Allsopp's research and teaching interests focus on instructional methods for students with learning and behavioral problems and how technology can be used to enhance preservice teacher preparation and inservice teacher professional development. He is a Consulting Editor for *Remedial and Special Education*.

Cindy L. Anderson, Ph.D., Assistant Professor, Master of Arts in Teacher Leadership, Roosevelt University, Chicago, Illinois. Dr. Anderson's research interests are technology and learning standards for students with disabilities and the integration of technology into

teacher education. She is Co-Editor of the Technology and Media (TAM) Division newsletter, Past President of the Special Education Technology Special Interest Group (SETSTIG) of the International Society of Technology in Education, and Vice President of the Assistive Technology Committee for the Society for Information Technology in Teacher Education (SITE).

Kevin M. Anderson, Ed.D., Executive Director, Instructional Services, Kenosha Unified School District No. 1, Kenosha, Wisconsin. Dr. Anderson's research and writing interests focus on the integration of technology into standards-based classroom instruction. He is Co-Editor of the Technology and Media (TAM) Division newsletter, past Board member of TAM, and a past Area Coordinator for Phi Delta Kappa.

Tamarah M. Ashton, Ph.D., Associate Professor, Department of Special Education, California State University, Northridge, Northridge, California. Dr. Ashton's primary teaching and research interests involve teacher education, learning disabilities, assessment, and assistive technology. She serves on the Executive Board of the Council for Educational Diagnostic Services (CEDS) of the Council for Exceptional Children as Research Chair and as Associate Editor for Assistive Technology for the *Journal of Special Education Technology*.

M. Nell Bailey, M.A., Project Director, RESNA Technical Assistance Project. Ms. Bailey's areas of interest include the provision of technical assistance, program implementation and evaluation. She is Associate Editor for Education and Policy for the journal *Assistive Technology*, and she is Topic Coordinator for the policy track at the RESNA Annual Conference. In addition, she serves on several national advisory boards regarding technology for people with disabilities.

Laura J. Ball, Ph.D., CCC-SLP, Assistant Professor, Speech-Language Pathologist; Augumentative Communication Specialist, Munroe-Meyer Institute; University of Nebraska Medical Center, Omaha, Nebraska. Dr. Ball has clinical and research interests in augmentative and alternative communication and motor speech disorders impacting children and adults.

Richard Banks, Chief Technology Officer (CTO), EASI: Equal Access to Software and Information, Menomonie, Wisconsin. Mr. Banks became proficient on using assistive technology because of his own limited eyesight. He works tirelessly to disseminate knowhow on accessible information technology to schools and universities through EASI's onsite and on-line workshops. He spent six months in Thailand establishing accessible technology for Thai university students with disabilities.

Brenda Bannan-Ritland, Ph.D., Associate Professor, Instructional Technology, George Mason University, Fairfax, Virginia. Dr. Bannan-Ritland's research interests include utilizing Web-based technologies for instruction and training, particularly focusing on constructivist learning environments and emerging design-based research processes.

Michael M. Behrmann, Ed.D., Helen A. Kellar Professor of Special Education, Director of the Helen A. Kellar Institute for Human disAbilities, Graduate School of Education, George Mason University, Fairfax, Virginia. In his 24 years at George Mason, Dr. Behrmann has obtained over $15 million in grants, contracts, and gifts for training, technical assistance, and research. His research in assistive technology enables individuals with disabilities to function in the world of school, work, home and community, includes applications such as Web access; computer-based instructional materials, expert systems, virtual reality; and innovations in personnel development, including online learning and distance education. He was a founding member of the Technology and Media (TAM) Division of the Council for Exceptional Children.

David R. Beukelman, Ph.D., CCC-SLP, Barkley Professor of Communication Disorders, University of Nebraska, Lincoln, Nebraska. He is the Director of Research and Education, Communication Disorders Division, Munroe-Meyer Institute; University of Nebraska Medical Center, Omaha, Nebraska. Dr. Beukelman has authored the primary textbook in augmentative and alternative communication, in addition to several other texts related to augmentative and alternative communication and motor speech disorders. He has also authored several computer software programs, including *Cue-Write*, a program to support writers with spelling disabilities.

Denise V. Bilyeu, M.S., CCC-SLP, Speech-Language Pathologist; Agumentative Communication Specialist, Munroe-Meyer Institute; University of Nebraska Medical Center, Omaha, Nebraska. Mrs. Bilyeu has 11 years of experience in augmentative and alternative communication. She has worked as an alternative and augmentative communication consultant for area school districts, with specializations in the areas of literacy and technology in the classroom.

A. Edward Blackhurst, Ph. D., Professor Emeritus, Department of Special Education and Rehabilitation Counseling, University of Kentucky, Lexington, Kentucky. Dr. Blackhurst has conducted research on numerous applications of technology in special education, including use of communication satellites, computer-assisted instruction, expert systems, telecommunications, technology productivity tools, hypermedia, assistive technology, Web-based instruction, high-tech futures, conceptual models, competency-based instruction, history, and pre- and inservice technology training. He is Past-President of the Association for Special Education Technology and the Teacher Education Division (TED) of the Council for Exceptional Children (CEC). He was the recipient of TED's Excellence in Teacher Education Award and the Career Distinguished Leadership Award from the Technology and Media (TAM) Division of CEC.

Cathy Bodine, Ph.D., CCC-SLP, Assistant Professor, Section Head, Department of Rehabilitation Medicine and Director of Assistive Technology Partners Department of Physical Medicine and Rehabilitation, University of Colorado Health Sciences Center, Denver, Colorado. Dr. Bodine is a Senior Consultant to the Colorado Department of Education's Special Education Services Unit where she is responsible for 67 teams of assistive technology specialists working within Colorado's schools. She serves on the Board of Directors for RESNA, and is a contributing editor to *Exceptional Parent* and the *Journal of Assistive Technology Outcomes and Benefits*.

Randall Boone, Ph.D., Professor, Department of Curriculum and Instruction, University of Nevada Las Vegas, Las Vegas, Nevada. Dr. Boone's research and teaching interests focus on instructional design and technology accessibility issues for persons with disabilities. He is co-editor of the *Journal of Special Education Technology*.

E. Amanda Boutot, Ph.D., Assistant Professor, Department of Special Education, University of Nevada, Las Vegas. Dr. Boutot coordinates the program in Mental Retardation/Severe Disabilities and co-coordinates the concentration in Autism at the graduate level. Her research interests include socialization and inclusion for children with autism. She is active in several CEC divisions and has been a member of the Autism Society of America for 12 years.

Gayl Bowser, M.Ed., Coordinator, Oregon Technology Access Program; Assistive Technology Specialist, Oregon Department of Education, Roseburg, Oregon. Ms. Bowser is the Coordinator of the Oregon Technology Access Program, which is operated by the Oregon Department of Education. She has been recognized by many awards for her work, including: Oregon Council for Exceptional Children's Teacher of the Year, Technology and Media (TAM) Division's Service Award, and was recognized as a Distinguished Educator by the Milken Family Foundation.

Monica R. Brown, Ph.D., Assistant Professor, Department of Special Education and Communication Disorders, New Mexico State University, Las Cruces, New Mexico. Dr. Brown's research and teaching interests focus on preparing teachers to use technology with a social justice orientation that ensures equitable access and use for all students.

Pam Campbell, Ph.D., Associate Professor, Department of Special Education, University of Nevada, Las Vegas, Las Vegas, Nevada. Dr. Campbell's research interests focus on teacher preparation, school renewal, collaborative practice, and using technology to improve instruction for all students. She is a member of the International Council for Learning Disabilities (CLD), as well as the Teacher Education (TED) and Technology and Media (TAM) Divisions of the Council for Exceptional Children.

Diana Foster Carl, M.A., the Director of Assistive Technology Services at Region IV Education Service Center, Houston, Texas. Ms. Carl's interests focus on building the capacity of public school personnel to provide quality services in the area of assistive technology, so that when students with disabilities need assistive technology to access the curriculum, they receive appropriate devices and services. She is the lead facilitator of the Texas Assistive Technology Network, a collaborative project between the twenty educational service centers in Texas and the Texas Education Agency, and is a founding member of the Quality Indicators for Assistive Technology (QIAT) Consortium.

Brian Castellani, Ph.D., is an Assistant Professor of sociology at Kent State University, in Kent, Ohio. He teaches undergraduate courses in sociology. His research interests focus on the sociology of complexity and medical sociology.

John Castellani, Ph.D., is an Associate Professor the Division of Education, Technology for Educators Program, Johns Hopkins University, Baltimore, Maryland. He is also the program director for the Maryland State Department of Education partnership grant for assistive technology at the Center for technology in Education. Currently he serves as President of the Technology and Media (TAM) Division of the Council for Exceptional Children.

Norman Coombs, Ph.D., EASI: Equal Access to Software and Information, Laguna Hills, California. Dr. Coombs, though blind, helped pioneer Rochester Institute of Technology's distance learning program, which led to his earning several awards, including the New York State CASE Teacher of the Year Award. As Chief Executive Officer (CEO) of EASI, he works to assist schools and universities make their information and computer systems fully accessible to students and teachers with disabilities.

Robert M. Corso, Ph.D., Visiting Professor, Department of Special Education, University of Illinois at Urbana-Champaign. Dr. Corso currently serves as the Project Coordinator for the Center on the Social and Emotional Foundations for Early Learning. His research interests include collaborative services between early intervention, Early Head Start, and child care personnel, and culturally competent early childhood services. He currently heads up the evaluation activities of the Hilton/Early Head Start Training Program.

Lindy Crawford, Ph.D., Assistant Professor of Special Education at the University of Colorado at Colorado Springs. Dr. Crawford teaches courses in applied behavior analysis, classroom assessment, and educational research and statistics. Her research interests include: student performance on large-scale tests of writing, effective instructional practices for English language learners, and the reliability and validity of alternate assessments.

Bridget Dalton, Ed.D., Chief Education Officer and Senior Research Scientist at CAST, a not-for-profit educational research and development organization. She obtained her doctorate in reading, language and learning disabilities from Harvard Graduate School of Education, where she served as a lecturer in education. Prior to joining CAST, Bridget chaired the language and literacy graduate program at the University of Guam and directed the College of Education Literacy Center. Bridget has served as co-editor of *Reading Online*, IRA's peer-reviewed electronic journal. Her research focuses on literacy, technology, and struggling readers.

Daniel K. Davies, M.A., Founder and President, AbleLink Technologies, Colorado Springs, Colorado. Mr. Davie's research and technology development efforts focus on technology use by people with mental retardation. Among other activities, he is President-Elect of the Technology SIG for the American Association on Mental Retardation.

Dave L. Edyburn, Ph.D., Associate Professor, Department of Exceptional Education, University of Wisconsin-Milwaukee, Milwaukee, Wisconsin. Dr. Edyburn's research and teaching interests focus on the use of technology to enhance teaching, learning, and performance. He is Co-Principal Investigator of a federally funded project designed to measure the outcomes of assistive technology. He is a Past President of the Technology and Media (TAM) Division of the Council for Exceptional Children and the Founding President of the Special Education Technology Special Interest Group (SETSTIG) of the International Society of Technology in Education. He is the editor of *Remedial and Special Education* and *Special Education Technology Practice* and serves of the editorial board of several professional journals.

Judith G. Fein, M.A., served as the federal project officer for programs that include assistive technology for children and adults with disabilities, personnel preparation, arts for children with disabilities as well as research for children with disabilities. She is primarily interested in promoting the use of assistive technology to enhance the independence of people with disabilities.

Gail Fitzgerald, Ph.D., Associate Professor, School of Information Science and Learning Technologies, University of Missouri-Columbia. Dr. Fitzgerald's research and development interests focus on electronic performance support systems for students with emotional/behavioral disabilities and interactive, case-based, multimedia instruction in teacher preparation. She was awarded the 1995 TAM Service Award by the Technology and Media (TAM) Division of the Council for Exceptional Children.

Douglas Fuchs, Ph.D., Nicholas Hobbs Professor of Special Education and Human Development, Vanderbilt University, Nashville, Tennessee. Dr. Fuch's research focuses on reading instruction to enhance achievement across the achievement distribution, in preschool through high school. He directs Vanderbilt University's Reading Clinic, is the past co-editor of *The Journal of Special Education* and currently serves on the editorial boards of 10 educational psychology, special education, and general education journals.

Lynn S. Fuchs, Ph.D., Nicholas Hobbs Professor of Special Education and Human Development, Vanderbilt University, Nashville, Tennessee. Dr. Fuch's research focuses on classroom assessment and instructional practices for students with reading and mathematics disabilities. She is the past co-editor of *The Journal of Special Education* and currently serves on the editorial boards of 10 educational psychology, special education, and general education journals.

Joseph Calvin Gagnon, Ph.D., Assistant Professor, Graduate School of Education, George Mason University, Fairfax, Virginia. Dr. Gagnon's research includes effective mathematics instruction and technology-based practices for students with emotional disabilities and learning disabilities. He also conducts research on curriculum, assessment, and accountability policies in day treatment programs, residential schools, and juvenile corrections.

James Emmett Gardner, Ph.D., Professor of Education in the Special Education Program, University of Oklahoma, Norman, Oklahoma. His research and writing interests include instructional applications of technology with at-risk students and students with mild disabilities. Some of his recent attention has been directed at examining strategies that special

and general educators can apply to integrate the World Wide Web into curriculum domains and instructional activities, and the role of technology to enhance thematic units. He is a Past President of the Technology and Media (TAM) Division of the Council for Exceptional Children and a member of the editorial board of the *Journal of Special Education Technology*.

Cindy L. George, Special Projects Coordinator, Kellar Institute for Human disAbilities, George Mason University, Fairfax, Virginia. Ms. George has been Principal Investigator on numerous federally funded grant projects focusing on the development of assistive technology products. Currently, she is an adjunct instructor and assistive technology certificate coordinator at George Mason as well as an outside consultant for various private organizations and assistive technology manufacturers.

Len Haines, Ph.D., Professor, Department of Educational Psychology and Special Education; Assistant Dean, Undergraduate Programs, College of Education, University of Saskatchewan, Saskatoon, Saskatchewan, Canada. Dr. Haines' central research interest has been technology support for collaborative planning and teamwork, including the design of computer software to support teams in instructional planning for students with special needs, transition planning, inclusion, interagency teams, and the collaborative process itself.

Carol L. Hamlett, M.S., Research Associate, Department of Special Education, Vanderbilt University, Nashville, Tennessee. Ms. Hamlett has been involved for the past 20 years in the development of software for use in instruction and assessment of elementary-aged students in the areas of reading, spelling, and math.

Ted S. Hasselbring, Ed.D., William T. Bryan Professor of Special Education Technology, University of Kentucky, Lexington, Kentucky. Over the past 20 years, Dr. Hasselbring has conducted research on the use of technology for enhancing learning in students with mild disabilities and those who are at-risk for school failure. He has authored more than 100 book chapters and articles on learning and technology and services on the editorial boards of six professional journals. Dr. Hasselbring is also the author of several computer programs, including Scholastic's *READ 180*.

Jane Hauser is a program analyst with the Division of Research to Practice in the Office of Special Education Programs in the U.S. Department of Education, Washington, DC. Her work currently focuses on technology for students with disabilities, research-to-practice issues, and strengthening the delivery of technical assistance to support improved learning environments for children with disabilities.

Kyle Higgins, Ph.D., Professor, Department of Special Education, University of Nevada, Las Vegas, Las Vegas, Nevada. Dr. Higgins's research and teaching interests focus on the use of technology as an instructional tool for students with disabilities and the design and development of educational software to meet the specific educational needs of students with disabilities. She is co-editor of the *Journal of Special Education Technology*.

Shannon Hilliker Ph.D. student in the Department of Educational Theory and Practice at the University of Albany, Albany, New York. Her research and teaching interests involve teacher training with technology. Her area of specialization is working with English to speakers of other languages (ESOL) teachers in the field to integrate media in their classrooms.

Richard Howell, Ph.D., Associate Professor and Special Assistant to the Vice Provost, University of New Mexico, Albuquerque, New Mexico. Dr. Howell's research interests focus on the multicultural design issues in online teaching and learning. He is currently responsible for online initiatives and curriculum development at the University of New Mexico. He is a past chairperson of the Robotics and Mechatronics special interest group of the Rehabilitation Engineering Society of North America.

Mary Blake Huer, Ph.D., Professor in the Department of Human Communication Studies, California State University, Fullerton, California, and Fellow of the American Speech-Language-Hearing Association. Her areas of expertise and publications focus on speech acoustics and cross-cultural communication patterns. She is the author of the *Nonspeech Test*, an assessment tool for early language, and is the Associate Editor of *Language, Speech, and Hearing Services in the Schools*. She is the first Chair of the International Committee of the International Society of Augmentative and Alternative Communication.

Tara L. Jeffs, Ph.D., Assistant Professor, Special Education, East Carolina University, Greenville, North Carolina. Dr. Jeffs is the Director of the Assistive Technology Lab at East Carolina University and she is involved in teaching courses in the Assistive Technology Certificate Program. Her research and teaching interests focus on assistive technology and teacher preparation. She has written numerous articles on integrating assistive technologies into the classroom.

Marci Kinas Jerome, M.S., Administrative Faculty, Assistive Technologist, Kellar Institute for Human disAbilities, George Mason University, Fairfax, Virginia. Ms. Jerome's professional interests include the integration of assistive technology into classroom curricula, universal design for learning, special education policy, and distance education technology for teacher training.

Elizabeth A. Lahm, Ph.D., Director, Wisconsin Assistive Technology Initiative, Oshkosh, Wisconsin. Dr. Lahm's research and training interests focus on teacher competencies to improve assistive technology practices that increase student benefits from assistive technology, and data-based practices that demonstrate assistive technology outcomes. She serves on the Council for Exceptional Children Subcommittee on Knowledge and Skills, and is a Past President of the Technology and Media (TAM) Division of the Council for Exceptional Children.

Colin J. Laine, Ed.D., Director of the Centre for Communicative and Cognitive Disabilities and the Centre for Assistive Technology, the University of Western Ontario, London, Canada. Current research and teaching interests focus on the use and impact of assistive technology on the development of effective written communication by individuals with communication impairments. Dr. Laine has received several research and teaching awards, including the Sam Rabinovitch Award for Excellence in Research and held numerous offices including Canadian Delegate to the World Council for Gifted and Talented Children.

Shelly J. Lane, Ph.D., OTR/L, FAOTA, Department of Occupational Therapy, School of Allied Health Professions, Virginia Commonwealth University, Richmond, Virginia. Dr. Lane's research focuses on play, assistive technology, and sensory processing in infants and young children with disabilities. She has worked with the Let's Play Projects for several years as Director and Research Consultant. Other teaching and advisement responsibilities address neuroscience applications to occupational therapy, research methods, and grant writing. She has been a Content Editor and Specialist for F.A. Davis Publishing, and most recently holds second editorship for the book, *Sensory Integration: Theory and Practice* (2nd ed.). Dr. Lane is a Fellow of the American Occupational Therapy Association and was a certified Assistive Technology Provider (ATP).

John Langone, Ph.D., Professor and Head in the Department of Special Education, University of Georgia, Athens, Georgia. Dr. Langone is also Past President of the Technology and Media Division (TAM) of the Council for Exceptional Children. His research interests include developing and measuring the effects of innovative technology solutions for use in higher education, including video examples of effective teaching practices of special educators. Dr. Langone has been awarded a number of federally funded grants in the areas of flexible delivery systems in teacher education, secondary education/transition to adulthood and special education technology. He is a consistent contributor to the professional literature, authoring three books and numerous chapters and articles.

Rena B. Lewis, Ph.D., Associate Dean for Faculty Development and Research, College of Education, San Diego State University, San Diego, California. Dr. Lewis' research interests in special education center around the ways in which technology can be used to enhance the literacy skills of students with learning disabilities. She is a frequent contributor to the professional literature and the author of several textbooks including *Teaching Students with Special Needs in General Education Classrooms* (7th ed.) with Donald H. Doorlag.

Barbara L. Ludlow, Ed.D., Professor, Special Education Programs, Department of Educational Theory and Practice, West Virginia University, Morgantown, West Virginia. Dr. Ludlow's research and teaching interests address development and evaluation of innovative models of teacher education using technology-mediated instruction to reach prospective and practicing teachers at a distance. She is an Associate Editor of the *Journal of Special Education Technology* and *Teacher Education and Special Education*.

Paula Maccini, Ph.D., Associate Professor, Department of Special Education, University of Maryland, College Park, Maryland. Dr. Maccini's research and teaching interests focus on teaching mathematics to secondary students with learning disabilities and emotional/behavior disorders. She is particularly interested in methods for teaching math in alternative settings for students with mild disabilities.

David B. Malouf, Ph.D., is a research analyst with the Division of Research to Practice in the Office of Special Education Programs in the U.S. Department of Education, Washington, DC. His work focuses on technology for students with disabilities and on the inclusion of students with disabilities in large-scale assessments and standards-based reform.

Nancy Meidenbauer, M.S., Project Coordinator, RESNA Technical Assistance Project. Ms. Meidenbauer's interests have focused on the assistive technology equipment recycling and financial loan programs developed by the state Tech Act projects. In addition, Ms. Meidenbauer coordinates the production on reports and information products regarding the Technical Assistance Project.

Maureen Melonis, M.N.S., CCC-SLP, Senior Instructor, Assistant Director, Education Coordinator, Assistive Technology Partners, Department of Physical Medicine and Rehabilitation, University of Colorado Health Sciences Center, Denver, Colorado. Her research and training interests are focused around assistive technology, teaming, consultation and collaboration in assistive technology. She has served as education coordinator for the Colorado Assistive Technology Project (the Tech Act) and has supported the development of an assistive technology infrastructure systems change movement in the state of Colorado.

Carla Meskill, Ed.D., is Associate Professor, Department of Educational Theory and Practice, at the University of Albany. Her research and teaching explores new forms of technology use in language education. Her area of specialization is in computer assisted language learning, the design and evaluation of multimedia language teaching environments, and the use of media in language classrooms.

Susan G. Mistrett, MSEd., Center for Assistive Technology, University at Buffalo, the State University of New York, Buffalo, New York. Research and teaching interests focus on assistive technology and universal design applications that promote development through play. Outcomes of her work include identification of best practices for the integration of technology into existing programs in order to maximize the independence and participation of children with disabilities in home, education, and community settings. She has authored articles, book chapters, web sites, and training curricula that focuses on assistive technology for young children.

Beth Mineo Mollica, Ph.D., Scientist, Center for Applied Science and Engineering and Associate Professor, Department of Linguistics, University of Delaware, Wilmington, Delaware. Dr. Mineo Mollica develops and evaluates assistive technology devices and strategies for people with significant disabilities, with her research focusing primarily on language representation issues. As the director of the Delaware Assistive Technology Initiative, she facilitates improved technology access and utilization for people with disabilities in Delaware via training, technical assistance, and advocacy at both systemic and individual levels. Dr. Mineo Mollica is active on a number of state and national committees and boards. She recently concluded a three-year term as Editor of the journal *Assistive Technology*.

Seunghun Ok, M.S., Graduate Research Assistant, Helen A. Kellar Institute for Human disAbilities, George Mason University, Fairfax, VA. Mr. Ok is interested in assistive technology applications for people with disabilities, especially those in Korea, his home country, where assistive technology is not yet in place.

Cynthia M. Okolo, Ph.D., Professor, Department of Counseling, Educational Psychology, and Special Education; Michigan State University, East Lansing, Michigan. Dr. Okolo's research interests are in the areas of technology, literacy, and history instruction for students with mild disabilities. She directs a doctoral program in assistive technology and is a Past President of the Technology and Media (TAM) Division of the Council for Exceptional Children.

Howard P. Parette, Ed.D., Professor and Kara Peters Endowed Chair in Assistive Technology, Department of Special Education, Illinois State University, Normal Illinois. He has published extensively on children with special needs, with emphasis on assistive technology applications for children with disabilities and their families. In recent years, he has focused particular attention on cross-cultural applications of assistive technology. He is the current Editor of *Assistive Technology Outcomes and Benefits*.

Carrie A. Prentice, M.S., CCC-SLP, Speech-Language Pathologist, Quality Living, Inc., Omaha, Nebraska. Mrs. Prentice specializes in augmentative and alternative communication for children and adults. Currently, she provides evaluation and treatment for adults with acquired and degenerative disabilities, along with training for family and support staff on how to maximize communication and learning potential using augmentative and alternative communication.

Penny R. Reed, Ph.D., Consultant in Special Education and Assistive Technology, Juneau, Wisconsin. Dr. Reed's interests are primarily in helping school districts and other educational agencies to implement legal, efficient, and cost-effective assistive technology services. Dr. Reed developed and served as Director of the Wisconsin Assistive Technology Initiative (WATI). She has been active in the Technology and Media (TAM) Division of the Council for Exceptional Children, serving as President in 2000-2001. Dr. Reed received the 1992 TAM Leadership Award.

Gladene Robertson, Ph.D., Associate Professor (retired), Department of Educational Psychology and Special Education, University of Saskatchewan, Saskatoon, Saskatchewan, Canada. Dr. Robertson's career has been focused on a quest toward the goal of effectively communicating the importance of honoring the individuality of every learner. Effective inclusionary teachers, collaborative teaming, adaptive instruction, as well as change theory have dominated her interests, her teaching, and her practice.

David H. Rose, Ed.D., Co-Executive Director, CAST, Wakefield, Massachusetts. Dr. Rose specializes in developmental neuropsychology and in the universal design of learning technologies. Dr. Rose helped found CAST in 1984 to expand opportunities for students with disabilities through the development and innovative application of computer technology. With Dr. Anne Meyer, he is the author of *Teaching Every Student in the Digital Age: Universal Design for Learning* (Association for Supervision and Curriculum Development, 2002) and *Learning to Read in the Computer Age* (Brookline Books, 1999).

Dianne Rothenberg, M.S., Co-Director, Early Childhood and Parenting Collaborative, College of Education, University of Illinois at Urbana-Champaign. Her research interests include Internet use by parents, families, and early childhood educators. Formerly Co-Director of the ERIC Clearinghouse on Elementary and Early Childhood Education, Ms. Rothenberg is currently project coordinator for the Illinois Early Learning Project and the Prekindergarten Research in Progress Database Project, and Associate Editor of *Early Childhood Research & Practice*, the first peer-reviewed, Internet-only journal in early childhood education.

Amy G. Ruffino, MS OT, Occupational Therapist, Center for Assistive Technology, University at Buffalo, the State University of New York, Buffalo, New York. Research and teaching interests are in the areas of early intervention and pre-school practice and application of assistive technology to the birth through five populations. Additional interests are play development and universal design applications.

Rosa Milagros (Amy) Santos, Ph.D., Assistant Professor, Department of Special Education, University of Illinois at Urbana-Champaign. Dr. Santos' research interests include issues that relate to the impact of culture, race, and language in the delivery of services to young children with disabilities and their families. Her research focuses on family support services, parent-child interactions across cultures, development of intercultural competence of early childhood service providers, and using technology in personnel preparation. She serves on several editorial boards and is currently a Member-At-Large, Division of Early Childhood (DEC) of the Council for Exceptional Children.

Jennie I. Schaff, Ph.D., Assistant Professor, Special Education, State University of New York at Geneseo, Geneseo, New York. Dr. Schaff's research and teaching interests focus on assistive technology and augmentative and alternative communication. Specifically, she is interested in strategies used to teach children to utilize such technologies.

Marcia J. Scherer, Ph.D., Director, Institute for Matching Person and Technology; Senior Research Associate, International Center for Hearing and Speech Research (a joint program of the University of Rochester and National Technical Institute for the Deaf/Rochester Institute of Technology); Associate Professor of Physical Medicine and Rehabilitation, University of Rochester Medical Center. Dr. Scherer has authored and edited several books and many research papers on assistive technology. She is a Fellow of the American Psychological Association in Rehabilitation Psychology as well as in Applied Experimental and Engineering Psychology. She is also a Fellow of the American Congress of Rehabilitation Medicine.

Carolyn Sitko, MEd., was Research Officer at the Centre for Communicative and Cognitive Disabilities, Faculty of Education, the University of Western Ontario, London, Canada, for 12 years. Her work included disseminating research and practical information to special educators through publications and workshops.

Merrill Sitko, Ph.D., Professor Emeritus, Centre for Communicative and Cognitive Disabilities, Faculty of Education, the University of Western Ontario, London, Canada. Dr. Sitko's interest in research and teaching about the effective uses of technology for facilitating writing and problem solving in students with learning and other disabilities led to the establishment of Centres for Assistive Technology. He held the Endowed Chair in Communication Disabilities and received the Sam Robinovitch Award for Excellence in Research.

John Slatin, Ph.D., Director of the Accessibility Institute at the University of Texas at Austin with a joint appointment as a Professor in the Department of English and and the Division of Rhetoric and Composition. Among his many professional and personal interests, his recent research has focused on a a broad range of issues related to the challenges of making the World Wide Web accessible to everyone, including people with disabilities. He is co-author of the book, *Maximum Accessibility* (2003), a practical guide to Web accessibility strategies, standards, and policies.

Sean J. Smith, Ph.D., Assistant Professor, Department of Special Education, University of Kansas, Lawrence, Kansas. Dr. Smith's research and teaching interests focus on the integration of technology into the lives of students with disabilities, specifically the engagement of teachers to enhance technology use. He is Co-Principal Investigator on a U.S. Department of Education funded project to examine the use of technology by people with cognitive disabilities and an Associate Editor of the *Journal of Special Education Technology*.

Debra Sprague, Ph.D., Associate Professor, Graduate School of Education, George Mason University, Fairfax, Virginia. Dr. Sprague's research interests focus on the innovative use of technology to support teaching and learning. She currently serves as Editor of the *Journal of Technology and Teacher Education*. She is also the Principal Investigator of a Preparing Tomorrow's Teachers for Technology (PT3) grant.

Skip Stahl, M.S., Senior Associate, CAST, Wakefield, Massachusetts. Mr. Stahl is nationally recognized for his training efforts using CAST's Universal Design for Learning model. He has helped numerous school districts and state education agencies develop proactive strategies for meeting the needs of all learners using technology. Mr. Stahl chaired the technical panel for the National File Format, a U.S. Department of Education-funded initiative to establish a voluntary national standard for accessible digital instructional materials for students with disabilities. He writes a regular column for *Counterpoint*, a publication of the National Association of Directors of Special Education.

Nicole M. Strangman, Ph.D., Technical Writer, CAST, Wakefield, Massachusetts. A bench scientist-turned-writer, Dr. Strangman is interested in the connections between neuroscience and education. She is an author on numerous CAST publications, including *Teaching Every Student in the Digital Age: Universal Design for Learning*. While editorial assistant for *Reading Online* she developed the "Teachers' Voices" article series.

Matt Tincani, Ph.D., Assistant Professor, Department of Special Education, University of Nevada, Las Vegas. Dr. Tincani's research and teaching interests include augmentative and alternative communication for children with autism and positive behavioral supports. He is a member of the Council for Children with Behavioral Disorders, and has served on the Executive Council of the Association for Behavior Analysis.

Gerald Tindal, Ph.D., Professor and Director of the Behavioral Research and Teaching (BRT) as well as Area Head of Educational Leadership, University of Oregon, Eugene, Oregon. He teaches courses that focus on measurement systems for general and special education teachers and administrators. His work includes both curriculum-based measurement of basic skills and concept-based instruction and problem solving in secondary content classrooms. For the past decade, Dr. Tindal has conducted research on student participation in large-scale testing. This work includes investigations of test accommodations, teacher decision-making using curriculum-based measurement, and extended assessments of basic skills. He publishes and reviews articles in many special education journals and has written several book chapters and books on curriculum-based measurement.

Alan VanBiervliet, Ph.D., Professor, Department of Health Behavior and Health Communication, University of Arkansas for Medical Sciences, Little Rock, Arkansas. Dr. VanBiervliet has 27 years of experience developing, evaluating, and disseminating digital technologies for persons with disabilities. His first professionally distributed computer program, a multimedia language development program for persons with severe disabilities, was published in 1977. During the past 24 years he has continuously received external funding for 37 research and development projects via federal, state and private sources. He has received numerous national and international awards for his work.

Michael L. Wehmeyer, Ph.D., Associate Professor, Department of Special Education; Director, Kansas University Center on Developmental Disabilities; Associate Director, Beach Center on Disability, University of Kansas, Lawrence, Kansas. Dr. Wehmeyer's research and teaching interests focus on self-determination and the education of students with cognitive disabilities. He is Co-Principal Investigator on a U.S. Department of Education-Funded project to examine the use of technology by people with cognitive disabilities and on the editorial board of the *Journal of Special Education Technology*.

Cheryl A. Wissick, Ph.D., Associate Professor, Programs in Special Education, College of Education, University of South Carolina, Columbia, South Carolina. Dr. Wissick's research and teaching interests focus on the integration of technology using thematic units and the Web into the curriculum. She is also interested in the development of activities using agent-based technology. She has been actively involved with the field of special education for the past 20 years. Currently she is the Treasurer of the Technology and Media (TAM) Division of the Council for Exceptional Children and the Special Education Technology Special Interest Group (SETSIG) of the International Society of Technology in Education.

Joy Smiley Zabala, Ph.D., ATP, an internationally recognized professional developer and consultant in assistive technology and leadership. Dr. Zabala's interests focus on collaborative processes in assistive technology selection, acquisition, and use. She is the developer of the SETT Framework, a collaborative decision-making tool, and is co-founder of the Quality Indicators for Assistive Technology (QIAT) Consortium. She is President-Elect of the Technology and Media (TAM) Division of the Council for Exceptional Children, facilitates the QIAT listserv, co-chairs the Technology Desk of the Division for International Special Education and Services (DICES) of the Council for Exceptional Children, and is the TAM representative on the organizational board of the European Schools Project.

Section 1

Historical, Policy, and Legal Foundations

1

Historical Perspectives about Technology Applications for People with Disabilities

A. Edward Blackhurst

People with disabilities and unique talents have benefited greatly over the years from advances in technology. For example, the development of the audiometer permitted a more accurate evaluation of hearing; the Perkins Brailler enabled quick transcription of braille symbols for people who are blind; programmed instruction enhanced the learning of students experiencing difficulty with academic subjects; machines that can produce speech sounds have helped facilitate communication with children who cannot talk; systematic approaches to classroom management have reduced problems encountered by students with behavior disorders; specially designed keyboards have enabled people with physical disabilities to use computers; and computer-based information systems have facilitated enrichment programs for students with unique gifts and talents.

This chapter describes some of the forces that have shaped current concepts about technology applications in special education and related practices. The chapter is not a review of the literature, nor is it a historical treatise. Rather, it represents the author's personal perspectives about ways to view technology, the role technology plays in the field of special education, and some of the forces that have impacted on the development of technology applications. The information presented reflects the author's perspectives as a "participant observer" in a host of technology-related special education projects over a period of 44 years. Because a knowledge of history can help

us understand current practices, avoid past mistakes, and plan improvements, the content is presented from an historical perspective.

Those interested in more detailed historical and descriptive information might want to examine the references cited in this chapter, others in this book, as well as comprehensive books and articles on the topic (e.g., Aldinger, Warger, & Eavy, 1995; Alliance for Technology Access, 2001; Bain & Leger, 1997; Behrmann, 1984, 1988; Beukelman & Mirenda, 1998; Blackhurst, 1965, 1978, 1997, 2001; Blackhurst & Cross, 1993; Blackhurst, Hales, & Lahm, 1998; Blackhurst & Hofmeister, 1980; Boone & Higgins, 1992; Bowe, 1984; Cavalier & Ferretti, 1996; Chambers, 1997; Church & Bender, 1989; Church & Glennen, 1992; Cook & Hussey, 2002; Computer Museum History Center, 2003; Council for Exceptional Children, 1987; Flippo, Inge, & Barcus, 1995; Galvan & Scherer, 1996; Golden, 1998; Goldenberg, Russell, & Carter, 1984; Hasselbring, 1994; Hofmeister, 1984; Inge & Shepherd, 1995; Johnson, 1987; Lance, 1973; Lewis, 1993; Lindsey, 2000; Ludlow & Duff, 1998; Male, 1994; Meers, 1998; Nazzaro, 1977; Parette, 1997; Polsson, 1999; Ray & Warden, 1995; Rose & Meyer, 2000; Scherer, 1993, 2004; Silverman, 1995; Slaton & Lacefield, 1991; Taber, 1983; Thorkildsen, 1994; Woodward & Cuban, 2001).

In addition, the Connecticut State Department of Education has prepared a number of useful bibliographies related to technology applications in special education that can be accessed via the World Wide Web (Web). Topics include assistive technology (www.ctserc.org/library/actualbibs/AssTech.pdf), augmentative and alternative communication (www.ctserc.org/library/actualbibs/Augmentative.pdf), and computers and special education (www.ctserc.org/library/actualbibs/Computers8398.pdf). Descriptions about projects related to virtual reality in special education are also available on the Web (www.ori.org/educationvr.html).

Further, timelines of many technology-related milestones are provided by Blackhurst and Edyburn (2000). Organized according to seven chronological periods, the technology milestones in their article are presented in six different threads: legislation, events, people, products, publications, and technology in society. That resource, in addition to Nazarro (1977), has been drawn upon for many of the specific dates and topics that are included in this chapter.

Perspectives about the Impact of Technology

For many years, technology has been applied to a number of major problems in special education, with highly significant results. This section highlights some of them.

The Pre-Computer Age

Because of the allure of high-tech, sophisticated devices, the impact of earlier accomplishments is frequently overlooked. Table 1 contains a sampling of some of the technology-related contributions from the pre-computer age.

The Impact of Computers

From a more contemporary view, following are just a few of the ways in which technology is being used with children and adults who have disabilities. Many of these applications are the direct result of the invention of the microprocessor and resultant microcomputers in the late 1970s.

Table 1. Pre-Computer Technology Milestones That Impacted Special Education

Year	Event
1808	The precursor of braille is developed as a series of raised dots for sending military messages at night.
1834	The braille code, using six dots, is published by Louis Braille.
1863	A socket with a suction cup is developed to attach a lower-limb prosthesis.
1874	The audiophone bone conduction amplifier is invented.
1892	The braille typewriter is developed.
1900	The first electrical amplifying device for people with hearing impairments is invented.
1913	Printed letters are translated to musical tones for blind readers using the Optophone prototype.
1914	The Tadoma method is developed for teaching children who are deaf and blind; the Simplex Hearing Tube, which used a funnel to catch sound, is invented.
1916	The intelligence quotient (IQ) is introduced with the publication of the Stanford-Binet Scale of Intelligence.
1920	A human emotional response is conditioned by Watson in an experimental setting.
1926	Pressey develops a teaching machine that uses programmed instruction; a phonograph audiometer is developed to identify hearing impairments.
1928	Radios are distributed to citizens who are blind by the American Foundation for the Blind; seeing eye dogs are introduced to the United States.

(continued next page)

Table 1. Pre-Computer Technology Milestones That Impacted Special Education (continued)

Year	Event
1930	A standard report form is developed for eye examinations.
1934	The printing visagraph is developed to enlarge printed pages and put them into raised form; the Gault Teletactor amplifies speech vibrations so that people who are deaf can receive them tactually; Talking Books for the blind are produced on long-playing records.
1935	The Waldman Air Conduction Audiometer is developed to detect hearing impairments.
1938	Pitch is translated into a visual image by the Coyne Voice Pitch Indicator.
1945	Improvements in prosthetic limbs are made to meet the needs of wounded World War II veterans.
1947	The Perkins Brailler is developed; printing of large-type books is initiated by the American Printing House for the Blind.
1949	Speech is transformed to visual patterns by the cathode ray translator.
1952	Students who are blind use the Stenomask to dictate lecture notes while listening.
1953	The megascope is invented to project and magnify printed material.
1954	B. F. Skinner publishes *The Science of Learning and the Art of Teaching*.
1960	Lumsdaine and Glaser publish *Teaching Machines and Programmed Learning*.
1962	Mager publishes *Preparing Objectives for Programmed Instruction*.
1965	Mobility for people who are blind is facilitated through the invention of the Kay Binaural Sensor; studies are performed using token economies.
1966	The laser cane is developed for use by people who are blind.
1967	The *National Society for the Study of Education 66th Yearbook* is devoted to programmed instruction.
1968	A device is invented for compressing speech to more than 320 words per minute without distortion.
1971	The Optacon enables people who are blind to convert ink print to tactile impressions of letters.
1972	A braille writer of pocket size is developed; the Kay Spectacles, which enable people who are blind to determine the precise location of obstacles, are developed as mobility aids.
1974	A braille calculator is developed; reading material can be magnified 25 times and displayed on a TV screen using the Visualtek Miniviewer; the electronic blackboard is developed to transmit writing over telephone lines for display on TV screens.
1975	A talking calculator is developed to provide audio output; speech synthesizers help persons with impaired speech to make spoken sentences; spectrograms of speech can be frozen on a TV monitor using the speech spectrograph display; Cybercom permits those with severe disabilities to communicate via electric typewriter and message board operated by a pneumatic switch; speed of recorded speech can be regulated using the Variable Speed Control Disc; Individualized Education Programs (IEP) are mandated for students enrolled in special education programs in P.L. 94-142.

- Computer-assisted and multimedia instruction for children with learning difficulties

- Synthetic speech production for non-vocal children

- Assistive and adaptive equipment for those with physical disabilities, sensory impairments, communication disorders, and learning disabilities

- Translation of printed text into spoken text for people with visual impairments and reading disabilities

- Use of virtual reality to train students how to operate electric wheelchairs

- Computer-generated IEPs

- Electronic communication for sharing special education information

- Computerized databases of information about assistive technologies

- Expert computer systems to assist decision making of special education teachers and researchers

- Devices to enable the enlargement of text materials for those with visual impairments

- Voice recognition systems to enable people who cannot write to produce written text

- Computer systems that can be used to search the world's literature about special education and related services

- Robotic arms that can be used to assist people who are paralyzed

- Internet-based performance support systems to enable teachers to manage unacceptable behavior of students

- Fax machines and Telecommunication Devices for the Deaf (TDDs) that enable people with severe hearing loss to communicate via printed text over telephone lines

- Use of communication satellites and compressed interactive video to provide preservice and inservice education to special educators and related services personnel

- Telecommunication systems to enable students with disabilities to communicate over the Internet

- Universal design for learning that can provide access to instructional content and support for learners with a wide array of educational needs

Numerous other examples could be provided. One thing seems clear, however: Most researchers and other authorities who are knowledgeable about technology have concluded over the years that technology has the potential for dramatically improving the quality of education and the quality of life for people with disabilities, as evidenced by the citations at the end of this chapter.

Perspectives about the Technology Continuum

To many people, the term "technology" conjures up visions of computers and other high-tech devices that are often viewed as being very expensive and very complicated to use. Often, such perspectives focus solely on hardware and equipment, overlooking the role of procedures that relate to the delivery of technology services but do not involve the use of equipment or devices.

For teachers, a useful perspective is to view technology as a tool that can be used to solve problems in the education of their students. It is helpful to think about a continuum that ranges from high-tech to no-tech solutions to problems. For example, high-tech solutions are those that involve the use of sophisticated devices, such as computers and interactive multimedia systems. Medium-tech solutions include the use of less complicated electronic or mechanical devices such as video cassette players and wheelchairs. Low-tech solutions are less sophisticated and can include things such as adapted spoon handles, Velcro fasteners, or raised desks that can accommodate a wheelchair. Finally, no-tech solutions are those that do not require devices or equipment. These might involve the use of very systematic teaching procedures or the contributions of related services personnel such as physical or occupational therapists.

In making decisions about the type of technology tools or supports a particular student might require, a good approach is to start with the no-tech solutions and then work up the continuum as needed. For example, in teaching home economics to a student with one arm, it might be better to teach the student how to wedge a mixing bowl into a drawer and hold it with a hip while stirring than to purchase an expensive medium-tech electric mixer that is equipped to stabilize the mixing bowl while it is being operated. That solution is cheaper and less intrusive than the special mixer. It also enables the student to function in a variety of environments where stabilizing mixers are not available.

Too often, when making technology decisions in IEP meetings, there is a tendency to start at the upper end of the technology continuum when, in fact, it is better to start at a lower point. For example, when making IEP decisions about students whose handwriting is difficult to recognize, it is not uncommon to hear recommendations that the student should be provided with a laptop computer to take from class to class (cost: $800-$3,000). In reality, an electronic keyboard with memory that can be downloaded into a desktop computer later in the day may be more appropriate (cost: about $300). While the student in this example may eventually require a laptop computer, the electronic keyboard may be a better place to start.

Perspectives about Types of Technology

Technology professional development programs have often triggered negative reactions among potential participants, as reflected by this teacher's comments in 1985, when informed that her school would be required to develop a technology plan, a component of which would require inservice training for all school personnel:

I really hate having to learn how to use a computer. I'm no good with machines and I really don't want to spend the time learning how to use one. I'd rather spend my inservice hours on improving my teaching skills. I don't need to know how to operate a computer to be a good teacher.

Resistance to computers, as reflected in the above statement, has diminished as computers have become easier to use and have become more pervasive in our society. Inservice training also has improved and become more readily available, and those entering professional positions have become fluid technology users as a result of early exposure to a wide array of devices and equipment in both homes and schools.

Often, technology applications in schools have tended to focus on the operation of equipment such as projection devices, audio and video recorders, and computers. In the mid-1960s, however, a trend emerged that has changed the way professionals perceive technology applications in education. At that time, educators began considering the concept of *instructional technology*.

After considerable deliberation, a Congressional Commission on Instructional Technology (1970) concluded that technology involved more than just hardware. Thus, the Commission concluded that, in addition to devices and equipment, instructional technology also involves a systematic way of designing and delivering instruction. At about the same time, Haring (1970) reached a similar conclusion when he examined the use of instructional technology in special education.

These distinctions were further defined 10 years later in a comprehensive review that concluded that there were two types of technology applications in special education: media technology and systems technology (Blackhurst & Hofmeister, 1980). The former focused on the use of various devices, while the latter focused primarily on systematic approaches to instruction.

With the rapid development of microcomputer technology in the early 1980s, increased research on instructional procedures, and the invention of new devices and equipment to aid individuals with health problems, physical disabilities, and sensory impairments, the ensuing years bore witness to a very dramatic evolution. As a result of exploring such developments over more than a quarter of a century, a view of technology has evolved that places the various approaches into perspective. This view is a broad one in which six types of technology are recognized: the *technology of teaching*, *instructional technology*, *assistive technology*, *medical technology*, *technology productivity tools*, and *information technology* (Blackhurst, 1997; Blackhurst & Lahm, 2000).

Technology of Teaching

The technology of teaching refers to instructional approaches that are systematically designed and applied in very precise ways, such as the following:

Example of Technology of Teaching

Ann is teaching letter recognition to her preschool students with disabilities. She has presented the letters of the alphabet to her students and identified those that the students are unable to recognize. She selects groups of two unidentified letters for each student.

Her classroom is organized into learning centers. She decides to imbed instruction on letter recognition into the natural activities that are conducted in the learning centers. She constructs felt letters for use on the flannel board in the Book Center, selects blocks with the letters for the Fine Motor Center, and writes the letters on the dry-erase board in the Writing Center.

After systematically orienting each student to one of the target letters, she says, "Look! What letter?" and then waits 3 seconds for a response. If students answer correctly, Ann provides verbal praise (e.g., "Very good! That was an 'H'.") Students are instructed to wait if they do not know the answer. If they don't provide a response after the 3-second delay, Ann names the letter: "This is an 'H'." If they answer incorrectly, they are told, "No. Wait if you don't know."

As the students get used to the procedure, they gradually associate the name of the letter with its shape and are able to name it correctly before the 3-second delay is up. When they are able to answer correctly on three consecutive presentations, another letter is introduced.

The above example comes from the research of Ann Blackhurst (1997), who successfully taught letter recognition to several of her preschool students with disabilities. This technology of teaching, known as *constant time delay*, is one of a number of response prompting strategies that research has shown to be effective with students who have disabilities (Wolery, Ault, & Doyle, 1992).

Technologies of teaching refer to instructional approaches that are systematically designed and applied in very precise ways. Many are embellishments and extensions of the work of B. F. Skinner (Greer, 1991). Although there are different technologies of teaching, most include the use of very well-defined objectives, precise instructional procedures based upon the tasks that students are required to learn, small units of instruction that are carefully sequenced, a high degree of teacher activity, high levels of student involvement, liberal use of reinforcement, and careful monitoring of student performance. Another feature shared by technologies of teaching is that they are based on theories of learning and theories of instruction. They also have been validated through empirical research (Algozzine & Ysseldyke, 1992; Lovitt, 1995).

Among the many successful examples of technologies of teaching are the application of applied behavior analysis (Wolery, Bailey, & Sugai, 1988) for teaching social and academic skills (Alberto & Troutman, 1995); direct instruction of academic skills (Carnine, Silbert, & Kameenui, 1990); teaching students how to apply learning strategies (Deshler & Schumaker, 1986); teaching special education majors at a university via adjunct auto-instruction (Renne & Blackhurst, 1977); and teaching special educators via competency-based instruction (Blackhurst, 1977, 2001).

In most cases, technologies of teaching can be applied without the use of computers or other instructional media. Sometimes, however, software and multimedia programs can be developed that have been based on technology of teaching principles. Examples include the use of computer-controlled video anchored instruction programs to teach problem solving (Hasselbring, Goin, & Wissick, 1989) and the use of constant time delay to teach the memorization of spelling words (Stevens,

Blackhurst, & Slaton, 1991), abbreviations (Edwards, Blackhurst, & Koorland, 1995) and math facts (Bausch, 1999). Bausch (1999) also used an alternate keyboard with students who had learning disabilities, thus illustrating how assistive technology and instructional technology can be combined to facilitate the application of the technology of teaching.

Instructional Technology

Although there are differing opinions about the nature of instructional technology, the Commission on Instructional Technology (1970) provided the following definition:

Instructional technology is a systematic way of designing, carrying out, and evaluating the total process of learning and teaching in terms of specific objectives, based on research in human learning and communication, and employing a combination of human and nonhuman resources to bring about more effective instruction. (p. 199)

Typical applications of instructional technology may use conventional media such as videotapes, computer-assisted instruction, or more complex systems, such as hypermedia-based anchored instruction programs and the Web.

It is important to note the various components of the above definition and to realize that technology is really a tool for the delivery of instruction. In this conceptualization, technological devices are considered as means to an end and not an end in and of themselves. Use of technology cannot compensate for instruction that is poorly designed or implemented.

Assistive Technology

Assistive technology employs various types of services and devices to help people with disabilities function within the environment. Assistive technologies include mechanical, electronic, and microprocessor-based equipment, non-mechanical and non-electronic aids, specialized instructional materials, services, and strategies that people with disabilities can use either to (a) assist them in learning, (b) make the environment more accessible, (c) enable them to compete in the workplace, (d) enhance their independence, or (e) otherwise

improve their quality of life. These may include commercially available or "homemade" devices that are specially designed to meet the idiosyncratic needs of a particular individual (Blackhurst & Cross, 1993). Examples include communication aids, alternative computer keyboards, adaptive switches, and services such as those that might be provided by speech-language pathologists, physical therapists, rehabilitation engineers, and occupational therapists.

Medical Technology

The advances constantly being made in medical technology continue to amaze. In addition to seemingly miraculous surgical procedures that are technology-based, many individuals are dependent upon medical technology to stay alive or otherwise function outside of hospitals and other medical settings.

The twentieth century was marked by a wide range of medical achievements and the development of a variety of remarkable devices to facilitate the health and vitality of people. These ranged from the 1914 development of the low-tech Simplex Hearing Tube that used a funnel to catch sound and transmit it to the ear to facilitate hearing, to the high-tech cochlear implant that can be surgically implanted to enable some people with severe auditory impairments to hear sounds.

Many complex machines were also developed for use by medical personnel in diagnosing and treating a variety of physical conditions. These include treatment of visual loss via laser surgery, continuous glucose monitoring for people with diabetes, cardiac pacemakers for those with heart conditions, implantation of electrodes in the brain to control epilepsy, and the use of robotic arms to minimize the invasiveness of various surgical procedures (Hales, 1999). In addition, a number of very specialized devices also were developed to help people with unique medical problems to stay alive. Terms such as "technology-dependent" or "medically fragile" emerged to describe individuals with such needs (Batshaw & Perret, 1992).

It is necessary for some individuals to receive periodic treatment that is provided via machines. An example is weekly dialysis treatments for those whose kidneys do not function properly. Periodic blood platelet transfusions may be required for others, such as in the case of people with sickle cell anemia.

Other children and adults require more constant use of technologies in order to ensure their survival. For example, some people lack the muscle control to breathe. Devices, called ventilators, are used to perform mechanical breathing for those individuals. A ventilator is attached to a tube that has been inserted into the person's neck via a tracheostomy. The ventilator can be adjusted to mix air and oxygen, if needed, to operate at the appropriate rate and pressure level for each individual. "Trach tubes" must be cleaned on a regular basis in order to keep the airway clear. Suction machines are sometimes used to assist with this process. Other machines are used to mist medication into the trach tube for those who may require respiratory therapy.

Special equipment also may be necessary to assist those who are unable to eat independently. Body supports are needed for those who cannot maintain an upright position while eating. Feeding tubes may be necessary for those who cannot take food orally. A nasogastric tube that is inserted through the nose into the stomach may be required for some, while a gastronomy tube that is inserted directly into the stomach may be required for others.

Some people with heart conditions may require constant monitoring of their circulatory systems. A device, called a pulse oximeter, can be attached to a finger or toe to monitor the heart rate and the oxygen content in the blood. This device, no larger than a small bandage, feeds data to a display that can be set to sound an alarm if an abnormal reading is detected. It also can store information in a computer.

But not all medical technologies are at the high-tech end of the continuum. For example, a colostomy bag is a low-tech device that can be used to collect body wastes for those who have had surgery required to reroute the colon. The colostomy bag is worn over an opening on the abdomen.

"Bionic" extremities have been developed and robots have been developed to enable people to feed themselves by controlling the actions of robots with their voices (Morris,

1985). Experiments are continuing on developing devices that use electronic stimulation of the muscles to elicit movement in nonfunctional limbs in an effort to enable those who are paralyzed to regain their ability to walk. As knowledge and technology continue to improve, and microchips become increasingly smaller and more powerful, it is anticipated that even more remarkable medical technologies will be developed in the twenty-first century.

Technology Productivity Tools

As the name implies, technology productivity tools are computer software, hardware, and related systems that enable us to work more effectively and efficiently. For example, computer software such as database programs can be used to store and rapidly retrieve information; word processing programs can be used to easily edit text material; Fax machines can facilitate the transmission of written documents over long distances; expert system computer programs can aid in decision making, such as the educational placement of students with disabilities; and videoconferencing facilities can reduce the need for travel.

Information Technology

Information technologies provide access to knowledge and resources on a wide range of topics. The Internet and its Web component is the most prominent example of information technology. Not only can the Internet provide information to professionals who provide special education services, Web sites can be used by people with disabilities to facilitate learning, productivity, personal enrichment, and the use of leisure time.

The most notable information technology for professional educators is the Educational Resources Information Center (ERIC) system, which enables people to search much of the world's literature related to all areas of education. ERIC was established in 1966, and was operated until the end of 2003 by the National Library of Education under a grant from the U.S. Department of Education. At the time this chapter was written, there was uncertainty about the structure and operation of the ERIC system, since a decision was made by the funding agency to redesign it. The redesign was scheduled to be completed in 2004. The primary resources of the ERIC system as they existed at the end of 2003 will be described, since many of them will, in all likelihood, remain available, regardless of the structure of the ERIC system.

People in the ERIC system reviewed and abstracted articles in educational journals and other educational publications and entered them in an electronic database, which contains more than a million abstracts. Users searching for information about an educational topic can retrieve the abstracts by using combinations of descriptors. ERIC can be accessed via the Web at www.eric.ed.gov, by using CD-ROMs that contain the ERIC abstracts, or through conventional printed documents, such as *Resources in Education* (RIE) and *Current Index to Journals in Education* (CIJE).

If the number on an abstract retrieved via an ERIC search includes "ED," the full text of the article can be retrieved from one of more than 900 libraries that contain microfiche of those articles, or they can be purchased from the ERIC Document Reproduction Service. ERIC also produced *ERIC Digests*, two-page summaries of topics of current interest. These were produced at the rate of about 100 per year. Currently, there are more than 2,400 *ERIC Digests* available.

Sixteen ERIC Clearinghouses provided a host of specialized information about a variety of educational topics, including the Clearinghouse on Disabilities and Gifted Education, which was operated by the Council for Exceptional Children (CEC).

When conducting searches of the ERIC database, it is necessary to use descriptors that were assigned to each abstract as it was entered into the database. These descriptors can be combined with words like "AND," "OR," and "NOT" to broaden or narrow a search.

Although the ERIC database is very comprehensive, a typical ERIC search MAY NOT retrieve all the information related to a special education topic. The CEC-ERIC Clearinghouse abstracted articles and collected information about abstracts that are not included in the main ERIC collection due to limitations that were placed on the size of the main ERIC system. The excess information was collated into the *Exceptional Child Education Resources* (ECER) database and print publication. There are more than 80,000 abstracts in the ECER collection, only one-half of which are in the main ERIC collection. The print version of ECER is located in most education libraries, while the electronic form of the database is available on CD-ROM. Therefore, when conducting an ERIC search for information on a special education topic, it is important to search the ECER database as well as the ERIC database to increase the likelihood of retrieving the most all-encompassing information. It will be interesting to see how comprehensive the redesigned ERIC system will be with respect to abstracts of publications related to special education.

An Illustration

Each of the above technology types has significant implications for the delivery of special education services in and of itself. However, they may also be used in combination. Take, for example, the case of Carrie, a fifth grader.

Using Multiple Technologies

Carrie had a horseback-riding accident that damaged her spinal cord. She has breathing difficulties and is unable to use her hands to operate a computer keyboard. Carrie must use a respirator to help her breathe (*medical technology*). She also uses a voice-operated computer (*assistive technology*) that delivers instruction from a software program that was designed to deliver spelling instruction (*instructional technology*) using a constant time delay response prompt fading instructional procedure (*technology of teaching*). Her teacher stores progress reports in an electronic gradebook program and uses a word-processing program to prepare progress reports for Carrie's parents (*technology productivity tool*). She also uses the Web to conduct ERIC searches related to assistive technology and to obtain information about resources that she can use to improve Carrie's instruction (*information technology*).

While the above example may be somewhat extreme, it serves to place the various types of technology into perspective. In reality, it is more likely that only one or two types of technology would be used simultaneously.

Perspectives about Federal Initiatives

Over the years, the federal government has played a pivotal role in stimulating technology applications in special education. This stimulation has been in the form of federal laws and regulations that have included technology mandates and funding to support a wide variety of technology research and development, training, and service activities.

Legislated support for technology can be traced back to 1879, when $10,000 in federal funds were allocated to the American Printing House for the Blind to produce braille materials. Table 2 contains a list of some of the more prominent public laws (P.L.) related to technology.

Of the above laws, the following four—and their amendments—have had the greatest impact for technology applications for students with disabilities.

IDEA, the Individuals with Disabilities Education Act (P.L. 94-142 and its amendments), guarantees the right of all children with disabilities to a free and appropriate education in the least restrictive environment. From a technology standpoint, IDEA requires that assistive technology be considered for each student for whom an IEP is developed. This requirement places greater emphasis on assistive technology for students with disabilities than was the case prior to the enactment of that legislation. School personnel are now required to develop policies and procedures for meeting this provision of the law.

At the time this chapter was written, Congress was in the process of revising IDEA. By the time this book is published, the reauthorization process should have been completed. In all likelihood, changes will have been made in the law and the federal regulations for its implementation. Access to that information should be available from the Department of Education Web site at www.ed.gov.

P.L. 99-506 amended the Rehabilitation Act of 1973 by adding Section 508 to that act. Section 508 ensures access to computers and other electronic office equipment in places of federal employment. The guidelines ensure that users with disabilities can access and use the same databases and applications programs as other users. Users with disabilities also will be able to manipulate data and related information sources to attain the same results as other users, and will have the adaptations needed to communicate with others on their system.

P.L. 101-336, the Americans with Disabilities Act, *broadened the definition of those who are considered to have disabilities. It also broadened the types* of agencies and employers covered by Section 508 requirements and mandates additional protections, such as accessible public transportation systems, communication systems, and access to public buildings. These requirements are opening many avenues of employment for people with disabilities who were previously excluded from office work because of inaccessible equipment.

P.L. 100-407, the Technology-Related Assistance for Individuals with Disabilities Act, provided funds to states to develop systems for a variety of technology assistance to children and adults with disabilities and their parents and guardians. Specifically, the purpose of P.L. 100-407 is to enable states to conduct needs assessments, identify technology resources, provide assistive technology services, and conduct public awareness programs, among others.

The "Tech Act," as it has come to be known, provided definitions of assistive technology devices and services. Those definitions were slightly modified in the reauthorization of P.L. 105-17, The Individuals with Disabilities Education Act (IDEA), to make the wording of the definitions applicable to children with disabilities in schools. As defined in Section 300.5 and 300.6 of IDEA:

The term "assistive technology device" means any item, piece of equipment, or product system, whether acquired commercially off the shelf, modified, or customized, that is used to increase, maintain, or improve the functional capabilities of a child with a disability. The term "assistive technology service"

Table 2. Major Federal Legislation Related to Technology

Year	Legislation
1879	P.L. 45-186 provided funds to the American Printing House for the Blind to produce braille materials
1904	P.L. 58-171 promoted circulation of reading matter among people who were blind
1920	P.L. 66-236 extended vocational rehabilitation services previously authorized for World War I veterans to civilians
1936	P.L. 74-732 authorized persons who were blind to operate vending stands in federal buildings
1958	P.L. 85-905 allocated federal funds for the purchase of captioned films and distribution of them through Schools for the Deaf
1963	P.L. 88-164 provided funds to train teachers for all disabilities and establish research and demonstration projects to study methods for educating exceptional children
1968	P.L. 90-247, Elementary and Secondary Education Amendments, expanded the instructional media program to include production and distribution of educational media for use by individuals with disabilities
1973	P.L. 93-112 guaranteed rights to education and employment through section 504 of the Rehabilitation Amendments
1975	P.L. 94-142 guaranteed the rights of all children with disabilities to a free and appropriate public education
1983	P.L. 98-199 amended P.L. 94-142 to provide additional emphasis on parent education and preschool, secondary, and postsecondary programs for children and youth with disabilities
1986	P.L. 99-506 amended the Rehabilitation Act of 1973 by adding Section 508, which required accessibility to computers and other electronic office equipment in places of federal employment
1987	P.L. 99-457 amended the handicapped amendments of 1986, Part G, and established the Technology, Educational Media and Materials program for the purpose of enhancing research and development advances and efforts
1988	P.L. 100-407, The Technology-Related Assistance Act for Individuals with Disabilities (Tech Act), provided funding for statewide systems and services to provide assistive technology devices and services to individuals with disabilities
1990	P.L. 101-476, Education of the Handicapped Amendments, included technology provisions for students with disabilities
1990	P.L. 101-336, American with Disabilities Act, defined protections for individuals with disabilities and mandated accessibility
1990	P.L. 101-431, Television Decoder Circuitry Act, required built-in closed caption decoders in all new television sets with 13 inch screens (or larger) manufactured or sold in the United States after July 1, 1993
1996	P.L. 104-104 mandated that telecommunication systems and devices must be accessible for individuals with disabilities and provided funds for schools and libraries to access telecommunications at special rates (e-rate)

(continued next page)

Table 2. Major Federal Legislation Related to Technology (continued)

Year	Legislation
1997	P.L. 105-17, Reauthorization of the Individuals with Disabilities Education Act, mandated that every IEP team consider assistive technology when planning for the individualized educational needs of students with disabilities
1998	P.L. 105-394 extended funding of the 1988 Tech Act to assist states in promoting awareness about assistive technology, provide technical assistance, outreach, and foster interagency coordination
2001	P.L. 107-110, No Child Left Behind Act, revised the 1965 Elementary and Secondary Education Act providing incentives to use technology in the education of students and their teachers

means any service that directly assists a child with a disability in the selection, acquisition, or use of an assistive technology device. Such term includes —

(A) the evaluation of the needs of such child, including a functional evaluation of the child in the child's customary environment;

(B) purchasing, leasing, or otherwise providing for the acquisition of assistive technology devices by such child;

(C) selecting, designing, fitting, customizing, adapting, applying, maintaining, repairing, or replacing of assistive technology devices;

(D) coordinating and using other therapies, interventions, or services with assistive technology devices, such as those associated with existing education and rehabilitation plans and programs;

(E) training or technical assistance for such child, or, where appropriate, the family of such child; and

(F) training or technical assistance for professionals (including individuals providing education and rehabilitation services), employers, or other individuals who provide services to, employ, or are otherwise substantially involved in the major life functions of such child. (www.ed.gov/offices/OSERS/Policy/IDEA/the_law.html; pp. 8-9.

Space limitations preclude a thorough explication of the many technology-related projects that have been supported by the federal government through discretionary funds provided to various government agencies. The federal agency that has been the most active in supporting technology initiatives for people with disabilities is the Office of Special Education Programs (OSEP) in the Office of Special Education and Rehabilitative Services in the U.S. Department of Education (www.ed.gov/about/offices/list/osers/osep/about.html).

Recognizing the need for persons who have the knowledge and skills necessary to implement technology applications in special education, the Research to Practice Division in OSEP has supported numerous projects over the years to fund technology training programs for teachers, administrators, leadership personnel, and parents.

Many of the technology advances that have occurred over the years would not have been possible without federal support. Legislators and professionals in the executive branch of the federal government should be commended for their past support of technology initiatives and should be strongly encouraged to continue their efforts. The results of past federal initiatives have paid rich dividends to people with disabilities. Likewise, valuable technology initiatives, too numerous to mention here, have been developed over the years by state legislatures.

Perspectives about the Impact of the SEIMC Network

The early 1960s saw a dramatic growth of public school programs for students with disabilities. As the number and types of such programs expanded, it became necessary to improve access to instructional materials, media, and technology by special education teachers. In 1964, the federal government funded two prototype Special Education Instructional Materials Centers (SEIMCs) to explore ways to make instructional technologies more accessible to special education teachers. The viability of the SEIMCs was quickly recognized, and a national network of centers was established by the mid-1960s. (See the December, 1968, special issue of *Exceptional Children* for more details.) The SEIMC Network eventually consisted of 14 regional SEIMCs, four Regional Media Centers for the Deaf, the Council for Exceptional Children (CEC) ERIC Clearinghouse, a Network Coordinating Office, and numerous affiliated state and local centers covering the entire United States and trust territories.

The primary focus of the SEIMC Network was to provide practical information and resources to support the instruction of students with disabilities. Centers in the network performed a variety of functions, including the loan of instructional media and materials, dissemination of related information, development and evaluation of instructional materials, inservice training of teachers, materials information storage and retrieval, and the development of locally accessible Instructional Materials Centers.

Over the ensuing years, the SEIMC Network was disbanded as special education teacher preparation programs improved, state and local instructional support systems became more viable, and commercial vendors provided more instructional materials, The network produced a lasting legacy, however. Following are several of the more notable outcomes:

- In response to the need for a practical journal for special education teachers, *TEACHING Exceptional Children* was conceptualized by SEIMC Network personnel and the first issue was produced in the fall of 1968 (Blackhurst, 1968). Published by CEC, that journal continues to be distributed to the more than 50,000 of its members and to most major professional libraries.

- SEIMC personnel established the Association for Special Education Technology (ASET) as a Special Interest Group of the Association for Educational Communications and Technology (AECT) in 1972.

- ASET published the first issue of the *Journal of Special Education Technology* (JSET) in March, 1978.

- ASET affiliated with CEC as its Technology and Media (TAM) Division in 1984 and received its official division charter in 1989. TAM has become the major professional organization for people interested in technology applications in special education.

- Responsibility for the publication of JSET was assumed by TAM. The journal has become the major outlet for the publication of professional articles and research reports related to special education technology.

- A large number of professional personnel emerged from the SEIMC Network who have become researchers, teacher educators, policymakers, and leaders who are advocates for the use of technology in special education.

Many of the current uses of technology-particularly instructional technology-in special education can trace their roots to work that was initiated in the SEIMC Network. These include activities associated with computer-assisted instruction, distance education, accessing electronic databases of information to support instruction, anchored instruction, multimedia instructional programs, and the use of communication satellites and telecommunication systems for delivering instruction.

Perspectives about the Role of Theory, Research, and Practice

A goal of the authors of the chapters in this book is to base their content and recommendations on research evidence, to the greatest extent possible. Due to the relative recency of many technology applications, however, the empirical research base that can be called upon for this purpose is rather small.

However, there are many different types of research. For example, much of the information presented in this chapter is based on historical research. Information later in the chapter is based on an accumulation of years of basic research related to human development.

In lieu of a comprehensive research base, several of the concepts presented in this book are derived from theories. As illustrated in Figure 1, there are strong interrelationships among theory, research, and practice.

In the simplest definition, theories are speculations and principles that can be used to explain or predict phenomena. Good special education teachers, for example, use techniques based upon theories of learning and theories of instruction when teaching their students.

A theory also can be used to generate hypotheses that can be tested by research. The results of such research may provide evidence that supports the theory, which, in turn, strengthens the theory. On the other hand, research may produce results that cause the theory to be revised, or rejected. Thus, there is a strong interrelationship between theory and research.

Considerable research is conducted in laboratory settings where researchers can exert control over the variables they want to study. It is easier to manipulate variables in the psychology lab or educational clinic than in classrooms. However, it is critical that theories be tested in the real world (e.g., classrooms, community settings, and the workplace) to see whether or not they work.

Theory and research, then, serve as the foundation for classroom practices. In return, the results of research conducted in labs and in classrooms can have an impact on the development and revision of theories of learning and instruction. Following is an example of the relationship between a theory of learning, applied research, and classroom practice related to instructional technology:

Figure 1. The relationships among theory, research, and practice.

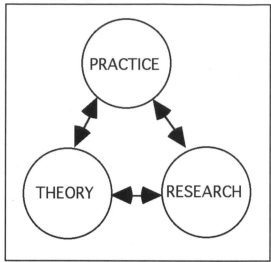

Example of the Relationships among Theory, Research, and Practice

There is a theory that students progress through a series of stages: (a) They learn new knowledge or skills during the acquisition stage of learning; (b) After initial learning takes place, they move to the proficiency stage where they improve their speed or fluency in responding; (c) In the generalization stage they apply what they have learned in other contexts; (d) Retention and memory are addressed in the maintenance stage; and (e) Adaptation of what they have learned to new circumstances occurs in the application stage (Haring, Lovitt, Eaton, & Hansen, 1978).

A special education teacher, Ima Wonder, was interested in applying the theory about stages of learning to the selection of computer software for instructing her students in math. As a result, she selected tutorial software for students who were in the acquisition stage of learning. She used drill and practice software in the proficiency stage. Educational games were used as her students moved into the generalization stage. She applied testing software in the maintenance stage; and problem-solving software was used in the application stage.

Ms. Wonder found that her students performed successfully at each stage; therefore, she obtained data that supported the theory about stages of learning. She also developed stronger faith in the validity of the theory and was more likely to apply it again to math and the other subjects she taught.

The above example is an illustration of an action research project. Teachers are encouraged to conduct such research within their classrooms because they can contribute to the evaluation of theories and provide data that can support their instructional efforts.

Additionally, the application of theory can reduce the possibility of making incorrect instructional decisions. For example, one of the most frequent mistakes teachers make when integrating computer software into the curriculum is to use inappropriate software for their students' learning stage. The biggest culprit is the use of drill and practice, instead of tutorial, software when the student is in the early acquisition stage of learning. Attention to theories of learning and theories of instruction can help to reduce such errors and result in more effective instruction.

Not only are theories useful for guiding the selection and use of computer-assisted instruction, they are extremely useful to those who develop computer-based teaching materials. For example, theories about situated cognition (Cognition and Technology Group at Vanderbilt Learning Technology Center, 1993a, 1993b) have led to the development of hypermedia programs that include video examples that serve as conceptual anchors for learners. Research has shown that such programs are both effective in teaching children (Hasselbring et al., 1989) and in providing pre- and inservice training for professionals (Blackhurst & Morse, 1996). Further, theories about near-errorless teaching procedures, such as the constant time delay response prompting procedure, have led to the development of computer software for teaching spelling to students with learning disabilities (e.g., Edwards et al., 1995; Stevens et al., 1991).

The Role of Conceptual Models

Sometimes, theories are used to generate conceptual models, which are often represented as graphical figures that display variables and their interrelationships, as illustrated in Figure 1. Conceptual models have many practical implications for practitioners, including the following:

- Models can serve as the conceptual underpinning for a given set of activities.

- They can provide a graphic representation of the variables associated with the topic of interest and their interrelationships.

- Models can help to simplify and explain complex phenomena.

- They may give direction to the sequence of action steps needed to successfully complete an activity.

- They facilitate communication among staff who use them and are helpful in communicating information about the topic of interest to others.

- They are useful in helping to define needed policies, procedures, and activities and for assigning job responsibilities.

- Some planning models can be used to define activities, events, constraints, sequences, and timelines that can then be used for project planning and monitoring.

- Conceptual models can be used to identify elements of an activity that require evaluation.

Model building is consistent with the earlier conceptualization about the use of systematic approaches for the design of instruction presented in the sections related to instructional technology and the technology of teaching. The literature contains a number of useful theoretical models that have implications for special educators. In addition to the model that will be presented later in this chapter, see, for example, models for diagnostic teaching (Cartwright & Cartwright (1972), designing special education personnel preparation programs (Blackhurst, 1977), using progressive time delay with students who have severe developmental disabilities (Gast & Schuster, 1993), making decisions about assistive technology (Scherer, 2004; Zabala, 1995), and designing special education continuing professional development programs (Blackhurst, 2001).

With respect to the value of theory, one thing seems clear: The most effective special educators are those who have a thorough grounding in theories of learning and instruction and use them to guide their instructional activities. These educators are able to articulate a rationale for their teaching procedures; they exhibit self-confidence in their abilities; they are comfortable and secure in discharging their professional responsibilities; and, most important, their students learn.

A number of conceptual models are included in this book. Some are represented graphically, others are expressed in narrative descriptions. The next section of this chapter presents a theoretical perspective that can be used to guide the planning and delivery of special education services with an emphasis on considerations that relate to the use of technology. When examining that model, and others in this book, reflect on the above points to see how they relate to the application of the concepts represented in each model.

A Functional Perspective about Technology

Unfortunately, many decisions about applications of technology in special education are "device driven." That is, as new devices appear on the market, it is not uncommon to find consumers, parents, vendors, and professionals advocate strongly for their acquisition and use with different students—often with less than satisfactory results (cf. Bell, Rylance, Bliss, & Blackhurst, 2000). Instead of getting caught up in the allure of devices and new products with intriguing features, a more appropriate perspective is to make decisions about the use of technology based upon functions that the prospective users must perform in response to demands that are placed upon them from the environment.

Human Functions to Consider

Following are descriptions of seven areas of human function that can be considered when making decisions about the design and delivery of special education, technology applications, and related services. Examples are provided to illustrate some of the technology devices and services that can be used to respond to demands associated with each function.

Existence

Functions associated with existence are those basic responses that are needed to sustain life. They include eating, elimination, bathing, dressing, grooming, and sleeping. Special education services, particularly those for preschool children and individuals with severe disabilities, may focus on teaching children to perform such functions. Further, special devices such as adapted eating utensils, dressing aids, adapted toilet seats, button hooks, and grooming aids may be provided to assist children in performing those functions. Assistance in using such devices may also be provided by occupational therapists.

Communication

The reception, internalization, and expression of information, such as visual and auditory reception, oral and written expression, and social interaction are functions included in the category of communication. Communication aids, speech synthesizers, captioned video, telephone amplifiers, hearing aids, picture boards, writing and drawing aids, pointers, and alternative input and output devices for computers reflect some of the devices that can be used to facilitate communication. Augmentative communication services, social skills training, and the services of speech-language pathologists and audiologists might be needed to support communication functions.

Body Support, Protection, and Positioning

Some children need assistance to maintain a stable position or support or to protect portions of their body, such as standing, sitting, alignment, stabilizing, and preventing injury from falls. Braces, support harnesses, slings, prone standers, furniture adaptations, and protective headgear are some of the useful devices in this functional category, as are the services of a physical therapist. Other medical personnel also may provide supporting services for functions in this category.

Travel and Mobility

Functions in this category include the ability to move horizontally, vertically, or laterally, such as crawling, walking, using stairs, lateral and vertical transfers to and from chairs and beds, and navigating the environment. Wheelchairs, special lifts, canes, walkers, scooters, specially adapted tricycles, and crutches can be used to support these functions. Vendors of such products and specialists, such as those who provide mobility training for children who are blind, may be called upon to provide training and other services associated with this category.

Environmental interaction

The environment can be adapted or the person can adapt to the environment. This category includes functions associated with these adaptations as seen in the performance of many of the activities of daily living, both indoors and outdoors. Examples of functions include driving, food preparation, operation of appliances, and alteration of the living space.

It may be necessary to make a number of modifications to school facilities to accommodate functions in this category. For example, enlarged door knobs, automatic door openers, special switches for controlling computers, remote-control devices, grabbers to reach items on high shelves, chalkboards and desks that can be raised so that a student in a wheelchair can use them, hand-operated automobile driving controls, and ramps to accommodate wheelchairs may be required. Often, assistive technology specialists are called upon to provide help with environmental adaptations, and rehabilitation engineers can design and fabricate special adaptations to the environment.

Education, Transition, and Rehabilitation

Functions in this category include those associated with school activities and preparing for new school settings or post-school environments, including employment. Activities related to this area include assessment, learning, access to the general education curriculum, creative and performing arts, using instructional materials, and preparing for new environments, among others. Solutions to functional problems in this category may include adapted instructional materials, educational software, computer adaptations, community-based instruction, creative arts therapy, and other related services.

Special education teachers and general education teachers, speech-language pathologists, rehabilitation counselors, psychologists, and others may be involved in providing direct services to students. In addition, numerous technologies may be used within the context of schools, such as computer-assisted instruction, audio instructional tapes, print magnifiers, book holders, assistive technologies, and other materials and equipment that can facilitate learning.

Sports, Fitness, and Recreation

Functions associated with group and individual sports, physical fitness, hobby and craft activities, and productive use of leisure time are included in this category. The services of a person trained in adapted physical education may provide a valuable resource in this area. Programs such as Special Olympics, adaptive aquatics and adaptive horseback riding also relate to this function. In addition, a wide array of equipment and devices can facilitate functions in this category, including balls that emit audible beeps so that children who are blind can hear them, specially designed skis for skiers with one leg, braille playing cards, modified workout machines, and wheelchairs for basketball players who cannot walk or run.

Many more examples of technology services and devices could be provided, but the above should be sufficient to illustrate the importance of attending to human functions when planning and implementing special education, technology applications, and related services. Consistent with this perspective, it is more relevant to focus on the functions that a student can perform and those in which difficulty is experienced than to focus on a diagnostic label or disability category when planning special education services. Such an orientation enables teachers and those providing related services to more directly address a child's needs.

A Unifying Functional Model

As noted earlier, IDEA requires that assistive

technology be considered for each student with an IEP. As described in the section on federal initiatives, the specific language in IDEA addresses the concept of "function." The definition of assistive technology devices includes the phrase, *improve functional capabilities of a child with disabilities*. The definition of assistive technology services includes this requirement: *The evaluation of the needs of such child, including a functional evaluation of the child in the child's customary environment.*

Nowhere in the federal legislation is an explanation given about the meaning of *functional capabilities* within the context of the legislation or what a *functional evaluation* is. It is the perspective here that the seven functional areas described above provide a framework for considering assistive technology devices and for structuring assistive technology evaluations, thus providing a way to meet the intent of the legal mandates of IDEA. The model described in this section expands on this notion by illustrating how decisionmaking about technology can be made within a context of human function.

When decisions are being made about the provision of special education services, the real issue is the problem the child has in functioning within his or her environment. For example, a preschooler with cerebral palsy may lack the fine muscle control that will permit her to fasten buttons so that she can get dressed independently. A boy with a visual impairment may be unable to use printed material that is being used for instruction in an English class. Another student, due to unknown causes, may be unable to solve math problems. Similarly, a child who has been in an automobile accident may have sustained a severe head injury that has impaired her ability to speak clearly.

In each of these cases, an environmental demand has been placed on the child to perform some function that he or she finds difficult to execute because of a set of unique circumstances or restrictions in functional capability caused by a lack of personal resources. For example, these children lack the physical or mental capability to button, read, calculate, or speak.

All of us face situations daily in which environmental demands are placed on us. Our goal is to understand the processes involved and relate them to the lives of exceptional children who face more complex and restrictive situations. It is necessary to know a variety of things, such as the nature of the demands that are being placed on the student from the environment and how those demands create the requirements to perform different human functions, such as learning, walking, talking, seeing, and hearing. It is also important to know how such requirements are—or are not—being met by the student and how factors such as the student's perceptions and the availability of personal resources such as intelligence, sight, hearing, and mobility can affect the responses the student can make. In addition, it is important to understand how availability of external supports, such as special education, different types of therapy, and technology can impact the student's ability to produce functional responses to the environmental demands.

Although each child is unique, the common challenge is to identify and apply the best possible array of special education, technology, and related services that will provide support, adjustment, or compensation for the child's functional needs or deficits. A variety of responses may be appropriate. For example, Velcro fasteners may be used to replace buttons on garments for the child having difficulty with buttoning. Braille or audio materials may be provided for the child who cannot read conventional print. The student who has difficulty calculating may require specialized, intense direct math instruction, while a computerized device that produces speech may enable the child who cannot talk to communicate.

The unifying functional model displayed in Figure 2 was developed to illustrate the different elements of life associated with a functional approach to special education and related services, including the provision of various technologies. When examining this model, note that the items in each box are meant to be illustrative, not all-inclusive.

The following example illustrates the various elements of the model, their interrelationships, and how the model can serve as a framework for making decisions about technology: Joe is a high school sophomore with learning disabilities, who is planning to attend college.

Figure 2. A unifying functional model.

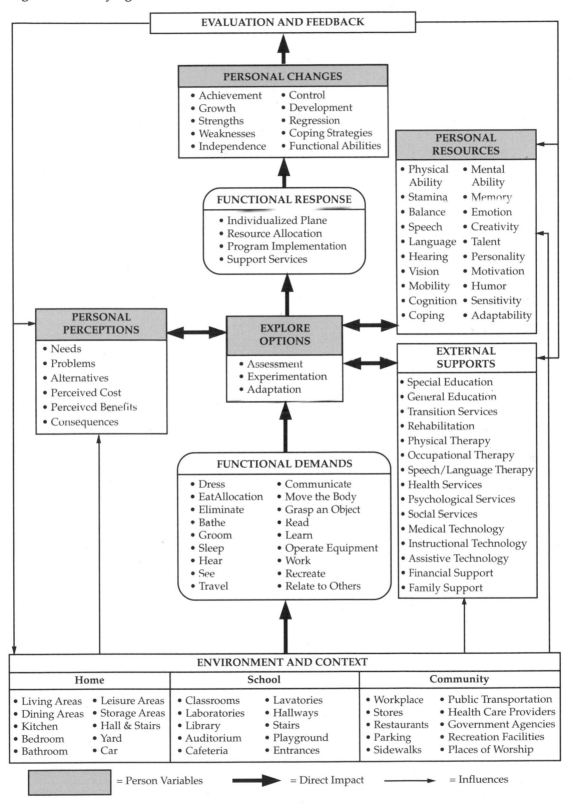

Although he has above-average intellectual ability, Joe experiences difficulty with written composition and spelling, plus his handwriting is difficult to read. His reading rate is slow, and he experiences some difficulty in comprehending written material, but his understanding of spoken information is excellent. Joe receives most of his education in general education classes with support from a special education resource teacher, who also consults with Joe's other teachers about ways to ensure that Joe will succeed in his college preparatory courses. Those responsible for developing a transition plan for special education also have been involved in making decisions about ways to best prepare him for his college experience.

Application of the model begins with the box at the bottom of Figure 2, labeled *environment and context*. Those involved in transition planning for Joe are concerned with two environments. One is his prospective college environment, the other is his current high school environment. The context is that he will eventually find himself in an academic setting that requires certain skills that must be applied independently. He must develop those skills and learn how to apply them while he is still in high school.

The environment and context place *functional demands* on all of us. Although a host of issues could be addressed related to the demands placed on Joe, those related to technology will be highlighted here, since that is the focus of this book. The demands placed on Joe will include the ability to read and comprehend the written materials that he will encounter in college. Due to the amount of reading that is required, he will have to be able to read that material quite rapidly. He also will have to prepare written compositions, reports, and answers to examination questions. Furthermore, it will be incumbent upon him to prepare written materials that are legible and have correct spelling.

In preparing to make responses to environmental demands, people *explore options* that will enable them to respond in a constructive fashion. This typically involves assessments, experimentation with different options, and making adaptations. In Joe's case, a variety of technology-based options might be considered

to assist him in meeting the demands described. For example, to increase his reading rate, speed reading programs or the use of machines designed to increase reading speed, such as tachistoscopes (Blackhurst, 1967), may be explored. The possibility of obtaining books recorded for people with visual impairments or reading difficulties as an alternative to reading might be considered. Another option would be to use a scanner to convert printed text to computer files that could be read aloud through speech synthesis. The use of hand-held spelling checkers and word-processing computer programs that incorporate spell checking features might be pursued. The possibility of obtaining instruction in the use of learning strategies to help him develop good study habits, such as those described by Deshler and Schumaker (1986), also might be investigated.

One's *personal perceptions* play a big part in exploring response options and deciding which option to accept. For example, some people may perceive that a need exists or that they have a problem; others may not. People also have perceptions about the psychological, physical, and monetary costs of different alternatives and their consequences.

A second factor in making decisions about response strategies relates to the *personal resources* that people have available to them. These relate to their abilities in areas such as physical functioning, cognitive ability, intelligence, motivation, speech, and other personal dimensions that can be used in producing actions.

A third factor influencing decisions relates to the *external supports* a person has available. Supports are resources available to assist individuals in responding to environmental demands. For example, family members can provide both emotional and physical support. They may also be able to provide interpretations of their child's or a sibling's personal perceptions when a disability interferes with the ability to communicate reactions and preferences. Social service agencies can provide supportive services, such as instruction about ways to cope with environmental pressures. Health insurance agencies can sometimes provide financial support for the purchase of assistive and adaptive devices.

Finally, special education and transition services are another major form of external support, as are the use of technology devices and the delivery of various technology services.

To continue with the example, in the area of personal perceptions, Joe realizes that he has a problem with reading, composition, spelling, and handwriting. He also has a fierce desire to do things for himself and "to fit in" with his fellow students.

In the area of personal resources, Joe and his teachers know that, although he has several learning problems, he is bright enough to master course content. He is particularly adept at learning and remembering information that is presented orally.

In exploring options for external supports, Joe decides against the scanner and speech synthesizer due to the complexity and cost of the equipment, the time involved in scanning text and converting it to computer files, and the possibility that its use might draw undue attention on the part of other students to his problems. Although this might be a sound option later, the decision is made to start with other options that appear more realistic at the moment. (Note that this also is an example of employing the technology continuum as part of the decisionmaking process.)

The *functional response* is the result of the assessment, experimentation, and decision making that was just described. In Joe's case, this will be instruction about how to efficiently use a tape recorder to play back and learn from audio tapes of recorded texts. (This option was selected because Joe could qualify for the federal Talking Book program sponsored by the National Library Service for the Blind and Physically Handicapped at the Library of Congress, lcweb.loc.gov/nls/nls.html, that would enable him to obtain audio recordings of books he would be using in college.) It also was decided to provide instruction on how to use a word-processing computer program that is equipped with a spelling checker, text-to-speech converter, and grammar checker. His resource teacher also will teach him how to use learning strategies to facilitate studying. These provisions are written into the transition plan that is incorporated into his IEP, the special equipment and software is located, instruction

about its use is implemented, and Joe incorporates its use into his school activities.

As a result of the functional response to the environmental demand, *personal changes* occur. Such changes may be dramatic or subtle, depending upon the nature of the environmental demand, the decisions that were made, and the nature of the resources that were expended and the supports provided. Thus, following evaluation after the implementation of the transition goals within his IEP, it was found that Joe improved his ability to function in his current academic environment by using audiotapes and computer software productivity tools to participate in his classes.

Feedback (as represented by the arrows emanating from the *evaluation and feedback* element of the model) also may lead to the selection of additional technologies. For example, word prediction software and the use of macro programs that automatically type frequently used words and phrases may be added to his repertoire. As Joe matures and gains confidence in his abilities, he may elect to experiment with scanning devices that will enable him to convert printed text to audio formats. In addition, as he demonstrates success to his family, their perceptions may change, resulting in their provision of additional external support for his use of technology.

As illustrated, the process represented in the functional model becomes a dynamic one, in which demands constantly change, as do personal perceptions, personal resources, external supports, and examination of alternative solutions. The result is changing functional responses to the environmental demands that lead to personal changes which, in turn, have the potential for modifying all of the other factors illustrated in the model.

As presented in this two-dimensional format, the model represents a "snapshot" of a person's situation at a single moment in time. As such, it does not reflect the fact that changes are constantly occurring in each component and that those changes have the potential for impacting on the other components and, subsequently, on other functional responses made by the individual.

The final feature to note in the model is the shaded areas in Figure 2. These represent personal variables. As just noted, the model, as presented here, is two-dimensional. However, the central focus is the individual and the decisions that are involved in assisting that individual in responding to environmental demands. That process is clearly complex, encompassing more than two dimensions.

Implications of the functional model. Several implications can be drawn from the unifying functional model in Figure 2. For example, it places the various types of technology devices and services into proper perspective: namely, as external supports. It helps us understand how a person functions, the factors that are important in making decisions, and how the decisions that are made can impact on the individual. It also identifies many of the factors that should be taken into consideration when making decisions about the nature of services that are provided to a given student. In addition, it illustrates interrelationships of component factors and their potential for influencing each other. Although the model does not define cause-and-effect relationships, it does help us realize that many factors are involved and that they interact in complex ways.

The model provides direction for those making referrals for technology (and other) services. The individuals who make referrals should be aware of the model and its components. Furthermore, they should be encouraged to obtain as much information as possible about the various factors included in the model and provide data about them as part of the referral process.

The model can also guide prereferral activities, assessment, and instructional planning activities. By attending to the various factors in the model, and others that may be added, those assessing children who have been referred for technology services can identify variables that should be evaluated for their potential impact on a person. Assessments of those variables, in turn, should generate data that can aid in making decisions about the types of technology and related services that could help an individual respond successfully to environmental demands. Finally, such decisions should result in incorporating technology services in the IEPs for students enrolled in special education programs.

Source of the model. The functional model described here evolved from more than 25 years of research and development activities by Melichar (1978). Although the model was originally developed to guide the delivery of assistive technology services (Melichar & Blackhurst, 1993), it has become clear since the model was conceptualized that it can be used to guide the delivery of *all* special education and related services.

The original model is explained in more detail, with examples of its application to people with different types of disabilities, in an introductory special education textbook (Blackhurst & Berdine, 1993). It also has been used to as a framework for aligning technology with transition competencies (Blackhurst, Lahm, Harrison, & Chandler, 1999), and has been described as a way to make decisions about a broad array of technologies for people of different ages with disabilities (Blackhurst & Lahm, 2000). Its most recent revisions were performed by members of the University of Kentucky Assistive Technology Project and are reflected in the description presented here.

Personal Perspectives about the Future

When I first wrote about the implications of high technology for special education more than 35 years ago (Blackhurst, 1965), it was fun speculating about what the future might hold. Although some of the devices I speculated about eventually were developed in one form or another, I missed the mark badly on others because I did not anticipate the development of personal computers and the many marvelous applications that were developed as extensions to them.

In projecting future technology developments as we move further into the twenty-first century, only a few things can be said with some certainty: On the high-tech side, microprocessors will continue to get smaller and faster; telecommunication systems will be developed with greater capacity and speed; costs of computers and related equipment will decline; software developers will develop "smarter" software; computer memory and file storage requirements will increase; interconnectivity among classrooms and schools will improve; and products will be developed that we cannot even conceptualize at the present time.

On the no-tech side, people will become more knowledgeable about the various technologies and their application; more attention will be paid to the implications of technology when planning IEPs for individual students; technology specialists and support systems will become more available in schools; more technology inservice training programs will be provided for special education teachers and related personnel; colleges and universities will add instruction about technology for people who are preparing for special education positions and those who are involved in providing related services. All of these high-tech through no-tech developments auger well for special education programs and for people with disabilities who will be the users of technology and the recipients of technology services.

From a hardware and software standpoint, ingenious computer scientists, creative engineers, clever software programmers, and "talented tinkerers" have produced—and will continue to produce—an amazing array of low-tech to high-tech devices that can help people who have severe medical problems to stay alive and function in our society, enable people who have difficulty speaking to communicate, let people who cannot hear use telecommunication systems, provide children who have difficulty learning with effective instruction, help people who cannot see listen to machines that can read for them, assist people who have limited muscle control to operate machinery and appliances, and aid people who cannot walk in moving from place to place,

Basic research conducted at Duke University, and reported in the following excerpt from an article by Weiss (2003, p. A3), provides just a glimmer of what the future might hold.

Monkeys Move Robotic Arm with Thoughts

Scientists in North Carolina have built a brain implant that lets monkeys control a robotic arm with their thoughts, marking the first time that mental intentions have been harnessed to move a mechanical object.

The technology could someday allow people with paralyzing spinal cord injuries to operate machines or tools with their thoughts as naturally as others today do with their hands. It might even allow some paralyzed people to move their own arms or legs again, by transmitting the brain's directions not to a machine but directly to the muscles in those latent limbs....

The...monkeys, with wires running from their brains to a robotic arm, were able to use their thoughts to make the arm perform tasks. Before long...they will upgrade...so they can transmit their mental commands to machines wirelessly....

The new work is the first in which any animal has learned to use its brain to move a robotic device in all directions in space and to perform a mixture of interrelated movements, such as reaching toward an object, grasping it and adjusting the grip strength depending on how heavy the object is.

The implications of similar future research endeavors for people with various types of physical disabilities should be apparent.

Finally, it should be noted that many of the current technology applications and practices in special education reflect the "state of the art." A major challenge facing us is to move those applications to the point where they reflect the "state of the science." We must continue to conduct research and study the application of technology devices and services in objective ways so that we can make informed decisions about their use.

Acknowledgment: Preparation of this chapter was supported, in part, by the Department of Special Education and Rehabilitation Counseling, University of Kentucky, and by the National Assistive Technology Research Institute, which is supported by Cooperative Agreement #H327G000004 from the Research to Practice Division, Office of Special Education Programs, U.S. Department of Education. The information presented in the chapter does not necessarily reflect the official position of the University of Kentucky or the U.S. Department of Education.

References

Alberto, P. A., & Troutman, A. C. (1995). *Applied behavior analysis for teachers* (4th ed.). Columbus, OH: Merrill.

Aldinger, L. E., Warger, C. L., & Eavy, P. W. (1995). Expert systems software in special education. *TEACHING Exceptional Children, 27*(2), 58-62.

Algozzine, R., & Ysseldyke, J. (1992). *Strategies and tactics for effective instruction.* Longmont, CO: Sopris West.

Alliance for Technology Access. (2001). *Computer resources for people with disabilities: A guide to exploring today's assistive technology* (3rd ed.). Alameda, CA: Hunter House.

Bain, B. K., & Leger, D. (Eds.). (1997). *Assistive technology: An interdisciplinary approach.* New York: Churchill Livingston.

Batshaw, M. L., & Perret, Y. M. (1992). *Children with disabilities: A medical primer.* Baltimore: Paul H. Brookes Publishing Co.

Bausch, M. E. (1999). *A comparison of standard computer keyboard input to alternate keyboard input when using the constant time delay response prompting procedure during computerized mathematics instruction.* Unpublished doctoral dissertation, University of Kentucky, Lexington.

Behrmann, M. (1984). *Handbook of microcomputers in special education.* San Diego, CA: College-Hill Press.

Behrmann, M. (1988). *Integrating computers into the curriculum: A handbook for special educators.* San Diego, CA: College-Hill Press.

Bell, J. K., Rylance, B., Bliss, T., & Blackhurst, A. E. (2000). Caroline never smiles. In T. Bliss & J. Mazur (Eds.), *Elementary and middle school teachers in the midst of reform: Common thread cases* (pp. 57-84). Upper Saddle River, NJ: Prentice Hall Simon and Shuster.

Beukelman, D. R., & Mirenda, P. (1998). *Augmentative and alternate communication: Management of severe communication disorders in children and adults* (2nd ed.). Baltimore: Paul H. Brookes Publishing Co.

Blackhurst, A. (1997). *Teaching letter recognition to preschool children with and without disabilities using constant time delay via embedded instruction.* Unpublished masters thesis, University of Kentucky, Lexington.

Blackhurst, A. E. (1965). Technology in special education - some implications. *Exceptional Children, 31*, 449-456.

Blackhurst, A. E. (1967). Tachistoscopic training as a supplement to reading instruction for educable mentally retarded children. *Education and Training of the Mentally Retarded, 2*, 121-125.

Blackhurst, A. E. (1968). Dissemination: TEACHING exceptional children. *Exceptional Children, 35*, 315-317.

Blackhurst, A. E. (1977). Competency-based special education personnel preparation. In R. D. Kneedler & S. G. Tarver (Eds.), *Changing perspectives in special education* (pp. 156-182). Columbus, OH: Charles E. Merrill.

Blackhurst, A. E. (1978). Using telecommunication systems for delivering in-service training. *Viewpoints in Teaching and Learning, 54*, 27-40.

Blackhurst, A. E. (1997). Perspectives on technology in special education. *TEACHING Exceptional Children, 29*(5), 41-48.

Blackhurst, A. E. (2001). Designing technology professional development programs. In J. Woodward & L. Cuban (Eds.), *Technology, curriculum and professional development: Adapting schools to meet the needs of students with disabilities* (pp. 138-186). Thousand Oaks, CA: Corwin Press.

Blackhurst, A. E., & Berdine, W. H. (Eds.) (1993). *An introduction to special education.* New York: HarperCollins.

Blackhurst, A. E., & Cross, D. P. (1993). Technology in special education. In A. E. Blackhurst & W. H. Berdine (Eds.). *An introduction to special education* (3rd ed., pp. 77-103). New York: HarperCollins.

Blackhurst, A. E., & Edyburn, D. L. (2000). A brief history of special education technology. *Special Education Technology Practice, 2*(1), 21-35.

Blackhurst, A. E., Hales, R. M., & Lahm, E. A. (1998). Using an education server software system to deliver special education instruction via the World Wide Web. *Journal of Special Education Technology, 13*(4), 78-98.

Blackhurst, A. E., & Hofmeister, A. M. (1980). Technology in special education. In L. Mann & D. Sabatino (Eds.), *Fourth review of special education* (pp. 199-228). New York: Grune and Stratton.

Blackhurst, A. E. & Lahm, E. A. (2000). Foundations of technology and exceptionality. In J. Lindsey (Ed.) *Technology and Exceptional Individuals* (3rd ed, pp. 3-45). Austin, TX: PRO-ED.

Blackhurst, A. E., Lahm, E. A., Harrison, E. M., & Chandler, W. G. (1999). A framework for aligning technology with transition competencies. *Career Development for Exceptional Individuals, 22*(2), 153-183.

Blackhurst, A. E., & Morse, T. E. (1996). Using anchored instruction to teach about assistive technology. *Focus on Autism and Other Developmental Disabilities, 11*, 131-141.

Boone, R., & Higgins, K. (Eds.). (1992). *Multimedia: TAM topical guide #1*. Reston, VA: Council for Exceptional Children.

Bowe, F. G. (1984). *Personal computers and special needs*. Berkeley, CA: Sybex.

Carnine, D. W., Silbert, J., & Kameenui, E. J. (1990). *Direct instruction reading* (2nd. ed.). Columbus, OH: Merrill.

Cartwright, G. P., & Cartwright, C. A. (1972). Gilding the lily: Comments on the training-based model. *Exceptional Children, 39*(3), 231-234.

Cavalier, A. R., & Ferretti, R. P. (1996). Talking instead of typing: Alternate access to computers via speech recognition technology. *Focus on Autism and Other Developmental Disabilities, 11*, 79-85.

Chambers, A. C. (1997) *Has technology been considered? A guide for IEP teams*. Albuquerque, NM: The Council of Administrators of Special Education.

Church, G., & Bender, M. (1989). *Teaching with computers: A curriculum for special educators*. Boston, MA: College Hill Press.

Church, G., & Glennen, S. (1992). *The handbook of assistive technology*. San Diego, CA: Singular Publishing Group.

Cognition and Technology Group at Vanderbilt Learning Technology Center. (1993a). Anchored instruction and situated cognition revisited. *Educational Technology, 33*(3), 52-70.

Cognition and Technology Group at Vanderbilt Learning Technology Center. (1993b). Integrated media: Toward a theoretical frame-work for utilizing their potential. *Journal of Special Education Technology, 12*(2), 75-89.

Commission on Instructional Technology. (1970). *To improve learning: A report to the President and the Congress of the United States*. Washington, DC: U.S. Government Printing Office.

Computer Museum History Center. (2003). *Timeline of computer history*. Available at www.computerhisory.org/timeline/index.page.

Cook, A. M., & Hussey, S. M. (2002). Assistive technologies: Principles and practice (2nd ed.). St. Louis, MO: Mosby.

Council for Exceptional Children (1987). *ERIC/SEP Project on interagency information dissemination*. Reston, VA: Author.

Deshler, D. D., & Schumaker, J. B. (1986). Learning strategies: An instructional alternative for low-achieving adolescents. *Exceptional Children, 52*(6), 583-590.

Edwards, B. J., Blackhurst, A. E., & Koorland, M. A. (1995). Computer-assisted constant time delay prompting to teach abbreviation spelling to adolescents with mild learning disabilities. *Journal of Special Education Technology, 12*(4), 301-311.

Flippo, K. F., Inge, K. J., & Barcus, J. M. (1995). *Assistive technology: A resource for school, work and community*. Baltimore: Paul H. Brookes Publishing Co.

Galvan, J. C., & Scherer, M. J. (1996). *Evaluating, selecting, and using appropriate assistive technology*. Gaithersburg, MD: Aspen.

Gast, D. L., & Schuster, J. W. (1993). Students with severe developmental disabilities. In A. E. Blackhurst & W. H. Berdine (Eds.), *An introduction to special education* (3rd ed., pp. 454-491). New York: HarperCollins.

Golden, D. (1998). *Assistive technology in special education: Policy and practice*. Albuquerque, NM: The Council of Administrators of Special Education.

Goldenberg, E. P., Russell, S. J., & Carter, D. J. (1984). *Computers, education and special needs*. Reading, MA: Addison-Wesley.

Greer, R. D. (1991). Teaching practices to save America's schools: The legacy of B. F. Skinner. *Journal of Behavioral Education, 1*(2), 159-164.

Hales, D. (1999, November 28). Medical miracles in a microchip. *Parade: The Sunday newspaper magazine*, New York: Parade Publications.

Haring, N. G. (1970). The new curriculum design in special education. *Educational Technology, 10,* 24-31.

Haring, N. G., Lovitt, T. C., Eaton, M. D., & Hansen, C. L. (1978). *The fourth R: Research in the classroom.* Columbus, OH: Merrill.

Hasselbring, T. S. with the Cognition and Technology Group at Vanderbilt. (1994). Multimedia environments for developing literacy in at-risk students. In B. Means (Ed.), *Technology and educational reform: The reality behind the promise* (pp. 23-56). San Francisco: Jossey-Bass Inc.

Hasselbring, T. S., Goin, L. I., & Wissick, C. (1989). Making knowledge meaningful: Applications of hypermedia. *Journal of Special Education Technology, 10,* 62-72.

Hofmeister, A. (1984). *Microcomputer applications in the classroom.* New York: Holt, Rinehart, and Winston.

Inge, K. J., & Shepherd, J. (1995). Assistive technology applications and strategies for school system personnel. In K. F. Flippo, K. J. Inge, & J. M. Barcus (Eds.), *Assistive technology: A resource for school, work and community* (pp. 133-166). Baltimore: Paul H. Brooks Publishing Co.

Johnson, D. L. (1987). Computers in the special education classroom. New York: CBS College Publishing.

Lance, W. D. (1973). Technology and media for exceptional learners: Looking ahead. *Exceptional Children, 44,* 92-97.

Lewis, R. B. (1993). *Special education technology.* Pacific Grove, CA: Brooke Cole Publishers.

Lindsey, J. (Ed.) (2000). *Technology and exceptional individuals* (3rd ed.). Austin, TX: PRO-ED.

Lovitt, T. C. (1995). *Tactics for teaching* (2nd ed.). Englewood Cliffs, NJ: Merrill/Prentice Hall.

Ludlow, B. L., & Duff, M. C. (1998). *Distance education and tomorrow's schools.* Bloomington, IN: Phi Delta Kappa Educational Foundation.

Male, M. (1994). *Technology for inclusion: Meeting the special needs of all students* (2nd ed.). Needham Heights, MA: Allyn & Bacon.

Meers, D. T. (1998). *Using the Internet to support teachers in the management of students with challenging behaviors.* Unpublished master's thesis, University of Kentucky, Lexington.

Melichar, J. F. (1978). ISAARE: A description. *AAESPH Review, 3*(4), 259-268.

Melichar, J. F., & Blackhurst, A. E. (1993). *Introduction to a functional approach to assistive technology.* Training module. Lexington, KY: University of Kentucky, Department of Special Education and Rehabilitation Counseling.

Morris, B. (1985). *The world of robotics.* New York: W. H. Smith Publishers.

Nazzaro, J. N. (1977). *Exceptional timetables: Historic events affecting the handicapped and gifted.* Reston, VA: Council for Exceptional Children.

Parette, J. P. (1997). Assistive technology devices and services. *Education and Training in Mental Retardation and Developmental Disabilities, 32*(4), 267-280.

Polsson, K. (1999). *Chronology of events in the history of microcomputers.* Available at: www.islandnet.com/~polsson/comphist.htm

Ray, J. R., & Warden, M. K. (1995). *Technology, computers, and the special needs learner.* Albany, New York: Delmar.

Renne, D. J., & Blackhurst, A. E. (1977). The effect of adjunct auto-instruction in an introductory special education course. *Exceptional Children, 43,* 224-225.

Rose, D., & Meyer, A. (2000). Universal design for learning. *Journal of Special Education Technology. 15*(1), 67-70.

Scherer, M. J. (1993). *Living in the state of stuck: How technology impacts the lives of people with disabilities.* Cambridge, MA: Brookline.

Scherer, M. J. (2004). *Connecting to learn: Educational and assistive technology for people with disabilties.* Washington, DC: American Psychological Association.

Silverman, F. H. (1995). *Communication for the speechless* (3rd ed.). Needham Heights, MA: Allyn & Bacon.

Slaton, D. B., & Lacefield, W. E. (1991). Use of an interactive telecommunications network to deliver inservice education. *Journal of Special Education Technology, 11,* 64-74.

Stevens, K. B., Blackhurst, A. E., & Slaton, D. B. (1991). Teaching memorized spelling with a microcomputer: Time delay and computer-assisted instruction. *Journal of Applied Behavior Analysis, 24,* 153-160.

Taber, F. M. (1983). *Microcomputers in special education: Selection and decision making process.* Reston, VA: Council for Exceptional Children.

Thorkildsen, R. (1994). *Research synthesis on quality and availability of assistive technology devices: Technical Report No. 7.* Eugene, OR: National Center to Improve the Quality of Tools for Educators, University of Oregon. Available at: idea.uoregon.edu/ ~ncite/ documents/techrep/other.html)

Weiss, R. (2003, October 13). Monkeys move robotic arm with thoughts. Lexington, KY: *Lexington Herald Leader,* p. A3.

Wolery, M., Ault, M. J., & Doyle, P. M. (1992). *Teaching students with moderate and severe disabilities: Use of response prompting procedures.* White Plains, New York: Longman.

Wolery, M., Bailey, D. B., & Sugai, G. M. (1988). *Effective teaching: Principles of applied behavior analysis with exceptional students.* Boston, MA: Allyn & Bacon.

Woodward, J., & Cuban, L. (Eds.). (2001). *Technology, curriculum and professional development: Adapting schools to meet the needs of students with disabilities.* Thousand Oaks, CA: Corwin Press.

Zabala, J. (1995). *The SETT framework: Critical issues to consider when making informed assistive technology decisions.* Washington, DC: ERIC Document Reproduction Service (No. ED 381 962).

2

Comprehensive Statewide Programs of Technology-Related Assistance

M. Nell Bailey, Nancy Meidenbauer, Judith Fein, and Beth Mineo Mollica

The Assistive Technology Act of 1998 (P.L. No. 105-395, 112 Stat. 3627) promotes access to assistive technology equipment and assistive technology services for children and adults. Specifically, the Act provides states with federal discretionary grants to assist in the operation of State Assistive Technology (AT) Act Projects. These state AT Act projects maintain "comprehensive statewide programs of technology-related assistance for individuals with disabilities of all ages" (P.L. No. 105-394, 112 Stat. 3632). This terminology is central to an understanding of the intent of this law, which, foremost, is to promote "consumer-responsive" assistive technology programs in states. According to the AT Act, for a state to fulfill the mandate of being consumer-responsive, its assistive technology program must be "equally available to all individuals with disabilities residing in the State, regardless of their type of disability, age, income level, or location of residence in the State, or the type of assistive technology device or assistive technology service required" (P.L. No. 105-394, Stat. 3632). Thus, the law explicitly provides equal access for infants and children, as well as adults. Further, the term "consumer-responsive" requires assistive technology programs to be "easily accessible" and to respond to an individual's AT requirements "in a timely and appropriate manner."

In 2003, all 50 states[1] and the District of Columbia, Puerto Rico, American Samoa, Guam, the Commonwealth of the Northern Mariana Islands, and the U.S. Virgin Islands operated consumer-responsive assistive technology projects funded by federal dollars. The National Institute on Disability and Rehabilitation Research (NIDRR), in the Office of Special Education and Rehabilitative Services of the U.S. Department of Education, administers the federal AT Act program.

Under the AT Act, state AT Act projects must focus on achieving progress in five goal areas: employment, health care, community living, education, and telecommunications/information technology. The act also seeks to build the capacity of other organizations to provide AT equipment and services.

History of the Assistive Technology Act

As mentioned, the goal of the AT act is to increase access to assistive technology devices and services for individuals of all ages and across all types of disabilities. The act is based on its predecessor, the Technology-Related Assistance for Individuals with Disabilities Act of 1988 (P.L. No.100-407, "Tech Act"), and the amended Tech Act, passed in 1994 (P.L. No. 103-218). The Tech Act was the first federal law that focused exclusively on making assistive technology more readily available to persons

---

[1]States in this chapter refer to all 50 states and outlying areas—the District of Columbia, Puerto Rico, American Samoa, Guam, the Commonwealth of the Northern Mariana Islands, and the U.S. Virgin Islands.

with disabilities, and was the first legislation to define the terms "assistive technology device and assistive technology services" (Fein, 1996, p. 1).

In the text of the original legislation, Congress laid out the findings and purposes of this important federal law. The Tech Act noted that technology had become a "powerful force" in the lives of Americans and that it provided "important tools" to perform tasks quicker and easier. The law indicated that "for some individuals with disabilities, assistive technology is a necessity that enables them to engage in or perform many tasks." Specifically, assistive technology "enabled some individuals with disabilities to have greater control over their lives" and participate in their community more fully. Congress also emphasized that when individuals use assistive technology, the costs for early intervention, education, and other services can be reduced (P.L. No. 100-407).

Congress found that many people with disabilities did not have access to assistive technology. Specifically, the Tech Act identified a serious lack of (a) resources to fund assistive technology devices and services, (b) trained personnel to help ensure proper use of these devices and services, (c) information to individuals who could benefit from these technologies, and (d) coordination among public and private programs, particularly to ensure good transitions between programs and activities (P.L. No. 100-407).

The Tech Act attempted to address many of these concerns through state technology-related assistance programs designed to increase availability and funding for assistive technology, encourage coordination among state agencies, and promote public awareness about the use of assistive technology equipment and services.

Impact of the First Federal Assistive Technology Law on National and State Legislation

The Tech Act broke new ground by being the first federal law to define assistive technology devices and services. The impact of the act on other federal laws was seen in 1990 when these new assistive technology definitions were included in the Individuals with Disabilities Education Act Amendments of 1990 (IDEA). Adding these definitions to IDEA increased access to assistive technology devices and services, through school systems, for children and youth with disabilities (Assistive Technology and the Individualized Education Program, 1992, p. 4). Moreover, these definitions reinforced existing special education law, which requires provision of assistive technology as needed for a free appropriate public education (FAPE).

Even further, in 1997 when IDEA was reauthorized, a requirement was added that every individualized education program (IEP) for students must consider assistive technology as one of many "special factor considerations." This special factor requirement means that every IEP team at a school must look at the assistive technology needs of each student when designing a specific education plan for that student.

Today, the AT Act of 1998 continues to build on the many successes of the Tech Act in providing expanded access to assistive technology equipment and services. State AT projects identify and work to permanently overcome barriers that prevent individuals with disabilities from accessing assistive technology.

The AT Act of 1998 also has made state government more accessible to individuals with disabilities by requiring states receiving federal funding to comply with Section 508 of the Rehabilitation Act. Section 508 mandates that the federal government must procure and provide accessible electronic and information technologies. As applied to state governments, Section 508 requires that state electronic and information technologies be accessible to state employees and the public.

Additionally, each state project has a protection and advocacy (P&A) program for assistive technology to provide individual and systems legal representation and advocacy. P&A services can be particularly useful to parents and educators who are seeking legal precedents and advice when trying to obtain assistive technology for students.

Structure of the Assistive Technology Act

AT Act Paves Way for Increased Provision of Assistive Technology Devices and Services

The AT Act has a three-fold purpose mirrored by its three sections: Title I, Title II, and Title III. Under Title I, the AT Act provides federal grants to states to support capacity building and advocacy activities and provide statewide programs of technology-related assistance for children and adults. Also under Title I, NIDRR is authorized to award grants to fund separate technical assistance projects that aid assistive technology organizations and individuals with disabilities. Four technical assistance projects are currently funded. These projects address issues ranging from legal advocacy assistance, including access to relevant court cases archived on the Internet, to the creation of a national assistive technology Web site, which offers up-to-date information on many types of assistive technology.

Under Title II, the AT Act authorizes national activities that include the coordination of federal research efforts, evaluations of federal efforts on assistive technology, and training of state and federal employees on making technology, including information technology, accessible to employees and the public. The AT Act also advocates for more widespread incorporation of "universal design" principles into products and services. Universal design is a term that describes products or systems that are directly usable by most individuals with disabilities without requiring adaptation.

Under Title III, the AT Act provides federal funds to states and nonprofit groups for the operation of alternative financing programs, such as loans or other funding options to individuals with disabilities and their families for the purchase of assistive technology. Under Title III, the AT Act also funds a technical assistance program to help states set up and operate state assistive technology financial loan programs.

The AT Act requires the governor of each state to designate a lead agency for the Title I AT Act Project in that state. The lead agency is responsible for coordinating AT Act activities, which extends from preparing the grant application for Title I federal funds to promoting the goals of the AT Act. The lead agency also assumes responsibility for the fiscal and administrative management of the AT Act grant in the state. Often this lead agency in a state delegates the programmatic implementation of the AT Act to a division or department within the lead agency or to a nonprofit organization. The lead agency typically has been a vocational rehabilitation agency, a university center for excellence, or a nonprofit agency.

In 1989, the first states in the nation were awarded assistive technology grants under the Tech Act. Nine states were awarded Title I grants to operate assistive technology programs, and awards to additional states were granted each year until the last one was funded in 1995 (see Table 1 for lead agencies, agencies responsible within each state for programmatic implementation of the AT Act, and the year the state received a Title I federal grant for assistive technology.

Title I – State Grant Programs

The essential elements of Title I—Sections 101, 102, and 104—are designed to help states provide access to assistive technology equipment and services for individuals with disabilities. For fiscal year 2002, federal funding for all Title I activities was $24.3 million, with additional funding provided by state governments.

Operation of State Assistive Technology Projects – Section 101

Under Section 101 of Title I of the AT Act of 1998 (P.L. No. 105-394), the federal government provides continued grants to states for a specified time period (through fiscal year 2004) for the operation of state AT Act projects. As described previously, one major goal of the AT Act is to support capacity building and advocacy activities to assist states in maintaining permanent, statewide programs of technology-related assistance. Overall, Title I requires states to perform the following specific activities:

1. Support a public awareness program that provides information related to the availability and benefits of assistive technology devices and services, and is linked to a national public Internet site.

Table 1. Lead Agencies and Agencies Responsible for Programmatic Implementation of the Tech Act as of 2/03

State	Lead Agency	Agency Responsible for Programmatic Implementation	Name of Assistive Technology Project
1989 States			
Arkansas	Department of Workforce Education	Rehabilitation Services	Arkansas Increasing Capabilities Access Network (ICAN)
Colorado	University of Colorado Health Sciences	Center for Excellence	Colorado Assistive Technology Project (CATP)
Illinois	Office of Rehabilitation Services	501(c)(3) Entity	Illinois Assistive Technology Project
Kentucky	Department for the Blind	Department for the Blind	Kentucky Assistive Technology Service Network (KATS)
Maine	Department of Education	Department of Education	Maine Consumer Information and Technology Training Exchange (CITE)
Maryland	Governor's Office for Individuals with Disabilities	Governor's Office for Individuals with Disabilities	Maryland Technology Assistance Program (MD TAP)
Minnesota	Department of Administration	Department of Administration	Minnesota System of Technology to Achieve Results (STAR) Program
Nebraska	Department of Education	Division of Vocational Rehabilitation	Nebraska Assistive Technology Project
Utah	Utah State University	Center for Excellence	Utah Assistive Technology Project
1990 States			
Alaska	Division of Vocational Rehabilitation	Division of Vocational Rehabilitation	Assistive Technologies of Alaska
Indiana	Family and Social Services Administration	501(c)(3) Entity	Accessing Technology Through Awareness in Indiana (ATTAIN) Project
Iowa	University of Iowa	Center for Excellence	Iowa Program for Assistive Technology (IPAT)
Massachusetts	Commission for the Deaf and Hard of Hearing	Commission for the Deaf and Hard of Hearing	Massachusetts Assistive Technology Partnership (MATP)
Mississippi	Department of Rehabilitation Services	Office of Vocational Rehabilitation	Mississippi Project Success Through Assistive/Rehabilitative Technology (START)
Nevada	Department of Human Resources	Rehabilitation Division	Nevada Assistive Technology Collaborative
New Mexico	Department of Education	Division of Vocational Rehabilitation	New Mexico Technology Assistance Program
New York	Governors Office	Office of Advocate for the Disabled	New York State Technology Related Assistance for Individuals with Disabilities (TRAID) Project

(continued next page)

Table 1. Lead Agencies and Agencies Responsible for Programmatic Implementation of the Tech Act as of 2/03 (continued)

State	Lead Agency	Agency Responsible for Programmatic Implementation	Name of Assistive Technology Project
North Carolina	Department of Health and Human Resources	Division of Vocational Rehabilitation	North Carolina Assistive Technology Project
Oregon	Disabilities Commission	501(c)(3) Entity	Oregon Technology Access Through Life Needs Project (TALN)
Tennessee	Department of Human Services	Division of Rehabilitation Services	Tennessee Technology Access Project (TTAP)
Vermont	Department of Aging and Disabilities	Agency of Human Services	Vermont Assistive Technology Project
Virginia	Department of Rehabilitative Services	Department of Rehabilitative Services	Virginia Assistive Technology System (VATS)
Wisconsin	Department of Health and Family Services	Division of Supportive Living	Wisconsin Assistive Technology Program (WisTech)
1991 States Delaware	University of Delaware	Center for Applied Science and Engineering	Delaware Assistive Technology Initiative (DATI)
Georgia	Department of Labor	Vocational Rehabilitation Program	Georgia Tools for Life
Hawaii	Department of Human Services, Vocational Rehabilitation and Services for the Blind Division	501(c)(3) Entity	Hawaii Assistive Technology Training & Service (HATTS) Project
Louisiana	Department of Health and Hospitals	501(c)(3) Entity	Louisiana Assistive Technology Access Network (LATAN)
Missouri	Governor's Council on Disability	Governor's Council on Disability	Missouri Assistive Technology Project
Montana	Department of Health and Human Services	University of Montana, Rural Institute on Disability	MonTech Program
New Hampshire	University of New Hampshire	Center for Excellence	New Hampshire Technology Partnership Project
South Carolina	University of South Carolina	School of Medicine	South Carolina Assistive Technology Project
1992 States Connecticut	Department of Vocational Rehabilitation	Department of Social Services	Connecticut Assistive Technology Project
Florida	Department of Education, Division of Vocational Rehabilitation	501(c)(3) Entity	Florida Alliance for Assistive Services and Technology (FAAST)
Idaho	University of Idaho Department of Career	Center for Excellence	Idaho Assistive Technology Project

(continued next page)

State	Lead Agency	Agency Responsible for Programmatic Implementation	Name of Assistive Technology Project
Michigan	Development, Rehab Services	Disability Rights Coalition	Michigan TECH 2000 Project
New Jersey	Department of Labor and Employment, Division of Vocational Rehabilitation	Protection and Advocacy, Inc.	New Jersey Technology Assistive Resource Program (TARP)
Ohio	Ohio State University	Ohio State University	Assistive Technology of Ohio
Oklahoma	Oklahoma State University	Wellness Center	Oklahoma ABLE Tech
Pennsylvania	Temple University	Center for Excellence	Pennsylvania's Initiative on Assistive Technology (PIAT)
South Dakota	Department of Human Services, Division of Vocational Rehabilitation	South Dakota Assistive Technology Project	DakotaLink
Texas	University of Texas at Austin	Center for Excellence	Texas Assistive Technology Partnership
West Virginia	Division of Rehabilitation Services	Center for Excellence	West Virginia Assistive Technology System (WVATS)
1993 States Alabama	Rehabilitation Services	Rehabilitation Services	Alabama Statewide Technology Access and Response (STAR) System for Alabamians with Disabilities
Am. Samoa	Department of Human Resources	Division of Vocational Rehabilitation	American Samoa Assistive Technology Project (ASATS)
California	Department of Rehabilitation	Department of Rehabilitation	California Assistive Technology Systems (CATS)
District of Columbia	Department of Human Services, RSA	University Legal Services	Assistive Technology Project for the District of Columbia (ULS/ATP)
Kansas	University of Kansas	Center for Excellence	Assistive Technology for Kansans Project
North Dakota	Department of Human Services	Division of Vocational Rehabilitation	North Dakota Interagency Program for Assistive Technology (IPAT)
Puerto Rico	University of Puerto Rico, Central Administration	University of Puerto Rico	Puerto Rico Assistive Technology Project
Rhode Island	Department of Human Services	Office of Rehabilitation Services	Rhode Island Assistive Technology Access Project (ATAP)
Washington	University of Washington	Center for Excellence	Washington Assistive Technology Alliance (WATA)
Wyoming	University of Wyoming	Center for Excellence	Wyoming's New Options in Technology (WYNOT)

(continued next page)

Table 1. Lead Agencies and Agencies Responsible for Programmatic Implementation of the Tech Act as of 2/03 (continued)

State	Lead Agency	Agency Responsible for Programmatic Implementation	Name of Assistive Technology Project
1994 States Arizona	Northern Arizona University	Center for Excellence	Arizona Technology Access Program (AzTAP)
Guam	University of Guam	Center for Excellence	Guam System for Assistive Technology (GSAT)
Com. of Northern Mariana	Governor's Developmental Disabilities Council	Governor's Developmental Disabilities Council	System of Technology-Related Assistance for Individuals with Disabilities (STRAID)
1995 State Virgin Islands	University of the Virgin Islands	Center for Excellence	U. S. Virgin Islands Technology-Related Assistance for Individuals with Disabilities (TRAID)

2. Promote interagency coordination that improves access to assistive technology devices and services for individuals of all ages who have disabilities.
3. Provide technical assistance and training, including the development and implementation of laws, regulations, policies, practices, procedures, or organizational structures that promote access to assistive technology devices and services.
4. Provide outreach support to community-based organizations that provide assistive technology devices and services to individuals with disabilities or that assist individuals in using assistive technology, including individuals from underrepresented and rural populations.

States and outlying areas funded under the AT Act also may perform optional activities such as (a) establishing an alternative state-financed system for the purchase of assistive technology devices and services, (b) providing technology demonstrations, (c) distributing information about how to finance assistive technology devices and services, (d) operating a technology-related information system, (e) participating in interstate activities, and (f) creating public-private partnerships pertaining to assistive technology.

Protection and Advocacy Systems – Section 102

Section 102 of Title I authorizes funding for state protection and advocacy systems, which provide legal advocacy to assist individuals with disabilities in accessing assistive technology devices and services. Grants are awarded by NIDRR to an entity in each state that provides protection and advocacy services through the systems established under the Developmental Disabilities Assistance and Bill of Rights Act. Under the AT Act of 1998, federal assistance for protection and advocacy will be provided for six years.

Technical Help for State AT Act Projects and Individuals with Disabilities – Section 104

Section 104 authorizes the operation of technical assistance programs to assist state AT Act projects and persons with disabilities in developing increased access to assistive technology. The four technical assistance programs currently operated under Section 104 are:

1. A national assistive technology Web site, www.assistivetech.net, operated by the Georgia Tech Center for Assistive Technology and Environmental Access. This site offers detailed product information on different types of assistive technology.
2. The RESNA Technical Assistance Project, which assists the 56 state AT Act grantees in

developing effective, consumer-controlled systems for assistive technology. The RESNA Technical Assistance Project also collaborates with other organizations to provide services to the states. Internet access to the RESNA Technical Assistance Project is at www. resna.org/taproject.

3. A National Assistive Technology Advocacy Project operated by Neighborhood Legal Services, Inc. This project provides technical assistance to protection and advocacy agencies, other agencies, and individuals seeking legal assistance on accessing assistive technology. The Web site for this project (www. nls.org) also offers a technical assistance resource library with precedent-setting court documents and administrative decisions on assistive technology.

4. A data collection project, the Assistive Technology Data Collection and Reporting Project, which is operated by InfoUse (www. infouse.com/atdata/web-based.html). InfoUse and Research Triangle Institute, a subcontractor to InfoUse, designed, tested, and are implementing a Web-based performance reporting system to collect data from State AT Act Projects for the National Institute on Disability and Rehabilitation Research.

Title II - National Activities

Title II provides for increased coordination of federal efforts related to assistive technology and universal design through the Interagency Committee on Disability Research (ICDR), which is chaired by NIDRR. Title II also authorizes funding for joint research projects by ICDR member agencies, special grants related to universal design concepts, and grants for organizations and agencies that work on assistive technology policies.

Title III – Alternative Financing Mechanisms

Title III authorizes federal grants to establish or expand alternative financing programs for the purchase of assistive technology by individuals with disabilities. Under Title III, the Alternative Financing Program (AFP), financing projects have been established in 16 states with the support of federal funds, which are matched by state funds. (Note: Some states also operate different types of financing programs for assistive technology without federal assistance.) The federally financed alternative financing programs may use the following types of mechanisms: (a) a low-interest loan fund; (b) an interest buy-down program; (c) a revolving loan fund; (d) a loan guarantee or insurance program; (e) a program operated by a partnership among private entities for the purchase, lease, or other acquisition of assistive technology devices or services; and (f) another mechanism that meets the requirements of this program. A loan guarantee is the most common type of financing program offered by Title III state grantees.

Appropriations for Title III alternative financing programs have increased since the federal funding for these programs began in federal fiscal year 2000. In that year, six states received the first federal grants, a total of $3.8 million, which were awarded by NIDRR. In fiscal year 2001, $13.6 million was awarded to 14 states for the continuation or establishment of alternative financing projects. The states receiving the federal grants over the two years were Arizona, Arkansas, Florida, Illinois, Kansas, Kentucky, Louisiana, Maryland, Michigan, Missouri, Nevada, Oklahoma, Pennsylvania, Utah, Virginia, and Wisconsin.

Under Section 306 of Title III, the federal government also funds an Alternative Financing Technical Assistance Project, which assists states that are operating Title III alternative financing programs. This technical assistance project is operated by RESNA, and administered by NIDRR. RESNA provides assistance to states in preparing applications for grants under Title III, and assists grant recipients in the development and implementation of alternative financing programs.

Selected Accomplishments of State AT Act Projects to Advance the Lives of Persons With Disabilities

Capacity Building

State AT Act projects work with persons with disabilities to identify needs and overcome barriers to acquiring assistive technology. To further these goals, state AT Act projects have successfully promoted policies and legislation that have expanded access to assistive technology devices and services, increased funding sources, created new programs, and improved the timeliness of the provision of services and devices for people with disabilities. Consequently, the focus of state AT Act projects extends beyond the provision of devices and services to children and adults with disabilities by devoting much of their time to capacity building, which substantially increases the capability of other state agencies, nonprofit groups, and consumer groups to provide more assistive technology services and equipment to those with disabilities.

Capacity building by state AT Act projects has been accomplished through many varied activities such as grant awards, consumer and advocate educational programs, training sessions, and other actions. Through capacity building work, state AT Act projects further their reach by ensuring that more individuals with disabilities are informed about, and are able to access, assistive technology and information technology. Congress has encouraged the capacity building work of states by listing this activity among the major purposes of the AT Act.

The capacity building efforts by state AT Act projects have concentrated on five main areas—employment, community living, telecommunications and information technology, education, and health care—as mandated by the AT Act of 1998. After describing regional capacity building, this chapter will discuss the specific work of state AT Act projects that have not only increased direct services to individuals with disabilities but have increased the ability of other organizations to provide more assistive technology equipment and services.

Specific Assistive Technology Work by State AT Act Projects to Assist Individuals with Disabilities

This section examines the ways in which state AT Act projects are aiding children and adults in accessing AT devices and services for use in employment, community living, telecommunications and information technology, education, and health care. During the past 12 years, state AT Act projects have developed comprehensive AT plans to meet the complex needs of individuals with disabilities. AT Act projects have worked in partnership with persons with disabilities, other state agencies, and advocacy groups to identify needs, develop plans, and access funding and resources for the provision of high- and low-tech AT devices and services.

As stated in the previous section, capacity building by state AT Act projects has been woven into many aspects of their programs. A prime example of an important capacity-building activity of many state AT Act projects has been a significant change in "practice" that benefits infants and toddlers. Thus, state AT Act projects have worked with state officials to ensure that AT is included in many states' early intervention services for children with disabilities. Some state AT Act projects have also helped pass state legislation that mandates screening for hearing problems in newborns and the provision of necessary followup services. This early identification of hearing problems will allow services and assistive technology to be provided at a very early age, to help ensure a child's normal development (Rehabilitation Engineering and Assistive Technology Society of North America, 1999).

Throughout the nation, other policies and practices have been changed in numerous ways to better assist those with disabilities in accessing assistive technology equipment and services. This section highlights some of the policy and practice changes that individual states have accomplished. Examples of the work of state AT Act projects provide a roadmap for exploring the ways in which assistive technology is expanding school, work, and community experiences for individuals with disabilities. Because of space constraints, only the activities of one or a few states are described below for each of the five goal areas, but many other states may be doing similar work. The activity is summarized first, followed by individual state's actions.

Education

Obtaining Needed Assistive Technology for Students

Children often have difficulty obtaining needed assistive technology for use at school. Teachers and administrators who have limited experience in using assistive technology may be reluctant to subscribe to or investigate its usefulness.

Maryland

The Maryland Technology Assistance Program (MD TAP) created a nonprofit organization to act as a bargaining and purchasing agent for Maryland educational entities when they are purchasing assistive technology for students. This new cooperative organization has produced more than $600,000 in discounts and savings for its members by conducting large bids, negotiating statewide buys, and serving as middleman for some devices and software. In addition, the Maryland Assistive Technology Cooperative has helped break a psychological barrier that implied that assistive technology was too expensive for schools. The result is that more students can receive needed assistive technology equipment. The use of assistive technology equipment in school enhances a student's ability to learn and to interact with teachers and other students.

Transferring Assistive Technology with the Student

Once assistive technology is obtained for a student, it is important to ensure that the technology stays with the student as he or she moves to new educational or vocational environments. Three measures undertaken by state AT Act projects provide exemplifies the ways in which states are addressing this concern.

Oklahoma

Oklahoma's AT Project, ABLE Tech, worked with the Oklahoma Commission on Children and Youth to secure a mechanism for transferring of assistive technology between state agencies and school districts. With the new transfer policy, students do not lose the use of technology they have mastered when they advance to other environments. The policy provides for the seamless transfer of assistive technology when students move between agencies, for example, when a student goes from a special education classroom to vocational rehabilitation. ABLE Tech worked directly with the taskforce from the Oklahoma Commission on Children and Youth to complete this effort.

Wyoming

Wyoming's AT Project, WYNOT, and its Protection and Advocacy Agency worked with the Department of Education to develop a cooperative agreement among preschools and other schools to transfer assistive technology equipment with the student as he or she enters grade school. An earlier agreement with the Department of Vocational Rehabilitation had eased transition and equipment ownership issues for older students who are moving from high school to work settings.

Educating Parents, School Officials, and Advocates on Children's Rights to Assistive Technology

State AT Act projects have worked to ensure that parents, educators, and advocates are informed about a school system's responsibilities for providing assistive technology to children with disabilities. State AT projects have developed multistage programs to educate various audiences about assistive technology.

North Dakota

North Dakota's Interagency Project for Assistive Technology (IPAT) developed a three-step approach to addressing awareness, proper use, and integration of assistive technology in schools around the state. First, IPAT published *Technology for All: A Guide to Solving the Puzzle*, which outlined a planning process for assistive technology purchasing. IPAT developed these materials in response to a request from school administrators and staff for a comprehensive, schoolwide plan to purchase assistive technology for students.

Next, IPAT produced an 18-minute videotape, *Know Your Rights to Assistive Technology in Education*, to help parents of students with disabilities obtain the assistive technology that their students need. The video mirrors information in IPAT's statewide assistive technology guide. These products were developed in conjunction with the North Dakota Department of Public Instruction.

Lastly, IPAT provided training for attorneys regarding the public school systems' responsibility for assistive technology. The North Dakota Bar Association sanctioned the training by awarding it continuing legal education credits. The presentation and credits were offered over Interactive Video Network as well as self-study via videotape.

Training Initiatives for Students with Disabilities and Professional Service Providers

Education initiatives by state AT Act projects also include efforts to provide education and training for younger students and for professionals in health care and nonprofit agencies in areas related to assistive technology. Some state training programs have worked on high-tech skills for students through varied approaches and methods, while others have provided opportunities for service professionals to better serve persons with disabilities by becoming certified as assistive technology practitioners.

Oregon

Oregon Technology Access for Life Needs (TALN) has worked to establish a high-tech training program for middle school and high school students to provide job skills and assistive technology skills for increased employment opportunities and a successful transition from high school. These training programs are funded by the Vocational Rehabilitation Division; the programs are designed to equip 9th- through 12th-grade students with disabilities with the skills needed to enter high-tech jobs after high school graduation. TALN provides assistive technology expertise, training, and equipment loans to the schools. In turn, the school districts provide modified curriculum, community outreach, and placement with local industries.

Utah

For more than two years, the Utah Assistive Technology Program has provided competency-based training to 55 service providers in state and private agencies and consumer organizations. Trainees gain specific skills and competencies outlined by the AT Practitioner credentialing program of the Rehabilitation Engineering and Assistive Technology Society of North America (RESNA). The goal of this professional development program is to offer increased quality care for consumers.

Employment

Providing Tax Incentives

State legislatures may pass laws to give tax relief or funding help to employers that provide assistive technology devices or work accommodations for individuals with disabilities. State AT Act projects have worked with state legislators to enact model programs in this area.

Iowa

The Iowa Partnership for Assistive Technology (IPAT) helped develop a bill that gives tax credits to Iowa small businesses that provide assistive technology devices or workplace accommodations for individuals with disabilities. The new technology tax credit covers 50% of the first $5,000 paid for devices or modifications with a cap of $2,500. The tax credit is available to a business each tax year. The state's Assistive Technology Tax Credit Act provides a hiring incentive for Iowa's small businesses to hire, retain, and accommodate employees with disabilities, who in turn offer a pool of dependable, productive, and qualified workers.

The tax credit is available to businesses that have 14 or fewer employees, or to small businesses with gross receipts from the preceding tax year of $3 million or less. About 70,000 businesses in Iowa-90% of all businesses-have fewer than 20 employees.

Ohio

Assistive Technology of Ohio staff helped develop legislation passed by the Ohio General Assembly to assist businesses in providing workplace modifications for persons with disabilities. The legislation provides state funding to small businesses for reduced-rate loans for workplace accommodations. These loans can be used to make modifications that facilitate the hiring or improve the accommodation for consumers with disabilities. Additionally, the loans may be used to assist Ohio businesses in complying with the Americans with Disabilities Act.

Loan Programs to Purchase Assistive Technology

Loan programs offered through state AT Act projects (under Title I) and local or regional banks provide an important resource for many people seeking to purchase assistive technology at a cost they can afford. Currently, 32 states offer some type of financial loan program that provides loans at low interest rates to individuals with disabilities. As mentioned in the previous section on Title III, 26 state AT Act programs currently are recipients of federal grants to operate affordable financing programs for the purchase of assistive technology.

Assistive technology frequently purchased through these programs includes vans or vehicle modifications, wheelchairs, adapted computers, and other equipment that assists individuals with disabilities in obtaining or maintaining employment or in increasing their mobility or adaptability in a home, school, or community environment. The following information illustrates some of the ways in which states are assisting individuals with disabilities through financing programs.

Puerto Rico

The Puerto Rico Assistive Technology Program (PRATP) found that a lack of financial aid for the purchase of assistive technology was one of the biggest barriers faced by people with disabilities when trying to acquire an assistive technology device for employment or other purposes. To help solve this problem, PRATP members contacted a local bank to develop a low-interest loan program. The collaborative venture, Program Impulse to the Future, was begun in October 1999 and allows assistive technology consumers to acquire needed devices with low interest loans.

Kentucky

Kentucky's Assistive Technology Loan Corporation (KATLC), created by the Kentucky General Assembly in 1996, began a collaboration with a bank for a low-interest loan program for assistive technology equipment and services. The loan program, begun in May 2000, assists Kentuckians with disabilities in acquiring assistive technology to obtain or maintain employment, pursue their education, and improve their quality of life. KATLC worked with Fifth Third Bank of Kentucky to provide loans between $500 and $25,000 at a fixed rate of 6% for up to 10 years.

Helping Individuals Maintain Agricultural Careers After Disability

A lack of awareness of some types of assistive technology, particularly for use in careers in which service providers and related agencies' staff have little experience, can be a serious drawback to individuals who want to re-enter these job fields after an injury or disability. States have teamed with nonprofit agencies to provide better opportunities for those who wanting to regain employment in farming occupations.

Wisconsin

Vocational Rehabilitation (VR) counselors, county agricultural extension agents, and insurance company staff in Wisconsin received training in the use of assistive technology for farmers with disabilities. This training was needed because most of these professionals knew little about assistive technology options in farming. WisTech, the AT Project in Wisconsin, contracted with the state's Easter Seals AgrAbility program to provide training. The AgrAbility training targeted this group because VR counselors, agricultural agents, and Worker's Compensation Insurance adjusters typically recommend that a person in a farming occupation who becomes disabled due to a farming accident or after acquiring an age-related disability leave farming and begin another occupation.

Since receiving the training, VR staff are reporting an increase in the number of individuals they are rehabilitating as farmers or agricultural workers. VR and private insurance agencies also are agreeing to fund more assistive technology, based on the success of farmers who are using assistive technology.

Community Living

Helping Agencies Reach Rural Areas

Outreach to rural or underserved populations of individuals with disabilities is a primary focus of the AT Act of 1998. State AT Act projects have devised creative programs to address this pressing need for assistive technology. The two states described here have implemented successful outreach programs to underserved populations.

Minnesota

Minnesota's AT Project, a System of Technology to Achieve Results (STAR), provides funding to volunteer groups who can deliver assistive technology services and devices in rural regions of the state. STAR provides funds through Community Action Network (CAN) grants. The capacity building of local agencies has been increased through the development of these rural access points for assistive technology. The ultimate goal of the program is to ensure that the assistive technology needs of individuals with disabilities are addressed by skilled personnel located within 50 miles of their homes.

In state fiscal year 2000-2001, the CANs also brought more that 60 assistive technology training classes and clinics to their regions, serving over 1,700 Minnesotans, free of charge. Each CAN that received a grant from STAR has leveraged between $10,000 and $50,000 in additional support for their activities during a two-year period.

New Jersey

The New Jersey Assistive Technology Resource Program (TARP) continued the expansion of its Latino outreach efforts. This includes collaboration with community-based organizations in Latino communities and outreach to churches and bilingual educators to raise awareness about access to assistive technology. In June 2000, TARP, in collaboration with community-based organizations, held a Latino Summit Conference that offered information on several program and issue areas, including access to assistive technology.

Efforts to Increase Home Accessibility

Recognition of the need for improved physical access to homes brought together home builders, private groups, agencies, and State AT Projects. Collaborations have produced home-building legislation that requires disability-friendly homes.

Vermont

Vermont became the first state to assist persons with disabilities in gaining easier physical access to many new homes that will be built by developers. The Vermont Assistive Technology Project (VATP) initiated efforts aimed at state legislation that requires all new one-, two-, and three-family housing units built on speculation to include disability access features. These housing units include townhouses and condominiums. The increased physical access will help ensure more "visitable" homes, which refers to homes that are not only accessible to guests with disabilities visiting the homes of nondisabled hosts, but those that can be easily adapted to the future needs of the nondisabled residents.

Access features now mandated by Vermont law include wider doorways, accessible hallways, and bathrooms on the first floor with doorways wide enough for wheelchair users to enter. VATP worked on a task force, which included several state agencies, private groups, and a contractors' association, to effect passage of the law that requires the new disability access. The legislation, passed in April 2000, also directs VATP to work with many groups to create and disseminate educational materials explaining the new construction standards and the advantages of visitable homes.

Assistive Device Lemon Laws

The purchase of assistive technology can be expensive. State AT Act project staff throughout the country have found that persons with disabilities may be seriously sidelined by the failure of these complex devices, such as power wheelchairs, when a retailer or manufacturer refuses to fix the chair appropriately. Consequently, state AT Act projects have worked with other organizations to encourage state legislators to pass laws to require repair or replacement of defective assistive technology. Currently, 38 states have assistive technology lemon laws that protect constituents with disabilities.

New Mexico

The New Mexico Technology Assistance Program (NMTAP) led a bipartisan cooperative involving the New Mexico Governor's Office, Republican and Democrat legislators, and citizens throughout New Mexico to pass the Assistive Device Lemon Law. This law created a one-year warranty on all assistive devices "used for major life activities." To qualify as a "lemon" the devices must have been repaired four times or have been out of service for 30 cumulative days. If after attempts to repair the device, it is still not fixed, the consumer has the option of getting a full refund of the purchase price or a replacement. The law also includes a provision that it is the manufacturer's responsibility to provide a loaner replacement devices or reimburse for a temporary replacement of the device for the duration of the repair period. This law is typical of the legislation passed in other states. These laws help people with disabilities from getting stuck with an assistive device that does not work, one that is a "lemon."

Getting Assistive Technology to Those Who Need It

Many state AT Act projects have promoted the development of some type of equipment loan, equipment exchange, or equipment recycling program to provide access to assistive technology at reduced or no cost. In addition, a number of related programs have been developed by private organizations throughout the country. Some recycling programs directly sell or donate second-hand equipment, or they refurbish the equipment, such as computers or power wheelchairs, and make it available through donation or sale to individuals with disabilities and their families. Also, to decrease the cost of buying new equipment some states have organized buying cooperatives to buy new assistive technology in bulk orders, thereby reducing the cost of the equipment. State AT Act projects and nonprofit groups also provide assistive technology equipment demonstration centers where individuals with disabilities can try out different assistive technologies.

District of Columbia

The University Legal Services Assistive Technology Program (ULS/ATP) for the District of Columbia teamed with the DC Center for Independent Living (DCCIL) to administer a community-based equipment recycling and lending program. This program was established to increase the options for acquiring assistive technology by individuals with disabilities. The program receives donations of used equipment, refurbishes the equipment, and then lends these devices on a first-come, first-serve basis to individuals with disabilities who have no other means of obtaining such assistive technology.

Georgia

Georgia Tools for Life, and the Association of Georgians with Disabilities developed an assistive technology buying cooperative to reduce the cost to consumers for assistive technology devices. A cooperative allows goods to be purchased in greater volume at lower, dealer prices. This ensures that new technology is an attainable reality for many persons with disabilities. Volume buying for the cooperative includes many types of items such as scooters, alternative and augmentative communication (AAC) devices, and lifts for vans.

Telecommunications/Information Technology

Electronic and Information Technology Accessibility for Individuals with Disabilities

State AT Act projects have worked to ensure access to electronic and information technology for individuals with disabilities. Technology makes government accessible on the Internet to many people, including those with disabilities. Under Section 508 standards of the federal Rehabilitation Act, states are mandated to offer Internet and information technology accessibility for state government Web sites and programs. The following information on two state AT Act projects illustrates the ways in which states are complying with this mandate.

West Virginia

West Virginia Assistive Technology System (WVATS) staff collaborated with an interagency group, designated by the governor of West Virginia, to produce accessibility standards for the Web sites of state agencies. Most state agencies now have incorporated Web accessibility standards into their sites. WVATS staff monitor Web sites for compliance with access standards and offer suggestions for improvement to new sites or sites not meeting these standards.

South Carolina

The South Carolina Assistive Technology Project (SCATP) took the lead with South Carolina legislators in establishing the South Carolina Access to Information Technology Partnership and Coordinating Committee in June 2000. The

Coordinating Committee was co-chaired by the South Carolina School for the Deaf and the Blind and the Office of Information Resources. The committee examined methods for providing better access to electronic and information technology for the state's citizens with disabilities. The partnership developed a statewide Web accessibility training plan, and a state policy and Web accessibility implementation plan.

The Coordinating Committee also established five pilot centers to model multiple means of access to information technology for people with disabilities. SCATP continues to provide training and technical help to those who are responsible for promoting and helping people use these centers.

Health Care

Health care issues and assistive technology intersect at many levels for individuals with disabilities. In this area, state AT Act projects advocate for better access to assistive technology devices and services through working with public and private agencies on health care coverage. Also, AT Act projects strongly encourage changes in assistive technology coverage in the policies of federal government programs (for example, Medicaid and Medicare). Changes in federal programs often propel similar changes in private health care programs, which can result in increased coverage of needed assistive technology for more individuals. This section provides information on the ways that three state AT Act projects have helped make significant contributions to health care access in assistive technology through policy changes and advanced telemedicine services.

Changing Medicaid Policy to Include Communications Devices

Louisiana
Louisiana's AT Project, Louisiana Assistive Technology Access Network (LATAN), facilitated the development of criteria and a checklist to be used when recommending an augmentative and alternative communication (AAC) device for Medicaid coverage. The criteria and checklist were adopted as part of Medicaid policy and procedures for use with individuals of all ages who needed AAC devices. LATAN now provides training on criteria, AAC assessments, and Medicaid procedures to speech therapists, case managers, rehabilitation counselors, Medicaid personnel, and others involved in the provision of AAC.

Providing Telemedicine Services
Health care services often are difficult to access for individuals with disabilities who live in remote locations. Telemedicine services can offer consultations from off-site locations. This has been used by states to combat a shortage of AT experts, who can conduct assistive technology assessments via telemedicine systems.

Guam
The Guam System for Assistive Technology Project (GSAT) partnered with the University of Pittsburgh to use live video off-island telemedicine to conduct preliminary assistive technology assessments. Particularly in geographic areas that do not have enough local assistive technology evaluators, telemedicine provides an innovative method whereby experts can conduct initial assistive technology assessments from distant locations. The GSAT telemedicine program is providing important, accessible assistive technology services for persons with disabilities in Guam.

Texas
The Texas Technology Access Project worked with advocates and health care professionals to foster legislation that established a telemedicine pilot program for rural areas in Texas. This program provides Medicaid reimbursement for telemedicine services, including those provided by assistive technology service providers. Under this program, people with disabilities in remote sites in the state will receive care and consultation for their assistive technology needs from assistive technology experts at central health facilities.

Lessons Learned

In the 13 years since the first assistive technology law was passed, staff of state AT Act projects have amassed considerable information about better ways to provide assistive technology. Seven key points summarize important lessons learned from the work accomplished by state AT Act projects and may serve as a guide for future advancements.

1. Change takes time. Although a person with a disability may desperately need to acquire assistive technology today, a need does not translate into a policy change that will provide instant access to assistive technology. Professionals can work for increased access to assistive technology for several years before any actual results happen. For example, the state AT Act project in Arkansas worked for nearly 10 years before Medicaid agreed to cover durable medical equipment and assistive technology for adults with disabilities.

2. Collaboration with other public and private agencies is important. The synergy created by group efforts expands the reach and benefits of any single organization. Collaborative efforts also increase the likelihood of success in policy and legislative efforts.

3. The involvement of consumers and family representatives enriches an organization's efforts and activities. Such involvement makes services more consumer responsive and more likely to meet the needs of the intended audiences.

4. Early involvement in a state's planning process is important. Being "at the table" early in local, state, and national discussions on disability issues helps ensure that technology is incorporated into policy decisions for employment, education, and independent living.

5. Sustainability is an elusive word. Nothing is permanent. Changes that were made and services that were expanded sometimes can be undone because of budget and other fiscal crises. Although some states are receiving assistive technology funding from their state legislatures and other entities, it is usually a one-time (one-year) appropriation and does not necessarily lead to program permanency.

6. A need will always exist for assistive technology information and support. As new technologies are developed, more people acquire disabilities, and services are fragmented, there will continue to be a need for a central place that people with disabilities can learn about assistive technology devices and services.

7. Success stems from an unqualified commitment to increasing access to assistive technology and is not dependent on the type of lead organization that handles the project. Successful efforts have come from all types of lead agencies such as vocational rehabilitation agencies, university centers for excellence, and nonprofit agencies.

In the past 13 years, both successes and failures of state AT Act projects have been shared at assistive technology conferences, through organizations of state AT Act projects, and through the work of Technical Assistance Projects for assistive technology. The experiences of state AT Act projects have helped other states in crafting policies, procedures, legislation, and practices to provide more types of assistive technology equipment and services to individuals with disabilities.

References

Assistive Technology Act of 1998, Pub. L. No. 105-394.

Fein, J. (1996). A history of legislative support for assistive technology. *Journal of Special Education Technology, 12,* 1-3.

Individuals with Disabilities Education Act, Pub. L. No. 105-17.

Rehabilitation Engineering and Assistive Technology Society of North America. (1999, January). *Assistive Technology Act of 1998,* Pub. L. No. 105-394. (The TAP Bulletin: a publication of the RESNA Technical Assistance Project.) Arlington, VA: Author.

RESNA Technical Assistance Project. (1992). Assistive technology and the individualized education program. Arlington, VA: author.

Technology-Related Assistance for Individuals with Disabilities Act of 1988, Pub. L. No. 100-407.

Technology-Related Assistance for Individuals with Disabilities Act of 1988, as amended, Pub. L. No. 103-218.

3

A Federal Program to Support Innovation and Implementation of Technology in Special Education

David B. Malouf and June Hauser

The Promise of Technology

Increased demands are being placed on educational programs for students with disabilities. The requirement for a free appropriate public education in the least restrictive environment that was established by P.L. 94-142 in 1975 was just the beginning of this trend. More recently, expectations have been raised further by legal mandates requiring that students with disabilities have access to the general education curriculum, be included in assessments and accountability, and achieve to high academic standards (The Individuals with Disabilities Education Act Amendments of 1997; The No Child Left Behind Act of 2001). Clearly, a high bar has been set, and all available resources and methodologies must be used if we are to achieve these challenging goals for the students we serve.

One type of resource that may enable special education to meet these challenges is technology, including assistive technology and instructional technology. Specifically, assistive devices have been shown to help students with disabilities increase their independence by learning to communicate more effectively, to

control their environments, and to achieve greater mobility (Burnette, 1990; Derer, Polsgrove, & Rieth, 1994; Todis, 1996; Todis & Walker, 1993). Instructional technology has also been demonstrated to enhance students' learning and meaningful participation in classroom activities by enabling teachers to tailor instruction to individual student needs and to supplement and/or enhance effective instruction (Higgins & Boone, 1993; Okolo, Bahr, & Rieth, 1993; Woodward & Carnine, 1993; Woodward & Rieth, 1997).

Technology also can support practitioners in administrative and managerial tasks, such as making assessment tasks more precise and manageable or facilitating individualized program planning (Fuchs, Fuchs, & Hamlett, 1993). Technology is also finding increased use as a vehicle for delivering and expanding professional development opportunities for practitioners and families (Blackhurst, Hales, & Lahm, 1998; Foegen & Hargrave, 1999; Gallagher & McCormick, 1999; Meyen, Tangen, & Lian, 1999; Paulsen, Higgins, Miller, Strawser, & Boone, 1998).

Congress recognized the importance of technology to enhance educational results for students with disabilities when it passed the 1997 amendments to the Individuals with Disabilities Education Act (IDEA). These amendments introduced a provision requiring that teams responsible for developing an individualized education program (IEP) must consider whether the child requires assistive technology devices and services. This was not the first time IDEA

Authors' Note: The opinions expressed in this chapter are those of the authors and do not necessarily reflect the positions or policies of the U.S. Department of Education; official endorsement neither is implied nor should be inferred.

acknowledged the importance of technology. Approximately ten years prior to the 1997 amendments, Congress authorized a funding program under IDEA to support technology research, development, innovation, and utilization. This chapter discusses this funding program and some of the work it has supported.

Barriers to Achieving the Benefits of Technology

Despite dramatic progress in the development and availability of technology for students with disabilities, it can be argued that technology has not lived up to its potential for these students. This assertion is consistent with some recent reexaminations of the value of technology in education in general (Norris, Soloway, & Sullivan, 2002), and of the issue of implementing new educational practices (Elmore, 1996). But there are also special considerations when technology and the needs of students with disabilities are involved (Hutinger, Johanson, & Stoneburner, 1996; Lesar, 1998; McGregor & Pachuski, 1996; Wehmeyer, 1999).

For example, Todis (2001) described a two-year qualitative study of alternative and augmentative communication (AAC) devices in classroom and home use. Although a number of benefits were achieved, several barriers and problems were also encountered. For example, parents, students, and schools sometimes had different goals and priorities involving the use of devices. Devices were sometimes incompatible with the physical or social environment, or required responses that were difficult for the students. Teachers were sometimes unable to incorporate devices into their programs of instruction; in fact, in some cases the devices were disruptive for both teachers and students.

At a more general level, Cuban (2001) proposed a number of factors that may impede meaningful use of technology in both general and special education. These include cultural beliefs about the nature of schooling; unclear and competing goals for education; organizational structures in districts, schools, and classrooms; and cultures of teaching. Thus, political factors and resource limitations all interact to constrain the adoption of educational innovations such as educational technologies. Even

if resources and administrative support are provided, the process of developing and adopting innovative educational uses of technology may be slow and sporadic.

In addressing the development and implementation of technology, it is important that a range of factors be understood and addressed. Factors of implementation, such as awareness, training, funding, and administrative support, must be explored along with factors of design, such as device capability, usability, and costs. And, technology must never be considered in isolation, but always in the context of the needs it is intended to meet and the contexts in which it is intended to function.

A Program of Federal Support for Innovation and Implementation of Technology for Students with Disabilities

History of Federal Support for Students with Disabilities

Federal support for the use of technology to assist individuals with disabilities dates back more than a century (Fein, 1996). In 1879, Congress passed the Act to Promote the Education of the Blind to provide embossed books and tangible apparatus for blind students. This law is still on the books, and over the years the services it supports have been broadened to encompass newer electronic technologies. In 1958, Congress passed the Captioned Films for the Deaf Act, which provided for captioning films and distributing them through agencies serving the deaf. Federally supported work begun the 1960s eventually led to closed-captioned television, and federal support in the 1970s led to the development of the Kurzweil reading machine (Hauser & Malouf, 1996).

Given the technological revolution that flourished in the 1980s, it is not surprising that this decade witnessed several major legislative developments related to the use of technology for people with disabilities. These laws included the Technology-Related Assistance for Individuals with Disabilities Act of 1988 (the Tech Act), which established federal definitions for assistive technology device and assistive technology service and authorized grants to increase the availability and use of assistive technology in the states. The assistive technology definitions in this law became standard and were later used in the Individuals with Disabilities Education Act (IDEA).

At about the same time that the Tech Act was enacted, the 1986 amendments to the Education of the Handicapped Act (EHA; later entitled the Individuals with Disabilities Education Act or IDEA) established the Technology, Educational Media, and Materials (TMM) program (Part G) to advance the use of new technology, media, and materials in the education of students with disabilities through such activities as research, development, and dissemination. The budget for Part G in fiscal 1987 was $4.7 million. With successive amendments and reauthorizations, EHA/IDEA broadened its provisions related to technology, and additional funds were appropriated for technology. The 1997 reauthorization of IDEA merged the Part G TMM program with the Part F Instructional Media program to produce a single discretionary program entitled the Technology Development, Demonstration, and Utilization; and Media Services program.

This long history of federal programs and provisions has been shaped by a recognition of technology's potential for benefiting individuals with disabilities. The laws have been intended to ensure that the necessary services and products are available for these benefits to be achieved. In addition, there has been a corollary recognition that federal support for research and development is needed to promote the development of new technologies and to study the best uses of technology. Thus, federal funds have historically been used to support the development of new media technologies for the blind, new captioning technologies, and a variety of other technologies.

The TMM Agenda

In 1990, the Office of Special Education Programs (OSEP) in the U.S. Department of Education established a strategic agenda to guide investments in the TMM program for improving educational results (U.S. Department of Education, 1992). OSEP introduced the national technology program agenda after involving stakeholders from across the nation in a year-long agenda-building process. The overarching goals for technology inquiry were identified as: fostering lifelong learning; encouraging participation in diverse educational, domestic, work, and community environments; promoting equity in opportunity for individuals with disabilities; and enabling individuals with disabilities to be productive and independent. To achieve these goals, the agenda put forth four program commitments by which the use of technology would be advanced for all categories of disability. These commitments were:

- Enable the learner across environments by fostering the creation of state-of-the-art instructional environments, both in and out of school

- Promote effective policy at all levels in government, schools, and businesses

- Foster use through professional development by training and supporting teachers, administrators, parents, and related-service personnel

- Create innovative tools by encouraging the development of varied and integrated technologies, media, and materials

For over a decade, this agenda has served as the touchstone of OSEP's technology research and development efforts. The agenda provides a coherent framework for linking research with implementation, and underscores the importance of examining and improving access to information and support. The agenda has stimulated the exploration of issues related to providing innovative technology tools that enable students to learn across educational and classroom settings.

Retrospective Studies

OSEP commissioned a group of researchers to review past TMM project investments in order to improve future practice (Okolo, Cavalier, Ferretti, & MacArthur, 1995). These researchers identified five broad categories of focus:

- **Assistive technology**–projects that look at how to compensate for or otherwise address special student needs

- **Technology and instruction**–projects related to instructional design, literacy, mathematics, social studies, science, and early childhood education

- **Technology and assessment**–projects about assessment of academic skills, videodisc assessments, behavioral assessment, expert systems for decision support, and eco-behavioral assessment

- **Future applications**–projects that analyze trends in hardware and software developments for individuals with disabilities

- **Implementation and dissemination of technology applications and services**– projects that examine how technology is used in educational and clinical settings, models of technology integration, centers to disseminate information about technology, and staff development efforts

These authors acknowledged the diversity of topics and issues addressed in the projects funded under this program and the potential benefits for students with disabilities. They called for expanded efforts to disseminate the resulting products and promote their use in practice, and recommended increased emphasis on programmatic, high-quality research.

Examples of How Technology Can Improve Educational Outcomes for Students with Disabilities

Over the years that OSEP funds have supported technology research and innovation, certain patterns have emerged concerning how technology can enhance educational programs and outcomes for students with disabilities by providing access to the classroom and the curriculum and by supporting learning once access is attained. These patterns have evolved as technologies have improved and as we have developed a more complete understanding of how technology can contribute to the educational process for these students.

Technology to Provide Access to the Regular Classroom and the General Curriculum

The 1997 reauthorization of IDEA extended the principle of "access" to include not only physical access to the school and classroom, but also access to the general curriculum. Fur-

ther, this access is not simply exposure, but is intended to allow students to participate and progress in the general curriculum. Assistive technology has long been recognized as a tool for gaining physical or sensory access to schools (e.g., through the use of motorized wheelchairs, hearing amplification devices). Now technology should be recognized as a means for gaining curricular access as well.

Students who are deaf or hard of hearing, for example, are increasingly placed in general education classrooms. At middle school and high school levels, these classrooms are characterized by large volumes of academic information being conveyed orally through teacher lectures and student discussions. The C-Print system, developed at the National Technical Institute for the Deaf (NTID) at the Rochester Institute of Technology (RIT), provides real-time translation of speech to text by means of a classroom "captionist," who uses speech-recognition software and a keyboard-based abbreviation system to produce transcriptions and class notes (Stinson, Elliot, McKee, & Francis, 2000). A similar service is provided by the Remote Realtime Online Captioning service operated at Minot State University, which uses the Internet to allow remote captionists to provide captions and class notes (Remote Realtime Online Captioning: Overview, n.d.).

For students with visual impairments, the challenges center around providing access to information that is presented visually. While some visual information can be adequately described verbally, the standard academic curriculum is replete with examples of graphic, symbolic, or other types of visual information that are essential to learning but are difficult to translate into words. An example may be found in the graphing calculators that are typically required when students begin to study algebra and that can provide important support in acquiring math concepts. A project at Automated Functions in Virginia developed a Multiple Output Graphing Scientific Interactive Calculator (MOGSIC) that uses speech, stereo sound, and a haptic mouse to convey mathematical functions that would otherwise be presented graphically (Morford, n.d.).

For students with learning or academic skill deficits, electronic books provide access to curricular materials by presenting text in adaptable ways (e.g., variable sizes, auditory or visual) combined with embedded resources (e.g., linked illustrations and definitions) (Anderson-Inman & Horney, 1997). Project Intersect at the University of Oregon has developed a digital library of electronic texts on a variety of curricular topics (The Intersect Digital Library, n. d.). Further, in 2002, OSEP funded a project at the Center for Applied Technology (CAST) to develop a voluntary national file format for instructional materials to be delivered in an accessible electronic format (U.S. Department of Education, 2002).

Technology to Support Learning

Technology provides a promising means for helping students with disabilities learn challenging academic skills and content. Although it is still common to see educational software that applies a drill-and-practice model of instruction, recent work has demonstrated that technology can provide broader and more varied support for learning both basic skills and complex information. Thus, there has been increased application of research on learning which supports principles such as providing explicit instruction and strategic support, building on preexisting knowledge, and providing for transfer and generalization (Bransford, Brown, & Cocking, 1999). Moreover, theories of constructivism, anchored instruction, situated learning, and cognitive apprenticeship have all influenced the development of technology-based approaches to special education instruction (Hauser & Malouf, 1996).

Interesting examples of technology to support learning can be found in the Read 180 program developed at Vanderbilt University (Hasselbring, 1999) and distributed by Scholastic, Inc., and the Transitional Mathematics program developed at the Washington Research Institute (Woodward & Stroh, 2004) and distributed by Sopris West. These products, which received some or all of their development funds from the OSEP technology program, are intended to address skill deficits in reading or mathematics through the application of technologies such as computers, CD-ROM, multimedia, and the World Wide Web. Both products attempt to develop basic skills while at the same time cultivating more advanced and complex skills. They accomplish these multiple purposes by drawing upon a variety of theoretical and empirical resources, such as research on learning, instructional design, and strategy instruction, and various formulations of constructivism. In addition, they combine technology-based instruction with conventional instruction to capitalize on the advantages of each. Both products have substantial research bases and have also been shaped by extensive tryouts in classroom settings. In their eclectic and pragmatic approaches, they may represent a new generation of technology-based approaches to instruction for students with special needs.

Another shift in the use of computers in education may be found in the increased use of computers as learning "tools" to support learning rather than as "tutors" (or conveyors of content) (Hauser & Malouf, 1996). Computers of increasing power are combined with technologies such as CD-ROMs, DVDs, and the World Wide Web to offer ever more powerful learning tools. Examples are the TELE-Web project at Michigan State University (TELE-Web Aids Reading and Writing Skills, 1998), Kid Tools at the University of Missouri (Fitzgerald & Semrau 2000), and Draft:Builder developed by EDC (Corley, Follansbee, Hoffman, Lorin, & Zorfass, 2002) and marketed by Don Johnston. These applications are relatively free of content, compared with Read 180 and Transition Mathematics, and instead provide support for the development of skills determined by the curriculum and instruction in the specific classroom.

How the Program Supports Technology Research and Innovation

While research and development efforts have provided considerable evidence to document the positive results of technology and have suggested implementation approaches, questions remain regarding utilization of technology. To address these issues, a number of OSEP's current investments are building upon past work in exploring technology as an intervention. Technology-based strategies that assist students in achieving meaningful participation and independence are being considered across various educational settings. These strategies emphasize how technology is integrated into the full range of school-related activities–its use, the effects of using assistive and instructional technology on a broad range of results, and how the environment of schools either facilitates or hinders the use of technology. This means looking at change on multiple levels-not just in the classroom, but throughout the educational system, including at the school, district, state, and federal levels (Means et al., 1993). At the local level, this may include the perspectives of curriculum, professional development, and technical assistance. Systemic factors may include the extent to which policy and planning support accessibility, availability, and effective application of the technology. The pattern of looking at technology as an intervention has emerged in current projects in a variety of ways. The following are examples of innovative OSEP-funded efforts that hold promise for shaping the future.

Steppingstones of Technology Innovation for Students with Disabilities

After reviewing projects supported by the OSEP technology program, Okolo et al. (1995) suggested that projects be funded in phases to provide adequate support for design/test iterations and for behavioral research evaluations. An additional consideration was suggested by authors such as Gersten, Morvant, and Brengelman (1995), who argued that specific attention needed to be paid to the process of implementing innovations, as otherwise successful interventions might fall into disuse in a surprisingly short period of time. In response to these considerations, OSEP established a grant competition in 1998 entitled Steppingstones of Technology Innovation for Students with Disabilities. Projects in this priority are designed to focus research on implementation as well as the effectiveness and sustained use of a technology-based approach. The stepping stone framework embodies the notion of technology as a complex intervention by building into its design an understanding of implementation and the work that needs to be done to ensure utilization. There are three phases of possible work:

- **Phase 1–Development.** Projects develop and refine a technology-based approach and test its feasibility for use with students with disabilities.

- **Phase 2–Research on effectiveness.** Projects select a promising technology-based approach that has been developed in a manner consistent with Phase 1 and subject it to rigorous field-based research and evaluation to determine effectiveness and feasibility in educational or early intervention settings.

- **Phase 3–Research on implementation.** Projects select a technology-based approach that has been evaluated for effectiveness and feasibility and study its implementation in multiple settings to acquire an improved understanding of the range of contexts in which the approach can be used effectively and the factors that determine its effectiveness and sustainability in that range of contexts.

Futures Studies

In the early 1980s it was recognized that such "new" technologies as videodiscs and microcomputers, when used in instructional settings, were showing promise for children with disabilities. Use of these technologies not only could improve educational opportunities, but also could increase future career potential. For OSEP, it appeared an opportune time to fund projects that would analyze trends in hardware and software developments to keep abreast of cutting edge technologies. Therefore, beginning in 1984 and every three to five years since, OSEP has examined "futures" technology from a variety of fields (e.g., business, military, medicine).

Early studies focused on specific technology applications, seeking those at a stage where they could be adapted for children with disabilities. But in time, the focus shifted to classroom instruction and how technology could be used as a tool to improve instruction and access to the general education curriculum. A focus on the needs of the learner was deemed critical, particularly since cutting-edge technologies can be exciting and there could be a tendency to use technology for its own sake when it is good instruction that is important, not the technology.

The first study focused on research and applications of simulation, artificial intelligence, and robotics (Moore, Yin, & Lahm, 1985). At that time, computer simulation appeared to present the fewest technical barriers to instruction. As a result, OSEP funded projects that used simulation (in the form of software and video) to teach work-related social competence. At the same time, OSEP continued to support basic research on the use of robotics and artificial intelligence.

An ensuing study examined specific disabilities and matched them with particular technologies (Middleton & Means, 1991). Scenarios were written about what barriers existed to adapting technology to a person's needs and what it would take to bring certain technologies into the marketplace. In looking at virtual reality, for example, the study saw the technology moving out of research and development in phases. In 1991 it predicted that within three to five years, more advanced forms of virtual reality would move into industry and the military, then into entertainment and into some higher education settings (most likely into medicine, science, and computer science), and, finally, into schools at the kindergarten through 12th grade level. Today, we see virtual reality, once considered an expensive toy, showing potential to be used in physical rehabilitation, in treatment of phobias, and in training teachers in a virtual classroom.

In 2002, OSEP's annual Technology Project Directors' Conference focused on technology futures, based on the issues that arose in five commissioned papers. The papers' topic areas ranged from the science of learning and data mining to what the classroom of 2006 would look like. To ground the conference discussions, the focus was on possible implications for future research, for personnel development, and for development of new approaches and products (Hauser, 2001). The discussions seemed to echo a sense that we now have more of a say about the future of technology than we once did. Suggestions included:

- Make it easier for school systems to move research-based practices into the classroom by identifying models of best practices and

create new instructional strategies tailored to incorporate technology into the general education classroom.

- Coordinate funding efforts among OSEP and other federal agencies.

- Make sure sustained supports are in place to ensure implementation.

- Promote more collaboration between general and special educators in implementing technology-based approaches and to improve future instructional programs for students with disabilities.

- Put systems in place to more effectively teach teachers to use assistive and instructional technology efficiently.

Research on Assistive Technology

Assistive technology can play a critical role in increasing access to the general education curriculum. Research has shown that, for students with disabilities, technology can improve education outcomes by increasing access to learning opportunities. Yet, there is often a gap between the research and implementation of technology. Classroom change takes time, and new technologies must be adapted to suit a broad range of needs and a variety of settings.

To gain insight into effective strategies that reduce these potential barriers, an initiative was undertaken to synthesize information from projects that have developed and/or studied approaches to selecting and using assistive technology, training parents, and providing local programs to support the appropriate uses of assistive technology. Information was derived from a review of 47 assistive technology projects including 36 supported by OSEP and 11 supported by other federal agencies. An analysis of the projects (Gruner et al., 2000) led to a recommendation that the following seven principles be considered in making decisions about the selection and use of assistive technology with children with disabilities:

- **Provide leadership**. This principle recognized that a critical element in sustaining any educational intervention is a strong, overarching vision. Such a vision is the foundation for an agreed-upon set of goals and objectives that foster a sense of commitment to the intervention.

- **Support collaboration**. This highlights the teamwork necessary to promote and sustain change in practical settings. In implementing effective interventions, teachers, students, family members, administrators, researchers, and policy makers all have an important contribution to make.
- **Monitor impact**. The focus here is to help projects track tangible indicators of results and focus on effectiveness.
- **Build capacity**. Sustainability is the benchmark of success in any capacity-building effort. Ideally, according to this principle, effectiveness arises out of building the capacity of service providers who provide similar services.
- **Reduce fear and become comfortable with technology**. Fear of assistive technology was a common theme–fear of cost, how to use the technology, the complexity. In many cases, fears could be alleviated through general awareness of what was available, how other projects or schools were using technology, and clear expectations of hoped-for outcomes.
- **Acknowledge diversity**. It is important for service providers to be sensitive to different cultural values and norms and how they affect the approach to and use of technology. Related to this is the need for a realistic understanding of access to the technology itself, particularly for whose who live in remote, physically hard-to-reach areas.
- **Focus on supporting student learning**. Technology is merely a tool, and the ultimate goal is to use that tool to support student learning and achievement.

The National Assistive Technology Research Institute (NATRI) located at the University of Kentucky

While AT devices foster access to the classroom and learning, certain factors may limit their widespread use. One such factor is awareness. School districts may not have access to the latest information about technology or know where to go to get it. Another factor is financial. Purchasing materials requires knowledge, trained personnel, time, money, and planning. Without such elements in place, students may not gain timely access to AT devices. Training is another factor, not just for the child using the technology but for practitioners, who need to understand how to use a full continuum of technology in the classroom. School districts still are learning how best to provide students the technology they need and are seeking alternative and cost-effective means to gain access to key technologies.

To gain a more comprehensive understanding of AT use, OSEP funded the National Assistive Technology Research Institute at the University of Kentucky to examine factors related to the use of AT services in the schools.

The center is studying the use of AT in a range of states and local school districts and considering what factors enhance or impede decision making, planning, acquisition, maintenance, training, and instruction in the use of AT. The project is examining such issues as the percentage of children using AT devices and services, school district policies, IEP practices, training, instruction, and student outcomes. It also is looking at the extent to which institutions of higher education are providing instruction to develop AT knowledge and skills among students preparing for careers in the schools. Results of the work will be disseminated in ways that will assist researchers, policymakers, administrators, and practitioners in developing or improving AT policies and practices for students with disabilities.

Tots 'N' Tech: Research Institute on the Use of Technology in Early Intervention at Jefferson University and Arizona State University

Technology has shown great potential in supporting the growth and development of infants and toddlers with disabilities. The years from birth to three are especially pivotal (Mistrett et al., 2001). During this period, young children make important gains in mobility, communication, social awareness, and cognitive understanding. At this time, children's development is tied to interaction with those who care for them. So the potential of technology shows promise not only in supporting the child's development, but also in enhancing caregivers' ability to meet the child's needs. Technology also can enable children to engage in the same activities as their peers who are not disabled.

Yet, the research knowledge base on this topic has been limited. Thus, evidence of the use and effectiveness of assistive technology for this population is, in the main, anecdotal and practitioner-oriented, and comprehensive research on the subject is sparse.

Recognizing this, OSEP funded a major initiative in this area. Tots 'N' Tech: Research Institute on the Use of Technology in Early Intervention is a collaborative effort between Thomas Jefferson University in Philadelphia and Arizona State University to study the use of assistive technology devices and services with children birth to three. The project views families as the center of their children's learning and development and sees the potential of technology to promote children's learning and participation within family settings. Project objectives include:

• Examining the potential for AT devices and services to contribute to children's learning and participation within the activities and routines of natural settings;

• Identifying critical factors associated with positive outcomes for families and their infants and toddlers;

• Translating research results for families and early intervention service providers.

How the Program Supports Technology Implementation

Technology as an educational intervention is complex. Its implementation requires more than attention to one or two elements but must address a framework of related elements if enduring change is to be realized. In most cases, full implementation of technology requires a comprehensive look at integrating the technology into the curriculum, into instruction, and into the educational setting with substantive policy and professional development support.

In 1983, OSEP funded the National Assistance Project for Special Education Technology (NAPSET) to help local school districts plan for the advent of technology in their schools. Many of the findings from this project were precursors to the much more

intense and in-depth implementation work OSEP projects do today.

The project took into account the level of use of technology in the special education department and a district's readiness to make change. It found that districts where knowledge and skills were at very low levels of use were most successful when they focused on raising general level of awareness and interest in the technology and on implementing a concrete practice. Districts at moderate to higher level of use were most successful when they focused on developing management systems and writing long-range plans for integrating technology into the curriculum. Where resources or district support were lacking, it was critical for teams to address these issues first before moving on to the implementation and institutionalization of innovations.

The complexities of implementation arose in many subsequent projects. In 1995, OSEP initiated a review of five collaborative technology research projects that were studying technology strategies that supported access to the general education curriculum. The cross-project analysis reinforced the components of effective technology integration (e.g., planning, professional development, integrating technology into the curriculum, technical assistance, student outcomes, and evaluation).

The Center to Link Urban Schools with Information and Support on Special Education and Technology (LINK•US)

What we know now echoes and expands the findings of earlier studies and reinforces the continued potential of technology implementation. Just as our past research efforts now represent a body of knowledge, implementation projects represent an opportunity to turn that knowledge into practice. Now, instead of looking specifically at technology and its use, we look at broader approaches within the context of a district, concentrating on building internal capacity, on institutionalized change, and on scaling up.

An embodiment of this pattern of work is the LINK•US center at the Education Development Center, Inc., a five-year project funded by OSEP. The overall project goal was to improve outcomes for students with disabilities by having general and special education teaching personnel integrate a range of technology tools into a standards-based curriculum. LINK•US provided key school district personnel with technical assistance to design, conduct, and evaluate ongoing professional development (Zorfass, 2000). This presumed upfront such key implementation factors as involvement of key leaders from both general and special education and resources allocated to support district initiative. Followup support by local trainers supported the necessary work and helped the districts "own" the initiative. The project found that just implementation is not enough:

- If the goal is institutionalized change and scaling up, scale-up strategies must be considered in the beginning when the initative is designed;

- The initiative needs successive rounds of implementation–the first round is merely the pilot; and

- Scaling up must go hand in hand with building capacity of leaders–a trainer-of-trainers or coaching model.

As a result of its five-year effort, the project developed the STAR Tech Professional Development Program–**S**upporting **T**eachers to **A**chieve **R**esults by Integrating **Tech**nology into the Curriculum (Zorfass, Shaffer, & Rivero, 2003). The technical assistance is guided by the following principles: all professional development activities must be aligned with key district initiatives (e.g., language and literacy improvement) and all activities must be directed at improving results for students.

Model implementation mirrors the critical elements of many successful implementations, creating a learning community with practitioners, providing hands-on help for teacher inquiry on integrating technology, and supporting key leaders.

As an integral part of the model, collaboration between general and special education teaching personnel is encouraged. Such collaboration is supported by district facilitators, administrators, and related service providers. Collaborative school-based teams design, implement, and reflect on the best methods and procedures to integrate technology into ongoing instruction. Teams use an established process for looking at the work of three focal groups of students (students with IEPs, students at risk for failure, and typically developing students) over time. The process involves determining each student's abilities and needs, identifying clear goals related to standards, generating instructional strategies that meet the needs of diverse learners, determining how technology can support learning, and designing assessments. In evaluating the success of such a model, it is important to determine the extent to which teachers institutionalize this process and sustain the use of technology.

Family Center on Technology and Disability

As technology is implemented across settings, the perspectives of multiple stakeholders regarding its usability may affect success. Therefore, as researchers and developers create new technology approaches, the needs and abilities of every individual whom the child will encounter while using the technology must be addressed.

One of the most significant stakeholder groups is the child's family. Thus, the potential of technology may be hindered when families are not trained to integrate use of the assistive device in naturally occurring activities. Professionals are responsible for helping children and their families select and acquire assistive technology devices and services, as well as instructing them in their use.

The Family Center on Technology and Disability, housed at the Academy for Educational Development (AED), is an example of an OSEP center designed to support families by providing readily accessible information about technology. At the core of the center's approach is a partnership with other national organizations who serve families of children with disabilities. Rather than serving families directly, the center's emphasis is on identifying partners who, through their ongoing work with families, can serve as intermediaries in dissemination. These partners disseminate information and provide support to their constituents, thereby broadening the reach of the center.

Summary

The IDEA provision to consider assistive technology in the development of IEPs reflects a growing body of knowledge that has demonstrated the power and potential of technology to enhance the lives of children with disabilities. However, to guarantee that technology will be used consistently and effectively for its intended purposes requires much more than simply recommending a particular tool, putting the tool into the student's or educator's hands, or providing a staff development workshop for teachers. Appropriate use of technology requires that effective technologies be available and that educators understand how these technologies will interact with myriad contextual factors to benefit students with disabilities.

By recognizing the complexity of this issue, the OSEP technology program has produced a strand of inquiry that has evolved from a focus on usefulness–the potential of technology to alleviate a student need–to a focus on both usefulness and utilization. Program research attempts to illuminate contextual factors that both impede and facilitate the use of technology. The success of technology in helping students progress ultimately will depend on how well a full range of technology and contextual factors are addressed.

References

Anderson-Inman, L., & Horney, M. (1997). Electronic books for secondary students. *Journal of Adolescent and Adult Literacy, 40*(6), 486-491.

Blackhurst, A.E., Hales, R.M., & Lahm, E.A. (1998). Using an education server software system to deliver education coursework via the World Wide Web. *Journal of Special Education Technology, 13*, 78-98.

Bransford, J. D., Brown, A. L., & Cocking, R. R. (Eds.). (1999). *How people learn: Brain, , experience, and school.* Washington, DC: National Academy Press.

Burnette, J. (1990). *Assistive technology design in special education.* Reston, VA: The Council for Exceptional Children.

Corley, P., Follansbee, R., Hoffman, B., Lorin, L., & Zorfass, J. (2002). *Draft:Builder.* [Computer software]. Volo, IL: Don Johnston Inc.

Cuban, L. (2001). Why are most teachers infrequent and restrained users of computers in their classrooms? In J. Woodward & L. Cuban (Eds.), *Technology curriculum and professional development: Adapting schools to meet the needs of students with disabilities* (pp. 121-137). Thousand Oaks, CA: Corwin Press, Inc.

Derer, K., Polsgrove, L., & Rieth, H. (1994). A survey of assistive technology applications in schools and recommendations for practice. *Journal of Special Education Technology, 13*, 62-80.

Elmore, R. F. (1996). Getting to scale with good educational practice. *Harvard Educational Review, 66*, 1-26.

Fein, J. (1996). A history of legislative support for assistive technology. *Journal of Special Education Technology, 13*, 1-3.

Fitzgerald, G., & Semrau, L. (2000). The development of KidTools. In C. Wissick (Ed.), Book and Software Review Column. *Journal of Special Education Technology, 15*(3), 41-44.

Foegen, A., & Hargrave, C.P. (1999). Group response technology in lecture-based instruction: Exploring student engagement and instructor perceptions. *Journal of Special Education Technology, 14*, 3-17.

Fuchs, L.S., Fuchs, D., & Hamlett, C.L. (1993). Technological advances linking the assessment of students' academic proficiency to instructional planning. *Journal of Special Education Technology, 12*, 49-62.

Gallagher, P.A., & McCormick, K. (1999). Student satisfaction with two-way interactive distance learning for delivery of early childhood special education coursework. *Journal of Special Education Technology, 14*, 32-47.

Gersten, R., Morvant, M., & Brengelman, S. (1995). Close to the classroom is close to the bone: Coaching as a means to translate research into practice. *Exceptional Children, 62*(1), 52-66.

Gruner, A., Fleming, E., Carl, B., Diamond, C.M., Ruedel, K.L.A., Saunders, J., Paulsen, C., & McInerney, M. (2000). *Final report: Synthesis on the selection and use of assistive technology.* Contract Number HS97017002. Washington, DC: American Institutes for Research.

Hasselbring, T. S. (1999). *Read 180* [Instructional software and other media and print materials]. New York: Scholastic Inc.

Hauser, J. (2001). Preface to the special issue. *Journal of Special Education Technology, 16*(4), 5-6.

Hauser, J., & Malouf, D.B. (1996). A federal perspective on special education technology. *Journal of Learning Disabilities, 29*(5), 504-511.

Higgins, K., & Boone, R. (1993). Technology as a tutor, tool, and agent for reading. *Journal of Special Education Technology, 12,* 28-37.

Hutinger, P., Johanson, J., & Stoneburner, R. (1996). Assistive technology applications in educational programs of children with multiple disabilities: A case study report on the state of the practice. *Journal of Special Education Technology, 13,* 16-35.

The Individuals with Disabilities Education Act Amendments of 1997, Public Law 105-17, 105th Congress, 1997.

The Intersect Digital Library. (n.d.). Retrieved May 28, 2003, from intersect.uoregon.edu/

Lesar, S. (1998). Use of assistive technology with young children with disabilities: Current status and training needs. *Journal of Early Intervention, 21,* 146-159.

McGregor, G., & Pachuski, P. (1996). Assistive technology in schools: Are teachers ready, able, and supported? *Journal of Special Education Technology, 13,* 4-15.

Means, B., Blando, J., Olson, K., Middleton, T., Morocco, C.C., Remz, A.R., & Zorfass, J. (1993). *Using technology to support education reform.* Washington, DC: U.S. Government Printing Office.

Meyen, E., Tangen, P., & Lian, C.H.T. (1999). Developing online instruction: Partnership between instructors and technical developers. *Journal of Special Education Technology, 14,* 18-31.

Middleton, T., & Means, B. (1991). *Final report: Exploring technologies for the education of children with disabilities.* Contract Number HS89027001. Menlo Park, CA: SRI International.

Mistrett, S., Hale, M.H., Diamond, C.M., Ruedel, K.L.A, Gruner, A., Sunshine, C., Berman, K., Saunders, J., & McInerney, M. (2001). *Final report: Synthesis on the use of assistive technol-ogy with infants and toddlers (birth through age two).* Contract Number HS97017002. Washington, DC: American Institutes for Research.

Moore, G.B., Yin, R. K., & Lahm, E. A. (1985). *Robotics, artificial intelligence, computer simulation: Future applications in special education.* Contract Number 300-84-0135. Washington, DC: Cosmos Corporation.

Morford, R. (n.d.). *Final report: Multiple output graphing scientific interactive calculator (MOGSIC).* Award Number H327A980007. Falls Church, VA: Automated Functions, Inc.

Norris, C., Soloway, E., & Sullivan, T. (2002). Examining 25 years of technology in education. *Communications of the ACM. 45*(8), 15-18.

The No Child Left Behind Act of 2001, Public Law 107-10, 107th Congress, 1st Session 2001.

Okolo, C.M., Bahr, C., & Rieth, H. (1993). A retrospective view of computer-based instruction. *Journal of Special Education Technology, 12,* 1-27.

Okolo, C.M., Cavalier, A.R., Ferretti, R.P., & MacArthur, C.A. (1995, January). *Projects funded by the technology, media, and materials program, 1986-1994: What have we learned?* Unpublished manuscript.

Paulsen, K.J., Higgins, K., Miller, S.P., Strawser, S., & Boone, R. (1998). Delivering instruction via interactive television and videotape: Student achievement and satisfaction. *Journal of Special Education Technology, 13,* 59-77.

Remote Realtime Online Captioning: Overview. (n.d.). Retrieved May 28, 2003, from www.ndcd.org/realtime/overview.html

Stinson, M.S., Elliot, L., McKee, B., & Francis, P. (2000). The C-Print real-time speech-to-text support service. *Volta Voices, 8,* 16-22.

TELE-Web Aids Reading and Writing Skills. (1998). *New Educator, 4*(1). Retrieved June 1, 2003, from ed-web3.educ.msu.edu/NewEd/Spring98/Default.htm

Todis, B. (1996). Tools for the task? Perspectives on assistive technology in educational settings. *Journal of Special Education Technology, 13,* 49-61.

Todis, B. (2001). It can't hurt: Implementing AAC technology in the classroom for students with severe and multiple disabilities. In J. Woodward & L. Cuban (Eds.), *Technology curriculum and professional development:*

Adapting schools to meet the needs of students with disabilities (pp. 27-46). Thousand Oaks, CA: Corwin Press, Inc.

Todis, B., & Walker, H. (1993). User perspectives on assistive technology in educational settings. *Focus on Exceptional Children, 26*, 1-16.

U. S. Department of Education. (November 15, 2002). *Voluntary national standard for accessible digital instructional materials to be developed*. [Press Release]. Washington, DC: Author.

U.S. Department of Education. Office of Special Education Programs. (1992). *The technology, educational media, and materials strategic program agenda for individuals with disabilities*. Washington, DC: Author.

Wehmeyer, M.L. (1999). Assistive technology and students with mental retardation: Utilization and barriers. *Journal of Special Education Technology, 14*, 48-58.

Woodward, J., & Carnine, D. (1993). Uses of technology for mathematics assessment and instruction: Reflection on a decade of innovations. *Journal of Special Education Technology, 12*, 38-48.

Woodward, J., & Rieth, H. (1997). A historical review of technology research in special education. *Review of Educational Research, 67*, 503-536.

Woodward, J., & Stroh, M. (2004). *Transitional mathematics*. Longmont, CO: Sopris West Publishing Company.

Zorfass, J. (June, 2000). *Providing technical assistance at the local level: Lessons learned*. Presentation at the annual meeting of the OSEP Technical Assistance and Dissemination Project Directors, Washington, DC.

Zorfass, J., Shaffer, C. G., & Rivero, H. K. (2003). *Leading indeed: Guidelines to implement the STAR tech professional development program*. Contract #HS97-02-2001. Newton, MA: Education Development Center.

4

Assistive Technology and the IEP

Penny Reed and Gayl Bowser

The provision of assistive technology to a child with disabilities is one component of the child's overall educational program. Educational services for children and youth with disabilities age 3-21 are governed by Part B of the Individuals with Disabilities Education Act (IDEA)[1]. The primary purpose of IDEA is to ensure that a free and appropriate public education (FAPE) is provided to children with disabilities who have been determined to need specially designed instruction (i.e., special education). The law pertaining to the education of children with specifically identified disabilities was first

---

[1] Part C of IDEA deals with the education of children from birth to age 3. Many, but not all, of the assistive technology requirements of Part B also apply to Part C. The following references to assistive technology are included in Part C of IDEA. "With regard to early intervention services each of those services for which the child is eligible is of consideration by the IFSP team in determining the services necessary to the outcomes, goals, and, overall development/progress of the child. IDEA describes those early intervention services, which include assistive technology in section. 303.12 (20 U.S.C. 1401(1) and (2); 1432(4)) "Therefore, it is within the determination or consideration of early intervention services that assistive technology is actually considered with regard to Part C and IFSP development. This consideration may too occur in the IFSP review." (20 U.S.C. 1436).

enacted by Congress in 1975 (P.L. 94-142) and has periodically been updated since then with new reauthorizations. As did previous legislation, the 1997 reauthorization of the Individuals with Disabilities Education Act (IDEA '97) requires that each child who is identified as needing special education must have an Individualized Education Program (IEP) that is planned at least once each calendar year.

The term *IEP* refers to the entire program of instruction and support services that is designed to meet the unique educational needs of a child with a disability. In this chapter both the IEP meeting and the resulting IEP document will be addressed. Together these formalize and define a free appropriate public education for a student with a disability (Yell, 1998). Regulations and guidelines for including assistive technology in the IEP will be discussed in both the context of the meeting and the resulting document. In order to appropriately and effectively include assistive technology, a clear understanding of the overall IEP process is necessary.

IDEA '97 emphasizes progress in the general education curriculum and holds schools to a high level of responsibility for developing and implementing valid and beneficial IEPs (Drasgow, Yell, & Robinson, 2001). This high level of responsibility includes the requirement that the IEP:

1. include measurable annual goals
2. specify how progress toward meeting the annual goals will be measured

AT & the IEP/Reed & Bowser **61**

3. include services needed to advance appropriately toward attaining the annual goals

The school must regularly inform the parents of each student who receives special education services of their child's progress toward meeting the annual goals and the extent to which this progress is adequate to enable the child to achieve those goals (Drasgow et. al., 2001). Progress on meeting the goals must be reported with the same frequency as progress is reported for students who do not receive special education. IDEA '97 also communicates a clear requirement that the IEP must be revised if a child fails to make progress toward the annual goals (Clark, 1999).

One of the significant components of IDEA '97 is the requirement that each IEP team considers five special factors, including the child's need for assistive technology (IDEA 34 CFR § 300.346 (a)(2)(v) [Authority: 20 U. S. C. § 1414(d)(1)(A) (d)(3)]. Overall, the goal of IDEA '97 was to improve the effectiveness of special education services and increase the benefits to students to the extent that such benefits are necessary to achieve measurable academic progress (Eyer, 1998). For many students assistive technology can be the key to achieving such progress (MacArthur, 1999; Todis & Walker, 1993).

IDEA has required school districts to provide assistive technology since 1990. It may be included in the IEP as part of an annual goal, short-term objectives, or one of the related services or supplementary aids and services that are needed in order for the student to advance toward the attainment of annual goals and make progress in the general curriculum. In addition, the school district is required to provide the assistive technology for use at home or in other settings if the IEP team determines that FAPE can only be achieved if it is provided in those settings. The mandate for provision of assistive technology by school districts as stated in IDEA '97 is as follows:

300.308 Assistive Technology

(a) Each public agency shall ensure that assistive technology devices or assistive technology services, or both, as those terms are defined in 300.5-300.6, are made available to a child with a disability if required as a part of the child's—

(1) Special education under 300.26;
(2) Related services under 300.24; or
(3) Supplementary aids and services under 300.550(b)(2).

(b) On a case-by-case basis, the use of school-purchased assistive technology devices in a child's home or in other settings is required if the child's IEP team determines that the child needs access to those devices in order to receive FAPE. (34 CFR § 300.308 [Authority: 20 U. S. C. § 1412(a)(12)(B)(i)])

IDEA '97 has both procedural and substantive requirements. Procedural requirements are those components of the law that require schools to follow specific steps, such as including the child's parents in the development of the IEP, conducting complete and individualized evaluations, and determining the appropriate educational placement. Substantive requirements address the required contents of the IEP to ensure that the program confers meaningful educational benefit to a student. (Drasgow et. al., 2001). This discussion of AT and the IEP will include both procedural and substantive requirements.

Definition of Assistive Technology Devices and Services

Assistive technology was first defined in law as a part of the Technology Related Assistance Act of 1988 (P.L. 100-407). The definition was very broad and addressed individuals of all ages. The definition for assistive technology devices in IDEA '97 is identical to that definition, except that it specifically addresses children:

300.5 Assistive Technology Device

As used in this part, "assistive technology device" means any item, piece of equipment, or product system, whether acquired commercially off the shelf, modified, or customized, that is used to increase, maintain, or improve functional capabilities of children with disabilities. (34 CFR § 300.5 [Authority: 20 U. S. C. § 1401(1)])

By definition, assistive technology includes all items that, when used, increase, maintain, or improve functional capabilities. These functional capabilities include seeing, hearing, communicating, moving about in the environment, reading, writing, completing simple or complex tasks of daily living, and much more. Because the definition contains the word technology there is a widespread misconception that assistive technology always means computers or computer-based devices. Conversely, some practitioners believe that there is too much focus on more complicated assistive technology devices and try to combat that by drawing attention to "low-no tech" tools (Purcell & Grant, 2002). To develop both effective and legal individualized plans for assistive technology use, the IEP team must keep in mind that the definition of assistive technology encompasses all items that an individual uses to improve function. The Assistive Technology Checklist (see Figure 1)(Wisconsin Assistive Technology Initiative, 2004), and the Assistive Technology Consideration Quick Wheel (Council for Exceptional Children, 2002) are two tools designed to help increase the IEP team's awareness of the full range of assistive technology. Assistive technology services are also specifically defined in IDEA. The definition is as follows:

Figure 1. Computer access as assistive technology checklist. Used with permission of the Wisconsin Assistive Technology Initiative (2004).

Computer Access
- Keyboard w/ accessibility options
- Word prediction, abbreviation/expansion to reduce keystrokes
- Keyguard
- Arm support (e.g. Ergo Rest)
- Track ball/track pad/ joystick w/ on-screen keyboard
- Alternate keyboard (e.g. IntelliKeys, Discover Board, TASH)
- Mouth stick/Head Master/Tracker w/ on-screen keyboard
- Switch with Morse code
- Switch with scanning
- Voice recognition software
- Other:

300.6 Assistive Technology Services
Any service that directly assists a child with a disability in the selection, acquisition, or use of an assistive technology device. Such term includes:
(A) the evaluation of needs including a functional evaluation of the child, in the child's customary environment;
(B) purchasing, leasing or otherwise providing for the acquisition of assistive technology devices by children with disabilities;
(C) selecting, designing, fitting, customizing, adapting, applying, maintaining, repairing, or replacing of assistive technology devices;
(D) coordinating with other therapies, interventions, or services with assistive technology devices, such as those associated with existing education and rehabilitation plans and programs;
(E) training or technical assistance for a child with a disability, or where appropriate that child's family; and
(F) training or technical assistance for professionals (including individuals providing education and rehabilitation services), employers or others(s) who provide services to employ, or are otherwise, substantially involved in the major life functions of children with disabilities. (34 CFR § 300.6 [Authority: 20 U.S. C. § 1401(2)])

The purpose of clearly defining assistive technology services is to ensure that any assistive technology devices included in a child's IEP are provided, are kept in working order, are integrated into the child's overall educational program, and are supported by individuals who are trained to operate them and teach the child to use them.

Composition of the IEP Team

IDEA '97 requires that the IEP team complete all tasks related to evaluating a student with a disability, determining the student's eligibility for special education and related services, and developing, reviewing, and revising the IEP. The IEP team must include the parents in addition to specific qualified professionals. Parents are clearly intended to be active participants in the development of the IEP and integral to the discussion and planning. The make-up of the IEP team is designed to promote collaboration among all individuals involved with the child's educational program (Council for Exceptional Children, 2000).

By statute, the IEP team must be composed of:

- *The child's parents;*

- *At least one of the child's regular education teachers;*

- *At least one special education teacher or where appropriate, special education provider of the child;*

- *A local education agency (LEA) representative who:*
  - *– is qualified to provide or supervise specially designed instruction;*
  - *– is knowledgeable about the general education curriculum; and*
  - *– is knowledgeable about the availability of LEA resources;*

- *An individual who can interpret the instructional implications of evaluation results, who can be one of the members described in 2-4 above;*

- *At the discretion of the parents or LEA, other individuals who have special knowledge or expertise about the child including related services personnel, as appropriate; and*

- *The child, when appropriate. (34 CFR § 300.344 [Authority: 20 U. S. C. § 1414(d)(1)(B])*

The IEP team has full responsibility to plan a program that will ensure FAPE. While there is no requirement that one person must know everything about the child and the assistive technology that might help that child, collectively IEP team members must hold the necessary knowledge and skills to appropriately address all aspects of the student's program, including assistive technology. For some IEP teams this may be a challenge. Lahm and Sizemore (2002), in a survey of educators, speech language pathologists, occupational therapists, assistive technology suppliers, and assistive technology practioners, found that 83% of them agreed that their education did not adequately prepare them to provide assistive technology services. If members of

the IEP team are not sufficiently knowledgeable to address assistive technology concerns, one or more additional team members who have the requisite knowledge may be added. Team members added to provide assistive technology expertise should have specific knowledge about assistive technology for the areas of concern that were identified during the evaluation.

The IEP Meeting

The IEP meeting is convened after a child has been determined to be eligible for special education services. The IEP team's duty is to plan an individualized program that meets the child's unique educational needs. The IEP team must address both specially designed instruction and any related services or supplementary aids and services that the district will provide to meet those needs (Bateman & Linden, 1998).

The IEP meeting generally begins with an overview of evaluation results and a discussion of progress that the student has made during the previous year. This information will be included in the IEP document to designate the child's present level of performance. The child's current abilities, the problems that interfere with the child's education, and the implications of this information form the basis of the annual goals that will then be developed (Gorn,1999). The child's current use of assistive technology should be part of the discussion of the present level of performance. For example, if a child who experiences difficulty in writing, write: six words a minute with a pencil and 20 words a minute with a portable word processor, it is important to include this information in the discussion of present level of performance since it may help the team determine the child's need for assistive technology for writing.

Along with annual goals based on present level of educational performance, the IEP team must develop either short-term objectives or benchmarks for the student. Benchmarks are indicators of the amount of progress toward a goal that a student is expected to make within specified segments of the school year, whereas short-term objectives are discrete skill components of an annual goal (Drasgow et. al., 2001).

Figure 2 offers examples of benchmarks and short-term objectives for a child who uses an augmentative communication device with four vocabulary choices for simple communication tasks. Both benchmarks and short-term objectives are measurable intermediate steps between the present levels of educational performance and the annual goals.

Once the annual goals with accompanying benchmarks or short-term objectives have been determined, the IEP team must discuss the specific services that the school will provide. These may include related services or supplementary aids or services that the student will need in order to master the projected annual goals. They may also include support for the staff members who help to educate the student. As stated previously assistive technology may be included as part of (a) goals and objectives, (b) related services or (c)supplementary aids and services. In addition, it may also be included under supports for staff. Goals and objectives address changes in the student's performance. Related services are those actions taken by adults that are required in order for the child to benefit from the educational program. Supports for staff are the training, assistance or other actions needed by the educators who provide the individualized instruction (Bowser & Roberts, 2003).

Focus on Planning in the IEP Meeting

The purpose of the IEP meeting is to discuss a student's unique needs and plan a program of intervention that will meet those needs. All team members are required by IDEA to spend time discussing and planning to meet that child's needs. The way in which IEP meetings are conducted varies greatly from state to state, from district to district, and even from school to school. The nature of the discussion and its effectiveness are impacted by many factors including proximity of members, style of communication (written, verbal, and nonverbal, and the quality of team process employed) (Lytle & Bordin, 2001). One process for conducting IEP meetings that lends itself well to consideration of assistive technology is that described by Reed (1997). In this process, all IEP team members, including parents, come to

Figure 2. Sample IEP annual goal, short-term objectives, and benchmarks for a student who uses an augmentative communication device.

Annual Goal: Jasmine will communicate independently without prompts from adults.

Short-Term Objectives for Communication

- Jasmine will use her communication device to correct a miscommunication without prompting from an adult for 80% of all possible opportunities on five consecutive days.
- Jasmine will use her communication device to initiate a conversation without prompting from an adult at least three times daily on five consecutive days.
- Jasmine will use her communication device to request information from a peer without prompting from an adult at least once daily on five consecutive days.

Benchmarks for Communication

- Jasmine will independently initiate communication, request information and correct miscommunications 25% of all possible opportunities on five consecutive days.
- Jasmine will independently initiate communication, request information and correct miscommunications 50% of all possible opportunities on five consecutive days.
- Jasmine will independently initiate communication, request information and correct miscommunications 75% of all possible opportunities on five consecutive days.

the IEP meeting prepared to discuss the student but without having written any draft goals. They may bring test scores, samples of work, ideas, or observational data that they think may prove useful. Discussion is divided into four separate steps:

1. The team discusses and records long-term goals, hopes and dreams for the child.

2. The team discusses and records what the child is able to do in relation to those goals.
3. The team determines what the child should be able to do one year from now in relation to those goals.
4. The team identifies the services that the child will need in order to have a good chance to accomplish those goals in one year.

Throughout an IEP meeting that uses the above format, the discussion is recorded in such a way that all team members can see the results of the discussion as it takes place. This may be on a flip chart, an overhead projector or a projected computer screen. Any IEP team members may think of things that need to be added or changed throughout the discussion. That can occur as long as everyone is aware of it and agrees with the addition or change. Step 1 begins by asking the parents to share their long term goals for their child. This simply frames the discussion and assures that the parents are active participants early in that discussion. When the process is finished, the information in Step 2 becomes the Present Level of Performance. The information in Step 3 becomes the Annual Goals. The information in Step 4 is a compilation of items that will need to be written on the IEP form under Related Services, Supplementary Aids and Services, Supports for Staff or as part of the methods and materials under specific goals. Discussion of assistive technology may naturally occur in any of the steps; however, it is during Step 4 that this discussion most frequently occurs.

When a system such as this is used, the result is that the meeting is effectively used to plan, parents are equal and full participants, and everything that is written in the IEP is directed at achieving long-term goals. Figure 3 offers a sample of IEP planning charts developed using this system.

Consideration of Assistive Technology Need

No matter how the meeting is conducted, the IEP team's discussion must include consideration of the following special factors:

1. *when appropriate, strategies, including positive behavioral interventions, strategies, and sup-*

Figure 3. Sample charts developed using the IEP planning process.

Hopes and Dreams
- Get a driver's license
- Graduate from high school
- Buy a car
- Get a welding certificate
- Have my own apartment

What the Student Can Do
- Can answer sample driver's test questions orally
- Has finished all required classes except English, math and internship.
- Has taken welding in shop classes
- Knows basic addition and subtraction facts
- Can do simple practical math with a calculator
- Can write paragraphs of five sentences or less using a talking word processor

What the Student Could Do in a Year
- Pass the written driver's test
- Create and follow a simple budget
- Visit technical colleges with welding programs
- Purchase items from a simple shopping list using a calculator to total amounts and make purchase decisions
- Write descriptions of welding jobs and products of up to two pages using outlining software and a talking word processing program
- Open a bank account and save a portion of allowance/earnings

Accommodations and Services That Will Be Needed
- Modified driver's test
- Talking word processing software
- Concept mapping/outlining software
- Calculator for all practical math problems
- AT training for new staff

ports for children whose behavior impedes their learning or that of others;
2. *the language needs related to the IEP of a child with limited English proficiency;*

3. *the provision of instruction in Braille and the use of Braille for a child who is blind or visually impaired, unless the IEP team determines, following evaluation of the child's reading and writing skills, needs, and appropriate media (including future needs for instruction in Braille or the use of Braille), that such instruction is not appropriate;*
4. *the child's communication needs; for a child who is deaf or hard of hearing, the language and communication needs, opportunities for direct communications with peers and professional personnel in the child's language and communication mode, academic level and full range of needs, including opportunities for direct instruction in the child's language and communication mode; and*
5. *whether the child needs assistive technology devices and services. (34 CFR § 300.346 (a)(2)(v) [Authority: 20 U.S.C. § 1414(d)(3) and (4)(B) and (e)])*

If, in considering these special factors, the IEP team determines that a child needs a particular device or service in order to receive FAPE, the IEP team must include a statement to that effect on the IEP (34 CFR § 300.346 (a)(2)(v) [Authority: 20 U.S.C. § 1414(d)(1)(A]).

Some of the required special factors apply only to specific situations, such as "a child whose behavior impedes his learning or that of others" or "a child who is blind or visually impaired." There is no such restriction on the requirement to consider the need for assistive technology devices and services. Every IEP team must answer the question "Is there assistive technology which is needed for this child to receive a free and appropriate public education or to benefit from the educational program we have designed?"

It is important to note that the requirements for Braille and for communication needs also lead to a discussion of assistive technology. Students who use Braille may use things such as electronic notetakers or specialized computers and software that fits the definition of assistive technology for vision impairments. Other students who cannot use their voices to communicate effectively may use electronic voice output devices to speak for them. Such devices are also considered assistive technology.

Neither the federal statutes nor federal regulations provide any guidance about how the IEP team is to implement the requirement to consider assistive technology. Most IEP forms developed by states and local education agencies across the United States have listed the special factors on the IEP form. In most cases, the IEP team must check a box to indicate that it has considered whether the child needs assistive technology (Edyburn, 2002). The quality of that consideration may vary highly, depending upon the knowledge of the IEP team (Golden, 1998; Lahm & Sizemore, 2002).

While IDEA '97 requires that assistive technology be considered for all children with disabilities, many educators have little experience in implementing this requirement. For example, in a survey of Oregon educators, over 40% of those surveyed had never participated in considering assistive technology during an IEP meeting (Bowser, 1997).

Since 1990, numerous print and web resources have been developed to help both parents and professionals learn more about assistive technology and the IEP process (Bowser & Reed, 1995; Chambers, 1997; RESNA Technical Assistance Project, 1992; Texas Assistive Technology Network, 2002).

In order to examine the IEP team's role in considering the need for assistive technology, it is helpful to look at a definition of consideration. *The American Heritage Dictionary* (2001) defines "consider" as, "to think about carefully and seriously," "to form an opinion about," or "to look at thoughtfully." Team members cannot "think carefully" about something unless they know something about that subject. Therefore, it is critical that someone on each IEP team knows about the assistive technology the child might need (Reed & Bowser, 1998). In addition, individuals who work directly with the child may make less expensive, more practical suggestions if they are familiar with assistive technology themselves rather than relying on recommendations from a more formal evaluation conducted by an external team. Behrmann and Schepis (1994) found that the more removed the assistive technology evaluators were from the daily setting, the more expensive and complex their recommendations for assistive technology.

Another aspect of assistive technology consideration is that the IEP team must identify assistive technology services that might be needed to support the child's assistive technology use. Such services include training and technical assistance and supports to school personnel. In order to appropriately consider assistive technology services, the IEP team members need to know how their school district provides these services. Are there key individuals who have been identified within the district? Is there an assistive technology team? If so, is there a referral process to initiate services from the AT Team? Training or technical assistance for professionals has been mandated since 1990. In IDEA '97, this is further expanded to include, "supports for school personnel." If in their consideration, IEP team members determine that assistive technology is warranted, the team must consider what training or support the direct service providers need and document how it will be made available (34 CFR § 300.347 [Authority: 20 U.S.C. § 1401(2)]).

To help IEP team members and others, indicators of high quality consideration of the need for assistive technology have been developed (Zabala et al. 2000). When all of the following factors are present as the IEP team considers assistive technology, the likelihood that appropriate decisions will be made increases (Zabala et. al. 2000).

1. Assistive technology devices and services are considered for all students with disabilities regardless of type or severity of disability.
2. The IEP team has the knowledge and skills to make informed assistive technology decisions.
3. The IEP team uses a collaborative decision-making process based on data about the student, environments, and tasks to make assistive technology determinations.
4. A continuum of assistive technology devices and services is explored.
5. Decisions regarding the need for assistive technology devices and services are based on access to the curriculum and the student's IEP goals and objectives.
6. Decisions regarding the need for assistive

technology devices and services and supporting data are documented.

Further, several assistive technology programs have developed guidelines to help IEP teams make good decisions about assistive technology and to document those decisions. Included in these are:

- Boston Public Schools, Student Access Map (SAM): www.boston.k12.ma.us/teach/technology/emmanuel.asp

- Georgia Program for Assistive Technology: www.gpat.org

- Oregon Technology Access Program: www.otap-oregon.org

- Texas Assistive Technology Network: www.texasat.net

- Wisconsin Assistive Technology Initiative: www.wati.org

Transition Planning and Assistive Technology in IEP Development

Beginning when a student is 14 years of age, IDEA requires that the IEP team start to plan for the student's transition from school to life in the community. When the child is 14, this planning takes the form of developing goals and objectives that relate to postsecondary education, vocational training, integrated employment (including supported employment), continuing and adult education, adult services, independent living, or community participation (34 CFR § 300.29 [(Authority: 20 U.S.C. 1414(d)(1)(A) and (d)(6)(A)(ii)]). When the student reaches the age of 16 and each year that the student remains in school after that, a specific transition plan must be developed by the IEP team (34 CFR § 300.347(b)(1) [Authority: 20 U.S.C. 1414(d)(1)(A) and (d)(6)(A)(ii)]). This transition plan includes transition benchmarks as well as goals for learning. Benchmarks typically included in a transition plan are steps such as obtaining a driver's license, applying to institutions of higher education, applying for vocational rehabilitation services, contacting an independent living facility, or other steps appropriate to the student's individual needs (Wehmeyer & Lawrence, 1995)

The transition plan focuses on the specific actions that the student and/or the student's support network will take in order for the student to make a smooth transition from school to post-school settings. IDEA requires that the IEP team be expanded to include all those service providers and advocates for the student who can be of assistance when he or she is no longer receiving school services. Often the student identifies several new team members such as a trusted friend, a grandparent, a minister, or a case manager from another agency, who participate as IEP team members. One important member of an IEP team for a student who uses assistive technology is a person who can help identify new assistive technology that may be needed due to specific characteristics of the setting to which the student is transitioning (Anctil, 1998). Whether the student is transitioning to a post secondary education setting or a community setting the environmental demands will be very different than the school setting. Once technology is identified, any needed support for its use will need to be identified and included in the transition plan.

Much has been written about the importance of self-determination and self-advocacy as students prepare to transition out of the public school system (Direction Services, 1997; Kelker & Holt, 1997; Powers, 1996; Storms, De Stefano & O'Leary, 1996; Wehmeyer & Kelchner, 1995). Curricula have been developed and used to train students in specific self-determination skills (Wehmeyer, Agran, & Hughes, 1998). However, it is not just the training of the student, but the response from the adults with whom the student interacts that is critical. Thus Abery and Stancliffe (1996) found that the nature of the interactions between the IEP team members and the student is one of the critical factors in acquiring self-determination. Thoma (1999) recommended specific strategies for supporting students as they acquired the ability to speak for themselves. These include helping them prepare for their IEP meetings, allowing them to decide who should participate, and helping them focus on needed supports rather than trying to fit into existing programs. Assistive technology is one type of support that can make it possible for young adults to be successful in environments that might not otherwise be open to them.

Scherer (1991) has studied adults who use technology and those who eventually abandon technology use. Three aspects of AT use must be considered to prevent technology abandonment: the milieu in which the person uses or will use assistive technology, the personality of the user, and the characteristics of the specific technology. In order to ensure continued use of successfully adopted assistive technology after the student leaves school, the transition team must include support and assistive technology services, as defined in IDEA, in the IEP. Failure to do so typically results in abandonment of the assistive technology within one year of transition from school services (Anctil, 1998).

In all aspects of planning for the future, students must be able to clearly and confidently articulate their choices and interests, even when the adults in their life do not agree (Steere & Cavaiuolo, 2002). With regard to assistive technology, the student must know what assistive technology exists, how it works, and when it might be beneficial. Exposure to appropriate assistive technology along with the necessary training and sufficient time to become proficient with the technology are critical as students prepare for transition. The following is a list of resources that IEP teams might use to help a student develop self determination skills related to the use of assistive technology:

- Hey! Can I Try That?
  www.edtechpoints.org

- Self Determination Student Information Guide: www.wati.org/atandtransition.htm

- Self directed IEP: www.ldonline.org

- Transition and self-advocacy:www.ldonline.org/ld_indepth/transition/transition_self_advocacy.html

When the management, repair, and maintenance of assistive technology is one of the areas of concern, the IEP should include provisions for putting together a transition portfolio to accompany the student when he or she exits school. A transition portfolio can be an effective support for the student who may not always be able to self-advocate or communicate his or her wishes or interests (Demchak & Greenfield, 2000). A list of the contents of a portfolio for management of assistive technology and forms to gather that information are available to download from the Wisconsin Assistive Technology Initiative (www.wati.org/atandtransition.htm).

Required Components of the IEP Document

The purpose of the IEP document is to summarize the agreements made during the IEP meeting. Thus, it describes the needs of the student, delineates the specific annual goals and short-term objectives or benchmarks, specifies the educational programming and placements and describes how performance will be measured. Unfortunately, in the past IEPs have often been inadequate guides for classroom instruction (Smith, 1990b). However, IDEA requires that the completed IEP serve both as a tool for instructional planning and a tool for communication about the unique needs of the student, about the commitments of the school district, and about each person's role and responsibilities in implementing the plan (Kukic & Schrag, 1998).

If the child's educational program is questioned, the IEP document will come under close scrutiny. Drasgow et al. (2001) reviewed dozens of cases in which complaints had been filed and found that hearing officers or courts often ruled an IEP as invalid (a) if annual goals were so unchallenging that achieving them would not result in meaningful progress, (b) if evaluations were completed by personnel with no credentials to perform them, and (c) if the IEP did not address all areas of need identified during evaluation.

Much has been written about the process of IEP development (Bateman & Linden, 1998; Huefner 2000; Walsh, 2001,) and issues associated with legally defensible IEPs (Drasgow et al., 2001; Julnes & Brown 1993). Carl and Zabala (2002) offer the following top 10 critical elements in developing an IEP which includes assistive technology.

1. Develop measurable goals and objectives.
2. Base goals and objectives on the general curriculum first.

3. Focus on student performance outcomes and functional application of assistive technology.
4. Address the following questions.
   a. What are the instructional tasks that the student is expected to accomplish?
   b. What barriers exist for this student to be able to accomplish the required tasks?
   c. How does assistive technology help the student overcome barriers and accomplish instructional tasks independently?
   d. What is the range of supports provided to the student to overcome the barriers?
5. Write collaborative, integrated goals and objectives.
6. Write curriculum-based objectives. Then include assistive technology needed to accomplish that objective.
7. Generally use generic terminology for focusing on assistive technology features rather than using brand names.
8. Include a system of assistive technology devices to accomplish tasks rather than just one tool.
9. Be specific as to the role assistive technology will play in the plan.
10. Include assistive technology services and program supports to be provided in the IEP.

Purpose of the IEP Document

The IEP document is both an educational and a legal tool. It has several stacked functions, including:

- Communicating what was decided in the IEP meeting
- Committing district resources
- Providing the means to measure progress
- Guiding implementation for the year

Each of these functions is discussed in more detail in the following sections.

Communicating What Was Decided in the IEP Meeting

Once the process of developing an IEP has been completed, each person who contributes to the education of an individual child must be made aware of all the specifics of the plan and the part they will play in implementing it. For this reason, it is important that the IEP document offers a clear and complete description of the program. The plan insures that each person who attended the meeting has the same understanding of what will be implemented. However, many people who did not attend the meeting may be asked to take responsibility for some part of implementation and will, therefore, need a clearly written IEP document as a guide. For example, staff assignments are changed, new staff are hired, the student moves within the district or the student moves to a new district. When a child who is eligible for special education services moves from one school district to another, the new district must implement the existing IEP or hold a new IEP meeting to revise it. Additionally, school districts are in a strong position legally when the IEP teams design educational programs that are beneficial and clearly communicate the specifics of the plan.

A well-written IEP document is designed to clarify the instruction, services, and accommodations a child will need. The intent of IDEA is that the assistive technology devices and services that will be provided are described as clearly and as completely as possible. Thus, the type or features of the device which the student will use, the services that will be needed to support that use and the purposes for which it will be used should all be described in the IEP in such a way that everyone can understand the plan for AT use.

In some cases this may include the name of a specific assistive technology device, especially if the child has received extensive training on a device that has unique features. In other cases a more generic description may be more appropriate such as "talking word processing software" rather than the specific name of the software program.

Committing District Resources

By law, the IEP document must list all school district resources that will be provided to implement the plan for an individual child. This includes assistive technology devices and services that the IEP team incorporates in a program for a child with a disability.

While education agencies are committed to ensuring that devices and services listed on the IEP are made available to the child, this requirement does not mandate that all assistive technology be purchased with school district funds. Other funding sources may be utilized. However, it is not acceptable for a school district to refuse to provide needed assistive technology devices and services due to lack of funds.

Most of the decisions about how to document the provision of assistive technology devices and services are left to individual school districts. Such decisions include interpretations of the definition of assistive technology, instruction in documentation of the need for assistive technology on the IEP, and the use of assistive technology as either accommodations or modifications (Bowser, 2001). Many school districts have developed assistive technology operating guidelines to help in the development of IEPs that offer consistent levels of quality and clarity. Such model operating guidelines (Bowser, 2002) provide specific actions that each IEP team must take to meet the legal requirements of IDEA and ensure that the consideration of assistive technology during the IEP team meeting is adequate to ensure FAPE.

Providing the Means to Measure Progress

The IEP document should also be written in such a way that specific data can be collected about the student's progress toward meeting goals and objectives. Objective data increase the chance of seeing patterns and trends in the student's performance that can be used to develop more effective educational programs. There are many ways to collect data including interviews, review of products created by the student, direct observation and video taping (Reed, Bowser, & Korsten, 2002)

When an IEP team develops criteria to indicate that a goal has been met, the team should describe the type of change it hopes to see. Knowledge of research on the impact of assistive technology use can help a team set reasonable expectations. For example, MacArthur (1999) found that the use of text-to-speech and word prediction software resulted in improved spelling and legibility for four out of five students with learning disabilities. However, he found no difference in the length of the written material or the rate of composition. Therefore, goals for use of these type of assistive technology should probably not include increased length or rate of composition for a student with a learning disability unless specific data have shown this to be a reasonable expectation. Use of those same tools by a student with a motor impairment might result in a change in both speed and length of written products. Reasonable criteria should be set for the use of assistive technology based on the type of task for which the technology will be used and the expected rate of student progress.

Guiding Implementation for the Year

An IEP will not provide a free appropriate public education, unless it is implemented as written. It must contain sufficient information and direction for all educators who serve the student to implement it throughout the school year. For example, if the IEP requires that the student have classroom tests read to him either with assistive technology or by a person, all the student's teachers must be held responsible to make sure that this happens in their class. All of the teachers and related service providers involved in the child's educational program must understand that it is their responsibility to implement the IEP as written (LaPoint, 1997). In order to do this, they must have copies of the IEP and understand how to implement the goals (Menlove, Hudson, & Suter, 2001).

Content of the IEP Document

Both the federal government and individual states make rules about the specific form and content of the IEP document. That is IDEA '97 includes specific rules about what must be included in the IEP document. In addition, some states offer state forms that must be used by all IEP teams in that state. Other states require specific IEP content but leave decisions about format to individual education agencies.

In general, a good IEP clearly relates to the general education curriculum and shows how the student will progress in that curriculum. Historically special educators have been unfamiliar with the general education curriculum (Pugach & Warger, 1993). To ensure proper progress in the general education curriculum, general and special educators must work together.

IDEA '97 specifically requires that annual goals be measurable (IDEA 34 CFR §300.347 (a)

(2) [Authority: 20 U.S.C. § 1414(d)(1)(A) and (d)(6)(A)(ii)). This requirement is part of the law because Congress was concerned that previously annual goals had often been too abstract, broad, or vague (Drasgow et al., 2001). Lignugaris/Kraft, Marchand-Martella, and Martella (2001) make the case that annual goals must be precise in order to be measurable and suggest using the time tested pattern of four parts to each goal: (a) condition; (b) student's name; (c) clearly described, observable behavior; and (d) performance criteria. Measurable annual goals with their short-term objectives or benchmarks are the heart of the IEP. The use of assistive technology should be tied to these annual goals. Therefore, when assistive technology is included in an IEP, the document must clearly relate the assistive technology devices to specific annual goals or related services for which it will be used. Assistive technology should not be an add-on that is unrelated to the rest of the student's program. For example, it would not be appropriate to write a separate goal stating that a child will learn to activate a switch with no indication of what the child is using the switch to do.

An IEP must also show how the student will be supported in participating in state and district assessment. Such support may include assistive technology if it is allowed by the state and for a given test. Numerous states have developed extensive rules about the use of assistive technology during state and local assessments. Web sites, such as the following brief sample, that are maintained by state education agencies are helpful sources for these rules.

- California Department of Education Standards and Assessment Division www.cde.ca.gov/statetests
- Maine Department of Education www.state.me.us/education/mea/ meahome.htm
- Oregon Department of Education, Office of Assessment and Evaluation www.ode.state.or.us/asmt
- Texas Education Agency Texas Alternative Assessments www.tea.state.tx.us/ student.assessment/faq/sdaa.html

- Wisconsin Department of Public Instruction www.dpi.state.wi.us/dpi/oea/assessment.html

The 2001 reauthorization of the Elementary and Secondary Education Act reinforced the requirement that students with disabilities participate in state and local assessments (Elementary and Secondary Education Act, 2001). This law is commonly referred to as "No Child Left Behind" (NCLB). Under NCLB schools must test at least 95 percent of students with disabilities. NCLB requires that test scores of students with disabilities be reported along with their nondisabled peers and be included in decisions as to whether the school is making adequate yearly progress. It also requires that districts report the progress of all students who receive special education separately as a part of determining adequate yearly progress of the school and the school district.

IDEA requires that each IEP must indicate when a modification or an accommodation will be used (IDEA 34 CFR §300.347 (a) (2) [Authority: 20 U.S.C. § 1414(d)(5)(i)]). An accommodation is a change in how a student accesses and demonstrates learning, but it does not substantially change the instructional content. A modification, on the other hand, is a change in what a student is expected to learn and demonstrate (Walsh, 2001). The difference between accommodations and modifications is critical because modifications change the essential content that a student needs to know for successful performance in high-stakes state and district assessments whereas an accommodation does not (Green & Sireci, 1999). The use of an assistive technology device in assessment may be either an accommodation or a modification depending upon the task for which it is used. Consider the use of text-to-speech software to read test questions and provide auditory feedback as the student answers the questions. If the test is a reading test, use of text-to-speech would be a modification of the task. However, if the test is to determine a student's ability to solve a science problem, the use of the same software may be an accommodation.

Since they were first required in 1975, IEP documents reviewed by experts have shown several problems (Huefner, 2000). These include a lack of adequate training for teachers in developing IEPs, inadequate use of team processes, rote compliance with the paperwork requirements with no thought to purpose and outcome, and excessive demands on teacher time (Smith, 1990a). Other problems include minimal coordination with the general education curriculum (Lipsky & Gartner, 1996), poor connection between assessment data and instructional goals (Smith & Simpson, 1989), and failure to write measurable goals and objectives that can be used to evaluate and monitor student achievement (Yell, 1998). All of these problems can impact the effective inclusion of assistive technology in the IEP. To ensure that the IEP document does provide a framework for implementation, teams sometimes develop an additional action plan that describes how implementation will be provided to help the child meet annual goals and short term objectives. While not required by IDEA, such a plan helps to clearly designate responsibility for actions described in the IEP and set the stage for ongoing data collection.

Because students frequently struggle with multiple aspects of a task such as writing, technology alone rarely addresses all of the student's writing needs (Fennema-Jansen, 2001). When teams develop implementation plans for assistive technology users, instruction in the use of strategies must usually be combined with instruction in the use of the technology. Plans for offering training in technology use to professionals often accompany the training for an individual student. Figure 4 offers an example of an implementation plan for a student's use of assistive technology for writing.

Summary

The IEP forms the basis of the student's educational program. Discussion during the IEP meeting should flow from identification of present level of educational performance to the setting of measurable annual goals with accompanying objectives or benchmarks. Assistive technology may be included in all discussion, but must be addressed during the specific consideration of the child's need for assistive technology that is required as one of the Special Factors.

Figure 4. Sample implementation plan for a student using assistive technology for writing.

Implementation Plan for Jeremy to Meet Writing Goal. (*Note: The class is learning to use the 6 + 1 Traits for Writing.*)

Student Concerns:
- Following instruction on using ideas, content and organization strategies, Jeremy will use outlining/diagramming software to practice.
- Following instruction on finding the "Voice" for his writing, Jeremy will use text-to-speech software to help him decide what "sounds' right to him.
- Following instruction on word choice strategies and conventions, Jeremy will use his speaking spellchecker in addition to the classroom word wall.
- Following instruction on sentence fluency, Jeremy will use text-to-speech software to listen to his writing for fluency.
- When presenting his written work to the class, Jeremy will choose multimedia software to present main ideas.

Environmental Concerns:
- Jeremy will sit on the left side of the room near the computer bank.
- Jeremy will keep his speaking spell checker in his desk.
- The special education program will provide all needed software and supplies for Jeremy's classroom.

Staffing Concerns:
- The assistive technology consultant will train Jeremy's teacher and two paraprofessionals in the use of the selected text-to-speech software and outlining/diagramming software.
- The special education teacher will provide Jeremy with direct one-to-one instruction on the use of multimedia software daily for four days.
- The Title I reading paraprofessional will work with Jeremy in pull-out training for three weeks to help him use the software
- The general education teacher will allow Jeremy to work with the computer software following all sessions on using ideas and content and organization strategies and on instruction on sentence fluency.

A child's IEP document describes the services that a school district will provide to ensure that the child receives a Free and Appropriate Public Education. If an IEP is not specific enough, the plan is open to a wide variety of interpretations and confusion is likely. In order to create a plan with as much clarity as possible, the IEP team may ask the following two questions:

- Will the teachers, educational assistants, related service providers and administrators who did not attend this meeting, but will be working with this student, understand what we want them to do?

- If this student moved to a new school district, would the people in that district be able to understand and implement our plan?

When an IEP team takes the time to ensure that assistive technology services are described in a clear manner in the appropriate places in the plan, each person on the student's educational team can better understand what is needed for successful implementation. This helps to improve the student's education as well as reduce conflict.

The Quality Indicators for Assistive Technology Services (QIAT Indicators) for Inclusion of Assistive Technology in IEPs offer guidance to help the team and the educational agency effectively describe the role of assistive technology in a child's IEP (Zabala et al., 2000).

1. The education agency has guidelines for documenting assistive technology needs in the IEP and everyone on the IEP team is aware of them.
2. Assistive technology is included in the IEP in a manner that provides a clear and complete description of the devices and services to be provided and used.
3. Assistive technology is used as a tool to support achievement of IEP goals and objectives as well as participation and progress in the general curriculum.
4. IEP content regarding assistive technology use is written in language that describes measurable and observable outcomes.
5. All services needed to implement assistive technology use are documented in the IEP.

Additional discussion of the QIAT Indicator Areas can be found in Chapter 10 of this book.

IDEA'97 requires that the IEP team consider assistive technology needs in the development of every IEP. Once the IEP team has reviewed assessment results and determined that assistive technology is needed for provision of FAPE, the IEP document must reflect the team's determination in as clear a fashion as possible.

References

Abery, B., & Stanclife, R. (1996). The ecology of self-determination. In D. Sands & M. Wehmeyer (Eds.). *Self-determination across the life span: Independence and choice for people with disabilities* (pp. 111-146). Baltimore: Paul H. Brookes.

American Heritage Dictionary (4th ed.) . (2001). New York: Dell Publishing.

Anctil, T. (1998). Framing the transition Iissues, TechTransmitter, *1*(2), 1-2

Bateman, B.D., & Linden, M.A. (1998). *Better IEPs: How to develop legally correct and educationally useful programs (3rd ed.).* Longmont, CO: Sopris West.

Behrmann, M.M. & Schepis, M.M. (1994). Assistive technology assessment: A multiple case study of three approaches with students with physical disabilities during the transition from school to work. *Journal of Vocational Rehabilitation, 4*(3), 202-210.

Bowser, G. (1997). Unpublished survey. Roseburg: Oregon Technology Access Program.

Bowser, G. (2001), Assistive technology questions for administrators, *Oregon Department of Education Bookshelf CD.* Salem: Oregon Department of Education.

Bowser, G. (2002). *Assistive Technology; Sample operating guidelines for school districts and IEP teams.* Roseburg: Oregon Technology Access Program.

Bowser, G., & Reed, P. (1995). Education TECH Points for assistive technology Planning. *Journal of Special Education Technology, 7*(4), 325-338.

Bowser, G., & Roberts, D. (2003). *Documenting services on the IEP: A guide for related service providers,* Roseburg: Oregon Technology Access Program

Carl, D., & Zabala, J. (2002). *AT and the IEP: Building a solid foundation.* Paper presented at Closing the Gap Preconference, Minneapolis, MN.

Chambers, A.C. (1997). *Has technology been considered? A guide for IEP teams.* Reston, VA: The Council of Administrators of Special Education and the Technology and Media Division of the Council for Exceptional Children.

Clark, S. G. (1999). Assessing IEPs for IDEA compliance. *Education Law Report, 137,* 35-42.

Council for Exceptional Children. (2000). *Developing educationally relevant IEPs: A technical assistance document for speech-language pathologists.* Reston, VA: Council for Exceptional Children.

Council for Exceptional Children. (2002). *Assistive technology consideration quick wheel.* Arlington, VA: Author.

Demchak, M.A., & Greenfield, R.G. (2000). A transition portfolio for Jeff, a student with multiple disabilities. *Teaching Exceptional Children, 32*(6), 44-49.

Direction Services (1997). *After school – then what?: A resource guide for transition planning.* Portland, OR: Direction Services.

Drasgow, E., Yell, M.L., & Robinson, T.W. (2001). Developing legally correct and educationally appropriate IEPs. *Remedial and Special Education, 22,* 359-373.

Edyburn, D. (2002). Assistive technology and the IEP, *Special Education Technology Practice,* 4(3), 15-21

Eyer. T.L. (1998). Greater expectations: How the 1997 IDEA Amendments raise the basic floor of opportunity for children with disabilities. *Education Law Report, 126,* 1-19.

Fennema-Jansen, S. (2001). Measuring effectiveness: Technology to support writing. *Special Education Technology Practice, 3*(1), 16-22.

Golden, D. (1998). *Assistive technology in special education: Policy and practice.* Reston, VA: The Council of Administrators of Special Education and the Technology and Media Division of the Council for Exceptional Children.

Gorn, D. (1999). *What do I do when? The answer book on special education law.* Horsham, PA: LRP Publications.

Green, P.C., & Sireci, S.G. (1999). Legal and psychometric policy consideration in the testing of students with disabilities. *Journal of Special Education Leadership, 12*(2), 21-28.

Huefner, D.S. (2000). The risks and opportunities of the IEP requirements under IDEA '97. *Journal of Special Education, 34*(4), 195-204.

Individuals with Disabilities Education Act, Amendments of 1997, Public Law No. 105-17†§602, U.S.C. 1401 {On-line} www.ed.gov/ofices/OSERS/IDEA/the_law.html

Julnes, R.E., & Brown, S.E. (1993). Legal mandate to provide assistive technology in special education programming. *West's Education Law Quarterly, 2(4),* 552-563.

Kelker, K & Holt, R. (1997). *Parents' Guide to transition: What happens after high school?* Billings, MT: Parents, Let's Unite for Kids

Kukic, S., & Schrag, J. (1998). *IEP connections for a dynamic, living and practical process.* Longmont, CO: Sopris West.

Lahm, E.A., & Sizemore, L. (2002). Factors that influence assistive technology decision making. *Journal of Special Education Technology, 17*(1), 15-25.

LaPoint, S.L. (1997). Student progress as a determinate of FAPE. In G. Reusch (Ed.), *Special education law and practice,* (pp.1-23). Horsham, PA: LRP Publications.

Lignugaris/Kraft, B., Marchand-Martella,

N., & Martella, R.C. (2001). Strategies for writing better goals and short term objectives or benchmarks. *Teaching Exceptional Children, 34*(1), 52-58.

Lipsky, D.K., & Gartner, A. (1996). Inclusive education and school restructuring. In W. Stainback & S. Stainback (Eds.), *Controversial issues confronting special education: Divergent perspectives* (pp. 3-15). Boston: Allyn & Bacon.

Lytle, R., & Bordin, J. (2001). Enhancing the IEP team: Strategies for parents and professionals. *Teaching Exceptional Children, 33*(5), 40-44.

MacArthur, C.A. (1999). Word prediction for students with severe spelling problems. *Learning Disability Quarterly, 22*(3), 158-172.

Menlove, R.R., Hudson, P.J., & Suter, D. (2001). A field of IEP dreams: Increasing general education teacher participation in the IEP development process. *Teaching Exceptional Children, 33*(5), 28-33.

Powers, L (1996). *Take charge for the future,* Portland, OR: Oregon Health Sciences University

Pugach, M.C., & Warger, C.L. (1993). Curriculum considerations. In J.I. Goodlad & T.C. Lovitt (Eds.), *Integrating general and special education.* (pp. 125-148). New York: McMillan.

Purcell, S.L., & Grant, D. (2001). *Assistive technology solutions for IEP teams.* Verona, WI: IEP Resources.

Reed, P. (1997). *Let's put the planning back in Individualized Educational Programs.* Retrieved January 13, 2004 from *www.wati.org/bestpractices.htm*

Reed, P., & Bowser, G. (1998, Fall). Considering the need for assistive technology. *TAM Connector*(10)1.

Reed, P., Bowser, G., & Korsten, J. (2002). *How do you know it? How can you show it?* Oshkosh, WI: Wisconsin Assistive Technology Initiative.

RESNA Technical Assistance Project, (1992). *Assistive technology and the individualized education program.* Washington, D.C.: RESNA Technical Assistance Project.

Scherer, M. (1991). *Matching people with technologies,* Webster, NY: Scherer Associates

Smith, S.W. (1990a). Comparison of Individualized Education Programs (IEPs) of students with behavioral disorders and learning disabilities. *The Journal of Special Education, 24*, 85-110.

Smith, S.W. (1990b). IEP's in special education: From intent to acquiescence. *Exceptional Children, 57*(1), 61-74.

Smith, S.W., & Simpson, R.L. (1989). An analysis of individualized education programs (IEPs) for students with behavioral disorders. *Behavioral Disorders, 14*, 107-116.

Steere, D.E., & Cavaiuolo, D. (2002). Connecting outcomes, goals, and objectives in transition planning. *Teaching Exceptional Children 34*(6), 54-59.

Storms, J., De Stefano, L., & O'Leary, E. (1996). *Individuals with disabilities education act: transition requirements.* Eugene, OR: Western Regional Resource Center

Texas Assistive Technology Network (2002, April). *Considering Assistive Technology in the IEP Process.* Retrieved January 8, 2004, from *www.texasat.net*

Thoma, C.A. (1999). Supporting student voices in transition planning. *Teaching Exceptional Children, 31*(5), 4-9.

Todis, B., & Walker, H. (1993). User perspectives on assistive technology in educational settings. *Focus on Exceptional Children, 26*, 1-16.

Walsh, J. M. (2001). Getting the "big picture" of IEP goals and state standards. *Teaching Exceptional Children, 33*(5), 18-26.

Wehmeyer, M.L., Agran, M., & Hughes, C. (1998). *Teaching self-determination to students with disabilities: Basic skills for successful transition.* Baltimore: Paul H. Brookes.

Wehmeyer, M.L., & Lawrence, M. (1995). *Whose future is it anyway?: A student-directed transition planning process.* Arlington, VA: The Arc, 13-17.

Wisconsin Assistive Technology Initiative (2004). *Assistive technology checklist.* Oshkosh: Wisconsin Assistive Technology Initiative. Retrieved January 8, 2004 from *(www.wati.org/at_check_list.htm)*

Yell, M.L. (1998). *The law and special education.* Upper Saddle River, NJ: Merrill/ Prentice Hall.

Zabala, J., Bowser, G., Blunt, M., Hartsell, K., Carl, D., Korsten, J., Davis, S., Marfilius, S., Deterding, C., McCloskey-Dale, S., Foss, T., Nettleton, S., Hamman, T., & Reed, P. (2000). Quality indicators for assistive technology services in school settings. *Journal of Special Education Technology, 15*(4), 25-36.

Section 2

Access for Diverse Populations

5

Cultural Research in Special Education Technology

Howard P. Parette, Mary Blake Huer, and Alan VanBiervliet

Interest in special education technology first emerged more than three decades ago (Haring, 1970). Since that time, the field of special education has witnessed a continual evolution of the use of assistive technology (AT) by children with a wide range of disabilities and educational needs. AT service delivery impacts the lives of all children with disabilities and their families, including those from diverse cultural backgrounds, who often have unmet needs (McInerney, Osher, & Kane, 1997). Unfortunately, there is little literature and only a few data-based studies of the use of AT with children with disabilities and their families from diverse cultural backgrounds. While the topic of culture has received growing attention from educators in the emerging educational milieus of the twenty-first century, empirical research focused on the impact of culture on the use of AT has not kept pace. With a goal of focusing attention on this area, this chapter reviews, discusses, and introduces various parameters related to cultural research and special education technology.

In commenting on the challenges to the field of AT in the new millennium, Cheek, Denny, and Rice (2000) noted "We need to know how our culture is represented, how that culture is portrayed in particular ways, and how one culture is represented to the exclusion of others" (p. 459). Similarly, in a recent analysis of disability policies, Silverstein (2000) pointed out that sensitivity to the cultural backgrounds of individuals with disabilities is em-

bedded in the language of federal legislation that has been accepted as a basic tenet of disability policy in the United States. In developing systems of comprehensive AT service delivery, the Technology Related Assistance for Individuals with Disabilities Act of 1988 (P.L. 100-407) and its reauthorization (The Assistive Technology Act of 1998, P.L. 105-394) acknowledged the importance of addressing underserved and underrepresented populations (Association of Tech Act Projects, 2000). Similarly, the Individuals with Disabilities Education Act Amendments of 1997 acknowledged both the increasing numbers of students from non-Euro-American backgrounds [§687(c)(7)(A)] in public education as well as the disproportionate number of children with disabilities from culturally diverse backgrounds who are served in special education settings [§687(c)(8)(B)].

Such increases in students' culturally diverse backgrounds have, and will continue to have, a dramatic impact on America's special education service system (The Changing Face of Education, 2000), including AT service delivery. Therefore, it is important to focus on: (a) what we know now about the impact of cultural parameters on service delivery; (b) what we need to discover about cultural diversity and AT use by children and their families; (c) available empirically based AT studies; and (d) preparations for a future when new and emerging AT will become available to assist families and professionals.

Cultural Parameters That May Impact Service Delivery in Special Education Settings

Numerous professionals have noted that understanding the cultural values of the many diverse groups represented in our public school systems is essential for creating partnerships that result in optimal educational outcomes (Harry, Grenot-Scheyer, Smith-Lewis, Park, Xin, & Schwartz, 1995; Lamorey, 2002). Focusing on the definition of the word *culture* is a useful starting point. Unfortunately for professionals working with students with disabilities and their families, there is wide variability in the definition of culture. For example, an early work by Kroeber and Kluckhohn (1952) identified more than 200 definitions of culture. Culture has been broadly defined as a common set of beliefs, values, behaviors, and communication patterns that are shared by a particular group of people and learned as a function of social membership (Miraglia, Law, & Collins, 1999; Soto, 1994; Soto, Huer, & Taylor, 1997). It has also been described as a lens through which individuals see themselves in relation to others and the world (Battle, 2002; Soto et al., 1997). In examining the similarities of the definitions offered in the literature, Bodley (1994) suggested that culture involves at least three components: what people *think*, *do*, and *produce*. With regard to AT decision-making, all participants in the process bring their own unique ways of thinking about and perceiving the world around them. Each participant may behave in a very different way, based on previous learning and the expectations of individuals and specific cultures within their various environmental settings. They also produce, or develop, unique strategies, processes, and tangible products that reflect their unique learning and backgrounds.

Bodley (1994) also noted that culture consists of several properties, it is: (a) *shared* (i.e., others within the culture have agreed upon or accept the values/beliefs/practices); (b) *learned* (i.e., over time by participation within the culture); (c) *symbolic* (i.e., anything that is taken to mean something beyond what it is; the symbols have been agreed upon by members of the culture); (d) *transmitted cross-generationally* (i.e.,

from individual/s to individual/s); (e) *adaptive* (i.e., it is flexible to change to varying degrees); and (f) *integrated* (i.e., it permeates the behaviors and activities of individuals within a particular cultural group). Bodley (1994) presented an overview of the varying conceptual interpretations of culture that have guided the research investigations in anthropology and related disciplines. One parameter that may be focused upon to a greater extent is related to an improved understanding of the various and shifting concepts of culture as held or perceived throughout the service delivery processes within educational settings.

Variability in Cultural Positioning

The complexity of culture is such that individuals involved in AT decision-making may have a variety of cultural positions at varying points in time during the decision-making process. For example, an individual may be (a) *monocultural* (i.e., his or her interactions with others tend to be based on their own individual cultural backgrounds or their perceived similarity to others) (Smart & Smart, 1992; Soto, 1994); (b) *bicultural*, or identifying with two cultural groups and interact comfortably with both (Hanson, Lynch, & Wayman, 1990); or (c) *multicultural* (i.e., identifying with the value systems of more than two groups). In addition, individuals are also affected by the process of *acculturation* that involves the extent of accommodation to a newly introduced culture experienced by an individual (Kalyanpur & Harry, 1999).

Studies have described frameworks for acculturation, suggesting a continuum along which an individual's responses can range from immersion in one's traditional culture, to a bicultural or "dualistic" orientation, to immersion in or accommodation to the host culture (i.e., atraditional (Ramirez & Castaneda, 1974) or overacculturation (Leung, 1988). Soriano (1995) differentiates between acculturation and assimilation, arguing that acculturation is biculturalism, or the capacity to function in both the traditional and the host or mainstream culture, whereas assimilation refers to absorption into the mainstream. The process of acculturation varies markedly across individuals, particularly in the United States where there is an overarching national culture "as well as ethnic and other subsocieties and institutions" (Banks, 1997, p. 6). For example, an individual will belong to the U.S. culture, or macroculture, which includes many microcultural groups, each participating in the macroculture to varying degrees while simultaneously retaining aspects of the respective microcultures (Kalyanpur & Harry, 1999). Factors such as "race, ethnicity, nationality, language, social status, and geographic location are key ingredients to the pattern of identity that emerges" (Kalyanpur & Harry, 1999, p. 4). Compounding the problem is the fact that individuals often develop affiliations with professional groups and organizations, including state entities (e.g., public schools), that have their own unique norms and expectations (Bullivant, 1993). Affiliation with the norms and expectations of these groups will also vary depending on the degree of socialization and nature of experiences that have occurred within and across groups.

In an early publication, Bowles and Gintis (1976) noted that the majority of individuals involved in public school processes are disadvantaged socially given that they are required to consume and value the cultural products produced by others (e.g., team decision-making strategies, curriculum). Thus, the cultural products typically presented to children with disabilities and their families are those reflecting Euro-American, middle class values (Benner, 1998; Kalyanpur & Harry, 1999). As a result, as Carolan (2001) noted, successful school experiences occur to the extent that students, families, and professionals adhere to a primarily Euro-American "prescribed set of cultural content delivered through a narrowly defined curriculum and set of behaviors."

Both students with disabilities and their families have historically been expected to adapt to what has been offered, with the expectation that this would perpetuate relationships among groups in the social system (Bowles & Gintis, 1976). However, educators have recognized that dissonance occurs when efforts to provide services operate under the assumption that children with disabilities and their families must adapt to the products and processes created by others that diverge markedly from their own. This recognition has led researchers to advocate for "cultural reciprocity," or shared understanding of the cultures of professionals and families (Kalyanpur & Harry, 1999). The usefulness of a model of cultural reciprocity will be discussed to a greater extent later within this chapter. First, it is important to review current AT use by children and their families.

Cultural Diversity and AT Use by Children and Their Families

The influence of the parameter of culture on AT use by children and their families has come more sharply into focus because of a growing recognition of the importance of (a) family-centered practice in special education generally (Bruder, 2000; Shelton & Stepanik, 1994); and (b) family involvement in educational decision-making, AT decision-making specifically (Hutinger, 1994; Judge & Parette, 1998; Parette & Anderson, 2001; Parette & Angelo, 1998). As noted in the reauthorization of the Individuals with Disabilities Education Act of 1997 (IDEA) (P.L. 105-17):

> Over 20 years of research and experience has demonstrated that the education of children with disabilities can be made more effective by strengthening the role of parents and ensuring that families of such children have meaningful opportunities to participate in the education of their children at school and at home. [§1400(c)(5)(B)]

Such strongly held professional recommendations echo the concerns of P.L. 100-407 which mandates that AT services for individuals with disabilities representing different cultures, religious beliefs, languages with a variety of dialects, socioeconomic classes and levels of education, as well as varying degrees of acculturation and assimilation must be ethnically and culturally tailored (Bailey, 1991). This signals a shift from child centeredness in AT decision-making that has predominated professional thinking for years (see, e.g., Church & Glennen, 1992; Flippo, Inge, & Barcus, 1995; King, 1999) toward an emphasis on family-centeredness (see, e.g., Judge & Parette, 1998; Parette & Brotherson, 1996). Recognizing cul-

Figure 1. Influences on acculturation during assistive technology decision-making.

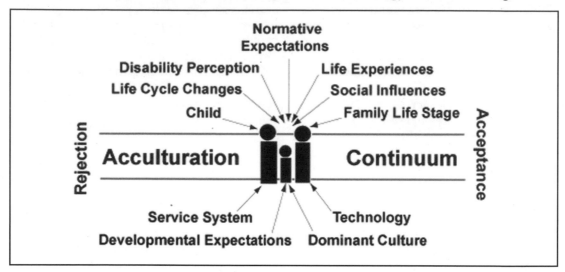

tural issues as central to delivering appropriate AT devices and services for a particular child is especially important in the AT decision-making process to ensure that devices are not abandoned (Briegel, 2000; Phillips & Zhao, 1993). Numerous culturally relevant factors have been shown to result in abandonment. Studies have examined the impact of life-style and culture on the rehabilitation process and device usage (Becker & Kauffman, 1988; Gitlin, Luborsky, & Schemm, 1998; Murphy, Scheer, Murphy, & Mack, 1988; Scheer & Luborsky, 1991). These studies have identified a dynamic interaction between varying aspects in the life of an individual with disability, including (a) differences in device acceptability due to psychological and normative, age-related physical and psychological traits; (b) stage in the life cycle; and (c) stage in the life of the family (Luborsky, 1991; Murphy, 1990).

Family Factors Affecting AT Decision-Making

Early models of AT assessment typically focused on child, school, and technology factors (Parette & Hourcade, 1997). Thus, the traditional approach of AT emphasized the student and the classroom in the AT decision-making process (Institute for Matching Person and Technology, 2002; Reed & Bowser, 1998; Williams, Stemach, Wolf, & Stanger, 1995; Wisconsin Assistive Technology Initiative, 1998; Zabala, 1998). By contrast, current models of

assessment emphasize the process of assessment involving a multidisciplinary, collaborative team approach, and all follow an ecological, functional assessment approach (Bromley, 2001). Three of the current models are designed for school and other environmental settings (Bromley, 2001): (a) Student, Environment, Tasks, and Tools (SETT) (Zabala, 1998); (b) Lifespace Access Profile (LAP) (Williams et al., 1998); and (c) the Matching Person and Technology (MPT) (Institute for Matching Person and Technology, 2002). As noted in Figure 1, a family is affected by a wide range of culturally relevant forces. Only a few are discussed in the following sections: (a) acculturation, (b) social influences, (c) developmental expectations, and (d) life experiences.

Acculturation

Acculturation is a powerful determinant of attitudes and behaviors and affects many aspects of child and family functioning (Smart & Smart, 1992). Damen (1987) defined acculturation as a process involving the internalization of knowledge necessary to function in a particular societal group. This process involves disengaging from the world view, learning new ways to meet old problems, and shedding ethnocentric evaluations (Damen, 1987). As Ruiz (1981) described acculturation, it involves giving up "old ways" and adopting "new ways." Another definition suggests that acculturation is the degree to which people from a particular culture display behavior that is more like the behavior exhibited by persons in the dominant culture (Torres-Davis & Trivelli, 1994).

Wide ranges of individual acculturation effects have been demonstrated in various health-related attitudes and social behaviors (Kunkel, 1990; Pomales & Williams, 1989; Ponce & Atkinson, 1989; Sutton, 1999; Wells, Hough, Golding, & Burnam, 1987). The influences of such factors must be considered by team members during AT decision-making, as family members will tend to fall along a continuum, ranging from strong affiliation with their own unique culture and its values and beliefs, to alignment with Euro-American culture.

With regard to AT use, acculturation influences the extent to which family members are familiar with and may be responsive to particular devices and services developed or provided by Euro-American professionals (Parette, Huer, & Scherer, 2004). In contemporary American society, people have increasingly become acculturated to the daily use of technology (e.g., use of electronic alarm clocks, DVDs, CD players, and automatic teller windows). Further, many people are also not as fearful of computers and other sophisticated technology devices as may have been the case a decade ago.

Families from various cultural backgrounds also will have been affected to varying degrees by their exposure to technology. However, it is critical for professionals to understand the extent to which families members currently use technology, a component of the MPT model (Institute for Matching Person and Technology, 2002). Such understanding will: (a) provide insights into the comfort with which the family may be able to discuss specific AT solutions considered during team processes; (b) help recognize the priorities, concerns, and resources of families during AT decision-making; and (c) enable the selection of devices from a more culturally sensitive perspective.

Barerra (1993) noted that the acculturation process can result in significant stressors on family members, especially when behaviors associated with competence in one environment differ from those in other environments. Persons within specific cultures will be influ-enced to use AT by acculturation factors in varying degrees dependent on many factors. These include geographic and social isolation of the family from exposure to technology (Torres-Davis & Trivelli, 1994). For example, families from very rural areas may not have been exposed to information about or seen assistive devices used by young children prior to meeting with professionals during team decision-making processes. Such lack of technology familiarity may have a significant effect on their willingness to use AT. Conversely, families who reside in urban areas may have had considerably more exposure to and information about AT, influencing their ability to make decisions using a broader knowledge or experiential base than families from rural settings. A more thorough discussion of issues related to the impact of assistive devices on family functioning is found in Parette and Angelo (1998).

Social Influences

Professionals who work with families must also recognize that cultural factors are influenced by situational, or social factors. This can result in family agreement with professionals that recommended interventions are appropriate while choosing not to implement the recommendations in specific settings (VanBiervliet & Parette, 1999). For example, if core family values reflect deep respect for the role of teachers in the education of the child, there may be reticence on the part of the family to disagree openly with a particular teacher during AT decision-making (Roseberry-McKibbin, 1995).

Neither cultural nor psychosocial aspects of AT use have been fully examined to date. Some qualitative reports of technology use (Becker & Kaufman, 1988; Sheer & Luborsky, 1991; Stein, 1979) have suggested a dynamic interaction between AT and user factors, such as (a) differences in AT acceptability as a function of age-related normative psychological and physical capabilities; (b) changes in the life cycle of the individual; and (c) family life stage (Luborsky, 1991; Smith-Lewis & Ford, 1987). Also, motivation to use AT may be influenced markedly by the presence of a disability and its concomitant emotional effects (Turner & Noh, 1988). The extent to which these factors affect most families is unclear and has yet to be systematically examined in empirical studies.

Of particular importance to some users of AT and their families is the social and personal stigma associated with persons who are visibly different in appearance or behavior (Luborsky, 1993). While professionals may agree that use of AT for a particular child is necessary, the family may feel that its use will result in social stigma (Parette & Scherer, 2004). Thus, there may be a powerful perceived need on the part of the family that preserving its self-esteem and prestige as whole persons within a particular cultural context is more important than the potential of AT to increase independent functioning of the child. For example, studies have noted the social impact of assistive device use among African-American family members in public settings, suggesting that some families prefer not to be the focus of public attention (Parette, Brotherson, Hoge et al., 1996; Smith-Lewis, 1992). Thus, it is important that professionals consider the level of community acceptance anticipated by family members prior to asking them to implement AT in community settings.

Lund (1986) noted that families may be reluctant to initiate interventions when changes in family routines are anticipated. Other studies have described consumers or family members choosing not to use specific AT devices due to quality of life issues (Brotherson, Oakland, Secrist-Mertz, Litchfield, & Larson, 1994; Parette, Brotherson, Hoge, & Hostetler, 1996) or visibility of disability (Kaufert & Locker, 1990), even though improved functioning might result from AT use. These motivational factors may not be due to the inherent traits of the AT or of the disability, but may be more a function of the social contexts of device usage (Ainlay, Becker, & Coleman, 1986). As Parette (1998) noted, "sensitivity to these factors does not mean ignoring them out of deference, but rather talking about the family's concerns, checking them out, and helping family members weigh the benefits for the child against the social costs" (p. 199).

Social contexts are also important given that families from different cultures have preferences for certain communication styles. High-context cultures (e.g., Asian, Native, Hispanic,

and African-American) often place greater emphasis on information provided through the (a) situational context, (b) relationships of persons involved in the interactions, and (c) physical and/or nonverbal cues (Hall, 1974; Lynch, 1997). Low-context approaches (e.g., those preferred by many Euro-American professionals during AT decision-making), on the other hand typically place greater importance on concise verbal communication, with an emphasis on getting to the point quickly (Hecht, Anderson, & Ribeau, 1989). Professionals should be aware of such differences in communication styles, and strategies for communicating information should be developed to be sensitive to family preferences (DeGangi, Weitlisbach, Poisson, & Stein, 1994; Parette, 1997; Soto et al., 1997).

Developmental Expectations

Another important influence on the family during AT decision-making is the life course of the child and family. Luborsky (1993) described the life course as culturally defined expectations of stages and transitions for the socially defined individual. Numerous authorities have reported that developmental milestones across cultures vary markedly (Edwards, Gandini, & Giovaninni, 1996; Levy, 1996; Miller, 1979). Developmental expectations across the lifespan may influence the responsiveness of children with disabilities and family members when AT devices are prescribed (Harry et al., 1995; Kalyanpur & Harry, 1999). For example, expectations across cultural groups for such basic skills as walking, talking, and dressing vary by as much as a year or more, thus affecting family (and professional) perceptions of the relative importance of such skills during AT decision-making.

Life Experiences

Given that families have had differing experiences with AT, it is reasonable to assume that such experiences—both positive and negative—may influence their perceptions of and willingness to use AT (Luborsky, 1991, 1993; Scheer & Luborsky, 1991). These experiences in social, cultural, and lifetime contexts result in the development of personal themes over time both by the AT user and the family that potentially affect the focus of evaluations, interventions, and resulting experiences (Luborsky, 1993). It has been noted that beliefs and attitudes gain power from past experiences that influence the comprehension of subsequent events (Nespor, 1987). Thus, if families have had prior positive experiences with the AT decision-making process, and are comfortable participating in these processes, they may be far more comfortable (and effective) than families who have not had such experiences and who may rely heavily on professional judgments (e.g., families from high-context cultures who see professionals as authorities and show them great deference in making decisions about interventions).

Legal Mandates

While the previous few sections have focused on family factors affecting AT decision-making, the literature reveals that other factors may also impact decision-making during the educational intervention processes. The historical origins for the varying legal mandates that affect children with disabilities and their families are of particular importance.

Service providers may gain greater understanding of the actions of families during AT decision-making through a study of legal mandates within different countries around the world. Kalyanpur and Harry (1999) presented a scholarly examination of special education in the context of mainstream U.S. American culture. In particular, they outlined how core American values were reflected in legal policy. For example, in the Individuals with Disabilities Education Act of 1990 (IDEA) (P.L. 101-476) the American value of equality is reflected in the expectation that parents and service providers develop partnerships in the education decision-making process. Similarly, the principle of due process of law is based on the value of individualism.

Kalyanpur and Harry (1999) suggest that dissonance may often occur during when family members are asked to participate in decision-making when strongly held values exist regarding the importance of social hierarchies versus social equity. Various legal mandates offer a lens through which a broader understanding of culture and family reactions during AT decision-making processes may be

attained. For example, a special issue of *Teaching Exceptional Children* presented legal mandates for special education services including immigrants in the United States (Al-Hassan & Gardner III, 2002) and children in Mexico (Shepherd, Contreras, & Brown, 2002), Taiwan (Kang, Lovett, & Haring, 2002), Israel (Meadan & Gumpel, 2002), Canada (Dworet & Bennett, 2002), and South Korea (Park, 2002). A careful examination of time periods over which each country witnessed the emergence of legally sanctioned access to special education services, and funding for such, provides insight into issues pertaining to access to educational services in various countries. Alternative explanations for beliefs and traditions reflect examples of cultural differences between the family and the professional service provider.

Overview of AT Culture Studies

Relatively little research has been done specifically in the area of culture and its influence on AT decision-making. The importance of considering cultural factors was emphasized by Soto (2000) who noted, "Social and cultural factors underlie all clinical activities. Failure to recognize and take these social and cultural factors into account can diminish the effectiveness of clinical services, even in the presence of state-of-the-art technology or the best clinical procedures" (p. 2). Scherer (1996) presented case studies of individuals with disabilities having needs for or who use AT, and has explored issues related to the AT decision-making processes. She notes that "The individual's cultural identity and the values and norms of that culture should be considered" (p. 124). Similarly, Scherer indicates that specific cultural factors affect AT decision-making, including (a) whether or not AT is forced on the individual, (b) prior experiences/expectations, (c) social settings in which the device will be used, (d) public response to the device, (e) attitudes toward the device, and (f) perceptions of the extent to which the device is helpful or restricting. Such considerations are inherent in the MPT assessment process (Institute for Matching Person and Technology, 2002), which takes into account cultural and attitudinal influences on resource selection and use of AT devices. As noted by

Scherer (personal communication, September 17, 2002):

> *the importance of the MPT process isn't just about finding the right assistive technology for a consumer, it is about a person-centered process that takes a consumer through a progression of steps to become more comfortable with his/her disability and more independent in all areas of his/her life.*

Cultural Studies and AAC

The most intense examinations of cultural influences on AT decision-making have been conducted in the area of augmentative and alternative communication (AAC) that the largest cross-cultural AT study to date was a U.S. Department of Education Special Project reported by Parette and VanBiervliet (2000). The investigators sought to create a knowledge base (Parette, VanBiervliet, Reyna, & Heisserer, 1999) as the foundation for an interactive CD that could be used during AAC decision-making with families across cultures. Family members (*n*=58) from Native-American, Hispanic, Asian, and African-American communities, professionals (*n*=32), and vendors (*n*=5) participated in focus groups and gave voice to issues related to AAC in the process of developing the knowledge base. All focus groups were video- and audio-tape recorded, transcribed, and analyzed by AAC researchers.

Resulting family voices were organized around the themes of (a) building family and professional partnerships, (b) respecting family values and ethnicity, and (c) helping families to use AAC devices. Professional voices were organized around the themes of (a) communication style, (b) specific information needs, (c) values, (d) teaming, and (e) implementation/training. Information generated by participants, coupled with extensive reviews of the literature, and expert and consumer panel input (see Parette & VanBiervliet, 2000), resulted in a state-of-the-art CD that has received four major media competition awards to date. Tables 1 and 2 present findings of the study that may have implications for AT decision-making generally, and issue areas that should be explored in future research investigations.

Only a few data-based studies on families receiving AAC interventions within culturally diverse populations have been published (Huer, 2000; Huer, Parette, & Saenz, 2001; Huer, Saenz, & Doan, 2001; Parette, Brotherson, & Huer, 2000). Although the specific objectives of these studies vary, all reflect as a common theme the importance of understanding the impact of ethnicity/culture from family members, or others, within different cultural groups. For example, in a "graphics symbols" study (Huer, 2000), three aided graphic symbol sets used in AAC (Blissymbols, DynaSyms®, and Picture Communication Symbols) were examined. Although family members of AAC users did not serve as the participants during this study, 147 adults, whose languages included Chinese, Spanish, or English, and who identified themselves as African-American, Chinese-American, European-American, or Mexican-American participated. A questionnaire containing graphic symbols with translated referents (in English, Mexican Spanish, and Mandarin Chinese) was rated on a 7-point scale of iconicity. Results suggested that individuals from different cultural/ethnic groups perceived graphic symbols introduced into AAC interventions differently.

Two data-based studies focused on families from within two different communities (Huer, Parette, & Saenz, 2001; Huer, Saenz, & Doan, 2001)—families within the Mexican-American and the Vietnamese-American communities. Huer, Parette, et al. (2001) reported results based on "conversations" with families (in Spanish) within the Mexican-American community. Seven family members of children with disabilities participated in two focus groups. Each family member's child was enrolled in an AAC intervention program in the public school. After a content analysis of all the focus group conversations, general perspectives expressed by family members were identified. The purpose of the "conversations" project was to collect information for identifying and understanding issues influencing AAC practices within a Mexican-American community. In brief, the families indicated that they: (a) felt respect for professionals; (b) emphasized the performance of simple tasks by their children; and (c) sought AAC devices that speak in Spanish.

Table 1. Issues in Augmentative and Alternative Communication (AAC) Device Decision-Making Imperatives for Professionals as Expressed by Families

Theme	Summary of Focus Group Findings
Communication Style	• Minimize use of jargon that limits communication with families • Communicate their discomfort with AAC devices • Communicate the extent of their involvement in learning to use AAC devices if they are uncomfortable with a device under consideration
Specific Information Needs	• Provide more information about AAC devices (range of devices available, critical features, maintenance, support, funding process, warranties) • Clearly communicate information about AAC device ownership • Allow family to watch other children using AAC devices prior to purchase • Clearly communicate information about short-term AAC device alternatives during repair periods and waiting period for initial receipt of device
Family Values	• Show sensitivity to family's expectations for the child • Demonstrate recognition of and sensitivity to immediate and future needs of the child and the family • Recognize that families have no background in parenting children with disabilities • Understand the realities of family life, demands, and routines • Recognize that some children and families have had a range of past experiences using AAC devices and that these experiences influence their needs and priorities • Consider compact and easily transportable devices for smaller children • Examine the child's home environment before prescribing devices • Show sensitivity to the terminology used when discussing children • Recognize that child and family preferences for devices differ from those of service professionals
Family Values	• Understand that children with similar symptoms are unique individuals from different families and therefore should not be discussed collectively as a group • Recognize the child's need for "personal space" during AAC technology interventions
Teaming	• Recommend AAC devices based on objective rather than subjective experiences • Demonstrate experience and comfort with the use of AAC devices • Show sensitivity to and provide options for the child and family during repair intervals • Recognize that professional recommendations are based on short-term contact with the child (versus the lifetime contact of the family) • Consider age-appropriate recommendations • Validate family concerns • Include family members in meetings and ensure family ownership of the intervention process

(continued next page)

Table 1. Issues in Augmentative and Alternative Communication (AAC) Device Decision-Making Imperatives for Professionals as Expressed by Families (continued)

Theme	Summary of Focus Group Findings
Teaming (continued)	• Ensure that new team members are familiar with the past work of the team • Communicate concerns regarding the child and AAC devices • Acknowledge family members for their work in identifying resources • Provide guidance for better decision making • Recognize that the child may refuse to participate in evaluations by using a defense mechanism as a response to new team members • Realize the importance of the primary caregiver in the development of child/team member rapport during evaluations • Establish rapport with child prior to assessment • Adapt child assessment procedures where necessary • Clearly understand that insurance companies base decisions on evaluation information provided by teams • Provide information about timelines of the AAC device assessment process • Ensure that child has continued access to the AAC device from time of rental to actual delivery to the family • Ensure that the AAC device is not taken away after the child has had hands-on experiences and shows a preference for and the ability to use the device • Ensure that the AAC device is not selected for use by others in lieu of individualizing selection of a device to meet the needs of the child and family
Training	• Provide opportunities for hands-on experiences • Demonstrate competence in use of AAC devices • Show sensitivity to the inordinate amount of time families must wait to receive toll-free technical assistance callbacks • Show sensitivity to the family's needs for repeated training sessions in order to learn to use the AAC device effectively • Recognize that vendors provide varying levels and quality of family support • Provide user-friendly, accessible training and support materials prior to purchase of the AAC device and thereafter • Create parent support groups for dissemination of information and training • Ensure continuity of AAC programming across natural and community settings (e.g., ordering, receiving, learning to use) • Provide instruction for appropriate use of the AAC device to siblings in the family if the device is intended for home usage • Clearly communicate the extent to which professionals will train the child and the family (including siblings and extended family) to use the AAC device • Teach families how to teach their children to use AAC devices

Note: Based on focus group discussions with families reported in: Parette, H. P., Brotherson, M. J., Hoge, D., & Hostetler, S. A. (1996, December). *Family-centered augmentative and alternative communication issues: Implications across cultures.* Paper presented to the International Early Childhood Conference on Children with Special Needs, Phoenix, AZ. © 1996 by Howard P. Parette. Reprinted with permission.

Table 2. Issues in Augmentative and Alternative Communication (AAC) Device Decision-Making Imperatives for Intervention Team Members as Expressed by Professionals

Issue	Implications for Teams
Communication Style	*Families and Professionals should:* • Maintain open lines of communication across settings • Be open-minded • Avoid assuming defensive postures *Professionals should:* • Avoid jargon and gear language to listeners
Specific Information Needs	*Professionals should:* • Communicate the role of the family in AAC device decision making
Values	*Professionals should:* • Share a common value—wanting the child to learn—with the family • Value family insights • Value family members as team participants • Value insights of all persons who work with the child on a daily basis • Recognize that child/family bonds exist even in absence of regular contact • Recognize that families are limited by financial, educational, and physical constraints *Families should:* • Accept reality of disabilities and children's limitations • Be patient and not demand rapid results after an AAC device has been implemented
Teaming	*Professionals should:* • Consider family needs to ensure appropriate selection of AAC devices • Respect family needs, concerns, and priorities • Recognize that families display varying degrees of willingness to participate in AAC device implementation across time (acculturation) • Establish trust with family members • Collaborate with family members and establish consensus • Meet regularly with family members • Celebrate positive daily changes resulting from AAC device implementation with family members • Recognize that child factors may have have a greater impact on success with AAC devices for some children than family commitment • Recognize that the evaluation process may include unjust elements—optimum devices may not be feasible due to funding constraints • Clearly communicate expectations regarding AAC devices • Not have preconceived ideas regarding AAC devices • Clearly specify goals for the child • Examine a range of AAC devices • Have expertise with AAC devices recommended • Be aware that AAC device options are increasing in the midst of decreasing funding availability
Implementation and Training	*Families want professionals to:* • Provide social support through family support groups • Train family members in the use of AAC devices in community settings • Make loaner AAC devices available after evaluations • Provide training targeting integration of AAC device into home and community

(continued next page)

Table 2. Issues in Augmentative and Alternative Communication (AAC) Device Decision-Making Imperatives for Intervention Team Members as Expressed by Professionals (continued)

Issue	Implications of Teams
Implementation and Training (continued)	*Professionals want families to:* • Commit time to AAC device implementation • Understand that AAC device success corresponds to time commitment given by families

Note: Based on focus group discussions with families reported in: Parette, H. P., Brotherson, M. J., Hoge, D., & Hostetler, S. A. (1996, December). *Family-centered augmentative and alternative communication issues: Implications across cultures.* Paper presented to the International Early Childhood Conference on Children with Special Needs, Phoenix, AZ. © 1996 by Howard P. Parette. Reprinted with permission.

Huer, Saenz, et al. (2001) reported results from a survey of Vietnamese-Americans. Although the study group did not represent family members of children receiving AAC services, they did respond to questions about the use of AAC by children in their community. For example, they responded to questions about the use of pictures, gestures, and/or computers for communication by children who could not speak. Using a 29-item survey questionnaire in both English and Vietnamese, the attitudes of Vietnamese-Americans (*n*=43) towards children with disabilities were examined. Responses provided information about the extent of their beliefs about disabilities and their choice of the Vietnamese language versus the English language during everyday activities. Finally, the survey provided information about the extent of their acculturation since moving to the United States.

New and Emerging Technologies to Assist Families and Professionals

Family Learning Styles

The assistive technology assessment, prescription, and implementation processes involve a partnership between families and professionals gathering and sharing large amounts of information. Typically, families, regardless of their cultural background, are unfamiliar with the purpose, functioning, and pros and cons of specific assistive technologies, particularly in the early stages of AT planning. Therefore, much of the AT professional's role is to serve as an educator about AT in relation to the needs of the family and child.

Cultural groups tend to have some learning style elements that distinguish them from other cultural groups. Reminding educators of the connection between culture and learning style, Guild (1994) points out that effective educational practices stem from an understanding of the way individuals learn, including the effect of one's culture upon learning. Dunn and Griggs (1995) noted that within cultural groups, individuals differ significantly from each other; therefore, it is equally important to identify and respond to the individual's learning style preferences. Specifically, they emphasized that educators need to be aware of three critical factors: (a) universal principles of learning do exist; (b) culture influences both the learning process and its outcomes; and (c) each individual has unique learning style preferences that affect his or her potential for achievement.

When working with families, AT professionals must modify their educational approaches from child learning to adult learning strategies, as adults learn differently than children. For example, the adult learning literature points out that adults: (a) have a need to know why they should learn something; (b) have a need to be self-directing; (c) bring to the learning situation a background of experience (including cultural experiences) that is a rich resource upon which to build new knowledge and skills; (d) become ready to learn when they experience a need to know in their life situations; and (e) by virtue of life and work experiences have a task-centered or problem-centered orientation to learning (Knowles, 1996). For these reasons, it is important to design family AT education activities that incorporate the following strategies and concepts: base AT education on valid needs of the family; present training with as many user-controlled options for learning as possible; provide training as close to the time it is needed as possible; do not provide a large amount of information and tell the family they need to know the information for future use; and focus activities on "doing" something with information rather than simply "knowing" the information.

Information and Educational Technologies

AT professionals must employ a variety of teaching strategies to accommodate family learning style preferences and needs. It is important to consider employing a variety of media, capitalizing on the unique strengths of each medium. It is always best to design alternative activities to reach the same objective and give participants the option of selecting those activities that best meet their preferred learning style.

A number of recent developments in communication and education technology that provide important new educational approaches for tailoring education to individual needs. Some of these approaches, such as emails about implementation progress, a CD-ROM with interactive learning or activities, or a Web site describing an AT device and vendor options, might be supplemental to face-to-face meetings. Others, such as an interactive educational program, may be used to replace a meeting or for family members who could not attend a

meeting. This combination of face-to-face and computer based delivery of information is called *blended learning* (Valdez, 2001). Often referred to as "the best of both worlds," blended learning is a powerful, flexible strategy that can enhance the learning experience. For example, assessment information may be reviewed in a face-to-face meeting with the family and a CD-ROM or Web site could be accessed for information about alternative technologies during the meeting. These digital resources could include examples of several persons using the AT in multiple settings and talking about their experiences. The family could then use the CD-ROM or access the Web site from home for additional information, to refresh what they learned, or to use the information in an interactive task. The family and AT professional could communicate regularly via phone or email.

Digital technologies provide a number of new opportunities for enhancing the individualization of AT processes, user control, and range of learning options then previously available. A wide range of high-quality digital information can be stored in compact mediums, such as DVDs, or via the Web and be retrieved via a click of the mouse. With properly designed resources, AT professionals could create an instructional program tailored to a particular family that includes imagery and video clips that are culturally appropriate. The family members could choose parts of the instructional programs they want to watch and view them from home as well.

Another strategy is to provide a variety of on-screen instructional or information guides. These characters can represent individuals from

Figure 2. Illustration of peer guide features incorporated into *Take Control: Multimedia Guide to Spinal Cord Injury Volume 1 Program* (VanBiervliet & McCluer, 1996). Reprinted with permission.

various cultural or ethnic groups and provide unique perspectives on the information presented. The guides can present information via digital videos, audio narration, pictures and text. *The Check Rock and Roll Interactive CD-ROM* uses on-screen digital guides to provide information about pressure ulcer prevention (Paulsen & Creasey, 1999). This program includes five on-screen peer guides with spinal cord injuries who represent individuals with various characteristics. The user can click on a peer button, listen to a description of the guide's experiences, and even select questions to ask the guide. Several easy-to-use interactive activities, including a skin damage meter, a turning schedule clock, and a pillow placement task, are available for applying the information to practical tasks. Users can also tailor information to meet their own needs by selecting learning paths or tracks, one for persons with paraplegia, the other for persons with tetraplegia.

The Take Control: Multimedia Guide to Spinal Cord Injury Volumes 1-4 CD-ROM programs also used the peer guide concept and provide multiple learning paths (VanBiervliet, 1999, 2002) (see Figure 2). The programs can be used in many ways, as tutors, as learning games, and as encyclopedias on spinal cord injury. Take Control is designed to provide both a guided path for the learner and an opportunity for the learner to explore the information in any order or at any depth. On-screen peers serve as program guides. The peer guide periodically appears on screen to provide instructions and personal experiences and to offer words of encouragement. The guides include persons from a variety of walks of life and sociocultural backgrounds. Prior to selecting a guide, the guide can be "interviewed" by the user. Each guide has an accompanying biographical sketch and a brief digital movie in which the guide introduces him/herself in their own words.

Vignettes, or short personal stories, are another powerful tool for individualizing digital programs. *The Families, Cultures and Augmentative and Alternative Communication CD-ROM* contains video vignettes of family members from five different cultural groups who discuss their experiences with the AT processes (VanBiervliet & Parette, 1999, 2002) (see Figure 3). These digital movies have accompanying on-screen narration in English or Spanish, so users can read along if desired. The program features mothers, fathers, grandparents and extended family members talking about their experiences with this communication technology. For example, an aunt from a Navajo village talks about her family's desires to have the images on her nephew's communication system displayed using earth-tone colors that are more representative of their culture rather than less familiar primary colors. A woman of Philippine heritage talks about how the food pictures depicted are not the foods her family eats. Others discuss the difficulty of incorporating the communication technology into their family lifestyles. Finally, interactive games are available to provide alternative means of accessing information and to reinforce concepts and content presented.

Maximizing Access

Good instructional design is accessible design. No responsible educator would knowingly create an instructional program that students or family members could not use simply due to their racial or cultural heritage. It is equally inappropriate, as well as perhaps a violation of federal and state laws, to create a computer-based program that cannot be used by students or family members with disabilities. Computer program accessibility does not just happen; design considerations must be factored into all stages of the development process. Retrofitting or revising a program to incorporate appropriate access after it has been released is far more expensive than planning for maximum accessibility from the initial development stages. For example, using larger text sizes (16 or 18 point) to enhance readability is easy to do at the beginning of development but may require a total redesign of the program later on (Arditi, 1999). An important point of view is that accessibility is user-centered, whether the user is a student or a family member; it is not program or document-centered (Slatin & Rush, 2003). Thus, it defines accessibility as an aspect or quality of the individual user's experience of the resource, not a property of the document itself. Accessibility is defined in terms of the user's ability to

Figure 3. Illustration of vignettes incorporated into the *Families, Cultures, and AAC Program* (VanBiervliet & Parette, 1999). Reprinted with permission.

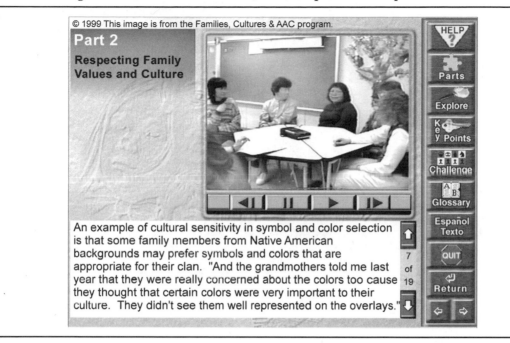

© 1999 This image is from the Families, Cultures & AAC program.

Part 2

Respecting Family Values and Culture

HELP
?

Parts

Explore

Key Points

Challenge

Glossary

Español Texto

QUIT

Return

An example of cultural sensitivity in symbol and color selection is that some family members from Native American backgrounds may prefer symbols and colors that are appropriate for their clan. "And the grandmothers told me last year that they were really concerned about the colors too cause they thought that certain colors were very important to their culture. They didn't see them well represented on the overlays."

7 of 19

access and use the program and its resources as effectively as someone without a disability. Developers who incorporate access solutions may find that these modifications bring benefits to the wider populations as well. The principles of universal design or maximum accessibility, that is, designing to meet the needs of as many users as possible, provide a new dimension for improving the usability of educational software for all persons.

In order to achieve maximum accessibility, it is important that program developers have a better understanding of how people with disabilities will experience the program. Involving persons with disabilities in all phases of design and evaluation helps to avoid unnecessary program barriers and reduce costs. Incorporating a few simple features greatly increases the number of people who can use an application. For educational programs, Universal Design can be viewed as providing multiple representations of content, providing multiple options for expression and control, and providing multiple options for engagement and motivation (Center for Applied Special Technology, 2002). Providing multiple representations of content involves providing essential informa-

tion in redundant formats such as an auditory narration accompanied by text and images (see Figure 4). An example of providing multiple options for control is to enable keyboard options for mouse movements and selections. Options for engagement include presenting content in multiple learning styles, such as guided and exploratory styles, and offering multiple levels of depth or detail on topics.

Digital Divide

Computer and Internet use has spread rapidly across all demographic groups and geographic regions. Americans are increasingly using the Internet and computers at home, work, school, and other locations for an expanding variety of purposes. Such increased use is occurring for people regardless of income, education, age, race, ethnicity, or gender (National Telecommunications and Information Administration, 2002). For example, the rate of growth in Internet use among African-Americans and Hispanic-Americans (33% and 30%, respectively) over the past few years surpassed the growth rates for Euro-Americans or Asian-Americans (approximately 20%). However, although the gap between the Internet connected and uncon-

Figure 4. Illustration of multiple access features incorporated into the *Families, Cultures, and AAC Program* (VanBiervliet & Parette, 1999). Reprinted with permission.

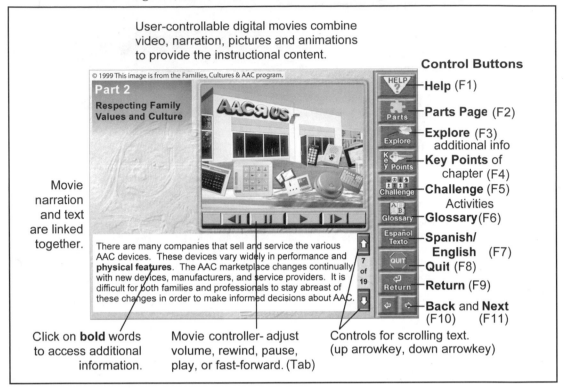

nected is narrowing at a rapid pace, for many the gap will remain. Many of the persons with the greatest needs, such as the very poor, persons with low literacy, the homeless, persons with disabilities, and elderly also have the least access to information technology. Providing access to information to these groups has been an ongoing challenge. AT professionals must be cautious in their recommendations regarding the use of the computers and the Internet for providing AT information. First they must ascertain the family's access and ability to use computers and the resulting information. Computers are available for public use in libraries, community centers, and senior centers. Free or low-cost classes on using computers and the Internet are also offered in most communities. However, even if access is readily available, computer technology may still not be an appropriate educational approach due to learning preferences and computer skills. Therefore, AT professionals must be prepared to provide information in formats that are appropriate to individual family needs.

Implications

Within this chapter we have discussed the importance of understanding various cultural issues related to family-centered approaches when introducing AT. In addition, we have summarized contemporary studies and strategies incorporating family factors related to AT decision-making. Finally, new and emerging technologies have been introduced to give a snapshot of future interventions. Based on our reviews of the various literatures, we feel that the greatest implications for future applications may result from a model that includes the concept of cultural reciprocity.

Simply being aware of cultural influences on AT decision-making is not enough to ensure collaboration with families and effective decision-making. Awareness is merely the framework for such collaboration (Kalyanpur & Harry, 1999). It is equally important to provide strength to the collaborative relationship with families by having knowledge about the beliefs and values that undergird the varying perspectives of all parties. Kalyanpur and Harry

(1999) suggest a four-step process for professionals to develop a "posture of cultural reciprocity" (p. 118). We feel that by combining the four-step process with knowledge of emerging technologies and a family-centered approach, cultural reciprocity may be achieved. A description of these steps and examples are presented below.

Step 1. Identification of the cultural values embedded in the professional's interpretation of the family and/or student's AT needs or in the recommendation for service.

This step essentially requires the professional to ask "why" a specific perception is held. For example, an Asian student with a physical disability is reticent to make eye contact with and respond verbally when addressed by adults. Even when efforts are made by adults to "build rapport," the student still displays a perceived inability or unwillingness to demonstrate these important developmental skills. At this point, the professional should ask him/herself why these skills are deemed important. If the professional is from a Euro-American cultural background, the perception may simply be that eye contact and verbally responding to adult communication initiations are important in both the classroom and daily interactions with others.

Step 2. Determining whether the family recognizes and values these assumptions, and if not, how their perception differs from that of the professional.

In this second step, the family is approached and the professional presents his or her perception of the "issue" to the family. This become problematic in working with families across cultures, as some families may require an interpreter for interactions with school personnel to occur. When interpreters are used, some families are uncomfortable discussing family matters in the presence of others. They may also feel that probing questions from professionals are intrusive (Chan, 1985; VanBiervliet & Parette, 1999; Zuniga, 1992). Resources for working with interpreters are readily available elsewhere as issues related to working with interpreters are beyond the scope

of this chapter (see, e.g., Lynch & Hanson, 1998; VanBiervliet & Parette, 1999). Once appropriate contact is made with the family, the professionally held perception should be presented in a culturally sensitive way to the family for their consideration and response. In this example, the family may reveal that they see nothing wrong with the child's behaviors and that such behavior is typical of children in Asian family settings.

Step 3. Acknowledging and giving specific respect to any cultural differences identified, and fully explaining the cultural basis of the professional assumptions.

In this phase, the professionals should explain to the family their assumptions and beliefs and how they are different (Kalyanpur & Harry, 1999). In this example, the professional would clarify that eye contact is important during communication interactions, and that verbal responses to adult communicative initiations are important. Further, the professional would note that failure to demonstrate these behaviors leads one to believe that the student has not heard what has been said to him or her, and that disrespect is communicated by not making eye contact. The professional must also acknowledge that the family feels that (a) lack of eye contact communicates deference to and respect for authority figures, and that (b) children are taught to listen and not draw attention to themselves by responding to adults.

Step 4. Determining the most effective way to adapt professional interpretations or recommendations to the value system of the family.

For example, through discussion and collaboration, all parties work out an alternative solution that is acceptable to professionals *and* the family. In this student's case, both professionals and family members agree that acceptable outcomes are for the teacher to be certain that the child has "heard" the teacher when addressed and that the information has been "processed" (i.e., the child understands the communication initiation and provides a response that assures the professional that communication has taken place).

This process acknowledges that all cultures possess diverse cultural sets, often conflicting symbols, rituals, stories, and guides to action. This is also true of all institutions in the United States, including special education (i.e., there is a subsystem of culture in special education within the larger education system) (Kalyanpur & Harry, 1999). Special education as a system reflects a culture of sets of behavior that have become ingrained in the behavior of the professionals who work with families. When conflicts with existing cultural sets occur in the school setting, students with disabilities and their families must employ a cultural tool-kit (Swidler, 1998) to mediate the conflicts. This tool-kit provides individuals with the tools for constructing different strategies of action in response to conflicts, or environmental demands. Both individuals and groups actively use different tools from this kit to do different things in different situations.

Summary

Culture is and will continue to be an important factor in AT decision-making. Unfortunately, until recently, practitioners in the field have paid little attention to the potentially powerful influences of culture on the behavior of persons with disabilities, their families, and the professionals who work with them. While our understanding of the impact of culture on AT service delivery is just beginning to unfold, this awakening suggests the complexity of effective AT decision-making. It is unreasonable to assume that any professional will ever be able to completely understand the myriad influences, including cultural, that affect a particular individual with a disability and his or her family at a point in time when AT is being considered by a team. The real challenge for professionals is to consider as many potential influences as possible during the AT decision-making process and to make informed decisions based on careful examination of these influences. The issues discussed in this chapter, coupled with the promise of new and emerging technologies designed to assist professionals and families, may assist better use of our existing resources in the years ahead, and better assist persons with disabilities in becoming effective users of AT.

References

Ainlay, S. C., Becker, G., & Coleman, L. (1986). *The dilemma of difference: A multidisciplinary view of stigma*. New York: Plenum Press.

Al-Hassan, S., & Gardner III, R. (2002). Involving immigrant parents of students with disabilities in the educational process. *Teaching Exceptional Children, 34*(5), 52-58.

Arditi, A. (1999). *Making text legible: Designing for people with partial sight*. Retrieved December 12, 2002, from www. lighthouse.org/ print_leg.htm.

Association of Tech Act Projects. (2000). *Providing outreach to rural and underserved persons about assistive technology*. Retrieved September 18, 2002, from atto. buffalo.edu/registered/ATBasics/Foundation/Laws/atap.pdf.

Bailey, N. M. (1991). Reach out and touch: Serving the un- and under-served. *A. T. Quarterly, 2*(5), 9-10.

Banks, J. A. (1997). *Teaching strategies for ethnic studies* (6th ed.). Needham Heights, MA: Allyn and Bacon.

Barerra, I. (1993). Effective and appropriate instruction for all children: The challenge of cultural/linguistic diversity and young children with special needs. *Topics in Early Childhood Special Education, 13*, 461-487.

Battle, D. E. (2002). *Communication disorders in multicultural populations* (3rd ed.) Boston: Andover Medical.

Becker, G., & Kaufman, S. (1988). Old age, rehabilitation, and research: A review of the issues. *The Gerontologist, 28*, 459-468.

Benner, S. (1998). *Special education issues within the context of American society*. Belmont, CA: Wadsworth.

Bodley, J. H. (1994). *Cultural anthropology: Tribes, states and the global system*. Mountain View, CA: Mayfield.

Bowles, S., & Gintis, H. (1976). *Schooling in capitalist America: Educational reform and the contradictions of economic life*. New York: Basic Books.

Briegel, A. R. (2000). Assistive technology assessment: More than the device. *Intervention in School and Clinic, 35*, 237-243.

Bromley, B. E. (2001). *Assistive technology assessment: A comparative analysis of five models*.

Conference Proceedings. CSUN'S Sixteenth Annual International Conference Technology and Persons with Disabilities. Retrieved September 19, 2002, from www.homemods.org/library/pages/ATAssess.htm.

Brotherson, M. J., Oakland, M. J., Secrist-Mertz, C., Litchfield, R., & Larson, K. (1994). Quality of life issues and families who make the decision to use a feeding tube for their child. *Journal of the Association for Persons with Severe Handicaps, 20,* 202-212.

Bruder, M. B. (2000). Family-centered early intervention: Clarifying our values for the new millennium. *Topics in Early Childhood Special Education, 20,* 105-115, 122.

Bullivant, B. M. (1993). Culture: It's nature and meaning for educators. In J. Banks & C. McGee-Banks (Eds.), *Multicultural education: Issues and perspectives* (2nd ed., pp. 29-47). Needham Heights, MA: Allyn and Bacon.

Carolan, B. (2001). Technology, schools and the decentralization of culture. *First Monday, 6*(8). Retrieved August 26, 2002, from: www.firstmonday.dk/issues/issue6_8/carolan/

Center for Applied Special Technology. (2002). *CAST's three principles of universal design for learning.* 1998. Retrieved December 12, 2002, from www.cast.org/udl/UniversalDesignforLearning361.cfm.

Chan, S. (1985, April). *Reaching out to Asian parents.* Paper presented at the Annual Convention of the Council for Exceptional Children, Anaheim, VA.

Cheek, E. H., Denny, R. K., & Rice, G. E. (2000). Technology, exceptional individuals, and the coming millennium. In J. D. Lindsey (Ed.), *Technology and exceptional individuals* (3rd ed., pp. 459-462) Austin, TX: Pro-Ed.

Church, G., & Glennen, S. (Eds.). (1992). *The handbook of assistive technology.* San Diego, CA: Singular.

Damen, L. (1987). *Culture learning: The fifth dimension in the language classroom.* Reading, MA: Addison-Wesley.

DeGangi, G. A., Wietlisbach, S., Poisson, S., & Stein, E. (1994). The impact of culture and socioeconomic status on family-professional collaboration: Challenges and solutions. *Topics in Early Childhood Special Education, 14,* 503-520.

Dunn, R., & Griggs, S. A. (1995). *Multiculturalism and learning style: Teaching and counseling adolescents.* Westport, CT: Praeger.

Dworet, D., & Bennett, S. (2002). A view from the North: Special education in Canada. *Teaching Exceptional Children, 34*(5), 22-27.

Edwards, C. P., Gandini, L., & Giovaninni, D. (1996). The contrasting developmental timetables of parents and preschool teachers in two cultural communities. In S. Harkness & C. M. Super (Eds.), *Parents' cultural belief systems: Their origins, expressions, and consequences* (pp. 270-288). New York: Guilford Press.

Flippo, K. F., Inge, K. J., & Barcus, J. M. (1995). *Assistive technology. A resource for school, work, and community.* Baltimore: Brookes.

Gitlin, L. N., Luborsky, M. R., & Schemm, R. L. (1998). Emerging concerns of older stroke patients about assistive device use. *The Gerontologist, 38*(2), 169-180.

Guild, P. (1994). The culture/learning style connection. *Educational Leadership, 5*(8), 16-21

Hall, E. T. (1974). *Handbook for proxemic research.* Washington, DC: Society for the Ontology of Visual Communications.

Hanson, M. J., Lynch, E. W., & Wayman, K. I. (1990). Honoring the cultural diversity of families when gathering data. *Topics in Early Childhood Special Education, 10,* 112-131.

Haring, N. G. (1970). The new curriculum design in special education. *Educational Technology, 10,* 24-31.

Harry, B., Grenot-Scheyer, M., Smith-Lewis, M., Park, H. S., Xin, F., & Schwartz, I. (1995). Developing culturally inclusive services for persons with severe disabilities. *The Journal of the Association for Persons with Severe Handicaps, 20,* 99-109.

Hecht, M. L., Andersen, P. A., & Ribeau, S. A. (1989). The cultural dimensions of nonverbal communication. In M. K. Asante & W. B. Gudykunst (Eds.), *Handbook of international and intercultural communication* (pp. 163-185). Newbury Park, CA: Sage.

Huer, M. B. (2000). Examining perceptions of graphic symbols across cultures: A preliminary study of the impact of culture/ethnicity. *Augmentative and Alternative Communication, 16,* 180-185.

Huer, M. B., Parette, H. P., & Saenz, T. (2001). Conversations with Mexican-Americans regarding children with disabilities and augmentative and alternative communication. *Communication Disorders Quarterly, 22,* 197-206.

Huer, M. B., Saenz, T., & Doan, J. H. D. (2001). Understanding the Vietnamese-American community: Implications for training educational personnel providing services to children with disabilities. *Communication Disorders Quarterly, 23,* 27-39.

Hutinger, P. (1994, Summer). Study shows assistive technology produces positive effects, makes recommendations for future efforts. *ACTTive Technology, 9*(3), 1, 3, 4, 6.

Individuals with Disabilities Education Act Amendments of 1997, P. L. 105-17. (June 4, 1997). 20 U.S.C. § 1400 et seq

Institute for Matching Person and Technology. (2002). *Matching person and technology assessment process.* Retrieved September 24, 2002, from members.aol.com/impt97/mptdesc.html.

Judge, S. L., & Parette, H. P. (1998). Family-centered assistive technology decision making. *Infant-Toddler Intervention, 8*(2), 185-206.

Kalyanpur, M., & Harry, B. (1999). *Culture in special education. Building reciprocal family-professional relationships.* Baltimore: Brookes.

Kang, Y., Lovett, D., & Haring, K. (2002). Culture and special education in Taiwan. *Teaching Exceptional Children, 34*(5), 12-15.

Kaufert, J., & Locker, D. (1990). Rehabilitation ideology and respiratory support technology. *Social Science and Medicine, 6*(19), 609-618.

King, T. W. (1999). *Assistive technology: Essential human factors.* Boston: Allyn and Bacon.

Knowles, M. (1996). Adult learning. In R. Craig (Ed.), *The ASTD training and development handbook* (4th ed., pp. 253-264). New York: McGraw-Hill.

Kroeber, A. L., & Kluckhohn, C. (1952). Culture: A critical review of concepts and definitions. *Papers of the Peabody Museum of American Archaeology and Ethnology (Vol. 47).* Cambridge, MA: Harvard University.

Kunkel, M. A. (1990). Expectations about counseling in relation to acculturation in Mexican-American and Anglo-American student samples. *Journal of Counseling Psychology, 37,* 286-292.

Lamorey, S. (2002). The effects of culture on special education services. Evil eyes, prayer meetings, and IEPs. *Teaching Exceptional Children, 34*(5), 67-71.

Leung, E. K. (1988, October). *Cultural and acculturational commonalities and diversities among Asian Americans: Identification and programming considerations.* Paper presented to the Ethnic and Multicultural Symposium, Dallas, TX. (ERIC Document Reproduction Service No. ED 298 780)

Levy, R. I. (1996). Essential contrasts: Differences in parental ideas about learners and teaching in Tahiti and Nepal. In S. Harkness & C. M. Super (Eds.), *Parents' cultural belief systems: Their origins, expressions, and consequences* (pp. 123-142). New York: Guilford Press.

Luborsky, M. R. (1991). Adaptive device appraisal by lifelong-users facing new losses: Culture, identity, and life history factors. In F. Hafferty, S. C. Hey, G. Kiger, & D. Pfeiffer (Eds.), *Translating disability: At the individual, institutional, and societal levels* (pp. 361-366). Salem, OR: Society for Disability Studies and Willamette University.

Luborsky, M. R. (1993). Sociocultural factors shaping technology usage. Fulfilling the promise. *Technology and Disability, 2*(1), 71-78.

Lund, N. J. (1986). Family events and relationships: Implications for language assessment and intervention. *Seminars in Speech and Language, 7,* 415-431.

Lynch, E. W. (1997). Developing cross-cultural competence. In E. W. Lynch & M. J. Hanson (Eds.), *Developing cross-cultural competence. A guide for working with young children and their families* (2nd ed., pp. 47-89). Baltimore: Brookes.

Lynch, E. W., & Hanson, M. J. (1998). (Eds.). *Developing cross-cultural competence. A guide for working with young children and their families* (2nd ed.). Baltimore: Brookes.

McInerney, M., Osher, D., & Kane, M. (1997). *Improving the availability and use of technology for children with disabilities.* Washington, DC: Chesapeake Institute of the American Institutes for Research. Retrieved

September 6, 2002, from www.air.org/techideas.pdf.

Meadan, H., & Gumpel, T. (2002). Special education in Israel. *Teaching Exceptional Children, 34*(5), 16-20.

Miller, D. L. (1979). *Mother's perception of Indian child development.* Unpublished research report, Institute for Scientific Analysis, San Francisco.

Miraglia, E., Law, R., & Collins, P. (1999). *A baseline definition of culture.* Retrieved August 6, 2002, from www.wsu.edu:8001/vcwsu/commons/topics/culture/culture-definition.html.

Murphy, R. (1990). *The body silent.* New York: Norton.

Murphy, R. F., Scheer, J., Murphy, Y., & Mack, R. (1988). Physical disability and social liminality: A study in the rituals of adversity. *Social Science and Medicine, 26,* 235.

National Telecommunications and Information Administration. (2002*). A nation online: How Americans are expanding their use of the Internet.* U.S. Department of Commerce. Retrieved September 15, 2002 from www.ntia.doc.gov/ntiahome/dn/index.html.

Nespor, J. (1987). The role of beliefs in the practice of teaching. *Journal of Curriculum Studies, 19,* 317-328.

Parette, H. P. (1998). Cultural issues and family-centered assistive technology decision-making. In S. L. Judge, & H. P. Parette (Eds.), *Assistive technology for young children with disabilities: A guide to providing family-centered services* (pp. 184-210). Cambridge, MA: Brookline.

Parette, H. P. (1997). Assistive technology devices and services. *Education and Training in Mental Retardation and Developmental Disabilities, 32,* 267-280.

Parette, H. P., & Anderson, C. L. (2001). Family and related service partnerships in home computer decision-making. In L. J. Krueger (Ed.), *Computers in the delivery of special education and related services. Developing collaborative and individualized learning environments* (pp. 96-113). New York: Hayworth.

Parette, H. P., & Angelo, D. H. (1998). The impact of assistive technology devices on children and families. In S. L. Judge, & H. P.

Parette (Eds.), *Assistive technology for young children with disabilities: A guide to providing family-centered services* (pp. 148-183). Cambridge, MA: Brookline.

Parette, H. P., & Brotherson, M. J. (1996). Family participation in assistive technology assessment for young children with disabilities. *Education and Training in Mental Retardation and Developmental Disabilities, 31*(1), 29-43.

Parette, H. P., & Hourcade, J. J. (1997). Family issues and assistive technology needs: A sampling of state practices. *Journal of Special Education Technology, 13,* 27-43.

Parette, H. P., & VanBiervliet, A. (2000). *Culture, families, and augmentative and alternative communication (AAC) impact: A multimedia instructional program for related services personnel and family members.* (Final report for U.S.D.E. Contract No. H029K50072). Cape Girardeau, MO: Southeast Missouri State University. Retrieved August 22, 2002, from cstl.semo.edu/parette/homepage/finalreport.pdf

Parette, H. P., Brotherson, M. J., & Huer, M. B. (2000). Giving families a voice in augmentative and alternative communication decision-making. *Education and Training in Mental Retardation and Developmental Disabilities, 35,* 177-190.

Parette, P., Huer, M. B., & Scherer, M. J. (2004). Effects of acculturation on assistive technology service delivery. *Journal of Special Education Technology, 19*(2), 31-41.

Parette, P., & Scherer, M. J. (2004). Assistive technology use and stigma. *Education and Training in Developmental Disabilities, 39*(3), 217-226.

Parette, H. P., Brotherson, M. J., Hoge, D. R., & Hostetler, S. A. (1996, December). *Family-centered augmentative and alternative communication issues: Implications across cultures.* Paper presented to the International Early Childhood Conference on Children with Special Needs, Phoenix, AZ.

Parette, P., VanBiervliet, A., Reyna, J. W., & Heisserer, D. (Eds.). (1999). *Families, culture, and augmentative and alternative communication (AAC). A multimedia instructional program for related service personnel and family members.* Retrieved August 22, 2002, from cstl.semo.edu/parette/homepage/database.pdf.

Park, J. (2002). Special education in South Korea. *Teaching Exceptional Children, 34*(5), 28-33.

Paulsen D. F., & Creasey, G. H. (1999, September). *Check, Rock & Roll: Pressure ulcer prevention using interactive multimedia.* Paper presented at: 16th Annual Conference of the American Association of Spinal Cord Injury Nurses, Las Vegas, NV.

Phillips, B., & Zhao, H. (1993). Predictors of assistive technology abandonment. *Assistive Technology, 5,* 36-45.

Pomales, J., & Williams, V. (1989). Effects of level of acculturation and counseling style on Hispanic students' perceptions of counselors. *Journal of Counseling Psychology, 36,* 79-83.

Ponce, F. Q., & Atkinson, D. R. (1989). Mexican-American acculturation, counselor ethnicity, counseling style, and perceived counselor credibility. *Journal of Counseling Psychology, 36,* 79-83.

Ramirez, M., & Castaneda, A. (1974). *Cultural democracy, bicognitive development and education.* NY: Academic Press.

Reed, P., & Bowser, G. (1998, November). *Education tech points: A framework for assistive technology planning and systems change in schools.* Paper presented at the CSUN Conference on Technology and Persons with Disabilities, Los Angeles, CA.

Roseberry-McKibbin, C. (1995). *Multicultural students with special language needs.* Oceanside, CA: Academic Communication Associates.

Ruiz, R. A. (1981). Cultural and historical perspectives in counseling hispanics. In D. W. Sue (Ed.), *Counseling the culturally different. Theory and practice* (pp. 186-215). New York: Wiley & Sons.

Scheer, J., & Luborsky, M. (1991). The cultural context of polio biographies. *Orthopedics, 14,* 1173-1181.

Scherer, M. J. (1996). *Living in the state of stuck. How technology impacts the lives of people with disabilities* (2nd ed.). Cambridge, MA: Brookline.

Shepherd, T. L., Contreras, D., & Brown, R. (2002). Special education in Mexico: One community's response. *Teaching Exceptional Children, 34*(5), 8-11.

Silverstein, R. (2000). An overview of the emerging disability policy framework: A guidepost for analyzing public policy. 85 Iowa Law Review 1691.

Slatin, J. M., & Rush, S. (2003). *Maximum accessibility.* Boston: Addison-Wesley.

Smart, J. F., & Smart, D. W. (1992). Cultural changes in multicultural rehabilitation. *Rehabilitation Education, 6*(2), 105-122.

Smith-Lewis, M. (1992). *What is mental retardation? Perceptions from the African American community.* Unpublished manuscript. Hunter College, New York.

Smith-Lewis, M. R., & Ford, A. (1987). A user's perspective on augmentative communication. *Augmentative and Alternative Communication, 3,* 12-17.

Soriano, M. (1995). Latinos in rehabilitation: Implications for culturally appropriate counseling. *NARPPS Journal, 19*(2), 67-72.

Soto, G. (1994). A cultural perspective on augmentative and alternative communication. *American Speech-Language-Hearing Association Special Interest Division 12, 3*(2), 6.

Soto, G. (2000). "We have come a long ways" AAC and Multiculturalism: From cultural awareness to cultural responsibility. *Augmentative and Alternative Communication, SID 12 Newsletter, 9*(2), 1-3.

Soto, G., Huer, M. B., & Taylor, O. (1997). Multicultural issues. In L. L. Lloyd, D. H. Fuller, & H. H. Arvidson (Eds.), *Augmentative and alternative communication* (pp. 406-413). Boston: Allyn and Bacon.

Stein, H. F. (1979). Rehabilitation and chronic illness in American culture. *Journal of Psychological Anthropology, 2,* 153-176.

Sutton, L. (1999). *Feed a cold, starve a fever: An exploration into the relationship between culture, belief, and health.* Masters thesis, University of Massachusetts-Amherst. Retrieved January 7, 2003, from members.tripod.com/random_sage/intro.htm.

Swidler, A. (1998). Culture and social action. In P. Smith (Ed.), *The new American cultural sociology* (pp. 171-187). Cambridge: Cambridge University Press.

Technology-Related Assistance for Individuals with Disabilities Act of 1988, P. L. 100-407.

(August 19, 1988). 29 U.S.C. 2201 et seq.: *U. S. Statutes at Large, 102*, 1044-1065.

The Assistive Technology Act of 1998, P.L. 105-394. (November 13, 1998), 112 STAT. 3627.

The Changing Face of Education. (2000, March). *Communicator.* Retrieved August 7, 2002, from www.naesp.org/comm/c0300.htm.

Torres-Davis, A., & Trivelli, L. U. (1994). *Project Reaching Out: Technology training for Hispanics with disabilities.* Arlington, VA: RESNA.

Turner, R. J., & Noh, S. (1988). Physical disability and depression: A longitudinal analysis. *Journal of Health and Social Behaviour, 29,* 23-27.

VanBiervliet, A. (1999). Multimedia and SCI: Educational strategies for the 21st century. *Topics in Spinal Cord Injury Rehabilitation, 5*(3), 33-49.

VanBiervliet, A., & McCluer, S. (1996). *Take Control: Multimedia guide for spinal cord injury Volume I* [CD-ROM]. Little Rock: Arkansas Spinal Cord Commission and Program Development Associates, Inc.

VanBiervliet, A., & Parette, H. P. (2002). Development and evaluation of the *Families, Cultures and Augmentative and Alternative Communication* (AAC) multimedia program. *Disability and Rehabilitation, 24*(1-3), 131-143.

VanBiervliet, A., & Parette, H. P. (1999). *Families, cultures, and AAC* [CD-ROM]. Little Rock, AR: Southeast Missouri State University and University of Arkansas for Medical Sciences.

Valdez, R. J. (2001) *Blended learning: Maximizing the impact of an integrated solution.* Retrieved December 12, 2002, from www.sanantonio-astd.org/ElrngDocs/blended_learning.pdf.

Wells, R. B., Hough, R. L., Golding, J. M., & Burnam, M. A. (1987). Which Mexican Americans underutlilize health services? *American Journal of Psychiatry, 144,* 918-922.

Williams, W. B., Stemach, G., Wolfe, S., & Stanger, C. (1995). *Lifespace access profile: Assistive technology assessment and planning for individuals with severe or multiple disabilities* (rev. ed.). Irvine, CA: Lifespace Access Assistive Technology Systems.

Wisconsin Assistive Technology Initiative. (1998). *Assessing students' needs for assistive technology: A resource manual for school district teams.* Amherst, WI: Author.

Zabala, J. (1998). *Ready, SETT, Go! Online workshop.* Retrieved January 7, 2003, from www2.edc.org/NCIP/Workshops/sett3/index.html.

Zuniga, M. E. (1992). Families with Latino roots. In E. W. Lynch & M. J. Hanson (Eds.), *Developing cross-cultural competence. A guide for working with children and their families* (pp. 151-179). Baltimore: Brookes.

6

Access Granted: Achieving Technological Equity in the 21st Century

Monica R. Brown

Information/educational technology (IT/ET) holds the promise of enabling access to information irrespective of a person's social situation (Greenhill, 1998). Unfortunately, particular groups (e.g., students from culturally and linguistically diverse backgrounds (CLD), students with disabilities, female students, students from poverty households) of students have a greater likelihood of experiencing disadvantage with the introduction of IT/ET into the classroom than others (Ammann, 2001; Becker & Sterling, 1987; Bhargava, 2002; Brunner & Bennett, 1997; Greenhill, 1998; Gorski, 2000; National Center for Education Statistics (NCES) (2000). Thus, existing studies suggest that female students (Bhargava, 2002; Brunner & Bennett, 1997; Butler, 2000; Fletcher-Flinn & Suddendorf, 1996), students from CLD backgrounds (Gorski, 2000; Henry, 1997; Zakariya, 1984), and students with disabilities (Burgstahler, 1995; Heinisch, n.d.; Lewis, 1997; Lewis, Harrison, Lynch, & Saba, 1995) may not be receiving the benefits of IT/ET in the classroom to the same extent that their peers do.

Identification of the above groups implies that they are in some way the source of the problem by diverting attention from the broader and, usually, systemic sources of the problem back to the individual. Of crucial importance to addressing inequities and access to IT/ET is the identification and minimization, if not elimination, of broader influences that assist in perpetuating these socially constructed barriers. Being identified as a female student, a student from a CLD background, and/or a student

with a disability does not causally imply that the student will be disadvantaged in accessing IT/ET. However, some students from each of these groups will experience inequalities (i.e., parity with regard to access to technology and attitudes toward technology) and inequities with regard to IT/ET access and use in the form of barriers such as teacher attitudes, scarce resources at school and home, instructional practices, and student attitudes (Brown, 2000, 2002; Brown, Higgins, & Hartley, 2001; Greenhill, 1998). Discriminatory barriers are maintained and largely function in an external relationship to the groups being disadvantaged (Dwyer, 1997). Thus women, individuals from CLD backgrounds, students with disabilities, and students from poverty households, along with other arbitrary groupings, are defined by a relationship to an external "norm" or "mainstream" (i.e., Caucasian, middle class male students) that possesses none of these identifications (Greenhill, 1998).

Based on a 1999 survey, *Teachers' tools for the 21st century: A report on teachers' use of technology;* The National Center for Education Statistics, (NCES, 2000) found that limited access to technology is widespread. Technology can bring opportunities to students that would be impossible otherwise, but this can only occur if we begin to address many, if not all, of the barriers (e.g., resources, resources between schools, curriculum/pedagogy, environment/classroom setting, home access and use, individualized instruction) that exist to access and use for some groups of students (e.g., female students, students with disabilities, students from CLD backgrounds, students from poverty households).

If technology is going to bring the potential to education for all students, it is important that we begin to narrow the divide that exists between mainstream students and students from traditionally disadvantaged groups. The remainder of this chapter is dedicated to identifying equity issues, discussing the impact of technology inequities on non-mainstream students, identifying barriers to equity, and making recommendations for remedying the inequities that exist with regard to instructional/educational technology access and use.

Equity Issues: The Technology Gap

When educational opportunities are not equal or equitable for all, regardless of race/ethnicity, gender, social status, or ability, it is natural to judge that as being unfair and to demand strategies to remedy those inequalities and inequities. Such an issue has arisen over the access and use of computers and the Internet.

In recent years, the investment in technology for K-12 public schools in the United States has grown astronomically (Yau, 1999). With this shift towards a technology-driven model of education comes many questions and concerns from those concerned with technology equity. They include: (a) Are traditionally underserved students receiving a fair or adequate share of technological resources in comparison with mainstream populations? (b) Are the teachers of these students receiving adequate training on the effective use of educational technology? (c) Are there specific uses of educational technology that are particularly effective for teaching traditionally underserved populations? If so, are they actually being employed for these students? and (d) Do these students have sufficient access to technology at home to aid their learning? (Yau, 1999).

Before these questions can be answered, it is important to acknowledge that access to technology is considered and measured in a variety of ways, including: (a) the ratio between the number of students at a school and the number of computers owned by the school; (b) the ratio between the number of students at a school and the number of computers that are operational in the school's classrooms; (c) the amount of time that students work on the computers; (d) the type and range of computer learning tasks that students are assigned at school; and (e) the availability of a computer for use at home or after regular school hours (Yau, 1999).

Demographic Factors in Technology Equity and Access

The literature on equitable access and use of technology indicates that technology has the power to polarize certain groups of students (e.g., students with disabilities, students from CLD backgrounds, female students, students from poverty households) and prevent them from participating equally in society (Bhargava, 2002; Brown, 2000; Brown et al., 2001; Brunner & Bennett, 1997; Burgstahler, 1995; Butler, 2000; Greenhill, 1998; Heinisch, n.d.; Henry, 1997; Koch, 1994; Lewis, 1997; Mark & Hanson, 1992; Rockman, 1995). Many of these students are placed at risk because they are already unlikely to graduate from high school or can be expected to leave high school without an adequate level of basic skills because the risk factors (i.e., low achievement, low social status, poor attendance, and attendance at schools with large numbers of students living in poverty) make it more difficult for the students to graduate. Although great strides have been made to narrow the divide between those with and those without access to technology, the fact remains that there is an ever widening gap (Robyler, 2001; Yoder, 2001). These students become victims in the sense that the likelihood of reaching their full potential is diminished (Brown, 2000). The remainder of this section will include a discussion of the equity issues with regard to each of the above-identified groups.

Inequities Based on Gender

Historically, a gender gap has existed in technology (Mark & Hanson, 1992; Sadker, 1999). More recent literature on gender and computer technology (since 1992) indicates that a great deal of work has been done to address some of the past issues, but the fears of technology inequities still remain as much alive as they were in the 1980s and 1990s (American Association of University Women [AAUW], 1998). According to the AAUW report, girls of all ethnicities rate themselves significantly, "lower than boys on computer ability" (p. 4). The summary stated further that, "girls use computers less often outside of school and therefore, boys enter the classroom with more prior experience with computers and other technology than girls" (p. 4). If more attention is not paid to ensuring that girls receive advanced-level computer courses and technology access, they may be relegated to bystander status in the technological 21st century.

Inequities in and out of School

Mark and Hanson (1992) have identified three areas where there is clear gender inequity in learning with technology, (a) within the school environment, female students have less access to technology and the reasons why they use technology is much different than for males; (b) girls have more negative attitudes towards technology than boys do; and (c) male and female students view technology and computers as chiefly a male area. Greenhill (1998) found even greater inequity in the use of technology outside of the school environment. That is, boys were found to be more likely to have access and use a computer and other technologies at home. Table 1 presents evidence of the continued gender gap from the AAUW report and other sources.

Many factors have been identified (e.g., biases in software selection, teacher attitudes, student attitudes, lack of female role models) in past literature as contributing to these inequities. At the same time, research has also offered suggestions/tips on how to create more equitable technology environments and how to encourage technology use by all students, particularly female students (e.g., provide role models, integrate technology into all subject areas, use the Internet as a research tool, use technology in collaborative projects, make sure that students get equal time with the technology when they are paired at personal computers, review software for blatant biases, look for opportunities to showcase women in scientific and technical fields, host a summer camp for girls) (Bhargava, 2002; Brunner & Bennett, 1997; Koch, 1994; National Education Association [NEA], 1997).

The good thing about technology is that it is gender-neutral. That is, (a) it is not influenced by the appearance or manner of the user (NEA, 1997); (b) there is no inherent bias in the feedback or remediation offered by its applications; and (c) when integrated fully into the curriculum, it has appeal to those who like to problem solve, as well as those who like to work individually or collaborate (NEA, 1997). In a sense, it is an equalizing tool whose value is in its capacity to facilitate a more gender-equitable environment (NEA, 1997). But in order for technology to be the equalizing tool we think it can be, careful consideration must be given to what tools are selected and how they are incorporated into the classroom.

Race/Ethnicity and Access

Available statistics show that computer and Internet access in U.S. public schools has increased at a very steep rate over the past decade or so (Gorski, 2001; U.S. Department of Commerce, 2000; Yau, 1999). Thus, the number of computers available per student increased from a ratio of 1:125 in 1983 to 1:9 in 1995 (Glennan & Melmed, 1996), and then to 1:5 in 2000 (Cattagni & Westat, 2001; Smerdon et al., 2001). These statistics are based on "access" as defined by the ratio of the number of students to the number of computers. When "technology access" is defined by frequency of use of a school computer, some data indicate that students from CLD and poverty backgrounds are even less likely to have access to technology (NCES, 1997; Smerdon et al., 2001).

Likewise, schools are being connected to the Internet at an ever-increasing rate (U.S. Department of Commerce, 1999, 2000, 2002; Yau, 1999). The NCES (1997) reported that 78% of schools had Internet access, showing a sharp increase in school Internet access from 54% in 1994 to 90% in 1997. However, even with these increases in Internet access and use in U.S. public schools, there are still disparities (e.g., instructional) between mainstream and traditionally disadvantaged students (e.g., students from CLD backgrounds and students from poverty backgrounds).

Table 1. Evidence of Continued Gender Gap.

Evidence	Source
1. Female enrollment in computer programming courses still lags behind that of males.	AAUW, 1998; Durndell, Glissov, & Siann, 1995; Hanson, 1997
2. High school girls are less likely than boys to take physics and high-level computer classes and are still underrepresented in Advanced Placement (AP) computer science classes.	Durndell, Glissov, & Siann, 1995
3. Women remain underrepresented in computer technology careers.	Hanson, 1997
4. Girls continue to rate themselves lower than male students with regard to their self-perceptions and attitudes about computer ability.	Boser, Daughtery, & Palmer, 1996; Durndell, Glissov, & Siann, 1995; 1996; Hodes, 1995-1996; Mark & Hanson, 1992
5. Female students continue to be disproportionately represented among those who suffer computer anxiety.	Cooper & Stone, 1996
6. Sociocultural conditions reinforce girls' negative attitudes toward computers.	Koch, 1994; Mark & Hanson, 1992; Swanson, 1997
7. Male students use computers more at home and at school than female students, a practice that is reinforced by many parents.	Durndell, Glissov, & Siann, 1995; Greenhill, 1998; Koch, 1994; Mark & Hanson, 1992; Reinen & Plomp, 1997
8. Teachers may be transmitting, even unconsciously, the message that female students do not need to participate in computer technology.	Hanson, 1997; Koch, 1994; Reinen & Plomp, 1997
9. Using computers for games is widespread, and games that appeal to males continue to dominate game software.	NEA, 1997; Rockman, 1995
10. Fewer women than men are computer educators.	NEA, 1997; Reinen & Plomp, 1997
11. Teacher education programs remain problematic with regard to the amount of time they spend on examining gender issues in general, much less in technology specifically.	AAUW, 1998

Instructional Disparities

Racial/ethnic characteristics have a great deal to do with the kinds of computer use we find in the schools (Brown, 2000; Brown et al., 2001; Rockman, 1995). Instructional practices for CLD students and students from poverty households can be distinguished from the more am- bitious "best practices" found in wealthier areas (Rockman, 1995). That is, students in less wealthy schools receive a different, qualitatively poorer kind of instruction, using different materials and resulting in inequitable outcomes (Brown et al., 2001; Rockman, 1995). These students receive fewer assignments that incorporate hands-on and higher order thinking activities to engage the minds of the students and help them think critically and write better (Rockman, 1995).

Substantial disparities have continued to widen with regard to Internet and computer access and use, both when comparing African-American and Hispanic individuals against the national average and against Caucasian individuals (U.S. Department of Commerce, 2002, 2000). Some of the major findings reported in the literature include the following:

1. By the end of 1998, 37% of the classrooms in schools with CLD enrollments of 50% or more of the student body had Internet access, compared to 57% of those schools with less than 6% CLD enrollment did (NCES, 2000).
2. By 2000, only 23.5% of African-American households, and only 23.6% of Hispanic (Latino/a) households had Internet access (NCES, 2000), considerably lower than the 41.5% national average (NCES, 2000).
3. At annual incomes less than $15,000, Caucasian households (22.8%) and Asian households (39.4%) enjoy much greater percentages of computer ownership than African-American (11.5%) and Hispanic (12.5%) households in the same income bracket (U.S. Department of Commerce, 2000, 2002).
4. While about 70% of the teachers in schools in which the CLD students comprise less than 20% of the student body report having Internet access in their classrooms, only 51% of the teachers whose schools have 50% or more CLD student enrollment have that luxury (Smerdon et al., 2001).
5. The gaps widen. Between October 1997 and December 1998, the gap in Internet access between Caucasian and African-American households grew 5.1 percentage points; between December 1998 and August 2000, there was a 4-percentage point increase (U.S. Department of Commerce, 2000, 2002).
a. Caucasian and Hispanic households grew 4.7 percentage points between 1997 and 1998, and widened even further between 1998 and 2000 (5.3 percentage points) (U.S. Department of Commerce, 2002, 2000).
b. Between Asian-Pacific Islanders and Caucasians, the gap grew from 6.2 percentage points in 1998 to 10.7 percentage points in 2000 (U.S. Department of Commerce, 2002, 2000).
6. The divide between the African-American household Internet access rate and the national average rate increased 3.0 percentage points from December of 1998 to August of 2000 (U.S. Department of Commerce, 2000, 2002).
a. The divide between Hispanic households and the national average increased 4.3 percentage points in the same time period (U.S. Department of Commerce, 2002, 2000).

Although there is significant variation in Internet access and computer ownership within subgroups of these broad categories, Internet rates still fall well short of the national average of 42%, and households of CLD individuals had disparate rates of ownership compared to Caucasian households (U.S. Department of Commerce, 2000, 2002). Table 2 illustrates the percentage of growth in computer and Internet access among racial/ethnic groups.

Access and Use Among Individuals with Disabilities

Access to the information highway and other technology enhances communication and information for all individuals, but particularly for people with disabilities (Burgstahler, 1995). Unfortunately, many people with disabilities do not have access to the input and output alternatives that allow them to use the technologies (Burgstahler, 1995; Heinisch, n.d.; Lewis, 1997). In addition, there appears to be a discrepancy between the potential offered by computers in educational settings and the ways in which they are actually being used (Behrmann, 1988; Brown, 2000). Thus, the presence of computers in the schools does not necessarily mean that they are being used appropriately or to the best advantage for students with disabilities. Teachers need to be able to teach students basic computer technology as well as modifications for special applications. Students need to learn to be users of information and not just recipients of information (Geisert & Futrell, 1990; Lewis, 1997).

Technology has the potential to increase the rates of computer and Internet use among people with disabilities, but it can be an enor-

Table 2. Percentage of U.S. Households with Computer and Internet Access by Race/Ethnicity

Race/Ethnicity	Computer Access 1998	Computer Access 2000	Internet Access 1998	Internet Access 2000
Caucasian	46.6	55.7	29.8	46.1
African American	23.2	32.6	11.2	23.5
Asian, Pacific Islander	55.0	65.6	36.0	56.8
Hispanic	25.5	33.7	12.6	23.6

Source: U.S. Department of Commerce. (2000). *Falling through the net: Toward digital inclusion: A report on Americans' access to technology tools.* Retrieved November 5, 2000, from http://www.ntia.doc.gov/ntiahome/fttn00/Falling.htm.

mous barrier if products are not designed to be accessible. Research has identified some of the barriers that exist for people with disabilities, including: (a) information, (b) ignorance, and (c) the design and manufacture of the computers themselves (Burgstahler, 1995). Kaye (2000) reported that people with physical disabilities were less than half as likely to have computer access at home as people without physical disabilities (23.9% and 51.7%, respectively).

In their report, the U.S. Department of Commerce (2000) followed the concept used by the Americans with Disabilities Act (ADA) to define persons with physical and mental disabilities. According to ADA, a person with a disability as a person who has a physical or mental impairment that substantially limits one or more life activities. The major findings from the U.S. Department of Commerce (2000) study are outlined below. See Table 3 for information pertaining to computer and Internet access and use among individuals with disabilities.

1. People with a disability were only half as likely to have Internet access and computer use than those without disabilities.
2. Just under 25% of the people without disabilities have never used a computer, whereas close to 60% of people with disabilities have never used a computer.
3. Males with or without disabilities are more likely than females in the comparable populations to have Internet access at home. The difference between the group with disabilities and the group without

disabilities is larger for women than for men (48% and 55%, respectively).

4. In the comparison of persons who regularly use a personal computer (PC), women without a disability lag behind men with a disability in this category.

Two things are evident in the literature with regard to certain groups of students: (a) there are disparities in the access and use of computers and the Internet, and (b) when computers are used, it is uncertain whether the types and quality of instruction are such that students are fully benefiting from it. If technology is going to fulfill its promise for all students, all groups, especially those that have been traditionally underserved, they must receive more opportunities to access and use the technology. Additionally, the barriers that exist have to be identified, addressed, and eventually eliminated.

Barriers to Equity and Access

On a most basic level, teachers may be more likely to integrate computers and other technologies into classroom instruction if they have access to adequate equipment. However, there are typically barriers to access and equity in place that prevent teachers from effectively integrating the technology. These barriers can usually be grouped into five categories, (a) resources, (b) resources at school, (c) curriculum/pedagogy, (d) environment/classroom setting, and (e) attitudes (i.e., teacher and student) (Brown, 2000; Brown et al., 2001; Greenhill, 1998; Marginson, 1993), and identifying these

Table 3. Percentage of U.S. Households with Computer and Internet Access by Disability (Ages 16-24)

Category	Home Internet Access Nondisabled	Disability	Regular PC User Nondisabled	Disability
All	41.4	35.9	57.6	39.5
Male	41.5	34.8	54.8	35.5
Female	41.2	37.1	60.3	44.0
Caucasian	50.0	44.7	64.4	46.5
African American	No data	No data	No data	No data
Asian & Pacific Islander	48.3	No data	69.0	No data
Hispanic	21.6	No data	41.6	30.8

Note. "No data" in cells indicates that there was insufficient sample size to produce reliable estimates.

Source: U.S. Department of Commerce. (2000). *Falling through the net: Toward digital inclusion: A report on Americans' access to technology tools.* Retrieved November 5, 2000, from www.ntia.doc.gov/ntiahome/fttn00/Falling.htm.

categories makes it easier for teachers to advocate for strategies that will help them to minimize the influence of the barriers in their classroom environments. For example, if the teacher recognizes that the female students are underrepresented in computer science courses, teachers must develop programs at the school, district, and state level to increase girls' representation in those classes. We shall now turn our attention to examining the five barriers in greater detail.

Resources

Greenhill (1998) and Marginson (1993) identified resourcing as a key element in the provision of access to IT/ET. Thus, educational providers obtain IT/ET equipment at varying rates (i.e., slow and fast tracks), and the rate at which the equipment is obtained impacts on an individual's ability to gain access to information technologies, especially in the educational setting. The authors insist that educational environments, when appropriately managed and funded, can alleviate the disparities that exist among personal ownership of resources. Home-based educational resources are out of the scope of the government intervention, but addressing inequity and inequality within educational environments can contribute to more equitable distribution of IT/ET equipment

(Reinen & Plomp, 1997). To further compound the issue, inequality and inequity can be experienced at many levels. They are experienced between different schools, between individual students, and individually between the school and domestic environments (Greenhill, 1998). It is evident that the rate at which schools obtain access to information technologies and the disparity between poor and wealthy schools impacts on the students' ability to access and use informational/educational technologies.

Resources at School

Information and educational technology has transformed and continues to transform the schooling experience for many children. For others, this transformation has not occurred. Yau (1999) commented on the disparities between poor and wealthy schools indicating that no shortage of technology resources is apparent at the aggregate level, but that the distribution of those resources across different populations is a cause for concern. Neuman (1990) found that inner-city schools with higher enrollments than suburban schools create overcrowding and a scarcity of resources for students. Becker and Sterling (1987) agreed, noting that even though African-American students attended schools with about the same number of computers as Caucasian students, African-American students typically attended larger schools, so the ratio of students per computer was less favorable.

Children in rural and remote areas and children attending small or isolated schools have gained access to an expanded range of courses through the combination of IT and distance education (Greenhill, 1998; Kinser, Pessin, & Meyerholen, 2001). But, despite these improvements in opportunity provided by IT, not all children are benefiting from the access to new technology and improved communications infrastructures (Greenhill, 1998). Distance can exacerbate the barriers to acquiring appropriate IT resources. Thus, students in suburban and rural schools in low-income areas may experience inequities when the demand for access to IT resources exceeds the capabilities of funding sources (Greenhill, 1998).

Thus, consideration must be given to developing the most equitable strategies for funding IT/ET in schools, while being careful not to privilege schools that already have, potentially self-funded, technology resources and are considered "technologically ready" (Fletcher-Flinn & Suddendorf, 1996). Once schools have been identified as technologically ready, it is the responsibility of the classroom teachers to make sure students receive quality access and instruction.

Curriculum/Pedagogy

For students who do not have access to technology in the home, schools must also provide well-developed computer literacy curricula (Greenhill, 1998). In particular, curricula that focuses on the issues concerning the instruction of those students who have typically been underserved in terms of technology access and use. According to Waxman and Padron (1995), many of these students have different educational needs and technology is an effective tool for individualized learning, group interaction, managing and coordinating learning, expression, and knowledge production (Greenhill, 1998; Hopkins, 1991).

Educators must consider students' cognitive styles, expectations of technology, and academic learning time (Salerno, 1995), as well as classroom organization, and student grouping as instructional variables when planning to integrate technology into the curriculum.

Efforts must be made to use technology so that it is accessible to all students. This way students learn to tell the technology what to do rather than always doing what the technology tells them to do. Appropriate use of technology by different targeted groups (e.g., students with disabilities, female students, students from CLD backgrounds) should always be promoted (Brown, 2000).

Environment/Classroom Setting

The classroom setting provides an important environment for learning and skill acquisition to occur. Classrooms that incorporate IT into their makeup can either benefit or restrict the individual student's learning experience (Greenhill, 1998). Environments that incorporate IT are learner-focused and concerned with how technology can support the individual student's needs (Riley, Kunin, Smith, & Roberts, 1996). Additionally, the environments are capable of producing significant academic and social improvements in students (Christie & Sabers, 1989; Riley et al., 1996), as well as gains in achievement, higher test scores, and improved student attitudes (Wepner, 1991). Riley et al. also reported increased student enthusiasm and engagement, improved student retention and course completion, and increased job placements for students. All of these improvements are critical in that they are reflected in students' sense of social integration and bonding at school, leading to a decrease in the dropout rate for these students (Brown, 2000; Christie & Sabers, 1989).

Attitudes

Both overt and covert discrimination resulting from attitudinal behaviors continues to be a cause of disadvantage for many students (e.g., students from CLD backgrounds, students with disabilities, students from poverty households, female students) in the classroom (Dwyer, 1997; Ryan, 1997). Sutton (1991) found that teachers profess equity and equality in attitudinal surveys, but in reality use practices (e.g., using instruction based on a student's race/ethnicity, social status, ability, or gender) that are not equal or equitable.

At the rate at which technology changes, attitudes towards the technology itself may be as important as one's skills with a specific piece of technology. Chen (1985) found that gender was a consistent factor affecting computer attitudes. Male students generally had more positive attitudes toward computers and other technologies than did female students (Hess & Miura, 1985; Miura, 1987). While studies have examined ethnic differences in attitudes, and Griffin, Gillis, and Brown (1986) found that Caucasian students had more positive attitudes towards technology than students from CLD backgrounds (predominantly Hispanic).

If the 21st century is to be the decade when the technology gaps begin to consistently narrow between the typically disadvantaged students and the mainstream students, the above barriers must be addressed by those in positions to make decisions that impact on students' lives (Alden, n.d.). In addition, schools and classroom teachers must identify strategies for closing the gap that will be most effective with the students they are working with.

Closing the Gap

The digital divide is complex and lacks an easy solution. Solving the problem requires that schools and educators examine students' access to technology as well as technology equity and certain students (e.g., students with disabilities, students from CLD backgrounds, female students, students from poverty households) with regard to technology. Technology education teachers must meet and discuss equity issues relative to students with disabilities, students from CLD backgrounds, and female students. Various forums must be held, including workshops with outside facilitators and in-school meetings to discuss guidelines (Silverman & Pritchard, 1996). Further, all teachers must consider strategies (e.g., technology camps for girls) to attract more of the above students into technology classes including, if necessary, curriculum revisions or reorganization of computer labs.

It will take a coordinated national approach that provides pervasive access to technology, appealing content, and compelling role models before the equitable use of computers by children is achieved, including (a) strengthening national, state, and local leadership, (b) providing for funding for hardware, software, and connectivity, (c) improving technology, (d) developing and promoting new content, (e) training teachers, parents, and other caregivers, and (f) modeling successful programs (Chen, 2000). In addition to the previously mentioned suggestions, Brown (2000), Brown et al. (2001) and others have identified specific strategies (e.g., creating after-school programs, loaning technology to families, developing a technology plan) that can be used by school districts and/or school district personnel to ensure equitable access to technology for all students. Table 4 provides strategies school districts, administrators, schools, and teachers can use to ensure equitable access to technology.

Unequal access to technology remains a serious issue, just as it was in the 20th century. Solving these equity problems, whether gender, race/ethnicity, disability, or economically based, will take time and money. More importantly, it will take a commitment from both the public and school district personnel to reach the goal.

Conclusion

Until we enjoy universal access to technology, the Internet, and ideas on how to use them responsibly and productively, many people will continue to wield an unfair advantage in their learning environment, in the job market, and in their daily lives (Yoder, 2001). This unfair advantage creates a gap between those who have the advantage and those who do not, leaving a disproportionate segment of the population without access to technology (NCES, 2000; U.S. Department of Commerce, 1999, 2000, 2002; Yoder, 2001).

Schools lag behind workplaces, leisure places, and other realms of life in their access to new information technologies (Secretary's Conference on Educational Technology, 1995). Moreover, current technologies are not equitably distributed among different kinds of schools (e.g., rural, urban, suburban), certain groups of students (e.g., female students, students from CLD backgrounds, students with disabilities), and certain households (e.g., families living in poverty vs. wealthier households). Ensuring equitable access is the first step toward build-

Table 4. Strategies to Ensure Equitable Access to Technology

What School Districts Can Do
1. Seek high-tech business partners who often are interested in helping out local schools (NETC, 2000).
2. Write grants to receive public and private support.
3. Conduct special fund-raising events.
4. Seek hardware and software donations that meet your needs (Brown et al., 2001).
5. Identify what skills parents or guardians have that might be used in your programs.
6. Establish or join a consortium to help stretch resources even further.
7. Investigate ways to sell, donate, or trade-in old equipment (e.g., hold a garage sale).
8. Consider leasing equipment.
9. With many schools and a limited budget, explore networking options for local and state-wide use.

What District Administrators Can Do
1. Survey schools within district to determine differences in amount of equipment, type of equipment, and number and type of course offerings and whether these differences are substantial enough to constitute unequal access (Northwest Educational Technology Consortium [NETC], 2000).
2. Based on results of the survey, enact a district policy that outlines a minimum technology plan that offers all students the opportunity to become computer literate as defined by the district; be sure to require staff training and frequent assessment of the plan (NETC, 2000).
3. Develop a plan or set of strategies for assisting individual schools to meet the requirements of the district policy (NETC, 2000).

What Schools Can Do
1. Hold a lab night where students and parents work together at computers (provide child care) (NETC, 2000).
2. Schedule activities during the day for parents who are at home during the day, have other children at home during the evening, or have concerns about going out at night (Brown, 2000; Brown et al., 2001).
3. Have loaner equipment that can be borrowed for a specific amount of time; this could include laptops, instructional videos, and hand-held calculators (Education Commission of the States, 2000).
4. Have loaner instructional software (Brown, 2000; NETC, 2000).
5. Keep labs open before and after school, in the evenings, during the summer (in conjunction with summer school); use volunteers to staff and supervise these additional hours (Brown et al., 2001; NETC, 2000).
6. Seek funds (e.g., mini-grants) to serve groups with limited economic means.
7. Partner with the public library to make your equipment available to students during the summer (American Library Association (ALA), 1998).
8. Encourage students to use public library technology for after-school homework assistance and to take advantage of mentoring and tutoring programs (ALA, 1998).

What School Staff Can Do
1. Offer computer classes for staff so that all staff are competent computer users and can integrate computers at various skill levels (Brown, 2000; Brown et al., 2001; NETC, 2000).
2. Be advocates for equity; take notice and speak up when you see inequities in access or use. For example: (1) survey the location of computers within your school and monitor who uses them; (2) monitor use of the computer laboratory during free times; (3) monitor whether

(continued next page)

Table 4. Strategies to Ensure Equitable Access to Technology (continued)

all students have opportunities to go on "electronic" field trips or use networking to participate in collaborative projects; (4) monitor whether different groups of students are proportionally represented in interactive TV courses (NETC, 2000).

3. Develop a plan to integrate diverse uses of computers and other educational technology across the curriculum to help teachers find ways to use technology in their classrooms (Brown et al., 2001).

4. Identify a staff member who can help all teachers integrate the computer or other technology into their classrooms (NETC, 2000).

5. Locate computers in central supervised location(s) or have them available in all classrooms; if computers are located in a central area periodically monitor their use, post rules for use and enforce them; and if necessary, reserve special times for their use by underrepresented user groups (Brown, 2000; Brown et al., 2001; McKenzie, 1998).

6. Educate parents or guardians about the rewards of being computer literate. Suggestions for parents include: (a) listen to children when they want to talk about how they use computers at school and acknowledge their accomplishments; (b) if possible, purchase or borrow computer magazines; (c) if you have one, encourage use of home computer, especially for female children; (d) enroll children in computer camps and after-school programs and seek financial assistance if it's needed (Brown, 2000); (e) initiate talking about computers and other technology; (f) express high expectations of your children regarding technology, science, and mathematics (NETC, 2000).

7. Develop classes for parents to help them become computer literate (Brown, 2000).

8. Have parents and children work together on computer-based learning programs (NETC, 2000).

ing challenging learning environments at school (Secretary's Conference on Educational Technology, 1995).

Technology serves as a symbol of a school's ability to prepare an educated and qualified workforce. Local and state policymakers must tackle the more difficult issues of getting to the underlying educational needs, not just providing equal numbers of technology stations (Rockman, 1995). Further, school officials in decision-making positions, must ensure that technology, when used effectively, is used to provide appropriate and improved instruction for those students who need it most (Rockman, 1995). Additionally, resources are needed to provide support for students who are at risk for school failure (Greenhill, 1998; Rockman, 1995).

References

Alden, S.B. (n.d.). The role technology can play in preparing our children for the 21st century. Retrieved June 1, 2002, from *www.computerlearning.org/articles/Prepare.htm*

American Association of University Women. (1998). *Gender gaps: Where schools still fail our children*. Executive Summary. Retrieved March 18, 2003 from *www.aauw.org/research/GGES.pdf*

American Library Association. (1998). New report shows more libraries connect to the Internet, access still limited. American Library Association – Washington Office Newsline, 7(149). Retrieved June 12, 2000, from *www.ala.org*.

Ammann, T. (2001). Parents and cartoons help bridge Delaware's digital divide. *Learning & Leading with Technology, 28*(5), 42-47.

Becker, H.J., & Sterling, C.W. (1987). Equity in school computer use: National data and neglected considerations. *Journal of Educational Computing Research, 3*(3), 289-311.

Behrmann, M.M. (1988). *Integrating computers into the curriculum*. Boston: Little, Brown, and Company.

Bhargava, A. (2002). Gender bias in computer

software programs: A checklist for teachers. *Information Technology in Childhood Education Annual*, 205-218.

Boser, R., Daughtery, M., & Palmer, J. (1996). *The effect of selected instructional approaches in technology education on students' attitude toward technology.* Report from the Council on Technology Teacher Education, Reston, VA. (ERIC Document Reproduction Service No. ED 395 212)

Brown, M.R. (2000). Access, instruction, and barriers: Technology issues facing students at risk. *Remedial and Special Education, 21*(3), 182-192.

Brown, M.R. (2002). Multicultural education and technology: Perspectives to consider. *Journal of Special Education Technology, 17*(3), 51-55.

Brown, M.R., Higgins, K., & Hartley, K. (2001). Teachers and technology equity. *Teaching Exceptional Children, 33*(4), 32-40.

Brunner, C., & Bennett, D. (1997). Technology and gender: Differences in masculine and feminine views. *NASSP Bulletin, 81*(592), 46-51.

Burgstahler, S. (1995). *Access and equity for students with disabilities.* Testimony to the United States Department of Education Northwest Regional Forum on the National Plan for Technology in Education, Seattle, WA. Retrieved November 5, 2002, from *it.wce.wwu.edu/necc97/poster1/DoIt/WebWhacker/WW205.html*

Butler, D. (2000). Gender, girls, and computer technology: What's the status now? *The Clearing House, 73*(4), 225-229.

Cattagni, A., & Westat, E.F. (2001). *Internet access in U.S. public schools and classrooms: 1994-2000.* Washington, DC: U.S. Department of Education, Office of Educational Research and Improvement. National Center for Education Statistics.

Chen, M. (1985). A macro-focus on microcomputers. In M. Chen & W.J. Paisley (Eds.). *Children and microcomputers: Research on the newest medium* (pp. 87-107). Beverly Hills, CA: Sage.

Chen, M. (2000, fall/winter). Five commentaries: Looking to the future. *Children and Computer Technology, 10*(2), 168-180. Retrieved December 18, 2003, from *www.futureofchildren.org/usr_doc/vol10no2Commentary%2Epdf.*

Christie, N., & Sabers, D. (1989, March/April). *Using microcomputers to implement mastery learning with high-risk minority adolescents.* Paper presented at the annual meeting of the American Educational Research Association, San Francisco. (ERIC Document Reproduction Service No. ED 326 178)

Cooper, J., & Stone, J. (1996). Gender, computer-assisted learning, and anxiety: With a little help from a friend. *Journal of Educational Computing Research, 15,* 67-91.

Durndell, A., Glissov, P., & Siann, G. (1995). Gender and computing: Persisting differences. *Educational Research, 37,* 219-227.

Dwyer, P. (1997). "Outside the educational mainstream: Foreclosed options in youth policy" in discourse. *Studies in the Politics of Education, 18*(1), 71-85.

Education Commission of the States. (2000). *Technology: Equitable access in schools.* Denver: Author.

Fletcher-Flinn, C.M., & Suddendorf, T. (1996). Computer attitudes, gender and exploratory behaviour: A developmental study. *Journal of Educational Computing Research, 15*(4), 369-439.

Geisert, P.G., & Futrell, M.K. (1990). *Teachers, computers and curriculum.* Boston: Allyn and Bacon.

Glennan, T.K., & Melmed, A. (1996). *Fostering the use of educational technology: Elements of a national strategy.* Santa Monica, CA: Rand Corporation.

Gorski, P. (2000). The digital divide in 2000: A fact sheet. Retrieved July 15, 2002, from *curry.edschool.virginia.edu/centers/multicultural/resources/ddfacts.html.*

Gorski, P. (2001). *Multicultural education and the Internet: Intersections and Integrations.* New York: McGraw-Hill Higher Education.

Greenhill, A. (1998). *Equity and access to information technology shifting the source of the problem in the 21st century.* Paper presented to TASA Conference. Retrieved June 1, 2002, from *www.spaceless.com/papers/9.htm.*

Griffin, B. L., Gillis, M.K., & Brown, M. (1986). The counselor as a computer consultant: Understanding children's attitudes towards computers. *Elementary School*

Guidance and Counseling, 20, 246-249.

Hanson, K. (1997). *Gender, discourse, and technology*. Newton, MA: Education Development Center.

Heinisch, B.S. (n.d). Overcoming the barriers to computer use by individuals who have disabilities. The Research Center on Computing & Society. Retrieved November 5, 2002, from *www.southernct.edu/organizations/rccs/text-only/resources_t/research_t/adap_tech_t/equity_access_t/heinisch_t/overcoming*.

Henry, T. (1997). Computer access lags for minority students. Retrieved February 27, 1998, from *www.usatoday.com/life/cyber/tech/cta505.htm*.

Hess, R., & Miura, I. (1985). Gender differences in enrollment in computer camps and classes. *Sex Roles, 13*(3/4), 193-203.

Hodes, C. (1995-96). Gender representations in mathematics software. *Journal of Educational Technology Systems, 24*, 67-73.

Hopkins, M. (1991). Technology as a tool for transforming learning environments. *The Computing Teacher, 18*(7), 27-30.

Kaye, H.S. (2000). *Computer and Internet use among people with disabilities*. San Francisco: National Institute on Disability and Rehabilitation Research.

Kinser, J., Pessin, B., & Meyertholen, P. (2001). From the fields to the laptop. *Learning & Leading with Technology, 28*(5), 14-17, 48.

Koch, M. (1994). No girls allowed. *TECHNOS Quarterly, 3*(3). Retrieved May 9, 2002 from *www.technos.net/journal/volume3/3koch.htm*.

Lewis, R.B. (1997). Changes in technology use in California's special education programs. *Remedial and Special Education, 18*(4), 233-242.

Lewis, R.B., Harrison, P.J., Lynch, E.W., & Saba, F. (1995). Applications of technology in special education: A statewide study. *Learning Disabilities, 5*(2), 69-79.

Marginson, S. (1993). *Education and policy in Australia*. Cambridge University Press: Cambridge.

Mark, J., & Hanson, K. (1992). *Beyond equal access: Gender equity in learning with computers*. Newton, MA: Education Development Center. Women's Educational Equity Act Publishing Center Digest.

McKenzie, J. (1998). Creating technology enhanced student-centered learning environments. *From Now On, 7*(6), 1-14. Miura, I.T. (1986, April). *Understanding gender differences in middle school computer interest and use*. Paper presented at the annual meeting of the American Educational Research Association, San Francisco.

Miura, I. (1987). Gender and socioeconomic status differences in middle-school computer interest and use. *Journal of Early Adolescence, 7*(2), 243-253.

National Center for Education Statistics. (NCES). (1997). *The condition of education*. Washington, DC: United States Department of Education.

National Center for Education Statistics. (NCES). (2000). *Internet access in U.S. public schools and classrooms, 1994-1999*. Washington, DC: United States Department of Education.

National Education Association. (1997). *Technology briefs: Technology and gender inequity*. Retrieved May 9, 2002, from *www.nea.org/cet/briefs/05.html*.

Neuman, D. (1990). Beyond the chip: A model for fostering equity. *School Library Media Quarterly*, 158-164.

Northwest Educational Technology Consortium. (2000). *Equity in educational technology: Strategies for addressing access inequities*. Northwest Regional Educational Laboratory (NWREL). Retrieved December 15, 2003, from *www.netc.org*.

Reinen, J., & Plomp, T. (1997). Information technology and gender equity: A contradiction in terms? *Computer Education, 28*(2), 65-78.

Riley, R., Kunin, M., Smith, M., & Roberts, L. (1996). *Getting America's students ready for the 21st century: Meeting the technology literacy challenges. A report to the nation on technology and education*. Washington, DC: U.S. Department of Education.

Roblyer, M.D. (2001). Digital desperation: Reports on a growing technology and equity crisis. *Learning & Leading with Technology, 27*(8), 50-53, 61.

Rockman, S. (1995). In school or out: Technology, equity, and the future of our kids. *Communications of the ACM, 38*(6), 25-29.

Ryan, J. (1997). Student communities in a culturally diverse school setting: Identity, representation and association. *Discourse: Studies in the Cultural Politics of Education, 18*(1), 37-53.

Sadker, D. (1999). Gender equity: Still knocking at the classroom door. *Educational Leadership, 56*, 22-26.

Salerno, C. (1995). The effect of time on computer-assisted instruction for at-risk students. *Journal of Research on Computing in Education, 28*(1), 85-97.

Secretary's Conference on Educational Technology. (1995, March). *Issue 1: Access and equity.* Retrieved November 5, 2002, from *www.ed.gov/Technology/Plan/MakeHappen/Issue1.html.*

Silverman, S., & Pritchard, A.M. (1996). Building their future: Girls and technology education in Connecticut. *Journal of Technology Education, 7*(2), 41-54.

Smerdon, B., Cronen, S., Lanahan, L., Anderson, J., Iannottie, N., & Angeles, J. (2001). *Teachers' tools for the 21st century: A report on teachers' use of technology.* Washington, DC: National Center for Education Statistics.

Sutton, R.E. (1991). Equity and computers in the schools: A decade of research. *Review of Educational Research, 61*(4), 475-503.

Swanson, J. (1997). A conversation with Janese Swanson. In American Association of University Women, 1998. *Gender gaps: Where schools still fail our children* (p. 71). New York: Marlowe.

U.S. Department of Commerce. (1999). *Falling through the net: Defining the digital divide: Fact sheet.* Washington, DC: National Telecommunications and Information Administration, Economics and Statistics Administration (NTIA). Retrieved May 9, 2002, from *www.ntia.doc.gov/ntiahome/digitaldivide/factsheets/access.htm.*

U.S. Department of Commerce. (2000). *Falling through the net: Toward digital inclusion: A report on Americans' access to technology tools.* Washington, DC: National Telecommunications and Information Administration, Economics and Statistics Administration (NTIA). Retrieved November 5, 2002, from *www.ntia.doc.gov/ntiahome/fttn00/Falling.htm.*

U.S. Department of Commerce. (2002). *A nation online: How Americans are expanding their use of the Internet.* Washington, DC: National Telecommunications and Information Administration, Economics and Statistics Administration (NTIA). Retrieved November 5, 2002, from *www.ntia.doc.gov/ntiahome/fttn00/Falling.htm.*

Waxman, H., & Padron, Y. (1995). Improving the quality of classroom instruction for students at risk of failure in urban schools. *Peabody Journal of Education, 70*(2), 44-65.

Wepner, S. (1991, October/November). *The effects of a computerized reading program on "at-risk" secondary students.* Paper presented at the annual meeting of the College Reading Association, Crystal City, VA. (ERIC Document Reproduction Service No. ED 340 006)

Yau, R. (1999, Fall/Winter). Technology in K-12 public schools: What are the equity issues? The Mid-Atlantic Equity Center. Equity Review. Retrieved April 6, 2003, from *www.maec.org/pdf/techrev.pdf.*

Yoder, M.B. (2001). The digital divide: The problem and its implications. *Learning & Leading with Technology, 28*(5), 10-13, 50-51.

Zakariya, S.B. (1984). In school (as elsewhere), the rich get computers; the poor get poorer. *The American School Board Journal,* 29-32, 54.

7

English Language Learners and Technology

Carla Meskill and Shannon Hilliker

With the number of English Language Learners (ELLs) enrolled in U.S. schools on the rise, if a teacher has not yet encountered non-native speakers of English, chances are she soon will. For the 2001-2002 school year, for example, it was estimated that 4,747,763 Limited English Proficient (LEP) students were enrolled from pre-K to 12th grade in the nation's public schools. This represents a 95% growth rate since 1991 (www.ncela.gwu.edu/states/stateposter.pdf).

The commitment of professional educators and school personnel to understanding the strengths and needs of ELLs is essential for the success of this growing population. Current theory and practice indicate that complex, language-focused, socioculturally grounded instruction is called for. In these efforts the use of technology in ESOL (English to Speakers of Other Languages) instruction has become increasingly popular. This chapter outlines key concerns of the field and presents ways in which technologies are being used to complement ESOL instructional practices.

Who Are English Language Learners?

Often teachers hesitate to refer students for ESOL support. Uninformed teachers may even mistakenly label a child as having a disability because of their limited ability to communicate in English. Students who are learning English are not disabled. They simply need support in developing their academic language and literacy. "Academic literacy" as a goal for non-native speakers of English in US schools can be defined as "the sum of the vocabulary, grammatical constructions, and language functions that students will encounter and be required to demonstrate mastery of during their school years (kindergarten through Grade 12)" (Cummins, 2000, p. 541). Nevertheless ELLs are overrepresented in special education. Overrepresentation happens "when the percentage of minority students in special education exceeds the percentage of these students in the total population" (Zhang & Katsiyannis, 2002, p. 180). For example, in the state of California for the 1998-1999 school year, which incidentally was the school year following the passing of Proposition 227-legislation that dismantled bilingual programs in the state-ELLs were 27% more likely than English-proficient students to be placed in special education in elementary grades, and almost twice as likely in secondary grades (Artiles, Rueda, Salazar, & Higareda, 2002). Nationally, an under-representation of minority students in gifted programs also exists. Both overrepresentation in special education and underrepresentation in gifted programs happen in part due to the fact that while ELLs may be able to carry on a conversation and may seem to "know" the language, when it comes to academics, these same students often do not appear as able to function linguistically. And therefore are mistaken as needing special education when the real need is in the area of second language and literacy support.

In New York State, parents of ELLs are contacted via the Home Language Questionnaire (HLQ) in order to determine children's English and native language proficiency. The form deals with understanding, speaking, reading, and writing English and identifying the language in which student may be the most literate. The forms are available in English as well as any other language as needed. Along with proficiency measures, these survey data inform the school and the ESOL specialist about a child's level and needs. As a student progresses through proficiency levels, the amount of ESOL decreases and mainstream English language arts instruction increases. For example, at the beginning level, a student in grades K-8 is eligible for six hours of ESOL instruction a week while a student in grades 9-12 requires nine hours of ESOL support per week. At the intermediate level, all grades should receive six hours of service per week. Advanced and transitional ELLs receive three hours of ESOL instruction and three hours of ELA instruction per week (New York State: Instructional Components of Programs and Required Units of Study in Language Arts under CR Part 154).

In short, ELLs can receive a maximum of nine hours per week of specialized ESOL instruction for their language acquisition needs if they are properly identified, leaving a large portion of their school day in mainstream classrooms. With the growing numbers of ELLs in our schools, all school personnel need training and information to insure that ELLs get the most out of their education.

To achieve that goal, oftentimes teachers must advocate for their students. For example, teachers may need to advocate for ESOL, special education, and even mainstream students to have access to technology, to have their cultural differences understood and valued, to receive home and school interaction and support, and to have accommodations for tests. Understanding the culture and the needs of learners can help a teacher make her case and arrange for the needed accommodations.

Assessment is critical in this regard: first, when a child arrives to determine if he or she needs ESOL or special education support, and second, an ongoing basis to make sure the child's needs are being continually met via the support they are receiving. Teachers can advocate for children to make sure the testing is fair and/or the student gets the proper attention as a result of assessments. Tests must be appropriate and measure first- and second-language proficiency, and determine whether there is any disability such as physical, learning, or behavior problems (Baker, 1996).

What Is ESOL?

Although the ESL (English as a Second Language) profession is relatively young, it is rapidly developing and is becoming a highly respected. ESOL specialists in K-12 public schools are charged with working closely with ELLs and their families to ensure children learn the English language and gain the literacy skills they need in order to do well in school. The rate and success of second-language and literacy learning are strongly correlated with contextual and individual factors, including literacy in the first language. One of the key roles for the ESOL professional is to determine children's home literacy practices, their schooling before coming to the United States, their attitude and special skills when it comes to learning, and their special needs, strengths, and interests as individuals. The motivation to learn English is typically strong among immigrant families who see English as a key to academic and economic success (August & Hakuta, 1998). The ESOL teacher capitalizes on and makes every effort to sustain high levels of motivation to learn the language and how things are done in U.S. schools.

The ESOL teacher's role is to design content-area activities and to scaffold the learning and support learner activity at every opportunity. In ESOL classes, social collaboration is emphasized in solving problems and performing tasks that involve the language and concepts of the mainstream classroom. The language learning process greatly benefits from this mode of instructional activity and support (Gibbons, 2002).

In sum, serving ELLs involves a complex array of issues. ESOL instructional activity that supports English language and literacy development is equally complex as each child bringing a rich and wide-ranging set of experiences and dispositions to the learning. ESOL instructional practices that are considered optimal hinge on highly skilled ESOL professionals who design, orchestrate, and support the best environments and activities for this special population. In the next section, we present an overview of the many roles that computers can and do play in well-designed ESOL instructional activities. The bulk of the research cited was found in the leading journals in the field of language and technology as well as from the limited number of books and book chapters that address language and technology. If works pertained to instruction in a language other than English, and findings were deemed relevant to general aspects of learning an additional language, these were included as well.

Learning Language with Computers

Given that the purpose of ESOL instruction is to support children in their language and literacy development through the content areas, what role can and does technology play in the education of ELLs? Language theorists, researchers, and practitioners have tried to answer this question from varying perspectives leading to a flurry of theoretical speculation, a number of divergent empirical studies, and an enormous amount of practical application throughout the world. We begin our survey of English Language Learners and technology by providing some historical context for CALL (Computer-Assisted Language Learning): its beginnings, its concerns, and its directions.

Computer-Assisted Language Learning

In the late 1970s, when computing in education was becoming a practical reality, CALL was a source of great expectations and strong enthusiasms. As in the more general arenas of economics, medicine, and education in general, technology was perceived as a solution to most issues, especially poor U.S. performance in foreign language classes. Thus, the early days of CALL, foreign-language faculty were quick to appropriate mainframe computers for programmed grammar and vocabulary drills modeled chiefly after the traditional audio-tape-based language laboratory (Chapelle & Jamieson, 1983; Hart, 1981; Wyatt, 1982). The difference was that instead of audio, video, and animations, a student worked with text only and instead of having only themselves to rely on for correction, the computer provided feedback to learners regarding their responses.

In these early years of CALL, the notion of having an efficient machine undertake the practical drilling aspect of language learning was particularly attractive (Underwood, 1984). There was a certain "scientific" aspect to this form of CALL that, like its predecessor the analog audiotape language laboratory, was appealing to administrators and those outside of the language teaching profession. Language learning software sales pitches often included language related to freeing up the teacher for other, more important tasks while students did workbook-style exercises in the target language with the computer judging their work and providing instant feedback.

Such freeing up of the teacher and efficient, scientific learning, however, have yet to materialize on a scale and in the ways initially imagined. Rather, the trend was and has been far more experienced, dedicated language teachers to spend the additional time needed to integrate machines into the everyday curricular stream and to do more (not less) to supplement and actively support what students do while on the computer; in short, the demands on teachers were (and still are) greater, not fewer. Less experienced teachers tended to use machines as "electronic babysitters" (Branscum, 1992) and, to this day, in poorer schools with untrained teachers, the electronic babysitter syndrome persists (Technology Counts, 2001). In short, by no scientific magic have computing technologies revolutionized language learning.

From these beginnings, like conceptualizations of how languages are best learned, our understandings of roles for CALL in second-language teaching and learning have greatly evolved. From once viewing language learning as an act of memorization with a dose of special skill (a "gift"), we have come to understand that language acquisition involves a myriad complex social, psychological, neurological, and cultural aspects that are idiosyncratically related to each individual learner, the contexts of teaching and learning, and specific approaches language professionals apply. On a parallel track, CALL has evolved from being received as a tutor providing individualized practice through drills with feedback, to being conceived of as a tool for productive involvement in authentic uses of the target language for authentic purposes (Higgins, 1987; Meskill, 1999a; Perrone, Repenning, Spencer, & Ambach, 1998; Stevens, 1991). Currently, therefore, it is the contexts and processes of technology-supported ESOL instruction that constitute a core concern of language researchers and practitioners, not how individual learners drill on machines (Crookall, Colemen, & Oxford, 1992; van Lier, 2000; Wyatt, 1984). In short, CALL has moved from a focus on didactic teaching machines to viewing of computers as mediators of constructive language and literacy acquisition activity.

Drill and practice software continues to be used widely but, the time an ESOL professional spends working with learners is rarely a time for learners to work in isolation nor does lengthy drilling align with the foundations of second-language acquisition from which ESOL professionals operate. Rather, ESOL contact time is typically spent in intense sociocognitive activity that is seen as the locus for developing the complex of linguistic competencies and academic literacy needed for success in school.

Computers are one of many tools used to support such learning. As such, in today's ESOL classrooms children search the Internet, email, word process, desktop publish, play math games, create with presentation software, engage in simulation games, read talking books, write with story starters, and the like. These are the same tools native English speaker children use for their content-area courses, the difference being that in the ESOL classroom these tools are used to learn English through authentic content and processes (Meskill, Mossop & Bates, 1999; Meskill & Mossop, 2000a). Thus, ESOL teachers render these products-produced for purposes other than to teach English to ELLs-useful by repurposing. In short, it might be said that ESOL teachers operate according to the following premises:

- The machine is a slave of learning, not vice versa (Higgins, 1987).

- Human-human interaction is the key locus of learning (Pica, 1995).

- Technology is only as good as the uses to which a talented teacher puts it (Egbert, Chao & Hanson-Smith, 1999).

Further, it is the ESOL teachers shape the social learning environment and the activity within that environment. It is the manner in which they cast the role of the computer, and model and scaffold children's work on the computer, that ultimately counts towards ELLs' acquisition of language and literacy. As outlined earlier, this is complex instruction; it is complex learning, and the environments and processes whereby it takes place are worthy of close examination. Before turning to the anatomy of computer and ESOL environments, we will have a look at the kinds of technology tools ESOL teachers use and of some of the activities for which they use them.

What Do ESOL Teachers Do with Computers?

A comprehensive survey of technology-using ESOL teachers revealed that teachers use native speaker software-tools, games, and content-area software with their ELLs to reinforce the English language and literacy skills these children need (Meskill & Mossop, 2000a). Again, ESOL teachers do not teach the English language as a distinct subject; rather, they teach the English language through the content of social studies, science, math, and English language arts so that while children are learning the language, the are also learning and reinforcing the literacy skills and content they need to do well in school. The following outlines ESOL teachers' most frequently reported uses of technology for these purposes.

The following section examines issues and findings from close study of classroom processes and products involving ESOL professionals making use of technology to teach English language and literacy.

Table 1. Reported Uses of Technology by ESOL Teachers

Kindergarten Through Early Elementary Grades	*Emergent literacy:* Alphabet and spelling programs are used in developing basic literacy skills. Additionally, graphics programs are used to support learners in making connections between images and text. Graphics often serve as a springboard for discussion and beginning to write in the target language.
Elementary	*Literacy through stories:* Teachers use programs that allow students to choose environments and graphics to support the stories they write. There is preference for software that allows students to write, voice record their stories, and listen to the playback as they follow the text on the screen. Some use of book-length reading programs was also reported. Here, while reading the story, learners can access explanations and animations through hypertext links.
Elementary-Middle School	*Literacy through personal journal writing:* Word processing is used as the medium for interactive dialogue journals. Personal entries and responses are saved electronically.
	Literacy through content: Social studies, science, and math programs are used as part of interdisciplinary, theme-based activities. Multimedia encyclopedias and the Internet are also used for content research.
	Literacy through publishing: Word processors and desktop publishing packages are used to create booklets and newsletters. Multimedia presentation tools are also used by students to create slide shows and photo displays.
Upper-Elementary Through Middle School and High School	*Literacy through problem solving:* Interactive games and simulations are used in conjunction with content-based work. In such programs students make thoughtful choices based on their understanding of text and visual materials. These choices entail immediate consequences.
	Literacy through telecommunications: Email is used to connect students to other schools, to experts, and to shared problem-solving hubs. There is also a growing use of the Internet for accessing information relevant to students native language and culture, to the interests of individual students, and to support mainstream classroom work.
	High school autonomous use with integration across the curriculum: Computers are used as tools by students as they work on their own projects. When the system is networked, students are able to access their work in a variety of content areas from a number of locations in the school building and on the Internet.

Meskill, C., & Mossop, J. (2000). Technologies use with learners of English as a second language. *Journal of Educational Computing Research, 22*(3), 276-277.

In the Classroom-Processes and Products

Value of Joint, Productive Activity

The most valued and commonly employed approaches to ESOL instruction involve students in collaborative productive tasks that require communication (written, spoken, production, and reception) in the target language. This is not unlike the widely accepted view of human interaction and its discourse as the major locus of all learning (Rogoff, 1991; Tharp & Gallimore, 1988). Such principles have long been the hallmark of language education, including K-12 ESOL instruction (August & Pease-Alvarez, 1996; Johnson, 1995; Pica, 1995), and are grounded in the theoretical and empirical constructs of language input, output, and feedback (Krashen, 1985; Swain, 1985) considered necessary ingredients for the genre of active negotiation of meaning that is the primary locus of second language acquisition (Lantolf, 2000; Long, 1985; van Lier, 1996). As such, trained ESOL professionals design, implement, orchestrate, and support activities with, through, and around computers that are deliberately collaborative and authentic, and that focus on and reinforce the language ELLs require to do well in school.

As in the *SimEarth* example below, technology-using ESOL teachers set up a need and desire to communicate. They establish learner familiarity with the language and literacy skills necessary to successfully perform the computer-based task through carefully prepared and orchestrated activities that take place before learners approach the machines. These pre-computer tasks, along with on-computer, and post-computer tasks, all require both comprehension and production of language related to the content and processes of the learning activity. As such, ESOL teachers capitalize on every aspect of the instructional environment to practice and reinforce the language of school. During all three phases (pre- on- and post-) of the learning activity, the ESOL teacher exploits the moment, the here-and-now relevance (Krashen, 1982), to model, teach, focus, and reinforce elements of the English language. When the opportunity presents itself (most often while children are

working *on* the machines) the teacher relinquishes authority and allows the ELLs to introduce and control the topics of verbal exchanges. In all three contexts, the teacher continually scaffolds and directs learners' productive, authentic use of the words and concepts central to the lesson (e.g., the language of science in the example below). Finally, ESOL professionals continually provide challenges just beyond an individual learner's current level of ability; in the case of the on-machine time, this can mean noting what learners are doing on the screen and in their logbooks and pushing them to the next level of conceptual and linguistic sophistication.

At the middle school level where more challenging academic content represents the core concern of ESOL instruction, Martie Menzel of Indian River Schools, whose academic and language focus in the following scenario is science, is focusing on language to describe conditions (abstract and concrete) while learning vocabulary related to the science curricula her sixth and seventh graders need for their classes. She uses the popular simulation software *SimEarth* to focus learners' attention and activity on these learning goals. Prior to having her ELLs work with the *SimEarth* software, they are stepped through a carefully designed sequence of offline activities that introduce the syntactic forms, lexical items, and related concepts. These activities make use of worksheets, maps, reference books, the blackboard, and, most important, fellow students to learn, practice, and reinforce the language they will need to use while online. Also, and quite critically for the success of the SimEarth activity, Martie has designed an on-computer task learners are to accomplish, which carefully reviewed, discussed, clarified and committed to prior to turning on the machines. In the following instance, learners are to log in the status of their planets' atmospheric and geological conditions every five minutes. Sample logbook entries are reviewed, including the kinds of language forms and lexical items needed to compose an acceptable logbook entry. The grading of these entries is also discussed. Beyond the language and literacy practice required to undertake the task, Martie's aim in having the children build their planets on the computer is to take advantage of this rich, active context to scaffold and support their use of English as they work on the machine. Thus, Martie makes use of the machine to focus, highlight, anchor, and elaborate the language and concepts on the screen to engage her learners in speculative, constructive conversation about the physical, chemical, and biological composition of the planets they construct. As is evidenced in the following brief exchange, ELLs not only use the developing concepts and accompanying vocabulary of science in productive, authentic ways, they often do so as if they are in or part of these simulated worlds:

ELL: *Oh no! They destroyed all my oxygens!*

Teacher: *The oxygen just died?*

ELL: *Mm hm. Gotta get all these animals off the property so they won't destroy us.*

(Unpublished classroom transcript from Meskill, Mossop, & Bates, 1999)

Simulations such as *SimEarth* "fulfill a need by offering authentic safe environments in which learners could become proficient using the target language to carry out the multitude of activities constituting every life" (Murray, 1999, p. 306). Moreover, for language instruction, simulations provide a language/concept-rich environment in which to use English authentically (Crookall & Oxford, 1990), an aspect of simulations that the teacher above capitalizes on a great deal.

Research-Classroom Use

This overview of CALL began by pointing out that a great deal of research activity has been undertaken over the brief history of the discipline. Where as beginning research chiefly focused on the machine, the features of particular software, and individual students learning with the machine, of late a need has evolved the need to view computer use in language learning more broadly to encompass and account for the complexities of the classroom processes that support the language and literacy acquisition processes.

In either case, the primary question seems to be: Is there any tangible, conclusive evidence that language learners benefit from the use of computers? A tentative response to this question would be affirmative; CALL does no harm. Language learners learn as well using computers as they do without. Whether or not language learning with computers is in some way superior is a far more complex question, the answer to which is an unmitigated "that depends." The complex sociocultural, sociocognitive contexts of ESOL and technology instruction are only beginning to be examined and explained.

Motivating Active Involvement

The motivational quality of instructional computing for language learners has been widely and consistently documented (Cifuentes & Shih, 2001; Schofield, 1995; Stevens, 1991). The majorities of documented uses of technology are, however, most often lighthouse projects (a one of a kind demonstration of technology) and therefore tend to report increased enthusiasm/motivation with selected teachers under special conditions (Miller & Olson, 1998). As technology tools become fully integrated into the instructional stream, these initial spurts of enthusiasm tend to level off and the use of technology becomes a matter of course, not a special event.

Integrated and used thoughtfully and well, technology in ESOL can mobilize children to active involvement in the content, contexts, and discourses of school. For example, learning language through academic content has been found to be greatly facilitated when teachers include computer use as part of instruction (Adamson, Herron, & Kaess, 1995; Kasper, 2000; Meskill et al., 1999). Moreover, how things get done verbally in school can be nicely modeled using the computer as a springboard. In the following scenario, the ESOL teacher emphasizes the language of turn taking to beginning ELLs using the computer as a tool for doing so:

T: *Who's turn it is? Who's turn is it? (takes S2's hand off mouse)*

S: *My turn.*

T: *It's your turn? Whose turn is it S, is it S2's turn? Yes? Yes? Let's click on the pink button. Click on the pink button. Good. Now whose turn is it?*

S2: *It's his turn*

T: *It's his turn.*

(from Meskill & Ulitsky, 2001, p. 6)

The public nature of what appears on the computer screen and the consequent immediacy of concrete visual referents allow for frequent and powerful teachable moments (Meskill et al., 1999, 2000) while visually anchoring the target language in such as way that comprehension and, ultimately, acquisition of the forms and functions of the language are increased(Palumbo & Bermudez, 1994; Plass, Chun, Mayer, & Leutner, 1998). The visual aspect also reinforces a focus on form (Long, 1991) and the acquisition of vocabulary (Nikolova, 2002). It is also clear that weaker students do well with more visual, on-screen support options (Shea, 2000), along with teacher and peer support while working on the computer (Meskill & Mossop, 2000b; Meskill et al., 1999). The Internet, moreover, extends such opportunities to learn language (Warschauer, 1999), culture (Osuna & Meskill, 1998), and content (Cummins, 2000), with telecommunications eliciting more language learner writing/participation (Chun, 1994; Kern, 1995; Warschauer, 1997).

Learner Control

Csikszentmihalyi's (1991) emphasis on control in learning underscores the importance of student control of education processes generally; however, more specific to second-language acquisition processes is the issue of student control of the instructional conversation. Granting ELLs control of topic, or choice of what to speak about during instruction augments their sociocognitive/discoursal participation in instructional exchanges, thus increasing the likelihood of target language forms, structures, and, consequently, meanings to be negotiated and their patterns internalized. For instance, in the examples above, the ESOL teachers allow learners to control the pace and direction of what they do on the computer given the constraints of the language and literacy task assigned. This type of learner control over the timing and direction of an activity is desirable for productive language learning environments (Johnson, 1995).

The following illustrates the empowering aspect of a first-grade ELL using what is on the computer screen to establish control and to take a stand. The children's ESOL teacher, Cathy, has paired two learners: Juana has very limited English skills and has been paired with Chang who has stronger writing skills, but whose speaking skills are not as strong as Juana's. Chang is showing Juana how to compose a story using a story generator program. Juana has just clicked on the word "bull." The teacher (T) intervenes:

T: *Just one second. Let's take a look a that bull first of all. What would you say a bull is?*

C: *It's like a dog, but it just gots horns.*

J: *It's like a cow.*

T: *It is like a cow. Do you think it's a boy or a girl?*

C: *Girl.*

J: *Boy.*

T: *Well let's see. If it's a girl. What gives milk?*

Both: *Cow.*

T: *A cow. And a cow would be a girl. This . would be a boy. B for boy, B for bull. Here we have a bull. Would you like a bull in your story, Juana?*

J: *Dog.*

T: *Would you like a bull in your story?*

J: *No.*

(from Meskill et al., 1999, p. 20)

While the teacher appears to maintain control of the exchange, she is not in control of what goes on the computer screen. This is Juana's story, Juana's world, and Juana will decide what goes into her story, no one else. This is an important step to take in a new language – to assert a position – and is unlikely to have happened if Juana had not been in control of the machine. Later on Chang suggests Juana color the dog she has placed in her story brown. She insists she wants the dog to be black, and colors it black, again emphasizing her ownership of what is on the screen.

At more advanced levels, when ELLs explore hyperlinks to complete a well-designed task that is itself determined by their particular interests, the result is often active engagement in a process of acquiring and creating complex knowledge and its accompanying language (Warschauer, 1999). Moreover, the potential benefits of telecollobaration environments for language acquisition appear promising. The possibilities for less inhibited, time-independent, yet productive discourses are particularly attractive to those attempting to communicate in a newly learned language. There are ample opportunities for ELLs to learn a range of discourses while communicating with a wide range of individuals in their native language as well as in English. Research on computer-mediated communication indicates that the amount and quality of student participation and student-student interaction in computer-mediated conversations are consistently higher than in face-to-face learning contexts. Students in online collaborations also enjoyed more topic control than their live counterparts (see Kern, 1995; Sullivan & Pratt, 1996; Warschauer, 1996).

Family/Community Involvement

For ELLs, technologies represent a powerful medium for family/community involvement in their education. For example, many anecdotal accounts demonstrate the status benefits enjoyed by ELLs who use technology to present their culture, special areas of expertise, and their personal lives. In Cathy's early elementary classroom (above), parents and grandparents come to the class on a regular basis and use publishing software to construct bilingual stories with the children. These stories are shared with mainstream students, who thereby come to understand the value and power of knowing two languages. A number of other telecollaboration projects have extended the ELL audience and pool of conversation partners to local and international communities (see Cummins & Sayers, 1995). ELL participation in networked literature circles – whereby students in different physical locations read the same texts and discuss their reactions online – is also a means of empowering participation in rich sociocollaborative interaction.

In terms of products, ELL children take great pride in the products they create using computers (Meskill et al., 1999; Meskill & Mossop, 2000a, 2000b). The stories, presentations, booklets, and Web pages they design and construct demonstrate to others that, even though they may appear to have limited abilities in English, they are capable of doing tangible, thoughtful, quality work. Valuing these children's emerging native language and ad-

vanced literacy is also critical; ELLs come to U.S. schools knowing an enormous amount about the world that should be valued and mined as the foundation for their second-language literacy. Making connections to what ELLs know about their home cultures through the Internet is an effective use of the computer (Cummins & Sayers, 1995; Meskill et al., 1999, 2000).

Integration

Perhaps the most critical issue related to classroom uses of technology for language learning is that of integration into the regular classroom curricular stream. In his 2001 study of technology-rich schools, Cuban was able to locate only a limited number of educators who had successfully accomplished full, effective integration. In one of the successful integration cases he documented, the teacher (a two-way bilingual English-Spanish primary school teacher) had not only seamlessly integrated computers into instructional conversations per se, but also managed to bridge whole/part class activity around computers to more independent (solo or small group) work. The following scenario depicts Mrs. Rodrigues' class and the bridge she builds between activities that make use of the computers in her classroom:

> ...she holds up for the class, one at a time, large cut-outs of a triangle, square, circle, and rectangle.

> For each shape, Rodrigues asks the whole group what it is. Individual children yell out in Spanish and English whether it is a triangle or circle. She offers a "Muy bien!" followed by a warm "Good, Miguel." She then gives the cutout to each child to touch and pass on to a neighbor.

> Now Rodrigues turns to the computer monitor, where the same four shapes are displayed. She moves the cursor to each shape and then asks the class what each shape is. Again, a chorus of vigorous shouts in two languages fills the room, followed by bilingual compliments on the correct answers. Rodrigues then passes out to each child envelopes filled with smaller versions of the

four shapes. Calling the children's attention to the cursor on the screen, she clicks on a rectangle on the screen and asks the class to pull that shape out of the envelope. She does the same with a triangle and the other shapes until all the figures in the envelope are arrayed in front of each child. She then reviews with the class what each shape is...

Later in the morning when children choose which center they want to work in, visitors watch them clustered around two machines looking at "Millie's Math House." Two 4-year-olds, Lucinda and Maria, are whispering to each other. Maria points and Lucinda hits the keys when the computer voice asks aloud what size shoes are pictured: big, medium, small? The computers are left on all day, and they are in constant use by one or two preschoolers. "Stickybear's Early Learning Activities" and other multimedia software delight the children with animation and clever graphics. ..With an occasional interruption by an aide or Rodrigues, they largely work by themselves, teaching and learning from one another about what is happening on the screen.

(Reprinted by the permission of the publisher from *Oversold and Underused: Computers in the Classroom* by Larry Cuban, pp. 37-39, Cambridge, MA: Harvard University Press, Copyright© 2001 by the President and Fellows of Harvard College).

This is an excellent example of a teacher who has integrated computer use seamlessly into the context of a bilingual math lesson. That is, the role for the machine is incidental to the larger sociocognitive processes taking place around learning.

Language learning, like all learning, is highly context dependent, including the characteristics and life situation of individual learners and the like. ESOL professionals teach language through academic content, which itself carries implications for the kinds of discourse and processes that are appropriate for linguistic and conceptual development. Apart from studies examining the discourse of language learners paired at the computer (Levy & Hinckfuss, 1990; Meskill, 1993; Piper, 1986),

research on the actual discourse/learning dynamics of the computer-using language classroom are few. However, anecdotal accounts from classroom-based research do converge on the issue of the opportunities computers represent for English language learners to become experts in computing, thus providing an inroad to participation and enhancement of self-esteem that may not have otherwise been possible (Cazden, Michaels, & Watson-Gegeo, 1987; Johnson, 1985; Meskill & Mossop, 2000a).

Self-Study Opportunities

With computers, opportunities for independent practice with authentic English abound. Learners can talk with keypals on the other side of the globe, interact with peers from around the world while playing games (e.g., games.yahoo.com) or exploring MOOs (Multi-User Domain Object Oriented), visit virtual museums, malls, universities, libraries, and check the news as it happens in any part of the world. In the context of independent access to online learning resources, one of the ESOL teacher's many roles is to teach basic electronic literacy skills (below), ensure that each child has access to machines outside of school, and hold children accountable for these "fun" activities by assigning tasks for which they must produce evidence of their learning (e.g., written directions to a museum exhibit of their choice, a report on a MOO adventure, a summary of an online pool tournament, etc.). Likewise, if their online, out-of-class leisure activities involve reading electronic documents, a lesson in good reading strategies can apply; in the case of electronic documents this would include discussion of the various text support options available in electronic environments (e.g., change of view, font, and size for easier reading, use of various windowed dictionaries, identifying and accessing meaning-based links on the page versus tangential links, understanding how to save, send, and modify the text as needed, and, perhaps, most important, how to judge a text's credibility).

ESOL teachers often model this kind of critical thinking by reading a Web page out loud and using a series of questions and answers what good readers of electronic texts generally use:

- Who wrote it? Is this a credible individual?

- What is the purpose/agenda of this writer/ these writers?

- For what audience is the text intended?

- How does the text relationally fit with surrounding texts?

- What links or functions are available to support my understanding?

- What visual cues are present to support my understanding?

- What do I already know about the topic?

- Is this text reshaping this knowledge? How?

- What are the implications of this text beyond this Web site?

Continually addressing such questions involves highly literate thinking and problem solving and is central to contemporary electronic literacy.

The web offers opportunities for both receptive activities and interactive activities. Receptive activities include listening to audio files and/or viewing video files, lurking in various communications venues, reading electronic documents, and using search engines. The number of opportunities for this type of self-study is astounding (see, for example, World Languages at merlot.org).

Active activities include composing, responding to stimuli on the screen as directed, commenting on what one is doing and what others are doing on the screen, playing simulation games, engaging in a WebQuest, and creating Web pages. For example, online cloze exercises, like offline cloze exercises, are excellent tools to involve learners in deducing rules and regularities-both syntactic and semantic-of the target language. Such activities are widely published on the Web and free of charge. Cloze activities are popular in that mastering the target language comes both from very careful reading for both meaning and form and from the deductive processes involved in deciding the correct forms or words to complete a cloze passage.

Activities that involve ELLs in human-human communication include e-mailing, interacting with others in a MOO or MUD (Multimedia User Domain), interacting in a chatroom, contributing to an asynchronous discussion, and the like. In terms of motivation, these forms of recreational language-learning activity can be viewed as a potentially powerful means for ELLs to have safe, controlled contact with native speakers whereby they enjoy sufficient time and resources to work at both comprehending what native speakers write and composing appropriate responses in ways that simulate live conversation. One drawback is the quality of language used by native speakers in these telecommunications environments: the loose, informal nature of this "spoken text," for example, can mislead the non-native speakers' developing hypotheses about the syntactic and lexical systems of the target language.

Research on Individuals' Language Learning

The original notion that computers might teach learners languages more effectively and more efficiently than traditional classroom instruction harkens back to claims made by Berlitz audiotape advertisements; that is, given the *right* materials, anyone can learn languages. Individuals who exert sufficient perseverance to successfully learn a language without the support of live instruction are extremely rare. Nonetheless, the belief persists that somehow science can produce a means of fail-safe, effortless language acquisition through the application of technology. Learning an additional language beyond childhood requires a great deal of time, effort, and motivation, and only a small number of human beings are able to accomplish this on their own. Nevertheless, one of the focal uses of computers that was initially conceived and tenaciously pursued is the self-study, or "programmed learning," model whereby a learner works in tandem with carefully designed software to move through instructional sequences deemed necessary to master the target language. Today recognition of the key roles human mentoring and guidance play in language learning prevails as well as the preeminence of the tool role over the tutor role of technology (Egbert, Chao, & Hanson-Smith, 1999; Meskill, 1999a; Warschauer, 1999).

Nonetheless empirical research that focuses on the machine-learner dialog we as a primary site of language learning continues to be undertaken. For example, research has focused on the effectiveness of computer-assisted instruction in teaching specific language skills, including listening, (Dunkel, 1991); grammar (Swann, 1992); reading (Ercetin, 2003); writing (Pennington, 1993); pronunciation (Anderson-Hsieh, 1992); and vocabulary acquisition (Bland, Noblitt, Armington, & Gay, 1990; Kang, 1995). Learner characteristics in conjunction with computer-assisted language learning have also been studied (e.g., field dependence/independence; Chapelle & Jaimeson, 1983); and good computer-based language learning strategies use (Meskill, 1991a).

To date, very little research has focused on the effects of having vast amounts of reference and resource materials available to learners as they undertake learning a language. On a smaller scale, the impact of having access to contextual clues to meaning available on the computer screen has thus far proven positive (Bueno & Nelson, 1993; Chun & Plass, 1996; Shea, 2000), but has also been linked to how well individual learners make use of effective comprehension strategies (Meskill, 1991a; Ulitsky, 2000).

Electronic Literacy

Learners worldwide face the need to become fluent and literate in the language of telecommunications; in other words to become "electronically literate." For ESOL professionals, this additional set of literacy skills represents both new building blocks with which to construct English language and literacy skills and new challenges. As Hunt reasons, "[t]o prepare our students for tomorrow's world, we must teach them how to reason and communicate effectively through available technologies" (1993, p. 9), and there is no better venue for teaching new forms of literacy than the computer itself (Heath, 1990).

One of the most promising aspects of personal computing and telecommunications is the widespread use of computers outside of school. Indeed, the trend of students spending more time on computers at home than in school continues (Cuban, 2001; Technology Counts, 2001). As the number of hours children spend on computers continues to grow, so does access to fun, motivating, and empowering activities on the Internet, especially the means of interacting with others. Most students, including ELLs, now come to school fully skilled in operating the machine and managing content. In addition to rote mechanical and navigational skills, higher-level sociolinguistic skills are also at play in telecommunications (e.g., communication, construction, and research) (see Shetzer & Warschauer, 2000, for discussion of these electronic literacy skills).

These are skills that serve ELLs particularly well. In consort with their teachers, they can use electronic text in its range of forms to express and communicate-indeed, to demonstrate skills and abilities not readily displayed otherwise by virtue of limited speaking and writing abilities. Moreover, the interdependency of literacies would predict that having a well-developed electronic literacy serves to scaffold and augment the acquisition of subsequent language and literacy skills. Indeed, it is only a matter of time and appropriate research to uncover connections between the kinds of literacy practiced in electronic environments and print literacy learning, especially when new languages are involved (Warschauer, 1999; Meskill, Mossop, & Bates, 2000). For example, telecollobration environments force a shift in compensatory strategies that ELLs typically employ in face-to-face interaction to make up for missing vocabulary, structures, poor comprehension, and the like. An electronically literate person is expected to exercise effective written strategies that mark online discourse as unique from face-to-face interaction the most prevalent being the use of language that is clear and unambiguous to the person being addressed. For ELLs, online communication with others represents a golden opportunity to consider these elements fully within their own timeframe as they compose: Whom is being addressed? What does he or she know and not know? What is the clearest way to make my meaning known to them? What are the norms that native speakers apply when composing a similar message? When using an additional language, especially in face-to-face situations with native speakers, ELLs often lack the time to carefully consider and respond appropriately to these critical questions. Research on language learners using telecommunications has consistently demonstrated that learners benefit from that extra time (Kern, 1995; Warschauer, 1996).

Current research in second-language learning as well as telecommunications in a second language also examines the shifting social roles and range of discourses inherent in electronic literacy and the corresponding implications for second language (particularly English language) learners (Lam, 2000; Murray, 2000). This is an area crucial to K-12 ELL learning as the manner in which ELLs learn and use the English language independently online to negotiate their English-language identities and to become familiar with varying discourse practices carries implications for their language and literacy learning within the school environment. ESOL professionals ground and build on such foundations.

Future Directions

As Cuban (2001) documents, in the past 30 years of life with personal computers, education has experienced a very slow revolution. During this period of enthusiasm and experimentation, a great deal of emphasis has been, and still is, placed on the machine/the technology itself (e.g., the quest for the latest and greatest, the holy grail of the "killer app", the promise of transformation, the threat of falling behind, and the like). What we have learned in reflecting back on the inching-along progress of this revolution is that what matters most are thoughtful, knowledgeable, committed educators who make wise, informed decisions about how and why to make this "hand-me-down technology" (Meskill, 1999b, p. 460) work to best suit their goals, contexts of use, and, most urgently, the learners who depend on them for language and literacy instruction. While dearth of primary research that details the anatomy of effective- second language and literacy teaching with computers would indicate that such research is difficult to do, it is nonetheless critical for deepening our understandings of optimal uses and processes of technology use with ELLs. The electronic literacy skills with which ELLs are increasingly coming to school warrant attention as the way

these skills support language and literacy development in a second language potentially matter a great deal.

Conclusion

ESOL professional educators face numerous and complex challenges to face in supporting the English language and literacy development ELLs. As this review of key issues involved in teaching English Language Learners and technology has demonstrated, contexts for learning established and orchestrated by skilled ESOL professionals are critical to the technology and language-learning configuration. It is ultimately the teacher and fellow learners who stimulate, support, value, and sustain thought, action, and discourse through and around the machines. Skilled ESOL teachers tailor emphasis on those aspects of the target language they deem opportune for student learning at a given moment in their carefully designed activity. It follows that the most urgent agenda for CALL research is the study of such exemplary ESOL classroom practices and how such practices can be translated into effective professional development in uses of instructional technology.

Looking to the future, video and audio streaming will no doubt improve as will the overall speed and quality of access, presentation, and opportunities for intelligent and meaningful interaction with aural and visual content. While these features promise to enhance language teaching and learning, again, such technological features are only as good as their classroom application and integration. The more extensive language educators' resources are, the more opportunity they have to enrich the activities they design. To thoroughly and successfully mine the riches of these media, a great deal of media-related conceptual work, in tandem with a solid foundation in second-language learning, is a must (see Meskill, 2002). The vast and varied electronic resources in voices from around the planet now at our fingertips, combined with skilled, knowledgeable ESOL teaching professionals, spell a bright future for ELLs in U.S. schools.

References

Adamson, H., Herron, J., & Kaess, D. (1995). An experiment in using multimedia to teach language through content. *Journal of Intensive English Studies, 9*, 24-37.

Anderson-Hsieh, J. (1992). Using electronic visual feedback to teach suprasegmentals. *System, 20*(1), 51-62.

Artiles, A., Rueda, R., Salazar, J., & Higareda, I. (2002). English-Language learner representation in special education in California urban school districts. In D. Losen & G. Orfield (Eds.), *Racial inequity in special education* (p. 119). Cambridge, MA: Harvard Education Press.

August, D., & Hakuta, K. (Eds.). (1998). *Educating language-minority children*. Washington, DC: National Academy Press.

August, D., & Pease-Alvarez, L. (1996). *Attributes of effective programs and classrooms serving English language learners*. University of California, Santa Cruz: National Center for Research on Cultural Diversity and Second Language Learning.

Bland, S., Noblitt, J., Armington, S., & Gay, G. (1990). The naïve lexical hypothesis: Evidence from computer-assisted language learning. *Modern Language Journal, 74*, 440-450.

Branscum, D. (1992, September). Educators need support to make computing meaningful. *Macworld Special Edition*, 83-88.

Bueno, K., & Nelson, W. (1993). Collaborative second language learning with a contextualized computer environment. *Journal of Educational Multimedia and Hypermedia, 4*(2), 177-208.

Cazden, C. (1986). Introduction: Children and ESL. In P. Rigg & D. Enright (Eds.). *Children and ESL: Integrating perspectives* (pp. 9-21). Washington, DC: Teachers of English to Speakers of Other Languages.

Cazden, C., Michaels, S., & Watson-Gegeo, K. (1987). *Microcomputers and literacy project Final Report* (Grant No. G-83-0051). Washington, DC: National Institute of Education.

Chapelle, C., & Jaimeson, J. (1983). Language lessons on the PLATO IV system. *System, 11*(1), 13-20.

Chun, D. (1994). Using computer networking to facilitate the acquisition of interactive competence. *System, 22*(1), 17-31.

Chun, D., & Plass, J. (1996) Effects of multimedia annotations on vocabulary acquisition. *The Modern Language Journal, 80*(2), 183-198.

Cifuentes, L., & Shih, Y. (2001). Teaching and learning online: A collaborative between US and Taiwanese students. *Journal of Research on Computing in Education, 33*(4), 456-475.

Crookall, D., & Oxford, R. (1990). Linking language learning and simulation/gaming. In D. Crookall & R. Oxford (Eds.). *Simulations, gaming, and language learning* (pp. 3-24). New York: Newbury House.

Crookall, D., Coleman, D., & Oxford, R. (1992). Computer-mediated language learning environments: Prolegomenon to a research framework. *Computer Assisted Language Learning. 5*(1-2), 93-120.

Csikszentmihalyi, M. (1991). *Flow: The psychology of optimal experience*. New York: HarperCollins.

Cuban, L. (2001). *Oversold and underused: Computers in the classroom*. Cambridge, MA: Harvard University. Press.

Cummins, J. (2000). Academic language learning, transformative pedagogy, and information technology: Towards a critical balance. *TESOL Quarterly. 34*(3), 537-548.

Cummins, J., & Sayers, D. (1995). *Brave new schools: Challenging cultural illiteracy through global learning networks*. New York: St. Martins Press.

Dunkel, P. (1991). Computerized testing of nonparticipatory L2 listening comprehension proficiency: An ESL prototype development effort. *Modern Language Journal, 75*, 64-73.

Egbert, J., Chao, C., & Hanson-Smith, E. (1999). Computer-enhanced language learning environments: An overview. In J. Egbert & E. Hanson-Smith (Eds.), *CALL environments: Research, practice and critical issues* (p. 1-15). Alexandria, VA: TESOL Publications.

Ercetin, G. (2003). Exploring ESL learners' use of hypermedia reading glosses. *CALICO Journal, 20*(2) 261-282.

Hart, R. (1981). *Studies in Language Learning 3(1)*. The PLATO System and Language Study. [Special Issue].

Heath, S. (1990). *The fourth vision:* Literate

language at work. In A. Lundsford, H. Moglen, & J. Slevin (Eds.), *The right to literacy* (pp. 289-306). New York: The Modern Language Association.

Higgins, J. (1987). Artificial unintelligence: Computer uses in language learning. *TESOL Quarterly, 21*, 159-165.

Johnson, D. (1985). *Using computers to promote the development of English as a second language: A report to the Carnegie Corporation.* (ERIC Document Reproduction Service No. ED 278 211)

Johnson, K. (1995). *Understanding communication in second language classrooms.* New York. Cambridge University Press.

Kang, S. (1995). The effects of a context-embedded approach to second-language vocabulary learning. *System, 23*(1), 43-55.

Kasper, L (2000). New technologies, new literacies: Focus discipline research and ESL learning communities. *Language Learning & Technology, 4*(2), 105-128.

Kern, R. (1995). Restructuring classroom interaction with networked computers: Effects on the quality and characteristics of language production. *Modern Language Journal, 79*(4), 457-476.

Krashen, S. (1985). *The input hypothesis.* London: Longman.Lam, W. (2000). L2 literacy and the design of the self: A case study of a teenager writing on the Internet. *TESOL Quarterly, 34*(3), 457-482.

Lantolf, J. (2000). Introducing sociocultural theory. In J. Lantolf (Ed.), *Sociocultural theory and second language learning* (pp. 1-26). New York: Oxford University Press.

Levy, M., & Hinckfuss, J. (1990). Program design and student talk at computers. *CAELL Journal, 1*, 21-26.

Long, M. (1991). Focus on form: A design feature in language teaching methodology. In K. de Bot, D. Coste, R. Ginsberg, & C. Kramsch (Eds.), *Foreign language research in cross-cultural perspectives* (pp. 39-52). Amsterdam,The Netherlands: John Benjamins.

Long, M. (1985). Input and second language acquisition theory. In S. Gass & C. Madden (Eds.), *Input and second language acquisition.* (pp. 377-393). Rowley, MA: Newbury House.

Meskill, C. (1991). Multimedia and language learning: Assessing goals and system attributes. *Computer-Assisted English Language Learning Journal, 2*(2), 11-14.

Meskill, C. (1991a) The Role of Strategies A Advisement for On-line Language Learning Employing Interactive Videodisc. *System, 19*(3), 277-287.

Meskill, C. (1993) ESL and multimedia: A study of the dynamics of pairedstudent discourse. *System, 21*(3), 323-341.

Meskill, C. (1999a). *Computers as tools for sociocollaborative language learning.* In K. Cameron (Ed.), *CALL: Media, design and applications* (pp. 141-162). Amsterdam,The Netherlands: Swets & Zeitlinger.

Meskill, C. (1999b). Twenty minutes into the future. In J. Egbert & E. Hanson-Smith (Eds.), *CALL environments: Research, practice and critical issues* (pp. 459-469). Alexandria, VA: TESOL Publications.

Meskill, C. (2002). *Teaching and learning in real time: Media, technologies, and language acquisition.* Houston, TX: Athelstan.

Meskill, C., Mossop, J., & Bates, R. (1999). *Electronic text and English as a second language environments.* Albany, NY: National Research Center on English Learning and Achievement. Retrieved December 10, 2002, from *cela.albany.edu/esl/*index.html

Meskill, C., & Mossop, J. (2000a). Technologies use with learners of English as a second language. *Journal of Educational Computing Research, 22*(3), 265-284.

Meskill, C., & Mossop, J. (2000b). Electronic Texts in ESOL Classrooms. *TESOL Quarterly, 34*(3), 585-592.

Meskill, C., Mossop, J., & Bates, R. (2000). Bilingualism, cognitive flexibility, and electronic texts. *Bilingual Research Journal, 23*(2&3).

Meskill, C., & Ulitsky, H. (2001). *English language learners and technology: Challenges, constraints, and teacher strategies.* Paper presented at the annual meeting of the American Education Research Association, Seattle, WA.

Miller, L., & Olson, J. (1998). Literacy research oriented toward features of technology and classrooms. In D. Reinking, M. McKenna, L. Labbo, & R. Kieffer (Eds.), *Handbook of lit-*

eracy and technology (pp. 343-360). Mahwah, NJ: Lawrence Erlbaum.

Murray, D. (2000). Protean communication: the language of computer-mediated communication. *TESOL Quarterly, 34*(3), 397-421.

Murray, G. (1999). Autonomy and language learning in a simulated environment. *System, 27,* 295-308.

Nikolova, O. (2002). Effects of students' participation in authoring of multimedia materials on student acquisition of vocabulary. *Language Learning & Technology, 6(1), 100-122.*

Osuna, M., & Meskill, C. (1998). Using the World Wide Web to integrate Spanish language and culture: A pilot study. *Language Learning & Technology, 1*(2), 71-92.

Palumbo, D., & Bermudez, A. (1994). Using hypermedia to assist language minority learners in achieving academic success. *Computers in the Schools, 10,* 171-188.

Poster: The growing number of LEP students, 2001-2002. (n.d.). Retrieved December, 11, 2003 from www.ncela.gwu.edu/states/stateposter.pdf.

Pennington, M. (1993). A critical examination of word processing effects in relation to L2 writers. *Journal of Second Language Writing, 2,* 227-255.

Perrone, C., Repenning, A., Spencer, S., & Ambach, J. (1998). Computers in the classroom: Moving from tool to medium. *Journal of Computer Mediated Communication, 2*(3) Retrieved February 6, 2003, *www.esc.edu/dept/Annenberg/vol2/issue3*

Pica, T. (1995). Second language learning through interaction: Multiple perspectives. In D. Regan (Ed.), *Contemporary approaches to second language acquisition in social context* (pp. 9-31). Dublin, Ireland: University College Dublin Press.

Piper, A. (1986). Conversation and the computer: A study on the conversational spin-off generated among learners of English as a foreign language working in groups. *System, 14,* 187-198.

Plass, J., Chun, D., Mayer, R., & Leutner, D. (1998). Supporting visual and verbal learning preferences in a second language multimedia learning environment. *Journal of Educational Psychology, 90*(1), 25-36.

Rogoff, B. (1991). Social interaction as apprenticeship in thinking: Guidance and participation in spatial planning. In L. Resnick, J. Levine, & S. Teasley (Eds.), *Perspectives on socially shared cognition* (pp. 349-364). Washington, D.C.: APA Press.

Schofield, J. (1995). *Computers and classroom culture.* New York: Cambridge University Press.

Shea, P. (2000). Leveling the playing field: A study of captioned interactive video for second language learning. *Journal of Educational Computing Research, 22*(3), 243-263.

Shetzer, H., & Warschauer, M. (2000). An electronic literacy approach to network-based language teaching. In M. Warschauer & R. Kern (Eds.), *Network-based language teaching: Concepts and practices* (pp. 171-185). New York: Cambridge University Press.

Stevens, V. (1991). A study of student attitudes toward CALL in a self-access student resource centre. *System, 19*(3), 289-299.

Swain, M. (1985). Communicative competence: Some roles of comprehensible input and comprehensible output in its development. In S. Gass & C. Madden (Eds.), *Input in second language acquisition* (pp. 235-253). Rowley, MA: Newbury House.

Swann, P. (1992). Computer assisted language learning for English as a foreign language. *Computers in Education, 19*(3), 251-266.

Sullivan, N., & Pratt, E. (1996). A comparative study of two ESL writing environments: A computer-assisted classroom and a traditional oral classroom. *System, 24,* 1-14.

Technology counts 2001: The new divides. (2001). *Education Week, 20*(35).

Tharp, R., & Gallimore, R. (1988). *Rousing minds to life: Teaching, learning, and schooling in social context.* New York: Cambridge University Press.

Underwood, J. (1984). *Linguistics, computers, and the language teacher: A communicative approach.* Rowley, MA: Newbury House.

Ulitsky, H. (2000). *New methodology and media integration in Ukraine a study of teacher constraints, supports, and change in a developing country.* Unpublished Doctoral Dissertation, University at Albany. Van Lier, L. (1996). *Interaction in the language curriculum: Awareness, autonomy & authenticity.* New York: Longman.

Van Lier, L. (2000). Computers and pedagogy, *TESOL Quarterly, 34*(3), 617-625.

Warschauer, M. (1996). Comparing face-to-face and electronic discussion in the second language classroom. *CALICO Journal, 13*(1-2), 7-25.

Warschauer, M. (1997). Computer-mediated collaborative learning: Theory and practice. *The Modern Language Journal, 8*(1), 470-481.

Warschauer, M. (1999). *Electronic literacies: Language, culture, and power in online education*. Mahwah, NJ: Lawrence Erlbaum Press.

Wyatt, D. (1982). Computer-assisted instruction: Individualized learning in ESL/ESP. *English for Specific Purposes*, 58/59.

Wyatt, D. (1984). *Computers and ESL*. Orlando, FL: Harcourt Brace Jovanovich.

Zhang, D., & Katsiyannis, A. (2002). Minority representation in special education: A persistent challenge. *Remedial and Special Education, 23*(3), 180-187.

8

Proactive Accommodation: Web Accessibility in the Classroom

James Allan and John Slatin

The introduction of networked computers and other information technology has had profound consequences for education, transforming relationships between learners and instructors, among learners, and between class members and course materials (Slatin, 1992). Educators increasingly use computer technology, especially the World Wide Web and interactive multimedia, to heighten students' engagement in and responsibility for their learning. These technologies also hold unprecedented promise for students with disabilities to grow and learn alongside their peers. Too often, however, students with disabilities are denied the opportunity to participate as full and equal collaborators because online resources designed without regard for accessibility place insurmountable barriers in the way of their learning. No matter how visually appealing or highly interactive online resources may be; no matter how well they may satisfy state curriculum standards; if they are not accessible to all learners they fail a critical test of educational value.

Learning resources are accessible when students (or teachers, or parents) with and without disabilities can access and use them with equal effectiveness. Accessibility should, therefore, be an important consideration for educators designing or selecting online learning resources for their students. Making accessibility an important criterion requires no sacrifice of pedagogical effectiveness or aesthetic appeal. On the contrary, good design is accessible design, design that takes the needs of learners with disabilities into account from the outset and makes it a priority to meet those needs while creating intellectually engaging, pedagogically effective, and aesthetically rich learning experiences that challenge all participants to perform at their highest level. Integrating accessibility concerns into teaching and learning activities, whether those activities take place online or in a physical classroom, can also support larger pedagogical and curricular objectives, improving teaching effectiveness and enhancing learning for all students.

Enabling Participation

Putting the emphasis on participation places substantial burdens on the design and development of course materials, as Wenger (1998) and others have pointed out. Participation is important because learning is a fundamentally social process. Learners with disabilities need access to their classmates as well as to instructors and course materials. By the same token, the emergent learning community needs access to all its members, including those who have disabilities. (Just as course materials and classroom interactions are too often inaccessible to students with disabilities, so students with disabilities are too often inaccessible to their peers and their instructors. Accessibility is a two-way street.)

Benefits for Learners

Most of us are familiar with at least some version of Howard Gardner's theory of multiple intelligences (Gardner & Hatch, 1989) and the notion of multiple learning styles—visual, aural, kinesthetic, for example. And most of us take advantage of these different modalities to help bring important ideas home to our students, just as we use a variety of activities to foster learning: lecture, small-group discussion, quizzes, short-answer tests, research papers, lab experiments, and so on. These same pedagogical strategies go a long way toward enabling learners with disabilities to participate on equal terms with their peers. Multimedia can play a key role in this process–combining text with images, sound, video, and animation—provides multiple avenues for learning.

Accessibility in the Classroom

The growing importance of Web-based resources and other digital media in education calls for a new approach to the challenge of accommodating students, instructors, and parents who have disabilities. In the 30 years since passage of the Rehabilitation Act of 1973, accommodation has generally taken place after the fact. That is, textbooks and other paper-based course materials must be read onto audiotape or transcribed in braille, for example. Films and videos must be captioned for students who are deaf or hard of hearing or described for students who are blind; laboratory exercises must be adapted for students with motoric impairments; and so on. All this takes time—anywhere from a couple of days for simple materials to a couple of months for textbooks in the sciences or mathematics. As a result, students who depend on these alternative formats fall further behind the longer they are forced to wait, making an already difficult situation even worse. What Jerry Michalski (2002) calls the "law of convenience" kicks in: "Every additional step that stands between people's desires and the fulfillment of those desires greatly decreases the likelihood that they will undertake the activity."

All this changes with the advent of the World Wide Web as a major publishing medium in the early 1990s and the development of accessibility standards in the second half of the decade. No longer should it be necessary for students (or instructors) with disabilities to wait days or weeks or even months while essential course materials are converted to alternative formats. Textbooks can be published simultaneously in print and digital talking book editions (just as mass-market fiction and non-fiction are published as print and audiobooks). Further, online course materials can be designed so that they are accessible right out of the box from the outset, as it were, to students with and without disabilities. The result will be an improved learning experience—not just for students with disabilities, but for everyone.

As instructors, we should take care to ensure that online course materials are accessible in accordance with guidelines and standards at the institutions where we teach. But there is more to it than that. Student-authored Web pages must also be accessible, especially when these are to be produced collaboratively or made available to other students in the same or other classes; otherwise, students with disabilities will be excluded from collaborative activities, barred from learning from their peers. No less important, students who do not have disabilities will lose valuable opportunities to learn from peers who do unless they can participate equally. Requiring that student work be accessible means that accessibility must be part of the curriculum—not simply as a stand-alone module that can be added to or deleted from the schedule without affecting anything else, but as a point of entry into the intellectual and pedagogical concerns of the course.

Why Make Your Educational Web Sites Accessible?

Much has been written about why to make educational Web sites accessible (Hricko, 2003; Yu, 2003). We will only provide a short review of the legal requirements for Web accessibility.

Sections 504 and 508 of the Rehabilitation Act of 1973, respectively, refer to access to programs and activities of an organization, and access to telecommunication devices and services for persons with disabilities.

Section 504 applies to all federal agencies-including the Department of Education. The Department of Education has written rules (34 CFR 104) to ensure "equal access to programs and activities" provided by the department, including organizations that are part of the department's oversight responsibilities (i.e., schools and other educational institutions).

Section 504 states:

(a) No otherwise qualified individual with a disability in the United States, ..., shall, solely by reason of her or his disability, be excluded from the participation in, be denied the benefits of, or be subjected to discrimination under any program or activity receiving Federal financial assistance. (Section 504, 1973)

The application of this statute to educational institutions includes physical accessibility as well as accessibility to and participation in programs and activities provided by the institution (www.ed.gov/policy/rights/guid/ocr/disability.html). These may include use of the school's Web site for assignments, delivery of instruction, communication with instructors, and so on; coursework; school materials; textbooks; assistive technology for computers; as well as access to the school Web site and other communication by parents with disabilities.

While Section 504 requires that educational programs and activities must be accessible, it does not state how accessibility should be accomplished. This is where Section 508 comes in by providing an objective measure of the accessibility of telecommunication services (Web sites, online instruction and learning, etc.) through the standards established by the Access Board. These standards are also known as the Section 508 Standards (www.access-board.gov/sec508/guide/index.htm).

Another statute that applies to educational programs is Title II of the Americans with Disabilities Act of 1990 (ADA), which prohibits discrimination based on disability in public entities. The Title II regulation is in the federal code of regulations at 28 CFR 35.

The U.S. Department of Justice has released a letter indicating the applicability of the ADA to the Internet (Deval Patrick, Assistant Attorney General, Civil Rights Division, U. S. Department of Justice, letter to Tom Harkin, U. S. Senate, re: application of the ADA to "Web pages" on the Internet, September 9, 1996, 10 NDLR ¶ 240.). The most recent case

law regarding a public entity is the MARTA case (Vincent Martin et al. v. Metro. Atlanta Rapid Transit Authority, No. 1:01-CV-3255-TWT, at 34 (N.D. Ga. Oct. 7, 2002)), where U.S. District Judge Thomas Thrash specifically required accessibility to a Web site, as that Web site was the main means of providing "program" information to members of the public (see www.icdri.org/CynthiaW/martandlr.htm). Since public schools and other educational institutions are subject to Title II, if they have any program information, services, or instructional content that students are required to access on their Web sites, those sites and the contents must be accessible.

Already some states, such as Arkansas, Georgia, and Hawaii, are formally applying Section 508 Web accessibility standards to K-12 school Web sites (doe.k12.hi.us/technology/accessibilitymemo001208.htm; www.techarch.state.ar.us/domains/accessibility/policy/accesspol.doc; www.ncleg.net/gascripts/Statutes/StatutesTOC.pl?0168A).

Universities have also followed suit, notably Brown University (www.ilru.org/online/handouts/2003/Brown/Web_Resources.htm) and Michigan Virtual University (standards.mivu.org/standards/access/), as well as the Universities of Arizona, North Carolina-Chapel Hill, Texas, Washington, and others. (For example, see the University of Texas at Austin's Web Guidelines-Accessibility, at www.utexas.edu/Web/guidelines/accessibility.html).

What Technologies Should Be Accessible?

Instructional Web sites are like a hydra, a many-headed beast. The user as a human views the hydra as a whole beast. The hydra's body represents the pedagogical content of an instructional Web site. Instructional components/interfaces (e.g., Web page, discussion forum, email.) are the heads that the human must interact with in order to access the content. Any inaccessible component, like the hydra's teeth, imperils students' ability to learn from their interactions with pedagogical content.

While the mythical hydra had only seven heads, the hydra of instructional Web sites may have many more. These include but are not limited to:

- Course home page/login page
- Course information page (syllabus, reading list, grading system, etc.)
- Course resources (ancillary materials, instructor created materials)
- Pedagogical content
  - Lecture notes and similar text
  - Images and animations
  - Charts and diagrams
  - Tables
  - Multimedia
  - Audio
  - Video
  - Simulations
- Other content delivery technologies
  - Courseware (WebCT, BlackBoard, etc.)
  - PDF documents
  - PowerPoint presentations
  - Flash movies
  - Shockwave
- Communication/collaboration tools
  - Email
  - Instant messaging/chat
  - Discussion forum
  - Blogs (Web logs)
  - MUD/MOO
  - Web-based authoring
  - White board
  - Videoconferencing
  - Net meeting
  - WIKIs
- Assessment/evaluation
  - Quiz
  - Test
  - Survey

Seven Key Accessibility Issues

The primary interface for online courses is likely to be the World Wide Web. For this reason, being mindful of accessibility requirements when designing or writing instructional Web pages helps to ensure accessible content. We will not cover the Section 508 Web accessibility standards in detail (comprehensive treatments are available in Slatin & Rush, 2003, and Thatcher et al., 2002). Instead, we will concentrate on the requirements that are used most frequently and thus have the most impact on accessibility.

Each of the technologies listed in the previous section involves one or more of the following seven features that appear on Web pages:
- images
- color
- structure and style
- forms
- tables
- multimedia
- non-HTML content used on Web pages and/or delivered over the Web.

In the following sections of this chapter we will discuss the accessibility and pedagogical issues related to these features. Each section provides (a) a rationale for accessibility of the component; (b) rules for creating accessible content, together with examples of HTML code; and (c) pedagogical suggestions for integrating accessibility into student content creation to enhance learning by students with and without disabilities.

Images

Nearly every Web page contains images. They may be navigation controls (home button, next page button), decorative images with no content value, pictures or graphics used to provide content or illustrate a concept, or charts or graphs. Regardless of purpose, all images require an "alt" attribute in the <img> tag, also known as "alt-text." "Alt-text" is an alternative representation of an image describing its purpose or content. Missing or inappropriate alt text is one of the largest accessibility barriers and one of the easiest to fix.

Take a look at your Web page (or any other page if you do not have one). Imagine listening to that page as read by a screen reader—the software that students who are blind depend upon. What will those students hear when the screen reader encounters the images on your page? If those images have alt-text, the student will hear it; if there is no alt-text, the student will probably hear something far less meaningful. Suppose the page contains several graphical icons, including a calendar icon that links to the instructions for the current assignment. If the page includes alt-text for that icon, the screen reader will read it: the student will hear the phrase "Current Assignment," for example. But if the alt-text is not provided, the screen reader falls back on its default behavior: it reads the name and location of the icon itself (which might sound something like "slash images slash assicon dot gif," or, worse, "slash images slash nav twenty seven dot gif"). As a result, the student has to figure out the purpose of the icon using only the filename as a clue—and note that filenames like "nav twenty seven dot gif," which are quite common, give no clues at all!

Rules

For these reasons, text equivalents (alt-text) must be provided for all images and animations. The author of a Web page must provide the "alt" text. The accuracy and appropriateness of this alternative content depend on a few simple rules. These rules apply to images used for different purposes, for example, for navigation, for conveying information, for filling space, or for submitting forms, and so on.

In general:
- Every image must have a valid "alt" attribute (see Figure 1). Alt-text should not begin with phrases such as "Image of," "Photo of," and so on. Screen readers and conventional browsers automatically signal that images are present (for example, by adding the word "image" or changing the shape of the cursor).
- Use short clear "alt-text" for all images that carry information. Do not make it long, for example, "A button that has a red border

Figure 1. HTML source code showing "alt" attribute for "globe" image.

`<img src="some_path/ball.gif" alt="Earth" />`

with a blue background and the word HOME written in white letters, that links to the home page of this Web site." In this case, the alt-text should read simply, "Home," because sighted users see this word when they look at the image.

- The alt-text for an image link should tell the user the destination of the link. For example, an image linked to the "home page" of an instructional Web site (see Figure 2) should have alt="Home." Using the keyboard to select a link that a screen reader identifies by speaking the word "Home" is functionally equivalent to clicking an icon that displays the same word. Alt-text for image links should not contain the words "link to," "go to," or other similar language. Assistive technology and the browser already reveal this information to the user.

Figure 2. HTML source code showing "alt" attribute for image linked to "home page."

 Home

`<a href="index.html"><img src="some_path/ foo.gif" alt="Home" /></a>`

- Images that do not convey information or that are redundant to on-screen text should have alt=""; this is usually described as empty or null alt-text. For example: `<img src="spacer.gif" alt="" />` (Note: There is no space between ""). There is an important exception to this rule, however: ALL links that are images must have a non-empty alt attribute that indicates the link's destination. (For a technique that avoids creating redundant graphical and text links, see "Alt text for a link that contains both graphics and text," at www.utexas.edu/research/accessibility/resource/how_to/graphic/imagetextlinks/imagetextlink.html).

- Images whose purpose is to convey complex information (such as charts, graphs, etc.) usually require a more in-depth description than is appropriate for alt text. These descriptions may be provided in three ways:

Figure 3. HTML source code showing "longdesc" for a chart image.

<img src="AfrApePopulations.jpg" width="438" height="323" border="0" alt="African Great Ape Populations" **longdesc="greatape_description.html"**>

The description found in "greatape_discription.html" page would say:
African great apes description chart.
The chart "African Great Apes" is a histogram displaying estimated population sizes for all nine known subspecies of African great apes. All are currently listed by the International Union for Conservation of Nature and Natural Resources (IUCN) as endangered or critically endangered. The scientific and English common names and population sizes for each species or subspecies are listed below.

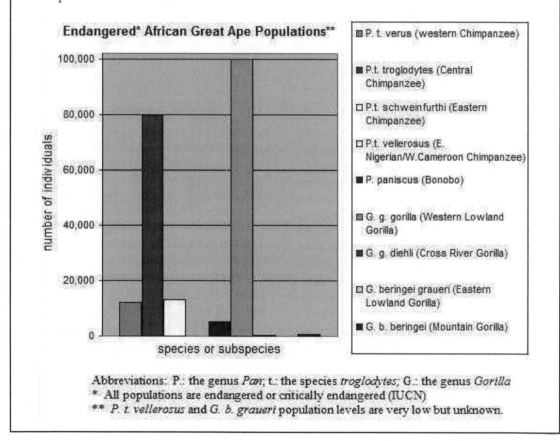

1. "inline" (that is, as part of the same page that includes the image)
2. via a link from the page that displays the image to a separate page containing the description
3. by using the "longdesc" attribute in addition to the alt-text, as shown in Figure 3. The page may also contain an accessible HTML table of the same information. (See the Table section below, for an expanded discussion of table accessibility).

Image Maps
Image maps (that is, images that contain several "hotspots" that link to other pages, usually on the same site) are often used to provide an elaborate graphical interface linking to sections of an instructional Web site. The rules for image maps are similar to those for images.

- Include alt text on the actual image referenced in the <map> element.
  <map name="us-map">

```html
<img src="../usmap.gif"
width="420"height="380" alt="Map of
United States" usemap="#us-map" />
```

- Include alt text on every <area> element used in the <map> (the <area> element defines the shape of the hotspot) specifying the purpose of each hot spot (e.g., Colorado, Texas).
```html
<area shape="polygon" coords="134, 15,
134, 82, 217, 82, 217, 15" href="#co"
alt="Colorado" />
```
- Use client-side image maps (server-side image maps are inherently inaccessible). If a page contains an image map, you can find out what kind it is by viewing the source code and searching for the word "ismap": this is the tell-tale sign that identifies a server-side image map. Client-side maps are identified by the word "usemap."

Image Buttons

Web authors sometimes choose to use an image button rather than the usual HTML "submit" button. As with all other images, it is important that the image buttons used in forms contain alt-text. The alt-text for image buttons follows the same principles as alt-text for images used in other ways, as discussed above.

- Each <input> element with attribute of type="image" must have alt-text specifying the purpose of the button as shown in Figure 4.

Pedagogical Applications for Writing Alt Text

The need to supply appropriate text alternatives and long descriptions is a good opportunity for students to develop their ability to write clear, concise statements that accurately express the meaning and convey the purpose of each image. Describing complex images clearly and accurately in a manner that leaves room for readers to form their own ideas about the images' meaning challenges students to articulate what such images represent and then write clear, informative descriptions that convey relevant information in a neutral manner. Such writing assignments call upon students to do several things, including:

- They must identify the image and articulate its purpose, if possible in a complete sentence, such as: "The blue arrow is a link to the next page."

- They need to compress that sentence as much as possible, reducing it to the shortest form that accurately conveys the purpose of the image to someone who cannot see it: "Next page."

- Invite peer review. Peer reviewers can be presented with a page that contains only the text alternatives and asked to answer some questions about the purpose of the various elements on the page based only on the text. Meanwhile, others can be asked to answer the same questions based only on the images.

- Students have to determine whether the concise text alternative (the alt-text) provides enough information about the image or what it represents to stand alone. If the answer is no, as it might be, for example, in the case of a chart or graph, a news photograph, or a painting, they should go on to describe the image clearly and accurately, perhaps following Adam Alonzo's guidelines for describing visual art or the National Braille Association's guidelines for describing maps, charts, diagrams, and other illustrations (see the Resources section for information on obtaining these guidelines). Again peer reviewers may be asked to answer questions based solely on the description, while others answer the same questions based only on the image.

Figure 4. HTML source code showing "alt" attribute for a form control button.

```html
<input type="image" src="button.gif"
alt="Search Now" />
```

Color

Every page also contains a variety of colors. The colors may be in the images on the page, in the background of the page, or in the text of the page. Information specifically conveyed by color is lost for people who are color blind or use monochrome displays.

Rules

The following rules help ensure accessibility and usability.

- Do not use color as the only way to convey information. For example, in a listing of 15 class meetings, three items are green. The sentence preceding the list states, "Classes in green are optional." Unless there is some other indication of "green" classes, such as other punctuation to highlight the information, it will be lost to people who are color blind, users of monochrome screens, or users of screen readers. Note: Changes in font type (Times to Arial), font weight (bold), or other attribute (italics) are not easily discerned by assistive technologies and may be dependent on the user's device, operating system, or browser. A better solution would be to say "Classes in green text and surrounded by angle brackets <> are optional." Then, besides making the text of the optional class meetings green, surround each item with angle brackets: for example, <Discussion of Chapter 7>. People using screen readers will hear "less Discussion of Chapter 7 greater," and will understand that this discussion meeting is optional.
- Ensure there is adequate contrast between text and background to make reading the pages as easy as possible. (See the Resources section for information about color selection, contrast, and legibility.)

Pedagogical Applications for Using Color
Color is an extremely important tool in the graphic designer's repertoire. Color may be used to convey information, to add emphasis, to guide the learner's eye to a specific area of the screen; to create a mood; to symbolize an abstract concept such as purity or grief. This rich variety of meaning may be lost for learners who cannot see color or those who have difficulty perceiving it accurately. This is why it is so important to avoid using color as the *only* means of conveying information. To put it another way, the fact that color's richness of meaning may be lost on some participants is the reason why web resources should seek additional ways to make apparent what color conveys.

Challenge students to identify things in the environment where color conveys information. Candidates might include signage, advertisements, weather maps, and so on. Once students have identified several examples, have them discuss whether the same information would be available in the absence of color. Make black and white photocopies of the materials collected by the students, then divide the students into groups. Give one group of students the colorful originals while the second group gets the same items in black and white. Then challenge both groups with questions whose answers depend on the way color is used in the materials. Of course the students in the black-and-white group will be unable to meet the challenge. Have the students discuss the role of color in these materials, and have them brainstorm ways to make it possible to answer the questions even in the absence of color. How could other aspects of the materials be enhanced or reinforced, or added, to provide the same information or create the same sense of engagement and appeal even for those who cannot see the color? Repeat these activities, this time challenging students to identify examples on the World Wide Web.

Forms

Web pages use forms to request information from the user, such as login name and password; or to allow the user to interact with the site, such as searching for information or responding to assessment items.

While the intent of a form control may be apparent visually through positioning, that same control may not have the same or any prompt text to a blind student using a screen reader. People using screen readers need to be told the purpose of an edit field or check box. In short, make the following demand explicit and unambiguous: "Tell me what this form control is for!"

Rules

The rules for accessible form controls are as follows:

- Visually associate each control with its prompt by positioning the prompt immediately adjacent to or immediately above the control. For radio buttons and checkboxes the prompt text should appear to the right of the element (see Figure 5). For other controls <textarea> and <input>, the prompt may appear immediately to the left or just above the item (see Figure 6).

• Make sure that each form control (text input, radio button, checkbox, select menu, textarea) is associated with its prompt by tagging each prompt with the <label> element and making the label element's "for" attribute match the "id" attribute of the form control. This explicitly (programmatically) associates the two elements, allowing assistive technology to find the appropriate prompt for a specific form control no matter the visual location or intervening HTML code. Note: Often tables are used for laying out forms to make them visually aligned. The table layout often confuses people who use screen readers. Using the <label> element allows visual formatting while aiding accessibility (see Figures 7 and 8).

• When there is no on-screen prompt, use the "title" attribute on the control.

Figure 5. HTML source code show placement of radio button form controls and on-screen text.

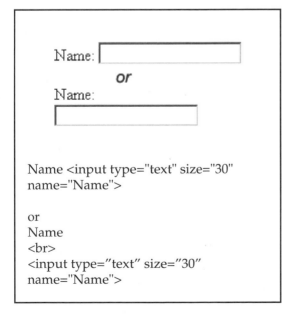

```
O Yes
O No

<input type="radio" name="visited"
value="0"> Yes
```

Figure 6. HTML source code show placement of text-input form controls and on-screen text.

```
Name: [                    ]
            or
Name:
[                    ]

Name <input type="text" size="30"
name="Name">

or
Name
<br>
<input type="text" size="30"
name="Name">
```

Figure 7. Table with lines to illustrate the separation of the prompt text from the actual form element.

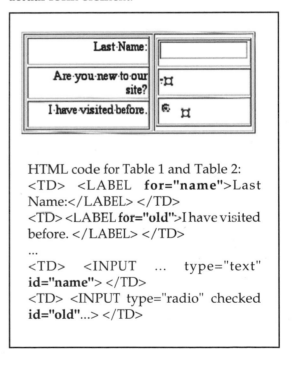

HTML code for Table 1 and Table 2:
<TD> <LABEL **for="name"**>Last Name:</LABEL> </TD>
<TD> <LABEL **for="old"**>I have visited before. </LABEL> </TD>
...
<TD> <INPUT ... type="text" **id="name"**> </TD>
<TD> <INPUT type="radio" checked **id="old"**...> </TD>

Figure 8. The same table but without lines to show actual display in a browser.

```
        Last Name: [                ]

Are you new to our site?

    I have visited before.  O
```

Figure 9. HTML source code showing "title" attribute for a radio-button with no on-screen text.

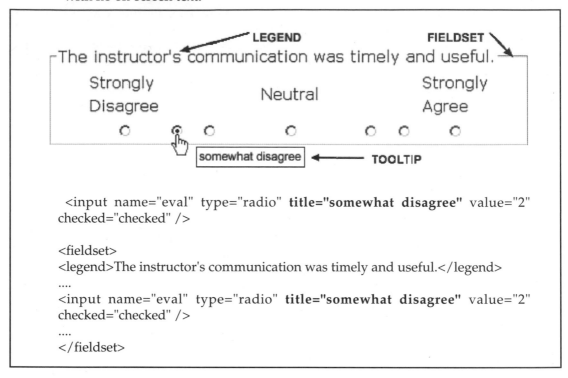

```
   <input name="eval" type="radio" title="somewhat disagree" value="2"
checked="checked" />

<fieldset>
<legend>The instructor's communication was timely and useful.</legend>
....
<input name="eval" type="radio" title="somewhat disagree" value="2"
checked="checked" />
....
</fieldset>
```

Figure 9 shows the mouse pointer pointing at a radio button that has no visual label. Because the "title" attribute was used, a "tooltip" showing the contents of the "title" will appear in some browsers. Screen readers will also read this information.

• For multiple radio buttons or check boxes, group the controls using the <fieldset> and <legend> elements.

This not only groups the radio buttons visually by drawing a box around them, but explicitly associates the contents of <legend> with each radio button. This is most useful in multiple-choice tests. Note: in Figure 9 the Web browser displays a box around the radio buttons to represent the <fieldset> element. The <legend> is the text that overlaps the top line of the box.

Pedagogical Applications for Creating Accessible Forms
Web-based forms are important tools for student work as well as for online tests and quizzes. For example, students may design forms to use as tools for online research. Focusing on accessibility issues can help students clarify the purpose and organization of the questionnaire or survey as a whole and of individual items.

As students determine the types of information they want to gather, they will also determine how best to ask for it. Some questions will require respondents to key in their answers–names and addresses, for example– whereas others will require them to select from a list of groups to which they might belong (age range or income level, for example). Substantive questions might be true/false; others might use a Likert scale to determine participants' attitudes. Each of these calls for a different type of form control, and each requires a slightly different accessibility technique. Using those accessibility techniques will enable students to ensure that respondents (a) understand how the survey is organized; (b) always know what question they are answering; and (c) understand what type of response is required. For example, as student researchers design their survey instruments, they are likely to arrange the questions in some sort of logical order. To make that order more apparent to respondents, especially respondents with visual impairments or learning disabilities, they should use the <fieldset> element to group related items and identify the groupings with the <legend> element. The <fieldset> and <legend> elements can be used in combination with other elements to make individual survey items accessible as well.

True/false questions, multiple-choice test items, and questions that use a Likert scale typically employ radio buttons. These are form controls used to select mutually exclusive options. But because these controls are used in different ways, they may look different on the screen. For example, making the true/false items accessible requires three things:

1. Using a <label> element for each radio button (<input> element of type="radio") allows sighted users to see and blind users to hear which choice indicates "true" and which indicates "false."

2. Using the <fieldset> element groups the true/false items with each other and with the item to which they respond.

3. Using the <legend> element within the <fieldset>, as shown in Figure 9, displays the prompt on the screen so that it is part of the <fieldset> (group) both visually and auditorially.

Together, these three techniques cause screen readers to speak the prompt together with each possible response (for example, "French fries are considered part of a healthy diet: true radio button not checked French fries are considered part of a healthy diet: false radio button checked").

Student researchers might use a Likert scale to elicit attitudes and ask respondents to weight their answers along a continuum from strongly negative to strongly positive. As in our previous example, they should use the <fieldset> element to create a group that contains the question (displayed via the <legend> element) and the possible responses. Each response is an <input> element of type="radio"; the radio

buttons are laid out horizontally along a single line. Explicitly labeling each option on a 5- or 7-point scale might create a screen so crowded with text that respondents with low vision or learning disabilities might become confused. Here, as Thatcher et al. (2002) has pointed out, the best choice might be to use the <label> element for only the two extreme options (i.e., strongly agree and strongly disagree). These labels would appear on the screen. The remaining options could be identified using each radio button's "title" attribute. There would be no screen text associated with these options. That is, the visual layout would make it clear to most sighted users that each button represents a point on the spectrum between strong agreement and strong disagreement. People using screen readers might well understand this in principle, but unless the student Web designers take specific steps to identify the options, blind respondents would hear only "radio button not checked radio button not checked radio button not checked." The solution is to use the <label> element to identify the options at either end of the range, and then use the "title" attribute for each radio button between the two end-points (see Figure 9, for example, title="somewhat disagree").

Sighted students can test forms created by students who are blind; similarly, blind students can test those created by students who see. And in a class where no blind students have enrolled, some students can act as "human screen readers," reading (or misreading) the form as a screen reader would while their peers verify the survey items and confirm that the correct options are associated with each item.

Page Structure and Style

The Web allows for the creation of unique interfaces to information based upon a defined set of structural components, such as hypertext links, forms, headings, tables, and so on. The use or misuse of these components may affect the accessibility and usability of the page. For example, assistive technology allows users to navigate a page by jumping from heading to heading, provided that the headings are marked up using the appropriate HTML structural elements <h1>, <h2>, etc. However, if text that looks like a heading has only visual formatting (larger font size, bold font, centered text) without the appropriate structural markup, the assistive technology will ignore the text when the user tries to navigate through the headings. Conversely, using structural markup simply to change the visual appearance of the page (as when designers use the <h1> element to display text in a large, bold font) may confuse people who depend on the headings to gain a sense of how the document is organized. The appearance of the structure can be changed to suit the visual aesthetic of the author by using Cascading Style Sheets (CSS).

Rules

The following rules help ensure accessibility and usability of the page.

- Use structural elements (headings, paragraphs, list, etc.) for their intended purpose.

- Avoid using HTML structural mark up <h1>, <blockquote>, etc.) for visual effects.

- Avoid using HTML presentational markup <style>, <font>, <center>, etc.) to simulate structural markup.

- Use relative units (%, em) to ensure scalability of page size, layout and textual content.

- Separate content from presentation.

- Provide a consistent page layout and navigational scheme for the entire site.

- Provide a page that describes the layout, navigational scheme, accessibility features, and other relevant information about the site. This is especially important for interactive applications such as discussion forums or other parts of the site that may have complex interfaces or be difficult to use.

Pedagogical Applications of Separating Content and Structure from Presentation and Layout

The idea that documents have structure often strikes inexperienced writers as difficult to understand, whether they are working on persuasive essays or lab reports. In addition, inexperienced writers often get so excited about their ability to control and change the visual appearance of their work that they neglect the substance of their arguments and their data. Focusing on accessibility can help students grasp the idea of structure and encourage them first to clarify their ideas and information and then use visual appearance to make those ideas more appealing and more understandable.

You can begin with the idea that every HTML document is contained within an HTML element; the beginning of that element is defined by the <html> ("open html") tag and the end is marked with the </html> tag ("close html"). Within these limits are at least two additional structural elements, the document head (<head>...</head>) and its body (<body>...</body>). Each of these in turn contains other elements, many of which can appear only in the <head> or <body>. For example, <meta> elements, which provide information about the document primarily for use by other computer programs, appear only between the <head> and </head> tags. Conversely, the <body> typically contains text divided into paragraphs (<p>...</p>). Related paragraphs might be grouped under section headings that show how the sections fit in the logical hierarchy (structure) of the argument or report. As in an outline, a level 1 heading (<h1>...</h1>) can contain second-, third-, even fourth-, fifth-, and sixth-level headings (<h2>...<h6>). In addition to text, each section may also include such structural elements as numbered and bulleted lists (<ol> and <ul>, respectively), data tables with <caption> elements and "summary" attributes, column and row headings, and data cells; images with alt text and long descriptions; forms that include fieldsets marking related items; <object> elements that contain multimedia files with their closed captions and audio descriptions; and so forth.

It may be useful to have students examine a series of Web pages to identify the differences between correctly used structural elements and other techniques such as the use of graphics or presentational markup (such as the "color" attribute or the bold (<b>) element) to create the mere appearance of structure. For example, it is still quite common to find Web pages that use a graphic containing bold lettering over a background color to mark off a section of the page visually; for example, there might be a line containing the single word "News" in large, bold, white letters against a green background. Human readers easily recognize that the page contains a section of "News" items. But people who use screen readers have no way to tell that this image defines a section within the logical organization of the page, as they would if an HTML header tag (i.e., <h2>News</h2>) was present.

In a subsequent exercise focusing on logical organization, students could go on to arrange various elements in the order that is best for them and their readers, and on choosing the most appropriate elements for specific purposes. For example, level three section headings should follow (and be contained within) sections defined at level two; there should be no level two sections inside sections marked as level three, and so on. Similarly, decisions about whether to use numbered or bulleted lists depend on whether the order of the list items matters or not, or even on whether readers will need an easy way, like a number, to refer to individual items.

In making these choices, students ensure that what they have written will be accessible to fellow students and others who use screen readers, for two reasons: (a) First, screen readers automatically identify elements such as headings, tables, lists, images, and links. This makes it possible for student readers (and authors!) to perceive how documents are organized and mobilize that perception to aid understanding. (b) Second, screen readers speak Web pages in the same order in which the elements of those pages appear in the "source documents;"-that is, the actual HTML code, no matter how those elements appear visually. Students who listen to the pages or use browsers that do not support Cascading Style Sheets (CSS) will not be distracted or confused by changes in the visual appearance of the page. (Reading their own work aloud is an excellent way for students to discover and correct logical problems, awkward phrases and sentences, or spelling and typographical errors.)

Once a Web page makes sense when it is read aloud, students can go on to experiment with visual appearance by using CSS to control the way individual elements look and even

where they are placed on the page (eventually, it will be possible to control the way elements sound as well). Experimenting with CSS can also help students understand how visual appearance contributes to or detracts from readers' understanding. For example, peer review exercises can help students understand the importance of choosing the appropriate structural elements and ordering them properly. Peer review activities based on pages that present the same material using different fonts, colors, borders, and so on, can make similar points about the role of visual appearance.

Web browsers such as Internet Explorer, Netscape Navigator, Opera, and others are designed to give these elements a "default" appearance on the screen. For example:

- a blank line will appear between paragraph elements by default.

- a level 1 heading (<h1>) will appear in a larger font than a level 2 (<h2>), and so on.

- table headings (<th> elements) will automatically appear in bold and be centered in their cells.

- each item or <li> element in a numbered list (<ol>) will be numbered automatically.

Tables

Tables are used for two purposes on the Web (a) to control page layout and (b) to present data. The following information applies only to data tables.

Data tables are designed for viewing columnar information. Effective visual formatting makes it easy for users to understand how data are related. As noted in our discussion of structural elements, visual formatting that does not make use of the structural markup provided for tables in HTML may create an accessibility barrier. In the absence of appropriate structural markup, assistive technology can only make a "best guess" as to which row or column heads are relevant to a particular cell. By contrast, when the author uses correct table markup, screen readers will announce the headings associated with each cell as the user navigates a table; this is true even in the case of complex tables.

Figure 10. HTML source code example of complex table.

The mean number of benthic invertebrates per m_ at two upper intertidal stations (Stations 1 and 2) in Baker Bay, Columbia River estuary, during February (no agal mat) and August (with agal mat) 1981				
	February (No agal mat)		August (With agal mat)	
Stations	1	2	1	2
Species				
Eteone dilatae	46.1	230.5	0.0	0.0
Neanthes limnicola	6.6	540.2	0.0	92.2

```
<tr>
    <td> </td>
    <th colspan=2 id="feb"> February<br>(No agal mat) </th>
    <th colspan=2 id="aug"> August<br>(With agal mat) </th>
</tr>
<tr>
    <th id="station" abbr="Station number">Stations</th>
    <th id="feb1" headers="feb station"> 1</th>
    <th id="feb2" headers="feb station"> 2</th>
    <th id="aug1" headers="aug station"> 1</th>
    <th id="aug2" headers="aug station"> 2</th>
</tr>
<tr>
    <th id="species" colpsan="5">Species</th>
</tr>
<tr>
    <th id="eteone" headers="species"><i>Eteone dilatae</i></th>
    <td headers="eteone feb station feb1"> 46.1</td>
    <td headers="eteone feb station feb2"> 230.5</td>
```

Rules

The following rules will help create accessible data tables.

Simple tables:

• Place column headings in the first row and place row headings in the first column.

• Use the <th> element for all heading cells.

• Use the "scope" attribute on all heading cells, specifying whether the heading refers to a column or a row e.g.,scope="row", scope="col". <th scope="col">English Name</th>

• Use the <caption> element and/or the "summary" attribute of the <table> element to provide additional information about the table.

Complex tables:

• Assign an id attribute to each heading cell (TH).

• Assign a string of two or more id's as the value of the "headers" attribute for each data cell <td> to say which heading cells are related to that data cell.

Grey cell in table shown in Figure 3: Based on the "headers" indicated in this cell, a screen reader would say "Eteone dilatae February (No agal mat) Station number 2 230.5"

• For each <table> element, include either a "summary" attribute or a <caption> element or both. The summary is not visible on the Web page, but assistive technology reveals the information to the user. The "summary" attribute provides additional detail about the purpose or structure of a table. This information may be readily apparent to people who can scan the table visually but would be difficult or tedious to discover by listening. A <caption> is explicitly associated with a table and is visible on the Web page. Caption is used to describe or add a title to a table. Because the <caption> element is part of the table, it "travels" with the table; that is, if it becomes necessary to move the table to a different location on the page, the caption will move along with it. This gives the <caption> element a clear advantage over other ways of titling tables (such as putting the table beneath a heading). See Figure 11.

- Do not include the number of rows and columns in the summary or caption; assistive technology knows this information and informs the user.

Pedagogical Applications of Accessible Data Tables

A Web page does not just present information, and a data table is more than a list of data. Like a chart or graph, the table creates a visual representation of relationships among data. As Cantor (2003) put it in a recent conference presentation, every cell "tells a story," and the challenge is to make that "story" accessible to students who cannot use the visual design to understand how the data are related to one another. As Cantor notes, we can use HTML markup to describe these relationships verbally so that people who use screen readers can hear the stories that people looking at the table can infer from what they see. These "data stories" are very short-just a single sentence, but sometimes this can be quite dramatic. Learning and using the HTML techniques that make these stories accessible to classmates who

Figure 11. African great ape populations illustrates a table with "caption" and "header cells" labeled.

Scientific Name	English name	Number
Pan troglodytes verus	Western Chimpanzee	12,000
P. t. troglodytes	Central Chimpanzee	80,000
P. t. schweinfurthi	Eastern Chimpanzee	13,000
P. t. vellerosus	E. Nigerian-W. Cameroon Chimpanzee	unknown
Pan paniscus	Bonobo	5,000
Gorilla gorilla gorilla	Western Lowland Gorilla	100,000
G. g. diehli	Cross River gorilla	200
G. beringei graueri	Eastern lowland (Grauer's) gorilla	unknown
G. b. beringei	Mountain gorilla	650

<TABLE summary="A chart giving the Latin and English names, and population sizes for endangered species of African Great Apes.">
<CAPTION> African Great Apes</CAPTION>

Source: Accessibility Institute: Graph and chart on same page. Available at www.utexas.edu/research/accessibility/resource/how_to/graphic/chartdesc_onpage/chartdesc_onpage.html. Accessed 28 November 2003.

use screen readers helps students understand the data more thoroughly, and can even provide a way to test whether both sighted and blind students understand the data in the same way.

Figure 12 below shows endangered species of African Great Apes. The top row contains three column headings: Scientific name, English name, and number [of apes that survive]. The first cell in each of the following rows contains the row heading, which shows the scientific name of a species. The English name appears in Column 2 and the number of known survivors is shown in Column 3. In HTML, the column and row headings would be defined with the <th> element and scope attribute (for example, <th scope="col">Scientific name</th> and <th scope="row">G.g.diehli</th>). The data cells are defined using the <td> element (for example, <td>200</td>). Someone looking at the table can see these relationships clearly. But a blind student who is listening to the page may not be able to keep track of information as easily.

After listening to part of the table shown in Figure 4, for instance, it may be difficult for the student to remember whether the number of surviving apes in a species comes at the beginning or end of the row. When students hear "G.g. diehli cross-river gorilla 200 G. beringei graueri eastern lowland (Grauer's) gorilla …," they may not be certain which species has only 200 remaining members. In other words, the story of the numbers has been lost.

Making the table accessible means making each story audible as well as visible. Students should be able to tell the story of any cell by using the column and row headers plus the data in the cell to write a one-sentence "story." Cantor (2003) notes that a data cell is one that refers to another cell in order to tell its story; a

Figure 12. African great ape populations.

African Great Apes		
Scientific Name	**English name**	**Number**
Pan troglodytes verus	Western Chimpanzee	12,000
P. t. troglodytes	Central Chimpanzee	80,000
P. t. schweinfurthi	Eastern Chimpanzee	13,000
P. t. vellerosus	E. Nigerian-W. Cameroon Chimpanzee	unknown
Pan paniscus	Bonobo	5,000
Gorilla gorilla gorilla	Western Lowland Gorilla	100,000
G. g. diehli	Cross River gorilla	200
G. beringei graueri	Eastern lowland (Grauer's) gorilla	unknown
G. b. beringei	Mountain gorilla	650

Source: Accessibility Institute: Graph and chart on same page. Available at www.utexas.edu/research/accessibility/resource/how_to/graphic/chartdesc_onpage/chartdesc_onpage.html. Accessed November 28, 2003. Used by permission.

header cell is one that helps other cells tell their stories. A blind student who listens to the table of endangered great apes and wonders about the number 200 can ask to "hear the story" told by that cell. If that student is using JAWS 5.0, what she hears is: "Column 8, row 3 number g.g. diehli 200." This is because the screen reader reports the column and row numbers followed by the column and row headers followed by the contents of the cell the student is interested in. So the student who listens to the table has to learn to fill in the gaps in the "story"; she can write it out: "In Column 8, Row 3, the great ape whose scientific name is g.g. diehli numbers (equals) 200." Of course this sentence should match the one that sighted students write about the same cell.

When students have to create their own data tables, they can use the same technique. That is, they can write a set of one-sentence stories about their data, then retell those stories using the appropriate HTML elements and attributes. Once they have written a cell's story as an sentence, they might highlight the words they want to use as column and row headers. Then they can mark up the row and column headers as <th> elements with scope="col" or "row" as needed.

The exercise could just as easily be reversed, so that students who are blind are challenged to write the sentences and create the HTML markup that makes these relationships visible to their sighted classmates, who in turn would verify their understanding by expressing the relationship in sentence form. Another exercise might focus on a problem we mentioned earlier: namely, that the use of layout tables to format discussion forums can present serious difficulties for people who depend on screen readers and are not familiar with the layout or structure of the forum. Advanced students might try their hand at redesigning the list of messages and replies in a discussion forum as a complex table, so that, for example, cells containing the subject line of a message can yield the story of who sent that message, when they sent it, and what thread or topic it belongs to. This can easily become a problem both in designing an accessible table and in using structural elements correctly and creatively.

Multimedia (Audio, Video)

Web pages designed for education often contain multimedia components in the form of downloadable or streamed audio and video files. These multimedia materials may present barriers to students with disabilities and to students whose native language is not the language of the multimedia content. Students who are deaf or hard of hearing may not be able to hear the audio content, students who are blind or have low vision may not be able to gather information that is not provided via the standard audio track, and students with attentional difficulties may find it difficult to identify the salient points of a fast-moving scene.

Yet, multimedia can be an extremely powerful device for learning, not just for students who see and hear and track information easily but for students with disabilities as well. Rather than avoid multimedia, it is a good idea to learn how to incorporate it into an overall strategy of inclusiveness. As a starting point, alternatives to auditory and visual information must be provided to ensure access.

Rules
The following rules help make multimedia content accessible:

- Include a text *transcript* for each informational audio file.

- Provide synchronized text equivalents (*captions*) for the audio content of a multimedia presentation.

- Provide synchronized *audio descriptions* of significant video information in multimedia presentations.

Multimedia content displayed on a Web page requires some tool or browser plug-in that "plays" the content. As a result, these tools must also be accessible.

Pedagogical Applications for Making Multimedia Accessible
Making multimedia accessible may require captions, audio descriptions, or both. These media equivalents must be synchronized with the multimedia. That is, captions appear as the words they transcribe are spoken; audio descriptions are timed to coincide with events on

screen and with pauses in the audio portion. Creating captions and audio descriptions enhances understanding both for the hearing and seeing students who do the transcribing and describing, and for the students who depend upon captions or descriptions for access to the material.

The first step in captioning is to prepare an accurate transcript of the audio portion of the multimedia material. This demands that students listen carefully (and often repeatedly) to the soundtrack, paying attention not only to what is being said but also to who is speaking as well as to any significant nonspeech sounds such as laughter, music, ringing telephones, and the like. It also requires correct spelling and appropriate punctuation.

The second step is to synchronize the transcript with the multimedia. This is where the transcript becomes a set of captions. This means that students must pay attention not only to who is speaking and what he or she is saying, but also to *timing*. They can also enhance their technical knowledge and skill by learning how to use tools like MAGpie from the National Center for Accessible Media (ncam.wgbh.org/webaccess/magpie/).

Preparing good audio descriptions requires students to watch the video material carefully and attentively. They must be able to identify the essential elements and significance of each scene; they must also be able to identify essential information that is only available visually, in order to determine whether audio description is necessary. (Audio description is not required if the primary soundtrack supplies the information necessary to comprehend the scene.) Students must then craft very brief yet accurate and informative descriptions that can be spoken during silences in the main soundtracks. Such silences often last only two or three seconds, so students are forced to pare descriptions to the bone while providing the information necessary to allow people to understand the material even when they are unable to see it. Students should work in pairs or small groups when transcribing the soundtrack, creating captions, or writing and recording audio descriptions. This can speed up the work while improving accuracy.

As with our previous examples, it is easy to test the effectiveness of captions and descriptions. For example, students who watch a captioned video with the audio turned off should be able to answer the same questions as students who watch the same video while listening to the soundtrack, whereas students who watch the same video with the sound turned off but without the captions will be unable to respond correctly. Similarly, students who listen to the audio description with the video masked should be able to answer the same questions as students who listen to the soundtrack while viewing the video, whereas students who listen only to the main soundtrack without being able to see the visual track will most likely be lost. (Comprehension is further increased if students themselves develop the questions and score the responses.)

Other Technologies (PDF, Flash, Movies, and so on)

HTML is still the primary language of the World Wide Web, but a growing amount of Web content is produced using other technologies. Some types of Web content require separate tools to display the content or allow users to interact with it. For example, documents in Adobe's PDF format require *Adobe's Acrobat Reader*; Flash movies require the *Macromedia Flash Player* or the Flash browser plug-in; and video and audio require players such as *Quicktime, RealOne, Windows Media Player*, or similar software. Each of these tools includes features that may lend themselves to a particular pedagogical need or technical concern, and each raises different accessibility issues and addresses them in a different way. It is important that content creators are aware of these issues: Besides making Web-based content accessible, it is essential that the tools chosen to display the content are accessible as well.

At a minimum, sites must provide a link to an accessible version of the viewer or player. That is, a page that includes a link to a document in PDF format must also include a link to an accessible version of the *Adobe Acrobat Reader* (www.adobe.com/products/acrobat/alternate.html) or a link to a resource page on the site that has a link to the accessible version of the reader. Additionally, the actual content of the PDF document must be accessible when used with the *Acrobat Reader* and assistive technology (See the Resources section for information about PDF accessibility).

Each of these tools must be accessible to the user's choice of assistive technology or operating system controls. That is, the tool's interface must be operable from the keyboard without requiring a pointing device (whether a conventional mouse or an alternative device such as a joystick, trackball, or head-mounted pointer). The tool must either work directly with the functions of the operating system or provide for assistive technology to access these functions. Additionally, the tools and their content may be embedded within the Web page or opened in a separate application window. User control of functions and features of embedded tools is severely reduced or nonexistent compared to the stand-alone version of the same tool. For example, the stand-alone application *RealPlayer* allows users to toggle audio descriptions and captions on and off, adjust movie size, adjust volume, and more—all from the keyboard without using the mouse. By contrast, the *RealPlayer* embedded in a Web page does not allow users to control these features at all.

The only sure way to check the accessibility of media players and other plug-ins is to test them on a variety of platforms with a variety of assistive technologies. Short of such testing, however, there are a number of things content creators can do to make an informed choice about the accessibility of the media players and other plug-ins their content may require. For information about the accessibility features of media players and similar products, check the product's Web page. Usually there is a link to information about accessibility features and resources. Some may even include information about how the product complies with Section 508 (for examples, see access.adobe.com or www. macromedia.com/macromedia/accessibility/tools/vpat/flash.html). Content creators should also examine the products themselves. Features to look for include menus that indicate keyboard shortcuts, Help files that include "accessibility" or "keyboard shortcuts" as a topic, or wizards that make content

accessible. It should also be noted that at this time versions of players/viewers accessible to screen readers are only available for the Microsoft Windows platform.

The bottom line is that instructional content must be accessible to students with disabilities regardless of the tool that displays it. In general, the burden of accessibility lies with the author or the content creator. The author has control over the accessibility of the content and can also exercise control over the choice of player required to access the content. There are a number of video formats, for example, as well as corresponding players; each format and player has some advantages and disadvantages in terms of accessibility, which content creators should factor into their decision making (for more on this point, see Slatin & Rush, 2003, especially Chapters 13 and 14). Many toolmakers provide guidelines or recommendations on how to create accessible content for their tools. For example, Adobe has a white paper entitled "How to Make Accessible PDF Documents," and a section of the Macromedia site (www. macromedia.com/macromedia/accessibility/) is devoted to accessibility features and content-creation guidelines for all of their products. Ultimately, authors' choices are constrained by the availability of accessible media players and other plug-ins. It is wise for content creators to inform themselves about the available options before creating content that cannot be provided in an accessible form.

Rules

The following rules help ensure accessibility when other technologies are included:

- The content must be accessible to students with disabilities, regardless of the content delivery format or tool required.

- At a minimum, sites must provide a link to an accessible version of the tool.

- Tools embedded within Web pages must be keyboard accessible, or the option to open the content in a stand-alone version should be provided.

Pedagogical Applications for Non-Web Technologies

Some classes require students to create animations using Flash or similar technologies. More frequently, students are asked to develop PowerPoint presentations to present their research findings or other information to their classmates. These animations and presentations may then be published to the class Web site (or in some cases on the students' own sites). Like conventional Web pages, these student-authored materials must be accessible. The pedagogical principles and exercises discussed above apply to these non-Web technologies, although the specific techniques may differ from the HTML examples offered. For example, the techniques for making Flash movies accessible are quite different from those for HTML, though the end result is comparable. There are also techniques for giving accessible presentations with PowerPoint (the Robert Wood Johnson Foundation's guidelines for presenters can be easily adapted to classroom use: see www.rwjf.org/grantee/howtoPlanMeeting_8.jhtml). It is also possible to publish PowerPoint slides to the Web in accessible format: there is a tool that converts PowerPoint files to accessible HTML; students and instructors should become familiar with the Microsoft Office Web Publishing Accessibility Wizard (see the Validation and Repair Tools section under Resources below).

Conclusion

The World Wide Web is a vibrant and multifaceted instructional environment. As we have seen, the materials and tools used for instruction and communication with students may be (and are required to be) made accessible to students and instructors alike. There are no secret weapons or incantations to tame the hydra, but we can practice accessible design. Unless accessibility is considered in all phases of instruction from inception to delivery, it is the students—not the hydra who will be incapacitated. This chapter presented a brief overview of how to make instructional content and tools accessible, regardless of whether the author is an instructor or student, and ensuring that the hydra interacts in a useful manner with a variety of computing platforms, formats, assistive technologies, and, most important, with all students and instructors.

We have only scratched the surface here. What lies beyond the scope of this chapter is the whole challenge of design, of putting the elements together in such a way as to create a rich and meaningful learning experience for all our students. We must note, too, that Web resources are only part of the picture. As the growing literature on Universal Design for Learning (UDL) (CAST, 2003) and Universal Instructional Design (UID) (UID.CA, 2003) suggests, accessible Web resources are most effective when they are part of a broad-based instructional strategy that aims at full inclusion and equal participation by students with and without disabilities.

References

Americans with Disabilities Act of 1990 (ADA). (1990). Retrieved August 10, 2003, from www.usdoj.gov/crt/ada/pubs/ada.txt.

Cantor A. (2003, November). *How to code accessible html data tables*. Presentation at 6th Annual Accessing Higher Ground Conference: Assistive Technology and Accessible Media in Higher Education, Boulder, Colorado.

CAST. (2003). *Universal design for learning*. Retrieved December 15, 2003, from www.cast.org/udl/.

Gardner, H., & Hatch, T. (1989). Multiple intelligences go to school: Educational implications of the theory of multiple intelligences. *Educational Researcher, 18*(8), 4-9.

Hricko, M. (2003). Understanding section 508 and its implications for distance education. In M. Hricko (Ed.), *Design and implementation of Web-enabled teaching tools* (pp. 25-46). Hershey, PA: Information Science Publishing.

Michalski, J. (2002). "The Law of Convenience." Retrieved December 11, 2003, from www.sociate.com/Topics/Convenience/convenience.shtml.

Rehabilitation Act of 1973. (1973). Retrieved August 10, 2003, from www.dot.gov/ost/docr/regulations/library/REHABACT.HTM.

"Section 504." (1973) Pub. L. No. 93-112 § 504, 87 Stat. 355, 394 (codified as amended at 29 U.S. C. § 794 (1994)). Retrieved August 10, 2004 from www.access-board.gov/enforcement/Rehab-Act-text/title5.htm

"Section 508." (1998) Pub. L. No. 105-220, 112 Stat. 936 (1998) (codified as amended at 29 U.S. C. 798). Retrieved August 10, 2004 from www.access-board.gov/enforcement/Rehab-Act-text/title5.htm

Slatin, J. (1992). Is there a class in this text? Creating knowledge in the electronic classroom. In E. Barrett (Ed.), *Sociomedia: multimedia, hypermedia, and the social construction of knowledge*. Cambridge, MA., and London: MIT. (pp.29-52).

Slatin, J., & Rush, S. (2003). *Maximum accessibility: Making your Web site more usable for everyone*. Boston, MA: Addison-Wesley.

Thatcher, J., Bohman, P., Burks, M., Henry, S. L., Regan, B., Swierenga, S., Urban, M., & Waddell, C. D. (2002). *Constructing accessible Web sites*. Birmingham, UK: Glasshaus.

UID.CA (2003). Universal instructional design. Retrieved December 15, 2003, from www.uid.ca/.

Wenger, E. (1998). *Communities of practice: Learning, meaning, and identity*. Cambridge (England): Cambridge University Press.

Yu, H. (2003). Web accessibility and the law: Issues in implementation. In Hricko M. (Ed.), *Design and implementation of Web-enabled teaching tools*. (pp. 1-24). Hershey, PA: Information Science Publishing.

Resources and Tools

(All URLs current as of August 2004)

Accessibility Guidelines and Standards

1. *Web Accessibility Initiative (WAI)*. A major activity of the World Wide Web Consortium, the WAI is a broad collaboration among industry, academic research, and members of the disability community to define standards and techniques for maximizing the accessibility of Web-based materials for all users; www.w3.org/wai.

2. *Web Content Accessibility Guidelines 1.0* (including checklist and techniques documents). These guidelines are the closest thing to a universally accepted standard for accessible Web content (this position may be challenged by the U.S. government's Section 508 standards; see below); www.w3.org/TR/WAI-WEBCONTENT/.

3. *Section 508 Final Standards*. These standards, which became effective on June 21, 2001, govern IT accessibility for all federal agencies and departments. The standards are making a significant impact in the private and nonprofit sectors as well as government; www.access-board.gov/news/508-final.htm. For additional information on Section 508, see www.section508.gov.

4. *SALT: Specifications for Accessible Learning Technologies*, by the National Center for Accessible Media in collaboration with the IMS Global Learning Consortium; ncam.wgbh.org/salt/.

5. *Making Educational Software and Web Sites Accessible*. Excellent, detailed guidelines for CD-ROM-and Web-based multimedia. The guidelines aim at education, but are much more broadly applicable. Site includes downloadable prototypes and information about accessibility issues related to specific development platforms. Originally published in 2000, the guidelines were updated in January 2003; ncam.wgbh.org/cdrom/guideline/.

6. *Distance Education: Access Guidelines for Students with Disabilities*. The California Community College System's comprehensive accessibility guidelines for its distance learning applications, published in 1999; www.htctu.fhda.edu/dlguidelines/final%20dl%20guidelines.htm.

7. *Designing Web Sites for People with Learning Disabilities*. Useful guidelines published by England's Society for People with Learning Disabilities. The document tries to practice what it preaches; www.learningdisabilities.org.uk/html/content/Webdesign.cfm.

8. *Guidelines for Signing Books*. Guidelines for the production of video-based stories in sign language developed by an international team

in the European Union. At www.sign-lang.uni-hamburg.de/SigningBooks/SBRC/Grid/d71/guide00.htm

9. *University of Texas at Austin Web Accessibility Guidelines*; www.utexas.edu/Web/guidelines/accessibility.html.

10. *A Developer's Guide to Creating Talking Menus for Set-top Boxes and DVDs*. Published in August 2003 by the National Center for Accessible Media, and available at no charge from ncam.wgbh.org/resources/talkingmenus/

Accessibility Resources

Books

11. Slatin J. & Rush S., (2002). *Maximum accessibility: Making your web site more usable for everyone*. Boston, MA: Addison-Wesley.

12. Thatcher J. et al. (2002). *Constructing accessible web sites*. Birmingham, UK: Glasshaus.

Online Information and Tutorials

13. Accessibility Institute. Includes "how-tos and demos" page, useful links, summaries of Accessibility Institute research, etc; www.utexas.edu/research/accessibility.

14. *Web Accessibility for Section 508*. The online accessibility course; www.jimthatcher.com/weebcourse1.htm.Thatcher's site includes other valuable information, including a comparison chart with side-by-side views of Section 508 requirements and related WCAG Checkpoints. www.jimthatcher.com.

15. Adaptive Technology Resource Center, University of Toronto. Wide-ranging research and development program related to adaptive technologies for persons with disabilities, including excellent work on Web and software accessibility; www.utoronto.ca/atrc/. See also the SNOW project site;snow.utoronto.ca/index.html.

16. National Center for Accessible Media (NCAM). NCAM has pioneered such im-portant developments as closed captioning and descriptive video service, and continues to conduct innovative research on ways to make video and other media both interactive and accessible. Free download of NCAM's MAGpie software for captioning and describing video; ncam.wgbh.org/.

17. WebAim. Web Accessibility in Mind. Tutorials, training, accessible simulations, laws, guidelines and more; www.Webaim.org/. The 508 checklist with success/failure criteria is especially helpful; www.Webaim.org/standards/508/checklist

18. WebSavvy. Useful tutorials and other information on accessible design, including Flash, from the University of Toronto; www.Websavvy-access.org.

19. *Describing maps, diagrams, charts, and illustrations*. Excerpted from the National braille Association Manual, 3d edition. Includes useful examples. Available at www.w3.org/2000/08/nba-manual/Overview.html.

20. *A Picture Is Worth 300 Words: Writing Visual Descriptions for an Art Museum Web Site*, by Adam Alonzo. Clear, concise, useful guidelines for describing complex images. Available at www.csun.edu/cod/conf/2001/proceedings/0031alonzo.htm.

21. Lighthouse International's guides to improved legibility through font selection and sizing, and effective use of color and contrast. *Simple Steps to More Readable Type through Universal Graphic Design* is available at www.lighthouse.org/bigtype/universal_graphic_design.htm. *Making Text Legible: Designing for People with Partial Sight* is available at www.lighthouse.org/print_leg.htm.

22. Safe Web colours for colour-deficient vision. Guidelines for selecting Web colors that work for people who have difficulty seeing certain colors. Excellent illustrations. By Christine Rigdon of British Telecom. Available at more.btexact.com/people/rigdence/colours/index.htm.

23. *Captioning FAQ*. A readable guide to closed

captioning by the Media Access Group at WGBH-TV in Boston, the PBS station that pioneered closed captioning for television in the early 1970s; main.wgbh.org/wgbh/pages/mag/services/captioning/faq/.

24. Trace Research and Development Center at the University of Wisconsin-Madison. Probably the leading center for research on information technology and people with disabilities; www.trace.wisc.edu.

25. International Center for Disability Resources on the Internet, Section 508 resource page. Substantial listing of government, industry, and academic resources related to federal accessibility standards as defined by Section 508 of the Rehabilitation Act; w w w . i c d r i . o r g / s e c t i o n _ 5 0 8 _resource_page.htm.

26. Microsoft's Enable site. Substantial site providing information about and access to many Microsoft tools for accessible design, plus links to many other resources, including information about Microsoft's Active Accessibility (MSAA) Application Programming Interface (API) for Windows; www.microsoft.com/enable.

27. UseIt! Web site maintained by Jakob Nielsen, a leading usability expert who has written some useful pointers about accessible design www.useit.com.

28. *Introduction to Flash Accessibility*, by Bob Regan, director of product accessibility at Macromedia, Inc. EASI Webcast. Links to audio-only and text transcript; available at easi.cc/media/flashp1.htm.

29. Macromedia's Flash MX Accessibility page includes links to training video and other resources for creating accessible Flash movies using Flash MX; www.macromedia.com/macromedia/accessibility/features/flash/.

Validation and Repair Tools

1. BOBBY, the automated accessibility checker. Comes in two versions, one on the Web and one stand-alone (Java-based_ application.

Stand-alone version can check a whole Web site; the online version checks one page at a time and has trouble with dynamically generated pages. No automated tool can possibly detect all accessibility problems. Humans are necessary!) Available at bobby.watchfire.com.

2. A-PROMPT. An evaluation and repair tool developed jointly by Toronto's Adaptive Technology Resource Center and Wisconsin's Trace Research & Development Center (see above). Available for download at aprompt.snow.utoronto.ca/. W3C's HTML Validation Service, available online via the WAI site at www.w3.org/wai.

3. The WAVE. Especially useful in helping sighted developers "see" ALT text and recognize the order in which items on their pages will be read by screenreaders and speaking browsers. Available at wave.Webaim.org

4. WebXACT. A new tool (June 2003) from Watchfire (publishers of Bobby), WebXACT integrates accessibility checking with other measures (includes checking for broken links, links to privacy policies, site statistics, etc.). The free online version checks one page at a time, and the company provides code for integrating this free checker into your own Web site. Available at Webxact.watchfire.com/.

5. Microsoft Office Web Publishing Accessibility Wizard. Developed by the Division of Education-Rehabilitation Services at the University of Illinois-Urbana-Champaign, this tool steps PowerPoint authors through the process of converting PowerPoint presentations into accessible Web-based presentations. Also works with MS Word; cita.rehab.uiuc.edu/software/office/.

6. The WAI's Evaluation and Repair Tools Working Group maintains a list of free and commercial evaluation and repair tools. The list is frequently updated. Available at www.w3.org/WAI/ER/existingtools.html.

Authoring Tools Reported to Provide at Least Some Support for Creating Accessible Content

1. IBM's Home Page Builder includes a configurable accessibility checker, and much of its extensive functionality is accessible from the keyboard; www-3.ibm.com/software/Webservers/hpbuilder/win/

2. Macromedia's Dreamweaver MX includes extensions for checking compliance with Section 508 and with general usability guidelines. If you turn on Accessibility Preferences, the authoring tool will prompt for ALT text, table markup, form labels, and other accessibility features; www.macromedia.com/macromedia/accessibility/

3. Access. Adobe. Information about accessibility features for Adobe products, including instructions on using *Acrobat 5* and *Microsoft Word 2000* to create accessible PDF documents; access.adobe.com *Acrobat Reader for Windows* with search and accessibility features is available at www.adobe.com/products/acrobat/alternate.html.

Tools for Captioning, Descriptive Video, etc.

1. MAGpie (Media Access Generator). Produced by the National Center for Accessible Media (NCAM) at WGBH (PBS) in Boston. Tool for producing closed captions, descriptive video, an so on, and outputting files in multiple formats, including QuickTime, RealPlayer, SMIL, and SAMI. Version 2.0 is currently in beta-testing; www.wgbh.org/ncam/.

2. Apple QuickTime Pro (widely available). Supports multiple tracks for video, audio, closed captioning, description, and so on. Limitation of current version is that captions, and so on, are all part of one QuickTime file and therefore not read by screen readers such as JAWS and Window-Eyes. Reportedly, this will be solved in the next version, which will also provide better support for SMIL (see above); www.apple.com/quicktime/products/.

3. SMIL. Synchronized Media Integration Language. A W3C specification for coordinating synchronized display of multiple media tracks such as video, audio, captions, descriptions, and so on. SMIL is an XML application; www.w3.org/AudioVideo/.

9

Information Training and Technical Assistance:
A Case Study of the Culturally and Linguistically Appropriate Services (CLAS) Institute Web Site

Rosa Milagros Santos, Robert M. Corso, and Dianne Rothenberg

The rise of the World Wide Web in the early 1990s opened the gates to a flood of up-to-date, cutting-edge information on early childhood special education (ECSE) that once was difficult to access. This kind of access via the Internet has added a new dimension to the teaching and learning process, whether it involves education and training provided by teacher educators, inservice trainers, or those engaged in technical assistance (TA). These groups of educators continue to need to know how to explain Internet use and Internet resources to service providers and future teachers.

This chapter discusses the growth of the Internet, demographic trends in Internet use, and the impact of technology and the Internet on professional development, particularly in ECSE. Specifically, we will describe the processes and lessons learned by the federally funded Early Childhood Research Institute on Culturally and Linguistically Appropriate Services (CLAS Research Institute) in its efforts to infuse an understanding of technology and the Internet into the information training and technical assistance staff members provided to facilitate ECSE teachers' and other professionals' development of cross-cultural competence. Finally, implications for research and teacher preparation and recommendations for future applications of technology are discussed.

Growth of the Internet

Over 10 years ago, in 1993, Internet use began to increase dramatically because of a new interface provided by the National Center for Supercomputing Application Mosaic (NCSA, developed at the University of Illinois at Urbana-Champaign) to the World Wide Web. According to one estimate, in June of 1993 about 130 Web sites were available on the Web (Gray, 1996). By 2002, more than 8 million Web sites (containing 800 million pages) were estimated to be online (National Telecommunications and Information Administration [NTIA], 2002). There are no reliable estimates as to how many currently available Web sites are devoted to education or to early childhood special education. However, it is clear that because of the phenomenal growth of the number of Web sites, the primary issue for educators has become one of learning to "drink from a fire hose" – that is, learning how to sift efficiently through the astounding amount of information available on the World Wide Web to find what they want and can use in their daily work.

Demographic Trends in Internet Use
Complicating the problems related to teaching and learning about using the Internet as a primary source of information for new (and experienced) Internet users are the clear indi-

cations that the digital divide continues. Digital divide is a term used to refer to the gap between people and learning communities who can make effective use of information technology and those who cannot (according to *First Quarter 2001 Global Internet Trends* from Nielsen/Netratings and reported by the Benton Foundation [Digital Divide Network Staff, Benton Foundation, 2001]). No consensus exists on the extent of the digital divide, but a few generalizations can be made. For example, in the United States at the present time, individuals from low-income homes, African-Americans, and Hispanics are less likely than their middle-class white and Asian-American counterparts to be Internet users.

At the same time, Internet use among traditionally underserved populations is increasing faster than among the general population. A recent report entitled *A Nation Online: How Americans Are Expanding Their Use of the Internet* (NTIA, 2002) is based on the September 2001 U.S. Census Bureau's Current Population Survey of approximately 57,000 households and more than 137,000 individuals in the United States. This study is considered highly reliable with regard to Internet use, broadband (high-speed Internet) distribution and use, and computer connectivity in general. Authors of *A Nation Online* found that as of September 2001, more than half of the nation's households were online. About 54% of the total population, or 143 million Americans, were using the Internet at that time at home-an increase of 26 million in just 13 months.

As illustrated, while still inequitable, Internet use is generally increasing for people regardless of income, education, age, race, ethnicity, or gender. Between August 2000 and September 2001, for example, Internet use among African-Americans and Hispanics increased at annual rates of 33% and 30%, respectively. By comparison, whites, Asian-Americans, and Pacific Islanders experienced Internet use annual growth rates of approximately 20% during these same periods (NTIA, 2002).

A problem related to the changing demographics of the diversity of individual Internet users, and one that impacts training, is that some government agencies and many nonprofit organizations (including some of the groups providing technical assistance or training in other areas) often are too close to the wrong side of the digital divide (Ryberg, Mowry, Saxrud, & Welbourn, 2002). That is, primarily because of limited resources, these groups are sometimes ill equipped to make use of the Internet at a high level and may not be in a position to be able to help others learning to use the Internet in their professional or student lives.

Groups offering technical assistance from a university setting may find themselves in a different position. High-speed, high-level usage of the Internet-routine in most university settings-may raise expectations about Internet use among TA providers that are unlikely to be met in non university settings, particularly in traditionally underserved rural and inner city areas. Therefore, technical assistance and training by university-based TA providers must be carefully planned-first, so that Web sites produced for underserved groups are easily accessible and friendly to users, and second, so that the training provided by university-based groups is based on a realistic understanding of the technology environment of the groups receiving technical assistance. Usually, this type of technical assistance must include what we call in this chapter "information training" for those who may be new to the Web or whose knowledge of the Internet is based only on casual use that may not have equipped them with the information skills needed to use Internet resources in their workplace.

With so many new users continuing to come online, training by technical assistance providers in information retrieval and use is likely to be needed for the foreseeable future if those who work in ECSE, specifically those who work with families, are to be equipped to make use of Internet resources in professional settings.

Infusing Internet Use into Professional Development Programs

Because of the growth in resources and available browsers, the use of the Internet has become ubiquitous in preservice training programs during the last decade. The Web has dramatically impacted professional development in the preparation of teachers

(Hains, Belland, Conceição-Runlee, Santos, & Rothenberg, 2000). For example, several states have adopted standards for technology as part of the certification requirements for teachers (e.g., the Illinois State Standards for Technology). Further, national accreditation organizations such as the National Council for Accreditation of Teacher Education (NCATE) and the Institute for Higher Education Policy (IHEP) have each developed standards or benchmarks related to the use of technology in higher education. For more information, see NCATE's *Standards for Technology in Teacher Preparation* (www.iste.org/standards/ncate/index.cfm) and IHEP's *Quality on the Line: Benchmarks for Success in Internet-Based Distance Education* (www.ihep.com/Pubs/PDF/Quality.pdf).

Teacher education programs include a range of technology options from courses delivered in part through Web-based course management programs, such as Black Board or Web CT, to courses offered entirely on the Internet, to entire teacher education programs offered long distance using the Internet and other forms of distance learning technology (Hains et al., 2000). The increase in distance learning options (particularly Web-based instruction) has changed teaching in higher education (IHEP, 1999), specifically for students preparing to be teachers, and particularly those living in rural communities (e.g., Collins, Schuster, & Grisham-Brown, 1999; Lock, 2001; Ludlow & Duff, 2002; Luetke-Stahlman, 1995). For example, students can complete, submit, and receive feedback on their assignments or projects entirely on the Internet. They can also take tests online. In-depth discussions among instructors, guest speakers, and students on specific topics can be conducted via live Internet chats or through listservs or message boards.

While some educators have approached the integration of technology and training with great caution and reluctance, others have been more willing to experiment with the ways to deliver content using distance-learning technology and the Internet in particular (e.g., Caro, McLean, Browning & Hains, 2002; Ludlow, 2002). While there is a growing knowledge base on the efficacy of such efforts, there is still much to be learned about the effectiveness of the use of technology in higher education. In 1999, IHEP published a review of original research on the efficacy of distance-learning offered in colleges and universities. Although they reported some evidence that students enrolled in courses offered through distance-learning options performed as well as their counterparts registered in classroom-based courses and rated their experiences favorably, IHEP also noted that the quality of the research upon which these results were based "is questionable and thereby renders many of the findings inconclusive" (IHEP, 1999, p. 18).

As a field we are still developing our understanding of what types of content can be delivered effectively via the Internet and the conditions under which optimal online learning can occur. For example, we need more experimentation and research on what technology would be most effective in teaching attitude-based skills, such as building healthy and reciprocal relationships with families of children with special needs as proposed by Barrera, Corso, and Macpherson (2003) and Kalyanpur and Harry (1999). We may learn that certain skills are best taught via traditional face-to-face interactions, or that different types of learners benefit from being able to take courses that use varying amounts of technology. For example, although Gallagher and McCormick (1999) found that students who participated in an ECSE course delivered through distance learning rated their experience as "acceptable," most indicated that given the option, they would have chosen a traditional face-to-face course offering.

Information Technology and Technical Assistance Paradigm

A new IT&TA paradigm is suggested in this chapter that acknowledges and builds on the roles of information, training in information use, and technical assistance in bringing about system or organizational change, particularly in the area of professional development. This paradigm helps to clarify the role of information in systemic change. The diagram in Figure 1 makes clear that reliable, research-based, high-quality information is a necessary (but not sufficient) basis for action or for changing behaviors. In this example, research-based information on child development, recommended

Figure 1. The information-training technical assistance (IT&TA) paradigm.

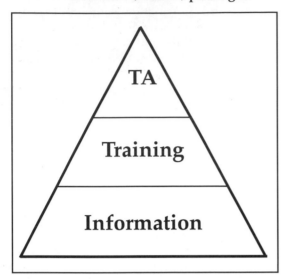

practices in early childhood special education, and early education are viewed as the core knowledge needed to make decisions and changes in the education of young children with special needs. Training, presented in the second level of the pyramid, is also needed to access, collect, and interpret the information that is necessary to implement change, and training also is a necessary condition or precursor (but again not sufficient in itself) to systemic change. Technical assistance (TA), which appears at the top of the Information Training and Technical Assistance (IT&TA) pyramid in Figure 1, represents targeted applications of expert knowledge and wisdom to local and/or specific situations.

The IT&TA paradigm can be helpful in thinking through issues related to personnel development and the role of the World Wide Web in this effort. The Internet and Web sites like the one created by the CLAS Research Institute and described in this chapter make clear contributions to all the parts of the IT&TA pyramid. Web sites are increasingly the repositories of the information needed to train personnel; learn about, meet, and report compliance with government regulations; find the resources needed for systemic change; share these resources with stakeholders; and record a program's progress in implementing systemic change.

The demographics of Internet use among various cultural, ethnic, and linguistic groups suggest that for many years to come learners with varied levels of expertise in Web use are likely to be enrolled in preservice courses and inservice trainings. With the diversity of online users constantly growing, for the foreseeable future we will continue to need to supply training so that those who work in ECSE are equipped to make use of important Internet resources.

Barriers to Internet Use

The World Forum on Community Networking estimated in 2002 that the proportion of English-language Web sites has decreased from 90% to less than 50% of the increasing number of Web sites over the last few years (www.globalcn.org/conf/montreal2002/en/t4_en.html). The result is that more resources than ever are available in languages other than English on the Web. Although this development has reduced one major barrier to Internet use among many linguistically diverse groups, language diversity on the Internet is still seriously limited in many topical areas. Despite the growth in the use of English in academic settings, English-only materials remain a barrier to information use by diverse groups of service providers.

In addition to access barriers related to the digital divide, the most commonly cited barriers to effective Internet use by an increasingly diverse, multicultural audience include language, literacy, and the lack of cultural diversity of resources on the World Wide Web (Taglang, 2001). Access is only part of the equation of effective Internet use by ECSE professionals. The ability to find and use Internet resources effectively comes with training and experience, and differs from the skills needed to use email, online shopping, or gaming. For example, skills related to evaluating the quality of information, citing and paying attention to copyright restrictions of Web documents, and skills related to downloading and printing out online documents assume greater importance in teaching and learning settings than in home or leisure use of the World Wide Web.

Key Issues in Information Training

To help teacher educators and trainers

engaged in preservice and inservice education understand the challenges posed by the Internet as a major information resource, we propose that four levels of training are needed to use Web resources effectively and to transfer what has been found or learned on the Web to realistic life and work situations (see Table 1).

Almost all training sessions involving the use of World Wide Web resources—whether these sessions last an hour or several days—address these levels of learning in some way. While training may focus on any one of these areas, at least some attention must be paid to the other areas in most workshops, training sessions, or presentations.

Table 1. Levels of Training Needed to Use Web Resources

Four Levels of Web Training
Level 1: Understanding of the basics of Internet use
Level 2: Proficiency in the use of Web navigation and searching skills
Level 3: Learning to evaluate and think critically about information found online
Level 4: Learning to use information and materials found online in offline settings

Level 1: Computer Basics.

This part of an information training workshop is the most likely to change in content over time as users' baseline knowledge continues to increase. For example, just a few years ago, a "computer basics" section of a workshop might cover the following topics: choosing an Internet provider; how to get help when you need it; how to save files and graphics; and how to find what you want on the Web. Now, a "computer basics" section of a workshop might include training on saving and printing different kinds of Web file formats, thinking critically about and evaluating information on the Web, understanding databases, and learning about search (and metasearch) engines.

Level 2: Web Navigation Skills.

Educators tell us that finding high-quality Web sites that are relevant to their information needs continues to be a central problem in using the Web. As a result, workshops typically include segments on using the browser's Bookmarks or Favorites feature, understanding file protocols, and how to locate or identify high-quality, relevant Web sites.

Level 3: Evaluation/Critical Thinking Skills.

A related topic is helping new Web users employ critical thinking skills to evaluate the information they find on the Web. That is, users need to know how to determine if the information they find on the Web is current, accurate, and comprehensive. They need to know what clues are likely to signal that a Web site may contain inaccurate or biased information, or information that views a topic from just one perspective.

Level 4: Transferability/Generalizability Skills.

This part of an information workshop can respond to questions such as, What can you do with the information you find on the Web? What copyright rules apply? And, How can you use this information offline?

Developing Cross-Cultural Competence: Building a Case for Effective Infusion of the Internet into Professional Development Programs

One of the content areas that holds great promise for teacher development supported through technology is the enhancement of cross-cultural competence of professionals in education (Gorski, 1999). This topic continues to receive increased attention in ECSE and early childhood education (ECE) in general because of the increasing number of young children and families from different cultural, ethnic, and linguistic backgrounds that are supported through schools, educational programs, and other service agencies (Lynch & Hanson, 2004). Encouraging the development of cross-cultural competence in teacher education is especially critical because of the racial, ethnic, and linguistic differences typical of the teachers and other professionals in most agencies and centers compared to the children and families they serve (Hanson, 2004). Furthermore, Gorski (1999) pointed out that the well-meaning but misconstrued approach to multicultural education through week- or month-long celebrations of specific ethnic or cultural groups, or all-encompassing diversity celebrations, makes developing the cross-cultural competence of school personnel even more critical.

Multiple approaches to acquiring cross-cultural competence have been proposed and reported to be effective (Hains, Lynch, & Winton, 2000). Programs that provide preservice and inservice students opportunities to participate in a series of coursework or seminars that focus on raising self-awareness and understanding of other cultural, ethnic, and linguistic groups have reported changes in student attitudes and better understanding of the topics (e.g., Derman-Sparks & Phillips, 1997; Ponterotto, Alexander, & Grieger, 1995). But few have used technology as a tool to facilitate the acquisition of cross-cultural competence. For example, Herbert, Mayhew, and Sebastian (1997) described a federally funded model program designed to prepare teachers to work with Native Americans with disabilities. This program infused multiple strategies, including distance learning, to address such topics as developing cultural sensitivity and conducting nonbiased assessments (Herbert et al., 1997). Hains and colleagues (2000) described some strategies teacher educators can implement using existing Web sites such as the CLAS Research Institute Web site that focus on issues related to diversity as a way to enhance learning about issues of culture and language in ECSE. Gorski (1999) pointed to a natural convergence of the Internet and multicultural teaching, writing, "the Web transcends virtually all other educational media in its capacity for facilitating intercultural, interactive and collaborative teaching and learning" (p. 2).

In the following section, we describe the process used by the CLAS Research Institute in developing an interactive Web site with a focus on facilitating potential users' development of cross-cultural competence. Lessons learned in the process of promoting cross-cultural competence via the Internet are discussed.

The CLAS Research Institute Web Site: A Case in Point

The CLAS Research Institute focused on increasing cross-cultural competence of ECSE personnel, emphasizing the World Wide Web as the primary medium for collecting and presenting materials intended to foster this competence. The project considered the preparation of Web-based resources and the provision of technical assistance and training to develop skills in accessing information as part of its primary mission. CLAS was a five-year (1997-2002), federally funded (through the Office of Special Education Programs, U.S. Department of Education), collaborative effort of the University of Illinois at Urbana-Champaign, The Council for Exceptional Children, the University of Wisconsin-Milwaukee, the ERIC Clearinghouse on Elementary and Early Childhood Education, and the ERIC Clearinghouse on Disabilities and Gifted Education. The primary purpose of the CLAS Research Institute was to identify, collect, evaluate, and provide information to promote effective and appropriate early intervention and preschool practices that are sensitive and respectful to children and families from culturally and linguistically diverse backgrounds. Training and technical assistance was also provided by the project to help early care providers and families access this information.

CLAS found that in order to work effectively with children and families whose culture and language are different from their own, service providers must: (a) understand what is culturally and linguistically appropriate for families; (b) appreciate the impact of culture, race, power, ethnicity, and language on the services provided to this nation's increasingly diverse populations; (c) become skilled enough to be able to gain access to information, techniques, and strategies that are current and research-based; (d) provide materials that are culturally and linguistically appropriate to families and early care providers; (e) acknowledge the culture and language of the children, families, and communities receiving the material; and (f) respect, reflect, and include the values, beliefs, customs, and traditions of the children, families and communities receiving services. To respond to these needs, ready access was needed to materials that have been evaluated as meeting current recommended practices and that had been evaluated as culturally and linguistically appropriate for the intended audiences, appropriately translated if available in more than one language, and presented effectively and without contributing to stereotypes.

During the five years of the project, the CLAS Research Institute solicited, collected, and cataloged over 4,500 materials from all over the United States (and its territories) that reflected the intersection of culture and language, disabilities or special needs, and child development. The vision for CLAS included making information about these materials available in a central Web site that could be accessed via the Internet from any location. The purpose of this database was to help build a knowledge bank that could foster a shift in thinking in the field of ECSE toward cross-cultural competence, by collecting and making available to early childhood practitioners as many relevant, culturally appropriate materials as possible.

Building a Web Site for Disseminating Information

Shortly after the project began, the CLAS Research Institute developed a Web site (clas.uiuc.edu) as its primary mechanism for informing consumers (e.g., practitioners, families, and researchers) about materials and practices available to early childhood special educators and the contexts in which they might select a set of materials or practices (see the CLAS Research Institute home page in Figure 2.)

Recognizing the four levels of competence necessary to successfully find, access, and use information from the World Wide Web (i.e., having computer basics, having Web navigation skills, having evaluation/critical thinking skills, and having transferability/generalizability skills), the CLAS Research Institute made several decisions. To address the first two levels, building a Web site that was easy to access and navigate as well as welcoming to culturally and linguistically diverse audiences was of great concern. Thus, as the CLAS Research Institute developed its Web site, the intent was to ensure that the search for and presentation of information and materials would be more than "user-friendly." The primary goal from the onset was to make a site that was "user-amorous," regardless of users' ability and experience with the Internet. To accomplish this goal, the project worked from the outset to engage early childhood professionals in using the Web site, visit frequently, and continue to provide feedback.

One of the essential elements in ensuring that the Web site was "user-amorous" to diverse groups of people was to create a site that was inviting to individuals whose primary language was not English. By the time a third

Figure 2. The CLAS early childhood research institute Web site's home page.

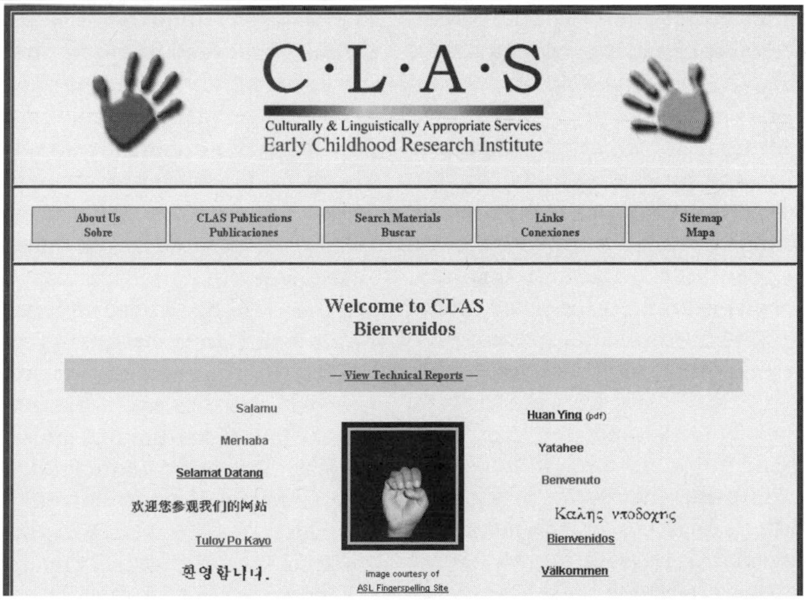

Figure 3. The CLAS early childhood research institute Web site's search page.

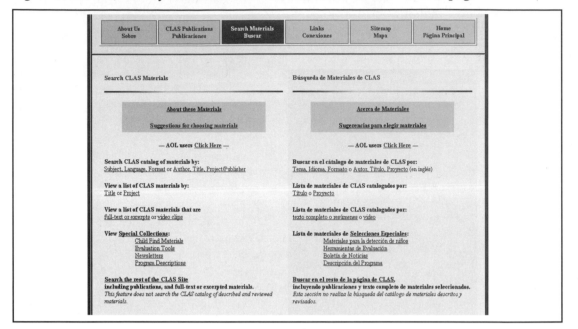

major revision to the CLAS Research Institute home page was made, based on feedback from its advisory board and staff, a home page was created that welcomed users in a variety of languages, including Tagalog, Navajo, Korean, Chinese, Russian, and American Sign Language (among other languages). The majority of the Web pages were made available in both English and Spanish soon after the project began. In addition, more than 30% of the materials in the searchable database were in languages other than English. These practices reinforced CLAS's commitment to diversity in both culture and language.

Another strategy for ensuring ease of use was to provide a database that had both predefined search terms and parameters, as well as a search function that allowed users to use terms outside of those provided. In this way, users were not required to have any prior knowledge of how of the database was developed or searched. Instead, users were provided simple check boxes to indicate the type of material they were looking for (e.g., child assessment, child guidance, early literacy, and transition), the format they were looking for (e.g., print, video, and audio) and the language in which they wanted the material. (A sample of the search page from the CLAS Research

Institute Web site may be found in Figure 3.) Once items were retrieved from the database, users had several options, including downloading materials or finding out how to access materials that were not available for downloading.

One of the most important considerations of the CLAS Research Institute was to help practitioners and families develop their evaluation and critical thinking skills. In addition to increasing awareness and access to the thousands of early childhood special education materials that have been developed in the last decade, the goal was to help those who came to the site to think critically about which materials they should select for their community. From many pages on the site Web users are prompted to view pages that outline criteria for selecting materials, for the purpose of helping those engaged in selection to reflect on the quality and appropriateness of the materials. These criteria were drawn from the recommended practices for ECSE as outlined by The Council for Exceptional Children's Division of Early Childhood (Odom & McLean, 1996) but also from the related fields of early childhood education (particularly from the National Association for the Education of Young Children's [NAEYC] Developmentally

Appropriate Practice in Early Childhood Programs Serving Children from Birth through Age 8, NAEYC, 1997) and cross-cultural and multicultural education. Additional information on the guidelines developed by the CLAS Research Institute to review materials is available in Fowler, Santos, and Corso (2005) and Santos, Corso, and Maude (in progress). In these publications, we describe the development of the process we used to review materials submitted to the CLAS Research Institute for their cultural and linguistic appropriateness.

In an effort to counteract a dominant perspective or an overly narrow approach, the CLAS Web site allowed for multiple viewpoints regarding a variety of topics such as perceptions of disability and the extent to which a disability is viewed as a deficit to be repaired. Currently, the dominant perspective focuses on "fixing" disabilities. However, not all cultural or linguistic groups subscribe to this viewpoint. To discuss related issues such as "When does intervention tamper with cultural beliefs or values?" or "What are the implications for interventionists?" or "Does professional training in EI/ECSE make the interventionist from a particular cultural or linguistic group an outcast from that group?" it is critical that everybody involved have a voice in understanding the issues and deciding the answer. Thus, it was important that a variety of input from diverse practitioners and families was involved in developing the Web site.

In addition, the CLAS Research Institute recruited a culturally, linguistically, and professionally diverse pool of field reviewers to write reviews of acquired materials from their unique perspectives (see Santos, Corso, & Maude, in progress). About 25% of the materials in the database include these critical reviews, which highlight the strengths and weaknesses of the materials. Finally, Web users were encouraged to share their individual perspectives about materials in the CLAS database using a form that gathered their comments and made them available at the end of the material. All of these activities were intended to heighten the critical thinking skills of the Web users and involve them in working with the materials.

To support Web users' acquisition of transferability/generalizability skills, the CLAS Research Institute Web site and trainings contained information related to how to use the information you find on the Web (e.g., what copyright rules apply, how to display appropriate materials on staff bulletin boards, and printing and distributing appropriate materials to parents). By helping practitioners and families understand the difference between copyrighted information materials and those that are in the public domain, project staff helped Web users think about strategies for effectively adapting or transferring the materials and resources on the Web to their communities. For each of the materials included in the database, information was provided about its copyright status. In addition, for materials about which the CLAS field reviewers wrote reviews, a section was included on the generalizability of the materials to help users consider the broad use of a material across multiple audiences.

Evaluating the CLAS Web Site

A great deal of effort was devoted to formative and summative evaluation of the design and usability of the CLAS Web site. Several evaluation studies were conducted in an effort to ensure that the Web site was easy to navigate (e.g., Corso, 2001). Based on data collected from these studies, several components were added to the site, including the predefined search terms for materials in the database, adding full texts or excerpts of the materials, and some video clips. These features allowed practitioners to read or view part of an item listed in the CLAS database before deciding to download or purchase it.

The evaluation studies also revealed several features that made accessing information through this medium difficult. For instance, some of the participants in the study reported that (a) the speed in accessing information was too slow when there were many graphics; (b) too much information on one page was discouraging; and (c) when there were multiple pages to search for information, searching became too complex. Specific feedback was solicited on improving the organization and clarity of the site and was used as a basis for changes to the site.

Despite these efforts, it became clear that many teachers would not access Web sites, such as the CLAS Research Institute site, without further training and technical assistance related to how to access information from the Internet. In one study, pre-training assessment questionnaires were administered to determine teachers' prior experience with computers and the Internet in one midwestern city (Corso, 2001). While access to the World Wide Web at home was high (82%), only 14% of the respondents indicated that they had access to the World Wide Web at work. Further, respondents reported using a computer at work mainly for word processing, while their primary use of the computer at home was for email. A large percentage of those who used the Internet did so for entertainment and shopping. Finally, few teachers reported using the Internet to support their work with children and families.

An instructional workshop for searching the CLAS Web site and other general World Wide Web searching skills was provided for participants who had had no such experience. Topics included understanding the basics of Internet use; building proficiency in the use of Web navigation and searching skills; learning to evaluate and think critically about information found online; and using the Web to find, evaluate, and access education-related information. As discussed earlier in this chapter, each of the four levels of Internet training was included.

After the instructional workshop, participants were asked to log on to the CLAS Web site to take part in a "hands-on activity instruction" to search for materials. Participants noted a marked increase in their ability to use the CLAS Web site and other sites that could support their work with young children and their families as a result of attending this workshop. It was clear that even in 2001 (when these studies were conducted) that many teachers would not access the information for work-related purposes without this type of training and technical support.

Additional evaluation efforts were conducted to try to determine who was coming to the CLAS Web site and what types of information and resources they were seeking. A "guestbook" accessible from the home page helped capture these data. A sample page of the CLAS Research Institute guestbook can be found in Figure 4. On several occasions during the project, the guestbook appeared as a "pop-up" window to encourage Web users to provide information about themselves. From these data the CLAS Research Institute staff were able to determine the background of responding users, as well as their reasons for visiting the site.

Figure 5 illustrates the self-reported cultural, ethnic, or racial backgrounds of the 1,160 Web visitors who responded to the CLAS guestbook from 2000-2002. As illustrated, a

Figure 4. The CLAS early childhood research institute Web site's guestbook.

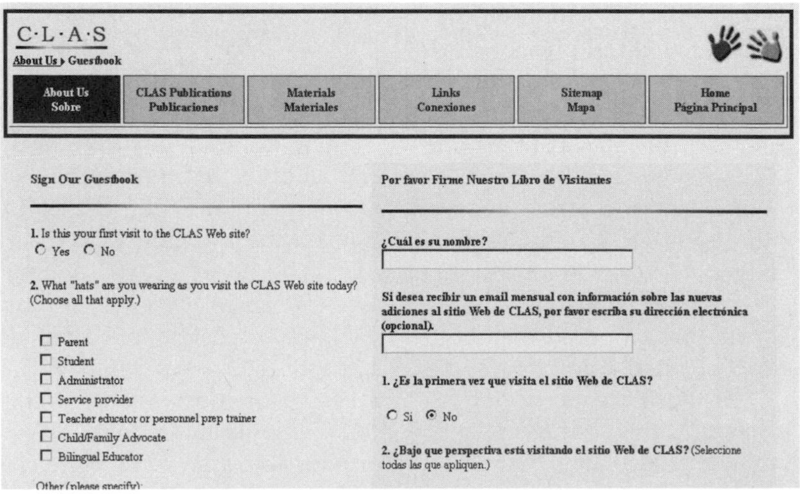

Figure 5. Percentage of self-reported cultural, racial, or ethnic backgrounds of the CLAS Early Childhood Research Institute collected from Web site visitors between 2000 - 2002 (*n*=1,160).

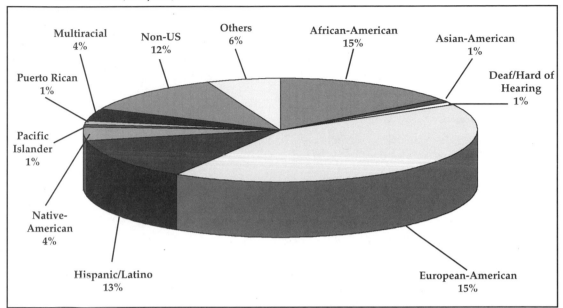

large percentage of the CLAS Research Institute Web visitors marked European-American (42%) as their cultural, ethnic, or racial background, followed by African-Americans (15%), and Hispanic or Latinos (13%). Other groups checked included Native Americans (4%) and Multiracial (4%), among others. These numbers suggest that the CLAS Research Institute Web site was reaching a wide and varied audience residing in the United States and in other parts of the world (non-U.S. respondents totaled 12%). Also of interest are the data presented in Figure 6, which show that over 80% of the respondents were first-time visitors.

Figure 7 graphically illustrates the reasons why Internet users visited the CLAS Research Institute Web site. Approximately 18% of the respondents noted that they visited the site to

Figure 6. Percentage of first-time visitors to the CLAS Early Childhood Research Institute collected between 2000-2002 (*n*=1,160).

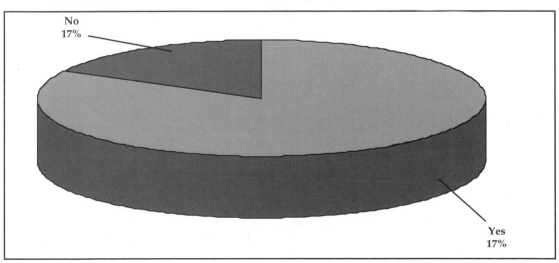

help them with their own professional growth. Additionally, a large percentage noted that they were looking for specific materials to help them with planning and program improvement and to share information with others. It is worth noting that a number of individuals (7%) who visited the Web site were looking for materials that are available in languages other than English.

Perhaps one of the most insightful pieces of information gathered related to how individuals learned about the CLAS Research Institute. In the early years of the project, a great

able by search engines) and by increasing the number of Web sites that linked to the CLAS Research Institute site. Specifically, the project queried teachers and interventionists to determine the search terms they would be most likely to use to find ECSE resources that are culturally and linguistically appropriate. Based on this input, metatags were added to the CLAS Web pages that increased the likelihood that the CLAS Research Institute would be among the top 10 sites retrieved in their search. Similarly, by increasing the number of organizations that linked to the site, the project in-

Figure 7. Reasons cited for accessing the CLAS Early Childhood Research Institute collected from Web site visitors between 2000-2002 (n=1,160).

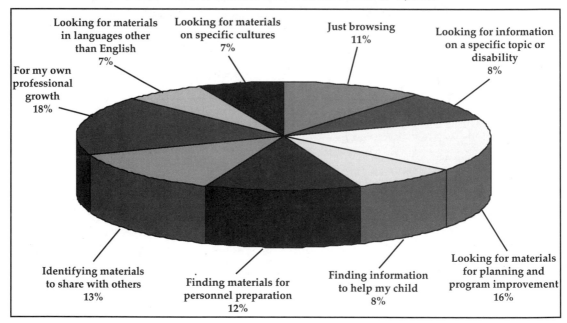

deal of effort was made to disseminate information about the Institute through traditional methods (e.g., conference presentations, newsletters, and press releases). Despite the resources devoted to sharing information about the site through these mechanisms, data collected as part of the evaluation revealed that the majority of those coming to the site located it by using Internet search engines or through links from other early childhood or special education Web sites. Subsequently, resources were directed to increasing the likelihood that a Web user would find the site through a search by using "metatags" (terms attached to Web pages that are not visible to users but search-

creased its exposure beyond those who had attended a certain conference or received a newsletter or brochure from the CLAS project. Figure 8 demonstrates the ways through which Internet users found the CLAS Research Institute Web site. Interestingly, 40% found the site through an Internet search, which supports the efforts the CLAS Research Institute took to create metatags as described above.

Based on the IT&TA framework described in this chapter, the CLAS Research Institute also worked to build partnerships with other training and technical assistance (T/TA) providers within the early childhood community. Thus, formal partnerships were forged with

Figure 8. Ways by which Web visitors found the CLAS Early Childhood Research Institute collected from visitors between 2000-2002 (*n*=1,160).

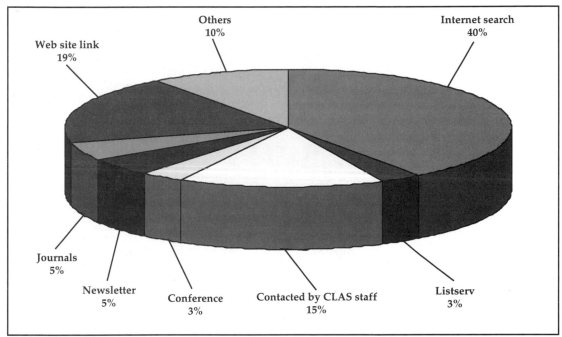

T/TA providers in early intervention, Head Start, and Early Head Start. In addition, the CLAS Web site project was featured in training sessions that served thousands of Early Head Start/early intervention teams. Through these efforts, a model linking information, training, and technical assistance was fostered not only within the CLAS Research Institute but also within the larger T/TA network that has historically maintained longer-term funding cycles than most federally funded projects.

Conclusion

One can make a strong case for "information training" as part of the information, training, and technical assistance continuum. One reason is that use of the Internet to find information of all kinds continues to accelerate, along with user expectations for finding significant information on the Internet (Horrigan & Rainie, 2002). A second reason is that the number of Internet users continues to increase at a rapid rate. Statistics from the National Telecommunications and Information Administration (2002) document the rate of growth of general Internet use in the United States as two million new Internet users per month. A third

and compelling reason is that many of these new Internet users are adults who had little or no exposure to learning about computers and the Internet in school.

The CLAS Research Institute Web site is an example of how to connect people who create information with people who need information—people who work directly with families or who are part of a training network. CLAS was successful in integrating Web site planning and growth with every other aspect of the project. Based on formative and summative evaluation to inform Web design and changes. Maintenance of the CLAS Web site is now supported through miscellaneous funds under the newly formed Early Childhood and Parenting Collaborative of the College of Education at the University of Illinois at Urbana-Champaign. Efforts are continuing to seek additional funding to update the site and database of materials and to provide information training to potential users.

There is much to learn about how to best provide training and technical assistance to early childhood special educators using the Internet, and a growing need to train personnel to facilitate their development of cross-cultural competence. The need for more information regarding effective programs addressing cross-cultural competence and programs that are delivered using the Internet also shows no sign of abating. The intent of this chapter has been to share information on the elements that came into play when the federally funded CLAS Research Institute implemented its information training and technical assistance system, with a focus on developing ECSE professionals' cross-cultural competence. This chapter describes one strategy among the many possible strategies that have to be taken to fully address this training area. We hope that sharing the lessons learned from the CLAS Research Institute's efforts will stimulate further investigation into this topic.

Finally, we highly recommend that emphasis be placed on designing and implementing rigorous scientific research into the efficacy of Internet-based training for students, teachers, and other service personnel. As increasing numbers of personnel preparation programs move to providing teacher training over the Internet, demonstrating these programs' efficacy and validity becomes doubly important. Projects and programs stand to benefit from such research efforts to extend, expand, and enhance preservice and inservice training for those providing service to diverse individuals with disabilities and their families.

References

Barrera, I., Corso, R. M., & MacPherson, D. (2003). *Skilled dialogue: Strategies for responding to cultural diversity in early childhood*. Baltimore: Paul H. Brookes.

Caro, P., McLean, M., Browning, E., & Hains, A. (2002). The use of distance education in a collaborative course in early childhood special education. *Teacher Education and Special Education, 25*, 333-351.

Collins, B. C., Schuster, J. W., & Grisham-Brown, J. (1999). So you're a distance learner? Tips and suggestions for rural special education personnel involved in distance education. *Rural Special Education Quarterly, 18*, 66-71.

Corso, R. M. (2001). *CLAS evaluation report*. Champaign, IL: CLAS Early Childhood Research Institute.

Derman-Sparks, L., & Phillips, C. B.. (1997). *Teaching/learning anti-racism: A developmental approach*. New York: Teachers College Press.

Digital Divide Network Staff, Benton Foundation. (2001). *Digital divide basics fact sheet*. Retrieved February 2, 2003, from www.digitaldividenetwork.org/content/stories/index.cfm?key=168.

Fowler, S. A., Santos, R. M., & Corso, R. M. (Eds.) (2005). *CLAS collection #1: Getting started: Culturally and linguistically appropriate screening, assessment and family information gathering*. Longmont, CO: Sopris West.

Gallagher, P. A., & McCormick, K. (1999). Students satisfaction with two-way interactive distance learning for delivery of early childhood special education coursework. *Journal of Special Education Technology, 14*, 32-47.

Gorski, P. (1999). Toward a multicultural approach for evaluating educational Web Sites. *Multicultural pavilion: Digital divide & E-learning*. Retrieved October 24, 2002, from curry.edschool.virginia.edu/go/multicultural/net/comps/eval.html.

Gray, M. K. (1996). *Internet growth summary*. Retrieved February 3, 2003, from icities.csd.uoc.gr/project/doc/Part%20II_Web_site_numbers.doc.

Hains, A. H., Belland, J., Conceição-Runlee, S., Santos, R. M., & Rothenberg, D. (2000). Integrating technology into personnel preparation. *Topics in Early Childhood Special Education, 20*, 132-144.

Hains, A. H., Lynch, E. W., & Winton, P. (2000). *Moving towards cross-cultural competence in lifelong personnel development: A review of the literature* (Technical Report #3). Champaign, IL: CLAS Early Childhood Research Institute.

Hanson, M. (2004). Ethnic, cultural, and language diversity in intervention settings. In E. W. Lynch & M. J. Hanson (Eds.), *Developing cross-cultural competence: A guide for working with young children and their families* (3rd ed. pp. 3-18). Baltimore: Paul H. Brookes.

Herbert, M. A., Mayhew, J. C., & Sebastian, J. P. (1997). The circle of life: Preparing teachers to work with American Indian students with disabilities. *Rural Special Education Quarterly, 16*, 2-9.

Horrigan, J. B. & Rainie, L. (2002). *Counting on the Internet: Most expect to find key information online, most find the information they seek, many now turn to the Internet first.* Retrieved January 2, 2003, from www.pewInternet.org/reports/toc.asp?Report=80.

Institute for Higher Education Policy [IHEP]. (1999, April). *What's the difference? A review of contemporary research on the effectiveness of distance learning in higher education.* Washington, DC: Authors. Retrieved: February 18, 2003, from www.ihep.com.

Kalyanpur, M., & Harry, B. (1999). *Culture of special education.* Baltimore: Paul H. Brookes.

Lock, R. H. (2001). Using Web-based information to facilitate inclusion practices in rural communities. *Rural Special Education Quarterly, 20,* 3-10

Ludlow, B. L. (2002). Web-based staff development for early intervention personnel. *Infants and Young Children, 14,* 54-64.

Ludlow, B. L., & Duff, M. C. (2002, March). Webcasting: A new technology for training special educators in rural areas. In *No child left behind: The vital role of rural schools.* Annual national conference proceedings of the American Council on Rural Special Education, Reno, NV.

Luetke-Stahlman, B.(1995). Deaf education on rural/remote areas: Using compressed/interactive television. *Rural Special Education Quarterly, 14,* 37-42.

Lynch, E. W., & Hanson, M. J. (Eds.), (2004). *Developing cross-cultural competence: A guide for working with young children and their families* (3rd ed.). Baltimore: Paul H. Brookes.

Odom, S. L., & McLean, M. E. (1996). *Early intervention/early childhood special education: Recommended practices.* Austin, TX: Pro-Ed.

National Association for the Education of Young Children [NAEYC]. (1997). *Developmentally appropriate practice in early childhood programs serving children from birth through age 8.* Washington, DC: Author. Retrieved February 23, 2003, from www.naeyc.org/resources/position_statements/daptoc.htm.

National Telecommunications and Information Administration [NTIA] and the Economics and Statistics Administration, U.S. Department of Commerce. (2002). *A nation online: How Americans are expanding their use of the Internet.* Washington, DC: Authors. Retrieved January 2, 2003, from www.ntia.doc.gov/ntiahome/dn/.

Ponterotto, J. G., Alexander, C. M., & Grieger, I. (1995). A multicultural competency checklist for counseling training programs. *Journal of Multicultural Counseling and Development, 23,* 11-20.

Ryberg, R., Mowry, D., Saxrud, K., & Welbourn, A. (2002). *Nonprofits in the information age.* Eau Claire, WI. Retrieved January 2, 2003, from www.digitaldividenetwork.org/content/stories/index.cfm?key=253.

Santos, R. M., Corso, R. M., & Maude, S. (in progress). *Increasing meaningful participation of diverse constituents: The CLAS experience.* Champaign, IL: CLAS Early Childhood Research Institutes.

Taglang, K. (2001). *Content and the digital divide: What do people want?* Retreived January 2, 2003, from www.digitaldividenetwork.org/content/stories/index.cfm?key=14.

Section 3

Assistive Technology

10

Quality Indicators for Assistive Technology Services in Schools

Joy Smiley Zabala and Diana Foster Carl

Quality Indicators for Assistive Technology Services (QIAT) is a set of descriptors of critical elements related to major functions involved in the provision of assistive technology services. Quality indicators have been developed and validated (Zabala, 2001, 2004) for six functions: Administrative Support, Consideration of Need, Assessment of Need, Documentation in the IEP (Individualized Educational Program), Implementation, and Evaluation of Effectiveness. In addition, quality indicators have recently been developed for Assistive Technology in Transition, and Assistive Technology Professional Development and Training. This chapter provides an overview of:

- The purpose, rationale, and need for QIAT

- The QIAT development process

- The basic principles of QIAT

- Quality indicators, intent statements, and common errors

- The QIAT Self-Evaluation Matrices

- QIAT research

- Ongoing QIAT activities

The Purpose and Rationale for QIAT

The primary purpose of Quality Indicators for Assistive Technology Services is to support thoughtful development, provision, and evaluation of assistive technology services for students with disabilities, regardless of where the services are provided or the specific model used to support service provision. In brief, QIAT supports the idea that the services should address not only the needs of students, but also the needs of family members and school personnel who work with students who require assistive technology devices and services to receive a free, appropriate, public education (FAPE).

The descriptors included in QIAT provide support for the development and delivery of assistive technology services of consistently high quality to all students who require those services to progress toward meeting their educational goals. QIAT can be used a guide for program improvement, that is, as a tool for increasing the quality and consistency of services. Rather than proposing or supporting any particular model of assistive technology service delivery, QIAT attempts to describe factors that should be overtly recognizable in some form in any service delivery system of high quality.

Although the quality indicators are not lists of competencies for service providers, it is understood that services of high quality require the preparation and availability of competent service providers. With this in mind, QIAT is expected to be useful not only to school personnel, families, and students with disabilities, but also to professors in colleges and universities, and professional developers as they go about preparing people to be involved in the provision of effective assistive technology services to students. Further, people who develop, implement, or monitor legislation, policies, or guidelines related to assistive technology should find QIAT a useful support in formulating equitable policies related to assistive technology services in schools and determining whether or not those policies are being appropriately implemented.

In order to understand the need for quality indicators, it is important to understand the history of assistive technology in educational policy and what research has shown about the delivery of assistive technology services and the impact of assistive technology upon the education of students with disabilities.

Assistive Technology in Educational Policy

As early as 1990, the Office of Special Education Programs (OSEP) at the United States Department of Education issued a policy letter requiring consideration of assistive technology during the development of IEPs for children with disabilities (Schrag, 1990). This directive indicated that the provision of a FAPE for all students with disabilities must include the tools needed for the student to benefit from educational opportunities. The requirement that schools provide assistive technology devices and services determined to be necessary was explicitly included when the Individuals with Disabilities Education Act (IDEA) was passed later that year. Thus, IDEA (P. L.101-476) not only mandated the provision of assistive technology devices and services if determined to be required for the provision of a FAPE, but also provided definitions of assistive technology devices and services (Individuals with Disabilities Education Act, 1990).

The reauthorization of IDEA in 1997 (P. L. 105-17) added the mandate that each IEP team consider each student's possible need for assistive technology devices and services during the development of the IEP (Individuals with Disabilities Education Act, 1997). This addition increased interest in the procedures and practices that school districts use to determine whether or not a student with disabilities requires assistive technology devices and services, and, if required, the nature of those devices and services.

Establishing the Need for Quality Indicators for Assistive Technology

Although federal policy mandates the consideration and provision of assistive technology devices and services, there is a continuing gap between what is required by policy and what consistently occurs in educational settings. This gap points to the need for guidance in assuring that assistive technology services of quality are available on a much broader scale.

Practitioners working to narrow the gap note that the ability of education agencies to develop and provide assistive technology services of consistently high quality has been complicated by at least three realities: (a) the complexity of issues and processes related to assistive technology; (b) large numbers of diverse individuals involved in the processes; and (c) lack of a unifying set of standards of descriptors to aid members of IEP teams and school districts in the development, provision, selection, and evaluation of quality assistive technology services (Bowser & Reed, 1995; Carl, Mataya, & Zabala, 1994; Zabala, 1995, 1996).

Research has confirmed the gap and identified major barriers to consistent, equitable implementation of policy related to assistive technology service provision (Hutinger et al., 1996; MacGregor & Pachuski, 1996; Todis, 1996; Todis & Walker, 1993).

In a qualitative study involving observation of thirteen students and interviews with their teachers, service providers, and family members, Todis and Walker (1993) found that devices tended to be underutilized for the educational goals for which they were intended, with the result that students were under-served and their educational results were not positively impacted on a consistent basis. They reported that all phases of assistive technology service delivery were complicated by a lack of understanding, communication, and planning between different school service providers and between school personnel and families. The researchers concluded that, beyond barriers identified in any one area, the most pervasive barrier was a lack of understanding of the interaction of the different factors that influence effective use of assistive technology use.

In a later report based on the same study, Todis (1996) examined the differing perspectives that family members and school personnel bring to the task of determining the assistive technology devices and services needed by students and discussed the difficulties of reaching consensus about what can and should be done. As in the previous report, she underscored the complexity of factors related to the provision of educational services to students with disabilities, particularly when assistive technology is involved, and called for closer examination of both intended and unintended results of the processes (or lack thereof) used to make decisions about assistive technology services.

MacGregor and Pachuski (1996) surveyed experienced assistive technology service providers in the state of Pennsylvania to determine their perspectives on staff training and preparedness to use assistive technology devices for educational purposes. The researchers concluded that there was a need for *interdisciplinary planning teams to develop carefully considered programs and supports for the use of assistive devices* (p. 14). This study, like the study done by Todis and Walker (1993), emphasized the need for careful planning and the importance of the interconnectivity of factors that influence the provision of assistive technology devices and services.

Hutinger, Johanson, and Stoneburner (1996) echoed the findings of the previous studies in their longitudinal case study research with children who were introduced to assistive technology in their very early years and who had continued to use technology for between three and eight years. They reported that the most frequently noted barriers to effective assistive technology service provision involved differing attitudes, knowledge and skills on the part of parents and service providers. In each of six cases, differing perspectives and attitudes of families and school personnel, differing knowledge and skills related to assistive technology, lack of alignment of goals and expectations, and lack of collaboration, were cited as he most common barriers to the effective use of assistive technology by students. As a result of their findings, Hutinger et al. (1996) called for increases in collaborative planning, staff training, parental support, equipment management, proactive support by administrators, and a clearly defined system of policies and procedures.

Clearly, practitioners and researchers concur that, in order to lower identified barriers and increase the consistency of quality assistive technology service delivery requires (a) addressing the differing perspectives, attitudes, knowledge, skills, and levels of preparedness of the many people who play a role in the consideration, development, delivery, and evaluation of assistive technology services in school settings; (b) increasing opportunities for school staff and family members of students with disabilities to learn about and participate in assistive technology processes; and (c) providing a systematic guide for planning, developing and delivering assistive technology devices and services.

Some local school districts have been able to employ and allocate personnel who have been specifically trained in leadership for the development and delivery of assistive technology services. However, a survey of districts in Oregon indicated that less than 15% of the districts in that state have been able to employ trained assistive technology leaders (Bowser, 1999). Though some organizations have provided training focused on building the capacity of school districts and individual service providers in various aspects of assistive technology service development and provision, these programs have been rare (Todis, 1996).

Regardless of these concerns and the training and support issues they raise, federal mandates require that efforts be undertaken to greatly increase the capacity of educators and family members to participate in the development, delivery, and evaluation of assistive technology services. In order to accomplish this effectively, the experiences of service providers and the findings of researchers indicate the need for a set of widely applicable, and generally accepted, indicators that could serve to guide the development, delivery, and evaluation of assistive technology services of consistently high quality.

Quality Indicators for Assistive Technology Services

The Development of QIAT

In response to the need for widely applicable, and generally accepted, indicators of quality assistive technology services, a small, diverse group of assistive technology leaders from across the country formed the QIAT Consortium and subsequently proposed a set of quality indicators for assistive technology services (Bowser, Korsten, Reed, & Zabala, 1999; Zabala et al., 2000). Although each individual involved in the original development of QIAT had a history of expertise and leadership in assistive technology in K-12 school settings at national, state, or local levels, the group was, by intention, geographically and professionally diverse (Zabala et al., 2000).

Extensive group processes resulted in the selection of four areas deemed important to the provision of assistive technology services for immediate development. They included: (a) Consideration of Need, (b) Assessment of Need, (c) Implementation, and (d) Evaluation of Effectiveness. Quality Indicators for Administrative Support and Documentation in the IEP were added the following year, and Quality Indicators for Assistive Technology in Transition and for Professional Development and Training in Assistive Technology were added in 2003.

Dissemination of the QIAT work began immediately after the initial drafts were developed. In order for QIAT to be valuable in a range of settings, development requires participation by people with a wide range of perspectives on assistive technology in different parts of the country. In addition to individual sharing by members of the original development team, four primary tools were used to invite and engage participation in the group's ongoing work. They included interactive conference presentations, development of the QIAT web site (www.qiat.org) and listserv, QIAT Summits, and publications in consumer journals and newsletters (Bowser et al., 1999). By taking advantage of any of these interactive opportunities, interested persons were able to receive information about QIAT, engage in critical discussion of the work, and provide input into the continuing work. Throughout the development of QIAT, people used these tools to make contributions that served as formative evaluation data that informed the revision and continued development of QIAT. In addition, the broad participation in the QIAT work also helped determine the perceived value of QIAT to people with differing attitudes, perspectives, understandings, and responsibilities. Thus, well over 2,000 written responses and untold hours of collegial conversation demonstrated that there was considerable interest in QIAT and that QIAT provided useful information to people concerned with the development and delivery of quality assistive technology services.

In December of 2000, an article published in the *Journal of Special Education Technology* (JSET), the research journal of the Technology and Media Division of the Council for Exceptional Children, detailed the development of QIAT and brought the QIAT work to the attention of the research community (Zabala et al., 2000). The article is available online in its entirety at jset.unlv.edu/15.4/Zabala/first.html.

Basic Principles

When reviewing or using QIAT, it is important to know the basic principles underlying all areas of QIAT: (a)It is essential that all assistive technology services developed and delivered by states or districts are legally correct according to the mandates and expectations of federal and state laws and are aligned to district policies; (b) Assistive technology efforts, at all stages, involve ongoing collaborative work by teams that include families and caregivers, school personnel, and other individuals and service agencies, as appropriate; and (c) Multidisciplinary team members involved in assistive technology processes are responsible for following the code of ethics for their respective professions.

While these principles are not restated throughout QIAT, they are so important that the QIAT Consortium believes that failure to respect them will severely compromise any efforts to provide quality assistive technology services.

QIAT is designed to be specifically applicable to educational settings at all levels.

Therefore, the term "education agency" is used throughout QIAT, rather than school, district, service provider, or some other more specific term, to avoid the assumption that QIAT applies to only one level or type of service provision. Though QIAT is intended for educational settings and is based upon the regulations of the United States, personal communications (A. Smaill, September 10, 2001; A. Knotts, February 10, 2003) and research in progress (Zabala, 2004) indicate that other countries and service agencies have found that, with minor adjustments pertinent to specific regulations and service plans, the content is valuable and useful in other settings as well.

The Structure of QIAT

QIAT includes quality indicators, intent statements, and common errors for each of eight areas believed to be important to the provision of consistent, effective assistive technology services. They include administrative support, consideration of need, assessment of need, assistive technology in the IEP, implementation, evaluation of effectiveness, transition, and professional development. In order to be easily remembered and readily applied, the quality indicators in each area are limited in number and are intentionally brief. The main idea of each indicator is underlined to add clarity, and intent statements have been added to provide additional information that can assist in understanding and applying the corresponding quality indicator.

The brief list of common errors that education agencies make when providing services in the corresponding area is provided to illustrate what services frequently look like in the absence of attention to quality indicators. They are included with the belief that by being aware of common errors, it may be possible to avoid them completely, or lessen their impact.

The first five areas included in QIAT, while critical to the equitable provision of quality services, refer to services that are provided directly to students. Each of these areas represents one of the major functions needed for adequate provision of assistive technology services.

The seventh and eighth areas included in QIAT are Assistive Technology Professional Development and Training, and Administrative Support. Each of these areas applied to a systemic function important to comprehensive assistive technology service provision at all levels of the education agency.

Quality Indicators for Consideration of Assistive Technology Needs

This area addresses the consideration of a student's possible need for assistive technology devices and services as an integral part of the educational process identified by IDEA '97 for referral, evaluation, and IEP development. Although assistive technology is considered at all stages of the process, the Consideration Quality Indictors are specific to the consideration of assistive technology in the development of the IEP as mandated by IDEA '97. In most instances, the quality indicators are also appropriate for the consideration of assistive technology for students who qualify for services under other legislation (e.g., 504, ADA).

1. Assistive technology devices and services are considered for all students with disabilities regardless of type or severity of disability.
   Intent: IDEA '97 is based on a child-centered process. That is, decisions regarding the need for assistive technology are determined by the unique educational needs of each individual student. Services cannot be determined based on categories.

2. The IEP team has the knowledge and skills to make informed assistive technology decisions.
   Intent: The IEP team members collectively use their skills to recommend assistive technology devices and services needed to remove barriers to student performance. When the assistive technology needs are beyond the knowledge and scope of the IEP team, support from other resources is sought.

3. The IEP team uses a collaborative decision-making process based on data about the student environment and tasks to determine assistive technology needs.

Intent: Although IDEA requires that the assistive technology needs of students be considered during the development of the IEP, it does not specify a process. The IEP team uses a process determined by the state or district to make informed decisions about the need for assistive technology. The process is communicated and used consistently across the district.

4. A continuum of assistive technology devices and services is explored.
   Intent: The IEP team considers a range of tools and strategies, including no tech, low tech and high tech to meet the educational needs of the student. Consideration is not limited to the devices and services currently available within the district.

5. Decisions regarding the need for assistive technology devices and services are made based on access to the curriculum and the student's IEP goals and objectives.
   Intent: After the IEP team determines the curricular tasks the student needs to complete and develops the goals and objectives, the team considers whether assistive technology is required to accomplish those tasks.

6. Decisions regarding the need for assistive technology devices and services and supporting data are documented.
   Intent: The IEP team determines whether or not assistive technology devices and/or services are needed. The IEP team uses something more than a check box to document the basis of the decision.

Common Errors in This Area:

• Assistive technology is considered for students with severe disabilities only.

• No one on the IEP team is knowledgeable regarding assistive technology.

• The team does not use a consistent process based on data about the student, the environments, and tasks to make decisions.

• Consideration of assistive technology is limited to those items that are familiar to team members or are available in the district.

• Team members fail to consider access to the curriculum and IEP goals in determining

if assistive technology is required in order for the student to receive FAPE.

• If assistive technology is not needed, the team fails to document the basis of its decisions.

Quality Indicators for Assessment of Assistive Technology Needs

This area addresses issues related to the determination of assistive technology devices and services are needed by a student in order to receive FAPE. Quality Indicators for Assessment of Assistive Technology Needs is a process conducted by a team, used to identify tools and strategies to address a student's specific need(s). The issues that lead to an assistive technology assessment may be very simple and quickly answered or more complex and challenging. Assessment takes place when these issues are beyond the scope of the problem solving that occurs as a part of normal service delivery.

1. Assistive technology assessment procedures are clearly defined and consistently used.
   Intent: Throughout the educational agency, personnel are well informed and trained about assessment procedures and how to initiate them. There is consistency throughout the agency in the conducting of assistive technology assessments.

2. Assistive technology assessments are conducted by a multidisciplinary team that actively involves the student and family or caregivers.
   Intent: The multidisciplinary team conducting an assistive technology assessment is comprised of people who collectively have knowledge about the abilities and needs of the student, the demands of the customary environments, the educational objectives, and assistive technology. Various team members bring different information and strengths to the assessment process.

3. Assistive technology assessments are conducted in the student's customary environments.
   Intent: The assessment process takes place in customary environments (e.g., classroom, lunchroom, home, playground) because of

the varied characteristics and demands those environments present. In each environment, district personnel, the student, and family or caregivers are involved in gathering specific data and relevant information.

4. Assistive technology assessments, including needed trials, are completed within reasonable time lines.
   Intent: Assessments are initiated in a timely fashion and completed within a time line that is reasonable as determined by the IEP team. The time line complies with applicable state and agency requirements.

5. Recommendations from assistive technology assessments are based on data about the student, environments, and tasks.
   Intent: The assessment includes information about the student's needs and abilities, demands of the environments, and educational tasks and objectives. It may include trial use of the technology in the environments in which it will be used.

6. The assessment provides the IEP team with documented recommendations about assistive technology devices and services.
   Intent: The recommendations from the assessment are clear and concise so that the IEP team can use them in decisionmaking and program development.

7. Assistive technology needs are reassessed by request, or as needed, based on changes in the student, environments, and/or tasks.
   Intent: An assistive technology assessment is available any time it is needed due to changes or when it is requested by the parent or other members of the IEP team.

Common Errors in This Area:

- Procedures for conducting assistive technology assessment are not defined, or are not customized to meet the student's needs.

- A team approach to assessment is not utilized.

- Individuals participating in an assessment do not have the skills necessary to conduct the assessment, and do not seek additional help.

- Team members do not have adequate time to conduct assessment processes, including necessary trials with AT.

- Communication between team members is not clear.

- The student is not involved in the assessment process.

- When the assessment is conducted by any team other than the student's IEP team, the needs of the student or expectations for the assessment are not communicated.

Quality Indicators for Documentation in the IEP

This area addresses documentation of assistive technology devices and services in the IEP. The Individuals with Disabilities Education Act of 1997 (IDEA '97) requires that the IEP team consider assistive technology needs in the development of each student's IEP. If the IEP team determines that assistive technology is needed to ensure provision of FAPE, the nature and extent of the devices and services to be provided and the roles role of assistive technology in the child's educational program must be clearly reflected in the IEP.

1. The education agency has guidelines for documenting assistive technology needs in the IEP, and everyone on the IEP team is aware of them.
   Intent: Education agencies give instructions to IEP teams on how IEPs should be written. These instructions include guidance about documentation of assistive technology needs. Districts give direction to IEP teams on how to document assistive technology as a related service, supplementary aid or service, goal, objective, and so on.

2. Assistive technology is included in the IEP in a manner that provides a clear and complete description of the devices and services to be provided and used.
   Intent: IEPs are written in such a manner that everyone who attended the IEP meeting and others who might need to use the information to implement the plan understand what is to be done. IEPs are clearly written with as little jargon as possible. They give a clear picture of the devices and services which the IEP team determined were necessary.

3. Assistive technology is used as a tool to support achievement of IEP goals and objectives as well as participation and progress in the general curriculum.

Intent: There should be a clear relationship between assistive technology devices and services included in an IEP and the goals and objectives developed by the team. Most goals and objectives should be developed before decisions about assistive technology use are made.

4. IEP content regarding assistive technology use is written in language that describes measurable and observable outcomes.

Intent: At the point of periodic review, the IEP is used to measure whether the district met its commitments and the whether the educational goals set for the child were appropriate. Content that describes measurable and observable outcomes for assistive technology allows the team to review the success of the plan.

5. All services needed to implement assistive technology use are documented in the IEP.

Intent: IDEA lists a variety of services (i.e., evaluating, customizing, maintaining, coordinating services, training for the child and family, technical assistance for professionals) that must be provided to support the child's use of an assistive technology device. IEPs that include assistive technology devices often fail because inadequate services are provided. It is important that the IEP includes services as well as devices.

Common Errors in This Area:

- IEP teams do not know how to include assistive technology in IEPs.

- IEPs including assistive technology use a "formula" approach to documentation. Thus, all IEPs are developed in similar fashion and the unique needs of the child are not addressed.

- Assistive technology is included in the IEP, but the relationship to goals and objectives is unclear.

- Assistive technology devices are included in the IEP, but no assistive technology services support the use.

- Expected results of assistive technology are not measurable or observable.

Quality Indicators for Assistive Technology Implementation

Assistive technology implementation pertains to the ways that assistive technology devices and services, as included in the IEP (including goals/objectives, related services, supplementary aids and services and accommodations or modifications), are delivered and integrated into a student's educational program. Assistive technology implementation involves people working together to support the student using assistive technology to accomplish tasks necessary for active participation in customary educational environments.

1. Assistive technology implementation proceeds according to a collaboratively developed plan.

Intent: Following IEP development, all those involved in implementation work together to develop a written action plan that provides detailed information about how the assistive technology will be used in specific educational settings, what will be done, and who will do it.

2. Assistive technology is integrated into the curriculum and daily activities of the student.

Intent: Assistive technology is used when and where needed to facilitate the student's access to the curriculum and active participation in educational activities and routines.

3. Team members in all of the child's environments share responsibility for implementation of the plan.

Intent: Persons working with the student in each environment know what to do to support the student using assistive technology.

4. The student uses multiple strategies to accomplish tasks, and the use of assistive technology may be included in those strategies.

Intent: Assistive technology tools are used when needed to remove barriers to participation and/or performance. Alternate strategies may include use of the student's natural abilities, other supports, or modifications to the curriculum, task, or environment. At times these alternate strategies may be more efficient than the use of assistive technology.

5. Training for student, family, and staff is an integral part of implementation.

   Intent: Determination of the training needs of the student, staff and family is based on how the assistive technology will be used in each unique environment. Training and technical assistance are planned and implemented as ongoing processes based on current and changing needs.

6. Assistive technology implementation is initially based on assessment data and is adjusted based on performance data.

   Intent: Formal and informal assessment data guide initial decisionmaking and planning for assistive technology implementation. As the plan is carried out, student performance is monitored, and implementation is adjusted in a timely manner to support student progress.

7. Assistive technology implementation includes management and maintenance of equipment and materials.

   Intent: For technology to be useful, it is important that equipment management responsibilities are clearly defined and assigned. Although specifics may differ based on the technology, general areas may include organization of equipment and materials, responsibility for acquisition, repair and replacement, and b surance that equipment is operational.

Common Errors in This Area:

- Implementation is expected to be smooth and effective without addressing specific components in a plan. Team members assume that everyone understands what needs to happen and knows what to do.

- Plans for implementation are created and carried out by one IEP team member.

- The team focuses on device acquisition and does not discuss implementation.

- An implementation plan is developed that is incompatible with the instructional environments.

- No one takes responsibility for the care and maintenance of assistive technology devices, so they are not available or in working order when needed.

- Contingency plans for dealing with broken or lost devices are not made in advance.

Quality Indicators for Evaluation of Effectiveness

This area addresses the evaluation of the effectiveness of assistive technology devices and services provided to an individual student. It includes data collection and documentation to monitor changes in student performance resulting from the implementation. Student performance is reviewed in order to identify if, when, or where modifications and revisions to the implementation are needed.

1. Team members share clearly defined responsibilities to ensure that data are collected, evaluated, and interpreted by capable and credible team members.

   Intent: Each team member is accountable for ensuring that the data-collection process determined by the team is implemented. Individual roles in the collection and review of the data are assigned by the team. Data collection, evaluation, and interpretation are led by persons with relevant training and knowledge. It can be appropriate for different individual team members to conduct these tasks.

2. Data are collected on specific student behaviors that have been identified by the team and are related to one or more goals.

   Intent: In order to evaluate the success of the assistive technology use, data are collected on various aspects of student performance. The behavior targeted for data collection is related to one or more IEP goal(s) (e.g., ability to accomplish the task, use of the technology, changes in student behavior).

3. Evaluation of effectiveness reflects the objective measurement of changes in the student's performance (e.g., student preferences, productivity, participation, independence, quantity, quality, speed, accuracy, frequency, or spontaneity).

   Intent: Expected changes in student performance are determined by the IEP team. The behavior targeted for data collection must be observable and measurable. Data that capture changes in student behaviors may be either quantitative or qualitative, or both.

4. Effectiveness is evaluated across environments, including during naturally occurring opportunities as well as structured activities.
   Intent: The team determines the environments where the changes in student performance are expected to occur and prioritizes appropriate activities for data collection in those environments.

5. Evaluation of effectiveness is a dynamic, responsive, ongoing process that is reviewed periodically.
   Intent: Scheduled data collection occurs over time and changes in response to both expected and unexpected results. Data collection reflects measurement strategies appropriate to individual student needs. Team members evaluate and interpret data during periodic progress reviews.

6. Data collected provide a means to analyze response patterns and student performance.
   Intent: The team regularly analyzes data to determine student progress and error patterns.

7. The team makes changes in the student's educational program based on data.
   Intent: During the process of reviewing data, the team determines whether program changes/modifications need to be made in the environment, tasks, and tools. The team acts on these decisions and makes needed changes.

Common Errors in This Area:

- An observable, measurable student behavior is not specified as a target for change.

- Team members do not share responsibility for evaluating effectiveness.

- An environmentally appropriate means of data collection and strategies has not been identified.

- A schedule of program review for possible modification is not determined before implementation begins.

Assistive Technology in Transition

Transition for assistive technology users addresses the ways that a student's use of assistive technology devices and services is transferred from one setting to another. Assistive technology transition involves people from different classrooms, programs, buildings, or agencies working together to ensure continuity in the student's assistive technology use and thereby avoid a loss of skill, independence, and/or function. It is critical that all participants in transition planning recognize that the student is the only one who does not change during the transition process.

1. Transition plans address the assistive technology needs of the student, including: roles and training needs of team members; subsequent steps in assistive technology use; and followup after transitions take place.
   Intent: The transition plan assists the receiving agency/team in successfully providing needed supports for the AT user. This involves the assignment of responsibilities and the establishment of accountability.

2. Transition planning for students using assistive technology empowers the student to participate at a level appropriate to age and ability.
   Intent: Specific self determination skills are taught that enable the student to gradually assume responsibility for participation and leadership in AT transition planning as capacity develops. Assistive technology tools are provided, as needed, to support the student's participation.

3. Advocacy related to assistive technology use is recognized as critical and planned for by the teams involved in transition.
   Intent: Everyone involved in transition advocates for the student's progress, including the student's use of assistive technology. Specific advocacy tasks related to AT use are addressed and may be carried out by the student, the family, staff members or a representative.

4. Needs related to using assistive technology in the receiving environment are determined during the transition planning process.

Intent: Environmental requirements, skill demands, and needed AT support are determined in order to plan appropriately. This determination is made collaboratively and with active participation by representatives from sending and receiving environments.

5. Transition planning for students using assistive technology proceeds according to a time line based on the complexity of student's needs.

Intent: Transition planning time lines are adjusted based on the specific needs of the student and differences in environments. Complexity of assistive technology needs and issues will affect the time required for planning and transition activities; therefore, transition planning for students who use assistive technology may need to start sooner.

6. The transition team addresses specific equipment and funding issues such as transfer or acquisition of assistive technology and needed manuals and support documents.

Intent: A plan is developed to ensure that the AT equipment, hardware, and/or software arrives in working condition accompanied by any needed manuals. Provisions for ongoing maintenance and technical support are included in the plan.

Common Errors in This Area:

- Lack of self-determination, self-awareness and self-advocacy on part of the individual with a disability (and/or advocate).

- Lack of adequate long range planning on part of sending and receiving agencies (timelines).

- Inadequate communication and coordination.

- Failure to address funding responsibility.

- Inadequate evaluation (documentation, data, communication, valued across settings) process.

- Philosophical differences between sending and receiving agencies.

- Lack of understanding of the laws and responsibilities across agencies.

AT Professional Development and Training

This area defines the critical elements of quality professional development and training in assistive technology. Assistive technology professional development and training efforts should arise out of an ongoing, well-defined, sequential and comprehensive plan. Such a plan can develop and maintain the abilities of individuals at all levels of the organization to participate in the creation and provision of quality assistive technology services. The goal of assistive technology professional development and training is to increase educators' knowledge and skills in a variety of areas including, but not limited to: collaborative processes; a continuum of tools, strategies, and services; resources; legal issues; action planning; and data collection and analysis. Audiences for professional development and training include students, parents or caregivers, special education teachers, educational assistants, support personnel, general education personnel, administrators, assistive technology specialists, and others involved with students.

1. Comprehensive assistive technology professional development and training support the understanding that assistive technology devices and services enable students to accomplish IEP goals and objectives and make progress in the general curriculum.

Intent: The Individuals with Disabilities Education Act (IDEA) requires the provision of a free and appropriate public education (FAPE) for all children with disabilities. The Individualized Education Plan (IEP) defines FAPE for each student. The use of AT enables students to participate in and benefit from FAPE. The focus of all assistive technology professional development and training activities is to increase the ability of students to accomplish IEP goals and objectives.

2. The education agency has an assistive technology professional development and training plan that identifies the audiences, the purposes, the activities, the expected results, evaluation measures, and funding for assistive technology professional development and training.

Intent: The opportunity to learn the appropriate techniques and strategies is provided for each person involved in the delivery of assistive technology services. Professional development and training are offered at a variety of levels of expertise and are pertinent to individual roles.

3. The content of comprehensive AT professional development and training addresses all aspects of the selection, acquisition, and use of assistive technology.

    Intent: AT professional development and training address the development of a wide range of assessment, collaboration and implementation skills that enable educators to provide effective AT interventions for students. The AT professional development and training plan includes, but is not limited to, collaborative processes; the continuum of tools, strategies, and services; resources; legal issues; action planning; and data collection.

4. AT professional development and training address and are aligned with other local, state, and national professional development initiatives.

    Intent: Many of the effective practices used in the education of children with disabilities can be enhanced by the use of assistive technology. The functional use of AT is infused into all professional development efforts.

5. Assistive technology professional development and training include ongoing learning opportunities that utilize local, regional, and/or national resources.

    Intent: Professional development and training opportunities enable individuals to meet present needs and increase their knowledge of AT for use in the future. Training in AT occurs frequently enough to address new and emerging technologies and practices and is available on a repetitive and continuous schedule. A variety of AT professional development and training resources are used.

6. Professional development and training in assistive technology follow research-based models for adult learning that include multiple formats and are delivered at multiple skill levels.

    Intent: The design of professional development and training for AT recognizes adults as diverse learners who bring various levels of prior knowledge and experience to the training and can benefit from differentiated instruction using a variety of formats and diverse timeframes (e.g., workshops, distance learning, followup assistance, ongoing technical support).

7. The effectiveness of assistive technology professional development and training is evaluated by measuring changes in practice that result in improved student performance.

    Intent: Evidence is collected regarding the results of AT professional development and training. The professional development and training plan is modified based on these data in order to ensure changes educational practice that result in improved student performance.

Common Errors in This Area:

- The educational agency does not have a comprehensive plan for ongoing AT professional development and training.

- The educational agency's plan for professional development and training is not based on AT needs assessment and goals.

- Outcomes for professional development are not clearly defined and effectiveness is not measured in terms of practice and student performance.

- A continuum of ongoing professional development and training is not available.

- Professional development training focuses on the tools and not on the processes related to determining student needs and integrating technology into the curriculum.

- Professional development and training are provided for special educators but not for administrators, general educators, or instructional technology staff.

Quality Indicators for Administrative Support

This area defines the critical areas of administrative support and leadership for developing and delivering assistive technology services. It involves the development of policies, procedures, and other supports necessary to sustain all aspects of effective assistive technology programs.

1. The education agency has written procedural guidelines that ensure equitable access to assistive technology devices and services for students with disabilities, if required for FAPE.

   Intent: The education agency has clear written procedural guidelines that provide equal access to assistive technology devices and services for all students. Access to AT is the same for all students regardless of abilities, economic status or geographic location. All district personnel are familiar with the procedural guidelines.

2. The education agency has clearly defined and broadly disseminated policies and procedures for providing effective assistive technology devices and services.

   Intent: District personnel in special education and general education are familiar with the policies and procedures in both special education and general education. The procedures are readily available at each campus and all school personnel know how to access the procedures.

3. The education agency has written descriptions of job requirements, which include knowledge, skills, and responsibilities for staff members who provide assistive technology services.

   Intent: The education agency has clear written statements of job requirements that address the necessary AT knowledge, skills, and responsibilities for all staff members. This includes all personnel from the classroom through the central office. This may be reflected in a position description, assignment-of-duty statement, or some other written description.

4. The education agency employs a range of personnel with competencies needed to provide quality assistive technology services within their areas of primary responsibility.

   Intent: The agency employs staff members from the classroom through the central office who have AT knowledge and skills commensurate with job requirements. Although classroom teachers, supervisors, and purchasing agents, for example, may need different knowledge and skills related to assistive technology, all must be knowledgeable for the system to work well.

5. The education agency includes assistive technology in the technology planning and budgeting process.

   Intent: Historically, the AT needs of the agency have either been separate or omitted. A comprehensive technology plan provides for the technology needs of all students in both general education and special education.

6. The education agency provides continuous learning opportunities about assistive technology devices, strategies, and resources for staff, family, and students.

   Intent: The training addresses the needs of the student, the family, and all the staff involved with the student. Ongoing training and technical assistance opportunities are readily accessible to all members of the IEP team. The training and technical assistance includes training on AT devices, strategies, and resources to support IEP goals and objectives.

7. The education agency uses a systematic procedure to evaluate the components of assistive technology services to ensure accountability for student progress.

   Intent: There is a clear systematic procedure with which all administrators are familiar and use regularly. This procedure is used consistently across the agency at both central office and building levels. The components of this process include budgeting, planning, delivery, and evaluation of AT services.

Common Errors in This Area:

- If policies and guidelines are developed, they are not known widely enough to ensure equitable application by all IEP teams.

- It is not clearly understood that the primary purpose of assistive technology in school settings is to support implementation of the IEP for the provision of a free appropriate public education (FAPE).

- Personnel have been appointed to head assistive technology efforts, but resources to support those efforts have not been allocated (time, a budget for devices, professional development, etc.).

- Assistive technology leadership personnel try to or are expected to do all of the assistive technology work and fail to meet expectations.

- Assistive technology services are established but their effectiveness is never evaluated.

The QIAT Self-Evaluation Matrices

The QIAT Self-Evaluation Matrices (QIAT Consortium Leadership Team, 2001) were developed in response to formative evaluation data indicating a need for a model to assist in applying QIAT (see Appendix A). The QIAT matrices are based on the idea that change does not happen immediately, but rather, moves toward the ideal in a series of steps that take place over time. The QIAT matrices use the Innovation Configuration Matrix (ICM) developed by Hall and Hord (1985) as a structural model. The ICM provides descriptive steps, ranging from the unacceptable to the ideal that can be used as benchmarks to determine the current status of practice related to a specific goal or objective and guide continuous improvement toward the ideal. Thus, it enables users to determine areas of strength that can be built upon as well as areas of challenge in need of improvement.

When the QIAT matrices are used to guide a collaborative self-evaluation conducted by a diverse group of stakeholders within an agency, the information gained can be used to plan for changes that lead to improvement throughout the organization in manageable and attainable steps. The matrices can also be used to evaluate the level to which expected or planned-for changes have taken place by periodically analyzing changes in service delivery over time. Similarly, when completed by an individual or a team, the results of the

self-evaluation can be used to measure areas of strength and plan for needed professional development, training, or support needed by the individual or team. However, when the matrices are used by an individual or a team, it is important to realize that the results can only reasonably reflect perceptions of the services in which that individual or team is involved and may not reflect the typical services within the organization. Since a primary goal of QIAT is to increase the quality and consistency of assistive technology services to all students throughout the organization, the perception that an individual or small group is working at the level of best practices may still indicate a need to increase the quality and consistency of services throughout the organization.

Since the descriptive steps included in the QIAT matrices are meant to provide illustrative examples, they may not be specifically appropriate, as written, for all environments. Therefore, people using the matrices may wish to revise the descriptive steps to align them more closely to specific environments. However, when doing this, care must be taken that the revised steps do not compromise the intent of the quality indictor to which they apply.

QIAT Research

Although the formative evaluation process used to the development of QIAT enhanced the probability that QIAT would be useful (Zabala et al., 2000), research efforts are in progress to determine the perceived validity and utility of the indicators to groups of people with acknowledged leadership, expertise, and experience in assistive technology from each of the groups for whom QIAT is intended (school district personnel, individual service providers, consumers and families, higher education personnel, and policy makers). The specific purpose of the investigation (Zabala, 2004) was to determine the degree to which the expert reviewers believe a need for quality indicators exists, the degree to which they perceive each of the quality indicators to be important to people with responsibilities, interests and perspectives similar to theirs, and the degree to which they believe QIAT will be useful in meeting the needs of others with similar responsibilities and perspectives. The study involves only the first six areas of QIAT since the last two were not yet developed when the research was initiated.

In brief, preliminary results indicate that greater than 85% of assistive technology leaders involved in the research believe each of the quality indicators is important to people with interests and responsibilities similar to their own. Further, results of the research indicate there is a strong need for quality indicators and that QIAT either is or will be very useful to themselves and others. In addition to reviewing QIAT for need, utility, and validity, the leaders involved in the investigation provided extensive qualitative feedback that will be instrumental in shaping revisions to QIAT that will be required over time in response to the changing needs of students, as well as changes in policies, expectations, educational tasks, and technology.

One revision, based on qualitative data gathered during the research, has already been accomplished. The area of Administrative Support, which pertains to the systemic provision of assistive technology services agency-wide, has been moved from the beginning of the QIAT document to the end where it is paired with the other systemic area, Professional Development. Although the wording of QIAT included in this chapter is current as of this writing, other changes will be made based on this research and input from the field. It is important to visit the QIAT web site (www.qiat.org) for periodic updates or additions.

Ongoing QIAT Activities

QIAT is and will always be a work in-progress that requires ongoing activities related to development and implementation. Thus, the version of QIAT contained in this chapter will, undoubtedly, change over time in response to the changing needs and tasks of students and those who love and support them, changes in the tasks expected of educational service providers, changes in the state of assistive technology service delivery, and, of course, the inevitable changes in technology. Flexibility and

fluidity based on strong principles and supported by research are paramount to the utility of QIAT. There are three major ways in which interested people become a part of the QIAT Community and be involved in the ongoing QIAT work.

Web Site

One of the most active methods for sharing and participating in QIAT work is through the QIAT web site, hosted by the National Assistive Technology Research Institute (NATRI) (Hasselbring & Lahm, 2000) at the University of Kentucky. The web site (www.qiat.org) contains not only the most current version of QIAT, but also drafts of QIAT at all stages. This provides a historical perspective that may be useful to researchers and others interested in how QIAT has evolved. The web site also contains resources and links that people involved in QIAT activities have found useful, information about upcoming QIAT conference sessions and work sessions, and a section about research related to quality assistive technology services.

Two opportunities for ongoing participation that are also found on the website are QIAT Summits and the QIAT List.

Summits

QIAT Summits are held every other year in different parts of the country. A QIAT Summit is not a conference, but a work session consisting of a series of activities during which participants work collaboratively in large and small groups to:

1. Deepen understanding of the purpose, scope, and potential uses of the quality indicators;
2. Discuss, develop, or plan for tools that can assist with implementation of the quality indicators, and,
3. Revise, refine, and expand upon the quality indicators as needed for comprehensive coverage and relevance.

Summits provide a way to expand the number of stakeholders who participate in the actual development and writing of the quality indicators and in the sharing and development of tools that support the application of QIAT, such as the QIAT Self-Evaluation Matrices. Anyone interested in assistive technology services is invited to attend. Costs are kept as low as possible. Summit participants are representative of all groups identified as potential consumers of QIAT work, including consumers, service providers, administrators, higher education professionals, and policy makers.

Details about the specific activities, participants, and results of previous QIAT Summits and the proposed focus and activities of upcoming Summits are available on the QIAT website (www.qiat.org).

QIAT List

The QIAT List is by far the most active and easily accessible ongoing opportunity for involvement in QIAT work. The QIAT List is an electronic mailing list supported by Listserv™ software and facilitated by Joy Zabala. The QIAT List was started in 1997 to facilitate widespread engagement in collegial conversation the about the quality indicators and topics related to their continued development. As QIAT work progressed, however, discussions broadened to focus not only on the indicators, but also on a range of topics that pertain to quality assistive technology services. Virtually any question or concern that any list participant cares to open to collegial conversation is appropriate for posting on the list. Thus, discussions on topics such as report writing, research, staff qualifications and certification, device specifics, state standards, and the selection, acquisition, and use of assistive technology tools are common on the QIAT List.

The QIAT List started in 1990 with two participants, had grown to over 360 participants by 2001 (Zabala, 2001). Currently over 950 people from across the United States and several other countries are subscribed to the QIAT List. Information about joining the QIAT List or viewing the archives of the thousands and thousands of messages that have been sent since the inception of the list is available on the QIAT web site (www.qiat.org).

Conclusion

QIAT began as a response to a need reflected in scholarly research and in the professional and personal experiences of consumers, service providers, and staff developers at both preservice and inservice levels. QIAT provides support for improvements in the quality and consistency of assistive technology services at every level, as evidenced by its reported use to shape practice at national, state, and local levels, as well as in higher education and research.

To date, the QIAT has been included in policy documents and operational guidelines at district and state levels. Numerous groups have used the QIAT Matrices to systematically evaluate assistive technology services and plan for incremental, continuous improvement. Many service providers have used QIAT to improve their services, to communicate the importance of the various aspects of assistive technology services to others, and as a tool to encourage collaboration throughout service delivery processes.

Several researchers around the country have used QIAT to guide various aspects of their research. Among the researchers making use of QIAT are those involved in the National Assistive Technology Research Institute (NATRI) at the University of Kentucky (Hasselbring & Lahm, 2000) to whom members of the QIAT Consortium serve as an advisory panel. Additionally, research about the application of QIAT will subsequently appear in scholarly literature, as several doctoral candidates are including QIAT in their dissertation research.

Whether or not guides such as QIAT, when consistently used for planning, delivering, and evaluating assistive technology services, contribute to changes in professional practices that lead to measurable changes in student participation and improved educational results is an important empirical question that needs to be answered. However, it is clear that without such guides, the probability that needed changes will occur is low.

There is much evidence, both research-based and practical, that underscores the importance of developing and sustaining consistent quality assistive technology services in educational settings. Perhaps the most compelling evidence is found in statements of those for whom QIAT is intended. A service provider said, "Having quality indicators is essential to effective assistive technology service delivery. They provide a frame of reference and a way for us to measure the quality of our efforts. The better and more systematic we are at addressing assistive technology needs, the more likely we are to improve student outcomes" (Zabala, 2002). The hope in this comment is found in the poignant words of an adult consumer who received no assistive technology services as a student, "I wish something of this nature had been available twenty years ago. Awareness...has grown but many still dwell in the dark ages. I hope that QIAT will bring light into their world..." (Zabala, 2002).

References

Blackhurst, A.E., & Lahm, E.A. (2000). Technology and exceptionality foundations. In J.D. Lindsey (Ed.), *Technology and Exceptional Individuals* (pp. 3-45). Austin, TX: Pro-Ed.

Blackhurst, A.E., MacArthur, C.A., & Byrom, E.M. (1987). Microcomputer competencies for special education professors. *Teacher Education and Special Education, 10*(4), 153-160.

Bowser, G., Korsten, J., Reed, P., & Zabala, J. (1999). Quality indicators for effective assistive technology services. *TAM Connector, 11*(5), 1-5.

Bowser, G., & Reed, P. (1995). Education TECH points for assistive technology planning. *Journal of Special Education Technology, 12*(4), 325-338.

Calculator, S., & Jorgenson, C. M. (1991). Integrating AAC instruction into regular education settings: Expounding on best practices. *Augmentative and Alternative Communication, 7*, 204-214.

Cook, A.M., & Hussey, S.M. (1995). *Assistive technologies: Principles and practice*. St. Louis, MO: Mosby.

Gray, S. (1997). AAC in the educational setting. In S.L. Glennen & D.C. DeCoste (Eds.), *Handbook of augmentative and alternative communication* (pp. 547-597). San Diego, CA: Singular Publishing Group.

Hall, G. E., & Hord, S. M. (1987) *Change in schools: Facilitating the process*. Ithaca: State University of New York Press.

Hasselbring, T.H., & Lahm, E.A. (2000). *University of Kentucky assistive technology research institute*. Unpublished manuscript, University of Kentucky, Lexington.

Hutinger, P., Johanson, J., & Stoneburner, R. (1996). Assistive technology applications in educational programs of children with multiple disabilities: A case study report on the state of the practice. *Journal of Special Education Technology, 13*(1), 16-35.

Individuals with Disabilities Education Act of 1990, PL 101-476. (October 30, 1990), Title 20, U.S.C. 1400 *et seq*.: U.S. Statutes at Large, 104, 1103-1151.

Individuals with Disabilities Education Act, Amendments of 1997, Public Law No. 105-17, ◊ 602, U.S.C. 1401 [On-line]. Available: www.ed.gov/offices/OSERS/IDEA/the_law.html

MacGregor, G., & Pachuski, P. (1996). Assistive technology in schools: Are teachers ready, able, and supported? *Journal of Special Education Technology, 13*(1), 4-15.

QIAT Consortium Leadership Team (2001). *The QIAT self-evaluation matrices*. Retrieved March 1, 2003, from *www.qiat.org*.

Schrag, J. (1990). *OSEP policy letter*. Washington, DC: U.S. Office of Education.

Todis, B. (1996). Assistive technology in educational settings. *Journal of Special Education Technology, 13*(2), 49-61.

Todis, B., & Walker, H.M. (1993). User perspectives on assistive technology in educational settings. *Focus on Exceptional Children, 26*(3), 1-16.

Zabala, J. S. (1996). SETTing the stage for success: Building success through effective use of assistive technology. *Proceedings of the Southeast Augmentative Communication Conference* (pp. 129-187). Birmingham, AL: United Cerebral Palsy of Greater Birmingham.

Zabala, J. (2001). *Exploring the effectiveness of an electronic mailing list for creating and maintaining a national conversation on assistive technology service provision in school settings*. Unpublished manuscript., University of Kentucky, Lexington.

Zabala, J. (2002). [Development and evaluation of quality indicators for assistive technology services]. Unpublished raw data.

Zabala, J. S. (2004). *Development and evaluation of quality indicators for assistive technology services*. Unpublished doctoral dissertation, University of Kentucky, Lexington.

Zabala, J., Bowser, G., Blunt, M., Hartsell, K., Carl, D., Korsten, J., Davis, S., Marfilius, S., Deterding, C., McCloskey-Dale, S., Foss, T., Nettleton, S., Hamman, T., & Reed, P. (2000). Quality indicators for assistive technology services in school settings. *Journal of Special Education Technology, 15*(4), 25-36.

Zabala, J., Carl, D., & Mataya, C., (1994). *What's the big IDEA?: Legal and practical aspects of assistive technology in school settings.* Professional development conducted at the Closing the Gap Conference on Technology in Special Education and Rehabilitation, Minneapolis, MN

Appendix A.

QIAT Self-Evaluation and Planning Matrix: Administrative Support

Quality Indicator	Unacceptable	Variations			Promising Practice
1. The education agency has written procedural guidelines that ensure equitable access to assistive technology devices and services for students with disabilities, if required by FAPE.	(1) No written procedural guidelines are in place.	(2) Written procedural guidelines for few components of AT service delivery are in place (i.e., assessment or consideration).	(3) Written procedural guidelines that address several components of AT service delivery are in place.	(4) Written procedural guidelines that address most components of AT service delivery are in place.	(5) Comprehensive written procedural guidelines that address all components of AT service delivery are in place.
2. The education agency has clearly defined and broadly disseminated policies and procedures for providing effective assistive technology devices and services.	(1) No policies or procedures disseminated and no plan to disseminate.	(2) A plan for dissemination exists, but has not been implemented.	(3) Procedures are disseminated to a few staff who work directly with AT.	(4) Procedures are disseminated to most agency personnel and generally used.	(5) Procedures are disseminated to all agency personnel and consistently used.
3. The education agency has written descriptions of job requirements, which include knowledge, skills, and responsibilities for staff members who provide assistive technology services.	(1) No job requirements relating to AT are written.	(2) Job requirements related to AT are written only for a few specific personnel who provide AT services.	(3) Job requirements related to AT are written for most personnel who provide AT services but are not clearly aligned to job responsibilities.	(4) Job requirements related to AT are written for most personnel who provide AT services and are generally aligned to job responsibilities.	(5) Job requirements related to AT are written for all personnel who provide AT services and are clearly aligned to job responsibilities.
4. The education agency employs a range of personnel with competencies needed to provide quality assistive technology services within their areas of primary responsibility.	(1) AT competencies are not considered in hiring, assigning, or evaluating personnel.	(2) AT competencies are recognized as an added value in an employee, but are not sought.	(3) AT competencies are recognized and sought for specific personnel.	(4) AT competencies are generally valued and used in hiring, assigning, and evaluating personnel.	(5) AT competencies are consistently valued and used in hiring, assigning, and evaluating personnel.

(continued next page)

QIAT Self-Evaluation and Planning Matrix: Administrative Support (continued)

Quality Indicator	Unacceptable	Variations			Promising Practice
5. The education agency includes assistive technology in the technology planning and budgeting process.	(1) There is no planning and budgeting process for AT.	(2) AT planning and budgeting is a special education function that is not included in the agency-wide technology planning and budgeting process.	(3) AT is sometimes included in the agency-wide technology planning and budgeting process, but is inadequate to meet AT needs throughout the agency.	(4) AT is generally included in agency-wide technology planning and budgeting process in a way that meets most AT needs throughout the agency.	(5) AT is included in the agency-wide technology planning and budgeting process in way that meets AT needs throughout the agency.
6. The education agency provides continuous learning opportunities about assistive technology devices, strategies, and resources for staff, family, and students.	(1) No learning opportunities related to AT are provided.	(2) Learning opportunities related to AT are provided on a crisis basis only. Learning opportunities may not be available to all who need them.	(3) Learning opportunities related to AT are provided to some individuals on a predefined schedule.	(4) Learning opportunities related to AT are provided on a predefined schedule to most individuals with some followup opportunities.	(5) Learning opportunities related to AT are provided on an ongoing basis to address the changing needs of students with disabilities, their families, and the staff who serve them.
7. The education agency uses a systematic procedure to evaluate the components of assistive technology services to ensure accountability for student progress.	(1) AT services are not evaluated.	(2) Varying procedures are used to evaluate some AT services. Procedures may or may not be based on student progress.	(3) A systematic procedure, sometimes linked to student progress, is inconsistently used to evaluate AT services.	(4) A systematic procedure, linked to student progress, is generally used to evaluate AT services.	(5) A systematic procedure, linked to student progress, is consistently used throughout the agency.

QIAT Self-Evaluation and Planning Matrix: Consideration of Need

Quality Indicator	Unacceptable	Variations			Promising Practice
1. Assistive technology devices and services are considered for all students with disabilities regardless of type or severity of disability.	(1) AT is not considered for students with disabilities.	(2) AT is considered only for students with severe disabilities or students in specific disability categories.	(3) AT is considered for all students with disabilities, but the consideration is inconsistently based on the unique educational needs of the student.	(4) AT is considered for all students with disabilities, and the consideration is generally based on the unique educational needs of the student.	(5) AT is considered for all students with disabilities, and the consideration is consistently based on the unique educational needs of the student.
2. The IEP team has the knowledge and skills to make informed assistive technology decisions.	(1) The team does not have the knowledge or skills needed to make informed AT decisions. The team does not seek help when needed.	(2) Individual team members have some of the knowledge and skills needed to make informed AT decisions. The team does not seek help when needed.	(3) Team members sometimes combine knowledge and skills to make informed AT decisions. The team does not always seek help when needed.	(4) Team members generally combine their knowledge and skills to make informed AT decisions. The team seeks help when needed.	(5) The team consistently uses collective knowledge and skills to make informed AT decisions. The team seeks help when needed.
3. The IEP team uses a collaborative decision-making process based on data about the student, environments, and tasks to make determinations.	(1) No process is established for IEP teams to use to make AT decisions.	(2) A process is established for IEP teams to use to make AT decisions, but it is not collaborative.	(3) A collaborative process is established but not generally used by IEP teams to make AT decisions.	(4) A collaborative process is established and generally used by IEP teams to make AT decisions.	(5) A collaborative process is established and consistently used by IEP teams to make AT decisions.
4. A continuum of assistive technology devices and services is explored.	(1) The team considers only one assistive technology device.	(2) The team only considers readily available technology.	(3) The team sometimes explores a continuum of AT devices and services but may not address all of the student's current needs (e.g., communication but not mobility).	(4) The team generally explores a continuum of assistive technology devices and services are based on all of the student's current and near-future needs.	(5) The team consistently explores the full continuum of assistive technology devices and services based on current and near-future needs.

(continued next page)

QIAT Self-Evaluation and Planning Matrix: Consideration of Need (continued)

Quality Indicator	Unacceptable	Variations			Promising Practice
5. Decisions regarding the need for assistive technology devices and services are made based on access to the curriculum and the student's IEP goals and objectives.	(1) Decisions about a student's need for AT are not connected to IEP goals or the general curriculum.	(2) Decisions about a student's need for AT are based on either access to the curriculum/IEP goals or the general curriculum, not both.	(3) Decisions about a student's need for AT sometimes are based on both the student's IEP goals and general education curricular tasks.	(4) Decisions about a student's need for AT generally are based on both the student's IEP goals and general education curricular tasks.	(5) Decisions about a student's need for AT consistently are based on both the student's IEP goals and general education curricular tasks.
6. Decisions regarding the need for assistive technology devices and services and supporting data are documented.	(1) Documentation of consideration of a student's possible need for AT devices and services is not in the IEP.	(2) Documentation of consideration of a student's possible need for AT devices and services is inconsistent and may be limited to a "yes/no" check box.	(3) Documentation of consideration of a student's need for AT devices and services is only included if AT is needed.	(4) Documentation of consideration of a student's need for AT devices and services generally is included whether or not AT is needed.	(5) Documentation of consideration of a student's need for AT devices and services consistently is included whether or not AT is needed.

Appendix A.

QIAT Self-Evaluation and Planning Matrix: Assessment of Need

Quality Indicator	Unacceptable	Variations			Promising Practice
1. Assistive technology assessment procedures are clearly defined and consistently used.	(1) No procedures are defined.	(2) Some assessment procedures are defined, but not generally used.	(3) Procedures are defined and used only by specialized personnel.	(4) Procedures are clearly defined and generally used in both special and general education.	(5) Clearly defined procedures are used by everyone involved in the assessment process.
2. Assistive technology assessments are conducted by a multidisciplinary team that actively involves the student and family or caregivers.	(1) A designated individual with no prior knowledge of the student's needs or technology conducts assessments.	(2) A designated person or group of individuals who have knowledge of technology, but not of the student's needs, environments, or tasks conducts assessments.	(3) A designated team with knowledge of assistive technology conducts assessments with limited input from individuals who have knowledge of the student's needs, environments, and tasks.	(4) A team whose members have direct knowledge of the student's needs, environments, and tasks, and of assistive technology generally conducts assessments.	(5) A flexible team formed on the basis of knowledge or expertise in the areas of the individual student's needs, environments, and tasks, and of assistive technology conducts assessments.
3. Assistive technology assessments are conducted in the student's customary environments.	(1) No component of the AT assessment is conducted in any of the student's customary environments.	(2) No component of the AT assessment is conducted in any of the student's customary environments; however, data about the customary environments are sought.	(3) Functional components of AT assessments are sometimes conducted in the student's customary environments.	(4) Functional components of AT assessments are generally conducted in the student's customary environments.	(5) Functional components of AT assessments are consistently conducted in the student's customary environments.
4. Assistive technology assessments, including needed trials, are completed within reasonable time lines.	(1) AT assessments are not completed within agency time lines.	(2) AT assessments are frequently out of compliance with time lines.	(3) AT assessments are completed within a reasonable timeline and may or may not include initial trials.	(4) AT assessments are completed within a reasonable timeline and include at least initial trials.	(5) AT assessments are conducted in a timely manner and include a plan for ongoing assessment and trials in customary environments.

(continued next page)

QIAT Self-Evaluation and Planning Matrix: Assessment of Need (continued)

Quality Indicator	Unacceptable	Variations			Promising Practice
5. Recommendations from assistive technology assessments are based on data about the student, environments, and tasks.	(1) Recommendations are not data based.	(2) Recommendations are based on incomplete data from limited sources.	(3) Recommendations are sometimes based on data about student performance on typical tasks in customary environments.	(4) Recommendations are generally based on data about student performance on typical tasks in customary environments.	(5) Recommendations are consistently based on data about student performance on typical tasks in customary environments.
6. The assessment provides the IEP team with documented recommendations about assistive technology devices and services.	(1) Recommendations are not documented.	(2) Documented recommendations include only devices. Recommendations about services are not documented.	(3) Documented recommendations may or may not include sufficient information about devices and services to guide decisionmaking and program development.	(4) Documented recommendations generally include sufficient information about devices and services to guide decisionmaking and program development.	(5) Documented recommendations consistently include sufficient information about devices and services to guide decisionmaking and program development.
7. Assistive technology needs are reassessed by request, or as needed, based on changes in the student, environments, and/or tasks.	(1) AT needs are not reassessed.	(2) AT needs are only reassessed when requested. Reassessment is done formally and no ongoing AT assessment takes place.	(3) AT needs are reassessed on an annual basis or upon request. Reassessment may include some ongoing and formal assessment strategies.	(4) AT use is frequently monitored. AT needs are generally reassessed if current tools and strategies are ineffective. Reassessment generally includes ongoing assessment strategies and includes formal assessment, if indicated.	(5) AT use is continually monitored. AT needs are consistently reassessed if current tools and strategies are ineffective. Reassessment consistently includes ongoing assessment strategies and includes formal assessment, if indicated.

QIAT Self-Evaluation and Planning Matrix: Assistive Technology in the IEP

Quality Indicator	Variations				
	Unacceptable				Promising Practice
1. The education agency has guidelines for documenting assistive technology needs in the IEP, and everyone on the IEP team is aware of them.	(1) The agency does not have guidelines for documenting AT in the IEP.	(2) The agency has guidelines for documenting AT in the IEP, but team members are not aware of them.	(3) The agency has guidelines for documenting AT in the IEP, but members of some teams are aware of them.	(4) The agency has guidelines for documenting AT in the IEP, and members of most teams are aware of them.	(5) The agency has guidelines for documenting AT in the IEP, and members of all teams are aware of them.
2. Assistive technology is included in the IEP in a manner that provides a clear and complete description of the devices and services to be provided and used.	(1) Assistive technology devices and services are not documented in the IEP.	(2) Some AT devices and services are minimally documented. Documentation does not include sufficient information to support effective implementation.	(3) Required AT devices and services are documented. Documentation sometimes includes sufficient information to support effective implementation.	(4) Required AT devices and services are documented. Documentation generally includes sufficient information to support effective implementation.	(5) Required AT devices and services are documented. Documentation consistently includes sufficient information to support effective implementation.
3. Assistive technology is used as a tool to support achievement of IEP goals and objectives as well as participation and progress in the general curriculum.	(1) AT use is not linked to IEP goals and objectives or participation and progress in the general curriculum.	(2) AT use is sometimes linked to IEP goals and objectives but not linked to the general curriculum.	(3) AT use is linked to IEP goals and objectives and sometimes linked to the general curriculum.	(4) AT is linked to IEP goals and objectives and is generally linked to the general curriculum.	(5) AT is linked to the IEP goals and objectives and is consistently linked to the general curriculum.
4. IEP content regarding assistive technology use is written in language that describes measurable and observable outcomes.	(1) The IEP does not describe outcomes to be achieved through AT use.	(2) The IEP describes outcomes to be achieved through AT use, but they are not measurable.	(3) The IEP describes outcomes to be achieved through AT use, but only some are measurable.	(4) The IEP generally describes observable, measurable outcomes to be achieved through AT use.	(5) The IEP consistently describes observable, measurable outcomes to be achieved through AT use.
5. All services needed to implement assistive technology use are documented in the IEP.	(1) Services needed to support AT use are not documented.	(2) Some services are documented, but they do not adequately support AT use.	(3) Services are documented and are sometimes adequate to support AT use.	(4) Services are documented and are generally adequate to support AT use.	(5) Services are documented and are consistently adequate to support AT use.

QIAT Self-Evaluation and Planning Matrix: Implementation

Quality Indicator	Unacceptable	Variations			Promising Practice
1. Assistive technology implementation proceeds according to a collaboratively developed plan.	(1) There is no implementation plan.	(2) Individual team members may develop AT implementation plans independently.	(3) Some team members collaborate in the development of an AT implementation plan.	(4) Most team members collaborate in the development of AT implementation plan.	(5) All team members collaborate in the development of a comprehensive AT implementation plan.
2. Assistive technology is integrated into the curriculum and daily activities of the student.	(1) AT included in the IEP is rarely used.	(2) AT is used in isolation with no links to the student's curriculum and/or daily activities.	(3) AT is sometimes integrated into the student's curriculum and daily activities.	(4) AT is generally integrated into the student's curriculum and daily activities.	(5) AT is fully integrated into the student's curriculum and daily activities.
3. Team members in all of the student's environments share responsibility for implementation of the plan.	(1) Responsibility for implementation is not accepted by any team member.	(2) Responsibility for implementation is assigned to one team member.	(3) Responsibility for implementation is shared by some team members in some environments.	(4) Responsibility for implementation is generally shared by most team members in most environments.	(5) Responsibility for implementation is consistently shared among team members across all environments.
4. The student uses multiple strategies to accomplish tasks and the use of assistive technology may be included in those strategies.	(1) No strategies are provided to support the accomplishment of tasks.	(2) Only one strategy is provided to support the accomplishment of tasks.	(3) Multiple strategies are provided. Students are sometimes encouraged to select and use the most appropriate strategy for each task.	(4) Multiple strategies are provided. Students are generally encouraged to select and use the most appropriate strategy for each task.	(5) Multiple strategies are provided. Students are consistently encouraged to select and use the most appropriate strategy for each task.
5. Training for student, family, and staff is an integral part of implementation.	(1) AT training needs have not been determined.	(2) Training needs are initially identified for student, family, and staff, but no training has been provided.	(3) Initial AT training is sometimes provided to student, family, and staff.	(4) Initial and followup AT training is generally provided to student, family, and staff.	(5) Ongoing AT training is provided to student, family, and staff, as needed, based on changing needs.

(continued next page)

QIAT Self-Evaluation and Planning Matrix: Implementation (continued)

Quality Indicator	Unacceptable	Variations			Promising Practice
6. Assistive technology implementation is initially based on assessment data and is adjusted based on performance data.	(1) AT implementation is based on equipment availability and the limited knowledge of team members, not on student data.	(2) AT implementation is loosely based on initial assessment data and rarely adjusted.	(3) AT implementation is based on initial assessment data and is sometimes adjusted, as needed, based on student progress.	(4) AT implementation is based on initial assessment data and is generally adjusted, as needed, based on student progress.	(5) AT implementation is based on initial assessment data and is consistently adjusted, as needed, based on student progress.
7. Assistive technology implementation includes management and maintenance of equipment and materials.	(1) Equipment and materials are not managed or maintained. Students rarely have access to the equipment and materials they	(2) Equipment and materials are managed and maintained on a crisis basis. Students frequently do not have access to the equipment and materials they require.	(3) Equipment and materials are managed and maintained so that students sometimes have access to the equipment and materials they require.	(4) Equipment and materials are managed and maintained so that students generally have access to the equipment and materials they require.	(5) Equipment and materials are effectively managed and maintained so that students consistently have access to the equipment and materials they require.

QIAT Self-Evaluation and Planning Matrix: Evaluation of Effectiveness

Quality Indicator	Unacceptable	Variations			Promising Practice
1. Team members share clearly defined responsibilities to ensure that data are collected, evaluated, and interpreted by capable and credible team members.	(1) Responsibilities for data collection, evaluation, or interpretation of data are not defined.	(2) Responsibilities for data collection, evaluation, or interpretation of data are assigned to one team member.	(3) Responsibilities for collection, evaluation and interpretation of data are shared by some team members.	(4) Responsibilities for collection, evaluation and interpretation of data are shared by most team members.	(5) Responsibilities for collection, evaluation and interpretation of data are consistently shared by team members.
2. Data are collected on specific student behaviors that have been identified by the team and are related to one or more goals.	(1) The team neither identifies specific changes in student behaviors expected from AT use nor collects data.	(2) The team identifies student behaviors and collects data, but the behaviors are either not specific or not related to IEP goal(s).	(3) The team identifies specific student behaviors related to IEP goals, but inconsistently collects data.	(4) The team identifies specific student behaviors related to IEP goals, and generally collects data.	(5) The team identifies specific student behaviors related to IEP goals and consistently collects data on changes in those behaviors.
3. Evaluation of effectiveness reflects the objective measurement of changes in the student's performance (e.g., student preferences, productivity, participation, independence, quantity, quality, speed, accuracy, frequency, or spontaneity).	(1) Effectiveness is not evaluated.	(2) Evaluation of effectiveness is based on something other than student performance, such as changes in staff behavior and/or environmental factors.	(3) Evaluation of effectiveness is based on subjective information about student performance.	(4) Evaluation of effectiveness is generally based on objective information about student performance from a few data sources.	(5) Evaluation of effectiveness is consistently based on objective information about student performance obtained from a variety of data sources.
4. Effectiveness is evaluated across environments including during naturally occurring opportunities as well as structured activities.	(1) Effectiveness is not evaluated in any environment.	(2) Effectiveness is evaluated only during structured opportunities in controlled environments (e.g. massed trials data).	(3) Effectiveness is evaluated during structured activities across environments and a few naturally occurring opportunities.	(4) Effectiveness is generally evaluated during naturally occurring opportunities and structured activities in multiple environments.	(5) Effectiveness is consistently evaluated during naturally occurring opportunities and structured activities in multiple environments.

(continued next page)

Appendix A.

QIAT Self-Evaluation and Planning Matrix: Evaluation of Effectiveness (continued)

Quality Indicator	Unacceptable	Variations			Promising Practice
5. Evaluation of effectiveness is a dynamic, responsive, ongoing process that is reviewed periodically.	(1) No process is used to evaluate effectiveness.	(2) Evaluation of effectiveness only takes place annually, but the team does not make program changes based on data.	(3) Evaluation of effectiveness only takes place annually and the team uses the data to make annual program changes.	(4) Evaluation of effectiveness takes place on an on-going basis and team generally uses the data to make program changes.	(5) Evaluation of effectiveness takes place on an on-going basis and the team consistently uses the data to make program changes.
6. Data collected provide a means to analyze response patterns and student performance.	(1) No data are collected.	(2) Data are collected on staff behavior or environmental factors rather than student performance.	(3) Data are collected on student performance, but data are not sufficient to allow necessary analysis.	(4) Data are collected on student performance and are generally sufficient to allow necessary analysis.	(5) Data are collected on student performance and are consistently sufficient to allow necessary analysis.
7. The team makes changes in the student's educational program based on data.	(1) Program changes are never made.	(2) Program changes are made in the absence of data.	(3) Program changes are loosely linked to student performance data.	(4) Program changes are generally linked to student performance data.	(5) Program changes are consistently linked to student performance data.

11

Teaming and Assistive Technology in Educational Settings

Cathy Bodine and Maureen Melonis

What Is a Team?

A team is defined as an identified group of two or more people who interact dynamically, have complimentary skills, are committed to a common purpose, set of performance goals and approach for which they hold themselves mutually accountable (Katzenbach & Smith, 1993; Parette & Brotherson, 1996; Paris, Salas, & Cannon-Bowers, 2000). A more fundamental definition of teaming can be found in the preface to Rainforth and York's 1997 edition of *Collaborative Teams for Students with Disabilities*. Jennifer York's son Sam provided a succinct and credible definition of teaming by sharing his 7-year-old perspective: "Teaming means you work together, no matter what. You do it because you'll come up with better ideas. And, if (or when) you disagree, you just figure it out-without fighting" (Rainforth, York-Barr, 1997). The concept of teaming is prolific with numerous research articles describing the characteristics of effective teams (Cummings, 1981; Dyer, 1984; Friedlander, 1987; Larson & Lefasto, 1989; Sundstrom, DeMeuse, & Futrell, 1990). Quite frankly, we believe Sam got it right on his first try!

Too many skills and too much knowledge are required to function independently in the complicated and fast-paced world of education and assistive technology. The individual model is no longer supported in the public school environment. Educators' jobs are more complex than ever before and much is expected of them. Teachers and related services personnel are required to rapidly respond to the needs of a diverse and ever-changing school population, rapidly changing technology, and demands for excellence and accountability from all segments of society (Fullan, 1993). Individuals must work collaboratively as a team in order to stay abreast of rapid changes in assistive technology, to meet work demands, and to stay current on other relevant topics such as child development, disability topics, funding and legislation. It is no longer a question of whether we should work as a team, but rather what are the strategies that make teamwork most effective. Teaming has evolved during the past century and is now recognized as the preferred means to accomplish common aims. Teaming allows groups of people to come together around mutual goals to meet the specific needs of a child through a collaborative relationship.

There are literally thousands of books, articles and Web-based resources filled with information on the value of teams, the stages of teaming, and the inherent benefits of using teaming as an organizational process. In this chapter we have chosen to summarize those findings, beginning as early as 1933, through today. Each of these authors has something important to contribute as we outline strategies and ideas designed to make the assistive technology teaming process more effective within today's educational environment. We will begin the chapter with a discussion of the evolution of legislation and teaming concepts, followed by an overview of how teams have evolved, the role of team members, and how the educational model effects teaming. We will provide strategies to build and maintain effective teams by outlining some typical team pitfalls as well as creative solutions.

Evolution of Teaming

The concept of working as a team is not new. Some of our earliest history lessons focus on individuals coming together, as a team to build safe communities, gather food and raise children. The past forty or so years have shown a significant upsurge in the literature on teaming with numerous articles stressing the value of teaming within business and the education communities. Of particular interest are the different rationales chosen by the two communities for establishing teams. In the business world, teaming has been adopted because it is viewed as the most economic method to accomplish goals. Unlike the educational model, which views teaming as a "helping" model, the American business community has adopted new ideas about organizational teaming and management in order to improve quality, productivity, and profits (Deming, 1982; Peters & Waterman, 1982).

The fiscal realities facing educators and administrators today, however has resulted in almost the opposite reaction by schools. Teaming is most likely viewed as creating an economic hardship, rather than as a useful productivity tool. The financial reality of paying for substitutes; assistive technology devices and services that might be recommended by the team, and the perception that teaming is a potential waste of valuable professional time, has left its hallmark on administrative decision-making regarding the use of teams. Additionally student outcomes over time (e.g., higher achievement, employment following emancipation from school) have yet to be successfully correlated with educational spending within the states.

Whatever one's personal thoughts about our current political climate and the changes occurring within our educational systems, including school-based accountability, one potential outgrowth of a standards-based education is the recognition that the provision of appropriate assistive technology devices and services has the potential to raise student achievement. Our 20 years of assistive technology and teaming experience in Colorado has taught us to recognize that collaborative/transdisciplinary teams do a much better job of matching technology to the student than any other strategy we have tried.

The Value of Teams

For students who use assistive technology to be successfully included within the life of their school, teamwork must play a critical role. Instead of viewing the classroom through the lens of "my class" or "your class" all teachers, related services personnel, and paraprofessionals must share responsibility for each classroom and the learning of all students. For students to come together, the adults must come together. Individual team members must not establish their personal value based on titles or degrees, but on a shared desire to ensure all students are contributing members of their classroom. Establishing equal parity for all team members is an essential component for true collaboration (Downing, 2002; Idol, Nevin, & Paolucci-Witcomb, 1994; Rainforth & York-Barr, 1997; Walter-Thomas, Korinek, McLaughlin, & Williams, 2000).

The implicit rationale for a team approach to special education decision-making is the belief that group decision-making provides a safe-guard against individual errors in judgment, enhances adherence to due process requirements, and stimulates beneficial group interactions so that particular "mindsets" do not prevail. (Kaiser & Woodman, 1985).

Much has been written about the value of teaming within school reform literature and team organization has emerged as one of the most powerful methods for reforming American public education in the 1990s. Teaming is an enabling reform that fosters collegiality and interpersonal affiliation because it facilitates communication and collaboration; team organization is far more than an instructional innovation. It changes the professional and interpersonal dynamics for everyone involved. Teaming is viewed as a transformational mechanism within educational reform (Erb & Doda, 1989).

Developmental and Legislative Foundations for Assistive Technology Teams

Public Law 94-142, the Education of All Handicapped Children Act, passed by Congress in 1975, now codified as the Individuals with Disabilities Education Act (IDEA) and amended in 1997, mandated not only that school districts provide assistive technology devices and services in order for children with disabilities to receive a "free and appropriate education," it also mandated the provision of teams as the core of decision-making procedures in special education. The precise way in which these professional teams should be developed and organized, who would serve on them, how they were to go about their assessment and placement decision-making processes, was left up to the individual states to determine. Consequently, there is great variability among teams throughout the United States. Further confusion was created by the many different names for these teams, including assessment teams, child study teams, evaluation and placement committees, planning and placement teams, school appraisal teams, and assistive technology teams (Clark, 1994; Pfeifer, 1981).

The law stipulates the use of teams in the assessment process as well as during implementation of services. Specifically, section 121 a 532 (e) -142: "The evaluation is made by a multidisciplinary team or a group of persons, including at least one teacher, or other specialist, with knowledge in the area of the suspected disability." In addition, Section 121 a 533 (3) mandates cooperation to "insure that the placement decision is made by a group of persons, including persons knowledgeable about the child, the meaning of the evaluation data, and the placement options."

Also, embedded within the IDEA is an acknowledgment that educational personnel must collaborate with one another and with families of children. Parents are included as integral members of the team. Thus, the act guarantees parents the right to participate in developing their child's individualized educational program (IEP), yet many parents still find themselves in passive or reactive roles (Salisbury, 1992).

Legislation for early intervention also refers to and requires teaming. Federal legislation, PL 99-457, Part H, now Part C, requires that early intervention teams work with family members of infants and toddlers in the development of the individualized family services plan (IFSP) and that states conduct activities leading to interagency collaboration both at the state and local level to provide a comprehensive coordinated system of services to infants and toddlers and their families.

With regard to assistive technology, teams are also mentioned in the legislation. The amendments of 1997 required every IEP team to consider each student's need for assistive technology during the IEP process as part of the Special Factors requirement (IDEA, 1997). Further, in order to consider the need for assistive technology, at least one person on the IEP team must have awareness of assistive technology. If the team determines that assistive technology is necessary for a student to receive a free and appropriate education (FAPE), the school must provide it.

But what does "consideration" mean? When considering a student's need for assistive technology, four general conclusions can be reached.

1. Current interventions (whether no tech, low tech or high tech) are working and nothing new is needed, including assistive technology.
2. Assistive technology has already been selected (or there has been a trial with assistive technology) and it is known to work.
3. New or different assistive technology should be tried.
4. The IEP team does not know enough to make an immediate decision. In this case, more information must be obtained, typically through an assistive technology evaluation process (adapted from www.wati.org).

The IDEA reauthorization of 1997 also gives the IEP team the authority to select individual accommodations and modifications needed for a child with a disability to participate in state and district wide assessments of student achievement. This includes alternate assessments if it is determined the student will be unable to successfully participate in the standard assessment process.

Types of Teams

In order to understand teams and their level of functioning, it is important to have a clear understanding of the types of teams that exist as well as the stages that most teams progress through.

Multidisciplinary

Multidisciplinary teams have historically been based on the medical model of intervention. On multidisciplinary teams, professionals from several disciplines, including the assistive technology specialist, work independently of each other (Fewell, 1983). That is, while they may share the same space, and even work side by side, they function separately and interact minimally (Clark. 1994).

On multidisciplinary assistive technology teams, members present information specific to their area of expertise to the other members of the team and make specific recommendations regarding educational services based on their area of expertise. For example, reports provided during the IEP meeting where each professional has evaluated the child independently with an assessment tool specific to their discipline, and then shares their report and recommendations during the IEP meeting. The recommendations are also implemented individually. By design, professionals on multidisciplinary teams function as independent specialists. Thus, for the most part, they work independently and in isolation from one another (Bennett, 1982; Fewell, 1983).

Interdisciplinary

Interdisciplinary teams are composed of parents as well as professionals from several disciplines. Often each professional is responsible for his or her own area of expertise and the part of the IEP related to that area. Unlike multidisciplinary teams, these teams are characterized by formal channels of communication that encourage team members to share their information and discuss individual results (Fewell, 1983; Peterson, 1987).

In the educational setting, interdisciplinary teams are often more effective than multidisciplinary teams because members share ideas with each other and decisions are reached through greater collaborative interaction. Interdisciplinary teams can also have inherent problems because team members do not always share the same language nor do they always have a clear understanding of the expertise of their fellow members. Many teams have discovered that sharing terminology does not always result in shared meaning (Howard, 1982).

Interdisciplinary teams typically meet in person to share assessment results and recommendations. Once their recommendations are made various professionals and para professionals within the local school or classroom provide follow-up and implementation on an individual basis.

Transdisciplinary/Collaborative

The transdisciplinary model is an outgrowth of dissatisfaction with the old medical model, fragmented among different specialty areas that are deficit-based, reactive, and remediation-oriented (Downing & Bailey, 1990). The transdisciplinary/collaborative team model has been supported as preferable by a number of observers in special education (Giangreco, 1986; Hutchinson & Haring, 1982; Kahler & Carlton, 1982; Rainforth, York et al. 1997). In this model, the teams attempt to form a more unified approach to working together, with professionals often crossing boundaries of expertise and information sharing (Sarason & Lorentz, 1998).

Transdisciplinary teams are family-centered, collaborative, and form the basis for service delivery as well as assessment and planning. Individuals, including parents, siblings and community members who are familiar with the student, exchange knowledge, information, and skills and then the intervention plan is carried out. During the decision-making process, the collective sharing and wisdom of the group allows for the creation of many alternatives for educational services. The goals of the services relate to the whole student rather than discipline specific goals.

More recent literature (Rainforth & York, 1987; Rainforth, York-Barr, 1997; Thousand & Villa, 1992) details the value of the collaborative team. Similar to transdisciplinary teams, collaborative teams are defined by Kagan (1991) as: organizational and inter-organizational structures sharing resources, power and authority and bringing people together to share common goals that cannot be accomplished by a single individual or organization working independently. Collaboration is an interactive process that enables people with diverse expertise to generate creative solutions to mutually defined problems (Clark, 1994; Idol, Nevin, & Paolucci-Witcomb, 1994; Kagan, 1991).

Johnson, Johnson, and Maruyama (1983), in a meta-analysis of over 521 studies, suggest irrefutable support for the belief that joint efforts to achieve goals promote positive relationships, psychological health, and social competence:

Cooperation is an inescapable part of our lives. It is built into our biology and is the hallmark of our species. Cooperation is the building block of human evolution and progress. It is the heart of interpersonal relationships, families, economic systems, and legal systems...Understanding the nature of interdependent systems and how to operate effectively within them is an essential quality of future citizens (p. 167)

Teamwork and cooperation is the preferred method of interaction among most experts. Even in the animal world, cooperative teaming allows for protection and survival. Both in the animal world and among humans, collaborative team members share equal status. Within the transdisciplinary model, there is a belief that everyone on the team, including family members, the individual with the disability, and his or her peers has contributions to make that are valuable. The individualized needs of the child create a common goal or interest and unites members so they can create the best educational solution with the child. Team members share responsibility in decision-making by consensus as well as in implementation and subsequent outcomes. Depending upon which tasks are being addressed, the number of team members contributing may vary. Parity, shared responsibility, commitment, trust, respect, and willingness to work toward consensus are among the basic tenets of collaborative teamwork (Larson & Lefasto, 1989). A summary of the evolution of teaming concepts is presented in Table 1.

In 1933, John Dewey defined reflective thinking as "the kind of thinking that consists in turning a subject over in the mind and giving it serious and consecutive consideration" (Dewey, 1933). The use of a collaborative/transdisciplinary model exemplifies this notion of serious and consecutive consideration. By sharing diverse perspectives, collaborative teams have the potential to greatly increase the breadth and quality of solutions, including assistive technology, developed to address educational, social, and other issues that emerge for children with disabilities as they traverse their day (Rainforth, York-Barr, 1997). In addition, the practice of collaboration lends itself to collegial support and problem solving on an ongoing basis.

The Development of Collaborative Teams in Colorado

Teams are not static entities. Instead they are constantly evolving and changing based on the dynamics of each member as well as the team as a whole. Within Colorado, we have observed an evolution in assistive technology teams throughout the state over the past 19 years.

The Colorado Department of Education Special Education Services Unit (CDE-SESU) initiated the Colorado Statewide Augmentative/Alternative Communication (SWAAC) program in 1983 in response to an increasing need to serve students who used or needed to use augmentative/alternative communication (AAC) devices. Beginning with just 25 school-based professionals who first received formal training in 1986 in the use of augmentative/alternative communication devices and serving just 63 students, the teams have pro-

Table 1. Evolution of Teaming Concepts: Further Reading

Decades	Concepts	Source
1950s-2002	**Group Interaction and Group Development** Beginning in the early 1950s, group dynamics and group development became an area of study. Since then, numerous studies have been conducted to verify that groups move through distinct stages that can be identified and described.	Abelson & Woodman, 1983 Bales, 1950 Brophy, 1998 Butler & Maher, 1981 Cissna, 1984 Cummings, 1981 Doda, 1989 Dule et al., 1999 Dyer, 1984 Erb & Doda, 1989 Fleming & Monda-Amaya, 2001 Freeman, Miller et al. 2000 Friedlander, 1987 Garner, 1995 Kuypers, Davies et al., 1986 Tuckman & Jensen, 1977 Yoshida, Fenton et al. 1978
1970s-1990s	**Multidisciplinary Teams** Based on the medical model of intervention. Multidisciplinary team members function independently of each other. They may share space, and may even work side-by-side, but they function separately and interact minimally. Members present information specific to their area of expertise and make recommendations based on their own specialty area. Recommendations are also implemented individually.	Fewell, 1983 Kaiser & Woodman, 1985 Pfeifer, 1981 Smith & DiBacco, 1974 Yoshida, 1980
1980s-2002	**Interdisciplinary** Interdisciplinary teams are composed of professionals from several disciplines and include the family as an equal member of the team. Formal channels of communication that encourage team members to share information and discuss individual results characterize these teams. Inherent problems include lack of understanding of other team members' disciplines and difficulties developing shared meanings based on terminology.	Bennett, 1982 Clark, 1994 Courtnage & Smith-Davis, 1987 Crow & Pounder, 2000 Downing & Bailey, 1990 Elksnin, 1997 Hinojosa, Bedell et al., 2001 McCallin, 2001 McClelland & Sands, 1993
1990s-today	**Transdisciplinary/Collaborative Teams** Teams attempt to form a more unified approach to working together. Team members often cross boundaries of expertise and information sharing. Individuals exchange knowledge, information, and skill with those assigned to carry out the intervention plan. During the decision-making process, the collective sharing and wisdom of the group allows for the creation of many alternatives for educational services. The goals of the services relate to the whole student rather than discipline-specific goals. These teams are family-centered, collaborative, and form the basis for assessment, planning, and service delivery.	Downing & Bailey, 1990 Elksnin, 1997 Idol et al., 1994 Kagan, 1991 Rainforth & York, 1997 Sarason & Lorentz, 1998 Thousand & Villa, 1992 Paris & Salas, 2000 Parette, 2000 Walther-Thomas, 2000

gressed from using a multidisciplinary model to today's transdisciplinary approach.

By 2004, the SWAAAC teams had grown to over 500 members representing 67 teams throughout Colorado. A 1.5 million dollar assistive technology loan bank had been established and an advisory group formed to conduct statewide needs assessments and to provide support to the Colorado Department of Educations SWAAAC teams.

The focus has shifted to building capacity in local communities around assistive technology devices and services with distance and local educational opportunities open to all (including families and students). At the time of this writing, team members have on loan over 450 devices each week; are conducting local assistive technology assessments on an as-needed basis and assist their local IEP teams to consider and procure assistive technology devices and services for over 80,000 special education and Section 504 eligible students. In addition, a matrix of necessary core and expanded competencies has been developed based on discipline-specific (e.g., ASHA, AOTA) and special education (NASDSE) assistive technology-recommended competencies. These competencies are being used to guide the future development and education of all assistive technology team members in Colorado.

The articulated values of the SWAAAC teams were adapted and adopted in 2001 from Rainforth and York (1997), as follows.

1. Equal participation in the collaborative assistive technology teamwork process by the student, family member, and by all disciplines deemed necessary for individuals to achieve their specific educational goals

2. Consensus decision-making about priority assistive technology related goals and objectives to all areas of functioning: school, home, work, play and the community

3. Consensus decision-making about the type and amount of assistive technology support required from related services personnel

4. Attention to assistive technology related needs for motor, communication, language, curricular needs, seating and positioning, cognitive development, sensory and perceptual access, and learning style

5. Infusion of assistive technology knowledge and skills from different disciplines into the intervention design

6. Role release to enable the assistive technology team members most directly involved to develop the confidence and competence necessary to facilitate active learning and effective participation in all environments

7. Collaborative problem solving for implementing assistive technology strategies for successful learning and communication across environments

Team Development

In general, anyone who has a direct interest in the growth and development of a particular student with a disability, including their family members, may legitimately serve as a member of an assistive technology team. Each member serves a critical and ongoing role within the life and development of the student utilizing assistive technology devices and services. But what factors are most critical when establishing successful assistive technology teams? The following section outlines a number of important considerations relative to establishing teams and assuming team member roles.

Planning for Change

Establishing a collaborative culture represents a major shift for many schools. Change often results in significant emotional turmoil for most individuals immersed in the change process, often including changes in individual roles and in service delivery. According to Likert (1967), expect it to take as much as five years for a major systems change to filter through and become the norm in an organization.

The organizational change literature suggests the following six elements are essential for effective organizational change: shared leadership, a coherent vision, comprehensive planning, adequate resources, sustained implementation, and continuous evaluation, and improvement (Walter-Thomas, Korinek, McLaughlin, & Williams, 2000).

Complicating systems changes efforts is that every team operates within a larger institutional setting or context, a point that is particularly highlighted in the special education literature (Smith & DiBacco, 1974). The extent to which administrators perceive value in and

Figure 1. Five Factors to Consider Prior to Developing an Assistive Technology Team: A Preliminary Survey

(a) Describe the extent to which administrators and staff are concerned about the need for an assistive technology team.
(b) What are the attitudes and values of school personnel toward utilizing a team approach to enhance assistive technology service delivery?
(c) What is the likelihood that administrators will commit resources to the team, such as personnel, release time, access to information, and financial support?
(d) What other changes are currently occurring in the organization that may facilitate or hinder the development of an assistive technology team (e.g., staffing changes)?
(e) Clearly identify the potential negative side effects of a team approach (e.g., resentment or jealousy of team members) within your building or district.

support the team process significantly impacts the team's ability to function. Pfeifer (1981) found two areas that emerged as major self-perceived issues for educational teams: (a) too constrictive a set of team roles and goals, and (b) functioning under extensive pressure with minimal support. Pfeiffer noted that the following variables have a major impact on the functioning of teams: added time to engage in the team process, how the larger system perceives the role of the team, and the extent to which the team's goals receive recognition and support (Pfeifer, 1981).

In many educational settings throughout the United States, school systems are organized according to a top-down model. Decisions about changes in procedures and daily practice usually come from the top of the organization, the superintendent or the board of education, and are passed down a military style "chain of command" to principals and then to teachers. The teachers in most schools are organized in separate departments with high degrees of role differentiation and specialization, and they often see themselves as belonging to complete territorial units within the school and not as members of a cooperative team (Garner, 1995).

In the long run, perhaps the most effective strategy for team development is the simultaneous adoption of the top-down and bottom-up processes, involving both high-level administrative support for the team-work concept and careful attention to the selection and training of team members (Clark, 1994). In Colorado, we have enjoyed significant and ongoing support for many years from our Director of Special Education at the State level and from the vast majority of district administrators. Clearly, administrative support is a basic factor in effective teaming and collaboration (Fullan & Hargreaves, 1996; Larson & Lefasto, 1989). Table 2 outlines some key considerations relative to administrative support for assistive technology teams.

When administrative support is lacking, planning time, professional development, staff commitment, and the overall success of the team is negatively effected. When leadership at the administrative level is present it helps to ensure that various facets of the change process is considered prior to implementation. Most critical is consideration of the long- and short-term consequences of enacting a new model of practice. At the building level, principal involvement is critical for the development and ongoing work of collaborative communities to be successful (Stoll, 1991).

Table 2. Taxonomy of Variables Influencing AT Team Performance

Factors	Description	Examples	Applicable Interventions
Contextual factors	Variables in the environment in which the team activity is embedded	Culture Climate Training/education systems Reward systems Information system Legislation	Team selection Task design Training Goal setting
Structural factors	Variables primarily from sources external to the team, but may include some internal to the team (e.g., team organization)	Physical environment Organizational arrangements Technological systems Budgets Team proximity Dedicated time	Task design Training Team organization
Team design factors	Variables inherent in the team makeup	Work design Task interdependence Team size/composition Leadership	Team selection Task design Training
Process factors	Variables inherent in the team itself and how the team functions	Boundary management Task cohesion Performance norms Communication Team interactions Potency/team self-efficacy Team spirit	Team selection Task design Training-team building, communication, etc.
Contingency factors	Variables from sources internal and external to the team	Team Mission/goals Resource availability Procedural requirements Rules of operation, managing or decision-making Administration support or change	Task design Training

Developing an Effective Team

An important part of team development is for potential members to truly understand the concept of teaming and its potential benefits. A commitment by the educational administration is also crucial to developing the infrastructure necessary to ensure the success of the team. Team members need to develop an understanding of how to work together in partnership to accomplish their shared vision. Important skills include team building, consensus building and shared decision-making, creating an open and trusting environment, negotiating, and compromising.

Maher and Hawryluk (1983) suggested five factors that should be considered before developing a team to facilitate educational service delivery: (a) the care and concern evidenced by administrators and staff about the need(s) being addressed by a team approach; (b) the attitudes and values of school personnel toward using a team approach to improve educational service delivery; (c) the reality that resources will allocated to the team by administrators such as personnel, release time, access to information, and other financial support; (d) other changes going on within the organization that may impact the development of a team (e.g., staffing changes); and (e) the possible negative side effects of a team approach (e.g., team members struggling with interpersonal issues about a team approach). Effective teaming and collaboration is best supported when there is a strong plan, mutual goals, effective communication, clarity with team roles, and competent leadership. Team members must have an equal voice in decision-making and time available for open discussions of concerns and suggestions (Downing, 2002).

The Role of Team Members

In general, anyone who has something to contribute and who wants to be on a student's educational team can and should become a member. Historically, the makeup of teams has usually been determined by matching the student's abilities to the professional who had training or expertise in the student's particular disability (Rainforth, York-Barr, 1997). Yet, training and certification in a given disability does not ensure training or credibility in assistive technology devices and services. In other words, being a licensed speech pathologist does not mean the professional has sufficient training in augmentative/alternative communication (Beukelman & Mirenda, 1998). The most effective support for a given student will probably be a combined effort from a number of people, both those familiar with AT and those unfamiliar with AT. The blending of all team members' skills and knowledge leads to a more holistic program for the student (Downing, 2002; Downing & Bailey, 1990).

Effective parental involvement programs acknowledge that parents are a child's earliest and most influential teachers. "Attempting to educate the child without parental support is akin to trying to rake leaves in a high wind" (Taylor, 2000, p. 69).

Early assessment techniques developed to determine the appropriateness of AT for a student with a disability have been roundly (and properly) criticized for their narrow view and failure to include families in the process. A comprehensive AT assessment model involves families throughout the AT process and incorporates collaboration and individualization. It is critical not only during the assessment process, but throughout the lifespan of AT usage, to understand the relationship between the family and the incorporation of AT into the life of the student (Parette & Brotherson, 1996).

Recognizing and Managing Dysfunctional Teams

From time to time, teams exhibit dysfunctional behaviors or act in nonproductive ways. Some conflict is normal and even positive as it can move a group forward if handled appropriately. Sharing different opinions, vantage points, and knowledge bases often results in more creative and comprehensive solutions. However, dysfunctional behavior can escalate into a dysfunctional team. Dysfunctional behavior may include such symptoms as disorganized meetings, no clear agenda or established goals, inability to make decisions or take action, formation of cliques and alliances, hidden agendas, lack of trust, defensiveness, and so on. Role ambiguity, overlap, and conflict are also areas identified as potentially problematic on special education teams (Butler & Maher, 1981; Ulrey, Hudler, Marshal, Wuori, & Cranston, 1987; Yoshida, 1980).

Some teams experience dysfunction due to an imbalance of power and influence. Often one team member maintains more influence, perhaps due to perceptions of authority. The perception of power and status can also affect the role of parent's on a team. Parents may believe they have limited status or power. They can be intimidated by the process, the use of jargon, and by the perceived unwillingness of professionals to include them equally within the team process. (Hermary & Rempel, 1990; McClelland & Sands, 1993; Yoshida, 1980).

When Problems Occur

There are two primary types of issues influencing effective team functioning typically titled structural and relational. Structural issues refer to issues surrounding the organization of the team and expectations for functioning within the organizational model. Structural factors to consider include: who is on the team, proximity (or location and distance between members), how the team is actually set-up or structured, and the types of service delivery models used by the team. It also includes the bigger agenda of the team. The teams primary goal and purpose and how team resources are managed combine to create structure for a team (Beukelman & Mirenda, 1998; Blackstone, 1990; Salas, Dickenson, Converse, & Tannenbaum, 1992).

Relational issues as one might expect, refers to the relationships among team members. Relational issues to consciously consider, include the individual interactions and dynamics of team functioning. The interdependence and social norms of the group, as well as how the team communicates and interacts are also relational issues that must be taken into account for effective team functioning. Teams members frequently struggle with decision making, interdependence, conflicts, and troubling behaviors such as imbalances in power among members. It is not unusual for teams to spend a great deal of time thinking about structural issues with much less emphasis placed on relational issues. Quite frankly, it is much easier to blame structural issues as the "problem" rather than address core relational factors that are impeding team progress and development.

Blackstone (1990) and others (Paris, Salas, & Cannon-Bowers, 2000; Paulus, 2000) discussed both structural and relational factors and their importance to clinicians. Structural factors that impede service delivery include: insufficient funding, team composition, center-based evaluations, lack of a team approach, insufficient time, workload levels and lack of follow-up and pull-out therapy services. Structural problems often appear in the form of confusion about the purposes of the team or how it operates (team instability); the perception that services are delivered inequitably (only demanding families receive service); long lag times between referral and service delivery; team meetings that are contentious, disorganized and consume too much time; and, ultimately, less-than-adequate outcomes for the assistive technology end-user.

In summary, structural issues include:
- The model(s) of service delivery that regulates the functioning of the team

- Team goals and purposes
- Team membership or composition
- Team referrals and how that process is organized
- Service organization and delivery
- Resource management
- How and who runs the team meetings (Beukelman & Mirenda, 1998, p. 126).

Relational issues encompass the interactions among team members. They directly impact how the team functions and the quality and quantity of work produced. To truly assess relational performance of a team, it is necessary to think about the dynamic, multilevel nature of teamwork—including the relationships among team members. When teams struggle with relational issues, members are uncomfortable with basic interactions and often seek to avoid situations where they might feel vulnerable. For example, many teams struggle with fully including families on the assistive technology team. This may be due to cultural differences-including school cultures that dismiss parents as troublesome or ineffective team members; or it may be simply because many assistive technology team members are uncomfortable with their level of assistive technology expertise and feel obligated to demonstrate an "expert" role in front of parents.

Other relational issues may have to do with individual personalities. Team behaviors tend to evolve over time and occasional conflicts can and do occur. If team members are not prepared to address relational issues directly, team processes, decision-making and ultimately the individual success of assistive technology end-users are seriously impacted.

In summary, relational issues include:
- Frequent violation of the implicit and/or explicit social norms of communication established by the group
- Not feeling it is safe for team members to express their feelings and opinions

Table 3. Taxonomy of Variables Influencing AT Team Performance

Factors	Description	Examples	Applicable Interventions
Contextual factors	Variables in the environment in which the team activity is embedded	Culture Climate Training/education systems Reward systems Information system Legislation	Team selection Task design Training Goal setting
Structural factors	Variables primarily from sources external to the team, but may include some internal to the team (e.g., team organization)	Physical environment Organizational arrangements Technological systems Budgets Team proximity Dedicated time	Task design Training Team organization
Team design factors	Variables inherent in the team makeup	Work design Task interdependence Team size/composition Leadership	Team selection Task design Training
Process factors	Variables inherent in the team itself and how the team functions	Boundary management Task cohesion Performance norms Communication Team interactions Potency/team self-efficacy Team spirit	Team selection Task design Training-team building, communication, etc.
Contingency factors	Variables from sources internal and external to the team	Team Mission/goals Resource availability Procedural requirements Rules of operation, managing or decision-making Administration support or change	Task design Training

Adapted from Beukelman and Mirenda, 1998; Paris, Salas, & Cannon-Bowers, 2000.

- Unequal or dysfunctional interactions among members
- Inability to give and receive criticism, resolve conflicts, and view the world from others' perspectives
- Decision-making processes that cause members to feel devalued or marginalized
- Members who regularly dominate meetings and interactions
- Lack of creative problem-solving skills
- Freeloading, perpetual lateness, or work avoidance by members
- Lack of positive interdependence (all for one, one for all); (Beukelman & Mirenda, 1998, pp. 126-127)

Both structural and relational issues affect team performance and, unfortunately, are often ignored until it is too late. It is critical that team members spend time up front organizing the team and reaching consensus on how the team will function and how it will be structured. This will prevent significant problems later. The structure that each team adopts is dependent on its long-term goals and may even change over the life of the team. Essential

Table 4. Task and Team Competency Types

| | Competency Types | |
	Task	Team
Specific	*Task-specific* competencies: performing teamwork behaviors for a specific task or situation (e.g., interaction required for a task, knowledge of the specific role responsibilities for a particular team).	*Team-specific* competencies relate to a specific team and influence the performance of that team (e.g., knowledge of teammates' characteristics, team cohesion).
Generic	*Task-generic* competencies are transportable and can be used for other task (e.g., planning skills, interpersonal skills, communication).	*Team-generic* competencies are, in principle, transportable from one team to another and can influence the performance of any team that an individual serves on (e.g., communication skills, attitudes toward teamwork).
	Competency Alignments	
Task specific/ team specific	Needed when team membership is stable and the number of tasks is small.	*Example:* Assessment of motor skills for switch access
Task specific/ team generic	Needed when team members perform a specific team task, but do not work consistently with the same teammates.	*Example:* AT team assessment that includes the regular education teacher and the parents
Task generic/ team specific	Needed when team membership is stable, but the tasks vary.	*Example:* Assisting teachers to prepare students who use assistive technology for a once-a-year field trip
Task generic/ team generic	Needed where team members work on a variety of teams, as well as on a variety of tasks.	*Example:* IEP teams, planning committees, curriculum committees

Adapted from Paris, Salas, & Cannon-Bowers, 2000.

to preventing dysfunction is monitoring team dynamics through observation and periodic assessments of team function. Surveys such as, "How Are We Doing as a Team," or others like it, can help the team address problems before they escalate and interfere with team function (Thousand & Villa, 1992). Such surveys typically address both structural and relational issues, and allow team members to step back from day-to-day team tasks to analyze issues that may present a problem. The survey process is intended to guide team members' thinking about the key things that make teams work, whether or not they are doing them, and whether what they are doing could be improved. The evaluation process is not intended to rate how effective each team is, but rather to help each group critically reflect on what has been effective for them and what they would like to do differently in the future. The participatory nature of the evaluation process encourages the use of the evaluation as a learning tool and allows the perspectives of different team members to be expressed.

Team performance has typically been considered to be a function of the average skill level of the individuals on the team (see Tables 3 and 4). However, while it is critical to the success of the team to demonstrate individual competencies, individual competencies are not enough (Paris, Salas, & Cannon-Bowers, 2000; Salas, Dickenson, Converse, & Tannenbaum, 1992). Thus, teaming skills are as important, if not more so than individual skill levels. Training efficiency can be maximized by combining individual and team skills training into a single training design and by allocating the appropriate amount of individual skills training relative to team skills training. Skills that are targeted for training should meet specific criteria: (a) empirically demonstrated to have an effect on team success, (b) are difficult to learn, (c) require more than simple repetition for development, (d) require practice to prevent their loss, and (e) may be infrequently required, but are essential for survival (Dyer, 1984, in Paris, Salas, & Cannon-Bowers, 2000). Team training is more than just team building. It is not enough to train specific assistive technology related competencies and simply hope team members will magically figure out how to operate as a team.

Within the realm of assistive technology, teamwork is the cooperative effort of a group of professionals, peers and family members, working toward meeting a collective goal such as defining appropriate assistive technology solutions and services for students with disabilities. This is achieved through defining the roles and responsibilities of each team member and providing a climate that is conducive to the efficient operation of those roles and responsibilities (Dyer, 1984; Mendelsohn, 1998).

The importance of conflict and how to understand and deal with it is of primary importance to healthy teams. Several observers suggest that conflict is a function of both inadequate preparation for teamwork and of poorly defined models for team collaboration and decision-making (Abelson & Woodman; 1983; Butler & Maher, 1981; Moore, Fifield, & Spira, 1989; Ulrey, Hudler, Marshall, Wuori, & Cranson, 1987). To minimize the impact of conflict within the team process, it is extremely important to establish group norms. Ideally this should be done during the planning phase of a team. Group norms can be viewed as the "rules of the team." For example, teams should establish a process for dealing with conflict or disagreements. Remember on a team, members are working toward consensus rather than one person's viewpoint. For example, the team may decide (in advance) that if a conflict occurs, those in disagreement will have the opportunity to present their viewpoint, using positive, nonjudgmental language, to the rest of the team members. Members will proactively discuss the issue(s) and work together to create a solution. Teams may also want to decide, prior to a conflict arising, at what point or when, a mediator might be useful should the team become stuck when trying to resolve a conflict.

Group norms can also include scheduling team activities on a regular basis that allow relationships to develop naturally. For example, a number of the Colorado teams have chosen to meet once monthly for a quick meal and an opportunity to work on specific team activities. These activities might include: developing process forms, discussing policies and/or best practices, learning a new piece of equipment, etc. The most important point of these get togethers is that it allows team members to develop trust and respect for each other. It creates a safe climate for learning and minimizes future conflict development.

When conflicts do occur, it is critical that team members respect each other—both publicly and privately—and that all members agree to work proactively to develop an equitable solution as quickly as possible. Minimizing conflict and maximizing collaborative work models should be a high priority for all team members.

Other examples of group norms include clearly defined roles and responsibilities. Each "position" on the team should be documented and responsibilities assigned. For example, if the role of Team Coordinator is identified as an important role of the group, the team should work together to discuss exactly what the position entails and how much time it will most likely require. Specific responsibilities of the team coordinator should also be highlighted and written down, so everyone on the team is fully aware of the role and responsibility of the Team Coordinator position. This activity should be repeated for each team position, so everyone has the opportunity to contribute, discuss and agree on individual team member roles and responsibilities.

It is never too late to address these issues. Even if you are a member of a longstanding assistive technology team, it is a good idea to set aside dedicated time to discuss both structural and relational team components. It is also entirely appropriate to make changes within these areas of your team. Remember, excellent teams are constantly evolving and changing-- in large part, because those participating on great teams are open to change and willing to pay attention to those things that will enhance the overall functioning of individual team members and the team itself.

Need for Educational Programs to Teach Teaming Skills

According to the literature, one factor that contributes to the success of teams in the educational environment is to model teaming within professional and family-centered training programs. There is a significant need to develop both preservice and inservice training opportunities to teach the collaborative team process, as these skills are not traditionally presented in discipline-specific programs.

Courtnage and Smith-Davis (1987) surveyed 360 special education programs at U.S. colleges and universities. They found 48% had no interdisciplinary team training opportunities. Of the 188 institutions with interdisciplinary programs, only 39 reported their departments offered inservice training to schools or other agencies. Yoshida (1983) reported less than 35% of teachers surveyed received either preservice or inservice preparation in team process or the types of decisions teams make. During the past decade some models of combined general and special education teacher education programs have begun to appear in the literature (Meyer & Biklen, 1992). However, even in a field where the law has mandated team functioning, there is limited information available and perhaps most importantly, minimal practice models are available for professionals to emulate.

Future of Collaborative Teams

Few professionals are taught teamwork skills at the preprofessional level. In an ethnography with physiotherapists, (Hilton, Morris, & Wright, 1995) concluded that poor understanding of roles, skills, and expectations caused team conflict and subsequent failure. Professionals must be taught team skills as undergraduates if they are to become success-ful practitioners in team-based settings (Bricker & Widerstrom, 1996; Hilton, Morris, & Wright, 1995; Pounder, 1998).

Organizational context exerts a tremendous influence on teams. Organizational context includes such things as the collective values of the organization and the nature of tasks teams are engaged in. The clarity of the team's mission and the extent to which the team is allowed to operate autonomously directly impact how well teams function. Honest feedback on individual and team performance and the extent to which rewards and consequences are contingent on these performances directly correlate to the productivity and success of the team. Training, consultation and support availability for teams along with a physical environment that promotes positive and productive interactions among team members can do much to influence the outcomes of a team approach (Bricker & Widerstrom, 1996).

Lamorey and Ryan (1998) conducted a national survey of 195 professionals to examine the relationship between current theories and actual practices of multidisciplinary, interdisciplinary, and transdisciplinary (collaborative) special education teams. Barriers to effective team functioning included: (a) administrative obstacles, (b) need for team members to develop collaborative skill sets, (c) difficulty in communication, and (d) lack of competence. The authors found only moderate levels of parental involvement across all team types. Further, the therapists tended to use educators to support their interventions and to obtain information (Lamorey & Ryan, 1998) rather than approaching parents and other caregivers for information.

When we observe students learning with the support of a teacher, or teachers working with their students, we are much more likely to attribute the performance to individual contributions. In other words, we do not take collaboration and teamwork for granted in education and continue to question its appropriateness from a number of angles. Accepted as normal practice in the private sector and other public sector work (e.g. health and social services), leadership through teamwork is still a novelty in education, throwing up challenges to the relationship between the "hero" principal and teachers as autonomous professionals (Hall, 2001). Few professional education programs address team working issues and still fewer consider these issues might be addressed in a multi-professional educational context (Freeman, Miller, & Ross, 2000).

Criteria for Effective Teamworking

There must be a commitment to two aspects of being a team member: the practice of collaborative care and attention to being a team member. There must also be recognition of different levels of role understanding and their importance in the development of negotiated role boundaries. Equal value must be assigned to each professional's contribution both to the development of the student and to the individual professional's development. Team members must acknowledge the complexity of communication, including a belief that communication involves wide discussion and negotiation to develop a team understanding of the individual student. It must also be assumed that professionals learn both skills and knowledge from other team members-including the family and the student with a disability (Freeman, Miller, & Ross, 2000).

In spite of the promise of transdisciplinary/collaborative teaming, problems remain. In a synthesis of collaboration issues addressed by numerous authors, Pounder (1998) identified and described some of the problems associated with collaboration:

1. Collaborative change versus the persistence of schools (especially with regard to established methodologies)
2. Resource gains versus the perceived costs of collaboration
3. Professional interdependence versus norms of professional autonomy
4. Shared influence versus shared accountability

These tensions may limit the viability and promise of collaborative teaming.

Summary

Educationally based teams have evolved dramatically during the past forty years. We have learned that for teams to function successfully there must be administrative support, a commitment to the team process by all members, focus on structural and relational issues and the willingness to engage in a pattern of continual improvement. Teams must support shared knowledge and be willing to engage in ongoing training activities, including time spent on learning how to function as a team and as an individual member of a team.

We also know within the field of assistive technology, teams must include the individual with a disability and his or her family within the assessment and selection process in order for technology to be fully adopted by the end-user (Galvin & Scherer, 1996; Phillips & Zhao, 1993). Our primary goal as an assistive technology team member in an educational setting is to enable students with disabilities to achieve a free and appropriate education by including assistive technology devices and services when and where they are needed. It should also include a commitment to ensuring students exceed expectations! This can be achieved most readily when team members share a common purpose and commitment to the team process.

References

Abelson, M. A., & Woodman, R. W. (1983). Review of research on team effectiveness: Implications for teams in schools. *School Psychology Review, 12*, 125-136.

Bennett, F. C. (1982). The pediatrician and the interdisciplinary process. *Exceptional Children, 48*, 306-314.

Beukelman, D. R., & Mirenda. P. (1998). *Augmentative and alternative communication: Management of severe communication disorders in children and adults.* Baltimore: Paul H. Brookes.

Blackstone, S. (1990). Populations and practices in AAC. *Augmentative Communication News, 3*(4), 1-3.

Bricker, D., & Widerstrom, A. (1996). *Preparing personnel to work with infants and young children and their families.* Baltimore: Paul H. Brookes Publishing Co.

Butler, A. S., & Maher, C. A. (1981). Conflict and special services teams: Perspectives and suggestions for school psychologists. *Journal of School Psychology, 19*, 62-70.

Clark, P. G. (1994). *Learning from education: What the teamwork literature in special education can teach gerontologists about team training and development.* Annual Meeting of the Association for Gerontology in Higher Education, Cleveland, Ohio, Association for Gerontology.

Clark, P. G. (1994). Social, professional, and educational values on the interdisciplinary team: Implications for gerontological and geriatric education. *Education Gerontology, 20*, 35-51.

Cummings. T.G. (1981). Designing effective work groups. In P. Nystrom & W. Starbuck (Eds.), *Handbook of organizational design* (Vol. 2, pp. 250-271). Oxford, UK: Oxford University Press.

Deming, E. (1982). *Out of crisis.* Cambridge: Massachusetts Institute of Technology, Center for Engineering Study.

Dewey, J. (1933). *How we think: A restatement of the relation of reflective thinking to the educative process.* Boston: Houghton Mifflin Company.

Downing, J., & Bailey, B. R. (1990). Sharing the responsibility: Using a transdisciplinary team approach to enhance the learning of students with severe disabilities. *Journal of Educational and Psychological Consultation, 1*, 259-278.

Downing, J.E. (2002). *Including students with severe and multiple disabilities in typical classrooms: Practical strategies for teachers* (2nd ed.). Baltimore: Paul H. Brookes.

Dyer, J. L. (1984). Team research and team training: A state-of-the-art review. *Human Factors Review*, 285-319.

Erb, T. O., & Doda, N. M. (1989). *Team organization: Promise – practices and possibilities.* Washington, D.C., National Education Association.

Fewell, R. R. (1983). The team approach to infant education. *Educating handicapped infants: Issues in development and intervention.* Rockville, MD: Aspen.

Freeman M., Miller, C, & Ross, N. (2000). The impact of individual philosophies of teamwork on multi-professional practice and the implications for education.

Journal of Interprofessional Care, 14(3), 237-247.

Friedlander, F. (1987). The ecology of work groups. In J. Lorsch (Ed.), *Handbook of Organizational Behavior* (pp. 301-314). Englewood Cliffs, NJ: Prentice-Hall.

Fullan, M. (1993). *Change forces: Probing the depths of educational reform.* London: Burgess Science Press.

Fullan, M., & Hargreaves, A. (1996). *What's worth fighting for in your school?* New York: Teachers College Press.

Galvin, J. C., & Scherer, M. (1996). *Evaluating, selecting, and using appropriate assistive technology.* Gaithersburg, MD: Aspen Publishers, Inc.

Garner, H. (1995). *Teamwork in education and child care.* Boston: Allyn & Bacon.

Giangreco, M. F. (1986). Delivery of therapeutic services in special education programs for learners with severe handicaps. *Physical and Occupational Therapy in Pediatrics, 6*(2), 5-15.

Hall, V. (2001). Management teams in education: An unequal music. *School Leadership and Management, 21*(3), 327-341.

Hermary, M. E., & Rempel, J. (1990). Parental and staff perceptions of individual programming teams: Collaboration in and beyond the conference. *Education and Training in Mental Retardation, 25*, 25-32.

Hilton, R. W., Morris, D. J. & Wright, A. M. (1995). Learning to work in the health care team. *Journal of Interprofessional Care, 9*, 267-274.

Howard, J. (1982). The role of the pediatrician with young exceptional children and their families. *Exceptional Children, 48*, 316-322.

Hutchinson, T. A., & Haring, N. G. (1982). Serving exceptional individuals. *Theory Into Practice, 21*(2), 82-87.

Idol, L., Nevin, A., & Paolucci-Whitcomb, P. (1994). *Collaborative consultation* (2nd ed.). Austin, TX: Pro-Ed.

Johnson, D.W., Johnson, R. T. and Maruyama, G. (1983). Interdependence and interpersonal attraction among heterogeneous and homogeneous individuals: A theoretical reformulation and meta-analysis of the research. *Review of Educational Research, 53*, 5-54.

Kagan, S. L. (1991). *United we stand: Collaboration for the child care and early education services.* New York: Teachers College Press.

Kahler, M. L., & Carlton, G. R. (1982). Educating exceptional students: A comprehensive team approach. *Theory Into Practice, 21*(2), 88-96.

Kaiser, S. M., & Woodman, R. W. (1985). Multidisciplinary teams and group decision-making techniques. *School Psychology Review, 14*, 457-470.

Katzenbach, J. R., & Smith, D. K. (1993). The discipline of teams. *Harvard Business Review, 71(2)*, 111-120.

Lamorey, S., & Ryan, S. (1998). From contention to implementation: A comparison of team practices and recommended practices across service delivery models. *Infant-Toddler Intervention, 8,* 309-331.

Larson, C. E., & M. J. Lefasto, M. J. (1989). *Teamwork: What must go right / What can go wrong.* Newbury Park, CA: Sage.

McClelland, M., & Sands, R. G. (1993). The missing voice in interdisciplinary communication. *Qualitative Health Research, 2*, 74-90.

Mendelsohn, R. (1998). Teamwork–The key to productivity. *Journal of Management in Engineering, pp.* 22-25.

Meyer, L., & Biklen, D. (1992). *Inclusive Elementary and Special Education Teacher Programs.* Syracuse:Syracuse University, Division for the Study of Teaching and Division of Special Education and Rehabilitation.

Moore, K. J., Fifield, M. B., Spira, D. A., & Scarlato, M. (1989). Child study team decision making in special education: Improving the process. *Remedial and Special Education, 10*(4), 50-58.

Parette, H. P., & Brotherson, M.J. (1996). Family participation in assistive technology assessment for young children with mental retardation and developmental disabilities. *Education and Training in Mental Retardation 31,* 29-43.

Paris, C. R., Salas, E., & Cannon-Bowers, J. (2000). Teamwork in multi-person systems: A review and analysis. *Ergonomics, 43*, 1052-1075.

Paulus, P. B. (2000). Groups, teams andcreativity: The creative potential of idea-generating groups. *Applied Psychology: An International Review, 49*, 237-262.

Peters, T. and R. Waterman (1982). *In search of excellence: Lessons from America's best-run companies.* New York: Harper & Row.

Peterson, N. (1987). *Early intervention for handicapped and at-risk children: An introduction to early childhood special education.* Denver:Love.

Pfeifer, S. I. (1981). The problems facing multidisciplinary teams: As perceived by team members. *Psychology in the Schools, 18*, 330-333.

Phillips, B., & Zhao, H. (1993). Predictors of assistive technology abandonment. *Assistive Technology, 5*, 36-45.

Pounder, D. (1998). Promises and pitfalls of collaboration: Synthesizing dilemmas. In D. G. Pounder (Ed.), *Restructuring schools for collaboration: Promises and pitfalls* (pp. 173-180). Albany: State University of New York Press.

Rainforth, B., & York, J. (1987). Integrating related services in community instruction. *Journal of the Association for Severe Handicaps, 12*, 190-198.

Rainforth, B., & York-Barr, J. (1997). *Collaborative teamwork for students with severe disabilities: Integrating therapy and educational services* (2nd ed.). Baltimore: Paul H. Brookes.

Salas, E., Dickinson, T. L., Converse, S. A., & Tannenbaum, S. I. (1992). Toward an understanding of team performance and training. In R. Swezey & E. Salas (Eds.), *Teams: Their training and performance* (pp. 3-29). Norwood, NJ: Ablex.

Salisbury, C. (1992). Parents as team members: Inclusive teams, collaborative outcomes. In B. Rainforth, J. York & C. Macdonald, (Eds.), *Collaborative teams for students with severe disabilities: Integrating therapy and educational services* (pp. 43-66). Baltimore: Paul H. Brookes.

Sarason, S. B., & Lorentz, E.M. (1998). *Crossing boundaries.* San Francisco: Jossey-Bass, Inc.

Smith, K. E., & DiBacco, J. (1974). The multidisciplinary training team: Issues and problems. *Journal of School Psychology, 12*, 158-167.

Stoll, L. (1991). School effectiveness in action: Supporting growth in schools and classrooms. In M. Ainscow, (Ed.), *Effective schools for all*. London: David Fulton Publishing.

Sundstrom, E., DeMeuse, K. P., & Futrell, D. (1990). Work teams: Applications and effectiveness. *American Psychologist, 45*(2), 120-133.

Taylor, G. (2000). *Parental involvement: A practical guide for collaboration and teamwork for students with disabilities*. Springfield, IL. Charles C Thomas Publisher Ltd.

Thousand, J., & Villa, R. (1992). Collaborative teams: A powerful tool in school restructuring. In R. Villa, J. Thousand, W. Stainback, & S. Stainback (Eds.), *Restructuring for caring and effective schools: An administrative guide to creating heterogeneous schools* (pp. 73-108). Baltimore: Paul H. Brookes.

Ulrey, G., Hudler, M., Marshall, R., Wuori, D., & Cranston, C. (1987). A community model for physician, educator, parent collaboration for management of children with developmental and behavioral disorders. *Clinical Pediatrics, 26*, 235-239.

Walter-Thomas, C., Korinek, L., McLaughlin, V. L. & Williams, B. T. (2000). *Collaboration for inclusive education*. Needham Heights, MA: Allyn and Bacon.

Yoshida, R. K. (1980). Are multidisciplinary teams worth the investment? *School Psychology Review, 12*, 137-143.

Yoshida, R. K. (1980). Multidisciplinary decision-making in special education: A review of the issues. *School Psychology Review, 9*, 221-227.

12

Students with Learning Disabilities Using Assistive Technology in the Inclusive Classroom

Tamarah M. Ashton

Inclusion is no longer a trend. It is reality. With teachers having more demands than ever before placed on their time and expertise to make curriculum meaningful to all students (Harden & Rosenberg, 2001), it is little wonder that the term assistive technology often seems like a scary word to them (Maushak, Kelley, & Blodgett, 2001). Instead, assistive technology should be seen as "the great equalizer" (Wyer, 2001) rather than "just one more thing" with which teachers must contend.

Defining a Segment of the Special Education Technology Discipline

The term assistive technology seems almost foreign to many general educators, making them often think of students with severe disabilities who require the use of elaborate switch options or expensive, adaptive equipment-something the "specialist" will take care of (Quenneville, 2001). Along the same lines, many educators hold the misperception that all assistive technology devices are computerized, unaffordable, and require extensive training before they can be incorporated into someone's life (Ashton, 2000).

In reality, however, the assistive technology for students with learning disabilities can be something as inexpensive as a pencil grip or as simple as a straight edge to keep their writing lined up on the page. Many software programs have also been designed with the unique needs of learning disabilities in mind (e.g., *Simon Sounds It Out*, Don Johnston, 1994), and still other programs that were originally designed for a general audience (e.g., *Inspiration®*, Strategic Transitions, 1999; *WiggleWorks*, Scholastic, 1996) have been adopted for use with students with learning disabilities.

The federal definition of assistive technology with which most educators are familiar is the following: "any item, piece of equipment, or product system, whether acquired commercially off the shelf, modified, or customized, that is used to increase, maintain, or improve functional capabilities of individuals with disabilities" (IDEA, 1990). The intent of each element of the definition will be explored in an effort to fully understand how it might impact the life of an individual with a disability; in the case of this chapter, specifically, we will examine the elements through a lens of learning disabilities.

1. Any item, piece of equipment, or product system-The operative word in this phrase is any. While any might be referring to an elaborate computer setup costing thousands of dollars, it might also be referring to a far less expensive piece of word prediction software such as *Co:Writer* (1992-2002), or any other item that might assist someone in

learning (e.g., tape recorder, alternative keyboard).

2. Whether acquired commercially off the shelf, modified, or customized-The commercial market has developed many innovative products to improve the lives of individuals with disabilities, but it is important to remember that teachers, family members (Male, 2002; Parette & McMahan, 2002), and the students themselves, are often capable of modifying an item found in any classroom into something that may be especially helpful for a student with learning disabilities. For example, cassette tape recordings of a particularly difficult social studies or science textbook may be useful for a number of students. Most classrooms have at least one tape recorder available and parents are often willing to volunteer their time to modify these types of material.

3. Used to increase, maintain, or improve functional capabilities – I wrote this book chapter on a computer with the use of a word processing program. This is improving my functional capabilities. I could write everything out by hand, dictate it to someone else, or even use a typewriter. But since I have a computer readily accessible, why would I choose another method? I am faster with a keyboard, I can readily change errors, and I am able to quickly change the order of material and store it as I find necessary.

This is exactly what assistive technology does for people with disabilities. Whatever device or strategy they are using helps them do something faster or even at a higher level than they could achieve without it. For a student with a learning disability, an example could be a talking calculator. The student might be able to do the arithmetic in her head or by hand, but if number reversals are common or the auditory confirmation is helpful, why not use that assistive technology item to improve her functional capability? And keep in mind that in the inclusive classroom, others might benefit as well.

For the purposes of this chapter, King's (1999) definition of assistive technology will be used to operationalize the term in a broad sense. It is important to remember throughout that our focus is on learning disabilities:

- *Assistive means helping, supporting, and aiding in accomplishing practical functions, tasks, or purposes for persons of all ages. Individuals who use AT may include anyone. These persons may have a variety of special needs, disabilities, limitations, and/or challenges that limit their participation in life and thus require supportive functions from other humans and from special tools and devices.*

- *Technology means reliance on simple as well as potentially highly complex tools, devices, and equipment, and on related industrial processes, which may be mechanical, electronic, electromechanical, or hydraulic in nature (or combinations of these features) – as well as the strategies, methods, and techniques that the human must bring to the interaction to make tools and devices operate to accomplish a purpose (p. 14)*

Outlining a Systematic Methodology for Locating Relevant Literature

This next section will present a selected review of the literature on the use of assistive technology by students with learning disabilities in inclusive settings. Two major areas of the research will be investigated:

1. examples of promising assistive technology practices for students with learning disabilities and how they might be used in the general education classroom

2. how teachers are trained to provide access to the curriculum for all students using assistive technology

To establish reasonable parameters for the review, the research was delimited in three important ways. First, only research studies of elementary school students and programs were included, distinguishing grades 1 through 6 for consideration. Second, only empirical evaluative studies were included to emphasize research findings as opposed to opinion articles. Finally, the search extended no further back than 1995.

After an initial search, it became apparent that the second criterion, only empirical evaluative studies, had to be altered to include a variety of published reports. To date, little research has been conducted on the use of assistive technology by students with learning disabilities in the inclusive classroom. This review then, will serve as an overview and will include examples of implementation in the field considered best practice at this time.

The literature search was begun with a collection of journal articles (published between 1995 and 2002) acquired through earlier research. Next, among these papers, references to additional published work were collected. A computer search of current literature was also conducted through the ERIC and Academic Search Elite Databases using descriptors such as *assistive-technology, learning-disabilities, inclusion*, and *general education*. Additionally, hand searches were conducted in the 2000-2002 issues of *Exceptional Children, Journal of Learning Disabilities, Journal of Special Education Technology, Learning Disability Quarterly, Learning Disabilities Research and Practice, Teacher Education and Special Education*, and *Teaching Exceptional Children*. Pertinent documents that emerged from these searches were also reviewed and are included in the analysis.

Analyzing What We Know – An Interpretive Review of the Literature

This discussion will be divided into two separate areas: (a) examples of promising assistive technology practices for use in the general education classroom, and (b) teacher training – providing access to the general education curriculum for all students.

Promising Assistive Technology Practices for Use in the General Education Classroom

The literature contains a number of examples of assistive technology applications found successful when working with students with learning disabilities (e.g., Babbitt & Miller, 1996; Lewis, Graves, Ashton, & Kieley, 1998; MacArthur, 2000; Okolo, Cavalier, Ferretti, & MacArthur, 2000; Raskind & Higgins, 1995; Thompson, Bethea, Rizer, & Hutto, 1998), but the inclusive classroom was not usually the location where the research took place. In many cases, however, it is easily conceivable that these same uses of assistive technology would be just as successful in an inclusive environment and would most likely benefit many gen-

eral education students as well. Perhaps the focus should be on how to make learning accessible to all students (Barry & Wise, 1996; Messerer, 1997), rather that viewing assistive technology as special accommodations for special students. Indeed, "if curriculum designers recognize the widely diverse learners in current classrooms and build in options to support learning differences from the beginning, the curriculum as inherently designed can work for all learners" (Hitchcock, Meyer, Rose, & Jackson, 2002, p. 12). This view would also take the responsibility off the general educator's shoulders to add something to the curriculum (Langone, 1998). That is, the assistive technology item or procedure would become just another way to help many instead of one.

According to Rainforth (1996), the most advantageous strategies for successful inclusion "parallel the best practices in general education reform and restructuring" (p. 2). Therefore, the following literature is highlighted to demonstrate how the use of assistive technology can enhance the achievement of students (Merbler, Hadadian, & Ulman, 1999) with learning disabilities. All of these articles examine at least one type of assistive technology. Most of them cite examples of software and other items that were not necessarily designed for use only with special education students; general education students were the original target of many of these items, so why not show their demonstrated "assistiveness" for all learners?

Assistive technology using the language arts as an example. Howell, Erickson, Stanger, and Wheaton (2000) examined a computer-based program (*IntelliTools Reading*, 2001) for improving the reading of first-grade students considered at risk for reading difficulties. The prototype (developed using *IntelliPics, IntelliTools*, 1994, and a beta version of *IntelliTalk II, IntelliTools*, 2000) was used for purposes of this study. In almost all areas, students using *IntelliTools Reading* significantly improved their reading abilities.

Many such programs are available today including *Readable Stories* (Laureate Learning Systems, 1996); *Reading Lesson* (Attainment, 2000); *Start-to-Finish Books* (Don Johnston, 1994); *Stories & More* (Edmark, 2000); and *WiggleWorks* (Scholastic, 1996). Some target a special education or at-risk audience, others do not. In the area of learning disabilities, these programs are usually considered assistive technology because they assist the learner in improving one or more skills in reading. If they can assist a child with a learning disability, consider how they might also benefit students who are not labeled, but who are struggling to master specific reading concepts. This opens a new door for the general educator. She now has at her disposal a tool that can potentially benefit many; it is no longer something extra she has to remember to include in the daily schedule for just one student.

Similarly, many teachers with technological expertise are beginning to learn how to create their own EBooks. EBooks are simply electronic versions of books that typically include a number of ways to maneuver within the text. For example, some EBooks read aloud for the user, whereas others have pop-up glossaries. Some students might need to have the text highlighted word by word as they progress through a passage, while others might prefer to have the entire document presented in a larger font size.

Cavanaugh (2002) explains how to begin the process of creating one's own EBooks and how to find EBooks online that others have already created. Her theory is that because most EBooks have built-in accommodations (e.g., text-to-speech capabilities, extra practice activities), this makes them accessible, effective, and easy to use in the general education classroom. Because research has shown that features such as text-to-speech may greatly increase the reading comprehension of students with learning disabilities in reading (e.g., Higgins & Raskind, 2000), they are becoming a popular addition to instruction. Others have found conflicting results (Faris-Cole & Lewis, 2001), but with future improvement in the technology, the promise of success is still very real.

Because EBooks allow each student to set up his or her own profile of preferences, teachers have a tool that can be used by a number of students within any inclusive classroom. For example, if one student needs to have additional practice with spelling the vocabulary words from the story, that activity can be selected. This can take place while the student at the next computer is listening to the entire story being read aloud one more time. This flexibility of the tool itself allows for individualization of instruction that could never be achieved with just one teacher and an entire classroom of students.

Word processing programs are another type of program related to the language arts that have garnered much attention in the literature (e.g., De La Paz, 1999; Lewis, Ashton, Happa, Kieley, & Fielden, 1999; Montgomery, Karlan, & Coutinho, 2001). Of particular focus have been the variations in spellcheckers and their appropriateness for use with students with learning disabilities. (In these instances, spellcheckers can be considered assistive technology for students with learning disabilities.) For example, Montgomery et al. (2001) found that, overall, spellcheckers are not effective in providing the target word the student is trying to spell. If the word is included in the list of possible options, it is rarely first in that list. However, Lewis et al. (1999) using *Write This Way* (Hartley, 1993) noted that even though the correct word might not be first in the generated list, students with learning disabilities were able to detect the correct spelling regardless of placement in the list 94% of the time. Because most students attempt to spell words phonetically, this is an important finding. The majority of spellcheckers are created to correct typographical errors, not misspellings. It is only logical, therefore, that students' first choice for their selected word is not included.

Since it is so likely that students with learning disabilities are able to locate the word being sought, it only follows that general education students would also be able to locate the correct word from among a list of possible choices. For this very reason, teachers, special as well as general educators, have adopted the CHECK strategy (Ashton, 1999), an independent method for checking a document's spelling errors. The steps of CHECK are listed in Table 1.

In another area of computer software that deals with written language, Sturm and Rankin-Erickson (2002) studied the effects of hand-drawn versus computer-generated concept mapping on middle school students with learning disabilities. A no-map support group was

Table 1. Steps of the CHECK Strategy

CHECK	√ Check the beginning sound of the word. √ What other letter(s) could make that beginning sound?
HUNT	√ Hunt for the correct consonants. √ Have you included all the consonants in the rest of the word?
EXAMINE	√ Examine the vowels. √ What other vowel(s) could make the same sound(s)?
CHANGES	√ Changes in suggested word lists may give hints. √ What words are being suggested? Is that the one you're looking for?
KEEP	√ Keep repeating steps one through four. √ Need help? Try dictionaries and asking others for assistance.

also included. The assistive technology applied was *Inspiration* (Strategic Transitions, 1999). This software program is designed to assist writers in the prewriting stages. Specifically, it assists students in brainstorming and outlining their ideas. The program can toggle between a traditional outline and a concept map formation of the information input by the student. Although the program was not designed with special education students in mind, many special educators have found it to be beneficial in helping students with learning disabilities expand on their original concept for a story or report.

Specifically, Sturm and Rankin-Erickson (2002) showed that essays produced in the hand- and computer-mapping conditions scored significantly above the pretest writing samples on three factors: (a) number of words, (b) number of T-units, and (c) holistic writing scores. Additionally, students' attitudes toward writing were dramatically more positive in the computer-mapping condition as compared to the students who used no maps or who drew their maps by hand.

All of the examples above demonstrate how general educators might be able to incorporate items such as software programs (Duhaney & Duhaney, 2000; Howell et al., 2000; Lewis et al., 1999; Montgomery et al., 2001); strategies (Ashton, 1999); and EBooks (Cavanaugh, 2002) into a typical daily classroom routine. Instead of taking instructional time away from the entire class to teach a strategy to a student with learning disabilities, that same strategy is usable by all students in the classroom. Further, software programs or some of their specific elements can be thought to benefit any student who might need their assistance, not just the one or two with IEPs that outline their mandated use.

Teacher Training -Providing Access to the General Education Curriculum

For readers who are familiar with the workings of Universal Design for Learning (UDL), much of what has been presented thus far may not sound new or unique. Indeed, it is not. UDL is a term coined by the Center for Applied Special Technology (CAST) in the late 1990s. Why then have we rarely seen it addressed in the learning disabilities literature? Most discussion surrounding UDL seems to primarily focus on those students with the most severe challenges, particularly physical in nature. With the emphasis on accessing the general education curriculum in IDEA '97 and national and state content standards now in place for all students (Jitendra, Edwards, Choutka, & Treadway, 2002), a universally designed system for learning and teaching is the only way for the inclusive classroom to survive, let alone thrive.

The way in which teachers are trained to work in inclusive classrooms plays an important role in how they approach the use of assistive technology and students with learning disabilities. Most general education teacher training programs include only one class dealing with special education, typically a survey course that takes students on a "one disability a week" journey. Characteristics of disabilities are covered, legislation is a focus, and issues such as assessment, behavior management, and assistive technology are only briefly mentioned. If general educators have only a textbook definition of assistive technology when beginning their careers, how can they be expected to incorporate assistive technology for students with learning disabilities, let alone try to adapt it to meet the needs of all students?

After the passage of IDEA '97, the Knowledge and Skills Subcommittee of the Council for Exceptional Children developed assistive technology competencies for special educators (Council for Exceptional Children, 1998). These include 51 essential knowledge and skill competencies covered across eight categories. The categories are 1) Philosophical, Historical, and Legal Foundations of Special Education; 2) Characteristics of Learners; 3) Assessment, Diagnosis, and Evaluation; 4) Instructional Content and Practice; 5) Planning and Managing the Teaching and Learning Environment; 6) Managing Student Behavior and Social Interaction Skills; 7) Communication and Collaborative Partnerships; and 8) Professionalism and Ethical Practices. Following this, the International Society for Technology in Education (ISTE) published its own comprehensive National Educational Technology Standards for Teachers (2000) consisting of six categories encompassing 23 general competencies. ISTE's categories are 1) Technology Operations and Concepts; 2) Planning and Designing Learning Environments and Experiences; 3) Teaching, Learning, and the Curriculum; 4) Assessment and Evaluation; 5) Productivity and Professional Practice; and 6) Social, Ethical, Legal, and Human Issues.

After reading these lists, it becomes quite clear that any special educator would have a difficult time mastering all of these competencies. Because the specific nature of assistive technology adaptations into the classroom can be challenging for any teacher (Bryant & Bryant, 2003; Friend & Bursuck, 2002; National School Boards Association and the Office of Special Education Programs, 1997; Sax, Pumpian, & Fisher, 1997; Warger, 1998), a focus of training must be on how to effectively consider and maneuver within the realm of assistive technology. In brief, "essential for all teachers is the knowledge of procedures for determining if a software program or assistive device has potential for a student or a class of students" (Lahm & Nickels, 1999, p. 60).

Unfortunately, very few models of training are available to prepare educators to use technology in today's schools (Ludlow, 2001). All teachers are expected to help students understand and appropriately use their assistive technology devices, teach students to keyboard and use a computer, including the Internet, and then use all of those technologies in their teaching. The following literature is cited to highlight the disparities in current training programs and the need for a revision in how technology is incorporated into that training.

Lombardi and Hunka (2001) asked teachers in the second, third, and fourth years of their teacher training programs to evaluate their perceived degree of competence and confidence when working with special education students. Across the three years of training, approximately 10-20% of the students felt competent and confident, 10-40% felt competent but not confident, another 25-35% were confident but felt they weren't competent, and finally, 25 to almost 50% felt neither competent nor confident. These numbers are discouraging in and of themselves. To make matters worse, it is highly unlikely that these preservice teachers would have felt any more competent or confident in dealing with assistive technology.

In a related study, Cook (2002) qualitatively analyzed the comments of 181 undergraduate preservice general educators. Although not measured in exactly the same manner as Lombardi and Hunka (2001), the overall implications of the results are similar. Respondents most frequently mentioned personal characteristics, dispositions, and talents as their strengths. Traits they probably realized they possessed when deciding to become teachers. Unfortunately, they cited their weaknesses as teaching experience, teaching training, and instructional knowledge and skills. Some of these perceived weaknesses might simply be due to the fact they hadn't yet been in charge of their own classrooms. However, if they felt they had instructional deficits, how could they possibly be any stronger in their abilities to use and teach various technologies?

Anderson and Petch-Hogan (2001) hit on a very obvious, yet critical point when they conducted an exploratory study designed to measure changes in awareness of preservice special educators concerning students with disabilities and the use of technology. Not surprisingly, results suggested that participation in a technology-rich field experience (e.g., Bauer & Ulrich, 2002; Miller, Brown, & Robinson, 2002) increases the likelihood that students will (a) increase their knowledge of the use of technology for students with disabilities, (b) use their knowledge of technology to facilitate student learning, and (c) incorporate technology as a tool into their teaching.

These results point to another avenue for further improvement of teacher preparation; not only do training programs need to rethink and revamp the way in which technology knowledge and skills are incorporated, they must also consider the knowledge and skills of the master teachers and mentors with whom these preservice teachers are entrusted for practica and student teaching. Consider the following scenario: A preservice teacher who doesn't feel confident about a particular aspect of his training (e.g., assistive technology) is completing his final student teaching placement. He is placed with a supervisor who isn't any more comfortable with assistive technology and doesn't focus on any type of technology in her teaching. This preservice teacher will become a credentialed teacher without having experienced technology in the classroom and will most likely continue not to incorporate it into his future classrooms.

Defining a Research Agenda: What Do We Need to Know?

Inclusion is no longer a trend; it is reality. That is how this chapter began. Is that statement true? Is inclusion really here? If it is, why do we have so many unanswered questions? Did we place implementation before information? None of these questions can be answered or

fully addressed within the scope of this chapter, nor can the past be changed simply with a few keystrokes. What is important now is to identify the areas in which we need further information and develop a plan for getting answers to our questions.

Three main areas of need have evolved from this discussion: (a) There is a critical need to incorporate assistive technology into preservice training for both general and special education teachers. (b) Inservice teachers, in both special and general education, require that same type of training to continually update their knowledge and skills and be able to work with student teachers as well as mentor new teachers. (c) More specific research is needed on the use of assistive technology in inclusive classrooms. This chapter will conclude by briefly considering each of these areas.

Preservice Training

A UDL must be taught in any preservice teacher training program today. No matter what credential, certificate, or license teachers are planning to obtain, they will be working with students with disabilities. Most frequently, students with learning disabilities. The face of special education is changing, and the way we identify the existence of a learning disability will follow a very different procedure, but the fact that all kinds of students with all types of learning needs will be present in the general education classroom is not going to change in the foreseeable future.

Teachers in training have a great deal of content information to learn and many, many competencies to achieve. By guiding them toward incorporating a UDL, each of these areas becomes part of a comprehensive, cohesive whole rather than a list of unrelated tasks to check off when completed. With such training, new teachers will be able to think of assistive technology in terms of its "assistiveness" for all students, not something special or extra that needs to be added to their checklist.

Inservice Training

How do we create the same vision for teachers who are already on the job? While altering the way in which preservice training is delivered may seem like a daunting task, changing the mindsets of experienced professionals is practically insurmountable. According to Cutter, Palincsar, and Magnusson (2002), there is one more step we must take before we can even begin to think of changing mindsets – investigating meaningful ways of assisting teachers to critically reflect upon and revise their instructional practices. We cannot afford to leap to implementation without enough information. Forcing teachers to learn something they perceive as unnecessary will prove a fruitless endeavor.

Research

Without measuring effectiveness, how can we expect new teachers, and especially their more experienced counterparts, to incorporate assistive technology into their classrooms? The answer is, we can't! Much further research is necessary to validate the use of assistive technology with students with learning disabilities in inclusive environments. Until it can be shown that specific tools and strategies can be successfully incorporated into a general education setting, few teachers will be willing to attempt it on their own. Not only must the assistive technology be shown to work for students with learning disabilities, it must be evident that its use is not disruptive to other students or to classroom procedures and routines, and is relatively easy for teachers to use.

Then and only then will teachers feel free to venture into new territories. Only then will we be able to say that a true Universal Design for Learning can work. All students must be seen as individuals. All students must have available to them the services and materials they need to succeed. If inclusion is here, we had better find a way to achieve its original intent – equal access to a universal, but individual, schooling.

References

Anderson, C. L., & Petch-Hogan, B. (2001). The impact of technology use in special education field experience on preservice teachers' perceived technology expertise. *Journal of Special Education Technology, 16*(3), 27-44.

Ashton, T. M. (1999). Making technology work in the inclusive classroom: A spell CHECKing strategy for students with learning disabilities. *Teaching Exceptional Children, 32*(2), 24-27.

Ashton, T. M. (2000). Assistive technology. *Journal of Special Education Technology, 15*(1), 57-58.

Attainment. (2000). *Reading lesson* [computer software]. Verona, WI: Author. [www.attainmentcompany.com].

Babbitt, B. C., & Miller, S. P. (1996). Using hypermedia to improve the mathematics problem-solving skills of students with learning disabilities. *Journal of Learning Disabilities, 29*(4), 391-401, 412.

Barry, J., & Wise, B. J. (1996). Fueling inclusion through technology: Students with disabilities can rise to new heights with assistive technology. *School Administrator, 53*(4), 24-27.

Bauer, A. M., & Ulrich, M. E. (2002). "I've got a Palm in my pocket:" Using handheld computers in an inclusive classroom. *Teaching Exceptional Children, 35*(2), 18-22.

Bryant, D. P., & Bryant, B. R. (2003). *Assistive technology for people with disabilities*. Needham Heights, MA: Allyn & Bacon.

Cavanaugh, T. (2002). EBooks and accommodations: Is this the future of print accommodation? *Teaching Exceptional Children, 35*(2), 56-61.

Center for Applied Special Technology. Information available at www.cast.org/.

Cook, B. G. (2002). Inclusive attitudes, strengths, and weaknesses of pre-service general educators enrolled in a curriculum infusion teacher preparation program. *Teacher Education and Special Education, 25*(3), 262-277.

Council for Exceptional Children. (1998). *What every special educator should know: The international standards for the preparation and certification of special education teachers* (3rd ed.). Reston, VA: Author.

Cutter, J., Palincsar, A. S., & Magnusson, S. J. (2002). Supporting inclusion through case-based vignette conversations. *Learning Disabilities Research & Practice, 17*, 186-200.

De La Paz, S. (1999). Composing via dictation and speech recognition systems: Compensatory technology for students with learning disabilities. *Learning Disability Quarterly, 22*, 173-182.

Don Johnston. (1992-2002). Co:Writer [computer software]. Wauconda, IL: Author. [www.donjohnston.com].

Don Johnston. (1994). *Simon sounds it out* [computer software]. Wauconda, IL: Author. [www.donjohnston.com].

Don Johnston. (1994). *Start-to-finish books* [computer software]. Wauconda, IL: Author. [www.donjohnston.com].

Duhaney, L. M. G., & Duhaney, D. C. (2000). Assistive technology: Meeting the needs of learners with disabilities. *International Journal of Instructional Media, 27*(4), 393-401.

Edmark. (2000). *Stories & more series* [computer software]. Redmond, WA: Author. [www.riverdeep.net/edmark/].

Faris-Cole, D., & Lewis, R. (2001). Exploring speech recognition technology: Children with learning and emotional/behavioral disorders. *Learning Disabilities: A Multidisciplinary Journal, 11*(1), 3-12.

Friend, M., & Bursuck, W. D. (2002). *Including students with special needs: A practical guide for classroom teachers* (3rd ed.). Needham Heights, MA: Allyn & Bacon.

Harden, B., & Rosenberg, G. (2001). Bringing technology to the classroom. *ASHA Leader, 6*(14), 5-6.

Hartley Courseware. (1993). *Write this way* [computer software]. Dimondale, MI: Author. [www.nol.net/~athel/org/har.html].

Higgins, E. L., & Raskind, M. H. (2000). Speaking to read: The effects of continuous vs. discrete speech recognition systems on the reading and spelling of children with learning disabilities. *Journal of Special Education Technology, 15*(1), 19-30.

Hitchcock, C., Meyer, A., Rose, D., & Jackson, R. (2002). Providing new access to the general curriculum: Universal design for learning. *Teaching Exceptional Children, 35*(2), 8-17.

Howell, R. D., Erickson, K., Stanger, C., & Wheaton, J. E. (2000). Evaluation of a computer-based program on the reading performance of first grade students with potential for reading failure. *Journal of Special Education Technology, 15*(4), 5-14.

Individuals with Disabilities Education Act, 20 U.S.C. § 1400 et seq. Originally entitled the Education for All Handicapped Children Act.

IntelliTools. (2001). *IntelliTools reading* [computer software]. Petaluma, CA: Author. [www.intellitools.com].

IntelliTools. (2000). *IntelliTalk* II [computer software]. Petaluma, CA: Author. [www.intellitools.com].

IntelliTools. (1994). *IntelliPics* [computer software]. Petaluma, CA: Author. [www.intellitools.com].

International Society for Technology in Education. (2000). *National educational technology standards for teachers.* Eugene, OR: Author.

Jitendra, A. K., Edwards, L. L., Choutka, C. M., & Treadway, P.S. (2002). A collaborative approach to planning the content areas for students with learning disabilities: Accessing the general curriculum. *Learning Disabilities Research & Practice, 17*, 252-267.

King, T. W. (1999). *Assistive technology: Essential human factors.* Needham Heights, MA: Allyn & Bacon.

Lahm, E. A., & Nickels, B. L. (1999). Assistive technology competencies for special educators. *Teaching Exceptional Children, 32*(1), 56-63.

Langone, J. (1998). Managing inclusive instructional settings: Technology, cooperative planning, and team-based organization. *Focus on Exceptional Children, 30*(8), 1-15.

Laureate Learning Systems. (1996). *Readable stories* [computer software]. Winooski, VT: Author. [www.laureatelearning. com/].

Lewis, R. B., Ashton, T. M., Haapa, B., Kieley, C., & Fielden, C. (1999). Improving the writing skills of students with learning disabilities: Are word processors with spelling and grammar checkers useful? *Learning Disabilities: A Multidisciplinary Journal, 9*(3), 87-98.

Lewis, R. B., Graves, A. W., Ashton, T. M., & Kieley, C. L. (1998). Word processing tools for students with learning disabilities: A comparison of strategies to increase text entry speed. *Learning Disabilities Research & Practice, 13*, 95-108.

Lombardi, T. P., & Hunka, N. J. (2001). Preparing general education teachers for inclusive classrooms: Assessing the process. *Teacher Education and Special Education, 24*, 183-197.

Ludlow, B. L. (2001). Technology and teacher

education in special education: Disaster or deliverance? *Teacher Education and Special Education, 24,* 143-163.

MacArthur, C. A. (2000). New tools for writing: Assistive technology for students with writing difficulties. *Topics in Language Disorders, 20*(4), 85-100.

Male, M. (2002). Technology for inclusion: *Meeting the special needs of all students* (4th ed.). Needham Heights, MA: Allyn & Bacon.

Maushak, N. J., Kelley, P., & Blodgett, T. (2001). Preparing teachers for the inclusive classroom: A preliminary study of attitudes and knowledge of assistive technology. *Journal of Technology and Teacher Education, 9,* 419-431.

Merbler, J. B., Hadadian, A., & Ulman, J. (1999). Using assistive technology in the inclusive classroom. *Preventing School Failure, 43*(3), 113-117.

Messerer, J. (1997). Adaptive technology: Unleashing the power of technology for all students. *Learning and Leading with Technology, 24*(5), 50-53.

Miller, D., Brown, A., & Robinson, L. (2002). Widgets on the Web: Using computer-based learning tools. *Teaching Exceptional Children, 35*(2), 24-28.

Montgomery, D. J., Karlan, G. R., & Coutinho, M. (2001). The effectiveness of word processor spell checker programs to produce target words for misspellings generated by students with learning disabilities. *Journal of Special Education Technology, 16*(2), 27-41.

National School Boards Association and the Office of Special Education Programs. (1997). *Technology for students with disabilities: A decision maker's resource guide.* Washington, DC: Office of Special Education and Rehabilitative Services, U.S. Department of Education.

Okolo, C. M., Cavalier, A. R., Ferretti, R. P., & MacArthur, C. A. (2000). Technology, literacy, and disabilities: A review of the research. In R. Gersten, E. P. Schiller, and S. Vaughn (Eds.), *Contemporary special education research: Syntheses of the knowledge base on critical instructional issues* (pp. 179-250). Mahwah, NJ: Lawrence Erlbaum.

Parette, P., & McMahan, G. A. (2002). What should we expect of assistive technology?: Being sensitive to family goals. *Teaching Exceptional Children, 35*(1), 56-61.

Quenneville, J. (2001). Tech tools for students with learning disabilities: Infusion into inclusive classrooms. *Preventing School Failure, 45*(4), 167-170.

Rainforth, B. (1996). Related services supporting inclusion: Congruence of best practices in special education and school reform. *Consortium on Inclusive Schooling Practices Issue Brief, 1*(2). Available at www.asri. edu/ CFSP/brochure/related.htm

Raskind, M. H., & Higgins, E. (1995). Effects of speech synthesis on the proofreading efficiency of postsecondary students with learning disabilities. *Learning Disability Quarterly, 18,* 141-158.

Sax, C., Pumpian, I., & Fisher, D. (1997). Assistive technology and inclusion. *Consortium on Inclusive Schooling Practices Issue Brief, 2*(1). Available at www.asri. edu/ CFSP/brochure/asstech.htm

Scholastic. (1996). *WiggleWorks* [computer software]. New York: Author. [www. scholastic.com/].

Strategic Transitions. (1999). *Inspiration* [computer software]. Aurora, ON, Canada: Author. [www.strategictransitions. com].

Sturm, J. M., & Rankin-Erickson, J. L. (2002). Effects of hand-drawn and computer-generated concept mapping on the expository writing of middle school students with learning disabilities. *Learning Disabilities Research & Practice, 17,* 124-139.

Thompson, A. R., Bethea, L. L., Rizer, H. F., & Hutto, M. D. (1998). *Students with disabilities and assistive technology: A desk reference guide.* Jackson, MS: Project START.

Warger, C. (1998). *Integrating assistive technology into the standard curriculum.* Arlington, VA: ERIC Clearinghouse on Disabilities and Gifted Education.

Wyer, K. (2001). The great equalizer: Assistive technology launches a new era in inclusion. *Teaching Tolerance, 19,* 1-5.

13

Assistive Technology and Students with Mild Disabilities: From Consideration to Outcome Measurement

Dave L. Edyburn

During the past 20 years, the use of technology in special education has evolved considerably. While the development and maturation of the discipline is obvious, many components of the field are still in their infancy. Assistive technology for students with mild disabilities is one such example.

Despite the explosion of products and developments in the marketplace, to-date, the profession has been slow to recognize the need to integrate state-of-the-art technology into special education programs and services for students with mild disabilities. Evidence for this position may be found in the literature. Thus, ERIC and Google searches using the descriptors "assistive technology" and "mild disabilities" yield very few articles (Behrmann, 1994; Bryant, Bryant, & Raskind, 1998; Edyburn, 2000a; Raskind, Higgins, Slaff, & Shaw, 1998), book chapters (Okolo, 2000), or conference papers (Edyburn, 1996; Edyburn & Smith, 2000). In addition, minimal attention is devoted to assistive technology applications for individuals with mild disabilities in leading assistive technology textbooks (Bryant & Bryant, 2003; Cook & Hussey, 2002; Male, 2003; Scherer, 2004).

This situation is curious. Given the high incidence of mild disabilities, why has so little effort and attention been devoted to the use of assistive technology by students with mild disabilities? One possible explanation suggests that this component of the field is still in its infancy. Support for this position can be garnered from a historical viewpoint as well as from a policy perspective.

Historically, assistive technology devices and services have been associated with individuals with physical and sensory impairments whose needs were moderate or severe. As special educators were introduced to assistive technology in the forms of alternative keyboards, switches, and Braille printers, the application of these tools for students with mild disabilities was not readily apparent. However, new language in the Individuals with Disabilities Education Act (IDEA) Amendments of 1997 (Public Law 105-17) required that assistive technology be considered when planning the individualized educational program (IEP) of all students with disabilities. Thus, the 1997 reauthorization of IDEA can be viewed as a marker event defining a new era relative to mild disabilities and assistive technology (Edyburn, 2000a).

This chapter will provide an in-depth review of research, policy, and practice relative to the use of assistive technology by students with mild disabilities. In addressing a broad array of issues from consideration to outcome measurement, the chapter is organized in four sections: Foundations, Assistive Technolology Consideration, Interventions, and Outcomes. Each section begins with a description of the relevant topics, followed by a critique of current practice, concluding with recommendations for new directions that will enhance the use and effectiveness of assistive technology for students with mild disabilities. While the challenges confronting the discipline are significant, the current state of affairs provides significant opportunities.

Foundations

Given the interdisciplinary nature of assistive technology service delivery, it is essential to have a shared understanding of the conceptual foundations that support our work. This section is designed to provide a common frame of reference concerning mild disabilities and assistive technology.

An introduction to four related topics will start the discussion: an overview of definitions, incidence, and common characteristics associated with mild disabilities. Next comes a review of types of technology and the legal foundations that lend legislative support to facilitating technology use by persons with disabilities, followed by a brief introduction to assistive technology. A critique of current practices will conclude this section along with recommendations for new directions in foundations of assistive technology for students with mild disabilities.

Definitions, Incidence, and Common Characteristics Associated with Mild Disabilities

In academic contexts, mild disabilities are typically considered to include learning disabilities, emotional/behavioral disorders, and mental retardation. These disabilities are defined as follows in the IDEA '97 Final Regulations (§300.7 Child with a disability):

Learning Disabilities
(10) Specific learning disability is defined as follows: (i) General. The term means a disorder in one or more of the basic psychological processes involved in understanding or in using language, spoken or written, that may manifest itself in an imperfect ability to listen, think, speak, read, write, spell, or to do mathematical calculations, including conditions such as perceptual disabilities, brain injury, minimal brain dysfunction, dyslexia, and developmental aphasia. (ii) Disorders not included. The term does not include learning problems that are primarily the result of visual, hearing, or motor disabilities, of mental retardation, of emotional disturbance, or of environmental, cultural, or economic disadvantage. (Authority: 20 U.S.C. 1401(3)(A) and (B); 1401(26))

Emotional/Behavioral Disorders
(4) Emotional disturbance is defined as follows: (i) The term means a condition exhibiting one or more of the following characteristics over a long period of time and to a marked degree that adversely affects a child's educational performance: (A) An inability to learn that cannot be explained by intellectual, sensory, or health factors. (B) An inability to build or maintain satisfactory interpersonal relationships with peers and teachers. (C) Inappropriate types of behavior or feelings under normal circumstances. (D) A general pervasive mood of unhappiness or depression. (E) A tendency to develop physical symptoms or fears associated with personal or school problems. (ii) The term includes schizophrenia. The term does not apply to children who are socially maladjusted, unless it is determined that they have an emotional disturbance. (Authority: 20 U.S.C. 1401(3)(A) and (B); 1401(26))

Mental Retardation
(6) Mental retardation means significantly subaverage general intellectual functioning, existing concurrently with deficits in adaptive behavior and manifested during the developmental period, that adversely affects a child's educational performance. (Authority: 20 U.S.C. 1401(3)(A) and (B); 1401(26))

To monitor the prevalence of disabilities in K-12 schools, IDEA requires an annual child count. This means that each state is responsible for collecting data each year about the number of children served in special education. These data are aggregated across districts within the state and reported to the federal government. The Office of Special Education (OSEP) at the U.S. Department of Education is required by Section 618 of the Individuals with Disabilities Education Act (IDEA) to collect the data and make an annual report to Congress. This report is known as *The Annual Report to Congress on the Implementation of the Individuals with Disabilities Education Act.*

The most recent report, The Twenty-Fourth Annual, released for the year 2002, is available online at: www.ed.gov/about/reports/annual/osep/2002/index.html. As has been the case historically, the most recent data indicate that the majority (68.8%) of students receiving special education services have mild disabilities (LD, ED/BD, MR). As we turn our attention to technology, it is important to keep in mind that we are discussing the assistive technology needs of approximately 4 million students, ages 6-21, with mild disabilities (U.S. Department of Education, 2002).

Meese (2001) summarizes the characteristics often associated with mild disabilities as follows: cognitive characteristics (intellectual ability, attentional deficits, memory and thinking skills); academic characteristics (reading, language arts, mathematics) and social-emotional characteristics. The majority of students with mild disabilities receive special education services in general education classrooms. However, specialized instruction can also be provided in a resource room or in a self-contained special education classroom depending on each child's needs and the severity of the disability.

Types of Technology

Left undefined, the term technology is often synonymous with computers. Blackhurst (1997) has suggested that four different forms of technology are relevant to special education and rehabilitation: the technology of teaching, medical technology, instructional technology, and assistive technology.

Briefly, the *technology of teaching* involves the pedagogy that we utilize in designing instruction and learning environments for individuals with disabilities. *Medical technology* involves new experimental treatments, prostheses, wheel chairs, lifts, and so on. *Instructional technology* covers software and hardware that is specifically designed to enhance teaching and learning. Finally, *assistive technology* are those devices and services that enhance the performance of an individual with a disability by enabling him/her to complete tasks more effectively, efficiently, and independently than otherwise possible.

While all four defintions are relevant to special education technology, within the contexts of schooling and mild disabilities, this review will focus broadly on the technology of teaching, instructional technology, and assistive technology. Given that the defining characteristics of mild disabilities involve cognition, the relationship between educational or instructional technology and assistive technology is a critical factor in capturing the potential of technology for individuals with mild disabilities. Further, increased attention must be focused on the technology of teaching and how curriculum, instruction, and assessment can be made cognitively accessible for students (Edyburn, 2000a).

Legal Foundations

The fields of special education and rehabilitation have had a long-standing interest in technology and the potential it holds for individuals with disabilities (Blackhurst, 1997; Blackhurst & Edyburn, 2000; Fein, 1996; Hannaford, 1993). One of the first public policy documents to draw attention to the potential of technology was *Technology and Handicapped People* (Office of Technology Assessment, 1982). This report introduced readers to specialized technology tools, how they served a specific individual, and the impact they had on the person's life. These real-life stories served as powerful illustrations of the potential of technology for individuals with disabilities.

As a result of these early success stories, and others that would be collected and shared in subsequent years, the argument was advanced that public investment in research and development in the area of technology and disability could reap significant dividends in the form of improved communication skills, expanded mobility and independence, as well as an increase in the number of individuals gainfully employed and therefore contributing to the tax base. Indeed, the argument for the benefits of technology for individuals with disabilities was so persuasive that a series of federal laws was enacted to provide ways to capture the potential of technology on an ever-increasing scale.

Thus, federal legislation has emerged in which the potential of technology for individuals with disabilities has been consistently advanced. Most notably, this includes the Technology Related Assistance for Individuals Act (The Tech Act), passed in 1988 and the 1997 reauthorization of the Individuals with Disabilities Education Act. Thus, in the relatively brief span of 15 years since the publication of *Technology and Handicapped People* (Office of Technology Assessment, 1982), Congress was effectively persuaded by the success stories to stimulate change by utilizing federal policy and major funding initiatives as a mechanism to foster the rapid expansion of research, development, and adoption of technology by individuals with disabilities. As a result, the potential of technology for individuals with disabilities has been recognized and valued as an area of national investment.

Defining Assistive Technology Devices and Services

Two dimensions of assistive technology are recognized in federal law (IDEA '97 Final Regulations): assistive technology devices and assistive technology services. The definitions were originally developed as part of the 1988 Tech Act legislation and subsequently have been cited or incorporated into all technology and disabilitiy legislation (i.e., Americans with Disabilities Act, 1990; The Individuals with Disabilities Education Act Amendments, 1997; Telecommunications Act of 1996; The Assistive Technology Act of 1998). In reading the following definition of an assistive technology device, pay careful attention its encompassing nature:

§300.5 *Assistive technology device.*

As used in this part, Assistive technology device means any item, piece of equipment, or product system, whether acquired commercially off the shelf, modified, or customized, that is used to increase, maintain, or improve the functional capabilities of a child with a disability. (Authority: 20 U.S.C. 1401(1)

While many believe the term assistive technology applies only to computers, in reality, assistive technology devices (e.g., adaptive feeding instruments, wheelchairs, vision aids) have a long history in the fields of special education and rehabilitation. For example, current estimates suggest that there are over 25,000 assistive technology devices designed to enhance the life functioning of individuals with disabilities (AbleData, 2003). Given that the operational word is the definition is any, some

have argued that the definition is so broad that it could include anything (Edyburn, 2003a). Others have noted that the definition simply reflects the fact that assistive technology solutions may involve no technology (no-tech) (like a strategy), low technology (lo-tech) like a pencil grip, or high technology (high-tech) like computer-based tools.

A second definition advances a critical component involved in the effective use of assistive technology. That is, success is dependent not only on having access to a device, but also on factors involving selection, acquisition, and use of a tool. These ideas are codified in the following definition of assistive technology services:

§300.6 *Assistive technology service.*

As used in this part, Assistive technology service means any service that directly assists a child with a disability in the selection, acquisition, or use of an assistive technology device. The term includes – (a) The evaluation of the needs of a child with a disability, including a functional evaluation of the child in the child's customary environment; (b) Purchasing, leasing, or otherwise providing for the acquisition of assistive technology devices by children with disabilities; (c) Selecting, designing, fitting, customizing, adapting, applying, maintaining, repairing, or replacing assistive technology devices; (d) Coordinating and using other therapies, interventions, or services with assistive technology devices, such as those associated with existing education and rehabilitation plans and programs; (e) Training or technical assistance for a child with a disability or, if appropriate, that child's family; and (f) Training or technical assistance for professionals (including individuals providing education or rehabilitation services), employers, or other individuals who provide services to, employ, or are otherwise substantially involved in the major life functions of that child. (Authority: 20 U.S.C. 1401(2)

The definitions of assistive technology devices and assistive technology services provide a comprehensive perspective on processes that enable individuals with disabilities to acquire and use assistive technologies that enhance functional capabilities.

Critique of Current Practices

Current practice reveals little evidence of widespread use of assistive technology by students with mild disabilities. The literature provides a context for understanding the evolution of events and issues that have contributed to the current state of affairs.

In the mid-1980s, one of the common applications for computers in special education focused on the use of drill and practice software to remediate deficits in knowledge of basic facts and concepts (Bahr & Rieth, 1991). A landmark work by Russell, Corwin, Mokros, and Kapisovsky (1989) called into question this widespread practice by challenging educators to move beyond drill and practice to use technology in ways that provided access to higher-level thinking skills. As a result, the profession gained a sensitivity about using technology to engage students with disabilities in meaningful, respectful, and developmentally appropriate tasks (Gardner, Taber-Brown, & Wissick, 1992).

During the 1990s, technology applications began to move away from computer-assisted instruction to focus on the use of technology to enhance personal productivity. For example, it was during this period that we began to realize that some off-the-shelf tools (e.g., word processors, spelling checkers) did not appear to meet the unique needs of some students with mild disablities (Dalton, Winbury, & Morocco, 1990; MacArthur, 1996, 1998, 1999, 2000; MacArthur, Graham, Haynes, & De La Paz, 1996). As a result, productivity tools that were created for other disabilities, (for example, word prediction was originally created for individuals with physical and health impairments who tired easily from the effort involved in keyboarding) found new application for students with learning disabilities who had difficulty writing because of the challenges of spelling. Likewise, text-to-speech applications, originally developed for individuals who were blind, were recognized as relevant for individuals with reading disabilities. Thus, the profession began to focus efforts on locating appropriate assistive technology tools that could enhance learner productivity (Behrmann, 1994; Edyburn, 2000b).

In the late 1990s and early 2000s, education experienced considerable reform through the adoption of academic content standards and associated accountability testing. The importance of helping students with disabilities achieve high academic standards was clearly stated in the 1997 reauthorization of IDEA. However, while inclusion offered physical access to general education classrooms, students with disabilities were encountering significant difficulties related to cognitive access to the curriculum (Edyburn, 2002b). As a result, special educators have devoted increased time and energy to issues associated with accessible curriculum design (Burke, Hagan, & Grossen, 1998; Dacey Eichleay, & McCauley, 2002; Hitchcock, Meyer, Rose, & Jackson, 2002; King-Sears, 2001; Wehmeyer, Lattin, & Agran, 2001). As we learn more about the need for an accessible curriculum, assistive technology for students with mild disabilities takes on renewed importance.

While difficult for many people to appreciate at the time, the passage of the No Child Left Behind (NCLB) Act of 2001 (P.L. 107-110) is emerging as a defining landmark event in American education. Advanced primarily as an education accountability act, the law requires states to develop curriculum standards, standardized assessments of students' performance in meeting these standards, emphasis on helping all students to read by the end of grade three, and sanctions for consistently low-performing schools.

Due to the emphasis in NCLB on the scientific-based evidence underlying educational practice, educational research is receiving a degree of attention it has seldom seen. In the context of NCLB, the current research base for assistive technology and students with mild disabilities is clearly inadequate. However, the literature is very clear about the following: Assistive technology has considerable potential for students with mild disabilities (Behrmann, 1994; Edyburn, 2000a; Lewis, 1998; MacArthur & Malouf, 1990; Raskind, 1993; Wehmeyer, 1999); the effectiveness of technology is enhanced when it is implemented along with principles of effective instruction (Ellis & Sabornie, 1986; Larsen, 1995; Lieber & Semmel, 1985); and school administrators and policies can facilitate or inhibit the acquisition and use of technology by students with mild disabilities (Goldman, Semmel, Cosden, Gerber, & Semmel, 1987; Higgins & Zvi, 1995; Okolo, Rieth, & Bahr, 1989).

A final issue impacting current practice relative to the provision of assistive technology devices and services to students with mild disabilities is a perceived reluctance by administrators to provide assistive technology for students with high incidence disabilities. The problem has been described as follows:

> *Jimmy's handwriting is not legible; therefore he needs a laptop computer. Though such a claim and solution may be certified by an IEP team, the budgetary implications of this mandate, when applied to a high-incidence population, have created an environment in which adminstrators are reluctant to approve requests for assistive technology for students with mild disabilities, given the fact that they have 50 students like Jimmy within their building. (Edyburn, 2000a, p. 5)*

As we will discuss in subsequent sections, this issue is complex and has critical implications for utilizing a professional knowledge base relative to assessment, intervention, and outcome of assistive technology use by students with mild disabilities. At its core, the example above raises questions about the nature of assistive technology for students with mild disabilities, how we determine who needs it and who does not, and simultaneously paralyzes decision making as we ponder the sheer size, cost, and commitment of serving high-incidence populations. Individually and collectively, these issues serve as obstacles in the process of capturing the potential of assistive technology for students with mild disabilities.

New Directions in Foundations of Assistive Technology for Students with Mild Disabilities

Significant advances within the specialty area of assistive technology for students with mild disabilities will not be possible without major advances relative to three foundational topics. First, the implications of models that clarify the role of technology in enhancing performance need to be explored. Second, given concerns about cognitive functioning as one of the primary characteristics of mild disabilities, additional work is needed to understand the role of cognitive prostheses. Third, new tools for addressing a question deeply embedded in the assistive technology consideration process, remediation vs. compensation, must be developed to enhance decision-making. Each of these topics will be discussed briefly to highlight their importance in setting new directions for the foundations of assistive technology for students with mild disabilities.

Models for understanding the role of technology in enhancing performance.
The potential of technology for individuals with disabilities has long been recognized in the special education and rehabilitation communities (Blackhurst, 1997). To understand why this is the case requires insight into the relationships among the concepts of impairment, disability, handicap, and assistive technology:

> *... defines an impairment as "any loss or abnormality of psychological, physical, or anatomical structure or function." A disability results when the impairment leads to an inability to "perform an activity in the manner or within the range considered normal for a human being (e.g., difficulties in communicating, hearing, moving about, or manipulating objects). A handicap results when the individual with an impairment or disability is unable to fulfill his or her normal role. According to these definitions, a handicap is not a characteristic of a person; it is a description of the relationship between the person and the environment... This approach provides an important perspective on the role of assistive technologies in reducing the handicapping effects of disabilities. Describing persons with disabilities in this way also emphasizes functional outcomes, instead of focusing on limitations, and assistive technologies are employed primarily to contribute to successful functional outcomes for persons with disabilities. (World Health Organization, 1980, quoted in Cook & Hussey, 1995, p. 5)*

Thus, assistive technology offers a means for enhancing functional performance when a person with a disability is unable to perform an activity that can normally be completed by

Figure 1. Wile's model of human performance technology. Adapted from: Wiley, D. (1996). Why doers do. *Performance and Instruction*, 25(2), 30-35.

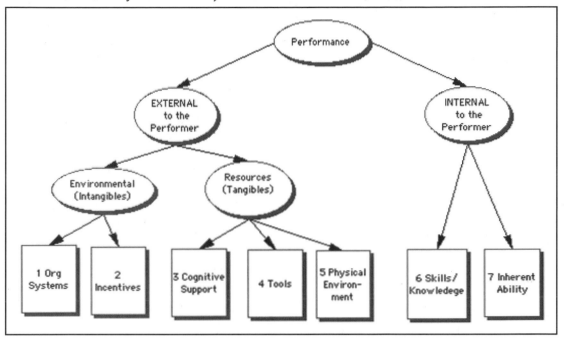

other people. Hence, the essence of assistive technology efforts centers on the individual, with the primary consideration being improved performance:

> [The] assistive technology selection system has as its emphasis using what function is available (human component) to accomplish what is desired (activity) in a given context (place, environment, people). We are not concerned as much with remediation of a disability as we are with enabling functional results and helping the individual to achieve what he or she wants to accomplish. Functional results require that we maximize the skills of the person with a disability. This places human performance at the center of our system. (Cook & Hussey, 1995, p. 46)

Cook and Hussey point out a subtle but essential question for members of an IEP team to discuss as part of the assistive technology consideration process: When do we recognize the limitations of instructional or remediation strategies to enable an individual to achieve a specified level of performance and when do we decide that assistive technology can be utilized to enable the indi-

vidual to achieve a functional level of performance?

When designing interventions to enhance human performance, conceptual models can inform our understanding of the contributions and limitations of assistive technology for individuals with disabilities (Edyburn, 2002b; Lenker & Paquet, 2003). Indeed, many theorists have advanced models that attempt to describe the individual components affecting human performance in a variety of tasks (Baily, 1989; Gilbert, 1978; Mager, 1992; Rossett, 1992; Spitzer, 1991).

In an effort to synthesize the many dimensions that have been identified by theorists as contributing to performance, Wile (1996) studied five common models of human performance technology and sought to reconcile their differences through a normalization process. A graphic illustrating the relationships among the components of Wile's model is presented in Figure 1.

Wile's analysis suggests that performance can be affected by seven variables: (1) organizational systems, (2) incentives, (3) cognitive support, (4) tools, (5) physical environment, (6) skills/knowledge, and (7) inherent ability.

These variables can be viewed as part of two classes: those that are internal to the performer (#6 & #7) and those that are external (#1, #2, #3, #4, #5). Further, the external variables can be understood as part of environmental factors, or intangibles (#1 & #2) and resources, or tangibles (#3, #4, & #5). Performance problems may be traced to a single variable or a combination. In Wile's estimation, the variables are sequenced by ease of remediation, that is, problems related to organizational system variables (#1) are easier to impact than problems associated with intrinsic abilities (#7).

Traditionally, poor performance has been considered the result of inadequate training (#6) or a deficit within the individual (#7) that made a person unsuitable for a given task. However, as the model illustrates, a range of factors, such as poor working conditions (#1, #5) or lack of incentives (#2), may also be valid explanations of poor performance. This model helps us understand that technology is not a simple panacea for remediating performance problems. For example, if the real issue is that the individual lacks the incentive to complete an academic task (#2), performance may not improve despite the availability of a technology tool (#4). Likewise, when a tool (#4) is only available in one environment (#5), the model explains why performance gains will be limited.

When a student with mild disabilities encounters a difficulty in the academic environment, Wile's model illustrates the array of interventions that should be assessed. For example, when a student has demonstrated chronic inability to memorize the multiplication facts such that it is interfering with his performance in math class, teachers have a number of options to explore. Since the child's IQ (#7) suggests that he is capable of memorizing the facts, changes in instructional interventions (#6) are warranted. Changes in the organizational structure may also be considered (#1) (i.e., reduce the number of problems to practice, alter the types of instructional materials used, or change teachers to find a more compatible personality or classroom structure), as well as changes in settings (#5) or incentive/motivational strategies (#2). If all of these interventions do not enhance the student's performance in applying his knowledge of multiplication facts, two variables deserve further investigation: (#3) cognitive support and (#4) tools. In this case, it appears obvious that the child's performance relative to using multiplication facts in the math classroom could be enhanced with the use of a multiplication table (#3) or a calculator (#4). By understanding the many variables that affect performance we are less likely to mistakenly view technology as a panacea for performance problems.

Models of human performance can contribute to the development of performance support strategies that utilize technology. Specifically, in Wile's model, variables #3 (cognitive support) and #4 (tools) suggest the value of identifying devices and tools that augment and extend cognitive functioning as a strategy for enhancing performance.

Cognitive Prostheses

A second new direction that must be addressed by the field of assistive technology for students with mild disabilities involves the concept of cognitive prostheses. Most readers will be familiar with physical prostheses (e.g., replacement of a limb lost in an accident). Applications of technology that extend human cognitive performance have been referred to as "cognitive technologies," "intelligence extenders," "cognitive workbenches," or "mental prostheses" (Office of Technology Assessment, 1982).

To date, little attention has been devoted to the development and use of cognitive prostheses for students with mild disabilities (Bohman, 2004; Edyburn, 1991, 2000a; Rowland, 2004). Part of the reason may be the influence of the historical view that knowledge is synonymous with memory. This explains, for example, the extensive focus in education on committing information to memory and the expectation that an educated person is someone who knows extensive bodies of knowledge without having to rely on external sources. A second reason may be the relatively recent development of technologies that serve as storage devices (e.g., speed dial for storing and dialing telephone numbers; programmable buttons on the car radio for recalling your favorite radio stations). Also consider the use of the World Wide Web and the many tools that can be used for creating, storing, retrieving, sorting, manipulating, and displaying information.

When considering the assistive technology needs of students with mild disabilities, additional research and development is necessary to identify devices and tools that augment and extend cognitive functioning as a strategy for enhancing performance. As we will see in the following examples, students could be using many different types of cognitive prostheses, but the abundance of questions about technology-enhanced performance makes decision making difficult.

A few years ago a local assistive technology specialist contacted me to see if I could help. The parents of a fifth-grade child who was struggling with mastering math facts had taken issue with recommendations by the school staff and the assistive technology team that the child should be allowed to use a calculator to complete her assignments. The assistive technology team felt this was an appropriate use of assistive technology, but the parents interpreted this recommendation to mean that the school staff had "given up" on their child. They felt that allowing their daughter to use a calculator to complete her math work would be "cheating."

I have pondered this example a great deal and I am not sure I am any closer to providing a convincing response today than when the situation first occurred. However, it really does not matter what I think. As I understand the discipline of special education technology, it appears to me that we (collectively, the discipline) do not have an answer to these parents' concerns. That is, where are the guidelines that dictate that all avenues to teach a child must be exhausted prior to the introduction of assistive technology? How do we know whether or not a child has the cognitive capabilities for learning the information? What alternative learning strategies have been used to help the child master the content? Should direct instruction continue while a child is taught how to use of a performance aid? If assistive technology is permitted, what will be the consequences of this device dependency? Finally, how do we distinguish who can and cannot benefit from a cognitive prosthesis? After all, wouldn't all students get higher test scores if they could look up the answers? Is that fair?

There is considerable prejudice against tools that *appear* to provide competitive advantage to students who some believe should "simply try harder." We also hold to the historical notion that the child doesn't *know* the information if s/he has to rely on an external source. This response takes us down a path where the only knowledge that is valued is the kind we hold in our head and fails to recognize the frailty of memory or the reality that knowledge is of two types: the kind you know and the kind you know how to find (Boswell, 1887).

As we continue to measure the outcome of education in forms that equate knowledge with memory, we are perpetuating discrimination against individuals with disabilities that involve cognition. By arguing that it is not fair that some students are allowed to use a cognitive prosthesis, we illustrate our arrested development that fair means everyone gets the same thing rather than everyone gets what he or she needs (Welch, 2000). It is vitally important that these issues are addressed in order for cognitive prostheses to be an acceptable form of assistive technnology for students with mild disabilities.

Remediation vs. Compensation
Theorists (Cook & Hussey, 1995, 2002; King, 1999) have raised the same issue that befuddled the parents and IEP team in the example about calculator use. That is, how do we decide if the best course of action is remediation (i.e., additional instructional time, different instructional approaches) or compensation (i.e., recognizing that remediation has failed and that compensatory approaches are needed to produce the desired level of performance)? Perhaps it is not coincidental that these theorists are therapists by training and thus are used to making decisions about functional performance. The importance is placed on can I do it? rather than how I do it. For example, if I cannot complete certain tasks without my right arm, additional therapy may be an option if I am recovering from surgery, but not if I have had an amputation. The benchmarks to guide decision-making about remediation and compensation are much clearer in situations involving mobility and sensory impairments. Unquestionably,

compensatory approaches are often used because there simply are no other ways to complete the task.

Unfortunately, few guidelines are available to guide decision-making about assistive technology for learning (Edyburn, 2002c). If a child has repeatedly failed a test of essential knowledge (e.g., adding fractions, states and capitals, presidents of the United States, parts of a plant), how much failure data do we need before we have enough evidence that the child cannot perform the task? When do we intervene? And, what do we do? Under what conditions does a student demonstrate that s/he needs a cognitive prosthesis to gain access to a given body of essential knowledge? The assistive technology theorists suggest we have a critical decision to make: remediate or compensate.

Teachers are extremely comfortable with the options associated with remediation: re-teach the information, use alternative instructional strategies, break the tasks down into smaller parts to analyze what the child knows and what components are problematic, reduce the number of items that must be completed, provide additional practice, engage in one-on-one tutoring, and so on. If this approach always worked, we would never meet students who could not read independently beyond the second-grade level or students who failed to master the basic math facts.

At some point in the educational process, special educators must recognize the need for compensatory approaches. That is, we have to provide compensatory interventions when a student's academic history illustrates a pattern of failure given typical instructional strategies (e.g., a fourth grader with learning disabilities failed to learn the names and capitals of the 50 states, now we expect him to learn the names of all the American presidents). If a known characteristic of a disability is that a student has difficulty processing and retrieving information, then why doesn't the IEP team's consideration of assistive technology result in the recommendation of the Web search engine Ask Jeeves (www.askjeeves.com)? Functionally, this would allow a child to look up the answers to anything s/he does not know. If our goal is to enhance educational performance, Ask Jeeves provides a compensatory approach for the student to meet specific objectives by accessing information s/he does not remember.

The argument that Ask Jeeves is assistive technology graphically illustrates how much we do not know about assistive technology as a cognitive prosthesis (Bohman, 2004; Edyburn, 1991, 2000a; Rowland, 2004). Some obvious questions include: Who needs it? What are the benefits associated with its use? What are the drawbacks to its use? Further, this provocative example highlights the need for frameworks to guide decision making when considering the adoption assistive technology. How much failure data is needed to trigger a decision to de-emphasize remediation approaches and increase the use of compensatory approaches that enhance a child's functional performance?

Despite the current educational reform rhetoric about high academic standards, educational practice prefers to hold time constant. That is, if all students are to achieve a given educational standard, time should vary to allow for different rates of learning. However, we prefer to hold time constant (e.g., one-day lessons, two-week units) moving onto the next topic despite the extreme variance in performance within a class.

When time is held constant, it is impossible to make claims about all students achieving high standards without changes in instruction. This is a confusing factor about the current standards movement. Many teachers and administrators believe high standards mean one-size fits all relative to curriculum, instruction, and assessment. This misunderstanding translates into classroom practices that seek to produce high academic performance by locking all the variables: time, content knowledge, instructional approach, learning activities, methods of assessment, and ultimately performance. Proponents of NCLB revel in the belief that failure is not an option. However, when all the variables are locked, it seems that failure is the only option.

The importance of enhancing academic achievement suggests an urgent need to explicitly address a question deeply embedded in the assistive technology consideration process: remediation vs. compensation. While teachers and therapists tend to view this as an either/or question, it may be more fruitful direction to ask what percentage of effort should be devoted to each (Edyburn, 2003b). Why isn't the use of Ask Jeeves an appropriate assistive technology tool for a student? After all, if time is to be held constant (e.g., a one-week unit) and traditional instruction has generally failed to produce acceptable levels of academic performance, the performance theorists (Wiley, 1996) suggest that the only other variables to manipulate to enhance performance involve altering the tools or the cognitive supports.

Somewhere there is an invisible line demarcating the boundaries and relationships among teaching (can I claim that I have taught if you haven't learned?), learning differences, expectations and standards, and technology-enhanced performance. If a fundamental characteristic of a mild disability is difficulty learning, it behooves the profession to respond with a deeper understanding of assistive technology for learning in order to ensure that children and youth are receiving the free appropriate public education (FAPE) to which they are entitled.

We will now turn our attention to issues associated with assessing the need for assistive technology and the decisions associated with assistive technology consideration.

Assistive Technology Consideration

While assistive technology assessment procedures have been in place in many school districts since the early 1980s, the 1997 reauthorization of IDEA mandates consideration of assistive technology. Since IEP teams must document their efforts to consider assistive technology for each student, in this section we will examine the requirement for assistive technology consideration along with resources that facilitate the process. In addition, we'll offer a critique of current practices and suggest recommendations for new directions relative to consideration of assistive technology for students with mild disabilities.

Issues Involved in Consideration
As noted earlier, in a brief 15-year period, a series of laws established a matrix of federal policies advancing the acquisition and use of technology for individuals with disabilities. Two factors contributed to the passage of these laws: (a) the apparent value of technology already available in the marketplace for individuals with disabilities and (b) the exceedingly small number of people who were benefiting from existing technology. As a result, federal policy has been used as a mechanism for capturing the potential of technology on an ever-increasing scale.

The concept of assistive technology consideration is a rather recent development. Its origin can be traced to the Individuals with Disabilities Education Act Amendments of 1997 (Public Law 105-17), which contained a requirement for IEP teams to consider assistive technology in the development of an IEP: "The IEP Team shall—(v) consider whether the child requires assistive technology devices and services" [Section 614 (d)(3)(B) Consideration of Special Factors].

Whereas some observers believed this language reflected a new federal policy, Golden (1998) argued that it simply formalizes a previous responsibility:

> The IDEA requires schools to provide AT if it is needed for a student to receive a free appropriate publication education (FAPE). FAPE can include a variety of services such as special education, related services, supplementary aids and services, program modifications or support for school personnel. AT, just like other components of FAPE, must be provided at no cost to parents. The specific IDEA requirement for schools to provide AT is as follows:

> 300.308 Assistive Technology
> Each public agency shall ensure that assistive technology devices or assistive technology services or both, as those terms are defined in 300.5 - 300.6 are made available to a child with a disability if required as part of a child's (a) Special education under 300.17; (b) Related services under 300.16; or (c) Supplementary aids and services under 300.550(b)(2). (Golden, 1998, p. 4)

Golden's analysis highlights a critical issue: free appropriate public education (FAPE).

Schools are required to provide assistive technology for students who need such tools, if they are necessary for the student's participation in and benefit from a free appropriate public education. The historical implications of this requirement are unquestioned in the context of mobility (e.g., a powered wheelchair) and communication (e.g., an augmentative communication system). However, the requirement now explicitly covers all disabilities. In the context of high-incidence disabilities, the consideration requirement often raises a budgetary red flag for administrators. For example, does every student with poor handwriting need a laptop computer? If so, where will the funds come from to pay for this educational need? If everyone cannot have a laptop, who will decide who can benefit from one and who cannot?

The requirement to consider assistive technology has spawned a tremendous need in the field for training and resources. Several noteworthy resources have been developed to facilitate the intent as students, parents, teachers, administrators, and technology specialists engage in the consideration process.

The SETT Framework, created by Joy Zabala (1995), focuses the attention of IEP teams on the Student, the Environment, the Tasks required for active participation in the activities of the environment, and then the Tools need for the student to address the tasks. SETT was designed to facilitate gathering and organizing data to enhance assistive technology decision-making. This model has been widely adopted and implemented due to the intuitive nature of the four core areas, its ease of use in assessment and decision-making, and the fact that the student is the initial and primary focus. In addition, this model illustrates how changes in the environment or the task can fundamentally alter the need for tools.

Chambers' (1997) book, *Has Technology Been Considered? A Guide for IEP Teams,* is an acknowledged key resource on the topic of assistive technology consideration. Chambers observed that the 1997 reauthorization of IDEA required that assistive technology be considered, but that the legislation offered no guidelines on how to implement this requirement. This book is an outcome of her research which involved a delphi study of assistive technology experts and focus groups with trainers and consumers of assistive technology services. A valuable component of Chambers' work is a model outlining a sequence of questions that should be discussed by an IEP team. As a result of engaging in the proposed process, Chambers argues that teams will automatically generate the documentation of their assistive technology consideration efforts on behalf of a child.

As school districts seek to implement assistive technology on a systemic basic, an analysis developed by Golden (1999) may be used to sensitize administrators to the gap between students currently using assistive technology and the potential number of students who could benefit (see Table 1). To arrive at an estimate of the size of the population of students receiving special education who could potentially benefit from assistive technology, Golden came up with conservative projections of the number of students who should be using assistive technology using the diagnostic categories in the state of Missouri. Her estimates were based on the types of educational needs students typically have in academic areas, study skills, daily living, leisure/recreation, and program accessibility as well as the types of assistive technology that are available to address such needs. The purpose of this exercise is to offer some benchmarks for schools to use in a programmatic evaluation of whether they are adequately addressing students' assistive technology needs (e.g., if your school has a number of students with visual impairments who are not using any assistive technology, you should find out why). The concept of expectancy benchmarking offers some intriguing possibilities for guiding the assistive technology consideration process.

The Assistive Technology Consideration Quick Wheel (AT Quick Wheel) is a small manipulative wheel that offers hands-on access to a generic list of assistive technology for a variety of tasks. One side of the wheel lists federal definitions of assistive technology devices and services. The other side provides information about a variety of resources including books, journals, newsletters, and Internet sites. Both sides include a generic list

Table 1. Anticipated Assistive Technology Use

Disability	% Expected AT Use
Deaf and Hard of Hearing	100%
Blind and Visually Impaired	100%
Physical Disability	100%
Deaf/Blind	100%
Multiple Disabilities	100%
Traumatic Brain Injury	50-75%
Autism	50-75%
Learning Disability	25-35%
Health Impairment	25-35%
Cognitive Disability	25-35%
Speech/Language Disorder	10-25% *
Emotional Disability	10-25%

* Most students who need and/or use augmentative communication devices have an identified disability other than "speech/language," thus the lower projected usage for this diagnostic category.

Source: Golden, D. (1999). Assistive technology policy and practice. What is the right thing to do? What is the reasonable thing to do? What is required and must be done? *Special Education Technology Practice, 1*(1), 12-14.

of assistive technology tools to consider in a variety of academic areas, including mechanics of writing, computer access, math, and reading. The AT Quick Wheel was created by Penny Reed in collaboration with the IDEA Local Implementation by Local Administrators (ILIAD), the Technology and Media (TAM) Division of the Council for Exceptional Children, and the Wisconsin Assistive Technology Initiative (WATI). Despite the generic nature of the advice, to date, more than 400,000 copies of the AT Quick Wheel have been distributed, making it the most widespread assistive technology decision support tools.

Critique of Current Practices

This section analyzes the current state of affairs relative to assessing the need for assistive technology for students with mild disabilities. Topics to be discussed include lack of professional preparation for engaging in the consideration process, inadequate tools for supporting decision-making, limitations of current assessment models, and a lack of data to monitor the effectiveness of the assistive technology consideration mandate.

The current teacher certification standard for technology in many states simply involves completing a three-credit course in educational technology that may or may not cover assistive technology. In most special education certification programs, coursework in assistive technology is an elective rather than a required course. As a result, there is little evidence to indicate that professionals receive adequate preparation for selecting and using assistive technology through their preservice preparation (Edyburn, 2003a).

Less than half the states have a certificate or graduate program that offer advanced training with an emphasis on assistive technology. This situation is problematic since the mandate to consider assistive technology essentially added four million students with high-incidence disabilities to the assistive technology caseload. Over the past six years there has been no discernable increase in the number of AT specialists prepared or hired in response to the federal mandate. As a result, there is little evidence that school districts have adequately trained personnel in every school building to provide leadership on the issues associated with assistive technology (Edyburn, 2003a).

The paradox of assistive technology consideration (Edyburn, 2000a): "How can I consider assistive technology if I don't know what is available?" paralyzes many school-based assistive technology teams. The result is the inability to effectively implement the consideration mandate. The tremendous success of the AT Quick Wheel illustrates the urgent need for new tools to assist IEP teams in the assistive technology consideration decision-making process.

Given the lack of a data collection mandate in the federal law, no accurate figures are available concerning the number of students who use assistive technology. This means that it is not known how many students remain unaffected by the federal consideration mandate as a result of being unserved or underserved. Shocking evidence of this problem was revealed in a recent report analyzing 341 IEPs in a large urban school district when only six IEPs were found to mention the provision of assistive technology (Borsuk, 2004). Potentially the lack of assistive technology consideration illustrates legal exposure relative to the provisions of FAPE since chronic underachievement could be potentially mitigated by the use of assistive technology.

Research is urgently needed to test the validity of Golden's (1999) expectancy benchmarking approach as a basic tool for evaluating programs to ensure compliance with the federal mandate for assistive technology consideration. Additional research is needed to provide baseline data about the number of students using assistive technology and the kinds of assistive technology they use (Moser, 2003).

Most policies and procedures for assessing the need for assistive technology devices and services are based on a deficit model. That is, a student must fail and be noticed in order for a teacher to initiate a referral. There are many parallels between the special education and the assistive technology referral models. As a result, the assistive technology referral and evaluation system is subject to the same inherent limitations as the special education referral and evaluation system: inefficiency, significant delay in the provision of intervention services, high cost, and inadequate emphasis on monitoring and follow-up after the initial evaluation. Hence, current assistive technology assessment models are problematic for meeting the needs of students with high-incidence disabilities (Edyburn, 2000a). Thus, it may be necessary to revisit the historical precedent found in prereferral intervention models in the early 1980s, which were developed in response to the large numbers of students with mild disabilities being referred to special education with the belief that effective interventions could be designed for the general education classroom that would assist the target student as well as a peer group of other low-performing students.

In conclusion, there is little evidence to suggest that the mandate to consider assistive technology has resulted in widespread use of appropriate assistive technology by students with mild disabilities. Several factors have been cited that impair the efficacy of current assessment models. In the next section, we will present a series of recommendations for new directions in assistive technology assessment and consideration that may improve access to assistive technology devices and services for students with mild disabilities.

New Directions in AT Assessment and Consideration for Students with Mild Disabilities

The challenges described in the previous section provide the basis for the following recommendations. The purpose is to outline a series of initiatives that have the potential to address the assistive technology needs of students with mild disabilities who are currently unserved and underserved while improving the performance of those students who currently use assistive technology.

Perhaps it is time to rethink the term *assistive technology* and consider replacing it with the term *technology-enhanced performance*. Current assistive technology service delivery systems have over-emphasized tasks associated with selection of assistive technology and devoted little effort to enhanced functional outcomes. Morphing the concept of assistive technology into an updated form allows a subtle shift in emphasis. That is, it matters little what form the technology comes in (i.e., low-tech, high-tech), rather what matters is that appropriate tools have been acquired and are used to enhance functional performance. Refocusing our attention from the stuff of assistive technology to the results will signal a developmental maturation of the profession. Further, the concept of technology enhanced performance eliminates the artificial boundaries between technology use by individuals with disabilities versus technology used by nonhandicapped peers.

As mentioned above, limited evidence suggests that teachers and administrators are being adequately prepared to assume their decision-making roles relative to using technology to enhance educational achievement. There is a severe shortage of personnel preparation programs to provide advanced training in assistive technology. And state and federal leadership and resources are sorely needed for preservice and inservice personnel preparation. In short, particular emphasis on using assistive technology to enhance the educational performance of students with mild disabilities, a population of approximately four million students, is a critical national need.

According to the National Assessment of Educational Progress (NAEP), only one third of American students are performing at the proficient level in reading and math at the fourth grade level (National Center for Educational Statistics, 2003). This means there is a significant population of students with and without disabilities who could benefit from interventions that use technology to enhance performance. When the majority of students are failing to achieve appropriate functional levels of performance, questions must be raised about how we do business. One response is to suggest the implementation of a screening system, comparable to the special education Child Find mandate, that identifies students with performance problems and provides prereferral interventions that involve compensatory technology applications. Without a screening system that systematically identifies struggling students and engages them in diagnostic assessment to determine if appropriate technology tools can enhance their performance, we run the risk of perpetuating discriminatory assistive technology assessment practices that provide assistive technology only to those students with advocates who challenge the system.

Finally, the intent of the assistive technology consideration mandate will not be met until new tools are available that allow non-assistive technology specialists to understand the array of possibilities for addressing deficits in academic performance. Presently, assistive technology specialists serve a gatekeeping function. That is, we restrict access to assistive technology products until a person has passed through our assessment system. Teachers, administrators, and parents are in desparate need of easy-to-use decision-making tools that help them identify categories of products that may be useful for individual or groups of struggling students. Members of the assistive technology community need to capture their individual and collective wisdom and package their mental diagnostic models in forms that allow others to navigate our knowledge base and locate appropriate types of technology supports.

We will now turn to issues associated with interventions. That is, what are specific ways that assistive technology can be used by students with mild disabilities?

Interventions

Historically, the application of assistive technology for individuals with disabilities has been most notable for physical impairments. As the sophistication of technology grew in the twentieth century, considerable advances were made in the utilization of technology to compensate for sensory impairments (i.e., vision, hearing). Only recently has the notion of assistive technology been extended into areas of cognition, a topic of critical concern for individuals with mild disabilities. In this section, we will explore issues associated with reconceptualizing the forms of assistive technology and the implications of such rethinking when designing interventions. To conclude, a critique of current practices will be provided along with recommendations for new directions concerning assistive technology interventions for students with mild disabilities.

Two databases are widely recognized as authoritative sources for locating information about assistive technology: Closing the

Gap Solutions Database (www.closing thegap.com/solutions/) and AbleData (www. abledata.com/). While these databases are comprehensive, users will discover that the taxonomies used for classifying assistive technologies with potential value for students with mild disabilties are considerably broad (e.g., learning) and therefore inadequate to provide guidance on specific devices or interventions.

To remedy this situation, specialized sources for locating AT for students with learning disabilities have emerged. For example, Richard Wanderman, an adult with a learning disability, maintains the LD Resources Web site (www.ldresources.com/) with a wealth of information and offers his personal perspective on the value and use of specific tools. Further, Learning Disabilities and Assistive Technology is a Web site (www.gatfl.org/ldguide/) maintained by a project known as Georgia Tools for Life. This site offers a valuable interface for IEP teams in defining academic performance problems in reading, math, and writing; exploring potential instructional strategies; and providing links to detailed product information.

A third area of work involves the definition of learner productivity toolkits. Technology toolkits have been advanced as a technology integration strategy (Gardner & Edyburn, 2000) as well as an assistive technology prereferral intervention (Edyburn, 2000a). Several examples have been developed that illustrate the value of this strategy for helping students, teachers, administrators, and parents start the journey of locating appropriate assistive technology, Tools for Living with Learning Disabilities (www.ldonline.org/ld_indepth/technology/ccld_assistive_technology.html); and Customizing Technology Solutions for College Students with LD www. ldonline.org/ld_indepth/technology/customizing_technology.html).

As noted earlier when discussing the general literature base on assistive technology and mild disabilities, the research base on the effectiveness of technology for students with mild disabilities is small. For many years, this was due to the focus on instructional technology applications. Readers interested in starting points for accessing the research in specific academic applications of technology and students with mild disabilities are encouraged to consult the following references:

- Writing (Daiute & Morse, 1994; De La Paz, 1999; Lewis, Graves, Ashton, & Kieley, 1998; MacArthur, 1999, 1998, 1996; McNaughton, Hughes, & Ofiesh, 1997; Morocco, Dalton, & Tivnan, 1992; Vacc, 1987; Zhang, 2000).

- Spelling (Berninger et al. 1998; Dalton et al, 1990; Edwards, Blackhurst, & Koorland, 1995; MacArthur et al. 1996; Montgomery, Karlan, & Coutinho, 2001).

- Reading (Baker, Gersten, & Scanlon, 2002; Bangert-Drowns & Pyke, 2001; Boone & Higgins, 1993; Dawson, Venn, & Gunter, 2000).

- Behavior (Cafiero, 2000; Denny & Fox, 1989; Epstein, Willis, Conners, & Johnson, 2001; Manion, 1986; Strein & Kachman, 1984; Wetzel, 2001).

- Math (Browder & Grasso, 1999; Butler, Miller, Lee, & Pierce, 2001; Hasselbring, Goin, & Bransford, 1988; Hasselbring, Goin, & Wissick, 1989; Maccini, Gagnon, & Hughes, 2002; Woodward, 1995; Woodward & Carnine, 1993).

- Social studies (Okolo, & Ferretti, 1996).

Critique of Current Practices

Most schools have two parallel systems for supporting technology. Assistive technology devices are managed by assistive technology specialists for students with disabilities. While network coordinators and technology specialists manage the instructional technology (IT) infrastructure for students without disabilities. There are considerable differences between these two systems in terms of power, authority, and control (i.e., you can't put that adaptive software on the network because it will make the network crash ...). It is relatively rare to find a school where IT and AT have been integrally linked in ways that support the success of all students. Thus, assistive technology staff are challenged to work within the larger context of a school district.

What does assistive technology look like? Historically, assistive technology has taken various forms and is most widely associated with applications that help individuals who are blind, visually impaired, deaf, hard of hearing, or physically impaired. As mentioned, applications of technology that serve as cognitive prostheses are considerable less accepted and understood. For example, for a student with short- and long-term memory problems documented on his IEP, can the search engine Ask Jeeves (www.askjeeves.com) serve as a cognitive prosthesis to help him complete test items he does not know or remember? Or, could the *Job Coach* (www.attainment company.com/) be programmed to remind him of the sequence of steps for completing a task? Is the software product *Inspiration* (www.inspiration.com) AT or IT? Are text-to-speech products only for students with disabilities or could all students benefit from having the computer read selected words or whole passages?

Over the past 15 years, the marketplace has made outstanding advances that challenge us to rethink the form, function, and purpose of assistive technology. When human performance is the primary focus, the definition of assistive technology is necessarily broad as we seek to use any conceivable resource to enhance a person's performance. Whereas the application of assistive technology is obviously apparent in situations involving impairments that limit mobility, sensory perception, and communication, what does it mean to enhance the performance of a learner?

One model of learning suggests that learners pass through a series of stages in the process of acquiring knowledge (Haring, Lovitt, Eaton, & Hansen, 1978; Hasselbring & Bottge, 2000; Mindscape, 1988). The *entry level* is characterized by the learner performing the targeted task infrequently or not at all. During the *acquisition* stage, the learner performs the task initially at 0-25% accuracy and moves to more advanced level where the task is per*formed with 65-80% accuracy. At the next stage, proficiency*, the learner seeks to develop fluency (high rate and high accuracy), in performing the task. Retaining a high level of accuracy and rate is the primary consideration of the *maintenance* stage. At the *generalization* stage, the learner is encouraged to transfer his/her knowledge to new settings as a means of applying what has been learned to new situations. Finally, the *adaptation* stage is characterized by problem solving as the learner's knowledge is applied to novel problems. Hasselbring and Bottge (2000) have noted that the stages of acquisition and proficiency are particularly problematic for students with special educational needs.

While technology can be used in every stage of the learning process (i.e., applications of technology that enhance teaching and learning), it is when technology is utilized in ways that make a difference (quantifiable or qualitative) in performance that makes it function as assistive technology. For example, consider a student with learning disabilities who participates in an inclusion science class and is having difficulty balancing chemical equations. His teacher, concerned about the student's poor performance, has created a spreadsheet that structures the procedure into a series of steps and provides feedback to the student when he enters a value into an equation. While such an intervention might be considered "just good teaching," in the performance support literature it is considered a "job aid." In the context of high-incidence disabilities, it is an example of an instructional support strategy. For some students, this intervention will serve a transitional function helping them to understand the concept in more concrete terms and once they "get it," they will no longer utilize the spreadsheet but will be able to compute the calculations by hand, on paper, like most of their classmates. However, for other students, the spreadsheet is an example of assistive technology. The value of assistive technology is clear when assessing the student's performance under two conditions: completion of a specific task with the assistive technology and completion of the same task unaided.

At this point, it is important to highlight the distinction between instructional goals and functional outcomes. Wile's (1996) model of human performance discussed earlier helps us see the critical distinction between instructional technology and assistive technology. As long as the educational team seeks to employ various teaching and learning strategies, the application of technology is clearly instructional: we are explicitly seeking to enhance a student's skills and knowledge (see #6 in Figure 1); an intrinsic variable that affects performance. Indeed, such has been the historical emphasis of education: to increase the information and knowledge that we intrinsically carry with us. The value of such knowledge is clear in terms of portability and ready access.

Advances in the marketplace will continue to challenge the special education community to reconceptualize assistive technology. Consider the following descriptions of selected products. Could any of these products be listed on an IEP to enhance the functional performance of a student with a mild disability?

- If a student has difficulty remembering to perform various tasks, perhaps the IEP team should explore Ms. Reminder (www. iping.com) which allows reminders to be sent via email, phone, fax, and pager.

- If a student is unable to read a content area textbook, perhaps the team should explore the value of a text-to-speech tool like Readplease (www.readplease.com). Or, the student should perhaps be given access to online multimedia instruction like BrainPop (www.brainpop.com), which presents the information in audio and video formats. Or, should the student be given access to online instructional materials where the information can be read to the student (starchild. gsfc.nasa.gov/).

- If a student has difficulty completing multi-step math problems, perhaps the team should explore WebMath (www.webmath.com/) that allows the user to enter a wide array of mathematical statements and see step-by-step directions as well as the correct answer.

- If a student has difficulty engaging in the research process to prepare a report, perhaps the team should consider the use of Karnak (www.karnak.com), which allows users to enter topics and have the Web agent locate the best available information on the topic and send the results back via email.

The changing face of assistive technology is problematic for many teachers, administrators, and policy makers. First, consider the federal definition of assistive technology that begins with the word *any*. If assistive technology is anything that enhances functional peformance, how can we deny including tools like Ask Jeeves on the IEP? Once we make a commitment to determining that a student needs this assistive technology, the federal definition of assistive technology services comes to the forefront. This means we may also be required to purchase the student a laptop computer so s/he can access Ask Jeeves. Further, it is not unreasonable to request wireless Internet access since the student will have to access the Internet in all his/her classes throughout the school building.

New Directions in AT Interventions for Students with Mild Disabilities

The scarcity of assistive technology interventions for students with mild disabilities described in the previous section provides the basis for the following three recommendations.

Theoretical constructs

Rather than emphasizing the differences between assistive and instructional or educational technology, let us focus on clarifying the theoretical constructs associated with using technology to enhance teaching, learning, and performance. For example, why is the software product *Inspiration* assistive technology for a student with a disability but instructional technology for everyone else? And, how does the design of learning environments and instructional materials that utilize principles of universal design impact the need for assistive technology? Theoretical models that unify these disparate constructs will reduce the artificial boundaries that have emerged among these related disciplines and contribute to important advances in research, practice, and development.

Universal design

A second new direction for assistive technology interventions for students with mild disabilities focuses on universal design considerations for the general education classroom. The current educational system is based on a sorting mechanism to determine who can and cannot do specific academic tasks. This paradigm is in urgent need of change considering that 67% of the students are not achieving the anticipated levels of proficiency (National Center for Educational Statistics, 2003). Increasing our understanding of the continuum of academic differences is vital to designing learning environments and instructional materials that anticipate and value diversity in ways that allow all students to be academically successful.

Decision-Making Tools

Finally, the intent of the assistive technology consideration mandate will not be met until tools are available that allow non-assistive technology specialists to understand the array of possibilities for addressing deficits in academic performance. Presently, assistive technology specialists serve a gatekeeping function. That is, we restrict access to assistive technology products until a person has passed through our assessment system. Teachers, administrators, and parents are in desperate need of easy-to-use decision-making tools that help them identify categories of products that may be useful for a single individual or groups of struggling students. Members of the assistive technology community have to capture their individual and collective wisdom and package their mental diagnostic models in a form that allows others to navigate their knowledge base and locate appropriate types of technology supports. Recent work by Armstrong (2003) is a promising example of efforts to construct a palette of universal design, instructional technology, and assistive technology tools to facilitate learning a specific instructional goal (e.g., reading a map).

Outcomes

In this section, current work associated with assistive technology outcomes will be profiled. Recent efforts to define and measure assistive technology outcomes will be highlighted. In addition, a critique of current practices and offer recommendations for new directions concerning assistive technology outcomes relative to students with mild disabilities will be provided.

In contrast to the abundance of measures and indicators that document the acquisition of technology, typically, less information is available on the impact of assistive technology. To remedy this situation, the current context of increased accountability and desire for understanding the value of technology investments, three national research centers have been established. Their agenda is to substantially increase the knowledge base surrounding assistive technology and its effective use by individuals with disabilities.

First, the Office of Special Education Programs (OSEP) funded the National Assistive Technology Institute based at the University of Kentucky. This center is charged with conducting AT research, translating research into AT practice, and providing resources to improve the delivery of AT services. To-date a number of policy studies have been completed and current work is focused on collecting data in a ten-state project to ascertain the nature of assistive technology in schools. To learn more about this center, visit the NATRI home page: natri.uky.edu.

A second federal agency has also been concerned about assistive technology and has funded priorities to advance a research agenda concerning assistive technology outcomes. In October 2001, National Institute on Disability and Rehabilitation Research (NIDRR) funded two, five-year, research centers to address the gap in data collection efforts concerning assistive technology outcomes, as well as the paucity of measurement instruments and strategies. The ATOMS (Assistive Technology Outcomes Measurement System) Project is based at the University of Wisconsin-Milwaukee and CATOR (Consortium for Assistive Technology Outcome Research) is housed at Duke University. Additional information about the research, development, and dissemination activities of each of these projects can be found at their respective websites: www.atoms.uwm.edu/ and www.atoutcomes. org/.

What is meant by outcome? In focus group research conducted by the ATOMS Project (Edyburn, 2003d), assistive technology service directors generated the following list of variables that might be measured to understand the outcomes associated with assistive technology use:

- Change in performance/function (body, structure, activity)
- Change in participation
- Usage, and why or why not
- Consumer satisfaction (process, devices)
- Goal achievement
- Quality of life
- Cost

In the past, single measures (e.g., satisfaction) have served as the proxy for the outcomes associated with assistive technology use. However, lists like the one generated by the ATOMS Project above raise interesting questions about whether or not the construct of assistive technology outcome can be measured in a single dimension or whether it is a complex multidimensional construct. This issue relates significantly to the question: Whose outcome?

DeRuyter (1995, 1997) posed the following questions about whose outcome to measure? If a client reports high satisfaction with a device, is that sufficient outcome data? And, if the client is satisfied with a device, what if discernible differences in performance or participation cannot be measured? Are these outcomes more or less important than the outcomes a funding source is interested in? Indeed, much work remains to be done to understand the values held by stakeholders concerning AT outcomes and how these values might be transformed into weights within a measurement system in order to give priority for certain factors within the outcome model. Finally, the importance of self-determination needs to be reconciled with competing values associated with the measurement of assistive technology outcomes.

The ATOMS Project has identified the following design, measurement, analysis, and decision-making factors that must be addressed when creating outcomes systems to measure the impact of assistive technology: (a) developing appropriate research designs, (b) standardizing performance tasks, (c) standardizing the data collection and coding process, (d) analyzing results using standardized metrics and benchmarks, and (e) enhancing the reliability and validity of decision-making. This model for measuring the outcomes of assistive technol-

ogy has also been applied to the academic content areas of reading (Edyburn, 2004), writing (Edyburn, 2003e), and math (Edyburn, 2003f). In the sections that follow, each component is described in the context of trying to answer the question: How does one measure the outcomes of assistive technology in reading?

Conceptual Foundations

Historically, not being able to read meant someone had to read everything for you. Personal readers and books on tapes are examples of the limited palette of compensatory strategies that have been made available to individuals with a reading disability. The concept of using technology to read everything for you is not an idea that has received extensive consideration in the professional literature; such ideas appear more common in science fiction. As a result, there is an urgent need for theoretical foundations to guide the development and use of reading assistive technologies.

Two recent works provide important frameworks for filling a void in the area of assistive technology for struggling readers. Dyck and Pemberton (2002) advanced a model for making decisions about text adapatations and outlined the theoretical rationale for five types of text adaptations: bypass reading, decrease reading, support reading, organize reading with graphic organizers, and guide reading. Inspired by the Dyck and Pemberton model but disappointed that assistive technology was not critical to the proposed interventions, Edyburn (2003b) created a taxonomy of text modification strategies that highlighted both instructional and assistive technology interventions. These preliminary efforts are encouraging for both research and practice in understanding the application of assistive technology in reading.

Developing Appropriate Research Designs

Central to the definition of assistive technology is the expectation of enhanced performance. Smith (2000) outlines a theoretical view known as time series concurrent and differential (TSCD) approach, which involves a series of performance measures of an individual when s/he is completing a specific task, with assistive technology and without assistive technology.

Figure 2. Smith's TSCD model for isolating the difference between performance with AT and without AT.

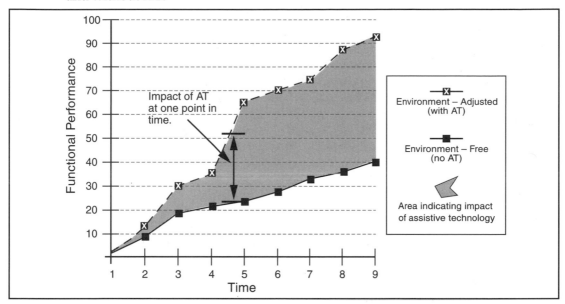

The results reflect a pattern that shows improved performance in both conditions; however, the performance with assistive technology is significantly greater than the performance without AT. The differences between the two measurements isolate the specific impact of assistive technology and provide evidence of the impact and outcome over time (see Figure 2).

The general utility of using this approach in research seeking to measure the outcomes of assistive technology for reading is unknown. While the approach is potentially useful and practical for measuring component skills of the reading process (e.g., reading rate, comprehension questions answered correctly), measuring less discrete components of the reading process (e.g., reading enjoyment) is problematic. At this time, for example, it is not known what the optimal time period is for data collection (daily, weekly, monthly) to yield measures that are sensitive enough to demonstrate change. Nonetheless, this research design appears highly compatible with existing instructional practices to warrant further consideration. In addition, the design will permit the collection of data from students without disabilities, which will contribute significantly to subsequent performance benchmarking efforts.

Alternatively, A-B-A single-subject research designs will reveal important patterns of performance for an individual during baseline (without AT), intervention (with AT), and reversal to baseline concerning any number of variables (e.g., minutes spent reading, comprehension questions answered correctly). While this methodology is essential for making decisions about the effectiveness of specific assistive technology for an individual student, it has limitations for informing general professional practice.

Identifying high-quality research methodology for reading assistive technology research is critical. The ongoing controversy surrounding the National Reading Panel (2000) report, the subsequent debates and critiques of research methodology for defining best practice (Block & Pressley, 2002; Kamil, Mosenthal, Pearson, & Barr, 2002), concerns about what types of data count as evidence of reading achievement (Murphy, Shannon, Johnston, & Hansen, 1998), and the use and misuse of research in policy making (Pressley, 2002; Smith, 2003) are instructive for guiding our embryonic efforts in establishing a useful research base that will inform classroom practice.

Standardizing Performance Tasks
Reading performance is often assessed through

informal reading inventories, curriculum-based assessments, and standardized tests. Typically, assessments of reading involve a variety of skills (letter and word recognition, vocabulary, reading rate, and comprehension (e.g., literal, inferential, critical). While several standardized measures of reading achievement are commonly used, no single test is a recognized standard. As a result, measuring the outcomes of reading assistive technology will be more problematic than assessment of outcomes of assistive technology for math and writing that have standardized representative tasks to facilitate comparison of performance between students.

Standardizing the Data Collection and Coding Process

A routine measure of reading comprehension involves answering assorted questions about the material a person has read. While the nature of the comprehension questions varies from assignment to assignment, comprehension question taxonomies illustrate a fairly standard set of questions (e.g., main idea, fact retrieval, inferential). Typically, data are collected on the percentage of comprehension questions answered correctly. Standardizing comprehension question sets in multiples of 5 or 10 to permit conversion to percentage appears desirable.

Two recent advances in the measurement of reading performance offer significant potential for standardizing the data collection and coding process associated with measuring the outcomes of reading assistive technologies. The Dynamic Indicators of Basic Early Literacy Skills (DIBELS) are a set of standardized, individually administered measures of early literacy development (dibels.uoregon.edu/). The 1-minute fluency assessments allow teachers to gather important curriculum-based assessment data on students' pre-reading and early reading performance. Another innovation in the area of measuring reading performance is the Lexile Framework for Reading (www.lexile.com/), a computation metric used to assess the difficulty of text and the skill of the reader. The purpose is to predict the difficulty an individual reader will have with a given text in an effort to match the reader with appropriate materials for reading instruction.

Analyzing Results using Standardized Metrics and Benchmarks

Exceptional performance in reading is usually characterized by high rates of fluency and comprehension. Scores on standardized reading assessments are typically transformed into percentiles to illustrate how an individual's performance compares with that of others similar in age. While grade equivalents are sometimes used, they have been abandoned by the profession due to their technical inadequacy and significant potential for misuse.

The Matthew Effect (Stanovich, 1986) is a well documented effect in reading education. Based on a Biblical metaphor about the rich getting richer and the poor get poorer it means that while young children may display small differences in reading ability, over time the differences become much larger such that effective readers exponentially become more proficient and learn more whereas poor readers fall further behind. Understanding the long-term net effect of a reading disability has significant implications for analyzing the results of data collected concerning the use of reading assistive technology. That is, while text-to-speech technology may provide short-term improvement in reading comprehension, will such gains be adequate for closing the achievement gap with non-handicapped peers? If not, what does this mean for measuring the outcome of the assistive technology? If reading assistive technology shows promising potential in short-term gains, should this trigger intensive assistive technology-based remedial interventions to try and close the multi-year gap?

One problem inherent in current single subject design research in assistive technology involves expectancy. That is, there are few guidelines by which gains in performance can be judged. For example, the performance evidence illustrated in Figure 2 suggests that significant progress is being made. However, without normative evidence, it is unclear whether the performance gap is being closed. A theoretical model by Deshler and colleagues (2001) graphically illustrates how the performance gap grows over time (see Figure 3). This situation has profound implications for

Figure 3. Deshler and colleagues, (2001) theoretical model of the cumulative deficit in performance experienced by some students with disabilities.

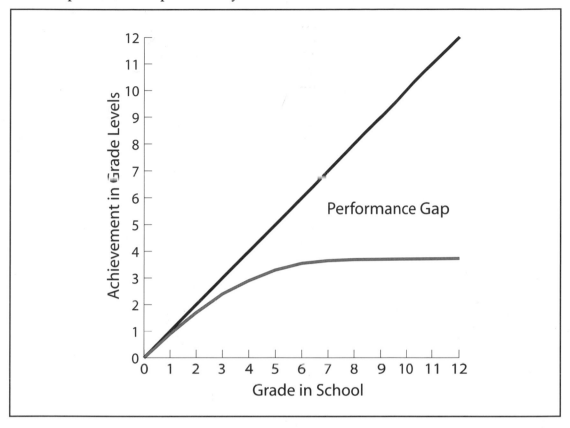

decisions about the potential role of assistive technology in closing achievement gaps, when to take snapshots of performance, and how to decide if performance is truly enhanced.

Enhancing Reliability and Validity of Decision-making

Reading education is concerned with two primary skills sets: learning to read (grades K-3) and reading to learn (grades 4 and beyond). Students with disabilities often demonstrate developmental delays that limit the benefit they receive from typical reading instruction in the early grades and end up being penalized throughout the rest of their academic career because their reading skill sets are not at grade level as the curriculum utilizes a one-size-fits-all reading-to-learn model in grades 4 and beyond. At the present time, little is known about how much failure data has to accumulate before educators recognize that a child is unable to read and in need of reading assistive

technologies. Edyburn (2003a) has argued that this is probably not either/or issue, but rather a question of what percentage of time/effort should be devoted to instruction and what percentage of time/effort reading compensation technologies should be provided so that the student can have access to the information.

As reading assistive technology performance data are collected, analysis should reveal several factors that will inform decision-making. First, does the graph indicate that reading performance with assistive technology is higher than performance without assistive technology? If so, the case can be made that the assistive technology is an effective intervention for enhancing performance. If not, the data suggest a need for additional training or a for a different intervention.

Second, do the data reflect that the student is able to meet the performance standard (i.e., 80% comprehension)? If so, the case can be made that the reading assistive technology effectively compensates for the person's disability. If the performance standard is not met, on the other hand, the IEP team must explore whether additional time is needed for developing mastery, whether additional interventions must be applied concomitantly, or whether a different intervention is needed.

Finally, can high levels of performance be maintained over time? That is, will the routine use of the assistive technology result in consistent high-quality performance in reading? In other words, is there any evidence that the assistive technology for reading is closing the achievement gap known as the Matthew Effect (Stanovich, 1986)?

This section has described some of the recent work by the ATOMS Project relative to measuring the outcomes of assistive technology in the context of academic learning tasks, common areas of difficulty for students with mild disabilities. There is an urgent need for significant philosophical and theoretical work regarding the nature of assistive technology for enhancing academic performance. We will now turn our attention to a critique of current practices.

Critique of Current Practices

Current law and regulations governing assistive technology involve only two definitions: assistive technology devices and assistive technology services. These components are but two legs of a three-legged stool. Missing from assistive technology federal policy is an emphasis on the purpose of assistive technology; that is, to enhance performance.

In my work with teachers, parents, and administrators, I have found that assistive technology is viewed by some as blank-check legal mandate that requires schools to purchase devices and services based with the *hope* that they will work for a specific student. Since federal regulations do not specify a process that involves systematic collection and evaluation of data, assistive technology consideration decisions are frequently made without evidence that assistive technology *actually* improves a students' academic performance. Without data and decision-making guidelines, however, it is not possible to equitably discern who can benefit from specific assistive technologies and who

cannot. This is not an acceptable procedure with high-incidence mild disabilities given the potential population of four million students. As a result, there is an urgent need for research and development to create protocols for measuring assistive technology outcomes and understanding rubrics for decision-making.

In this context it is important to distinguish between "claims of effectiveness" and statements that can be supported by evidence and subsequently verified. That is, just because someone says a device is effective for a specific child does not mean everyone agrees with the statement. As a result, all statements about assistive technology effectiveness should be treated initially, simply, as claims.

Routine scrutiny of each claim concerning the effectiveness of assistive technology is a nondiscriminatory professional practice. That means that vendors are not held to a higher standard simply because they are a for-profit organization versus the standard independent engineers would have to meet to show the effectiveness of their product. Similarly, that means that parents are not required to present more "proof" than a professional to support a request for assistive technology devices and services.

To judge the validity of a claim that assistive technology is effective, the evidence must be reviewed. The challenges associated with collecting evidence to support claims of effectiveness appear to pass through a developmental process with distinct phases: (a) exploratory phase, (b) descriptive phase, and (c) empirical phase. In the sections that follow, these concepts will be elaborated on, along with a description of the types of data often cited in support of a claim.

Exploratory Phase

The exploratory phase is often associated with new product development. Two benchmarks can be observed in the exploratory phase, intuition and observation. Evidence that is described with statements like "I just know it works" requires deferring to the judgment of the individual, parent, teacher, or product designer. As a result, this type of evidence may be more properly referred to as intuition.

A second benchmark is observation. This type of evidence is gathered from observers watching the assistive technology in use and drawing personal conclusions that "It appears to help."

Neither of these two benchmarks uses formal data collection procedures since the value of the assistive technology appears obvious. As a result, evidence gathered in the exploratory phase is seldom considered scientific and, therefore fails to offer convincing proof that the assistive technology is effective. However, experience in this phase may lead to more systemic data gathering in subsequent phases.

Descriptive Phase

The descriptive phase represents an advance in the type of evidence that is presented in support of an effectiveness claim. Two types of data are generally found in the descriptive phase, anecdotal evidence and case studies.

Anecdotal evidence involves gathering stories and critical incidents that can be used to make an argument that the assistive technology is effective. Often these types of data are used to inform purchasing decisions when the assistive technology is inexpensive since the efforts required to collect data are commensurate with the cost of the technology (i.e., a hand-held spelling checker). A shortcoming of anecdotal evidence is that it is generally unconvincing due to the impressionistic nature of the data and the lack of comprehensive or systematic procedures for collecting the data. Nonetheless, reports using anecdotal evidence have the potential to inform subsequent research by identifying key variables that impact the effective use of assistive technology.

Case studies, another method of data collection, generally focus on a single individual. Since case studies typically employ systematic procedures for data collection and analysis, the results often present evidence that have some credibility in scientific circles; even though the findings may or may not be replicable. Questions may also be raised concerning whether or not the observer was impartial.

Critics of evidence gathered in the descriptive phase often cite the inadequate sample size for basing decisions. However, the descriptive phase of evidence-based practice represents an important developmental benchmark in the search for reliable information about the effectiveness of assistive technology. As such, it signals a transition between sources of information that involve personal ways of knowing and more scientific approaches that involve systematic commitment to data collection and analysis.

Empirical Phase

The empirical phase typical involves well-designed research studies that seek to gather quantifiable data for statistical analysis. Three types of data sources can be observed in the empirical phase: group studies, research synthesis, and meta-analysis.

Group studies are a basic tool for researchers who seek to identify differences as a result of specific treatments or interventions. While group design studies are common in general education, in special education differences in disabilities make this measurement technique of limited use. As a result, few group studies have been conducted in assistive technology due to fundamental challenges involved in identifying appropriate samples.

Research synthesis is a process of analyzing patterns across a body of research studies. Typically, therefore, this approach is of limited use during the emergent period of growth of a research knowledge base (Edyburn, 2000c). For the field of special education technology, the requirements involving an adequate number of studies of which to make generalizations are a technical as well as a developmental problem.

Meta-analysis is a specific statistical procedure that computes an effect size about an intervention across a body of research to try to understand the effectiveness of the intervention. While Swanson (1999) has reported an effect size for technology use by students with disabilities as .77 (highly effective), for the reasons noted in the preceding areas, to date, meta-analysis has had limited application in the field of assistive technology.

Historically, empirical research has been the gold standard for proof concerning the effectiveness of a specific intervention. As a result, this standard has been incorporated into NCLB legislation. Despite outcries about the inappropriateness of such a standard for special education research, it highlights how sorely lacking the nature of assistive technology outcome data is. Research on the effectiveness of assistive technology is neither sophisticated nor adequate, and as a result, we know much less about the outcomes of assistive technology than necessary.

New Directions in Assistive Technology Outcomes for Students with Mild Disabilities

If local, state, and federal educational policies are to be informed by data, considerable commitment will be necessary to establish data collection protocols as a means of collecting valid and reliable data concerning the use of technology by students with mild disabilities. Specifically, much remains to be learned about the number of students with disabilities who use assistive technology, whether or not certain disability groups are underserved, and whether or not progress is being made in achieving the intent of the federal mandate to consider assistive technology. Given the size of the high incidence population with mild disabilities, discussions about the outcomes of assistive technology most necessarily will have to include issues of cost.

Little information is available about the relationship between student performance problems and the use of assistive technology to contribute to measurable gains in performance and achievement. Considerable efforts are needed to develop procedures and expectations about technology-enhanced performance. Finally, attention must be devoted to issues associated with interpreting assistive technology outcome data to ensure reliable and valid decisions are made about the selection, use, and effectiveness of assistive technology for students with mild disabilities.

Fuhrer (1999) provides a thoughtful summary of the historical context of assistive technology outcomes, including his impressions of the relatively slow response of the profession to ask questions about the effectiveness of assistive technology or seek methods to measure outcomes. Much remains to be learned about the value and impact of assistive technology for students with mild disabilities.

Conclusion

At the outset of this chapter I posed a question: Given the high incidence of mild disabilities, why has so little effort and attention been devoted to the use of assistive technology by students with mild disabilities? With few exceptions, the majority of the works published in this area have emerged since the 1997 IDEA reauthorization.

The lack of effort and attention devoted to assistive technology for students with mild disabilities may be understood as a lack of preparation. That is, currently we do not have adequate professional preparation programs, theoretical models, research-validated interventions, service delivery systems, or outcome measurement systems in place to meet the legal mandate or achieve its intent of providing all students with disabilities, including students with mild disabilities, access to appropriate assistive technology that enhances functional performance. Indeed, much more work is needed relative to the use of technology as a cognitive prosthesis.

The lack of preparation has created an urgent need for leadership and action on a comprehensive research, policy, and practice agenda to ensure that students with mild disabilities have routine access to appropriate assistive technology devices and services. Given the potential technology holds for approximately four million students, ages 6-21 with mild disabilities, only time will tell if we also lack commitment.

Acknowledgment

This work was supported in part by Grant # H324H990144 from the Office of Special Education and Rehabilitation Services, U.S. Department of Education, and Grant # H133A010403 from the National Institute on Disability and Rehabilitation Research, U.S. Department of Education to the University of Wisconsin-Milwaukee. Points of view or opinions stated in this chapter do not necessarily represent official agency positions.

References

AbleData. (2003). *Search for assistive technology products*. Available from: www.abledata.com/text2/search.htm

Armstrong, K. (2003). Location of specific places on a map: Assistive technology for learning. *Special Education Technology Practice, 5*(4), 24-27.

Bahr, C.M., & Rieth, H.J. (1991). Effects of cooperative, competitive, and individualistic goals on student achievement using computer-based drill-and-practice. *Journal of Special Education Technology, 11*(1), 33-38.

Baily, R.W. (1989). *Human performance engineering* (2nd ed). Englewood Cliffs, NJ: Prentice Hall.

Baker, S., Gersten, R., & Scanlon, D. (2002). Procedural facilitators and cognitive strategies: Tools for unraveling the mysteries of comprehension and writing process, and for providing access to the general curriculum. *Learning Disabilities Research and Practice, 17*(1), 65-77.

Bangert-Drowns, R.L., & Pyke, C. (2001). A taxonomy of student engagement with educational software: An exploration of literature thinking with electronic text. *Journal of Educational Computing Research, 24*, 213-234.

Behrmann, M.M. (1994). Assistive technology for students with mild disabilities. *Intervention in School and Clinic, 30*(2), 70-83.

Berninger, V., Abbott, R., Rogan, L., Reed, E., Abbott, S., Brooks, A., Vaughan, K., & Graham, S. (1998). Teaching spelling to children with specific learning disabilities: The minds ear and eye beat the computer or pencil. *Learning Disability Quarterly, 21*(2), 106-122.

Blackhurst, A. E. (1997). Perspectives on technology in special education. *Teaching Exceptional Children, 29*(5), 41-48

Blackhurst, A.E., & Edyburn, D.L. (2000). A brief history of special education technology. *Special Education Technology Practice, 2*(1), 21-35.

Block, C.C., & Pressley, M. (2002). *Comprehension instruction: Research-based best practices*. New York: Guilford Press.

Bohman, P. (2004). Cognitive disabilities part 1: We still know too little and we do even less. Retrieved on October 7, 2004 from: www.webaim.org/techniques/ articles/cognitive_too_little/

Boone, R., & Higgins, K. (1993). Hypermedia basal readers: Three years of school-based research. *Journal of Special Education Technology, 12*(2), 86-106.

Borsuk, A. (2004, March 23). Report faults MPS on special ed efforts. *Milwaukee Journal Sentinel*, pp. 1B-2B.

Boswell, J. (1887). *Life of Johnson*. New York: Harper and Row.

Browder, D.M., & Grasso, E. (1999). Teaching money skills to individuals with mental retardation: A research review with practical applications. *Remedial and Special Education, 20*, 297-308.

Bryant, D.P., & Bryant, B.R. (2003). *Assistive technology for people with disabilities*. Boston: Allyn & Bacon.

Bryant, D.P., Bryant, B.R., & Raskind, M.H. (1998). Using assistive technology to enhance the skills of students with learning disabilities. *Intervention in School and Clinic, 34*(1), 53-58.

Burke, M.D., Hagan, S.L., & Grossen, B. (1998). What curricular designs and strategies accommodate diverse learners? *Teaching Exceptional Children, 31*(1), 34-38.

Butler, F.M., Miller, S.P., Lee, K., & Pierce, T. (2001). Teaching mathematics to students with mild-to-moderate mental retardation: A review of the literature. *Mental Retardation, 39*, 20-31

Cafiero, J.M. (2000). Technology-based solutions for positive behavioral support, *Closing the Gap, 19*(4), 1, 28-29, 34-35, 39.

Chambers, A.C. (1997). *Has technology been considered? A guide for IEP teams*. Reston, VA: CASE/TAM.

Cook, A..M., & Hussey, S.M. (1995). *Assistive technologies: Principles and practice*. St. Louis, MO: Mosby-Year Book, Inc.

Cook, A.M., & Hussey, S,M. (2002). *Assistive technology: Principles and practices* (2nd ed.). St. Louis, MO: Mosby.

Dacey, M., Eichleay, K., & McCauley, J. (2002). The Student Access Map (SAM): Ensuring access to the general curriculum. *Closing the Gap, 11*(3), 1, 8, 9, 23.

Daiute, C., & Morse, F. (1994). Access to knowledge and expression: Multimedia writing tools for students with diverse needs and strengths. *Journal of Special Education Technology, 12*(3), 221-256.

Dalton, B., Winbury, N.E., & Morocco, C.C. (1990). "If you could just push a button:" Two fourth grade boys with learning disabilities learn to use a computer spelling checker. *Journal of Special Education Technology, 10*(4), 177-191.

Dawson, L., Venn, M.L., & Gunter, P.L. (2000). The effects of teacher versus computer reading models. *Behavioral Disorders, 25*(2), 105-113.

Denny, D., & Fox, J. (1989). Collecting and analyzing continuous behavioral data with the TRS-80 model 100/102 portable laptop computer. *Journal of Special Education Technology, 9*(4), 183-189.

DeRuyter, F. (1997). The importance of outcome measures for assistive technology service delivery systems. *Technology and Disability, 6*, 89-104.

DeRuyter, F. (1995). Evaluating outcomes in assistive technology: Do we understand the commitment? *Assistive Technology, 7*, 3-8.

De La Paz, S. (1999). Composing via dictation and speech recognition systems: Compensatory technology for students with learning disabilities. *Learning Disability Quarterly, 22*, 173-182.

Deshler, D.D., Schumaker, J.B., Lenz, B.K., Bulgren, J.A., Hock, M.F., Knight, J., & Ehren, B.J. (2001). Ensuring content-area learning by secondary students with learning disabilities. *Learning Disabilities Research and Practice, 16*, 96-108.

Dyck, N., & Pemberton, J.B. (2002). A model for making decisions about text adaptations. *Intevention in School and Clinic, 38*(1), 28-35.

Edyburn, D.L. (2003c). Assistive technology and evidence-based practice. *ConnSense Bulletin.* Available online: www. connsense bulletin.com/edyatevidence.html

Edyburn, D.L. (2003d). Measuring assistive technology outcomes: Key concepts. *Journal of Special Education Technology, 18*(1), 53-55.

Edyburn, D.L. (2003e). Measuring assistive technology outcomes in writing. *Journal of Special Education Technology, 18*(2), 60-64.

Edyburn, D.L. (2003f). Measuring assistive technology outcomes in mathematics.

Journal of Special Education Technology, 18(4), 76-79.

Edyburn, D.L. (2002a). Cognitive rescaling strategies: Interventions that alter the cognitive accessibility of text. *Closing the Gap, 21*(1), 1, 10-11, 21.

Edyburn, D.L. (2002b). Models, theories, and frameworks: Contributions to understanding special education technology. *Special Education Technology Practice, 4*(2), 16-24.

Edyburn, D.L. (2002c). *Remediation vs. compensation: A critical decision point in assistive technology consideration* [An essay]. Available at: *www.connsensebulletin.com/edyburnv4n3.html*

Edyburn, D.L. (2000a). Assistive technology and mild disabilities. *Focus on Exceptional Children, 32*(9), 1-24.

Edyburn, D.L. (2000b). Learner productivity: Supporting students with special needs in inclusive settings. *Closing the Gap, 19*(1), 20-22.

Edyburn, D.L. (2000c). 1999 in review: A synthesis of the special education technology literature. *Journal of Special Education Technology, 15*(1), 7-18.

Edyburn, D.L., & Smith, R.O. (2000, October). *Technology, teacher training, and mild disabilities.* Paper presented at the 18th annual Closing the Gap conference, Minneapolis, MN.

Edyburn, D.L. (1996). *Assistive technology for students with mild disabilities.* LRP Educational Technology Conference and Expo '96, San Francisco, CA, August 4-7.

Edyburn, D.L. (1991). Fact retrieval by students with and without learning handicaps using print and electronic encyclopedias. *Journal of Special Education Technology, 11*(2), 75-90.

Edwards, B.J., Blackhurst, A.E., & Koorland, M.A. (1995). Computer-assisted constant time delay prompting to teach abbreviation spelling to adolescents with mild learning disabilities. *Journal of Special Education Technology, 12*(4), 301-311.

Ellis, E.S., & Sabornie, E.J. (1986). Effective instruction with microcomputers: Promises, practices, and preliminary findings. *Focus on Exceptional Children, 19*(4), 1-16.

Epstein, J.F., Willis, M.G., Conners, K., & Johnson, D.E. (2001). Use of a technological prompting device to aid a student with attention deficit hyperactivity disorder to initiate and complete daily tasks: An exploratory study. *Journal of Special Education Technology, 16*(1), 19-28.

Fein, J. (1996). A history of legislative support for assistive technology. *Journal of Special Education Technology, 13*(1), 1-3.

Fuhrer, M. (1999, November). *Assistive technology outcomes research: Impressions of an interested newcomer.* Paper presented at the International Conference on Outcome Assessment in AssistiveTechnology, Oslo, Norway. Available online at: *www.utoronto.ca/atrc/reference/atoutcomes/newcomer/index.html*

Gardner, J.E., & Edyburn, D.L. (2000). Integrating technology to support effective instruction. In J. Lindsey (Ed.). *Technology and exceptional individuals* (3rd ed., pp. 191-240). Austin, TX: Pro-Ed.

Gardner, J.E., Taber-Brown, F.M., & Wissick, C.A. (1992). Selecting age-appropriate software for adolescents and adults with developmental disabilities. *Teaching Exceptional Children, 24*(3), 60-63.

Gilbert, T.F. (1978). *Human competence: Engineering worthy performance.* New York: McGraw Hill.

Golden, D. (1998). *Assistive technology in special education: Policy and practice.* Reston, VA: CASE/TAM.

Golden, D. (1999). Assistive technology policy and practice: What is the right thing to do? What is the reasonable thing to do? What is required and must be done? *Special Education Technology Practice, 1*(1), 12-14.

Goldman, S.R., Semmel, D.S., Cosden, M.A., Gerber, M.M., & Semmel, M.I. (1987). Special education administrators' policies and practices on microcomputer acquisition, allocation, and access for mildly handicapped children: Interfaces with regular education. *Exceptional Children, 53*(4), 330-340.

Hannaford, A.E. (1993). Computers and exceptional individuals. In J. D. Lindsey (Ed.), *Computers and exceptional individuals* (2nd ed., pp. 3-26). Austin, TX: Pro-Ed.

Haring, N.G., Lovitt, T.C., Eaton, M.D., & Hansen, C.L. (1978). *The fourth R: Research in the classroom.* Columbus, OH: Merrill.

Hasselbring, T.S., & Bottge, B.A. (2000). Planning and implementing technology programs in inclusive settings. In J.D. Lindsey (Ed.), *Technology and exceptional individuals* (3rd ed., pp. 91-113). Austin, TX: Pro-Ed.

Hasselbring, T.S., Goin, L.I., & Bransford, J.D. (1988). Developing math automaticity in learning handicapped children: The role of computerized drill and practice. *Focus on Exceptional Children, 20*(6), 1-7.

Hasselbring, T.S., Goin, L., & Wissick, C. (1989). Making knowledge meaningful: Applications of hypermedia. *Journal of Special Education Technology, 10*(2), 61-72.

Higgins, E.L., & Zvi, J. (1995). Assistive technology for postsecondary students with learning disabilities: From research to rractice. *Annals of Dyslexia, 45*, 123-142.

Hitchcock, C., Meyer, A., Rose, D., & Jackson, R. (2002). Providing new access to the general curriculum: Universal design for learning. *Teaching Exceptional Children, 35*(2), 8-17.

Kamil, M.L., Mosenthal, P.B., Pearson, P.D., & Barr, R. (2002). *Methods of literacy research.* Mahwah, NJ: Lawrence Erlbaum.

King. T.W. (1999). *Assistive technology: Essential human factors.* Boston: Allyn & Bacon.

King-Sears, M.E. (2001). Three steps for gaining access to the general education curriculum for learners with disabilities. *Intervention in School and Clinic, 37*(2), 67-76.

Larsen, S. (1995). What is quality in the use of technology for children with learning disabilities. *Learning Disability Quarterly, 18*(?), 118-130.

Lenker, J.A., & Paquet, V.L. (2003). A review of conceptual models for assistive technology outcomes research and practice. *Assistive technology, 15*(1), 1-15.

Lewis, R.B. (1998). Assistive technology and learning disabilities: Today's realities and tomorrow's promises. *Journal of Learning Disabilities, 31*(1), 16-26, 54.

Lewis, R.B., Graves, A.W., Ashton, T.M., & Kieley, C.L. (1998). Word processing tools for students with learning disabilities: A comparison of strategies to increase text entry speed. *Learning Disabilities Research and Practice, 13*(2), 95-108.

Lieber, J., & Semmel, M.I. (1985). Effectiveness of computer application to instruction with mildly handicapped learners: A review. *Remedial and Special Education, 6*(5), 5-12.

MacArthur, C.A. (2000). New tools for writing: Assistive technology for students with writing difficulties. *Topics in Language Disorders, 20*(4), 85-100.

MacArthur, C.A. (1999). Word prediction for students with severe spelling problems. *Learning Disabilities Quarterly, 22*(3), 158-172.

MacArthur, C.A. (1998). From illegible to understandable: How word prediction and speech synthesis can help. *Teaching Exceptional Children, 30*(6), 66-71.

MacArthur, C.A. (1996). Using technology to enhance the writing processes of students with learning disabilities. *Journal of Learning Disabilities, 29*(4), 344-354.

MacArthur, C.A., Graham, S. Haynes, J.A., & De La Paz, S. (1996). Spelling checkers and students with learning disabilities: Performance comparisons and impact on spelling. *Journal of Special Education, 30*(1), 35-57.

MacArthur, C.A., & Malouf, D.B. (1990). Microcomputer use in educational programs for mildly handicapped students. *Preventing School Failure, 34*(2), 39-44.

Maccini, P., Gagnon, J.C., & Hughes, C.A. (2002). Technology-based practices for secondary students with learning disabilities. *Learning Disability Quarterly, 25*(3), 247-261.

Mager, R.F. (1992). *What every manager should know about training.* Belmont, CA: Lake Publishing Co.

Manion, M.H. (1986). Computers and behavior disordered students: A rationale and review of the literature. *Educational Technology, 26*(7), 20-24.

McNaughton, D., Hughes, C., & Ofiesh, N. (1997). Proofreading for students with learning disabilities: Integrating computer and strategy use. *Learning Disabilities Research & Practice, 12*(1), 16-28.

Male, M. (2003). *Technology for inclusion: Meeting the special needs of all students.* Boston: Allyn & Bacon.

Meese, R.L. (2001). *Teaching learners with mild disabilities: Integrating research and practice.* Belmont, CA: Wadsworth/Thomson Learning.

Mindscape. (1988). *Curriculum methods for mastery. Or, how to make education special for all learners.* Glenview, IL: author.

Montgomery, D.J., Karlan, G.R., & Coutinho, M. (2001). The effectiveness of word processor spell check programs to produce target words for misspellings generated by students with learning disabilities. *Journal of Special Education Technology, 16*(2), 27-41.

Morocco, C.C., Dalton, B., & Tivnan, T. (1992). The impact of computer-supported writing instruction on fourth-grade students with and without learning disabilities. *Reading & Writing Quarterly, 8*(1), 87-113.

Moser, C. (2003). *The 1994 and 1995 NHIS Phase II Disability Followback Survey Child Questionnaire: A critical analysis of the data and its implication for future AT survey research.* Unpublished doctoral dissertation, University of Wisconsin-Milwaukee.

Murphy, S. Shannon, P., Johnston, P., & Hansen, J. (1998). *Fragile evidence: A critique of reading assessment.* Mahwah, NJ: Lawrence Erlbaum.

National Center for Educational Statistics. (2003). National assessment of educational progress: The nation's report card. Retrieved on November 15, 2003 from: *nces.ed.gov/nationsreportcard/*

National Reading Panel. (2000). *Teaching children to read: An evidence-based assessment of the scientific research literature on reading and its implications for reading instruction.* Washington, DC: U.S. Department of Health and Human Services.

Office of Technology Assessment. (1982). *Technology and handicapped people.* Washington, DC: U.S. Government Printing Office.

Office of Technology Assessment. (1988). *Power on! New tools for teaching and learning.* Washington, DC: U.S. Government Printing Office.

Okolo, C.M. (2000). Technology for individuals with mild disabilities. In J.D. Lindsey (Ed.), *Technology and exceptional individuals* (3rd ed., pp. 243-301). Austin, TX: Pro-Ed.

Okolo, C.M., & Ferretti, R.P. (1996). Knowledge acquisition and technology-supported projects in the social studies for students with learning disabilities. *Journal of Special Education Technology, 13*(2), 91-103.

Okolo, C.M., Rieth, H.J., & Bahr, C.M. (1989). Microcomputer implementation in secondary special education programs: A study of special educators', mildly handicapped adolescents', and administrators' perspectives. *Journal of Special Education, 23*(1), 107-117.

Pressley, M. (2002). What I have learned up until now about research methods in reading education. In D.L. Schallert, C.M. Fairbanks, J. Worthy, B. Maloch, & J.V. Hoffman; (Eds.), *51st yearbook of the national reading conference* (pp. 33-45). Oak Creek, WI: National Reading Conference.

Public Law 107-100. (2001). No Child Left Behind Act of 2001.

Public Law 105-394. (1998). The Assistive Technology Act of 1998.

Public Law 105-17. (1997). Individuals with Disabilities Education Act Amendments of 1997.

Public Law 104-104. (1996). Telecommunications Act of 1996.

Public Law 101-336. (1990). Americans with Disabilities Act.

Public Law 100-407. (1988). Technology-Related Assistance Act for Individuals with Disabilities Act.

Raskind, M. (1993). Assistive technology and adults with learning disabilities: A blueprint for exploration and advancement. *Learning Disability Quarterly, 16*(3), 185-196.

Raskind, M.H., Higgins, E.L., Slaff, N.B., & Shaw, T.K. (1998). Assistive technology in the homes of children with learning disabilities: An exploratory study. *Learning Disabilities: A Multidisciplinary Journal, 9*(2), 47-56.

Rossett, A. (1992). Analysis of human performance problems. In H.D. Stolovitch & E.J. Keeps, (Eds.), *Handbook of human performance technology* (pp. 97-113). San Francisco: Jossey Bass.

Rowland, C. (2004). Cognitive disabilities part 2: Conceptualizing design considerations. Retrieved on October 7, 2004 from: www.webaim .org/techniques/articles/conceptualize/.

Russell, S.J., Corwin, R., Mokros, J.R., & Kapisovsky, P.M. (1989). *Beyond drill and practice: Expanding the computer mainstream.* Reston, VA: Council for Exceptional Children.

Scherer, M.J. (2004). *Connecting to learn: Educational and assistive technology for people with disabilities.* Washington, DC: American Psychological Association.

Smith, F. (2003). *Unspeakable acts, unnatural practices: Flaws and fallacies in "scientific" reading instruction.* Portsmouth, NH: Heinemann.

Smith, R.O. (2000). Measuring assistive technology outcomes in education. *Diagnostique, 25,* 273-290.

Spitzer, D. (1991). *Introduction to instructional technology* (2nd ed.). Boise, ID: Boise State University.

Stanovich, K.E. (1986). Matthew effects on reading: Some consequences of individual differences in the acquisition of literacy. *Reading Research Quarterly, 21,* 360-407.

Strein, W., & Kachman, W. (1984). Effects of computer games on young children's cooperative behavior: An exploratory study. *Journal of Research and Development in Education, 18*(1), 40-43.

Swanson, H.L. (1999). Instructional components that predict treatment outcomes for students with learning disabilities: Support for a combined strategy and direct instruction model. *Learning Disabilities Research and Practice, 14,* 129-140.

U.S. Department of Education. (2002). Annual report to congress on the implementation of the Individuals with Disabilities Education Act (pp. II-18-20). Retrieved on Retrieved March 23, 2004, from: www.ed.gov/about/reports/annual/osep/2002/section-ii.pdf.

Vacc, N.N. (1987). Word processor versus handwriting: A comparative study of writing samples produced by mildly mentally handicapped students. *Exceptional Children, 54*(2), 156-165.

Wehmeyer, M.L. (1999). Assistive technology and students with mental retardation: Utilization and barriers. *Journal of Special Education Technology, 14*(1), 48-58.

Wehmeyer, M.L., Lattin, D., & Agran, M. (2001). Achieving access to the general education curriculum for students with mental retardation. *Education and Training in Mental Retardation and Developmental Disabilities, 36,* 327-342.

Welch, A.B. (2000). Responding to student concerns about fairness. *Teaching Exceptional Children, 33*(2), 36-40.

Wetzel, K. (2001). Reaching students with emotional disabilities. *Learning and Leading with Technology, 29*(2), 22-27.

Wile, D. (1996). Why doers do. *Performance and Instruction, 35*(2), 30-35.

Woodward, J. (1995). Technology-based research in mathematics for special education. *Focus on Learning Problems in Mathematics, 17*(2), 3-23.

Woodward, J., & Carnine, D. (1993). Uses of technology for mathematics assessment and instruction Reflection on a decade of innovations. *Journal of Special Education Technology, 12*(1), 38-48.

Zabala, J. (1995). *The SETT Framework: Critical areas to consider when making informed assistive technology decisions.* Retrieved on January 20, 2003 from: www.joyzabala.com.

Zhang, Y. (2000). Technology and the writing skills of students with learning disabilities. *Journal of Research on Computing in Education, 32*(4), 467-478.

Section 4

Disability-Specific Technology Applications

14

Growing and Learning Through Technology: Birth to Five

Susan G. Mistrett, Shelly J. Lane, and Amy G. Ruffino

The role of infants, toddlers and young children is to actively explore their environments and thereby develop the abilities to participate and learn within them. That assistive technology (AT) supports are unique for this younger age is recognized and reflected in the laws that mandate AT consideration. This uniqueness must also be reflected in early childhood practice; doing so requires that we adjust our vision of the appropriate tools necessary to meet the needs of this developing population. With this aim in mind, this chapter is designed to provide definitions and examples of AT use specific to this population; present AT devices and services frameworks specific to the AT needs of babies and young children, and link this to the International Classification of Functioning, Disability, and Health (ICF) framework that is more global and applicable across rehabilitative interventions and the age span.

The reader will quickly note that the evidence supporting the effectiveness of application of AT devices and services for babies and young children is greatly underdeveloped; the depth and breadth of research we need is simply not yet available. Examples of matrices that can structure the development of specific outcomes, and subsequently form an evidence base for practice, are presented. AT has great potential to improve the quality of life for very young children. We are all challenged to better understand how to use AT with this population, and, perhaps more critically, to develop the evidence needed to substantiate the effectiveness of this intervention.

Part I: What Is Assistive Technology for Young Children?

Early Childhood Development

The growth and development of children from birth through age 5 represents a remarkable stage of a child's life, during which gains in mobility, cognitive understanding, communication, social awareness, and activity are unmatched at any other period. Right from birth, infants use their abilities to explore, and eventually control, their environments. They gather information about the faces they see, sounds and language they hear, and objects and actions around them (Morton & Johnson, 1991). In this period of development, growth is continuous and dynamic, resulting in functional abilities to move freely in environments, communicate with others, and learn about relations of people and things in those environments. The goal of young developing children is to continually enhance and improve their emerging abilities that eventually lead to becoming independent. This is realized by actively participating in daily activities and routines within home, community and education environments.

Given the uniqueness of each child's experiences and development, growth is measured against developmental benchmarks that together lead to independent function. These milestones are perceived as indicators of skills sets gained and direction towards future skills. Although skills within developmental domains appear to be discrete, they overlap. When a child's progression towards independence slows, additional support may be indicated. Young children with developmental delays or disabilities that interfere with the physical exploration of their environment may be profoundly affected by diminished capabilities for sensory and motor interactions (Kaplan-Sanoff, Brewster, Stillwell, & Bergen, 1988). For example, a child without sight who is unable to see a toy will not be motivated to move towards it. This condition, therefore, interferes with all areas of development.

Interventions may diminish the impact of these delays and afford children continued opportunities to interact. Interventions can take many forms. For instance, they may be educational assistance or specialized training for the development of skills. They may also take the form of physical items that assist children in participating in family activities by supporting what they are able to do while reducing or circumventing the barriers that their disabilities present. These supports are regarded as technology as they make it easier for children to join in. We all know of technologies that make things easier for people. Things like alarm clocks that help us wake at the appropriate time and microwave ovens that make popcorn quickly with no mess are examples of such technologies. For all people, technology makes things easier; for people with disabilities, technology makes things possible. Technology used to help people with disabilities to participate more fully in life's activities is known as assistive technology (AT). For young children AT enables the ability to play, move, and communicate in order to participate in everyday activities. If a child is unable to sit up and play, a chair with a tray can be his assistive technology; if he has trouble seeing, glasses can assist him to see better. AT can include such common devices as well as more specialized ones. Picture/symbol boards assist children with limited ability in speaking to communicate; switch-adapted toys help children who are unable to physically manipulate a toy to play; items such as wedges, pommels, floor chair and tables support options for positioning with young children. A means to an end, rather than an end in itself, the usefulness of any particular AT tool can be expected to change over time as children continue to develop and their strengths and needs change (Mistrett et al., 2001).

What Does This Mean for Young Children?

AT has shown considerable promise in supporting the inclusion of young children with disabilities by helping to provide successful opportunities for them to engage in developmentally appropriate activities that otherwise might not be available to them.

The use of AT encompasses multiple purposes relevant to young children with disabilities and their families. Some examples may be found in Table 1.

Technology can be used to facilitate the child's access to and involvement in the environment, as when a toy is adapted to make it possible for a child to operate it or when a walker provides the means for exploration. AT can provide opportunities to promote fine-motor, gross-motor, or communication skill development circumventing the barriers that disabilities present. The use of AT with infants and young children is often a critical element in enhancing the child's ability to explore, learn, and play, leading to the development of self-efficacy (Robinson & Fieber, 1988; Sullivan & Lewis, 2000).

Technology can also be used to facilitate parental care giving. Helping children to be more independent, to require less assistance, can be of enormous help to both parents and children. For example, a seating arrangement that allows a child to sit independently and use her hands to manipulate toys on a front tray frees the parents from continuously holding their child upright. With this seating support, parents can face their child and interact with her and the toys.

Babies and young children may not be regarded as having functions that compel the use of AT as they are developing and combining skills that will lead to independence. Functional abilities such as manipulating a toy may begin with the child exploring a batting motion that causes a hanging toy to move and practicing it until the batting has achieved its purpose. This learned skill is then generalized and the child begins to make other things move with

Table 1. What AT Can Do for Young Children with Disabilities and Their Families

AT with young children can be used to:
Support the acquisition of new skills by providing access to new opportunities in all developmental domains.
Create supportive environments in which children can reach their maximum potential.
Increase independence in activities of daily routines.
Empower families and caretakers to facilitate development by giving them tools with which to work.
Increase the quality of life for young children and their families.

other actions of his or her body (Solano & Aller, 2000). If children with disabilities are denied the opportunity to bat at a toy or generalize such movement, they may never acquire the higher skills of grasp, transference and manipulation. The use of AT to support a child's initial movement toward a toy can facilitate that aspect of the child's development and minimize potential delay.

In Figure 1, AT has been used to support Dominic, who is blind, in accessing objects. Favorite toys and play materials have been linked to the overhead gym, keeping them within reach and within an accessible space. Typically developing children are encouraged to reach, bat, hold and move toys against each other within this play scenario. They depend on their sight to motivate interest to explore toys with their hands and feet; Dominic must use his other senses. Several technologies have been employed to assist and motivate him in this activity: the semi-circular pillow (Boppy®) supports his head and brings his shoulders forward, bringing his hands closer to midline and in a position to reach; the overhead gym is adapted by adding links to bring the toys closer to Dominic's hands. These supports, the pillow, overhead gym and links, are considered AT as they create an environment that provides opportunities for Dominic to locate toys in spite of his lack of vision, keep the toys within easy and understandable reach, and encourage Dominic to successfully explore the objects in front of him.

Assistive technology is not only the *item(s)* but also the *modifications* to the item, and/or the *strategies* for using items. Together, items, adaptations, and strategies make "it" AT. In sum, assistive technologies then are those items that make it possible for children with disabilities to participate. To develop a better understanding of the definition of AT as applied to young children, the following questions addressing the purpose of the AT may be useful:

- Does it (the AT) help to maintain what the child can do?

- Does it make it easier for the child to _____ (eat, play, explore); things that were too difficult before?

- Does it provide the needed support to increase the child's capabilities?

- Does it have certain features that result in better access by a child?

- Does its use result in increased opportunities for independence and exploration?

- Is it necessary for the child to participate? Does it extend participation? Without it what would the child's level of participation be?

AT is not always specialty items, those designed specifically for children with disabilities, particularly when applied to the needs of this youngest population. An assortment of items readily available from commercial sources, off-the-shelf, is particularly useful for a child with a disability, or may require simple modifications to increase their independent use. The most favorable commercial items are those that include features permitting them to be customized for the child. For instance, some electronic toys have sound controls or repositioning features.

Definitions of Assistive Technology for Young Children

Recognizing the need for such technologies, federal legislation that supports the development and education of children with disabilities-the Individuals with Disabilities Education Act (IDEA)-in 1990, first included definitions of AT devices and services as appropriate in programs designed for children with disabilities, ages birth to 21. Recent administrations have recognized and promoted AT's potential impact on individuals with disabilities: "...increasing access to assistive technologies... will help to increase the ability of Americans with disabilities to integrate into the workforce and promote increased access into daily community life. These technologies are helping to defeat dependence, frustrations and isolation" (New Freedom Initiative, 2001).

As noted above, AT definitions include both devices and services that improve the abilities of individuals with disabilities to engage in everyday activities, thereby normalizing life experiences. The federal definitions of AT devices and services from the 1997 Reauthorization of IDEA (P.L. 105-17) are presented below:

Assistive Technology Device is defined as: 'Any item, piece of equipment, or product system, whether acquired commercially off the shelf, modified, or customized, that is used to increase, maintain, or improve functional capabilities of a child with a disability.' [20 U.S.C., 1401, SECTION §300.5]

Assistive Technology Service is defined as: 'Any service that directly assists a child with a disability in the selection, acquisition, or use of an assistive technology device. Such term includes—(A) the evaluation of the needs of such child, including a functional evaluation of the child in the child's customary environment; (B) purchasing, leasing, or otherwise providing for the acquisition of assistive technology by such child; (C) selecting, designing, fitting, customizing, adapting, applying, maintaining, repairing, or replacing of assistive

technology devices; (D) coordinating and using other therapies, interventions, or services with assistive technology devices, such as those associated with existing education and rehabilitation plans and programs; (E) training or technical assistance for such child, or, where appropriate, the family of such child; and (F) training or technical assistance for professionals (including individuals providing education and rehabilitation services), employers, or other individuals who provide services to, employ, or are otherwise substantially involved in the major life functions of such child.' [20 U.S.C., 1401, SECTION §300.6]

This AT definition, used by most federal, state, and local institutions has wide implications for education and rehabilitation. It is broad by design in order to meet the AT needs of persons with disabilities across the lifespan. Much has been written about its potential impact on the functionality of persons of varying disabilities-the ability to improve independence, to compensate for limitations that disabilities present, and to create new opportunities for participating in work, school, and community settings. Historically, AT has been regarded as rehabilitative or prosthetic in nature, with its ultimate aim to provide the means for continued independence and the ability to earn a livelihood. This traditional vision does not support the role of young children who are very dependent on caregivers and do not earn an income. However, independence and social competence are part of the process of "becoming" prior to adulthood.

Although the law clearly includes a wide range of "commercial to customized" options, general perceptions of AT in its first decade have focused primarily on those technologies specifically designed to address the significant needs of individuals with low-incidence disabilities-items such as powered wheelchairs to provide independent transportation, communication devices for children without verbal abilities, Braille embossers to print out computer files in a readable format for people who are blind, assistive listening devices to intensify hearing abilities, and so on. The reality of this can be seen in the available research on AT effectiveness that will be reviewed later in this chapter. Although many of these specialized AT devices have kept their promise of increasing the independence of a small population of youth and adults with significant disabilities, they do not begin to meet the trans-generational technology needs of people with differing abilities who wish to participate in the full scope of life's activities. Further exploration into technology solutions for individuals with moderate and mild impairments to participate in routine daily tasks is needed more than ever as community access barriers diminish.

Assistive Devices

The usefulness of "commercially off-the-shelf, modified, or customized" items, especially as they pertain to the needs of young developing children, should also be examined. Features of commercial items may act to support the child's functional capabilities and, therefore, respond to the federal definition of AT. In looking closer at the broad definition of AT devices, it becomes clear that both the sources of technology items and their assistive intent are included. (Technology Source) "… any item, piece of equipment, or product system, whether acquired commercially off the shelf, modified, or customized …"

It may not always be appropriate for very young children to use technologies such as adapted computers, power wheelchairs, and complex communication devices—devices frequently considered to be at the heart of assistive technology. While some research suggests that children as young as 3 years of age can successfully use some high tech devices (Butler, 1988), young children and their families may not be ready for these specialized devices or find them to be "inappropriate" as children are in an ever-changing state of development in their first five years. As noted above, most existing research on this population has focused on "customized" AT; that is, devices specifically designed to compensate for the deficits of individuals with disabilities. The use of AT with young children may be limited because it is perceived to be primarily a high tech tool for learning, and more appropriate for older children (Sullivan & Lewis, 2000). In fact, leaders in the field of technology use with students

with disabilities such as the Center for Applied Special Technology also define AT as "applications (either hardware or software) designed specifically to assist disabled individuals in overcoming barriers" (Rose, 2001). Studies mainly ignore the use of "off-the-shelf, or modified" items by young children, and yet they may be more advantageous to the dynamic state of development in the early years. AT for this population must be child- and family-responsive, should require minimal training for its use, be readily available and enhance the child's participation in the routines within his or her natural environments (Mistrett et al., 2001). Because of their simplicity and availability, many AT devices for this age group are often not seen as "assistive," and little importance is attributed to their role in promoting development and independence (Sullivan & Lewis, 2000).

Is it the purpose of the item that makes it AT? The second part of the AT definition addresses this question. (Assistive Intent) "that is used to increase, maintain, or improve functional capabilities of a child with a disability."

If we understand that AT can make it possible for a young child to move, eat, play, sit, communicate, and interact, we make the definition more relevant to young children who are in the process of developing these skills and engaging in these activities. Although still used to "increase, maintain, and improve functional capabilities," AT for this age group can look very different. A product can be defined as assistive technology by the way it is used (Edyburn, 2000). For example, a bowl with a curved lip to contain food, a toy with easy-to-use buttons, or a tricycle with a molded seat providing postural support can all be seen as AT if they can "assist" a child's capabilities.

As devices used by adults are often used to rehabilitate functional abilities, those for growing children should be used to develop the foundation for functional activities. Given the rapid growth in this age group, we should not wait until the child misses developmental milestones, but can preventively use AT to support the child by bypassing immediate barriers to participation.

AT Services

Beyond these components of the AT devices, the AT services component of the law defines the adaptations and strategies (training, coordination, etc.) that extend the use of the item and help facilitate performance with the device. Both devices and services must be provided to increase, maintain, and improve child outcomes. AT services are of equal importance as they wrap around the device providing strategies that ensure its appropriate use. It is this combination of a responsive device with sound participation strategies that creates opportunities for increased participation and independence.

Legislative Program Components for Young Children (Parts B and C)

Legislation to ensure special education programs for children with disabilities has continually been expanded since the inception of the Education for the Handicapped Act (EHA) in 1974. The education needs of preschool children were addressed in 1986, which resulted in state programs for children ages 3 to 21. At that time, new mandates directed states to establish early intervention programs to support the needs of families with infants and toddlers with disabilities, ages birth through two. Table 2 indicates the timeline of relevant legislation. Assistive technology mandates are noted as well beginning with the reauthorization of the special education law known as the Individuals with Disabilities Education Act (IDEA) in 1990.

Although both Early Intervention (Part C) and Preschool Programs (Part B) address the needs of young children, they do so through significantly different processes and outcomes. Programs primarily differ in the recipients of service (family vs. child), the focus of the program (development vs. education) and the location of services. Emphasis in the language of the law has been added to ensure that services are provided in the most normalized environments, where the child would typically be if the disability did not exist. Although the way services are provided differs from state to state, basic components are mandated within both parts.

Part C: Early Intervention Programs for Children (Birth to 3) and Their Families

Recognizing the positive impact of intervention early in the lives of children, early intervention services often begin at the birth of a child. As the needs of infants and toddlers cannot be separated from those of their families, these programs regulated by Part C of IDEA focus on providing interventions that empower the family's ability to respond to the developmental needs of their children (Bronfenbrenner, 1975; Dunst, 1985; Rappaport, 1981, 1987). To do so, an Individualized Family Service Plan (IFSP) is developed, whereby families and professionals work together to identify desired outcomes and interventions that can help families support their children in achieving these outcomes. These family-centered programs focus on the development of the child and can include families with children who are at risk for developing future disabilities. The use of technology is consistent with best practice in early intervention programs as it can provide successful opportunities for development. In general, recommended best practices for young children include intervention strategies that are family-centered, home and/or community-based, and provided within the context of family life (Edelman, 1999).

Part B: Preschool Programs for Children (3 to 5)

Part B/Section 619 of IDEA regulates that preschool services focus on the ability of children with disabilities to benefit from education programs. Although families remain essential members of Individualized Education Program (IEP) development, services are now child-centered and are most frequently provided at either inclusive or specialized education centers. Services focus on the interference of the disability with the child's ability to benefit from the education program. Some states have designed "seamless" programs that address the needs of families and children birth through 5, while others address the specialized needs of children birth to 3 and 3-5 through different state agencies.

Natural Environments

Where services are provided for young children is also addressed by the IDEA legislation.

Table 2. Relevant Legislation Affecting Children with Disabilities for Children Birth to Five (with Emphasis on Assistive Technology)

Year	Title of Law	Significance
1968	Handicapped Children's Early Education Assistance Act, P.L. 90-538	Provided funds for developing programs in early education for children with disabilities (birth to 6 years of age) and their families
1972	Economic Opportunities Amendments, P.L. 92-424	Mandated that Head Start services include 10% children with disabilities
1975	Education for the Handicapped Act (EHA), P.L. 94-142	Mandated public special education to children with disabilities, 5 -21
1986	Amendments to Education for the Handicapped Act (EHA), P.L. 99-457	Mandated preschool special education for children 3-5 years of age; created Part H to develop birth to 3 early intervention programs
1990	Americans with Disabilities Act, P.L. 101-336	Further civil rights mandates for equal opportunity and equal access to public accommodations and opportunities
1990	Amended EHA as Individuals with Disabilities Education Act (IDEA), P.L. 101-476	Identified AT devices and services included in public education. Stipulated that AT be detailed on individual IEPs
1995	Head Start reauthorized; Early Head Start is created	Early Head Start (EHS), a new initiative for low-income pregnant women and children from birth through 3; includes 10% children with disabilities
1997	IDEA Amendments of 1997, P.L. 105-17	Part H renamed to Part C for early intervention. Required that AT devices and services be considered for each child

For all children, "natural environments" are settings that are natural or typical for an eligible child's age peers who have no disabilities, including the home and community settings in which children without disabilities participate (34 C.F.R. § 303.12). The goal is to enable the child with disabilities to be maximally engaged in, and benefit from, the same naturally occurring learning opportunities as would children without disabilities. The "natural learning environments" for infants and toddlers include home and community settings that afford learning opportunities as part of daily living (Dunst, Hamby, Trivette, Raab, & Bruder, 2000).

This concept of providing services in the child's "natural environments" evolved from least restrictive environment mandates and reflects the Part C mandate of family-centered services. Acknowledging that these first years are a time in which children's development is intrinsically tied to their interactions with those who care for them. It is from their caregivers that children first learn how to participate in daily events, communicate their wants and needs, and interact with individuals and materials (Mistrett etal, 2001). Since everyday opportunities to explore environments and interact with people lead to early learning experiences, it is critical that children participate to the greatest extent possible in natural learning opportunities inherent in the family's routines.

In general, infants, toddlers and preschoolers encounter many activities on a daily basis. Some are planned, such as preschool education programs, library story times, swimming classes, or playground activities. Many more occur within daily family activities as the child participates in rides in the car, going food shopping with a parent, or accompanying an older sibling to a ball game. Others "just happen" as part of daily life, like finding a field of flowers or going to a friend's home with a new kitten. Spontaneous and routine experiences can be just as important as a planned activity in promoting and enhancing a child's development. Findings show that, on average, children participate in more than 150 different settings as part of their family and community lives, which in turn provide more than 200 kinds of different learning opportunities (Dunst & Bruder, 1999). Therefore, increasing the number of activities in which a child can successfully engage, and increasing the opportunities for engagement in a variety of settings, significantly increases the child's learning opportunities (Dunst, Bruder, Trivette, Raab, & McLean, 1998). AT can provide necessary supports for successful participation in learning activities.

Least Restrictive Environments
The concept of natural environments extends to preschool education programs that maximize the participation of children with disabilities in all of the activities in the program. Young children with disabilities must receive their education program supports in the "least restrictive environments" (LRE) where they would attend school if they did not have a disability. IDEA requires that individuals with disabilities be educated to the maximum extent appropriate with individuals who are nondisabled. The removal of an individual from the regular education environment occurs only if the nature or severity of the disability is such that education in general education classes with the use of "supplementary aids and services" cannot be achieved satisfactorily. Assistive technologies are included here as they "enable children with disabilities to be educated with nondisabled children" ... in accordance with LRE mandates. [IDEA Section 612(a)(5)]. A continuum of alternate placement options must be made avaiable if the general education classroom is not an appropriate placement. LRE benefits for children with disabilities, as well as children without disabilities, are both education and community-based.

Inclusive opportunities provide children with disabilities age-appropriate peer models that stimulate their development and learning. Children without disabilities demonstrate more positive attitudes toward disabilities after being involved in integrated opportunities in school and out. Families benefit as transitions, transportation, and needed coordination are reduced. Finally, service providers benefit from a reduction in duplication of services and sharing of resources.

Acknowledging the increase in learning opportunities in community environments where all children participate, service locations have shifted from being provided primarily in centers for children with disabilities to home and community environments. In fact most recent data indicate that 68% of EI services are provided in the family's home and 36% of pre-school children with disabilities were served in typical early childhood settings (U.S. Department of Education, 2003). Both figures reflect an increase in services provided in natural environments.

IDEA Program Components Supporting AT Services
How the selection and use of AT with young children with disabilities is coordinated within their service delivery systems is important. The following section addresses program components that affect the delivery of AT services. As defined in Table 2, the provision of AT devices and services was guaranteed to children with disabilities as part of special education and civil rights legislation. Additionally, the U.S. Department of Education's Office of Special Education Programs (OSEP) establishes policy documents that describe the department's interpretation of IDEA or the regulations that implement it.

Mandated Consideration of Assistive Technology in IEP Development
The provision of AT devices and services was considerably strengthened with the IDEA (1997) mandate to "consider" AT for every child with a disability. Within the development of the IEP, the team must consider whether the child requires assistive technology devices and services. By including the consideration requirement, the law clearly intended to en-

courage district personnel to learn first hand about what works and what does not. Therefore, in order to consider technology for a student, team members must become aware of the technologies and their applications and reduce their reliance on outside "experts." The students may actually benefit in the long run as school district personnel are best equipped to understand the demands of the environment, or the time available, or the skills of the personnel in that environment, and so on (Reed, 2000).

Although AT is not specifically stated as a special consideration in IFSP development for children birth to 3, its inclusion is understood in the Part C regulations where it is "within the determination or consideration of early intervention services that assistive technology is actually considered with regard to Part C and IFSP development" where "all appropriate services determined by the IFSP team must be provided." AT is one of the Early Intervention services that a state is required to provide to a child. The IFSP must include a specific statement of all early intervention services necessary to meet the unique needs of the child and the family to achieve the identified outcomes. (IDEA, 20 U.S.C. 1436(d)).

State Assistive Technology Policy
Federal legislation mandates what the states must do, but not how they will do it. Many states have addressed the AT needs of children with disabilities and have developed AT policies and procedures for their use. A recent survey of state directors of special education on AT policies (NATRI, 2001) found that 86% of directors believe that AT policies are necessary to guide the delivery of assistive technology services. In fact, 50% were circulating state-developed AT policies to local school districts.

Policies can include definitions of technologies and services, assessment and training guidelines, and documentation on the IFSP/IEP. Procedures describe steps to be followed to identify, acquire, and evaluate the use of devices including use at home, conflict resolution and transition of devices to other education environments. State AT policies can support the clarification of related policies for specific populations. For example, in 1999, the New York State Department of Health, the lead agency for their Early Intervention Program, released a memo that addressed the appropriate selection and use of assistive technology devices and services for children eligible for the Early Intervention Program.

Provision of Assistive Technology
to Children
Despite the tremendous potential of AT devices and services for enhancing the development and quality of life for young children and their families, the potential of technology has not been realized. In reviewing annual IDEA reporting data (U.S. Department of Education, 1998, 1999, 2000, 2001, 2002, 2003) on the number of AT services provided to young children, an underutilization trend is apparent. Data from 1997 through 2001 indicate that less than 4% of infants and toddlers (0-3) in early intervention programs had an AT device or service on their IFSP. Thus, despite efforts to increase awareness of the potential of AT, the numbers have remained largely unchanged. Even though data are required by each state related to child count, placement, personnel, and exiting data for the preschool (3-5) population, data on the number of AT services provided are not required. Thus, it is unclear how many preschool-aged children in need of AT are receiving devices and services.

While these data may reflect a substantial under-reporting of use (U.S. Department of Education, 1998), these low rates of utilization strongly suggest that AT devices and services have not been used to their fullest extent, even though they are endorsed by legislation designed for young children. There is much work to be done to improve access to the full continuum of AT devices and services for young children and their families. Under reporting and/or under utilization may result if service providers perceive that only "customized" devices (designed for children with disabilities) are synonymous with AT and see "off-the-shelf" and "modifications" not as AT but as the common items they have always used in their therapeutic and educational services. Table 3 suggests several possible reasons for the low use of AT with this population.

The apparent low use of AT is a significant policy issue. More significant are the missed opportunities for enhancing the development

Table 3. Hypotheses and Implications of Low Use of AT for Young Children Birth to Five

Hypothesis	Implication
1. Fear that use of AT will interfere with children developing the function themselves.	1. Develop and disseminate materials that address these concerns in ways that reflect sensitivity and cultural competence.
2. High rate of abandonment of high-tech devices.	2. Conduct research into the underlying causes for abandonment of devices with this population.
3. Providers do not know about available AT.	3. Provide education regarding uses of AT with children birth to 5 years of age.
4. Low-tech devices not thought of as AT, or not paid for under state regulations.	4. Provide education regarding the full range of devices.
5. Lack of readily available providers due to geographic barriers – rural.	5. Explore Internet and telehealth strategies for recommending and supporting AT.
6. Payment source not available.	6. Review mandates for provision of AT and funding policies for service coordinators and providers.
7. Insurance covers needed devices so provision not reported as Part C.	7. Clarify policies regarding reflecting all devices and services on IFSPs regardless of funding source.
8. Insurance does not pay as device is not considered to be medically necessary.	8. Provide information on successful strategies for insurance coverage on devices and services to support use of the device.
9. Devices not available to meet individual needs.	9. Provide information regarding needed technology and software to potential developers of new devices.

Note: Adapted from Robinson, 2001.

of young children with disabilities and easing the demands of care for parents that low use represents. The missed learning opportunities to bat at a mobile, use a ride-on toy, or drink a cup of juice that could be addressed with some simple AT solutions hold potential long-term developmental consequences.

Barriers to AT Use

Demographics

The demographics of families such as race, primary language, and income influence technology use (National Center for Education Statistics, 2001). Limited financial resources, knowledge, and training are other commonly cited barriers. Family values, their perceptions of the child's abilities and behavior, and device preferences, as well as other information about daily routines, also greatly impact how and what technology is used (Armstrong & Jones, 1994; Parette & Hourcade, 1996). Finally, the everyday realities of cost, ease of use, and availability are factors that often cause families to prefer low tech AT over high tech devices (Horn & Warren, 1987; Mistrett, 2000).

Lack of Knowledge

Most studies indicate that service providers feel they lack the knowledge necessary to identify appropriate AT, to use it to create successful learning opportunities, to locate funding sources, to justify needs, and to effectively advocate for its use (Espe, 1998; Lesar, 1998; Parette, Hourcade, & Van Biervliet, 1993). Even providers with years of experience feel unable to keep pace with technological advances (Erin, Daugherty, Dignan, & Parson, 1990). Although the use of AT is increasing (Male, 1997), the lack of awareness and the lack of training continue to act as major barriers to providers using AT (Izen & Brown, 1991; MacGregor & Pachuski, 1996; Thorkildsen, 1994). As a result, parents express frustration that service providers lack necessary knowledge to make AT determinations (Goldman, Lowman, Bryen & Lemanowicz, 2000) sustaining the impression that IFSP and IEP teams are often unprepared to make AT decisions (Bowser & Reed, 1995; Hutinger, Johanson, & Stoneburner, 1996; McGregor & Pachuster, 1996). Bryant, Erin, Lock, Allen, and Resta (1998) list the following factors as barriers to developing teacher preparation:

- limited access of university faculty to technology

- limited incentives and opportunities for faculty to develop courses

- limited funding for new initiatives

Additional barriers may include:

- faculty lack of knowledge about AT and its benefits

- lack of AT requirements in national certification programs, including early childhood and special education programs

Changing Needs of Children and Families

Given the dynamic state of development as characteristic of young children, the application of appropriate technologies requires timely and strategic interventions. A young child may require upright seating supports if he is not independently sitting by 8 months of age. Independent sitting is a typical milestone achieved between approximately 6 and 8 months of age, and allows the child to socially interact and communicate, to better view and manipulate toys placed in front of him, and to prepare for future independence in eating, bathing, and play routines. In addition, the family's percep-

tions of the child's abilities are elevated when they see him in an age-appropriate position. If we look to current funding systems to provide "customized" seating solutions, it may take up to 6 months for the device to be received (WNY LEICC, 1999). As a result, several scenarios are possible when the device finally arrives: the child's development is further delayed as he has been denied the support for an additional six months, the child has physically outgrown the device, the child is now independently sitting and no longer needs the device, or the child now needs different supports for standing or mobility. In the latter case, the wait begins all over again.

Availability of Assistive Technology

Children and families need immediate access to appropriate devices as they grow. Technology must be available to support emerging abilities. Systems are required that are responsive to the needs of this youngest population. Identifying and locating technology supports that can be immediately applied is essential. Loan libraries and closets have been reported to be cost-effective and responsive in meeting the diverse and changing needs of individuals with disabilities (Burke, 1997; RESNA, 2003). While many states offer a variety of devices though Tech Act projects, few include substantial inventory with a range of AT for young children.

Part II: Frameworks for Using Assistive Technology with Babies and Young Children

This section provides a foundation for the use of AT with infants and young children, beginning with an established framework, the International Classification of Functioning, Disability, and Health (ICF) (ICF, 2001) used in adult rehabilitation, and moving on to separate frameworks developed to conceptualize the use of AT devices and services with young children. Frameworks provide us with a way to think and talk about the parallels and differences in the use of AT for this young population of individuals with disabilities and AT as it is used with older children and adults. ICF offers a universal language for talking about all aspects of rehabilitation, including AT. It is

Figure 2. Interactions between the components of ICF (2001).

	Part 1: Functioning and Disability		Part 2: Contextual Factors	
Components	Body Functions and Structures	Activities and Participation	Environmental Factors	Personal Factors
Domains	Body Functions and Structures	Life Areas (tasks, actions)	External Influences on Functioning and Disability	Internal Influences on Functioning and Disability
Constructs	Change in Body Functions (physiological) Change in Body Functions (anatomical)	Capacity Executing Tasks in a Standard Environment Performance Executing Task in the Current Environment	Facilitating or Hindering Impact of Features of the Physical, Social, and Attitudinal World	Impact of Attributes of the Person
Positive Aspect	Functional and Structural Integrity	Activities Participation	Facilitators	Not Applicable
	Functioning			
Negative Aspect	Impairment	Activity Limitation Participation Restriction	Barriers/Hindrances	Not Applicable
	Disability			

Note: Figure 2, Interactions between the components of ICF, has been reprinted with permission of the World Health Organization (WHO), and all rights are reserved by the organization.

used in reference to AT in the adult population, and fits well with our own conceptualization of how AT can and should be used with young children. Thus, using this framework puts AT with children into the same language arena as other rehabilitation efforts, allowing both consumers and funders to understand what we are talking about.

The ICF Framework

Although other frameworks have been proposed as a basis for understanding the application of AT (e.g., SETT, Zabala, 1995; HAAT, Cook & Hussey, 2002), using the ICF to frame what is known about the potential of AT for children has some benefits. Because it defines function and disability in the context of an individual's environment, it is very consistent with these more focused frameworks as well

with the laws described earlier that mandate AT devices and services for this population. Additionally, the ICF offers a means to look not just at disability, but also at ability, health, and wellness. Thus, it provides a structure for examining the evidence that exists for the use of AT with children. As can be seen in Figure 2, the ICF is divided into two parts: Functioning and Disability, and Contextual Factors.

While a thorough discussion is beyond the scope of this text, we will look at the ICF briefly as it applies to the use of AT. Meant to be applied not just to individuals with disabilities but to all people, the ICF begins by looking at these components of body structure and function that impact person's ability to participate in age-appropriate activities, across all life arenas. The framework provides guidance to look at differences in body structure and function,

Figure 3. AT device framework.

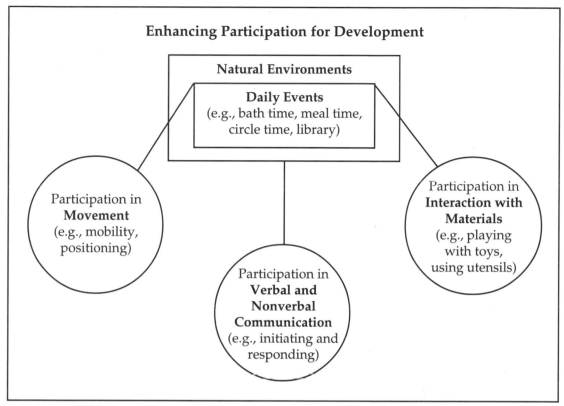

Enhancing Participation for Development

Natural Environments

Daily Events
(e.g., bath time, meal time, circle time, library)

Participation in **Movement** (e.g., mobility, positioning)

Participation in **Verbal and Nonverbal Communication** (e.g., initiating and responding)

Participation in **Interaction with Materials** (e.g., playing with toys, using utensils)

Note: Adapted from Mistrett et al., 2001. Reprinted with permission.

and considers how these differences may impact activities and participation, leading to impairment or disability. For instance, with young children with disabilities it considers how the disability impacts the child's capacity to engage in age-appropriate activities across all appropriate environments. In addition, the ICF includes a look at the strengths the child (and family) brings to the child's ability to engage in activities.

Part 2 of the ICF examines the context of functioning and disability, beginning with the immediate environment and moving beyond to include the environment more generally. Also included here are personal factors that can and do influence functioning. In Part 2 facilitators and barriers to functioning are examined. AT is noted to be a facilitator of functioning. When appropriately used, these devices and services, as defined earlier in this chapter, alter the individual's ability, capacity, and performance, as defined by ICF.

In the following AT Device and Service Frameworks we will see some of the same terminology. As you read through this next section, with its direct application to the use of AT with infants and young children, consider how well it links with and overlaps the concepts presented in the ICF, a universal language for looking at health and disability.

AT Device Framework

The AT Device Framework reflects the natural environments of the child, and the ability of that environment to support children's innate capacity to grow and develop that is shaped by the learning opportunities they are afforded. Just as every child is unique in terms of preferences and involvement in activities, every family has its own habits, rituals, and traditions. The purpose of early childhood programs is to maximize the active participation of children with disabilities by providing services that support their continuous growth and development. AT is one such service.

This framework considers the activities and how children play and learn, specific activities they enjoy, and expectations for participating is valuable for determining if and how AT can benefit a particular child. Technologies on their own are not effective unless they are adapted in their use to suit a child's and family's individual needs and resonate with the family's life style (Judge & Parette, 1998). The emphasis of AT use with young children goes well beyond simply matching the devices and services to the child's abilities and disabilities, to reflecting the broader goals of helping the child to grow and develop independence while reducing stress and empowering the family. By using AT with a child, we help to balance his or her interest in new explorations by adding supports where needed.

There are three primary ways in which young children participate in their daily activities: (a) through movement, (b) through communication, and (c) through interaction with materials (Lane & Mistrett, 2001). Each is described below with examples of specific AT supports.

Movement

Movement refers to body positioning and mobility. For young children with disabilities such as cerebral palsy or other orthopedic impairments, the issue may be uncontrolled body movement or, alternatively, an inability to initiate or sustain appropriate positioning or movement. Children with sensory impairments may require supports to safely move through and interact within environments. Any toddler who cannot sit up independently will require support in order to be comfortably and safely maintained in that position and to engage in a learning activity. Many devices are available to help.

Positioning Items

Some children with disabilities may have difficulty changing and maintaining different positions when they play. The positions that a child can use greatly influence the level and quality of play. Children who, at 10 months of age, are unable to sit independently are typically positioned lying on their backs. Clearly, such a position greatly limits participation in a variety of activities. For example, gravity makes it challenging for such children to bring their hands together to play, and visual gaze of the world is limited to what is hanging above. By being supported in sitting, children can watch their hands as they interact with toys and can more readily engage in a wider variety of routines and activities. Devices such as booster chairs, bath seats, and Rifton corner chairs can be used to support a child's ability to sit up (see Figure 4).

A range of AT supports and play strategies are available to help children in other positions: semi-reclined (sling seat, Boppys™,) side-lying (towels, E-Z lyers), prone (wedges, towels), kneeling (floor tables, stairs), sitting (Boppys™, corner chairs, Sassy Seats), and standing (Exersaucer; see Figure 5) are just a few devices that support various positions. Families report that such readily available positioning devices often better meet an active family's needs by providing options that are easy to transport, can be used in more than one environment, and support more than one position.

Mobility Items

Other children may need assistance in moving to explore their environments, a critical component of development. Commercial devices that encourage and support children to move can be found. Many families prefer to use items that appear less stigmatizing. For example, walkers (see Figure 6) can be fashioned from well-designed commercial items such as shopping carts and activity centers on wheels where the child stands behind and pushes. They can provide adequate support for many children and can be further adapted, if necessary, with weights to make them more stable, or Velcro can be applied around the wheels, which on low carpets will adhere and slow the walker. Being certain that their IFSP/IEP team agrees that such modifications are safe, given the skills and needs of the child, allows the use of such off-the-shelf options.

Low rocking and riding toys are other options that allow children to experience movements in supported positions. Easy-to-use climbing and sliding equipment for young children and other items such as well-designed swings for backyard play may be found in local stores with features that enhance independence. By pointing out certain design features to look for, families are assisted in selecting commercial items that can meet their children's needs.

Communication

Interactive communication between infants and caregivers starts much earlier than the onset of a child's speech and is critical to the normal development of language and social abilities. Some children with disabilities may need assistance to recognize and/or respond appropriately to communication cues. They may require supports to express their needs and preferences in ways that are easily understandable. In addition, when a child's acquisition of a language system is delayed, a communication-based approach where all IFSP/IEP team members apply the same communication strategies throughout the program should be encouraged (Wilcox, 1989).

Communication AT Items

Devices that use recorded messages to incorporate language into play and other daily activities provide a way for a child to use a voice to communicate. The ability to initiate is very powerful. Devices that offer single or multiple message choices are also available. Often used with photos and full-color or line drawings, they help children to select what they want to say. Some communication devices (*e.g., LITTLEmack, Say It/Play It* and *CheapTalk*) can act as a switch interface to control a computer software program (see Figure 7). They can also be used to include a message that is heard when a toy is activated. This strategy can be used to enhance opportunities for pretend play for nonverbal young children.

Interaction with Materials

Interaction with materials involves seeing, hearing, touching, holding, tasting, smelling, and moving things in the environment. For an infant, the active materials list may be relatively short, including such things as clothes, blankets, and toys, because the infant's exposure is limited to materials given directly to him or her. As the child matures however, the materials list grows quickly. By the time children can move around independently, they have access to everything in their environment. Many items

and tools that children use to participate in daily activities can be found commercially or adjusted for use with minor adaptations (see Section IV).

Switches, Adapted Battery-Operated Toys, and Interfaces

These specialized AT items make it possible for children to turn a toy on and off with a movement of a body part against a switch (see Figure 8). A variety of switches meet the unique abilities and interactive needs of children. They are a flexible option as any commercially available battery-operated toy, game, or appliance can be adapted for use with a switch. By employing special interfaces such as battery adapters, timers, latch devices, and series adapters, service providers can assist families in identifying ways in which children can develop and extend cause-effect relationships and play cooperatively with brothers and sisters. When adapting toys to be used with a switch, a family can be given a single battery-operated toy and a battery adapter. Service providers can show family members how to insert the adapter to modify the toy for switch use. With this know-how families can now adapt any battery-operated item, and often report that their children have begun using switches to activate several additional toys and household items.

Computer Hardware and Software

AT options also include computer peripherals and appropriate software for children who can benefit from computer activities (see Figure 9). Activities can include access to books, drawing programs, and real-life simulations where a child can successfully interact with the aid of the computer. In supporting the use of available resources, software programs can be suggested and Web sites identified for families who have Internet access. Families can download a variety of software programs to review for their children's use. CD-ROMs are available that can be used by both Macintosh and Windows platforms, and many of these commercial programs can be easily adapted or used by all children. A single switch connection (which reduces computer control to a single key), the use of a touch window (where the child simply presses any place on the screen to operate the computer), or a large track ball to control the mouse are often the most appropriate input devices for young children.

In each of the three participatory areas- movement, interaction with materials, and communication-observation is a precursor to exploration and active participation. Often children observe, think, and learn about activities in their environments both before and during exploration and active participation. The overarching goal of AT use with young children with disabilities is to expose them to natural learning opportunities that are as numerous and as varied as those to which children without disabilities are exposed.

The AT device framework offers therapists and educators a way to apply the AT concepts to all environments by examining the strengths and needs of the child in three critical areas of function necessary for participation in any event. It links to ICF conceptually and yet puts AT into this framework as a facilitator of function in these areas and a means to overcome the barriers that disabilities can construct. Further the use of a framework guides practitioners in all fields in implementing the laws that mandate consideration and trials of AT for young children by focusing attention on areas of functioning. The use of such a framework helps assure us that we are in fact meeting the needs of caregivers and children.

AT Service Framework

The AT Service Framework lays out the steps associated with selecting, using, and evaluating AT. Determining what AT (if any) may support a child's drive towards independent participation in everyday activities begins the process. The second step involves trial (and error) with AT items and strategies. Keeping track of success and failure for both devices and strategies at this step forms the evidence for practice. The evaluation of success is the last step, both for child and family and for development of evidence. The framework is cyclical as each evaluation leads to further examination of participatory activities where AT can be considered. The framework considers the natural environments of the child, the routines and activities embedded into the natural environment, the child's abilities, preferences, and needs, and what has already been tried (see Figure 10).

As can be seen in Figure 10, AT service is an iterative process, linked tightly to AT device choice. As child outcomes are reached or accomplished, providers look again at both the device and the service; one or both may need to be adapted. The two frameworks, presented separately here, are integrated in practice and this is how it must be to meet the needs of the child and the family. A case study (Lewis) illustrating the application of these frameworks is presented later in this chapter.

Part III: What Do We Know Abouot Assistive Technology for Children?

Summary of Available Evidence

Considerable anecdotal, and some empirical, evidence exist supporting the use of AT with children of all ages. At this point it is well accepted that AT must be considered, and when appropriate, incorporated into the lives of even the youngest children with disabilities. The relevant laws governing this have already been discussed. Technology offers opportunities for all children to extend control to new environments. For children with disabilities, AT gives them access to untried experiences. Using a combination of empirical and anecdotal results from their work, Lane and Mistrett (1996, 2001; Mistrett & Lane, 1995) have indicated that when children with disabilities are supported by assistive technology in play, their play becomes more complex, they interact more often with materials and people, and they become more playful. This suggests that the play potential in these children is not being tapped, and further that the use of AT as a tool for intervention supports and promotes the development of this early childhood occupational role. This early exposure to a wide variety of "typical" play activities that is facilitated through the application of assistive technology ideas also appears to decrease symptoms of passivity in children with disabilities (Lane & Mistrett, 2001).

Empirical reports of positive changes following implementation of customized (specially designed) AT have noted a number of

Figure 10. AT service framework.

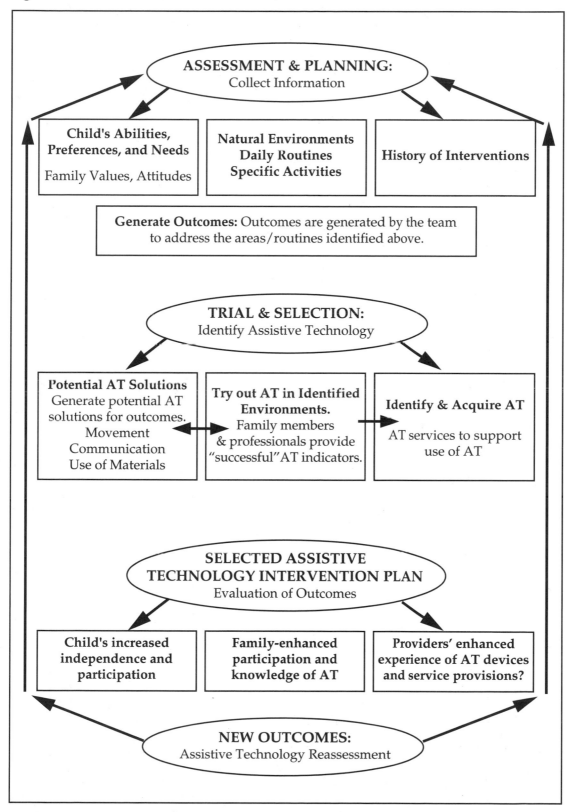

positive outcomes from the use of such things as use of computers, mobility devices, and communication aids in forestalling the development of learned helplessness and learning deficits (Behrmann & Lahm, 1984; Butler, 1986, 1988; Douglas, Reeson, & Ryan, 1988; Dudgeon, Massagli, & Ross, 1997; Robinson, 1986; Strommen, Revelle, Medoff, & Razavi, 1996; VanTatenhove, 1987; Wilds, 1989). Outcomes ranged from those related to the ease and accuracy of use for specific input devices (e.g., Strommen et al.), to improved eating and drinking skills (Hulme, Shaver, Acher, Mullette, & Eggert, 1987), to long- term outcomes such as high school completion and advancement to higher education (Dudgeon et al.).

Research also demonstrates strategies to augment existing play abilities or compensate for limitations imposed by disabilities by using AT applications (Behrman, 1984; Brinker & Lewis, 1982; Swinth, Anson, & Deitz, 1993). Further, AT may lay the foundation for transition to the use of other adaptive devices such as computers and augmentative communication devices. In fact, AT may be the only means by which some children with significant disabilities can be engaged in a physically and socially responsive environment. Thus, AT can make it possible for children to act on and receive a response from the environment (Sullivan & Lewis, 1993, 2000), offering them a means of interacting with both their material and human (caregiver) environments. At the same time it also allows for better caregiving (Daniels, Sparling, Reilly, & Humphry, 1995). Mistrett, Constantino, and Pomerantz (1994) documented increased social interaction with peers when AT was used in an inclusive preschool classroom. Thus, together these reports, both empirical and anecdotal, indicate that AT has the potential to extend all abilities of young children with disabilities by giving them access to their material and human environments in ways that might not have been present before.

Although we have fair support for the contention that assistive technology can be used to successfully influence children's attainment of a number of skills, we do not have a great deal of information on any single skill, any specific activity, any specific environment, or the use of specific strategies. What benchmark(s) indicate "success" and promote the abilities of children as they engage in the activities of childhood? A question such as this requires the development of additional evidence about the efficacy of assistive technology with children.

Further, we are making some assumptions about generalizability when we use some of the studies cited above because of they type of research design they represent. Designs employing single-subject methodology or case-study methods are not necessarily intended to be generalized to larger populations. The best design for generalization to a specific population is that of a randomized controlled trial (RCT). However, to date there are no RCTs published on the application of AT to babies and young children with disabilities.

Stepping back from these issues to a larger view of the problem, we find ourselves faced with the question of how we develop an evidence basis for AT practice, grappling with the process of defining specific outcomes to indicate success for the AT intervention.

Some Basics on Evidence-Based Practice

The concept of evidence-based practice (EBP) is an extension of evidence-based medicine, which has been defined as "the conscientious, explicit, and judicious use of current best evidence in making decisions about the care of individual patients. The practice of evidence based medicine means integrating individual clinical expertise with the best available external clinical evidence from systematic research" (Gray, 1997, p. 9). Thus, it is not completely research-based but a merging of knowledge bases from research and clinical practice. As such, it lends itself well to the field of assistive technology, where both clinical knowledge and research exist. Further, using evidence bases for our practice can lead to less uncertainty in the implementation of practice, and greater accountability.

In using EBP a sequence of activities can be described that defines the process. The sequence is spelled out in Table 4. The first thing we need to do is to develop a specific question. The examination of AT outcomes must look not only at the AT "device" or tools, but must also include what has been called the strategies earlier in this chapter, and the child's environment or

Table 4. Steps in Searching for Evidence

Overview: Evidence-Based Practice Steps
1. Develop a specific question.
2. Search the literature for relevant articles.
3. Evaluate the evidence for validity and usefulness.
4. Implement findings.

context as is indicated in all of the frameworks discussed previously.

A question about the use of AT with young children might be something like:

Customized Technology: To read her favorite story, Malika can use the available computer version with a connected switch to turn pages. What switch style offers the greatest success to this four year old with cerebral palsy?

This question asks about a device, but does not address strategy. To address strategy other questions would need to be asked. For instance, how close does Malika need to be to the monitor; where should the switch be placed for easiest access and for understanding causality; how should Malika be positioned and supported to use the switch and so on. The practitioner must decide which to question first, the device or the strategy.

Commercial or Modified Technology: Joey and his older brother enjoy playing cars. What commercially available booster seat will support independent seating for this 18-month-old child with low tone so he and his brother can play cars on the floor? Would modifications allow this commercial seat to be used?

Again, this question focuses on the seating device, not the strategies for playing. The strategies must be an integral and critical component of any intervention. Thus, a subsequent question could be crafted to address play strategies and Joey's unique skills, needs and preferences.

Because it is not always possible to find the exact answer to a question, practitioners need to be prepared to either broaden or narrow the search process. For instance, with the high tech question posed above, it may be necessary to look at switch style use for all preschool children with physical disabilities and then draw inferences to the specific group of children with cerebral palsy. Even though the literature does not hold the answer to the exact question posed, it is likely some useful information can be found. This process of looking for information related to the question, if information directly answering the question is not available, can be viewed as scaffolding the knowledge of the service provider and supporting the use of AT devices and services in intervention.

Next, a review of the literature is necessary to determine what evidence is available. The literature on the use of AT with infants and young children does not contain a huge number of studies on effectiveness, and those that do exist vary greatly in their approach, the population under study, and outcome measurements used. The relevant articles will need to be sought out, using the search strategies learned from previous trips to the library. If help is needed developing a search strategy, ask a librarian.

As information is located that addresses the question(s) asked, it must be evaluated for its usefulness, pertinence to the question, and validity. One means of doing this is to determine the rigor of the studies identified. Within the evidence-based literature, levels of evidence have been defined that provide guidance on how to interpret the rigor of research. Levels of evidence range from Level I, in which a study is generally taken to be a randomized control trial, through Level V, in which the study reflects expert opinion. The goal is of course to find the best available evidence, even though this may not always be at Level I. In fact, in the current literature on the use of AT with young children it is unlikely that any Level I studies will be found. Levels of evidence were originally defined by Fletcher and Sackett as part of a Canadian Task Force (1979). A basic version of the levels is presented in Table 5.

In the final step, the findings are implemented. If the information located does not

Table 5. Levels of Evidence

	Levels of Evidence
I.	Evidence from systematic review of multiple well designed randomized controlled trials
II.	Evidence from multiple or individual cohort or ecological studies
III.	Evidence from multiple or individual case
IV.	Evidence from case
V.	Opinions of respected authorities, based on clinical evidence, descriptive studies or reports of expert committees.

Source: Canadian Task Force on the Periodic Health Examination: The periodic health examination.

answer the question exactly it will be necessary to determine what was learned, and how this new knowledge can be put to work. Finally, it is appropriate to ask what more needs to be known to really understand the interventions that are being proposed. This is where every clinician and educator becomes a researcher. When the information is not available, it becomes our responsibility to begin to develop the information base we need to substantiate our interventions. The use of AT with children, particularly young children, is one area where the research is limited.

A number of excellent books, articles, and Web pages address evidence-based practice (e.g., Dawes, Davies, Gray, Mant, Seers, & Snowball, 1999; Gray, 1997; Helewa & Walker, 2000; Sackett, Rosenberg, Gray, Haynes, & Richardson, 1996; Sackett, Richardson, Rosenberg, & Haynes, 2000). Practitioners interested in this topic should seek more information in these resources.

Summary of Current Outcome Measures
Given this information, and the summary provided earlier in this chapter, the current knowledge about AT for children can be summarized.

Unfortunately, this information is limited and, when the quality of the material available is examined, it quickly becomes apparent that it is largely not at level I, but instead tip the scales at level IV and V.

The literature does indicate that there is some use of play and/or playfulness (viewed as a primary activity of childhood) as an outcome measure (Behrman, 1984; Brinker & Lewis, 1982; Lane & Mistrett, 1996, 2002; Mistrett, 2000; Swinth, et al., 1993). Although play is the very thing babies and young children ought to be spending their time doing, it is too often not a funded, or fundable, outcome measure. The empirical evidence summarized earlier also indicates that the following are used to measure outcomes that relate directly to something the baby or young child is doing:

• Use of computers, mobility devices, and communication aids (e.g., Behrmann & Lahm, 1984; Butler, 1988; Douglas, Reeson, & Ryan, 1988; Robinson, 1986; VanTatenhove, 1987; Wilds, 1989).

• As a transition to the use of other adaptive devices such as computers and augmentative communication devices (e.g., Wilds, 1989).

• Access modes to the computer or electronic device (e.g., Behrmann, 1984; Glickman, Deitz, Anson, & Stewart, 1995; Revelle & Medoff, 2002; Strommen, Razavi, & Medoff, 1992; Strommen, Revelle, Medoff, & Razaui, 1996; Swinth et al., 1993).

• Oral motor performance (e.g., Hulme et al., 1987).

• Changes in communication skills (e.g., Schepis, Reid, Behrmann, & Sutton, 1998).

• Literacy (e.g., Steg, 1983).

• Caregiving (e.g., Daniels et al., 1995).

• Social interaction (e.g., Mistrett et al., 1994).

• Cause and effect (e.g., Butler, 1988; Sullivan & Lewis, 1993, 2000).

This list is not meant to be all inclusive, nor to address all the potential outcome measures published. Instead, it is designed to suggest that there is a wide array of possible outcome measures. One trick is to develop a measurable outcome, and to actually measure it. The second, more daunting task, consists of measuring the how and why of participation, the use of physical supports (the device(s)) and what makes it work for the child and family (the strategies). Much of the available literature on the use of AT with young children is not empirical, but instead presents models for intervention, or theoretical concepts related to the use of AT. While it reflects the combined use of devices and services (strategies), measurable outcomes are minimal. This field needs more empirical research to support the application of this intervention tool, AT devices and service, to this young population of children, or the funding needed to continue to support development through AT will become increasingly unavailable.

A further challenge in the search for measurable outcomes is to make them meaningful. AT must be integrated into a child and family's daily routines and activities to support functional outcomes. It is only by establishing specific outcomes that we can begin to generate the evidence we need to justify using AT services and devices with young children. Setting and measuring AT specific outcomes that are pertinent to family routines and child activities will provide a way to track successes. These specific outcomes may or may not be included on a formal document such as the IEP or IFSP but should be recorded by one or more team members and reported on with input from the family and team.

Part IV: Types of Assistive Technology for Children

Attempts to order and classify AT has resulted in various categories of functional purpose. One of these is use or application. Lewis (1993) suggests that AT devices are used to augment, bypass or compensate for disabilities. Cavalier, Ferretti, and Okolo (1994) suggest that AT acts as either a prosthesis or a scaffolding tool that supports the acquisition of a new skill. Finally, RESNA relates AT to devices that respond to positioning, computer access, environmental control, augmentative and assistive communication, assistive listening, visual aids, mobility, computer-based instruction, physical education, recreation, leisure and play, and self-care (RESNA, 1992).

Another popular way to analyze AT items is to group them by complexity into low- vs. high-tech. " Low tech" items are described as simple, lacking moving parts, and limited in function (Langone, Malone, & Kinsley, 1999; Mann & Lane, 1995). In contrast, " high-tech" items are complex, multifunctional, and include moving parts (and electronics) (Langone et al., 1999; Mann & Lane, 1995).

Relating these categorization attempts to the federal definition of AT devices, there appears to be a broad correlation of the low tech examples to those that are commercial, off-the-shelf or modified. These are generally more available, less costly and require less training for their use (Angelo, 1997; Mistrett et al., 2001). High-tech devices, on the other hand, are seen to be those that are customized or designed specifically for individuals with disabilities. These generally require a specialist to locate, require extensive training, and can be highly personalized.

Although reports of positive outcomes resulting from the implementation of high tech AT exist, they may not be the most developmentally appropriate for young children with disabilities. In fact, they may act to further isolate the child. Mistrett (2000) found that when a range of options were offered to families, over 70% of the AT devices selected were low tech.

Low-tech/off-the-shelf or modified items may also be popular because some parents of infants and toddlers with disabilities are not "ready" for high-tech/customized interventions (Horn & Warren, 1987). One reason may be the "newness" of the child's diagnosis, and some parents' hesitancy to call attention to the disability with an unusual or specialized device. In other cases, the child's functional limitations may appear to be more a function of age than of disability, and the need for a customized intervention, therefore, may not be apparent. Thus, some children may reap greater benefits from off-the-shelf or modified options simply because the parents are more likely to use them.

Increased Scope of "Commercial, Off-the-Shelf" Assistive Technology Items

Influenced by the following practices, the field of commercial, off-the-shelf items appropriate for use by children with disabilities has expanded in recent years, making them readily available to families and caregivers. These products often prove to be excellent choices for young children because they are less costly and easier to obtain and use than customized products. There is a broad scope of items with features that extend their use to more children. Several trends have influenced this growth:

- Items such as suction-based bowls, sippy cups, and curved handle spoons have been "borrowed" from catalogs for children with disabilities as parents and other consumers found their design to be useful for all children, at least for a limited time during development.

- The use of some items may not be the intended use but can support activity and participation in new ways. For example, a child needing sitting support to play on the floor with his brother may benefit from the use of a commercial "booster chair" intended to raise chair height at a dining table. By placing it on the floor, the booster chair provides secure support with the additional benefit of a "tray" to hold toys and books. The addition of a swim foam "noodle," cut to fit under the knees, may offer just enough support to negate the need for a customized floor sitter, at least for a while.

- The passage of the Child Safety Protection Act (CSPA) resulted in the creation of the U.S. Consumer Product Safety Commission which established safety regulations in 1995 for toys that include small parts. For example, small balls and marbles are banned for sale if intended for children under three. This has resulted in the design of products with larger simplified features, making more toys and other items accessible to all children.

- The introduction of electronic components has increased the accessibility of many items (electronic toys, talking books and electric toothbrushes); pressing a single button can result in engaging sounds, lights, movement and full enjoyment.

- Universal design standards in the 1990s resulting from civil rights legislation have led to the identification of goods and environments that encourage participation of a broad range of individuals. Many new products have been designed with features that make their use successful by a wider range of children. Examples of readily available products include toys with clear picture labels on large buttons, voice-activated toys, curved and large-handled utensils, and textured books, to name a few.

We propose that any of these devices can be classified as AT devices when they are used to "increase, maintain, or improve functional capabilities" of children by allowing them increased opportunities to participate in everyday learning activities.

Modifications to Commercial Products

Early childhood professionals use a collection of materials (grips, Velcro, etc.) to adapt products. Sharing these methods and materials with families can promote the child's active involvement in routine activities. For example, a child not speaking at two years of age may use a set of pictures secured on a place mat to communicate during mealtimes. The service provider works with the family to identify relevant symbols, develop a choice-making process and a system of enhanced communication, and prepare the mat. With this knowledge, the family may change the pictures as appropriate. "A low tech device may have as much value as a high tech one if families find the device has enhanced their child's functioning, independence, and quality of life" (Judge & Parette, 1998, p. 3).

Several types of materials used for modifications and specific examples of their use are described below. Note the combination of commercial and specialty items.

Stabilizing

These materials support play by holding a toy within the child's reach or vision. Often toys that stay "in one place" are easier to use. Use them to hold a jack-in-the-box in place or connect a communication device to a crib.

- Tempo loop (Commercial)

- Dycem (Kapable Kids, Fred Sammons, Abilitations)
- Grip Liner; mug mats (Rubbermaid; Commercial)
- Velcro; Dual Lock (Commercial)
- Suction cups (Commercial)
- Cookie sheets for magnets
- Anti-roll crayons
- Weighted cups

Attaching

These materials are used to bring items closer to the child, making reaching, grasping, and playing less "work".

- Links (Right Start, Discovery Toys, Commercial)
- Snaps on fabric tape (Fabric store)
- "Stringers" or Magic Shoelaces
- Elastic Straps (Fabric store; other commercial)
- Attach-And-Play (Safety First; local)

Extending, Building Up

These materials are used to build up certain access features. They help children press too-small buttons or keys, hold puzzle pieces, or make brushes and markers easier to hold.

- Enlarged spoon handles
- Plasticine (Commercial)
- Magic Model Clay (Crayola)
- Popsicle sticks
- Cylindrical foam (Fred Sammons)
- Sponge rollers (Commercial)
- Knobs on puzzles
- Film Canisters with "X'd" ends

Highlighting Materials

These materials are used to highlight/enhance certain areas on toys, making them easier to locate. Change the appearance or feel of the toy pieces. Try highlighting certain areas or masking others. They help to simplify toy design and facilitate independent play by children

- Tape: painters, colored vinyl, colored masking tape
- Colored Velcro tape
- Wikki sticks
- Glued yarn, colored glue
- Black or contrasting color cloth for masking; cardboard templates, etc.

Confining

These materials prevent a toy from moving too far away from a child, out of the child's reach or vision. They help a child to control his immediate play environment.

- Hula-hoops (Commercial)
- Box tops
- Planter bases (Commercial)
- Lasagna pan
- Box top
- Placemats with dish outlines
- Containers, boxes, Tupperware for sorting

Other items can be used to create play areas which confine several toys. Their use may particularly benefit children with visual or physical impairments.

- Inflatable boats
- Tents
- Play environments-gardens, forts, castle, etc.
- Cribs, bathtubs, laundry baskets

Assistive devices manufactured and sold only by specialized vendors of items designed for use by persons with disabilities—items that would seldom be used by children without disabilities—would have the lowest level of availability and the highest level of complexity. Generally, these are devices that require the expertise of an early intervention, special education or assistive technology specialist to identify. Some items designed specifically for young children with disabilities require little training (i.e., single switches attached to toys) while others may require a great deal of training on the part of the caregivers, the child, or both (Dynavox®; computers and software). Many items in this category provide for highly programmable features to meet the unique needs of individual users, making their high tech complexity worthwhile (e.g., single- or multiple-choice augmentative communication devices, mobility systems, and adaptive computer peripherals). Since these devices are not

Table 6. Examples of Ranges of Technologies for Movement, Interaction, and Communication

	Commercial	Modified	Customized
Movement: Floor Sitting	Boppy®, Exersaucer®, Booster seat as floor seating system	Booster chair used as floor seat with side and pommel supports	Rifton corner chair, bath seat
Interaction: Toy Play	Toys designed with large, colorful, easy-to-press buttons	Toy buttons modified with added textures, making them easier to differentiate	Specialized toys (e.g., Dome Alone); switch-adapted toy
Communication: Provide Speech Output	Talking Picture Frames; Yack-Back	Pictures, photos, symbols on PVC frame	A message recordable device (e.g., CheapTalk)

designed for general use, they are not readily available at local stores.

A range of AT solutions should be offered to families that will address participation of children in specific activities. A combination of commercial and customized products is often the best solution.

Table 6 illustrates a range of AT solutions to common movement, interaction, and communication needs for participation in daily routines. Individualized AT solutions will take into consideration the abilities and preferences of the child as well as the attitudes and experiences of the family.

When using technology effectively with families with children with disabilities, the following factors contribute significantly to its success:

1. Child and family outcomes form the basis of the AT intervention. Technology is selected according to an activity specific to daily routines; it passes the "what for" test.
2. The selection and use of the AT fits the family's value system and lifestyle.
3. The entire IFSP/IEP team works together to identity outcomes and to select, use, and monitor the technology solutions. Families are full partners in the decision-making process.
4. If possible, commercial items are tried first as they are more like to be used in natural activity settings
5. Technology is changed frequently as the child/family needs change or as new technologies emerge. Access to an AT lending system appears to be a critical component to promoting the use of AT as it affords the family an immediate opportunity to try a variety of assistive technology supports. (Adapted from Todis, 1996)

Part V: Selecting and Using Assistive Technology with Children

Working with the Team

Team participation is critical to appropriate provision of AT to young children. The importance of professionals and family members working together for a common outcome has been emphasized repeatedly in the literature. Team approaches, which pool the expertise of all participants and in which members extend across traditional disciplinary boundaries, may be the most effective way to deliver AT services for children with needs in several areas; it is possible that no one individual or discipline will have all of the information available regarding the range of assistive devices that may be helpful for a child (Smith, Benge, & Hall, 1994).

Family participation in decision making and identifying AT solutions is essential. Just like all other services, AT should address the family's stated outcomes and be implemented within the context of the child's daily routines. Decisions about the use of AT by families involved in early intervention programs are influenced by both internal and external factors (see Table 7).

Table 7. Factors Influencing Decisions About AT Use

Internal factors include the family/caregivers	External factors include
• attitudes toward AT	• child's environment(s)
• value of the AT tools	• consistency of routines
• perception of the abilities, preferences, and barriers to participation that the child experiences	• activity level, persons present, skills of providers and available materials
• involvement in the child's program	
• expectations for the child's development	

Table 8. Questions to Consider When Building Partnerships Between Families and Professionals

Questions
Have all family members/caregivers been included in the AT selection and implementation process?
Are family preferences for times and locations for interactions considered?
Have family priorities, values, and cultural beliefs and perspectives been considered in every aspect of the AT selection and implementation process?
Are there opportunities for the family to be involved in the ongoing evaluation of the AT devices and/or services?
Are the family's changing needs addressed during the AT selection and implementation process?

In recent years growing appreciation for cultural diversity has advanced the quality of service delivery to various populations. When working with families, other team members must be culturally competent and provide service within the context of lifestyles and values of the family. There is clear evidence that attention to cultural and ethnic concerns during the decision-making process is linked to a family's willingness to participate in assistive technology device implementation (Parette, Brotherson, Hoge, & Hostetler, 1996). Table 8 presents some questions to consider when building and expanding partnerships with families.

When to Consider AT

As should be clear at this point, AT is opening doors to enhance opportunities for children with disabilities to participate in home, school, and community environments. Failure to consider the role of assistive technology limits the ways in which young children with disabilities and their family members can participate in daily routines and activities. A critical concept of AT is to continuously support the child's development by providing tools that address the challenges that may limit his or her ability to play with toys, communicate, participate, and explore the environment. As noted earlier, this is consistent with the framework presented in the ICF, and is reflected in the AT Device Framework. For example, AT can provide opportunities to promote fine-motor, gross motor, or communication skill development for young children by circumventing the barriers that disabilities present. AT devices alter the accessibility of the environment, putting control back into the hands of the user. AT services make use possible. And, new skills generate new experiences that result in gains in

Table 9. Guiding Questions for Considering AT

Questions
Is the child able to functionally communicate with adults and peers within reasonable expectations for his/her age?
Is the child able to sit, stand, and move about the environment freely as appropriate for age and developmental level?
Is the child able to perform self-help activities such as feeding, dressing, and toileting at a level appropriate for age and developmental level?
Is the child able to engage in developmentally appropriate play with toys and others or participate in developmentally appropriate academic and recreational activities with peers?

(Adapted from the State of New York Department of Health Early Intervention Memorandum 99-1)

all levels of functioning (Campos, Kermoian, & Witherington, 1996).

Assistive technology should be considered as an option for young children and their families anytime a child has difficulty participating. Table 9 lists several guiding questions to help determine if the implementation of AT devices and/or services is warranted.

As always, it is essential to take into account the child's age as well as current and expected developmental levels when answering the guiding questions. If the answer to any of these questions is "no," it is appropriate to consider AT devices and services as an intervention.

The process of considering and selecting appropriate assistive technologies is dynamic and should be revisited on a regular basis. As we have seen, the usefulness of a particular AT device or service changes as children develop, and their interests, abilities and needs change. Additionally, the availability of technology changes quickly, and new AT options should be explored periodically as appropriate devices and services become available.

Assistive technologies can and should be considered when changes occur in the child or in the environment. More specifically, AT should be considered when children get "stuck" – when they are no longer progressing toward meeting functional outcomes or when current interventions are not working to reach the desired outcomes. Below are three examples of when AT should be considered: as a result of changes in the child, as a result of

changes in the environment, and as a result of changes in the availability of technology.

John

John is a three-year-old child who has many friends in the preschool classroom. His teacher has noticed that even with significant physical disabilities, John has been increasingly able to use his arms and hands for daily activities. However his endurance is poor because a great deal of effort is required for each activity. John has a personal aide for periods of time during each school day. Each day one of the children is assigned a "Job Helper" duty such as turning off the lights in the room when they leave for the playground, passing out napkins during snack, and feeding the classroom goldfish. Parents and the preschool teacher would like to be able to give John more to do in the classroom, allowing him to contribute to and participate in classroom activities like the other children. To do so, John requires additional supports. His family and teacher need ideas for how technology could assist John in participating in several classroom activities.

An example of a situation in which AT should be considered due to *changes in the child* can be seen with John. John is showing changes in body function and in his interest to actively paricipate. By identifying the specific activities for participation, AT supports for positioning and interacting with relevant materials in each activity can be identified and tried.

Tamika

Tamika is a 4-year-old girl who enjoys books and stories and playing with puzzles. She has been receiving speech and language pathology and occupational therapy services in her home for the past two years. She has made steady gains in her ability to communicate using word approximations, gestures, and sign language and is able to communicate effectively with her parents and older brother. However, Tamika continues to have great difficulty making her needs and desires known to people outside her current environments. Looking ahead, Tamika's family has enrolled her in an integrated preschool program, set to begin in three months.

Tamika is an example of a situation in which AT should be considered due to *changes in the environment*. There is a need to increase the environments in which she can use her communication skills, and to identify new interactive opportunities and a responsive communication system for increased participation. Tamika and her family will need to try a variety of portable augmentative communication devices to assist Tamika in communicating with individuals across a variety of environments.

Jay

Jay is a two-and-a half-year-old boy who, despite near age-appropriate cognitive skills, has significant limitations in his expressive language abilities. Currently, Jay is using several small photo albums to make his needs and desires known to his family. His mother and speech therapist have put together one photo album for morning routines, one for mealtime, one for play time, and another for bedtime routines. Jay is able to indicate his needs within these contexts by pointing to photos. Due to the high cost of a suitable communication device for Jay in the past, it has not been possible to try out or purchase the appropriate technology. However, a multilevel communication device, appropriate to meet Jay's changing needs, is now available for loan along wiht a discount on the purchase price.

An example of a situation in which AT should be considered due to *changes in the availability of technology* can be seen with Jay. Using such a device will greatly increase Jay's ability to communicate in a variety of settings, which in turn, will positively impact his ability to participate in more activities. Due to the change in the availability of technology, Jay and his family can now try out a new device, and if it works, they can start the process to purchase this more appropriate and efficient communication system for Jay.

Examples of the Assistive Technology Decision-Making Process Using Matrices

The following is a case study that illustrates the AT Device and Service Frameworks. The process starts with activities within the routine events the child participates in within home and child care environments as the arenas for AT devices and services. Finding out where and how families play, work, and live, specific activities they enjoy, and how each member participates, is valuable for determining if and how AT can benefit a particular child and his or her family. Likewise, finding out how the child learns best, what environments are most conducive to learning, and what most interests the child, will determine if and how AT can benefit a particular child in his/her educational environment. As we have noted earlier, technologies are not effective on their own unless they are paired with strategies and adapted in their use to suit a child's and family's individual needs and resonate with the family's lifestyle and/or educational environment.

Lewis

Lewis is a two-and-a half-year-old boy who lives with both his mother and grandmother. He has been involved in his community's early intervention program since he was six months old. Lewis has general developmental delays in all areas: motor, cognitive, speech and language, social emotional skills and self-help limitations are evident. Lewis sits all by himself, crawls on the floor to get to certain objects, and is beginning to stand behind a small chair and push it. He enjoys taking objects out of containers and then banging them together, and is just beginning to understand that by pushing a button on a toy, he can make something happen – the musical jukebox is his favorite toy! He points and uses gestures with some sounds to indicate what he wants. His mother reports that Lewis needs an adult to engage him in new play activities. He currently receives occupational therapy, physical therapy, speech and language pathology services, and special instruction in his home. Lewis's mother is starting Lewis in a neighborhood preschool program two mornings per week once he is three years old. She wants to have supports in place before he starts.

Assessment and Planning: Collect Information

Based on this new information and Lewis' current level of performance, a meeting was held with the family, the therapists, and educator involved with Lewis. The team discussed the best approach to support him to begin preschool in six months. Along with the services at the preschool, the team wants to consider what AT supports he may need that will better enable Lewis to participate fully in his new preschool environment. Background information provided a baseline for Lewis. Ongoing dialogue among Lewis' caregivers and service providers was used to gather essential information regarding his mother and grandmother's perspectives and beliefs concerning AT, their desired level of involvement in the AT device and service decisions, and the family priorities, strengths, and needs. Interview, observation, and past experiences provide the service providers with additional information regarding Lewis and his family's interests and strengths. Current documentation contributed by everyone was used to gain information specific to all developmental areas, including gross- and fine-motor skills, cognitive levels, learning styles, communicative abilities, and social/emotional performance levels. The family and team members made several visits to the preschool Lewis will be attending to gather information about the environment, routines, and activities within these routines. The preschool staff was also helpful in sharing information about daily activities and the expectations for children in the program.

A matrix based on the information gathered in the assessment and planning stage was developed to identify and track Lewis' participation levels and to determine specific activities where AT should be considered. Environments in which Lewis would find himself, and the routines and activities associated with these environments that were considered high priority by the team, were included in the matrix. Lewis was observed during the first week of school. Figure 11 reflects only one routine activity – Outside Play – identified by the family and team. Prior to generating outcomes for Lewis, information about what is currently happening and what the team would like to see happen is identified for each activity within outside play. The family and team prioritized areas of concern in an effort to focus intervention. The routine of outside play with peers was selected as one area to target based on the family's desire for Lewis to be involved and play with children his own age, Lewis' interest in other children, and the frequency with which Lewis will have opportunities to participate in this activity in preschool.

All team members, including the preschool staff, determined that the outcomes generated ("What we'd like to see happen") should realistically be achieved after Lewis had attended his preschool program for two months. All outcomes were agreed upon by the team.

Trial and Selection: Identify Assistive Technology

In the trial and selection phase the family and team generated a list of potential AT options that encompassed mobility, communication, and the use of materials to address each of the identified outcomes. Strategies for using the potential devices during the specific activity of outside play were discussed and, following the initial brainstorming session, a list of the "best" AT devices and strategies to meet Lewis' and his family's needs was recorded on the expanded AT options matrix (see Figure 12). The professionals were able to acquire some of the devices for a trial period from a local lending library. Items not available for loan in the community were leased from a local vendor for a trial period of 60-90 days.

Figure 11. Matrix.

Routines	Activities	What Is Happening Now?	What We'd Like To See Happen	How Will We Know When We Have Been Successful? (Outcomes)
Outside Play	Playground	Sits and watches other children – little initiation Difficulty using standard equipment (e.g., swing, slide) Enjoys playing in sandbox	Initiate interactions with peers occasionally Be able to access sandbox and other playground equipment	Lewis initiates an interaction with a peer one time per day during outside play each week. Lewis chooses between three options for outside play (sandbox, swing, bubbles) each day. Lewis' classroom teacher demonstrates the ability to implement the necessary technology for Lewis to make choices during outside play.
	Go for a Walk	Unable to walk distances greater than 10 feet Enjoys being pushed in umbrella stroller, but he is too big for it and is beginning to protest when placed in it	To take part in walks with peers Have an appropriate means of mobility	Lewis participates in walks with peers each time this activity is performed using appropriate mobility device.

The team designated a member to observe Lewis using the AT and collect information on how each specific device and strategy worked toward meeting the established outcomes. For example, several varieties of a single-message output device as well as a number of walkers were tried prior to the final family and team decision. Data collection provided evidence of Lewis' ability to use the devices and strategies, and was used to support the written justification for the acquisition of the devices. Upon reviewing the reports, the team submitted the necessary justifications for the purchase of the assistive devices to the local early intervention office. Within three months of submitting the request, Lewis had received the devices.

The devices included an adapted swing, a floor sitter, posture walker, a switch-operated bubble blower, and three one-step communicators. Additionally, the occupational therapist used thermoplastic materials and foam to build up handles on sand toys and bubble wands. The speech and language pathologist worked with Lewis' family, special instructor, and preschool teacher to create several communication boards and to record messages for outside play activities.

Selected Assistive Technology Intervention Plan: Evaluation of Outcomes
The family and team constructed a plan for the set up and implementation of each of the AT devices in Lewis' natural environments. The plan included when the device was to be used, how it would be introduced to Lewis, and who was responsible for device set up and training

Figure 12. AT options matrix for Lewis.

Environment	Preschool
Routine	Outside play
Activity	Playing on playground: Swings, sand play, bubble play
Outcome/s	Lewis initiates an interaction with a peer one time per day during outside play each week.
	Lewis has at least three options that he can access each day for outside play (sandbox, swing, bubbles).

Areas to consider	AT Options		
Movement supports (positioning + mobility)	Adapted swing on playground	Adapted "floor seat" seat for sandbox and bubble play	Mobility aid (walker) for navigating short distances on playground
Interaction with materials supports	Built-up handles on sand toys and bubble wand	Switch-operated bubble blower (used with LITTLEmack)	Bubble blower with handle that activates blower
Communication supports	Communication picture board for each specific outdoor play activity	Single-message communication device (LITTLEmack) to call peers names on playground	Multiple-message device for sand and bubble activities

of both Lewis and his caregivers. A plan was written for the preschool environment as well as for home. Several of the team members were versed in the use of the selected devices and were able to train the family and remaining team members, including the preschool staff, in device use and basic problem solving. In addition, the AT devices that Lewis was using were demonstrated to the children in the preschool classroom during "show and tell." Careful monitoring of AT use was planned.

Outcomes were re-examined, and it was decided that an additional three-month period was needed before reevaluation of the goals. At this point Lewis would have been using his AT devices in his preschool environment for approximately five months.

Three of the four outcomes written for Lewis measure a change in his independence within his daily activities. One measures the family and preschool staff's increased knowledge and comfort with the implementation of technology. In addition to these documented outcomes, several service providers generated therapeutic outcomes to measure specific functions of device use. For example, the physical therapist wrote the following outcome: "Lewis will propel himself 10 feet using a walker on a flat grassy area two times during each outside play session." At the end of the specified period, data were gathered on all outcomes and a meeting was held with the family, team and preschool staff to discuss progress and to determine if new activities would require additional supports.

New Outcomes: Assistive Technology Re-Assessment

Upon evaluation of the outcomes several issues regarding future directions of device use were discussed and new outcomes were generated. The new outcomes focused on Lewis gaining independence and the family and classroom staff demonstrating improved confidence and knowledge of AT devices. The family and team decided that in the next six-month period they would explore a communication device with more choices that Lewis could use across several home and classroom environments. Additionally, Lewis would be expected to begin using the walker to navigate to/from specific areas in the preschool building as well as use it in community environments such as the local shopping mall. They also determined that the handles on some of the play materials in the pretend play area in the preschool as well as some of Lewis' toys at home needed to be built up for easier use. Once again, outcomes were generated for each of these new areas and a plan was put in place for their implementation.

Summary

That the AT needs are unique for this younger age is recognized and reflected in the laws that mandate AT consideration. While AT for young children shares some similarities with AT for adults, adjustments in one's vision of the appropriate tools is necessary to meet the needs of this developing population. To emphasize both the overlap and the critical differences between AT for the very young and AT for older children and adults, we presented frameworks specific to the AT needs of babies and young children (AT Devices and Services Frameworks), and linked this to the ICF, a framework that is more global and applicable across rehabilitative interventions and the age span.

As illustrated, the evidence supporting the effectiveness of application of AT Devices and Services for babies and young children needs greater breadth and depth. Examples of matrices that can structure the development of specific outcomes, and subsequently form an evidence base for practice, were presented. AT has great potential to improve the quality of life for very young children. The challenge to professionals is to know how to use AT with this population, and to provide the needed evidence of its effectiveness.

References

Americans with Disabilities Act of 1990, 42 U. S. C. § 12101 *et seq.* (2000).

Angelo, J. (1997). *Assistive technology for rehabilitation therapists.* Philadelphia, PA: F.A. Davis.

Armstrong, J. S., & Jones, K. (1994). Assistive technology and young children: Getting off to a great start! *Closing the Gap, 13*(3), 1, 31-32.

Assistive Technology Act of 1998, 29 U. S. C. § 3001 et seq. (2000).

Behrmann, M. M. (1984). A brighter future for early learning through high tech. *The Pointer, 28,* 23-26.

Behrmann, M., & Lahm, E. (1984). Babies and robots: Technology to assist learning. *Rehabilitation Literature, 45*(7), 194-201.

Bowser, G., & Reed, P. (1995). Education TECH points for assistive technology planning. *Journal of Special Education Technology, 12*(4), 325-338.

Brinker, R. P., & Lewis, M. (1982). Making the world work with microcomputers: A learning prosthesis for handicapped infants. *Exceptional Children, 49*(2), 163-170.

Bronfenbrenner, U. (1975). Is early intervention effective? In B. Frielander, G. Sterrit, & G. Kirk (eds.), *Exceptional infant: Vol. 3 Assessment and intervention* (pp. 449-475). New York: Brunner/Mazel.

Bryant, D. P., Erin, J., Lock, R. Allen J. M. & Resta, P. E. (1998). Infusing a teacher preparation program in learning disabilities with assistive technology. *Journal of Learning Disabilities, 31,* 55-66.

Burke, C. (1997). A summary of assistive technology equipment recycling: A comparison and feasibility study. *Technology and Disability, 7,* 175-182.

Butler, C. (1986). Effects of powered mobility on self-initiated behaviors of very young children with locomotor disability. *Developmental Medicine and Child Neurology, 28,* 325-332.

Butler, C. (1988). High tech tots: Technology for mobility, manipulation, communication, and learning in early childhood. *Infants and Young Children, 1*(2), 66-73.

Butler, C., Okamoto, G., & McKay, T.M. (1983). Powered mobility for very young disabled children. *Developmental Medicine & Child Neurology, 25,* 472-474.

Campos, J. J., Kermoian, R. & Witherington, D. (1996). An epigenetic perspective on emotional development. In R. Kavanaugh, B. Zimmerberg, & S. Fein (Eds.), *Emotion:*

Interdisciplinary perspectives (pp. 119-138). Mhawah, NJ: Erlbaum.

Canadian Task Force on the Periodic Health Examination. (1979). The Periodic health examination. *Canadian Medical Association Journal, 121(9)*, 1193-1254.

Cavalier, A. R., Ferritti, R. P., & Okolo, C. M. (1994). Technology and individual differences. *Journal of Special Education Technology, 12(3)*, 175-181.

Cook, A. M. & Hussey, S. M. (2002) (2nd Edition). *Assistive Technologies: Principles and Practice.* New York: Mosby.

Daniels, L. E., Sparling, J. W., Reilly, M., & Humphry, R., (1995). Use of assistive technology with young children with severe and profound disabilities. *Infant-Toddler Intervention, 5*, 91-112.

Dawes, M., Davies, P. T., Gray, A. M., Mant, J., Seers, K., & Snowball, R. (1999). *Evidence-based practice: A primer for health care professionals.* Philadelphia: Churchill Livingstone.

DeRuyter, F. (1995). Evaluating outcomes in assistive technology: Do we understand the commitment? *Assistive Technology, 7*, 3-16.

Digest of educational statistics, 2001 12/01/01 nces.ed.gov/pubs2002/digest2001/tables/dt427.asp

Douglas, J., & Ryan, M. (1987). A preschool severely disabled boy and his powered wheelchair: a case study. *Child: Care, Health and Development, 13*, 303-309.

Douglas, J., Reeson, B., & Ryan, M., (1988). Computer microtechnology for a severely disabled preschool child. *Child: Care, Health, and Development, 14*, 93-104.

Dudgeon, B. J., Massagli, T. L., & Ross, B. W. (1996). Educational participation of children with spinal cord injury. *American Journal of Occupational Therapy, 51*, 553-561.

Dunst, C. J. (1985). Rethinking early intervention. *Analysis and Intervention in Developmental Disabilites, 5*, 165-201.

Dunst, C. J., & Bruder, M. B. (1999). Increasing children's learning opportunities in the context of family and community life. *Children's Learning Opportunities Report, 1(1)*, 1-3.

Dunst, C. J., Bruder, M. B., Trivette, C. M., Raab, M., & McLean, M. (1998). *Increasing children's learning opportunities through families and communities early childhood research institute: Year two progress report.* Asheville, NC: Orelena Hawks Puckett Institute.

Dunst, C. J., Hamby, D., Trivette, C. M., Raab, M., & Bruder, M. B. (2000). Everyday family and community life and children's naturally occurring learning opportunities. *Journal of Early Intervention, 23(3)*, 151-1664.

Edelman, L. (1999). *Being a kd: Supports and services in everyday routines, activities, and places* (videotape), Denver: Colorado Department of Education, Western Media Products.

Education for All Handicapped Children Act of 1975, 20 U. S. C. § 1401 *et seq.* (1975).

Education for All Handicapped Children Act Amendments of 1986, P.L. 99-457, 20 U.S.C. x 1400 et seq.

Edyburn, D. L. (2000). Assistive technology and students with mild disabilities. *Focus on Exceptional Children, 32(9)*, 1-23.

Erin, J., Daugherty, W. Dignan, K., & Parson, N. (1990). Teachers of visually handicapped students with multiple disabilities: perceptions of adequacy. *Journal of Visual Impairment& Blindness, 84*, 16-20.

Espe, J.O. (1998, March). *Creating school based assistive technology teams in rural states: An inservice training model.* Paper presented at CSUN 1998 Conference, Los Angeles, CA.

Glickman, L., Deitz, J., Anson, D., Stewart, K. (1996). The effect of switch control site on computer skills of infants and toddlers. *American Journal of Occupational Therapy, 50*, 545-553.

Goldman, A., Lowman, J., Bryen, D. N., & Lemanowicz, J. (2000). *Assistive technology use by students in Pennsylvania. Brief Report #1.* Philadelphia: Institute on Disabilities/UAP, Temple University.

Gray, J. A. M. (1997). *Evidence-based healthcare.* New York: Churchill Livingstone.

Helewa, A., & Walker, J. M. (2000). *Critical evaluation of research in physical rehabilitation: Towards evidence-based practice.* Philadelphia: W. B. Saunders

Horn, E. M., & Warren, S. F. (1987). Facilitating the acquisition of sensorimotor behavior with a micro-computer mediated teaching system: An experimental analysis. *Journal of the Association for the Severely Handicapped, 12*, 205-215.

Hulme, J. B., Shaver, J., Acher, S., Mullette, L., & Eggert, C. (1987). Effects of adaptive seating devices on the eating and drinking of children with multiple handicaps. *American Journal of Occupational Therapy, 41*, 81-89.

Hutinger, P., Johanson, J., & Stoneburner, R. (1996). Assistive technology applications in education programs of children with multiple disabilities: A case study report on state of the practice. *Journal of Special Education Technology, 8*(1), 16-35.

Individuals with Disabilities Education Act Amendments of 1990, P.L. 101-476, 20 U.S.C. § 1400 *et seq.*

Individuals with Disabilities Education Act Amendments of 1997, P.L. 105-17, 20 U.S. C. § 1400 *et seq.*

Izen, C. L., & Brown, F. (1991). Education and treatment needs of students with profound, multiply handicapping, and medically fragile conditions: A survey of teacher's perceptions. *Journal of the Association for Persons with Severe Handicaps, 16*, 94-103.

Judge, S. L., & Parette, H.P. (1998). *Assistive technology for young children with disabilities: A guide to family-centered services.* Cambridge, MA: Brookline Books.

Kaplan-Sanoff, M., Brewster, A., Stillwell, J., & Bergen, D. (1988). In D. Bergen (Ed.), *Play as a medium for learning and development: A handbook of theory and practice* (pp. 137-161). Portsmouth, NH: Heinemann.

Lane, S. J., & Mistrett, S. G. (1996a). Play and assistive technology issues for infants and young children with disabilities: A preliminary examination. *Focus on Autism and Other Developmental Disabilities, 11*(2), 96-104.

Lane, S. J., & Mistrett, S. G. (1996b). Technology: Can and should it be used for early intervention? In S. Lane (Ed.), *Technology for the pediatric therapist* (pp. 191-209). Philadelphia: F. A. Davis.

Lane, S. J., & Mistrett, S. G. (2002). Let's play! Assistive technology interventions for play. *Young Exceptional Children, 5*(2), 19-27.

Langone, J., Malone, M., & Kinsley, T. (1999). Technology solutions for young children with developmental concerns. *Infants & Young Children, 11*(4), 65-78.

Lesar, S. (1998). The use of assistive technology with young children with disabilities: Current status and training needs. *Journal of Early Intervention, 21*(2), 146-59.

Lewis, R. B. (1993). *Special education technology: Classroom applications.* Pacific Grove, CA: Cole Publishing Co.

Male, M. (1997). *Technology for inclusion: Meeting the special needs of all students* (3rd ed.). Boston, MA: Allyn & Bacon.

Mann, W. C., & Lane, J. P. (1995). *Assistive technology for persons with disabilities* (2nd ed.). Rockville, MD: American Occupational Therapy Association.

McGregor, G., & Pachuski, P. (1996). Assistive technology in schools: Are teachers ready, able, and supported? *Journal of Special Education Technology, 13*(1), 4-15.

Mistrett, S. G. (2000). *Let's play! Project final report* (Final Report to OSERS, No. H024B50051). Buffalo: State University of New York at Buffalo, Center for Assistive Technology.

Mistrett, S. G., Constantino, S.M., & Pomerantz, D. (1994). Using computers to increase the social interactions of preschoolers with disabilities at community-based sites. *Technology and Disability, 3*(2), 148-157.

Mistrett, S. G., & Lane, S. J. (1995). Using assistive technology for play and learning: Children, from birth to 10 years of age. In W.C. Mann & J. Lane (Eds.), *Assistive technology for persons with disabilities* (pp. 131-163). Rockville, MD: American Occupational Therapy Association

Mistrett, S. G., Hale, M.M., Diamond, C.M., Ruedel, K.L.A., Gruner, A., Sunshine, C., Berman, K., Saunders, J., & McInerney, M. (2001). *Synthesis on the use of assistive technology with infants and toddlers (birth through age two).* Office of Special Education Programs. Washington, DC: U.S. Department of Education, Division of Research to Practice.

Moore, H., McQuay, H., & Gray, J. A. M. (Eds.). (1995). Evidence-based everything. *Bandolier, 1*(12), 1.

Morton, J., & Johnson, M. H. (1991). CONSPEC and CONLEARN: A two-process theory of infant face recognition. *Psychological Review, 98*, 164-181.

National Assistive Technology Research Institute (NATRI). (2001). Assistive Technology Policies of State Departments of

Education: The Baseline Investigation. Retrieved January 20, 2004, from: natri.uky.edu/resources/reports/polsea.html.

New Freedom Initiative. (February 1, 2001). Forward by George Bush. Department of Health and Human services. Retrieved January 20, 2004, from:www.hhs.gov/newfreedom/

Office of Special Education and Rehabilitative Services. (1989). *OSERS News in Print*, (2)1.

Oxford Center for Evidence Based Medicine (2001, May). Oxford Centre for Evidence-based Medicine Levels of Evidence. Retrieved January 10, 2004, from:www.cebm.net/downloads/Oxford_CEBM_Levels_5.rtf

Parette, H. P., Brotherson, M. J., Hoge, D. R., & Hostetler, S. A. (1996, December,). *Family-centered augmentative and alternative communication issues: Implications across cultures.* Paper presented to the International Early Childhood Conference on Children with Special Needs, Phoenix, AZ.

Parette, H. P., & Hourcade, J. J. (1996, April). *Best practices in identifying assistive technology from a cultural perspective.* Paper presented to the meeting of the Council for Exceptional Children, Orlando, FL.

Parette, H. P., Hourcade, J. J., & Van Biervliet, A. (1993). Selection of appropriate technology for children with disabilities. *Teaching Exceptional Children, 25*(3), 18-22.

Rappaport, J. (1981). In praise of paradox: A social policy of empowerment over prevention. *American Journal of Community Psychology, 9*, 1-25.

Rappaport, J. (1987). Terms of Empowerment/exemplars of prevention: Toward a theory for community psychology. *American Journal of Community Psychology, 15*(2), 121-128.

Reed, P. (2000). Assistive technology legislation. Retrieved December 11, 2002, from: atto.buffalo.edu/registered/ATBasics/Foundation/Laws/atlegislation.php

RESNA Technical Assistance Project. (1992). *Assistive technology and the individualized education program.* Washington, DC: RESNA Press.

RESNA Technical Assistance Project. (2003). AT connections. Retrieved January 22, 2003, from: www.resna.org/taproject/at/equiploan.html

Revelle, G.L., & Medoff, L. (2002). Interface design and research process for studying the usability of interactive home-entertainment systems by young children. *Early Education & Development, 13*, 423-434.

Robinson, C. (2001). *AT ACCESS – Assistive technology access for children and communities early: Status and strategies* (OSEP Grant Proposal CFDA 84-327X). Denver, Colorado: University of Colorado, Department of Psychiatry & Colorado Psychiatric Health.

Robinson, C., & Fieber, N. (1988). Cognitive assessment of motorically impaired infants and preschoolers. In T. Wachs & R. Sheehan (Eds.), *Assessment of young developmentally disabled children* (pp. 51-62). New York: Plenum Publishing Co.

Robinson, L. M. (1986). Designing computer intervention for very young handicapped children. *Journal of the Division for Early Childhood, 10*(3), 209-215.

Rose, D. H. (2001). Testimony: Hearing on education technology. Committee on Appropriations, Subcommittee on Labor, Health and Human Services, and Education. Retrieved January 12, 2003, from:www.cast.org/udl/index.cfm?i=2020

Sackett, D. L., Richardson, W. S. Rosenberg, W. M. C., & Haynes, R. B. (2000). Evidence-based medicine: How to practice and teach ebm. (2nd ed.). London: Churchill-Livingstone.

Sackett, D. L., Rosenberg, W. M. C., Gray, J. A. M., Haynes, R. B., & Richardson, W. S. (1996). Evidence-based medicine: What it is and what it isn't. *British Medical Journal, 312*, 71-72.

Schepis, M. M., Reid, D. H., Behrmann, M. M., & Sutton, K.A. (1998) Increasing communicative interactions of young children with autism using a voice output communication aid and naturalistic teaching. *Journal of Applied Behavior Analysis, 31*, 561-578.

Section 504 of the Rehabilitation Act of 1973, 29 U. S. C. § 479(a) (2000).

Section 508 of the Rehabilitation Act of 1973, 29 U. S. C. § 479(d) (2000).

Smith, R., Benge, M., & Hall, M. (1994). Technology for self-care. In C. Christiansen (Ed.), *Ways of living: Self-care strategies for special needs* (pp. 379-422). Rockville, MD: American Occupational Therapy Association.

Solano, T., & Aller, S. K. (2000, June). Tech for tots: Assistive technology for infants and young children (Part 1). *Exceptional Parent Magazine*, 44-47.

State of New York Department of Health, 1999 memorandum 99-1. Retrieved January 7, 2004, from: www.health.state.ny.us/nysdoh/eip/99_1.pdf

Steg, D. R. (1983). Long term gains from early intervention through technology: An eleven year report. *Journal of Educational Technology Systems, 11,* 203-214.

Strommen, E.F., Razavi, S., & Medoff, L.M. (1992). This button makes you go up: Three-year-olds and the Nintendo controller. *Applied Ergonomic, 2,* 409-413.

Strommen, E.F., Revelle, G.L., Medoff, L.M., & Razavi, S. (1996). Slow and steady wins the race? Three-year-old children and pointing device use. *Behavior & Information Technology, 15,* 57-64.

Sullivan, M.W., & Lewis, M. (1993). Contingency, means-end skills, and the use of technology in infant intervention. *Infants and Young Children, 5*(4), 58-77.

Sullivan, M.W., & Lewis, M. (2000). Assistive technology for the very young: Creating responsive environments. *Infants and Young Children, 12*(4), 34-52.

Swinth, Y., Anson, D., & Deitz, J. (1993). Single-switch computer access for infants and toddlers. *American Journal of Occupational Therapy, 47,* 1031-1038.

Technology Related Assistance Act for Individuals with Disabilities, 29 U. S. C. x 2201 et seq. (1994) (repealed, P.L.105-394, Nov. 13, 1998).

Thorkildsen, R. (1994). Research synthesis on quality and availability of assistive technology devices (Tech. Rep. No. 7, ED386855). Eugene; University of Oregon, National Center to Improve the Tools of Educators.

Todis, B. (1996). Tools for the task? Perspectives on assistive technology in educational settings. *Journal of Educational Technology, 13*(2), 49-61.

U.S. Department of Education. (1998). *Twentieth annual report to congress on the implementation of the Individuals with Disabilities Education Act.* Washington, DC: U.S. Government Printing Office.

U.S. Department of Education. (1999). *Twenty-first annual report to congress on the implementation of the Individuals with Disabilities Education Act.* Washington, DC: U.S. Government Printing Office.

U.S. Department of Education. (2000). *Twenty-second annual report to congress on the implementation of the Individuals with Disabilities Education Act.* Washington, DC: U.S. Government Printing Office.

U.S. Department of Education. (2001). *Twenty-third annual report to congress on the implementation of the Individuals with Disabilities Education Act.* Washington, DC: U.S. Government Printing Office.

U.S. Department of Education. (2002). *Twenty-fourth annual report to congress on the implementation of the Individuals with Disabilities Education Act.* Washington, DC: U.S. Government Printing Office.

Van Tatenhove, G. M. (1987). Teaching power through augmentative communication: Guidelines for early intervention. *Journal of Childhood Communication Disorders, 10*(2), 185-199.

Wilcox, M.J. (1989). Delivering communication-based services to infants, toddlers and their families: Approaches and models. *Topics in Language Disorders, 10*(1), 68-79.

Wilds, M. L. (1989). Effective use of technology with young children. *NICHCY News Digest, 13,* 6-7.

World Health Organization. (2001). *International classification of functioning, disability and health.* Geneva, Switzerland: World Health Organization.

Zabala, J. (1995, March). *The SETT framework: Critical areas to consider when making informed assistive technology decisions.* Paper presented at the Florida Assistive Technology and Media Division of Council for Exceptional Children, Orlando, FL.

Zabala, J. (n.d.). *Get SETT for successful inclusion and transition.* Retrieved January, 8, 2004, from:www.ldonline.org/ld_indepth/technology/zabalaSETT1.html

15

Technology Use and Students with Intellectual Disability: Universal Design for All Students

Michael L. Wehmeyer, Sean J. Smith, and Daniel K. Davies

The "promise" of technology presented in the Technology-Related Assistance for Individuals with Disabilities Act of 1988 (e.g., Tech Act) was that use of such technology would "enable individuals to: (A) have greater control over their own lives, (B) participate in and contribute more fully to activities in their home, school and work environments, and in their communities, (C) interact to a greater extent with nondisabled individuals, and (D) otherwise benefit from opportunities that are taken for granted by individuals who do not have disabilities" (p. 1044). People with and without disabilities universally value the goals of greater control and self-determination, inclusion and participation in school or community, and enhanced social inclusion. However, for some people with disabilities, the Tech Act's promise of technology to support these valued outcomes has remained largely unrealized. This is the case for adults and students with intellectual disabilities[1] (Wehmeyer, 1998, 1999). This chapter overviews the potential of technology (primarily electronic and information technologies) to support students with intellectual disabilities to achieve in and out of the classroom. The first section overviews changing conceptualizations of intellectual disability and discusses the role of technology to address the needs of people with intellectual disabilities, including a discussion of specific characteristics of people with intellectual disabilities that impact technology use. The second section examines the role of technology to enhance school and community outcomes for this population. The final section discusses issues pertaining to future technology development and implementation to ensure that students with intellectual disabilities can benefit.

From Programs to Supports: A Functional Definition of Mental Retardation

The 9th Edition of the American Association on Mental Retardation (AAMR) handbook on definition and classification of mental retardation (Luckasson et al., 1992) introduced a functional definition and classification system intended to link the classification of "mental

---

[1] We have elected to use the term *intellectual disability* instead of mental retardation when we can. While the latter remains the most widely used, there is a growing dissatisfaction with that term within the field. Intellectual disability is gaining popularity in the United States and is widely used internationally. We will use the term *mental retardation* in relation to specific definitions and eligibility criterion, but will use *intellectual disability* in other situations.

retardation" to a system of supports and move the diagnostic process away from its historic reliance on levels of deficit as identified by performance on an IQ test. Further, in this edition of the AAMR classification manual, mental retardation is defined not as something a person has or something that is a characteristic of the person, but instead as a state of functioning in which limitations in functional capacity and adaptive skills must be considered within the context of environments and supports. According to this perspective, "mental retardation is a disability only as a result of this interaction" (Luckasson et al., 1992 p. 10); that is, only as a result of the interaction between the functional limitation and the social context, in this case the environments and communities in which people with intellectual disability live, learn, work and play.

AAMR's reconceptualization of mental retardation places considerable emphasis on the interaction between the person with the disability and the context in which that person lives, learns, works, or plays. Why is this important for consideration by educators interested in technology? By defining the disability as a function of the reciprocal interaction between the environment and the student's functional limitations, the focus of the "problem" shifts from being a deficit within the student to identifying and designing of supports to address the individual's functioning within that context, with an enhanced focus on adaptations, accommodations, and modifications to the context. Technology, in turn, becomes a critical support tool not only to accommodate for a student's limitations (e.g., using an augmentative communication device with synthesized speech if the student is not able to speak), but also to apply principles of Universal Design for Learning to implement curricular and instructional modifications. We will discuss these areas, but before doing so, it is important to consider the degree to which students with intellectual disability use technology and to examine barriers that limit such access.

Technology Utilization and Students with Intellectual Disability

Overall there is only limited information available about the degree to which students with intellectual disability use technology. One study has provided important and useful information. The Arc, a national organization on intellectual disabilities, conducted a national survey of parents/family members regarding technology use by their family member with an intellectual disability (Wehmeyer, 1999). The survey consisted of five areas of questions focusing on the use of technology for a specific purpose: (a) Mobility Technology Devices, (b) Hearing and Vision Technology Devices, (c) Communication Technology Devices, (d) Home Adaptations, and (e) Environmental Control and Independent Living Devices. An additional set of questions tapped into the student's use of personal computers. Specifically, the survey solicited information about technology use in each functional area and computer use and availability, unmet needs with regard to each of the functional areas and computer use, barriers to technology use, training to use the technology, and satisfaction with technology use.

With regard to computer use, 68% of respondents indicated there was a computer in their home, and an additional 15% indicated that their son or daughter had access to a computer in another environment, mostly in school programs. When asked to identify what the student with an intellectual disability did with the computer, most noted educational activities. For respondents whose family member did not use computers either at home or elsewhere, 78% indicated that they believed that their family member could benefit from a computer. Although a wide array of assistive devices were used by students with intellectual disabilities, the most striking finding was that in four of the five use-specific areas, the percentage of students who could potentially benefit from assistive devices but did not currently have access to such devices was greater than the percentage of students who currently used such devices. The most frequently cited barrier to computer use was the cost or lack of funds, followed by the lack of training available, lack of information about what the computer could do to benefit the family member, the complexity of the device, and the lack of assessment.

In summary, technology was generally underutilized by students with intellectual disabilities. In most functional-use areas, more students who might benefit from assistive technology devices did not have them than students who did. Device cost, training, assessment, and complexity were identified as primary barriers. Encouragingly, however, 83% of students had access to a computer somewhere, although the range of activities for which these computers were used were limited.

Characteristics of Learners with Intellectual Disability That Impact Technology Use

The Arc's study focused mainly on barriers external to the learner, like funding, training, or maintenance. However, one of these external barriers, device complexity, is in essence a function of learner characteristics and the abilities students bring to bear in using technology. Characteristics of learners with intellectual disabilities include impairments in memory, language use and communication, abstract conceptualization, generalization, and problem identification/problem solving, which impact the design of effective technology-based educational supports. While students with intellectual disabilities may also have associated physical and sensory impairments that contribute to difficulty using technology, our focus here is on characteristics that are directly related to cognitive functioning. If physical adaptations are also required, such as adapted keyboards, magnified monitors, and so forth, the design of such adaptations should consider these characteristics and the recommendations described in this chapter to ensure accessibility for students with intellectual disabilities.

In general, to promote technology use by students in this population, educators need to consider numerous issues, such as the simplicity of the technology, the capacity of technology to support repetition, consistency in presentation and device use, and the capacity of the technology to provide information about and direction for device use in multiple modalities, including, in particular, audio and graphical representations and, in general, infusing Universal Design features into technology. In the following paragraphs, these characteristics are discussed within the context of several functional limitations commonly associated with intellectual disabilities.

Memory and Ease of Operation

Mainstream technology interfaces are often complex as developers seek to provide users with a wide array of program features. Too often this occurs at the expense of simplicity of use: Thus, while many students without cognitive disabilities may find these interfaces challenging, their complexity often renders the technology system unusable by students with intellectual disabilities. For example, students with memory impairments may not be able to recall multistep operations or navigate menu systems to locate desired program features, even following extensive training.

When considering technology supports for students with memory limitations, great care must be taken to present intuitive interfaces without overwhelming students with too many options. Often it is better to provide a single, consistent approach to performing a program function than providing multiple methods for accomplishing the same task. For example, in most Windows-based word processing systems, computer users can copy and paste text in a variety of ways: highlighting the text and selecting from the text toolbar and dropdown menu "Edit," "Copy," "Edit," "Paste;" highlighting the text and clicking on the "Copy" icon on the toolbar, followed by the "Paste" icon; or highlighting text and right clicking on the highlighted text, then selecting "Copy" and "Paste" from that menu. Such a range of options may be too complex for some students with intellectual disability for whom it may be simpler to stick to one modality (e.g., using the icons on the toolbar) across multiple task activities. In general, devices that require users to memorize long sequences of commands to succeed present barriers for students with intellectual disabilities.

Language and Communication

The language involved in technology use is often not consistent with that of everyday communication. Terminology used in some technology systems is often complex and may introduce new definitions of common terms. For example, a menu in a computer program, while conceptually similar ("an array of choices") to the common use of menu at a restaurant, may confuse a user with intellectual disability. Many examples of these language-related barriers can be identified by considering the terms used in common software applications (e.g., File, Tools, Window, Break, Drive). Use of terms with multiple meanings and abstract metaphors (e.g., files, folders) can pose barriers to people with intellectual disabilities, who respond to language based on a more literal, concrete representation of the world.

While many communication issues pertaining to technology use by persons with intellectual disabilities relate to the above discussion on language, simply the assumption by technology developers that all users can read introduces an even more significant obstacle to technology use by students with intellectual disabilities and others with reading comprehension difficulties. Although the technology field is increasingly embracing the use of more universally accepted graphics such as pictograms and emoticons to communicate information, most software and devices continue to rely primarily on text to present program options and provide instructions to users.

Conceptualization Skills and Abstract Thinking

It is likely that most students with intellectual disabilities will have some level of difficulty understanding the abstract concepts and metaphors used in technology devices. An example from the previous section referred to the use of the file-and-folder metaphor in computers. Beyond the need to conceive of virtual files and folders, computer users must also conceptualize the virtual location of these files within a computer directory. Indeed, many mainstream novice computer users have difficulty retrieving computer files due to their lack of understanding of "locations" and of "electronic" data storage.

Other technologies present their own challenges to the capacity of students with cognitive impairments to think abstractly. Communication devices often include customizable

pictures or text buttons that, when pressed, "speak" the indicated word or phrase. To provide added functionality, most of these devices include a feature that allows the user to create different overlays, or layers, so that more words or phrases can be accessed. For example, a typical device may have 16 buttons that can be programmed to speak a designated phrase. But an additional switch allows the user to activate another layer of programming so that the same 16 buttons can speak entirely different phrases. Many of these devices are not usable by students with intellectual disabilities due, in part, to the inability to conceive of these different "layers."

Other examples may be as simple as failure to recognize or understand the meaning of when the computer cursor arrow turns into a hand icon when placed over a click-able element of a Web site, or understand the difference between a single click, a double click, or a right-click. Even the most basic of software features—such as in the practice of disabling or "graying out" buttons when they have no practical use—often are too subtle to be recognized by users with cognitive disabilities. In summary, there seems to be an inherent tendency in technology development to add more features to a system or device. The result is usually an interface that requires relatively high levels of cognitive ability to navigate the system.

Problem Identification and Problem Solving

Using technology on a regular basis often requires problem identification and problem solving by the technology user, areas in which students with intellectual disability may have difficulty. This may be due to typical learning curves related to the acquisition of knowledge and skills to use a program or device, lack of experience with the technology, excessive complexity, poor interface design, program or system bugs and failures, conflicts with other technologies, or other possible situations. Many technology users rely on their ability to generalize previous learning to problem solve unexpected occurrences. However, many students with intellectual disabilities have limited ability to generalize learning from one situation to another and, therefore, do not develop the "workaround" strategies that typical users of technology develop to overcome problems.

Developing technology that never encounters unexpected errors is, essentially, impossible. However, given the difficulty many students with intellectual disabilities have responding to unexpected errors, it is imperative that a high priority be placed on identifying highly reliable technology supports for these students. Device failure is often a function of device complexity. That is, the more complex a device is and the more features it has, the more likely it is to have unexpected errors. At times it may be more important to identify less complex devices with fewer features if they provide the benefit of greater reliability. Moreover, many devices apply, in essence, a one-strike-and-you're-out approach whereby one error (wrong key stroke, push wrong button, etc.) results in the failure of the user's session. For example, the value of a dialogue box that asked you to confirm a selection (deletion, exit) becomes evident when you inadvertently hit the "Exit" icon without having saved an ongoing activity. The dialogue box allows you to select "Cancel" and does not immediately delete unsaved work. Students with intellectual disabilities need devices that minimize the potential for error but also allow errors to occur without dire consequences.

Technology's Role in Enhancing School and Community Outcomes for Students with Intellectual Disabilities

The previous sections illustrated that technology (assistive as well as electronic and information) is, in general, underutilized by students with intellectual disabilities and identified those characteristics of learners with intellectual disability that impact technology use. The remainder of the chapter overviews potential solutions to these barriers and features that address cognitive accessibility issues. We have opted to limit this discussion to electronic and information technologies for several reasons. First, even though many assistive technologies have not been adequately evaluated with students with intellectual disabilities, there is a

substantive literature base indicating that students with intellectual disability can benefit from utilization of "traditional" assistive technologies such as augmentative and alternative communication devices (Abrahamsen, Romski, & Sevcik, 1989; Romski & Sevcik, 1997), micro switches (Datillo, 1987; Lancioni, O'Reilly, & Basili, 2001), and mobility devices (Nochajski, Tomita, & Mann, 1996) across multiple domains, including home, school, and the community. Readers are directed to other sources that provide more detailed information with regard to these devices. Second, electronic and information technologies have the potential to significantly alter the types of instructional experiences and learning opportunities afforded to students with intellectual disabilities. In view of school reform efforts that focus on student progress and accountability in the general curriculum, discussed next, these technologies become particularly important.

Technology, Access to the General Curriculum, and Inclusion

The 1997 IDEA amendments contained statutory language requiring each student's IEP to include statements describing how the child's disability affects his or her involvement with and progress in the general curriculum, measurable goals to enable the child to be involved with and progress in the general curriculum, and services, program modifications, and supports necessary for the child to be involved in and progress in the general curriculum. The intent of these mandates was to ensure that all students have access to a challenging curriculum, are held to high expectations, and are included in school accountability mechanisms. IDEA regulations defined the "general curriculum" as "the same curriculum as for nondisabled children" (*Federal Register*, 1999, p. 12592). Specifically, the general curriculum refers to the formal curriculum adopted by state and local education agencies, a curriculum usually designed under the auspices of standards-based reform efforts across the country.

Although the IDEA mandates for access to the general curriculum clearly intend all students to have access to and progress in the general curriculum, to date there has been only limited focus on promoting such access for students with intellectual disability (Wehmeyer, Lance, & Bashinski, 2002; Wehmeyer, Lattin, & Agran, 2001). One of the primary means to ensure such access in these models is to focus on incorporating principles of Universal Design into instructional materials and methods.

Universal Design for Learning

One of the primary means by which technology can be applied to promote access is to apply principles of Universal Design to the design and development of curricular materials, thereby making them more usable by all students. Principles of Universal Design have been identified as important in technology device design so that a wider array of people can use a given device. The Trace Center identified seven principles of Universal Design to consider when designing assistive technology (see www.tracecenter.org/ for detailed information). Designing technology devices with principles of Universal Design in mind is intended to address many of the barriers to technology use identified in the earlier section of this chapter. Similarly, applying these same principles to the design, development, and presentation of curricular materials can ensure that students with intellectual disability have access to content information. Most content, particularly in core academic areas, is presented through print-based mediums (textbooks, worksheets) and lectures. Students who cannot read well or who have difficulty with memory or attention, including students with intellectual disabilities, do not have "access" to the content presented through these mechanisms and, thus, will not have the opportunity to learn the content. Applying principles of Universal Design to curriculum development can address this barrier by providing curriculum adaptations (e.g., modifications to how the content is represented, how it is presented, or how students engage with the content).

Bowe (2000) noted that Universal Design should be distinguished from simply using assistive technology to provide access to the general curriculum for students. The use of assistive technology comes after curriculum materials have been developed and, in most cases, after teachers have planned instruction. The advantage to Universal Design for Learning is that it takes place before materials are made and teachers decide how to teach. That is, access is built in from the beginning, thus eliminating the need for many adaptations.

Most people think of Universal Design only as captioning videos, offering digital documents so students can change the font face, size, or color, or providing texts on computer disks so that students can listen to them through screen reading software. Providing flexible materials is certainly an important part of Universal Design for Learning. However, for students with intellectual disabilities to access the general curriculum, educators must apply the principles of Universal Design to other aspects of the learning experience as well. Bowe (2000) looked at the application of Universal Design principles to education, which include:

(a) *Equitable use:* Materials can be used by students who speak various languages, address a variety of levels in cognitive taxonomies, providing alternatives that appear equivalent and, thus, do not stigmatize students.

(b) *Flexible Use:* Materials provide multiple means of representation, presentation and student expression.

(c) *Simple and Intuitive Use:* Materials are easy to use and avoid unnecessary complexity, directions are clear and concise, and examples are provided.

(d) *Perceptible Information:* Materials communicate needed information to user independent of ambient conditions or user's sensory abilities, essential information is highlighted and redundancy included.

(e) *Tolerance for Error:* Students have ample time to respond, are provided feedback, can undue previous responses, can monitor progress, and are provided adequate practice time.

(f) *Low Physical and Cognitive Effort:* Materials present information in chunks that can be completed in a reasonable time frame.

Designing educational materials and technology used in instruction with principles of Universal Design in mind is critically important for students with intellectual disabilities and presents an obvious role for technology in promoting access. Additionally, technology can be used to "augment" the curriculum (Wehmeyer, Sands, Knowlton, & Kozleski, 2002). Curriculum augmentation involves expanding the curriculum to teach students cognitive strategies or learning-to-learn strategies that enable them to better engage in the academic task. A number of such strategies are appropriate for use by students with intellectual disabilities, including self-regulation or student-directed learning strategies (Agran, King-Sears, Wehmeyer, & Copeland, 2003) that teach students to be more strategic learners. Technology can be applied to support these types of activities.

For example, Davies, Stock and Wehmeyer (2002) evaluated the impact of a palmtop PC-based software program, *Visual Assistant*, used by students to support learning through antecedent cue regulation, self-instruction, and self-monitoring/evaluation strategies. *Visual Assistant* is a multimedia software program designed to run on a Windows CE platform that allows users to view step-by-step picture sequences along with audio instructions at their own pace. Audio instructions and digital pictures can be created to customize the system. Activities are task-analyzed according to the training and support needs of each user. Digital pictures and audio instructions are then downloaded into the software for each step in the task. Each task can be represented on the palmtop computer screen with an icon that users press to initiate task instructions. After a task is selected, the picture for the first step is displayed and the first audio instruction is played. After completing the step, the user presses a "Done" button, which loads the next step picture, and the user presses a "Play" button to hear the associated audio instruction.

Davies et al. (2002) examined the use of the Visual Assistant with 10 participants with intellectual disabilities receiving community-based vocational supports or enrolled in a community-based transition program. Participants were more independent (requiring fewer external prompts) and more productive (making fewer errors) when using the palmtop PC-based software program. In essence, this device served as an accommodation to enable students to augment the curriculum and

apply strategies that enable them to succeed in the curriculum.

Finally, technology can play a meaningful role in promoting the inclusion of students with intellectual disabilities in general education classrooms in several ways. Promoting progress in the general curriculum, as discussed above, will itself result in greater inclusion in the general education classroom. Assistive technologies, such as augmentative or alternative communication devices, provide alternative means for students with intellectual disabilities to interact with their peers without disabilities, as well as to participate in classroom learning activities. Many devices can promote peer interactions by providing a topic of conversation between the student with intellectual disabilities and a peer. Technology devices like palmtop PCs are socially desirable and can facilitate social interactions.

Promoting Access and Inclusion: Features of Technology

As discussed in the previous section, technology can be a powerful tool for promoting access and inclusion, but educators and others need to be aware of differences in technologies that might impact this success. This section discusses some of the features of electronic and information technologies to consider when identifying technology to promote access and inclusion for students with intellectual disabilities.

General Issues

Using technology effectively in educational settings requires successful operation of all related hardware, the applicable operating system, one or more particular software programs (e.g., Web browser, word processor), and so forth. Barriers can exist at any or all of these points in the system, and any one of them might make the entire system inaccessible to students with cognitive disabilities. Universal Design principles, as discussed previously, can help make the technology system accessible to students across a range of disability categories. Major technology providers have made steady progress in providing "accessibility options" within computer operating systems, thanks in large part to the work of the Trace Center. These generally involve user-controlled features related to use of the keyboard, mouse and display screen, which can be adjusted to ease barriers introduced by various disabilities. While most of these features target persons with vision, hearing, or physical impairments, several are also useful to students with intellectual disabilities. For example, Microsoft's *Windows XP* includes a series of features primarily for people with physical disabilities called StickyKeys, ToggleKeys, and FilterKeys. FilterKeys can be used to cancel consecutive keystrokes and play a sound when a key has been successfully struck. Other examples include SoundSentry (which provides on-screen cues when computer sounds are made), controls to adjust the display contrast and font size, and keyboard controls for mouse movement. While these options were not designed specifically to address accessibility for students with intellectual disabilities, they can become part of the solution to make technology usable by these students. For instance, some students with intellectual disability may have difficulty making quick, clean key-presses. In that case, the FilterKeys feature may be useful to avoid unintended multiple key strokes on the same key. In addition to these features on traditional desktop platforms, newer platforms provide greater opportunity for access for students with intellectual impairments.

Palmtop and Other Platforms

Palmtop computers are becoming more and more prevalent in daily life. These devices have a variety of features that make them more user friendly than traditional desktop systems, including touch screen interfaces (that replace mouse and keyboard use), built-in audio recording, playback capacity, and so forth. Additionally, their portability provides the potential for powerful, computer-aided assistance in a wide variety of community settings, and their use of mainstream hardware platforms has potential to keep costs down compared to the high cost of dedicated assistive technology hardware devices.

However, some characteristics of palmtop computers tend to be barriers to students with intellectual disabilities and, therefore, need to be noted. For one, a confusing variety of hardware units are available with a variety of software interfaces requiring fairly sophisticated conceptualization, learning, and retention skills. Another barrier to students with intellectual disability is the relatively small touch screen (the entire screen size for these devices generally does not exceed 2.5 by 3.5 inches). While touch screen interfaces often have a high level of intuitiveness (i.e., directly tapping on a desired option without having to navigate first with at mouse), the limited availability of display space requires software developers to provide controls and other tap-able areas that are extremely small. This allows many features and options to be displayed on screen at any time but also limits access to students with more severe intellectual disabilities due to the cluttered screen and the need for very precise tapping to activate controls.

Advocating for mainstream technology developers to incorporate accessibility features in their systems through universal access approaches is the long-term solution. One interim approach involves using an operating system "shell" program that masks the complexity of the mainstream interface, thus enabling students with intellectual disabilities to access the features and programs of the technology they need via a much simplified user interface. Examples of these programs exist for palmtop as well as desktop computers.

Several approaches for simplifying access can be seen in the software application, *Pocket Voyager*, developed by AbleLink Technologies (www.ablelinktech.com). This software is designed to improve access to palmtop computers specifically for people with intellectual disabilities. The application "sits on top" of the mainstream palmtop computer operating system (i.e., Windows CE and its upgrades) to provide a simplified user interface (see Figure 1). When this software is launched on a Pocket PC palmtop computer, the physical buttons and controls on the hardware unit itself are either deactivated or re-programmed such that when one is pressed, the system automatically returns to the familiar *Pocket Voyager* interface. In addition, an interface is provided for teachers to create large, multimedia buttons on screen for any application loaded on to the palmtop computer. Therefore, the only icons/controls that appear on screen are the ones created in

Figure 1. *Pocket Voyager* **customizable desktop.**

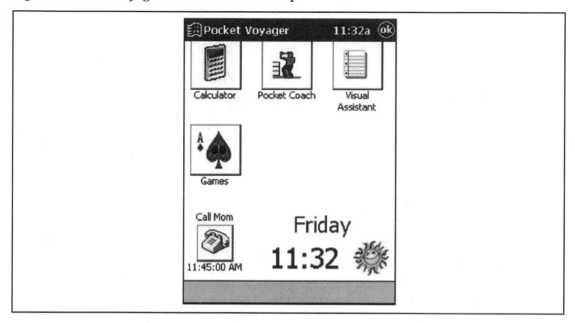

this way, thus eliminating much of the potential for confusion and unintended activation of programs. To set up an on-screen multimedia button, teachers can designate a custom picture or icon to display on the button, and can record an audio message that further identifies its purpose ("Tap here again if you want to play Solitaire."). When first tapped, a multimedia button plays the identifying message; when tapped again, the designated application launches. To further enable access, buttons created on screen in *Pocket Voyager* are large enough to be tapped by the user's finger, foregoing the need for a stylus.

Input Devices

Although new platforms such as Palmtop PCs are increasingly available, the desktop computer remains the most common system with which students interact, and computer keyboard and mouse remain the most typical input devices. On the surface, basic mouse use seems fairly straightforward: you see something on the screen and click on it. However, a step most mainstream users take for granted is the capacity to conceptualize the relationship between mouse movement on the desk and cursor movement on the screen. While this is not an insurmountable obstacle for many students with intellectual disabilities, it may require some orientation and the opportunity to practice before relying on mouse use as an input method. Advanced mouse inputs typically involve double clicking, right-clicking and drag-and-drop interfaces. These may require a higher level of cognitive ability that makes the features behind these inputs inaccessible to some students with severe intellectual disabilities. Additionally, one must know when to use one of these alternate mouse input techniques. Therefore, it may be wise to minimize their use in systems intended for use by these students.

Keyboard use is largely dependent on a person's literacy skills, often a barrier for students with intellectual disabilities. Additionally, keyboards require a degree of fine-motor skill control, visual-perception skills, and the ability to understand multistep concepts (e.g., CONTROL + ALT + DELETE). Alternative keyboards and keyboard overlays have been developed primarily to address physical access issues. Some of these have been designed to improve access for young children whose cognitive skills have not yet fully developed, or for use with specialized hardware or software.

Keyboard inputs are primarily made for entry of content, as well as for computer navigation (e.g., use of text menus to access controls and features). Emerging voice recognition systems, such as ScanSoft's *Dragon Dictate* and *IBM's ViaVoice*, hold promise for addressing barriers to keyboard use for some students with intellectual disabilities. These systems allow users to control both computer navigation (e.g., "open *Microsoft Word*") and provide content input (e.g., write letters). However, as is typical in most powerful computing technologies, the complex user interfaces that have been developed to provide access to the wide array of available features in voice recognition systems pose a barrier to individuals with cognitive disabilities. An option for students with intellectual disabilities may be a scaled down version that provides a simplified, consistent interface at the expense of eliminating some features.

Touch screens, which are becoming increasingly popular in some specialized computer systems, such as in shopping mall or university kiosks, provide an opportunity to improve access to computers for students with intellectual disabilities. Essentially, a touch screen can provide much of the same functionality as a computer mouse, but without having to make the cognitive connection between mouse and cursor movement. Touch screens do have limitations in terms of advanced inputs like double clicking and the drag-and-drop interface.

Computer-Mediated and Multimedia Instruction

Yet another means to improve classroom and school access and inclusion for students with intellectual disabilities is to utilize computer-mediated and multimedia instructional techniques. Although in its infancy in direct application with this population, multimedia instruction utilizing CD-ROM, DVD-ROM, or the Internet has experienced tremendous growth with students without disabilities as well as students with learning and attention disabilities (Wissick, 2001). We define multimedia to include applications that use multiple formats to present information, including text, graphics, and video and/or audio information, and thus link multimedia and computer-mediated instruction with efforts to incorporate Universal Design principles into instructional materials. For many, this includes hypermedia (interactive linking) and hypertext (nonlinear organization).

The power of multimedia lies in its capacity to place difficult and/or important concepts and information in a meaningful context for the learner. A recent example of this is *Read 180* (see www.scholastic.com), which applies the principles of anchored instruction to assisting students with reading comprehension. *Read 180* provides the opportunity to break down the reading process for improved comprehension with the assistance of whole-group instruction, direct instruction, and independent computer-mediated instruction offering intensive, individualized skills practice. For example, using a CD-ROM, students are provided a context for the book they are about to read via audio and video clips, graphic animation, slides, and text. The interactivity of the software also allows for ongoing practice, the opportunity to repeat any segment, a start-and-stop function to return to portions of the CD-ROM the next day, and other multimedia components.

Increasingly, multimedia applications for students with disabilities are being documented as an effective intervention for school as well as work-based simulation. For example, Okolo, Bahr, and Rieth (1993) examined the efficacy of multimedia-designed projects for students with learning disabilities in the social studies curriculum. Others (Higgins & Boone, 1993; Wissick, 1996; Wissick & Garner, 2000) also emphasize the benefits of multimedia applications to improve academics for students with learning disabilities. Through the use of multimedia software and related applications, teachers are finding the power of using a brief video clip to reinforce a specific passage, words, or ideas being introduced in a lesson. The flexibility of the audio, video, or animated illustration allows teachers and students ongoing access to retrieve the multimedia example multiple times if the student requires repeated exposure and practice.

With the recent advancements in CD-ROM and especially DVD technologies, student and teacher immediate access to interactive "anchors" only continues to improve, altering the way teachers use the technology in instruction. For example, in today's classroom easy access to a specific video clip via a CD-ROM or DVD-ROM is quickly replacing the traditional VHS tape and the VCR. Similarly, their ease of use and increasingly affordable cost of digitized pictures and video are enhancing the simulations educators can create to mimic authentic situations, therefore increasing application for individuals with disabilities. For instance, a job coach can easily capture the critical components of a task via a digital video camera. This could then be transferred to a CD-ROM for a student to review to enhance understanding of what the job requires as well as the skills needed to be successful. Thus, the available multimedia components continue to alter how educators can better prepare individuals with intellectual disabilities for gaining social and vocational skills to enhance their transition to community-based employment and living.

While the potential exists, for the most part little attention has been paid to the opportunities that multimedia may offer for providing training and other types of supports to students with intellectual disabilities in school- and community-based settings. Although researchers have examined the power of simulation with students with intellectual disabilities for almost two decades (Nietupski, Hamre-Nietupski, Clancy, & Veerhusen, 1986), a significant difficulty of these previous simulations was the inability to effectively simulate the targeted setting. With the advent of multimedia applications, teachers are now able to import real-life photographs and video into computer-based instructional programs, thus enhancing classroom-based instruction with stimuli that are virtual representations of those found in targeted settings. For example, Wissick et al. (1992) evaluated the effectiveness of a training program that used a computer-mediated, interactive, videodisc-based simulation. Specifically, these researchers evaluated the effectiveness of the simulation in decreasing the "extra actions" (e.g., moving up and down an aisle more than once) participants took to locate items within a simulated grocery store, thus improving their efficiency in shopping. The multimedia simulation was associated with a decrease in the number of extra actions it took participants to locate target items.

Langone, Shade, Clees, and Day (1999) examined the effectiveness of a multimedia instructional program to impact the generalization of match-to-sample skills of students with intellectual disabilities to a targeted setting. The multimedia program included photographs depicting target stimuli (i.e., cereal boxes as they appear on grocery store shelves) in an attempt to increase the likelihood that the selection of specified cereal boxes would generalize to grocery stores in the community. Their findings strongly suggested that discriminations established in a multimedia instructional setting generalize to the community-based grocery store.

As mentioned earlier, combining multimedia applications with handheld personal data assistants (PDAs) or Palmtop computers is one of the next advances of multimedia use with individuals with intellectual disabilities. Palmtop or PDA innovations (i.e., access to the Internet, cell phone capacity, use as a digital camera) will only increase the direct application of this multimedia and further expand the authentic experience we can provide to support the learning of the students with intellectual disabilities.

Internet Access and Browser Use

Finally, with regard to promoting school and community success, the potential of the Internet and the World Wide Web to benefit students with intellectual disability seems particularly promising. Like other aspects of computer and software access, however, access to the Internet is restricted for many people with intellectual disabilities. For a variety of reasons, many of them discussed earlier, Web browsers currently used to access the World Wide Web are not useable by most students with intellectual disability.

Researchers and developers at AbleLink Technologies (Davies, Stock, & Wehmeyer, 2001) developed a cognitively accessible Web browser, called *Web Trek* (depicted in Figure 2). The browser was designed to provide an accessible interface to support users with intellectual disabilities to perform the most common Internet tasks, such as entering a URL address, searching the Internet, saving favorite sites, and returning to favorite sites. The

Figure 2. *Web Trek* **browser.**

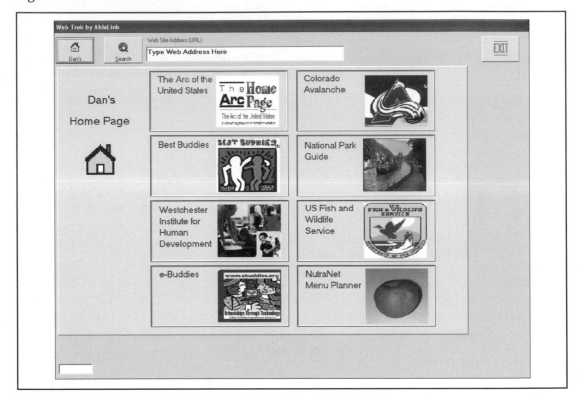

browser contains several features to ensure accessibility:

- *Audio prompting.* Two types of audio prompting are used. The first is a type of "button talk," whereby a message is played describing the use of a button when the cursor arrow is placed over it (without clicking). This is similar to the balloon help that displays the name or function of a button when the mouse is moved over it in most Windows applications. The second type is "error minimization" cueing, in which a message is played following a user-initiated event (e.g., a click) to guide the user to the next-most-likely step in a task.

- *Reduced screen clutter.* Only basic features being used, plus a few others such as a print or exit button, are provided on the *Web Trek* interface, minimizing screen clutter. Also, buttons or other on-screen features are only displayed when they have a use, as opposed to simply being "grayed out."

- *Personalization and customization.* The *Web Trek* displays the user's name on the Start button and Start Page as well as a digital picture of the user. In addition, buttons and controls can be displayed or hidden based on the needs of the particular user.

- *Use of graphics.* *Web Trek* uses a picture-based search process. To provide enhanced direction, graphics or buttons are provided in combination with audio prompts that reference the graphic.

- *Error minimization methodologies.* This broad category of development features includes anything that reduces opportunities or chances for making errors. Examples include all of the methodologies listed above, as well as design considerations such as consistent placement of familiar buttons from screen to screen and automating steps when possible.

Adolescents with intellectual disabilities were able to use the *Web Trek* browser to select web pages and to navigate to preferred sites with greater independence and fewer errors than required using a typical browser (e.g., *Microsoft Explorer*) (Davies et al., 2001). Further, all participants reported that it was a pleasurable experience for them to use the Internet and demonstrated their enjoyment by asking to do so again. Participants were interested in the results of their Internet searches; in all instances they were able to find information and pictures about the topics they searched for. Every participant expressed a desire to either continue after the evaluation session was over, or to return to continue another day (Davies et al., 2001).

Conclusions

True to the promise of the Tech Act, the advent of widely available, reasonably priced electronic and information technologies holds considerable promise to support students with intellectual disabilities in overcoming limitations presented by their cognitive disabilities. Technology developers herald the emergence of multimedia devices that combine the features of current day Palmtop PCs, mobile telephones, computers, digital cameras, and global satellite data devices into one portable, inexpensive device. Such devices could support a person with intellectual disability to navigate his way through the community without fear of becoming lost and open up avenues for greater employment and community inclusion opportunities. Such devices could also provide self-directed prompts to support people with intellectual disabilities across work, living, and school settings. The possibilities are almost limitless. However, if one looks at the degree to which earlier generations of technologies benefited people with intellectual disabilities, it is evident that unless new and emerging technologies attend to some of the issues we have discussed here – issues involving simplicity, flexibility and intuitiveness of use, redundancy and error minimization, and cognitively accessible input mechanisms-these new technologies may fall short of their promise.

Educators can play a role in linking students with intellectual disabilities to technologies that promote access and inclusion by being aware of these issues and assisting students and families in identifying devices that demonstrate the features described here. Sometimes simple adaptations, such as installing a touch screen, can make a previously inaccessible device available for students. Teachers who are aware that computer operating systems are too complex for students with intellectual disabilities can work with district software decision-makers to ensure that accessible (but age-appropriate) software programs become available to computer users. While not always marketed as cognitively accessible, teachers who know what features to look for can identify universally designed instructional materials that would be of use by students with intellectual disabilities. In so doing, educators can deliver the promise of technology for students with intellectual disabilities.

There are several important next steps for research. First, an examination of the literature base suggests that in far too many cases issues pertaining to the characteristics of people with intellectual disabilty were of secondary or concern in the evaluation of the use and impact of technology. With only a few exceptions, technology devices have not been designed or evaluated with the access needs of people with intellectual disability in mind. Only a handful of studies address issues of technology use pertaining to cognitive impairments, and none, to our knowledge, have actually evaluated the relative importance of the various principles of Universal Design on technology use by students with intellectual disability. Future studies need to go beyond the basic "can this work with this person or these people" design and examine not only the impact of technology on particular functional areas, but indeed to examine the multiple factors that impact that technology use, including environmental factors, factors related to the individual user, and factors pertaining to the device's design.

The issue of research design and the general quality of the research in this area is a second area of needed attention. There are too few studies that use more rigorous research designs or conduct longitudinal research that can provide causal linkages between technology use and more positive outcomes.

Finally, the movement from a deficits focus to a functional definition of mental retardation places much more importance on technology to improve the functioning of individuals with intellectual disability, and the research base needs to move from documenting how individual deficits impact technology use to how technology can enhance cognitive abilities and enable people to succeed. We are to a point where our knowledge of cognitive abilities and our capacity to design technology to impact those abilities are both advanced enough that yesterdays science fiction scenario can become today's technology support. Digital wireless telephony and Internet technologies; global positioning data and devices capable of utilizing these data; portable, powerful computers with accessible input/ output capacities; nanotechnology; personal digital assistants: The potential to benefit the lives of people with intellectual disability is significant. These technologies can augment cognitive abilities ranging from memory and attention, to computation and decision-making skills.

A recent report examining areas of research need with regard to technology and intellectual disability, Rizzolo, Bell, Braddock, Hewitt, and Brown (2003) noted that:

> Large scale, longitudinal studies are necessary to assess the need for, access to, and utilization of assistive technology in the states for this population. Additional studies are needed to identify the outcomes of technology use by people with ID/DD and their families, and by provider agencies and direct support professionals, including cost-benefit analyses. Additional studies are needed to examine whether assistive devices or services can reduce the need for personal assistance for persons with ID/DD. (p. 39)

There is a promising start to achieve the promise of technology for students with intellectual disability, but much remains to be done to make that promise a reality.

Authors' Note: The development of this chapter was supported by NIDRR Grant # H133A010602 awarded to the University of Kansas, Beach Center on Disability. The opinions and conclusions expressed here do not, however, necessarily represent the views of the U.S. Department of Education. Additionally, a number of the products overviewed in the chapter are produced and marketed by AbleLink Technologies, with whom chapter author Dan Davies is affiliated. This use is not intended to market any specific product, but simply to provide illustrations of the types of modifications that might benefit students with mental retardation. When other products exist, we have highlighted them instead of or in addition to an AbleLink product.

References

Abrahamsen, A.A., Romski, M.A., & Sevick, R.A. (1989). Concomitants of success in acquiring an augmentative communication system: Changes in attention, communication and sociability. *American Journal on Mental Retardation, 93*, 475-496.

Agran, M., King-Sears, M, Wehmeyer, M.L., & Copeland, S.R. (2003). *Teachers' guides to inclusive practices: Student-directed learning strategies.* Baltimore: Paul H. Brookes.

Bowe, F. G. (2000). Universal design in education: *Teaching nontraditional students.* Westport, CT: Bergin & Garvey.

Davies, D., Stock, S., & Wehmeyer, M. L. (2001). Enhancing independent Internet access for individuals with mental retardation through the use of a specialized web browser: A pilot study. *Education and Training in Mental Retardation and Developmental Disabilities, 36*, 107-113.

Davies, D.M., Stock, S., & Wehmeyer, M. L. (2002). Enhancing independent time management and personal scheduling for individuals with mental retardation through use of a palmtop visual and audio prompting system. *Mental Retardation, 40*, 358-365.

Federal Register, (1999, March 12). Washington, DC: U.S. Government Printing Office.

Higgins, K., & Boone, R., (1993). Technology as a tutor, tools, and agent for reading. *Journal of Special Education Technology, 12*(1), 28-37.

Lancioni, G.E., O'Reilly, M.F., & Basili, G. (2001). Use of microswitches and speech output systems with people with severe/ profound intellectual or multiple disabilities: a literature review. *Research in Developmental Disabilities, 22*, 21-40.

Langone, J., Shade, J., Clees, T. J., & Day, T., (1999). Effects of multimedia instruction on teaching functional discrimination skills to students with moderate/severe intellectual disabilities. *International Journal of Disability, Development and Education, 46,* 493-513.

Luckasson, R., Coulter, D.L., Polloway, E.A., Reiss, S., Schalock, R.L., Snell, M.E., Spitalnick, D.M., & Stark, J.A. (1992). *Mental retardation: Definition, classification, and systems of supports.* Washington, DC: American Association on Mental Retardation.

Nietupski, J., Hamre-Nietupski, S., Clancy, T., & Veerhusen, S. (1986). Guidelines for making simulation an effective adjunct to in vivo community instruction. *Journal of the Association of Persons with Severe Handicaps, 11,* 12–18.

Nochajski, S. M., Tomita, M. R., & Mann, W. C. (1996). The use and satisfaction with assistive devices by older persons with cognitive impairments: A pilot intervention study. *Topics in Geriatric Rehabilitation, 12,* 40–53.

Okolo, C. M., Bahr, C. M., & Rieth, H. J. (1993). A retrospective view of computer-based instruction. *Journal of Special Education Technology, 12*(2), 1-27.

Rizzolo, M.C., Bell, R., Braddock, D., Hewitt, A., & Brown, C. (2003). *Emerging technologies for persons with intellectual and developmental disabilities.* A paper presented at the 2003 ARC of the United States National Goals Conference, January 7, 2003.

Romski, M.A., & Sevcik, R.A. (1997). Augmentative and alternative communication for children with developmental disabilities. *Mental Retardation and Developmental Disabilities Research Reviews, 3,* 368–386.

Technology-Related Assistance for Individuals with Disabilities Act of 1988, PL 100-407. (August 19, 1988). Title 29, U.S.C. 2201 et seq: *U.S. Statutes at Large,* 102, 1044-1065.

Wehmeyer, M. L. (1998). National survey of the use of assistive technology by adults with mental retardation. *Mental Retardation, 36,* 44-51.

Wehmeyer, M. L. (1999). Assistive technology and students with mental retardation: Utilization and barriers. *Journal of Special Education Technology, 14*(1), 50–60.

Wehmeyer, M. L., Lance, G. D., & Bashinski, S. (2002). Promoting access to the general curriculum for students with mental retardation: A multi-level model. *Education and Training in Mental Retardation and Developmental Disabilities, 37,* 223–234.

Wehmeyer, M. L., Lattin, D., & Agran, M. (2001). Promoting access to the general curriculum for students with mental retardation: A decision-making model. *Education and Training in Mental Retardation and Developmental Disabilities, 36,* 329-344.

Wehmeyer, M. L., with Sands, D. J., Knowlton, H. E., & Kozleski, E. B. (2002). *Teaching students with mental retardation: Providing access to the general curriculum.* Baltimore: Paul H. Brookes.

Wissick, C.A. (1996). Multimedia: enhancing instruction for students with learning disabilities. *Journal of Learning Disabilities, 29,* 494-503

Wissick, C. A., (2001). Book and software review. *Journal of Special Education Technology, 16*(4), 46-48.

Wissick, C.A., & Garner, J. (2000). Multimedia or not to multimedia? *Teaching Exceptional Children, 32*(4), 34-43

Wissick, C. A., Lloyd, J. W., & Kinzie, M. B. (1992). The effects of community training using a videodisc-based simulation. *Journal of Special Education Technology, 11*(4), 207-222.

.

16

Classroom Technology for Students with Learning Disabilities

Rena B. Lewis

One of the highest and least accessible shelves in my office houses my "archives" collection. It serves as a repository for dusty books and journals that I've accumulated throughout my career – and that I'm too nostalgic to part with. It includes the textbook for the first special education course I took when I started my master's degree in the early 1970s (the first edition of Samuel A. Kirk's *Educating Exceptional Children* dated 1962), the first book on learning disabilities that I read (Doris J. Johnson & Helmer R. Myklebust's 1967 *Learning Disabilities*), and the text that taught me about phonics in my first graduate reading course (William S. Gray's 1960 revised edition of *On Their Own in Reading*).

That same shelf is also home to the September 1982 special issue of *BYTE* magazine on "Computers and the Disabled." This issue of "The Small Systems Journal" as *BYTE* was called, speaks in dated language ("the disabled") and features obsolete, if not arcane technology products (e.g., the software programs *WordStar* and *VisiCalc*, TRS-80 and Osborne computers, RGB monitors, and daisy wheel printers). However, the articles related to assistive technology admirably presage the future. For example, in "Let There Be Talking People Too," Mark Dahmke describes the design of a speech synthesis system to aid people with communicative disorders. In "Computers Play a Dual Role for Disabled Individuals," Greg Vanderheiden pleads the case for

adapting "microcomputers" to allow access to standard software for persons with disabilities. The article "Adaptive-Firmware Card for the Apple II" by Paul Schwejda and Greg Vanderheiden describes one early access device, the adaptive firmware card, a precursor to contemporary technologies such as *Ke:nx* and the *IntelliKeys* keyboard. Other articles discuss the programming language Logo and its use as a learning and communication tool for children with disabilities, talking computer "terminals" for individuals with visual impairments, software to translate standard text to Braille, and a review of an early voice recognition device for the Apple II computer.

We have come a long way since that special issue of *BYTE* in the early 1980s. We have moved from thinking about the potential of adapting microcomputers to assist persons with disabilities to the birth and early years of a new field, assistive technology. However, it is important to remember that assistive technology is a young field, just beginning its third decade. Over that brief period, we've encountered several overlapping stages: (a) early unbridled optimism, (b) experience-based realism, (c) the search for effective practices for classroom computer use, and (d) the challenges we face today and the hopes we carry forward to the future. In the next section, I discuss each of these stages, providing greatest attention to effective practices.

The Early Days of Giddy Exuberance

The early days of the field of assistive technology were filled with hope, promise, and an almost unbridled optimism about the potential of technology to change the lives of persons with disabilities for the better. Consider the words of Dolores Hagen, founder of the Closing the Gap organization, publication, and conference, as she introduces the proceedings from the first Closing the Gap conference:

> *Today's technology can bring speech to the non-vocal, Braille or speech to the blind and telephone use to the deaf. It can also remove the pencil and paper blockade for the learning disabled, provide environmental control for the physically handicapped and dramatically improve the quality of life for the mentally disabled.* (Hagen, 1985, p. 2)

Florence M. Taber is no less enthusiastic in the introduction to *Microcomputers in Special Education*, the first textbook published on assistive technology:

> *...the educational forecast for the future is that the microcomputer will be an essential part of every classroom. If used to its capacity, all students will learn at their own individual rates ... Each individual will be able to learn through approaches designed specifically for him or her.* (Taber, 1983, p. 1)

Michael M. Behrmann and Liz Lahm echo these sentiments in their Foreword to the Proceedings of the *National Conference on the Use of Microcomputers in Special Education*, the first conference on the topic sponsored by the Council for Exceptional Children (CEC). They say:

> *Computer usage in special education is a natural extension of instruction because of the many similarities among the characteristics of computers, instructional methods used in special education, and the learning characteristics of handicapped children. These similarities include the ability to individualize and to provide needed repetition and the computer's infinite patience in drill and practice ...* (Behrmann & Lahm, 1984, p. v)

Enthusiasm Tempered by Experience: Teachers Speak Out

While experts were extolling the great potential of computers for transforming the lives of persons with disabilities, teachers and other pioneering professionals were beginning to experiment with the use of technology to improve teaching and learning in preschool, elementary, and secondary classrooms. Special education teachers and administrators alike were enthusiastic about the benefits of technology. In one series of studies, my colleagues and I at San Diego State University investigated the views of special education professionals in the state of California toward the usefulness of computers and other technologies in school programs for students with disabilities (Lewis, 1997; Lewis, Harrison, Lynch, & Saba, 1994; Lewis, Lynch, Harrison, & Saba, 1988). A total of 302 teachers and 292 administrators were surveyed in 1987; the study was repeated in 1994 with 189 teachers and 149 administrators from the same districts. The benefits of technology identified by at least 40% of each of these groups were the following:

- Students can proceed at their own pace
- Computer-based instruction can be varied for individual students
- Immediate feedback is provided
- Enthusiasm for school in general increases
- Students' self-concept improves
- Engaged time and time on task increase
- Students learn about things to which they otherwise would not be exposed
- Academic performance improves
- Students learn more quickly

However, both teachers and administrators also identified barriers to technology use. In 1987, the major problem identified by administrators was the small number of computers available for instruction. In 1994, administrators' concerns had changed to the costs of computers, software, and assistive devices; the need for hardware repair and replacement; and the need to provide training to teachers (Lewis, 1997). In both years, teachers who identified themselves as computer users were primarily concerned about software, particularly the need for more high-quality software and the difficulties encountered with software-computer incompatibilities. The 1987 study also identified a small group of teachers ($n = 87$) who were not computer users. The main reason for their nonuse was lack of access: Either (a) hardware and software were not available to them, or (b) availability was so limited that computer use was not practical (Lewis, Dell, Lynch, Harrison, & Saba, 1987).

Experienced technology-using special education teachers in the 1987 study offered a number of recommendations to colleagues thinking about implementing technology programs in their classrooms. The five overriding suggestions identified by the teachers are listed below along with selected teacher quotations.

1. Don't be afraid of technology; jump right in and learn how to use it. As one teacher said, "Don't be afraid to begin. The students teach you as you go along. One doesn't need to be mechanical (I'm not) to use the computer."
2. Begin slowly; it takes time and planning to set up a classroom technology program. At first glance, this second recommendation appears contradictory to the first. It isn't. A teacher explained: "Go slow! Get familiar with one specific area of technology and branch out as you feel more comfortable. Don't try to learn it all at once."
3. Don't use technology just as a reward or a leisure activity. "It is important to start students with good programs they feel challenged with and enjoy. Do not use it as a 'babysitting' device-but an educational/discovery device. The students will surely perk up!"
4. Technology is not a panacea; do not expect miracles. Teachers were full of praise for technology but that praise was not unrealistic. Here's one teacher's advice: "Don't assume that the device, software, etc., will do the job alone. You still need to monitor, evaluate, and teach. No program can replace good teaching. It can only support that teaching."
5. Technology is a powerful tool in the hands of effective teachers. "Raise your expectations – the kids will probably top them." (Lewis, Dell et al., 1987, pp. 68-71)

The Search for Effective Practices

As computers became more common in classrooms, teachers and researchers turned their attention to the search for effective practices in instructional uses of technology. These efforts were spurred by support from the Office of Special Education Programs (OSEP) of the U.S. Department of Education. As Hauser (2001) explains, OSEP has provided funding for more than 20 years to "projects using technology to improve outcomes for children with disabilities" (p. 5). The paragraphs that follow describe two OSEP-funded projects that I directed: the Enhancing Writing Skills Project (Lewis, 1998; Lewis, Ashton, Happa, Kieley, & Fielden, 1998/1999; Lewis, Graves, Ashton, & Kieley, 1998) and Project LITT (Literacy Instruction Through Technology) (Lewis, 1999/2000, 2000, 2003).

Enhancing Writing Skills Project

This project was designed to study the effects of using word processing tools to enhance the writing skills of students with learning disabilities in grades 4 through 12. The word processing tools under investigation included speech synthesis, text-entry tools such as word prediction, and editing tools such as spelling and grammar aids. The major research question was whether tools such as these increase the writing speed, quantity, quality, and accuracy of students with learning disabilities and their attitudes toward the writing process.

As discussed in the grant final report (Lewis, 1998b) for the Enhancing Writing Project, separate pretest-posttest control group experimental studies were conducted in each year of the project. In Year 1 (1994-1995), four text-entry strategies were compared: keyboarding instruction, alternative keyboards, word prediction, and word prediction with speech synthesis. The Year 2 study, conducted in 1995-1996, investigated the effects of two types of text-editing tools, spelling and grammar aids, with and without speech synthesis. The Year 3 study, conducted in 1996-1997, investigated speech synthesis under three conditions: when available (a) at all times versus, (b) only during text entry, versus (c) only during the editing/revising stages of writing.

The major conclusion arising from this series of studies was that word processing programs and tools enhance some, but not all, aspects of the written language performance of students with learning disabilities. In general, word processing has the most impact upon the accuracy of students' writing, allowing students with poor handwriting and spelling skills to improve the appearance of their work and to decrease the frequency with which misspelled words appear. There are also important differences among the various word processing tools in their effectiveness in aiding students and in their acceptability to both students and teachers.

Word prediction appears to be the most promising strategy for improving the text-entry speed of students with learning disabilities as they make the transition from writing by hand to writing on the computer. When used for a 20-week period, word prediction allowed students to achieve a typing speed equal to 82% of their handwriting speed. In previous research (MacArthur & Graham, 1987), students transitioning to keyboarding achieved a keyboarding speed only half that of their handwriting speed.

The question of whether to teach *keyboarding skills* to students with learning disabilities is an important one. It can be argued that, although it takes time for students to learn a systematic method of interacting with the standard keyboard, efforts will eventually pay off because students will have a quick, efficient strategy for text input. The results of Study 1 suggested that efficient keyboarding skills cannot be acquired in one school year, at least using the interventions we employed. That is, after 20 weeks, students who did not receive keyboarding instruction achieved the same speed (in relation to their initial handwriting rate) as those who did. It is possible that practice with keyboarding may be as beneficial as systematic keyboarding instruction, at least in the short term.

Spelling checkers appear to be effective editing tools for students with learning disabilities, although grammar checkers do not. However, it is difficult to draw conclusions about the value of grammar checking tools for this population for two reasons. First, grammar checkers are rarely included as a feature in word processing programs designed for students in grades 4 through 12, the target population in this project. Second, in the one word processor meeting requirements for Study 2, the algorithms underlying the grammar checker relied upon text with correctly spelled words. Students with learning disabilities are unlikely to write text that is free of misspelled words.

The findings relative to the addition of *synthesized speech* to word processors are contradictory and difficult to explain. In Study 1, students who used word prediction with speech were the most successful in decreasing the most common type of spelling error. Those were nonreal word errors (e.g., "thar" for "there") as opposed to real word errors (e.g., "to" for "two"). In Study 2, students who used spelling checkers with speech were the most successful in making corrections in misspelled words when the spelling checker was unable to suggest the correct option; similar results were obtained in Study 3. However, in Study 3, spelling checkers appeared to have a much more positive effect on students' writing quality and accuracy than synthesized speech. When the speech feature of the word processor under study (Write:OutLoud) was activated, little change was seen in the performance of elementary-grade students. Students in the secondary grades also did not improve and, although it is difficult to draw firm conclusions from the small number of secondary students included in the sample, they appeared to experience declines in performance. One possible explanation is that speech acted as a distraction to older students, drawing their attention away from the conceptual aspects of the writing task.

Research results must always be viewed as tentative until they are confirmed by other investigators. However, it is also important to translate research results into guidelines that can inform practice. To that end, this set of tentative recommendations is offered.

1. Combine good writing instruction with word processor use. Use the writing-as-a-process model and teach students strategies for planning, editing, and revising. Also teach strategies for using the word processor and its features such as spelling checkers.
2. When selecting a word processing program or tool, consider these factors:

- *Ease of use*. The student's skill levels must be the first concern in evaluating ease of use. However, it is also important to consider the demands placed on the teacher. An approach that requires a great deal of teacher time and effort is not likely to be used with any regularity.
- *Capabilities of the computer*. Determine whether the computer has sufficient power and memory to run a given program quickly and efficiently.
- *Acceptability to the student*. Like any other instructional material, software programs and computer devices should be age-appropriate. The best judges of this are the students themselves; they are the experts who must determine if something is too juvenile or too different to fit within their comfort zone.

3. Consider using a word prediction program such as Co:Writer to increase text-entry speed. This program is not a word processor; it is used in addition to a word processor. When the student types the first letter of a word, programs like Co:Writer attempt to predict the word being entered and list several alternatives. If the correct word is not displayed, the student types the second letter to see a second array of choices. The process continues until the correct word is available for selection.

4. Choose a word processor with a spelling checker. Select a program such as Write:OutLoud that has been found effective with students with learning disabilities. If no information is available about a program, use samples of students' work to evaluate the effectiveness of the spell checker.

5. Remember that spelling checkers are not perfect.

- Spelling checkers don't recognize "personal" words. Choose a program that lets you add to the spelling dictionary. Add students' and teachers' names, the name of the school and its teams, and other words as needed.
- Spelling checkers don't recognize "real word" errors. The biggest problems are homonyms and careless errors (e.g., "the" for "they").
- Spelling checkers suggest alternatives but the correct word isn't always there. Encourage students to systematically change the spelling of the word so that the spelling checker can recognize it.
- Some students can't read the words that spelling checkers suggest. Consider a word processor with speech.
- Spelling checkers are an aid to spelling, not a replacement for spelling instruction.

6. Be wary of grammar checkers. Before using a word processor with a grammar checker, evaluate the checker carefully to determine if it detects errors accurately and provides help messages that are intelligible and useful to students.

7. Speech synthesis is more likely to be helpful to younger students than to older students. When using a word processor with speech, carefully evaluate its effects on students' writing performance.

8. Balance concerns about writing speed with other benefits. Word processing increases legibility, a potentially important benefit even if speed decreases. Tradeoffs may be necessary. Approaches that offer improved writing accuracy and quality do not always improve writing speed.

9. Think about combining approaches. For example, some students may benefit from using word prediction with a program that offers a powerful spelling checker.

10. Whatever approach is selected, monitor the student's progress and reevaluate, as necessary. As with any other instructional intervention, ongoing assessment of the student's progress provides information about the effectiveness of the intervention and alerts the teacher to the need for change if the student is not experiencing success.

Project LITT

The purpose of this three-year project was to study the effectiveness of a new type of reading software-hypermedia-based children's literature (or, as it is often called, talking storybook software)-in improving the literacy skills of students with learning disabilities. Lewis (2000b) explains:

Sometimes called talking storybooks, these programs read stories aloud in realistic digitized speech, colorful graphics accompany the text, and students often have opportunities to interact with both text and graphics. Example programs are those in the Living Books series by Mattel Interactive (formerly Broderbund), Disney's Animated Storybooks, and Scholastic's WiggleWorks series. (p. 8)

Thus, this new generation of software provides students opportunities to interact with engaging narratives using rich, colorful illustrations; music, sound effects, and realistic digitized speech; and features such as speech- and hypermedia-enhanced text that support the reading process for poor readers. The major research question of interest was whether this type of software is a useful instructional tool for improving the reading skills of students with learning disabilities.

As described in the grant final report (Lewis, 2000a), the five interrelated studies in the project focused on characteristics of hypermedia-based children's literature in relation to students' learning needs (Study 1), learning strategies employed by students with learning disabilities in interactions with this type of software (Study 2), types of instructional supports needed to maximize reading gains students receive from hypermedia-based children's literature (Study 3), the effectiveness of this software in improving reading skills of students with learning disabilities (Study 4), and the effectiveness of bilingual versions of this software in improving the reading skills of students with learning disabilities who are English language learners (Study 5). Study 1 was conducted in the first year of the project (1996-97), Studies 2 and 3 in the second year (1997-98), and Studies 4 and 5 in the third year (1998-99).

It is clear from the results of Study 2 of Project LITT that, when students with learning disabilities engage in unstructured interactions with talking storybook software, their reading performance is not enhanced. When left to direct their own interactions with this software, students chose to spend the majority of their time engaged with non-reading aspects of the program. This lack of attention to the instructional task was reflected in their minimal gains in reading recognition skills in Study 2: only 2.4 words per program.

When structured support was provided to students in Study 3, their time on task increased as did the gains they made in reading skills. In fact, the number of words learned per talking storybook program appeared directly related to the amount of instructional support provided. As support increased through four levels, similar increases were seen in number of words learned: 4.8, 6.8, 8.8, and 9.6 words per program.

The high-support instructional strategies developed and refined in Study 3 were tested in typical special education classrooms in Studies 4 and 5. In Study 4, 19 special education teachers provided high instructional support to 56 students with learning disabilities. In Study 5, 3 bilingual special educators provided high instructional support to 11 bilingual students with learning disabilities. Although students learned from their interactions with the talking storybook programs, their gains were not as great as those that occurred in Study 3. One explanation is that the instruction delivered by classroom teachers was less intense than that delivered by project staff in Study 3.

One of the most encouraging findings from Project LITT's research is that talking storybook software is a useful option for teachers to consider including in classroom reading programs for elementary-grade students with learning disabilities. Although students who interacted with these programs in Study 4 did not experience greater gains on norm-referenced measures of reading than students who continued with their regular reading programs, neither were their gains inferior. Talking storybook programs, as part of the total reading program, contributed to students' overall reading skills development.

Another important consideration is that teachers reported student gains in reading fluency and self-confidence. Unfortunately, however, we did not measure these critical variables. Further research on the use of talking storybook programs should include assessment of reading speed and fluency as well as student self concept and self confidence.

Special education teachers of students with learning disabilities had several opportunities throughout Project LITT to share their insights about talking storybook software. Following are the major recommendations teachers offered for the selection of software appropriate for use in classroom reading instruction.

1. Talking storybooks are typically rich and engaging programs that appeal to students, keep their attention, and motivate them. However, beware of programs with more entertainment than educational value.
2. Select programs that are enhanced versions of excellent storybooks for children. Don't settle for poor or mediocre children's literature just because it is available on a CD-ROM disc.
3. Give preference to programs that focus on the story (rather than on dazzling graphics, superfluous hot spots, or unrelated activities).
4. Choose programs that are appropriate for students' ages in content, text, graphics, and narration. Avoid programs where one element (e.g., the content of the story) is clearly discrepant from another element (e.g., the graphics).
5. Consider the readability level of the story and other characteristics of the text (e.g., appearance, interactivity).
6. Carefully evaluate the graphical components of the program and whether they enhance or diminish the reading experience.
7. Whenever possible, select programs that are both age- and skill-appropriate for students.
8. Select programs with useful instructional features such as writing activities; avoid programs where game-like activities interfere with the story.
9. Look for programs where teachers can control important instructional parameters such as the size of the text and the speed at which text is read aloud.

In addition to suggesting that great care be taken in the selection of talking software programs, teachers made two other important recommendations. The first was that talking storybook programs should be incorporated as one part—but only one part—of the classroom reading program. Students enjoy the programs, they are motivated to interact with them, and they appear to benefit from that interaction. However, talking storybooks alone are not a complete reading program. They are best seen as an engaging addition to instruction, one that increases students' enthusiasm for the reading process.

The second major recommendation was that high instructional support is necessary for students to benefit from talking storybook programs. Without supervision and support, students will not attend to the reading task. Teachers found that the high support conditions used in Study 4 and 5 were successful in focusing students' attention on the task and thereby providing them with the opportunities needed to interact with the text portions of the talking storybook programs.

Current Challenges and Portents for the Future

There are many excellent summaries of the state of the art of assistive technology for students with learning disabilities. These include Edyburn's 2000 article "Assistive Technology and Students with Mild Disabilities" and the *ERIC Digest* entitled *Assistive Technology for Students with Mild Disabilities: Update 2002* by Behrmann and Jerome (2002). Another source is Lewis (1998a). Also important are current reviews of the research literature such as that of MacArthur, Ferretti, Okolo, and Cavalier (2001). Individuals interested in thinking about the future of assistive technology should consult the Fall 2001 special issue of the *Journal of Special Education Technology*. In short, these summaries and reviews point to a number of promising paths for the practitioners and researchers in the field of assistive technology to travel. I comment briefly on two of these in the next paragraphs.

One notion that has been proposed to improve classroom instruction for students with learning disabilities is the introduction of toolkits for teaching and learning. For example, Edyburn (2000) describes an assistive technology core toolkit for classrooms that would include tools to address the needs of typical students with mild disabilities. Edyburn provides the following description of a toolbox for students with difficulty in writing:

> *The "traditional toolbox" that teachers have used to deal with this instructional problem has included textbooks, reference books,*

paper, and pencil. In contrast, a "technology toolbox" offers possibilities such as handheld spelling checkers, predictive word processors, talking word processors, electronic thesaurus, prewriting software, concept mapping software, graphic writing environments, telecommunications, desktop publishing tools, web publishing, and video production tools. (p. 13)

This represents an important paradigm shift. Instead of each individual student having to demonstrate that he or she has a problem severe and persistent enough to warrant allocation of assistive technology resources, those resources are available to all students as part of a responsive instructional environment.

Universal design is a similar notion. Rather than retrofitting a curb, a restroom, or a textbook after the fact to allow access for everyone, it makes better sense to incorporate universal access as one of the specifications of the basic design. Rose (2001), in a recent testimony to the Senate Appropriations Committee, identified three areas of technology that are critical to efforts for improving educational services for students with disabilities. In addition to continued development of new assistive technologies, Rose recommended:

• Digital Curricula. *Most existing classroom technologies are still print based—making it very difficult to use assistive technologies, and even more difficult to individualize the curriculum in ways that are necessary for students with disabilities. I recommend that the congress provide support and legislation so that every piece of curriculum is made available in digital format so that it can be easily customized and made accessible for all students.*

• Universal Design of Learning Technologies. *As new technologies are developed for schools, they should be made accessible to all of the students in the school, right from the start. Congress should support efforts to make guidelines for universal design of such technologies and provide leadership in purchasing, maintaining, and disseminating such technologies in all of its programs. (pp. 66-67)*

Finally, among the "archives" collection in my office is an article that a colleague and I wrote in the early 1980s about the future of special education (Cegelka & Lewis, 1983). The accuracy of this article's predictions is not important. What is important are the values that undergird the questions that we asked. Those values persist and the questions continue to challenge us:

• *How can we assure equity in access to technology and other advances to all members of the population, including those at the lower ends of the economic continuum?*

• *How can we best reduce the dissonance between cognitive disability and the high-technology society?*

• *How do we maintain personal privacy in an era of expanding information systems with their attendant stores of lifespan data?*

• *How do we balance the prevention of disability with our expanded capacity for the preservation of life?*

• *How can we provide a supportive environment to offset the effects of disability without denying the individual control over his or her destiny?*

• *What do we mean by human dignity and, above all, how do we nurture and sustain it?* (pp. 71-72)

References

Behrmann, M., & Jerome, M. K. (2002). *Assistive technology for students with mild disabilities: Update 2002.* Arlington, VA: ERIC Clearinghouse on Disabilities and Gifted Education.

Behrmann, M. M., & Lahm, L. (Eds.). (1984). *Proceedings of the national conference on the use of microcomputers in special education.* Reston, VA: Council for Exceptional Children.

Cegelka, P. T., & Lewis, R. (1983). The once and future world: Portents for the handicapped. *The Journal for Special Educators, 19*(4), 61-73.

Computers and the disabled. [Special issue]. (1982). *BYTE, 7*(9).

Dahmke, M. (1982). Let there be talking people too. *BYTE, 7*(9), 6, 8.

Edyburn, D. L. (2000). Assistive technology and students with mild disabilities. *Focus on Exceptional Children, 32*(9), 1-24.

Gray, W. S. (1960). *On their own in reading* (rev. ed.). Glenview, IL: Scott, Foresman.

Hagen, D. (1985). Introduction. In M. Gergen, & D. Hagen (Eds.), *Computer technology for the handicapped: Proceedings from the 1984 Closing the Gap conference* (pp. 2-3). Henderson, MN: Closing the Gap.

Hauser, J. (2001). Preface to the special issue. *Journal of Special Education Technology, 16*(4), 5-6.

Johnson, D. J., & Myklebust, H. R. (1967). *Learning disabilities: Educational principles and practices.* New York: Grune & Stratton.

Kirk, S. A. (1962). *Educating exceptional children.* Boston: Houghton Mifflin.

Lewis, R. B. (1997). Changes in technology use in California's special education programs. *Remedial and Special Education, 18,* 233-242.

Lewis, R. B. (1998a). Assistive technology and learning disabilities: Today's realities and tomorrow's promises. *Journal of Learning Disabilities, 31,* 16-26, 54.

Lewis, R. B. (1998b). *Final report. Enhancing the writing skills of students with learning disabilities through technology: An investigation of the effects of text entry tools, editing tools, and speech synthesis.* San Diego, CA: San Diego State University, Department of Special Education. (ERIC Document Reproduction Service No. ED 432 117)

Lewis, R. B. (1999/2000). Literacy skills for students with learning disabilities: Are talking storybooks effective? *Closing the Gap, 18*(5), 1, 8, 33.

Lewis, R. B. (2000a). *Final report. Project LITT (Literacy Instruction Through Technology): Enhancing the reading skills of students with learning disabilities through hypermedia-based children's literature.* San Diego, CA: San Diego State University, Department of Special Education. (ERIC Document Reproduction Service No. ED 438 648)

Lewis, R. B. (2000b). Musings on technology and learning disabilities on the occasion of the new millennium. *Journal of Special Education Technology, 15*(2), 5-12. [Reprinted on the Web as part of the *Journal of Special Education Technology* ejournal; available: jset.unlv.edu/15.2/Lewis/first.html

Lewis, R. B. (2003). Reading software for students with learning disabilities. In D. D. Matthews (Ed.), *Learning disabilities sourcebook* (2nd ed., pp. 461-478). Detroit, MI: Omnigraphics.

Lewis, R. B., Ashton, T. M., Haapa, B., Kieley, C. L., & Fielden, C. (1998/1999). Improving the writing skills of students with learning disabilities: Are word processors with spelling and grammar checkers useful? *Learning Disabilities: A Multidisciplinary Journal, 9,* 87-98.

Lewis, R. B., Dell, S. J., Lynch, E. W., Harrison, P. J., & Saba, F. (1987). *Special education technology in action: Teachers speak out.* San Diego CA: San Diego State University, Department of Special Education.

Lewis, R. B., Graves, A. W., Ashton, T. M., & Kieley, C. L. (1998). Word processing tools for students with learning disabilities: A comparison of strategies to increase text entry speed. *Learning Disabilities Research & Practice, 13,* 95-108.

Lewis, R. B., Harrison, P. J., Lynch, E. W., & Saba, F. (1994). Applications of technology in special education: A statewide study. *Learning Disabilities: A Multidisciplinary Journal, 5,* 69-79.

Lewis, R. B., Lynch, E. W., Harrison, P. J., & Saba, F. (1988). Effective classroom practices: What California teachers say about using technology with handicapped learners. In H. J. Murphy (Ed.), *Proceedings of the Third Annual Conference "Computer Technology/Special Education/ Rehabilitation"* (pp. 357-366). Northridge: California State University, Northridge.

MacArthur, C. A., Ferretti, R. P., Okolo, C. M., & Cavalier, A. R. (2001). Technology applications for students with literacy problems: A critical review. *The Elementary School Journal, 101*(3), 273-301.

MacArthur, C. A., & Graham, S. (1987). Learning disabled students' composing under three methods of text production: Handwriting, word processing, and dictation. *Journal of Special Education, 21,* 22-42.

Rose, D. H. (2001). *Testimony: Hearing on education technology.* Committee on Appropriations Subcommittee on Labor, Health and Human Services, and Education Hearing on Education Technology, July 25, 2001. Retrieved December 11, 2003 from:www.cast.org/udl/index.cfm?i=2020.

Schwejda, P., & Vanderheiden, G. (1982). Adaptive firmware card for the Apple II. *BYTE, 7*(9), 276, 278, 282-283, 286, 288, 291-294, 299, 302, 304, 306, 310, 312, 314.

Taber, F. M. (1983). *Microcomputers in special education.* Reston, VA: Council for Exceptional Children.

Vanderheiden, G. (1982). Computers play a dual role for disabled individuals. *BYTE, 7*(9), 136, 138-140, 142, 144, 146, 148, 150, 154, 156, 158-159, 162.

17

Using Technologies to Meet the Unique Needs of Students with Emotional/Behavioral Disorders: Findings and Future Directions

Gail Fitzgerald

Over the last decade, interest and exploration of the computer and related technologies have increased for educating children for the twenty-first century. Early efforts in special education technology focused on applications for students with mild disabilities who might benefit from effective software design and for students with physical and sensory disabilities needing adaptive devices and assistive technology for learning (Blackhurst, 1997; Fitzgerald & Koury, 2003). Later efforts shifted to exploring effective instructional technologies to maximize learning and to support students with mild disabilities in the general education environment (Woodward & Rieth, 1997). Throughout the history of special education technology, there has been little consideration, exploration, or research conducted on the uses of technologies to assist students with behavioral and emotional disorders (EBD). Little attention has been focused on the unique needs of this population or to any special applications that go beyond instructional programming for individuals with mild disabilities. A programmatic research agenda is long overdue that will define and document the potential for new technologies to assist youth with EBD.

According to the federal definition of emotional disturbance, students in this population manifest one or more of the following:

1. *Inability to learn which cannot be explained by intellectual, sensory, and health factors;*
2. *Inability to build or maintain satisfactory*

interpersonal relationships with peers and teachers;
3. *Inappropriate types of behavior or feelings under normal circumstances;*
4. *A general pervasive mood of unhappiness or depression; or*
5. *A tendency to develop physical symptoms or fears associated with personal or school problems.* (U.S. Department of Education, 1999, p. 12422)

Programmatic efforts for these children require more than teaching the curriculum of the school; other curricular needs include instruction in social skills, self-control, thinking and problem-solving skills, self-understanding and coping skills, and dealing with irrational thoughts and beliefs. Beyond emphasizing technologies for traditional learning, the challenge in special education technology is to explore ways of using new technologies to meet needs for personal change in what might be considered the "therapeutic" curriculum (Fitzgerald & Werner, 1996).

In summarizing the current literature and defining needs for a research agenda in EBD technologies, instructional contexts must be considered. Schools are changing and technologies are changing, and both are influenced by bimodal pressures. On the one hand, schools are held to higher levels of accountability for standards-based curriculum and school-wide assessment using statewide tests and requirements of the No Child Left Behind Act. Pressures are exerted on teachers to stick to the defined curriculum and to use mastery learning approaches. New software development initiatives provide standards-referenced, mastery learning materials to "guarantee" children's successful performance on state standards (Plato, 2004). Special educators have broadened their curricular scope to examine instructional practices and supports necessary for students to gain meaningful access to the core curriculum (Gersten, 1998) and to improve achievement for statewide testing.

On the other hand, new theories of learning suggest that schools have to reform to provide learner-centered instruction based on authentic learning experiences, problem-based instruction, higher-order thinking, and student-driven inquiry (Fulton, 2003; Jonassen, Howland, Moore, & Marra, 2003). Technology is changing to emphasize information-age skills such as finding and evaluating information through the Internet and using presentation tools to demonstrate learning. General education classrooms rarely use educational software now for mastery learning and have shifted to using computers for online, inquiry-oriented and collaborative learning projects (Means, 2001). Further, new technologies are used to support meaningful learning through technology-enhanced real-world learning contexts, electronic communication, visualization and analysis tools, scaffolds for problem solving, and opportunities for feedback, reflection, and revision (Bransford, Brown, & Cocking, 1999).

Although past research may have been conducted under traditional teaching and learning paradigms, current and future research has to recognize to a greater extent the contextual pedagogical variables surrounding the study of technology innovations. The issues facing the special education technology community interested in applications for youth with EBD are extremely complex: special applications, pressure for standards-based achievement, unique population needs, new paradigms for teaching and learning, and ever-emerging technologies.

To provide a framework for synthesizing past research and current applications and to identify a programmatic roadmap, an applications taxonomy is offered (see Figure 1). One dimension of the matrix lists the core deficits of the population, including cognition, behavior,

and affect. The second dimension lists broad categories of technology applications that are evidenced in schools today. These categories reflect traditional as well as emerging uses of technology, and represent a continuum ranging from traditional technologies of directed learning software and student use of computer tools (which reflect traditional views of teacher-centered teaching and learning paradigms) to new technologies involving constructivist learning environments and online, networked learning technologies (which reflect changing views toward student-centered teaching and learning paradigms). This matrix framework is used to discuss technology applications for students with EBD; few of these technology applications are described in the literature at this time. Descriptive or research articles were located and included in this synthesis for the applications appearing in standard font, whereas applications that have not been described in the literature for this population are listed in italics.

The research studies included in this review met the following criteria. First, preference was given to empirical studies utilizing appropriate quantitative, single-subject, or qualitative (case study, interview, or field observation) methodologies. Descriptive articles that did not report observations of implementation or articles that only offered position statements were not included. Second, articles were almost exclusively selected from peer-reviewed journals or published conference proceedings. Third, studies had to include participants with EBD and preferably identify results for this distinct group. Fourth, proposed interventions had to include technology for instruction, support for learning, or therapeutic goals for the participants. The literature search was conducted in relevant educational, psychological, and medical journals. The empirical articles were grouped for analysis into the matrix framework and descriptive articles were analyzed as emerging uses of technology.

Cognition

Learning

The traditional uses of technology—computer-assisted instruction (CAI) and computer-man-

Figure 1. A taxonomy of technology applications for youth with EBD.

		Directed Learning Applications	Computer Tool Applications	Constructivist Learning Environments	Online Learning Technologies
Cognition Learning, accessing, and using information and solving problems using a systematic approach.	Learning	Computer-assisted and computer-managed instruction. *Tutorials to support content area learning.*	Productivity tools such as word processors, spreadsheets, databases, graphic organizers, and presentation tools and other electronic data-gathering tools.	*Situated learning environments to support knowledge construction.*	*Information gathering and sharing via the Web.* *Electronic field trips.*
	Thinking and problem solving	*Tutorials for thinking and problem-solving strategies in the content areas.*	Performance support tools for learning strategies and thinking and problem solving strategies.	*Situated learning environments to support thinking and problem solving.*	*Learning circles/ E-Pals.* *WebQuests with structured problem solving.*
Behavior Learning and using appropriate and prosocial behaviors with self and others.	Personal and interactive behaviors	Computerized cognitive training. Biofeedback for anger and impulse control. *Tutorials in social skills, anger control, and other therapeutic curriculum.*	Performance support tools for planning, organizing, and using self-control skills for personal and interactive behaviors. *Handheld computers for recording self-monitoring.*	*Simulations involving personal decision-making, cooperative learning, or social skills.* *Interactive games requiring cooperation and/ or social skills.*	Cyber mentoring. Chat room interactions. Online therapy monitoring. Online cooperative games. Global exchanges.
Affect Identifying and changing unhealthy feelings and irrational thoughts and beliefs.	Moods, feelings, beliefs emotions	Biofeedback for managing stress and feelings. *Tutorials in cognitive restructuring, (e.g., changing moods, feelings, thoughts, and beliefs).*	Performance support tools for analyzing *moods, feelings, thoughts, and beliefs* and making plans to change.	*Simulations requiring analysis of moods, feelings, thoughts, and beliefs.*	E-mail communication with therapists. *Online therapy and support groups.*

Note. No descriptions of italicized applications were found in the literature that included students with emotional and behavioral disorders.

aged instruction (CMI)—focus on learning, broadly defined as the acquisition, retention, and use of information. The characteristics of the EBD disability affect, by definition, educational performance. However, programming emphasis has primarily been placed on behavioral manifestations of the disorder, thus neglecting adequate focus on learning of academic skills and curriculum content.

Although there is widespread belief among special educators that CAI/CMI have positive effects on the learning and behavior of students with EBD, empirical support is scant and compromised by poor research designs. At this time the most that can be said is that CAI/CMI offer great potential for assisting students with learning and on-task behaviors due to its novelty, software design features, and motivational capabilities (Fitzgerald & Koury, 1996). In a 2002 review of the literature on children with attention deficit/hyperactivity disorder (ADHD) Xu, Reid, and Steckelberg summarized that there was insufficient evidence to support positive effects of CAI, although results were included in the review for two students who demonstrated positive outcomes. Kleiman, Humphrey, & Lindsay (as cited in Xu et al., 2002) compared performance between paper/pencil and CAI/CMI instruction in math computation. The children with ADHD in this study did twice as many problems and spent more time working on math problems without loss of accuracy or speed; students strongly preferred the computer form of practice. However, serious methodological concerns were evident in the criteria for selecting children with ADHD and the statistical testing of differences (Xu et al., 2002).

Discussion in the literature with regard to learning outcomes related to CAI generally points to improvements in achievement as secondary to increased on-task behavior, longer periods of focus on CAI-delivered practice, and higher levels of task acceptance and motivation. There is some evidence that drill-and-practice CAI as compared to seatwork practice is an effective behavior management strategy for students in urban high schools as demonstrated by reductions in disruptive behaviors; however, no causality can be ascribed to CAI exclusive of other operating variables

(Din, 1996). Different characteristics of software, such as content, practice format, animation, difficulty, and peer participation, influence attending behavior and motivation for ADHD students (Ford, Poe, & Cox, 1993).

It is difficult methodologically to sort out the unique contribution that CAI makes to improved learning, as complex variables related to instructional strategies, content, and setting factors must be controlled to do so. In research conducted in real classrooms, better indicators of effective uses of CAI may be to examine the attitudes and motivations toward the learning by students engaging in varying instructional activities. The nature of the EBD disability is the overt rejection of tasks that are viewed as boring, unpleasant, unknown, or too difficult. Learning simply does not occur until the student commits to the task and becomes engaged.

A wide variety of computer tool programs available in educational software are heralded as supporting learning, easing the mechanics of instructional activities, providing training for "real-world" applications, and enabling students to be more independent (Edyburn, 2000). In the area of EBD, writers have suggested that word processing and journaling can enhance personal expression (Fitzgerald, 1994); production activities such as creating class newspapers or multimedia products can facilitate content learning, cooperative learning, and communication skills (Fitzgerald, 1994; Okolo & Ferretti, 1996); the construction of PowerPoint presentations may improve reading and language skills and interest in education (Murry, 2002); and creating and organizing information using nonlinear, hypermedia tools that are linked with alternative forms of media may increase understanding of information (Mayer & Leone, 2002). Descriptions of these applications are based on sound learning theories, anecdotal narratives, and findings with other populations.

Actual evidence of effectiveness is minimal however. Only one research article was located that investigated written expression with elementary students in a self-contained EBD class. Six students were involved in writing short paragraphs under two conditions: paper/pencil and word processing (Langone,

Levine, Clees, Malone, & Koorland, 1996). Using an alternating-treatment single-subject design the study compared outcomes on four dependent measures: spelling, punctuation, complete sentences, and ratings of paragraph quality. Measures did not include behavior ratings, observations, or time on task. The findings were equivocal for the six students varying across students and treatment conditions. When students were asked which condition they preferred, half preferred each condition; thus, no preference emerged. Participating teachers, however, perceived on-task behavior to be better with fewer disruptive behaviors in the computer writing condition. It should be noted that this study used older technology (Apple IIe computers, monochrome monitors, keyboard navigation, and a children's word processing program) and did not employ state-of-the-art hardware and software that may make word processing easier, more attractive, and more motivational. Consistent with other summaries, the technology was viewed only as a tool to be used within other instructional strategies to teach written expression.

Computer tools can also be used for knowledge construction by creating products. Current examples of knowledge construction tools in education are presentation software, hypermedia writing programs, and multimedia packages. In a descriptive research report, Wetzel (2001) summarized the extensive integration of computer tool programs into a self-contained classroom program for middle-school students with emotional disabilities. The setting was a Classrooms of Tomorrow Today program with training provided through a College of Education PT3 grant. The teacher received 90 hours of instruction in educational technology over two semesters and had five iBooks, two Macintosh desktop computers, a projection device, and wireless Internet service in her classroom. Over the course of the school year, her integration of technology expanded, she moved to more advanced applications, and students became more skilled and self-directed. A wide range of tool programs was implemented, including concept maps, multimedia presentations, word processing, iMovie production, graphic organizers, timeline tools, and charting and graphing programs. Students used the Internet to gather information for reports. Improvements in social skills, cooperative learning skills, and positive attitudes toward school were described. The extensive institutional support, teacher training, and teacher commitment to meaningful uses of technology were clear hallmarks of the success of the program.

While these applications show promising results in the descriptive literature, there is no empirical evidence that students with EBD disorders can or will successfully learn from these technologies. Pedagogy suggests, however, that hypermedia, computer writing, and multimedia production facilitate learning because of their advantages of flexibility, individualization, reduction in cognitive load, support for knowledge construction, multiple media formats, and increased motivation (Mayer & Leone, 2002). In particular, hypermedia has great potential to support learning. In general, hypermedia studies support moderate increases in learning across elementary to college-age students (Ayersman, 1996; Higgins, Boone, & Lovitt, 1996; Liu, 1998). Hartley (2001) found that general education high school students could learn strategies from hypermedia computer programs, but knowledge of the strategies did not improve achievement. It was hypothesized that learning to use a strategy has little value if the student never decides to use it. Thus, CAI and hypermedia can be effective instructional methodologies, but they are insufficient to support learning unless contextualized, applied, and generalized.

The literature suggests that use of tools alone is not likely to impact learning. To support learning, self-direction, and knowledge construction, the use of tools must be integrated into an instructional program. When tools are well integrated into effective instruction, they may enhance learning by reducing frustration, easing the construction process, helping to organize new information, increasing self-direction, and enabling more professional-appearing products. These are powerful uses of technology that are worthy of investigation to discern how to effectively teach, integrate, and generalize the use of tools for students with EBD. When students are able to utilize tools independently, learning can become more self-directed and increase feelings of competence and pride (Murry, 2002). The implications of these findings are important when considering decontextualized strategy instruction for students with EBD: strategy instruction must be integrated with content learning.

Anchored instruction is one form of a constructivist learning environment that situates learning in a meaningful context so students can develop deeper understanding and transfer of knowledge and skills outside of school (Gersten, 1988). A line of work at Vanderbilt University focused on the use of video anchors to situate problem-based scenarios in middle school math instruction (Cognition & Technology Group, 1990). No studies from this line of work focused on results with students with EBD, although some were typically included as members of low-achieving or remedial classes using the anchored instructional approaches (Bottge, Heinrichs, Chan, & Serlin, 2001; Hasselbring & Moore, 1996; Koury, 1996). Although no differential outcomes are described for the EBD population, results have been promising for improving math problem solving and motivation using the video anchors. Bottge et al. (2001) found a decrease in computational skills for remedial students and stressed the importance of continued explicit instruction on procedural skills in tandem with teacher-enhanced problem-solving instruction. This finding is consistent with other recommendations to embed the technology into an effective instructional program.

Thinking and Problem Solving

The EBD community has largely not embraced the use of computer technology for teaching thinking and problem-solving skills or other therapeutic goals. Although a plethora of printed curriculum materials exist in these areas, few include any use of technology other than videotapes. For example, commercial materials are available for teaching social skills, anger management, conflict resolution, and thinking and problem-solving skills. The instructional kits are primarily composed of teacher and student manuals, skill cards and worksheets, and sometimes audios or videos. Software is not available with most the

cognitive-behavioral curricula that could extend learning through practice, scenario-based problem solving, or cooperative learning activities.

In an overview of promising practices for students with EBD and behavior control problems, Fitzgerald (1994) suggested that commercial thinking skills programs and teacher-prepared multimedia scenarios could be used to teach and practice a problem-solving process. Generic problem-solving steps could be pre-taught and then practiced with materials as diverse as strategy games, adventure games, simulations, and role-playing scenarios. Three innovations to utilize the computer for teaching thinking and problem-solving skills have been described in the literature; however, they have limited empirical support.

In one application, a software version of a personal problem-solving guide was created and used as a part of a counseling process with students with special needs to do social decision making (Elias, Tobias, & Friedlander, 1994). The computerized guide was used to prompt students to enter responses to (a) describe the problem, (b) generate alternate solutions, (c) select alternative actions, and (d) generate an action plan. A helping professional, such as a school psychologist or counselor, provided assistance in completing the problem-solving activity over multiple sessions, and then used the action plan for role-playing and sharing the plan with others. The resulting action plans were used as informal contracts between the child and teachers in multiple settings. Thus, the computer-based activity provided structure to the problem-solving process, created opportunities for practice, and helped establish agreements between students and adults. The process was described as effective with middle- and high-school students and useful with individuals and groups. The authors believed the computer aided in the transportability of the approach across multiple settings and personnel.

Fitzgerald and Werner (1996) described two computer-based cognitive-behavioral interventions that used the computer to provide cognitive rehearsal and action planning. In one case study, a simple mediation essay was authored for a 9-year-old with severe aggression. The child's own language was used in developing the mediation essay to support internal speech. The program led the child through four behavioral questions and responses to: (a) What did I do wrong? (b) Why is it wrong? (c) What should I do? and (d) What will happen when I do this? The program consisted of a tutorial part for controlled practice, and a quiz part for checking correct responding and retraining if necessary. The computerized mediation essay served as a behavioral consequence where practice was required during preferred activity time. Using an A-B-C single-subject design in two classrooms, the overall intervention demonstrated immediate and lasting effectiveness. Because the procedures combined computerized behavioral rehearsal and a positive reinforcement system with consequences, the effect of the computerized component could not be isolated. However, it was evident that the child was able to carry out the computer practice independently and the intervention served to focus the student's attention on the behavioral choices and consequences.

A second cognitive-behavioral innovation was designed for a 12-year old with mild mental retardation and autistic-like behaviors. The procedure combined computer-based instruction with a self-management strategy called S.T.A.R. (Fitzgerald & Werner, 1996). S.T.A.R. is a mnemonic strategy that stands for "stop-think-act-results." The computerized strategy guided the student through a problem-solving process of stopping impulsive behavior, planning self-talk and positive alternatives, and recognizing positive outcomes for the behavior change. The computer program prompted the student through a series of action planning steps by making choices displayed through simple graphics and text and assembling a "plancard" for use in classroom situations. In this case study, the student was successful in creating action plans using the computer and liked creating the plans and printing out reinforcement coupons. However, the student was not successful in carrying out the plan independently. Additional support from teachers was necessary to implement the plan and do simple self-monitoring. Even so, because this form of computerized action planning provides structure and consistency in a motivating way, there is potential for this procedure to offer a step toward eventual independence in self-management.

Independent use of strategies provided through computer tools can be an important part of the change from external behavioral control to metacognition and internal control—important precursors to managing one's own behaviors. The strategies provide explicit frameworks to show students what needs to be done (Gersten, 1998), and the computer-based tools support personalized use. It is essential to integrate learning and practice with computer tools in the curriculum and classroom to achieve success with these approaches.

Behavior

Personal and Interactive Behaviors

Applications of technology in work with children/youth with ADHD have focused on behavioral manifestations of attending, impulsive, and disruptive behaviors. In the mid-1990s, two lines of research and development emerged utilizing computer-based activities to impact behavior-computerized cognitive training and biofeedback. These initiatives were aligned primarily with the disciplines of psychology and psychiatry and were based on the belief that the computer offered advantages for conducting cognitive training through randomization, delivery controls, and customization (Kotwal, Burns, & Montgomery, 1996). Studies during this period relied heavily on parent and teacher ratings and behavioral observations to assess change, and utilized single-subject experimental designs with very small sample sizes. Studies typically had insufficient controls to establish causal relationships among variables or prediction of impact. No evidence was found that these lines of research continued beyond the 1990s or that the approaches had much impact in educational settings. However, these technology-based interventions demonstrate the potential for using technology to assist children with behavior control issues. Therefore, further research with these approaches is warranted.

Cognitive Training

One form of computer-assisted cognitive training uses technological devices to prompt attending or task completion behaviors. These attention-training systems (ATS) started with battery-operated devices, and in later developments shifted to automated cues through a computer. DuPaul, Guevremont, and Barkley (1992) used a battery-operated device on student desks to implement a response-cost intervention whereby a red light was activated when the child was off task, and points were deducted from the accumulated total of points. The two children in this study showed improved attention and reduced levels of ADHD behaviors that exceeded success with the response-cost intervention by itself, but the singular contribution of the signaling device could not be ascertained due to multiple, concomitant contingencies in place.

Similarly, Evans, Ferre, Ford, and Green (1995) described a battery-operated hand-held control device that automated the delivery of token reinforcers and point deductions by a red light signaling system. Decreases in off-task behavior across multiple settings were demonstrated through an ABAB single-subject design. Researchers concluded that the signaling device contributed to the successful outcomes within an overall effective classroom management strategy, but several limitations were evident in interpreting the role that the technology played in the success of the procedure.

Given that the positive results in these studies are consistent with current research establishing the effectiveness of response-cost contingencies and attention training, the technology may provide a more efficient method of group administration of the intervention with immediate reinforcement. One of the central issues in attention training is maintenance of change following intervention. This concern is warranted. In a once-a-week ATS training program in a clinical setting over a 13-week period, five children with ADHD showed marked improvement in attending behavior during training, but the improvement deteriorated once the ATS was removed (Gordon, Thomason, Cooper, & Ivers, 1991). Gains in attentiveness were not maintained beyond the actual treatment phase. It is noteworthy that the one child who had inconsistent results had severe concomitant behavioral problems and possible manic-depressive illness. This finding raises concerns about generalizing findings, even when successful outcomes are evident, across the EBD spectrum of disorders.

The computer has also been used as a prompting device to cue students with ADHD to carry out and complete daily tasks. In one study carried out in an elementary school, a computer program was used by parents of children with ADHD to set up reminder prompts for daily tasks, such as taking medicine, getting school materials ready, and turning in homework. The prompts were printed out for children to take to school and self-monitor completion. Daily responses were entered into the computer at night and tracked through a progress monitoring system coupled with daily and weekly reward charts (Epstein, Willis, Conners, & Johnson, 2001). Effectiveness of the intervention was assessed using a single-subject reversal design. Outcomes were generally better in the school than home environment. In this application, the computer was not actually used as a cuing device, but rather as a planning and monitoring device used primarily by adults to bring structure to the goal-setting and management system.

Computer-delivered cognitive training directly targets the unique needs of children with EBD to gain self-control over impulsive behaviors. Two studies describe the use of the Captain's Log software (Sanford & Browne, 1988) that provides training and practice in skills such as attention, concentration, and problem solving. In these studies, a therapist provided individual training over a period of time. Success was reported with one student who received auditory discrimination (rhythm and tone), color discrimination/inhibition, scanning reaction, and stimulus reaction (inhibition and reaction time) training. Although there were inconsistencies between some of the items on the parent and teacher rating scales, ratings and narrative reports suggested an overall increase in on-task behaviors and reduction in disruptive behaviors at school (Kotwal et al., 1996). However, seven-month followup revealed some deterioration of the improvement.

The Captain's Log software was used in a similar study with four elementary-age children with severe EBD and ADHD (Slate, Meyer, Burns, & Montgomery, 1998). Training was intensive; each child received 64 half-hour sessions over a semester's duration. Computerized exercises included concentration and attention skills. Mixed results were found based on the various outcome measures. Results were generally positive for improvement in response control, control of impulsive behavior, control of hyperactive behavior, and attention based on direct tests, but inconclusive based on teacher ratings of behavior. Improvement in classroom behavior evaluated through a classroom point system was only evident for one of the four students. A relationship was found between success on the cognitive training exercises and degree of behavioral improvement.

These findings are limited by small sample sizes and lack of control of other confounding treatments, including pharmacological treatments, ongoing therapy, and behavior modification programs at school or treatment center classrooms. In the cognitive training area, it appears that computerized exercises can produce change in some of the core problems inherent in the EBD disability, but maintenance and generalization of improvements are questionable beyond the individual therapeutic setting. The viability of the computer-assisted cognitive treatment approach appears to be quite limited for use in educational settings.

Biofeedback

Work in the clinical area with biofeedback has demonstrated some success with reducing hyperactive behaviors by altering brain waves to increase inhibition for children with ADHD. This approach started in medicine but has recently been implemented in school settings (Xu et al., 2002). There are two types of biofeedback treatment. One process involves using electromyographic (EMG) feedback displayed through a meter to help the person learn to reduce muscle tension by "calming down." The other process provides electroencephalographic (EEG) feedback to help the person learn to control brain-wave activity, increasing the desired forms of brain activity and decreasing undesired forms of brain

activity. Based on case studies involving treatments lasting 5-27 months, claims have been made that EMG and EEG therapies are effective in producing brain wave changes to decrease motoric behaviors, increase attending, improve academic performance as measured by grades and achievement tests, and improve IQ scores (Linden, Habib, & Radojevic, 1996; Lubar, 1991; Tansey & Bruner, 1983). Common problems in these studies include failure to control for simultaneous treatments, possible bias in behavior raters, and failure to generalize into classroom settings (Xu et al., 2002).

There appears to be some promise in the use of biofeedback to help children and adolescents relax and lower stress, a goal often addressed during startup classroom activities. For example, Blanton and Johnson (1991) described a biofeedback treatment with children with ADHD delivered in a clinical setting. The three children participating in the study were able to relax using the biofeedback training. Using an alternating-treatment design, one of the children was simultaneously observed in the classroom and an increase in on-task behavior was documented.

An interesting group study with 63 elementary-aged children with ADHD compared the effectiveness of two forms of self-control training on perceptions and levels of self-control (Kaduson & Finnerty, 1995). One form of self-control training used cognitive-behavioral strategies (CB), the other used biofeedback (BF). Comparisons also included a control group who received no self-control training. Treatments were delivered in 10 one-hour group sessions. The CB training combined cognitive restructuring and behavioral rehearsal techniques by learning to use self-statements and preplanning strategies and by focusing on personal effort in academic tasks. The BF training focused on EMG controls to control muscle activity; children had to respond to audio and visual biofeedback to activate a remote-control road racing game by relaxation. The control group received no specific self-control training while engaging in board games (e.g., *Trouble, Sorry, Checkers*); game-playing behaviors were encouraged through modeling, role-playing, coaching, feedback, and discussion of game strategies.

A variety of measures were used, including a child self-report rating scale and a battery of parent checklists and rating scales completed at pre, post, and three-month followup. The results indicated there were no comparative differences on behavioral measures favoring any of the three conditions. Although the biofeedback condition displayed the largest improvement in the children's perception of self-control, their improved perception of self-control did not affect their behavior in the home setting. The control group was the only condition demonstrating improvement of hyperactive behaviors at home. Implications are that biofeedback can be an effective treatment approach focusing on self-esteem and/or self-control problems, but direct procedures involving practice of socialization skills in interactive games are more effective in reducing ADHD behaviors in home and school. Behavioral observation data were not available to interpret discrepancies in outcomes based on the various measures used.

In spite of methodological concerns, positive case reports suggest that biofeedback treatment approaches have therapeutic merit by addressing the core ADHD disabilities of hyperactivity, impulsivity, and inattentiveness. However, more research and development is needed to determine how to deliver biofeedback training within the school milieu. Before biofeedback becomes practical for educational uses, user-friendly biofeedback software applications have to be developed—ones that teachers can deliver within their group settings and ones that move the child to increased internal controls beyond the biofeedback mechanisms.

Calling their approach "affective computing," Steele and Steele (2002) suggest that computers in the future may be able to read the psychophysiology of a student through various wearable devices. The device would detect emotions and serve as a signal to the student that he/she is having an emotional reaction and needs to redirect his/her behavior to avoid an undesirable response. Similar to biofeedback training, the use of physiological devices must be integrated into instruction so that the student knows how to respond with alternative behaviors. Further, support is needed to

ensure that results can be generalized across time and settings and maintained through ongoing internal control mechanisms.

With advances in software design for children, increased classroom access to computers and hand-held devices, and higher computer skill levels for teachers and students, biofeedback is one line of technology application warranting further investigation. Although previous reports have focused on biofeedback with ADHD, other characteristics of EBD may respond to this approach by helping reduce anxiety and stabilize moods. Studies such as the Kaduson and Finnerty study (1995) comparing forms of computer-delivered, e.g. cognitive training and biofeedback, and non-computer cognitive training, are needed to determine the add-on value of technology in supplementing or delivering behavioral instruction.

Affect

Moods, Feelings, Beliefs, and Emotions
The area of greatest challenge and least development in the field of EBD is technology applications to address problems of moods, feelings, beliefs, and emotions. Certainly, some of the problem-solving tools or forms of multimedia expression described previously could be applied to these areas of affect. For example, if available, story scenarios could be used to facilitate discussion of concerns and solutions, similar to bibliotherapy. Computer-based simulations and virtual reality could be used in class discussions as the anchors to explore different problem solutions and outcomes. It is likely that teachers in classrooms are already doing this work as they utilize all possible methods of helping their students, but it is unlikely that these technology interventions are being developed and researched in any systematic way.

Two case vignettes with adolescents who used the Internet as a psychiatric tool have been reported in the literature (Bailey, Yager, & Jenson, 2002). The cases were meant to open up new discussion for practitioners on technology innovations on "old psychiatric wines in new digital bottles" (p. 1). The first case involved a socially isolated 15-year old boy who was comfortable with computers and spent most his out-of-school time in chat rooms on the Internet. Therapy moved from face-to-face therapy sessions to chat room sessions because the patient was more comfortable using online communication. Shared discussions about chat room interactions with the patient's online peers eventually led to forming some live as well as virtual friendships that were shared with the therapist. It appeared in this therapy case that the online communication facilitated contact, more open expression, and greater equality in communication.

The second case described therapy with a 17-year-old high school girl with anorexia nervosa. After previously participating in traditional medical and psychological counseling programs, she had slightly increased her weight, but she had not made progress in eating or activity patterns, compulsive behaviors, or other emotional aspects of the disorder. A multifaceted intervention program was set up focusing on medications, reduced exercising, a meal plan, outpatient therapy, office visits, bibliotherapy, and email communication with her psychiatrist. The threat of inpatient hospitalization was used for insufficient progress on the treatment plan. Outcomes of the intervention were reportedly very good; weight gain was maintained and other psychosocial goals were met. The patient valued the use of email in her treatment program. It appeared email communication increased the frequency and amount of contact, provided "on-demand" communication when needed (as opposed to scheduled sessions), allowed for relaxed expression of feelings outside of a face-to-face interaction, forced the patient to constantly deal with eating-related behaviors, provided a concrete log of treatment details, and opened up therapy sessions to discuss meaningful issues.

Two concerns identified for online therapies are confidentiality and security for storing messages long-term. Because of these complex issues, guidelines are needed for educators as well as therapists adopting the use of chat room and email communication as interventions. Because families are increasingly using the Internet to secure information and join self-help groups, it is anticipated that online communication will evolve as another mode for sharing information, guiding self-help initiatives, and providing personalized assistance. Educators may find, as suggested by Bailey et al. (2002), that "We may find much of worth in the simpler uses of computers for helping us connect with, stay in touch with, and provide care for our patients" (p. 9).

Emerging Uses OF Technology

Virtual Reality

Computer simulations can be helpful for developing social skills and interactive behaviors. One form of simulations—virtual reality—immerses the learner in a computer-generated environment that provides an experience as if it were real. Thus, within an animated 3-D environment, the learner can see, hear, touch, speak, manipulate objects, and interact (Jonassen et al., 2003). Virtual environments strive to be similar to real experiences and to provide opportunities for practice of skills under conditions close to actual situations in order to enhance transfer of training.

Development and testing of virtual reality applications in education are in their infancy. Muscott and Gifford (1994) describe two potential applications of immersive virtual reality to assist children with EBD—teaching prosocial skills and utilizing role-playing scenarios. Multiple learners can work together on a collaborative project in a virtual networked environment, thus learning and practicing social skills as they cooperate on solving the project. A simulated role-playing environment can be created with objects or "agents" within the simulation creating situations within which the learner has to make different choices and follow the consequences of those choices. If several students utilize a virtual environment simultaneously, they can try out different roles, choices, and outcomes.

The potential for providing realistic practice in virtual environments is apparent, but to date, no work has been reported in the literature with EBD populations. Given the high cost of software development and questions about hardware access and teacher skills to implement such applications, comparative research should focus on integrating simulations into the behavior change curriculum, skill outcomes, transfer of skills in authentic situations, and the benefits and added-value of the technology.

Cybermentoring

The Internet offers new modes of communication for persons across distance and settings: email, listservs, chat rooms, and video-conferencing. These forms of communication can be used to form relationships that have the potential to provide support and perspective in a natural way (Jonassen et al., 2003). Whereas relationship building is a central goal in working with children with EBD, the Internet opens up new possibilities for providing online support and guidance to children and adolescents either individually or in groups. One example is cybermentoring where students are linked to adult mentors to draw upon the real world for educational purposes. Cybermentoring brings far-ranging and specialized resources to the classroom and provides a way for adults from all walks of life to become engaged with education. Since cybermentors are engaged in real-world work and pursuits, they bring authenticity, new perspectives, and opportunities for collaboration to the relationship.

The Buddy Project is a cybermentoring program operated through an intermediate unit detention center (Kane, as cited in Jonassen et al., 2003). The program's goal is to return students to regular school environments. Cybermentoring is utilized as the means to encourage students to become lifelong learners, develop proficiency in technological skills, and motivate them to stay in school. Mentors are drawn from adults across the United States who are interested in working with youth but need flexibility in scheduling time; they include one or more scientists, attorneys, physicians, psychologists, government workers, and artists, and some of them are bilingual. Reported benefits from the Buddy Project that particularly meet the needs of students with EBD include reducing the isolation from adult contact for students in a detention center; providing support and advocacy; moving students toward career and personal goals; providing assistance in planning goals and steps to meet the goals; providing motivation and resources to succeed; providing security of a caring relationship; and

increasing regard for others from different races and cultures. Although outcomes from this program have not been published beyond project reports, the initial efforts demonstrate the doability of the innovation and warrant further description, replication, and empirical study.

As more work is done with cybermentoring programs and other forms of Internet communication, operational guidelines will be needed to provide monitoring by each student's special education team and to secure confidentiality of information.

Electronic Performance Support Systems

Electronic performance support systems (EPSS) offer tremendous potential for addressing the needs of children/youth for improving self-regulation, strategic learning, and self-determination. Providing tools for skill usage and teaching children how to modify the tools for use in other contexts increase the probability that they will transfer skills appropriately to similar situations and generalize the skills into nonsimilar situations (Gersten, 1998). Computer tools provide a nonintrusive method of learning and supporting the use of these skills, which in turn, increase the likelihood of success in school, home, and community environments. EPSS approaches are currently being developed for students with behavioral disorders with support from the U.S. Department of Education in a series of software products (Fitzgerald & Koury, 2001; Fitzgerald & Koury, 2003; Fitzgerald & Semrau, 1998).

The conceptual framework for the KidTools Support System (KTSS) is based on the innovative use of EPSS to assist children and youth in developing self-regulation, learning strategies, and school/transition skills using cognitive-behavioral approaches (see Figure 2). Recognizing the importance of ecological variables surrounding an innovation, the framework addresses multiple systems that impact the innovation (Biemiller & Meichenbaum, 1998; Luca & Oliver, 2001). Because interactive, complementary processes occur when a specific innovation is nested within an ecology, interventions in the ecology are likely to improve the successful adoption of the innovation (Peled, Peled, & Alexander, 1994). The ecological support components include orientation and training resources, online

Figure 2. Conceptual framework for *KidTools Support System*.

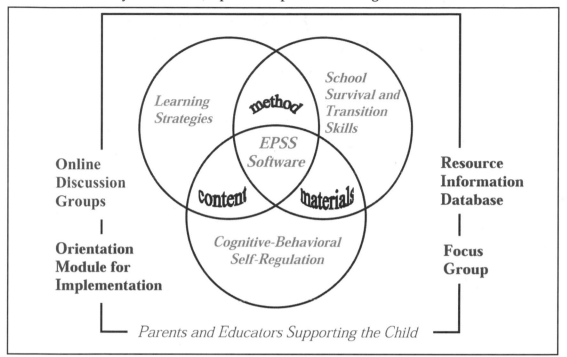

discussion groups for implementers, resource information databases about the strategies and tools, and periodic online focus group discussions.

The software programs provide easy-to-use template tools for elementary- and middle-school students to personalize for self-management, problem solving, school survival skills, and learning strategies. There are two titles in the series—KidTools and KidSkills—and each has two levels for ages 7-10 and 11-13. Children with behavioral disorders and their teachers from multiple sites have participated in field testing these programs. The newest software being developed in this series—Strategy Tools—aims at secondary students for building organizational, goal-setting, problem-solving, learning, and transition skills. All the software programs are similar in that they utilize the computer and online supports to meet the specialized needs of students with EBD: difficulties in learning and problem solving; managing personal and interactive behaviors; and managing moods, feelings, beliefs, and emotions.

The KidTools software consists of computerized templates based on cognitive-behavioral approaches to help students change cognitions (thoughts, beliefs, self-talk, cues) and behaviors (actions) within a problem-solving framework. Each program consists of approximately 20 easy-to-use behavior templates that are kid-friendly with colorful graphics, text-with-audio capabilities, and automatic recordkeeping. These tools help children plan for, create, and implement self-management skills in school settings. Tools include point cards, countoons, STAR card, monitoring cards, problem-solving cards, and contracts. To use the tools, children click on "hot words" or "hot boxes" on the template form to enter their personalized content and then print the completed form for use in their classrooms or homes. The tool bar on the template is consistent on all tools and allows the child to return to previous examples, erase entries and start over, print, and save entries by exiting. Internal recordkeeping features compile records of use and allow easy re-call of tools for editing. Figure 3 provides an example of the STAR card tool that helps

Figure 3. *KidTools* STAR card tool.©The Curators of the University of Missouri, a public corporation. All rights reserved.

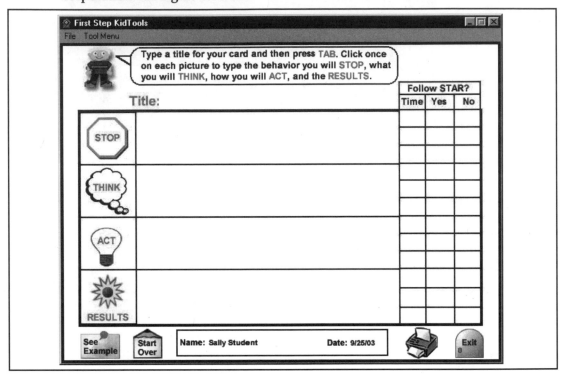

children stop and think about behaviors before acting impulsively.

The KidSkills software contains computerized template tools to help students develop organizational skills and to use learning strategies. The software consists of 32 organizational and learning strategy tools in the elementary- and middle-school versions. Tools are included for getting organized, doing homework, learning new content, organizing information, preparing for tests, and doing projects. The design features are identical to those in KidTools. Figure 4 provides an example of the KidSkills Big Picture strategy tool which helps children organize learning in a multistep project.

Prior to successful use of these tools, students must be instructed in how to use the strategies and also receive guided practice while using the tools. To support tool instruction, the KTSS series contains information databases to help teachers and parents learn about the approaches and how to implement the tools in educational settings. Each database provides overviews and rationales for the tools, examples

of completed tools, tips for implementation, and additional resources. Figure 5 displays an example of strategy information available in the information base program for teachers, Skill Resources, for the My Notes tool to help children learn new information. Additional systems supports are provided on the KidTools Web site at kidtools.missouri.edu. A future development includes a Strategy Coach Web site with resources for secondary-age youth. The purpose of this new support is to enable older students to learn the strategies independently without having to rely on adult instruction.

As the software was being developed, the programs underwent formative evaluation to ensure the interface was appropriate for young children (Fitzgerald, Watson, & Lynch, 1999) and that teachers and children could utilize the programs to facilitate behavior change (Fitzgerald, Lynch, Semrau, & Peng, 2000). Findings from formative evaluation led to technological changes in both KidTools and KidSkills to improve the editing and recordkeeping recall capabilities of the

Figure 4. *KidSkills* big picture tool.©The Curators of the University of Missouri, a public corporation. All rights reserved.

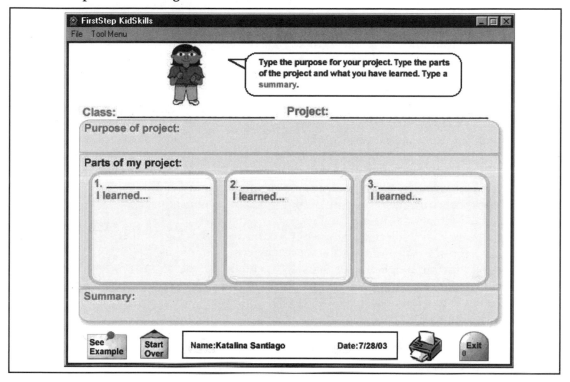

Figure 5. My notes tool rationale in *Skills Resources.*©The Curators of the University of Missouri, a public corporation. All rights reserved.

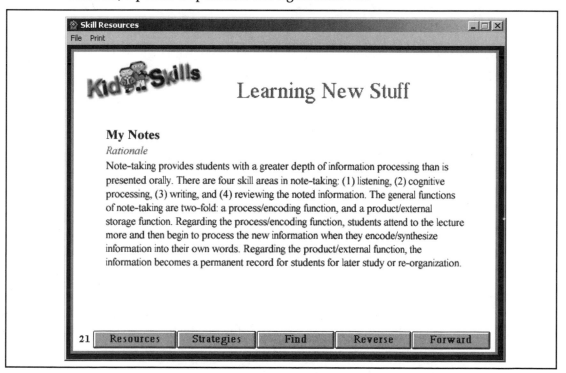

software to simplify text entry for children (Fitzgerald, Koury, & Peng, 2001). Usability studies with elementary- and middle-school students confirmed that they quickly learned to use the tools, modified the tools to meet personal needs, and perceived the tools as useful. Children and teachers in three states who used the software enthusiastically supported the programs. Children said KidTools is "cool" and it "helps you be better" because you pay attention to how you act. Teachers reported children were intrigued by the software and became independent with it. Many described behavior changes attributed in part to the tool approaches that help children think before they act (Fitzgerald, Koury, & Peng, 2002). Finally, mini-case studies emerging from action research projects with KidTools demonstrated success with initiating behavior change within teacher-managed behavior change procedures (Miller, Mitchem, Fitzgerald, Koury, & Hollingsead, 2004).

Although these approaches—EPSS tools and online learning supports—appear to have considerable potential for supporting behavior change, problem solving, and improved use of learning strategies for the EBD population, no complete field tests or empirical studies have been conducted to demonstrate their effectiveness. What is known, however, is that specialized technologies can be designed that offer the promise of improving behavior and learning outcomes for students with EBD by enhancing internalization and enabling access to support and information (Koury & Fitzgerald, 2003).

Summary and Future Research Directions

It seems clear, based on limited empirical findings and descriptions of emerging uses of technology for children and youth with EBD, that this specialized field is in its infancy. Referring back to the taxonomy presented in Figure 1, specialized applications for students with EBD were primarily found using directed learning approaches and computer tools. These technology applications included computer-assisted and computer-managed instruction in the content areas; computerized cognitive training; biofeedback for anger and impulse control

and for stress reduction; use of productivity tools to support academics, learning strategies, organizational skills, self-monitoring, and making personal change plans. These applications were delivered through the older technologies of directed learning instruction and using the computer as a tool for personal needs. There were no applications involving constructivist learning environments other than a description of future uses of virtual reality for social skills training and role-playing. The uses of online learning technologies included online communication with therapists for treatment monitoring and support and a cybermentoring program within education.

Many writers have described positive outcomes of technology with the EBD population, but research interest appears to be thin, fragmented, and not focused on therapeutic uses of technology. Most of the work in the area is directed towards academic/content learning or behavioral control. A decade ago, Fitzgerald (1994) described promising practices for integrating the computer into therapeutic instruction for students with EBD.

> It can be argued that the computer is the most powerful reinforcer in the educational environment for a majority of students with emotional or behavioral disorders. For those students who are reluctant learners due to motivational problems or cognitive deficits as well as for those students who have emotionally-based difficulties, the computer offers a personalized learning environment without the complications of adult interactions or behavioral control issues. Software can be creatively adapted to support instruction in thinking, problem solving, social interaction, and behavioral control skills. (Fitzgerald, 1994, p. 87)

To date, few of these specialized practices have been developed, implemented, or researched, and the potential of technology as a therapeutic tool remains unfulfilled. As recently as 2003, a description of a technology curriculum for students with EBD described narrow, out-of-date instruction of disjointed specific skills including "computer literacy and technology ethics, keyboarding and mouse skills, multimedia production, research, spreadsheets and databases, and word processing" (White, Palmer, & Huffman, 2003, p. 24). This technology curriculum was offered to students in a therapeutic day school as skills to be mastered without meaningful, authentic learning experiences or intentional programming to address their social, emotional, and behavioral needs. Such articles perpetuate ill-founded practices that are not linked to evidence or best practice.

The following statement by Carl Smith aptly defines the challenge facing all educators of children with EBD, as well as the special education technology community.

> *After what many of us consider years of neglect or an under-emphasis on the needs of students with emotional and behavioral disorders, we are at a critical juncture at which the needs of the children and families for and with whom we work are at the forefront of several national agendas. Perhaps the necessary, yet uncomfortable question we now face is whether we can, as a profession, deliver on our long-term, implied promises for improving the lives of these children and youth. (Smith, 2003, p. 11)*

Virtually all writers in this area express the belief that the computer is a powerful educational tool and describe promising practices for integrating meaningful uses of technology into the curriculum. Recognizing the limited development and empirical base of support for technology applications in EBD, attention must be given to designing and developing specialized applications to address their unique needs. This development work must be done as the first stage before implementation and empirical research can be conducted (Osher & Hanley, 2001). These applications have to provide authentic learning experiences based on learner-centered instruction and emphasize emerging uses of technology in the information age. As Ted Hasselbring stated, "We can't predict the future, but we can invent it" (2001). Invention is needed to develop tutorials and simulations to teach thinking, problem solving, social skills, and other therapeutic goals essential to successful daily living. Invention is needed to provide electronic performance support tools, links to Web-based information, and strategies

to enable students to move toward self-control, personal problem solving, and independence. Invention is needed to link students and families to available electronic resources and provide real-time access to support, mentoring, and habilitative programs. Invention is needed to utilize new technologies on the road ahead. Research will be complex and compromised by ecological variables and challenges inherent in the EBD population, but it is necessary to meet our obligations for empirically-based practice for this underserved population.

References

Ayersman, D. (1996). Reviewing the research on hypermedia-based learning. *Journal of Research on Computing in Education, 28*, 501-525.

Bailey, R., Yager, J., & Jenson, J. (2002). The psychiatrist as clinical computerologist in the treatment of adolescents: Old barks in new bytes. *The American Journal of Psychiatry, 159*, 1298-1304.

Biemiller, A., & Meichenbaum, D. (1998). The consequences of negative scaffolding for students who learn slowly— A commentary on C. Addison Stone's "The metaphor of scaffolding: Its utility for the field of learning disabilities." *Journal of Learning Disabilities, 31*, 365-369.

Blackhurst, A. E. (1997). Perspectives on technology in special education. *Teaching Exceptional Children, 29*(5), 41-48.

Blanton, J., & Johnson, L. (1991). Using computer assisted biofeedback to help children with attention-deficit hyperactivity disorder to gain control. *Journal of Special Education Technology, 11*(1), 49-56.

Bottge, B., Heinrichs, M., Chan, S., & Serlin, R. (2001). Anchoring adolescents' understanding of math concepts in rich problem-solving environments. *Remedial and Special Education, 22*, 299-314.

Bransford, J., Brown. A., & Cocking, R. (Eds.). (1999). *How people learn: Brain, mind, experience and school.* Washington, DC: The National Academies Press.

Cognition and Technology Group at Vanderbilt. (1990). Anchored instruction and its relationship to situated cognition. *Educational Researcher, 19*(5), 2-10.

Din, F. (1996). Computer-assisted instruction, students' off-task behavior and their achievement. *Education and Treatment of Children, 19,* 170-182.

DuPaul, G., Guevremont, D., & Barkley, R. (1992). Behavioral treatment of attention-deficit hyperactivity disorder in the classroom. *Behavior Modification, 16,* 203-225.

Edyburn, D. (2000). Assistive technology and students with mild disabilities. *Focus on Exceptional Children, 32*(9), 1-23.

Elias, M., Tobias, S., & Friedlander, B. (1994). Enhancing skills for everyday problem solving, decision making, and conflict resolution in special needs students with the support of computer-based technology. *Special Services in the Schools, 8*(2), 33-52.

Epstein, J., Willis, M., Conners, C., & Johnson, D. (2001). Use of a technological prompting device to aid a student with attention deficit hyperactivity disorder to initiate and complete daily tasks: An exploratory study. *Journal of Special Education Technology, 16*(1), 19-28.

Evans, J., Ferre, L., Ford, L, & Green, J. (1995). Decreasing attention deficit hyperactivity disorder symptoms utilizing an automated classroom reinforcement device. *Psychology in the Schools, 32,* 210-219.

Fitzgerald, G. (1994). Using the computer with students with emotional and behavioral disorders. *Technology and Disability, 3*(2), 87-99.

Fitzgerald, G., & Koury, K. (1996). Empirical advances in technology-assisted instruction for students with mild and moderate disabilities. *Journal of Research on Computing in Education, 28,* 526-553.

Fitzgerald, G., & Koury, K. (2003). *The effectiveness of technology-assisted instruction for students with mild and moderate disabilities.* Unpublished manuscript.

Fitzgerald, G., & Koury, K. (2001). *The Kidtools support system* (Project #H327A000005). Washington, DC: United States Department of Education: Office of Special Education Programs.

Fitzgerald, G., & Koury, K. (2003). *The Strategy Tools support system* (Project #H827A030044). Washington, DC: United States Department of Education: Office of Special Education Programs.

Fitzgerald, G., Koury, K., Miller, K., & Hollingsead, C. (2004). Beyond the innovation: System supports for the implementation of performance support software for children. In *Proceedings of Ed-Media World Conference on Educational Multimedia, Hypermedia, and Telecommunication.* Charlottesville, VA: AACE.

Fitzgerald, G., Koury, K., & Peng, H. (2002). User studies: Developing learning strategy tool software for children. In *Proceedings of Ed-Media 2002 World Conference on Educational Multimedia, Hypermedia, and Telecommunication* (pp. 510-515). Charlottesville, VA: AACE.

Fitzgerald, G., Lynch, J., Semrau, L., & Peng, H. (2000). User studies: Evaluating the use of EPSS tools for self-management by children. In *Proceedings of Ed-Media 2000 World Conference on Educational Multimedia, Hypermedia, and Telecommunication* (pp. 1301-1303). Charlottesville, VA: AACE.

Fitzgerald, G., & Semrau, L. (1998). *Virtual Resource Center in Behavioral Disorders* (Project #H029K70089). Washington, DC: United States Department of Education: Office of Special Education Programs.

Fitzgerald, G., Watson, P., & Lynch, J. (1999). EPSS in the classroom: Self-management tools for kids. In *Proceedings of Ed-Media 1999 World Conference on Educational Multimedia, Hypermedia, and Telecommunication* (pp. 1225-1226). Charlottesville, VA: AACE.

Fitzgerald, G., & Werner, J. (1996). The use of the computer to support cognitive-behavioral interventions for students with behavioral disorders. *Journal of Computing in Childhood Education, 7*(3/4), 127-148.

Ford, M. J., Poe, J., & Cox, J. (1993). Attending behaviors of ADHD children in math and reading using various types of software. *Journal of Computing in Childhood Education, 4,* 183-196.

Fulton, K. (2003). Redesigning schools to meet 21st century learning needs. *T.H.E. Journal, 30*(9), 30-36.

Gersten, R. (1998). Recent advances in instructional research for students with learning disabilities: An overview. *Learning Disabilities Practice, 13,* 162-170.

Gordon, M., Thomason, D., Cooper, S., & Ivers,

C. (1991). Nonmedical treatment of ADHD/hyperactivity: The attention training system. *Journal of School Psychology, 29*, 51-159.

Hartley, K. (2001). Learning strategies and hypermedia instruction. *Journal of Educational Multimedia and Hypermedia, 10*, 285-305.

Hasselbring, T. (2001). A possible future of special education technology. *Journal of Special Education Technology, 16*(4), 15-21.

Hasselbring, T., & Moore, P. R. (1996). Developing mathematical literacy through the use of contextualized learning environments. *Journal of Computing in Childhood Education, 7*, 199-222.

Higgins, K., Boone, R., & Lovitt, T. (1996). Hypertext support for remedial students and students with learning disabilities. *Journal of Learning Disabilities, 29*, 402-412.

Jonassen, D., Howland, J., Moore, J., & Marra, R. (2003*). Learning to solve problems with technology: A constructivist perspective.* Upper Saddle River, NJ: Merrill Prentice Hall.

Kaduson, H., & Finnerty K. (1995). Self-control game interventions for attention-deficit hyperactivity disorder. *International Journal of Play Therapy, 4*(2), 15-29.

Kotwal, D., Burns, W., & Montgomery, D. (1996). Computer-assisted cognitive training for ADHD. *Behavior Modification, 20*(1), 85-96.

Koury, K. A. (1996). The impact of preteaching science content vocabulary using integrated media for knowledge acquisition in a collaborative classroom. *Journal of Computing in Childhood Education, 7*(3/4), 179-197.

Koury, K., & Fitzgerald, G. (2003). *The KidTools Support System: Design and formative evaluation—An iterative process* (Technical Report). Columbia: University of Missouri-Columbia.

Langone, J., Levine, B., Clees, T., Malone, M., & Koorland, M. (1996). The differential effects of a typing tutor and microcomputer-based word processing on the writing samples of elementary students with behavior disorders. *Journal of Research on Computing in Education, 29*(2), 141-158.

Linden, M., Habib, T., & Radojevic, V. (1996). A controlled study of the effects of EEG biofeedback on cognition and behavior of children with attention deficit disorder and learning disabilities. *Biofeedback and Self-Regulation, 21*(1), 35-49.

Liu, M. (1998). The effect of hypermedia authoring on elementary school students' creative thinking. *Journal of Educational Computing Research, 19*, 27-51.

Lubar, J. (1991). Discourse on the development of EEG diagnostics and biofeedback for attention-deficit/hyperactivity disorders. *Biofeedback and Self-Regulation, 16*, 201-225.

Luca, J., & Oliver, R. (2001). Developing generic skills through on-line courses. In *Proceedings of Ed-Media 2001 World Conference on Educational Multimedia, Hypermedia, and Telecommunication* (pp. 1163-1164). Charlottesville, VA: AACE.

Mayer, M., & Leone, P. (2002). Developing untapped talents and fostering success with hypermedia. In L. K. Wilder & S. Black (Eds.) *Integrating technology in program development for children and youth with emotional or behavioral disorders* (pp. 47-65). Arlington, VA: Council for Children with Behavioral Disorders.

Means, B. (2001). Technology use in tomorrow's schools. *Educational Leadership, 58*(4), 57-61.

Miller, K., Mitchem, K., Fitzgerald, G., Koury, K., & Hollingsead, C. (2004). KidTools/KidSkills: Self-management, problem solving, organizational and planning tools for children. *Proceedings of the American Council on Rural Special Education (ACRES).*

Murry, F. (2002). Increasing reading and language skills with PowerPoint. In L. K. Wilder & S. Black (Eds.) *Integrating technology in program development for children and youth with emotional or behavioral disorders* (pp. 39-46). Arlington, VA: Council for Children with Behavioral Disorders.

Muscott, H., & Gifford, T. (1994). Virtual reality and social skills training for students with behavioral disorders: Applications, challenges and promising practices. *Education and Treatment of Children, 17*, 417-434.

Okolo, C., & Ferretti, R. (1996). The impact of multimedia design projects on the knowledge, attitudes, and collaboration of students in inclusive classrooms. *Journal of Computing in Childhood Education, 7*(3/4), 223-251.

Osher, D., & Hanley, T. (2001). Implementing the SED national agenda: Promising programs and policies for children and youth with emotional and behavioral problems. *Education and Treatment of Children, 24*, 374-403.

Peled, Z., Peled, E., & Alexander, G. (1994). An ecological approach for information technology: Intervention, evaluation, and software adoption policies. In E. Baker & H. O'Neil (Eds.), *Technology assessment* (pp. 35-61). Hillsdale, NJ: Lawrence Erlbaum Associates.

Plato Instructional Systems. (2004). www.plato.com/k12/instructional/.

Sanford, J., & Browne, R. (1988). *Captain's Log* [Computer Software]. Richmond, VA: Brain Train.

Slate, S., Meyer, T., Burns, W., & Montgomery, D. (1998). Computerized cognitive training for severely emotionally disturbed children with ADHD. *Behavior Modification, 22*, 415-437.

Smith, C. (2003). Meeting the behavioral and discipline needs of students with emotional and behavioral disorders: Are we missing the forest for the trees. *Beyond Behavior, 13*(1), 8-11.

Steele, M., & Steele, J. (2002). Applying affective computing techniques to the field of special education. *Journal of Research on Technology in Education, 35, 236-240.*

Tansey, M., & Bruner, R. (1983). EMG and EEG biofeedback training in the treatment of a 10-year-old boy with a developmental reading disorder. *Biofeedback and Self-Regulation, 8*, 25-37.

U.S. Department of Education. (1999). Assistance to states for education of children with disabilities and the early intervention program for infants and toddlers with disabilities: Final regulations. *Federal Register, 64*(48), CFR Parts 300 and 303.

Wetzel, K. (2001). Reaching student with emotional disabilities: A partnership that works. *Learning and Leading with Technology, 29*(2), 22-27.

White, C., Palmer, K., & Huffman, L. (2003). Technology instruction for students with emotional and behavioral disorders attending a therapeutic day school. *Beyond Behavior, 13*(1), 23-31.

Woodward, J., & Rieth, H. (1997). A historical review of technology research in special education. *Review of Educational Research, 67*(4), 503-556.

Xu, C., Reid, R., & Steckelberg, A. (2002). Teaching applications for children with ADHD: Assessing the empirical support. *Education and Treatment of Children, 25*, 224-248.

18

Physical Access in Today's Schools: Empowerment Through Assistive Technology

Cindy L. George, Jennie I. Schaff, and Tara L. Jeffs

In considering students with physical disabilities and their overall functionality within the school environment, an overwhelmingly long list of barriers arise that prevent their complete access to the school and its primary components. No longer is a school with stairs leading up to its entrance the only thing that prevents a school from being completely accessible to a student with physical disabilities. Considerations must be made beyond the physical outdoor environment to other, equally important areas of the educational environment such as classroom curriculum, indoor school and classroom physical surroundings, and the technological supports and alternatives that may help provide educational success. This chapter addresses these additional considerations within three main sections.

The first section concentrates on the academic successes of students with disabilities and the tools that may be used to increase their independence and access to the curriculum. How to create a classroom community in which all students are active participants and engaged is explored followed by a discussion on literacy and accessible learning environments.

The second section focuses on assistive technology for the goal of independent living, specifically within the school environment. In particular, we elaborate on transitions and mobility within the school while continually emphasizing the importance of independence for all students, including those with physical disabilities.

The chapter ends with a discussion of Universal Design and considerations needed for creating a barrier-free environment. Suggestions and evaluative ideas are recommended for those wishing to evaluate their own school environments for students with physical disabilities.

Academic Success

It is no surprise that students with physical disabilities experience an enormous spectrum of individual challenges within the academic setting. Past and present research reveals several recurring themes relevant to practitioners and researchers alike. These include (a) creating a classroom community, (b) building a literacy foundation for learning, (c) providing accessible learning, and (d) ensuring tools for lifelong learning. A closer examination of these themes provides a roadmap for continual understanding and improvement of current academic support systems and educational research involving students with physical disabilities.

Creating a Classroom Community
Within the classroom, the typically plans, organizes, and implements the essential components needed for optimum learning. In essence, the teacher establishes the classroom environment and facilitates a community that encourages active participation and in return yields academic success.

Current research on the predictors of successful inclusion consistently reports that teacher attitudes toward integration of students with disabilities reflect their perceptions of the specific disability as well as their beliefs about the instructional demands and management needs that the student will require (Rich, Linor, & Shalev, 1984; Scruggs & Mastropieri, 1996; Soodak, Podell & Lehman, 1998).

Preliminary research conducted by Frith and Edwards (1981) investigated perceptions and concerns of regular classroom teachers who were requested to take an increasing role in the education of students with physical disabilities. Thirty-two regular classroom teachers who had experience working with students with physical disabilities in their classrooms and 46 regular classroom teachers who had never interacted with students with physical disabilities were surveyed. Substantial differences were found between the two groups. For example, the number one concern for teachers with experience in working with students with physical disabilities was lack of materials, whereas the number one concern for teachers without experience in working with students with physical disabilities was toileting responsibilities. Frith and Edwards concluded that sustained interaction with students with physical disabilities appears to have a positive impact and can substantially alter the perceptions of classroom teachers. Thus, it appears that much apprehension of working with students with physical disabilities is likely due to uncertainty on the teacher's part. In order for students with physical disabilities to be successfully included into the classroom, up-front conversations (involving teachers, parents, student, and support professionals) about the student's needs, expectations, and educational resources are essential.

Hemmingson and Borell (2002) examined various types of barriers in both the physical and social aspects of school environments. Their findings suggest that the majority of barriers facing students with physical disabilities originate from the way in which the classroom environment or school activities are organized and carried out. If this is the case, then classroom teachers and school administrators must be aware of how their communication and teaching style facilitates or hinders a positive learning environment.

Hart and Williams (1995) researched the communicative behaviors and attitudes towards the inclusion of students with physical disabilities in the classroom. The results of the study identified four different communication roles assumed by instructors in the study and their impact on effective teaching. A short description of each follows:

The Avoider – displays communication avoidance and generally nervous behaviors in the presence of a student with a disability (p. 144). Avoidance may be manifested as physical separation from the student or failure to discuss a particular student's disability and disabilities in general. When instructors function as avoiders, they decrease their effectiveness by restraining their warmth and nonverbal immediacy, characteristics usually associated with effective teaching. In essence, avoiders gear their teaching toward able-bodied students only. (p. 145)

The Guardian – is overly protective of students with disabilities. Whether seeking to establish emotional, physical, or intellectual protection, some instructors tend to lower standards and separate students with disabilities from the rest of the class (p. 145). The tendency to favor the student with disabilities negatively affects the enthusiasm that students without disabilities have for the activity or the discussion often declines or disappears. Enthusiasm is generally considered an effective teaching characteristic. Guardians run a risk of allowing sympathy or misplaced concern to replace enthusiasm. Instructors who behave as guardians may send a false message that students with disabilities succeed only with breaks and assistance and that they need guardians to complete classroom assignments. (p. 147)

The Rejecter – rejects the ability of students with disabilities to be productive members of the class. This role differs from that of the guardian in that these instructors destroy the student's confidence or frustrate the student into withdrawing emotionally and academically. Instructors who behave as rejecters do not know how to deal with students with disabilities in the classroom and either ignore or verbally abuse them. (p. 147)

The Nurturer – is more at ease with students with disabilities. Instructors fulfilling this role facilitate an environment in which students with disabilities are supported and encouraged (p. 149). The nurturer displays an effective communicator style, using humor, self-disclosure, warmth, enthusiasm, and nonverbal immediacy. Although all nurturers do not employ each of the effective instructional characteristics, by functioning as nurturing instructors they may enact positive instructional characteristics when working with students with physical disabilities. (p. 150)

Students with physical disabilities are often treated differently and thus receive a different level of education (Hart & Williams, 1995). Such treatment has an adverse effect on the classroom environment. Therefore, it is imperative that we acknowledge instructional communication practices and adopt practices that facilitate equal treatment of those with disabilities in the classroom. Such practices begin with building a classroom community that promotes the attitude and belief that all students (a) should be treated as equals, (b) are capable of learning, and (c) should be provided with the best opportunities possible for academic success.

Hemmingson, Borell and Gustavsson (1999) researched the impact of teaching styles and learning for students with physical disabilities, concluding that teaching styles established the working pace in the classroom and, thus, influenced the amount of opportunity available for students with physical disabilities to participate in learning activities. In addition, they found that the explicit or implicit rules for how to do a certain learning activity, including the place, pace, and time, restricted student participation and often did not meet the needs of the student, thus, negatively influencing the opportunities open to students with physical disabilities to participate actively. For example, students could usually accomplish a learning task, such as writing, but not as fast, or in the same manner, as other students in the class (Hemmingson & Borell, 2002).

Students believe that active participation in classroom activities is the most important indicator of being a member of a class, whether they have disabilities or not (Williams & Downing, 1998). Teachers play an important role in facilitating such membership by adapting lessons, integrating assistive technologies, and providing choice in school activities (Hemmingson & Borell, 2002; Knight & Wadsworth, 1993). It is the teacher's responsibility to ensure opportunities for students to engage in learning. Such opportunities can be created for students with physical disabilities through activities that encourage and promote their becoming valuable class members, using flexible modifications/adaptations, and integrating innovative assistive technologies. Examples of classroom assistive technology include such things as magnetic rulers, online calculators, 3-D electronic manipulatives, computer simulation programs, Velcro strips, plastic guards, trays or plates with partitions, robotic arms/workstations, and online communications. Computer adaptations within the classroom might include such assistive technologies as keyguards, expanded keyboards, mini keyboards, track balls, joysticks, sticky keys, scanning software, various switches and Morse code switch systems.

The most important step in creating a successful inclusive classroom environment for all students is for teachers to have adequate information about the students' needs, strengths, and goals and ideas for making appropriate adaptations/accommodations (Hemmingson & Borell, 2002). Thus, the learning environment is dependent on information and cooperation among teachers, parents, school support professionals and school administrators (Hemmingson & Borell, 2002; Rich et al., 1984; Scruggs & Mastropieri, 1996; Soodak et al., 1998). That is, it is not only that the teacher establishes the classroom environment and facilitates a community that encourages active participation and in return yields academic success. Such a task should be accomplished through effective communication between all parties vested in the educational success of the student with physical disabilities.

Building a Literacy Foundation for Learning

Literacy is the backbone of all academic learning. If a student has mastered basic literacy skills, all other academic content areas are approachable. Without such mastery, therefore, the doors of learning new content area knowledge are often blocked. Current research demonstrates the importance of such skills from beginning of school on through adulthood. Despite the importance of literacy skills, Browning (2002) notes that a lack of literacy (reading and writing) skills in individuals with physical disabilities has been well documented in the research literature dating as far back as the 1950s. Typically, functional curriculum involving self-help skills are offered for students with physical disabilities with little or no emphasis on building reading and writing skills (Foley, 1993). Light and Kelford Smith (1993) found that priorities voiced by parents of children with physical disabilities were focused on their desire for their children to achieve physical independence. Similarly, reading and writing are often considered low priorities in relation to other activities (Browning, 2002).

In reviewing the research on literacy development of children with physical disabilities, Browning (2002) identified influential factors, including the key role that parents and professionals play in providing a literacy-rich environment. These key players are encouraged to engage the child in daily literacy experiences and provide access to technology that motivates and facilitates the child's efforts to read and write. Such an environment provides opportunities for the child to explore and interact with various forms of text materials essential to obtaining early literacy skills. Browning notes that research demonstrates a strong connection between priorities, expectations, and the provision of opportunities.

Technological Interventions for Literacy

Contemporary instructional approaches for students with physical disabilities evolve from understanding the characteristics and challenges of these students. For the purpose of this chapter, only technological interventions will be explored. Examples include the use of audio books, electronic books, and text-to-speech programs, word processing programs, spelling and grammar checks, word prediction programs, outlining and concept mapping software, and speech recognition. Studies involving the implementation of assistive technologies in developing and building literacy skills are limited and leave little doubt that more research is needed. Yet, much is to be learned from existing research and the implications for students with physical disabilities.

Audio Books

Audio books provide readers with an opportunity to use their listening skills to enjoy a good book. Such books are provided without written text. Audio books are often professional recordings of best-selling novels and children stories on cassette tapes. Audio books can be purchased in most bookstores and/or checked out at public libraries. In addition, a non-profit national organization, the Recording for the Blind & Dyslexic (RFBD), provides parents, students, and teachers a clearinghouse of audio cassette tapes, not only of popular books but of commonly used textbooks. Both parents and teachers can easily integrate audio books into the home and school environment, thus creating a curiosity and appreciation for literature among children. Audio books are very beneficial to students with physical disabilities because they eliminate the sometimes awkward task of holding, manipulating, and viewing a standard book.

Electronic Books

Electronic books are books that are available in digital form. Digital form or electronic text allows the reader to view the text within a computer application, e-book reader, or personal digital assistant (PDA). These books come in various formats (CD ROM, DVD, and online). Although the first available electronic books were text only, as technology has advanced, these books often include multimedia text enhancements such as synchronized text with high-quality audio speech, sounds, and animations for optimal interactivity. Electronic books provide the reader with options to customize the reading environment. Many offer the ability to expand or collapse large amounts of information making it easier for users to see overall structure and access only necessary or desired information. Other features such as navigation, search, font size, bookmarks, and notes allow the reader with physical disabilities to meet their unique needs.

Text-To-Speech Programs

Text-to-speech programs support reading and writing through the use of visual and auditory stimuli, sometimes referred to as bimodal reading. The primary function of text-to-speech software is to convert text to speech output, allowing readers to use both their auditory and visual skills. In essence, text-to-speech programs enable the user to see text that is displayed on a computer screen and simultaneously hear it spoken aloud.

Text-to-speech software provides many options and features. Universal text readers perform text reading in many computer applications, allowing users to complete tasks such as researching on the Internet, reading email, and writing and editing reports with greater ease. Other text-to-speech systems combine the use of a scanner and optical character recognition (OCR) technology to convert printed text into electronic text, thus transferring any printed materials such as student workbooks, tests, and textbooks into a computer for reading. Text-to-speech software is backed by research as providing support for less skilled readers and eliminating word recognition difficulties so more effort can be focused on reading comprehension (Montali & Lewandowski, 1996; Wepner, 1990). Text-to-speech programs may benefit students with physical disabilities by providing them with a multimodal approach to reading and writing along with customizable options to enhance study skills. Many text-to-speech programs offer valuable tools such as audible spellchecking, voice notes, highlighting features and invaluable electronic dictionaries.

Word Processing Programs, Spelling and Grammar Check

Word processing programs are widespread in today's homes, schools, and society in general. Word processing provides the learner with features for spelling and grammar correction commonly referred to as spelling and grammar checks. Such features may improve spelling, grammar usage, writing motivation, and build vocabulary (MacArthur, 1999). Word processing has been found to be most beneficial for students who have physical difficulties with handwriting and for students with severe spelling deficits (Outhred, 1989). In combination with alternative keyboards, word processing can open the world to writing for some students with physical disabilities.

Word Prediction Programs

Word prediction software provides the user with a list of words after a word has been typed. Word lists are based upon previous words used in the sentence and/or grammatically correct word choices for sentence completion. Such lists can be customizable to meet the user's needs. For example, users can select the number of word guesses that they would like displayed at one time. In addition, words list can be listed horizontally, vertically, or in black/white contrast for easier viewing. Word prediction software can benefit students with physical disabilities in many ways, including:

- Reducing the number of keystrokes required to type a specific word. Instead of typing each letter of a word, the user selects the word through a list of word choices, thus possibly reducing fatigue.

- Automatic spacing and capitalization, thereby reducing the amount of energy spent on writing format.

- Reducing the number of spelling errors.

- Increasing vocabulary usage.

- Increasing grammatical accuracy and sentence structure.

Word prediction programs ease the demands of writing by diminishing the focus on spelling and grammatical structure and increase overall writing productivity. Several studies have shown that word prediction can improve the quality and quantity of writing for students with disabilities (Higginbotham, 1992; Lewis, Graves, Ashton, & Kieley, 1998; MacArthur, 1998; Swiffin, Arnott, & Newell, 1987).

Outlining and Concept Mapping Software

Graphic organizers, concept maps, and structured overviews have been used in the learning process for over two decades to assist students in maintaining focus on a topic and creating clear and concise relationships between various types of information. In particular, outlining and concept mapping software enhances the overall structure and quality of reading and writing. Concept mapping software can be beneficial for students with physical disabilities by providing a manipulative and customizable shell or holding place for collecting, organizing, and interacting with information needed to complete literacy activities.

Speech Recognition

Speech recognition software allows a user to use a computer by speaking into it. There are two types of speech recognition software: discrete speech and continuous speech. *Discrete speech* software requires the user to speak slowly, pausing after each word. This type of software can be very beneficial for users who require extra time for language processing and word retrieval. *Continuous speech* allows the user to speak naturally, using phrases or sentences. As technology advances with faster computer processors, more RAM memory, advanced sound cards, and high-efficiency microphones, the effectiveness and use of speech recognition software is also improving.

Although not effective for everyone, speech recognition provides an alternative to the standard keyboard through the use of voice commands. For some users with physical disabilities, speech recognition is easier and require less energy to use than other alternative input devices such as switches, alternative keyboards, and onscreen keyboards.

Advantages of speech recognition include the generation of text quickly and accurately. In a study conducted by Kotler and Tam (2002) involving individuals with physical disabilities (ages 19-35) using discrete speech software, the most frequently noted advantages were faster speed of text generation compared to other access methods and hands-free use of the computer. All participants in the study felt that speech recognition was appropriate for word processing. De La Paz (1999) found that users were able to achieve success in writing tasks that normally would be unsuccessful, due to the ability to bypass weak written language/spelling skills.

Disadvantages of speech recognition include frustration of unacceptable recognition accuracy. For example, Kotler and Tam (2002) found that the most frequently noted disadvantages included limited support for applications, fatigue, and lack of confidentiality. Additional disadvantages found by De La Paz (1999) were the frustration of articulating ideas, and editing and revising writing products.

Although many individuals have been successful using speech recognition software for their computer needs (this author included), many have not, and research has yet to prove its effectiveness.

Literacy Wrap-Up

In order to build literacy skills, children need an environment rich in reading materials and opportunities to interact with text, drawing and writing tools. The more opportunities children have to access verbal and written language, the more chances they have to develop literacy skills (Browning, 2002). For some students with physical disabilities such interaction and exposure can be challenging, however. For example, difficulties may arise in holding books, turning pages, obtaining visual proximity, and manipulating paper and pencil. Technology such as the tools described above can provide the needed assistance for children with physical disabilities to access literacy materials and develop the foundation for all future learning.

Providing Accessible Learning

According to Lewis et al. (1998), assistive technology has two fundamental purposes. "First, it can augment an individual's strengths so that his or her abilities counterbalance the efforts of any disabilities. Second, technology can provide an alternate mode of performing a task so that disabilities are compensated for or bypassed entirely" (p. 17). Through assistive technology and instructional accommodations, learning can become more accessible. Learning activities and environments must be closely analyzed to facilitate active participation and increase chances for success for students with physical disabilities (Knight & Wadsworth, 1993). Examples of accommodations include note takers, lab assistants, group lab assignments, cooperative learning groups, extended time on tasks and assignments, alternative testing arrangements, course materials available in various formats, tape recorders, computer with special devices, and access to research resources on the Internet.

Providing a child physical access to a computer system does not ensure academic success. In most cases even computer stations need some type of accommodation or assistive technology to guarantee access and productivity. For example, students may benefit from repositioning the keyboard and monitor, key guards, expanded keyboards, mini keyboards, trackball, joysticks, sticky keys, scanning software, switches, and Morse code-activated switches. Higgins and Boone (1996) stress that the key to selecting effective technology is making the right match between the technologies, commonly faced challenges of the individual, and the requirements needed for successful implementation.

For the purpose of this chapter, accessible learning practices and examples will be discussed within the science and math classroom. Through this discussion, accommodations, effective teaching practices, and common assistive technologies that facilitate accessible learning will be shared.

The Science Classroom

The science classroom commonly provides hands-on learning activities for students to explore and apply learning concepts. If not carefully thought out, planned, and organized by the classroom teacher for some students with physical disabilities, such activities can create frustration and prevent participation. According to Mastropieri and Scruggs (1993), the first and foremost thing science teachers need to remember is that each student, with or without disabilities, is an individual. Therefore, it is through careful matching of a student's individual strengths/weaknesses and academic interests to the science curriculum/learning activities that a student will find success and academic achievement. Mastropieri and Scruggs suggest that the following effective teaching strategies be included in the science classroom:

- Daily and weekly review
- Clearly stated objectives
- Information delivered in a clear and succinct manner-SCREAM variables:

  – Structure
  – Clarity
  – Redundancy
  – Enthusiasm
  – Appropriate pace
  – Maximize student engagement
- Guided practice
- Independent practice
- Formative evaluation

These strategies in conjunction with assistive technologies that are often found in the science classroom (e.g., trays with partitions, Velcro strips, plastic guards, measuring wheels, robotic workstation, and use of electronic communications) can provide accessible learning in the science classroom.

The Math Classroom

The math classroom commonly uses manipulatives, paper-and-pencil practice, calculators, and geometric models to teach important concepts. Such learning activities can create challenges for students with physical disabilities to fully participate alongside their peers. To diminish such challenges alternatives include the use of math software tools, computer-aided drafting and design (CADD) to replace pencil-and-paper practice, and the use of electronic manipulatives to enable students with physical disabilities to explore three-dimensional objects with their symbolic representations.

Innovative learning resources are also available online (via the Internet). One example is "An Internet-Based Curriculum on Math and Aeronautics for 4th-7th-Grade Children with Physical Disabilities." The project involves creating online lessons and activities on math and aeronautics with the aim of improving education and career options for children with physical disabilities. A combination of a newly developed math program, existing curricula, available materials and assistive technologies, and the use of the Internet will support these interactive math experiences for students across the nation (Kraus, 1998).

Essential components of making learning accessible involves attention to such things as classroom scheduling, flexible curriculum supports, and accessible and strategically placed equipment and technologies within the classroom or school environment. Other considerations to facilitate accessible learning include alternative formats for class materials and teaching practices that accommodate for learners' differences and individual needs.

Ensuring Tools for Lifelong Learning

As students with disabilities progress through the educational system and into the adult world, opportunities for accommodations and support seem to diminish (Hemmingson & Borell, 2002; Stewart, Law, Rosenbaum, & Willms, 2001). It is essential that practitioners and researchers realize the need and demand for a shift in service delivery from teaching transition skills to providing opportunities and experiences that promote self-determination (Stewart et al., 2001). In these efforts, it is essential that young adults are aware of the tools available for lifelong learning. This can be accomplished through collaborative planning and interactive decision making involving a network of people/resources and engaging youth with physical disabilities in making their own decisions on what is needed to be successful. Such decisions might include the use of assistive technologies to gain self-confidence and become self-reliant and responsible citizens.

Assistive Technology for Independent Living

The role that assistive technology plays in integrating students with physical disabilities in educational environments is significant. As outlined earlier in this chapter, research and "best practice" support the use of assistive technology in schools for providing accessible course materials and alternate teaching strategies as well as providing an accessible means to participate in class activities and assignments (Browning, 2002; Hemmingson & Borell, 2002; Knight & Wadsworth, 1993). Thus, students who successfully use their assistive devices may have the potential to work better beside their classmates as equals and become active members of the class environment. However, the complex orthopedic and health needs of students with physical disabilities greatly im-

pact these experiences and create additional goals and objectives for independent living. Thus, assistive technology may play an equal, if not a more crucial role in providing access for students to successful experiences that enable personal growth.

Today's schools provide independent living experiences through services such as (a) vocational coursework for supporting career options; (b) related services for supporting self-help, mobility, or communication skills; and (c) extracurricular activities for supporting social skills, recreation, and a sense of community. The extent to which these services are successful in fulfilling the needs of individual students who have varied physical and health issues remains a question. For these students, school services not only require individualization to meet child-specific goals and objectives through increased knowledge, time, and responsiveness on the part of school personnel, but continued support and research from all related disciplines for sound methods of implementation.

The following review of the literature shows research evidence of the effectiveness of assistive technology as a successful implementation strategy for addressing specific areas of independent living: self-help, social skills, transition, and mobility. The ways in which these assistive technologies impact an individual's functional independence are diverse and often connect and/or encompass multiple areas of school-related activities (Browning, 2002; Hemmingson & Borell, 2002; Knight & Wadsworth, 1993).

Self-Help Skills at School

All children begin school with a range of the self-help skills required for becoming more independent. Typical kindergartners still have bathroom accidents, are often unable to tie their shoes or button their coats, and frequently find it difficult to express their desires and needs without impulsive interruptions, tears, or physical outbursts. Children who have physical disabilities enter school with an even greater range of self-help skills. Because these children either have motor skills that are restricted by limited or distorted movement or completely lack movement in their motor repertoire, they need greater assistance in skills often expected from kindergartners such as toileting, eating, and communicating. Thus, schools not only find it necessary, as required by law (IDEA, 1997), to address these deficit areas. Teachers as well as classroom assistants are to provide instruction and assistance to children who are identified as having a deficit in areas of self-help, as noted within each child's Individualized Educational Program (IEP).

To better understand the needs of school-aged children and the effects on the delivery of therapy services, Pollack and Stewart (1998) conducted a study involving parents, teachers, and school-aged children with physical disabilities. Results from a published interview battery known as the Canadian Occupational Performance Measure (COPM) with all three groups of participants showed two specific trends, suggesting that (a) in general, children's self-help issues lessened in priority as they got older; and (b) children with less severe disabilities indicate a greater number of problems. Discussions to explore why children with less severe disabilities report greater problems suggested that perhaps higher expectations are placed on these children, with more latitude for problems to arise. A second, more in-depth interview was conducted with only parents and teachers. Results revealed that self-help difficulties in children with physical disabilities are indeed most significant, with teachers tending to place higher priority on these skills than parents (e.g., communications, toileting, eating).

In addition to problem identification, Pollack and Steward's second objective was to look at perceptions and expectations of related service providers (i.e., therapists). In general, they found that parents, teachers, and students alike value team involvement and communication. As defined in the IDEA '97 Law and Regulations (Part A: Sec. 602. Definitions):

The term 'related services' means transportation, and such developmental, corrective, and other supportive services (including speech-language pathology and audiology services, psychological services, physical and occupational therapy, recreation, including therapeutic recreation, social work services,

counseling services, including rehabilitation counseling, orientation and mobility services, and medical services, except that such medical services shall be for diagnostic and evaluation purposes only) as may be required to assist a child with a disability to benefit from special education, and includes the early identification and assessment of disabling conditions in children.

Related service personnel are the persons who most likely are evaluating and providing assistive devices support independent self-help by students with physical access issues. Stoller, (1998) depicts the influence that assistive devices have on early human development (see Figure 1). She shows the relationship between technology and human development along with information on skill development and low-tech solutions for school personnel who work with children with disabilities.

The literature shows that these related service fields (e.g., physical therapy, speech pathology, occupational therapy) extensively use assistive technology to augment their services. Examples for occupational therapists include support to enhance neurodevelopmental therapy (Law, Russell, Pollack, Rosenbaum, Walter, & King, 1997) and to provide environmental control (Williams & Loebl, 1995). For physical therapy the literature focuses on the use and benefits of various assistive technology to improve physical therapy goals for students (Herman-Hilker, Hilker, & Levine, 1995). Speech pathology has of late, been inundated with assistive technology ranging from low-tech solutions to more complicated augmentative communication devices and their use in the world of telecommunications (Simpson, 1998).

Despite the growing presence of assistive technology in the research literature, it appears that the actual implementation within the schools is still insufficient. In a recent study, Hemmingson and Borell (2002) found that students with physical access issues were restricted from school activities. For example, many problems identified by students through interviews focused on the typical school activity of changing classes. Specifically, this process created barriers for these students when they had to

Figure 1. The influence of assistive devices of the developmental cycle of human occupation.

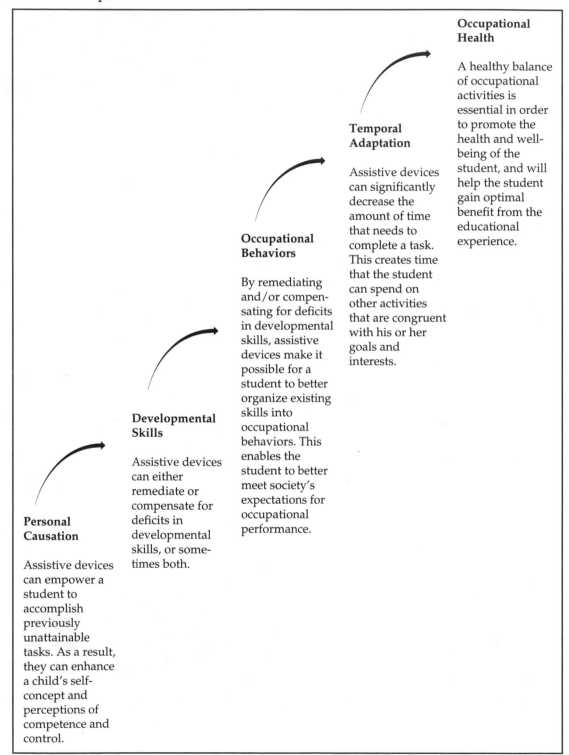

Occupational Health

A healthy balance of occupational activities is essential in order to promote the health and well-being of the student, and will help the student gain optimal benefit from the educational experience.

Temporal Adaptation

Assistive devices can significantly decrease the amount of time that needs to complete a task. This creates time that the student can spend on other activities that are congruent with his or her goals and interests.

Occupational Behaviors

By remediating and/or compensating for deficits in developmental skills, assistive devices make it possible for a student to better organize existing skills into occupational behaviors. This enables the student to better meet society's expectations for occupational performance.

Developmental Skills

Assistive devices can either remediate or compensate for deficits in developmental skills, or sometimes both.

Personal Causation

Assistive devices can empower a student to accomplish previously unattainable tasks. As a result, they can enhance a child's self-concept and perceptions of competence and control.

Adapted from: Stoller, L.C. (1998). *Low-tech assistive devices: A handbook for the school setting.* Farmington, MA: Therapro.

transfer to different floors, change buildings, or carry books, computer equipment, and other assistive technologies through the school environment. The incidence of these problems increased with student age, supporting the notion that as students move up in grades toward high school, they tend to move about the school building more often. While solutions for reducing these barriers can also be found in the literature (Schaff & George, 2002) in the form of various equipment and implementation strategies, it cannot be overstressed that professional competence is an essential component in the successful inclusion of students with physical disabilities.

Social Skills

Being socially competent is an art we all strive for. It often determines how our needs are met, how our relationships with others progress, and how our feeling of belonging is maintained. Social skills are so important that friendship itself is identified as one of the most basic aspirations parents have for their school-age children (Ontario Association for Families of Children with Communication Disorders, 2002). Individuals of all ages struggle with social skills, so much so that there are endless numbers of support groups, consultant organizations, training packages, and writings on the topic.

Children from preschool to high school are inundated with different social situations that they are expected to deal with in appropriate ways. Children with physical disabilities often have issues that limit their ability to participate in social situations (Hemmingson & Borell, 2002). For example, they may have communication deficits that hinder their ability to talk with peers. Physical conditions may restrict them from playing on the floor, listening to music, or throwing a ball. Children who are limited visually may find it difficult, if not impossible, to actively participate in reading books, taking pictures, or playing sports.

All children should have fun, make friends, and be social. Therefore, integrating children with disabilities into school-related social situations should be equally important as their access to academics. Play is essential for a healthy developing child. Play itself is a pre-

requisite to most adult life activities, and self-esteem and self-concept benefits for all people are widely found in the literature. Yet play and physical activity is often denied to children with disabilities for reasons ranging from fear of injury to the inability to locate physical access solutions. Limiting play and recreational activities due to physical access restrictions is no longer a valid practice, however. There are numerous means of physical access to almost any recreation or leisure activity from modifications of rules and procedures to assistive technologies that enable full or partial participation in recreation activities.

In support of individuals with physical disabilities participating in sports and recreation, the American Academy of Orthopedic Surgeons (AAOS) has created a chart relating potential sports and recreation activities with individuals who have various functional disabilities (see Figure 2). Surgeons noted with each functional disability area whether that sport activity would be appropriate in terms of participation, and if so, how it should be approached, recommended, individualized, adapted, or not recommended. Numerous assistive technologies are now available for making the adaptations and individualizations suggested by the AAOS. Assistive technologies that may be suitable for enabling children in physical education classes as well as extracurricular events need to be fully researched and tried in an effort to completely integrate all children into the social, physical, and health benefits of sports, recreation, and leisure activities.

School is often the first environment where children are challenged socially. Here they meet and have to interact with strangers; they have to share materials, attention, and time; and they must manage it all within a structured environment that is controlled by someone else. Several studies have tested positive social interactions using computers with young children. In 1989, Spiegel-McGill, Zippiroli, and Mistrett researched the need for adaptations in play materials to enhance social opportunities. They observed play between children with and without disabilities during three staged situations: without interactive manipulatives, with computers, and with

Figure 2. Sports and recreation participation possibilities for individuals with selected functional disabilities

Sports & Recreation

Participation Possibility Chart

	Archery	Bicycling	Canoeing/Kyaking	Fishing	Golf	Sailing	Skiing (downhill)	Table Tennis
Amputations								
Upper Extremity	A	R	A	R	A	R	R	R
Lower Extremity (AK)	R	R	R	R	R	R	A	R
Lower Extremity (BK)	R	R	R	R	R	R	R	R
Cerebral Palsy								
Ambulatory	R	R	R	R	R	R	A	R
Wheelchair	R	I	R	R	I	R		R
Spinal Cord Disruption								
Cervical	A		A	R		R	A	A
High Thoracic (T1-T5)	R		R	R	A	R	A	R
Low thoracolumbar (T6 - L3)	R		R	R	A	R	A	R
Lumbosacral (L4-sacral)	R	R	R	R	R	R	R	R
Neuromuscular Disorders								
Muscular dystrophy	A	I	I	R	R	R	I	R
Spinal muscular atrophy	A	I	I	R	R	R	I	R

Key: **R** =Recommended   **A** =Adapted   **I** =Individualized   **NR** =Not Recommended
       Blank =No information or not applicable

Adapted from: Participation Possibilities Chart, The American Academy of Orthopedic Surgeons.

remote-controlled robots. Computers appeared to facilitate social interactions with children who were identified as having moderate to severe social deficits. In 1994, similar study was conducted involving researchers from the previous study (Mistrett, S. G., Constantino, S. Z., & Pomerantz, D.). This project, also involving 4- and 5-year-olds with physical disabilities and peer playmates, resulted in a greater demonstration of the computer as a social facilitator.

During adolescence, students with disabilities, like their peers, are dealing with increased social needs. However, those with physical disabilities are not as likely to be socially independent (Pollack & Stewart, 1998). A comparison study of young adults with and without physical disabilities, ages 18-25, showed that those with physical challenges had a significantly higher rate of severe social difficulties (Thomas & Bax, 1988).

For these reasons, school personnel should be keenly aware of the importance of implementation strategies and assistive technologies that promote social competence for their students. Social training can be a component of the educational schedule for students who require more intense, direct instruction. However for those who need little encouragement and can make their own generalizations into multiple environments and situations, it can be transparent and integrated naturally throughout the school day.

Transition

The movement from school to adulthood, whether to a postsecondary institution, vocational training establishment, group home living environment, or work, is a huge step for all young persons. Students who have physical disabilities find themselves in even more extreme circumstances. A recent qualitative study sampling 34 individuals experiencing transition (Stewart et al., 2001) reported that they all felt extremely unprepared and inapt for the adult world they were entering. They described the adult world as having two different divisions: those with disabilities and those without. This distinction was significant for these young people and their parents, for it sets the attitudinal differences among the general population, affecting the social and institutional environments around them. It was also noted that environments such as health care, social services, and transportation all abruptly change once an individual becomes 21 years old. Services as well as assistive technology devices are seldom transitioned in a smooth fashion, if transitioned at all. These youth expressed a need to be directly involved in the tools and supports necessary for a more fluid transition into adulthood.

Mobility Within Schools

Historically, assistive technology has played a crucial role in mobility. Accounts of wheelchairs for individuals with disabilities can be found as far back as the sixteenth century (Sawatzky, 2002). King Phillip II (1595) of Spain used a rolling chair with footrests so that other persons could move him about. Stephen Farfler, a watchmaker who was paraplegic, built his own personal manual wheelchair when he was 22 in 1655 (see Figure 3). John Dawson, known as the wheelchair maker, invented a wheeled chair in 1783 that was used throughout that era by individuals who could not walk. By the time the United States had gone through two world wars, sending soldiers home with disabilities, wheelchairs and other ambulatory aids such as walkers, crutches, and mobility canes became more widely used (Bledsoe, 1980). However, it was not until the passage of the Education for All Handicapped Children Act (P.L. 94-142) in 1975 that mobility services and assistive technology became part of the education of children with physical disabilities.

Within the past 25 years, research has sup-

Figure 3. Stephen Farfler's wheelchair (1655).

ported assistive technology for independent mobility. Inman, Loge, and Leavens (1995) identified multiple sources of research demonstrating that self-locomotion plays a significant role in developing spatial perceptual abilities; that is, the localization of one's being in space. These cognitive abilities are not only necessary for mobility but also for other independent living activities such as self-help skills, vocational tasks and social interactions (Tefft, Guerette, & Furumasu, 1999). In addition, spatial abilities provide a foundation for skills needed in academic areas such as astronomy, geography, and geometry (Saads & Davis, 1997). Thus, for students who have a physical disability that limits their independent mobility, the goal for self-locomotion and spatial perceptual development becomes essential.

Individuals who have more severe orthopedic disabilities commonly use wheelchairs for mobility. It has been customary for the rehabilitation team involved in the treatment of these individuals to include the use of manual wheelchairs. For adults who are unable to self-propel, motorized wheelchairs are often used to achieve independent mobility. However, access to powered mobility by children is often limited to only those who successfully pass a hierarchy of a subjective set of prerequisite readiness skills. These skills seem to have been used arbitrarily to focus on the features and function of the powered wheelchairs available at the time. Thus, readiness was determined by the flexibility of powered chairs instead of the needs of children (Kangas, 2002; McNeal, 1994).

The focus of readiness, prerequisites, and trends toward approaching powered mobility for children are beginning to change. Research is supporting these changes by providing evidence that children as young as 11 months old can safely learn to operate motorized chairs (Jaffe, Butler, Hays, & Everard, 1986). Butler (1986) further supported the use of such mobility by indicating that power did not stop a young child's typical walking potential nor did it lessen the desire an older child has for walking as a form of ambulation for short distances.

Recent research has been conducted to develop various methods for teaching children to drive either prior to acquiring a powered chair or when receiving a powered chair. Inman et al. (1995) studied the use of virtual reality technology that has been successful in training airline pilots and astronauts, driving skills to teach children with orthopedic limitations the operation of motorized wheelchairs. The training involved a virtual reality system requiring children to be seated in powered wheelchairs positioned on rollers to simulate real movement during the training sessions. The children also wore a helmet–like technology that provided both visual and auditory displays of virtual experiences. Preliminary results showed that the system was most successful with young children who have orthopedic disabilities not accompanied by secondary limitations such as mental retardation.

Another indication of change is the shift towards powered mobility training that more resembles natural environments and supports given children in typical ambulation. Some rehabilitation professionals feel strongly that it is only when a child has powered mobility that ability can be proved. According to Kangas (2002), "it is the point of delivery of the chair at which treatment really begins. Training is treatment" (p. 2). She identifies six principles of training that should be taken into consideration when children acquire powered mobility:

1. Familiar environment, small space, parents first
2. Immediate success and independent control
3. Control of speed
4. Going and stopping vs. forward (turning as going, not circling)
5. Switch site/access
6. Forward direction/no reverse at first

Another growing interest in the field of mobility is the use of prosthetic technologies. Play is an essential piece of the curriculum for children in early childhood classrooms. All types of play (sensorimotor, social, constructive) contribute to the skills necessary to become an independent member of society. However, play most often requires movement, and for children who are limited by orthopedic disabilities, movement in play is hindered. Studies involved in providing support through prosthestic and orthotics to children during play are plentiful (Morris & Naumann, 1996; Parker, Naumann, & Cleghorn, 1993). Access to these mobility aids has resulted in successful participation as children are being integrated into play, not only in the classroom but also in physical education activities and during recess on playgrounds.

Despite all of the technology available to children with physical disabilities, mobility still remains a primary concern for students with these challenges. In a study by Pollack and Stewart (1998), parents, teachers, and students, independently identified mobility as the most significant problem in school, and this opinion appeared constant for students across all age groups. Further investigation into the reasons behind this concern should be conducted. Questions related to consumer knowledge, device access, geographical location, and assistive technology funding should all part of the investigation. This equation should also include consideration of successful implementation of assistive technology when the technologies are *not* balanced, leaning more towards person-centered solutions, therefore fixing the person, rather than adaptations necessary in the environment as a whole.

Education and Access to the Education Setting

One of the best predictors of academic achievement for students with disabilities is the opportunity for them to actively participate in instruction and the instructional environment (McDonnell, Thorson, McQuivey, & Kiefer-O'Donnell, 1997). Researchers have attempted to define what is meant by an effective instructional environment (Brophy & Good, 1986; McDonnell et al., 1997). While no uniform definition exists, findings have provided a detailed synthesis of organizational classroom strategies that maximize both the learning potential and classroom access for students with disabilities (Brophy & Good, 1986; McDonnell et al., 1997).

With the push in the disability field toward full inclusion, research on students with disabilities has typically focused on the individual student's needs rather than on the school environment itself (Hemmingson & Borell, 2002). The role that the physical environment plays in the participation of students with disabilities cannot be overstressed. However, this role is typically overlooked in the literature. The majority of studies that address physical access to school and classroom environments suggest that architectural barriers and inadequate access to assistive technologies are a great hindrance to overall accessibility (Parrett & VanBiervliet, 1990).

Universal Design

Throughout the twentieth century, the concept of Universal Design has evolved and developed. While the term was developed in reference to the outside and physical environment, its definition has grown to encompass inside environments, as well as academic and technology products. Universal Design was created as a result of the barrier-free movement in the 1950s which initiated a period of change in both public policies and in design of common environments. Initially, physical barriers were identified as a significant obstacle to individuals with physical and mobility impairments. Universal Design, a worldwide movement, is based on a foundation of beliefs that all environments, instruction, and products should be designed taking into consideration the needs of the greatest array of possible users (Connell, Jones, Mace et al., 2002). Other terms that are commonly used interchangeably with Universal Design include design for all, barrier-free environments, inclusive design, and lifespan design.

Universal Design is based on the following premises:

1. Being human entails varying abilities. These abilities are not unique conditions but common characteristics of physical and intellectual change that occurs in the typical lifespan.
2. If an environmental design works well for an individual with a disability, that same design will work well for an individual without a disability.
3. An individual's ability to function in the physical environment with a sense of autonomy, control, and comfort affects this same individual's self esteem and greatly affect his or her well-being.

Table 2. Accessibility Legislation Precursors to Universal Design

Legislation	Description
Architectural Barriers Act of 1968	Mandates that all buildings created, constructed, changed, or leased with the use of federal monies be made accessible be free of what was perceived as the most significant obstacle to employment for people with disabilities.
Section 504 of the Rehabilitation Act of 1973	This was the first civil rights law for people with disabilities. This act, which made it illegal to discriminate on the basis of disability, applied to federal agencies, public universities, federal contractors, and any other institution or activity receiving federal funds.
The Education for Handicapped Children Act of 1975	Also referred to as the Individuals with Disabilities Education Act, or IDEA, this act guarantees a free, appropriate education for all children with disabilities. This act has had an effect on educational programs, including the facilities in which they were conducted.
The Fair Housing Amendments Act of 1988	This act expanded the coverage of the Civil Rights Act of 1968 to include families with children and people with disabilities. The act requires that accessible units be created in all new multifamily housing with four or more units, both public and private, not just those receiving federal funds. Accessibility Guidelines were issued by the U.S. Department of Housing and Urban Development in 1991 to facilitate compliance.
The Americans with Disabilities Act of 1990 (ADA)	Awakened public awareness of the civil rights of people with disabilities. This law prohibits discrimination in employment, access to places of public accommodation, services, programs, public transportation, and telecommunications. Physical barriers that impede access must be removed wherever they exist. The ADA includes a uniform nationwide mandate that ensures accessibility regardless of local attitudes. The Architectural and Transportation Barriers Compliance Board (Access Board) issued Accessibility Guidelines for accessible design in 1991. These guidelines were adopted with modifications by the U.S. Department of Justice and became the enforceable ADA Standards for Accessible Design.
The Telecommunications Act of 1996	This act mandates that telecommunications services and equipment and customer premises equipment be "designed, developed, and fabricated to be accessible to and usable by individuals with disabilities, if readily achievable." It applies to all types of telecommunications devices and services, from telephones to television programming to computers.

Note: Adapted from Connell, Jones, Mace et al., 2002, Center for Universal Design, School of Design, North Carolina State University.

4. Usability and aesthetics are compatible. (Adapted from Connell, Jones, Mace et al., 2002, Center for Universal Design, School of Design, North Carolina State University.)

The onslaught of legislation supporting the design of public environments to meet the needs of individuals with disabilities began in the late 1960s. See Table 2 for a detailed description of the legislation dealing with accessibility that laid the foundation for universal design.

Universal Design in the School Environment

Access to the school environment for students with disabilities is of critical concern. Consider the following two scenarios of Jacqueline, a 12-year-old girl with athetoid cerebral palsy diagnosed at birth. Jacqueline has no functional use of her legs and has limited and spastic movements with her arms. She uses a sip and puff power wheel chair to move around her environments. First, she moves through her day in an inaccessible school environment (scenario #1) followed by a description of this same girl's school day in a universally designed and fully accessible environment (scenario #2) .

Scenario #1: Jacqueline is taken to school each day by one of her parents. She is unable to take the school bus because there is no way for her to get onto the bus without someone lifting her out of her wheelchair and carrying her into a seat and there is no way to get her wheelchair onto the bus unless someone lifts the chair; also there is no extra room for the wheelchair to be stored once on the bus.

At school, Jacqueline has to take herself around to the back of the school building in order for her to be able to enter the school since there are no curb cuts allowing Jacqueline to get up onto the front walkway to the school in her wheelchair. Once Jacqueline gets to the back door of the school, she has to wait for someone to open the door for her. Finally inside, Jacqueline makes her way down the narrow hallways of the school. She has to be careful not to bump into any kids, lockers, or anything else in the hallway. Most of the time, Jacqueline says that she simply waits by the door until the bell rings and the kids are in class, so that she can more easily and safely make her way to the classroom.

In the classroom, Jacqueline's teacher helps her to take off her coat, and then the teacher hangs up her coat and puts her bag and lunch away. Jacqueline cannot reach the coat rack, nor can she open the classroom refrigerator or locker because of the limited space and ways in which they open.

School begins with first period, which is computer lab. Jacqueline is unable to go to the computer lab because it is on the second floor and there are no elevators. Instead, she stays in the classroom and works at her desk while waiting for the rest of the class to come back. When the class returns, Jacqueline participates in her English class. Today the students are doing book report presentations, and when Jacqueline's turn arrives, the teacher simply tells her to do her presentation from her desk since "the aisles to the front of the room are too tight or else we will have to make everyone move their desks."

Before lunch, Jacqueline needs to use the bathroom. She is accompanied to the bathroom and assisted by an aide working at the school. At home, Jacqueline can transfer herself to the toilet; however, because of space limitations in the school bathroom, which does not allow for her wheelchair to even enter, Jacqueline must rely on the aide.

Recess is spent with Jacqueline seated in her wheel chair beside the teachers outside on the playground as she watches her classmates play on the equipment. After recess, Jacqueline concludes her day in her classroom with her classmates. However, she must leave early (even though the last subject of the day is her most difficult, science), because if she does not, she will have to dodge too many individuals in the hall and will be late for her parents to pick her up since she has to again maneuver herself around the school building to get back to the front where she is picked up. Sometimes she must sit and wait for someone to come and open the door for her.

Scenario #2. Jacqueline is picked up each morning by the school bus. The bus driver lowers the lift at the back of the bus and Jacqueline maneuvers herself onto the lift, which is then raised.

Once on the bus, Jacqueline's wheelchair snaps into an automatic secure lock that allows for total safety while the bus is in motion. Once at school, Jacqueline gets off of the bus after the lift is lowered and maneuvers herself up the curb cut onto the sidewalk and to the school main doors.

Once inside, Jacqueline makes her way down the wide hallways of the school. Her friends can even walk beside her because of the width of the hallway which allows for other students to walk around them.

In the classroom, Jacqueline takes off of her coat and hangs it on a coat hook that is at her shoulder height when she is seated in the wheelchair. She then puts her lunch away in the refrigerator, which opens to the side, allowing for optimal positioning and placement of her lunch, while she remains seated in her wheelchair.

School begins with first period, which is computer lab. Jacqueline takes the school elevator to the second floor. Next, she returns to the classroom and participates in her English class. The students are doing book report presentations, and when Jacqueline's turn arrives, she reverses her wheelchair away from her desk and maneuvers herself forward down a center aisle in the classroom, allowing her easy access to the front to deliver her presentation.

Before lunch, Jacqueline needs to use the bathroom. She takes herself to the bathroom and transfers herself to the toilet in the spacious and accessible school restroom.

At recess, Jacqueline remains in her wheelchair but maneuvers herself into the wheelchair-accessible swing. In this swing, she is seated beside her friends on other swings and is able to swing while remaining in her wheelchair. If she chooses not to swing, she can use her wheelchair and go up and down ramps onto and off of the jungle gym. After recess, Jacqueline concludes her day in her classroom with her classmates, and goes home on the same bus that she came to school on.

Environmental Adaptations and Considerations

Clearly Jacqueline's school days are very different, depending on which school she is attending. The two previous scenarios are true stories of one young girl before and after she attended a barrier-free or universally designed school. The difference in Jacqueline's ease of activity between when she attended the school in Scenario #1 and the school in Scenario #2 is tremendous. Just as monumental was the difference in this young girl's self-esteem after she began her new school. Jacqueline's grades improved, her motivation improved, her friendships and social activities changed drastically for the better, and overall, Jacqueline was a much happier young adult.

The remainder of this chapter discusses different environmental factors that were mentioned in the previous scenarios. Additionally, a series of general considerations are listed for those wishing to evaluate, change, or closely examine their current situation.

Accessible Transportation

Transportation to and from school is often overlooked among school personnel. If there is no accessible transportation immediately available, parents usually take on the role of transporting a child in a wheelchair, for example. to and from school.

Consider the following with regards to a student's mode of transportation to and from school:

1. Is the current method of transport for the student to and from school ideal?
   a. Does the student travel in a manner most similar to other students in the school system?
   b. If not, is it for transport accessibility reasons?

2. Is the student able to independently or with as little support as possible get into and out of the vehicle?
   a. If the student requires assistance, is it as minimal as possible? Or is it for such things as lifting and carrying?
   b. Ideally, any support is precautionary or for safety reasons, more than for actual lifting and carrying.

3. Is the method of transport safe? Are there:
   a. Locks for wheelchairs on busses or in vans?
   b. Safety belts
   c. Ramps or lifts for wheelchairs instead of stairs (see Figure 4)
   d. Secure location for walkers, quad-canes, crutches, or any other assistive technologies

School Grounds

From the moment the student gets off of the

Figure 4. School bus with wheelchair lift.

bus, van, or out of their parent's vehicles, he or she is on the school grounds. Making the grounds accessible and barrier-free is critical for both starting the student's day on a positive note and, just the same, ending it on a positive note. Ease of transport into and out of the school building is a necessary consideration when looking at the overall accessibility of the school environment.

Curb cuts are a good example of a necessary accommodation for those who can not step up 6-12 inches off of the ground for reasons such as lack of strength, use of a wheelchair or for safety reasons for someone who is visually impaired and cannot identify a drop-off or step-up depending on where he or she is coming from. For the same reason, ramps are necessary for those who have difficulty or are unable to climb stairs.

The placement of automatic door openers to assist those with limited strength or who are in a wheelchair and cannot open a door while simultaneously backing up the wheelchair and holding the door for entrance into the school. Also, for a student with a broken arm, or for a teacher on crutches carrying a bag of school supplies and lesson plans, automatic door openers are of great help (see Figure 5).

Consider the following with regard to the accessibility of entering and exiting a school:

1. Are the school grounds, driveway, and sidewalks level and without potholes or other obstacles that can cause safety or inaccessibility issues?

   a. Walk from the front door of the school to the back playground or to another school door while blindfolded (with a spotter, of course) and identify obstacles that could be a safety hazard.

   b. Try the same exercise using a wheelchair and identify any obstacles preventing you from accessing a certain location.

     i. Is there a step up to the playground?

     ii. Is there a step down from the front door?

2. Are there alternatives to all stairs and curbs?

   a. Are there curb cuts?

   b. Are there ramps?

3. Are there automatic door openers for those who are unable to open the doors manually?

Figure 5. Door with automatic door opener.

4. Are the doorways wide enough to allow an individual in a wheel chair comfortable entering and exiting through the doorway?

Inside the School

Once inside the school building, there are numerous considerations for ease of access. Making the inside of the school as safe as possible is of extreme importance. Additionally and ideally, the school environment will be as comfortable and as inviting as possible. In such an environment, space is generous for mobility and socialization, and the entire school is accessible to all students.

Consider the following with regard to the accessibility of maneuvering around and throughout the school environment:

1. Are the hallways wide enough to allow for an individual in a wheelchair to transport him or herself (or to be transported) during a busy time without feeling overwhelmed or crowded?

2. Are all doorways at least 35 ½ inches wide to allow for ease of entering and exiting if in a wheelchair?
3. Are there automatic buttons for the water fountains, toilets, soap dispensers, and doorways?
4. Does the bathroom allow for enough room for transfers to take place from a wheelchair to a toilet?
a. Does the bathroom allow for enough room for this transfer and for an aide's presence and assistance, if necessary?
5. Are their alternatives to steps within the school building (i.e. an elevator, ramps, stair lifts)

Classroom Setup

When designing a classroom with accessibility, a couple of key concepts must be kept in mind. First and foremost, is the space within the classroom set up to allow for optimal performance by all students within the class? Is there enough room between desks, lockers, and various classroom stations so that an individual in a wheelchair can easily maneuver from one place to another? The setup of the classroom is of primary concern. This also includes placing necessary items, including coat racks, shelving and bulletin boards, at a reachable level for an individual who remains seated and functioning from a wheelchair.

Consider the following with regard to setting up an accessible classroom environment:

1. Does the classroom set-up allow for ease of transport from all locations to all other locations for individuals in wheelchairs, on crutches, with walkers, etc.?
2. Are all shelving, coat hooks, and lockers at a reachable level for an individual in a wheelchair so that he or she need not rely on the assistance of a teacher or another student?
3. Do lockers and refrigerators open so that an individual in a wheelchair can actually open the door and still either take something out or put something in independently?
4. Are all bulletin boards, artwork, signs, etc., at eye level for someone in a wheelchair?
5. Are doorways wide enough for comfortable entrance and exit using a wheelchair (usually 35 ½ inches)?

School Playground

There are many options for designing a playground to meet the needs of an individual with a disability. Considerations similar to those applied to other areas of the school environment are necessary. For example, it is necessary to consider whether or not the design of the playground allows an individual with a disability with as much independence as possible.

1. Is the playground designed to allow an individual with a disability to participate in the various activities? (see Figure 6)
a. Another way of asking this is: Is there more for an individual with a disability to do than to sit beside a teacher while the remainder of the students play on a playground or play basketball, etc.?
2. Are there alternatives to steps?
a. Ramps, lifts?
3. Is the environment designed with safety in mind? Is the ground concrete with potholes or is it comprised of a foam outdoor floor, or covered with soft wood chips?

Conclusion

A plethora of considerations need to be made when evaluating the accessibility of a specific environment specifically, a school environment. In addition, the time that it takes and the costliness of such changes are often extensive. However, time and money are far outweighed by the benefits of providing each student with as many opportunities for independence as possible. For with independence comes self-esteem, self-belief, socialization, academic improvements, and above all, the association of school as a safe and comfortable place.

In considering the accessibility of school environments for students with physical disabilities, areas that merit consideration include, but are not limited to, the physical outdoor environment, the inside environment, the school curriculum, and technology that promotes social and academic engagement in the school setting.

Upon identifying these areas, it is necessary to address any barriers. Within this chapter, a variety of methods have been suggested

Figure 6. Accessible playground for individuals with disabilities.

for targeting these accessibility areas, ranging from high technological solutions to low and no tech solutions. These solutions pertain to the use of various equipment and implementation strategies. However, the importance of professional competence cannot be underestimated as an essential component to the success of students. While no uniform solution exists in addressing these issues, what is imperative is for educators and all school personnel to remember that there is a way to overcome each and every barrier. Some solutions may not come as readily or easily as others, but determination and dedication to equal access to the school environment for all students is imperative.

References

Bledsoe, C.W. (1980). Originators of orientation and mobility training. In R.L. Welsh & B.B. Blasch (Eds.), *Foundations of orientation and mobility* (pp. 581-624). New York: American Foundation for the Blind Press, Inc.

Brophy, J.E., & Good, T.L. (1986). Teacher behavior and student achievement. In M.C. Wittrock (Ed.), *Handbook of research on teaching* (3rd ed., pp. 328-275). New York: MacMillan.

Browning, N. (2002). Literacy of children with physical disabilities: A literature review. *Candian Journal of Occupational Therapy, 69*, 176-82.

Butler, C. (1986). Effects of powered mobility on self-initiated behaviors of young locomotor disabled children. *Developmental Medicine Child Neurology, 28*, 325-332.

Connell, B.R., Jones, M., Mace, R., Mueller, L., Mullick, A., Ostroff, E., Sanford, J., Steinfield, E., Story, M. & Vanderheiden, G. (2002). Principles of Universal Design. Retrieved January 25, 2004, from Center for Universal Design, School of Design, North Carolina State University Web site: www.design.ncsu.edu/cud/univ_design/princ _over view.htm

De La Paz, S. (1999). Composing via dictation and speech recognition systems: Compensatory technology for students with learning disabilities. *Learning Disability Quarterly, 22*, 173-182.

Foley, B. E. (1993). The development of literacy in individuals with severe congenital speech, a motor impairment. *Topic in Language Disorders, 13*, 16-32.

Frith, G. H., & Edwards, R. (1981). Misconceptions of regular classroom teachers about physically handicapped students. *Exceptional Children, 48*, 182-185.

Hart, R. D., & Williams, D.E. (1995). Abled-bodied instructors and students with physical disabilities: A relationship handicapped by communication. *Communication Education, 44*, 140-154.

Hemmingson, H., & Borell, L. (2002). Environmental barriers in mainstream schools. *Child: Care, Health, & Development, 28*, 57-63.

Hemmingson, H., Borell, L., & Gustavsson, A. (1999). Temporal aspects of teaching and learning implications for pupils with physical disabilities. *Scandinavian Journal of Disability Research, 1*, 26-43.

Herman-Hilker, S. L., Hilker, D. F., & Levine, S. P. (1995). Achievement of physical therapy goals as a result of assistive technology use. *Proceedings of the RESNA 1995 Annual Conference, Vancouver, British Columbia.*

Higginbotham, D.J. (1992). Evaluation of keystroke saving across five assistive communication technologies, *Augmentative Alternative Communication, 8*, 258-272.

Higgins, K., & Boone, R. (1996). Special series on technology: An introduction. *Journal of Learning Disabilities, 29*, 340-343.

Inman, D., Loge, K. & Leavens, J. (1995). Virtual reality solutions for children with physical disabilities. *Proceedings of the*

MASEVR 2nd International Conference. Retrieved December 30, 2002, from: *www.ori. org/~vr/publications/masevr-95.html.*

Jaffe, K. M., Butler, C., Hays, R. M., & Everard, D.H.S. (1986). An innovative motorized wheelchair for young disabled children. *Journal of the Association of Children's Prosthetic-Orthotic Clinics, 21*(3), 46.

Kamenetz, H. L. (1969). *The wheelchair book. Mobility for the disabled.* Springfield, IL: Charles C. Thomas.

Kangas, K. (2002, March). Powered mobility training for children with complex needs. Proceedings of the 18th International Seating Symposium. Retrieved December 30, 2003, from: www.cw.bc.ca/sunnyhill/ SeatMob/index.htm.

Knight, D., & Wadsworth, D. (1993). Physically challenged students. *Childhood Education, 69*, 211-215.

Kotler A.L., & Tam, C. (2002). Effectiveness of using discrete utterance speech recognition software. *Augmentative and Alternative Communication, 18*, 137-146.

Kraus, L. E. (1998). Teaching mathematics to students with physical disabilities using the world wide web: The planemath program. *Proceedings from CSUN Conference.* Available online www.csun.edu/cod/conf/1998/ proceedings/csun98_073.htm.

Law, M., Russell, D., Pollack, N., Rosenbaum, P., Walter, S., & King, G. (1997). A comparison of intensive neurodevelopmental therapy plus casting and a regular occupational therapy program for children with cerebral palsy. *Developmental Medicine & Child Neurology. 39*, 664-670.

Lewis, R.B. (1998). Assistive technology and learning disabilities: Today's realities and tomorrow's promises. *Journal of Learning Disabilities, 31*, 16-26.

Lewis, R.B., Graves, A.W., Ashton, T.M., & Kieley, C.L. (1998). Word processing tools for students with learning disabilities: A comparison of strategies to increase text entry speed. *Learning Disabilities Research & Practice, 13*, 95-108.

Light, J., & Kelford Smith, A.K. (1993). Home literacy experience of preschoolers who use ACC systems and of their nondisabled peers. *Augmentative and Alternative Communication, 9*, 10-25.

MacArthur, C.A (1998). Word processing with speech synthesis and word predication: Effects on the dialogue journal writing of students with learning disabilities. *Learning Disability Quarterly, 21*, 151-166.

MacArthur, C.A. (1999). Overcoming barriers to writing: Computer support for basic writing skills. *Reading and Writing Quarterly, 15*, 169-192.

Mastropieri, M. A., & Scruggs, T.E. (1993). *A practical guide for teaching science to students with special needs in inclusive settings.* Austin, Texas: Pro-Ed.

McDonnell, J., Thorson, N., McQuivey, C., Kiefer- O'Donnell, R. (1997). Academic engaged time of students with low-incidence disabilities in general education classes. *Mental Retardation, 35*(1), 18-26.

McNeal, D. R. (1994). RERC on technology for children with orthopedic disabilities. *Technology and Disability, 3*, 307-314.

Mistrett, S. G., Constantino, S. Z., & Pomerantz, D. (1994). Using computers to increase the social interactions of preschoolers with disabilities at community-based sites. *Technology and Disability, 3*(2), 148-157.

Montali, J., & Lewandowski, L. (1996). Bimodal reading: Benefits of a talking computer for average and less skilled readers. *Journal of Learning Disabilities, 29*, 271-279.

Morris, A. R., & Naumann, S. (1996). Human Movement Research Program, The Hugh MacMillan Rehabilitation Centre. *Development of a pediatric above-knee endoskeletal running prosthesis.* Retrieved December 28, 2002, from the Department of Veterans Affair Web site: www.vard.org/prog/96/ch01/ pr96020.htm.

Ontario Association for Families of Children with Communication Disorders (OAFCCD). (2002). *The social consequences of failure in communciation.* Retrieved December 28, 2002, from:www.oafccd.com/factshee/fact 74.htm.

Outhred, L. (1989). Word processing: Its impact on children's writing. *Journal of Learning Quarterly, 22*, 262-264.

Parett, H.P., & VanBiervliet, A. (1990). A prospective inquiry into technology needs and practices of school-aged children with disabilities. *Journal of Special Education Technology, 10*, 199-206.

Parker, K., Naumann, S., & Cleghorn, W. L. (1993). Human Movement Research Program, The Hugh MacMillan Rehabilitation Centre. *Analysis of a pediatric ankle-foot orthosis.* Retrieved December 28, 2002, from the Department of Veterans Affair Web site: www.vard.org/prog/93/ch11/pr93290.htm.

Pollock, N., & Stewart, D. (1998). Occupational performance needs of school-aged children with physical disabilities in the community. *Physical & Occupational Therapy in Pediatrics, 18*(1), 55-68.

Rich, Y., Linor, M., & Shalev, M. (1984). Perceptions of school life among physically disabled mainstreamed pupils. *Educational Research, 26,* 27-32.

Saads, S., & Davis, G. (1997). *Spatial abilities, Van Hiele levels and language use in three-dimensional geometry.* Retrieved December 28, 2002, from: www.soton.ac.uk/~crime/publications/gdpubs/PME1997.html.

Sawatsky, B. (2002). *Wheeling in the new millennium: The history of the wheelchair and the driving forces in wheelchair design today.* Retrieved December 28, 2002, from: www.wheelchairnet.org/WCN_WCU/SlideLectures/Sawatzky/WC_history.html.

Schaff, J., & George, C. (2002). "Don't high school students need assistive technology, too?" *Special Education Technology Practice, 4*(3), 22-25.

Scruggs, T.E., & Mastropieri, M.A. (1996). Teacher perceptions of mainstreaming/Inclusion, 1958-1995: A research synthesis. *Exceptional Children, 63,* 59-74.

Simpson, J. (1998). *How people who use electronic augmentative and alternative communication devices utilize telephony* [A Rehabilitation Engineering and Research Center on Universal Telecommunications Access Report]. Retrieved December 28, 2002, from:www.icdri.org/JeniferS/how_people_who_use_electronic_au.htm.

Soodak, L.C., Podell, D.M., & Lehman, L.R. (1998). Teacher, student, and school attributes as predictors of teachers' responses to inclusion. *The Journal of Special Education, 31,* 480-497.

Spiegel-McGill, P., Zippiroli, S. M., & Mistrett, S. G. (1989). Microcomputers as social facilitators in integrated preschools. *Journal of Early Intervention, 13,* 249-260.

Stewart, D.A., Law, M.C., Rosenbaum, P., & Willms, D.G. (2001). A qualitative study of the transition to adulthood for youth with physical disabilities. *Physical & Occupational Therapy in Pediatrics, 21,* 3-21.

Stoller, L. C. (1998). *Low-tech assistive devices: A handbook for the school setting.* Farmington, MA: Therapro.

Swiffin, A.L., Arnott, J.L., & Newell, A.F. (1987). Adaptive and predicative techniques in communication prosthesis. *Augmentative Alternative Communication, 3,* 181-191.

Tefft, D., Guerette, P., & Furumasu, J. (1999). "How important is mobility for your child?" *Exceptional Parent, 29,* 40-43.

Thomas, A. P., & Bax, M. C. O. (1988). The social skills difficulties of young adults with physical disabilities. *Child: Care, Health, and Development, 14,* 255-264.

U.S. Department of Education. (1997). *Nineteenth annual report to Congress on the implementation of the Individuals with Disabilities Education Act.* Washington, DC: Author.

Wepner, S. (1990). Computers, reading software, and at-risk eighth graders. *Journal of Reading, 34*(4), 264-268.

Williams, B., & Loebl, D. (1995). Case study: Adapting a TV/VCR control for a person with severe developmental disability. *Technology and Disability, 4,* 287-294.

Williams, L. J., & Downing, J.E. (1998). Membership and belonging in inclusive classrooms: What do middle students have to say? *The Journal of the Associations for Persons with Severe Handicaps, 23,* 98-110.

19

Accessible Information Technology and Persons with Visual Impairments

Richard Banks and Norman Coombs

People with visual impairments primarily comprise those who are blind or who have low vision. A significant difficulty for this special population is the difficulty in reading print material. As print material proliferated more and more in the last 500 years, the impact of this impairment became more debilitating. Only a limited amount of information was available in large print and even less could be obtained in Braille. As a result, there was a rapidly growing body of information that persons with visual impairment were unable to access independently.

Recently, since the beginning of the Information Age, more and more information has been produced in a digitized format, which means that it can be displayed in many different modes. The computer with special adaptive computer software and hardware permits information to be displayed in ways that is accessible to individuals with impairments. With its potential to reverse much of the negative effects of print impairments, this information access revolution has been called "liberation technology." Indeed, it is the most empowering tool to impact this special population in several centuries.

When implemented thoughtfully in schools and universities, access to information creates the most level learning platform that special students have had in modern times. By the same token, when teachers and staff fail to make the necessary adaptations, students will suffer from worse barriers than before. In employment, as computers become ubiquitous, adapting them for employees with disabilities has the potential to significantly reduce the deplorable unemployment rate for this population. In the activities of daily living, people have access now to newspapers, magazines, increasing numbers of books, and all kinds of public information ranging from store ads, to media program schedules, phone numbers, online banking and an ever-growing list of resources that are routinely part of people's lives today.

Society's treatment of people with visual impairments has also changed over this time period. At one time people with disabilities were hidden from view; either cared for by family or warehoused by the state in institutions with minimal care. Society treated them with a combination of prejudice, discrimination, and paternalism. The vision of a blind man begging on the street with a tin cup was not an uncommon occurrence. As wounded veterans returned home from the wars of the twentieth century, they felt that their country owed them a better life than what was widely available to them. Further, during the Civil Rights Movement people who were variously disadvantaged and discriminated against insisted that they be treated more fairly and that they be given more control over their own lives. Paternalism was not enough; they demanded empowerment. At the same time, a host of technological inventions made it possible for people with disabilities to do more things for themselves, thereby depending less on assistance from others. Information technology is one of the recent innovations that has the potential to increase the independence of people with visual impairments.

Adaptive Computer Hardware and Software

Adaptive or assistive software and hardware refers to tools that provide alternative display modes to the traditional computer display, making that information accessible to users who are blind or who have severely restricted vision. This includes screen reading software that turns the display into synthetic speech and screen enlargement software that can greatly increase the size of items on the monitor. It also includes refreshable Braille displays, providing tactile access to what was displayed on the screen. Braille embossers provide hard copy Braille similar to the output of a printer. Further, optical scanners enable users who are visually impaired to input text from a print document into the computer where it becomes accessible. People with visual processing disabilities or cognitive disabilities have frequently found that screen enlargement and screen reader programs help them to comprehend information better. Users with motor impairments that otherwise prevent their using a standard computer now have access to alternative input devices such as on-screen keyboards, alternative keyboards, alternative mice, and voice recognition. In this chapter, we will focus on adaptive computer technologies are used by individuals who are blind or who are visually impaired.

Synthetic Speech

The arrival of the personal computer on the commercial scene was soon followed by synthetic speech hardware and software that turned text into computer code, which the hardware then interpreted as phonetic sounds. Speech synthesis is the artificial generation of the spoken word through computer-based hardware and software. A speech engine is a software program that runs on your computer and translates text into speech in real time. Synthetic speech, which has an unlimited vocabulary, employs mathematical algorithms to translate text into phonemes, which are the basic components of speech. These are rapidly assembled to generate sounds for letters, words, and phrases.

The earliest hardware products such as the Votrax, Echo, DecTalk, and their accompanying software, tended to mangle the pronunciation of many words. For example, it was common for a word like "Bible" to sound like "bibble" or "twofold" to be pronounced as "twofold." It took practice to understand the sounds as words in the first place, but, in addition, the listener had to learn to accommodate for the garbled pronunciations as well. Over the following years, the software that controlled the pronunciation improved especially as computer memory and speed also increased. Eventually, as sound cards have become a standard feature in personal computers, programmers have developed software synthesizers that function through the sound card and speakers, that are part of the computer right off of the shelf, so special hardware is no longer necessary.

Screen Reader

The screen reader is software that enables someone who is blind to have nearly total control of a computer. Many screen readers can be installed so that they start automatically, giving the user control of the computer when it is turned on. The screen reader coexists in memory with other software packages such as word processors, spreadsheets and Web browsers. The screen reader enables the user to hear keystrokes as they are entered at the keyboard and also lets the user hear what is displayed on the monitor. It is highly configurable and can be set up to meet specific requirements. For example, it can be set to read by letter, word, or line. Or it can be configured to read any portion of the screen with a single keystroke. This is useful for rapidly reading small segments of the computer screen, such as the program title, menu bar, current word or line. The screen reader can also read the entire contents of the monitor from top to bottom without interruption or without needing constant directions from the user.

Screen readers can be configured to work with many of off-the-shelf commercial applications software and can be programmed to automatically monitor and then read selected portions of the screen. For example, if a dialog box pops up on the screen, the screen reader can be programmed to automatically read the entire contents of the box, only the title, the default selection in the box, or whatever is required. The software usually comes with special configurations to work with common word processors, databases, spreadsheets, browsers, and other software.

Users who are blind find the mouse difficult or impossible to use, so they run the system through keystrokes instead. The operating system has built-in keyboard commands that give them control of both the operating system and all applications. A screen reader user has to learn both the special keystrokes that control the operating system and other keystrokes that give control of the features of each application. Fortunately, most software based on the graphical user interface have a common look and feel and use the same standard keystrokes for similar activities.

One of the most important features offered by today's screen readers is known as screen review mode. When the software is placed in this mode, the user can utilize the arrow and other navigation keys to reread what is on the screen or on parts of the screen without moving the actual cursor or focus. Users who can see are able to look around the display without moving the computer cursor, and users who are blind also need this ability. Further, the user has more than one window open at a time; it is possible to move between them with keystrokes.

The screen reader software also enables the user to manage such sound features as volume, rate, and pitch. It also provides control of the punctuation level and enables the selection of whether it speaks all punctuation, some punctuation, or none. It can be configured to pronounce numbers either as full digits or as decorative characters, and to indicate capital letters by using a higher pitch or by saying "capital." A sample of the host of commands for reading available in a screen reader include: Speak current character, Speak prior character, Speak next character, Speak current word, Speak prior word, Speak next word, Spell current word, and so on.

There are also special commands for special applications like spreadsheets. For example, the software can be configured to read row and column titles as the user moves from one cell to another. Although many programs work effectively with screen readers, not all applications are friendly to speech output. You should contact the vendor of any application (or any adaptive equipment) that does not work with your screen reader and make them aware of the incompatibility. Before making significant investments in software or hardware, users should determine that it is compatible with screen reader technology, or be sure it can return be returned for a full refund if the applications conflict.

Besides outputting the contents of a display to a speech synthesizer, screen reader programs can output the information through a refreshable Braille display. This is a hardware device that is usually attached to the bottom edge of the keyboard. It has a number of pins that can be raised and lowered in the shape of Braille characters. Sometimes the strip displays 20 characters or even an entire line of the monitor display at once. A button on the strip lets the user manipulate the refreshable display to reflect different portions of the monitor's content. Refreshable displays are expensive, but they can be indispensable if the user requires extremely accurate knowledge of what is on the screen. It is especially helpful if the speech output is not clear as to exactly what letter is being spoken.

Braille Embosser

A Braille embosser is the equivalent of a printer. That is, instead of putting ink on a page, the embosser makes Braille dots on special-quality Braille paper. To output Braille on an embosser, the user requires special translation software. Braille consists of a code of six dots that represent the alphabet and some other symbols. In addition, it includes a large number of standard shorthand abbreviations, which help to reduce the size of the output, as Braille is quite bulky. The translation software not only replaces the shape of a print letter with a set of dots, it also includes many of these shorthand abbreviations. Further, because of the bulk of Braille, a line of Braille does not contain as much as does a line of print. The translation software has to reformat the document for Braille output.

Braille Note Takers

Numerous Braille-based note takers are currently available for users who are blind, have low vision, or are deaf and blind. These devices are similar in many ways to pocket computers or Palm Pilots. Braille note takers use a Braille keyboards for input instead of a computer keyboard. Because Braille is a code of six dots, the keyboard consists of six input keys plus a few special command keys such as the "enter" key. The user presses a combination of keys simultaneously to make a single Braille character or abbreviation. Output can be either refreshable Braille or synthetic speech.

Braille note takers typically include word processing, calendar, phone list, print functions, and Internet capability. Most also offer direct compatibility with mainstream operating systems and permit documents created on a personal computer to be transmitted to the note taker for use on the road. This also works in reverse, allowing the user to create documents on the note taker and send them to the desktop computer.

Screen Magnification

Screen magnification software enables the personal computer to increase the size of the characters and images displayed on its video screen. Most screen magnification programs now also feature speech output and can provide magnification and speech at the same time. The typical magnification program is a memory-resident utility that is run immediately after the operating system is loaded. Adaptive software that is loaded right after system start allows the user to immediately take control of the computer.

A typical magnification software program can magnify the video display from about 2x to 20x. Magnification packages track the mouse and cursor, following it around the screen, which helps users to remain oriented within the document. Orientation in the document can be a significant problem. When the display content is enlarged many times, the computer monitor becomes, in effect, only a window peering into a small portion of that display. Some standard features that facilitate user orientation include letting the user set markers at different points in the display such as in the center and four corners. A keystroke will then move the focus to the selected point. Another feature leaves the display normal in the background while a selected portion of the display is enlarged in the foreground. Users can also alter font type, as well as foreground and background colors. Having the ability to hear the text spoken in synthetic speech while simultaneously looking at it in enlarged font assists many people with visual and cognitive processing disabilities as well as those with limited vision.

Optical Scanner and Optical Character Recognition

The scanner and optical character recognition software (OCR) provides possible access to print materials. While increasing numbers of books are created and available in electronic formats, much information is still only available in hard copy print. The scanner takes a picture of a print page. OCR software "looks" at that picture and attempts to break it down into letters and numbers, which then can be stored in the computer as text that can be manipulated in word processors, displayed on the monitor, or output through a speech synthesizer.

Flatbed scanners are readily available and relatively inexpensive. Most of them interface with personal computers using a standard SCSI or USB port. Besides connecting the scanner and computer, the user needs to install the drivers for the scanner that came packaged with it. After the OCR software that came with the scanner has been loaded, and the computer is ready to scan and read documents. Finally, special integrated scan and read applications that walk the user through the process of scanning, using OCR, storing the output, as well as reading it. For example, this software can inform the user who is blind when a scanned document is top-side up or sidewise and automatically correct it as necessary. The vendors providing these integrated packages also provide a stand-alone computer and scanner that can be run without having to know the computer operating system or the intricacies of screen reading software.

Creating Accessible Electronic Texts

Creating accessible electronic text materials for people with visual impairments is relatively simple, especially if the content itself is fairly simple and is being presented in a straightforward manner. More complex formats as well as documents including mathematics, images, tables, charts and graphics may require some special consideration.

Adaptive software has become very complex and sophisticated and is potentially able to handle complex content. However, especially in school situations, the creator has to be aware that the user with a disability may not be skilled enough in the intricacies of the adaptive software to be able to benefit from some of its more advanced features.

Word Processor Documents

All of the adaptive software types discussed in this chapter can be used easily to both write and read word processed documents. However, a screen reader turns text into speech but cannot analyze a picture, For example, creators should include a picture label and, frequently, also include a text description for users who are blind. Graphs are also pictures and, therefore, require a label and text description. If the graph requires the user to be able to analyze it in some detail, a text description may be inadequate. In such cases, it may be necessary to provide a tactile hard copy of the graph. We will deal with tactile graphic production later in the chapter.

Content that is prepared in columns poses a potential problem. Screen reading software normally reads from left to right across the entire screen. While the screen reader has the power to enable a user to deal with this format, avoiding it will guarantee that even a user with limited skill in using special software can access the document. However, when the content can actually be presented more clearly in a column format, its use is recommended. Charts and tables pose a similar problem. Therefore, columns and rows should be clearly labeled, and the table should be preceded by a brief summary or description of what the user will encounter.

If a document containing several columns will be output to hard copy Braille, it may create yet another problem. Because Braille is so large and bulky, all the columns may not fit across the Braille page, causing items from the right-hand columns to be placed on the next line under left-hand columns. Sometimes using landscape Braille embossing will solve the problem. If not, the material may have to be formatted differently for Braille output.

Creating Documents by Scanning Hard Copy

Scanners come in a wide range of prices and quality, but their cost is now generally very reasonable. A flatbed scanner works better than a handheld scanner. If the scanner will be used to scan large quantities of material, a higher speed scanner is recommended. The optical character recognition software that accompanies all scanners is also generally of a high quality. Scanning large quantities of loose sheets can be facilitated by adding an automatic feeder. When scanning a bound book, it is important to place it on the scanner surface as flat as possible to avoid losing text near the binding. It is also important that it be placed carefully to avoid accidentally including text a facing page.

The first thing to do after the document has been scanned is to run a spell checker on it. This will catch many of the OCR errors. For total accuracy, someone will need to proof it. If the OCR has introduced many errors into the document, inputting the document by hand could consume less time than correcting a badly corrupted text.

Adobe Portable Document Format (PDF)

PDF has become a common and popular way to provide documents. In the past, these documents could not be read by screen reading software, as they were essentially pictures of text, and not actual text, and as we have seen, screen readers cannot interpret images. Recently, however, Adobe has provided several solutions to this problem. One partial, imperfect solution is to use OCR software to analyze the image and attempt to recognize the text and create an accessible text document. However, the results of OCR analysis of a document are usually less than perfect, so to get an accurate document, someone has to manually correct the resulting product. The better solution is to create a file that will save both the text and an image of the text. Adobe has worked with the major screen reader vendors to enable their products access to the actual text in the PDF file. Having the actual text available also means that anyone can now do a word search of a PDF document to locate information quickly. Accessible PDF materials can only be produced by using a recent version of Acrobat, using any other software that will output a PDF document will not result in an accessible product. Moreover, having PDF documents also depends on the user who is blind having access to a recent version of the screen reading software. Unless content providers using PDF have the technical know-how to be certain that an accessible product will result, they should also create the document in another accessible format to guarantee its availability to a person with visual impairments.

Spreadsheets

Spreadsheets facilitate producing materials in a two-dimensional format. Screen reading software, however, functions best when interpreting linear, one-dimensional content. But the power of modern screen reader software enables it to aid a person who is blind in navigating a spreadsheet and understanding its contents. Actually, content that is conveyed audibly, unless it is stereophonic in nature, favors a linear presentation. The problem resembles the old image of the four blind men looking at an elephant, each grasps a part of it and misses the whole picture. When someone who is blind, encounters a spreadsheet, he or she hears the data one item at a time. On the other hand, someone with normal vision sees the whole and then analyzes the individual items in that context and must build a mental image of the whole part by part to get a complete understanding. Even when the screen reader can look at individual cells rather than reading across the entire line from left to right, the user who is blind has to put in extra effort to make sense of what the screen reader is verbalizing.

The person creating a spreadsheet can do several things to make understanding easier for the person who has visual impairments. If the user receives a brief explanation and overview of the spreadsheet, the task of constructing the mental image of the whole is simplified.

Such an explanation should include specifying which rows and columns contain row and column headings. Becoming familiar with the headers and their location is the first step in understanding the content. The creator should also avoid using unnecessary blank cells merely for format purposes. Otherwise, someone moving from cell to cell looking for content will waste a lot of time encountering blank cells. If the spreadsheet is used in an instructional situation, the student could benefit from being warned in advance that spreadsheets will be used as part of content delivery. This would allow the student to study the screen reader documentation beforehand to become familiar with its features.

Users with visual limitations using screen magnification software are in a similar situation. While they may be looking at more than one cell at a time, they may still only be looking at a small portion of the spreadsheet on the computer display. Thus, providing an overview of the spreadsheet in advance and avoiding unnecessary blank cells will help these users also. While outputting simple spreadsheets to hard copy Braille or in very large print is not a problem, outputting larger spreadsheets may distort the formatting and make the content meaningless.

PowerPoint/ Presentations

Normally, PowerPoint is not thought of as a means of providing electronic text. However, because it is used so widely and because the presentation itself is frequently shared with the audience, it is worth discussing briefly.

As of the writing of this chapter in late 2002, JAWS, the screen reader produced by Freedom Scientific, handles both the creation of and reading of PowerPoint slides quite well. Other screen reading software have severe problems accessing it. However, there is one rather simple solution. One of the choices in PowerPoint is to export the slides to other formats. If the presentation is exported to Word, for example, its text portions will become accessible to any screen reader.

Creating Hard Copy Mathematics and Tactile Graphics

Creating mathematics in electronic text is difficult because of the limitation of the ASCII computer code itself. Many mathematic symbols, especially in more advanced math, cannot be represented by the computer character set. Commonly, this is overcome by providing a graphic of the missing symbol. However, as we have seen, the screen reader cannot handle these symbols.

One solution would be to verbalize the symbol as well as displaying it, but complex math does not readily lend itself to a spoken presentation. Scholars have conducted research to find the best way to speak math formulae in order to be understood accurately. If this had been successful, it could have been adapted to being spoken by a synthesizer from the electronic document. The researchers had a reader in one room, while a listener was in the next room wearing a headset to listen to his colleague. The listener wrote down what he understood. Even after repeated trials, the results were still dismal. Complex math statements are extremely difficult to describe accurately. For this reason, the courts have ruled that, for students who read Braille, the school must provide complex technical information in Braille.

Even producing math in Braille is much more complicated than one might expect. Braille is a code of six dots, which imposes restrictions on what it can express conveniently. In addition, Braille is linear, whereas most math and technical material involves subscripts and superscripts, making it two-dimensional. The reader sees the formula as two-dimensional. Braille has symbols indicating that an item is either subscript or superscript, but it is all on a level line. Thus, the reader has to try to imagine what it should look like. However, the technical Braille problem was that Braille did not have symbols for many math items.

Dr. Abraham Nemeth, a blind mathematician, devised a special Braille notation for math, which is now the standard in North America. To produce technical Braille requires a Braillist who knows both math and Braille. As noted above, software to facilitate outputting Braille from an electronic document, can deal with both the standard Braille code and the specialized Nemeth Braille math code. However, this is complicated in two ways. First there are fewer letters across a Braille page, which requires reformatting the document. If this is done automatically by the software, it may make a mess out of important format features. Second, most Braille documents are written in a kind of standard shorthand. Inserting math into this shorthand is always a disaster. The software has to be told when to use shorthand Braille or when to switch to using the Nemeth Braille code. In many cases, the production of complex hardcopy Braille math should be outsourced to a vendor specializing in its creation rather than struggling with it without the specialized knowhow to do it efficiently.

Hard-copy tactile graphics are required in some technical courses to represent drawings, graphs, maps, and similar materials. Not only can a computer display give detailed graphs, drawings and maps, the computer also permits zooming on a particular region. It can use colors and shading to indicate special information and can give it a three-dimensional appearance. In such instances, not only will an alternative text tag for the image be inadequate, frequently a lengthy description will fail to convey important features. Hard copy tactile graphics can be an advantage but, as we will see, it is still lacking when compared to the visual displayed on the monitor.

Information conveyed by color and texture is difficult to translate into equivalent haptic information. Even the most skilled professional does not know how to make tactile representations of many such maps that are as informative to blind readers as the visual maps are to sighted readers. There are several problems. One is that haptic perception is much less detailed than visual perception. Another is that most people who are blind have little experience in reading tactile pictures. It is difficult to make tactile pictures that are very detailed without simultaneously making them confusing to blind readers. First, the creator of the tactile materials must simplify the complexities, and second, students who are blind must learn how to understand tactile materials.

Before looking at the electronic production of tactile graphics, it should be mentioned that a tactile representation of drawings, graphs, and maps can be created using common craft materials, for example, cutting and pasting paper, cardboard, string, metal foil, and so on, onto a heavy paper base. Heavy acrylic paint can be squirted through a syringe to make into intricate patterns of raised lines. The paint dries in about an hour. Some of the materials used to make the molds are common materials found in any home or school.

Several manufacturers of Braille printers sell computer programs that permit a user to print out graphic images. The owner or potential purchaser of a Braille printer should contact the dealer or manufacturer for information about such programs. Some programs allow a user to print graphs of functions on Braille printers. These programs may be used by blind people and are likely to be useful in advanced math and science. Sighted computer users can design graphics on almost any computer graphics program and can add Braille through the use of Braille Font packages available from Braille translation software vendors. Prof. Marie Knowlton, University of Minnesota, has modified a version of the MacPaint program for the Macintosh to include Braille fonts and useful tools for making graphics for blind people. Print hard copy images made with any of these programs may be transferred to swell paper from which tactile pictures can be obtained. The most efficient Braille embosser for producing tactile graphics is the Tiger Advantage by ViewPlus Technologies, which allows anyone, with or without sight, to create graphics using standard computer software and to output it in raised dot tactile graphics. The Tiger is only one of several tools developed by Dr. John Gardner, a physicist at Oregon State University who lost his sight in mid-career. Gardner has found the Science Access Project and is the recipient of several grants from the National Science Foundation.

Providing hard copy tactile graphics is not enough. The visually impaired person will benefit from training in using tactile instructional materials and will also be helped if provided with an overview and orientation points before starting to examine it. Most people who are born blind or who lose their sight at an early age have great difficulty understanding information presented in two-dimensional tactile pictures. Sighted children have to learn about parallax, representation of three-dimensional objects by two-dimensional projections, and use of spatial position in such things as maps and graphs. Children who are blind seldom have access to comparable tactile pictures and, therefore, do not develop these concepts. As a consequence, they often have great difficulty with topics such as geometry and function graphs that are typically taught using two-dimensional pictures.

The concept of using computers to facilitate access to two-dimensional information by people who are blind was pioneered by Dr. Donald Parkes, University of Newcastle, Australia, with the Nomad tablet. The Nomad is a touch-sensitive digitizing pad with a built-in voice synthesizer attached to a computer through a standard serial port connection. A tactile picture is mounted on the Nomad pad, and information about various portions of the picture is contained in an electronic file in the computer. When a user presses on some part of the picture, and information about that region is sent from the computer to be spoken by the speech synthesizer on the Nomad.

The Nomad is currently being sold in the United States by the American Printing House for the Blind. They also sell Nomad pictures with accompanying computer files that they have made to illustrate several subjects studied by blind children. Users can also prepare their own pictures by any method and program in the information using software tools supplied with the Nomad. Anybody, sighted or blind, who can use a computer can prepare these computer maps.

Dr. Parkes has recently introduced two new computer programs that greatly extend the usefulness of the digitizing pad. AudioCAD is a computer graphics design program usable by both blind and sighted users. Blind users can design some things using voice and others using audio information, but AudioCAD is most useful when used with the Nomad or other digitizing pads. The initial version of AudioCAD supports the Nomad and the Edmark TouchWindow. The TouchWindow is available from commercial computer hardware vendors and dealers who sell AudioCAD.

The other new program from Dr. Parkes is AudioPIX. This program allows blind or sighted users to construct computer files identifying various objects on tactile pictures mounted on either the Nomad or other supported digitizing pads.

Creating Accessible Online Content (Web, Email and Chat)

If the adaptive technology opened the Information Age to people with visual impairments, the advent of the Internet has opened the entire world for them to explore, enjoy, and enhance their lives and employment.

Web Accessibility

Before considering Web accessibility in a formal manner, readers are encouraged to try the following experiment to get an idea of a non-technical, more "human" perspective on Web pages. Be sure your computer shows a Web page. Use the browser's Internet option settings to turn off the display of images and pictures. Refresh the page, and the graphics should all disappear. Move your mouse out of reach and use the tab key to move from link to link on the page.

If the Web page is relatively accessible, when you tab to a link where there had been a graphic, there will now be a text label explaining the graphic. For example, where there had been a picture of the library acting as a link to library information, the word "library" should now appear. If the page was not designed and built with accommodations for users with disabilities, much of the information and many of the hyperlinks will no longer be accessible. Screen readers, which help users with visual impairments "read" what is on a computer screen, can only read text, not images. Therefore, hyperlinks that are graphics or icons, for example, will become "black holes" if they do not have appropriate text tags included. Some words that appear on the Web are, in fact, graphics of words rather than text that a screen reader can interpret. Without text tags, these elements can also be lost to users with disabilities. Consider a Web page that is crammed with information, requiring you to look at it a second or third time to understand it. Now imagine the problems this sort of page presents for someone with low vision, poor color perception, or a learning disability.

The solution to providing access to the Web is not to make boring Web pages, but to learn how to use Web design tools to make attractive pages while still providing maximum accessibility for users with a wide range of disabilities.

In 1997 the World Wide Web Consortium (W3C), the international body that oversees the protocols and operations of the Internet, created the Web Accessibility Initiative (WAI). It has created a number of recommendations and tools including its Web Accessibility Guidelines and its Quick Tips. (This chapter will use the tips to briefly outline creating accessible Web content.) Newly released Section 508 standards, set forth by the Federal Access Board, offer an alternative for addressing accessibility of Web pages. The standards of Section 508 went into effect in June 2001 and are a federal procurement mandate for federal Web pages. However, Section 508 is also being widely accepted as a minimum standard to ensure accessibility.

WAI Ten Quick Tips – www.w3.org/wai

1. **Images & animations**. *Use the alt attribute to describe the function of all visuals.* Adding a text label to all images is by far the most useful and important feature you can implement to improve the accessibility of your Web pages. Screen reading software for the blind can output text to a synthesizer but cannot speak an image. The software usually indicates that there is a graphical element on the page, which, at least, lets the user know that there is something there. The HTML code for including an image and the added text tag looks like: <IMG src="NORM-PRO.JPG" alt="My Photo">. If you are using a WYSIWYG (what you see is what you get) editor, you will never see the HTML code. When you input the information for the image, you will usually see a text input box pop up. Probably you have always ignored it. Next time, try typing in a short label for the image. Providing access to your Web images can be just this simple.

2. **Image maps**. *Use client-side Map and text for hotspots.* There are both client-side and

server-side image maps. The server-side maps are not readily accessible to adaptive software. However, the server-side image maps require implementation by a system operator, and these are falling out of use. The hot spots on image maps are essentially images. You can add text labels to the hot spots making them totally accessible for screen reading software.

3. **Multimedia**. *Provide captioning and transcripts of audio, descriptions of video, and accessible versions in case inaccessible formats are used*. Audio is inaccessible to people who are Deaf. Providing a text transcription will permit these individuals to access the information. Non-disabled users frequently like to print transcripts so they can study the material and add personal notations to it. The audio of video is likewise not available to the Deaf. Transcriptions are not adequate in this case. Having the text displayed simultaneously with the pictures is usually necessary for full understanding of the video. Internet streaming captioning is required in this case. Video descriptions for users who are blind may also be necessary. When the voice track of a video does not adequately carry the meaning of the video, a video description must be added. However, because video can communicate both visually and verbally, it can provide information in redundant modalities and increase accessibility. This dual communication frequently also facilitates communication across cultural and linguistic barriers.

4. **Hypertext links**. *Use text that makes sense when read out of context. For instance, do not use "click here."* When a user who is blind is navigating a Web page, he or she cannot use the mouse. The tab key will jump the point of focus on the screen from link to link on the page. If there is text content between hot spots, the synthesizer does not read that during navigation but speaks the next link as it gets highlighted. If the text for the link does not make sense out of context, what the blind person hears has limited meaning. Using "click here!" is a famous example of what to avoid.

5. **Page organization**. *Use headings, lists, and consistent structure. Use CSS for layout and style where possible*. A well-organized page goes a long way to convey meaning. Pages that are cluttered make understanding harder for everyone. This is especially true for users with low vision, with learning disabilities, with cognitive problems, users of foreign languages, and so on. Simple pages layout where all ingredients reinforce the central message work best. When possible, use the same organization for all or most of the pages on your site. Once someone understands your general layout, new pages are more readily understood. The other layout comments in this tip are relevant only to those writing actual HTML code. The more pages are designed according to basic HTML code guidelines, the greater likelihood that adaptive software can handle the page. If your main Web master sets up templates for the Web, cascading style sheets (CSS) can be implemented to take care of many format issues permitting you to forget about them. Many WYSIWYG editors are notorious for writing cluttered code. FrontPage is among the worst. The real problem with cluttered code is that if you go to add access HTML features later, the page code can make this frustrating and difficult. Therefore, be sure to include access features when you first design a page using your WYSIWYG editor.

6. **Graphs and charts**. *Summarize or use the longdesc attribute*. The simple text label used for images cannot begin to describe a complex graphic. Instead, you need some way to provide a longer description. The same is true for graphs and charts. There is a feature in the most recent HTML standards for writing long descriptions, but no browser currently this feature. However, you can put a link on the page to a "text description." Besides explaining the item for users who are blind, the text description will help anyone having trouble understanding the graph or chart, including learners with cultural and language barriers.

7. **Scripts, applets, and plug-ins**. *Provide alternative content in case active features are inaccessible or unsupported*. Teachers with some technical know-how frequently want to add a little dazzle to their material to make it

more attractive and to reduce boredom for the students. Not only does this frequently present problems for students using special adaptive software, it probably does not function well for students with older browsers and with slow connections. The caveat here is to make a point of providing such more "creative" content in some alternative format as well.

8. **Frames**. *Label with the title or name attribute.* Older browsers, text browsers, and older adaptive technology were not able to handle frames. Now, they can usually be accommodated. It is important to provide titles for frames. Visually, a page with frames uses the frames to convey some information such as one part of the screen being navigation links and another part being main content. The user of a screen reader does not get that context. A frame title like "navigation frame" can convey the same meaning.

9. **Tables**. *Make line-by-line reading sensible. Summarize. Avoid using tables for column layout.* Screen reading software reads from left to right across a page. Therefore, columns are turned into meaningless garble unless they make sense if read from left to right, such as in:

> hotel $100
> food $50

Recent screen reading software has the ability to read the HTML behind the computer monitor and to decolonize a Web page.

10. **Check your work**. *Validate the HTML. Use evaluation tools and text-only browsers to verify accessibility.* Accessibility experts maintain that validating the HTML code is the first and most important thing to do. Adaptive technology frequently cannot interpret poor HTML. Your Web authoring software will have the ability to validate your page's HTML. There are also accessibility validation tools. If you go on the Web to: www.cast.org/bobby and submit the URL for a page, Bobby will return an analysis of your page. Bobby is far from perfect, but it is a terrific place to start. Look at your pages with a text-only browser. Turn images off on your own browser, and look at your page. Finally, find some students with disabilities and use them as a focus group to help you test your pages.

Email and Internet Chat

Traditional email is totally accessible to users with visual impairments and adaptive technologies as it is essentially plain text. The addition of font, color, and format features are no problem for adaptive software to interpret. However, embedding images into a message does create a problem, as does attaching an image file. Therefore, when this done, it needs some description or explanation for users who are blind. Actually, email has proven a wonderful tool to help people with visual impairments increase contact with friends. If a person who is blind receives printed or handwritten paper mail, someone has to read it to that person. Email, in contrast, permits keeping in touch with friends totally independently, by means of assistive technology.

Online chat rooms are extremely popular with a portion of the public. Unfortunately, none of the generally available chat room systems is accessible using a screen reader. Either the screen reader does not speak the room content or it reads the entire screen content over and over every time something new is posted. A couple of chat room systems are in prototype development but they are not yet available. Instant messaging systems such as AOL Instant Messenger do have special scripts to facilitate access provided by the major screen reader vendors.

Summary

Digitized information is essentially display independent. While it is usually prepared to be output to a computer monitor or printer, it offers amazing flexibility in how it is used and permits being tailored to individual tastes and special needs. For example, the information can be displayed in extremely large fonts; it can have its foreground and background colors altered; it can be "spoken" by a speech synthesizer; it can be output to a printer using large font; it can be displayed with refreshable Braille; and it can be used to produce hard copy Braille on a Braille embosser. Information technology, when joined to special adaptive hardware and software, goes a long way to transcend the print disability endured for centuries by people with visual impairments.

Resources

*AbleData online database.*Sponsored by the National Institute on Disability and Rehabilitation Research, U.S. Department of Education, is an excellent online resource on adaptive computer products as well as a host of other assistive devices. Web: www.abledata.com/.

American Council of the Blind, a national membership organization. 1155 15th Street, NW, Suite 1004 Washington, DC 20005; (202) 467-5081; (800) 424-8666; Fax: (202) 467-5085; Web: www.acb.org.

American Foundation for the Blind 11 Penn Plaza, Suite 300, New York, NY 10001; (212) 502-7755; Web: www.afb.org.

American Printinghouse for the Blind, Braille publishing and source for daily living products, P.O. Box 6085, Louisville, KY 40206; (502) 895-2405; Fax: (502) 899-2274; (800) 223-1839 toll free; Web: www.aph.org.

National Federation of the Blind, a national membership organization. 1800 Johnson Street, Baltimore, MD 21230; (410) 659-9314; Web: www.nfb.org.

Hardware and Software

Ai Squared provide screen magnifier software. P.O. Box 669, Manchester, VT 05255 (802) 362-3612 Fax: (802) 362-1670; Email: zoomtext@aisquared.com; Web: www. aisquared.com.

ALVA Access Group Inc., provides refreshable Braille displays and both a screen reader and a screen magnifier for Mac as well as PC. 436-14th Street, Suite 700, Oakland, CA 94612; (888) 318-2582; Fax: (510) 451-0878; Email: info@aagi.com Web: www.aagi. com/.

Duxbury Systems Inc. provides Braille translation that translates text for output to Braille embossers. 435 King Street,Littleton, MA 01460; (978) 486-9766; Fax: (978) 486-9712 Email: duxbury@world.std.com; Web: www.duxburysystems.com.

Enabling Technologies provides several Braille embossers, 1601 Northeast Braille Plaza. Jensen Beach, FL 34957; (561) 225-3687; Fax: (561) 225-3299; Email: enabling@brailler. com; Web: www.brailler.com.

Freedom Scientific Inc. provides Braille displays, Braille embossers, screen reader and screen magnification, and many other products for people with visual impairments and learning disabilities. 11800-31st Court North, St. Petersburg, FL 33716; (800) 444-4443; Fax: (813) 528-8901; Email: info@freedom scientific.com; Web: www.freedom scientific .com.

GW Micro Inc., provides screen reader software. 725 Airport North Office Park. Fort Wayne, IN 46825 (219) 489-3671; Fax: (219) 489-2608 Email: support@gwmicro.com Web: www.gwmicro.com.

HumanWare Inc. provides refreshable Braille displays, Braille note taker and screen reader software. 6245 King Road, Loomis, CA 95650; (800) 722-3393; Fax: (916) 652-7296; Email: info@humanware.com; Web: www. humanware.com.

IBM Special Needs Center provides Home Page Reader, a talking Web browser. P.O. Box 1328; Boca Raton, FL 33429; (800) 426-4832; Email: snsinfo@us.ibm.com; Web: www.ibm.com/able.

ViewPlus Technologies produces the Tiger Advantage embosser and other scientific and math accessibility products. 1853 SW Airport Avenue, Corvallis, OR 97330 (866)836-2184; Fax: (541)738-6505; Email: info@viewplus.com; Web: www. viewplustech.com.

Web Accessibility Resources Bobby, is the best-known Web accessibility checker. Web: bobby.watchfire.com/bobby/html/en/index.jsp.

Rehabilitation Act Section 508 Web accessibility standards. Web: www.access-board.gov// 508.htm. World Wide Web Consortium Web Accessibility Initiative. Web: www.w3.org/wai.

Technology and Disability Conferences

Accessing Higher Ground (annual conference) - Assistive Technology and Accessible Media in Higher Education, University of Colorado at Boulder. Web: www.colorado.edu/sacs/ ATconference.

California State University Northridge, Technology and Persons with Disabilities (CSUN) (annual conference). Web: www.csun.edu/cod/.

Closing the Gap (annual conference on assistive technology and special education). Web: www.closingthegap.com.

Technology and Disability Online Training

EASI (Equal Access to Software and Information) provides 8 month-long, instructor-led online courses; completion of any five will lead to a Certificate in Accessible Information Technology given in partnership with the University of Southern Maine. P.O. Box 818, Lake Forest, CA 92609; (949) 916-2837; Fax: (949) 916-1013 Web: www.rit.edu/~easi.

VATU (Virtual Assistive Technology University) provides online courses in assistive technology for undergraduate or graduate credit through the University of Southern Maine, College of Education and Human Development. Web: www.alltech-tsi.org/initiatives/vatu/index.htm.

ALLTech/The Spurwink Institute Pineland Farms, 60 Pineland Drive, New Gloucester, ME 04260; (207) 688-4573; Fax: (207) 688-4036; Web: www.usm.maine.edu/alltech/what.htm.

Technology and Disability Internet Resources

The value of connecting with resources on the Internet is that they can be kept up-to-date in a way that is not possible for print resources.

AHEAD (American Association on Higher Education and Disabilities): Web: www.ahead.org.

DO-IT (Disabilities, Opportunities, Internet working, and Technology): Web: www.washington.edu/doit.

EASI (Equal Access to Software and Information): Web: www.rit.edu/~easi.

NCAE (National Center on Accessible E-Learning): Web: easi-elearn.org.

NCAM (National Center on Accessible Media): Web: ncam.wgbh.org.

NLS (National Library Service, Library of Congress): Web: lcWeb.loc.gov/nls/nls.html.

RFB&D (Recording for the Blind and Dyslexic): Web: www.rfbd.org

Trace Research and Development Center: Web: www.trace.wisc.edu

WebAIM (Keeping Web Accessibility in Mind): Web: www.Webaim.org

20

Assistive Technology in Education for Students Who Are Hard of Hearing or Deaf

Marcia J. Scherer

Hearing has been characterized as occurring on three psychological levels: (a) The *social or symbolic level*, which is the capability to receive and understand language (in other words, to communicate with others), (b) the *signal or warning level*, which enables individuals to respond to such cues as a fire alarm, and (c) the *level of fundamental "connectedness,"* which gives people the sense of being in touch with the surrounding environment even though perhaps not consciously aware of such sounds as people moving around the classroom, noise outside, and so on (Davis, 1997). It is the last level, the fundamental sense of connectedness, that gives quality to life and defines the world as being "alive." This "quality to life," this fundamental connectedness, and how it can be enhanced by today's technologies in light of current educational practices, are the themes of this chapter.

At a physical level, hearing loss can occur as a result of damage to any part of the ear: outer, middle, or inner ear (Dugan, 1997; Medwetsky, 2002; Mencher, Gerber, & McCombe, 1997; Myers, 2000; Scheetz, 2001). It can occur in only one ear or in both. When the damage or obstruction is in the outer or middle ear, the person experiences a *conductive* hearing loss. Ear wax build-up or infection of the auditory canal in the outer ear can lead to conductive loss. This typically results in a loss of hearing in the low-frequency ranges (the lower pitched, deep sounds) that provide volume but are less important for speech understanding. Middle-ear problems include

perforation of the eardrum and infection. Conductive hearing losses usually do not result in severe losses, and a person with this type of hearing loss can customarily use a hearing aid well since sound amplification of speech is the key intervention.

Sensorineural hearing losses commonly result from damage to the sensory apparatus (hair cells of the inner ear or the nerves that supply it) or to the auditory centers of the central nervous system by disease (for example, due to high fever and reactions to medications), trauma (including noise) and, most commonly, age-related losses in sensorineural sensitivity. Damage to the inner ear result in *sensorineural* loss, and the person will likely experience difficulty with high-frequency, high-pitched sounds such as with the soft consonants *s*, *f*, and *sh*. These hearing losses can range from mild to profound and even with amplification to increase the sound level, a person with a sensorineural hearing loss may perceive distorted sounds. The ability to clearly understand speech is diminished because parts of words and sentences are missed. There will also be a reduced ability to enjoy television and radio. Sometimes successful use of a hearing aid is not possible.

A combination of conductive and sensorineural losses means that a problem occurs in both the outer or middle and the inner ear. This results in *mixed* hearing loss. The fourth type of hearing loss is *central* hearing loss, which results from damage or impairment to the nerves or nuclei of the central nervous system, either in the pathways to the brain or in the brain itself.

Hearing loss is generally described as mild, moderate, severe, or profound, depending upon how well a person can hear the intensities or frequencies most associated with speech (see Table 1). Hearing loss is most commonly evaluated through audiometric tests that use pure tone and/or speech stimuli. Audiometers are calibrated according to established standards and variance from these norms are considered to represent hearing loss. Sound is measured both by its loudness or intensity (measured in units called decibels, dB) and its frequency or pitch (measured in units called hertz, Hz).

The threshold of "normal" hearing is denoted as an intensity of 0dB. Each 3-dB increase represents a doubling of the sound intensity. Hearing loss is also measured in dB. A person with a 25-dB hearing loss would not hear a sound below 25dB in intensity (McFadyen, 1996, p. 145).

Nonauditory factors, such as personal and social experiences, combine with hearing loss to result in a highly unique perception of the meaning of that loss to the individual (Schirmer, 2001; Thomas, 1985). Because the influence of such nonauditory factors is difficult to measure, audiologic recommendations can sometimes seem to miss the desired mark.

Educational Implications of Hearing Loss

While the term "hearing impairment" is often used generically to describe a wide range of hearing losses, including deafness, the regulations of the Individuals with Disabilities Education Act (IDEA) define hearing impairment and deafness separately. This is also the case for deaf-blindness, but the services for this disability are very specialized and will not be discussed in this chapter. Hearing impairment is defined by IDEA as "an impairment in hearing, whether permanent or fluctuating, that adversely affects a child's educational performance."

A major obstacle for individuals with severe hearing loss is the fact that sensory disabilities are considered to be "low incidence." Thus, they comprise a small proportion of the general population and even among students with disabilities, they are a minority. Focusing on those aged 6 to 21, the U.S. Department of Education (1998) reported that during the 1996-97 school year, 68,766 (or 1.3% of all students with disabilities) received special education services under the category of hearing impairment. However, the number of children with hearing loss is undoubtedly higher, since many of these students may have other disabilities as well and may be served under other categories.

A child with a hearing impairment can generally respond to auditory stimuli, including speech. Deafness, on the other hand, is defined as "a hearing impairment that is so severe that the child is prevented from receiving sound in all or most of its forms and is impaired in processing linguistic information through hearing, with or without amplification" (U.S. Department of Education, 2001). Generally, only children whose hearing loss is greater than 90dB are considered deaf for the purposes of educational placement, but this can vary according to the state in which the child lives. The chart on the next page lists ranges of hearing loss in dB with associated listening difficulties.

While hearing loss or deafness in itself does not affect a person's intellectual capacity or ability to learn, most children who are either hard of hearing or deaf require some form of special education services in order to receive an adequate education.

Technologies and Accommodations

Assistance available to children with hearing loss under IDEA includes a variety of supports: language and auditory training, amplification systems, services of an interpreter for students who use manual communication, favorable seating in the classroom to facilitate speechreading, captioned films/videos, assistance of a notetaker (who takes notes for the student so the student can focus on the teacher and instructional material displayed to the class), instruction for the teacher and peers in alternate communication methods (such as sign language), and counseling for personal development.

Within any given range of hearing loss, strategies to enhance the data input to students

Table 1. Functional Difficulties Associated with Various Degrees of Hearing Loss

Degree of loss	Description	Functional Listening Difficulties for Students
0-25 dB	Normal	None
26-40 dB *Speech area (consonants)*	Mild Hard of hearing	Students may experience difficulty in group settings and situations involving soft or distant speech. Language delays possible. Environmental accommodations may be sufficient.
41-55 dB *Speech area (vowels)*	Moderate Hard of hearing	Students may experience difficulty in groups; conversation must be loud to be heard. Language and learning difficulties are evident. Environmental accommodations, hearing aids, assistive listening devices, special education placement, and counseling may be beneficial.
56-70 dB *Baby crying*	Moderate/severe	Students experience difficulty understanding conversations in many situations. Will benefit from a hearing aid(s), assistive listening devices, and special education placement.
71-90 dB *Vacuum cleaner*	Severe "deaf"	Students will not hear conversational speech. Speech and language difficulties are obvious. Will benefit from a hearing aid(s) and special education placement.
91+ dB *Phone ringing, lawnmower*	Profound "Deaf"	Students may hear loud noises but are more aware of vibration. Vision is primary means of communication (sign language, captioning, text telephone [TDD] use).

Adapted from: *Connecting to Learn: Educational and Assistive Technology for People with Disabilities* (p. 27), by M.J. Scherer, 2004, Washington, DC: APA Books.

across different situations of communication difficulty include assistive technologies.

An assistive technology (AT) for a person with hearing loss can be the key to being connected to the world. It may be something as simple as a vibrotactile pager, flashing timer, strobe light alarm, and a dial on a telephone to amplify the sound being received. Hearing aids, which come in a variety of styles are one of the most common devices used by persons with hearing loss. Assistive technologies for

people with hearing loss fall into many categories, and each will be discussed in turn.

Alerting and Signaling Devices

These devices are designed to get the individual's attention through a flashing or strobe light or vibration and may be used in conjunction with a very loud sound. They include timers, alarms (fire, smoke, gas), pagers, alarm clocks, and signals that the doorbell or phone is ringing. Service animals are also trained to alert individuals with hearing loss to a variety of environmental sounds, including ringing doorbells and telephones, alarms, and so on.

Devices to Amplify Sound in Group Situations and Large Areas

To improve listening in large areas such as classrooms, theaters, and large meeting rooms, may be equipped with wireless assistive listening systems. There are three major types. FM systems use radio frequencies set aside by the Federal Communications Commission (FCC) to allow for the transmission of sound from a microphone to a receiver (set to the same radio frequency) connected to earphones or hearing aids. FM systems are useful when the microphone can be placed close to the sound source. For example, a speaker during a professional meeting may be asked to clip the microphone on her belt so that her speech is directly inputed into the receiver. Other large areas may use an audio induction loop or infrared systems, which use infrared light to transmit sound. All systems require the person with hearing loss to have a receiver.

Telephone Devices

The sound from a telephone can be amplified through built-in volume controls, in-line amplifiers, and add-on portable amplifiers (good for traveling). Persons with severe and profound hearing loss may require a Telecommunications Device for the Deaf (TDD) or teletypewriter (TTY) in order to be able to converse with another person. A TDD/TTY allows the use of a standard phone. They work like this:

TTYs are made up of a typewriter-like display. The visual display may be in the form of printed characters on paper, an alphanumeric display, or both. To use a TTY, you place the telephone handset on the coupler and type the message you wish to send. When you press letters on the keyboard to type in the message, a series of tones are generated. There is a different set of tones for each character. Those tones that form the typed message are sent over the telephone lines to the telephone on the other end of the line. This telephone also must be linked to a TTY so that the message can be decoded and

displayed. The latest models of TTYs have a voice carry-over (VCO) mode so that the hard of hearing person can speak the message but receive the answer on the TTY. (Dugan, 1997, p. 54)

While the teletypewriter has been called by several names, including telecommunication device for the deaf or text telephone, the national organization, Telecommunications for the Deaf, Inc., has taken a firm stand and endorses the acronym of "TDD" to represent all text telephones (www.netac.rit.edu/publication/tipsheet/TDDa.html).

Cagle and Cagle (1991) have developed a book of TDD etiquette and abbreviations that are recommended for any new TDD user. If a TDD user wishes to speak to someone without a TDD, relay services can be used. Since 1993, relay services have become available in each state. A person with hearing loss calls a relay service via a TDD and a hearing operator receives the message over a TDD. The operator then telephones the other party and relays in voice what was said by the TDD user. The TDD operator types the voice response into the TDD. When using a relay service, it's important to talk to the operator just as you would to the person with whom you are conversing. The relay operator will type or voice verbatim messages and responses.

Other resources for communicating over distances include cell phones, digital wireless phones, two-way messaging, Web meetings, and e-mail.

Telecommunications Devices and Accommodations to Telecommunication Technologies

Devices in this category apply to such media as radio, television, and CD/DVD/stereo systems. For persons with mild to moderate hearing loss, such devices can be connected to hearing aids through an induction loop system or earphones. For persons with severe and profound hearing loss, closed and open captioning displays what is said in text that flows along the screen and can be read.

The Telecommunications Act of 1996 requires manufacturers and service providers of telecommunication equipment to address the

Table 2. Communication Difficulties and Corresponding Strategies

Communication Difficulty	Strategies for Students with Hearing Loss	Strategies for Communicating with Students with Hearing Loss
Noise	The student should focus complete attention on the speaker, particularly attending to people's faces and nonverbal communication signals. If necessary, move to a quieter place and avoid as much distraction as possible.	Remove any unnecessary background noise (e.g., turn off radio, tv). Face the person as you speak and make sure you have the person's attention before speaking. Speak slowly and clearly: do not exaggerate mouth movements, do not chew gum, do not obscure your lip movements. Raise your voice slightly, but do not shout. If you asked to repeat something, rephrase your response (and add facial expression or nonverbal cues). Position yourself in front of a blank wall (or, one with an uncomplicated background) so the light is on your face with no glare is in the person's eyes.
Distance between speaker and listener	The student should move as close to the speaker as possible. An assistive listening device may also be helpful. Situate yourself in an area with as little background noise as possible with an unobstructed view of the speaker's face and body movements.	Face the audience and speak slowly and clearly. Raise the level of your voice. Use gestures and nonverbal cues as much as possible. If an Interpreter is accompanying a person with hearing loss, speak directly to the person and not the Interpreter.
Multiple speakers	The student should tell other people s/he has a hearing problem and request that they speak one at a time, slowly, and clearly. Try to position yourself so that you have a view of as many speakers' faces as possible. Let the conversation flow naturally, but ask specific questions about what you missed rather than saying, "What?" Ask people to rephrase, rather than repeat, what they said.	Each speaker should face the person with hearing loss when speaking and speak naturally. Make sure each speaker speaks slowly, clearly, and one at a time. The area should be well lit and each speaker should be clearly visible to the person with hearing loss. A person with hearing loss should face away from any windows so as to avoid glare. When an Interpreter is present, speak to the group and not to the Interpreter.
Low light levels	The student should move as close to the speaker as possible. Or, move to an area with better lighting. Take advantage of all existing light by positioning yourself to clearly see the speaker's face.	Obtaining more light is essential. Or move to an area with better lighting, if possible. Face the speaker when talking. Raise your voice level, but do not shout.

(continued next page)

Table 2. Communication Difficulties and Corresponding Strategies (continued)

Communication Difficulty	Strategies for Students with Hearing Loss	Strategies for Communicating with Persons with Hearing Loss
Complex information	The student should ask for written cues, if this is feasible, on a blackboard, chart paper, etc.. Request a brief verbal outline of key points.	Handouts prepared ahead of time outlining the communication are very helpful. New or unusual words, acronyms, etc. should be defined. Say what you are going to say, say it, and summarize what you've said. To check for understanding, monitor the listener's facial expressions. If an Interpreter is present, speak to the audience and not the Interpreter.

Adapted from: *Connecting to Learn: Educational and Assistive Technology for People with Disabilities* (pp. 28-29), by M.J. Scherer, 2004, Washington, DC: APA Books.

access needs of people with disabilities when they design and fabricate equipment. In 1997, the FCC approved adding to the Telecommunications Act of 1996 a mandate to close caption virtually all U.S. television programming by 2006. Manufacturers and service providers must also evaluate the accessibility, usability, and compatibility of relevant equipment and services and give persons with disabilities access to telephones, cell phones, pagers, and operator services. This is inclusive of providers of voicemail or an interactive menu service that has replaced many receptionists.

Captioning

Captions are translations of the spoken word into text that looks like subtitles on the screen, thus allowing people who are deaf and hard of hearing to read what they cannot hear. There are two kinds of captioning, open and closed. *Open captions* are permanently part of the picture and always visible on the screen whereas *closed captions* have to be "opened" in order to be visible. Decoders may be attached to TVs built prior to 1993; TVs with 13-inch or larger screens manufactured after July 1993 for sale in the United States must have a built-in decoder chip. According to the National Captioning Institute (www.ncicap.org), closed captions are converted to electronic codes placed on videotapes or inserted into the regular television signal (specifically on Line 21, a portion of the picture not typically visible). There are 525

horizontal lines in a television picture; line 21 is at the top just before the start of the picture-information-carrying lines. Thus, captions do not obstruct key parts of the picture. They typically are white letters against a black background, and their size is proportional to television screen. On a 19-inch screen, for instance, captions are 0.5 inches high.

To "open" the captions requires a decoder or a television with the built-in caption decoder chip. This service is free to anyone, and no special service is required to subscribe to in order to receive the captions. A program or video that has been captioned will have a (CC) symbol or registered service mark of the National Captioning Institute.

There are many forms of captions. *Real-time captioning* is the simultaneous appearance of captions while the speaker is talking. This is most frequently seen with live speeches and lectures. The image of the speaker appears on a screen and the captions along the bottom. Real-time captioning uses trained stenotype operators or other individuals specially trained. Researchers at the National Technical Institute for the Deaf have developed a training system that uses a laptop computer and requires only specialized training in learning and using an abbreviation system (e.g., Stinson & McKee, 2000).

Live-display captioning is used when a copy of a script and/or videotape is available in advance. The text of the program is transcribed and stored on a computer disk, and the prepared captions are displayed as line-by-line rolling text that is synchronized with the accompanying speech or recorded audio.

The FCC Caption Decoder Standard of 1991 as revised in 1992 as EIA-608 (WGBH Media Access Center, 2004) included specifications that caption decoders be capable of displaying seven colors to be used for either foreground or background (although a standard black background must always be a user-selectable option). One of the more popular choices for this option has been color-coding of speaker identification.

Newer products include personal captioning systems, which pick up text provided by a captioned transmission system and display it with a pair of eyeglasses with clip-on captioning display attached. The captions seem to float in front of the eye.

Captions for television viewers who are deaf can provide more than just a transcription of speech and indicate information that can be heard, but is not spoken like laughter and music and a person's manner of speaking. These features can greatly enhance learning.

As shown in Table 3, people with more severe hearing loss require a combination of sophisticated technologies. Many require a tolerance for fidgeting with gadgets, asserting their needs for assistive listening devices, and becoming accustomed to being inconvenienced in exchange for being connected.

The quality of AT, which varies widely, is related to the characteristics of AT devices and how devices match the needs of persons with disabilities.

Effects of Hearing Loss on the Learner and Learning

According to the National Information Center for Children and Youth with Disabilities in 2000 (www.nichcy.org), children with hearing loss may have difficulty in learning vocabulary, grammar, word order, idiomatic expressions, and other aspects of verbal communication. By age four or five, most children who are deaf are enrolled in school on a full-day basis and do special work on communication and language development. Students with hearing loss:

use oral or manual means of communication or a combination of the two. Oral communication includes speech, speechreading and the use of residual hearing (this may include use of hearing aids and/or assistive listening devices). Manual communication involves signs and fingerspelling (and requires the presence of a sign language interpreter to facilitate communication between hearing and non-hearing persons). Total Communication, as a method of instruction, is a combination of the oral method plus signs and fingerspelling: (Information Center for Children and Youth with Disabilities, 2001)

Learners with hearing, as well as vision, loss are becoming increasingly dependent on technologies. In fact, the majority of the information they receive is now technology-based, delivered via telecommunications or computer-based technologies. This makes literacy all the more important. For deaf persons, captioning or speech-to-text systems are commonplace; people with vision loss can choose among synthetic speech, electronic magnification, optical character recognition (OCR) technologies, and Braille technology.

Despite progress, specialized needs and preferences regarding technologies continue to be understudied in all levels of education for individuals with hearing or vision loss (e.g., Ramsey, 1997). Other areas in need of research include (a) an analysis of the influences on successful and unsuccessful outcomes from these technologies and (b) identification of strategies and tools that result in the most appropriate match of person and technology, training in its use, and optimal use of the technology.

People react to changes in their physical and sensory capabilities according to their personality and personal attitudes, history of social relationships and background experiences, lifestyle preferences, established interpersonal networks and communication needs, judgment and outlook regarding perceived capabilities and functioning in a variety of situations, and the adjustment patterns they have established to deal with loss and change (e.g., Scherer, 1996, 2000). The characteristics of the environments in which they typically find themselves

Table 3. Degree of Hearing Loss and Recommended Technologies

Degree of Loss	Alerting Systems	Group Settings/ Large Areas	Telephone	Media
0-25 dB *normal hearing*	None	None	None	None
26-40 dB *mild loss; hard of hearing*	None	Large-area listening systems	Telephone amplifier	TV/radio amplifying head sets, amplified telephone
41-70 dB *moderate/ severe loss; hard of hearing*	Flashing lights for ringing doorbell, phone. Flashing lights on fire, smoke, gas alarms	All above plus personal amplifier	All above	All above plus television listening devices (FM, infrared, audio loop)
71+ dB *severe; deaf*	All above plus vibrating alarm clock	All above plus Sign Language Interpreting services	All above plus text telephone or relay services	Closed captioning (useful for all degrees of loss, but essential for severe loss)

Adapted from: *Connecting to Learn: Educational and Assistive Technology for People with Disabilities* (p. 14), by M.J. Scherer, 2004, Washington, DC: APA Books.

(including the physical or built environment as well as the attitudes of the people within them) also exert a strong influence on how people react to their hearing and vision loss. One of the biggest factors in determining such reactions is the nature and severity of the loss, at what age it occurred, and whether there is associated pain or additional illnesses or injuries.

Many individuals with hearing loss find it helpful to socialize and learn from others who have hearing loss as it can be less fatiguing and guarantees shared experiences. There is a vast literature on the benefits of social support and having access to others who understand from first-hand experience one's everyday obstacles and frustrations (e.g., Pillemer & Suitor, 1996; Yalom, 1995). It can be reassuring, and it lets people know that they are not alone in what they are feeling and perceiving. Support groups

have also been found to be very helpful in modeling and sharing new strategies for communication. Internet and Web-based communications can be key means of support for students with hearing loss who find themselves isolated from peers in an inclusive educational environment.

Learners have varying characteristics and preferences. To maximize each learner's educational success, ideally, instruction and learning environments would allow learners to select from an array of options those that best suit their unique characteristics and goals. The loss of hearing affects the ways in which individuals can take in data. And without data, meaningful information cannot be obtained or understood completely.

Table 4: Psychosocial Challenges Resulting from Hearing Loss

Psychosocial Learning Challenges	Psychosocial Behavioral Challenges
Lack of exposure to film dialogue and information presented in other verbal media	Less general information about the world and interpersonal communication styles
Lack of exposure to verbal information and cues (e.g., voice inflection, verbal indicators of mood and affect)	Confusion and misunderstandings due to lack of perception of verbal clues to conversational affect and meaning

Educational Uses of Assistive Technology

The ultimate goal of using AT for school-age children is accessing education and participation in academic and social activities. The instructional goals for school-age children with disabilities are defined in the child's individualized education program (IEP). IDEA requires that AT be included in the IEP. As the quality and availability of AT increases, this requirement will become more important to consider.

While AT requirements will assist school-age children in meeting their educational goals, such requirements place financial and time burdens on the school system. Thus, as the demand for AT increases, acquiring AT has not necessarily become easier. This is due to several factors, including one or a combination of the following barriers:

• Lack of awareness of AT by students, parents and school personnel

• Lack of teacher and student training in the most appropriate and optimal use of AT

• Lack of AT funding and/or knowledge about access to funding

• Administrative requirements in schools such as not allowing AT to leave the classroom

Approximately 20,000 AT devices are currently available (www.abledata.com). Because there are so many devices, it is essential that teachers and specialists know how to locate and select appropriate devices for students. Only appropriate devices can be expected to result in a student's enhanced academic and social experiences. Locating AT devices can be facilitated by using such online resources as Abledata, which is supported by the U.S. Department of Education (www.abledata.com).

Determining the Most Appropriate Assistive Technology Devices

Determining student goals and preferences and then selecting the AT device that best matches them requires a comprehensive assessment of student, milieu/environments, and technology features. After a trial period of use, after training, and once the student uses the technology in actual situations and natural settings, feedback should be sought on how well the technology is performing for a given student and how the student has changed in capability and academic performance. Such practice is being evidence-based and measuring outcomes of the technology as an intervention. Evidence-based practice is required in IDEA. It is used in preschool, K-12, postsecondary, and vocational education.

Tools are available to help school districts improve the assistive technology services they provide. One such tool is the Educational Tech Points (Bowser & Reed, 1995), where each tech point represents a point in the process of referral, evaluation, and development of the IEP. An assessment packet developed by the Wisconsin Assistive Technology Initiative is organized around functional categories with a continuum of devices to consider (Lynch & Reed, 1997).

Another assessment tool, the SETT framework (Zabala, 1995), is designed to serve as a team-driven aid to gather and organize data on the student, environment, and tasks associated with assistive technology decisions.

Although these resources offer a excellent starting point, they may not meet the comprehensive needs of all students, however. For example, additional information is often needed from other resources in order to comprehensively address psychological and social issues. Nevertheless, these tools are responses to an unmet need: The availability of a systematic framework from which to build good policies and practices for matching students with the most appropriate assistive and educational technologies for their use is being viewed as increasingly fundamental to the provision of quality services.

The focus here will be on the Matching Person and Technology Model (MPT) and accompanying assessment process (Scherer, 1998). However, the measures mentioned above should be examined, as should many other measures and assessment processes, as they may be more appropriate for a given evaluation need. When selecting a measure, however, it is important to ensure that it meets the criteria for being a quality tool.

Matching Person and Technology (MPT) Model and Assessment Process

The MPT process consists of a series of instruments developed to address and organize the many influences that impact on the use of assistive, access, instructional and educational technologies including psychological and social factors (Scherer, 1995a, 1995c, 1998).

The MPT process has been designed to apply to students in secondary, postsecondary, and lifelong learning. It pays particular attention to the characteristics of the technology user: strengths and needs, goals and preferences, level of motivation and readiness, expectations and mood, and lifestyle factors. This information is then balanced with the characteristics of the milieu/environments in which the technology will be used, along with the features and functions of the technology itself. The MPT is a practical and research resource to identify the most appropriate technology for a person in light of the user's needs and goals, barriers that may exist to optimal technology use, areas to target for training for optimal use, and the type of additional support that may enhance use. It has been designed to organize

information efficiently and thoroughly while achieving an optimal match of student and technology. Efforts to develop an interactive CD-based training program in the use of the MPT process, as well as computerized scoring and interpretations have been achieved (Scherer & Cushman, 2002) and these materials will be available in June 2005.

The MPT process is best used with complex technologies and where a choice is available. After the person has received the most appropriate technology for his or her use, the MPT forms are administered one or more times post-AT acquisition to assess changes in perceived capabilities, subjective quality of life, and psychosocial factors such as self-esteem, mood, self-determination, and social participation and support.

The MPT process is both a personal and collaborative (user and provider working together) assessment, and the paper-and-pencil measures can be used as interview guides. A range of assessments are offered, ranging from a quick screen, to specialized evaluations (which can be completed in approximately 15 minutes) to a comprehensive assessment (which can be completed in 45 minutes by someone trained and experienced in using the forms).

The results can help provide the rationale for funding (Kemp, Hourcade, & Parette, 2000) and training, demonstrate improvement in skills over time, organize information about the needs of a particular student (e.g., Albaugh & Fayne, 1996; Albaugh, Piazza, & Schlosser, 1997), and provide insights into factors that contribute to (or detract from) the use of the desired technology. With such insights, educators can diagnose and intervene in potential or existing problem areas and, thus, better ensure that the use of the technology will enhance a student's educational experience.

The Matching Person and Technology Model/theory emerged from a grounded theory research study (Scherer, 2000, 2002). To operationalize the model and theory, an assessment process consisting of several instruments was developed from the experiences of technology users and non-users through participatory action research. Items emerged from characteristics differentiating the actual experiences of users and non-users and they have

Table 5. Steps of the Matching Person and Technology Process

Step One: Initial Worksheet for the *Matching Person and Technology (MPT)* Model is first used to determine initial goals that the professional and the user have established, including possible alternative goals. Second, potential interventions supportive of these goals are written in the space provided on the form. Third, any technologies needed to support the attainment of the goals are recorded.

Step Two: History of Support Use is used to identify technologies used is the past, satisfaction with those technologies, and those that are desired and needed but not yet available to the consumer. The professional and consumer complete this form collaboratively.

Step Three: The consumer is asked to complete his or her version of the appropriate form depending on the type of technology under consideration (general, assistive, educational, workplace or healthcare). The user form may serve as a guide for an oral interview, if that seems more appropriate. The professional completes the professional version of the same form and identifies any discrepancies in perspective between the professional's and the consumer's responses. Discrepancies become a topic for discussion and negotiation.

Step Four: The professional discusses with the user factors that may indicate problems with his or her acceptance or appropriate use of the technology.

Step Five: After problem areas have been noted, the professional and the consumer work to identify specific intervention strategies and devise an action plan.

Step Six: The strategies and action plans are committed to writing, for experience has shown that plans that are merely verbalized are not implemented as frequently as written plans. Written plans also serve as documentation and can provide the justification for any subsequent actions, such as requests for funding or release time for training.

held up well in additional research studies. Thus, based on the results of measurement standards applied to date, the MPT assessments have been determined to have reasonable inter-rater reliability and validity (Scherer, 1995b, 1999; Scherer & Craddock, 2002).

The importance of ensuring a client-centered approach, and relevant assessment process to match person and technology, is highlighted in the increasing corpus of research on technology use (Blackhurst & Edyburn, 2000; Edyburn & Gardner, 1999). For example, when examining reasons for technology abandonment or discontinuation of use, consumers are less likely to use recommended devices when their needs are neither fully addressed nor understood during the technology selection process (Cook & Hussey, 2002). Educators and other professionals who partner with consumers in the technology assessment and selection process will have preserved the highly valued "personal touch" as well as having helped more learners experience the excitement which accompanies success in accessing information (e.g., Lahm & Sizemore, 2002).

Table 6 lists IEP steps and how the MPT assessment forms can inform each step as well as the full IEP process.

Regarding the last step, it is important to regularly review with IEP team members, teachers, the student, and family: (a) how well the student is performing academically and socially; (b) the progress in achieving the goal(s) with the technology; and (c) the need and desirability of considering any additional technologies, accommodations, or supports for the student (Golden, 1998; Judge & Parette, 1998; Kelker, Holt, & Sullivan, 2000).

Table 6. How the IEP Steps and the MPT Assessment Process Work Together

AT assessment focusing on the user of the AT	Use Assistive Technology Device Predisposition Assessment (Form 4-1, Person) and/or Educational Technology Predisposition Assessment (Form 5)
Consideration of a continuum of AT devices or an ET with trials in customary environments	Use Assistive Technology Device Predisposition Assessment (Form 4-1, Device) and/or Educational Technology Predisposition Assessment (Form 5)
Selection of AT and or ET and development of a plan for its integration • designation of who will do what and where • training needs • device maintenance, support, etc.	Use data from ATD PA/ET PA
Documentation of evaluation procedure • specifying needs and preferences of the user and their importance • describing how the student's disability interferes with important academic activities and goals • noting what is presently being used and what has been tried • describing the features of the selected AT or ET, describing why it is better than alternatives and why it will meet the needs	Use the sum of information from completed MPT assessment forms
Regular review of • goals and achievements • device needs • necessary environmental accommodations	Re-administer forms and use post-technology matching to assess outcomes of the process. For the ATD PA, use Forms 4-2, Person, and 4-2, Device, as they have been specifically designed as follow-up measures

In summary, the MPT process contributes to evidence-based practice by promoting G.O.O.D. practice:

• Get the information

• Organize the information

• Operationalize and implement the steps in the process of matching the student with desired supports

• Document, revisit and update the effects of the supports

Appendix A on page 410, lists many Web sites with information that may prove highly useful in getting information. Then the MPT process can be used to organize obtained information in light of the student's characteristics and those of the environments in which the student will use technology.

It is important to always keep in mind that the MPT process and forms are not intended to evaluate teacher performance, but to foster and evaluate technology users' development, achievement, and satisfaction.

After the student is matched with technology and the device is selected, training is often required for optimal use of a device. Such training may not only involve the student, but also parents and key teachers. While many devices are easy to learn to use, others are more complex. Often few educators have received training, leaving everyone confused and frustrated when a device fails to operate according to expectations.

Perhaps a student has stopped using a device when all it may require to become useful again is a small adjustment or modification or an upgrade to match the student's developmental advancement (e.g., Scherer, 2000, Scherer & McKee, 1994). Consideration might be given to selecting a peripheral or additional or ancillary devices, making the necessary adjustments and upgrades, and so on, until the student finds the device usable again. Sample key considerations regarding the process of selection, accommodation, and usability include the following:

Selecting the technology or other support

- What will best suit this student's needs and preferences? A technology? Additional personal assistance? A combination?

- What is the most cost-effective choice?

- What is the most empowering choice for this student?

- Have the options been prioritized and has it been documented why one product or feature is preferable to another?

Accommodations

- Has trial use occurred in the settings of use?

- Is the technology being used as intended?

- Does the technology require customizing or other adaptations to the student?

Use

- Has the technology has been assembled correctly?

- Is the technology being used as intended?

- Does the student have changing needs that need to be evaluated?

- Have there been changes in the settings of use?

- Will the student be transferring to another school (or out of school) and is a plan in place for that transition?

The ultimate test of the effectiveness of a device is how well it fits the user. A key indicator of the quality of the match between person and technology is the frequency with which devices are abandoned or go unused. At times it appears that a device is perfect for a given student, but later it is found that the student stopped using it altogether, avoided use from the beginning, or is using it only in limited situations. If the student is supposed to use it 50% of the day, but only uses it 25% of the day, that discrepancy must be addressed. Why is that happening?

Based on earlier research (e.g., Scherer, 2000), when the use of a device interferes with other activities or needs satisfaction, it may be viewed as ineffective and then becomes abandoned. Consumers themselves may be unwilling to request training or other assistance. While many remain uninformed about the options available to them, others are not accustomed to being assertive and may hesitate to ask for the assistance to which they are entitled.

In cases where the device itself was satisfactory, survey respondents often report changed priorities or needs that led to the need to begin the process again of evaluating the characteristics and resources of the person, the characteristics and requirements of the milieu/environments, the characteristics of the technology, and the technology selection, accommodation, and usability (Cushman & Scherer, 1996).

While there are many benefits to be gained by using technologies, they have the potential to limit and isolate as well as to enable, liberate, and connect their users (Scherer, 1994, 2003; Scherer & Frisina, 1994). Some ATs, particularly the very high-tech ones, highlight a person's differences and set AT users apart as looking "different." While many individuals are grateful for their ATs, some feel stigmatized by them and even resent the need to use them. One student with hearing loss interviewed by the author felt personally stigmatized by a peer wearing a body hearing aid. She described this as follows.

"When I was growing up, another boy in school was hearing impaired. He could hear a little better than me ... he used to wear one of those hearing aids that you attach to your body. I could never tolerate that kind of thing. People look at you. And being a girl with those little bumps right there... He was the only other hearing impaired person, and we avoided each other."

Without even wearing a hearing aid herself, this student perceived the stigma of the AT as spreading to her because of having a similar hearing loss with the hearing aid user.

Summary and Recommendations

A student's performance and participation cannot be reduced to various and separate features of that individual. Nor is it possible or desirable to separate people's characteristics from the context, environments, and situations in which they perform and participate. As this chapter has shown, a person's optimal technology use and subsequent benefits are best achieved when multiple elements are addressed and their interactions are considered.

Certain product design considerations can help ensure technologies are usable by people with hearing loss as well as those students with other disabilities. *Universal design* refers to designing a product for use by a wide range of individuals with and without disabilities (e.g., Bowe, 2000; Connell et al., 1997; Vanderheiden & Tobias, 2002). Universal design focuses on the characteristics of the product (device) and the characteristics of the user. Matching these satisfactorily is called *ergonomics*, or the process of determining the quality of the match of product's characteristics and the user's characteristics. In universal design the focus is on the product ("how can we design this product so it can best be used by people with sensory, cognitive and mobility disabilities?"); in ergonomics the focus is on the unique individual user ("How easily and comfortably can Jim operate this device?").

Today, a student with a disability can use many of the same devices and educational and information technologies as students without disabilities when universal design principles are followed. By removing unnecessary barriers to technology use and access to information, students' self-reliance and independence, self-determination, and empowerment are enhanced.

With tight budgets and the need to help an increasing number of students, inappropriate matches of student and technology as well as technology non-use are luxuries we can no longer afford. We must reduce this abandonment and non-use rate, increase the literacy of all students, and help those with special needs succeed in participating in the larger society.

References

Abledata, (www.abledata.com) Retrieved February 2, 2004.

Albaugh, P.R., & Fayne, H. (1996). The ET PA for predicting technology success with learning disabled students: Lessons from a multimedia study. *Technology & Disability*, 5, 313-318.

Albaugh, P.R., Piazza, L., & Schlosser, K. (1997). Using a CD-ROM encyclopedia: Interaction of teachers, middle school students, library media specialists, and the technology. *Research in Middle Level Education Quarterly*, 20(3), 43-55.

Blackhurst, A.E., & Edyburn, D.L. (2000). A brief history of special education technology. *Special Education Technology Practice*, 2(1), 21-35.

Bowe, F.G. (2000). *Universal design in education.* Westport, CT: Bergin & Garvey.

Bowser, G., & Reed, P. (1995). Education tech points for assistive technology planning. *Journal of Special Education Technology*, 12, 325-338.

Cagle, S.J., & Cagle, K.M. (1991). *Ga and Sk etiquette: Guidelines for telecommunications in the deaf community.* Bowling Green, OH: Bowling Green Press.

Connell, B.R., Jones, M., Mace, R., Mueller, J., Mullick, A., Ostroff, E., Sanford, J., Steinfeld, E., Story, M., & Vanderheiden, G. (1997).

The principles of universal design. Raleigh: North Carolina State University, Center for Universal Design. Available at www.design.ncsu.edu/cud/univ_design/princ_overview.htm

Cook, A. M,, & Hussey, S. M. (2002). *Assistive technologies: Principles and practice, second edition*. St. Louis, MO: Mosby.

Cushman, L.A. & Scherer, M.J. (1996). Measuring the relationship of assistive technology use, functional status over time, and consumer-therapist perceptions of ATs. *Assistive Technology, 8*, 103-109.

Davis, H. (1997). *Hearing and deafness: A guide for laymen*: New York: Murray Hill Books.

Dugan, M.B. (1997). *Keys to living with hearing loss (Barron's keys to retirement plunning)*. Hauppauge, NY: Barron's Educational Series.

Edyburn, D.L., & Gardner, J.E. (1999). Integrating technology into special education teacher preparation programs: Creating shared visions. *Journal of Special education Technology, 14*(2), 3-20.

ERIC Clearinghouse on Disabilities and Gifted Education. (2002). *What is universal design for learning?* Arlington, VA: Author. Retrieved November 22, 2002, from http://ericec.org/digests/e586.html.

Golden, D. (1998). *Assistive technology in special education: Policy and practice*. Albuquerque, NM: Council of Administrators of Special Education (CASE)/Technology and Media Division (TAM) of the Council for Exceptional Children.

Individuals with Disabilities Education Act, Amendments of 1997, Public Law No. 105-17, § 602, U.S.C. 1401 [Online].Available: www.ed.gov/offices/OSERS/IDEA/the_law.html.

Judge, S.L., & Parette, H.P. (1998). *Assistive technology for young children with disabilities: A Guide to family-centered services*. Cambridge, MA: Brookline Books.

Katsiyannis, A., & Conderman, G. (1994). Section 504 policies and procedures: An established necessity. *NASSP Bulletin, 78*(565), 6-10.

Kelker, K.A., Holt, R., & Sullivan, J. (2000). *Family guide to assistive technology*. Cambridge, MA: Brookline Books.

Kemp, C.E., Hourcade, J.J., & Parette, H.P.

(2000). Assistive technology funding resources for school-aged students with disabilities. *Journal of Special education Technology, 15*(4), 15-24.

Lahm, E. A., & Sizemore, L. (2002). Factors that influence assistive technology decision-making. *Journal of Special Education Technology, 17(1)*, 15-25.

Lynch, J., & Reed, P. (1997). *AT checklist*. Wisconsin Assistive Technology Initiative (WATI). Retrieved April 28, 2003 from http://www.wati.org/pdf/atcheck1.pdf.

McFadyen, G. (1996). Aids for hearing impairment and deafness. In J. Galvin & M. Scherer (Eds.), *Evaluating, selecting and using appropriate assistive technology* (pp. 144-161). Gaithersburg, MD: Aspen Publishers, Inc.

Medwetsky, L. (2002). Central auditory processing. In J. Katz (Ed.), *Handbook of clinical audiology* (5th edition, pp. 495-509). Baltimore: Lippincott Williams and Wilkens.

Mencher, G.T., Gerber, S.E., & McCombe, A. (1997). *Audiology and auditory dysfunction*. Boston: Allyn & Bacon.

Myers, D.G. (2000). *A quiet world : Living with hearing loss*. New Haven, CT: Yale University Press.

National Captioning Institute. (www.ncicap.org). Retrieved January 28, 2004.

National Information Center for Children and Youth with Disabilities. (2001). *General Information about deafness and hearing loss*, Fact Sheet Number 3 (FS3). Washington, DC: Author. (www.nichcy.org).

Pillemer, K.,& Suitor, J.J. (1996). It takes one to help one: Effects of status similarity on well-being. *Journal of Gerontology, 51B*, S250-257.

President's Commission on Excellence in Special Education. (2002, July). A new era: Revitalizing special education for children and their families. Retrieved December 17, 2003 from www.ed.gov/inits/commissionsboards/whspecialeducation/reports.html.

Ramsey, C.L. (1997). *Deaf children in public schools: Placement, context, and consequences*. Washington, DC: Gallaudet University Press.

Rehabilitation Act of 1973. 29 U.S.C. Section 794.

Scheetz, N.A. (2001). *Orientation to deafness (second edition)*. Boston: Allyn & Bacon.

Scherer, M. J. (1994). Recommendations to the

Department of Education that emerged from the national symposium on educational applications of technology for persons with sensory disabilities. In *Smithsonian 1995 ComputerWorld Awards*. [Online]. Retrieved November 12, 2003 from innovate.si.edu/1995/nominee/ ea29.htm

Scherer, M.J. (1995a, March). Fitting *technology to your students' learning styles*. Invited presentation for the conference, Design for Excellence, San Diego, CA.

Scherer, M.J. (1995b, March). *Assessing the outcomes of teaching to students' learning styles*. Invited presentation for the conference, Design for Excellence, San Diego, CA.

Scherer, M.J. (1995c, March). *How educational technology enhances learning for the deaf*. Invited presentation for Project Needs, San Diego Public Schools, San Diego, CA.

Scherer M.J. (1996). Outcomes of assistive technology use on quality of life. *Disability and Rehabilitation, 18*, 439-448.

Scherer M.J. (1998). *The Matching Person and Technology (MPT) Model manual and accompanying assessment instruments (third edition)*. Webster, NY: Institute for Matching Person & Technology, Inc.

Scherer, M.J. (1999). Matching students and teachers with the most appropriate instructional and educational technologies. In B.Rittenhouse & D. Spillers (Eds.), *The electronic classroom: Using technology to create a 21st century curriculum* (pp. 143-164). Wellington, New Zealand: Omega Publishers, Inc.

Scherer, M.J. (2000). *Living in the state of stuck: How technology impacts the lives of people with disabilities, Third Edition*. Cambridge, MA: Brookline Books.

Scherer, M.J. (Ed.). (2002). *Assistive technology: Matching device and consumer for successful rehabilitation*. Washington, DC: APA Books.

Scherer, M.J. (2004). *Connecting to learn: Educational and assistive technology for people with disabilities*. Washington, DC: APA Books.

Scherer, M.J,. & Craddock, G. (2002). Matching Person & Technology (MPT) assessment process. *Technology & Disability [Special issue]: The Assessment of Assistive Technology Outcomes, Effects and Costs, 14*, 125-131.

Scherer, M.J., & Cushman, L.A. (2002). Deter-

mining the content for an interactive training programme and interpretive guidelines for the Assistive Technology Device Predisposition Assessment. *Disability & Rehabilitation, 24*, 126-130.

Scherer, M.J., & Frisina, D.R. (1994). Applying the Matching People with Technologies Model to individuals with hearing loss: What people say they want and need from assistive technologies. *Technology & Disability: Deafness and Hearing Impairments, 3*(1), 62-68.

Scherer, M.J., & McKee, B.G. (1994). Assessing predispositions to technology use in special education: Music education majors score with the "Survey of Technology Use." In M. Binion (Ed.), *Proceedings of the RESNA'94 annual conference* (pp. 194-196). Arlington, VA: RESNA Press.

Schirmer, B.R. (2001). *Psychological, social, and educational dimensions of deafness*. New York: Allyn & Bacon.

Stinson, M., & McKee, B. (2000). *Speech recognition as a support service for deaf and hard-of-hearing students: Adaptation and evaluation* (Year 2 annual progress report to the Spencer Foundation). Rochester, NY: NTID.

Telecommunications Act of 1996, Pub. LA. No. 104-104, 110 Stat. 56 (1996).

Thomas, A.J. (1985*). Acquired hearing loss: Psychological and psychosocial implications*. San Diego, CA: Academic Press.

U.S. Department of Education, Office of Special Education and Rehabilitative Services (OSERS). (2001). *Twenty-third annual report to Congress on the implementation of the Individuals with Disabilities Education Act*. Washington, DC: Author.

U.S. Department of Education. (1998). *To assure the free appropriate public education of all children with disabilities: Twentieth annual report to Congress on the implementation of the Individuals with Disabilities Education Act*. Washington, DC: Author.

Vanderheiden, G., & Tobias, J. (2002). *Universal design of consumer products: Current industry practice and perceptions*. Retrieved December 17, 2002, from trace.wisc.edu/docs/ud_consumer_products_hfes2000/.

WGBH Media Access Group. (2004). TechFacts:

Information about captioning for video professionals, volume 2 - The lowdown on upgrades: FCC standards, digital and pal encoding equipment. Retrieved 2 February 2, 2004, from http://main.wgbh.org/wgbh/pages/mag/resources/archive/techfacts/cctechfacts2.html.

Yalom, I. (1995). *The theory and practice of group psychotherapy* (4th edition) New York: Basic Books.

Zabala, J. S. (1995). *The SETT framework: Critical areas to consider when making informed assistive technology decisions*. Houston, TX: Region IV Education Service Center. (ERIC Document Reproduction Service No. ED381962).

Table 7. Key Web Resources

The following is a representative, but not comprehensive, sample of key resources for obtaining further information on the topics in this chapter. Web sites were chosen based on the probability that they would routinely be updated and that the URL would not change.

Organizations with a Focus on Children with Disabilities

Alliance for Technology Access (ATA): The ATA is a network of community-based resource centers, developers, vendors, and associates dedicated to providing information and support services to children and adults with disabilities, and increasing their use of standard, assistive, and information technologies. *www.ataccess.org*

Council for Exceptional Children (CEC): CEC is the largest international professional organization dedicated to improving educational outcomes for individuals with exceptionalities, students with disabilities, and the gifted. The organization provides a number of services, including professional development resources, journals and newsletters on new research findings, classroom and information services. *www.cec.sped.org*

RESNA (Rehabilitation Engineering and Assistive Technology Society of North America): RESNA is an interdisciplinary association of people with a common interest in technology and disability. Membership is open to all interested persons, and includes rehabilitation technology researchers, rehabilitation engineers, occupational therapists, physical therapists, speech-language pathologists/audiologists, educators, suppliers and manufacturers, end-users and advocates, policy specialists, and a variety of other rehabilitation and health professionals. *www.resna.org.*

European counterpart: *Association for the Advancement of Assistive Technology in Europe (AAATE), www.fernuni-hagen.de/FTB/aaate.htm*

Australian counterpart: The Australian Rehabilitation and Assistive Technology Association (ARATE), *www.e-bility.com/arata/index.shtml.* Special Interest Group, Human Perspectives of Technology (HPT), focuses on
- provision of the most appropriate and desired interventions that have the greatest likelihood of success, consumer use, and consumer satisfaction
- the person or user's technology preferences, including:
    - how well the technology meets the user's goals, needs and lifestyle
    - the user's perpective on different types of technology
    - how to promote effective use of technology
    www.e-bility.com/arata/sigs_humanperspectives.shtml

Product Information

ABLEDATA is the premier source for information on assistive technology products and resources featuring an online product catalog. It is sponsored by the National Institute on Disability and Rehabilitation Research, U.S. Department of Education: *www.abledata.com*

AbleNet offers practical products and creative solutions for teaching children with disabilities: *www.ablenetinc.com*

AT Network is dedicated to expanding the accessibility of tools, resources, and technology that will help increase independence, improve personal productivity, and enhance quality of life. Offers information and links to sites organized by function, group, and topic and an online journal published twice a month: *www.atnet.org/news/index.html*

(continued next page)

Table 7. Key Web Resources (continued)

Web Sites on Key Legislation

Individuals with Disabilities Education Act Amendments (IDEA) of 1997:
The IDEA, passed in 1975, changed the lives of children with disabilities by legislating inclusive education measures, giving all children an equal opportunity to excel academically. This 1997 act strengthens academic expectations and accountability for the nation's 5.8 million children with disabilities and bridges the gap that has too often existed between what children with disabilities learn and what is required in the regular curriculum. IDEA was reauthorized in late 2004 and the following Web site will have the new legislation: *www.ed.gov/offices/OSERS/IDEA*

Assistive Technology Act of 1998. The full text of this legislation to support programs of grants to states to address the assistive technology needs of individuals with disabilities may be accessed through the National Center for the Dissemination of Disability Research (NCDDR) Web site: *www.ncddr.org/relativeact/statetech/ata98.html*

Section 508 of the Rehabilitation Act of 1973. Federal employees and the public can access resources for understanding and implementing the requirements of Section 508 through this Web site: *www.section508.gov*

No Child Left Behind Act of 2001 (P.L. 107-110). Known in short as NCLB, this is the reauthorization of the Elementary and Secondary Education Act of 1965. The full text of NCLB can be accessed at: *www.ed.gov/legislation/ESEA02.* The NCLB Web site is: www.nclb.gov. *A general index of U.S. legislation related to education can be accessed at: www.ed.gov/legislation/*

Government Sites

Disabilityinfo.gov is a comprehensive federal Web site of disability-related government resources: *www.disabilityinfo.gov*

National Center for the Dissemination of Disability Research (NCDDR) in the U.S. Department of Education funds a variety of high-level research and knowledge dissemination projects to advance knowledge related to disability issues: *www.ncddr.org/index.html*

National Council on Disability (NCD) is an independent federal agency making recommendations to the President and Congress on issues affecting 54 million Americans with disabilities: *www.ncd.gov/*

National Information Center for Children and Youth with Disabilities (NICHCY) provides information on disabilities and disability-related issues with a special focus on children and youth (birth to age 22). Anyone can use their services—families, educators, administrators, journalists, students: www.nichcy.org/

National Rehabilitation Information Center (NARIC) collects and disseminates the results of federally funded research projects. NARIC's literature collection, which also includes commercially published books, journal articles, and audiovisuals, averages around 200 new documents per month. NARIC is funded by the National Institute on Disability and Rehabilitation Research (NIDRR) to serve anyone, professional or lay person, who is interested in disability and rehabilitation issues, including consumers, family members, health professionals, educators, rehabilitation counselors, students, librarians, administrators, and researchers: *www.naric.com*

(continued next page)

Table 7. Key Web Resources (continued)

Office of Special Education and Rehabilitative Services (OSERS), U.S. Department of Education provides a wide array of supports to parents and individuals, school districts, and states in three main areas: *special education, vocational rehabilitation, and research: www.ed.gov/offices/OSERS/index.html*

Measurement and Assessment

Assistive Technology Outcomes is dedicated to the development, evaluation, and application of valid, reliable, and sensitive outcome-measure tools to enable AT practitioners to determine the cost effectiveness of their services, to gauge the value of providing assistive technologies, and to select the best technology from an array of choices: *www.utoronto.ca/atrc/reference/atoutcomes/index.html*

Institute for Matching Person & Technology. Homepage for information about the Institute as well as the Matching Person & Technology assessment process and accompanying assessments: *members.aol.com/IMPT97/MPT.html*

Quality Indicators for Assistive Technology (QIAT) is a nationwide grassroots group that includes hundreds of individuals who provide input into the ongoing process of identifying, disseminating, and implementing a set of widely applicable Quality Indicators for Assistive Technology Services in School Settings: *www.qiat.org*

Student, Environment, Tasks, Tools (SETT) framework is a guideline for gathering data in order to make effective assistive technology decisions: */www2.edc.org/NCIP/ workshops/sett/SETT_home.html*

Wisconsin Assistive Technology Initiative (WATI) is a statewide project funded by the Wisconsin Department of Public Instruction to help school districts develop or improve their assistive technology services. WATI also works with birth to 3 programs through a grant from the Wisconsin Birth to 3 Program: *www.wati.org/*

Web Site Search Engines for Finding Other Resources and International Sites

Altavista, www.altavista.com

Google, www.google.com

(Just type in your need, product category, and so on)

21

Technology and Autism: Current Practices and Future Directions

Matt Tincani and E. Amanda Boutot

More than ever, technology is an integrated part of instruction for children with disabilities. Technology has been incorporated into classrooms to teach a variety of academic skills, ranging from notetaking (Boyle, 2001) to math problem solving (Bottge, Heinrichs, Chan, & Serlin, 2001). For example, learners with low-incidence disabilities, including autism, have been increasingly exposed to technology in the classroom and community. Technology interventions for children with autism include voice output communication aids (VOCAs) to address speech difficulties and a range of hardware and software programs to teach academic skills and enhance classroom participation (Mirenda, Wilk, & Carson, 2000). This chapter describes current best practices in technology interventions for students with autism and investigates future directions in applications and research.

Autism Overview

To understand the technology needs of children with autism, it is useful to review the unique characteristics of the disorder. Autism and related disorders afflict roughly 20 of every 10,000 children (National Research Council, 2001). In recent years, the incidence of autism in the U.S. population has surged. The number of children served under the autism category of the Individuals with Disabilities Education Act (IDEA) grew from approximately 5,500 in 1992 to approximately 65,500 in 2000 (U.S. Department of Education, 2001). Autism impairs social interaction and communication in young children, and produces repetitive and stereotyped patterns of behavior. Children with autism often fail to make eye contact, to use spontaneous speech, or to develop age-appropriate social relationships with peers and caregivers. Further, they frequently engage in repetitive or stereotypic behaviors (e.g., rocking, hand flapping), adhere to nonfunctional routines and rituals, and display a lack of symbolic or imaginative play (American Psychiatric Association, 2000). Readers interested in additional information on the characteristics of children with autism and effective teaching strategies are encouraged to consult Bondy and Sultzer-Azaroff (2002), Koegel and Koegel (1995), and Maurice, Green, and Luce (1996).

Most persons with autism have some degree of mental retardation (Wing, 1996). Of all the deficits that can occur as a result of autism, impairment in communication is often the most devastating. Approximately 50% of children identified with autism will remain functionally mute in adulthood (Peeters & Gilbert, 1999). Communication skills are critical to the successful participation of children with autism in inclusive classrooms, home, and community settings. Therefore, technology intervention for children with autism has focused heavily on the development of augmentative and alternative (AAC) communication systems for children with limited speech abilities.

Technology and Augmentative and Alternative Communication (AAC)

A variety of AAC systems are available to assist children with autism in communicating, including sign language, voice-output communication aids (VOCAs) and other electronic devices, and picture-based systems (see Mirenda, 2002, for a review). Generally, these systems fall into two types: unaided and aided. Unaided systems, such as sign language, do not require a device. Aided systems, in contrast, require the user to carry or have a device available. Because of this chapter's focus on the use of technology, we will describe the characteristics and potential advantages and disadvantages of aided AAC systems only. Examples of aided systems include VOCAs, picture boards, and picture exchange systems.

A VOCA is a device that produces prerecorded voice output when the user activates a switch (Romski & Sevcik, 1997). The switch may be activated by pressing a button, typing on a keyboard, or touching a picture symbol on a touch-sensitive screen. Devices vary considerably in terms of technological sophistication and complexity of use. On the lower end of the spectrum are single-button devices that play only one prerecorded message. These tools are often appropriate for children with severe or profound disabilities, for whom the use of multiple-key devices may prove difficult. On the higher end of the spectrum are tools that employ sophisticated microcomputers and touch screens. Recent advances in computer technology, including the introduction of personal digital assistants (PDAs), have increased the use of high-tech VOCAs. These devices are often hand-sized computers that may be carried on a belt or strap, allowing the user to activate thousands of words and sentences. An advantage of more sophisticated VOCAs is the potential to engage in complex communication; however, users may require extensive instruction before they achieve fluency.

Research outcomes for VOCAs suggest that many users acquire independent, functional use of the devices (Romski & Sevcik, 1997; Schlosser, 1999). VOCAs allow children with autism who cannot talk to make their needs and wants known to those around them.

Further, children with autism who learn to communicate functionally may experience a number of additional benefits, including increases in spontaneous communication (Dyer, 1989) and reductions in inappropriate behavior (Durand & Carr, 1992). Finally, the recent introduction of sophisticated computer devices allows some users to engage in complex, reciprocal conversation with peers and adults.

Despite many advantages, several potential disadvantages are associated VOCAs. First, because they are battery-powered, they are subject to dead batteries, break downs, and other technology-related mishaps. Second, VOCAs are often costly to purchase, placing them out of range for children without the necessary financial resources. Further, the user is essentially "voiceless" without the VOCA; if a device breaks down or the child leaves it at home or at school, she has no way to communicate. Finally, if the child is out of hearing range of a listener, or the setting is noisy, his message may not be heard by those around him. To avoid some of these problems, parents and teachers must be vigilant about maintaining batteries, conducting the necessary maintenance, and making sure the device is with the child at all times.

In contrast to high-tech VOCAs, low-tech AAC devices include picture boards and picture exchange systems. Picture-boards are laminated sheets of paper with a series of picture symbols printed on them, to which the user points to communicate a want or need. The picture symbols may represent a variety of items and activities of importance to the user ("drink," "bathroom," "take a break," etc.). An advantage of these devices over VOCAs is that they are not subject to technology-related breakdowns. A major potential disadvantage is that if the listener is not within close proximity to the child, or is not looking at the child, the child's message may not be heard. Further, successful use of a picture board requires the child to cleanly point to picture symbols. This skill is difficult for some children with autism to acquire (Bondy & Frost, 1994).

Picture exchange systems are another low-tech AAC option for children with autism. The Picture Exchange Communication System (PECS)(Bondy & Frost, 2002) is the most widely used picture-based AAC system for children with autism (National Research Council, 2001). PECS is an instructional system for teaching a child who cannot talk to approach a listener and to exchange a picture symbol to make a need or want known. The PECS system is unique because it breaks down the teaching process into discrete phases, beginning with the basic picture exchange and progressing to the formation of sentences. Although the PECS system is very popular, only three published studies support its efficacy for children with autism (Bondy & Frost, 1994; Charlop-Christy, Carpenter, LeBlanc, & Kellet, 2002; Schwartz, Garfinkle, & Bauer, 1998). While the results of these initial studies are favorable, further research is needed to confirm the benefits of the system.

To summarize, both high- and low-tech AAC devices enable children with autism to express their wants and needs and, in some cases, to engage in reciprocal conversation. While high-tech AAC devices have been cost prohibitive for many children, the cost of many of these devices is beginning to decrease. Additionally, financial assistance to purchase such devices is available in many communities (Mirenda et al., 2000). Low-tech devices are an attractive alternative for some children. One system in particular, PECS, has gained popular acceptance and is supported by initial research studies.

Beyond communication deficits, children with autism often need extra assistance with academics, including reading and writing, and social skills. The next section describes technology interventions to teach academics and social skills.

Technology, Academics, and Social Skills Instruction

Because autism affects children's language and intellectual abilities to a significant degree, academic performance and social skills are also affected. The increasing presence of personal computers in classrooms allows teachers to incorporate software into academic and social skills instruction. Surprisingly, despite the use of computers in many special education classrooms, few studies have systematically examined the effects of computer-assisted instruction for children with autism.

Chen and Bernard-Opitz (1993) compared the effects of computer-assisted instruction and personal instruction on the enthusiasm, compliance, and learning of four children with autism. Overall, they found greater enthusiasm and compliance for computer-assisted instruction, but learning rates for computer-assisted instruction and personal instruction varied across subjects. Because the researchers did not specifically describe the content of the computer-assisted lessons, it is difficult to pinpoint which aspects of the instruction enhanced children's enthusiasm and compliance. Still, the study tentatively supports the positive benefits of computer-assisted instruction.

Heimann, Nelson, Tjus, and Gillberg (1995) also found positive outcomes for computer-assisted instruction. They examined the effects of a software program on the language skills of 30 children with autism, mixed disabilities, and without disabilities. The program taught children to develop basic reading and writing vocabularies and to create simple sentences. Specific outcome measures in the study included reading, sentence imitation, phonological awareness, and communication. On average, each group, including the children with autism, improved their language skills significantly across all outcome measures using the software program.

In another study investigating computer-assisted instruction, Hagiwara and Smith Myles (1999) used a personal computer to create interactive social stories for three children with autism. Social stories (Grey, 1995) have been a popular intervention for teaching children with autism to interact appropriately with others. A social story describes a pretend social situation to a student and gives cues for how to behave appropriately. Researchers measured the effects of the interactive social stories on children's appropriate behavior, including compliance with a hand-washing task, and on-task behavior. Unlike the previous studies, Hagiwara and Smith Myles found that multimedia social stories did not have a consistent positive impact on the acquisition of target skills or the generalization of skills to different environments.

As illustrated, studies have found mixed evidence in favor of computer-assisted instruction for children with autism. More research is needed to confirm the benefits of technology-based instruction, and to understand how technology may be used to enhance academic and social skills. Still, based on limited evidence, the following tentative conclusions about the benefits of technology for children with autism can be reached.

First, for children with autism who have limited speaking and writing skills, computer keyboards may provide an effective alternative for the expression of literacy skills. Heimann et al. (1995) successfully used a computer keyboard to develop literacy and communication skills for a group of children with autism.

Second, children with autism may prefer computer-assisted instruction to teacher-delivered instruction because of the interactive and game-like nature of some software programs. Chen and Bernard-Opitz (1993) found that children with autism were more enthusiastic about computer-assisted instruction, as measured by observer ratings.

Third, although not addressed directly in these studies, computer-assisted instruction may be more cost-effective because it allows the classroom teacher to work with a greater number of students. Of course, this benefit is offset by the costs of purchasing and maintaining computers.

Collectively, these benefits suggest that computers may be a useful instructional tool for children with autism.

Using Technology in the Home

A critical component of an effective educational program is that it provides for generalization of skills across settings (Stokes & Baer, 1977). Often, the most important generalization setting is the home. For assistive technology devices to be functional, therefore, children with autism must be able to use them in the home as well as the school (Lindsay, 2000). When a child's IEP includes the use of a technological device, such as a voice-output device, the educational team must consider how the device will be adopted successfully in the home. Important issues arise with regard to availability, family comfort and training, and

functionality of the device (Bothersome & Cook, 1996).

Availability
Technology equipment is often prohibitively expensive for families to purchase without assistance, and often schools do not allow equipment to be checked out. This leads to problems with skill acquisition and generalization. If the child can only use his device at school, he misses critical opportunities to communicate in the home and community. Many states operate technology loan programs through the Technology-Related Assistance for Individuals with Disabilities Act Amendments of 1994 (also known as the Tech Act [P.L. 103-218]), allowing families to utilize equipment in the home and community. However, some states that do not provide this service (Turnbull & Turnbull, 2001). When devices are available for checkout, problems arise with availability of specific devices, waiting lists are often long for families wishing to use specific items, or the items may be old or damaged.

The issues of availability, waiting lists, and up-to-date or properly functioning equipment may be more easily addressed at the local level. One way to offset issues of availability would be for schools to obtain grant money to fund an assistive technology lending library for the families they serve (see Brewer, Achilles, & Fuhriman, 1995; Ruskin & Achilles, 1995, for lists of funding sources).

Family Comfort and Training
Another issue related to the use of assistive technology in the home stems from the heterogeneity of families of children with autism. While some families may be familiar and comfortable using a particular piece of equipment, others may be confused by it, or feel uncomfortable using it. Parents from differing cultures may be intimidated or confused by the special education process (Al-Hassan & Gardner, 2002), and may have diverging views on the use of technology. Parent's perceptions of technology have been found to vary based on personal experiences, training, socioeconomic status, and cultural beliefs and traditions (Downing, 1999). For example, if family members do not use technology on a daily basis either at home or work, they may find

such equipment intimidating or unnecessary. On the other hand, families who have access to and frequently use technology in their daily lives may find it more appealing and less intimidating.

If a technology device is to be successfully adopted in the home, educators must be sensitive to parents' unique goals and expectations (Parette & McMahan, 2002). For example, if the family does not buy into the use of the device, it is unlikely that they will follow through on its use. In addition, many devices require specialized training. Families need to receive this training and to have access to assistance after school hours when they have questions or something goes wrong with the device. If families feel that they are not supported in the use of a specialized piece of technology for their child, they are less likely to support its use, and the child is less likely to use it effectively in the home and community. Finally, problems may arise with the comfort level of family members relative to the use of assistive technology. In the case of a VOCA or other augmentative communication device, for example, family members may feel self-conscious about the use of such an item in the community.

Schools need to be aware of issues related to family comfort and training in order to provide the support and training necessary to help families feel more comfortable in the use of the device. In addition, teachers need to take the time to listen to families and be aware of cultural differences that may impact the family's comfort level with technology. In so doing, schools can greatly improve the possibility that the equipment will be used, and used appropriately, in the home and community.

When a technology device is included as part of a student's educational program, the following steps are recommended to increase the family's acceptance of the device:

1. Explain fully why the educational team recommends the use of a technology device. Parents may perceive their child's limited communicative abilities (e.g., gestures, simple words) to be adequate. Give examples of how the device may be used to enhance the student's functioning in home and community settings. For example, the student might use a VOCA to order food

when the family is out for dinner or to ask permission to go outside to play. Do not assume that parents understand the utility of an assistive device just because team members recommend it.

2. Be sensitive to the parents' goals and expectations for assistive technology. Team members and parents may have different expectations about the level of independent functioning the student will be able to achieve with the device. The team should set realistic expectations for use of the device at home and address goals that are consistent with the family's desires and expectations.

3. Assess parents' sociocultural views and their experiences with technology. Some parents have limited experiences with technology in their daily lives or are uncomfortable with technology. Team members should ask if parents are comfortable with a device, or if they have any prior experience using technology (e.g., personal computers, PDAs). Parents who are inexperienced or uncomfortable with technology may need extra assistance and training.

4. Demonstrate how to use the device, allow for practice, answer questions, and give feedback. Given the sophistication of some devices, parents may not understand the basics of operation. Rather than simply telling the parent how to use the device, be sure to model for them how the device is operated. Parents will also need training on how to teach their child to use the device. If possible, visit the home and demonstrate the teaching procedures necessary for the child to acquire effective use of the device at home. Remember to give frequent positive feedback and encouragement, especially at first.

5. Conduct ongoing assessment of progress in technology use in the home. Do not assume that introduction of a device is sufficient to maintain its use over an extended period. A team member should touch base with the parent at least monthly to assess the child's use of the device at home. In some cases an assistive technology support person may be available to conduct followups, in other cases the responsibility for doing so may fall to the special education teacher or speech pathologist.

Periodic retraining may be necessary for parents to maintain use of the device.

Functionality of Device

When deciding on the type of assistive technology to be used by a child with autism, professionals need to consider the home environment. Conducting an ecological assessment in the home and community where the child will most likely use the device will allow the school to make an equipment decision that is appropriate for all environments (Lindsey, 2000). An ecological assessment "results in a list of skills that a particular student needs in order to function in settings in which she currently participates and those in which she will participate in the future" (Scheuerman & Webber, 2002, p. 16). In other words, an ecological assessment provides information about which skills within a particular environmental setting or activity that the child must have to be as independent as possible.

An ecological assessment also identifies factors within the environment that may contribute to the success or failure of an intervention system and types of supports that may promote success. For example, if Spanish is the primary language spoken at home, an ecological assessment would identify the need for a VOCA programmed to speak in Spanish. Ecological assessment would also identify the Spanish vocabulary words used most frequently by the student in the home setting.

Technology and Teacher Training

Assistive technology services for children with disabilities are mandated by IDEA-1997 (P.L. 101-476; Hartsell, 2000). Many children, especially those with limited communication abilities, have IEP goals and objectives that include the use of assistive technologies (Mirenda, Wilk, & Carson, 2000). When making technology decisions for students, many teachers are concerned about their own experience with and knowledge of particular devices. Teachers are more likely to use devices with which they are comfortable. Unfortunately, these devices are not always the most suitable for students (Heimann, Nelson, Tjus & Gillberg, 1995; Romanczyk, Weiner, Lockshin, & Ekdahl, 1999).

In addition, educational teams may make decisions for technology use that do not take into consideration the teacher's ability, or lack thereof, to use particular devices.

Since teachers will be responsible for teaching these students to use technology devices, it is essential that they are adequately trained in a variety of technology choices for children with autism (Hagiwara & Smith-Myles, 1999). Such training may be provided on an as-needed basis from a school district technology team, during inservice trainings or through conferences provided at the local, state, or national level. Ongoing training and support are recommended to ensure that teachers are up-to-date on the use of technology with students with autism (Webb, 2000). It is also recommended that teachers receive specific training on the use of devices prior to attempting to teach the device's use to students (Mirenda, 1997). Families may also need training on the use of a particular device, and teachers are often in the best position to offer this training. Therefore, it is essential that teachers feel comfortable and well trained in the use of a device so that they can, in turn, help families use the device. Finally, general education teachers who will be working with technology should also be trained on the use of devices. Again, this responsibility is likely to fall on the special education teacher.

Future Directions

A major issue in the use of technology with children with autism spectrum disorders is the lack of relevant research in the field. Gaps in the research literature can have negative consequences for practitioners, who often look to the literature to get ideas on what devices are available and how to use them effectively with students. Additionally, the absence of a solid research base leads practitioners to implement technology strategies that are not research proven, which may be ineffective or even detrimental. It is imperative that researchers and practitioners in the field of autism begin to produce relevant and meaningful research on the use of technology for children with autism and their families so that efficacy and appropriateness of use can be determined. Below we outline areas of where research is needed in the areas of computer assisted instruction and augmentative and alternative communication (AAC).

Computer-Assisted Instruction

Overwhelmingly, the existing research on the use of technology by children with autism has focused on augmentative communication devices. Although computer-assisted instruction has been shown to improve the motivation and skill development of children with autism in reading, and speech, and has led to reduction of aberrant behaviors (Chen & Bernard-Opitz, 1993; Heimann et al., 1995; Parsons & LaSorte, 1993), this research is dated, with some studies more than 10 years old. Current research is needed to explore the use of computer assisted-instruction for children with autism in all content areas as well as for improved speech and reduction of inappropriate behaviors. Research questions in future studies may address the effects of computer-assisted instruction on various academic skills; student and teacher preference of computer-assisted instruction; and the generality of learning gains from computer-assisted instruction to other skills and settings.

This is the age of technology, and it appears that computers are not a luxury, but a necessity in today's classrooms. Therefore, it is expected that we will begin to see an increased number of software programs available for teachers, as well as parents, to develop IEPs, behavior plans, picture-cued schedules, and communication boards for data collection and progress reporting. Educators in the field of autism should watch closely the increased use of these programs to discern those that are of greatest value to themselves and their students.

Augmentative and Alternative Communication Devices

Given the static nature of the speech and communication deficits of persons with autism, the use and availability of high-tech AAC devices is also expected to continue to expand. Many effective devices are currently commercially available; more are expected in the coming years. For this reason, it is critical that research be conducted on the efficacy of such devices, both new and old. While research on the use of AAC devices is prevalent in the literature, less research involves people with autism specifically. This gap in the literature must be narrowed if teachers are to select devices that are appropriate and useful for their students.

References

Al-Hassan, S., & Gardner, R. (2002). Involving immigrant parents of students with disabilities in the educational process. *Teaching Exceptional Children, 5*(2), 52-58.

American Psychiatric Association. (2000). *Diagnostic and statistical manual of mental disorders, fourth addition, text revision.* Washington, DC: American Psychiatric Association.

Bondy, A., & Frost, L. (1994).The picture exchange communication system. *Focus on Autistic Behavior, 9,* 1-19.

Bondy, A., & Frost, L. (2002). *The picture exchange communication system.* Newark, DE: Pyramid Educational Products.

Bondy, A., & Sultzer-Azaroff, B. (2002). *The pyramid approach to education in autism.* Newark, DE: Pyramid Educational Products.

Bothersome, M.J., & Cook, C.C. (1996) A home-centered approach to assistive technology provision for young children with disabilities. *Focus on Autism and Other Developmental Disabilities, 11*(2), 86-96.

Bottge, B.A., Heinrichs, M., Chan, S., & Serlin, R.C. (2001). Anchoring adolescents' understanding of math concepts in rich problem-solving environments. *Remedial and Special Education, 22,* 299-314.

Boyle, J.R. (2001). Enhancing the note-taking skills of students with mild disabilities. *Intervention in School and Clinic, 36,* 221-224.

Brewer, E. W., Achilles, C. M., & Fuhriman, J.R. (1995). *Finding funding: Grantwriting and project management from start to finish* (2nd ed.). Thousand Oaks, CA: Corwin Press.

Charlop-Christy, M. H., Carpenter, M., Le, L., LeBanc, L. A., & Kellet, K. (2002). Using the picture exchange communication system (PECS) with children with autism: Assessment of PECS acquisition, speech, social-communicative behavior, and problem behavior. *Journal of Applied Behavior Analysis, 35,* 213-231.

Chen, S.H.A., & Bernard-Opitz, V. (1993). Comparison of personal and computer-assisted instruction for children with autism. *Mental Retardation, 31,* 368-376.

Downing, J.E. (1999). *Teaching communication skills to students with severe disabilities.* Baltimore: Paul H. Brookes Publishing Co., Inc.

Durand, V. M., & Carr, E. G. (1992). An analysis of maintenance following functional communication training. *Journal of Applied Behavior Analysis, 25,* 777-794.

Dyer, K. (1989). The effects of preference on spontaneous verbal requests in individuals with autism. *Journal of the Association of Persons with Severe Handicaps, 14,* 184-189.

Grey, C. (1995). Teaching children with autism to "read" social situations. In K. Quill (Ed.), *Teaching children with autism: Strategies to enhance communication and socialization* (pp. 219–242). New York: Delmar.

Hagiwara, T., & Smith Myles, B. (1999). A multimedia social story intervention: Teaching skills to children with autism. *Focus on Autism and Other Developmental Disabilities, 14,* 82-95.

Hartsell, K. (2000). *Assistive technology: What is it? And when do we provide it?* (Available from the Georgia Project for Assistive Technology, 528 Forest Parkway, Suite C, Forest Park, GA 30297).

Heimann, M., Nelson, K.E., Tjus, T., & Gillberg, C. (1995). Increasing reading and communication skills in children with autism through an interactive multimedia computer program. *Journal of Autism and Developmental Disorders, 25,* 459-480.

Koegel, R.L., & Koegel, L.K. (1995). *Teaching children with autism: Strategies for initiating positive interactions and improving learning opportunities.* Baltimore: Paul H. Brookes.

Lindsay, J. D. (Ed.). (2000). *Technology and exceptional individuals* (3rd ed.). Austin, TX: Pro-Ed.

Maurice, C., Green, G., & Luce, S.C. (1996). *Behavioral intervention for young children with autism: A manual for parents and professionals.* Austin, TX: Pro-Ed.

Mirenda, P. (1997). Functional communication training and augmentative communication: A research review. *Augmentative and Alternative Communication, 13,* 207-225.

Mirenda, P. (2002). Augmentative and alternative communications systems. In A. Bondy &

L. Frost, *A Picture's worth: PECS and other visual communication strategies in autism* (pp. 43-66). Bethesda, MD: Woodbine House.

Mirenda, P., Wilk, D., & Carson, P. (2000). A retrospective analysis of technology use patterns of students with autism over a five-year period. *Journal of Special Education Technology, 15*(3), 5-16.

National Research Council. (2001). *Educating children with autism.* Washington, DC: National Academy Press.

Parette, P., & McMahan, G. A. (2002). What should we expect of assistive technology: Being sensitive to family goals. *Teaching Exceptional Children, 35*(1), 56-61.

Peeters, T., & Gillberg, C. (1999). *Autism: Medical and educational aspects.* London: Whurr.

Public Law 101-476 (1990). *Federal Register, 54,* 35210-35271.

Parsons, C., & LaSorte, D. (1993). The effect of computers with synthesized speech and no speech on the spontaneous communication of children with autism. *Australian Journal of Human Communication Disorders, 21,* 12-31.

Romanczyk, R., Weiner, R., Lockshin, S., & Ekdahl, M. (1999). Research in autism: Myths, controversies, and perspectives. In D. Berkell Zager (Ed.), *Autism: Identification, education, and treatment* (2nd ed., pp. 23-61). Mahway, NJ: Lawrence Erlbaum Associates.

Romski, M. A., & Sevcik, R. A. (1997). Augmentative and alternative communication for children with developmental disabilities. *Mental Retardation and Developmental Disabilities Research Reviews, 3,* 363-368.

Ruskin, K.B., & Achilles, C.M. (1995). *Grantwriting, fundraising, and partnerships: Strategies that work!* Thousand Oaks, CA: Corwin Press.

Scheuerman, B., & Webber, J. (2002). *Autism: Teaching does make a difference.* Belmont, CA: Wadsworth

Schlosser, R. W. (1999). Comparing the efficacy of interventions in augmentative and altnernative communication. *Augmentative and Alternative Communication, 15,* 56–68.

Schwartz, I. S., Garfinkle, A. N., & Bauer, J. (1998). The picture exchange communication system: Communicative outcomes for young children with disabilities. *Topics in Early Childhood Special Education, 18,* 144-159.

Stokes, T.F., & Baer, D.M. (1977). An implicit technology of generalization. *Journal of Applied Behavior Analysis, 10,* 349-367.

Technology-Related Assistance for Individuals with Disabilities Act Amendments of 1994, P.L. 103-218.

Turnbull, A., & Turnbull, R. (2001). *Families, professional, and exceptionality: Collaborating for empowerment* (4th ed.). Upper Saddle River, NJ: Merrill-Prentice Hall.

U.S. Department of Education. (2001). *Twenty-third annual report to congress on the implementation of the Individuals with Disabilities Education Act.* Washington, DC: Author.

Webb, B.J. (2000). Planning and organizing: Assistive technology resources in your school. *Teaching Exceptional Children, 32*(4), 50-55.

Wing, L. (1996). *The autistic syndromes.* London: Constable.

22

Augmentative and Alternative Communication: Infusing Communication in an Academic Setting

Laura J. Ball, Denise V. Bilyeu, Carrie Prentice, and David R. Beukelman

Communication among teachers and students is an intrinsic component of learning. When students experience such severe communication disorders that they cannot meet their daily communication needs, participation in educational and social activities is severely reduced and learning and social engagement are limited. Therefore, it is the goal of school personnel and families to support the communication effectiveness of students so that they can participate consistently in educational experiences. Educational goals involve the development of communication proficiency as well as a wide range of knowledge and skills. Although we typically think of communication as speaking, reading, and writing, the National Joint Committee for the Communicative Needs of Persons with Severe Disabilities (1992) provides a much more complete definition:

> Any act by which one person gives to or receives from another person information about that person's needs, desires, perceptions, knowledge, or affective states. Communication may be intentional or unintentional, may involve conventional or unconventional signals, may take linguistic or nonlinguistic forms, and may occur through spoken or other modes. (p. 2)

Children and youth who are unable to meet their daily communication needs through traditional speech, listening, reading and writing require alternative communication support.

This chapter focuses on augmentative and alternative communication (AAC) strategies for facilitating the interaction skills of students with severe speech and/or language disabilities. The American Speech-Language-Hearing Association (1989) has defined AAC as "an area of clinical practice that attempts to compensate (either temporarily or permanently) for the impairment and disability patterns of individuals with severe expressive communication disorders (i.e., the severely speech-language and writing impaired)" (p. 107).

Any student for whom gestural, speech, and/or written communication are temporarily or permanently inadequate to meet the various daily communication needs is likely to benefit from AAC interventions. Severe communication disorders result from a range of developmental, physical, cognitive, or social impairments. For many children, severe communication disabilities are chronic; hence, they will require AAC support throughout their lives. Other children eventually learn to communicate using natural speech. However, even for these children, AAC is necessary as a means of communication that facilitates language development, social engagement, and academic participation until they learn to speak well enough so that they can be understood (Glennen & DeCoste, 1997).

The needs and capabilities of children and youth with severe communication disabilities vary considerably. Thus, a review of the communication patterns of students from kindergarten through high school reveals the range of communication needs that must be met using AAC strategies and technology. These needs range from simple naming and requesting to complex conversations, public speaking, and sophisticated writing. Further, individual students who use AAC technology demonstrate a wide range of capability. For example, physically, some are able to use their hands to interact with a traditional or modified keyboard, while others can only control a single switch. Linguistically, some are able to read word choices and spell unique messages, while others have such limited literacy skills that they must interact with objects, pictures, or drawings that represent single words or complete messages. To accommodate this range of needs and capability, a wide variety of different AAC technology has been developed and is commercially available.

AAC Technology Components and Sample Devices

AAC technology contains five primary components: access method, symbol (symbolic representation: e.g., gestures, photographs, objects, spoken words, Braille), user display, output, feedback, and display for the student (see Table 1). The access method refers to the means of controlling a particular technology. Children with sufficient motor control can directly select an item (word, letter, or drawing) by touching it. Those with limited physical ability may use a light beam or a head mouse to directly select preferred items using head movement. Finally, those with very limited motor ability may control the technology with a single switch, while a cursor/indicator on the technology scans an array of the available options. Symbol refers to how meaning or language is depicted on the AAC technology. For example, pictures, drawings, or alphabet may represent words and phrases. Output refers to the information delivered from the student to the listener. Feedback refers to the information provided to the student using AAC so that she/he may monitor what messages have been selected. Display refers to the manner in which communicative choices are presented to the

student. These may be in a static/stationary (e.g., object, printed symbol) or dynamic/changing format (e.g., computer monitor, picture/symbol array). AAC is composed not of a single technology, but rather a "system" of multiple communication components. As mentioned, these components are integrated to create an AAC system with a single goal: to enhance communication (American Speech-Language Hearing Association, 1991).

To familiarize the reader with a range of AAC technology, several devices will be described, along with a brief summary of the needs and capabilities of the students who might use such technology. Table 1 lists AAC technology categorized in the manner presented for this text. Each category will be discussed in detail.

Figure 1 shows several AAC devices that are similar because they contain a limited number of words and messages that are prerecorded (digitized) using the voice of another child or adult. These AAC devices are all specified by Category 1 in Table 1. The total recording capacity of these devices ranges from a few seconds to about 8 minutes. The messages are represented by objects, pictures, drawings, or printed word; depending on the language capability of the student. Using these devices, students do not generate unique messages by spelling individual words; therefore all messages must be predetermined and prerecorded for communication in specific contexts with specific people.

An example, the BIGmack® Communicator (Ablenet, Inc.), stores a single message that is activated by pressing the large button on top. Beginning communicators who are learning to name items, request choices, greet others, or request assistance use the BIGmack®. Another example included in this group of devices is the Cheap Talk 8© (Enabling Devices), which can store up to eight messages. Technology such as this allows the beginning communicator to be more actively involved in choice making activities. Examples of AAC technology from this category include the BIGmack®, Cheap Talk 8© (Enabling Devices), Take or Place N Talk© (Enabling Devices), Step by Step Communicator® (Ablenet, Inc.), HipTalk Plus© (Enabling Devices), TalkTrac® (Ablenet, Inc.),

Table 1. Categories of AAC Technology Based on Student Needs

AAC Technology	Category 1	Category 2	Category 3	Category 4
Access Method	Direct	Direct Scanning	Direct Scanning	Direct Scanning
Symbol Presented to Student	Objects Picture Symbols Photographs Line Drawings	Picture Symbols Photographs Line Drawings Orthography	Picture Symbols Digital Photos Orthography	Picture Symbols Digital Photos Orthography
Display Presented to Student	Static	Static Dynamic	Static Dynamic	Dynamic
Feedback Presented to Student	Tactile Auditory	Tactile Auditory Visual	Tactile Auditory Visual	Tactile Auditory Visual
Message Format Presented to Listener	Digitized Speech	Digitized Speech	Synthesized Speech	Synthesized Speech
Capacity	Single array Up to 8 minutes	Multiple array 8 – 60 minutes	Single array Extensive memory	Multiple array Extensive memory

Note. Dependent upon the AAC technology category, students who use AAC receive forms of feedback from the technology and may be presented with various forms of visual/tactile displays. The visual/tactile display may also take different forms of symbolic representation and presentation of message to the listener. If a particular student's needs are evaluated, and goals developed accordingly, the most appropriate AAC technology category may more readily be determined. From this, the range of particular devices that meet the student's needs may be narrowed.

Figure 1. Selected AAC devices from category 1.

BIGmack® Communicator
(Ablenet, Inc.)

**Cheap Talk 8©
Communicator**
(Enabling Devices)

Take or Place N' Talk©
(Enabling Devices)

**Step-by-Step
Communicator®**
(Ablenet, Inc.)

Hip Talk Plus©
(Enabling Devices)

TalkTrac®
(Ablenet, Inc.)

Mini Com©
(Enabling Devices)

Take N Talk Go! Board©
(Enabling Devices)

Sequencer©
(Mayer-Johnson, Inc.)

One by Four Talker
(Attainment Company, Inc.)

Mini-MessageMate
(Words+, Inc.)

Mini-Com© (Enabling Devices), Take or Place N' Talk Go! Board© (Enabling Devices), Sequencer© (Mayer-Johnson, Inc.), One by Four Talker (Attainment Company, Inc.), and Mini-MessageMate (Words +©, Inc.) (see Figure 1).

Figure 2 contains several AAC devices that are similar to those described above, but can store from 8 to 60 minutes of prerecorded messages. For this technology (see Table 1, Category 2), the messages (words, phrases and sentences) must also be pre-selected by the AAC team and must be prerecorded by a naturally speaking child or adult. The individual messages can be represented using pictures, drawings, or traditional orthography, depending on the language and literacy level of the student. Given the number of different words and phrases that can be stored in this technology, longer messages can be formulated through combinations of prerecorded messages. Further, the individual messages can be activated in a variety of ways, including directly touching the locations with the fingers, activating them with a head-mounted stick, or using an eye safe laser (Zygo, Inc.). Also, the various messages can be scanned by a cursor so that the child can indicate her or his choice by activating a single switch. Another distinguishing factor of this technology group is the ability to store messages in levels (grouped in sets/pages). This allows thematic vocabulary arrangement that may be quickly accessed according to the activity or environment. One example, the Macaw device, introduces students to message formulation by allowing them to actively combine symbols in meaningful sequences. Because of the multiple page arrangement, message formulation can be accomplished in several functional environments without re-recording vocabulary. Students using this technology are learning to expand their language skills beyond simple naming and requesting. Figure 2 illustrates examples of AAC technology from this category, including the Great Green MACAW (ZYGO Industries, Inc.), DigiCom2000 (The Great Talking Box Company), Mighty/Mini MO™ (Dynavox, LLC), 7-level Communication Builder© (Enabling Devices), Tech/Speak (AMDi), Easy Talk, MessageMate 40 (Words +©, Inc.), ChatBox (Prentke Romich Co.), Falck VocaFlex Colour (Saltillo), and SpringBoard (Prentke Romich Co.).

Figure 3 contains a group of AAC devices that are fundamentally different from those described above. Instead of using prerecorded (digitized) speech, they have the capability to generate synthesized speech. Messages are stored or formulated using standard letter-by-letter spelling or individual word selection. Once the message is formulated and a "speak" command is activated, the technology produces a computer-generated (synthesized) voice. This strategy allows children to produce any message (single word, phrase, sentence, or narrative) that they wish; the device will speak the message. The message is spoken using a synthesized voice sounding like a male, female, or child. This technology is also unique in that messages are primarily accessed using a traditional keyboard that is either organized alphabetically (A through Z layout) or as a conventional computer keyboard (QWERTY layout). Messages are formulated using letter-by-letter spelling or by retrieving words or phrases that have been stored using an abbreviation such as "rmb" for the device to produce the word "remember" or typing "hh" for the device to produce "hi, how are you." In addition, this technology may contain word prediction capability; that is, as messages are formulated, the technology predicts a group of words (4-10 choices) that anticipate the intended message. If the technology accurately predicts an intended word, the student chooses that word, rather than spelling the entire word. The technology then attempts to predict the next word in the intended message, and so on. Word prediction and abbreviation expansion assist students in creating messages more rapidly, helping them to produce timely communicative interactions. This technology is used with persons who are skilled literate communicators. Figure 3 contains examples of AAC technology from this category (see Table 1, Category 3), including the DynaWrite™ (Dynavox, Inc.), LightWRITER™ (Toby Churchill, Ltd.), EZ Keys™ (Words +©, Inc.), Link Plus (Assistive Technology, Inc.), Dubby (Tash, Inc.), and Cresspeaker® MAXX II (Crestwood Communication Aids, Inc.).

Finally, Figure 4 contains a very sophisticated group of AAC devices (see Table 1, Category 4) that combine many of the features

Figure 2. Selected AAC devices from category 2.

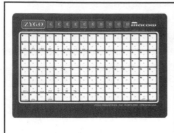

Great Green MACAW
(ZYGO Industries, Inc.)

Digicom2000
(The Great Talking Box)

Mighty/Mini Mo™
(Dynavox Systems, LLC)

7-Level Communication Builder©
(Enabling Devices)

Tech/Speak
(AMDi)

Easy Talk
(Sym Systems)

MessageMate 40
(Words+, Inc.)

ChatBox
(Saltillo, Inc.)

SuperTalker™
(Ablenet, Inc.)

Springboard
(Prentke Romich Company)

Faulk VocaFlex Colour
(Falck A/S)

adVOCAte
(Zygo Industries, Inc.)

described in the previous three groups. This technology produces synthesized speech output, allowing for the generation of unique messages. Many of the devices also have the capability to include a limited amount of pre-recorded (digitized) speech. As opposed to the technology in the previous group, these devices can support the communication efforts of young children, youth, and adults, because individual words and phrases can be represented by electronic drawings, printed words, and/or can be spelled on a letter-by-letter basis. This technology also contains word prediction capability.

Students control these devices by directly selecting individual locations with their fingers, head mouse, joystick, trackball, expanded keyboard, Morse code, or other alternative access options. They may also scan an array of choices and make the desired selection by activating a single switch. An example, the DM4™ (Dynavox, LLC) AAC device, enables the student to communicate by actively combining symbols and alphabet into functional messages. Prerecorded messages may be used for common songs, the Pledge of Allegiance, and so on. Students using this technology are participating in classroom activities, communicating with friends, and learning sophisticated language. Some items in this group include software programs that may be utilized with computer-based communication technology, allowing the student access to standard computer functions in addition to their communication options. Figure 4 shows examples of AAC technology from this category, including the DM4™ (Dynavox, LLC), DV4™ (Dynavox, LLC), Vanguard II (Prentke Romich Co.), Pathfinder (Prentke Romich Co.), Speaking Dynamically Pro Software, Talking Screen Software, Handheld Impact (Enkidu Research), Chat PC II (Saltillo Corp.), Mercury (Assistive Technology, Inc.), Say-it!SAM™ (Words+©, Inc.), e-talk (The Great Talking Box Co.), and Enkidu Tablet XL Impact (Dynavox, LLC).

Figure 3. Selected AAC devices from category 3.

DynaWrite™
(Dynavox Systems, LLC)

LightWRITER™
(ZYGO Industries, Inc.)

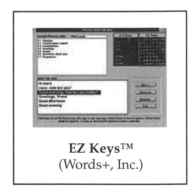

EZ Keys™
(Words+, Inc.)

Link Plus
(Assistive Technology, Inc.)

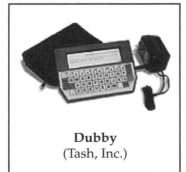

Dubby
(Tash, Inc.)

Crespeaker® MaxxII
(Crestwood Communication Aids, Inc.)

Figure 4. Selected AAC devices from category 4.

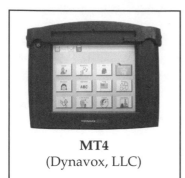

MT4
(Dynavox, LLC)

DV4
(Dynavox, LLC)

Vanguard II
(Prentke Romich Company)

Pathfinder
(Prentke Romich Company)

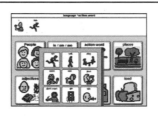

**Speaking Dynamically Pro
Application Software**
(Mayer-Johnson, Inc.)

Talking Screen
(Words+, Inc.)

Enkidu Handheld Impact
(Dynavox, LLC)

Chat PC
(Saltillo, Inc.)

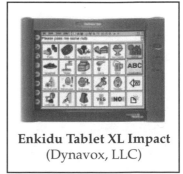

Mercury
(Assistive Technology, Inc.)

e-talk family
(The Great Talking Box)

SayIt!SAM™
(Words+, Inc.)

Enkidu Tablet XL Impact
(Dynavox, LLC)

AAC Service Delivery in the School Setting

In this section, we will first look at the overall goals of AAC in school, incidence of children with AAC, and the delivery of services by collaboration among a broad range of individuals.

Overall Goal of AAC in Schools

The goal of AAC is to maximize a student's potential in academic, social-emotional, and vocational pursuits by enabling functional communication. The academic component of AAC within the educational setting provides students with the opportunity to share information, ask questions, participate in discussions and other learning activities, and practice new skills. The social-emotional component provides students the opportunity to develop individual aspects of personality, express attitudes, select friends, and participate in preferred activities. Finally, the vocational component of AAC in the student's educational experience develops individual capabilities, therefore facilitating transitions from an educational setting to a vocational/volunteer setting, and from the role of student to the role of autonomous adult.

AAC Demographics in Schools

Demographic research reveals that 8 to 12 persons per 1,000 experience such profound speech disorders that they are unable to meet their daily communication needs using natural speech (Beukelman & Ansel, 1995). Survey results indicate that approximately 0.3-1% of school-age children are identified as having severe communication disabilities (Matas, Mathy-Laikko, Beukelman, & Legresley, 1985). These authors also reported that 3-5% of students certified for special education experience complex communication needs that would benefit from AAC. According to one study, 47% of speech-language pathologists in the public schools served children with AAC needs at some time during the school year (Simpson, Beukelman, & Bird, 1998). Research data are sparse regarding the demographics of implementation of AAC in the public schools.

Teachers are responsible for providing students with severe communication disabilities and their nondisabled peers with similar educational experiences. This includes presenting students with opportunities and the tools necessary to be active participants in the educational process. Communication plays a fundamental role in this process. For students with severe communication disabilities, AAC services support communication interactions at school, in the community, and at home.

Support for AAC in Schools

Delivery of AAC services to students in schools in the United States has long been a multidisciplinary activity in which speech-language pathologists play active roles as communication specialists (Beukelman & Mirenda, 1992). Idol, Paolucci-Whitcomb, and Neven (1986) present a comprehensive definition of collaboration:

> *Collaboration is an interactive process that enables people with diverse expertise to generate creative solutions to mutually defined problems. The outcome is enhanced, altered, and produces solutions that are different from those that the individual team members would produce independently. The major outcome of collaboration is to provide effective programs for students with needs within the most appropriate context, thereby enabling them to achieve maximum constructive interaction with their non-handicapped peers. (p. 1)*

A collaborative team approach involves utilizing individuals with diverse experiences to achieve mutual goals (Snell & Janney, 2000). The advantage is that team members rely on each other for expertise and reduce the burden of new learning for each member. By adhering to a collaborative approach, AAC team professionals also often eliminate duplication of services and reduce the time that the student is removed from "typical" school experiences. Table 2 illustrates suggestions for optimal roles for each team member, however the make-up of each team and various members' strengths will dictate optimal performance.

In order for a collaborative approach to be effective, the team must have regular face-to-face interactions, individual accountability, agreed-upon and exclusive responsibilities, mutual goals, and a structure for addressing

Table 2. Roles of Select AAC Team Members in Educational Settings

Note. Abbreviations represent: M= manager, or the person with the primary responsibility for the item. A = assistant, or the person who provides instructional assistance or supports for the item. C = consultant, or person who supports managers and assistants in implementation.

	Classroom Teacher	Educational Paraprofessional	Speech Pathologist	AAC Specialist	Motor Therapist	Parents	Peers
Vocabulary Selection	M	A	A	C		A	A
Language Development	A		M				
Functional Communication, Classroom	M	A	A	C		A	A
Speech/Language Intervention			M	C			
AAC Device Selection	C		A,C	M	A	A	
AAC Device Vocabulary Programming	A	M	A,C			A	
AAC Device Setup & Troubleshooting			A	M			
AAC Device Programming Training			A	M			
AAC Device Organization	C		A	M			
Monitoring Physical Access	M	A	A		C	A	
Classroom Arrangement	M						
Designing Functional Alternative Modalities (Non-device)	A	A		M	A	A	
Curriculum Modification	M		C	C			
Supporting Individual Participation & Independence		M					A
Coordinating Communication Effectiveness Feedback With Team	M	A	C		A	A	
Team Member Liaison (Family)	M	A					
Transition & Setup In Daily Activities		M					A

issues, performance and monitoring (Hunt, Soto, Maier, Muller, & Goetz, 2002). An AAC collaborative team may be comprised of any or all of the following: the student who uses AAC, peers, family members, classroom teacher, resource teacher, special education liaison, speech/language pathologist, occupational therapist, physical therapist, psychologist, educational paraprofessional, school administrators, vision consultant, hearing consultant, and/or medical personnel. Depending upon the unique situation of an individual student, the intensity of involvement of team members varies. In the sections below, typical roles of selected team members are described.

Teacher Roles on the AAC Team

The roles of certain AAC team members (i.e., speech-language pathologists, occupational therapists and physical therapists) have been well defined in the literature (Locke & Mirenda, 1992). In isolation or outside of the classroom, these professionals may not be able to deliver optimal AAC services to address the student's educational goals. Little information has been reported in the literature about the role of teachers on AAC teams. Locke and Mirenda (1992) surveyed special education teachers to obtain information describing their roles/responsibilities on teams delivering AAC services. Thirty-seven percent of special education teachers acted as team leaders, and all reported numerous other roles and responsibilities. Traditional "teacher roles" that were documented included adapting curriculum for AAC implementation, preparing and maintaining documentation, writing goals and objectives, assessing cognitive abilities, acting as liaison between school team members and parents, assessing social capabilities and providing for ongoing skill development. Less traditional duties assumed by teachers included developing appropriate vocabulary for students' communication systems, determining students' motivation and attitudes toward their AAC systems, and determining their students' communication needs.

Educational Paraprofessional Roles on the AAC Team

Educational paraprofessionals are integral in the inclusive education of students who use AAC. They may support the entire classroom, or assist a single student using AAC in a one-to-one capacity. In a one-to-one capacity, the paraprofessional assists the single student who uses AAC to whom they are assigned. Encouraging and coaching communication between the student using AAC and peers is a primary focus of the paraprofessional. This is often difficult because their close proximity with the student using AAC leads to a tendency to interact directly with the student and then "translate" to others, rather than requiring individual communication attempts/interactions. The "entire classroom" approach allows the paraprofessional to assist the classroom teacher and other students. This may allow them to make better use of their time, allow the student using AAC greater independence, and provide the classroom teacher with additional assistance.

Because of their daily involvement with the student using AAC, paraprofessionals are often excellent informants about a student's limitations and progress within specific lessons and classroom activities. They assist the team in selection of vocabulary to support educational and social interactions, and may enter/program this vocabulary into the AAC technology. In some instances, the paraprofessional may facilitate transitions across grade levels by providing necessary information about the student's past and current communication and learning strategies (Beukelman & Mirenda, 1992). Paraprofessionals take directions from other team members and work at realizing these recommendations. Some examples include (a) setting up AAC equipment, (b) assisting with transitions among activities and environments, (c) entering/programming vocabulary into the AAC technology, and (d) modifying the communication options for successful inclusion. Paraprofessionals have the unique challenge of providing support (scaffolding) for the student in the classroom, while at the same time ensuring opportunities for increased independence.

Parent Roles on the AAC Team

Along with teachers, parents play a vital role on the collaborative AAC team. To achieve a successful educational experience for the child and to maintain an effective system at home, teams are sensitive to the needs of the students' families. When family needs, preferences, and priorities are identified and honored during the assessment and implementation process, the family is more likely to be supportive of the team's goals. According to Angelo, Jones, and Kokoska (1995), "the family's willingness to support recommendations and implement AAC interventions continues to be an important variable in predicting successful outcomes" (p. 194). For example, family involvement has been shown to be essential in vocabulary selection for a student's AAC system (Carlson, 1981; Fried-Oken & More, 1992; Light, Beesley, & Collier, 1988; Yorkston, Dowden, Honsinger, Marriner, & Smith, 1988; Yorkston, Fried-Oken, & Beukelman, 1988); in facilitator training (Beukelman, 1991; Light et al., 1988); and in literacy learning (Koppenhaver, Evans, & Yoder, 1991). Most important, throughout a child's education, family members play an essential role in maintaining consistency and providing information about the components of their child's AAC program (Berry, 1987).

One important role of parents is to convey their educational concerns to the collaborative AAC team members. In this way, the team may collaborate to prioritize goals, giving consideration to the parent's concerns. Angelo, et al. (1995) surveyed mothers and fathers of young children (3-12 years) who used AAC for speaking and/or writing. The top concerns of mothers included integrating the child's technology into the community, developing community awareness and support for children who use AAC, obtaining computer access for their child, planning for future communication needs, and finding trained professionals to work with their child. In addition, fathers cited a strong desire for more education and understanding of how to use their child's technology, how to teach their child, and how to utilize the AAC system in the home environment. Finally, families of adolescents and adults who use AAC voiced many of the same concerns (Angelo, Kokoska, & Jones, 1996). Specifically, mothers most often expressed concerns about their child having social opportunities with nondisabled peers, as well as with other persons using AAC. Fathers concerns included integrating the child's technology into educational settings and obtaining computer access for their adolescent.

Peer Roles on the AAC Team

Peer interaction is vital for social growth, and developing peer relationships is often challenging for students who use AAC. Peer relationships range in significance for students who use AAC. At one end of the spectrum, peers may simply be part of the world around the student using AAC; at the other end, peers may be an integral component of the AAC support system. Overall, nondisabled children who have interacted with children with disabilities report more positive attitudes toward AAC than children who are less familiar with disabilities (Beck & Dennis, 1996; Blockberger, Armstrong, O'Conner, & Freeman, 1993; Beck, Kinsburg, Neff, & Dennis, 2000). Gender has also been found to influence peer attitudes. That is, nondisabled boys display a less positive attitude than nondisabled girls toward children who have disabilities and children who use AAC (Beck & Dennis, 1996; Beck et al., 2000; Blockberger et al., 1993; Rosenbaum, Armstrong, & King, 1986).

Communication Considerations for the Student Who Uses AAC

In the following section, we will discuss the unique communication challenges of students who use AAC and offer suggestions for enhancing their communicative competence.

Communicative Competence

Just as other students develop and refine their communication skills as they grow, students who use AAC must work to achieve their level of communicative competence. According to Light (1989), the wide range of skills that individuals who use AAC must learn to become competent communicators with their AAC technology include linguistic, operational, social, and strategic skills. In addition, communicative competence encompasses personal characteristics, partner characteristics, and environmental factors. In order to understand the complexity of using an AAC system well, it is important to understand each of the skills that contribute to competence.

According to Light (1989), linguistic skills include receptive and expressive abilities in the native language spoken by the family and broader social community. For students who use AAC, linguistic skills include the additional task of learning the language (linguistic code) of their AAC system (e.g., single-meaning symbols, multi-meaning icons, forms of text). Operational skills refer to the technical skills required to use the AAC system effectively. For example, the student must know how to physically access his/her system (via hands, single switch, head pointer, etc.) and how to navigate through the system's features and vocabulary to construct messages. Social skills, in turn, refer to knowledge, judgment, and skills in the social linguistic rules of interaction. For example, social skills would include the ability to initiate, maintain, and terminate interactions with a communication partner. These skills also include the ability to use an AAC system to express language functionally (e.g., requesting, protesting, sharing information, seeking information, commenting). Finally, strategic skills refer to compensatory strategies employed by students who use AAC. These skills are used to overcome communication breakdowns and technology limitations so that they may engage effectively with unfamiliar listeners. For example, communication breaks down when the message is misunderstood. The student now has the option of repeating the same message, rephrasing the message using different vocabulary, or selecting a message on his or her AAC technology that cues the listener regarding the intended topic.

Taking all of these skills into consideration, it becomes clear that students who use AAC must deal with many concerns simultaneously in order to be effective communicators. Many of these skills are learned most effectively through practice in the student's natural environment than through drill or isolated therapy. In other words, a student becomes a competent communicator by attempting and refining skills based on the situations that arise daily across a variety of environments.

Light (1988) identified four communication domains to consider when providing AAC services, including the communication of wants/needs, transfer of information, communication for social closeness, and etiquette.

Communication of Wants/Needs

Educators and families readily understand the importance of communicating wants and needs. A student develops independence by regulating his or her own physical state (e.g., requesting to use the restroom) and directing his or her learning needs (e.g., asking to be moved in order to see the blackboard). As important as it is to express wants and needs, however, communication for learning involves more than simply requesting.

Information Transfer

A student who uses AAC must process information and engage in interaction by sharing information. This includes academic content (e.g., what planets are part of the solar system), as well as personal information, experiences, and opinions that shape a student's knowledge base. Teachers and educational paraprofessionals typically contribute information about vocabulary needed to share information related to academic activities.

Social Closeness

Communication to establish and maintain social closeness includes a range of "small talk," asking questions of others, and expressing interest in others and their activities. Messages used to develop social closeness differ considerably from the messages used in academic participation. Parents and peers typically contribute information about the vocabulary of social closeness.

Etiquette

Messages to communicate etiquette include expression of apology, thanks, and appreciation. As students grow older, their expressions of etiquette increase and become more sophisticated. It is necessary for the AAC team to include etiquette messages that are age, and context, appropriate for the student. Table 3 illustrates school environmental examples of the four communication domains described by Light (1988).

Assessment of Social Needs

Several tools have been developed to support

Table 3. School Setting Examples Illustrating Light's (1988) Four Communication Domains

	Wants & Needs	Social Closeness	Information Transfer	Etiquette
Classroom	Signaling lack of understanding during an activity	Asking a peer to work in a group	Answering a question posed by the teacher	Saying "thank you " to a student for helping with a group assignment
Hallway	Asking directions to the nurse's office	Greeting a fellow student	Giving a visitor directions to the office	Saying "excuse me" in the hallway when needing extra room
Cafeteria	Ordering lunch in the cafeteria	Offering to share their dessert with another student	Telling the cook about a food allergy	Saying "yes, please" when offered a second food helping
Playground	Telling the teacher he/she needs help to get on the slide	Complimenting a friend for making a basket during a game	Explaining playground rules to a new student	Apologizing for bumping into a classmate when standing in line

educational staff in analyzing the social networks of students who use AAC. Making Action Plans (MAPS) (Pearpoint, Forest, & O'Brien, 1996), Circles of Friends (Snow & Forest, 1987), and Planning Alternative Tomorrows with Hope (PATH) (Pearpoint, O'Brien, & Forest, 1993) were introduced in the 1980s and 1990s to document levels of social engagement of students with disabilities and to track changes in their social networks. More recently, Social Networks (Blackstone, 2003) has been proposed as a strategy to document and guide the development of social relationships for children and adults who use AAC. Tools such as those mentioned provide school personnel with systematic strategies to focus on the social needs of students with severe disabilities.

Communication Patterns in the School Setting

Communication patterns in schools are primarily teacher directed, and as a result somewhat different from conversational patterns in other contexts. For a student who uses AAC, these interaction patterns have direct implications on selection of vocabulary, strategies for managing increased message complexity during ongoing instructional activities, and the integration of the student into instructional contexts (e.g., classroom setup, educator style). Studying communication patterns in first-, third-, and fifth-grade classrooms, Sturm and Nelson (1997, p. 270) identified 10 unofficial "rules" that guide interactions:

1. Teachers mostly talk and students mostly listen, except when the teacher grants them permission to talk.
2. Teachers give cues about when to listen closely.
3. Teachers convey content about things and procedures about how to do things.
4. Teacher talk gets more complex in the upper grades.
5. Teachers ask questions and expect specific responses.
6. Teachers give hints about what is correct and what is important to them.
7. Student talk should be brief and to the point.
8. Students should ask few questions and keep them short.
9. Students talk to teachers, not to other students.
10. Students can make a limited number of spontaneous comments, but only about the process or content of the lesson.

These rules have implications for students who use AAC and participate in large-group instructional learning situations. That is, knowledge of these rules dictates the type of message the child is expected to produce (e.g., brief, content-specific, teacher-directed), the manner in which the message is produced (e.g., combined whole message and word-by-word message creation capability), and the vocabulary needs that may be anticipated either on the AAC technology or through other means (e.g., flip chart, white board, vocabulary list).

According to Beukelman and Mirenda (1998), communication patterns among students in small cooperative learning groups closely resemble a peer conversational interaction. That is, while communication patterns in large-group, teacher-led instruction are quite predictable, the communication patterns and the vocabulary used in small-group activities are much less predictable. Providing generic messages on an AAC system may enable participation in the cooperative learning group situation without being content-specific. To ensure active participation of the student who uses AAC, the teacher may consider providing additional direction regarding roles of the group members.

Simpson (1996) noted that the communication of students who use AAC technology in classrooms varies considerably; however, three predominant patterns were observed during one-to one interactions: Students communicated (a) primarily with their teachers, (b) primarily with their educational paraprofessionals, or (c) equally among teachers, educational paraprofessionals, and peers. An environmental assessment of the type of interactions, instructional styles, peer involvement, and student expectations that apply will help determine vocabulary and other communication needs to facilitate one-one interactions (Beukelman & Mirenda, 1992).

Messaging/Vocabulary

Students who use AAC need to have access to a variety of messages. Some messages need to be produced in a "timely manner (e.g., "I'm fine, thanks, how are you?" "Excuse me, please"). Some messages need to be urgent (e.g., "Help!" "Stop that!"). Some messages

need to relate to the content of classroom instruction (e.g., current president of the United States, parts of a plant, or mathematical terminology). Some messages need to be novel (e.g., "last night I had a bad dream about a monster") while others can be somewhat anticipated (e.g., "last night I had a dream"). Finally, some messages are long and detailed (e.g. story about a birthday party, description of a hospital stay, trip to the zoo). In order to accommodate the varying nature of these messages, students who use AAC must have different message types available in their system.

In order for the AAC team to store appropriate messages in the AAC technology, a range of informants is required. Teachers control most of the interactions in the classroom; therefore they are great informants about the vocabulary to be included in their students' AAC systems. Family members provide important information about vocabulary related to personal experience outside of school that the student may wish to communicate with teachers and peers. Peers can provide unique age-appropriate messages, including small talk and slang. Finally, speech language pathologists often provide vocabulary related to social interaction and social closeness. In addition, they usually take the lead role in organizing, representing, and personalizing the vocabulary of a particular student.

AAC and Classroom Arrangement

Frequently, students who use AAC are positioned in the rear or side of the classroom, so that other assistive technology, such as a wheelchair or computer, can be accommodated (e.g., with space, electrical power, room for the paraprofessional). Unfortunately, this is rarely the best learning situation for the student. Instead, organizing the classroom so that the student using AAC is positioned near the teaching center results in greater interactions and classroom participation, as the teacher can use the instructional materials to support communication. For example, the teacher may use pictures, charts, a white board, or objects to teach a lesson. The teacher may then ask students using AAC to respond by pointing (e.g., with hands, eyes, a light) to their desired response. Often it is useful to organize the classroom with a "wide" center aisle or a wide aisle along the side of the classroom. In this way, students who use AAC have access to the teaching center(s). Additional classroom accommodations may include using cut-out desk tops or tables, using tables with adjustable height, providing a vertical work surface with a tilt, placing chalk boards low and positioned away from the wall, and arranging hardware in a low position (e.g., door knobs, light switches, coat racks, pencil sharpeners).

Curriculum and AAC

Until recently, teachers faced the challenge of teaching students who use AAC without a set curriculum. This resulted in "splinter" skill development (Fuller, Lloyd, & Schlosser, 1992; Glennen, 1997). In today's more inclusive atmosphere, students with special needs are integrated into general education classrooms. Using the general curriculum allows teachers to access existing resources rather than creating new ones. However, care should be taken to ensure that if a specific curriculum is followed, emphasis continues to be placed on the student's communication by incorporating AAC within classroom interactions. Inclusion of the student who uses AAC in the general curriculum creates a structure for peer interactions and support, and generates a competitive spirit with peers (Sturm, 1998). When looking at the educational goals of students who use AAC, it is important to remember that the goals of these students remain unchanged from those of their peers (e.g., obtaining general knowledge about the solar system). However, because of specific challenges, objectives towards obtaining these goals may need to be altered. Personalized educational programs as mandated by federal law (e.g., PL 94-142), is a means by which families, students and school personnel may achieve educational success for the student who uses AAC.

Once a student's social, communication, and academic goals have been determined, educators can coordinate their efforts by establishing clear goals and objectives. Calculator and Jorgensen (1991) proposed guidelines for developing integrated goals and objectives, stating that they should: (a) specify functional outcomes, (b) use natural settings, (c) clearly identify outcomes, (d) be measurable, (e) teach AAC skills as part of larger skill clusters, and (f) reflect implementation of the objectives in the environment (and with the people) which are functional and appropriate to the stated goal (and to the particular student). For example, a nonintegrated objective might read, "While seated at a table across from a classmate and instructed to 'hit the switch', John will do so at a rate at least 50% faster than his present average performance." On the other hand, an integrated objective might read, "While working at a table with a peer, John will indicate a desire to take a turn by using any communication mode available to him on 4 out of 5 consecutive occasions." In the latter example, goals and objectives are both functional and related to the general curriculum.

Participation Model

Beukelman and Mirenda (1998) developed a framework for making decisions and developing goals/objectives for including students who use AAC in general educational programs, the Participation Model. Within this model, they proposed four variables that educators and support staff may manipulate to develop a participation pattern in the classroom that fits the individual needs and capabilities of each student who uses AAC: integration, independence, academic participation, and social participation.

First, consider the level of integration. Beukelman and Mirenda (1998) define the term as "the physical presence of a student with disabilities in a general classroom attended by same-age peers" (p. 396). Students may be fully integrated, selectively integrated, or not integrated.

A student's independence can by gauged along a continuum (Independent -->Independent with Setup --> Assisted), with the goal for all students using AAC technology being maximum independence.

Students who are *Independent* are able to participate in activities with no assistance. Students who are *Independent with Setup* may require appropriate environmental and technical assistance with educational materials and their AAC technology, but then participates independently. Other students are *Assisted* in terms of AAC technology and classroom participation. For many students who use AAC, independence in the school environment is dependent upon the support staff working with the student (e.g., to independently participate in geography class, the appropriate vocabulary needs to be programmed ahead of time).

Within the Participation Model, *academic participation* is discussed in terms of four descending levels. *Competitive academic participation* is when students using AAC are measured by the same standards as their peers, although workloads may be adjusted. *Active academic participation* is when the expectations for students using AAC are adjusted, although the general content remains the same. *Academic involvement* is when the expectations and content are adjusted. Finally, *no academic participation* is when the students are excluded from learning activities entirely.

Along with academic participation, the school environment serves as a medium for social participation. As with all students, students who use AAC most likely define a great deal of their social self by school life. Differing from typical students, students who use AAC may not have other social interactions outside of their family. The Participation Model defines the levels of *social participation* in the same manner as academics (i.e., competitive, active, involved, none). This, *competitively social* students participate actively in social interactions and influence their peer group. Students who are *active participants* are involved in social interactions, but do not influence the peer group directly. *Socially involved* students are typically passive participants and may attend classes, but do not affect their peers. Finally, unfortunately, there are also students who have *no social participation* and limited access to their peers and any extracurricular activities.

Both academic and social participation are in some part determined by the student's abilities. However, the extent of a student's inclusion or exclusion from social and academic venues is also dependent upon the staff and peers at the school, and the family. Educational staff and family members must encourage social participation regardless of the academic participation level. Beukelman and Mirenda

(1998) submit that barriers to opportunity include those of policy, practice, attitude, knowledge and skill. Removal of academic or social barriers to achieve inclusion and higher levels of participation may require changes in school rules, access accommodations, peer and staff training and/or other changes.

If inclusion is not accomplished, negative results may occur, including (a) lack of continuity of educational programs (resulting in splinter skills, gaps, oversights, and redundancies), (b) reduced peer interactions (resulting in decreased desire to compete with peers to learn), (c) diminished peer instruction (diminishing opportunities to participate in cooperative learning groups), (d) negative self-image (and negative impressions of the student who uses AAC from a peer, family, and teacher perspective), in addition to (e) legal ramifications from the school system's lack of compliance with public law. In summary, the primary reasons for including students who use AAC into the general curriculum are to provide them with enriched educational and social benefits obtained from the classroom setting (Beukelman & Mirenda, 1998).

Curriculum Accommodations

Academic participation can only take place in the presence of accommodations for a student's unique input and output needs. Altering the means of input to the student and output acceptable to the teacher (e.g., expected product, adaptive equipment) are in which educators can make adaptations for a student who uses AAC.

Output Accommodations

Most often, output accommodations alter the amount of product expected from a student, or the mode in which the student presents the product. For example, a student with athetoid cerebral palsy may be capable of typing on a regular keyboard and providing the same type of written assignment that other classroom students are expected to provide. However, due to the extent of the student's motor difficulties, it may require an excessive amount of time to complete the assignment. In situations such as this, modifications to the length and/or format may be prudent. For example, it may be possible for the student to complete a shortened written assignment, and then provide the remainder of the answers verbally (using a specific AAC device). Time constraints may also arise because of a student's physical and medical needs. For example, a student who requires tube feeding three times daily will likely miss classroom instruction and work time. Such scheduling conflicts may also result in the need for shortened or amended assignments.

Accommodations may also include supplemental communication strategies in addition to the AAC technology. Although a particular student can competently use AAC technology to communicate, he or she may not be able to utilize it in all situations. This may occur when the student becomes involved in a group activity that requires changing the configuration of the classroom. For example, during a hands-on art activity the student may not be able to sit in his or her wheelchair where the AAC technology is mounted, or may have difficulty accessing the technology because of a lack of physical support. Also, educational staff may have difficulty keeping up with programming new vocabulary during curriculum content shifts. When this occurs, the student may need to access communication in a different manner. For example, a teacher may write key vocabulary words on a flip chart in the front of the room during a lecture. This allows the student who uses AAC to refer to the flip chart (using eye gaze, pointing, etc.) to answer and ask questions. This illustrates an essential principle in AAC services, that of an *AAC system*, which permits students to have access to communication alternatives in addition to a single AAC device. A student may be able to use AAC technology and also use several alternative strategies and/or techniques when the technology is unavailable or inefficient.

Input Accommodations

This type of accommodation alters the means by which materials are presented to the student who uses AAC. For example, a student with hearing impairment may require a written copy of lecture notes. Likewise, to aid comprehension of vocabulary, concepts, and stories in a preschool classroom, several adaptations may be made. Some examples include simplification of story plots, stories with a repeated line (e.g., the line from the story *The*

Very Hungry Caterpillar [Carle, 1986]: "But he was still hungry!"), repetition of stories, use of props during story telling, drama, use of pantomime, signs and gestures, follow up activities to reinforce vocabulary and concepts, and use of sign language and communication devices (West, Bilyeu & Brune, 1996). To assist in language and cognitive development, educators may provide information to students in multiple modalities, facilitating a student's comprehension of curricular content.

Academic Expectations

In a survey of a group of adults using AAC, McNaughton, Light, and Arnold (2002) reported themes emerging in communications regarding academic expectations. A predominant theme indicated that these individuals "made their greatest academic progress when expectations were high and that too often the expectations of special education teachers were low and the educational activities provided were inappropriate" (p. 72). The implications for use of the curriculum as a measure of accountability, attainment of established goals and objectives, and continually evaluating the changing current and future needs of a student using AAC are weighty.

Lue (2001) sees use of a curriculum as providing the teacher with a framework for skills students should master at various stages, and an accountability measure for meeting educational standards. When developing goals, determining academic progress, and interacting in each classroom activity, a teacher's high expectations of the student who uses AAC are imperative. The ChalkTalk program (Culp & Effinger, 1996), for example, provides a framework and suggestions to assist AAC team members in developing appropriate goals, assessing levels of success, and maintaining continuity in the presence or absence of a standard curriculum.

Literacy Skills and AAC

Literacy skills (reading and writing) are instrumental in facilitating participation in today's society. For a person who uses AAC, the development of literacy skills can lead to the ability to utilize complex communication systems (see Table 1, Categories 3 & 4), academic success, social involvement, volunteerism, and employment. Students who use AAC often have impaired language systems, limited literacy skill practice, and an underestimated literacy learning potential. Subsequently, they lag behind their peers in the development of literacy skills. In a striking example, Berninger and Gans (1986) reported that approximately 50% of students with cerebral palsy and normal intelligence demonstrated reading skills significantly below grade level.

Students who use AAC, especially those with physical disabilities, often do not participate in activities that support the emergence of literacy skills. Similarly, students with severe motor impairments rarely interact with or use writing tools (Koppenhaver, Evans, & Yoder, 1991) and are reliant upon others to provide literacy experiences for them. If little adaptive equipment is available, "normal" literacy experiences may be inaccessible to the child (Light, Kelford-Smith, & McNaughton, 1990). For example, a child with significant motor involvement may be motivated to read a book and look at the pictures, but may have difficulty turning the pages. Without the help of another person or adaptive equipment, the child will be unable to interact with the book.

Another contributing factor to the poor literacy skills of persons who use AAC is the limited availability of instructional time combined with the presence of other superseding needs. A student's time at home and at school is often taken up with physical, therapeutic, and medical concerns. Light et al. (1990) asked parents of students with severe speech and physical impairments to rate specific priorities for their children. Literacy was rated as a low priority and physical needs as a high priority. Because other needs are more urgent and perhaps greater; students with severe disabilities often become adults with poor literacy skills. Koppenhaver, Coleman, Kalman, and Yoder (1991) cite the research on emergent literacy and emphasize the following:

1. The process of learning to read and write is a continuum that begins at birth.
2. Reading, writing, speaking and listening abilities develop concurrently and inter-relatedly, rather than sequentially.
3. The functions of literacy are as integral to literacy learning as the forms.

4. Children learn written language through active engagement with their world.

Students who use AAC have specific needs that differ from those of typical students. However, when planning interventions or teaching strategies; these four conclusions should be considered. Students need exposure to and interaction with literacy materials. For example, allowing a student to illustrate his or her own text by utilizing a computer drawing program permits the student to be an active participant in the writing process. Although the end product may differ from that of peers, the creative process is more important than the actual end product.

Literacy Intervention

Literacy intervention for students who use AAC can be divided into two categories, provision of physical access to literacy and provision of cognitive access to literacy. *Physical access to literacy* and literacy materials simply means making the necessary accommodations for the student to manipulate and get into literacy materials. Quite often, physical access accommodations that have been made for a communication system also allow a student to access literacy materials. For example, a student who accesses a DynaVox (see Table 1, Category 4) by scanning a display and then selecting intended messages by activating a switch may use the same switch setup and scanning to write spelling words on a computer with a similar scanning function. Additionally, physical access may involve the transfer of printed materials to a computer program. The student can then read at his or her own pace, and independently turn the pages of text by activating a switch. In addition, the use of an alternate keyboard may enable a student with poor motor control to use the same word processor as his or her peers in the classroom.

Another accommodation for students who use AAC involves *cognitive access to literacy* and literacy materials (e.g., utilizing or creating materials at a level commensurate with the student's language and cognitive abilities). Some examples include (a) rewriting the text of a book that contains vocabulary and grammar so that the child may understand, (b) using picture symbols familiar to the child to accompany text and allow independent reading, (c) utilizing a talking word processor to read text and highlight word by word so that the student may follow along, and (d) creating a picture dictionary on the computer so that students can look up words they do not know how to spell. Enhancing cognitive access to literacy provides students a means by which they can become active participants in the learning process. Table 4 illustrates literacy enhancement technology applications for students who use AAC.

While creating physical and cognitive access to literacy is essential, creating literacy opportunities may be an overriding factor. Simple tasks such as reading shopping lists, reading street signs, writing in calendars, writing thank-you notes, drawing pictures, listening to stories, singing songs, rhyming words, and reading labels may be embedded into daily routines, as they are for typically developing children.

Pierce and McWilliam (1993) created a list of "Top Ten Emergent Literacy Opportunities for Preschool AAC Users," which included the following: (a) proper positioning for the child to see print and pictures, (b) incorporating speaking siblings or other peers during story reading for increased interaction and role modeling, (c) using repeated readings, (d) providing a variety of adaptive surfaces and prewriting and drawing toys with which the child may in engage in scribbling or drawing, (e) providing a communication signal for a child to request interaction with literacy events and artifacts, (f) providing adapted books to promote independent access to literacy, (g) increasing parent and teacher awareness of emerging literacy events and activities, (h) using "interactive" storybooks that offer high- and low-tech access to asking and answering questions about stories and re-telling stories, (i) adapting literacy-related drawing/writing artifacts to increase independent access and practice for children, and (j) using all types of assistive technology to promote emerging literacy skills in the preschool population. Teachers must be aware of these 10 opportunities and how they may be readily implemented using a variety of strategies within their classroom.

Vocabulary appropriate for literacy learning is vital to the academic success of a student who uses AAC. During book readings and other literacy activities, vocabulary that allows the student who uses AAC to participate in the activity is necessary. For example, quick phrases such as "turn the page," "let me see," "read it again," and "that's funny," allow students to control their own situation with typical communicative interactions. Also, including the names of characters, locations, and activities of reading assignments in AAC technology supports participation in literacy activities. Figure 5 illustrates two examples of vocabulary prepared for students using AAC for different sports activities.

Finally, a common goal important to students who use AAC is to learn how to access/use the Internet. For children and adults with disabilities, the Internet has been called "the great equalizer. Scott Palm (1996, personal communication with David Beukelman), an adult with cerebral palsy who uses AAC technology, has referred to the Internet as "a giant AAC system" for persons with and without disabilities. With the advancements in technology, all students now use the Internet for learning. By accessing the World Wide Web, students who use AAC have opportunities that might not be available otherwise. Some of these include the ability to advance their education, purchase goods and services, interact with greater numbers of people, mentor others who use AAC, volunteer, and ultimately become employed.

A study conducted to obtain information and opinions about employment experiences, access, and barriers by a group of adults using AAC (McNaughton et al., 2002) showed that adults using AAC identified technology, particularly access to the World Wide Web, as a strategy they often use to obtain employment. Further, everybody reported use of computers in the workplace and one half stated that computer expertise was an essential requirement of their job.

Supporting Educational Personnel: Providing Information "Just in Time"

When students use AAC technology in an integrated educational setting, the learning requirements by the educational staff are extensive; therefore, the instructional

Table 4. Literacy Enhancement Technology for AAC Implementation: Physical & Cognitive Access Capabilities

Technology (Software and Hardware)	Physical Access	Cognitive Access
Talking word processor (e.g., Intellitalk, Write: OutLoud, WYNN, WiVox)	• Highlights word by word to assist with visual tracking • Enables student to turn pages independently with mousing or switch click	• Reads text aloud • May provide picture symbol representation • Utilizes auditory spell checking • Highlights word by word when reading • Reads back text so that students can stay on topic
Alternate keyboard (e.g., Intellikeys with Overlay Maker, Discover: Board, Big Keys, King Mini)	• Allows student to type in larger or smaller key area • Keys may be arranged to fit the student's needs • Entire words or phrases can be programmed to reduce keystrokes and fatigue	• Pre-literate students can independently write using picture symbols • May provide word banks
Organizational software (e.g., Draft Builder, Inspiration/Kidspiration)		• Provides structure and organization • Provides topic suggestions • Develops vocabulary, semantic relationships
Adapted Mouse or Track Ball (e.g., Head Mouse, Headmaster Plus, Tracker 2000, Joystick Plus, Rollerball II, Micropoint)	• Provides access to software	
Symbol-based writing software (Writing With Symbols 2000, Picture IT, Pix Writer, WYNN, Clicker 4)		• Provides symbol based reading structure • Reads text and highlights word by word • Provides word bank support
Word prediction software (Co:Writer 4000, WriteAway 2000, Prototype, KeyREP)	• Reduces fatigue • Reduces keystrokes • Speeds message generation	• Provides spelling suggestions • Includes "talking" spell checker • Provides appropriate semantic choices (grammatical structure) • May provide auditory preview
Touch Screens (Touch Window, Gemini, Mercury, Tough Talker, Optimist II)	• Allows direct point access	• Make selections directly on the screen -- no intermediate steps or devices

(continued next page)

**Table 4. Literacy Enhancement Technology for AAC Implementation: Physical &
Cognitive Access Capabilities (continued)**

Technology (Software and Hardware)	Physical Access	Cognitive Access
Switch-based computer interfaces (ClickIt, Discover: Switch, Switch Click)	• Provides mouseless access to all types of point-and-click software • Enables software to have scanning access	
On-Screen Keyboards (handsOff, Discover:Screen, WiViK, SofType)	• Provides full computer functions with only mouse movements • Provides word prediction (reducing fatigue & keystrokes)	• Provides word banks • Provides word prediction • May provide auditory preview

expectations on the AAC team leaders are considerable.

For example, consider the needs of a typical first-grade teacher. She or he may have a student with special education certification in the classroom once every three years. She/ he has a student who uses AAC technology once every seven years. The school district has several options with regard to preparing this teacher. First, the district might schedule a generic in-service program or two each year for all teachers. Second, the district might provide no instruction in AAC for general education teachers, assuming that support personnel (e.g., speech language pathologist, AAC specialist, occupational therapist) will provide all of the expertise necessary. Or, the district might provide "just-in-time" information to teachers who will have students using AAC in their classroom during a given school year. Such information would be targeted toward the particular student and the specific AAC technology the student uses. In this model, every effort is made to bring the AAC team together as part of this process, so that teachers, paraprofessionals, and support staff can learn and plan together.

This "just-in-time" instructional opportunity must take several factors into account. First, each student and his or her technology will be somewhat different. Second, teachers vary in their preferred strategies, some preferring large-group, teacher-lead instruction, some

preferring small-group, teacher-lead instruction, some preferring small group, student-lead instruction, and yet others preferring independent learning. Third, the learning styles of AAC team members vary. Thus, research (Beukelman et al., 2002) has shown that some AAC team members are primarily "mastery learners," who are motivated to learn simply because they enjoy the content. Others are primarily "performance learners," who are motivated to learn in order to perform a specific task (e.g., learn just enough about AAC technology to complete an assigned task). Finally, others are primarily "social learners," who learn in order to be respected by and included in a group (e.g., AAC team). Recognition of these learning motivation strategies among team members may clarify the methods used in instruction. Some will prefer to learn new information alone, some prefer to learn in small groups, and others prefer to learn through direct instruction. Respect for various learning preferences on a team produces the most effective team dynamics.

Additional strategies have been proposed for assisting classroom teachers and paraprofessionals in obtaining information necessary to include a new student who uses AAC in classroom activities. Mentorship is one way to gain knowledge of a particular student. The student's teacher from the previous year may mentor the current teacher, who in turn mentors the next teacher, providing planning,

Figure 5. Examples of AAC vocabulary pages for preschool and school-age activities.

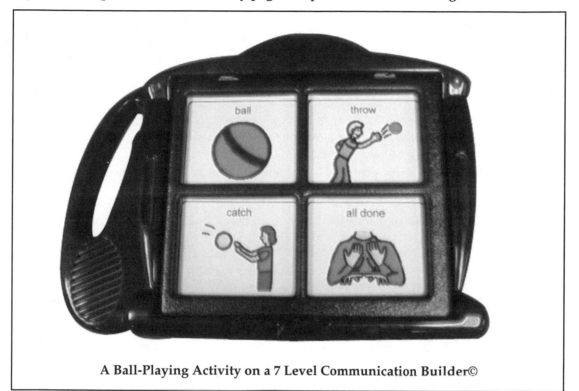

A Ball-Playing Activity on a 7 Level Communication Builder©

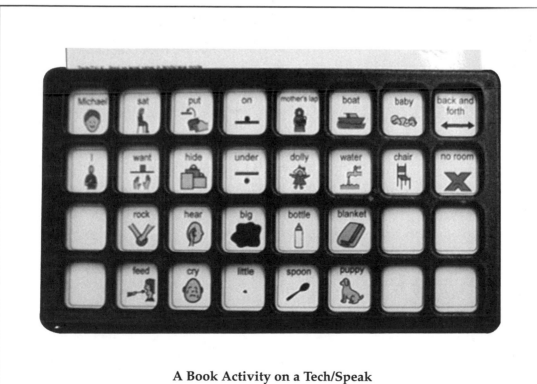

A Book Activity on a Tech/Speak

implementation, and assessment ideas. Another mentorship relationship may involve one teacher who has extensive or recent experience with students who use AAC and the teacher with little experience who will/does have a student with AAC in his or her classroom.

Time must be scheduled for regular AAC team meetings in which all members contribute to the development of strategies and ideas for achieving goals. According to a recent study (Hunt et al., 2002), greater AAC team engagement resulted in greater social and academic participation of students who use AAC in general education classrooms. AAC team support services are added as needed by the various team members. It is important to attempt to prevent the situation where consultants make suggestions and leave a single team member responsible for carrying them out. Instead, AAC team members should be brought into the classroom to observe each activity and provide necessary training, including specific examples for success. For example, parents may be in a situation to most readily program new vocabulary into an AAC device while helping their child with homework. Team members must not necessarily maintain their "traditional" roles. Flexibility in roles and responsibilities are important, and roles at any given time are dependent upon the student's current and future needs. With regular AAC team meetings, all may disseminate information and support each other.

Additionally, the teacher must be provided with sufficient non-classroom time (in addition to regular class planning time) with AAC team members (or alone) to enable cooperative team implementation of strategies. The responsibilities of each team member may increase or decrease as necessary for each goal, accommodation, or activity. All collaborative team members are used for classroom implementation (e.g., teachers, student, peers, family members, educational paraprofessionals, therapists) of each goal.

Conclusions

This chapter has discussed various aspects of implementing AAC technology for facilitating communication within an educational environment. Many topics have only highlighted issues of great concern for educators. Research is limited on implementation of AAC within an academic setting and examination of outcomes of such interventions, indicating an open path for future research. Existing research has indicated, however, that students with severe communication disorders benefit from use of AAC in their educational programs. Research has only begun to examine the types of AAC technology most suited to use by children both inside and outside of educational environments (Drager, Light, Speltz, Fallon, & Jeffries, 2003). Additional examination of the communication patterns of students who use AAC in various classroom activities and environments will yield greater understanding of the optimal organization for student participation.

Finally, ongoing technological advances are accompanied by newer, more efficient means of achieving communication and participation. One example that holds much promise for assisting students who use AAC is the "wireless" classroom, in which students may compose written and spoken messages, which are then sent though a wireless network to the teacher or other educational personnel. Also, the educational personnel may create communication displays with new vocabulary and send them to various students' communication systems directly through the wireless network. Advances in the technology used within an academic environment, as well as ongoing changes in students' needs, combine to result in evolving research directions.

Acknowledgements: This work was supported in part by the Munroe-Meyer Institute for Genetics and Rehabilitation and the Barkley Trust. The authors wish to thank the persons who use the ACC, their caregivers, and the educational personnel with whom we have collaborated for their contributions. "This publication was produced in part under Grant #H133E980026 from the National Institue on Disability and Rehabilitation Research (NIDRR), U.S. Department of Education. The opinions expressed in this publication are those of the grantees and do not necessarily reflect those of the NIDRR or the Department of Education."

References

AbleNet Inc., *BIGmack® Communicator* [AAC Device]. Minneapolis, MN: 1081 Tenth Avenue SE, 55414-1312.

AbleNet Inc., *Step by Step Communicator®* [AAC Device]. Minneapolis, MN: 1081 Tenth Avenue SE, 55414-1312.

AbleNet, Inc., SuperTalker® progressive communicator [AAC Device]. Minneapolis, MN: 1081 Tenth Avenue SE, 55414-1312.

AbleNet Inc., *TalkTrac®* [AAC Device]. Minneapolis, MN: 1081 Tenth Avenue SE, 55414-1312.

AMDi, *Tech/Speak* [AAC Device]. Hicksville, NY: 200 Frank Road, 11801.

American Speech-Language-Hearing Association (1989). Competencies for speech-language pathologists providing services in augmentative communication. *ASHA, 31,* 107-110.

American Speech-Language Hearing Association (1991). Report: Augmentative and alternative communication. *ASHA, 33* (Supplement 5), 9-12.

Angelo, D., Jones, S., & Kokoska, S. (1995). Family perspective on augmentative and alternative communication: Families of adolescents and young adults. *Augmentative and Alternative Communication, 11,* 193-201.

Angelo, D. H., Kokoska, S. M., & Jones, S. D. (1996). Family perspective on augmentative and alternative communication: Families of adolescents and young adults. *Augmentative and Alternative Communication, 12,* 13-20.

Assistive Technology, Inc., *Link Plus* [AAC Device]. Newton, MA: 7 Wells Avenue, 02459.

Assistive Technology, Inc., *Mercury* [AAC Device]. Newton, MA: 7 Wells Avenue, 02459.

Attainment Company, Inc., *One by Four Talker* [AAC Device]. Verona, WI: P.O. Box 930160, 53593-0160.

Beck, A. & Dennis, M. (1996). Attitudes of children toward a similar-aged child who uses augmentative communication. *Augmentative and Alternative Communication, 12,* 78-87.

Beck, A. R., Kingsbury, K., Neff, A., & Dennis, M. (2000). Influence of length of augmented message on children's attitudes toward peers who use augmentative and alternative communication. *Augmentative and Alternative Communication, 16,* 239-249.

Berninger, V. & Gans, B. (1986) Language profiles in nonspeaking individuals of normal intelligence with severe cerebral palsy. *Augmentative and Alternative Communication, 2,* 45-50.

Berry, J. (1987). Strategies for involving parents in programs for young children using augmentative and alternative communication. *Augmentative and Alternative Communication, 3,* 90-93.

Beukelman, D. (1991). Magic and cost of communicative competence. *Augmentative and Alternative Communication, 7,* 2-10.

Beukelman, D., & Mirenda, P. (1992). *Augmentative and alternative communication: Management of severe communication disorders in children and adults.* Baltimore: Paul H. Brookes Publishing Co.

Beukelman, D. & Ansel, B. (1995). Research priorities in augmentative and alternative communication. *Augmentative and Alternative Communication, 11,* 131-134.

Blackstone, S., & Hunt-Berg, M. (2003). *Social networks.* Monterey, CA: Augmentative Communication, Inc.

Blockberger, S., Armstrong, R., O'Connor, A., & Freeman, R. (1993). Children's attitudes toward a nonspeaking child using various augmentative and alternative communication techniques. *Augmentative and Alternative Communication, 9,* 243-250.

Calculator, S., & Jorgensen, C. (1991). Integrating AAC instruction into regular education settings: Expounding on best practices. *Augmentative and Alternative Communication, 7,* 204-214.

Carle, Erich. (1969). *The Very Hungry Caterpillar.* New York: Penguin Philomel.

Carlson, F. (1981). A format for selecting vocabulary for the nonspeaking child. *Language, Speech, and Hearing Services in Schools, 12,* 140-145.

Crestwood Communication Aids, Inc., *Cresspeaker® MAXX II* [AAC Device]. Milwaukee, WI: 6625 N. Sidney Place, Dept. 21F, 53209.

Crick Software, Inc., *Clicker 4* [Computer Software]. Bellevue, WA: 50-116th Ave SE, Suite, 211, 98004.

Culp, D., & Effinger, J. (1996). *ChalkTalk: Augmentative communication in the classroom.* Anchorage, AK: The Assistive Technology Library of Alaska.

Don Johnston, Inc., *Co:Writer® 4000* [Computer Software]. Volo, IL: 26799 West Commerce Drive, 60073.

Don Johnston, Inc., *Draft Builder®* [Computer Software]. Volo, IL: 26799 West Commerce Drive, 60073.

Don Johnston, Inc., *Write:OutLoud®* [Computer Software]. Volo, IL: 26799 West Commerce Drive, 60073.

Drager, K., Light, J., Speltz, J., Fallon, K., & Jeffries, L. (2003). The performance of typically developing 2 1/2-year-olds on dynamic display AAC technologies with different system layouts and language organizations. *Journal of Speech, Language, and Hearing Research, 46*(2), 298-312.

Dynavox Systems, LLC, *Mighty/Mini Mo™* [AAC Device]. Pittsburgh, PA: 2100 Wharton Street, Suite 400, 15203.

Dynavox Systems, LLC, *DynaWrite™* [AAC Device]. Pittsburgh, PA: 2100 Wharton Street, Suite 400, 15203.

Dynavox Systems, LLC, *DM 4™* [AAC Device]. Pittsburgh, PA: 2100 Wharton Street, Suite 400, 15203.

Dynavox Systems, LLC, *DV 4™* [AAC Device]. Pittsburgh, PA: 2100 Wharton Street, Suite 400, 15203.

Enabling Devices, *Cheap Talk 8©* [AAC Device]. Hastings-On-Hudson, NY: 385 Warburton Ave., 10706.

Enabling Devices, *HipTalk Plus©* [AAC Device]. Hastings-On-Hudson, NY: 385 Warburton Ave., 10706.

Enabling Devices, *Mini-Com©* [AAC Device]. Hastings-On-Hudson, NY: 385 Warburton Ave., 10706.

Enabling Devices, *Take or Place N' Talk©* [AAC Device]. Hastings-On-Hudson, NY: 385 Warburton Ave., 10706.

Enabling Devices, *Take or Place N' Talk Go! Board©* [AAC Device]. Hastings-On-Hudson, NY: 385 Warburton Ave., 10706.

Enabling Devices, *7 Level Communication Builder©* [AAC Device]. Hastings-On-Hudson, NY: 385 Warburton Ave., 10706.

Enkidu Research, *Handheld Impact* [AAC Device]. Pittsburgh, PA: Dynavox Systems, LLC, 2100 Wharton Street, Suite 400, 15203.

Enkidu Research, *Tablet XL Impact* [AAC Device]. Pittsburgh, PA: Dynavox Systems, LLC, 2100 Wharton Street, Suite 400, 15203.

Falck A/S, *Falck VocaFlex Colour* [AAC Device]. Millersburg, OH: Saltillo Corporation, 2143 Township Road 112, 44654.

Freedom Scientific Inc., *WYNN™* [Computer Software]. St. Petersburg, FL: 11800 31st Court North, 33716-1805.

Fried-Oken, M., & More, L. (1992). An initial vocabulary for nonspeaking preschool children based on developmental and environmental language scores. *Augmentative and Alternative Communication, 8,* 41-56.

Fuller, D., Lloyd, L., & Schlosser, R. (1992). Further development of an augmentative and alternative communication symbol taxonomy. *Augmentative and Alternative Communication, 8,* 67-74.

Glennen, S. (1997). Augmentative and alternative communication assessment strategies. In S.L. Glennen & D. DeCoste (Eds.), *The handbook of augmentative and alternative communication* (pp. 149-192). San Diego, CA: Singular Publishing Group.

Glennen, S., & DeCoste, D. (1997). *Handbook of augmentative and alternative communication.* San Diego, CA: Singular Publishing Group.

Greystone Digital Inc., *BigKeys* [Alternative Computer Keyboard]. Huntersville NC: P.O. Box 1888, 28078.

Hunt, P., Soto, G., Maier, J., Muller, E., & Goetz, L. (2002). Collaborative teaming to support students with augmentative and alternative communication needs in general education classrooms. *Augmentative and Alternative Communication, 18,* 20-35.

Idol, L., Paolucci-Whitcomb, P., & Neven, A. (1986). *Collaborative consultation.* Austin, TX: PRO-ED.

Information Services Inc., *WriteAway 2000 @ home* (v. 3.2) [Computer Software]. Newton, MA: Assistive Technology, Inc., 7 Wells Avenue, 02459.

Inspiration Software, Inc., *Inspiration®* (Version 7) [Computer software]. Portland, OR: 7412 SW Beaverton-Hillsdale Hwy, Suite 102, 97225.

Inspiration Software, Inc., *Kidspiration® 2*

[Computer software]. Portland, OR: 7412 SW Beaverton-Hillsdale Hwy, Suite 102, 97225.

IntelliTools®, Inc., *ClickIt!* ® [Computer Software]. Petaluma, CA: 1720 Corporate Circle, 94954.

IntelliTools®, Inc., *IntelliKeys* [Alternative Computer Keyboard]. Petaluma, CA: 1720 Corporate Circle, 94954.

IntelliTools®, Inc., *IntelliTalk® III* [AAC Computer Software]. Petaluma, CA: 1720 Corporate Circle, 94954.

IntelliTools®, Inc., *Overlay Maker* [Computer Software]. Petaluma, CA: 1720 Corporate Circle, 94954.

King, D. L. (1993). *Speaking Dynamically Pro Application Software* [AAC Computer Software]. Solana Beach, CA: Mayer-Johnson, Inc., P.O. Box 1579, 92075.

Koppenhaver, D., Coleman, P., Kalman, S., & Yoder, D. (1991). The implications of emergent literacy research for children with developmental disabilities. *American Journal of Speech-Language Pathology, 1(3),* 38-44..

Koppenhaver, D.A., Evans, D.A., & Yoder, D.E. (1991). Childhood reading and writing experiences of literate adults with severe speech and motor impairments. *Augmentative and Alternative Communication, 7,* 20-33.

Kortz, D. (1998). The importance of home and school connections. *ASHA Special Interest Division 12 Newsletter, 7(4),* 6-7.

Light, J. (1988). Interaction involving individuals using augmentative communication systems: State of the art and future directions for research. *Augmentative and Alternative Communication, 4,* 66-82.

Light, J. (1989). Toward a definition of communicative competence for individuals using augmentative and alternative communication systems. *Augmentative and Alternative Communication, 5,* 137-144.

Light, J., Beesley, M. & Collier, B. (1988). Transition through multiple augmentative and alternative communication systems: A three-year case study of a head-injured adolescent. *Augmentative and Alternative Communication, 4,* 2-14.

Light, J., Kelford-Smith, A., & McNaughton, D. (1990, August). *The literacy experiences of preschoolers who use augmentative and alternative communication systems.* Paper presented at the biennial meeting of the International Society for Augmentative and Alternative Communication, Stockholm, Sweden.

Locke, P., & Mirenda, P. (1992). Roles and responsibilities of special education teachers serving on teams delivering AAC services. *Augmentative and Alternative Communication, 8,* 200-214.

Lue, M. (2001). *A survey of communication disorders for the classroom teacher.* Boston: Allyn and Bacon.

Madentec Limited, *Discover Board®* [Alternative Computer Keyboard]. Alberta, Canada: 9935-29A Avenue, Edmonton, T6E 5H5.

Madentec Limited, *Tracker™ One* [Alternative Computer Access Device]. Alberta, Canada: 9935-29A Avenue, Edmonton, T6E 5H5.

Madentec Limited, *Discover: Switch®* [Alternative Computer Access Device]. Alberta, Canada: 9935-29A Avenue, Edmonton, T6E 5H5.

Madentec Limited, *Discover: Screen®* [Alternative Computer Keyboard]. Alberta, Canada: 9935-29A Avenue, Edmonton, T6E 5H5.

Matas, J., Mathy-Laikko, P., Beukelman, D., & Legresley. (1985). Identifying the nonspeaking population: A demographic study. *Augmentative and Alternative Communication, 5,* 249-256.

Mayer-Johnson, Inc., *Sequencer©* [AAC Device]. Solana Beach, CA: P.O. Box 1579, 92075.

Mayer-Johnson, Inc., *Writing with Symbols 2000™* [Computer Software]. Solana Beach, CA: P.O. Box 1579, 92075.

McNaughton, D., Light, J., Arnold, K. (2002). "Getting your wheel in the door:" Successful full-time employment experiences of individuals with cerebral palsy who use augmentative and alternative communication. *Augmentative and Alternative Communication, 18(2),* 59-76.

National Joint Committee for the Communicative Needs of Persons with Severe Disabilities (1992). Guidelines for meeting the communication needs of persons with severe disabilities. *ASHA, 33* (Suppl. 5), 1-8.

Origin Instruments Corporation, Head Mouse® Extreme [Alternative Computer Access

Device]. *Grand Prairie, TX: 854 Greenview Drive, 75050-2438.*

Origin Instruments Corporation, SofType™ [Alternative Computer Keyboard Software]. *Grand Prairie, TX: 854 Greenview Drive, 75050-2438.*

Pearpoint, J., Forest, M., & O'Brien, J. (1996). MAPs, Circles of Friends, and PATH: Powerful tools to help build caring communities. In S. Stainback & W. Stainback (Eds.), *Inclusion: A guide for educators* (pp. 67-86). Baltimore: Paul H. Brookes Publishing Co.

Pearpoint, J., O'Brien, J., & Forest, M. (1993). *PATH.* Toronto, ON, Canada: Inclusion Press.

Pierce, P. & McWilliam, P. (1993). Emerging literacy and children with severe speech and physical impairments (SSPI): Issues and Possible Intervention Strategies. *Topics in Language Disorders, 13*(2), 47-57.

Prentke Romich Company, *ChatBox* [AAC Device]. Wooster, OH: 1022 Heyl Road, 44691.

Prentke Romich Company, *Headmaster Plus* [Alternative Access Device]. Wooster, OH: 1022 Heyl Road, 44691.

Prentke Romich Company, *SpringBoard* [AAC Device]. Wooster, OH: 1022 Heyl Road, 44691.

Prentke Romich Company, *WIVIK 3 On-Screen Keyboard* [Alternative Computer Keyboard Software]. Wooster, OH: 1022 Heyl Road, 44691.

Prentke Romich Company, *Vanguard II* [AAC Device]. Wooster, OH: 1022 Heyl Road, 44691.

Prentke Romich Company, *Pathfinder* [AAC Device]. Wooster, OH: 1022 Heyl Road, 44691.

Prentke Romich Company, *Wivox* [Alternative Computer Software]. Wooster, OH: 1022 Heyl Road, 44691.

Riverdeep Interactive Learning Ltd., *TouchWindow®* 15 or 17 [Alternative Computer Access Device]. Boston, MA: 399 Boylston Street, 02116.

Rosenbaum, P., Armstrong, R., & King, S. (1986). Children's attitudes toward disabled peers: A self-report measure. *Journal of Pediatric Psychology, 11*, 517-530.

Saltillo Corporation, *Chat PC II* [AAC Device]. Millersburg, OH: 2143 Township Road 112, 44654.

Scherer, M.J. (1996). *Living in a state of stuck.* Cambridge, MA: Brookline Books.

Simpson, K. (1996). *Interaction patterns of four students with severe expressive communication impairments in regular classroom settings.* Unpublished doctoral dissertation, University of Nebraska-Lincoln.

Simpson, K., Beukelman, D., & Bird, A. (1998). Survey of school speech and language service provision to students with severe communication impairments in Nebraska. *Augmentative and Alternative Communication, 14*(4), 212-221.

Slater Software Inc., *Picture It* [AAC Computer Software]. Guffey, CO: 351 Badger Lane, 80820.

Slater Software Inc., *PixWriter* [Computer Software]. Guffey, CO: 351 Badger Lane, 80820.

Snell, M. E. & Janney, R. (2000). *Teachers' guides to inclusive practices. Collaborative Teaming.* Baltimore: Paul H. Brookes.

Snow, J., & Forest, M. (1987). Circles. In M. Forest (Ed.), *More education integration: A further collection of readings on the integration of children with mental handicaps into the regular school system.* (p. 176). Downsview, ON, Canada: G. Allan Roeher Institute.

Sturm, J. (1998). Educational inclusion of AAC users. In D. Beukelman & P. Mirenda (Eds.), *Augmentative and alternative communication: Management of severe communication disorders in children and adults* (pp. 391-424). Baltimore: Paul H. Brookes.

Sturm, J., & Nelson, N. (1997). Formal classroom lessons: New perspectives on a familiar discourse event. *Language, Speech, and Hearing Services in Schools, 28*, 255-273.

Sym Systems, *Easy Talk* [AAC Device]. Millersburg, OH: Saltillo Corporation, 2143 Township Road 112, 44654.

Tash, Inc., *Dubby* [AAC Device]. Richmond, VA: 3512 Mayland Ct., 23233.

Tash, Inc., *USB Mini* [Alternative Computer Keyboard]. Richmond, VA: 3512 Mayland Ct., 23233.

Tash, Inc., *USB King* [Alternative Computer Keyboard]. Richmond, VA: 3512 Mayland Ct., 23233.

Tash, Inc., *Switch Click* [Alternative Computer Access Device]. Richmond, VA: 3512 Mayland Ct., 23233.

The Great Talking Box Company, *Digicom 2000* [AAC Device]. San Jose, CA: 2245 Fortune Drive, Suite A, 95131

The Great Talking Box Company, *EasyTalk* [AAC Device]. San Jose, CA: 2245 Fortune Drive, Suite A, 95131

The Great Talking Box Company, *e-talk* Family [AAC Device]. San Jose, CA: 2245 Fortune Drive, Suite A, 95131

Toby Churchill, Ltd., LightWRITER™ [AAC Device]. Portland, OR: Zygo Industries, Inc., P.O. Box 1008, 97207-1008.

Toby Churchill, Ltd., *adVOCAte*™ [AAC Device]. Portland, OR: Zygo Industries, Inc., P.O. Box 1008, 97207-1008.

TRAXSYS, *Roller II Joystick*. Volo, IL: Don Johnston, Inc., 26799 West Commerce Drive, 60073.

TRAXSYS, *Roller Plus Trackball*. Volo, IL: Don Johnston, Inc., 26799 West Commerce Drive, 60073.

West, C., Bilyeu, D., & Brune, P. (1996, November). *AAC strategies for the preschool classroom: Developing communication and literacy.* Short course presented at the annual convention of the American Speech-Language-Hearing Association, Seattle.

Words+©, Inc., *EZ Keys*™ [AAC Computer Software]. Lancaster, CA: 1220 W. Avenue J, 93534-2902.

Words+©, Inc., *MessageMate 40* [AAC Device]. Lancaster, CA: 1220 W. Avenue J, 93534-2902.

Words+©, Inc., *Mini-MessageMate* [AAC Device]. Lancaster, CA: 1220 W. Avenue J, 93534-2902.

Words+©, Inc., *Say-it!SAM*™ [AAC Device]. Lancaster, CA: 1220 W. Avenue J, 93534 2902.

Words+©, Inc., *Talking Screen* [AAC Computer Software]. Lancaster, CA: 1220 W. Avenue J, 93534-2902.

Words+©, Inc., *TuffTalker*™ [AAC Device]. Lancaster, CA: 1220 W. Avenue J, 93534-2902.

Yorkston, K., Fried-Oken, M., & Beukelman, D. (1988). Single word vocabulary needs: Studies from various nonspeaking populations. *Augmentative and Alternative Communication, 4,* 149.

Yorkston, K. M., Dowden, P. A., Honsinger, M. J., Marriner, N., & Smith, K. (1988). A comparison of standard and user vocabulary lists. *Augmentative and Alternative Communication, 4,* 189-210.

ZYGO Industries, Inc., *Great Green MACAW* [AAC Device]. Portland, OR: P.O. Box 1008, 97207-1008.

ZYGO Industries, Inc., *Micropoint*™ [Alternative Computer Access Device]. Portland, OR: P.O. Box 1008, 97207-1008.

ZYGO Industries, Inc., *Optimist II!*™ [AAC Device]. Portland, OR: P.O. Box 1008, 97207-1008.

ZYGO Industries, Inc., *ProtoType*™ [Computer Software]. Portland, OR: P.O. Box 1008, 97207-1008.

ZYGO Industries, Inc., *The Grid*™ [Alternative Computer Access Software]. Portland, OR: P.O. Box 1008, 97207-1008.

Section 5

Instructional Design

23

Teamwork Needs Technology

Len Haines and Gladene Robertson

Collaboration is a body contact sport (Kiesler & Cummings, 2002, p. 57).

Among us the habit of competition and individualism is so ingrained that we seem to have forgotten one of the basic laws of survival: Strength lies in community (Remen, 2000, p. 267).

Teamwork is a mandate for professionals who provide services and supports for students with special needs. Gone are the days when a special educator or other human service provider could function as the expert, as the one with the professional authority and exclusive knowledge to operate with autonomy and decide on the educational plan for a child with disabilities. The field of special education has progressively evolved toward a service model in which planning and decision making are conducted by teams that work together to design education programs, related services, and supports for students. More and more, parents and students themselves play a prominent role on these teams. Rather than being told what they and their child need, parents are increasingly seen as the first and lifelong educators of their child, the ones who are in for the long haul as professionals come and go. Similarly, children with disabilities play active roles on their own planning teams, progressively gaining in skills of self-determination and self-advocacy. More and more, teams are expected to work collaboratively; that is, to adopt a style of interaction through which each team mem-

ber is valued and given a voice. And more and more, teams are expected to enhance the quality of education and related services by drawing in needed expertise from across traditional boundaries between human service agencies. This is an era of collaborative teamwork.

While there are many compelling reasons for basing educational plans and programs for students with special needs on collaborative team decision making, this interconnected way of working poses some several prominent challenges: first, team members may enter the teamwork situation with diverse beliefs, attitudes, and experiences about ways of working with others; second, team members often need to learn to work together productively and efficiently; and third, due to their diverse professional and experiential makeup, team members are not routinely available to meet in person. Therefore, teams need to sustain their work over time and space, a necessity that Hinds and Kiesler (2002) have described as *distributed work*.

The purposes of this chapter are to investigate teamwork in a variety of contexts and to examine the benefits, barriers, and supports that exist within those contexts. Central to these inquiries is an exploration of the relationships between teamwork and technology. The writers operate from the fundamental premise that in order for teamwork to yield optimal outcomes, technology tools are needed to support collaborative interactions.

To achieve their purposes, the writers conducted database and Internet searches of the existing literature on teamwork, collaboration, and technology in education and special education. In the course of the research, a substantial body of knowledge and evidence outside the education literature was also accessed. The fields of business and science, particularly computer science and information technology, contain a rich knowledge base and an active research agenda on the relationships between collaboration and technology. Knowledge gained from these disciplines was used to inform efforts to better understand the optimal roles of teamwork and technology as they relate to programming for students needing special education services and supports.

The following questions reflect the writers' strategy for surveying the literature and the organizational plan for this chapter. What is meant by the terms *teamwork* and *collaboration*? What are the influences of human and technology contexts upon teamwork and collaboration? What are the barriers to effective teamwork, and what practices serve as supports? What models can guide the process of teamwork and collaboration? Can technology tools enhance the processes and products of collaborative teamwork? What guidelines could enhance the design and use of collaborative software in relation to students needing special education services and supports?

Contexts for Teamwork

Seeking Clarity

There is not always consensus in the literature on some of the concepts that are central to the present discussion. Therefore, in order to make explicit the understandings that underpin the terminology used in this chapter, some of the most important terms will be operationalized.

In developing a rationale for the place of technology in collaborative teamwork, the writers accept Friend and Cook's (2003) view of collaboration as the "style" of an interaction between or among two or more persons. They also concur with Platt's (1994) view of teamwork as a "process" within which there are a number of further internal processes, including communication, problem solving, decision making, conflict resolution, and maintenance.

The writers believe the processes of teamwork interact in complex ways, often being at once foundational and dependent on one another. Each of these internal processes, in turn, is made up of a number of skills. For example, the process of communication includes many elements such as active and passive listening; using statements to provide, seek, confirm, or clarify information; giving and receiving feedback; asking questions to seek, provide, confirm, or clarify information; and receiving and expressing information through nonverbal skills (Friend & Cook, 2003).

It is further contended, however, that in order for these processes and skills to evolve appropriately, efficient frameworks must be in place to guide and facilitate growth. Implementation of frameworks protects against old habits of interaction surfacing to undermine and reduce the efficacy of teamwork processes. The use of guides also helps to ensure that newly learned internal processes and skills are embraced and used. Technology can provide frameworks that help to keep collaborative processes on track. Technology can also help to see that the individuals involved in teamwork are aware of their roles and responsibilities when they engage in collaborative interactions.

Seeking Symbols

Well over a decade ago, when the original CoPlanner software was introduced, it provided opportunities for professional teams to become involved in computer-mediated planning as they moved from an initial concern about a student, through gathering information, reflecting on that information, teaching, and monitoring various aspects of a student's program. CoPlanner was based on a question-driven decision model and consisted of several components, each designed to support teams as they carried out collaborative work (Haines, Sanche, & Robertson, 1993). Worksheets, forms, text documents, reporting guides, tools (detailed methods for assessing and teaching), an email system, a security system, and user help were all components of CoPlanner as it evolved (Robertson, Haines, Sanche, & Biffart, 1997).

Early in the development phase of the software, when the research team was looking for a symbol of collaborative devotion, the manner in which flocks of Canada geese live and complete their migrations was chosen (Robertson, Haines, Sanche, & Holmund, 1993). Several traits of these creatures of nature reflect the characteristics of collaborative teamwork. Migrating geese, flying in their characteristic V formation, create a slipstream effect. There is more resistance for those leading the flock, so the geese take turns flying at point. All geese have the opportunity to glide in the slipstream, but also to share leadership. Geese honk encouragement to their leaders, and support the other members of the flock in the slipstream. A pair of geese always falls out of formation to accompany a sick or wounded bird to the ground. Above all, geese show great concern for the most vulnerable in the flock.

These traits, instinctive to geese, are also at the heart of human collaborative interactions. They help to foster the growth of the skills and knowledge that underlie the internal processes of communication and decision making. The characteristics symbolized by the geese give meaning to the frameworks that guide those processes. They reflect the types of commitment and behavior that must be exhibited by groups of people who desire to work together productively toward a common goal in environments where accountability and outcomes are shared. These are not the characteristics exhibited in organizations where individuals compete for personal gain and power. Yet they are the qualities exhibited by people who often win admiration in society. A truly collaborative team can be recognized through the willingness of team members to nurture each other toward something better than any one person could achieve alone.

Seeking Inspiration
A story told of a race, held as part of a Special Olympics meet, reflects the spirit of collaboration in a particularly meaningful way. As the event progressed, it appeared that the participants in the race were well matched. The runners formed a close-knit pack as they progressed around the track. Suddenly, one of the athletes lost footing and went down. Only for a moment did the race continue, for the rest of the runners stopped, turned back, and collectively saw to the welfare of the fallen one.

Once the unfortunate runner was up, all those taking part in the race proceeded toward the finish line arm in arm, hand in hand.

Whether this story is true or has developed as an urban legend, it teaches two important lessons. The first lesson is a revelation of the nature of true teamwork. In this story, the finish line is seen as a collective goal rather than a marker by which to judge the comparative skills of individuals. Second, what evolved in this collective kindness was a moving human experience of much greater depth and meaning than would have been witnessed in the completion of a traditional race.

Central to the beliefs of the writers of this chapter is the view that evolution toward collaborative teamwork in most organizations, regardless of whether technology is used to support the underlying processes and skills, requires a transformation in the traditional ways of professional interaction. In many cases, it also requires transformation of established approaches to human relationships within those workplaces. Moving successfully through significant change in organizations is an extremely complex process that may begin with the initiative of one individual and result in the metamorphosis of an entire profession. In order to fully understand the transformation process, it is helpful to engage in an examination of changes in more than one context. In the pages that follow, transformational changes will be tracked first through human contexts (individual, organizational, and professional) and then the discussion will turn to transformational changes in the context of technology.

The Evolution of Collaborative Contexts

From Personal Idea to Organizational Transformation
As individual people move through their careers, they are likely to attain general understandings of concepts related to their work much more frequently than they will experience a true passion for a particular idea. Yet, there are those times in people's lives when they encounter a thought that they know has the capacity to "change everything" about how they do their work and, perhaps, how

they lead their lives. At these moments, their understandings are not surface-level hunches about vague possibilities, but deep realizations that are seen with striking clarity. During such experiences, not only are the implications of the new thought comprehended, but also the power of what the idea could ultimately achieve is profoundly felt. At such times people may also realize that if their concept is fully embraced, it will trigger change processes that, in turn, will result in nothing short of a transformation. Further, they sense that the idea may not result in just the transformation of self, but that it may potentially initiate a much broader, communal transformation.

When a new concept is shared with colleagues, some may grasp their coworker's vision and begin to do their jobs differently. In turn, those colleagues may begin working together, nurturing, refining, and spreading the idea. However, many in the workplace may understand only the most elementary, superficial elements of the idea. A few may see the potential of everything around them being altered and collectively begin to embrace the change. As the idea gains popularity, the majority may be content to incorporate vocabulary related to the concept into their conversations and documents, while continuing to engage in unaltered behaviors and routines. To those with the passion falls the task of helping others to reach a collective, deep understanding of the new concept so that organizational or professional transformation may occur. For without wider organizational change, the individuals involved may not be able to avail themselves fully of what the initial, inspiring idea had the potential to offer.

Transforming Organizations

Transformation is defined in *Webster's Dictionary* as a "change in nature." It implies renewal, newness, and altering something until it becomes something else. For many, the word transformation may bring with it a sense of immediacy. However, Fullan (2002), in outlining six guidelines for understanding change, describes the road to transformation as the hard, day-to-day work of reculturing. He reminds us that transforming the culture of an organization means changing what people value and how they will work together to accomplish what they value in a way that leads to deep, lasting change.

Transformation is neither simple nor straightforward. It is not shape shifting for convenience. Transformation does not conform to static, linear formulas imposed by some members of the organization upon others in the group. Instead, it is a dynamic, messy process that both alters and draws its strength from the unique community in which the genesis of the transformation was sparked.

As the topic of this chapter is developed, some aspects of the transformational processes associated with adopting collaborative teamwork in educational decision making, as they occur in the wider context of school restructuring and reform, will be described. The role technology plays as a tool in this transformation will be addressed. In the latter discussion, another transformation; namely, the transformation of thinking that is necessary to enable educators to utilize technology will be acknowledged.

Transforming School Cultures

While effecting deep-level change in the culture of any workplace is a challenge, transforming school cultures is a particularly formidable task. Barth (2002) defines a school's culture as "a complex pattern of norms, attitudes, beliefs, behaviors, values, ceremonies, traditions, and myths that are deeply ingrained in the very core of the organization . . . that wields astonishing power in shaping what people think and how they act" (p.7). Attempting to change these cultures can, in Barth's (2002) view, be a futile process, creating only superficial differences. It is important to realize that the transformation currently referred to in the education literature as *restructuring* will not become a reality because it promises to make teachers better at meeting the learning needs of students or because it purports to shape better administrators whose styles are more egalitarian. The change process is far too complex and the inertia of the customary is far too strong for initiatives to blossom easily or often.

The truth is that most people, in most situations, resist change because they are more comfortable with the conditions they know than they are with the risk of initiating something new. This remains true even when those familiar conditions are not satisfactory. However, educators trying to alter aspects of their profession confront other factors besides the usual resistance to change inherent in human nature.

Not Every Initiative Is a Transformation

In Fullan's (2001) view, not only do educators face turbulent, uncertain environments, they also suffer "the additional burden of having a torrent of unwanted, uncoordinated policies and innovations raining down on them from hierarchical bureaucracies" (p. 109). While such a bombardment of initiatives and reforms can lead to anger and frustration, it can also rob any organization of vital energy. Each initiative and every reform demands time from school personnel. In addition, these numerous projects may each generate expectations and a series of imposed objectives.

In examining the implications of overloading working teams with goals, Robbins and Finley (2000) point out that, "The problem is that when confronted with a list of 20 to 30 objectives, the tendency of most sentient beings is to go into shock and do nothing for a period of recovery" (p. 39). Burdening people with what Fullan (2001) describes as "too many disconnected, episodic, piecemeal, superficially adorned projects" (p. 109) can create the same state of inertia. In such a state, incomplete tasks and unmet goals tend to accumulate, since addressing them is beyond the capability of the individuals in question. Robbins and Finley (2000) believe that "goals that are not being worked on at present tend to gnaw at one's mental innards" (p. 39), further decreasing productivity.

Some change within organizational structures is inevitable. Kanter (1997) reminds us that even excellence in company performance does not protect against change. She cautions against limited change but also speaks out against too much change, which she describes as capable of evolving into endless painful revolutions.

There is a price to pay in school districts where attempts are made to keep up with a number of trends simultaneously. Teachers, often exhausted by requests to adopt numerous changes in curriculum, methodology, and various work-related protocols, are unable to take on more. In these districts, most change may be seen as good, and proponents of change may oversell small alterations as transformations, further dissipating the personal and organizational energies of teachers and administrators.

While the "discomfort of disturbance" (Fullan, 2001, p. 114) is an inevitable part of change, excessive, disparate demands for change may overwhelm educators. One purpose of this chapter is to examine how technology can help to ensure that inclusionary schooling for children with special needs, effectively planned and carried out by teams of collaborating professionals, does not become a casualty of the excessive demands for reform being made on today's educators. Preventing this loss is exceedingly important.

Finding Our Way in Establishing Priorities

Criteria for sorting through the myriad of demands for reform in education may be almost as numerous as the demands themselves. In some cases, the criteria by which initiatives are prioritized are established through careful democratic processes. However, in other instances such criteria are loosely established or idiosyncratic to groups or individuals. For example, the personal preferences of administrators at various levels of the hierarchical structure of a school division or district may fast track one project over another. Depending on the degree of vertical management in the district, individual teachers may choose, in so far as possible, to direct their energies according to their personal interests. General educators may view the movement toward collaborative teamwork as just one of many initiatives. Special educators, on the other hand, are more likely to see collaborative interactions as indispensable vehicles to maximize children's fundamental rights to effective instruction, appropriate adaptation, and inclusive programs.

Inclusive schooling is in no sense a minor special education initiative. In its pure form, inclusion is a complex, complete transformation of traditional service delivery in education. Successful inclusion is dependent on effective collaborative teamwork in the workplace. Collaborative teamwork itself represents still another deep-level change from the traditional professional relationships in schools. From the perspective of special education, it is imperative that policy decisions affecting change are not left to chance. Part of the assurance that inclusion and collaboration will receive the consideration they deserve when teachers and administrators prioritize numerous initiatives lies in recognizing their importance to all educators. Sergiovanni (1994) has argued that our potential to move from the past to something new lies in viewing schools more as communities than organizations. In changing this perspective, the ties between people are altered from contractual links to connections based a commitment. "The bonding together of people in special ways and the binding of them to shared values and ideas are the characteristics of schools as communities" (Sergiovanni, 1994, p. 4).

Choosing to Transform Toward Collaborative, Inclusive School Cultures

The development of collaborative relationships among professionals working with special needs students is recognized as being of continuing importance (Dettmer, Thurston, & Dyck, 2002; Fishbaugh, 2000; Friend & Cook, 2003; Idol, Nevin, & Paolucci-Whitcomb, 2000; Johnston, Brosnan, Cramer, & Dove, 2000; Thomas, Correa, & Morsink, 2001; Thousand & Villa, 2000; Walther-Thomas, Korinek, MacLaughlin, & Williams, 2000). The pivotal role of collaboration in restructuring school cultures has been emphasized by Friend and Cook (2003) as follows:

> *Of all the many complex challenges facing schools in the early years of the twenty-first century, none is as demanding nor as critical as creating in education a culture of collaboration and ensuring that everyone who works there has the dispositions, knowledge and skills to collaborate.* (p. 2)

This quote speaks to the importance of creating a culture conducive to collaboration but also stresses the need for ensuring that those working in the established collaborative culture are able to do so effectively. Training individuals in the knowledge and skills of collaboration is essential to the success of the reculturation process that will move educators away from individualism and toward effective team planning and implementation. Figure 1 traces an

Figure 1. Dynamic transformation toward effective collaborative teamwork.

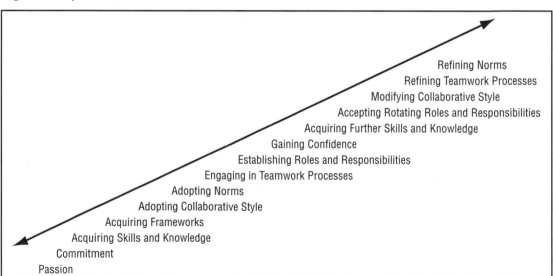

Each element of the transformation can be both foundational and dependent. Members, individually and collectively, meet and address shifting barriers while establishing new relationships as team members join and leave the team.

evolving collaborative culture. The processes depicted should not be considered as always occurring in this sequential fashion. The figure is not intended to indicate that with minimal amounts of modification and refinement a kind of team utopia can be achieved. For example, teams are established for different reasons and timeframes. Changing team membership means that individuals on the team may be at different stages of individual transformation, thus affecting the dynamics of the team and its impact on the larger organization.

Establishing Collaborative Cultures

Let us first consider some of the issues to be addressed in creating a culture of collaboration in school settings. In reminding us of the interactive duality of the cultural framework, Skrtic (1991) cites Pettigrew's (1979) cognitive perspective of organizational theory, which describes people creating culture and culture creating people. Reculturing toward collaborative teamwork may be viewed as just such a recursive process: the trained professionals who are implementing new ways of seeing and doing are, in turn, being sustained and inspired by the atmosphere of the collaborative culture they are creating.

Historically, teachers have often worked in conditions that leave them relatively isolated from their colleagues as they practice their profession. School cultures have traditionally seen professionals working side by side yet, often, behind closed doors. Expert consultants have made decisions about the programs and curricula of special needs children without significant input from those front line teachers who have been required to operationalize their suggestions.

A principal challenge to establishing collaborative approaches is the formation of an underlying school culture in which the views of those associated with a particular student are collectively honored and there is shared responsibility in planning and carrying out the student's program. Such a change is not surface level, but calls for a significant shift from accepted, habitual ways of interacting with others. It requires commitment to developing new ways of interrelating in the workplace that bring teachers to a place where working

together collaboratively becomes a comfort zone. Forms of working together should ensure that comfort is maintained – whether the colleagues with whom teachers work are within their own schools, from the wider school district, or from a range of other professional groups and agencies offering services and expertise that facilitate the development of optimal programs for children.

Platt (1994), in recognizing American culture as being conducive to individualism, believes that teamwork and functional multiagency systems in the field of health care are "so inconsistent with the traditions of American culture that they will not evolve without the specific planning of services and training of providers" (p. 9). Similar concerns and calls for planning and inservice could be expressed by educators when they attempt to establish local and interagency teamwork initiatives in school systems. As well as skills training, however, the success of moving to collaborative teamwork is partially dependent on the nature of those persons who first embark on teamwork initiatives within a particular school or school district.

Friend and Cook (2003) have stressed the importance of ensuring that those working in schools have the disposition, as well as the knowledge and skills, to collaborate. Thus the selection of team members and the provision of adequate training in collaborative skills are foundational to moving ahead to the transformations required.

Helping Providers to Develop Collaborative Skills

Finding those with the disposition to collaborate is viewed by Avery, Walker, and Murphy (2001) as an extremely important step in team building. They see motivation, energy, enthusiasm, drive, and interest as critical characteristics for building the responsible relationships and high performance needed for teams to function effectively. While Avery et al. (2001) acknowledge skills as another crucial factor; they believe that it is better, when forming teams, to seek out those with commitment to whom the necessary skills can be taught, than to choose those with skills for whom commitment may never emerge. The authors caution that, "Even highly skilled freeloaders will rapidly bring a team's performance level down" (Avery et al., 2001, p. 88).

Once committed teams are formed, training of skills requires careful consideration, since many underlying skills need to be honed to maximize interactional planning. With dedication and frequent opportunities to practice skills in nonthreatening situations, the skills of interpersonal communication, shared problem solving, managing resistance, and conflict resolution are developed over time. Team members can be helped to replace old ways of interacting with new, more efficient skills. This may be accomplished through in-depth inservice, followed by repeated structured opportunities to practice skills in school settings. Learning new skills is greatly enhanced by utilizing integrated peer coaching followed by debriefing with team members and the inservice provider. The result is a team that generates and feeds off its own empowerment. Manz, Neck, Mancuso, and Manz (1997) recognize that:

> The individualistic tendency to trust self more than the team is a challenge we must address and a mold that must be broken if we are to reap the benefits of teamwork. Going it alone may have been the rugged approach of the autocratic leaders of the past, but collaboration and teamwork is the progressive direction for the future. (pp. 15-16)

Learning From Business

Business has come to the realization that success in the new economy depends upon teamwork, both within and between organizations. This awareness was hastened some years ago by the Total Quality Management movement, most often associated with the ideas of W. Edwards Deming (Deming, 1986). Over a decade ago, Senge's (1990) seminal work on learning organizations enhanced understandings of how teamwork fits within broader organizational processes.

More recently, attention has shifted to the study of how teams can identify and create knowledge within organizations. The concept of intellectual capital, with components of knowledge, information, intellectual property, and experience that can be put to use to enhance productivity and innovation, has gained considerable attention in the business sector (Stewart, 1997). Knowledge management refers to the strategies by which intellectual capital is organized, delivered, and accessed (Malhotra, 1998). Managed knowledge enables the members of the organization to deal with current business challenges and effectively envision and create their future. Without access to managed knowledge, every situation is addressed based on what the individual or group brings to the task. With timely access to managed knowledge, in contrast, situations are addressed with a pool of understanding derived from experience in similar situations.

Intellectual capital and knowledge management concepts have the same importance in educational settings as in business environments. Intellectual capital consists of the knowledge and information of each team member, the past experiences of the team members, and the team members' knowledge of the skills and processes that support effective collaborative teamwork. Effective knowledge management means that knowledge is accumulated, properly organized, and available to share on an ongoing basis. Such management should ensure that foundational information regarding a student's learning and behavioral characteristics is available over time. This preservation of relevant information is particularly important to successive teams that plan children's programs from year to year. Children usually have a series of new teachers as they move through their schooling, agency involvements may vary from year to year, and consultative personnel on the team may change or be involved sporadically. Effective knowledge management is essential in safeguarding crucial information over time as well as ensuring that the information teams have at hand from previous cases can inform current team decision making. While there are many ways that knowledge management can be accomplished, technology offers enhanced options.

New ways of thinking have resulted in a transformation in how businesses conduct their work. As structures have changed from hierarchical to collaborative team arrangements, much attention has been directed toward creating and sustaining effective teamwork (Feteroll, Hoffherr, & Moran, 1993; LaFasto & Larson, 2001; Scholtes, Joiner, & Streibel, 1996). Popular team training manuals (e.g., Scholtes et al., 1996) address the process of teamwork by developing skills such as effective communication, collaborative decision making, and conflict resolution strategies. At the same time, working models and tools have been developed to provide a structure that guides team action.

The Development of Teamwork in Special Education

The encouraging promises offered to the business community by the concept of teamwork have been recognized by special educators for some time. Indeed, teams of one kind or another have been in use for decades. In their discussion of the development of team concepts in special education, Friend and Cook (2003) document teams serving the needs of students as early as 1950 and describe an increasing use of teams with the passage of time. The 1975 enactment of P.L. 94-142 mandated a team approach to assessment and decision making around programs for exceptional children. With the U.S. Department of Education Task Force (Will, 1986), came further recommendations to establish building-level support teams as a solution to escalating numbers of referrals, misclassifications, and the need to curb costs while maximizing opportunities for students. With time, the team concept became more common. Recognition of the value of teamwork gave rise to structured guides to team processes.

Indeed, prior to Will's (1986) pivotal article, Chalfant, Pysh, and Moultrie (1979) had already developed a model of in-school problem solving that incorporated specific training and a framework for carrying out prereferral team meetings. The TAT, or Teacher Assistance Team model, was designed to provide "a forum where classroom teachers can meet and engage in a positive, productive, collaborative, problem solving process to help students" (Chalfant & Pysh, 1989, p. 50).

The importance of collaborative teamwork has not diminished over the years. Thus, it remains mandated through the Individuals with Disabilities Education Act, IDEA, through which P. L. 94-142 was renamed and replaced (Vaughn, Bos, & Schumm, 1996). Friend and Cook (2003) recognize teamwork as the structure advocated most often for making changes that allow for greater teacher empowerment through shared decision making.

It has been some time since educators began to talk about the ways in which collaborative relationships among professionals working with special needs children could enhance effectiveness, However, the potential of the concept of teamwork has not been recognized in the field of education as clearly as it has been by the business community. This is true, even though some of the work originally intended for other environments has found its way into educational reform. The example of educators embracing the work of Senge (Senge, Cambron-McCabe, Lucas, Smith, & Kleiner, 2000) speaks to the fact that work originally designed for business has contributed significantly to other disciplines.

Unfortunately, new concepts in education often seem to be abandoned before they reach a level of deep understanding and the practices related to them can become fully implemented. Collaborative interaction is not old hat. In many respects, it has not yet been experienced in a pervasive manner. While there are pockets of change, there is not yet a widespread transformation. However, when transformed professional relationships do exist within school settings, they can be recognized by certain distinct qualities.

The Elements of Collaborative Teamwork
Friend and Cook (2003) have described six defining characteristics of collaborative relationships. First of all, engaging in collaborative relationships should be a choice, since "only the individuals involved can decide if a collaborative style will be used in their interactions" (Friend & Cook, 2003, p. 6). In other words, true collaboration occurs only on a voluntary basis. Second, collaboration requires that each participant's contribution be equally valued and that each member of a decision-making team have equal power in formulating decisions. It is essential to achieve this parity in particular collaborative activities even if the

parity is not present in other participant situations. Nothing exemplifies parity more than the concept of situational or distributed leadership (Idol, Paolucci-Whitcomb, & Nevin, 1986).

Goal sharing is the third, very important defining characteristic of collaboration. While not all goals need be shared, there should be a sufficient mutuality of purpose to keep the group functioning effectively. Shared goals may be general, such as formulating an optimal program for a student or a common belief in collaborative interaction, for "without a strong commitment to collaboration, the focus is likely to remain on the apparently disparate goals, and the matter is likely to become contentious" (Friend & Cook, 2003, p. 8).

The value of shared purposes for teams cannot be underestimated. Avery et al. (2001) believe that, "Lack of shared clarity about direction gets teams stuck" (p. 94). Further, Straus (2002) states:

When a group is in alignment about its direction (where it is trying to go), its commitment (the will it possesses to get there), and its capability (the skills and knowledge it has to complete its journey), there is a release of energy. Not only are team members energized by the process but so is the surrounding organization or community. (pp. 3-4)

The fourth defining characteristic discussed by Friend and Cook (2003) is the dependence of collaboration on shared responsibility and shared decision making. Responsibilities are not always equal, depending on the expertise required. However, the crucial decision making regarding the implementation of programs and the specifics of task completion must be equally shared. Sharing responsibility implies a clear definition of roles and it is in the delineation of roles and responsibilities that protocols and guidelines are extremely helpful. Technology, it will be argued, can make a powerful contribution in helping teams to establish and carry out clearly defined roles and responsibilities.

Friend and Cook (2003) include the sharing of resources and accountability for the outcomes of team planning as their final two defining characteristics of collaborative relationships. Each of these six team traits helps to shape powerful and enduring teams.

Helping Providers to Develop Norms of Conduct

The manner in which team members in education interact must be based on norms agreed upon by that particular team. Teams form, establish norms, and agree to work within the parameters of those norms. Norms may change through refinement but, as previously discussed, they may also become altered through the changing memberships within the team itself.

Platt (1994) delineates one process of interdisciplinary teams as being "an understanding, if not an agreement, on contextual rules, laws, norms, and roles and on ways to negotiate or establish changes in those rules, laws, norms, and roles" (p. 3). These directives toward "ways of behaving" are frameworks through which collaborative teamwork processes are achieved.

Friend and Cook (2003) remind us that, "The effectiveness of one team member has direct impact on the effectiveness of another and perhaps of the entire team" (p. 125). Avery et al. (2001) have stressed the importance of the willingness of all team members to give their best to the team and the impact of interrelational trust within the team structure:

a team performs to the level of its least invested member, not to the level of its most invested. . . . Group velocity increases in direct proportion to group members' confidence that they can interact with each other. Confidence soars when team-mates see each other maintaining the team's integrity or 'shape'. (p. 94)

However, it is not uncommon for individual political agendas to infiltrate legitimate team goals. When this occurs, the strategic plans of the group are drawn from the collectively-decided procedural focus on the student program. As far as possible, teams should be protected from personality conflicts and those who wish to promote personal agendas. In part, such protection is provided through training or inservice opportunities offered to team members so that they may learn the communication and problem solving skills that underlie collaboration. However, norms of conduct and procedures or frameworks for action help to keep planning groups professional, efficient, and on task.

Frameworks for Action

In addition to the norms of conduct we have already discussed, the value of following procedural protocols for team meetings in school settings has been recognized. These protocols function as stabilizing agents to ensure the focus and productivity of teams. Frameworks for brainstorming procedures (Dettmer et al., 2002; Osbourn, 1963) and decision making/problem solving (Tiegerman-Farber & Radziewicz, 1998; Vaughn et al., 1997) are well known. TAT meetings follow a specific protocol (Chalfant & Pysh, 1979, 1989; Walther-Thomas et al., 2000). Similarly, it is possible to distinguish several models of coteaching by the guidelines surrounding their use (Bauwens & Hourcade, 1995; Bauwens, Hourcade, & Friend, 1989; Cook & Friend, 1995; Dettmer et al., 2002; Vaughn, Schumm, & Arguelles, 1997). Further, educators throughout North America are familiar with the structure and procedures of a MAPs team meeting (Forest & Lausthaus, 1989; Vandercook & York, 1990). IEP teams can choose from a variety of procedures and formats to guide their decision-making processes (Salend, 2001; Sattler, 2001).

Frameworks, once mutually agreed upon, can be essential to maintaining the focus, effectiveness, and professionalism of teams over time. Without knowledge of communication and problem solving skills and without procedural guidelines, teams are at risk of losing the ability to plan, monitor, and maintain the most effective programs possible for the students they serve.

Early in this chapter, it was stated that the writers see technology as a major factor in facilitating the collaborative process. Technology has the potential to focus, clarify, expedite, and protect the process of teamwork. It can help educators to sort through the clamor of demands they face on a daily basis by revealing a clear path toward their collective goals as well as providing them with tools to reach those goals expediently. Technology

tools embedded in software can assist by objectifying problem solving beyond personal preference or opinion. Technology also has exciting potential in the area of knowledge management. Moreover, it can help to shape the interactional process in a way that builds the commitment of team members, thereby strengthening their confidence and infusing them with energy to embrace reculturation with dedication and a firm conviction about the benefits it has to offer. Teamwork needs technology. Next, more detail will be presented regarding how teamwork relationships and functions are affected once educators move collaboratively into technology contexts.

Technology Contexts

The exponential growth in computer technology and related innovations has been part of our lives for several decades. As hardware products shrink in size and expand in power, network capacity and interconnectivity have increased in speed and ease of use. Also, we live in an era of integration, both of hardware devices and software. Hardware devices continue to combine functions that were previously separate, such as cell phones and Internet access. Software products now combine and integrate functions, and link this functionality to the Internet. For example, Web browsers now combine email, chat, news, whiteboards, word processing, and more. These trends toward miniaturization, interconnectivity, multimedia, and functional integration will undoubtedly continue.

The technology trends noted previously are occurring at a time when the nature of teamwork is changing. In human services and education, the progressive philosophical move toward inclusive schools and integrated services linked to those schools (e.g., Dryfoos, 1994) has increased the teamwork mandate. At the same time, teams face difficult barriers in planning and delivering quality services to children and families. If collaborative planning teams are to live up to the high expectations of boosting the effectiveness of service provision, solutions need to be found to address these barriers. Advances in technology offer opportunities to address challenges to teamwork arising from distance and time. For example, if a team needs to make a decision about an assistive technology device to support a student's writing, team members could use chat software to brainstorm options and reach a consensus decision and an action plan, all without meeting in person. An added advantage of this approach is that each participant can retain for future reference an enduring record of the process and logic that led to the decision. If we know what resources a team requires to complete a task, we can find technology tools to support the process from a full array of workable, mutually agreeable options. This makes it imperative that teams share a deep understanding of the structure and process of teamwork.

Collaborative teamwork has emerged as an integral approach to work in the contemporary business and education workplace. Businesses have embraced team approaches to management and worker organization. Likewise, collaborative teamwork is increasingly the expected way of working within education in general and special education in particular. Yet, this interconnected and interdependent way of working faces many barriers in the context of an increasingly knowledge-based and global economy. There is need to arrive at a better understanding of how to make collaborative teamwork successful. Such enhanced understanding will recognize that collaborative teamwork is an essentially human enterprise driven by both social and cultural constructs. Technology tools can be used to support and even enhance teamwork. However, it is essential that there be a deep understanding of the intricacy of the relationships between technology and the human context it is intended to support.

Teamwork and Technology

In this section, the relationships between teamwork and technology will be explored. The discussion begins with considering characteristics of technology-supported teams in general: their composition and purposes, the challenges that arise from time and distance factors, and the technology options available to address these challenges. Then the outcomes of some studies that have addressed the effects of technology on teamwork will be examined. Much of the current knowledge base has arisen in the business, industry, and science and technology sectors. This profile of teamwork and technology is then considered relative to education teams that work together to design and deliver services and supports to students with special needs.

The Nature of Technology-Supported Teams

Teams are formed for many purposes. Team composition can range from few to many members, tasks can be described on a continuum from simple to complex, and duration of team engagement can vary from brief to ongoing (Fisher & Fisher, 1998). In some situations, the task that a team is addressing may require only quick, informal decisions involving several people in face-to-face sessions. However, teamwork is commonly pervasive and sustained, its members distributed in time and space (Sproull & Kiesler, 1991). In some cases, teams may have members who have never met face to face, yet their teamwork may encompass large projects that continue over a period of years. Decisions about the use of technology to support teamwork depend upon the composition of the team and the nature of its task.

Fisher and Fisher (1998) have described knowledge or work teams along several dimensions. Two of these are task duration and complexity (see Figure 2). The scope for teamwork may be either brief, with the team disbanding after its task is complete, or ongoing, with the team engaged in tasks that extend over time. Task complexity addressed by the team may range from a single operation, with a clear and simple goal, to multiple operations, with a complex task consisting of many subgoals.

The matrix in Figure 2 describes four broad types of teams. Natural work teams are small groups of individuals formed around natural work processes (i.e., work procedures that are a routine part of their jobs) in the same organizational unit. In education, such teams might consist of teachers who meet on a regular basis to coordinate curriculum delivery in a school. Crossfunctional teams conduct their work

Figure 2. Types of teams (adapted from Fisher & Fisher, 1998, p. 51).

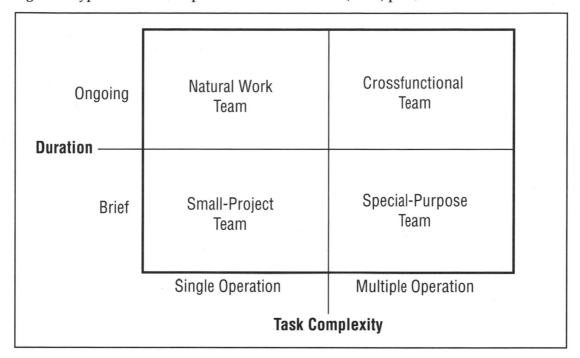

across multiple natural work teams. Their role is to address systemwide issues and coordinate ongoing activities. An educational example would be the work of a school division curriculum coordinating committee planning to implement a new curriculum initiative. Small-project teams are small natural work groups that are formed when needed to address confined tasks that require an immediate plan. In an education context, this type of team might be formed to identify new curriculum resources to be used within a school where a curricular plan has already been implemented. The fourth classification is the special-purpose team that would form to address a relatively complex task that needs to be accomplished in a confined time period. In the education example, such a team might form to design and deliver an IEP for a student. In a typical organization, a worker is a member of more than one type of team at the same time. Furthermore, roles on different teams are often interrelated, with the work of one team informing that of another.

Types of teams can also be considered relative to when and where they conduct their work. Figure 3 shows classifications of team interactions when time and location are considered (Johansen, 1988). This matrix offers

a useful framework for considering the types of technology needed to support the full range of team activities. When teams interact in the same location, they are said to be doing collocated work (Hinds & Kiesler, 2002). Collocated team interactions make the fewest demands on technology support, since physical presence allows the team to use an array of conventional tools (e.g., whiteboards, flip charts, and paper forms) to enhance understanding. This kind of teamwork may benefit from software that offers specific-purpose tools, such as shared displays and information-access software, to support the team's activities. Distributed synchronous interactions take place when team members interact at the same time, but are located in different places. In these situations, technology can assist teamwork by providing tools, such as chat systems and screen sharing, that allow team members to interact as naturally as possible. Asynchronous teamwork takes place in a shared location but at different times, thereby requiring ongoing task management. Related technology solutions include shared computers, team rooms, and project management software. The fourth type of team distribution, working together at different times and different locations (i.e., distributed team-

Figure 3. Time/space distribution of teamwork and related technology supports.

	Same place (collocated)	Different place (distributed)
Same time (synchronous)	**Face-to-face interactions** • team rooms • shared displays • specific-purpose tools (e.g.,voting,brainstorming)	**Distributed real-time interactions** • chat systems • screen sharing • videoconferencing • media spaces
Different time (asynchronous)	**Ongoing tasks** • team rooms • group displays • shared computers, calendars • project management software	**Communication and coordination** • email • electronic bulletin boards • list servers • project management software • schedulers

Time (left axis), Location (bottom axis)

work), places demands on team members to communicate and coordinate their work. Technology support tools include email, shared calendars, and electronic bulletin boards.

While these matrices help to convey some of the complexity and diversity of teams and teamwork, they do not reflect the fluidity that characterizes ongoing team interactions. Thus, meetings are often informal, unscheduled, and initiated by one person. People frequently come in contact with one another through casual interactions (e.g., coffee room meetings) and initiate and conduct conversations spontaneously. These meetings are facilitated by physical proximity, since collocated individuals can more easily connect with others present in their environment. Even in brief conversations much can occur, such as coordinating actions and exchanging information. For distributed teams, the lack of physical proximity means that other methods are needed to support mutual awareness and informal encounters.

Coupling is the extent to which teamwork tasks are interrelated and interdependent. It also refers to the amount of work that a team member can do before needing discussion, instruction, or information from other team members. In most team situations, people shift as needed between loosely and tightly coupled teamwork, moving fluidly between individual and group work. To manage this coordination, people need to maintain awareness of where others are working and what they are doing. Awareness allows people to recognize when it might be appropriate to collaborate with others and when to plan their next activity.

When collaborative teams work face to face, group members efficiently complete the task at hand by using collaboration skills and team norms to mediate their interactions, design the work plan, negotiate sharing of the task, and to help avoid or resolve conflict. They engage in task coordination to make agreed-upon events happen in the right order and at the right time. When team members work in close proximity, task coordination can be accomplished through explicit communication and the way tasks are shared. Awareness of others in proximity helps coordinate actions. On a larger scale, teams regularly revise group and individual tasks based on what the other team members are doing and have done, what they are still going to do, and what is left to do.

All of these factors contribute to an intricate impression of the complexity, multiplicity, and interconnectedness necessary for collaborative teamwork to function well. As teams move away from collocated work toward distributed interactions, the potential benefits of using technology to enhance teamwork increase, as do the barriers to successful teamwork. Indeed, in order for the potential benefits of technology to be realized, software solutions need to address and to support the intricacies of collaborative team interactions.

Technology Tools for Teamwork

There are many ways that technology can be deployed to support teamwork, from stand-alone computers in face-to-face team settings to networked computers using complex arrays of software to support distributed teams (see Figure 3). In fact, the study of computer-supported teamwork and the design of software to support collaboration have become active areas of research and development within information technology and business circles. Two key terms that can be used to access the extensive research and application literature are *computer-supported cooperative work* (CSCW) and *groupware*. In this section, we draw upon the literature in these two areas to provide a profile of current approaches to the design and use of technology to support teamwork.

CSCW has emerged as a field of study to examine the design and application of software to support teamwork. Researchers and developers working in this area are particularly interested in the nature of teams and teamwork because of the implications this understanding has for software design and use by teams. CSCW research draws on a diverse body of knowledge, including linguistics, social psychology, cognitive science, and computer science. Recent collections of this work (e.g., Hinds & Kiesler, 2002) reveal some of the depth of understanding that has emerged about group processes and the impact and limitations of technology in supporting teamwork.

Groupware refers to computer hardware and software that have been specifically designed to enhance teamwork (Johansen, 1988). Groupware design requires an understanding not only of how collocated teams work, but how teamwork changes when it becomes distributed and mediated by technology. In the section to follow, a description of how groupware can be used to support teams as they work in collocated and distributed situations is offered.

Broadly considered, groupware applications can be classified into the following categories: electronic mail/messaging; calendaring/scheduling; group document handling; workgroup development tools; group decision systems and meeting support; information sharing/conferencing products; and workflow management and business process design. These classes of groupware can be considered within the time-space matrix (see Figure 3) and the nature of the teamwork involved.

Synchronous collocated teams have the advantage of using groupware to augment conventional team tools and face-to-face interactions (Olson, Teasley, Covi, & Olson, 2002). An example is the team meeting room that supports interactive, continuous communication. Teams continue to benefit from the advantages of face-to-face interactions to coordinate their task activities and maintain awareness of other team members. However, groupware can also allow members to enter their work on computers and display individual or group products for the entire team to review or work on together. Specific-purpose tools may be used to guide workflow, brainstorming, or access to databases and other information sources to augment the knowledge base of the team.

For synchronous distributed teams, groupware needs to address problems of communication and task coordination that arise from lack of face-to-face contact. Since this type of distributed teamwork comes closest to reflecting the complexities of synchronous collocated teams, development work has been most aggressive in this area. Widely adopted solutions have included:

- chat systems that allow teams to network computers, conduct and store written dialogue, and exchange files

- screen sharing that allows teams to see the same objects and work on them together

- videoconferencing that allows team members to see and hear each other while working together

- media spaces that combine the above approaches

As Olson and Olson (2000) have reported, current generations of groupware solutions have fallen short in supporting the dynamic, tightly coupled work of remote teams. Studies (e.g., Kraut, Fussell, Brennan, & Siegel, 2002) have identified the following factors as difficult to address through the use of technology: initiating communication, frequency of communication, chance encounters, transitions from encounters to communication, conducting conversations, use of common ground, precise timing of cues, coordination of turn-taking, repair of misunderstandings, and maintaining task and team awareness.

Asynchronous collocation involves teams working together at the same place but at different times, with the team needing to sustain ongoing tasks when members are not face to face. Traditional team tools have involved sharing access to files and documents, including progress updates and notes to guide the work of other team members. Groupware solutions have included establishing of team rooms where workers can gather and shared computers that make use of specific-purpose planning tools such as team calendars, database and project management software, and collaborative writing and design tools. Sharing a work location allows team members to interact with the same objects, artifacts, and people without needing to rely on technology to gain this access. The challenge becomes one of maintaining continuity and coordination among team members in the absence of face-to-face interactions. Sproull and Kiesler (1991) have reported that in this situation technology solutions have involved providing general-purpose and specific-purpose tools to structure and manage team interactions. However, they caution against overstructuring these interactions through, for example, an automated calendar because structuring the group process requires prediction of the topics, kinds of social tasks, and strategies people will need to use. Such structure may not enable the flexible and spontaneous planning and revision that the task situation requires.

Asynchronous distributed teams interact at different times and different places. Accordingly, this kind of teamwork faces the greatest need for coordination and communication supports. Technology solutions have involved the use of such tools as document sharing and management, email, bulletin boards, and list servers. This kind of teamwork has been the focus of intensive study by researchers (see Hinds & Kiesler, 2002), who report both positive and negative outcomes when technology is used. Kiesler and Cummings (2002) concluded "the use of communication technology is likely to be most successful when work groups have already forged close relationships, so that existing feelings of alliance or commitment sustain motivation" (p. 69).

Just as the matrix in Figure 3 can assist in thinking about the kinds of teamwork groups engage in, it helps in identifying the technology needed to support teamwork in its various contexts. Yet the real issue is not finding which technology fits which team arrangement. The challenge is to identify and address the physical and social arrangements needed to help teams do their work productively. In brief, the need is for technology tools to support teams across many styles of teamwork: across time; across place; among casual and formal interactions; and between individual and group work.

The kinds of tools that are currently arising from the research on groupware can be illustrated by describing a current groupware development project. It should be remembered that groupware refers to a class of technology tools that support teamwork. Previously in this chapter it has been shown that these tools take many forms; their successful use depends on complex conditions related to team dynamics.

GroupLab at the University of Calgary's Department of Computer Science (www.cpsc.ucalgary.ca/grouplab/) conducts research into human-computer interaction and computer-supported collaborative work. Researchers at this unit (Greenberg & Roseman, in press) point out that as people move between their traditional teamwork patterns, groupware design has created gaps that compel users to switch from one groupware application to another. They define gaps as "the physical or perceptual boundaries within groupware that either distract participants from the work they are doing, or that block them from crossing the spatial, temporal, or functional boundaries inherent in collaborative work" (p. 3). They have described the development of groupware designed to achieve seamlessness, defined as mitigating or eliminating unnecessary obstructing perceptual seams or gaps. They argue that groupware designed as a room metaphor can nurture a wide range of natural team interactions within an environment that helps diminish technical gaps, and that supplies users with a conceptual model to reduce perceptual seams.

A room metaphor is a type of spatial model analogous to the physical rooms used by teams within a building. Rooms are bounded spaces that act as containers, items within a room have spatial locations and people can inhabit a collection of rooms. Such rooms typically include personal offices, shared rooms (e.g., breakout rooms and conference rooms), dedicated project rooms (open offices housing a team of 3-6 people where people can work together and leave artifacts), and public spaces for social interaction and casual work (e.g., coffee rooms, foyers, and commons). Greenberg and Roseman describe the room metaphor as a bounded space that allows partitioning, containment, and permeability. Within a virtual space, walls act as partitions that can create rooms to bring together and/or separate people and the tools they work with. Individual rooms act as containers for virtual people, furniture, tools for work and communication (e.g., telephones, overhead projectors), documents, and other artifacts that can support both individual and group activities. Finally, rooms are permeable, allowing people to enter, leave, and bring in or remove items.

These and other characteristics of the room metaphor were used in the design of a groupware product called TeamWave Workplace (Greenberg & Roseman, in press). While the technical details of the design are beyond the scope of this discussion, consideration of how the software facilitates asynchronous and synchronous work is of interest. When team members are present in a TeamWave room at the same time, they are automatically linked synchronously. The act of entering a room immediately connects all people within it, both for communication (e.g., a chat tool) and for work (e.g., applets and a background whiteboard). When people work asynchronously with this software, they can leave coordination documents for each other, such as to-do lists, action items, telephone logs, and vacation schedules. Virtual notes, reminders, and comments can be left on the whiteboard or written on "sticky notes" next to a relevant work object. The same artifacts work for both asynchronous and synchronous work. All room objects can be used either by a single user or by several users at the same time. Team members can work on tasks individually, and then share task artifacts with others, either asynchronously or synchronously. The transition between asynchronous and synchronous activity becomes a function of how people use the rooms and its tools, rather than a function of system constraints. Perhaps most importantly, the room metaphor capitalizes upon the daily experiences that humans share to provide software tools to support teamwork.

Despite what has been discovered about distributed teams, much remains to be learned. This discussion is concluded by considering some important questions that need to be addressed, both by researchers and designers of groupware and by teams who want to use technology to support their work.

- How can a sense of community and team commitment be fostered in electronic environments?
- What interpersonal skills are essential to distributed teamwork?
- What aspects of team process can be supported by technology and which cannot?
- When is it time to meet face to face, and when is it better to move to distributed options?
- How can communication among team members be suitably supported by technology?
- How can individual and group work be best coordinated in distributed environments?
- How can diversity among team members be acknowledged and supported?
- How can knowledge sources necessary for effective teamwork best be accessed and used?
- How can teams best monitor and adjust ongoing processes and tasks?

• How can distributed teams foster quality outcomes?

Benefits and Barriers of Technology for Teamwork

With the profile of technology tools for teamwork outlined in the previous section as a backdrop, we now consider the benefits and barriers arising from the use of technology to support teamwork. Our goal here is to avoid either unbridled enthusiasm or stifling pessimism about the potential that technology support can offer. In this way, we hope to arrive at a balanced consideration of strategies for technology support that are sensitive to the diverse needs and contexts of collaborative teams.

Electronic collaboration can result in benefits such as:

• Electronic team communication may reduce time needed for face-to-face meetings by enhancing project planning, coordination, and problem solving (Sproull & Kiesler, 1991, p. 30).

• There may be efficiency gains (accelerated and regularized information flow) and/or productivity gains (e.g., costs for coordination, scheduling, task assignments) (Sproull & Kiesler, 1991, pp. 4, 21-27).

• People may pay attention to different things, interact with different people, and depend on one another differently (Sproull & Kiesler, 1991, p. 4).

• There are opportunities for undominated dialogue, a weakening of the power relationship among team members (Sproull & Kiesler, 1991, p. 59).

• Access to knowledge sources and resources may enhance team planning or ongoing work (Robertson, Haines, Sanche, & Biffart, 1997, pp. 26-27).

• Technology planning frameworks and specific-purpose tools may enhance team purpose and process (Haines & Sanche, 2000, pp. 293-294).

• Individual work by team members may be enhanced through improved access to other team members and the products of the team's ongoing work (Harrington, 1993, p. 7).

Electronic collaboration can result in barriers such as:

• Electronic communication may reduce the strong interpersonal connections that foster the development of learning communities (Harrington, 1993, p. 9).

• Financial costs associated with hardware, software, and training may be prohibitive (Strassman, 1985, p. 82).

• Information overload may happen when information exchange is not contolled (Sproull & Kiesler, 1991, p. 115).

• Collaborative software systems may be so complex that many users cannot or will not use them (Johansen, 1988, p. 72).

• Individual team members may fail to participate, or may do so in an untimely fashion (Armstrong & Cole, 2002, p. 168).

• Electronic communication may not enable subtle, visible aspects (e.g., gestures, shared points of reference, turn-taking, repair of misunderstandings) of face-to-face interaction (Kraut, Fussell, Brennan, & Siegel, 2002, pp. 148-150).

• Electronic communication may reduce group conformity and convergence, leading to increased group conflict and time needed to resolve it (Sproull & Kiesler, 1991, p. 65).

• The information needed to maintain awareness of team, task, and the environment may overwhelm individuals and affect teamwork negatively (Kraut, Fussell, Brennan, & Siegel, 2002, pp. 152-156).

Identifying the benefits and barriers to the use of technology by collaborative teams can lead to insights into which technology tools to choose for specific team contexts and strategies for addressing the barriers that may be encountered in using those tools. It is important to note that any particular benefit or barrier may be altered by conditions that lead to more positive or negative outcomes. For example, among the barriers listed here, electronic communication was identified as a possible threat to establishing of learning communities. However, as pointed out by Harrington (1993), thoughtful and deliberate use of communication tools can lead to positive community building.

An extensive body of research identifies the challenges that traditional teams face in conducting their work productively (Friend & Cook, 2003); however, distributed teams face even more complexities (Hinds & Kiesler, 2002). Recent research in CSCW has clarified and emphasized the importance of respecting the complexity of teamwork and what we know and do not know about it, especially when technology, time, and distance are involved (Fisher & Fisher, 1998). At the same time, the research has revealed unique advantages of distributed environments. CSCW researchers have drawn extensively on the knowledge base built by cognitive scientists; for example, Festinger (1954) on social behavior in groups and Clark (1996) on the nuances of language.

The concept of awareness has gained prominence with CSCW researchers (e.g., Gutwin & Greenberg, in press; Weisband, 2002). However, this work has focused upon studying the mutual awareness of people's activity for the purpose of coordinating tasks and resources. What has not been evident in the CSCW literature, even in the work on awareness, is research on metacognition (e.g., Flavell, 1976, 1977, 1978) and strategic processes (e.g., Pressley & Levin, 1983). Metacognition refers to the awareness and control of one's thinking. It involves being aware of our thinking as we perform specific tasks and using this awareness to regulate what we are doing.

The concept of metacognition could make an important contribution to our understanding of team awareness at two levels: intraindividual and interindividual. At the intraindividual level, the focus would be upon each team member's awareness of the nature of the task and the processes and skills related to accomplishing the task. At the interindividual level, a metacognitive/strategic model would elucidate the structure of the team task and the processes and skills needed to work together to accomplish the task. In particular, such a model could foster team regulation through an "executive function;" that is, strategy activation, self-monitoring, and repair that guides the team in how to be productive and successful, and how to respond when problems arise.

Models for Teamwork and Technology

The primary means of fostering metacognition is to make the implicit explicit, thereby subject to awareness, reflection, and action. In the research literature on metacognition, this explicitness is often accomplished through exploration of mental models and self-talk procedures that structure and guide strategies to regulate processes and tasks (Flavell, 1976, 1977, 1978). A key tool to foster and guide explicitness has been the use of metacognitive questions; that is, questions purposefully designed and timed to trigger reflection and strategic action.

There has been no shortage of models proposed to guide teamwork and collaboration (Fishbaugh, 1997). In this section, two models, one representing team development and the other team operation are outlined. These models illustrate how explicitness can be accomplished to guide teamwork.

While descriptions of the stages of a group's developmental cycle vary, there is agreement on the broad characteristics of a team's evolution. Brill (1976) has described the following five stages:

1. Orientation (Forming): Members learn about each other and their team's purpose.
2. Accommodation (Storming): The team resolves issues of leadership, procedures, and goals.
3. Negotiation (Norming): The team sets role relationships, leadership roles, and processes.
4. Operation (Performing): Members align and work toward achieving the team goals.
5. Dissolution (Adjourning): Outcomes are evaluated and the team disbands.

Understanding the developmental cycle that teams follow offers an opportunity to raise this understanding to the level of awareness and action by designing tools and other supports to assist and regulate this development. It also offers the opportunity to build this knowledge into the design of groupware frameworks and tools to support this natural process.

In examining the operations that teams use to conduct their work, the present discussion is limited to problem solving. Essentially, the model described here is an elaboration of the fourth stage, or Operation level, of the Brill (1976) team development model. Once a team is functioning in an educational setting, the internal process of problem solving becomes very important. Friend and Cook (2003) describe six stages that characterize a team action cycle for problem solving:

1. Setting the problem-solving context (gather information on the current situation)
2. Identifying the problem (detail discrepancies between current and desired situations)
3. Generating potential solutions (propose a variety of means of addressing the discrepancies)
4. Evaluating potential solutions (identify positives and negatives, choose best options)
5. Implementing the solution (develop detailed plans, success criteria, and outcome evaluation)
6. Evaluating the outcome (decide on continuing, revising, or terminating the plan)

Earlier in this chapter, the value of frameworks for the collaborative process was discussed. Understanding the way teams operate to identify tasks and detail working plans offers an opportunity to design explicit planning frameworks and supports for the process. For example, the models outlined above could be readily supported by an array of decision-making and problem-solving tools specifically designed for each stage and strategically embedded in the model. This is the approach taken in the design of the *Coplanner* software described by Robertson et al. (1997) and by Haines and Sanche (2000). Likewise, a collaborative style could be facilitated through tools and supports designed to enhance processes of communication, problem solving, and consensus decision making.

In the next section, attention is focused on teams and teamwork in special education and the technology supports these teams might need. Of particular interest are the types of teams that typically operate in this area and the decision processes in which they engage.

Technology Support for Teamwork in Special Education

As in business and other organizational contexts, teamwork in special education covers a full range of types described in Figure 2. For example, special educators who coteach with classroom teachers engage in an informal, ongoing kind of teamwork, while these same professionals might serve together on a large interagency team designing an IEP in a formal way. The student-centered problem-solving teams as described by Friend and Cook (2003) are of particular interest because these types of teams have the most direct influence upon the design of instructional programs and related services and supports for students and families. Given the nature of this work, there seems to be a particular need for these teams to use technology to support their teamwork.

The use of technology in special education has been dominated by instructional software and by assistive technology devices and software (Male, 1997). Another area that has received considerable attention has been the development of IEP software and related special education information management systems. With reference to the latter, a great deal of emphasis in the design of software products has been placed upon compliance with regulations that govern the IEP process. To illustrate this point, an Internet search using the keywords "IEP software" was conducted and produced a large number of hits. Perusal of a selection of the product descriptions on the resulting Web sites yielded obvious similarities. The software features list below, taken from one Web site selected at random from the search, typifies this uniformity.

The software:

- Contains the forms recommended by the Department of Education, including the Assessment Summary Report, IEP and IFSP

- Facilitates the selection of clearly written, measurable, and content-specific annual goals and short-term objectives from curriculum banks

- Allows users to create their own benchmarks that meet their district's standards, and generates an individualized student progress report directly from the IEP goals and objectives

- Exports and imports data easily in the cross-platform Macintosh and Windows environment

- Provides a case management system that fully integrates special education information from the classroom to the district office and ultimately the State Department of Education

- Assists administrators with an integrated record- tracking system to help ensure that forms are completed to meet deadlines

- Ensures record confidentiality with advanced security functions

This description suggests an emphasis on filling out forms, administrative efficiency and compatibility, and compliance with regulations. Conspicuously missing in these products were technology tools specifically designed to support teams and the teamwork process.

Certainly, special education teams can and do use general-purpose tools such as email, file transfer, and chat programs to enhance teamwork (Male, 1997). However, this approach is subject to the barriers and limitations outlined in this chapter. In particular, these technology tools do not explicitly support a teamwork model or process since they are inherently free of content. Thus, current evidence strongly suggests that this approach is likely not as effective as it could be.

The *CoPlanner* software described earlier in this chapter has been explicitly designed to address the context and content of special education teams (Haines & Sanche, 2000; Robertson, et al., 1997; Sanche, Haines, & Robertson, 1994). This software application was originally built around a desktop metaphor and a stage model of team operation. The desktop metaphor was used to capitalize on users' familiarity with objects such as icons, folders, and menu bars. Likewise, familiar tools were part of the design:

worksheets, text documents, calendars with reminders, and forms. Further functionality was accomplished through templates, password security, external document aliases, and messaging with file transfer. The module concept allows the team to preformat a student file with folders and documents designed to suit the purpose of the team's planning (e.g., instruction, transition, assistive technology). The software design attempts to serve a metacognitive role through the use of a decision model, implemented in worksheet layouts, supported by guiding questions. For example, the decision model for the instructional planning module consists of stages labeled Identification, Information Gathering, Reflection, Teaching, Monitoring, and Reporting. Guiding questions (e.g., "What outcomes do you envision for this student?") provide a structure for each stage of the model. As the teamwork progresses, the folders that serve as document repositories can be accessed for a variety of purposes, including brainstorming guides, assessment tools, and IEP forms. The resulting student file becomes not only a guide for team planning activity, but also an archive of the decisions and actions that have transpired. Inherent in the *CoPlanner* design is the concept of knowledge management discussed earlier.

The *CoPlanner* software can be considered relative to the time/space distribution outlined in Figure 3. Clearly, the design best supports collocated teams, either at synchronous or asynchronous times. *CoPlanner* supports distributed teams only through email exchange and file distribution. Therefore, teams using a software product like *CoPlanner* would encounter many of the barriers that distributed teams face. Even in the context of collocated teamwork, more attention could be devoted within the *CoPlanner* software environment to strengthening teams as learning communities, to team development, and to a variety of collaboration process skills (e.g., conflict resolution, consensus decision making, and communication). To enhance distributed teamwork, *CoPlanner* could have a greater range of groupware tools including chat, shared screens, video conferencing, and bulletin boards available to the team. These features would work best when well integrated with the structure of software like *CoPlanner* to prevent the kinds of gaps and discontinuities that individuals can experience when using these tools.

One possible approach to integrating content with communication tools and resources would be a product like WebCT (www.webct.com). Although this web-based environment has been designed for distance delivery of courses, the array and flexibility of file sharing and communication tools offer interesting possibilities as an environment that could be crafted to enhance teamwork and collaboration. In the discussion that follows, principles and guidelines that would lead to more effective and efficient software support for teamwork are considered in more detail.

What might a more ambitious view of the future offer? The answer to this question lies at the juncture of active and passive approaches. It is possible to make greater demands than described in this chapter upon an ideal system of technology supports for teamwork. Technology supports must be viewed as offering much more than passive assistance in filling out forms. Quality teamwork is inquiry-oriented (Edyburn, 2000). It involves seeking knowledge and building shared knowledge, thereby co-constructing a complex, dynamic understanding of the team's mission, tasks, and actions. Technology supports that can help to build knowledge are needed. Such systems should be capable of actively drawing upon knowledge objects (Wiley, 2000) to create "if-then" scenarios and offer decision options, thereby serving a metacognitive role. Such "intelligent agent" technology (e.g., Horberg, 1995) would anticipate upcoming tasks and decisions based on the team's past decisions and actions. It would come to "know" the team and individual members of that team. Further, it would actively use this knowledge to respond at opportune times with questions, prompts, advice, and resources to the team and the evolving situation. In sum, groupware with active, intelligent components could go beyond simply supporting teamwork to transforming it.

Teamwork and Teamware: An Implementation Model

At the risk of introducing yet another coined term into what is already a bewildering array of vocabulary (Johansen, 1988), we proceed to outline some critical principles for the design and use of software to support collaborative teams. We prefer the term *teamware* to the prevailing term *groupware* because the component word *group* does little to capture the nature of the work that the software needs to support. On the other hand, the term *team* implies an organizing structure, an associated set of values and skills, and a process that distinguishes a team from a group.

In considering the implications for practice arising from this review, a three-level approach to teamware implementation is suggested (see Figure 4). The model has been cast in a pyramid shape to convey the principle of building-on. At the base level, the foundational task of building a culture of collaboration is of primary importance. Success at each other level depends on professionals, students, and parents sharing a set of values, and valuing this way of interacting and working together.

At the second level, the goal is to make explicit the frameworks, processes, and skills that guide and reflect teamwork. A first task here is to review and renew the special education service model to align it with the culture of collaboration. As pointed out earlier in this chapter, this step may require a great deal of work (see Figure 1), since traditional service models often reflect an underlying expert model of service delivery. Inherent in the design would be an explanation of the types of teams at different levels of the service model, their roles, and how they conduct their work. The developmental model (Brill, 1976) and the problem-solving model (Friend & Cook, 2003) described elsewhere in this chapter offer examples of how these structures can be made explicit and how tools can be designed to support the various activities of teams. In the problem-solving model, it is also important for teams to practice and refine their processes such as communication, consensus decision-making, brainstorming, and conflict resolution (Friend & Cook, 2003). Fluency with these processes and the

Figure 4. Three-level model of teamwork and technology.

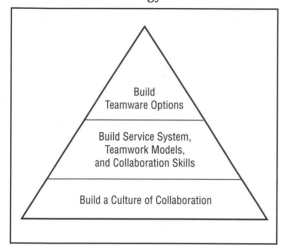

skills that underlie them is essential, especially when the added challenges of distributed work pose new barriers.

The third level of the implementation model should be built upon well-established teamwork at first and second levels (see Figure 4). Teamware should capture and represent the service system, types of teams, and the process of teamwork established at levels one and two. Care should be taken to create a dynamic balance between face-to-face meetings and use of technology options. The team should develop an orderly progression for the introduction of technology into the teamwork environment. Since many team members will be familiar with email and file exchange, teamware solutions could begin here. More sophisticated options such as whiteboards and chat systems can then be introduced cautiously, and carefully evaluated for their use and effectiveness.

Although a linear relationship among the three levels of the implementation model has been conveyed, it is recognized that these levels represent a more reciprocal relationship, and could be activated in parallel, stimulating the kind of recursive reculturing (Skrtic, 1991) described earlier in this chapter. For example, designing the teamwork model as a team would enhance building a culture of collaboration, and teamware tools could be introduced during the design of the teamwork model. It should be anticipated that implementation of team-

work and teamware will be highly idiosyncratic, requiring each team to design its own developmental pathway. The authors hope that the ideas presented in this chapter serve as a general heuristic for this process.

Conclusions

Collaborative teams have emerged as the preferred work units in today's professions and organizations. Collaboration is a style that these teams use as individuals interact with one another. Effective collaborative teamwork faces many obstacles; the most challenging barriers involve creating a culture of collaboration and conducting collaborative work across distance and time. Technology can be used to enhance the quality and productivity of collaborative teamwork. In particular, it can help teams to organize, plan, and communicate. However, introducing technology into the teamwork process requires careful planning and due regard for the complexities of teamwork, technology, and their interaction. Teamwork needs technology, because technology offers tools to diminish threats to efficiency and effectiveness, especially those arising from obstacles of time and distance. At the same time, technology needs teamwork because teams that use technology must be built upon a set of collaborative values, skills, and style of interaction to stand the greatest chance for success. Effective teamwork supported by technology offers encouraging promise for creating quality special education services for children and youth.

References

Armstrong, D., & Cole, P. (2002). Managing distances and differences in geographically distributed work groups. In P. Hinds & S. Kiesler (Eds.), *Distributed work* (pp. 167-189). Cambridge, MA: MIT Press.

Avery, C. M., Walker, M. A., & Murphy, E. (2001). *Teamwork as an individual skill: Getting your work done when sharing responsibility.* San Francisco: Berrett-Koehler.

Barth, R. S. (2002). The culture builder. *Educational Leadership, 59*(8), 6-11.

Bauwens, J., & Hourcade, J. J. (1995).

Cooperative teaching: Rebuilding the schoolhouse for all students. Austin, TX: Pro-Ed.

Bauwens, J., Hourcade, J. J., & Friend, M. (1989). Cooperative teaching: A model for general and special education integration. *Remedial and Special Education, 10*(2), 17-22.

Brill, N. (1976). *Teamwork: Working together in the human services.* Philadelphia, PA: Lippincott.

Chalfant, J. C., & Pysh, M. V. (1989). Teacher assistance teams: Five descriptive studies on 96 teams. *Remedial and Special Education, 10*(6), 49-58.

Chalfant, J. C., Pysh, M. V., & Moultrie, R. (1979). Teacher assistance teams: A model for within-building problem solving. *Learning Disability Quarterly, 2,* 85-95.

Clark, H. (1996). *Using language.* Cambridge: Cambridge University Press, 1996.

Cook, L., & Friend, M. (1995). Co-teaching guidelines for creating effective practices. *Focus on Exceptional Children, 28*(2), 1-12.

Deming, E. (1986). *Out of the crisis.* Cambridge, MA: MIT Press.

Dettmer, P., Thurston, L.P., & Dyck, N. (2002). *Consultation, collaboration, and teamwork for students with special needs* (4th ed.). Boston: Allyn & Bacon.

Dryfoos, J. (1994). *Full-service schools: A revolution in health and social services for children, youth, and families.* San Francisco: Jossey-Bass.

Edyburn, D. L. (2000). Collegial study groups: A strategy for creating shared visions of assistive technology outcomes. *Diagnostique, 25,* 327-348.

Festinger, L. (1954). A theory of social comparison processes. *Human Relations, 7,* 117-140.

Feteroll, E., Hoffherr, G., & Moran, J. (1993). *Growing teams: A down-to-earth approach.* Methuen, MA: GOAL/QPC.

Fishbaugh, M. (1997). *Models of collaboration.* Boston: Allyn & Bacon.

Fishbaugh, M. S. E. (2000). *The collaboration guide for early career educators.* Baltimore: Brookes.

Fisher, K., & Fisher, M. D. (1998). *The distributed mind: Achieving high performance through the collective intelligence of knowledge work teams.* New York: AMACOM.

Flavell, J. H. (1976). Metacognitive aspects of problem solving. In L.B. Resnick (Ed.), *The nature of intelligence* (pp. 231-235). Hillsdale, NJ: Erlbaum.

Flavell, J. (1977). *Cognitive development.* Englewood Cliffs, NJ: Prentice-Hall.

Flavell, J. H. (1978). Metacognitive development. In J. M. Scandura & C. J. Brainerd (Eds.), *Structural/process theories of complex human behavior* (pp. 213-245). Alphen aan den Rijn, Netherlands: Sijthoff & Noordoff.

Forest, M., & Lausthaus, E. (1989). Promoting educational equality for all students: Circles and maps. In S. Stainback, W. Stainback, & M. Forest (Eds.), *Educating all students in the mainstream of regular education* (pp. 43-57). Baltimore: Paul H. Brookes.

Friend, M., & Cook, L. (2003). *Interactions: Collaboration skills for school professionals.* Boston: Allyn & Bacon.

Fullan, M. (2001). *Leading in a culture of change.* San Francisco: Jossey-Bass.

Fullan, M. (2002). The change leader. *Educational Leadership, 59*(8), 17-20.

Greenberg S. & Roseman, M. (2003). Using a room metaphor to ease transitions in groupware. In M. Ackerman, V. Pipek, & V. Wulf (Eds.), *Beyond knowledge management: Sharing expertise.* Cambridge, MA: MIT Press. Retrieved from www.cpsc.ucalgary.ca/grouplab/.

Gutwin, C., & Greenberg, S. (in press). The importance of awareness for team cognition in distributed collaboration. In E. Salas, S. Fiore, & J. Cannon-Bowers (Eds.), *Team cognition: Process and performance at the inter- and intra-individual level.* Washington: APA Press. Retrieved from www.cpsc.ucalgary.ca/grouplab/.

Haines, L., & Sanche, R. (2000). Assessment models and software support for assistive technology teams. *Diagnostique, 25,* 291-306.

Haines, L., Sanche, R., & Robertson, G. (1993). Instruction CoPlanner: A software tool to facilitate collaborative resource teaching. *Canadian Journal of Educational Communication, 22,* 177-187.

Harrington, H. (1993). The essence of technology and the education of teachers. *Journal of Teacher Education, 44,* 1-15.

Hinds, P., & Kiesler, S. (Eds.). (2002).

Distributed work. Cambridge, MA: MIT Press.

Horberg, J. (1995). Talk to my agent: Software agents in virtual reality. *Computer-Mediated Communication Magazine, 2*(2), 3. Retrieved from: metalab.unc.edu/cmc/mag/1995/feb/horberg.html.

Idol, L., Paolucci-Whitcomb, P., & Nevin, A. (1986). *Collaborative consultation* Austin, TX: Pro-Ed.

Idol, L., Nevin, A., & Paolucci-Whitcomb, P. (2000). *Collaborative consultation* (3rd ed.). Austin, TX: Pro-Ed.

Johnston, M., Bronsnan, P., Cramer, D., & Dove, T. (Eds.). (2000). *Collaboration reforms and other improbable dreams.* Albany: State University of New York Press.

Johansen, R. (1988) *Groupware: Computer support for business teams.* New York: Macmillan.

Kanter, R. M. (1997). *On the frontiers of management.* Boston: Harvard Business School Press.

Kampwirth, T. J. (1999). *Collaborative consultation in the schools: Effective practices for students with learning and behavior problems.* Upper Saddle River, NJ: Merrill/Prentice Hall.

Kiesler, S., & Cummings, J. (2002). What do we know about proximity and distance in work groups? A legacy of research. In P. Hinds & S. Kiesler (Eds.), *Distributed work* (pp. 57-80). Cambridge, MA: MIT Press.

Kraut, R., Fussell, S., Brennan, S., & Siegel, J. (2002). Understanding effects of proximity on Collaboration: Implications for technologies to support remote collaborative work. In P. Hinds & S. Kiesler (Eds.), *Distributed work* (pp. 138-162), Cambridge, MA: MIT Press.

LaFasto, F., & Larson, C. (2001). *When teams work best.* Thousand Oaks, CA: Sage Publishing.

Male, M. (1997). *Technology for inclusion.* Needham Heights, MA: Allyn & Bacon.

Malhotra, Y. (1998). Tools@work: Deciphering the knowledge management hype. *Journal for Quality and Participation, 21*(4), 58-60.

Manz, C. C., Neck, C. P., Mancuso, J., & Manz, K. (1997). *For team members only: Making your workplace team productive and hassle-free.* New York: American Management Association.

Moore, G. A. (1991). *Crossing the chasm.* New York: Harper Collins.

Olson, G., & Olson, J. (2000). Distance matters. *Human-Computer Interaction, 15,* 139-179.

Olson, J., Teasley, S., Covi, L., & Olson, G. (2002). The (currently) unique advantages of collocated work. In P. Hinds & S. Kiesler (Eds.), *Distributed work* (pp. 113-135). Cambridge, MA: MIT Press.

Osbourn, A. F. (1963). *Applied imagination: Principles and procedures of creative problem-solving.* New York: Charles Scribner.

Pettigrew, A. (1979). On studying organizational cultures. *Administrative Science Quarterly, 24,* 570-581.

Platt, L.J. (1994). Why bother with teams: An overview. In R. Michael Casto & Maria C. Julia (Eds.), *Interprofessional care and collaborative practice: Commission on interprofessional education and practice* (pp. 3-10). Pacific Grove, CA: Brookes/Cole.

Pressley, M., & Levin, J. (Eds.). (1983). *Cognitive strategy research: Educational applications.* New York: Springer-Verlag.

Remen, R. N. (2000). *My grandfather's blessings.* New York: Riverhead Books.

Robbins, H., & Finley, M. (2000). *The new why teams don't work: What goes wrong and how to make it right.* San Francisco: Berrett-Koehler.

Robertson, G., Haines, L., Sanche, R., & Biffart, W. (1997). Positive change through computer networking. *Teaching Exceptional Children, 29*(6), 22-30.

Robertson, G., Haines, L., Sanche, R. (Producers), & Holmund, M. (Director). (1993). *Teamwork, technology and Teaching* (video tape). Saskatoon, SK: University of Saskatchewan.

Salend, S. (2001). *Creating inclusive classrooms: Effective and reflective practices* (4th ed.). Upper Saddle River, NJ: Merrill/Prentice Hall.

Sanche, R., Haines, L., & Robertson, G. (1994). Instruction CoPlanner: Computer technology supporting collaborative decision-making across the curriculum. *Journal of Technology and Teacher Education, 2,* 155-165.

Sattler, J. M. (2001). *Assessment of children: Cognitive applications* (4th ed.). San Diego, CA: Jerome M. Sattler, Publisher.

Scholtes, P., Joiner, B., & Streibel, B. (1996). *The team handbook.* Madison, WI: Joiner Associates.

Senge, P. (1990). *The fifth discipline: The art and practice of the learning organization.* New York: Doubleday.

Senge, P., Cambron-McCabe, N., Lucas, T., Smith, B., & Kleiner, A. (2000). *Schools that learn: A fifth discipline fieldbook for educators, parents, and everyone who cares about education.* New York: Doubleday.

Sergiovanni, T. J. (1994). *Building community in schools.* San Francisco: Jossey-Bass.

Skrtic, T. (1991*). Behind special education: A critical analysis of professional culture and school organization.* Denver: Love Publishing.

Sproull, L., & Kiesler, S. (1991). *Connections: New ways of working in the networked organization.* Cambridge, MA: MIT Press.

Stewart, T. A. (1997). *Intellectual capital: The new wealth of organizations.* London: Nicholas Brealey.

Strassman, P. (1985). *Information payoff: The transformation of work in the electronic age.* New York: Free Press.

Straus, D. (2002). *How to make collaboration work: Powerful ways to build consensus, solve problems, and make decisions.* San Francisco: Berrett-Koehler Publishers.

Thomas, C. C., Correa, V. I., & Morsink, C. V. (2001). *Interactive teaming: Consultation and collaboration in special programs* (3rd. ed.). Upper Saddle River, NJ: Prentice Hall.

Thousand, J. S., & Villa, R. A. (2000). Collaborative teaming: A powerful tool in school restructuring. In R.A. Villa & J. S. Thousand (Eds.), *Restructuring for caring and effective education: Piecing the puzzle together* (2nd ed.) (pp. 254-291). Baltimore: Brookes.

Tiegerman-Farber, E., & Radziewicz, C. (1998). *Collaborative decision making: The pathway to inclusion.* Upper Saddle River, NJ: Merrill/Prentice Hall.

Vandercook, T., & York, J. (1990). In W. Stainback & S. Stainback (Eds.), *Support networks of inclusive schooling: Interdependent integrated education* (pp. 95-122). Baltimore: Paul H. Brookes.

Vaughn, S., Bos, C. S., & Schumm, J. S. (1996). *Teaching mainstreamed, diverse, and at-risk students in the general education classroom.* Needham Heights, MA: Allyn & Bacon.

Vaughn, S., Schumm, J. S., & Arguelles, M. E. (1997). The ABCDEs of co-teaching. *Teaching Exceptional Children, 30*(2), 4-10.

Walther-Thomas, C., Korinek, L., McLaughlin, V. L., & Williams, B. T. (2000). *Collaboration for inclusive education: Developing successful programs.* Boston: Allyn & Bacon.

Weisband, S. (2002). Maintaining awareness in distributed team collaboration: Implications for leadership and performance. In P. Hinds & S. Kiesler (Eds.), *Distributed work* (pp. 311-333). Cambridge, MA: MIT Press.

Wiley, D. A. (Ed.), (2000). *The instructional use of learning objects.* Retrieved May 18, 2001, from reusability.org/read/chapters/wiley.doc

Will, M. (1986). Educating children with learning problems: A shared responsibility. *Exceptional Children, 52*, 411-415.

24

Designing Digital Materials for Students with Disabilities

Randall Boone and Kyle Higgins

Questionable Design

After almost 20 years of research, development, and user feedback, the operating system (OS) of the Macintosh computer finally addressed an annoying design flaw. When one wished to turn off the computer, a pull-down menu provided the options of Restart and Shut Down as adjacent menu options. A lazy finger on the track pad or careless mouse movement when intending to quit the computer easily resulted in a Restart rather than a Shut Down. This error placed the machine in an uninterruptible process of shutting down and then starting up all over, a two-minute departure from the user's intended goal. Actually, the design problem was not really fixed; the options of Restart and Shut Down remain adjacent to each other on the pull-down menu in the most current OS. However, when one selects Restart, a pop-up window appears, asking if the user really does want to restart, thus preventing the unintended outcome.

Within the Windows operating system, the design of the shut-down process has also drawn attention over the years. To exit or quit a computer that is running just about any version of the Windows OS, the user must first select the Start button, under which the option to quit is hidden; not exactly intuitive. Norman (1990) discusses what he calls knowledge in the head as opposed to knowledge in the world. While it can be expected that a computer user will bring some degree of user knowledge

(i.e., knowledge in the head) to the event, the design of the software should never provide cues that are unclear or illogical of what might be expected (i.e., the option to quit as part of a menu labeled start).

This chapter begins with these two examples of questionable design to illustrate that the issue of good design lies not only with the developers and users of educational software, but with the entire software industry -- even to the most basic and important software programs, the computer operating systems. Cooper (1999) gives a couple of explanations for this phenomenon of bad design: (a) the way programmers necessarily think in order to write good computer code has a detrimental effect on the design of the software products they create; and (b) software developers find it easier to convince users that the software is effective and easy to use than it would be to actually make the software effective and easy to use.

The first theory is based on a view of the design of digital materials as having two distinct design requirements, inside and outside. "The inside – must be written with technical expertise and sensitivity to the needs of computers. But equally clearly, the other side of software – the outside – must be written with social expertise and sensitivity to the needs of people...programmers can do the former, but it takes...designers to do the latter" (Cooper, 1999, p. 88). The second theory is supported by research on educational software indicating that developers for the most part do not engage in the formative evaluation phase of the instructional design process (Higgins, Boone, & Williams, 2000), nor do they consider interface with assistive devices (Golden, 2002) when creating educational software.

Dancing Bear-Ware

The metaphor of the dancing bear is a good lens for understanding the current state of the art of educational software and related digital materials. Cooper (1999) makes the observation that although the bear is really a terrible dancer and is doing nothing much more than shambling and shuffling from paw to paw, "the wonder isn't that the bear dances well but that the bear dances at all" (p. 26). For those who use digital technologies with students with disabilities, the wonder is not that a text-to-speech system works really well, but that the text-to-speech system works at all. Teachers are less concerned that the spell-check program does not explicitly help a student determine the correct substitute for a misspelled word, but that the program can actually find any of the misspelled words. In other words, educators are willing to adapt their teaching to fit inflexible software and often spend hours learning how to use a new program that does not include clear, easy-to-understand instructions. Similarly, students will return to work at a computer without complaint even after their work has been lost due to an inexplicable file saving process. These things are accepted as part of the price for seeing the bear dance.

Viewed as a cautionary tale, the dancing bear-ware story should motivate educators to demand software that provides more than this surface level of satisfaction. Educators rely on commercial software developers to produce quality educational materials. The belief is that these products have been properly designed, developed, and evaluated prior to being made available in the marketplace (Higgins et al., 2000). And while most software developers undoubtedly realize the importance of consulting with experts in the field of education, much software is still developed without consideration of important factors that are commonly found in the professional literature (Geisert & Futrell, 1995).

Lockard, Abrams, and Many (1997) identified three major areas of concern by educators about educational software: (a) the lack of a theoretical base for the instructional design of the software, (b) an overemphasis on technical concerns such as graphics and sound, and (c) a lack of interest for pedagogical issues. More specifically, for students with learning disabilities, Neuman (1991) found the following problems in the design of commercial educational software: (a) reading was difficult, (b) graphics were confusing, (c) keyboarding requirements were extensive, (d) presentation formats were not motivating, and (e) students had difficulty in understanding tasks, feedback, hints, and error messages.

And it is not as if the research base does not provide a significant amount of information regarding important components that should be incorporated into effective educational software to maximize learning outcomes for students with disabilities. For example, eight specific criteria were provided by Higgins et al. (2000) as part of a framework for evaluating educational software for students with disabilities: (a) feedback, (b) instructional design, (c) student needs, (d) teacher options, (e) software options, (f) screen design, (g) instructional options, and (h) sound. This checklist was suggested to allow "the educator to ascertain if the software publisher, at the very least, incorporated information concerning the learning characteristics of students with disabilities into a particular piece of educational software" (p. 114).

The history of educational software development for students with disabilities, in terms of instructional design, is not encouraging either. Ager (1986) found that less than 20% of educational software was considered to be satisfactory by teachers after the software was used by students with learning disabilities. A federally funded project in the late 1980s to improve the instructional design and use of software for students with disabilities concluded that publishers were reluctant to invest in the development of software specifically targeted to handicapped students because the market was not "lucrative" (Macro Systems, 1988). In research a few years later, Neuman (1991) determined that adequate study of the interactions of students with learning disabilities and their teachers with appropriate educational software was virtually nonexistent. Similarly, Zane and Frazer (1992) found that developers of educational software had little or no data to validate their claims regarding the impact of their software on student learning. Woodward and Noell (1993) found software development in special education to be constrained by "limited federal funding and the lack of a broad-based commercial market" (p. 160). Specific to students with learning disabilities, Larsen (1995) found that a theoretical framework for learning was missing from the design of most educational software. Moreover, Higgins and colleagues (2000) found educational software developers reluctant to discuss the instructional design process used in the development of their products. Thus, of 33 publishers contacted, 22 were unwilling to provide any information; and none was forthcoming with data from any formative or summative evaluation concerning any educational product.

So, how does this translate to the classroom where thousands of students are working and learning from digital materials every day? Williams, Boone, and Kingsley (2004) found that concern over instructional design of educational software was the top issue for computer-using teachers and educational specialists providing computer support in elementary, middle, and high schools. A Delphi method was used to determine how the current body of educational software was viewed by a group of more than 50 computer-using teachers and school district technology specialists. Of specific concern was the finding that, too often, teachers were adapting their lessons to accommodate the software they wanted to use because the software did not provide options to make it adaptable.

It is becoming increasingly clear that educational software developers are not doing any better in designing digital materials for students than the people at Apple or Microsoft have been in helping users quit their machines. Even though digital materials are now a permanent, although questioned (Cuban, 2001; Oppenheimer, 2003), fixture in classrooms around the world (Char, 1990; Heinich, Molenda, Russell, & Smaldino, 2002; Jeffries, 2000; Pastor & Kerns, 1997; Perkins, 1995; Shelly, Cashman, Gunter, & Gunter, 2002; Skinner, 2002; Tiu, Guglielmi, & Walton, 2002), a deficit of formative and summative evaluation data on commercial educational software products remains (Boone, Higgins, & Williams, 1997; Higgins et al., 2000; Lockard, et al., 1997). Tie this to the fact that most of the published research on educational software has been conducted, not with commercial software actually found in classrooms, but with software specifically created for the research projects (Rosenberg, 1997), and it gives cause for concern.

Access to Information Is Not Access to Learning

All digital materials for students with disabilities, including instructional software, have to be designed not only for optimum instructional delivery, but also for the closely related issue of accessibility. Accessibility in the context of design for learning should not be confused with accessibility as access to the material. Thus, Rose and Meyer (2002) explain that equating *access to information* and *access to learning* is a misreading of the terms.

Differentiating *learning* from *access* is an important feature in determining instructional design for digital content. For example, a student who is blind can achieve a certain level of access to printed materials that are provided in a digital format on a Web site through using a screen reader program that translates text into computer-generated speech. Depending upon the internal design of the digital file, however, the material may be more or less accessible. As the screen reader program processes the data from the digital file, it must separate content data from the display instructions. The screen reader will then provide a text-to-speech translation of what it has determined to be the content data. While the formatting tags of the hypertext markup language (HTML) may include adequate screen display directions, these directions alone may not provide a coherent and logical order for the text-to-speech output. As a result, the user will have access to the content, but perhaps not true accessibility for learning.

Moreover, simple access to the content when the digital version is an exact analog of the original (i.e., the format of the digital copy is the same as the original) may be insufficient if the student has a learning disability that is exacerbated by the design of a typical textbook. Again, simple access to the standard materials does not provide accessibility for learning.

Universal Design for Learning

Adaptability is the cornerstone of a relatively new instructional design concept for digital materials, universal design for learning (UDL). The term, *universal design*, originally referred to a design concept in architecture that provided for the divergent needs of special populations integrated into the original building design. The idea got past the problem of retrofitting, which often provided ineffective or inconvenient placements, aesthetic issues, and significant costs. It also provided the serendipity of accommodations, such as curb cuts, that were installed for people with disabilities but proved to be handy for others, such as people with strollers, shopping carts, and bicycles (Rose, 2000).

Making the leap from universal design in architecture to a universal design for learning is explained by Rose and Meyer (2002) from the Center for Applied Special Technologies (CAST), a leading proponent organization for UDL:

> The barriers inherent in printed textbooks had long excluded students with physical disabilities, students with visual impairments, and students with learning disabilities, among many others. It seemed ironic to us that legislators and architects were working very hard to ensure that educational buildings were universally accessible, but no such movement pursued universal accessibility for the methods and materials used inside the buildings – the curriculum. (p. 72)

A key issue in understanding UDL lies in the differences between access to information and access to learning. Thus, a basic premise of UDL is that a curriculum should "include alternatives that make the learning in it accessible and applicable to students with different backgrounds, learning styles, abilities, and disabilities" (Rose, 2000, p. 68).

Mainstream Design

The mainstream design world also may have a few things to teach educators about effective design of digital materials for students with disabilities. Norman (1990) provides four principles of good design for just about anything, from instruments in an airplane cockpit to the controls for a kitchen stovetop.

1. Visibility: the user can tell the state of the device and determine options for proceeding.
2. Conceptual model: the user observes consistency in the presentation of operations of the device within a consistent system image held by the user.
3. Mapping: the user can determine the relationships between actions and results, between controls and their effects, and between the system state and what is visible.
4. Feedback: the user receives full and continuous feedback about the results of actions.

Many complicated devices or systems with which we interact are quite easy to understand, sometimes even easier than less complicated devices, because they adhere to theses four principles. Norman uses the example of the automobile, with its many various operator functions and controls, as a much easier to learn and use system than a typical business phone system.

"What is good about the design of the car? Things are visible. There are good mappings between the controls and the things controlled. Single controls have single functions. There is good feedback. The system is understandable" (Norman, 1990, p. 22).

The phone system, on the other hand, has a structure that is less visible. "Mappings are arbitrary: there is no rhyme or reason to the relationship between the actions the user must perform and the results to be accomplished. The controls have multiple functions. The system … is not understandable; its capabilities aren't apparent" (Norman, 1990, p. 22).

Digital Is Different

Cooper (1999) refers to the absence of Norman's (1990) principles as *cognitive friction*, suggesting that cognitive friction is usually quite low in interaction with physical devices because of their smaller range of states. But this is not the case for interactive digital devices (i.e., anything that is controlled by a digital processor and that requires input from the user). For example, the worse thing that could happen with an accidental keystroke on a typewriter is an error on the paper you were writing. Compare this to an accidental keystroke on a word processor that might delete an entire manuscript. Thus, the outcome differences between SHIFT-X and CONTROL-X on a word processor could be the difference between adding a capital letter and deleting an entire paragraph. The opportunity for cognitive friction to have a negative influence on student performance with educational software and other digital materials is significant. The digital environment creates new responsibilities for the instructional designer.

Digital material or software? The title of this chapter uses the term digital materials although much of the discussion centers on educational software. Why two different phrases? Do they mean the same thing? Well, certainly, educational software is a type of digital material. However, there are some digital materials for educational purposes that are not really educational software. For instance, content saved in a digital, computer-readable file may not be considered software from a technical standpoint. But the digital data file needs a particular design, so that it can be displayed with accuracy and with a format that provides a consistency in usability.

The World Wide Web (WWW) is a good example of the overlap of software and digital content. The basic HTML file format on which the WWW operates consists of content that is displayed using a set of embedded formatting codes (i.e., tags). The interactive aspects of the Web, which look and act more like computer software, are generally built using any of several programming languages, such as JavaScript, Java, or Perl, that can be interpreted by a standard Web browser.

Accessibility
Accountability for all students' educational progress is clearly outlined in the 1997 Amendments to the Individuals with Disabilities Education Act (1997) (IDEA '97), which describes the requirements for access for students with disabilities to the general education curriculum. Circumventing the significant roadblocks to learning that exists in much print-based and ill-designed digital content commonly found in the curriculum has been of great concern to special educators. Looking at digital content, specifically, several efforts have been focused on accessibility. For example, the Bobby project (www.cast.org/bobby) at the Center for Applied Special Technology (CAST), the World Wide Web Consortium's (W3C) Web accessibility guidelines (www.w3.org/WAI/), Section 508 of the 1997 Rehabilitation Act (www.section508.gov), the Chaffee Amendment (1996) to the Copyright law, and the National Instructional Materials Accessibility Standard (NIMAS) report (2003), all seek to promote accessibility to digital content.

The Bobby Project, The W3C guidelines, and Section 508 all focus on content markup. Each provides a set of technical specifications that can be applied to the HTML files for Web pages. A rubric is provided to determine the degree to which accessibility is achieved by a Web page or Web site. The Chaffee Amendment and the NIMAS deal with print content. The Chafee Amendment requires publishers of certain print materials to make available a digital version of that content to serve persons with specific disabilities, including persons who are blind or are unable to read as a result of some physical limitation. The NIMAS seeks to provide a file format standard for the dissemination of the content materials that are covered under the Chaffee Amendment.

Instructional Design of Digital Materials

Over the years much has been determined about the instructional design of software for students with disabilities. A synthesis by Okolo, Bahr, and Rieth (1993) of instructional design research uncovered four factors important to effective delivery of computer-based instruction.
1. Effective software is designed to take best advantage of the particular constraints and affordances provided by the computer.
2. Effective software follows generic principles associated with effective teaching and learning.

3. Effective software incorporates a model of instruction that is appropriate for teaching a particular skill.
4. The degree of control the learner has over essential features of the software can impact the effectiveness of the software.

While these factors remain important today, clear directions for development of digital materials for students with disabilities are lacking. Certainly, there are pockets of potential. For example, anchored instruction (Bransford, Sherwood, Hasselbring, Kinzer, & Williams, 1990) and educational hypermedia and multimedia (Anderson-Inman & Horney, 1998; Anderson-Inman, Horney, Chen, & Lewin, 1994; Boone & Higgins, 1993; Higgins, Boone, & Lovitt, 1996; Horney & Anderson-Inman, 1999) have both shown degrees of effectiveness as educational platforms for specific instructional designs across a significant period of time and in a number of research situations, as briefly discussed below.

Anchored Instruction

As an instructional design, anchored instruction has been employed across a wide range of subject areas, learner populations, and media types. The basic focus of anchored instruction is to provide learners with authentic problem situations, often through video via some sort of media (e.g., videodisc, CD-ROM, DVD) as the "anchor" or context for learning. "The major goal of anchored instruction is to enable students to notice critical features of problem situations and to experience the changes in their perception and understanding of the anchor as they view the situation from new points of view" (Bransford, et al., 1990, p. 135). Bottge, Heinrichs, Mehta, and Hung (2002) investigated anchored math instruction for students with disabilities in general education classrooms, and the effect of anchored instruction on student and teacher interactions was explored by Glaser, Rieth, Kinzer, Colburn, and Peter (1999). Mechling and Langone (2000) evaluated the use of computer-based anchored instruction to increase photograph recognition by students with severe intellectual disability. The research on anchored instruction is providing a continuous data trail across time that will prove invaluable for developing effective instructional design of digital materials for students with disabilities.

Hypermedia and Multimedia

Much of the work with educational hypermedia and multimedia for students with disabilities has been focused on adapting textbooks and other materials from the regular education curriculum (Anderson-Inman & Horney, 1997, 1998; Boone & Higgins, 1993; Higgins & Boone, 1990a, 1990b). A wide range of supports and digital enhancements have been reported for both elementary (Boone & Higgins, 1993) and secondary students (Anderson-Inman & Horney, 1997; Higgins & Boone, 1990b). Many of these adaptations have been based on best practices from the professional literature. For example, a three-year study by Boone and Higgins (1993) of a hypermedia adaptation of a basal reading series incorporated (a) text-to-speech options, (b) an online dictionary for new vocabulary, (c) a graphical display for anaphoric elements, and (d) a specific questioning strategy for reading comprehension. While these studies have clear implications for instructional design within hypermedia/multimedia environments, "How students actually use hypermedia is an under-investigated research topic in special education" (Woodward, Gallagher, & Rieth, 2001, p. 9).

Currently, the National Center on Accessing the General Curriculum (NCAC) lists eight specific curriculum enhancements, most of which are doubly enhanced when implemented in a digital environment: (a) anchored instruction, (b) modified text, (c) text-to-speech, (d) manipulatives, (e) simulations/virtual reality, (f) technology tools, (g) concept maps, and (h) models (NCAC, 2003). The Web site (www.cast.org/ncac) provides an operational description along with a research bibliography for each enhancement.

Cognitive Processing

Looking at the instructional design of digital materials from a slightly different perspective, Mayer (2003) rejected a technology-centered approach, contending that "media environments do not cause learning, cognitive processing by the learner causes learning" (p. 137). Mayer's research was based on three instructional principles: (a) integrating pictures with words, (b) excluding irrelevant material, and (c) presenting words in a conversational style, which produced results in four instructional design methods.

1. *The multimedia effect:* information content presented in words and pictures was more effective than information presented in words alone.
2. *The coherence effect:* a multimedia explanation with extraneous material excluded was more effective than material with an embellished presentation.
3. *The contiguity effect:* it is more effective to present corresponding words and pictures near to, rather than far away from each other on the screen.
4. *The personalization effect:* multimedia explanations with the words presented in a conversational style, were more effective than a more formal style.

Mayer found these results to be true for both digital and conventional materials.

While Mayer's (2003) notion is well taken, that media environments are less important to learning than are the cognitive processes, Bransford, Brown, and Cocking (2000) offer a reminder that "learning theory does not provide a simple recipe for designing effective learning environments" (p. 131). They see technology being used best in five ways, four of which have direct ties to instructional design:

1. *Bringing exciting curricula based on real-world problems into the classroom.*
2. *Providing scaffolds and tools to enhance learning.*
3. *Giving students and teachers more opportunities for feedback, reflection, and revision.*
4. *Building local and global communities that include teachers, administrators, students, parents, practicing scientists, and other interested people. (p. 207)*

Along with their focus on specific learning opportunities that technology-based instructional design should incorporate, Bransford, and colleagues (2000) believe that good educational software is not yet the norm:

Software developers are generally driven more by the game and play market than by the learning potential of their products. The software publishing industry, learning experts, and education policy planners, in partnership, need to take on the challenge of exploiting the promise of computer-based technologies for improving learning. (p. 230)

Adapting Traditional Materials

With national longitudinal studies indicating that one in six children will encounter a problem in learning to read (National Center to Improve the Tools of Educators, 1996), the issue of accessibility of content and instructional design must be viewed as critical (Higgins, Boone, & Lovitt, 2002). Content-area textbooks are a prime example of access to materials but with limited access to learning. Sellers (1987) found 92% of students at the high school level were at the frustration reading level in their assigned textbooks. Similarly, Wait (1987) indicated that over half of the students using upper elementary content area texts were at their frustration reading level. Lovitt and Horton (1991, 1998) found that the majority of students with learning disabilities were unable to read their textbooks with the proficiency required to assimilate and integrate the information. Lovitt and Horton also found that the textbooks lacked the structure, coherence, unity, and audience appropriateness necessary for learning. Additionally, most textbooks have been found to lack learning scaffolds for a wide variety of learners (Boone & Higgins, 1993; Higgins et al., 1996).

Additional criticisms of content-area texts include (a) misleading titles and subtitles (Estes, 1982); (b) unrealistic levels for student background knowledge (McKeown & Beck, 1990); (c) reading level above the grade level for which they are written (Conrad, 1990); and (d) inclusion of interesting but ultimately unimportant details (Garner, Gillingham, & White, 1989).

A variety of methods for modifying textbooks have been proposed from the field of reading (Armbruster & Gudbrandsen, 1986; Readence, Bean, & Baldwin, 1998) and from special education (Higgins et al., 1996;

MacArthur & Haynes, 1995; Schumm & Stickler, 1991). Research indicates that digital versions of textbooks and related study guides can be successful instructional tools (Anderson-Inman et al., 1994; Boone & Higgins, 1993; Higgins et al., 1996; MacArthur & Haynes, 1995).

Schumm and Strickler (1991) identified nine successful textbook adaptations: (a) reading text aloud to students; (b) using related pictures, recording, or video; (c) constructing abridged versions of the text; (d) providing students with outlines or summaries; (e) using a multilevel approach in difficulty of text; (f) introducing key vocabulary in a prereading situation; (g) summarizing textbook information; (h) reducing the length of assignments; (i) slowing the pace of instruction; and (j) teaching students to take notes on key concepts and terms. Higgins and colleagues (2002) assert that most of these strategies can be implemented successfully in digital instructional materials. The overarching goal in the creation of what Boone, Higgins, Falba, and Langley (1993) termed digital cooperative texts is to make use of the best practices identified by research and incorporate them into the design of the digital materials.

Conclusion

Effective design in any endeavor is a difficult process that requires talent from many diverse sources. The design of digital materials, whether a computer-assisted instruction program, an anchored-instruction simulation, or an electronic text, is especially difficult. It must include not only an appropriate instructional design but also the basic design elements for identity (e.g., effective visual or auditory cues), interaction (e.g., clear navigation and feedback), and information (e.g., appropriate media choice, text vs. graphics) required for effective software (Mok, 1996). Cooper's (1999, p. 4) perspective on "why high-tech products drive us crazy" asks a simple question and is instructive to the instructional designer of digital materials for students with disabilities.

Question: "What do you get when you cross a computer with a _____?"

Answer: "You get something that acts like a computer."

Fill in the blank with "instructional materials" and the answer remains the same. The traditional instructional materials that were the basis for the instructional content are changed by the new medium. Good instructional design can be overshadowed by poor design for the digital environment.

Consequence of Bad Design

Specific indictments of software being widely used in America's schools are rare but not unknown. A good example is the presentation tool PowerPoint. Oppenheimer (2003) describes a classroom visit in which he is struck by an overemphasis on the tool and too little regard for the content as students prepared their PowerPoint presentations. "I was immediately struck by the clean graphics and digestible writing…But its content was no deeper than what one commonly sees in civics papers done elsewhere, with pencil and paper" (p. xii). The student whose presentation was being discussed estimated that he had spent 17 hours working on the project, only 7 of which went into research and writing.

Continuing with the same piece of software, Tufte's (2003) accusation is even more serious. He claims that the cognitive style of the PowerPoint presentation design is presenter-oriented and not focused on the content or the audience.

These costs result from the cognitive style characteristic of the standard default PP presentation: foreshortening of evidence and thought, low spatial resolution, a deeply hierarchical single-path structure as the model for organizing every type of content, breaking up narrative and data into slides and minimal fragments, rapid temporal sequencing of thin information rather than focused spatial analysis, conspicuous decoration and Phluff [sic], a preoccupation with format not content, an attitude of commercialism that turns everything into a sales pitch. (p. 4)

As evidence, Tufte provides as an instructive parody Lincoln's Gettysburg Address in

PowerPoint. In a slideshow format created through the automated help system provided in PowerPoint, Tufte shows how easily powerful ideas can be lost in translation to an inappropriate digital format. The idea that the design of a commonly used piece of software might actually be harmful from an educational standpoint is a difficult one with which educators must come to grips.

Digital Materials for Today and Tomorrow
It would be comforting to end this chapter with a clear sense of direction for designing digital materials for students with disabilities. Unfortunately, the knowledge base does not yet provide a clear and comprehensive picture.

Certainly, Rose's (2000) notion of universal design for learning is an admirable goal. But it is just that, a larger goal and not a design principle or instructional tactic that can be applied to the design of specific materials for learners with specific learning disabilities. The CAST Web site itself outlines several research-based "curriculum enhancements" as part of its National Center on Accessing the General Curriculum (2004). Included are familiar ideas such as anchored instruction, hypermedia/multimedia enhancements (e.g., modified text content), and text-to-speech output. Overlap these ideas with Mayer's (2003) findings concerning (a) use of text and graphics together, (b) proximity of related content, and (c) clear, precise narrative and a picture begins to form. Proven methods for adapting textbooks (Schumm & Strickler, 1991) give additional focus for modifying content (e.g., abridged text, outlines, summaries, multilevel narrative), and adapting instruction (e.g., vocabulary tasks, slowing pace, reduced assignment lengths) in a digital environment. These are all clear and positive steps on the road toward an instructional design paradigm for creating effective digital materials for persons with disabilities.

Even so, educators who are experienced with instructional applications of technology admit that the path forward is unclear. "Much remains to be learned about using technology's potential: to make this happen, learning research will need to become the constant companion of software development" (Bransford et al., 2000, p. 230). At the same time, warnings are made about unintended consequences that might be associated with software widely used in schools (Tufte, 2004), and voices from the computer software industry are calling out for improved design for all software (Cooper, 1999). Educators must consider all this, along with warnings from the mainstream design community with regard to the difficulty inherent in technology design, "… each new technology provides increased benefits. At the same time, added complexities arise to increase our difficulty and frustration" (Norman, 1988, p. 30).

The difficulties and frustrations are clearly documented within the literature and within the experiences of those who use digital materials in special education settings. It is to the benefits that the instructional design, software development, and special education communities must aspire.

References

Ager, A. (1986). Performance contoured programming: A structure for microcomputer-based teaching of individuals with severe learning difficulties. *Journal of the Association for Programmed Learning, 23*(2), 130-135.

Anderson-Inman, L. & Horney, M.A. (1997). Electronic books for secondary students. *Journal of Adult and Adolescent Literacy, 40*(6), 486-491.

Anderson-Inman, L., & Horney, M.A. (1998). Transforming text for at-risk readers. In D. Reinking, L. Labbo, M. McKenna, & R. Kieffer (Eds.), *Handbook of literacy and technology: Transformations in a post-typographic world.* Mahwah, NJ: Lawrence Erlbaum Associates.

Anderson-Inman, L., Horney, M. A., Chen, D., & Lewin, L. (1994). Hypertext literacy: Observations from the ElectroText project. *Language Arts, 71*(4), 37-45.

Armbruster, B. B., & Gudbrandsen, B. (1986). Reading comprehension in social studies programs. *Reading Research Quarterly, 21,* 36-48.

Boone, R., & Higgins, K. (1993). Hypermedia basal readers: Three years of school-based research. *Journal of Special Education Technology, 12*(3), 86-106.

Boone, R., Higgins, K., Falba, C., & Langley,

W. (1993). Cooperative text: Reading and writing in a hypermedia environment. *LD Forum, 19*(1), 28-37.

Boone, R., Higgins, K., & Williams, D. (1997). Supporting content area instruction with videodiscs and multimedia technologies. *Intervention in School and Clinic, 32*(5), 302-311.

Bottge, B., Heinrichs, M., Mehta, Z.D., & Hung, Y. (2002). Weighing the benefits of anchored math instruction for students with disabilities in general education classes. *Journal of Special Education, 35*(4), 186-200.

Bransford, J., Brown, A., & Cocking, R. (2000). *How people learn: Brain, mind, experience, and school*. Washington, DC: National Academy Press.

Bransford, J.D., Sherwood, R.D., Hasselbring, T.S., Kinzer, C.K., & Williams, S.M. (1990). Anchored instruction: Why we need it and how technology can help. In D. Nix & R. Spiro (Eds.), *Cognition, education, and multimedia*. Hillsdale, NJ: Lawrence Erlbaum.

Chaffee Amendment to the Copyright Act (1996). 17 U.S.C. Section 121.

Char, C. (1990). Interactive technology and the young child: Insights from research and design. *Center for Learning Technology Reports and Papers in Progress* (Report No. 90-2). (ERIC Document Reproduction Service No. ED 335 152)

Conrad, S. S. (1990. May). *Change and challenge in content textbooks*. Paper presented at the annual conference of the International Reading Association, New Orleans.

Cooper, A. (1999). *The inmates are running the asylum*. Indianapolis, IN: Sams.

Cuban, L. (2001). Why are most teachers infrequent and restrained users of computers in their classrooms? In J. Woodward & L. Cuban(Eds.), *Technology, curriculum and professional development* (pp. 121-137). Thousand Oaks, CA: Corwin Press, Inc.

Estes, T. (1982). The nature and structure of text. In A. Berger & H. A. Robinson (Eds.), *Secondary school reading: What research reveals for classroom practice* (pp. 85-96). Urbana, IL: ERIC Clearinghouse on Reading and Communication Skills.

Garner, R., Gillingham, M., & White, C.S. (1989). Effects of "seductive details" on macroprocessing and microprocessing in adults and children. *Cognition and Instruction, 6,* 41-57.

Geisert, P.G., & Futrell, M.K. (1995). *Teachers, computers, and curriculum*. Boston: Allyn and Bacon.

Glaser, C. W., Rieth, H. J., Kinzer, C. K., Colburn, L. K., & Peter, J. (1999). A description of the impact of multimedia anchored instruction on classroom interactions. *Journal of Special Education Technology, 14*(2), 27-43

Golden, D.C. (2002). Instructional software accessibility: A status report [Guest column]. *Journal of Special Education Technology, 17*(1), 57-60.

Heinich, R., Molenda, M., Russell, J., & Smaldino, S. (2002). *Instructional media and technologies for learning (7th ed.)*. Upper Saddle River, NJ: Pearson Education, Inc.

Higgins, K., & Boone, R. (1990a). Hypertext: A new vehicle for computer use in reading instruction. *Intervention in School and Clinic, 26*(1), 26-31.

Higgins, K., & Boone, R. (1990b). Hypertext computer study guides and the social studies achievement of students with learning disabilities, remedial students, and regular education students. *Journal of Learning Disabilities, 23*(9), 529-540.

Higgins, K., Boone, R., & Lovitt, T.C. (1996). Hypermedia text-only information support for students with learning disabilities and remedial students. *Journal of Learning Disabilities, 29*(4), 402-412.

Higgins, K., Boone, R., & Lovitt, T.C. (2002). Adapting challenging textbooks to improve content area learning. In M. Shinn, H. Walker, & G. Stoner (Eds.), *Interventions for academic and behavior problems II: Preventive and remedial approaches* (pp. 755-790). Bethesda, MD: National Association of School Psychologists.

Higgins, K., Boone, R., & Williams, D. (2000). Evaluating educational software for special education. *Intervention in School and Clinic, 36*(2), 109-115.

Horney, M.A., & Anderson-Inman, L. (1999). Supported text in electronic reading environments. *Reading & Writing Quarterly, 15,* 127-168.

Individuals with Disabilities Education Act (1997). 20 U.S.C. § 1400 *et seq.*

Jeffries, S. (2000). *An investigation into teacher education faculty technology usage.* Retrieved June 22, 2003, from New Mexico State University, Preparing Teachers for Tomorrow's Technology (PT3), pt3.nmsu.edu/educ621/steve1.html

Larsen, S. (1995). What is "quality" in the use of technology for children with learning disabilities? *Learning Disability Quarterly, 18*(2), 118-130.

Lockard, J., Abrams, P.D., & Many, W.A. (1997). *Microcomputers for twenty-first century educators.* New York: Longman.

Lovitt, T. C., & Horton, S. V. (1991). Adapting textbooks for mildly handicapped adolescents. In G. Stoner, M. R. Shinn, & H. M. Walker (Eds.), *Interventions for achievement and behavior problems* (pp. 439-471). Silver Spring, MD: National Association of School Psychologists.

Lovitt, T. C., & Horton, S. V. (1998). Strategies for adapting science textbooks for youth with learning disabilities. In E. L. Meyen, G. A. Vergason, & R. J. Whelan (Eds.), *Educating students with mild disabilities: Strategies and methods* (pp. 163-176). Denver, CO: Love Publishing.

MacArthur, C. A., & Haynes, J. B. (1995). Student assistant for learning from text (SALT): A hypermedia reading aid. *Journal of Learning Disabilities, 28*(3), 150-159.

Macro Systems (1988). *Improving the instructional design and use of general software for practical application with handicapped students* [Final report for contract #300-86-0063 to U.S. Department of Education]. (ERIC Document Reproduction Service No. ED 385 970)

Mayer, R.E. (2003). The promise of multimedia learning: Using the same instructional design methods across different media. *Learning and Instruction, 13*, 125-139.

McKeown, M. G., & Beck, I. S. (1990). The assessment and characterization of young learners' knowledge of a topic in history. *American Educational Research Journal, 27*(4), 688-726.

Mechling, L, & Langone, J. (2000). The effects of a computer-based instructional program with video anchors on the use of photographs for prompting augmentative communication. *Education and Training in Mental Retardation and Developmental Disabilities, 35*(1), 90-105.

Mok, C. (1996). *Designing business: Multiple media, multiple disciplines.* San Jose, CA: Adobe Press.

National Center to Improve the Tools of Educators. (1996). *Learning to read/reading to learn information kit.* Reston, VA: Council for Exceptional Children.

National Center on Accessing the General Curriculum. (2003). *NCAC publications: Directory at a glance.* Retrieved February 29, 2004, from www.cast.org/ncac/index.cfm?i=3117.

National Instructional Materials Accessibility Standard Final Report, (2003). Available from National Center on Accessing the General Curriculum: CAST.

Neuman, D. (1991). Learning disabled students' interactions with commercial courseware: A naturalistic study. *Educational Technology, Research, and Development, 39*(1), 31-49.

Norman, D. (1990). *The design of everyday things.* New York: Doubleday.

Okolo, C.M., Bahr, C.M., & Rieth, H.J. (1993). A retrospective view of computer-based instruction. *Journal of Special Education Technology, 12*(1), 1-27.

Oppenheimer, T. (2003). *The flickering mind.* New York: Random House.

Pastor, E., & Kerns, E. (1997). A digital snapshot of an early childhood classroom. *Educational Leadership, 55*(3), 42-45.

Perkins, D. (1995). *Software goes to school: Teaching understanding with new technologies.* New York: Oxford University Press.

Readence, J. E., Bean, T. W., & Baldwin, R. S. (1998). *Content area literacy: An integrated approach.* Dubuque, IA: Kendall/Hunt.

Rose, D. (2000). Universal design for learning [Associate editor column]. *Journal of Special Education Technology, 15*(1), 67-70.

Rose, D., & Meyer, A. (2002). *Teaching every student in the digital age: Universal design for learning.* Alexandria, VA: Association for Supervision and Curriculum Development.

Rosenberg, R. (1997). *The social impact of computers.* San Diego, CA: Academic Press.

Schumm, J. S., & Strickler, K. (1991). Guidelines for adapting content area textbooks: Keeping teachers and students content. *Intervention in School and Clinic, 27*, 79-84.

Section 508 of the Rehabilitation Act (1998). (29 U.S.C. 794d), as amended by the Workforce Investment Act of 1998 (P.L. 105-220).

Sellers, G. B. (1987). A comparison of the readability of selected high school social studies, science, and literature books (Doctoral dissertation, Florida State University). *Dissertation Abstracts International, 48*, 3085A.

Shelly, G., Cashman, T., Gunter, R., & Gunter, G. (2002). *Integrating technology in the classroom* (2nd ed.). Boston: Course Technology.

Skinner, R. (2002, May 9). *Tracking tech trends.* Retrieved June 28, 2002, from www.edweek.org/sreports/tc02/article.cfm?slug=35tracking.h21

Tiu, F., Guglielmi, J., & Walton, G. (2002, June). *Assessing a technology initiative: Lessons learned while integrating technology into teaching and learning.* Paper presented at the Annual International Forum of the Association for Institutional Research, Toronto, Canada.

Tufte, E.R. (2003). *The cognitive style of powerpoint.* Cheshire, CT: Graphics Press.

Wait, S.S. (1987). Textbook readability and the predictive value of the Dale-Chall, comprehensive assessment program, and cloze procedure (Doctoral dissertation, Florida State University). *Dissertation Abstracts International, 48*, 357A.

Williams, D., Boone, R., & Kingsley, K. (2004). Teacher beliefs about educational software: A delphi study. *Journal of Research in Teacher Education, 36*(3), 213-229.

Woodward, J., Gallagher, D., & Rieth, H. (2001). No easy answer. In J. Woodward & L. Cuban (Eds.), *Technology, curriculum and professional development* (pp. 3-26). Thousand Oaks, CA: Corwin Press, Inc.

Woodward, J., & Noell, J. (1993). Software development in special education. *Journal of Special Education Technology, 12*(2), 149-163.

Zane, T., & Frazer, C.G. (1992). The extent to which software developers validate their claims. *Journal of Research on Computing in Education, 24*(3), 410-419.

25

Electronic Performance
Support Systems

Jennie I. Schaff, Brenda Bannan-Ritland,
Michael M. Behrmann, and Seunghun Ok

As technology advances and computers are found on nearly every desk in nearly every office and in nearly every classroom around the country, an emerging technology called electronic performance support systems (EPSS) is increasingly being incorporated into both corporate and education environments. Perhaps the most familiar and simple embodiment of the EPSS concept is *Microsoft's Office Assistant*, the support mechanism embedded in word processing and other applications represented by a paperclip animated figure. The Office Assistant provides real-time prompts asking the user what exactly he or she hopes to accomplish within the open application and provides contextualized answers and help related to the given task.

While EPSSs are making their way into different software environments, and while technological advances are allowing such systems to perform a plethora of new and advancing tasks, these systems are only starting to emerge within the field of special education. This chapter will begin by defining EPSS and the rationale behind the development of such a tool. Next, we will argue for the presence of EPSS in special education, specifically for supporting students. Finally, we will describe and examine the design and development of an EPSS, *Literacy Explorer*, for use by students with disabilities.

Definition and Characterization of EPSS

An Electronic Performance Support System (EPSS) is a software platform or environment that provides an individual with the tools, including information, software, advice, guidance, and/or learning experiences needed to complete a specific task (Brown, 1996). These systems provide targeted performance support in real-time rather than providing extensive resources and training far removed from the context of the instructional or performance task. The end-result and goal of EPSS support is improved productivity with minimal external support by anything other than the EPSS system itself (Brown, 1996).

In trying to grasp the concept of an EPSS, consider the following example:

Craig is a 16-year-old student with learning disabilities, who has just entered high school. In middle school, he was in a self-contained learning disabilities class, however, in his new school he is in many mainstreamed classes.

One of the new classes that Craig is taking requires him to write a report on his most challenging middle school experience. The goal of this class, which is business-focused, is for the students to familiarize themselves with basic word processing and computer skills. Craig is expected to complete this assignment using a PC platform computer equipped with Microsoft Word. Using a PC computer is new to Craig because he has only used a Macintosh computer in the past.

Craig begins writing his report using Microsoft Word; however, he immediately experiences many difficulties. In the hour it takes him to write his paper, Craig ask his classmate, Bryan, for assistance ten times. Some of the questions that he asked Bryan include how to open a report template in Word, how to double space text, how to bold face the font, center text, italicize text, insert footnotes, and finally, how to save and print his paper. Besides asking Bryan, Craig asked his teacher for help with some of the problems.

The total assignment took Craig one hour. Bryan spent 35 minutes helping Craig, and the teacher spent 15 minutes helping Craig. Although the hour that Craig spent working was not excessive considering he was new to the software, Bryan and his teacher could have spent the cumulative 50 minutes that they spent helping Craig, doing their own work.

If Craig had known how to use Microsoft Office Assistant, it would have helped all three people in this scenario. Craig would have still needed to learn the answers to his questions but would have done so in a much more independent manner and therefore would have gained more confidence in his ability to manage word processing challenges. Bryan would not have been disturbed and would have accomplished his own work in a more timely manner and the teacher would have been able to spend more time assisting other students.

The *Office Assistant* allows the user to type in a question and provides a series of links to potential answers to that question. Eliminating the time other individuals contribute as well as reducing the time spent completing a task. An additional EPSS component related to the *Microsoft Office Assistant* is the capability to anticipate problems or questions that the user may have. For example, if it looks as though the user may be attempting to write a letter, the *Office Assistant* will pop up and ask if the user would like assistance writing a letter using the template that Microsoft has created for that specific type of letter writing.

Now, imagine the same scenario of Craig sitting at his computer attempting to write up a narrative about what he plans to do next summer for work:

Craig is at his computer and is in his word processing software, Microsoft Word. *As he is typing, he realizes that he needs to have his heading centered. Rather than disturbing his classmate, Craig types his question into the* Microsoft Office Assistant's *text bubble. In it, he types, "How do I center text?" He then clicks on the "Search" button to indicate that he would like the* Office Assistant *to provide him with potential answers to his question.*

In response to his question, a list of links to possible answers appears in the Office Assistant *space, the first of which is "Center Text." Craig clicks on this blue option (indicating a link to further information of "center text") and is then instructed with a step-by-step approach of how to center text. Craig can follow this sequence of steps while performing the actual task. Both sections of the application (the* Office Assistant *steps and the actual word processing application) remain open simultaneously. This allows Craig to implement the lesson being taught immediately, rather than learning them at one point and implementing them at another, such is often the case with conventional training and teaching methods.*

Person-to-Person Conventional Training Versus EPSS

The primary differences between face-to-face conventional teaching or training and electronic performance support systems can be seen in Table 1. Highlighting the main components these differences are the timing, adaptations to different users/learners, and the ongoing support components of each. For the purposes of this chapter and the relevance of the information to special education, the conventional training section incorporates conventional teaching methods including lectures, laboratories, and

Table 1. Comparing Conventional Teaching Methods and Electronic Performance Support Systems (adapted from Brown, 1996)

Factors for Comparison	Conventional Teaching Methods	Electronic Performance Support Systems
Timing of instruction: When does it occur?	Typically occurs before the individual is expected to complete work (i.e., lectures preceding labs and assignments)	Occurs as individual is completing a task
How is instruction related to the classroom?	Usually occurs in the classroom, isolated from the actual performance environment. Often students do not have the opportunity to apply what they learn within the classroom environment	Is totally integrated into the individual's classroom. Support happens in context; individuals request information when they need it
Does instruction adapt to individual learner differences?	Frequently does not adapt to individual learner differences. Teaching often seeks to create a single message for a homogeneous group of learners rather than recognizing that in teaching in a group, many messages are needed in many formats to impact a wide range of learners	Adapts to learner differences. Provides learners with different messages. It can support heterogeneous audiences, provide high-level concepts, step-by-step instructions, and/or decision support based on performer needs
Does instruction accommodate different learning styles?	Frequently cannot recognize differences in learning styles. Training is often focused on a single learning style because of the expense and time required to tailor instruction to different learning styles	Recognizes different learning styles. Allows performers to explore through browsing, learning in a sequential manner, or referring to electronic experts for guidance
Is instruction flexible or static?	Instruction is static. It often cannot accommodate changes in information, processes, or environment because it is created in advance.	Accommodates changes in instructional tasks and easily accommodates additional information
Is instruction ongoing?	Instruction is not ongoing; it has a beginning and end. Support is not always available when the individual is completing assignments or tasks	Instruction is ongoing. It is available whenever the learner needs it. It is built into the computer software system

seminars and compares such methods to the methods employed by an EPSS.

The Goal of EPSS

According to Gery (1991), the goal of an EPSS "is to provide whatever is necessary to generate performance and learning in the moment of need" (p. 3). Historically, such support has demanded significant human intervention, however, many instructional tasks can be additionally supported using an EPSS. Table 2 summarizes a variety of issues and questions that a special education student (and any student, for that matter) may have when faced with learning a new task. The second column lists the method in which a teacher can respond to such inquiries is found, whereas the third column includes the responses provided by an electronic performance support system.

EPSS in Education

Over the past 10 years, EPSS have provided many valuable and viable solutions to common human performance problems, including teacher professional development, corporate training, and technology problem solving (Bannan-Ritland, 2002; Gery, 1995; Laffey, 1995). As already mentioned, there has been increased presence of EPSS in corporate environments. However, EPSS technology brings burgeoning opportunities to the field of education. The prevalence of EPSS in the education setting is on the rise; however, it remains rather limited in scope. In the education setting, the majority of EPSSs are targeted toward supporting teachers rather than students (Northrup & Pilcher, 1998). Thus in a thorough literature review of EPSS in education, 46 articles were identified. Most of them targeted educators rather than students.

The few articles that did address EPSS and students with disabilities were specifically about one system entitled, *Literacy Explorer* developed at George Mason University, in Fairfax, Virginia. Through two Steppingstones to Technology grants from the United States Department of Education (H327A980035-99 & H327A000063) and a partnership between a number of organizations, including the Parent Education Advocacy Center in Fairfax, Virginia, *LiteracyAccess Online* was created to address the national and critical issue of literacy.

Literacy Explorer

Literacy Explorer is a World Wide Web-based electronic performance support system designed to enhance the reading facilitation abilities of parents, teachers, and tutors of students in 4th through 8th grade with or without disabilities (Bannan-Ritland, Egerton, Page, & Behrmann, 2000). *Literacy Explorer* is the core component of *LiteracyAccess Online* (LAO) Web site (www.literacyaccessonline.com), developed by faculty and students at George Mason University with funding from the Office of Special Education Programs in the U.S. Department of Education. As the EPSS component of the LAO site, the *Literacy Explorer* is designed to target the unique needs of struggling readers and their literacy facilitators, including teachers, parents, siblings, and tutors (Bannan-Ritland et al., 2000).

Development of Literacy Explorer

The design and development of *Literacy Explorer* has progressed through several phases, from initial analysis of the distinct problem of supporting literacy through identification of EPSS as a potential design solution and eventual development through multiple, iterative formative evaluation cycles. These integrated design and research processes have been characterized as the integrative learning design (ILD) framework described in detail by Bannan-Ritland (in press). The project involved a collaborative effort among professors, graduate students, parents, teachers, literacy and special education professionals that began as a Steppingstones to Technology Innovation for Students with Disabilities grant from the U.S. Department of Education

The major design and development effort related to *Literacy Explorer* was conceived of and implemented by several teams of master's and doctoral students who have worked on the project as a core part of their coursework in the Instructional Technology Immersion program (see immersion.gmu.edu) at George Mason University. This project-based collaborative

Table 2. Facing a Complex New Task (adapted from Gery, 1995)

The Question or Need	Response of Special Educator Without the Use of EPSS Technology	Response of Electronic Performance Support System
Why do this?	Explanation	Explanation Example and consequences
What is it?	Definitions Illustrations Descriptions	Definitions Illustrations Descriptions
What's related to it?	—	Available links
How do I do it?	Procedure Demonstration	Procedure Interactive advisors Structured paths (flowcharts, step charts, job aids, picture schedules) Demonstration
How or why did this happen?	Explanation	Explanation Example or demonstration
Show me an example	Examples	Examples
Teach me	Training Practice activities (if time and support available) Assessment or testing	Interactive trainingPractice activities with feedback Assessment or testing
Assist me	Advisors/teachers	Interactive advisors
Advise me	Structured paths, job/task aids, step charts, flow charts Monitoring systems	Structured paths, job/task aids, step charts, flow charts Monitoring systems with feedback
Let me try	Practice activities	Practice activities Simulation
Watch me	Observations	Monitoring systems
Evaluate me	Assessments or tests	Assessments or tests
Understand me	Oral feedback Written feedback	Feedback with scoring, judgment, or interpretation Monitoring systems tracking user actions or context
How does it work?	Explanation	Explanation

(continued next page)

Table 2. Facing a Complex New Task (continued)

The Question or Need	Response of Special Educator Without the Use of EPSS Technology	Response of Electronic Performance Support System
Why does it work like that?	Examples	Examples
Compare this or these for me	Comparative explanations or descriptions	Comparative explanations or descriptions
Predict for me	Descriptions	Descriptions or demonstrations of consequences
Where am I?	Teacher recollection	Monitoring systems Navigation systems Views of context ("you are here")
What next?	Directions, prompts, coaching	Directions, prompts, or coaching Lists of options or paths

Figure 1. The Literacy Explorer interface.

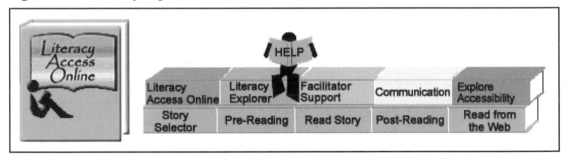

team experience provides an authentic context for learning instructional design and development with real clients and grant-supported tuition funding for students (Bannan-Ritland, 2001). Several graduate student teams led by professors in instructional design and special education created the initial designs, formatively evaluated those designs, and implemented revisions across six semesters.

The Literacy Explorer Interface

Through multiple phases, the *Literacy Explorer* has undergone revised versions of graphical and interactive user interface and associated elements. Specifically, qualitative and quantitative data collected through interviews, surveys, videotaping, and student artifacts were carefully analyzed and utilized in making revisions (Bannan-Ritland, 2001; Jeffs, 2000). Through each phase, the prototype matured and became functional. Currently, the site is undergoing extensive usability and accessibility testing to provide a comprehensive evaluation.

Literacy Explorer: Functionality

LiteracyAccess Online contains a variety of features and tools that are purposefully designed to provide support for literacy facilitators (e.g., parents, teachers, tutors, etc.) and children as they engage in the literacy process. As a primary component, the *Literacy Explorer* incorporates an EPSS-powered literacy tool into the LAO site. The most significant performance support features Literacy Explorer include providing the facilitator with specific

Figure 2. Screen print from story in Litearcy Access Online illustrates the array of performance support tools available to readers.

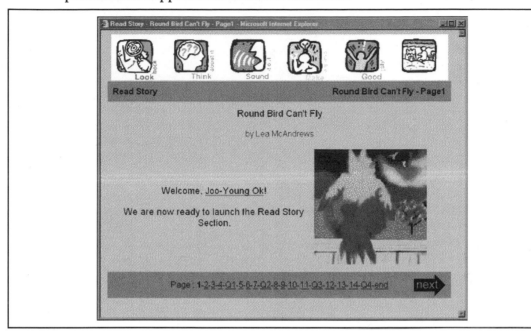

reading strategy guidance and implementing an adapted guided reading process as he or she is reading online with a child.

Real time support for the collaborative reading session is provided on each page of the "Read Story" section of the site, which comprises one component of *Literacy Explorer*. As highlighted on Figure 2, the six icons at the top of the screen provide the EPSS mechanism for the reading facilitator, detailing specific strategies that provide the facilitator with practical tips and language to use when reading with a child in a small pop-up window. For example, when the facilitator clicks on the icon for "Sound It Out," the prompt in Figure 3 assists the child in reading independently. Each EPSS strategy prompt was designed to support the facilitator's use of research-based reading, tutoring, and motivational strategies displayed. This prompt provides elaborative guidance to literacy facilitators highlighting scripted questions for them to use with the child (see Figure 3).

As the literacy facilitator and child progress through the stories, additional EPSS and related tools are available to assist the struggling reader. For example, prereading and postreading activities are provided that are structured to build prior knowledge, enhance

prediction and comprehension skills, as well as incorporate extension activities related to many of the stories. Pictures from a specific story are compiled in a prereading activity called "Picture Walk" to allow the child the opportunity to connect story information with previous knowledge and to use prediction skills, which are crucial for successful readers. Additional interactive features include highlighted words that provide immediate access to definitions, use of the word in a sentence, and audio pronunciation of the word through a pop-up dictionary support. More recently, LAO has registered as a *BrowseAloud* site, a browser plug-in by *textHELP!®*, which provides speech-enabled Web sites that register with the company. This text-to-speech capability is seamlessly integrated into the LAO Web site through the *BrowseAloud* downloaded to the user's desktop. This capability provides another form of performance support for children who need additional guidance in reading. In addition, research evidence suggests that all learners can benefit from the dual processing of text and audio (Mayer & Moreno, 2002).

"Read from the Web" and "Story Builder" are two additional EPSS features of *Literacy Explorer* (see Figure 4). In LAO, literacy

Figure 3. Highlighting scripted questions.

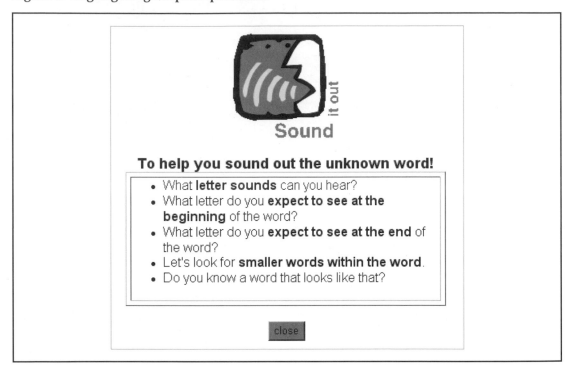

Figure 4. "Read from the Web" and "Story Builder".

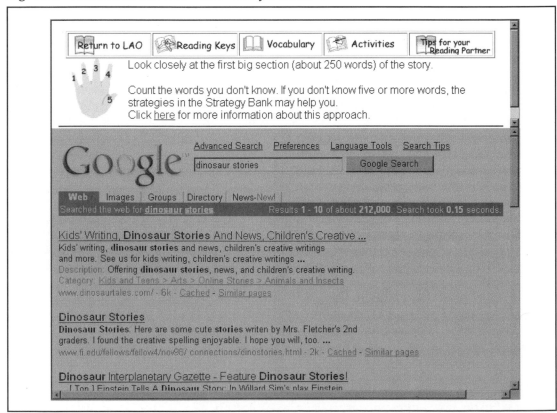

support is not limited to what is available within the site. The designers realized at the outset that the site needed to be flexible enough to apply reading strategies and supports to existing content from multiple sources for effective literacy development. As a result, reading content located through child-centered search engines were integrated into LAO. This design feature motivates children to read and write after locating material that is intrinsically motivating to them. The EPSS prompts remain accessible as the child searches for personally relevant material on the Web, allowing reading strategies to be used as he or she reads with a facilitator. Thus, virtually any literacy materials available on the Web can be used along with the performance support from this unique EPSS tool.

As illustrated in Figure 4, "Read from the Web" resides in the upper frame of the browser while the lower one is freed to be used to search the Web and look up any stories or literacy materials through the use of major search engines for children. Facilitators can then access LAO supports such as (a) reading strategies to help students figure out letters, words, and the meaning of what they are reading; (b) information on how to tell if given materials are too easy, just right, or too difficult; (c) access to a free online dictionary tool and a vocabulary list that can be developed while on the Web; (d) writing activities in which students can summarize the story, write their own story, or rewrite the ending to a story; and (e) strategies to help the facilitator guide the reader. All of these EPSS supports can be simplified to provide more detailed or in-depth information while still on the Web site chosen.

Perhaps one of the most innovative and generative activities on the site is the "Story Builder" which enables a child and facilitator to build their own "Literacy Explorer" story using text and pictures originally created or copied from the Web. The "Story Builder" feature automatically formats these created stories, up to 15 pages with 15 pictures, to

Figure 5. "Read from the Web" and "Story Builder".

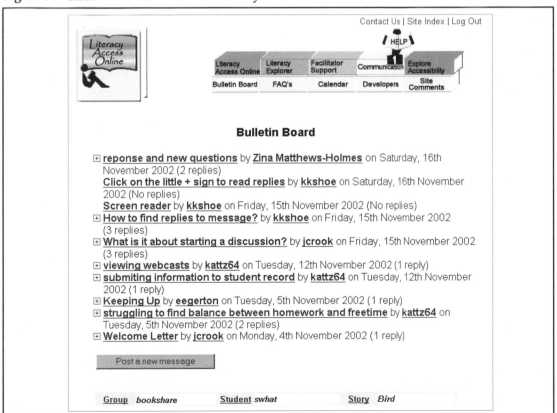

appear in the same manner as all other stories on the site, and stores them under the child's name in the database accessible only to the child and his or her facilitator. If the facilitator and child want to "publish" their story so other LAO users can try it out, "Story Builder" requires the Web address if the material was obtained from the Web, which enables copyright permission to be pursued before publication. This activity provides a high level of engagement and generative processing of information to encourage children's success in reading (Wittrock, 1991).

Although not a part of *Literacy Explorer*, LAO includes another important element that strengthens its power as an EPSS: the Bulletin Board, or BBS, in the Communication menu. The purpose of this asynchronous online community for literacy facilitators is to encourage communication among literacy facilitators as parents, teachers, tutors and others who are engaged in assisting children with or without disabilities in the reading process. Online communities have been used successfully in many fields and in many topic areas, but have not necessarily been viewed as a performance support mechanism. Preece (2000) characterizes an online community as consisting of some of the following components:

- *People who interact socially to satisfy their own needs;*

- *A shared purpose, such as an interest, need information exchange or service that provides a reason for the community;*

- *Policies, in the form of tacit assumptions, rituals, protocols, rules and laws that guide people's interactions; and*

- *Computer systems, to support and mediate social interaction and facilitate a sense of togetherness. (p. 10)*

LAO integrates the online community feature to provide a mechanism for community support to spontaneously form around the issue of children's literacy and disabilities. Several research studies are currently investigating this approach to supporting facilitators in their quest to support children. Online communities may be one of the best forms of elec-

Figure 6. The help figure in Literacy Access Online provides context sensitive help to readers.

tronic support as facilitators turn to each other for ongoing, dynamic guidance related to specific issues in children's literacy.

In addition, more "static" forms of support and information are also available for the facilitators. The "Facilitator Support" offers expert guidance in facilitation of the embedded literacy strategies and other resources available on the site. For example, in this menu segment facilitators can get help in preparing for upcoming sessions with the child, managing their own and their children's site accounts, and finding valuable information on reading and motivational strategies along with numerous other resources.

The Help Figure is a ubiquitous feature that appears on the main window. Along with the menu bar, the Help Figure is color-coded, indicating to the users their current location on the menu structure and providing responses to frequently asked questions about that section of LAO in a pop-up window when clicked.

To conclude this introduction of *Literacy Explorer*, Table 3 presents a summary of major supportive mechanisms surrounding Literacy Explorer as aligned with Gery's (1991) attributes of EPSS design.

Numerous Web sites are publicly available to provide support for EPSS (see table 4). EPSS Central provides a detailed description of EPSS as well as a plethora of other information pertaining to EPSS. EPSS World provides articles and other publications for support of such systems. With resources such as these, individuals who plan on implementing or

Table 3. Features of *Literacy Explorer* Aligned with Gery's (1991) Attributes of EPSS

Attributes of EPSS (Gery, 1991)	Design of *Literacy Explorer*
Integration of information, tools, and methodology for the user	Integrated features include: • Resources and links to reading approaches and assistive technology (information) • Structured guidance through reading session planner, note-taking strategy reminder, and decision support (tools) • Implemented theoretically hued reading strategies, tutorials to reading and tutoring strategies, process, and activity guidance (method)
Interactive advisory system that can accept, manipulate, monitor, and store data	Limited advisory system: • Accepts and stores notes/data on individual student capabilities for later reference by same or different facilitator • Accepts and stores information on negotiated goals for session and future objectives for facilitator/student reading session • Prompt use of strategies based on specific points in reading process
"Infobase" of information that usersw will inquire against, access, or have presented to do the job	Varying sources amounts of information by providing: • Central location where facilitators can find and use Web resources related to reading approaches and accessibility issues • Layers of information controlled by the facilitator related to reading strategies from simple hints, to text prompts, to elaborated explanations and finally, theoretical rationale
Various types of information organized and presented in multiple ways	Reliance on: • Both visual (iconic visual hints) and textual (prompts, explanations, and rationale) representation of information • Information on reading approach provided in tutorials, supplemental reading and on-demand during a reading session • Metaphor depiction of student's reading capabilities to help selection of appropriate Web readings
Different views on information	Customized information by providing: • Facilitator section to set up student profiles, explore strategies ahead of time or during session

Table 3. Features of *Literacy Explorer* Aligned with Gery's (1991) Attributes of EPSS (continued)

Attributes of EPSS (Gery, 1991)	Design of *Literacy Explorer*
Different views on information (continued)	• Facilitator access to previous session notes, goals, and progress, and ability to compare notes on a particular child • Student's primary focus is presented in central location on screen, colorful and large images; facilitator prompts are monochromatic and subtle so as not to distract the student's attention
Interactive productivity and application software	Additional software is implemented by incorporating: • Prompting of use of accessibility wizards included in Windows software • Accessibility applications such an text to speech and others to accommodate a wide range of users with various disabilities • Information on a wide range of interface elements geared toward specific disabilities • Session planner
Interactive training sequences	Implemented by including: • Small tutorials (skill builders) to support the reading process on topics such as word attack, phonics, write to read, and so on • Use of the prompting cues, session planner and the use of the Internet as a reading resource for specific support in the guided reading process
Monitoring, assessment, and feedback	Limited tracking mechanism that provides: • Information on student's progress, capabilities, and goals • End-of-reading session questionnaire to encourage facilitator to reflect on his or her own performance as a tutor • Tracking of site and reminding facilitators where they ended previous sessions • Consulting with a facilitator at the Communication section

Table 4. EPSS Resources on the Web

Web Site Name	Description	Web Site Address
EPSS Central	Detailed description of EPSS and its basic components, links to articles and other publications, information on EPSS design and development	www.pcd-innovations.com
EPSSWorld	Links to detailed information on EPSS, publications, and EPSS within various realms, including Web-based instruction and multimedia	www.epssworld.com
Electronic Performance Support Systems	"News and Views, What EPSS means to you"	www.stcpmc.org/archive/n&v/feat0598.html

using EPSS have great supports and resources. Specifically, individuals planning to use EPSS with individuals with disabilities, these resources are invaluable in providing support, and direction, as well as examples of how such implementation is most successful.

Conclusions

The use of EPSS holds great promise within special education environments. As seen in the discussion of Literacy Explorer, such tools provide children, parents, teachers, and other literacy facilitators with a just-in-time tool for literacy improvement. While the scope of research addressing EPSS in similar environments is limited, the potential of this type of system for supporting individuals with or without disabilities is limited only by the imagination of the instructional designers developing these sites.

Children and their reading facilitators benefit greatly from access to higher-level strategies, visual, text, and motivational supports, as well as engagement with reading content. The philosophy and structure of EPSSs hold great potential for those with special needs. The LAO site, the Literacy Explorers and corresponding multiple features and online community are an initial step toward exploring that potential.

References

Bannan-Ritland, B. (2003). The role of design in research: The integrative learning design framework. *Educational Researcher, 32* (1), 21-24.

Bannan-Ritland, B. (2002) Literacy Access Online: The development of an online support environment for literacy facilitators working with children with disabilities. *Tech Trends, 45*(2), 17-22.

Bannan-Ritland, B. (2001). An action learning framework for teaching instructiona design. *Performance Improvement Quarterly, 14* (2), 37-51.

Bannan-Ritland, B , Egerton, E., Page, J., & Behrman, M. (2000). Literacy explorer: A performance support tool for novice reading instructors. *Performance Improvement Journal, 39*(6), 47-54.

Brown, L. A. (1996). *Designing and developing electronic performance support systems*. Boston: Digital Press.

Gery, G. (1991). *Electronic performance support systems: How and why to remake the workplace through strategic application of technology*. Boston: Weingarten.

Gery, G. (1995). Attributes and behaviors of performance-centered systems. *Performance Improvement Quarterly. 8*(1), 47-93.

Jeffs, T.L. (2000). *Characteristics, interactions and attitudes of parent/child dyads and their user of assistive technology in a literacy experience on the Internet*. Unpublished doctoral dissertation, George Mason University.

Jonassen, D.H. (2000). Toward a design theory of problem solving. *Educational Research Theory & Development, 48*(4), 63-85.

Laffey, J. (1995). Dynamism in electronic performance support systems. *Performance Improvement Quarterly, 8*(1), 31-46.

Mayer, R.E., & Moreno, R. (2002). Aids to computer-based multimedia. *Learning & Instruction, 12*(1), 107-119.

Northrup, P. T., & Pilcher, J.K. (1998). *STEPS: An EPSS Tool for Instructional Planning*. Paper presented at the National Convention of the Association for Educational Communications and Technology, St. Lois, MO.

Preece, J. (2000). *Online communities: Designing usability, supporting sociability*. New York: John Wiley & Sons.

TextHelp website. (n.d.) Retrieved December 15, 2002, from www.texthelp.com/home.asp.

Wittrock, M.C. (1991). Generative teaching of comprehension. *Elementary School Journal, 92*(2), 169-184.

26

Assistive Technology and Universal Design for Learning: Two Sides of the Same Coin

David H. Rose, Ted S. Hasselbring, Skip Stahl, and Joy Zabala

Over the past decade, evolving technologies have revolutionized the way we do business, communicate, make war, farm, and provide medical treatment. New technologies are also transforming education, and in no domain more dramatically or successfully than in the education of students with disabilities.

Although the existing benefits of technology for students with disabilities are already widely recognized (e.g., Edyburn, 2003; Hasselbring & Glaser, 2000; Raskind & Higgins 1995; Rose & Meyer, 2002), the potential benefits are likely to be even more profound and pervasive than present practices would suggest. To ensure full realization of technology's potential for students with disabilities, the Office of Special Education Programs (OSEP) has funded two national centers that have a strong focus on technology: the National Assistive Technology Research Institute (NATRI) at the University of Kentucky and The National Center on Accessing the General Curriculum (NCAC) at CAST.

While both centers focus on the role of technology, their work is neither duplicative nor competitive. Rather, each is researching a distinct role for technology in improving education for students with disabilities, assistive technology (AT) and Universal Design for Learning (UDL), respectively. The question of how these two approaches can enhance and even support one another for the further benefit of students with disabilities is fundamentally important. We have engaged in early discussion of this issue with the National Center for Technology Innovation (NCTI) at the American Institutes for Research (AIR) and Pip Campbell and Suzanne Milbourne at Thomas Jefferson University, organizations whose OSEP-supported work is also at the forefront of technology in special education. In this article we provide a framework for further discussion of this significant issue by articulating the points of commonality and difference between AT and UDL.

Some individuals may see AT and UDL as identical, or conversely, antithetical. We believe that neither view is accurate but instead that AT and UDL, while different, are completely complementary—much like two sides of the same coin. We believe that advances in one approach prompt advances in the other and that this reciprocity will evolve in ways that will maximize their mutual benefits, making it essential that both approaches are pursued vigorously and distinctively. Through a better understanding and melding of AT and UDL, we believe that the lives of individuals with disabilities will ultimately be improved.

Two Roles for Technology: Assistive Technology and Universal Design for Learning

When most people imagine the role of technology for students with disabilities they think of AT. Relatively low-tech AT (like canes, wheelchairs, and eyeglasses) have been in place for a century, but the high-tech AT that has emerged over the last two decades has made a particularly dramatic impact on education, and has also captured the imagination of the public (Behrmann & Schaff, 2001; Edyburn, 2002). These newer technologies include diverse items such as electronic mobility switches and alternative keyboards for individuals with physical disabilities, computer-screen enlargers and text-to-speech readers for individuals with visual disabilities, electronic sign-language dictionaries and signing avatars for individuals with hearing disabilities, and calculators and spellcheckers for individuals with learning disabilities. The enormous power of such computer-based technologies to assist individuals with disabilities in overcoming barriers to educational access, participation, and progress is evident in the research base (Crealock & Sitko, 1990; Hebert & Murdock, 1994; MacArthur & Haynes, 1995; MacArthur, Haynes, Malouf, Harris, & Owings, 1990; Raskind & Higgins, 1999; van Daal & Reitsma, 1993; von Tetzchner, Rogne, & Lilleeng, 1997; Xin & Rieth, 2001).

In contrast to AT, universal design, although well established in architecture and other domains, is relatively new to education. One indication of this newness is the lack of clarity about what constitutes universal design in education, and a lack of differentiation from other approaches that address individual differences and disabilities. For example, there is frequent confusion about the relation between universal design in education and AT, in large part because both approaches depend significantly on modern technology (Bowser & Reed, 2000; Hitchcock & Stahl, 2003). Universal design (and particularly the branch that focuses on education, UDL) has goals similar to those of AT, including the overarching goal of increasing the access, participation, and progress of students with disabilities in our schools. However, the approaches differ in important ways.

The universal design approach is to create products and/or environments that are designed, from the outset, to accommodate individuals with a wider range of abilities and disabilities than can be accommodated by traditional applications. Rather than retrofitting ramps to existing buildings, the universal design movement in architecture educated architects in how to design buildings that are inherently accessible (Story, Mueller, & Mace, 1998). Such buildings tend to be more accommodating and flexible for all users.

In a related fashion, UDL seeks to educate curriculum developers, teachers, and administrators in how to design curricula and learning environments that from the outset make learning accessible to the widest range of students (Rose & Meyer, 2002). The focus of UDL is the learning environment rather than any particular student. Its purpose is to identify potential barriers to learning in a curriculum or classroom and to reduce such barriers through better initial designs, designs with the inherent flexibility to enable the curriculum itself to adjust to individual learners (Müller & Tschantz, 2003; Rose & Meyer, 2002).

Thus, although both AT and UDL rely on modern technology to improve education for students with disabilities, the technology tools used have a different site and mechanism of action. In AT, modern technology is employed at the level of the individual student to help him or her overcome barriers in the curriculum and living environments. With UDL, modern technology targets the curriculum itself; that is, technology is used to create curriculum and environments that, by design, lack traditional barriers to learning.

How Sharp Are the Distinctions Between Assistive Technology and Universal Design for Learning?

UDL and AT can be thought of as two approaches existing on a continuum. At the ends of this continuum, the two approaches are easily distinguishable. Toward the middle of the continuum, such easy distinctions are muddied, and there are greater points of interaction and commonality (Figure 1). Here we emphasize the interactions, because any comprehensive solution is likely to require attention to AT, UDL, and their effective integration. However, some crucial distinctions must also be understood.

Assistive Technology

Assistive technology is technology that increases, improves, or maintains the functional capabilities of students with disabilities.

Figure 1. The relationship between assistive technology and universal design for learning.

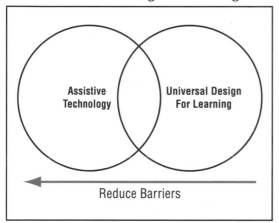

Reduce Barriers

Usually it is specifically designed to assist individuals with disabilities in overcoming barriers in their environment and in increasing their opportunities for independence. Because the intended consumers are usually individuals, specifically individuals with disabilities, AT can be carefully engineered, fitted, and adapted to the specific strengths and weaknesses of each person. In that regard AT is unique, personal (travels with the individual), customized, and dedicated.

Universal Design
Universal design is a process for designing general (i.e., used by everyone) products or structures in such a way as to reduce barriers for any individual (either with or without disabilities) and to increase opportunities for the widest possible range of users. Because the intended consumers are groups of individuals (i.e., a whole community), universal designs are engineered for flexibility, designed to anticipate the need for alternatives, options, and adaptations. In that regard, universal designs are often malleable and variable rather than dedicated. They are not unique or personal, but universal and inclusive, accommodating diversity.

Universal Design for Learning
The term UDL emphasizes the special purpose of learning environments—they are not created to provide information or shelter but to support and foster the changes in knowledge and skills that we call learning. While providing accessible spaces and materials is often essential to learning, it is not sufficient. Success requires that the components of pedagogy—the techniques, methods, scaffolds, and processes that are embedded in classrooms and curricula—are also accessible, and that the measure of their success is learning. The UDL framework is based in the neuroscience of learning, and its principles emphasize three key aspects of pedagogy: the means of representing information, the means for the expression of knowledge, and the means of engagement in learning (Rose & Meyer, 2002).

The Importance of Interaction and Integration of AT and Universal Design
In practice, universal design and AT often work in concert to achieve optimal and practical results (Hitchcock & Stahl, 2003). The following examples illustrate the value of integrating universal design and AT in architecture and the classroom, respectively.

Integration of Assistive Technology and Universal Design in Architecture
Consider the problem of mobility for the person with a physical disability. On the one hand, mobility can be viewed as primarily an individual problem—individual physical limitations create a unique, personal need for adaptation or enhancement. Such a view underscores the need for assistive solutions, solutions that are designed to help the individual to overcome his limitations, usually through application of technology. Electronic wheelchairs, wheeled walkers, and the like are examples. The advantage of such solutions is that they can be precisely tailored to the specific needs of the individual—adaptive seating for support, individual switch placement for control, and so forth.

On the other hand, mobility can also be viewed as an environmental problem—limitations in the design of the environment create physical barriers to mobility. A building that offers only stairs for moving between floors or rooms creates barriers for many individuals, including those who are using wheelchairs or wheeled walkers for mobility. Such a view underscores the need for a properly designed environment—one that provides alternatives like ramps and elevators. The advantage of such solutions is that they are universal, that is, they benefit not only a specific individual with a mobility barrier, but also many individuals, including nondisabled people, who are using baby carriages, carts, strollers, or pulling their luggage on wheels.

In reality, both the individual view and the environmental view are essential. If we focus only on the design of AT, we will inherit an environment that is so poorly designed and barrier-ridden that mobility will be limited for many individuals, creating a need for AT that is prohibitively extensive and expensive. The next generation of wheelchairs, for example, will be able to surmount barriers like stairs—a great advance—but they will cost many times more than existing wheelchairs, will be too cumbersome for many environments, and still face barriers like spiral staircases, ladders, and so on.

On the other hand, if we focus on universal designs at the exclusion of AT, we will fail to consider the customized adaptations that many people need and will build environments that are too complex and expensive. Many next-generation buildings, for example, will include ubiquitous moving walkways, but these will not adapt sufficiently for all individuals and will be prohibitively expensive and cumbersome for many buildings. Assistive technologies make universal designs more effective.

The most powerful and cost-effective solutions are ones that integrate these two approaches, yielding universal designs that are aware of the requirements of AT (e.g., buildings whose ramps have corners and inclines that are accessible to power wheelchairs) and AT that are aware of the affordances of universally designed buildings (e.g., wheelchairs that incorporate infrared switches to activate universally designed door and elevator buttons). Such integrated designs are not only more economical and ecological, they reflect the fact that disabilities are defined by the interaction between the environment and the individual.

Integration of Assistive Technology and Universal Design for Learning in the Classroom

Consider the problem for a student with a reading disability of mastering a history concept. Most history curricula pose significant barriers to such a student, especially the predominance of text. Most of the content is presented in text, and most of the assessment requires writing. This problem, too, can be viewed and solved in two different ways.

Taking an AT perspective, the problem can be considered an individual problem—it is clearly the individual student's reading disability that interferes with his or her ability to master the history content and demonstrate knowledge. This view fosters solutions that address the individual's weaknesses—remedial reading classes, special tutoring, and AT, for example. Of these, AT is particularly valuable because it provides independent means for the student to overcome his or her limitations by, for example using a spellchecker or audio version of the history book.

A UDL perspective, on the other hand, sees the problem as an environmental problem—the history curriculum's overreliance on printed text raises barriers to engagement and mastery for many students. This view fosters solutions targeting limitations in the curriculum rather than limitations in the student. Imagine a multimedia curriculum that provides digital, universally designed media that offer diverse options for viewing and manipulating content and expressing knowledge. Within such a flexible curriculum fewer students face barriers; digital text can speak aloud to reduce decoding barriers for students with dyslexia; digital images or video provide an alternative representation that reduces barriers in comprehension for students with language-based disabilities while providing descriptions and captions for students who are blind or deaf; and keyboard alternatives may reduce barriers in navigation and control for students with physical disabilities. These UDL solutions have the advantage of enhancing learning for many different kinds of students (Rose & Meyer, 2002).

In reality, both kinds of solutions are needed (Hitchcock & Stahl, 2003). In an educational setting, the disadvantage of exclusively using AT is that it is not integrated with the learning goals of a given lesson. If that is the case, AT may not be helpful, or may even interfere, from an educational standpoint. For example, a spellchecker would be a valuable AT for a student with learning disabilities in many situations, but in a lesson on spelling it would be counterproductive. The proper use of a spellchecker must be determined contextually, with an eye toward the goals of the lesson rather than merely the student's general access technologies (MacArthur, Graham, Haynes, & De La Paz, 1996).

At the same time, a purely UDL solution has the disadvantage that some built-in accommodations, particularly for students with low-incidence disabilities, are cumbersome, inefficient, or prohibitively expensive when included as an element of the basic curriculum. It is not necessary or advantageous to provide a screen reader or alternative keyboard with every piece of curriculum—students are better served by individual AT that has been adapted and fitted precisely to their own capacities and that can be used across many different pieces of curriculum without further adaptation or change of settings.

It is essential that universally designed curricula be aware of common assistive technologies and accommodate their features in the design process. For example, a UDL curriculum that is not aware of the requirements for keyboard equivalents in order to interface properly with single-switch access devices and alternative keyboards cannot provide universal access. Similarly, assistive technologies must be aware of the features built into universally designed curricula so that they are complementary and expansive rather than redundant. A text-to-speech technology that does not recognize common tagging features (like links or long descriptions) cannot provide adequate access to curricular materials.

In the past, there have been all too few examples of universally designed curricula, and even fewer examples of optimal linkages between such curricula and AT. We believe the future will bring many more. The next section provides a contemporary example of the kinds of progress that we anticipate.

The National Instructional Materials Accessibility Standard: An Example of the Current Linkage Between Universal Design for Learning and Assistive Technology

New developments in policy and practice are illuminating the educational landscape ahead and shaping the operational linkage between AT and UDL. One illustrative example is the recent inclusion of the National Instructional Materials Accessibility Standard (NIMAS) as part of the forthcoming Individuals with Disabilities Education Act (IDEA) reauthorization (NCAC, 2003; Rose & Stahl, 2003).

We begin this section by examining the policy supporting this new legislation, and the technological efficiencies it is designed to implement. We then discuss how the increased, timely availability of alternate accessible versions of textbooks, a development supported by NIMAS, promises to have a significant impact on the educational use of AT and relates to the integration of AT and UDL. Lastly, we address how this state of affairs may impact the education of students with disabilities now and in the future.

NIMAS and Current Policy and Technology Constraints on the Availability of Accessible Textbooks

As noted earlier, traditional print-based textbooks so prevalent in most classrooms pose barriers for many students with disabilities. While many students who are educated in general education classrooms can take advantage of the resources available in textbooks, these same resources are largely unavailable to students who cannot see the words or images on a page, cannot hold a book or turn its pages, cannot decode the text, or cannot comprehend the syntax that supports comprehension. These students may all require different supports to extract meaning from information that is book bound, and many require the retrofitting of print-based materials.

Two problems constrain the availability of accessible textbooks. The first is a problem of policy, the second a problem of technology.

Policy

Copyright laws provide publishers with the protection under which they produce, format, and distribute instructional materials. The content found in most textbooks used in K-12 classrooms is owned by individual or organizational rights holders who, not themselves publishers, grant fee-based permission to curriculum publishers to reproduce and use their materials. These permissions allow publishers to combine proprietary content with their own materials and distribute a product in an agreed-upon format or formats: print, audio book, CD-ROM, and so on. The original format for most K-12 textbooks is print, and traditionally it is this format for which publishers have secured and purchased copyright permissions. Unfortunately, when this is the case, legal agreements prevent publishers from providing more accessible versions of the materials.

However, students with disabilities and those supporting them have a legal means to acquire accessible versions of print textbooks by virtue of an existing copyright exemption. In September 1996, President Clinton authorized Section 121 of the United States Code, amending Chapter 1 of Title 17 and establishing a limitation on exclusive rights in copyrighted works. This legislative adjustment, commonly referred to as the Chafee Amendment (originally introduced by Senator John Chafee (R), Rhode Island) was specifically designed to create a legal conduit that would significantly enhance the flow of accessible, alternate format print works to the blind or other persons with disabilities. The Chafee Amendment copyright exemption was the culmination of efforts by disability advocates and the publishing community to create a mechanism that would obviate the need to seek, on a case-by-case basis, permission of the copyright holder every time a print work needed to be transformed into an alternate format for use by a person with a disability.

This exemption was designed as a relief valve for publishers and individuals with disabilities, allowing for the carefully monitored transformation of inaccessible materials into specialized formats for use by qualifying students (Perl, 2003).

Unfortunately, under current copyright law, only students with qualifying print disabilities may be provided with accessible braille, audio, or digital text versions of print materials without directly seeking permission from (and giving compensation to) the copyright holder. If the most conservative interpretation of the Chafee Amendment guidelines is applied, less than 5% of the nearly 6 million students who receive IDEA services and support would qualify to receive accessible instructional materials. In practice, there has been some flexibility in interpreting the Chafee Amendment guidelines, nevertheless the fact that the Chafee Amendment provides the only legal means of distributing accessible versions of proprietary materials to students with disabilities imposes a significant limitation when it becomes the basis for a compliance mandate in such expansive legislation as the IDEA.

The language in the current IDEA reauthorization includes a proposed modification to the copyright exemption that would allow publishers to provide digital files to authorized third parties specifically for the creation of accessible versions of textbooks for students with qualifying disabilities. This provision would include curriculum publishers within the Chafee exemption. While this modification would not expand access to these materials to a broader range of students than is presently identified under existing copyright law, it would significantly facilitate the flow of textbook files from producers to converters to users.

The significance of the inclusion of NIMAS in the IDEA as a mandate for both states and publishers cannot be overstated. It reflects widespread agreement among educators, disability advocates, and publishers, and it creates a precedent-setting national agenda by recognizing that instructional materials themselves, rather than the students using them, are in need of improvement. However, the fact that the right to accessible versions of print materials is extended to only a subset of IDEA-eligible students necessitates a more comprehensive alternative approach.

Technology

Beyond its application to IDEA-eligible students, the Chafee exemption created a new avenue for compliance with other federal mandates, including Section 504 of the Rehabilitation Act and the Americans with Disabilities Act. Since passage of the Chafee Amendment in 1996, special educators, disability service providers, advocacy organizations and new not-for-profits created specifically to take advantage of the copyright exemption began to actively transform print materials into accessible alternate versions. As these localized operations became more sophisticated and learned to exploit the potential of desktop computer technologies, textbooks became the content most often transformed. As a result, it is now common to find alternate format materials produced in schools and districts, postsecondary institutions, and regional education service centers nationwide. Not surprisingly, as more educational institutions have become equipped to create alternate format materials, students, their families and their advocates have increased their awareness of, and, subsequently, their requests for this content.

A variety of stakeholders—educators, national advocacy organizations, curriculum publishers, and others—have realized that the copyright exemption, originally designed to address individual instances of print inaccessibility, is increasingly being relied upon as the cornerstone for large-scale content transformation. This creates a problem because much like the architectural retrofitting referenced earlier, large-scale content transformation can be costly and time consuming and often results in an academic experience that is not equal to that provided to nondisabled students. Because the creation of these alternate editions begins with retrofitting and transforming an existing print version, each one represents a custom product. There is no economy of scale, no consistent quality control, no guarantee of efficient or timely delivery, and no guarantee of a consistent or harmonious interface with changing assistive technologies.

The National Instructional Materials Accessibility Standard: Integrating Policy and Technology

In the late 1980s, the Instructional Materials and Solutions Forum (convened by the American Foundation for the Blind) brought together approximately 40 national stakeholder organizations to address, among other things, the need for a scalable technological solution that would make the process of providing accessible, alternate versions more efficient, consistent, and timely. This initiative ultimately resulted in the creation of the National File Format Technical Panel in 2002 by the United States Department of Education, Office of Special Education Programs (Rose & Stahl, 2003). Charged with identifying the technical specifications for the NIMAS, the agreement reached by the technical panel in the fall of 2003 resulted in the identification of a technological format for source (publisher provided) files that will facilitate the efficient and consistent production of quality alternative formats. The inclusion of this recommendation in the reauthorization of IDEA reinforces the technical consensus with a national mandate for adoption (NCAC, 2003; Rose & Stahl, 2003).

The National File Format Technical Panel recommended that the NIMAS version 1.0 be an application of an XML-based (eXtensible Markup Language) standard. The National File Format Technical Panel recommended the DTBook element set, a component of the ANSI/NISO Z39.86. This recommendation aligned the NIMAS with the work being done concurrently by the DAISY consortium (www.daisy.org), the Open eBook Forum (www.openbook.org), and the IMS Global Learning Consortium (www.imsproject.org), thus ensuring cross-industry standards conformance.

The curriculum publishing community agreed to make available digital files containing all of the elements of the print textbooks (a combination of XML and PDF files), and further agreed to identify the XML components according to the NIMAS 1.0 standard. As a result of this consensus, third-party conversion organizations (Recording for the Blind and Dyslexic, American Printing House for the Blind, National Braille Press, etc.) and school districts will receive consistent, valid, and well-formatted digital source files from which to create accessible and student-ready versions. This will cut the conversion time—and therefore the distribution time—significantly. The promise of the NIMAS standard is that alternative versions will be made available to students at the same time that print versions are made available to their nondisabled classmates.

While this agreement will significantly streamline the conversion process by eliminating existing incongruities in publisher files, its true impact will likely be as a precedent-setting designation of the critical importance of separating content from its presentation. XML-based files remain malleable, their baseline component labeling (tags) can be extended to encompass a wide range of presentation needs, and content stored in this format can ultimately be transformed not only into accessible alternate versions, but into new, universally designed, enhanced learning editions as well.

The NIMAS standard is both a policy advance (an advance that ensures equitable access to educational materials for all students) and a technology advance (an advance in the publishing workflow that will lead to more efficient distribution for publishers and consumers alike). While NIMAS is not yet broadly based enough to be called a true universal design, it is clearly the foundation for future universal designs that will be based on it.

Current Integration of UDL and AT: Accessible Curriculum Content Increases the Efficacy of Assistive Technology

The increased availability of flexible and inherently accessible core curriculum materials under NIMAS will probably lead to an increased awareness of AT and a broadening of its use. The reason is that accessible information is not necessarily optimized for every potential user and, therefore, may prompt the use of AT. Consider, for example, familiar technological solutions for everyday tasks: word processing for writing and revision, spellchecking for editing, email for communication, financial software to reconcile our bank balances. Each requires the interplay between an application program (word processor, email or spreadsheet software) and the files that contain the information being rendered (word processing document, email message, or financial worksheet). These software applications may each be customized to fit the individual needs of a user, and AT is simply the magnification of that customization to accommodate needs that are not inherently addressed by the application itself.

To take another example, a Web page can be built to ensure the highest degree of accessibility according to the World Wide Web Consortium's Web Access Initiative Standards (www.w3.org/wai). But the capabilities of the browser—Internet Explorer, Netscape, Mozilla, Opera, Safari or others—supply the transformational energy needed to realize this accessibility. Assistive technology acts on accessible instructional materials in an identical fashion, and, much as there is a direct correlation between the capabilities and use of browsers and the availability and functions of Web pages, a similar relationship exists between AT and the materials it acts upon.

What will be the effect of NIMAS, a foundation for universal design, on AT? The availability of a universal file format will optimize AT in a number of ways, including a) all publishers will be producing a common format for access, greatly reducing the complexity of design for interfacing AT, b) every state and district will optimally accept and use materials in a common format, greatly reducing the complexity of training and support for the personnel who will administer and use AT, and c) every student who needs them will get high-quality digital accessible materials in a timely fashion, rendering their AT more effective for classroom learning with their peers. Complementarily, the availability of high-quality AT in the classroom will render these new materials immediately useful for students and their teachers, and will allow teachers, special educators, and AT professionals to concentrate on learning rather than production of accessible materials. While either universally designed materials or AT in isolation can be helpful, it is at the intersection of the two that information access, and, ultimately learning, becomes most individualized and appropriate.

The intrinsic flexibility of digital alternate format versions of textbooks supports transformations not previously possible. For example, accessible alternate versions of textbooks can be transformed into braille files ready to be sent to an embosser for the creation of printed braille. Alternatively, digital textbook files can be formatted for a refreshable braille display, or for display on a computer screen with instantaneous onscreen braille to text and text to braille conversion capabilities. This application allows teachers of the visually impaired, the majority of whom are sighted, to quickly and efficiently locate a paragraph, sentence, phrase, or even single word reference in a document—something that is very difficult to do with print braille. Similarly, subsections of a document can be translated to braille onscreen and either sent to a refreshable display print or an embosser, or translated into synthetic speech and saved as a portable audio (MP3) format. The alternate format (in this example, digital) provides the flexibility and the inherent transformative potential; the AT, refreshable braille display, synthetic speech, MP3 player, and so on allow the user (or those teaching them) to customize the experience for optimal benefit.

The schools, districts, and even states, that have begun to incorporate flexible digital versions of textbooks into their educational practice have increased their understanding of the importance and potential of AT devices and software. Because the emphasis on alternate format materials is on core curriculum resources, this awareness (and growing expertise) is extending well beyond special education and into general education classrooms. As a result, it is not as unusual as it once was to encounter a workshop on supported reading software during an institute for language arts teachers, and many schools are equipped with portable smart keyboards for word processing and text downloading; even MP3 players are no longer anomalies in the classroom—and they are not being solely used to store music.

The Future of Accessibility: Moving from Some Students to All Students

Existing copyright constraints limit the distribution of accessible alternate format materials, and thus fail to address the needs of all students with disabilities. But the establishment of the NIMAS and its inclusion in the IDEA reauthorization does create the foundation for that solution. The scope of current local efforts to use technology to create accessible alternative versions of core textbooks has highlighted the need while simultaneously exposing the inaccuracies and inefficiencies inherent in an uncoordinated approach. It has also illuminated the weaknesses in the present system, establishing the impetus necessary to promote widespread change.

The most effective approach to providing accessible versions of print textbooks entails the creation of a free market distribution model. In this model publishers would create alternative and accessible versions of print textbooks for direct distribution to states, districts, schools, and students at the same time that the print versions are made available. In this model, accessible (likely digital) versions could serve a broad range of students' needs, well beyond the needs identified in the narrow exemption from copyright laws granted by Chafee. The free market approach could eliminate the delay in the development and distribution of accessible digital versions that currently exists. However, in order for a free market system to become established, a number of conditions must be met.

First, education consumers (states, districts, schools) must demonstrate a willingness to pay for the value represented in the publishers' production and delivery of fully accessible instructional materials. If the growing array of state textbook adoption legislation, that is, legislation mandating the provision of accessible versions that go beyond requiring digital text files to the inclusion of graphical elements and easy-to-use navigation, is an indicator, the demand is beginning to be established.

Second, publishers must be able to reclaim the rights that have been exempted under the Chafee Amendment in order to facilitate production investments, including the acquisition of all rights required for reproduction and distribution of materials in digital formats. While nontrivial, obtaining these rights is made much more enticing if the intellectual property holders and the publishers perceive that adequate compensation is viable.

Third, the workflow that produces print textbooks has to be adjusted to accommodate the creation of digital versions, not as a deflection of core product development and manufacturing efforts but as a naturally occurring variation in the product cycle. Many of the large curriculum publishing companies have begun to move in this direction—some as a direct result of the NIMAS consensus—by establishing a digital workflow that can result in a number of published products, print textbooks and digital versions among them.

Fourth, third party conversion entities must prepare to meet an increased demand for their expertise. As commercial publishers move to establish a capacity to produce accessible digital versions for sale on the open market, organizations and companies that now perform the final step in the alternative format conversion, creating braille, digital audio or otherwise accessible editions, will find an increased demand for their skills as subcontractors or co-developers with curriculum materials producers.

None of these four conditions is felt to be unattainable, and the benefits to intellectual property holders, content developers, content conversion experts, and students with disabilities is readily apparent. Accessible digital versions would be provided to students with disabilities (who need them) and students without disabilities (who might prefer them). Intellectual property holders and content developers would be assured of adequate compensation and digital rights management. Content conversion experts would see their expertise in the development of alternative versions of instructional materials expand beyond the limited market in which they now exist into the broader educational enterprise. The NIMAS establishes an extensible foundation for moving this vision forward. This vision is moving toward a true universal design for learning.

Beyond Access —Towards the Learning Enterprise

While the stated purpose of determining the NIMAS specification was to facilitate the timely provision of accessible materials to students with disabilities, it is important to keep in mind that it is the nation's educational system within which these alternative versions will be provided. With that emphasis, the extent to which alternate, accessible versions of textbooks created from NIMAS-compliant source files enhance student achievement is a significant and very relevant question.

The answer to that question will require more research, research on outcomes (Edyburn, 2003). To date, flexible and accessible digital versions of core curriculum print textbooks have simply not been sufficiently available to measure their impact within the context of large-scale academic achievement. What is known, however, is that students with a wide range of disabling conditions—those who currently qualify as persons with print disabilities and those who do not—can benefit from universally-designed instructional solutions (Rose & Meyer, 2002).

A recent extensive summary of research in this area has been prepared by NCAC at www.cast.org/ncac (Strangman, Hall, & Meyer, 2003). Among many studies in this area are the following:

- Students with language-related disabilities showed positive effects for word recognition, comprehension, and fluency when using digital texts with synthetic, syllable- or letter name-level synthetic speech transformations (Elbro, Rasmussen, & Spelling, 1996).

- Students with attentional, organizational and learning disabilities have shown increased academic gain when exposed to technology-supported concept mapping strategies. (Anderson-Inman, Knox-Quinn, & Horney, 1996; Herl, O'Neil, Chung, & Schacter, 1999).

- Students who are deaf or hard of hearing show consistent academic gains when provided with the sequential text highlighting and supportive captions available with digital instructional materials (Andrews, & Jordan, 1997; McInerney, Riley, & Osher, 1999).

- Students with low cognitive abilities demonstrate increased functional skills when exposed to flexible technologies that maximize their strengths while helping to compensate for their weaknesses (Carroll, 1993; Wehmeyer, Smith, Palmer, Davies, & Stock, 2003).

The true promise of NIMAS is that it provides a flexible but sturdy foundation for curricula that embody UDL and capitalize on ATs to make that learning accessible to everyone. Realization of the promise of NIMAS will be apparent as a cultural shift for students with disabilities: the shift from a focus on access to a focus on learning. That critical shift will depend upon the continued evolution of an optimal interplay between UDL and AT.

The Future of Assistive Technology and Universal Design for Learning

We expect a continuing dialogue along the continuum of Universal Design for Learning and assistive technologies. As UDL matures, it will advance by incorporating many features now provided only by assistive technologies, in the same way that text-to-speech, spellchecking, and calculators can be routinely built into office word processing or that captioning is built into every television. As assistive technology matures, it will advance by assuming increasing connectivity with universal designs, taking advantage of the common structures (e.g., XML semantic tagging in a universally designed Web site) to provide highly individualized solutions that are not only sensory- and motor- but also cognitive- and linguistic-oriented. During this period of AT and UDL maturation and advancement, we must make every effort to ensure that these two fields develop symbiotically. When UDL and AT are designed to co-exist, learning for all individuals is enhanced.

In a world where we are very aware that understanding human behavior requires knowledge of the complex interaction between both cultural and individual development, we should not be surprised to find that fostering human learning will require access solutions that are optimal interactions between what is universal and what is individual.

References

Anderson-Inman, L., Knox-Quinn, C., & Horney, M. A. (1996). Computer-based study strategies for students with learning disabilities: Individual differences associated with adoption level. *Journal of Learning Disabilities, 29*(5), 461-484.

Andrews, J.F., and Jordan, D.L. (1997, February). *Special education technology for the next century.* Proceedings of the 1997 CSF/CEC and TAM Conference on Special Education and Technology, San Diego, California.

Behrmann, M., & Schaff, J. (2001). Assisting educators with assistive technology: Enabling children to achieve independence in living and learning. *Children and Families, 42*(3), 24-28.

Bowser, G., & Reed, P. (2000). Considering your child's need for assistive technology, *LD Online.* Retrieved January 15, 2004, from: www.ldonline.org/ld_indepth/technology/bowzer_reed.html.

Carroll, J.M. (1993). Creating a design science of human-computer interaction. *Interacting with Computers, 5*(1), 3-12.

Crealock, C., & Sitko, M. (1990). Comparison between computer and handwriting technologies in writing training with learning disabled students. *International Journal of Special Education, 5*(2), 173-183.

Edyburn, D.L. (2002). Models, theories, and frameworks: Contributions to understanding special education technology. *Special Education Technology Practice, 4*(2), 16-24.

Edyburn, D. L. (2003). 2002 in review: A synthesis of the special education technology literature. *Journal of Special Education Technology, 18*(3), 5-28.

Elbro, C., Rasmussen, I., & Spelling, B. (1996). Teaching reading to disabled readers with language disorders: a controlled evaluation of synthetic speech feedback. *Scandinavian Journal of Psychology, 37*, 140-155.

Hasselbring, T.S., & Glaser, C.H. (2000). Use of computer technology to help students with special needs. *Future of Children, 10*(2), 102-22.

Hebert, B. M., & Murdock, J. Y. (1994). Comparing three computer-aided instruction output modes to teach vocabulary words to students with learning disabilities. *Learning Disabilities Research & Practice, 9*(3), 136-141.

Herl, H. E., O'Neil, H. F. Jr., Chung, G.K.W.K., & Schacter, J. (1999). Reliability and validity of a computer-based knowledge mapping system to measure content understanding. *Computers in Human Behavior, 15* (3-4), 315-333.

Hitchcock, C., & Stahl, S. (2003). Assistive technology, universal design, universal design for learning: Improved learning opportunities. *Journal of Special Education Technology, 18*(4). Retrieved March 2, 2004, from: jset.unlv.edu/18.4T/hitchcock/first.html.

MacArthur, C. A., Graham, S., Haynes, J. A., & De La Paz, S. (1996). Spelling checkers and students with learning disabilities: Performance comparisons and impact on spelling. *Journal of Special Education, 30*, 35-57.

MacArthur, C. A., & Haynes, J. B. (1995). Student assistant for learning from text (SALT): A hypermedia reading aid. *Journal of Learning Disabilities, 28*(3), 50-59.

MacArthur, C. A., Haynes, J. A., Malouf, D. B., Harris, K., & Owings, M. (1990). Computer assisted instruction with learning disabled students: achievement, engagement, and other factors that influence achievement. *Journal of Educational Computing Research, 6*(3), 311-328.

McInerney, M., Riley, K., & Osher. D. (1999). *Technology to support literacy strategies for students who are deaf: Final report.* American Institutes for Research.

Myller, E., & Tschantz, J. (2003). *Universal Design for Learning: Four state initiatives, quick turnaround forum, project FORUM.* Alexandria, VA: National Association of State Directors of Special Education.

National Center on Accessing the General Curriculum. (2003). *National file format initiative at NCAC.* Retrieved January 15, 2004, from: www.cast.org/ncac/index.cfm?i=3138.

Perl, E. (2003). *Federal and state legislation regarding accessible instructional materials.* National Center on Accessing the General Curriculum. Retrieved January 15, 2004, from: www.cast.org/ncac/index.cfm?i=3122)

Raskind, M.H., & Higgins, E. (1995). Effects of speech synthesis on the proofreading efficiency of postsecondary students with learning disabilities. *Learning Disability Quarterly, 18*(2), 141-158.

Raskind, M. H., Higgins, E. L. (1999). Speaking to read: The effects of speech recognition technology on the reading and spelling performance of children with learning disabilities. *Annals of Dyslexia, 49*, 251-281.

Rose, D.H., & Meyer, A. (2002). *Teaching every student in the digital age: Universal Design for Learning.* Alexandria, VA: Association for Supervision and Curriculum Development.

Rose, D., & Stahl, S. (2003). The NFF: A national file format for accessible instructional materials. *Journal of Special Education Technology, 18*(2), 5-28.

Story, M.F., Mueller, J. L., & Mace, R. L. (1998). *The universal design file: Designing for people of all ages and abilities.* Raleigh: North Carolina State University, The Center for Universal Design.

Strangman, N., Hall, T., & Meyer, A. (2003). *Text transformations.* National Center on Accessing the General Curriculum. Retrieved January 15, 2004, from: www.cast.org/ncac/index.cfm?i=4864.

van Daal, V.H.P., & Reitsma, P. (1993, September). The use of speech feedback by normal and disabled readers in computer-based reading practice. *Reading and Writing, 5*(3), 243-259.

von Tetzchner, S., Rogne, S. O., & Lilleeng, M. K. (1997). Literacy intervention for a deaf child with severe reading disorder. *Journal of Literacy Research, 29*(1), 25-46.

Wehmeyer, M.L., Smith, S.J., Palmer, S.B., Davies, D.K. & Stock, S. (2003). Technology use and people with mental retardation. In L.M. Glidden (Ed.), *International review of research in mental retardation.* San Diego CA: Academic Press.

Xin, J. F., & Rieth, H. (2001). Video-assisted vocabulary instruction for elementary school students with learning disabilities. *Information Technology in Childhood Education Annual*, 87-103.

Section 6

Technology and Instruction

27

Integrating Technology in Standards-Based Instruction

Kevin M. Anderson and Cindy L. Anderson

This chapter takes a brief look at the current national emphasis on standards-based instruction and how technology may be integrated to provide more effective learning opportunities for students of all abilities. The first two sections of the chapter examine the basis for the standards movement and the instructional reform efforts coming from this initiative. Definitions of learning standards, the chronology of the development of subject-specific standards, and samples of state standards are included in these first sections.

The next major section of this chapter reviews the development of standards-based instruction at the classroom level. Standards are generally written in broad terms, so it is the responsibility of the local educator to determine appropriate instructional methods and assessment techniques to meet the needs of individual children. This section examines current efforts underway to make standards-based instruction appropriate for learners of all abilities.

The final section of this chapter examines the integration of technology into a standards-based learning environment. The major portion of this section is a case study showing how a team of teachers planned and implemented the integration of appropriate technology into an inclusive third-grade classroom.

Why the Current Push for Standards?

Historical Background

Since the publication of *A Nation at Risk* in 1983 (National Commission on Excellence in Education, 1983), public schools in the United States have been under increased scrutiny by politicians, business leaders, the media, and parents. A general perception was growing that schools were failing students by watering down curricula, lessening expectations, and using unskilled teachers. Numerous governmental and corporate leaders espoused the view that the general economic health of the country was dependent on how well students were doing in school. Whether any of these allegations were accurate was open to debate, but they certainly resulted in a closer examination of how schools were being run in the United States.

Numerous school reform efforts have resulted from this demand for new ways of conducting the business of educating children. Perhaps the most pervasive and wide-sweeping effort to improve schools has been the emphasis on developing rigorous standards of learning for students. According to Swanson and Stevenson (2002), standards-based reform initiatives promote an ambitious agenda in the sense that they aim to reach into individual classrooms, changing the nature of instruction with the ultimate goal of improving student learning.

Earlier educational initiatives attempted, largely unsuccessfully, to improve student performance indirectly through the imposition of funding formulas or formal regulatory requirements. Standards-based reform, on the other hand, is founded on a concrete model of educational practice that specifies new high-standards curricula and instructional techniques for the general classroom. The traditional work of education has been performed within individual classrooms that are substantially isolated from the teaching practices used in other classrooms, even within the same school. As a result, the technical core of instruction is surprisingly resistant to external influences for change. This loose coupling of organization and activity, policy and practice, can prove rather dysfunctional for schools attempting to enact systemic change in learning. The development of basic standards for learning for all students has the potential for tightening this coupling, resulting in the development of more consistent, appropriate learning opportunities.

Rather than holding students accountable to minimum acceptable levels of competency, the national standards-based reform movement calls for high standards for all students oriented around challenging subject matter, acquisition of higher-order thinking skills, and application of abstract knowledge to solve real-world problems (McLaughlin & Shepard, 1995). But more important, standards-based reform is based on a process-driven conception of educational change that explicitly links schooling inputs and policies to student outcomes through clearly defined mechanisms. That is, curriculum frameworks lay out the academic content students should know in given subject areas, while related policies provide the supports necessary to enact the reformed high-quality curriculum. These latter measures include the provision of curricular materials and other school resources, professional development to ensure that teachers have the requisite content knowledge and instructional abilities, and assessment and accountability systems to monitor and stimulate progress in student learning and achievement (Smith & O'Day, 1991). Rather than relying on funding channels or regulatory controls alone, as evidenced by the recently enacted No Child Left Behind legislation (United States Department of Education, 2003), standards-based reform aims to improve student learning by changing the core productive technologies of schooling—the academic content and pedagogical practices of classroom instruction. Educational historian Diane Ravitch (1995) asserts that just as standards have improved the daily lives of Americans so, too, will they improve the effectiveness of American education: "Standards can improve achievement by clearly defining what is to be taught and what kind of performance is expected" (p. 25).

In response to vigorous advocacy on the part of national participants, the states have rapidly adapted the tenets of standards-based reform to serve the needs of their own educational constituencies. According to M. Hayes Mizell of the Edna McConnell Clark Institute (Mizell, 2002), "we need standards not only to emphasize the academic purposes of schooling, but to provide school boards, superintendents, and principals with an anchor they can use to resist shifting currents" (p. 9). Although state approaches have varied considerably in terms of the strength of their responses and their specific routes to high standards, four coordinated forces impacting policy have emerged at the core of curriculum-driven agendas for change across the country: (a) Content Standards-detailed statements of the high-quality academic material students should learn; (b) Performance Standards-established levels of mastery students should be able to demonstrate over this content; (c) Aligned Assessments-statewide testing of students to measure their level of performance on the specified content, especially using performance-based methods; and (d) Professional Standards-training and certification requirements to ensure that teachers are sufficiently skilled as both pedagogists and subject-matter specialists to instruct a reformed, high-standards curriculum (Swanson & Stevenson, 2002). Researchers Robert Glaser and Robert Linn (1993) maintain that it might be only when reflecting upon the past that we note the importance of the current standards-based initiatives in American education:

> In the recounting of our nation's drive toward educational reform, the last decade of this century will undoubtedly be identified

as the time when a concentrated press for national education standards emerged. The press for standards was evidenced by the efforts of federal and state legislators, presidential and gubernatorial candidates, teacher and subject-matter specialists, governmental agencies, and private foundations . (p. xiii)

While standards-based initiatives across the country have developed out of different needs and expectations, common elements have emerged. According to McREL (Mid-Continent Research for Education and Learning) (Krueger & Sutton, 2001), standards-based instruction and assessment typically must do the following:

1. *Focus on the important concepts and skills that are critical to the understanding of important phenomena and relationships that can be developed over several age levels*
2. *Help students develop an understanding of these concepts and skills over several years in ways that are logical and that reflect intellectual readiness*
3. *Establish explicitly the connections among the concepts and skills in ways that allow students to understand both ideas and the connections among them*
4. *Assess and diagnose what students understand to determine the next steps in instruction.* (p. 51)

In addition, the practical impact of the application of high standards is neither failure rates nor social promotion, it is the use of multiple opportunities for students to demonstrate proficiency, and the steadfast refusal of teachers and administrators to label students as "proficient" when they are not (Reeves, 1998). Further, research from the National Center on Education Outcomes at the University of Minnesota (Thompson & Thurlow, 2001) stresses that students need to be part of the entire process of setting appropriate standards. By involving students in their own learning, standards-based programs will: (a) promote high expectations, (b) provide an accurate picture of education, (c) allow all students to benefit from reforms, (d) enable accurate comparisons of learning to be made, and (e) avoid unintended consequences of exclusion.

Timeline of the Development of Standards

Using the publication of *A Nation at Risk* (National Commission on Excellence in Education, 1983) as the unofficial beginning of the current standards movement in the United States, Table 1 highlights important events in the past two decades.

What Is Standards-Driven Reform?

Noting the diversity in learning styles and needs of students across the United States, educators do not expect all students to learn material in the same manner, using the same materials, and within the same time frame. Standards have been developed to allow teachers to meet these diverse needs without sacrificing the fundamental instructional requirements of an exemplary PK-12 education. For example, the authors of the National Science Education Standards (National Academy of Science, 1995) note that

Standards apply to all students, regardless of age, gender, cultural or ethnic background, disabilities, aspirations, or interest and motivation in science. Different students will achieve understanding in different ways, and different students will achieve different degrees of depth and breadth of understanding depending on interest, ability, and context. But all students can develop the knowledge and skills described in the Standards, even as some students go well beyond these levels. (p. 2)

These words, while written for a handbook dealing with science education, can be applied to instruction and assessment in any subject area. The key to using these standards well lies in providing rich, well-supported learning environments that respond to the unique educational needs of every student.

The essence of standards-based reform is the seemingly simple proposition that schools and school systems are to be held accountable for their performance, just as the students they serve are held accountable for theirs. This proposition seems to elicit three types of response from schools and school systems:

Table 1. Important Events in Standards-Based Reform Since 1983

1983	• *A Nation at Risk* is published by the National Commission for Excellence in Education.
1987	• The National Council of Teachers of Mathematics (NCTM) reviews curriculum documents and drafts math standards.
1989	• The nation's governors and President Bush adopt the National Education Goals for the year 2000. • NCTM publishes *Curriculum and Evaluation Standards for School Mathematics.* • Project 2061 of the American Association for the Advancement of Science (AAAS) publishes *Science for All Americans.*
1990	• The New Standards Project is formed to create a system of standards for student performance in a number of areas.
1991	• SCANS (Secretary's Commission on Achieving Necessary Skills) produces *What Work Requires of Schools.*
1992	• NCEST (National Council on Education Standards and Testing) releases its report *Raising Standards for American Education.* • Federal funding is provided to numerous organizations for the development of subject-area standards.
1993	• McREL publishes its first technical report on standards, *The Systematic Identification and Articulation of Content Standards and Benchmarks: An Illustration Using Mathematics.*
1994	• President Clinton signs into law Goal 2000: Educate America Act. • Standards are published for English/language arts (draft), visual arts, social studies, history, geography, and civics.
1995	• McREL publishes *Content Knowledge: A Compendium of Standards and Benchmarks for K-12 Education.* • The Third International Mathematics and Science Study (TIMSS) is conducted.
1996	• The second national "education summit" is held with 40 state governors and more than 45 national business leader in attendance. • Standards are released for foreign language, science, and English/language arts.
1998	• The Comprehensive School Reform Demonstration (CSRD) program provides $150 million for local schools to implement comprehensive school reform programs based on reliable research and effective practices and including an emphasis on basic academics and parental involvement.
1999	• TIMSS-Repeat collects data in 38 countries at the eighth-grade level in math and science.
2000	• NCTM revises the mathematics standards, publishing *Principles and Standards for School Mathematics.* • The International Society for Technology in Education (ISTE) publishes *National Educational Technology Standards for Students: Connecting Curriculum and Technology.*
2001	• The Elementary and Secondary Education Act (ESEA) is reauthorized, mandating sweeping changes for the nation's public schools in funding, student achievement accountability, and teacher quality.
2002	• States grapple with the funding, reporting, and testing requirements of the No Child Left Behind Act. (Marzano & Kendall, 1996)

1. *The "this, too, shall pass" syndrome, where teachers administrators begin counting their years until retirement;*
2. *The belief that this reform is just more of the same and can be addressed "if we just try harder;" or*
3. *The recognition that the reform is real and is here to stay, coupled with a sense of inefficacy because the capacity to respond- not the will-is sorely lacking. (Hickey, 2002, p. 48)*

According to Hickey, the first two responses are doomed to failure. The third provides at least a toehold from which the building of capacity can begin. But what does this mean and what steps are involved? Building school capacity means developing and infusing the skills, understandings, processes, and resources that enable a higher level of teaching and learning that permeates the school and results in sustained improvement in student performance.

Hickey, distinguished professor and director of the Center for Leadership in Education at Towson University, maintains that standards-driven efforts must be based on five key processes in order for student achievement to meet or exceed high standards of performance. These key processes are:

1. Understanding the target. *Experience shows that if there are 25 different classroom teachers, there will be 25 different understandings of what classroom outcomes should be, based on such factors as experience, depth of subject-matter knowledge, and sense of priority. Even if there is common agreement, other factors must be taken into consideration, such as do the students also understand the expected outcome and is the outcome the one that is being assessed?*

2. Teaching the indicators. *Where are the curriculum priorities set? Are state, district, and building priorities in alignment? The indicators set by the state cover a comprehensive set of goals and outcomes that have been determined by some process to be important for students to know and be able to do at each grade level. They are also the focus for most state assessment systems.*

3. Assessing the indicators. *State tests have become the driver for educational reform and school improvement, even though they are a most unsuitable vehicle for these purposes at the individual school level. Nevertheless, the state tests are important for political reasons, if not educational ones, and it is important for schools to base the assessment of classroom work on these indicators.*

4. Monitoring individual student progress. *Most teachers in most schools fail to monitor individual student progress effectively against the indicators being assessed, focusing instead on grading an assignment—whether or not it is related to the indicators and whether or not it reflects actual student learning (as opposed to simply meeting the requirements of the assignment). Additionally, what data are collected are rarely used to inform instruction and to make adjustments responsive to the needs of individual learners, nor are the results shared with other staff to enrich dialogue and reflection and contribute to making the schools a true learning community.*

5. Intervening when students are not succeeding. *If a teacher teaches and a student fails to learn, has real teaching actually taken place? This is the crucial linkage in the teaching-learning equation: assessing individual progress and providing appropriate interventions when a student fails to attain an outcome. When an intervention does occur, all too often it consists of more of the same. More is not needed; different is.* (Hickey, 2002, p. 48)

Defining Standards

So, what are standards and how would you know one if you saw one? General agreement specifies two types of standards: academic content standards and performance standards. Academic content standards typically describe what every student should know and be able to do in the core academic content areas. Content standards should apply equally to students of all races and ethnicities, from all linguistic and

Table 2. Examples of Standards from Delaware and Wisconsin

Standards/Benchmarks	Standards-Based Expectations (Partial Listing)
Delaware Content Standard	Requires students to: Construct, examine, and extend the meaning of literacy through listening, reading, and viewing
Delaware Performance Standard	Students demonstrate their understanding, meeting or exceeding the standard if their answer: • Accurately summarizes the story or nonfiction sequence • Identifies and discusses the characteristics of the type of literature • Identifies and explains technical elements of the language and how its was used in the story, giving supporting ideas to show a complete understanding of the selection • Chooses facts/details relevant to questions posed. (Anderson, Fiester, Gonzales, & Pechman, 1996)
Kenosha Language Arts Standard (Grade 5)	The student applies reading strategies to gain information and understanding
Kenosha Language Arts Benchmarks (Grade 5)	The student: • Uses arrangement of text/graphics to gain meaning • Uses strategies for accessing prior knowledge to understand the reading selection • Selects and uses appropriate reference tools to gain information • Takes action to understand text when meaning breaks down. (Kenosha Unified School District No. 1, 1999)

cultural backgrounds, both with and without special learning needs. Performance standards, on the other hand, try to answer the question: "How good is good enough?" In other words, they define how students demonstrate their proficiency in the skills and knowledge framed by the content standards.

Table 2 shows how districts may specify standards. Included are an example from Delaware's content and performance standards in reading and an example from Kenosha (WI) Unified School District's language arts standards and benchmarks (1999).

As illustrated in Table 2, terminology around learning standards varies from state to state and district to district. In fact, Douglas Reeves of the Center for Performance Assessment notes in *Making Standards Work* (Reeves, 1998) that "use of the word 'standards' to mean many different things is confusing and potentially destructive" (p. 16). Reeves suggests the

following common language in an effort to be clear and unambiguous about standards:

• *Academic Content Standards—The general expectations of what a student should know and be able to do. These are typically few in number and general in scope. Examples include:*

   a. Students will be able to design, conduct, analyze, evaluate, and communicate about scientific investigations.

   b. Students will know and understand properties, forms, changes in, and interrelationship of matter and energy.

   c. Students will communicate clearly and effectively about science to others.

• *Benchmarks—The specific expectations of student performance at critical levels of school, typically fourth, eighth, and twelfth grades. Examples include:*

   a. By Grade 4, students will identify and describe science-related problems or issues, such as acid rain and weather forecasting.

    b. By Grade 4, students will relate science information to local and global issues, such as world hunger and ozone depletion.

    c. By Grade 8, students will analyze the risks and benefits of potential solutions to personal and global issues.

    d. By Grade 12, students will analyze the costs, risks, benefits, and consequences of natural resource exploration, development, and consumption, such as resource management of forests and ground water pollution. (p.16)

Using this method, let's examine this sample content standard: "Students will relate physical materials, pictures, and diagrams to mathematical ideas."

There are many ways that a student can demonstrate that they meet this standard. For a younger student, it might include working and playing with blocks and creating some elementary mathematical relationships with them. For older students, it might include drawing pictures of a house and calculating the dimensions of their drawings. The point is that students demonstrate that they have met this standard not by responding to artificial multiple-choice questions involving pictures and mathematical concepts, but by engaging in realistic, interesting, and thought-provoking activities (Reeves, 1998).

In developing standards of expected learning, states and districts have often struggled with what it means to adopt standards. For example, Colorado has made it clear what its state learning standards mean for students:

Colorado's Standards DO:
- Reflect agreement among community members about the knowledge and skills students must have to graduate
- Hold each student to high performance standards in math, science, reading, writing, geography, history, and other subjects
- Build on best past and current practices
- Provide realistic expectations and appropriate learning opportunities for all students

Colorado's Standards DO NOT:
- Promote arbitrary classes, isolated curriculum, or "seat-time" spent in school

- Include fuzzy, unfocused minimum expectations or a watered-down curriculum
- Throw away graduation requirements and traditional grades, classes, or report cards
- Set unrealistic standards that prevent all students from succeeding (Anderson, Fiester, Gonzales, & Pechman, 1996).

No matter what terminology or approach is chosen for addressing learning standards, it is apparent that teachers are the key to achieving results based on these new challenging expectations. In fact, just being involved in the discussion and development of performance standards or benchmarks can have a positive effect on how instruction is impacted. Comments from the North Dakota State Language Arts Committee indicate that the impact of the project was best evidenced by the increased level of knowledge and understanding of standards for the English Language Arts Committee itself (Anderson, Fiester, Gonzales, & Pechman, 1996). In the district where the authors reside, teachers have been working on curriculum teams since the early 1990s to develop standards and benchmarks for each subject area and to align them with the state standards. As the district has moved forward in using the standards to report academic progress about student work to parents, those teachers who have been a part of the process have been the most enthusiastic and thorough about using the standards to guide instruction and assessment. Involvement definitely breeds familiarity, acceptance, and appropriate implementation.

The Impact of Standards for All Students

General Education

The use of standards-driven instruction can accomplish three important goals. First, committing to high academic standards makes the unequivocal statement that all students are expected to excel academically and will receive the help to do so. Second, standards setting and implementation engages parents and community members in discussion about what students should know and be able to do and strengthens the connections between state and local education reforms. Third, the development and implementation of standards involves classroom teachers, parents, and other members of the school community in the educational improvement process (Anderson, Fiester, Gonzales, & Pechman, 1996).

The following comments from participants in the development of standards-driven reform provide interesting insight into this process:

The standards make clear what we should be achieving at the end of each grade. – Linda Corner, Teacher in North Dakota

You have more teachers attuned to where you are trying to go and how it will cut across the various disciplines. – Clifton Reed, Massachusetts' Standards Setting Team Member

We asked the community to tell us what they expected us to do for them. As a result of that process, everything we do is tied into a standard, or we shouldn't be doing it. – Cynthia Bianco, Niagara City Schools Assistant to the Superintendent (Anderson, Fiester, Gonzales, & Pechman, 1996, p. 7)

Aligning Instruction and Assessment

In a standards-based curriculum, teachers design learning experiences to enable all their students to reach the level of understanding or skill described by applicable standards. Given the diverse backgrounds and interests of students in any classroom, teachers are challenged to present the content in an engaging and accessible manner and to make frequent assessments of the students' understanding.

Studying standards for student achievement is a critical element in the education of teachers by integrating the need for a solid understanding of content with experience in an array of instructional strategies. Ongoing professional development in both content and pedagogy is best done in connection with classroom practice and in collaboration with other teachers. In this way, teachers can practice how to determine what a student knows and share ideas on providing instruction that will enable students to achieve the standards.

Standards provide the link between instruction and assessment in the classroom. During the process of planning instruction and assessment, teachers develop achievement targets that are aligned with standards. Appropriate curriculum and instruction will support student progress toward these achievement targets as documented by assessments. When aligning instruction and assessment, teachers should consider five interrelated achievement targets:

• Knowledge students need to master

• Kinds of investigations and performance tasks students need to be able to design and complete

• Skills students must be able to demonstrate

• Products students must be able to create

• Attitudes toward the content area the teacher hopes students attain

Constructive teacher feedback that addresses specific qualities of student work enhances learning. At the beginning of a unit of study teachers should preassess student knowledge and skills. Based upon the preassessment results, teachers should design an instructional program that promotes successful learning experiences for each student. Assessment integrated within a unit should blend strategies such as performance tasks, informal assessments, journals, and more traditional paper-and-pencil tests that parallel daily classroom instruction. Teachers should also strive for assessments that ask students to apply concepts to real-world situations. In addition, assessments need to be fair to all students and accommodate a variety of developmental levels and learning styles.

Inquiry Learning

Inquiry-based learning is an excellent model to support standards. In inquiry-based classrooms, teachers support students as active learners as they explore, carefully observe, plan, and carry out investigations and research, communicate through varied methods, propose explanations and solutions, pose thoughtful questions, and critique their own investigative practices. Teachers in standards-driven, inquiry-based classrooms:

- *Concentrate on collection and use of evidence*

- *Act as facilitators or guides*

- *Help students benefit from mistakes*

- *Model inquiry behaviors and skills*

- *Use appropriate vocabulary*

- *Encourage dialogue among students and the teacher*

- *Pose thoughtful, open-ended questions and help student do the same*

- *Provide a rich variety of materials and resources for investigation*

- *Use raw data and primary sources of information*

- *Assist student with clear oral and written communication*

- *Allow students to expand upon previous inquiry activities. (Krueger & Sutton, 2001, p. 17)*

Inquiry-based learning is not always a hands-on experience. Reading, discussion, and research are good ways to practice inquiry when specific questions and evidence-based arguments are used. Further, a hands-on, inquiry-based experience can fail to help students learn the abilities and understandings of standards-driven inquiry if those learning goals are not explicitly addressed.

Effective Strategies

A variety of instructional methods should be used to reach students with high-quality, standards-based content. Such strategies should:

- *Address different student learning styles*

- *Encourage participation of under-represented students*

- *Support students in constructing their own understanding*

- *Challenge all students*

- *Encourage diverse student cooperation*

- *Encourage the use of inclusionary language in all classroom communication*

- *Involve parents in student learning. (Krueger & Sutton, 2001, p. 3)*

Effective teachers use questioning, classroom observations, interviews, and conferences to facilitate instruction and to inform classroom decisions. Observations framed around students' grasp of concepts, their dispositions toward learning, their communication abilities, and their group work contributions help teachers identify appropriate instructional strategies. The use of multiple means of assessment allows students to diversify thinking and response patterns. A wide variety of assessments can also facilitate classroom focus on standards-based experiences.

In making the transition to a standards-based classroom, teachers should consider the following questions:

1. Are assignments a "one-shot" affair, or do students have the opportunity to continuously revise and improve their work over the course of several days?

2. Are assignments rich in detail and complex in achievement, requiring several days to complete?

3. Do assignments dwell on a single set of knowledge in an individual subject, or do they integrate cumulative knowledge on a subject with several other academic disciplines?

4. When evaluating student work, is only a particular subject being considered, or is student proficiency demanded in every related academic subject?

5. Is the purpose of this activity to build a skill that will be tested in a different form at the end of the semester, or is the activity an opportunity for a student to demonstrate proficiency so that the assignment itself can become an assessment? (Reeves, 1998, pp. 104-105)

For each of these questions above, the contrast between traditional worksheets and standards-based assignments is stark. Meaningful instruction and assessment involving standards includes much more than rote memorization and regurgitation. When using standards effectively to plan daily instruction and cumulative assessments, teachers will find that students are learning and remembering much more and applying learning in better ways to real-world situations.

Special Education

Although standards are meant to apply to all children, the claim often rings hollow when applied to students with disabilities. Many teachers incorrectly assume that students with disabilities are unable to work toward proficiency because assignments need to be adapted to meet different learning abilities. Ysseldyke, Thurlow, and Shriner state in their report *Students with Disabilities & Educational Standards: Recommendations for Policy & Practice* (1994) that excluding students with disabilities from standards activities "perpetuates the myth of inherent differences between general and special education and continues the division among programs" (p. 13). One solution offered by the researchers is to develop one set of standards and expect widely varying student performance relative to them. Since student performance relative to the standards will always vary- regardless of whether students with disabilities are included- progress toward the standards should be based on some relative baseline measure, even the student's own personal baseline. "The expected range of performance is monitored for different students or student groups. Improvement over time toward set standards, but interpreted through initial performance or developmental level, presents an opportunity to include all students in efforts to adopt standards-based classrooms" (pp. 13-14).

Students with disabilities can learn the essential concepts embodied in standards-based instruction. Some students may need different presentations of the information; others may need less detail and lower levels of difficulty. To meet the needs of these students, educators can expand the standards to reflect the most basic levels of learning. By setting flexible learning goals and by working backwards from the content standards, an educator can determine where the student is in relation to achieving the standard and teach to the next horizon.

In a chemistry class, for example, the lesson may focus on balancing a chemical equation. Most of the students will work on demonstrating the changes mathematically. A student with significant disabilities who needs to have the content simplified may instead give an example and explain that matter doesn't simply "go away" when undergoing a chemical reaction. The concept is the same, but the level of difficulty and content differ.

When requiring compliance for the education of children with disabilities, there are implications for local policymakers and greater challenges for the team of professionals and parents who develop the IEPs. While they must determine the appropriate level of instruction, the curriculum can be too specific to adapt for students with a wide range of learning needs. Additionally, the IEP must address other identified educational needs. For example, a student with an emotional disorder may require instruction in social skills. However, as instruction on the curriculum narrows to the academic content described in the standards, instruction in social skills necessary to get and keep a job may be neglected. Finally, accommodations and modifications of materials and curriculum are often difficult for general classroom teachers to provide (Gajria, Salend, & Hemrick, 1994).

As part of developing standards for all students, teachers and administrators must keep in mind to:

- Expect each student to make progress

- Make fair comparisons among schools

- Examine current programs in order to identify needed changes

- Hold everyone in the system accountable for student achievement

- Encourage complete and accurate reporting of assessments

- Emphasize skills and knowledge for the world of work (Bechard, 2000).

Sample States' Responses

Various states have developed alternate assessments and eligibility prerequisites for student with disabilities (Thompson, Erickson, Thurlow, Ysseldyke, & Callender, 1999). These accommodations for students with disabilities have included the following:

1. Kentucky – Uses a portfolio organized by the child's teacher and scored by other teachers. Only students with severe cognitive disabilities are eligible to participate.
2. Maryland – Uses functional performance tasks, such as making a sandwich, that are videotaped by the teacher and scored by objective scorers. Only students identified with cognitive disabilities can participate.
3. Texas – Allows students with disabilities to take a variety of other tests, including tests from lower grade levels and simplified paper-and-pencil versions of their lowest-level tests. Students who are unable to physically participate in any of these tests are exempted from the testing program.
4. Colorado, Kansas, Missouri – Are piloting standards-based performance events, such as telling a story, which are scored by the student's teacher. Students with significant cognitive disabilities and those with other communication challenges, such as autism, are eligible to take these alternative assessments.

(Note: Changes in the testing of all children under the reauthorization of the Elementary and Secondary Education Act (ESEA), also known as the No Child Left Behind Act, may require states such as those above to make substantial changes to their assessment of children with disabilities.)

Implications of Including Students with Special Needs in Standards-Based Instruction and Assessment

In the policy brief "Students with Disabilities and Standards-Based Reform," Bechard (2000) outlines several recommendations for states and communities proceeding with standards-based reform. These recommendations include:

- Bringing standards-based instruction into institutions of higher education, given that special and general educators alike must take on new roles and collaborate as never before. For example, special educators must learn new content and be able to modify it. General educators must learn the essential concepts of that content and present them at different levels to a more diverse group of students. Teacher preparation programs typically have failed to train these groups of teachers to do these things.

- Providing support for the time and effort standards-based reform requires. This is particularly important for special education teachers where demands on time are already heavy.

- Implementing local policies that support building administrators who build leadership teams to examine school policies and programs and make change happen for all students.

Researchers from the National Center on Educational Outcomes at the University of Minnesota (Thompson & Thurlow, 2001) have pointed to several positive consequences of the participation of students with disabilities in standards-based instruction and assessment. From their surveys, at least two states noted that each of the following took place:

1. Accommodations for students receiving special education services have allowed these students to pursue a regular high school diploma.
2. Higher levels of parental awareness of standards and assessment have emerged, and expectations for students have increased.
3. Use of accommodations, including assistive technology, has increased.
4. Teacher attention to student achievement of skills included on assessments has grown.
5. District awareness of educational issues facing students with disabilities has increased.
6. State and district test scores have not dropped significantly as a result of the inclusion of students with disabilities.
7. Greater effort is being made to include special education personnel in staff development that addresses instruction toward standards.

Using Technology to Help Meet Standards

The use of instructional technology to meet learning standards empowers students by improving skills and concepts through multiple representations, enhanced visualization, and individualized and customized diagnoses, remediation, and evaluation. Using appropriate technology in the learning environment allows students more autonomy in practicing higher-order thinking skills and increases access to opportunities for students to select learning contexts and design investigations. Technology enriches the range and quality of investigations by showing multiple perspectives on abstract ideas and real-world problems. Calculators, spreadsheets, graphing programs, probeware, and programs modeling complex phenomena provide cognitive scaffolds to promote complex thinking, design, and learning. Such activities are often motivating because they are learner-focused and authentic, while encouraging critical thinking and creating lasting knowledge (Krueger & Sutton, 2001).

However, instructional technology will only have the desired impact if teaching moves toward more student-centered, inquiry-based practice, as discussed earlier. Indeed, teaching that reflects the current inquiry standards can be made even more effective by appropriate use of technology. Technology-rich, inquiry-based classrooms should have many of the following elements in place:

• Technology is viewed as an essential tool for gathering, storing, manipulating, analyzing, and displaying data

• Students of all abilities and diverse backgrounds are engaged and motivated

• Rich multimedia content is available that meets all students' distinctive learning needs

• Technology is used to augment communication by expanding audiences, creating powerful visuals and sounds through display media, and creating networks for exchange of information and collaboration (Rubin, 1996).

Teachers should assess all their students' needs to inform instruction, particularly for students with disabilities. Each student should be evaluated individually without generalizing, considering needs and preferences, facilities, and available technologies. Some accommodations that might be tried to meet the needs of all students include:

• Acquiring electronic control and collection devices for students with limited dexterity (puff switches, head switches, etc.)

• Using microscopes in conjunction with projectors for students who have visual impairments

• Finding accessible field sites, such as parks and wetlands with ramps and paved walkways

• Assigning individual FM units for students with hearing impairments

• Using closed-captioned videos and CDs

• Utilizing audio or tactile displays and text-reader software

• Using tables instead of desks to encourage students collaboration (Doran, Cawley, Parmar, & Sentman, 1995).

According to Caruso (2001), it is important to note the distinction between assistive technology and instructional technology. Assistive technology is not intended to instruct or teach but is used to increase access to instruction. Assistive technology may be paired with instructional technology to provide students with equitable access to appropriate learning opportunities and successes.

Assistive technology used for all students to meet academic standards may consist of radical, innovative devices for motor impairment or may be fairly common household items. Tape recorders, calculators, and word processors are all productive learning devices for students with learning disabilities. More sophisticated tools such as optical character recognition (OCR), talking calculators and word processors, and speech recognition systems are also effective in the right situation. What these technologies have in common is the ability to compensate for some of the limitations experiences by students with disabilities (Caruso, 2001).

Finding the right technology requires consideration of the intended user, the technology, the context in which the technology will be used, and how these variables fit together. Table 3 highlights a few of the ways

Table 3. Technological Applications for Students with Disabilities

Device	Function	Application
Word Processors	Corrects errors, moves copy, creates neat document	Useful for students with handwriting and spelling difficulties
Semantic Mapping	Diagrams ideas to help create an outline	Useful for visual learners and students who need help organizing material
Reading Pens	Miniature OCR system, but with only one word per time	Useful for students with trouble recognizing printed words
Personal Data Managers	Software or hardware to store information & dates	Useful for students with organizational or memory difficulties
Talking Calculators	Speak numbers, symbols, or operations as pressed	Useful for students who transpose numbers; helps catch errors
Speech Recognition	Changes spoken word to computer text	Useful for students who express themselves better aloud
Alternative Keyboards	Allow users to customize arrangement of keys	Useful for students who have trouble typing on standards keyboards

technology may be used for students of all abilities (Caruso, 2001).

Teaching and Assessing with Standards

Brain research has shown that long-term memory, or true learning, depends upon information that makes sense and has meaning to the learner. Without these connections, students' learning experiences simply add up to a collection of miscellaneous topics and unrelated facts. Integration of subject areas and standards often reveals an inter-dependency among the disciplines, helping students make sense of and understand new information. An example may be connecting a physics topic with physical education or sports to show how the laws of physics impact the movements of the body.

Thematic Learning

Thematic learning based on problem solving is one way to integrate and meet content standards. Integrating units based on a real-world problem can deepen students' understanding of concepts and content. In integrated problem-based units, students must find a fair solution to a problem by using multiple resources. Even in the face of increased standardized testing, integrated thematic units can meet the learning needs of students while preparing them for the requirements of state and local standards. According to Gordon F. Vars, emeritus professor of Teaching, Leadership, and Curriculum Studies at Kent State University, "Essentially you start with the kids and their concerns, both about themselves and with the world, and then you bring in the standards-what the adults want the kids to learn-and blend the two together. Find something the kids can relate to while getting the standards covered" (Allen, 2002, p. c).

Thematic lessons involving standards-based instruction and appropriate uses of technology share several components. Specifically, such lessons

- Allow students to play a role in an adult-level, real-world problem

- Require reinforcement of all four core academic standards-language arts, mathematics, science, and social studies

- Usually include the arts

- Reinforce the students' ability to understand any academic concept when they have an opportunity to put this knowledge to use in a real situation (Reeves, 1998).

Sample Thematic Unit Involving Standards

To help students become effective problem solvers, the classroom should present problems for them to investigate and solve. Further, to assess revised teaching methods, classroom instruction should include activities geared toward producing a performance product. This product could be three-dimensional, print-based, or computer-based (Anderson & Anderson, 2000).

Case Study

The following case study demonstrates how a team of teachers worked together to help all of their students produce performance products in order to meet their standards in language arts and mathematics.

Language Arts Planning

Ms. Carpenter wanted to develop an integrated unit for her third-grade classroom that was built around the theme of listening while incorporating the class focus on cultural influences of the community. She had recently purchased a CD-ROM version of *Why Mosquitoes Buzz in People's Ears* (Aardema, 2000) as an example of the culture of some of her students (see Figure 1). Ms. Carpenter wanted her plans to include all of her students with disabilities, so she asked for assistance in planning from her students' case manager, Mr. Antons. Together, they looked at the classroom goals and the individual benchmarks on all the IEPs of the students and mapped out activities in which all could participate during the unit. Table 4 shows the plan that the two teachers developed. This case study outlines how the two teachers, the sign language interpreter, and the paraprofessional working with the students with physical disabilities collaborated to develop and present the language arts and mathematics activities of the unit.

When Ms. Carpenter and Mr. Antons met, Ms. Carpenter shared with him that she wanted to create a thematic unit centered around fables that integrated classroom technology. She hoped to build the unit around the story *Why Mosquitoes Buzz in People's Ears*. Wanting to address all the needs in her classroom, Ms. Carpenter asked Mr. Antons to review the specific special needs within her classroom. The third-grade classroom included students with differing reading and writing skills, students with varying mathematics skill, one boy (William) who used a sign language interpreter due to hearing impairments, and one girl (Diane) who was in a wheelchair, paralyzed from the waist down and with limited fine-motor movement in her hands, the result of an accident with a three-wheeler.

The two teachers planned the language arts activities for the classroom. They first selected the appropriate standards from the national academic standards for language arts (National Council of Teachers of English and International Reading Association, 2001). Table 5 provides a listing of the language arts standards. For this lesson, Ms. Carpenter and Mr. Antons felt that the following standards should be included in the instruction:

- Standard 1
  (wide variety of print and non-print texts ...)
- Standard 2
  (literature from many periods and genre ...)
- Standard 3
  (apply a wide range of strategies ...)
- Standard 4
  (adjust the use of spoken, written, and visual language ...)
- Standard 5
  (wide range of writing strategies ...)
- Standard 6
  (knowledge of language structure and conventions ...)
- Standard 10
  (use of first-language fluency ...)

Language Arts Lesson

Ms. Carpenter created a context for the unit by having the students play the game "Telephone" to demonstrate how a message can be misinterpreted if it is not heard directly from the source and listened to carefully. She had previously consulted William's sign language interpreter about his participation in the activity. The interpreter suggested that she listen to the mes-

Figure 1. *Why Mosquitoes Buzz in People's Ears* **(CD-ROM).**

sage, then ask William to repeat it back to her using ASL sign language, so that he had to interpret the message from one source and translate it into ASL to pass on. The sign language interpreter would then translate William's interpreted message back into English to pass onto the next child. Sitting in her wheelchair, Diane would have no problem with the activity other than having other children lean towards her to speak to her and listen to her. The children enjoyed the activity and had a lively discussion about the very different message that was repeated by the last child.

Ms. Carpenter began the reading lesson by addressing the language arts standard for "appropriate use of vocabulary for different genre." She started by introducing the students to vocabulary words that might be encountered in reading *Why Mosquitoes Buzz in People's Ears*. Since much of the vocabulary in this book consists of the names of animals who appear in the story, Ms. Carpenter and Mr. Antons decided that this would be useful vocabulary to include in this instructional unit. To help the children learn the vocabulary, Mr. Antons suggested that the children develop a *Kidspiration* (Inspiration Software, Inc., 2000)

graphic organizer of the animal words by using pictures downloaded from the Internet to be labeled on their graphic. Since the program reads the text, Mr. Antons felt that the children could learn the vocabulary quickly by hearing the words spoken as they were written on the screen. However, this activity created problems for Diane, so Ms. Carpenter and Mr. Antons collaborated to help her with the use of the computer. With limited movement or strength in her hands, dragging a mouse and using keys on the keyboard were difficult actions for her. She was equipped with an *Intellikeys* keyboard that also had a switch attached for use when needed. Using this keyboard in conjunction with the overlay that functioned as an alternative keyboard, Diane could use *Kidspiration* to create her own graphic (see Figure 2). The paraprofessional assigned to Diane also helped to develop the graphic to allow Diane to keep up with the class.

Next, Ms. Carpenter presented the CD-ROM to her students as an example of an African folk tale. She connected the CD-ROM to the LCD panel and projected the images onto the screen in front of the classroom. Next, she assigned small groups to reread the story using the CD at one of

Table 4. Sample Learning Plan Developed by Ms. Carpenter and Mr. Antons

Classroom Activity	National Standard	Materials Needed	IEP Objective	Activity Modification	Materials to Be Developed
"Telephone"	Appreciate text	None extra	Listen to appreciate text	None needed except for William. Have sign language interpret translate to ASL	None
Vocabulary introduction	Use strategies to read text	Kidspiration Internet	Use strategies to read text; Use the Internet	None needed for William other than translation; Diane – Intellikeys keyboard with switch; others – Kidspiration's reading feature	Example graphic
Why Mosquitoes Buzz in People's Ears CD-ROM	Use different strategies to read different genres	CD-ROM	Using alternate inputs and reading	Set up ClickIt controls to CD-ROM for student and/or switch-activated story	ClickIt program - CD; Hyperstudio stack; review CD
Virtual zoo	Onomatopoeia as a strategy to interact with literature	Hyperstudio; Button List NBA; Speechviewer	Use onomatopoeia; use switch	Intellikeys keyboard; paraprofessional, sign language to interpret explanations	Example virtual zoo
Writing a fable	Knowledge of different genres	Draft: Builder; Co-Writer; Write OutLoud	Write fable; use Draft: Builder; Co-Writer; Write OutLoud	Paraprofessional to aid Diane in using software; sign language interpretation of explanation and videotaping of William's fable and aid in translation from ASL into print	Example fable and example of ASL-developed fable
Understanding symmetry	Geometry and problem solving	Microsoft Word; Hyperstudio, Intellimathics	Symmetry; using a switch; using Intellikeys	Hyperstudio NBA Button Lister	Hyperstudio Symmetrical objects stack; African mask

the six computers in her classroom. Mr. Antons had used *Hyperstudio©* (Knowledge Adventure, 2000) to develop an on-screen review activity with directions in a speaking textbox to accompany the CD. The children were able to open both programs, going between them to review parts of the story to answer the questions (see Figure 3). Mr. Antons programmed the stack to speak the children's responses to help those with reading and writing difficulties and for screen scanning, so that Diane could operate the activity. He also created a *ClickIt* (Intellitools, Inc., 1996) program to allow Diane to operate the CD. Since this activity was all text-based, William only used the services of his interpreter to supplement the activities.

Table 5. English/Language Arts Standards

1. Students read a wide range of print and non-print texts to build an understanding of texts, of themselves, and of the cultures of the United States and the world; to acquire new information; to respond to the needs and demands of society and the workplace; and for personal fulfillment. Among these texts are fiction and nonfiction, classic and contemporary works.

2. Students read a wide range of literature from many periods in many genres to build an understanding of the many dimensions (e.g., philosophical, ethical, aesthetic) of human experience.

3. Students apply a wide range of strategies to comprehend, interpret, evaluate, and appreciate texts. They draw on their prior experience, their interactions with other readers and writers, their knowledge of word meaning and of other texts, their word identification strategies, and their understanding of textual features (e.g., sound-letter correspondence, sentence structure, context, graphics).

4. Students adjust their use of spoken, written, and visual language (e.g., conventions, style, vocabulary) to communicate effectively with a variety of audiences and for different purposes.

5. Students employ a wide range of strategies as they write and use different writing process elements appropriately to communicate with different audiences for a variety of purposes.

6. Students apply knowledge of language structure, language conventions (e.g., spelling and punctuation), media techniques, figurative language, and genre to create, critique, and discuss print and non-print texts.

7. Students conduct research on issues and interests by generating ideas and questions, and by posing problems. They gather, evaluate, and synthesize data from a variety of sources (e.g., print and non-print texts, artifacts, people) to communicate their discoveries in ways that suit their purpose and audience.

8. Students use a variety of technological and information resources (e.g., libraries, databases, computer networks, video) to gather and synthesize information and to create and communicate knowledge.

9. Students develop an understanding of and respect for diversity in language use, patterns, and dialects across cultures, ethnic groups, geographic regions, and social roles.

10. Students whose first language is not English make use of their first language to develop competency in the English language arts and to develop understanding of content across the curriculum.

11. Students participate as knowledgeable, reflective, creative, and critical members of a variety of literacy communities.

12. Students use spoken, written, and visual language to accomplish their own purposes (e.g., for learning, enjoyment, persuasion, and the exchange of information).

(National Council of Teachers of English & International Reading Association, 2001, www.ncte.org/standards/standards.shtml)

Figure 2. Sample file created with *Kidspiration*.

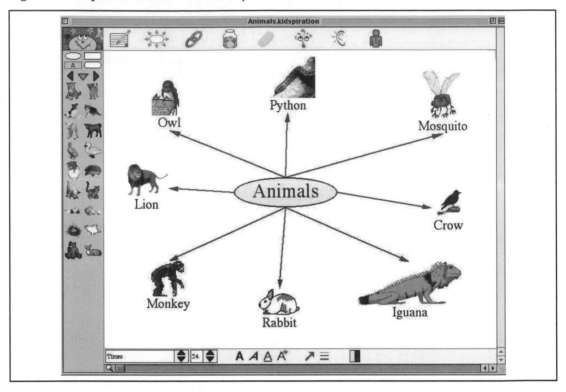

Figure 3. Sample file created with *HyperStudio*.

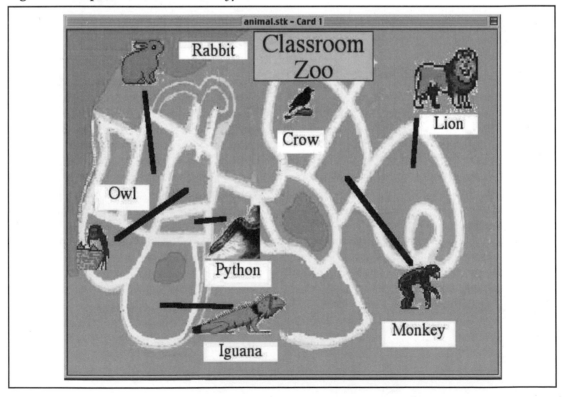

Why Mosquitoes Buzz in People's Ears was an excellent way for Ms. Carpenter to introduce the idea of onomatopoeia or the use of text to represent the sounds made by animals. After explaining how onomatopoeia works in literature and looking at the examples found on the CD, Ms. Carpenter asked the students to create their own examples of onomatopoeia by using *Hyperstudio* to create a virtual zoo. Using the animal pictures selected for the *Kidspiration* graphic, the children copied and pasted them into a zoo made with the tools used in *Hyperstudio* (see Figure 3). The children created a map of their zoo and placed buttons at the location of each animal. Then they wrote the text that they thought represented the sound that the animal made in a textbox. When the user clicked a button programmed to use *BlabberMouth NBA* (New Button Action) to read that text, the sound was made. *Blabbermouth NBA* uses speech synthesis to read the text and pronounces the sound according to phonetic rules, so it was necessary for the children to spell the sound properly according to phonetic rules, or the sound would not be made as they expected.

Mr. Antons reminded Ms. Carpenter that William might have trouble with this activity, given his lack of experience with sound. He made a sample stack with sounds typed in for closely related animals, so that William could use this as a model for completing his stack. Also, William's sign language interpreter programmed *IBM's Speechviewer* (International Business Machines, 2001) to judge the sounds made by the computer in William's stack. The interpreter recorded the sound of William's animals, so that as William typed closer and closer approximations of the interpreter's model, the balloon in the software got larger and larger, telling William that his animal sound was getting closer and closer to what it ought to sound like.

Diane needed to use her *Intellikeys* keyboard with the alternative keyboard overlay to use *Hyperstudio* to develop her stack. Each child in the class also used *Button Lister*, a *Hyperstudio NBA*, to make his or her stack accessible for Diane when she used her switch. The NBA programmed buttons to be scannable, so that Diane could activate them with her switch. It highlights one button at a time, so Diane used her switch to activate the button. Using this activity, the children addressed language arts standard 6 (see Table 5).

Ms. Carpenter felt that the CD provided a good way to address the standard of exploring different genres in literature by introducing the third graders to fables. After learning that a fable is a story in which animals are the characters who encounter a problem and resolve it, the children wrote their own fables for a book to take home to parents.

Mr. Antons reminded Ms. Carpenter that the children with reading and writing problems would struggle with the activity. He suggested that they use *Draft:Builder* (Don Johnston, Inc., 2001) to organize their fable. The program would not only help all the children organize their fables, it also included some additional features that aided students with reading and writing problems. For example, the speaking feature of the program helped the children who benefited from hearing text spoken. Using text-to-speech synthesis, the program read the words that the child needed to hear aloud. The program also worked with the word prediction program *Co Writer* (Don Johnston, Inc., 2001). If the student's spelling or vocabulary problems were severe, word prediction would display several words that made sense in the sentence. These words may be programmed to be read to the child, allowing the child to click on the word that was wanted. The draft of the fable could be imported into a talking word processor designed to help the poorer readers and writers. In this case, Mr. Antons suggested one that he was familiar with, *Write OutLoud* (Don Johnston, Inc. 2001).

Mr. Antons suggested using *Co-Writer* and *Write OutLoud* for Diane also. The two programs could be used with the *Intellikeys* mouse alternative and were scannable, allowing Diane to choose the best method for her to write her fable, either with the mouse alternative or by using her switch to select the letters and words for her fable.

Mr. Antons worked with the sign language interpreter to develop a method that would help William write his fable. In general, children with hearing impairments might not have problems writing fables of their own unless they also had reading and writing problems, as was the case with William. According to William's plan, he would sign his fable to the interpreter who used a digital videocamera to tape it and then burn it to CD format. Then, using the CD so that they could pause it when needed, they would work together to help put William's story into written format. Mr. Antons suggested that William also use *Co-Writer* to help him find vocabulary words to develop his story. His interpreter signed the predicted words to William if he did not know them, and he then judged which word he wanted for his fable. Then the sentences that William developed could be transferred to a word processor.

Language Arts Reflection

Ms. Carpenter and Mr. Antons reflected on the reading portion of their joint unit when it was finished. They were pleased that all the children were able to successfully interact with the story *Why Mosquitoes Buzz in People's Ears*. Mr. Antons reported that there were no problems for the students with reading and writing problems. The sign language interpreter and the paraprofessional reported that William and Diane were able to fully participate. Everyone was pleased that all of the students were able to successfully take part in the activity and work toward meeting their standards in language arts.

Mathematics Planning

Ms. Carpenter told Mr. Antons that their math curriculum would be introducing geometry concepts during the time she was using *Why Mosquitoes Buzz in People's Ears* to teach reading. Specifically, they would be addressing symmetry. She needed to address the national mathematics standards in geometry (see Table 6) that were appropriate to her students' grade level and curriculum, specifically the following two geometry standards: a) instructional programs should enable all students to analyze characteristics and properties of two- and three-dimensional geometric shapes and develop mathematical arguments about geometric relationships; and b) instructional programs should enable all students to apply transformations and use symmetry to analyze mathematical situations (National Council of Teachers of Mathematics, 2000). Mr. Antons noted that *Microsoft Word* had a feature called Autoshapes that would help her to draw symmetrical shapes for this lesson.

While helping Ms. Carpenter to plan the lesson, Mr. Antons suggested that they also address problem solving, in particular the national mathematics standard related to building new mathematical knowledge through problem solving. Mr. Antons suggested that since they were exploring the culture of Africa in their reading lessons, they could complement the cultural experience by using software to create symmetrical shapes for African masks. He suggested that tangrams, a concept with which the students were already familiar, be used to help children with learning problems build on knowledge they already had to help them understand symmetry.

Mathematics Lesson

Ms. Carpenter began the lesson by introducing the concept of symmetry. She wanted the children to distinguish between symmetrical objects and nonsymmetrical objects on a handout she developed using *Microsoft Word* and the Autoshapes function. At Mr. Antons' suggestion, and with his assistance, she copied and pasted the activity into *Hyperstudio*, so that she could have the children click on symmetrical objects and have the program judge the correctness of their choice. In this way, the activity would make use of *Hyperstudio*'s Button Scanner NBA and be accessible for Diane using her switch. Ms. Carpenter also typed directions that could be accessed and read with the *Blabbermouth NBA* to help the children who benefited from repeated directions. William received additional interpretation of the concept by his interpreter and assistance on difficult text that he could not read.

Next, at Mr. Antons' suggestion, Ms. Carpenter complemented her cultural theme by having the children create their own symmetrical objects. Since the class was reading an African folktale, she followed his suggestion that the children create symmetrical African masks from the tangram activity built into *Intellimathics* (Intellitools, Inc., 20021, 2002), a program designed to supplement math instruction, thus addressing the geometry standards that she wanted to cover. Following Ms. Carpenter's review of tangrams and her explanation of

Table 6. National Math Standards (NCTM)-Geometry and Problem Solving

Geometry
• Instructional programs PK-12 should enable all students to-
• Analyze characteristics and properties of two- and three-dimensional geometric shapes and develop mathematical arguments about geometric relationships;
• Specify locations and describe spatial relationships using coordinate geometry and other representational systems;
• Apply transformations and use symmetry to analyze mathematical situations;
• Use visualization, spatial reasoning, and geometric modeling to solve problems.
Problem Solving
• Instructional programs PK-12 should enable all students to-
• Build new mathematical knowledge through problem solving;
• Solve problems that arise in mathematics and in other contexts;
• Apply and adapt a variety of appropriate strategies to solve problems;
• Monitor and reflect on the process of mathematical problem solving. (National Council of Teachers of Mathematics, 2000, www.nctm.org/standards/standards.htm)

symmetry, Mr. Antons taught the class to use *Intellimathics*, which was accessible to Diane since it was designed to be used with *Intellikeys*. To do this activity, the children had to select, move, and rotate tangrams to create a mask. To be a symmetrical, each side had to mirror the other side, so the tangrams had to be positioned as mirror images of each other, thus addressing the problem-solving standards the two teachers wanted to address. Mr. Antons had made an example (see Figure 4), so that the children would understand what they were to do. Each child then developed his or her own African mask using *Intellimathics*. Mr. Antons and Ms. Carpenter made themselves available for additional explanations, as did William's interpreter and Diane's paraprofessional, both of whom had already been trained by Mr. Antons in using the software. An added feature was that the software spoke the words, thus helping those with reading and writing difficulties. Diane was be able to use her *Intellikeys* keyboard to create her African mask, while William received additional ASL translation as needed from his interpreter to complete his project.

Mathematics Lesson Reflection

The students in Ms. Carpenter's classroom made colorful African masks that the parents were pleased to see at open house. The masks showed the children's understanding and application of the concept of symmetry in the math curriculum. The sign language interpreter and Diane's paraprofessional were pleased that the masks their students made demonstrated an understanding of symmetry. Both teachers felt that the lesson was successful in demonstrating the students' grasp of the mathematics standards in problem solving and geometry.

Conclusion

Under the No Child Left Behind Act, schools must be accountable for student achievement related to state learning standards. Teachers must not only be familiar with these standards, but also with different teaching techniques for reaching them. The integration of technology into daily lessons provides students with a practical, hands-on method of connecting facts and conceptual information with real-world examples. As standards-based, thematic lessons are prepared, teachers need to consider the following questions:

Figure 4. Sample file created with *Intellimathics*.

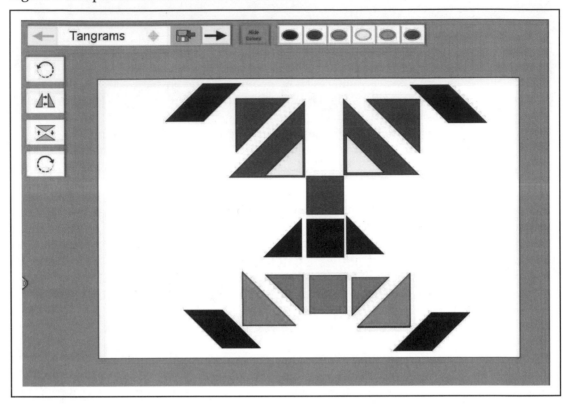

- What does it mean to meet the standard?

- What type of instruction best fits the standard?

- Are there multiple effective ways to teach and learn the material?

- What learning needs are required by students?

- What hands-on experiences provide the best concrete learning?

- What technology resources could help students learn the material?

- How can professional team members collaborate in the planning and teaching, especially for students with special needs?

- How can all students be actively involved in each lesson?

- What assessment(s) will show students learned and retained the material?

Setting classroom goals and objectives for student learning is not new in American education. What has changed is the new direct role played by federal and state governments in the establishment of learning standards for all students. Teachers must be knowledgeable about the required academic standards and how to best plan for teaching and assessing them. The use of multiple teaching methods, including the integration of instructional technology, will enable teachers to effectively reach all students under their direction.

References

Aardema, V. (2000). *Why mosquitoes buzz in people's ears* [Computer software]. New York: Scholastic, Inc.

Allen, R. (Ed.). (2002, Summer). Viewpoint. Focus on Integrated Curriculum. *ASCD*, pp. b-c.

Anderson, C.L., & Anderson, K.M. (2000). An introduction to *Kid Pix Studio Deluxe* and its potential for enabling students to meet high academic standards. *Special Education Technology Practice*, 2(4), 24-30.

Anderson, L., Fiester, L., Gonzales, M., & Pechman, E. (Eds.). (1996, Spring). *Improving America's Schools: A newsletter on issues in school reform*. Washington, DC: U.S. Dept. of Education.

Bechard, S. (2000). *Students with disabilities and standards-based reform*. Denver, CO: Mid-Continent Research for Education and Learning,

Caruso, G. (2001). Assistive technology: Finding the right fit. *Inside Education, 1*(4), 26-29.

Don Johnston, Inc. (2001). *Draft: Builder* [Computer software]. Volo, IL: Author.

Don Johnston, Inc. (2001). *Co-Writer 4000* [Computer software]. Volo, IL: Author.

Don Johnston, Inc. (2001). *Write OutLoud* (Version 3.0) [Computer software]. Author.

Doran, R., Cawley, J., Parmar, R., & Sentman, R. (1995). *Science for the handicapped*. Washington, DC: National Science Association.

Gajria, M., Salend, S. J., & Hemrick, M. A. (1994). Teacher acceptability of testing modifications for mainstreamed students. *Learning Disabilities Research & Practice, 9*(4), 236-243.

Glaser, R., & Linn, R. (1993). Forword. In L. Shepard (Ed.), *Setting performance standards for student achievement* (pp. xiii-xiv). Stanford, CA: National Academy of Education, Stanford University.

Hickey, M.E. (2002, September). Viewpoint: Building the capacity to make standards-driven reform work. *eSchool News*, p. 48.

Inspiration Software, Inc. (2000). *Inspiration* [Computer software]. Portland, OR: Author.

Inspiration Software, Inc. (2000). *Kidspiration* [Computer software]. Portland, OR: Author.

Intellitools, Inc. (2001, 2002). *Intellimathics* [Computer software]. Petaluna, CA: Author.

Intellitools, Inc. (1996). *ClickIt* [Computer software]. Petaluna, CA: Author.

International Business Machines. (2001). *Speechviewer (Version 3.0)* [Computer software]. Boston, MA: Riverdeep, Inc.

Kenosha Unified School District No. 1. (1999). *KUSD standards and benchmarks*. Kenosha, WI. Retrieved December 26, 2002, from: www.kusd.edu/lessons/sb/sb_toc.htm.

Knowledge Adventure. (2000). Hyperstudio (Version 4.2) [Computer software]. Torrance, CA: Author.

Krueger, A., & Sutton, J. (Eds.). (2001). *EDThoughts: What we know about science teaching and learning*. Aurora, CO: Mid-Continent Research for Education and Learning.

Marzano, R.J., & Kendall, J.S. (1996). *A comprehensive guide to designing standards- based districts, schools, and classrooms*. Aurora, CO: McREL.

McLaughlin, M., & Shepard, L. (1995). *Improving education through standards-based reform: A report by the national academy of education panel on standards-based education reform*. Stanford, CA: National Academy of Education.

Mizell, M.H. (2002). *Shooting for the sun: The message of middle school reform*. New York: The Edna McConnell Clark Foundation.

National Commission on Excellence in Education. (1983). *A nation at risk: The imperative for educational reform*. Washington, DC: United States Department of Education.

National Academy of Science. (1995). *Science education standards*. Washington, DC: National Academy Press.

National Council of Teachers of English and International Reading Association. (2001). *Standards for the English language arts*. Retrieved December 26, 2002, from: www.ncte.org/standards/standards.shtml.

National Council of Teachers of Mathematics. (2000). *Standards for school mathematics*. Retrieved December 28, 2002, from: www.nctm.org/standards/standards.htm.

Ravitch, D. (1995). *National standards in American education: A citizen's guide*. Washington, DC: Brookings Institution.

Reeves, D. B. (1998). *Making standards work: How to implement standards-based assessment in the classroom, school, and district*. Denver, CO: Advanced Learning Centers.

Rubin, A. (1996). Educational technology: Support for inquiry-based learning. In *Technology infusion and school change: Perspectives and practices*. Cambridge, MA: Technical Education Research Centers.

Shepard, L. (1995). *Improving education through standards-based reform: A report by the national academy of education panel on standards-based education reform.* Stanford, CA: National Academy of Education.

Smith, M.S., & O'Day, J. (1991). Systemic school reform. In S. H. Fuhrman & B. Malen (Eds.), *The politics of curriculum and testing (Politics of Education Association Yearbook, 1990)* (pp. 233-267). London: Taylor & Francis.

Swanson, C.B., & Stevenson, D.L. (2002). Standards-based reform in practice: Evidence on state policy and classroom instruction from the NAEP state assessments, *Educational Evaluation and Policy Analysis, 24*(1), 1-27.

Thompson, S., Erickson, R., Thurlow, M., Ysseldyke, J., & Callender, S. (1999). *Status of the states in the development of alternate assessments* (Synthesis Report 31). Minneapolis: University of Minnesota, National Center on Educational Outcomes.

Thompson, S., & Thurlow, M. (2001). *2001 State special education outcomes: A report on state activities at the beginning of a new decade.* Minneapolis: University of Minnesota, National Center on Educational Outcomes. Retrieved November 15, 2002, from: education. umn.edu/NCEO/OnlinePubs/2001State Report.html.

United States Department of Education. (2003). Retrieved December 31, 2003, from www.ed.gov/nclb/landing.jhtml

Ysseldyke, J., Thurlow, M., & Shriner, J. (1994). *Students with disabilities & educational standards: Recommendations for policy & practice* (Policy Directions No. 2). Minneapolis: University of Minnesota, National Center on Educational Outcomes. Retrieved November 15, 2002, from education. umn.edu/ NCEO/OnlinePubs/Policy 2.html.

28

Using Technology to Support Struggling Readers: A Review of the Research

Nicole Strangman and Bridget Dalton

Reading is arguably the most important academic skill for students to learn, influencing not only their success in school, but their eventual opportunities for employment, civic contribution, and personal enrichment. For many students, poor reading achievement constitutes a major barrier to learning and opportunity. The results of the 2003 U.S. National Assessment of Education Progress (NAEP) reading assessment document the enormity of the problem. Thirty-seven percent of tested 4th graders and 25% of tested 8th graders scored below basic reading achievement level on the NAEP reading assessment (National Center for Education Statistics, 2003). For a range of reasons including reading disability, learning disability, and physical disability, these students, unable to read and comprehend essential learning materials, will suffer impaired access, participation, and progress throughout the curriculum.

In this digital age, communicative media and forms are multiplying and increasing the literacy demands on students. Students must prepare for an environment where they will spend more time reading and using information on the Internet than they will reading from a printed book (Leu, 2000). While new media increase the need for more effective and more broadly defined literacy instruction, they also introduce a host of possibilities for strengthening literacy instruction and supporting struggling readers in the challenging task of reading for understanding in multiple genres, and for diverse purposes.

Digital technologies such as computer-mediated text, text-to-speech, speech recognition, hypermedia, and computer programs directed at specific reading skills, to name only a few, are an exciting new focus for literacy research. Digital technologies have the potential to support struggling readers in both a compensatory fashion, providing access to text (Edyburn, 2002a, 2002b, 2003), and a remedial fashion, helping students learn how to read with understanding (Rose & Dalton, 2002; Rose & Meyer, 2002). Although it can be difficult to choose between compensatory and remedial interventions (Edyburn, 2002b, 2003), these two methods of action can potentially have a valuable and mutually beneficial impact on struggling readers (Edyburn, 2003; Rose & Stahl, 2004).

The intent of this chapter is to provide an accessible introduction to the topic of technology to support struggling readers and identify the more promising technology-based literacy approaches based on a review of the research literature. The reviewed research includes studies specific to students with special needs and other studies not specific in this way but clearly focused on students with reading difficulties.

Research Methods

The literature search for this review encompassed articles (including but not limited to peer-reviewed articles) published between 1992 and 2002. For reviews of earlier research readers are directed to MacArthur, Ferretti,

Okolo, and Cavalier (2001), Okolo, Bahr, and Rieth (1993), and Torgesen and Barker (1995). Two methods were used to search the literature for publications relevant to reading and technology in education: manual browsing of a subset of journals known to publish research dealing wiht special education and keyword searches on the online PsychInfo database.

The following journals were manually searched: *Journal of Special Education Technology, Reading Research Quarterly, Journal of Literacy Research, Journal of Learning Disabilities, Learning Disabilities Research and Practice,* and *Exceptional Children.* Articles with the following keywords in the title or abstract were flagged for review: fluency, reading, phonemic awareness, vocabulary, comprehension, decoding, word attack, struggling readers, readers with disabilities, and technology.

PsychInfo searches were conducted using the following title/abstract/full text keywords: computer and reading, electronic and reading, concept map and reading, graphic organizer and reading, semantic map and reading, text-to-speech, technology and reading, video, videodisc, drill and practice and reading, software and reading, literacy and semantic map, literacy and concept map, literacy and graphic organizer, literacy and software, and literacy and technology. Search results were further restricted by selecting the following Limit Search options: English language, publication year 1992-2002, journal articles, preschool education, elementary education, elementary secondary education, primary education, intermediate grades, secondary education, middle schools, junior high schools, and high schools. The final round of searches was conducted in November of 2002. Although our search was strategic it nevertheless fell short of being comprehensive. Some relevant articles do not appear in this review because they were not identified in our search or could not be accessed in a timely fashion.

Articles were excluded using the following deletion criteria: topic area outside reading (e.g., spelling, writing, mathematics), intervention not involving technology, non-school setting, college or university setting, and focus outside of special education or struggling readers. Studies including the following specific sample populations were selected: students with learning disabilities, students with reading disability, students with below-average reading performance, students with autism, students with physical or mental handicaps, and students with deafness or hearing disability. Although some of these populations fall outside of special education, we believe that their members' status as struggling readers makes their inclusion appropriate for this review. Studies that used mixed samples including students outside these groups were also reviewed.

The following discussion will address the promising uses of technology for each major are of literacy: phonemic awareness, phonics/word recognition, vocabulary, fluency, comprehension, and engagement, culminating in a look at universal design and literacy learning.

Phonemic Awareness

Correlational studies have identified phonemic awareness as a strong predictor for early reading success (Goswami, 2000). And, the majority of students with reading disabilities have weakness in phonological processing (Liberman, Shankweiler, & Liberman, 1989; Stanovich, 1988; Torgesen, 1993). The National Reading Panel (NRP, 2000) confirmed the effectiveness of phonemic awareness instruction with not only normally progressing readers but also at-risk readers and readers with disabilities. It also spoke in favor of computer-based delivery methods, emphasizing, however, the need for further investigation, "More research is needed to determine whether and how PA might be taught more effectively using computers" (pp. 2-44). Although the Panel did not speak directly to the intersection of these two research strands, computers and special education, our review of the recent literature suggests there is promise in computer-based approaches to phonemic awareness training for students in special education.

While studies of computer and software programs for developing phonemic awareness are the most plentiful in the technology and special education research base the overall number of studies conducted in the last decade-seven-is still small. However, all seven studies support the effectiveness of training phonemic awareness on the computer. For example, a series of investigations by Wise, Olson, Ring, and Johnson (Olson, Wise, Ring, & Johnson, 1997; Wise & Olson, 1995; Wise, Ring, & Olson, 1999) demonstrates clear benefits of providing struggling readers (2nd to 5th grade) with literacy programs that emphasize explicit phonemic awareness instruction and practice on the computer. Common elements of these programs include computer time reading with speech and phonological decoding support and practice with computer software programs such as Phonological Analysis of Letters, NON (non-word reading), Marvin (articulatory awareness and sound manipulation), and Spello (manipulation of letters and sounds). These interventions have proven more successful than both regular instruction (Wise et al., 1999) and treatment controls involving comprehension strategy training and free time on the computer (Olson et al., 1997; Wise & Olson, 1995). Training that involved explicit instruction in sound manipulation was most effective. However, followup tests (Olson et al., 1997) suggest that students may need to spend more than the experimental 25 hours of training with these programs in order to make lasting gains in phonemic awareness.

Somewhat different forms of phonological awareness were emphasized in *DaisyQuest* and *Daisy's Castle*, two computer programs that use a game format to provide explicit tutorial instruction and practice in phonemic awareness. The versions used by Barker and Torgesen (1995) provided instruction in rhyme identification; identification of middle, beginning, and end sounds in words; recognition of words that can be formed from a series of phonemes presented as onset and rhyme; recognition of words that can be formed from a series of separately presented phonemes; and counting of sounds in words. First-grade poor readers who spent two weeks working with the computer programs made significantly greater gains on a computerized phonemic awareness test and a phoneme segmentation test than did students who received teacher-delivered phonemic awareness instruction instead. Comparisons to a control group that spent the same amount of time using math software were also significant, suggesting the effect was not due to engagement alone. Further, improvements on tests of phoneme elision, blending, and sound categorization were also greater than those of the control groups but did not reach significance.

A more recent investigation by Mitchell and Fox (2001) investigated the impact of *DaisyQuest* and *Daisy's Castle* computer programs with a group of kindergarten and first-grade at-risk readers. Their version of the software maintained the instruction and practice in rhyme identification and identification of middle, beginning, and end sounds in words but added instruction in phoneme segmentation and blending. A four-week daily regimen with the software was as effective as similar, teacher-delivered instruction at developing the trained skills as well as phoneme isolation. Both the computer and teacher regimens were superior to a control intervention involving work with math and drawing software.

Kerstholt, van Bon and Schreuder (1994) investigated different types of phonemic segmentation provided via the computer. Students with disabilities (mean age about eight years) were trained using just auditory stimuli provided by the experimenter (experimenter reads word to be named and provides oral feedback on student's response) or both auditory and visual stimuli (as the child pronounced each segment of the training word, the relevant grapheme was displayed on screen). Students in the two groups performed equally well on tests of phonemic segmentation, suggesting that for students with learning disabilities carrying out this type of task, auditory support may be sufficient.

The approaches discussed so far all represent examples of direct, explicit phonemic awareness instruction. However, attempts to indirectly improve phonemic awareness have also generally met with positive results. For example, Heimann, Nelson, Tjus and Gillberg (1995) reported that preschool students with autism or mixed handicaps made significant gains in phonemic awareness following three to four months of working with a multimedia computer program that teaches vocabulary and sentence creation. Students created sentences by pressing image icons on a keyboard, and the program used animation to illustrate them. It also provided feedback on sentence construction. Improvements in phonemic awareness were still apparent one semester after the intervention. Unfortunately, the meaningfulness of these findings is unclear given the absence of a control group.

Computer and software programs are not the only technologies with demonstrated effectiveness at improving phonological awareness. Two studies suggest that students with learning disabilities (age 9-18) can make significant and meaningful gains in phonological deletion by performing writing exercises with the use of discrete –but not continuous –speech recognition (Higgins & Raskind, 2000; Raskind & Higgins, 1999). Moreover, Raskind and Higgins (1999) established a causal relationship between the phonemic awareness gains and concomitant gains in word recognition, spelling, and reading comprehension. These improvements are impressive given that the sample included older students with disabilities, a population for which smaller effect sizes have been reported (National Institute of Child Health and Human Development, 2000). Control group comparisons suggest that the improvements were not tied to some kind of Hawthorne or halo effect. The basis for these improvements is unclear, even to the authors. Differences in the effectiveness of the two types of speech recognition suggest that bimodal sensory input is not itself supportive of phonological deletion gains. The authors suggest that the word-by-word dictation mode required for discrete speech recognition may cause students to attend more to individual words and their parts, particularly when comparing the speech recognition output to the intended input and making corrections.

The two negative findings from the literature both relate to the use of text-to-speech, (TTS), or synthetic computer speech. Olson and Wise (1992) found that below-average readers (grades 3-5) who over the course of a year spent time reading online with synthetic speech feedback showed no greater improvement on two phonological awareness in language tests than did students who instead of reading spent an equivalent amount of free time on the computer. Likewise, in an investigation by Elbro et al. (1996), students with reading disabilities or language disorders in grades 2 through 8 did not improve scores on phonemic awareness tests (phoneme deletion, phoneme synthesis, and syllable segmentation tests) after 40 sessions reading with syllable- or letter name-level synthetic TTS. Thus, it does not appear that TTS, at least in the context of simply reading digital text, is an effective approach for remediating phonemic awareness deficits.

As illustrated, the recent research literature speaks decidedly in favor of technology-based approaches to phonemic awareness instruction for students in special education. Nearly all of the studies we have found incorporated a control group enabling comparison to traditional and/or computer treatment comparisons, greatly strengthening the meaningfulness of the findings. Research studies suggest that computer-based explicit instruction emphasizing several combinations of skills can be successful. Given the NRP's observation that instruction focused on one or two skills is most effective, even greater effectiveness may be seen with technologies that provide more targeted instruction (NICHD, 2000). This is a worthwhile direction for future research.

Interestingly, the current literature provides evidence that not only explicit instruction but also indirect approaches can be effective, particularly those that involve writing activities with speech support. It is unlikely that a single approach to phonemic awareness instruction will succeed with all students. The best approach is for teachers to assess students' phonemic awareness before beginning phonemic awareness instruction. This will indicate which children need the instruction and which do not; which children need to be taught rudimentary levels of phonemic awareness, for example, segmenting initial sounds in words; and which need more advanced levels involving segmenting or blending with letters. (NICHD, 2000, p. 2-43). In the future, it will be important to tease out which approaches are most effective for which students.

Phonics/Word Recognition

Like deficits in other basic reading skills, deficits in phonics and word recognition can significantly impede reading comprehension both directly and, by monopolizing attentional resources, indirectly (Adams, 1990; Stanovich, 1988; Torgesen & Barker, 1995). Remediating such deficits is therefore an important priority for reading instruction, one with the potential to both prevent and remediate reading failure. Indeed, a strong research base suggests that phonics instruction can be an effective means of promoting reading growth for at-risk and struggling readers (NICHD, 2000).

As important as it is, phonics instruction, in isolation, is not an effective approach for promoting reading. Instead, it must be integrated into a systematic program of reading instruction. Given the heavy demands on teachers, any approach that can facilitate this integration would be extremely valuable. Technology has the potential to accomplish this by automating elements of phonics instruction and providing students the opportunity to practice independently with feedback-freeing teachers to focus on aspects of instruction for which they are essential.

Two technologies have primarily been investigated for the delivery of phonics instruction: computer programs/software and TTS. We will discuss these each in turn.

Text-To-Speech

The TTS literature, which is relatively sizeable, is full of contradictions regarding the effectiveness of this technology at promoting phonics and/or word recognition. Quite a few studies (Davidson & Noyes, 1995; Dawson et al., 2000; Elbro et al., 1996; Hartas & Moseley, 1993; Oloffson, 1992; Olson & Wise, 1992; van Daal & Reitsma, 1993) present evidence that the use of TTS before or while reading can improve students' ability to sight read and/or decode. Indeed, a few of them (Dawson et al., 2000; Elbro et al., 1996; Olson & Wise, 1992) document improvements surpassing those that occur when reading without TTS, spending free time on the computer, or receiving regular reading instruction. This kind of success has been reported with a range of student populations, including students with reading disabilities, language disorders, and below-average reading performance – but with a rather limited range of grade-levels, clustered around

grades 2 through 6. It is important to note that two of these studies are flawed in significant ways (Dawson et al. [2000] report an n of 4 and tested after only three sessions; Elbro et al. [1996] failed to randomize subject assignment). Also, Hartas and Moseley's (1993) intervention offered not only TTS but also supports such as a glossary and a playback function, confounding the results.

The majority of studies report no advantage of TTS over traditional approaches for improving students' decoding and/or sight recognition (Davidson & Noyes, 1995; Farmer et al., 1992; Lundberg & Oloffson, 1993; Montali & Lewandowski, 1996). Moreover, some of the studies cited above as reporting positive findings found no benefit on certain alternative measures or with certain group comparisons. For example, Dawson et al. (2000) noted that using TTS as a prereading model was better than not using any model at all but less effective than using a teacher model. For Elbro et al. (1996), replacing part of students' remedial instruction with practice reading with TTS significantly improved performance on tests of silent word reading and oral text reading but not oral word reading and oral nonword reading.

Reconciling these positive and negative findings is challenging given the extensive differences in study designs. Factors such as student population, type of TTS used, duration of the intervention, comparison condition, and experimental measures are all obvious potential influential factors. However, analysis of these factors does not provide a strongly arguable explanation for the differences in the literature. Possibly important, most of the studies reporting negative findings used word-level feedback, whereas many of those reporting positive findings used a mixture of several types (e.g., syllable and onset-rime feedback). In addition, several of the studies showing a strong positive impact of TTS (Elbro et al., 1996; Olson & Wise, 1992) had very long durations, suggesting that extended training favors positive results.

Worth commenting on here is research by Shany and Biemiller (1995) showing that the addition of audiotape-assisted reading practice (students listened and followed along

Figure 1. Students may click on a word or portion of the text and have it read aloud via text-to-speech (TTS).

CHAPTER 2

THE LAW OF CLUB AND FANG

Buck's first day on the Yea beach was like a nightmare. Every hour was filled with shock and surprise. He had been suddenly jerked from the heart of civilization and flung into the heart of things primordial. No lazy, sun-kissed life was this, with nothing to do but loaf and be bored. Here was neither peace, nor rest, nor a moment's safety. All was confusion and action, and every moment life and limb were in peril. There was imperative need to be constantly alert; for these dogs and men were not town dogs and men. They were savages, all of them, who knew no law but the law of club and fang.

with basal reader texts on tape) did not significantly improve third-and fourth-grade poor readers' performance on word or pseudoword reading tests. Nor were word recognition and phonics skills improved by teacher-assisted reading practice (where the teacher would help the student pronounce difficult words). This study strongly suggests two things. First, it is unlikely that the negative findings regarding TTS as a remediation tool are attributable to the speech's poor quality. Second, multisensory practice may be of limited effectiveness without a lengthy duration of practice or activities and/or supports focused on phonics/word recognition. Putting all this in perspective, the literature does not strongly support the use of TTS instead of traditional approaches for promoting phonics and word recognition. If teachers are willing to commit to longer and more intensive use of TTS, they might achieve more consistent and remarkable results. More likely, results will depend on a combination of direct instruction in phonics with extensive practice reading with TTS support.

A more elaborate application of TTS, "talking books," has also been investigated with regard to phonics/word recognition. Lewin (1997, 2000) twice investigated the effectiveness of talking book software for developing sight recognition/phonics skills in fourth grade poor readers. Neither study established any significant impact of the software on these skills. Both studies demonstrate word reading gains (on the Common Words Test, Key Word Test, and Phonic Knowledge Test), but some of the gains look modest, and Lewin does not provide statistical analysis of the gains or comparison to a nontechnology-based instruction control group. Thus, these two studies are not sufficient to draw any solid conclusions about the effectiveness of multimedia talking books relative to noncomputer-based methods. Interesting, however, in the 2000 study gains on all three measures were slightly higher for users of a basic software version than users of enhanced software that offered pronunciation hints (which could be made optional or mandatory) and five reinforcement activities to improve the use of reading cues and develop sight recognition of key vocabulary. A teacher taking part in the study observed that most students failed to access the pronunciation hints for their intended purpose as a device for considering alternative word identification strategies. This observation again raises the important point that struggling readers may not successfully utilize supports without proper instruction.

Computer and Software Programs

Computer and software programs have tended to incorporate more explicit forms of phonics and/or sight recognition training. For example, three groups (Marston et al., 1995; van den Bosch et al., 1995; Wentink et al., 1997) have investigated the effectiveness of computerized decoding training on word and/or pseudoword reading. Their findings are not entirely consistent. Marston et al. (1995) demonstrated a significant impact of computer-assisted instruction on word reading scores of third to fifth grade students with mild disabilities. Students who underwent computer training in decoding, sight word recognition, and comprehension significantly outperformed a nonequivalent control group (students in the control group were drawn from a broader range of grade levels) on word reading accuracy. In contrast, neither Wentink et al. (1997) nor van den Bosch et al. (1995) found a robust effect of computer training on word reading. In van den Bosch et al.'s study students with learning disabilities (mean nine years of age) scored equivalently on a word reading test with or without time-limited pseudoword naming training. In the Wentink et al. study (poor readers, age 8-12 years), this same kind of practice significantly improved only the reading of multisyllabic words. Again, reconciling these findings is not completely straightforward, but given that Marston et al. (1995) used a nonequivalent control group, their findings should probably be weighted less heavily.

Evidence regarding the impact of computer programs on phonics skills is equally divided. Although van den Bosch et al. (1995) reported significantly improved pseudoword reading, Wentink et al. (1997) were unable to show improvement. Thus, computer-based decoding training is not evenly supported by the literature with respect to either decoding or word recognition.

Computer-based phonemic awareness training is an alternative approach. The outcomes here have been more consistent (likely owing at least in part to a single group's repeated work in this area). Daisy Quest and Daisy's Castle are two game-format computer programs that provide explicit tutorial instruction and practice in phonemic awareness. Barker and Torgesen (1995) found that these programs were significantly more effective than phonological decoding or mathematics programs at developing first-grade poor readers' word identification skill. The programs also promoted gains in decoding, but these did not reach significance.

Barker and Torgesen's findings are generally consistent with a series of four studies by Wise, Olson and colleagues (Olson et al., 1997; Wise et al., 1999, 2000; Wise & Olson, 1995). These investigators have researched the effectiveness of computer-assisted phonological awareness training that complements small-group and one-on-one teacher instruction off the computer with the use of a variety of computer programs and reading on the computer with whole word or segmented speech feedback. Students with reading difficulties in grades 2 to 5 have been consistently shown to benefit from the training, making significantly greater gains in word and pseudoword reading than peers receiving similarly structured instruction focused on comprehension strategies (Olson et al., 1997; Wise & Olson, 1995; Wise et al., 2000) or normal instruction off the computer (Wise et al., 1999). Olson et al. (1997) also took the rare step of conducting maintenance tests one and two years after the conclusion of the original 30-hour intervention (Wise & Olson, 1995). Their findings indicate that the effects on phonological decoding persist for one year, disappearing by two years. It is not unreasonable to predict longer-lasting improvements with lengthier training time.

A few researchers have investigated the possibility of transfer effects from various other types of recognition training to word recognition. For example, Holt-Ochsner and Manis (1992) provided students with dyslexia (mean 13 years) with practice in semantic word recognition in the form of multimedia computer automaticity training games. The games required students to match words to definitions. After four training sessions with the games, students had made significant gains in word vocalization accuracy, suggesting that semantic-level word recognition training can affect the phonological level of word recognition. However, this study did not include any kind of control group. A second example is a study by Das Smaal et al. (1996) presenting evidence of transfer of training in multiletter unit detection to decoding and/or sight recognition skills. Comparisons in this case were made to a control group that spent an equivalent amount of time doing math and finger exercises on the computer.

Other Promising Approaches

Although sparse in the literature, a few other technological approaches are worth mentioning here. For example, Boone and Higgins (1993) investigated the benefits of multimedia texts as a supplement to a basal reading series for K-3 students. The texts differed across the three years of the study, offering vocabulary and decoding support in Year 1, additional semantic and syntactic support in Year 2, and comprehension strategies as well in Year 3 (see Vocabulary section). Looking at just the impact on low-ability readers, in most cases students' scores on the MacMillan Standardized Reading Test decoding and phonics subtest indicated that multimedia instruction and regular instruction produced equivalent gains. However, experimental instruction was more effective than traditional instruction in a few cases: for second graders in Year 1, for first graders in Year 2, and for third graders in Year 3. At the same time regular instruction was more beneficial for first graders in Year 1 and second and third graders in Year 2. The patchiness of these results may be a consequence of low statistical power—a study with a larger group of students might smooth out the inconsistencies. However, the relationship between grade level, beginning reading ability, and the effectiveness of various reading supports may be quite complex. In either case, multimedia lessons such as these are worth exploring further.

Speech recognition, although most frequently used to support the writing process, has been demonstrated to have a positive impact on word recognition/decoding skills. Two studies by Raskind and Higgins (Higgins & Raskind, 2000; Raskind & Higgins, 1999) sampling 12-and 14-year-olds with learning disabilities showed that using speech recognition to perform writing assignments and/or writing exercises promotes significantly greater gains on word recognition tests than does spending time on a nonreading computer activity (keyboarding). Both discrete and continuoous speech recognition were shown to be effective, with no significant difference between outcomes. Correlational data suggest that these improvements are tied to phonological awareness gains.

In conclusion, a variety of technologies has been enlisted as a means of providing training in phonics and/or sight recognition to students with special needs. Discrepant findings are a problem in several areas–most notably TTS and computerized decoding training. The most effective technological approaches seem to be computer-based phonemic awareness training and, somewhat unexpectedly, speech recognition. Other technologies such as supported multimedia reading lessons, computerized multiletter unit detection training, and computerized semantic word recognition training have also shown promise but need further research before widespread use can be advocated.

Vocabulary

Despite the major role of vocabulary in successful comprehension, research into vocabulary instruction is limited in scope and quality, as evidenced by the National Reading Panel's inability to find any studies of vocabulary instruction (with or without technology) meeting their criteria (NICHD, 2000). The Panel stressed the need for additional research in this area, particularly relating to students of different abilities and computer instruction. The Panel's conclusions are reinforced by a research-to-date survey of the literature. Two years after the report was published, there is still a very modest research base addressing these topics, with only a handful of studies targeting vocabulary as an outcome of even secondary interest.

Several different technological approaches have been taken to teaching vocabulary to struggling readers, ranging from basic, having students read text online (Swanson & Trahan, 1992), to elaborate, such as hypermedia study guides with an extensive array of supports (Boone & Higgins, 1993). Results have varied. The simple approach of reading text in digital but otherwise unaltered form appears to offer little advantage over reading printed text as a means for learning vocabulary (Swanson & Trahan, 1992). The addition of TTS to computerized texts offers greater potential, so far as it provides students with auditory cues to aid semantic retrieval that is unavailable when working alone with printed text. Indeed, Hebert and Murdock (1994) presented evidence that reading vocabulary, definitions, and sentences on the computer with digitized speech or TTS leads to greater vocabulary learning for students with language learning disabilities than does reading the same digital text without TTS. However, Elkind, Cohen, and Murray (1993) found no significant advantage to dedicating part of the typical reading period to reading on the computer with subsyllable-, word, and sentence-level synthetic TTS. Thus, the study's 28 sixth-grade students with dyslexia demonstrated equivalent three-month gains on the Gates-McGinitie Vocabulary test regardless of the treatment. Similarly, Davidson and Noyes (1995) reported that students with reading difficulties performed no better reading books on the computer with word- or page-level TTS than reading print versions offline to the teacher. There are numerous differences between these studies, but the differences between their comparison groups seem particularly significant. As a method for teaching vocabulary, reading words, definitions, and sentences on the computer may be more effective with TTS than without TTS, but spending time reading with TTS may not have any significant advantage over more traditional reading activities. This is clearly a question that merits further research.

Text-to-speech was one element of richly supported hypermedia texts investigated by Boone and Higgins (1993) in a three-year study. The texts were intended as lessons supplemental to the K-3 basal reading series that would provide systematic reading instruction. Thus, while the first-year texts incorporated

vocabulary and decoding support, new supports were added in each subsequent year of the study to target additional reading strategies and outcomes.

Specifically, Year 1 hypermedia texts incorporated vocabulary and decoding support: TTS, structural analysis of words, animated graphics, computerized pictures, definitions, synonyms, and digitized speech. Year 2 hypermedia texts additionally included syntactic and semantic support: graphical demonstrations of pronoun/referent relationships. Finally, Year 3 hypermedia texts additionally included comprehension strategies.

Students in the study were "ability grouped" into one of three categories (low, medium, or high) based on their pretest scores on the Macmillan Achievement Test (1983). Interesting, although vocabulary supports were maintained in the text across all three years, low-achievement students in the experimental treatment demonstrated a vocabulary advantage over their peers in the control group in only the first two years of the study. These findings suggest that supports should be integrated judiciously and with plentiful instruction about their effective use, particularly when working with struggling readers, who may find an abundance of options and features distracting and/or confusing.

The Boone and Higgins (1993) study might be interpreted as evidence in favor of a targeted approach to technology-based vocabulary instruction. It is true that less targeted approaches have met with limited success. A study by Raskind and Higgins (1999), for example, argues quite strongly against an approach combining writing exercises and speech recognition for improving the semantic organization of vocabulary. Students (mean 12.9 years of age) who did writing exercises on the computer with the use of TTS improved their scores on a Semantic Choice Task to the same degree as students who spent the same amount of time in a keyboarding class. An apparent contradiction to this line of reasoning, however, is Moore-Hart's (1995) evaluation of a hypermedia program, Multicultural Links, which combines a word processor with interactive hypermedia such as maps, annotations of multicultural books, minibiographies, and a multicultural calendar. Although not directly targeted at vocabulary, the program led to improved vocabulary normal curve equivalent scores from the California Achievement test. The students were fourth-and fifth-grade readers, including "a large number of below average readers." However, Moore-Hart's analysis did not distinguish between the performance of below-average students and the rest of the diverse sample.

Finally, Xin and colleagues have investigated video as a means of providing targeted vocabulary instruction (Xin, Glaser, & Rieth, 1996; Xin & Rieth, 2001). Their approach is to use a videodisc to anchor new vocabulary to a real-life context. In an evaluation of the method, Xin and Rieth (2001) found that students taught through the video-anchored instruction made significantly greater performance gains on a word definition test than did students taught with a traditional instruction approach (where print materials set the context). However, both groups made equivalent improvements in cloze sentence completion. Thus, while these findings support video-assisted vocabulary instruction as an effective tool, they also show that in some respects traditional methods can be used with nearly equivalent success.

Although studies investigating the effectiveness of technology-based methods for vocabulary improvement are of mixed quality and outcome, several approaches seem to be quite promising, most notably video-anchored instruction and supported hypermedia texts such as in the Moore-Hart (1995) and Higgins and Boone (1993) studies. However, our understanding of the effects of these approaches is far from complete, due to the frequent absence of controlled comparisons to traditional approaches. Since optimizing vocabulary instruction may require multiple approaches, it is important to continue to investigate such new methods.

Fluency

Naming-speed deficits are prominent in students with reading disabilities (as discussed in Wolf, Miller, & Donnelly, 2000). Wolf et al. (2000) argued that naming-speed deficits make a unique contribution to reading failure and

that they may be the source of reading failure for "treatment resisters." Unfortunately, fluency has received little attention in technology and special education research.

According to the National Reading Panel (2000), repeated oral reading with feedback has shown a consistent positive impact on fluency. However, it did not specifically comment on the effectiveness of computer-mediated oral reading practice. Although reading practice on the computer does not appear to have any advantage over equivalent forms of practice on paper (Swanson & Trahan, 1992), multisensory reading practice on the computer using TTS has generally shown promise.

Students from a variety of grade levels, reading with a variety of forms of TTS have been shown to improve oral fluency. For example, Dawson, Venn and Gunter (2000) observed oral fluency gains when seven- to eight-year old students with emotional and behavioral disorders listened to passages read by the computer with digitized TTS before attempting to read them themselves. Consistent with these findings, van Daal and van der Leij (1992) reported significant oral fluency gains when nine-year-old students below the expected reading-age level practiced reading words aloud on the computer with optional digitized, word-level speech feedback. van Daal and Reitsma (1993) reported that readers with disabilities (reading level-matched to readers in grades 3 and 4) demonstrated significantly improved oral word reading accuracy after eight training sessions with audio recorded speech feedback. Hartas and Mosely (1993) demonstrated improved oral fluency when older students with reading disabilities (grades 8-11) read books with the use of audiotaped word-, phrase- and full text-level TTS.

On the other hand, Farmer et al. (1992) found that 13- to 18-year-old students with reading disabilities reading short stories on the computer did not significantly improve word recognition speed when the stories were presented with whole-word synthetic TTS. It is tempting to conclude that digitized TTS is more effective than synthetic TTS for struggling readers. However, Elbro et al. (1996), who sampled students with reading disabilities and language disorders (grades 2 through 8), also demonstrated a significant improvement in oral reading fluency when students read aloud with synthetic, segmented TTS in place of regular remedial training (which included reading in groups, spelling to dictation, independent writing, and grammar exercises). And Oloffson (1992) showed that students with reading disabilities in grades 2 through 7 improved oral fluency when reading with synthetic, word-level TTS.

An alternative explanation for this one discrepancy is that it reflects the greater effectiveness of TTS reading practice with younger versus older readers. Farmer et al. (1992) sampled upper-elementary and high school students instead of the younger students targeted in other studies. Even so, what is lacking in this assemblage of research is solid evidence that students reading with TTS develop greater fluency than those engaged in other kinds of reading practice or training. Although Elbro et al. (1996) present evidence that reading with TTS leads to greater development of fluency than a traditional remedial program (which included reading in groups, spelling to dictation, independent writing, grammar exercises, etc.), Dawson et al. (2000), Farmer et al. (1992), and Oloffson (1992) were unable to demonstrate an advantage of reading with TTS over reading without TTS.

Books on tape are another method for providing students with multisensory reading practice. Shany and Biemiller (1995) reported that below-grade-level third- and fourth-grade students who took part in regular reading sessions where they listened to and followed along with a book on tape significantly improved reading speed and verbal efficiency (speed and accuracy of reading aloud) relative to a control group receiving regular reading instruction. These gains were equivalent to those made by students who engaged in teacher-assisted reading sessions. Letter naming speed and word naming speed were not improved, however, suggesting that this approach improved primarily contextual reading skills. While this seems to be a promising approach, it should be emphasized that the control group did not receive any additional practice outside of regular reading instruction, leaving open the possibility that the improvements that were seen were due to increased practice and not the books on tape per say. Many teachers offer TTS-supported reading practice in place of books on tape. Given the evidence to support TTS as a method for improving fluency, teachers may be justified in this practice.

Software and computer programs–both tutorial and drill and practice–are another potential tool for improving fluency. Wentink et al. (1997) presented findings showing significant effects of computerized training in time-limited pseudoword naming on fluency of word and pseudoword recognition. Poor readers who worked with the computer program made significantly greater fluency gains than peers who received no training. This is, however, the only straightforward, positive finding in our review of the literature.

Two studies reported no beneficial effect of computer training on fluency. Das-Smaal, Klapwijk, and van der Leij (1996) compared training in multiletter unit detection via a computer program to computerized math or finger exercises and found significant differences in gained accuracy but not speed of multiletter unit detection. Subjects were 9- to 10-year-old students with reading disabilities. Likewise, implementation of a computer support system for meaning, phonics, and fluency did not facilitate fluency gains for a mixture of second-language learners and students with dyslexia (Lynch, Fawcett, & Nicolson, 2000). These findings are, however, difficult to evaluate given the poor detail about the nature of the activities within the system.

Other findings are even less straightforward. Results reported by Holt-Ochsner and Manis (1992) may seem favorable to computerized fluency training, but the absence of a control group is problematic. Holt-Ochsner and Manis used two drill-and-practice computer games to train students with dyslexia to access word meaning more rapidly. Students working with the games developed not only faster semantic access but also more rapid word vocalization and improved automaticity for trained words. However, without a control group it impossible to establish whether this approach is more effective than alternatives. Findings by van den Bosch, van Von, and Schreiner (1995) underscored the importance of having an untreated control group. While investigating the effectiveness of two computer programs providing practice in pseudoword naming, these authors found that students who worked with one program significantly outperformed those working with the other on tests of pseudoword and word reading fluency. However, neither program produced a significant improvement in fluency relative to an untrained control group.

In conclusion, the research base proposes some solutions to the fluency deficits of students with disabilities; namely, multisensory reading practice mediated by talking computers. However, this approach needs to be compared to existing methods. This will be an important step in transforming what are promising findings into a persuasive argument for the equivalence or superiority of TTS/talking books over more traditional approaches. Evidence regarding computer programs directed at fluency is mixed and would benefit from the same kind of carefully controlled research.

Comprehension

The goal of reading instruction is to develop students who are able to read with understanding. Difficulties comprehending text may be due to students' weaknesses in any of the areas previously discussed—phonemic awareness, phonics and word recognition, vocabulary, and fluency. Comprehension also suffers if students have weaknesses related to background knowledge, text structure knowledge, reading strategies, metacognitive strategies, reading motivation and self-efficacy. Finally, comprehension of a particular text is also a function of the text characteristics, the task, and the larger sociocultural context.

Thus far, research on struggling readers' comprehension of digital texts has tended to focus on the potential to transform the text with learning supports targeted to student characteristics, such as decoding skill or level of background knowledge. There has been considerable interest in the use of TTS and digitized speech to either bypass or remediate decoding problems so that students may focus attentional resources on constructing meaning from the text. A second line of inquiry has

investigated the effects of providing additional representational supports to help students understand content, such as adding an online glossary, providing background material, or offering a summary of main ideas. A third line of inquiry has focused on how technology can support students' strategic learning and metacognition by providing information about, and, in some cases, prompting students to re-read the text, take notes, and apply strategies such as questioning and summarizing.

Computer Display of Text

Not surprisingly, there is no evidence that reading a text on screen versus print has a differential impact on comprehension for students with learning disabilities (Swanson & Trahan 1992).

Text-To-Speech and Digital Voice

Some studies employing TTS or digital voice to improve students' phonemic awareness, phonics, and/or fluency, have included measures of comprehension. The hypothesis is that by using TTS or digital voice students will have more fluent access to the text, thereby freeing up resources that can be allocated to comprehension. At a minimum, speech support may serve a compensatory function, ensuring students' access to the general education curriculum and age-appropriate reading materials. More ambitiously, it may also serve a remedial function if experience reading with TTS or digital voice transfers to improved comprehension of texts without speech support. The latter might occur as a result of more automatized word recognition skills, increased amount of reading, or a combination of both.

Some studies have shown that reading with speech feedback positively affects comprehension (Elbro, Rasmussen, & Spelling, 1996; Elkind, Cohen, & Murray, 1993; Lundgerg & Oloffson, 1993; Montali & Lewandoski, 1996), but only one found that improvement transferred to reading traditional text (Elbro et al., 1996). Elkind et al.'s study showed the powerful compensatory effect TTS may offer to middle school students with dyslexia. After reading literature with TTS for a semester, 70% of the students improved comprehension on a TTS-supported version of the Gray Oral Reading Test by approximately one grade level, and

40% realized even greater gains (two to five grade levels). However, no positive remedial effect was found when students were tested without TTS support. Important, 14% experienced a decrease in performance, perhaps due to kinesthetic-motor weakness, indicating that the benefit of this type of tool varies for students with different learner characteristics. The interaction with learner characteristics was also demonstrated in Lundberg and Olofsson's (1993) study of Scandinavian students with reading disabilities. They found that older students with reading disabilities (grades 4-6) improved comprehension when reading text with TTS support, while younger students (grades 2-3) did not. The teachers in the study offered a logical explanation for the differing results, suggesting that the older students were reading more difficult texts with a higher percentage of complex and multisyllabic words. Another explanation might be that the older students were better equipped to make decisions about targeting words for TTS support. Skill level is also a factor to be considered. Montali and Lewandoski (1996) compared the effects of text presentation (visual, auditory, and visual with voicing and highlighting) for average and less skilled readers. The bimodal presentation significantly improved comprehension of the less skilled readers.

In the only study to show a remedial effect, grade 2-6 Scandinavian students with reading and language disabilities read with TTS support 20 minutes a day for 40 days (Elbro et al., 1996). They demonstrated greater growth on a standardized reading assessment than a control group who received traditional reading remediation. A possible explanation for this finding is the difference in students' use of the TTS. Rather than simply clicking on a word for pronunciation, the word was presented broken into visual and auditory segments (either by syllable or by letter names), and the students had to generate their own pronunciation before clicking again and hearing the whole word. Thus, they had to actively work on decoding while reading connected text, synthesizing the word based on the first round of TTS support and then comparing their pronunciation with that of the text. The phonetic regularity of the Scandinavian language may also have been a factor.

On a related note, two studies have found that computer software designed to improve automatic word recognition for students with reading disabilities improves comprehension at the sentence level (Holt-Ochsner & Mannes, 1992) and passage level (Lundberg, 1995), respectively. Lundberg and Oloffson (1993) also reported a case study of a 15-year-old boy with severe reading disabilities and considered illiterate, who was able to read the newspaper and short stories after a year using the computer software.

In contrast to these studies, a number of researchers have found that TTS has no effect on comprehension (Farmer, Klein, & Bryson, 1992; Leong, 1995; Wise & Olson, 1995; Wise, Olson, Ring, & Johnson, 1998; Wise, Ring, & Olson, 2000). These studies differ from one another in important ways, and there do not appear to be common patterns that might explain the conflicting results. One explanation offered by van Daal and Reitsma (1993) is that students with learning disabilities do not access supports, even when warranted. This is an interesting point that deserves further study. And, as some studies indicate, it seems plausible that the effect of TTS will vary by learner characteristics such as reading ability and type of reading difficulty (e.g., students with weak word recognition skills and relatively stronger comprehension might benefit more from TTS than those with both weak decoding and weak comprehension). Further, since students are using TTS in a classroom literacy learning context, its effect might be mediated by the larger instructional context. Future research is needed to better understand for whom, and under what task and instructional conditions, TTS will support struggling readers' comprehension.

Hypertext with Learning Supports

At its most basic level, hypertext with TTS functionality allows students access to the content. However, students with reading difficulties struggle for many reasons other than weak decoding skills and dysfluent reading. For example, they may not have the requisite vocabulary or background knowledge to make sense of the text. Further, struggling readers tend not to be strategic in their approach to text. Thus, they often do not monitor their understanding and, unlike skilled readers, do not have a flexible repertoire of reading strategies that can be applied to diverse texts to accomplish varied reading purposes.

Several researchers have developed hypertexts that include various types of learning supports, some of them passive (e.g., a hyperlinked glossary), others interactive (e.g., prompts to apply a strategy, answer a question, or to take notes). These hypertexts also vary in relation to learner control. In some cases, students have control, deciding if and when to use supports; in other cases, control is mixed, with some supports controlled by the computer, others by the student (although it is possible for the computer to control all supports, we did not encounter any examples).

In a study of intermediate-grade, above- and below-average readers, Leong (1995) found no effects on comprehension for TTS; TTS with explanations of difficult words; TTS plus explanations of difficult words plus reading awareness prompts; and TTS with simplified passages. Boone and Higgins and colleagues have carried out a series of hypertext investigations. Although the results were variable across the three years of implementation, their study of hypermedia basal readers in grades K-3 demonstrates the promise of hypermedia designed to support the core literacy curriculum, especially for struggling readers (Boone & Higgins, 1993). The hypermedia texts included basal stories enhanced with vocabulary explanations and images, anaphoric reference, and comprehension questions with feedback to focus students' attention on the salient portion of the text if they selected the wrong choice. Low-achieving students in the experimental group significantly outperformed the control group on a standardized reading achievement test in grades K, 2 and 3 in Year 1, in grades 1, 2, and 3 in Year 2, and in grade K in Year 3.

Higgins, Boone, and Lovitt (1996) studied the effects of a hypertext study guide with links to explanatory information, links to simpler replacements for selected vocabulary and phrases, and comprehension questions with corrective feedback that had to be answered correctly before moving on to a new screen. Retention test scores for high school students with learning disabilities were highest for the lecture/hypermedia study guide group, followed by the study guide group, and by the lecture group. Remedial students in the hypermedia study guide or lecture/hypermedia study guide performed comparably, and more strongly than those in the lecture condition. However, none of these differences was significant, perhaps due to the small sample size.

In a study comparing the effects of two versions of a hypertext 10th-grade biology chapter, MacArthur and Haynes (1995) found that high school students with learning disabilities and low-achieving students demonstrated significantly greater comprehension with the enhanced version. The basic version presented the equivalent of the printed textbook in a digital format, with an online notebook. The enhanced version added TTS, an online-glossary, links between questions and text, main idea highlighting, and explanations summarizing key ideas.

Multicultural Links is a hypermedia program developed for upper-elementary students that provides multiple content resources about different cultures and is linked to a word-processing environment. In a year-long study of fourth- and fifth-grade students in an urban school with a high percentage of students reading below grade level, Moore-Hart (1995) found that students in the multicultural program with computers gained higher comprehension scores on the California Achievement Test than did students in the multicultural program-only group or the control group. However, it is not clear from the report whether these differences were significant.

Anderson-Inman and Horney have carried out a series of descriptive studies of supported hypertext learning with students with learning disabilities and other at-risk learners suggesting that students can productively use supports to accomplish school reading and studying (Anderson-Inman, Horney, Chen, & Lewin, 1994; Horney & Anderson-Inman, 1994; Horney & Anderson-Inman, 1999). They have developed a useful taxonomy of supports and identified patterns of reading and resource usage that have implications for hypertext design.

Computer Software

An alternative approach to hypertext, where learning supports are embedded in digital texts, is the development of a comprehensive technology-based program that includes direct instruction in the components of reading, often presented in a game-like format, as well as opportunities for reading digital text. One such example of a comprehensive program is RAVE-O (Retrieval, Automaticity, Vocabulary, Elaboration, and Orthography), a beginning reader intervention program developed by Maryanne Wolf and colleagues (Wolf, Miller, & Donnelly, 2000; Wolf, 2001). Designed to develop fluency and automaticity in reading disabled children with naming deficits (in addition to phonological deficits), the program is used in conjunction with a computer-based phonics program (Phonological Analyis and Blending program; Lovett et al., 1994). It includes on- and offline activities to develop fluency in the reading outcomes of word identification, word attack, and comprehension, while building automaticity in the underlying processes of visual recognition, auditory recognition, semantic development, and lexical retrieval. The program also addresses metacognitive and motivational issues, engaging students in positive experiences with language and encouraging them to reflect on improved competencies and success. The results have been impressive for beginning readers with reading disabilities, significantly improving reading comprehension in comparison to control groups in a series of studies (Wolf, 2001).

Two other comprehensive programs have also yielded positive comprehension results. Lynch, Fawcett, and Nicolson (2000) studied eight struggling readers' use of RITA, a computer-based literacy support system that includes curriculum-based activities in meaning, phonics, and fluency. Instructional plans targeted students' IEP goals, and students focused computer time on areas of need. These children significantly improved comprehension and demonstrated meaningful progress toward IEP goals. Another study of a computer-supported comprehensive literacy program for first-grade students resulted in greater comprehension compared to a control group, but the effect was only significant for males (Erdner, Guy, & Bush, 1998).

In summary, it is clear that technology has an important role to play in improving the reading comprehension of students with reading difficulties, from primary to high school levels. Particularly for older students who have already experienced the debilitating effects of poor reading on academic achievement, motivation, and self-efficacy, it is important to provide, at a minimum, digital versions of the core curriculum and literature with TTS support so that they have access to, and are able to participate in the general education curriculum. There is also promising evidence that hypertexts with embedded learning supports designed to actively engage students in reading for understanding are more productive learning environments for students with disabilities than traditional print. And, finally, there is strong support for comprehensive approaches that combine direct instruction in component skills and processes with reading of connected text. It seems reasonable to assume that students with reading disabilities will need a multifaceted approach to improving comprehension, and that the particular combination of supports and programs is best determined by an in-depth understanding of the learner, the task, and the context. While research focused on answering the "what works?" question is needed and important, it is equally important to pursue the question in relation to what works for whom and under what conditions.

Engagement

In their 2000 report on the scientific research in reading, the NRP addressed the same five literacy outcomes that we have discussed so far. We suggest that a sixth outcome, engagement, should be considered when evaluating the effectiveness of literacy instruction. There are at least two ways in which engagement is essential within the context of literacy and literacy instruction. First, engagement is a powerful determinant of the effectiveness of any given literacy approach. That is, if a student does not feel challenged and rewarded by instruction, it is unlikely that he or she will be fully motivated to work hard. Thus, engagement is in some sense a limiting factor with respect to the effectiveness of literacy instruction. Indeed, Lewin

(1997) argued that increased engagement, even in the absence of improvements in reading performance itself, is a powerful and independently worthwhile instructional outcome,

> . . . Researchers should also consider other benefits of the process such as improvements in confidence and attitude toward reading. If children discover the pleasures to be had in reading they will be inspired to continue to practice. This will undoubtedly have longer lasting benefits, even if the reading performance doesn't improve initially. (Lewin, 1997, p. 118)

The second respect in which engagement is vital relates to students' evolving feelings about reading itself. If students do not enjoy reading, skilled phonemic awareness, phonics and word recognition, vocabulary, fluency, and comprehension are of little purpose or consequence for them. Thus, in a second and broader sense, an effective literacy approach is one that generates excitement about reading itself. A student who likes to read will seek out opportunities to apply the literacy skills that he or she has developed outside of the present instructional context and outside of the classroom. Thus, in at least two important respects, engagement is a vital determinant of the outcome of reading instruction and students' ultimate place along the literacy spectrum.

What does the research base tell us about how to engage students in literacy learning and reading? Few investigators have actively and squarely addressed this issue in their research. Many are more concerned with controlling for technology's novelty effects. There is some legitimate concern on their part that technology may hold only fleeting appeal for students, thereby skewing experimental results over the shortterm (discussed in Mitchell & Fox, 2001). Numerous studies have found a positive impact of technology on student engagement (Heimann et al., 1995; Lewin, 1997, 2000; Lundberg & Olofsson, 1993; Montali & Lewandowski, 1996; Xin et al., 1996). In most of these cases, researchers have documented (based on interviews or observations) that students enjoy interacting and working with new technologies in the context of literacy instruction. In a couple of cases, increased task

engagement has actually been demonstrated. However, other researchers have reported no change in task enjoyment or motivation over the course of their technology interventions (Elkind et al., 1993; Moore-Hart, 1995). These two sets of studies are distinguished by their different time courses. Elkind et al. (1993) and Moore-Hart (1995) measured effects at much more extended time points (one semester and eight months, respectively) than the studies reporting positive effects on engagement (the studies cited above concluded after three sessions to four months). Collectively, therefore, these studies lend support to the argument that students' enthusiasm toward new technologies may be only short-lived.

Although the novelty and appeal of technology may diminish over time, technology nevertheless has the potential to revise students' outlook on learning and reading in lasting and fundamental ways. Thus, there is evidence to suggest that technology-based approaches can produce a lasting, favorable impact on students' regard for reading. Lewin (1997) reported that students enjoyed reading more after working with talking book software. Similarly, Moore-Hart (1995) suggested that students using an interactive hypermedia program to study literature and culture developed a more positive regard for both reading and writing. Elkind et al. (1993) found that students were more enthusiastic about reading after spending sessions reading with TTS. Adam and Wild (1997) noted that reluctant readers who used CD-ROM storybooks over the course of four weeks did not undergo any change in their regard for reading but did develop a higher regard for books and CD-ROM storybooks. These findings certainly put technology in a positive light and, as a whole, affirm the effectiveness of technology-based approaches in engaging students in literacy learning and reading. It may be tempting to draw the conclusion that technology-based approaches are in some way universally appealing to students. Indeed, this is pervasive enough an assumption–or at least a suspicion– that many investigators seem to anticipate and/ or control for the greater novelty and appeal of a technology-based approach. Although there is undoubtedly an element of truth to technology's widespread appeal, it would be a mistake to wholeheartedly trust in its validity. For example, Anderson-Inman and Horney (1998), found quite the opposite to be true in their study of hypertext reading patterns,

Although students generally liked using the program ("I liked this way of doing assignments and reading. It is really fun."), we saw little evidence to suggest they approached the hypertext materials with any excitement or reached any profound insights while using the programs. In general, students seemed to view reading in hypertext as just one more assignment. (Horney & Anderson-Inman, 1994, p. 90)

Likewise, a student probe conducted by Lewin (2000) suggested that use of basic talking book software did not affect students' regard for learning, whereas use of enhanced software actually lessened their reading enjoyment. The findings suggest that the high-ability readers in the group found reading insufficiently challenging when using the enhanced version.

We may need to look deeper than students' self-reported feelings to discover the true impact of technology on motivation. Most frequently, student interviews and poorly constrained observations and/or teacher reports have been used to investigate student engagement. For example, few of the studies we cited surveyed control groups on engagement measures–excluding the possibility of making comparisons between technology-based and more traditional approaches. Thus, even when outcomes are favorable, it is not clear that technology approaches are superior to existing ones. This line of research is deserving of more rigorous evaluation methods and more attention.

Beyond its bells and whistles, technology can offer features that hold great influence over student engagement, most notably choice and control. As discussed above, many of the digital texts investigated by researchers offer students the option of accessing alternative media such as speech and graphics (Higgins & Boone, 1993; Horney & Anderson Inman, 1994; Lewin, 1997; MacArthur & Haynes, 1995). Elkind et al. (1993) allowed students to select text and highlighting colors as well as reading speed and reading voice. Strangely, in very few cases (Olson & Wise, 1992; Wise et al., 1999) are students offered a choice of reading material, despite how common the practice is when reading off the computer.

Choice puts students more in control of their reading experience, which can have several benefits, as expressed by Lundberg and Oloffson (1993),

Here we would like to emphasize the fact that the readers are in control of the reading situation – they continuously monitor their own reading performance and have to decide when help is needed. The increased metacognitive awareness required might help to develop more active strategies also in reading comprehension. Computer-aided reading also removes much of the negative emotions associated with reading when the student discovers that texts are relevant and have personal significance. (p. 285)

By enabling the incorporation of supports and built-in feedback, digital learning environments offer an unprecedented opportunity for independent practice. Mitchell and Fox (2001), for example, allowed students to select from two computer programs and activities within those programs, and even allowed them to set their own learning goals—an empowering experience for students. And Lewin (1997) noted the motivating effect a talking book's feedback had on one student, who enjoyed not having to ask the teacher for help.

Universal Design and Literacy Learning

The research base offers a good measure of insight into ways that educators can harness technology to help prevent and/or remediate reading problems for students with special needs. However, there is a noticeable gap in the literature regarding a central issue in special education: Does one size fit all? The reality faced by most special education teachers is a mixed classroom of learners with different reading levels, language and cultural backgrounds, mental and physical abilities and disabilities, and preferences and interests. Is there a single instructional approach–be it for phonics, phonemic awareness, fluency, vocabulary, or comprehension—that can effectively support every student?

This is not an easy question to answer given the technical problems inherent in assembling a sufficiently large and diverse sample and navigating complex data analysis and interpretation. Thus, it is not surprising that few groups have sought to directly investigate it. However, when differences in responsiveness to literacy interventions are considered, the findings often challenge the notion of a one-size-fits-all approach. Thus, findings from several groups demonstrate that literacy interventions effective for one group of students are less effective or entirely ineffective for other groups of students (Boone et al., 1996; Heimann et al., 1995; Lynch et al., 2000). Heimann et al. (1995), for example, found differences in how students with autism and students with mixed mental disabilities fared using a multimedia computer program teaching vocabulary and sentence creation. This case might give the impression that such differences only occur between students from very different educational groups. In fact, this is not necessarily the case. When averaging responses, researchers may fail to notice differences within even a seemingly uniform group of students (Olson & Wise, 1992).

These research findings support the conclusion that many observers have already made on their own: that today's diverse classrooms demand a new approach to curriculum. Unfortunately, there is no ready-made solution for meeting the challenge of diversity. In its 2000 report, the NRP stated the problem well:

> As with any instructional program, there is always the question: "Does one size fit all?" Teachers may be expected to use a particular phonics program with their class, yet it quickly becomes apparent that the program suits some students better than others. In the early grades, children are known to vary greatly in the skills they bring to school. There will be some children who already know most letter-sound correspondences, some children who can even decode words, and others who have little or no letter knowledge. Should teachers proceed through the program and ignore these

> students? Or should they assess their students' needs and select the types and amounts of phonics suited to those needs? Although the latter is clearly preferable, this requires phonics programs that provide guidance in how to place students into flexible instructional groups and how to pace instruction. (NICHD 2000, pp. 2-96-2-97)

Teachers and students need an alternative to the one-size-fits-all approach (Edyburn, 2003a) but current instructional programs do not generally provide the necessary support to individualize teaching methods and/or materials. One promising model for curriculum change is Universal Design for Learning (UDL) (Orkwis & McLane, 1998; Rose & Meyer, 2002). UDL has its conceptual origins in universal design, an architectural movement that sought to accommodate the needs of users with disabilities by anticipating their needs at the design level. Resulting built-in features such as elevators and curb cuts had the unpredicted effect of improving usability not only for individuals with disabilities but for everyone. UDL extends this idea to education, offering a framework with which educators can rethink the curriculum with the strengths and needs of diverse students in mind. Taking advantage of the flexibility of digital materials, UDL asks that the curriculum—not the students—be adaptable.

The UDL framework draws upon the work of Lev Vygotsky (1962) and recent advances in the neurosciences regarding how the brain processes information. Thus, developments in brain research have illuminated for us that the three essential elements of learning identified by Vygotsky (recognition of the information to be learned, application of strategies to process that information, and engagement with the learning task) are overseen by three learning networks in the brain. Individual differences in these networks lead to considerable person-to-person differences in how students access, use, and engage with learning materials.

The principles of UDL call for particular kinds of flexibility in support of learner differences in recognition, strategy, or affect:

> to support diverse recognition networks, it is important to provide multiple means of representation;

to support diverse strategic networks, the learning environment should provide multiple means of expression within an apprenticeship model of learning; and

to support diverse affective networks, the learner should be provided multiple means of engagement. (Meyer & Rose, 1998; Rose & Meyer, 2002)

Universally designed curricula, therefore, include a range of options for accessing, using, and engaging with learning matter, made practical through the use of digital materials.

While UDL is still in the early stages on the road between concept and reality, elements of UDL can be seen in some in some of the existing experimental research and emerging technologies. Text-to-speech is a prominent example of a technological tool being used to support individual differences in recognition. Diverse students, including students with learning or reading disabilities, English-language learners, and students who fail to engage with reading, all struggle to achieve in reading and consequentially other subject areas. Text-to-speech offers these students an alternative for accessing essential content and learning vocabulary. At the same time, it can offer any student, even those proficient with text, the advantage of having redundant information that they can use to further hone essential reading skills such as phonemic awareness.

Technology makes it much easier for teachers to integrate multiple media into the classroom. In addition to speech, the research base offers innovative approaches to using images, animation, and video as part of literacy instruction. Images and animated graphics can be incorporated into digital texts as supplements to printed definitions, supporting vocabulary understanding and reading comprehension (Anderson-Inman et al., 1994; Boone & Higgins, 1993). Heimann et al. (1995) investigated a particularly interesting application of animation within a computer program. The computer program, which taught vocabulary and sentence creation, animated nouns, verbs, and sentences that students wrote, providing them with alternative representations for basic building blocks of text and their own writing attempts. Students working with the program made significant gains in phonemic awareness. An innovative video application by Xin and Rieth (2001) used video segments on the San Francisco earthquake of 1989 to anchor vocabulary instruction. The method was just as effective as a more traditional text-based approach.

Digital environments can also support strategic networks in novel ways. In order for students to master reading, like other complex skills, they require plentiful opportunities for supported practice. Students with multiple deficiencies need to practice with scaffolds in place so that they can focus on one skill at a time. Anderson-Inman and Horney (1998) have expressed exceptional confidence in digital materials' ability to meet this need, "the medium of hypertext is an ideal way to provide students with the support they may need in order to comprehend and appreciate good literature" (p. 280). These authors use the term "supported text" to describe texts that they have electronically altered to be more supportive of the reader by offering, for example, definitions, speech, pictures of vocabulary words, note-taking tools, selfmonitoring questions, and graphic organizer overviews.

Looking at this and other work within the literature, it is readily apparent that digital texts offer an excellent means to provide scaffolded reading practice. Lewin (2000), for example, described talking book software that offers TTS as well as optional or mandatory pronunciation hints. Hypermedia reading lessons developed by Boone and Higgins (1993) incorporate a rich set of scaffolds including vocabulary and decoding support in the form of speech, structural analysis of words, animated graphics, computerized pictures, definitions, and synonyms; syntactic and semantic support in the form of graphical demonstrations of pronoun/referent relationships; and comprehension support in the form of comprehension strategies. Pisha and Coyne (2001) report a positive student response to an online history textbook that offered multiple representations of content and strategic supports such as an online dictionary and Internet resources. In research currently underway at CAST, Dalton, Pisha, and colleagues have developed a series of universally designed

Figure 2. Instructional design and features of a universally designed scaffolded reading environment (Dalton et al., 2001).

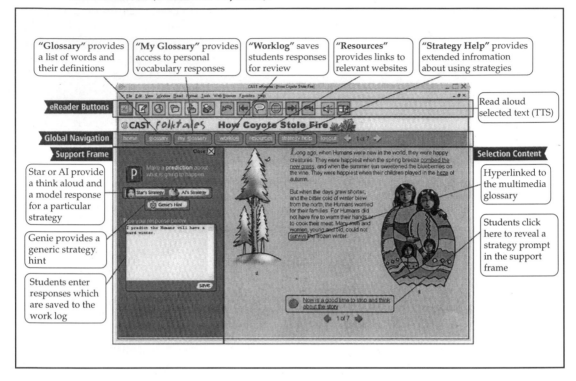

hypertexts for students (see Figure 2) with scaffolded strategic supports, representational supports, and embedded reflection and self-assessment (Dalton, Pisha, Eagleton, Coyne, & Deysher, 2002; O'Neil, 2001; O'Neil & Dalton, 2002; Rose & Dalton, 2002).

Anderson-Inman and Horney have done considerable research on the ways students interact with digital, supported text and have noted that students may not use resources effectively (Anderson-Inman, Horney, Chen, & Lewin, 1994; Horney & Anderson-Inman, 1999). Failure to access supports appropriately has been noted by others as well (Lewin, 2000). Tailoring the selection of supports to the student may help remedy this problem by ensuring that a student is working in an environment that is best suited to his or her needs and attentional capacity. Examples of individualized materials can be found in the literature. For example, teachers in Lewin's (2000) investigation of CD-ROM talking book software chose whether to make pronunciation hints optional or mandatory for different students.

In addition to choosing the kinds of supports needed, teachers can adapt materials. Edyburn (2003) references a variety of technologies, including TTS tools, that can be used to adapt text in different ways for different students. He discusses a process called cognitive rescaling where the cognitive difficulty of information is altered, and he describes simple tools such as the AutoSummary feature in *Microsoft Word* that can be used to accomplish this (Edyburn 2002a, 2003). Cognitive rescaling supports individual differences in recognition as well as engagement, as altering the readability of a text not only makes it more accessible to a student but also adjusts the level of challenge to an optimally motivating level (Edyburn, 2003).

Cognitive rescaling of text is just one example of how current technologies can be used to support individual student's needs in a UDL way. For example, Hay (1997) tailored a video-based research activity by providing video scripts with a vocabulary and presentation rate leveled to students' developmental reading abilities, commenting that "The individualization allows for students to receive the same information, but at appropriate levels. It levels the playing fields" (p. 65). The Primary Reading Manager described by Erdner et al. (1998) is another example. The software program allows teachers to set the level of difficulty and response time for computerized reading lessons on a student-to-student basis. Similarly, the SALT hypermedia program described by MacArthur and Haynes (1995) offers teachers the chance to modify text in such ways as highlighting main ideas and elaborating picture captions.

Of course, there is still the issue of deciding how to appropriately individualize materials. In this regard, research by Lynch et al. (2000) and Nicolson et al. (2000) is particularly relevant. These groups investigated the RITA system, designed to assist teachers in tailoring IEP activities. RITA offers suggestions for a personalized set of computer-based IEP activities based on students' pretest scores (Lynch et al., 2000; Nicolson et al., 2000). Findings suggest that use of the system can promote several reading skills. However, it is not clear whether the approach is effective for all students.

If the key to leveling the playing field in the classroom is to offer students multiple instructional approaches and materials, technology will undoubtedly be the key raw material. The research literature offers great examples of how technology can be used to flexibly support students' variable strengths and weaknesses. Ultimately, technology may enable teachers to adapt materials and tasks to the extent that they can meet every student's evolving needs, "Another benefit is the potential of software to constantly adapt to the needs of a child learning to read" (Lewin, 1997, p. 115). Technology's promise in this respect is still largely unexplored. Notable, among other things, is the general uniformity when it comes to methods of engaging students.

Conclusion

The technology and special education literature raises some exciting possibilities for improving the caliber and inclusiveness of reading instruction. For every critical reading skill there is a technology with demonstrated potential to help prevent and/or remediate learning failure. Foremost among these technologies are TTS, speech recognition, video, supported digital texts, and computer/software programs. Nevertheless, significant ambiguities in the research base limit progress in the field. To help resolve these ambiguities it is essential that researchers sample sufficiently large groups of students and wherever possible include appropriate control groups.

The research has made substantial progress in characterizing effective approaches for targeting vocabulary, fluency, phonics and word recognition, phonemic awareness, and comprehension. The field would greatly benefit from focusing the same level of attention on student engagement, itself a fundamental outcome of and influence on instruction. Another issue that needs to be squarely addressed is the role of pragmatic factors such as cost-effectiveness and ease of integration of technology into the curriculum. It may be that investigation of these factors will reveal the true advantages of technological approaches, which may offer a more practical approach for teachers.

Technology offers teachers the possibility of a more flexible teaching approach, one that accommodates students' need for individualized instruction and materials without overburdening teachers. An important direction for future research is the investigation of flexible approaches to reading instruction and learning, according to the principles of UDL. Supported, adjustable digital learning environments can help ensure that every teacher reaches the goal of leaving no child behind.

Taking a UDL perspective on the research literature, we encourage individuals to shift their way of thinking from identifying the best approach for literacy instruction to recognizing the value that different approaches may have for different students and different reading skills. In addition to answering persistent basic research questions, an important goal for the future will be to investigate ways to facilitate the integration of multiple approaches with existing classroom practice. Technology will no doubt play an essential role in that process.

Acknowledgment: We would like to thank Kristin Robinson for her assistance in conducting the literature search for this chapter.

References

Adam, N., & Wild, M. (1997). Applying CD-Rom interactive storybooks to learning to read. *Journal of Computer Assisted Learning, 13*, 119-132.

Adams, M. (1990). *Beginning to read: Thinking and learning about print.* Cambridge, MA: MIT Press.

Anderson-Inman, L., Horney, M. A., Chen, D., Lewin, L. (1994). Hypertext literacy: observations from the ElectroText Project. *Language Arts, 71*, 279-287.

Anderson-Inman, L., & Horney, M. (1998). *Tranforming text for at-risk readers.* In D. Reinking, M. McKenna, L. Labbo, & R. Kieffer (Eds.), *Literacy for the 21st century: Technological transformations in a post-typographic world* (pp. 15-43). Mahwah, NJ: Erlbaum.

Barker, T. A., & Torgesen, J.K. (1995). An evaluation of computer-assisted instruction in phonological awareness with below average readers. *Journal of Educational Computing Research, 13*(1), 89-103.

Boone, R., Higgins, K., Notari, A, & Stump, C. S. (1996). Hypermedia pre-reading lessons: Learner-centered software for kindergarten. *Journal of Computing in Childhood Education, 7*(1-2), 39-69.

Boone, R., & Higgins, K. (1993). Hypermedia basal readers: Three years of school-based research. *Journal of Special Education Technology, 12*(2), 86-106.

Dalton, B., Pisha, B., Eagleton, M., Coyne, P., & Deysher, S. (2001). *Engaging the text: Reciprocal teaching and questioning strategies in a scaffolded learning environment.* Final report to the U.S. Department of Education. Peabody, MA: CAST.

Das-Smaal, E. A., Klapwijk, M.J.G., & van der Leij, A. (1996). Training of perceptual unit processing in children with a reading disability. *Cognition and Instruction, 14*(2), 221-250.

Davidson, J., & Noyes, P. (1995). Computer-generated speech feedback as support for reading instruction. *Support for Learning, 10*(1), 35-39.

Dawson, L., Venn, M. L., & Gunter, P.L. (2000). The effects of teacher versus computer reading models. *Behavioral Disorders, 25*(2), 105-113.

Edyburn, D.L. (2003). Learning from text. *Special Education Technology Practice, 4*(3), 16-27.

Edyburn, D.L. (2002a April/May). Cognitive rescaling strategies: Interventions that alter the cognitive accessibility of text. *Closing the Gap, 1*, 10-11, 21.

Edyburn, D.L. (2002b). Remediation vs. compensation: A critical decision point in assistive technology consideration. *ConnSENSE Bulletin, 4*(3). Retrieved on January 21, 2004, from: www.connsense bulletin.com/edyburnv4n3.html.

Elbro, C., Rasmussen, I., & Spelling, B. (1996). Teaching reading to disabled readers with language disorders: A controlled evaluation of synthetic speech feedback. *Scandinavian Journal of Psychology, 37*, 140-155.

Elkind, J., Cohen, K., & Murray, C. (1993). Using computer-based readers to improve reading comprehension of students with dyslexia. *Annals of Dyslexia, 43*, 238-259.

Erdner, R. A., Guy, R. F., & Bush, A. (1998). The impact of a year of computer assisted instruction on the development of first grade learning skills. *Journal of Educational Computing Research, 18*(4), 369-386.

Farmer, M. E., Klein, R, & Bryson, S.E. (1992). Computer-assisted reading: Effects of whole-word feedback on fluency and comprehension in readers with severe disabilities. *Remedial and Special Education, 13*(2), 50-60.

Goswami, U. (2000). Causal connections in beginning reading: The importance of rhyme. *Journal of Research in Reading, 22*, 217-240.

Hay, L. (1997). Tailor-made instructional materials using computer multimedia technology. *Computers in the Schools, 13*(1-2), 61-68.

Hebert, B. M., & Murdock, J. Y. (1994). Comparing three computer-aided instruction output modes to teach vocabulary words to students with learning disabilities. *Learning Disabilities Research & Practice, 9*(3), 136-141.

Heimann, M., Nelson, K. E., Tjus, T., & Gillberg, C. (1995). Increasing reading and communication skills in children with autism through an interactive multimedia computer crogram. *Journal of Autism & Developmental Disorders, 25*(5), 459-480.

Higgins, E. L., & Raskind, M. H. (2000). Speaking to read: The effects of continuous vs. discrete speech recognition systems on the reading and spelling of children with learning disabilities. *Journal of Special Education Technology, 15*(1), 19-29.

Higgins, K., Boone, R., & Lovitt, T. (1996). Hypertext support for remedial students and students with learning disabilities. *Journal of Learning Disabilities, 29*(4), 402-412.

Holt-Ochsner, L. K., & Manis, F. R. (1992). Automaticity training for dyslexics: An experimental study. *Annals of Dyslexia, 42*, 222-241.

Horney, M. A, & Anderson-Inman, L. (1994). The ElectroText Project: Hypertext reading patterns of middle school students. *Journal of Educational Multimedia and Hypermedia, 3*(1), 71-91.

Horney, M. A., & Anderson-Inman, L. (1999). Supported Text in Electronic Reading Environments. *Reading and Writing Quarterly, 15*(2), 127-168.

Kerstholt, M. T., van Bon, W. H. J., & Schreuder, R. (1994). Training in phonemic segmentation: The effects of visual support. *Reading and Writing: An Interdisciplinary Journal, 6*(4), 361-385.

Leong, C. K. (1995). Effects of on-line reading and simultaneous DECtalk auding in helping below-average and poor readers comprehend and summarize text. *Learning Disability Quarterly, 18*, 101-116.

Lewin, C. (1997). Test driving: CARS: Addressing the issues in the evaluation of computer-assisted reading software. *Journal of Computing in Childhood Education, 8*(2/3), 111-132.

Lewin, C. (2000, June). Exploring the effects of talking book software in UK primary classrooms. *Journal of Research in Reading, 23*(2), 149-57.

Liberman, I. Y., Shankweiler, D., & Liberman, A. M. (1989). The alphabetic principle and learning to read. In D. Shankweiler & I. Y. Liberman (Eds.), *Phonology and reading disability: Solving the reading puzzle. International Academy for Research in Learning Disabilities Monograph Series, No. 6*. (pp. 1-33). Ann Arbor: University of Michigan Press.

Lovett, M., Barron, R., Forbes, J., Cuksts, B., & Steinbach, K. (1994). Computer speech-based training of literacy skills in neurologically impaired children: A controlled evaluation. *Brain and Language, 47*, 117-154.

Lundberg, I. (1995). The computer as a tool of remediation in the education of students with reading disabilities – A theory-based approach. *Learning Disability Quarterly, 18*(2), 89-99.

Lundberg, I., & Oloffson, A. (1993). Can computer speech support reading comprehension? *Computers in Human Behavior, 9*, 283-293.

Lynch, L., Fawcett, A. J., & Nicolson, R. I. (2000). Computer-assisted reading intervention in a secondary school: An evaluation study. *British Journal of Educational Technology, 31*(4), 333-348.

MacArthur, C., Ferretti, R. P., Okolo, C. M. & Cavalier, A. R. (2001). Technology applications for students with literacy problems: a critical review. *Elementary School Journal 101*(3), 273-301.

MacArthur, C. A., & Haynes, J. B. (1995). Student assistant for learning from text (SALT): A hypermedia reading aid. *Journal of Learning Disabilities, 28*(3), 50-59.

Marston, D., Deno, S. L., Kim, D., Diment, K., & Rogers, D. (1995). Comparison of reading intervention approaches for students with mild disabilities. *Exceptional Children, 62*(1), 20-37.

Meyer, A., & Rose, D. H. (1998). *Learning to read in the computer age*. Cambridge, MA: Brookline Books.

Mitchell, M. J., & Fox, B. J. (2001). The effects of computer software for developing phonological awareness in low-progress readers. *Reading Research and Instruction, 40*(4), 315-332.

Montali, J., & Lewandowski, L. (1996). Bimodal reading: Benefits of a talking computer for average and less skilled readers.

Journal of Learning Disabilities, 29(3), 271-279.

Moore-Hart, M. A. (1995). The effects of multicultural links on reading and writing performance and cultural awareness of fourth and fifth graders. *Computers in Human Behavior, 11*(3-4), 391-410.

Moseley, D., & Hartas, C. (1993). Say that again please: A scheme to boost reading skills using a computer with digitized speech. *Support for Learning, 8*(1), 16-21.

National Center for Education Statistics; (2003). *The nation's report card: Reading.* Retrieved January 22, 2004 from: nces.ed.gov/nations reportcard/reading/results2003/.

National Institute of Child Health and Human Development. (2000). Report of the National Reading Panel. *Teaching children to read: An evidence-based assessment of the scientific research literature on reading and its implications for reading instruction* (NIH Publication No. 00-4769). Washington, DC: U.S. Government Printing Office.

Nicolson, R., Fawcett, A., & Nicolson, M. (2000). Evaluation of a computer-based reading intervention in infant and junior schools. *Journal of Research in Reading, 23*(2), 194-209.

Okolo, C.M., Bahr, C.M., & Rieth, H.J. (1993). A retrospective view of computer-based instruction. *Journal of Special Education Technology, 12*(1), 1-27.

Olofsson, A. (1992). Synthetic speech and computer aided reading for reading disabled children. *Reading and Writing: An Interdisciplinary Journal, 4*(2), 165-178.

Olson, R. K., Wise B., Ring, J., & Johnson, M. (1997). Computer-based remedial traning in phoneme awareness and phonological decoding: Effects on the post-training development of word recognition. *Scientific Studies of Reading, 1*, 235-253.

Olson, R. K., & Wise, B. W. (1992). Reading on the computer with orthographic and speech feedback. *Reading and Writing: An Interdisciplinary Journal, 4*, 107-144.

O'Neill, L. (2001). Thinking readers: helping students take charge of their learning. *Exceptional Parent, 31*(6), 32-33.

O'Neill, L.M., & Dalton, B. (2002). Thinking readers part II: Supporting beginning read-ing in children with cognitive disabilities through technology. *Exceptional Parent, 32*(6), 40-43.

Orkwis, R., & McLane, K. (1998). *A Curriculum every student can use: Design principles for student access. ERIC/OSEP Topical Brief.* Reston, VA: ERIC/OSEP Special Project. (ERIC Document Reproduction Service No. ED423654)

Pisha, B., & Coyne, P. (2001). Jumping off the page: Content area curriculum for the Internet age. *Reading Online, 5*(4). Available: www.readingonline.org/articles/art_index.asp?HREF=pisha/index.html

Raskind, M. H., & Higgins, E. L. (1999). Speaking to read: The effects of speech recognition technology on the reading and spelling performance of children with learning disabilities. *Annals of Dyslexia, 49*, 251-281.

Rose, D., & Dalton, B. (2002). Using technology to individualize reading instruction. In C.C. Block, L. B. Gambrell, & M. Pressley (Eds.), *Improving comprehension instruction: Rethinking research, theory, and classroom practice* (pp. 257-274). San Francisco: Jossey Bass.

Rose, D., & Meyer, A. (2002). *Teaching every student in the digital age: Universal design for learning.* Alexandria, VA: Association for Supervision and Curriculum Development.

Shany, M. T., & Bielmiller, A. (1995). Assisted reading practice: Effects on performance for poor readers in grades 3 and 4. *Reading Research Quarterly, 30*(3), 382-395.

Swanson, H. L., & Trahan, M. F. (1992). Learning disabled readers' comprehension of computer mediated text: The influence of working memory, metacognition and attribution. *Learning Disabilities Research & Practice, 7*(2), 74-86.

Torgesen, J. K. (1993). Variations on theory in learning disabilities. In G.R. Lyon, D. B. Gray. J. F. Kavanaugh, & N. A. Krasnegor (Eds.), *Better understanding learning disabilities: New views from research and their implications for education and public policies* (pp. 153-170). Baltimore: Paul Brooks.

Torgesen, J. K., & Barker, T. A. (1995). Computers as aids in the prevention and remediation of reading disabilities. *Learning Disability Quarterly, 18*(2), 76-87.

Van Daal, V.H.P., & Reitsma, P. (1993). The use

of speech feedback by normal and disabled readers in computer-based reading practice. *Reading and Writing: An Interdisciplinary Journal, 5*(3), 243-259.

Van Daal, V.H.P., & van der Leij, A. (1992). Computer-based reading and spelling practice for children with learning disabilities. *Journal of Learning Disabilities, 23*, 186-195.

Van den Bosch, K., Van Bon, W.H.J., & Schreuder, R. (1995). Poor readers' decoding skills: Effects of training with limited exposure duration. *Reading Research Quarterly, 30*(1), 110-125.

Vygostky, L. (1962/1996). *Thought and language* (rev. ed.). Cambridge, MA:MIT Press.

Wentink, H.W.M.J., van Bon, W.H.J., & Schreuder, R. (1997). Training of poor readers' phonological decoding skills: Evidence for syllable-bound processing. *Reading and Writing: An Interdisciplinary Journal, 9*(3), 163-192.

Wise, B. W., & Olson, R.K. (1995). Computer-based phonological awareness and reading instruction. *Annals of Dyslexia, 45*, 99-122.

Wise, B. W., Olson, R. K., Ring, J., & Johnson, M. (1998). Interactive computer support for improving phonological skills. In J. Metsala & L. Ehri (Eds.), *Word recognition in beginning literacy* (pp. 189-208). Mahwah, NJ: Erlbaum.

Wise, B. W., Ring, J., & Olson, R.K. (1999). Training phonological awareness with and without explicit attention to articulation. *Journal of Experimental Child Psychology, 72*, 271-304.

Wise, B. W., Ring, J., & Olson, R.K. (2000). Individual differences in gains from computer-assisted remedial reading. *Journal of Experimental Child Psychology, 77*, 197-205.

Wise, B. W., & Olson, R. K. (1994). Computer speech and the remediation of reading and spelling problems. *Journal of Special Education Technology, 12*(3), 207-220.

Wolf, M., Miller, L., & Donnelly, K. (2000). The Retrieval, Automaticity, Vocabularly Elaboration, Orthography (RAVE-O): A comprehensive fluency-based reading intervention program. *Journal of Learning Disabilities, 33*(4), 375-386.

Xin, F., Glaser, C., & Rieth, H. (1996). Multimedia reading: Using anchored instruction and video technology in vocabulary lessons. *Teaching Exceptional Children, 29*(2), 45-49.

Xin, J. F., & Rieth, H. (2001). Video-assisted vocabulary instruction for elementary school students with learning disabilities. *Information Technology in Childhood Education Annual*, 87-103.

29

Writing Tools: Technology and Strategies for Struggling Writers

Merrill C. Sitko, Colin J. Laine, and Carolyn J. Sitko

Students with special needs, learning disabilities or other challenges often struggle and experience serious and persistent difficulties in written communication. They may have visual or auditory processing problems; motivational, emotional, and attitudinal issues; or disabilities that limit their control of the writing environment. While writing, they are often unaware of, or may fail to use efficient, appropriate cognitive, or linguistic information-processing strategies for learning, organization, and problem solving (Graham, Harris, MacArthur, & Schwartz, 1998; MacArthur, Ferretti, Okolo, & Cavalier, 2001). In order to overcome or compensate for such problems, students require well-designed instruction and assistance tailored directly to their needs in order to realize their true academic and personal potential in written communication

Technology, combined with effective instruction, may help teachers and caregivers to bridge the gap between the potential and the achievement of struggling writers by providing a rich, active, and highly individualized interaction between the student and the educational environment. Technology is becoming an increasingly important part of the general and special education experience for students with learning difficulties, since it offers students a different way of looking at themselves and their capabilities, and may help augment abilities and bypass or compensate for disabilities (Lewis, 2000; Male, 2003). Thus, students with special needs may feel empowered by adaptive and assistive technology, which can remove barriers and enable them to gain more equitable access to successful learning experiences and accomplish things not thought possible before (The Alliance for Technology Access, 2000). In the area of writing, motivating computer-based instruction allows reluctant writers to take control of their own learning and to develop a sense of confidence, ownership, and independence (Sitko & Sitko, 1996).

Many aspects of computer hardware and software provide tools for both teachers and students to facilitate and strengthen cognitive and linguistic strategies in writing. However, like any other instructional tool, technology alone is only a means for effective teaching (Gardner & Edyburn, 2000; Lindsey, 2000; Sitko & Sitko, 1995). Successful and realistic implementation of technology for struggling writers depends on:

- teachers' commitment, technology awareness, competence, and knowledge of effective pedagogical principles

- administrative support

- effective models, principles, and strategies of technology integration into the curriculum

- effective matching of curriculum writing goals, teaching philosophy, validated instructional procedures, appropriate technology applications. and students' individual learning strengths and needs.

This chapter will review research literature that examines how the features of current computer technology and the strategies used in implementing them can provide scaffolding to assist students with mild to moderate disabilities who struggle with written communication. The students in many of the studies have become more active, self-regulating and self-monitoring learners with more efficient writing strategies as a result of technology use. Empowering students with special needs to control their learning and writing through computer hardware and software is a prevalent theme in much of the research reviewed in this chapter.

Our search began with keywords in electronic databases such as ERIC and ProQuest Education Complete. Over the past five years, several papers have presented reviews, meta-analyses, anthologies, and commentaries from which one can gain a historical perspective as well as a reasonable foundation. In particular, Edyburn's reviews (2000, 2001, 2002a) provide a structure that can be a useful basis for further enquiry. His annual categorized reviews of the tables of contents of special education and technology journals have shown that a core of journals (3-7) have contained more than half the reliable published literature focusing on special education technology. We found the rest to be widely scattered. A second source (MacArthur et al., 2001) reviewed the literature on assistive technology and literacy, whereas MacArthur (2000) focused on a review of writing tools. Finally, a meta-analysis of writing interventions for students with learning disabilities (Gersten & Baker, 2001) provided insights into useful strategies for struggling writers. We also conducted a global search focusing on strategies for writing and on assistive "tools" (such as spelling checkers, word prediction, speech synthesis and speech recognition).

A pattern that emerges from studying papers from the past three to five years shows a burgeoning of studies that are not so focused on the technology per se. For instance, 22 articles dealt with assisting students in organizing their writing; however, only a few connect these strategies to the use of technology. This expansion of research on strategies is also noticeable in the abstracts of doctoral dissertations and conference proceedings. Historically, research on assistive technology has not fully utilized the growing research interest in strategies instruction.

Over the past decade almost 100 journal articles have been published on writing and technology per year, with only a few focusing on students with disabilities. Much of the information exists as unpublished academic work, professional articles, unresearched opinion, or anecdotal descriptions. Even some of the research-based papers focus on case studies that are personalized; or the variables are many and undefined, making a solid and common foundation for analysis and recommendations for practice questionable (Wong, 2001). However, the enthusiasm and experience of some teachers and students are impressive, and we have included reports found in online forums, resource collections, and the handouts and proceedings from recent special education technology conferences with the caveat that these do not necessarily represent empirical data.

Writing Difficulties

Models of writing (Bereiter & Scardamalia, 1987; Berninger & Swanson, 1994; Flower & Hayes, 1981; Hayes & Flower, 1987) suggest that writing involves a wide range of cognitive and linguistic skills, processes, and strategies, including:

- complex planning and selecting of goals, topics, and ideas
- generating and organizing information
- rich vocabulary and coherence
- audience awareness
- knowledge of the purpose and structure of genre
- comprehensiveness in story development
- engaging in an active recursive movement among planning, organizing, composing, editing, and revising processes
- knowledge of mechanics and conventions of punctuation, capitalization, spelling, and grammar
- reflective and strategic thinking
- problem solving, evaluation, and self-regulation of performance.

Writing is also a means of personal expression; hence the beliefs, motives, and intentions of writers impact their writing strategies and outcomes (Lavelle, Smith, & O'Ryan, 2002). Affective traits influencing the writing process include positive self-esteem, positive attitudes towards writing, belief in self-efficacy, confidence, emotions, attributions of success, and risk taking (Harris, Schmidt, & Graham, 1998; Lavelle et al., 2002; Sitko & Sitko, 1996).

Skilled writers are usually adept at the basic skills of written communication. However, communicating through written expression is problematic for many children and adults, especially so for those with learning, motor, sensory, or perceptual challenges, who often struggle with all aspects of writing skills. A number of researchers (cf. Adelman & Vogel, 1998; Bereiter & Scardamalia, 1987; Crealock & Sitko, 1990; Graham et al., 1998; MacArthur et al., 2001; Sturm & Rankin-Erickson, 2002) have identified a broad range of difficulties among reluctant writers in the areas of generating content, creating an organized structure, quickly and efficiently executing the mechanics of writing, making meaningful revisions to text, self-regulating their strategies, evaluating, forming, and reformulating goals.

In contrast to that of more skilled writers, the writing of students with writing difficulties is characterized as:

- minimizing the higher-level cognitive roles of planning, revising, reflection, and other self-regulation strategies in advance or during writing

- revealing difficulties in creating an organized structure

- relying on knowledge-telling writing strategies (i.e., quickly or impulsively telling what one knows from memory)

- displaying a lack of audience awareness

- having vocabulary gaps and relatively little content when composing

- struggling with quickly and efficiently executing the lower-level mechanics and conventions of spelling, punctuation, capitalization, and handwriting

In addition, the revisions of struggling writers are like "spot dusting," primarily limited to surface structure correction of mechanical errors. Writing products are less cohesive, omit important genre components and text structure, and are lower in overall quality (MacArthur et al., 2001). Reluctant writers further reveal a general lack of knowledge about writing, the writing process, and the criteria for good writing (Englert, Raphael, Anderson, Anthony, & Stevens, 1991; MacArthur, 2000).

Students who have felt unsuccessful in writing may have self-doubts; learned helplessness; negative attributions, attitudes, and emotions about writing; and be unwilling to try hard, certain that their written products are not worth the effort they expend (Harris et al., 1998; Sitko, McBride, & Sitko 1996). In their meta-analysis on writing interventions for students with learning disabilities, Gersten and Baker (2001) state that "On every conceivable measure of writing performance-including measures of both writing quality and quantity, and occurring across narrative and a range of expository text structures-students with learning disabilities write much more poorly than do students without disabilities" (p. 252).

The Process Approach to Writing

The process approach to writing, currently probably the most common instructional method of teaching writing skills, can accommodate a broad range of technology tools and strategies. This strategy is based on the theory (Bereiter & Scardamalia, 1987; Flower & Hayes, 1981; Graves, 1983; Hayes & Flower, 1987; Tomkins, 2000) that good writing must include the cognitive processes of:

- planning or prewriting-generating and organizing ideas and setting writing goals

- drafting -translating ideas into print

- postwriting or reviewing-evaluating, revising and editing written work.

It stresses constructivist, self-regulatory processes such as planning and revising, the importance of communicating or publishing to a writing audience, and establishing authentic reasons for learning to write. The process model recommends effective, individually tailored instruction in written communication skills as the need arises (Graham et al., 1998). In contrast, traditional models of writing instruction tend to focus more on the written products (Flower & Hayes, 1981), emphasizing mechanics and grammar over the content, process, and strategies involved in writing. A process-oriented teaching approach, as seen in the Writers' Workshop and whole-language approaches, places the learner and the learner's needs at the center of interactive community learning among teachers and students (Harris et al., 1998).

According to cognitive process models of writing, skilled or expert writers go through mental processes in a hierarchical and interactive or recursive manner during writing rather than one stage after another (Bruer, 1997; Flower & Hayes, 1981; Hayes & Flower, 1987; Tomkins, 2000). In addition, compared to novice writers, expert writers are more skilled in planning and creating goals, generating content, utilizing knowledge about text structure to organize compositions, accommodating audience, and diagnosing and revising problem areas in their writing (Bereiter & Scardamalia, 1987; Hayes & Flower, 1987).

Based on a process-oriented approach to writing, writing instruction for reluctant writers should be modeled on how expert or skilled writers write. Writing instruction for these students will take time and should be aimed at helping students internalize the writing process by teaching metacognitive awareness or a clear understanding of the organization of cognitive processes underlying the act of writing, as well as specific things the writer should do or think about throughout each phase of the writing process. In addition, teachers should model effective writing strategies, teach and support and scaffold students as they learn to improve their writing skills (Johnson, 2002).

Good process-oriented writing instruction should also be built on a diagnosis of the developing writer's problems and needs, and include instruction as needed in the lower-level transcription or mechanical skills. According to Graves (1985), the writing-process instructional approach for poor writers and those with learning disabilities should stress a meaning-centered approach first, and then, writing skills in the context of meaning. In their meta-analysis of teaching expressive writing to students with learning disabilities, Gersten and Baker (2001) conclude that "explicit teaching of critical steps in the writing process; adherence to a basic framework of planning, writing, and revision; and the provision of feedback-have reliably and consistently led to improvements in teaching expressive writing to students with learning disabilities" (p. 267). However, Roth (2000) emphasizes the strong attitudinal component that operates and mediates learning: thus, motivation to write must be a central feature of writing instruction for students with writing difficulties.

Strategy Instruction

Generating ideas, organizing, writing, revising, and publishing them into a coherent piece of writing are difficult skills for developing writers with or without disabilities. Strategies to help students with these skills across different types of writing tasks have been developed by a number of researchers (De La Paz, 1999; Englert et al., 1995; Harris, Schmidt, & Graham, 2002; Schumaker & Deshler, 1992; Sturm & Rankin-Erickson, 2002; Troia & Graham, 2002; Wong, Butler, Ficsere, & Kuperis, 1997). These researchers have found that students need both knowledge of the task-specific strategies successful writers use and the structure of various types of writing as well as procedures for putting the strategies into effect.

Strategy instruction attempts to teach students various cognitive and linguistic strategies or heuristics throughout the writing process, and self-regulation or control of learning strategies. According to Sturm and Rankin-Erickson (2002), strategy instruction "assists struggling writers by breaking down writing tasks and making the subprocesses and skills much more explicit" (p. 126). Strategy instruction programs also involve metacognitive training and instruction in skills necessary to implement, monitor, maintain, and generalize strategies (Roth, 2000).

Research involving strategy-oriented writing instruction for students with learning disabilities and writing problems has included several models. For example, self-regulated strategy development (SRSD) involves highly explicit, teacher-directed instructional stages that act as a framework or a "meta script" to assist students in developing knowledge about writing as well as the skills and strategies involved in the writing process, including planning, writing, revising, and editing. This extensive research program in elementary, middle and secondary classrooms and tutorial settings has revealed significant improvements in the quality of students' knowledge about and approach to writing, as well as self-efficacy and positive attitudes toward writing (Harris & Graham, 1996; Harris, Schmidt, & Graham, 2002; Troia & Graham, 2002).

The model incorporates several stages of instruction over a number of weeks in which the teacher scaffolds students' learning with a view to transferring responsibility for independent use of the target strategy to the students (De La Paz, 1999). These stages are:

1. Developing or activating students' background knowledge
2. Discussing the target strategy to be learned and obtaining students' commitment to learn
3. Teacher modeling of the strategy and self-regulatory statements
4. Mastery (memorization) of any strategy mnemonics or routines
5. Collaborative practice, in which teachers support the students' use of strategy in large or small groups of students
6. Independent practice, when instructional cues are gradually faded (Harris & Graham, 1996).

The SRSD model provides a structure within which teachers can help students learn strategies that are specific to the task at hand, whether those strategies assist with the process of writing (De La Paz, 1999) or the particulars of making the best use of the tools that technology can provide to support writers.

Another approach, the Cognitive Strategy Instruction in Writing (CSIW) program, uses "Think Sheets" and effective strategy instruction as prompts or cues to explicitly teach and direct writing strategies to students with learning disabilities during planning, organizing information, writing, editing, and revising (Englert et al., 1991; Englert et al., 1995; Graham et al.,1998). Teacher models and coaching are often used to help students internalize the strategies (Roth, 2000). Students in the Early Literacy Project (ELP) (Englert et al., 1995) for primary-grade students with mild disabilities were also taught to practice writing strategies and tools by working with partners or in small support groups in order to create a meaningful "collaborative space" for writing.

Learning strategies to assist students with learning disabilities with prewriting planning, writing and revising paragraphs, structured essays, and expository writing have been developed by a number of researchers (Ellis & Larkin, 1998; Graves, Semmel, & Gerber, 1974; Harris, Graham, & Mason, 2002; Schumaker & Deshler, 1992; Wong et al., 1997). The strategy steps or prompts in these studies were often encapsulated into a remembering device such as mnemonic which was representative of the writing process or task the strategy was designed to target.

How Can Technology Assist Students and Teachers in Addressing Writing Problems?

Technology offers many opportunities for enabling and supporting children and adults in improving writing skills. Technology has been integrated with effective strategies and models of instruction to enhance the writing of students with special needs.

Scaffolding Instruction

One useful educational strategy is "scaffolding;" that is, providing support to allow students to accomplish an activity that they would be unable to do without that support. Through scaffolding, instruction is offered in a manner that is sufficient to carry out a cognitive strategy or learning activity, with guidance or temporary structure and support diminished gradually as competence increases (Ellis & Larkin, 1998). Scaffolding instruction is important since, according to Vygotsky (1978) and others, instruction is most effective when it is aimed at a student's "zone of proximal development"-the area between what a learner can do independently (mastery level) and what he or she can accomplish with the support of a teacher or peer (instructional level) (Harris & Pressley, 1991). As Hogan and Pressley (1997) noted, scaffolding occurs through gradual increments in learning. Scaffolding can include such activities as explaining and demonstrating steps in a procedure, systematically developing prerequisite skills needed for a more demanding task, or identifying and correcting misconceptions.

Computer technology may provide teachers with tools for supporting students with writing difficulties as they explore and construct knowledge in personalized learning environments. With regard to technology and students with special needs, such "scaffolding" may be concrete through assistive or adaptive technology that permits students physical access to tasks that were previously inaccessible (The Alliance for Technology Access, 2000). Students with cognitive and/or physical disabilities can use the IntelliKeys programmable alternative keyboard (IntelliTools) with specially designed overlays that are streamlined to feature easy access to only those key functions required for particular types of software. Custom overlays created in Overlay Maker (IntelliTools), can guide and prompt a student through a series of steps in the learning process. Through a sequence of overlays, the I Can Write Series (IntelliTools) helps students learn to spell a particular word of interest to them, then other words using those same letters. Successive overlays can fade out the prompts. Students may move on to build sentences from categories of choices on templates. Whether temporary or permanent, such supports will change as students' skills and needs change. In the educational use of computers, support can come from several types of sources (Behrmann & Jerome, 2002). For example, certain features (like word prediction or cuing) inherent in the hardware or software being used may support the students' writing, or the environment may be structured to provide supports: in the physical setup of the computers to facilitate interactions or through props, strategy routines, or checklists.

A Computer-Assisted Writing Process Model

Computer-assisted writing instruction is a potentially powerful instructional tool in developing or improving the writing skills of students with serious writing difficulties. The Computer-Assisted Writing Process (CAWP) model assists reluctant writers and their teachers in developing written skills (Laine & Sitko, 2001; Sitko et al., 1996; Sitko & Sitko, 1999; Sitko, Sitko, & McBride, 1992). This highly structured, process–oriented model can be individualized to incorporate technology, if appropriate, at each stage in facilitating students' writing. While the structure of the model provides organizational tools to help students stay on track in developing their ideas, computer technology and specific strategies give them assistance and feedback in setting goals for their work and assessing their progress. Software such as concept mapping and outlining programs assists in the brainstorming and planning stages of writing. Keyboarding, spell check, thesaurus, word processing, word prediction, voice recognition and graphics programs help students through the mechanics and transcription of writing. Further, word counts, frequency lists, and computer analyses may generate numbers that students can focus on as concrete steps towards improving or revising their writing. The computer also seems to provide "neutral" input into the conferencing process between students and teacher. To a student who has struggled with writing over many years, the feedback from the computer may feel more like "information" and less like "criticism." The CAWP model may be used to increase students' metacognitive awareness of what is involved in writing, skill in mastering the writing process, and increased pride and ownership of the process and their own work. However, while technology may provide powerful tools to assist in the writing process, students still need specific training to know how and when to use technology effectively. In addition, they need to realize that they can achieve successful outcomes through their own efforts. It is only then that they will use the strategies.

The CAWP model assists students in addressing the writing process in manageable steps and using technology tools in a systematic and highly accountable way to set their own goals, write, and revise their work, and assess the results in a process they control. The purpose of the computer-assisted writing process is to establish a pattern of success. Most students in our research have experienced a long history of failure in writing in various instructional settings. Using the appropriate kind of program or assistive device, technology helps to remove that negative barrier between the teacher and the student and provides new tools and feedback to assist the students in becoming more self-reliant. As new computer hardware and programs have become available, they have been incorporated into the model so that students can take advantage of strategies and techniques that best meet their needs.

Once the purpose for writing has been established, the writing process in the CAWP model has been broken down into seven integrated, but separate, stages:

1. Computer Program Mastery-keyboarding, word processing basics, and any other "tools" the student will use
2. Brainstorming-generating and recording ideas
3. Planning-organizing ideas
4. Fast Draft-expanding the ideas into sentences
5. Proof reading Sequence-revision for content and form
6. Publishing-making the product appealing for the intended audience
7. Assessment and Goal Setting-evaluating the current project in light of previously decided goals and setting goals for the next project

Progress through these stages is emphasized and students are trained to recognize the stage on which they are currently working, distinct strategies to use in that phase, what they have already completed, and what stage comes next. The accountability built into the model keeps students focused on what they are trying to accomplish and their progress in achieving it. Figure 1 illustrates how the stages are related to each other and to technology.

Because this model is based on performing multiple revisions, students will likely spend more time and effort on their writing than they

Figure 1. Writing process model.

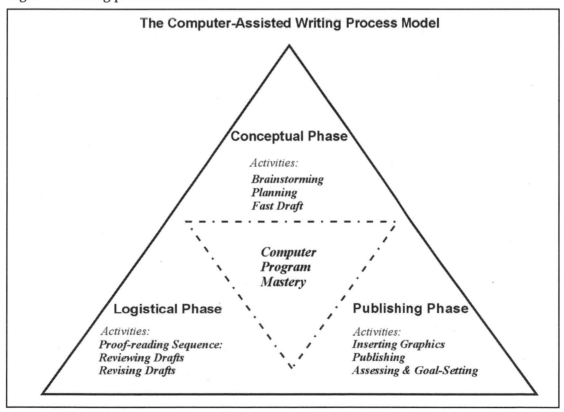

Writing Tools/Sitko, Laine, & Sitko **577**

have done in the past. It is important to elicit their cooperation by collecting baseline data, including previous assignments and writing samples, notes, formal and informal assessments. When students realize the need for improving their writing, participate in setting goals, and see tangible measures of what they do well and their improvement, the process sells itself. Some of the computer technology that can be incorporated the CAWP model is listed in Table 1.

Research using the CAWP model to assist struggling writers continues at the Centre for Communicative and Cognitive Disabilities www.edu.uwo.ca/cccd/.

Technology Tools for Reluctant Writers

Word processing was identified by Behrmann and Jerome (2002) as possibly "the most important application of assistive technology for students with mild disabilities" (p. 2) because of its potential for addressing barriers in mechanics, process, and motivation for writing. Mirenda and her associates (Mirenda, Wilk, & Carson, 2000) found that 75% of the requests for assistive technology to aid children with autism in British Columbia, Canada, over a five-year period from 1993-1998 were aimed at improving writing. McArthur and his colleagues (2001) proposed that the editing power of word processors for ease of revisions would encourage more revisions; this editing power combined with desktop publishing would assist the production of attractive publications with fewer errors; and the visibility of the screen and clarity of the product would facilitate collaboration among students.

Has the potential of technology to assist writing been realized? McArthur and his colleagues (2001) summarized research published in the period 1987-1999, examining the effects of word processing for students with literacy problems. Most studies (many with very small numbers of subjects), found no significant differences in the quality of writing with or without technology unless the technology was accompanied by instruction in specific strategies, particularly in revision, peer revision, and collaborative writing. In a three-year study, Lewis (1998) compared the effects of a number of text entry and editing tools on the writing skills of students with learning disabilities. Word processing had the most impact on the accuracy of the writing of students with learning disabilities in grades 4-12, especially the students with poor spelling skills. Her 10 recommendations for practitioners include features to consider when selecting writing technology and ends with this advice:

Whatever approach is selected, monitor the student's progress and re-evaluate as necessary ... ongoing assessment of the student's progress provides information about the effectiveness of the intervention and alerts the teacher to the need for change if the student is not experiencing success. (p. 9)

When choosing writing tools, it is important to match the features of the software with the skills and needs of each user, for there is no one-size-fits-all in special education technology (Laine, Sitko, Colwell, & Spence, 2002). Consider also the tools and customizable options available in standard word processors (Gilden, 2002; Marfilius, 2002).

Generating and Planning Ideas

Graphic Organizers

A great deal of research has been focused on the use of semantic maps, webs, and outlines to help students generate and/or recall and organize ideas (Anderson-Inman & Ditson, 1999; Ruddell & Boyle, 1989; Zipprich, 1995). According to Hall and Strangman (2002), "a graphic organizer is a visual and graphic display that depicts the relationship between facts, terms or ideas within a learning task" (p. 1). These authors describe many samples of graphic organizers and their uses. While their review of the literature focuses mainly on the use of graphic organizers in reading, they point to some common themes:

- Positive outcomes require the use of effective teaching practices.

- Graphic organizers can successfully improve learning when there is a substantive instructional context such as explicit instruction incorporating teacher modeling, independent practice with feedback, strategy instruction ... and concept teaching routines.

Table 1. Computer Tools for the Stages of a Writing Process Model

Writing Stage	Type of Tool	Sample Products
Computer Mastery	Typing tutorial or word prediction	*Type to Learn* (Sunburst) *Mavis Beacon Teaches Typing (Broderbund)* *Co: Writer 4000* (Don Johnston Inc.) *TextHELP* (TextHelp) *WriteAway 2000* (Information Services Inc) *WordQ* (Quillsoft)
	speech recognition	*Dragon Dictate* (Scansoft) Via Voice (IBM)
	alternative keyboards	*IntelliKeys* (IntelliTools)
	word processors which offer picture supports	*Clicker 4* (Crick Software) *IntelliTalkII* (IntelliTools) *Writing with Symbols 2000* (Mayer-Johnson)
Brainstorming and Planning	outliners	*DraftBuilder* (Don Johnson Inc.)
	graphic organizers	*Inspiration , Kidspiration* (Inspiration Software)
Fast Draft	portable keyboards	*AlphaSmart 3000, Dana* (AlphaSmart.Inc.) *DreamWriter* (Brainium Technologies) *Laser PC6* (Perfect Solutions)
	speech recognition	*Dragon Dictate* (Scansoft) *Via Voice* (IBM)
	word prediction	*Co: Writer 4000* (Don Johnston Inc.) *TextHELP* (TextHelp) *WriteAway 2000* (Information Services Inc) *WordQ* (Quillsott)
Proof Reading Sequence	spell checkers	Part of word processors like *IntelliTalkII* (IntelliTools) *Microsoft Word* (Microsoft) *TextHELP* (TextHelp) *WriteAway 2000* (Information Services Inc) *Write:OutLoud* (Don Johnson Inc.)
	text-to-speech	*IntelliTalkII* (IntelliTools) *TextHELP* (TextHelp) *WordQ* (Quillsoft) *WriteAway 2000* (Information Services Inc) *Write:OutLoud* (Don Johnson)
Publishing	desktop publishing	*Claris Works* (Claris) *Microsoft Publisher* (Microsoft)
	graphics or multimedia	*Hyperstudio* (Sunburst) *Kid Pix Deluxe* (Broderbund) *PowerPoint* (Microsoft)

- ... an interactive/collaborative approach involving teacher modeling, student-teacher discussion, and practice with feedback appears to be consistently correlated with learning improvement.

Behrmann (2002) suggests that the helpful low-tech tools of flow-charting, task analysis, webbing, and outlining also can be accomplished using graphic software-based organizers. "Such graphic organizers allow students to manipulate and reconfigure brainstormed ideas and color code and group those ideas in ways that visually represent their thoughts" (p. 1).

Plotnick (1997) lists the following advantages of computer mapping software:

- Ease of adaptation and manipulation – additions or changes are quick and easy

- Dynamic linking – items or groups of concepts can be rearranged with the links automatically updated

- Conversion – once the map is made, it can be converted to a text outline, a bitmap image and stored electronically

- Communication - digitized images can be sent in email or included in World Wide Web pages

- Storage – digital storage and retrieval takes less space

The most commonly used concept mapping software in education is *Inspiration* (Inspiration Software), first developed in 1988. Its successful use by students with learning disabilities for note-taking and studying has been documented extensively by Anderson-Inman and her group at the Center for Electronic Studying (Anderson-Inman & Ditson, 1999; Anderson-Inman & Horney, 1997). *Inspiration* provides students (grades 6 through adult) with two views or approaches for brainstorming and organizing ideas, a graphic view and a text view. In the graphic view, students can enter ideas, represent them with a graphic, link the ideas in any number of formats, label the links, and add and/or hide explanatory notes. A click of the mouse can transform this map to outline view, to show a textual representation of the ideas and their hierarchical organization. Students are thus able to work with both

a visual and verbal representation of their ideas (Chase, 2003). *Kidspiration* (Inspiration Software), with a text read-back feature, provides a simpler version of the program for students in grades kindergarten to 5. Many resources, including examples, tip sheets for writing strategies and templates are available through the *Inspiration* Web site (www.inspiration.com) and the Center for Electronic Studying, Computer-Based Study Strategies Web site (cbss.uoregon.edu/).

So far, we have more enthusiastic anecdotal reports than empirical evidence for the effectiveness of using these tools by struggling writers. During a one-month summer remedial program, 24 seventh- and eighth-grade students received instruction in writing strategies, *Inspiration* software, and word processors (Blair, Ormsbee, & Brandes, 2002). The students practiced keyboarding daily. The quantity and quality of the students' written products were tracked daily. Pre- and posttests of writing and attitudes were collected, and writing samples were solicited at the ends of Weeks 2 and 3. In addition, teachers kept daily logs of students' writing performance and attitude as well as observations on various strategies and techniques used and time spent planning for each assignment. One group was introduced to story webbing on Day 1 and *Inspiration* a "few" days later. The other half of the group received this instruction at the end of Week 2.

Given the time frame, the researchers were pleased with the modest improvement in writing quality, planning and attitudes to writing, as well as a substantial increase in the quantity of students' written product. However, it is disappointing that they report their results for the class as a whole, with no distinction between the two treatment conditions or details about the various tools and strategies employed by the students.

In their study of the effects of concept mapping on writing, Sturm and Rankin-Erickson (2002) used a repeated-measures-within-subject design in an eighth-grade classroom. All students in a class identified as needing reading support participated in the overall writing project, but data were collected for only the 12 students who were identified as having learning disabilities. Two baseline descriptive essays were produced by each student prior to instruction in concept mapping and composing. Students then received two weeks of instruction in hand-drawn and computer-generated mapping.

Students wrote two descriptive essays (one per week) in each of three treatment conditions: no mapping, hand mapping and computer mapping. Writing positions were randomized to control for order effects.

Results showed that, in general, students' writing improved both quantitatively (more T-units) and qualitatively (higher holistic scores) over time, regardless of condition. The authors surmise that the two weeks of strategy instruction given to the students about mapping, writing processes, and conventions prior to the treatment conditions provided students with a number of question prompts (posted in the classroom), which helped them to expand and organize their writing regardless of whether or not they used mapping tools (Sturm & Rankin-Erickson, 2002). While these are results all teachers would like to see, they do not really tell us whether or when computer mapping software is a more effective tool than others. If each group of students had received instruction in the relevant strategy just prior to the condition in which it was used, instead of at the beginning of the project, the effects of each condition might have been more evident. However, the logistics of carrying out such a procedure in a classroom would be quite difficult, as would a design comparing the two mapping strategies to a control group, if such a group could be assembled. The authors recommend further research employing single-subject designs to test the effects of mapping as a pre-writing strategy and to gain more specific information about those features and strategies that are most useful.

Students' attitudes to writing were significantly more positive when using computer mapping than when writing in other conditions. In fact, some students sought out additional opportunities to use computer mapping. The authors postulate that "for many students with learning challenges, the support of technology to complete a task may actually relieve some of the cognitive load; for others it may add to the enjoyment of the activity... For reluctant writers, a positive change in attitude toward writing, regardless of the reason, could be the first step toward improved writing skills" (Sturm and Rankin-Erickson, 2002, p. 136).

Outlines

Many word processing programs include an outlining tool to help writers organize their thoughts. *DraftBuilder* (Don Johnston Inc.) is an outlining tool designed to lead struggling writers (grade 3–12) through three key steps in creating a first draft: organizing ideas, taking notes and writing the first draft (Keller, 2002). Its split screen shows a visual map taking form on the right as the student adds concepts and ideas to the outline on the left. After students add notes to their outlines, they can drag them to the draft area where they may add more sentences and punctuation to complete their first draft. The program features color cuing and highlighting, speech feedback and spell checking. It also supports word prediction with *Co:Writer* (Don Johnston Inc.).

Research on how to enable middle school students to engage actively with information as they read and write has been conducted at the Education Development Center, Newton, Massachusetts, where "the analysis of the mountains of data collected has only just begun" (DraftBuilder, 2004, p. 1). Teachers of 6th and 8th grade classes implemented *Draft:Builder* as part of their social studies research units in the fall and spring of the school year. Typically the skills of students with learning disabilities, which were significantly different from those of normally achieving students in the first intervention, became indistinguishable from those of normally achieving students in the second intervention. Students in 6th grade, whose research skills were just developing, showed greater gains than did students in the 8th grade (Bob Follansbee, personal communication, November 3, 2004). It will be interesting to see how this tool affects the performance of struggling writers and their teachers.

One comprehensive software program that includes an outline feature is *WYNN* (*What You Need Now*; Freedom Scientific, Learning Group). This software is described by the developers as an active reading/writing environment that provides access to the writing process (Dalton

& Sember, 2002). Students can use the reading tools to scan books, articles, or Internet sites as they gather information; organize the information with the outline tool; and draft and revise their writing with the word prediction, spell check, and text read-back features. Implementation studies have provided some survey data to show that teachers and students with learning difficulties like the program and selectively use its features (Freedom Scientific, 2003; Garber, 2002). The reading features were favored, although many students also used the program to organize and draft written work. Of the teachers surveyed, 41% listed word processing as the most valuable feature. Students used the text to speech, audible spell check, and dictionary for feedback on their written work. Some frustration with the limitations of the program for formatting the written output has been expressed, with a few students and teachers remarking that they preferred other word processing programs for writing.

Prompts and Graphics

Other tools that are often used to aid writers include templates or documents prepared by the teacher so that students may work within the guidelines of an activity (Edyburn, 2002b). Word processors (such as *IntelliTalk II*, IntelliTools) with "locked" text allow students to add their own ideas without erasing the guidelines. We found little published research using this technique. Bahr and her associates (Bahr, Nelson, & Van Meter, 1996) compared the effects of two computer-based writing tools on the story-writing skills of nine fourth- through eighth-grade students with language-related learning disabilities. The first tool, a prompted writing feature in a word processor, allowed students to answer story grammar questions, then type stories using those responses as the plan; the second tool, a graphic story-writing program, allowed students to create graphic scenes, then type stories about those scenes. The students attended a series of after-school writing labs twice weekly for 11 weeks, using each tool for half of the writing sessions.

Group results did not clearly favor either tool; however, the researchers noted individual differences that they felt reinforced the concept that use of planning features should be linked to student needs. For example, students who had less internal organizational ability benefited from the computer-presented story grammar prompts and wrote less mature stories when using the graphics-based tool. Students with relatively strong organizational skills wrote more mature stories with the graphics-based tool. As with any technology, the needs and skills of the learner, the demands of the curriculum, and the nature of the learning environment all must be considered in order to find appropriate tools and strategies (Sturm & Koppenhaver, 2000).

Inputting Writing into Computers

Keyboards and Keyboarding

A number of studies noted the negative effect that slow keyboarding skills had on the production of writing using word processing (Lie, O'Hare, & Denwood, 2000; MacArthur et al., 2001; Painter, 1994). While a number of researchers have included keyboarding instruction in their studies (Lewis, 1998; Sitko et al., 1996; Wong, 2001), this variable is not always addressed. Thus, we found little research focusing on keyboarding instruction for students with writing difficulties. A study teaching systematic keyboard scanning to three elementary-school students with learning disabilities (Koorland, Edwards, & Doak, 1996) found no improvement over the students' previous "hunt-and-peck" strategies. An investigation into the rate of development of keyboarding skills in elementary school-aged children showed that students with identified learning disabilities learned keyboarding at a slower rate than children without disabilities, but skill in handwriting did not make a difference (Pisha, 1993). Access to a computer for homework assignments was also associated with improved keyboarding skills. Pisha suggests that after grade 3, students with learning disabilities should use computers for drill-and-practice of keyboarding and for completing meaningful assignments so that they will have access to tools to make writing a successful experience before disillusionment sets in. However, more is not always better. Concerns for injury-free keyboarding suggest limiting intensive practice to 15 minutes per session and emphasizing accuracy, not words per minute (Barksdale, 2003).

For students who are just beginning to learn to express their ideas in words, programs featuring pictures and grids that students can access by mouse, switch, or adapted keyboard to input words or phrases are described enthusiastically by many teachers and developers (Feit, 2002; Peake, 2002; Ray, 2002; Ziejdel & Fonner, 2002). These include programs like *IntelliPics* (IntelliTools), *IntelliPics Studio* (IntelliTools), *Clicker 4* (Crick Software), and *Writing with Symbols 2000* (Mayer-Johnson). Many examples of prepared templates can be shared by teachers at the producers' Web sites. We were unable to find research studies using these products, however.

Writing with technology requires access to computers, and many schools have invested in laptop computers or portable keyboards to increase students' opportunities to use them for writing (Belanger, 2000). While durability and relatively low cost are two of the attractions of portable keyboards, some of these keyboards also include features to aid writers with special needs (*AlphaSmart 3000*, AlphaSmart. Inc.: key response changes, spellcheck, word prediction; *LaserPC 6*, Perfect Solutions: speech feedback, display sizes). Enthusiasm is evident (Friedlander, 2002a, 2002b; Hamman & Griffin, 2002), but research is not documented.

Word Prediction

Models for writing portray it primarily as a problem-solving activity that includes "complex planning and evaluation processes, linguistic processes, and transcription processes" (MacArthur et al., 2001, p. 288). At its simplest level, students with impaired or emergent language skills are hampered by failure to recognize the words they wish to use (Bjaalid, Hoien, & Lundberg, 1995; Bruck, 1993). As a result, their written language is improved significantly through intervention in word finding, word fluency, and contextual cueing (Corrigan & Stevenson, 1994; Wiig & Semmel, 1980); and word prediction (Heinisch & Hecht, 1993; Laine & Follansbee, 1994; MacArthur, 1998a, 1998b). If, as Wiig and Semmel (1980) showed, word-finding skills can be assisted considerably through cueing, we need to consider how we can effectively assist cueing for low-language learners.

Assistance through word completion or word prediction has been extensively promoted in the past decade as a productivity tool for all. However, there appears to be distinct equivocation in the academic and professional literature of the past decade as to whether or not its use improves a writer's productivity significantly. As MacArthur (2000) stated "Development runs substantially ahead of research in this field" (p. 1). Vendors claim that specialty devices or programs can be installed easily and that word prediction is an agent to improved written expression – "one component . . . is the promise of increased worker productivity" (Bergeron, 1991, p. 130). Despite vendors' claims over the past decade of considerable positive results, the results of research into this area are limited and equivocal (cf. Burger, 1997; Koester & Levine, 1994a, 1994b; Lewis, Graves, Ashton, & Kieley, 1998; MacArthur, 1998a, 1998b, 1999; Treviranus & Norris, 1987; Venkatagiri, 1994). Much of this equivocation stems from too few cases being used in the studies; debatable designs that affect consistency and predictability of results; and debatable analyses upon which results are based (cf. MacArthur, 2000; Wong, 2001).

Little empirical research exists regarding the efficacy of implementing specialized access-to-writing systems to increase personal or professional written productivity for persons with disabilities (Wong, 2001). This is especially true of word prediction programs, whether operated manually (by keystroke) or orally (voice-activated); and of speech synthesis. A major problem is that many of the empirical studies were "small n" or single-case studies, thus discouraging any predictive interpretations of the results. Given the variances that exist within the category of "learning disability," the results found in single-case studies may be germane to only that case. For example, while the results in MacArthur's work often look impressive, it would be wrong to generalize them to the larger population.

In our own recent work (e.g., Colwell, 2000; Laine & Follansbee, 1994; Laine & Breen, 1996; Laine & Sitko, 2001), we have found the most common situation to be that young and poor readers are poor writers and that they are also poor problem solvers. Effective writers monitor their writing recursively, thus allowing them to make decisions (solve problems) continuously. However, little research has reported on the impact of using assistive writing tools on the problem-solving abilities of poor writers (Sitko & Sitko, 1996; Sitko et al., 1992). A major element is that poor writers do not possess effective word-finding skills (Laine, 2000, 1999; Wiig & Semmel, 1980). The challenge, therefore, is for writers to get past the "word-wall," or to access the "cues" that will enable them to do so. Thus the primary question remaining for any exploratory work is: whether or not tools, such as word prediction and speech synthesis, provide more immediate cuing to facilitate word finding and fluency (through word count) and flexibility (through variety of words used) – basic elements critical to effective written expression (Laine, 2000, 1999, 1998; Wiig & Semmel, 1980).

Speech Recognition (Oral Word Prediction)

There are two types of predictive dictionary: oral word prediction and manual word prediction. Laine and Wilkinson (1997) concluded that oral word prediction (speech to text) requires a higher cognitive functioning level as well as a good oral language ability for it to be an effective writing tool. Oral word prediction, sometimes referred to as "voice recognition" and "speech recognition," basically allows the user to speak to the computer; the software then converts the oral expression to algorithms, which are linked to particular letter/word patterns. This patterning is taught to the computer by the user reading a passage. The computer stores the "voice-file" and refines it through further use. The more one uses the program, the greater the efficiency of the software in recognizing one's speech patterns. But this form of input is not for everyone. Some programs like *Naturally Speaking* (Scansoft) – which simulates continuous speech – run too quickly for the low-functioning writer. Programs like *Dragon Dictate* (Scansoft) or *Via Voice* (IBM) are slower and simulate "discrete-speech," whereby each word is recognized independently of other words.

To use speech recognition effectively, the user needs to be able to recognize the words written. If corrections are not made, errors can build up in the voice file, thereby decreasing the efficiency of its use. Such programs also need faster-running machines to prevent the slow response to the spoken word from further frustrating the already impaired writer. Much of the literature on oral word prediction has focused on its technical aspects, especially the merits of continuous speech systems compared to discrete speech systems. Continuous speech systems may react too quickly for the low-functioning user to discern and correct errors "on-the-run," thus leading to differential use by any one group (e.g., Spence, 2002). Thus, providing a student who has language impairments with a sophisticated speech recognition system may create more of a barrier than an assistance.

By contrast, manual word prediction (keystroke-to-text) technology works by single keystroke. As each keystroke is made, a window containing a word list is modified to predict the word (or phrase) from the main dictionary. There are two distinct types of "word prediction" technology. One is not truly word "prediction" but rather word "completion." Here, the word list window changes as one types letters, but when one creates a space, the program (for example, *WriteAway2000*, Information Services Inc) does not predict the next word or phrase. However, other programs, such as *WordQ* (Quillsoft), do enable prediction based upon the word already typed and the sentence that has been emerging. One needs to determine which facility the user needs before purchasing. A second consideration is whether or not one wishes to use a program that is transparent, that is, one that will work in conjunction with a regular writing program, or that comes intact. While the former has the advantage of allowing the writer to use a writing program with which s/he is familiar, more than one program must be opened and familiar in order to gain effective use. Lower-functioning and younger writers may find greater facility in intact programs such as *Clicker4* (Crick Software) or *WriteAway2000* (Information Services Inc). Here the writer can focus on creating and editing the writing, then have the file exported to a more sophisticated program for particular formatting and refinement.

Several of the manual word prediction systems have attempted to incorporate increasingly large dictionaries; phrase and word lists; prefix and suffix panels; and larger phrase prediction based on either usage or through grammar rules. Such refinements may have made the programs more marketable to users who want to write more efficiently (a factor that is often advanced, but has never been proven), but they do not necessarily lead to an increase in productivity (Koester & Levine, 1994b; Kurtz, 2002; Venkatagiri, 1994), especially in populations with communicative and cognitive impairments. Given the client base, educators need a system that will encourage the user to find and use words and be able to use specific tools as needed rather than have them loaded continuously (albeit transparently).

What the literature and the studies at CCCD have shown is that more sophisticated programs are not necessarily beneficial. Also, far less is known empirically about the productive interaction between this technology and the user with disabilities, its role in learning, or its impact on independence and productivity than "common knowledge" would have us believe. At this point it is also imperative to consider literature that has examined and made comparisons among various "tools." Some of the tightest work originated with Heinisch and Hecht (1993). Most recently, Kurtz (2002) and Marfilius and Fonner (2003) have focused on word prediction. Marfilius and Fonner's chart is reprinted in Table 2 as it provides an overview of particular features important to any teacher when considering using this particular tool.

Both Kurtz' and Marfilius' papers are typical of an evolving focus-that of features of software and questions that relate directly to use in an inclusive education environment. Earlier work (e.g., Heinisch & Hecht, 1993), and work published through less education oriented journals (e.g., RESNA), focused more on the technical features, adequacy, and efficacy of the technology.

Revisions

Spelling Checkers
Spelling checkers may help students with writing problems to correct more errors, but they have significant limitations (Lewis, Ashton, Haapa, Kieley, & Fielden, 1999; MacArthur,

2000; MacArthur, Graham, Haynes, & De La Paz, 1996; Montgomery, Karlan, & Coutino, 2001). The greatest gains in error detection and correction appear to occur when the spelling checker is integrated with the word processor (McNaughton, Hughes, & Clark, 1997). However, there is great variation in the ability of word processors to identify correct choices for misspellings by poor spellers, especially writers with learning disabilities.

Building on earlier work, Montgomery and her colleagues (2001) analyzed the types of spelling errors made by students with learning disabilities and the rates of success of nine commonly used word processing programs in suggesting correct spellings. Results varied widely among programs, partly depending on the types of errors made. Efficiency of spell checkers increased as the phonetic error level or the bigram ratio of the misspellings (a statistical analysis of the ratio of syllable pairs to disyllable pairs) increased. However, none of the word processing programs was effective in placing the correct spelling first on the suggestion list, often not on the first screen or at all. Questions identified by this study include:

- Can detailed analyses of misspellings improve the algorithms used by spell-checking engines?

- Will spell-checking programs that incorporate common phonetic misspellings do a better job of identifying the target word for misspellings at lower phonetic error levels?

- Can spell checkers that integrate style/grammar checking do a better job of identifying misspellings, such as contextual and word spacing errors?

- Can students with learning disabilities be taught to modify their misspelling behaviors to increase the phonetic error level?

- Will a more detailed analysis of misspellings generate common phonetic errors that can be incorporated into strategies to improve the students' use of the spell checker as a compensation tool?

Most of the word processors tested by Montgomery are no longer available or have been replaced by later versions. Before expecting students to benefit from spell checkers, it is important to assess the ability of the selected word processing program to make appropriate suggestions for the students' misspellings. Since those suggestions will likely not be first in the list, students need to learn strategies for locating the correct spelling. Another serious limitation of spelling checkers is their failure to identify errors involving homonyms and other real words (MacArthur, 2000). Also, students with communications disorders may fail to recognize that certain correctly spelled words may be mistakenly identified as errors (Colwell, 2000). Some of these limitations may be overcome by providing students with particular strategies for using spell checkers (Ashton, 1999; McNaughton, Hughes, & Ofiesh, 1997), as suggested in Table 3.

Speech Synthesis

Probably the most used and most commented on assistive technology tool is text to speech (speech synthesis). To the myriad users with impaired writing skills, the ability of the computer to "read to me" has had, in our experience, more positive comments and impacts than any other single tool. Its versatility in the development of skills in both reading and writing makes it a tool that teachers can use more flexibly than word prediction.

Speech synthesis basically translates words typed by the user into speech and it "may help bridge the gap between what children want to express and what they have the skills to read and write" (MacArthur, 1996, p. 347). The features embedded in the technology are designed to assist users in detecting errors (e.g., misspelled words; incomplete or run-on sentences; grammatical errors) when they hear the sentences and words in addition to visually reading them and possibly missing details (Behrmann, 1994; Borgh & Dickson, 1992). The ability of students with learning disabilities "to detect errors auditorially is often significantly better than their ability to detect errors in written form" (Behrmann, 1994, p. 76), thus reducing the frustration of inaccurate decoding and allowing for more complete comprehension of text (Lundberg, 1995, as cited in Lauffer, 2002).

Several studies in the past decade that have focused on or included the use of speech synthesis (e.g., Borgh & Dickson, 1992; Olson & Wise, 1992; Raskind & Higgins, 1995; van Daal & Reitsma, 1993) have shown improvements in students' self-monitoring and editing of their writing. For example, Burenstein (1995) indicated that many students were able to recognize and correct more grammar and spelling errors after hearing their stories read back by the computer – a finding paralleling that noted by Spence (2002). Younger students have more difficulty with speech synthesis, as MacArthur (1998a) observed with respect to "practiced listening." As Forgrave (2002) stated, "It could be that younger students require more experience working with synthesized speech software before they are able to take full advantage of the benefits it can provide" (p. 123). Although 21 such studies have been published since 1995, many have used small samples or been single-case investigations. Further, results have also not been consistent across studies and none of them has been conducted over a long period (longer than one term or one academic year). As a result, Wong (2001) concluded that there have been too few studies to warrant any serious consideration of the implications of the findings.

When speech synthesis has been combined with word prediction (e.g., Colwell, 2000; MacArthur, 1998a, 1998b; Zhang, Brooks, Frields, & Redelfs, 1995), patterns of results are even more obscured. Yet, the researchers report that all participants appear to show an increase in accuracy over using word prediction alone. One must interpret the results cautiously. Thus, although there are numerous anecdotal reports, especially in professional periodicals, consistently documenting "the affective benefits of technology... it is much more difficult to find more objective evidence of attitude change [toward writing]" (Lewis, 2000, p. 8). Empirical evidence is inconsistent, and the results are missing the impact of long-term use by more than a small sample of users (cf. Graham & Harris, 1988; Lauffer, 2000). Lacking more conclusive evidence, from the anecdotal reporting, we can surmise that speech synthesis provides writers with bimodal feedback, which increases the chance that what has been written "makes sense"; encourages the writer to attend more to what has been written, which could result in

Table 2. Sorting Through Word Prediction Programs: Features

Sorting Through Word Prediction Programs: Features

Product Name	Platform						Selection Method			Auditory Feedback				Prediction Based On					Transparent Use		Appearance							Vocabulary Size	Custom Vocabulary						Additional	
	Mac	Win 95	Win 98	Win 2000	Win XP	Network Version	Typing Number	Clicking on Word	Scanning Option	Speaks Selected Word	Speaks Word Lists for Preview	Speaks Sentences	Highlight Words as Spoken	Alphabetical	Frequency of Use	Grammar	Phonetic	Custom Vocabulary	Works within other applications	Works Within Its Own Application	Change Font/Size	Adjust Number of Words Presented	Change Size of Prediction Window	Location of Prediction Window	Fixed/Dynamic Arrangement	Change Font Color	Change Background Color	Multiple Dictionaries/Max Size	Automatically Learns New Words	Uses a Key Stroke to Learn Words	Ability to Delete Custom Words	Ability to Add and Predict Phrases	Abbreviation Expansion	Use of Custom or Topic Dictionaries	Ability to Use Macros	Error Correction
Aurora 3.0	•	•	•	•	•	•	•	•		•	•			•	•	•	•	•	•		•	•	•	•	•	•	•	600,000	•	•	•	•	•	•	•	•
Co:Writer 4000	•	•	•	•	•	•	•	•	•	•	•	•	•	•	•			•	•		•	•	•	•	•	•	•	1,000-3,000 – 12,000-40,000	•	•	•	•	•	•	•	•
EZ Keys		•	•	•	•		•	•		•	•	•			•			•			•	•	•	•				5,000	•		•	•	•	•	•	
Gus		•	•	•	•		•	•						•	•						•	•	•	•				100,000								•
KeyRep		•	•	•	•			•		•	•				•						•	•	•	•				4 dictionaries								
PenFriend		•	•	•	•		•	•		•	•	•	•		•	•		•			•	•	•	•	•	•	•	500-2000-10,000			•	•	•	•		
PredictAbility		•		•	•		•	•							•			•			•	•		•		•	•	100 - 5000		•	•					
Predictor Pro		•	•	•	•		•	•	•	•	•		•	•	•			•	•	•	•	•	•	•	•	•	•	10,000	•		•	•	•	•		•
ProtoType		•	•	•	•		•	•	•	•	•		•	•	•			•	•	•	•	•	•	•	•	•	•		•			•	•	•		•
SoothSayer 3.0		•	•	•	•	•	•	•		•	•		•	•	•			•			•	•	•	•	•			11,000			•	•	•	•	•	•
Read & Write 7.0		•	•	•	•	•	•	•		•	•	•	•	•	•	•	•	•	•	•	•	•	•	•	•	•	•	31,000-44,000-81,000				•	•	•	•	•
Read & Write Mac	•							•											•	•	•			•		•										
WordSmith 3.0		•	•	•	•	•	•	•		•	•	•	•	•	•			•	•	•	•	•	•	•	•		•	31,000-44,000-81,000			•	•	•	•		•
WordQ		•	•	•	•	•	•	•		•	•	•	•	•	•			•		•	•	•	•	•	•	•		500-5000-10,500-15,000			•	•	•	•	•	•
WriteAway2000		•	•	•	•	•	•	•	•	•	•	•	•	•	•			•	•	•	•	•	•	•	•		•	600-2500-5000-8000			•	•	•	•	•	•

* Please note that some software programs may contain features not represented in this chart. This chart was created based on the use of the programs, demos or literature provided. This chart will be updated as information is shared with us.

© Copyright 2004   Scott Marfilius / marfilius@wi.rr.com   and Kelly Fonner   kfonner@earthlink.net greater time on task (Colwell, 2000; Spence, 2002), resulting in greater fluency – longer passages or more complex passages being written.

Implementing Technology and Writing Instruction

Two trends in education in North America today are making the search for tools for struggling writers more urgent. One is the desire for universal design for learning – meeting the needs of all learners in classrooms. The second is the adoption of American state and Canadian provincial achievement standards and "literacy tests" that students must pass in order to proceed or graduate from school. As we have described, a number of tools are available to help writers with special needs (Quenneville, 2001). Their usefulness depends on the match of their features to the needs of the learners and the ways in which they are implemented.

In one project in Toronto, Canada, "Language Labs" have been developed, which include reading and writing assistive technology to help students with learning disabilities. The writing tools include *Dragon Naturally Speaking Preferred* (Scansoft), *TextHELP Read & Write* (TextHelp), *Inspiration* (Inspiration Software), and the *LaserPC6* (Perfect Solutions) all together with *Microsoft Word*. The *Laser PC6* was chosen for use when a student could not come to the lab, as text to speech is common to all the software being used. According to survey results from the early-stage pilot project

in 18 middle and secondary schools with 38 language lab staff and 291 students responding, 82% of the teachers noted improvement in written output of the students, while 68% of the students felt they did better at written work when they used the lab. Other improvements included completion of assignments (74%) and self-esteem (85%) (Bingham, 2002).

The feedback we receive from the teachers and principals is absolutely wonderful. Students have improved their skills in their skill deficit areas, they can now complete work that they would never have been able to do, they are proud of their work, their marks have increased, self esteem has risen dramatically, behavior issues have decreased, attendance has increased. (Pillar, 2003)

Based on these results, the labs were expanded into 100 schools by the end of the 2002-2003 school year. It will be interesting to see what other data are reported, as surveys can be affected by what people feel is happening rather than by what truly is.

Another large-scale implementation project is *Begin With ME!* in Macomb, Michigan (Hardin & Miracola, 2003). This districtwide classroom-based project aims to bring educators from both special and general education together to help young writers. The project combines "simple, effective technology tools, good support strategies and motivating reasons to write to support good writing. These

Table 3. The CHECK Procedure

Check	Check the beginning sound of the word. What other letter(s) could make that beginning sound?
Hunt	Hunt for the correct consonants. Have you included all the consonants in the rest of the word?
Examine	Examine the vowels. What other vowel(s) could make the same sound?
Changes	Changes in suggested word lists may give hints. What words are being suggested? Is that the one you're looking for?
Keep	Keep repeating steps 1 through 4. Need help? Try dictionaries and asking others for assistance.

From Spell CHECKing: Making writing meaningful in the inclusive classroom; by Tamarah M. Ashton, *Teaching Exceptional Children*, 32, 1999, p. 25. Copyright 1999 by The Council for Exceptional Children. Reprinted with permission.

elements allow teachers to integrate technology into the writing process across the curriculum for all students" (Hardin & Miracola, 2003, p. 10). In a Universal Design for Access approach, assistive writing tools: talking word processors (*Write OutLoud*, Don Johnson Inc.), word prediction software(*Co: Writer 4000*, Don Johnston Inc.), visual organization software (*Kidspiration*, Inspiration Software), notetakers (*AlphaSmart*, AlphaSmart. Inc.), spell checkers and a variety of other low tech/no tech options, are available to all students at all times. Project designers have also been careful to include on-going support and training to educators, both on the technology involved, and on the strategies and process of writing. Multidisciplinary building support teams include a classroom teacher, a special educator, instructional and assistive technology support staff and the building principal.

Results of the preliminary study so far show that 58.7% of students who scored as "not proficient" on a standardized state assessment on the initial writing sample scored "proficient" on the final writing sample. In addition, students felt better about themselves as writers. Teachers reported significant growth in comfort about instructing writing to students with special needs, to the class at large, and to using technology in writing instruction. Finally, the researchers reported more collaboration among special and general educators throughout the district. It is encouraging to see the beginnings of whole school interventions which may eventually benefit all learners (Wehmeyer, Lattin, &Agran, 2001).

Research on Technology for Struggling Writers

Several findings regarding writing and technology still appear at issue in the literature. Key among them are:

1. Written language in language-delayed students is improved significantly through intervention in word finding, fluency, and flexibility (Wiig & Semmel, 1980), but even though these terms are used in many studies, there appear to be differing opinions about what they mean.

2. The use of cues in intervention facilitates or improves word recall and retrieval (e.g.,

German, 1991; Hutchinson, 1983; MacArthur, 1998a, 1998b; McGregor, 1989; Wing, 1990, Wong, 2001), but the word-finding efforts of language-delayed individuals also result in idiosyncratic patterns of expression in spontaneous speech and writing. Research results for one individual may not apply to another.

3. Such interventions facilitate language use better if used across the curriculum and in non-language class environments (Wiig & Semmel, 1980), but most empirical studies on technology tools for struggling writers have occurred within a clinical type framework.

4. Using word processing on computers is directly related to significant growth in writing ability and motivation for writing in children with severe learning disabilities (Colwell, 2000; Crealock & Sitko, 1990; MacArthur, 1998a, 1998b; Spence, 2002), but many studies have been conducted with small samples, thus their ability to generalize is questioned (e.g., Wong, 2001).

5. There is substantial literature supporting the use of speech synthesis with word processing (e.g., Cochran-Smith, 1991; MacArthur, 1998a, 1998b; Morocco & Neuman, 1986; Sitko et al., 1996; Spence 2002) to improve writing with adolescents with severe learning and language disabilities, but there is little evidence about differential effects in different instructional environments.

Lindsey (2000) identified several issues that classroom teachers and assistive technology (AT) advisors need to consider, including the following:

1. It is not enough to consider only what the student needs. We also need to consider the demands/outcomes of the curriculum and instructional priorities-"goodness-of-fit."

2. The effectiveness of any AT will be affected by the physical, social, and instructional setting in which it is placed, a factor that is especially important when considering the use of speech-to-text assistance. So, one must always ask whether the student will be able to use the AT and strategies proposed within the instructional environment in which he/she works.

3. What will be the impact of introducing and using AT, not only on the specific user but also on peers, teachers, and settings? Its implementation and use will modify many classroom routines and interactions.

4. What will be the possible impacts on policy and regulations of a student using AT for writing. Will it be allowed in one setting and disallowed in another? This issue continues in relationship to the use of AT in examinations (Kumar, 2003; Schleef 2003).

5. How will using AT for writing affect attitudes (e.g., is it "fair"? Welch, 2000)?

6. Teachers need to be adequately prepared. Lewis (2000) advises that teachers must be prepared not only on specific AT but also on how to use it in their teaching.

At best, the empirical literature shows that the relationship between the use of assistive technology and success with writing is equivocal. While certain variables (e.g., teacher, training, instructional contexts) interacting with the assistive technology are often acknowledged as confounding, they are mostly passed by or ignored (see Wong, 2001). MacArthur et al. (2001) noted that various factors need to be in place for most of the assistive technology to be effective. These features emanate from the teacher and the instructional context in which the students find themselves. These factors, clearly identified and found in numerous other papers, include:

1. An explicit structure-or model-of writing needs to exist in which the technology is used (see also Sitko et al., 1996).

2. Students must receive intensive training (see also, Wise, Olson, Ring, & Johnson, 1998), especially in word-processing/typing skills (see also Wong, 2001).

3. Teachers must instruct students in specific strategies for proficient writing and for effective use of the tools that the technology provides.,

4. Sufficient staff development must occur before the technology is introduced into the classroom with continuing and ongoing support afterwards. "Build it and they will come … is only true in baseball" (Garber, 2002, p. 1).

The more recent literature has "moved beyond media comparisons [to] … explicitly discussed specific instructional design features" (MacArthur et al., 2001 p. 296). For example, Wong (2001) states that for students with learning disabilities to capitalize on assistive technology, "they need prior or simultaneous instruction in a writing strategy contextualized in the writing process" (p. 365). This point is reiterated by MacArthur et al. (p. 298), who recommend that future research investigate the instruction that accompanies the use of any assistive "enhancement" as well as the type of enhancement and how the student uses it.

Isolating the interacting variables has thus far been elusive and the quality of research design and methodology have often been unsatisfactory (Smith, 2000; Wong, 2001). One factor that complicates the research into using technology to assist struggling writers is the evolving nature of technology: features of hardware and software described in research studies may have changed-and not necessarily for the better when it comes to serving the needs of students with disabilities. It becomes even more necessary for teachers to follow effective principles of writing instruction while at the same time watching out for and systematically documenting those features and techniques for using them that they observe to benefit their students. Given the number and transience of the variables that interplay when we write, the "whole" may defy any simple synthesis.

Conclusion

The use of technology as a tool has significant potential for increasing the quality of writing instruction provided to reluctant and developing writers in inclusive and specialized educational settings. Much work, teacher education, and systematic research still lies ahead before technology can be utilized with confidence and maximum effectiveness by classroom teachers and other educators. Future research and experimentation must continue to consider the most effective instructional strategies and administrative supports and models for integrating technology-based writing instruction and tools with other instructional writing activities and curricula for students with writing difficulties. With recent advances in multimedia, telecommunications, assistive technology, augmentative communication devices, word prediction, speech recognition and speech synthesis technologies, word processors and portable and other technologies, we can expect substantial growth in the classroom application of technology as a tool in writing instruction for reluctant writers.

Within this context, teachers, in particular, must see their role, not only as implementers of technology writing tools but as researchers and evaluators who carefully assess the impact on their students' knowledge, skills, and attitudes. When considering technology for writing instruction, we need to ask ourselves:

• What are the key features of the device or software program?

• How might I use this device or program, or others with similar features, to facilitate learning for reluctant writers?

• Is there a match between curriculum goals, my teaching philosophy, the nature of the learning environment, and the specific features of this technology and the individual strengths and learning needs, styles and interests of my reluctant writers?

• What pre-computer, computer and post-computer instructional writing activities and teaching strategies do I need to consider in planning lessons involving this technology?

• Under what conditions will a particular student best be able to use technology to facilitate writing?

Many questions and issues remain with respect to the efficacy and validity of technology tools in developing skills across various writing tasks and the diverse needs of struggling writers. However, technology offers many opportunities and tools for enabling, empowering, and supporting children and adults with writing difficulties. Technology, combined with appropriate and effective instruction, may help teachers bridge the gap between writing potential and actual writing performance by providing active, engaging, and successful writing activities and learning environments for reluctant writers.

References

Adelman, P.B., & Vogel, S.A. (1998). Adults with disabilities. In B.Y.L. Wong (Ed.), *Learning about learning disabilities* (2nd ed., pp. 657-701). San Diego, CA: Academic Press.

Alliance for Technology Access. (2000). *Computer and web resources for people for people with disabilities* (3rd ed.). Alameda, CA: Hunter House.

Anderson-Inman, L., & Ditson, L. (1999). Computer-based concept mapping: a tool for negotiating meaning. *Learning and Leading with Technology, 26*(8), 6-13.

Anderson-Inman, L., & Horney, M. (1997). Computer-based concept mapping: enhancing literacy with tools for visual thinking. *Journal of Adolescent and Adult Literacy, 40*(4), 302-305.

Ashton, T. (1999). Spell CHECKing: Making writing meaningful in the inclusive classroom. *Teaching Exceptional Children, 32*(2), 24-27.

Bahr, C., M., Nelson, N., & Van Meter, A.M. (1996). The effects of text-based and graphics-based software tools on planning and organizing of stories. *Journal of Learning Disabilities, 29*, 355-70.

Barksdale, K. (2003). *Safer keyboarding instruction: Fifteen principles of safer keyboarding instruction.* Retrieved February 2, 2003, from: www.speakingsolutions.com/news/.

Behrmann, M. M. (1994). Assistive technology for students with mild disabilities. *Intervention in School and Clinic, 30*(2), 70-83.

Behrmann, M., & Jerome, M. K. (2002). Assistive technology for students with mild disabilities: Update 2002. *ERIC Digest.* (Report No. EDO-IR-97-05). Arlington, VA: ERIC Clearinghouse on Disabilities and Gifted Education. (ERIC Document Reproduction Service No. ED463595)

Belanger, Y. (2000). Laptop computers in the K-12 classroom. *ERIC Digest.* (Report No. EDO-IR-2000-05. Syracuse, NY: ERIC Clearinghouse on Information and Technology, (ERIC Document Reproduction Service No. ED440644)

Bereiter, C., & Scardamalia, M. (1987). *The psychology of written composition.* Hillsdale, NJ: Erlbaum.

Bergeron, B. (1991). Challenges associated with providing speech recognition user interfaces for computer-based educational systems. *Collegiate Microcomputer, 9*(3), 129-143.

Berninger, V.W., & Swanson, H. L. (1994). Modifying Hayes and Flower's model of skilled writing to explain beginning and developing writing. In E.C. Butterfield (Ed.), *Children's writing: Toward a process theory of the development of skilled writing,* (pp. 57-82). Greenwich, CT: JAI Press.

Bingham, R. (2002). *Language lab research results.* Toronto, ON, Canada: Toronto District School Board.

Bjaalid, I. K., Hoien, T., & Lundberg, I. (1995). A comparison of components in word recognition between dyslexic and normal readers. *Scandinavian Journal of Educational Research, 39*(1), 51-59.

Blair, R. B., Ormsbee, C., & Brandes, J. (2002, March). Using writing strategies and visual thinking software to enhance the written performance of students with mild disabilities. In *No child left behind: The vital role of rural schools,* 22nd Annual National Conference Proceedings of the American Council on Rural Special Education (ACRES). Reno, Nevada. ERIC Clearinghouse on Disabilities and Gifted Education. (ERIC Document Reproduction Service No. ED463125)

Borgh, K., & Dickson, W. P. (1992). The effects on children's writing of adding speech synthesis to a word processor. *Journal of Research on Computing in Education, 24*(4), 533-544.

Bruck, M. (1993). Word recognition and component phonological processing skills of adults with childhood diagnosis of dyslexia: [Special Issue: Phonological processes and learning disability]. *Developmental Review, 13*(3), 258-268.

Bruer, J. T. (1997). Education and the brain: A bridge too far. *Educational Researcher, 26*(8), 4-16.

Burenstein, B. (1995). *Giving voice to student writing: Exploring the uses of speech recognition and speech synthesis in a writing curriculum. Final report.* Philadelphia, PA: Drexel Univ., Office of Computing Services. ((ERIC Document Reproduction Service No. ED395109)

Burger, S. R. (1997). *Spontaneous communication in augmentative and alternative communication (AAC): A comparison of dynamic display and Minspeak7.* Lafayette, IN: College of Wooster, Purdue University.

Chase, M. (2003). *The foundations and educational applications of visual learning: An Inspiration software white paper.* Retrieved February 1, 2003, from: www.inspiration.comvlearning/research/index.cfm.

Cochran-Smith, M. (1991). Word processing and writing in elementary classrooms: A critical review of the literature. *Review of Educational Research, 61*(1), 107-155.

Colwell, J. (2000). *The effect of word prediction and speech synthesis on the response journals of adolescent students with learning disabilities.* Unpublished master's thesis, The University of Western Ontario, London ON.

Corrigan, R., & Stevenson, C. (1994). Children's causal attributions to states and events described by different classes of verbs. *Cognitive Development, 9,* 235-256.

Crealock, C., & Sitko, M.C. (1990). Comparison between computer and handwriting technologies in writing training with learning disabled students. *International Journal of Special Education, 5*(2), 173-183.

Dalton, P., & Sember, M.A. (2002). Using WYNN 3 to teach process writing. *Proceedings of the CSUN Technology and Persons with Disabilities Conference.* Retrieved November 28, 2002, from: www.csun.edu/cod/conf/2002/proceedings/17.htm.

De La Paz, S. (1999). Teaching writing strategies and self-regulation procedures to middle school students with learning disabilities. *Focus on Exceptional Children, 31*(5), 1-16.

Draft:Builder: Research Retrieved January 12, 2004, from donjohnston.com/catalog/writecover/writecoverfrm.htm.

Edyburn, D. L. (2000). 1999 in review: A synthesis of the special education technology literature. *Journal of Special Education Technology, 15*(1), 7-18 .

Edyburn, D. L. (2001). 2000 in review: A synthesis of the special education technology literature. *Journal of Special Education Technology, 16*(2), 5-25.

Edyburn, D. L. (2002a). 2001 in review: A synthesis of the special education technology literature. *Journal of Special Education Technology, 17*(2), 5-24.

Edyburn D. L. (2002b, October). *Access to learning*. Preconference workshop presented at the 20th Annual Closing the Gap Conference, Minneapolis, MN.

Ellis, E.S., & Larkin, M.J. (1998). Strategic instruction for adolescents with learning disabilities. In B.Y.L. Wong (Ed.), *Learning about learning disabilities* (2nd ed., pp. 585-656). San Diego, CA: Academic Press.

Englert, C.S., Garmon,, A., Mariage, T., Rozendale, M., Tarrant, K., & Urba, J. (1995). The early literacy project: Connecting across the literacy curriculum. *Learning Disabilities Quarterly, 18*, 253-275.

Englert, C.S., Raphael, T.E., Anderson, L. M., Anthony, H. M., & Stevens, D. D. (1991). Making strategies and self-talk visible: Writing instruction in regular and special education classrooms. *American Educational Research Journal, 28*, 337-372.

Feit, S. (2002). Assessment: Key to diversifying instruction. *Proceedings of the CSUN Technology and Persons with Disabilities Conference*. Retrieved November 28, 2002, from: www.csun.edu/cod/conf2002/proceedings/70.htm.

Flower, L.S., & Hayes, J.R. (1981) Plans that guide the composing process. In C. H. Friderksen & J. F. Dominic (Eds.), *Writing: The nature, development, and teaching of written communication* (pp. 39-59). Mahwah, NJ: Erlbaum.

Forgrave, K. (2002). Assistive technology: Empowering students with learning disabilities. *The Clearing House, 75*(3), 122-127.

Freedom Scientific. (2003). *Independent research shows WYNN is a must-have tool for students*. Retrieved February 7, 2003, from: www.freedomscientific.com/wynn/RMC_Survey.asp.

Friedlander, B.S. (2002a). AlphaSmart 3000: An essential part of the AT toolkit. *Closing the Gap, 21*(1), 1, 18-19.

Friedlander, B.S. (2002b). Part II: AlphaSmart 3000: An essential part of the AT toolkit. *Closing the Gap, 21*(2), 1, 20.

Garber, S. (2002, October). *Making every student (and teacher) a WYNNer: The Howard County, MD Really Read Project*. Paper presented at the 20th Annual Closing the Gap Conference, Minneapolis, MN.

Gardner, J. E., & Edyburn, D. (2000). Integrating technology to support effective instruction. In J. D. Lindsey (Ed.), *Technology and exceptional individuals* (3rd ed., pp. 191-240). Austin, TX: Pro-Ed.

German, D. J. (1991). Analysis of children's word-finding skills in discourse. *Journal of Speech & Hearing Research, 34*, 309-316.

Gersten, R., & Baker, S. (2001). Teaching expressive writing to students with learning disabilities. *Elementary School Journal, 101*(3), 251-272.

Gilden, D. (2002). Beyond the accessibility wizard: MS Office provides more flexible low vision access. *Proceedings of the CSUN Technology and Persons with Disabilities Conference*. Retrieved February 2, 2003, from: www.csun.edu/cod/conf2002/proceedings/206.htm.

Graham, S., & Harris, K. R. (1988). Instructional recommendations for teaching writing to exceptional students. *Exceptional Children, 54*, 506-512.

Graham, S., Harris, K. R., MacArthur, C., & Schwartz, S. (1998). Writing Instruction. In B.Y.L. Wong (Ed.), *Learning about learning disabilities* (2nd ed., pp. 391-423). San Diego, CA: Academic Press.

Graves, A., Semmel, M., & Gerber, M. (1994). The effects of story prompts on the narrative production of students with and without learning disabilities. *Journal of Learning Disabilities, 17*, 154-164.

Graves, D.H. (1983). *Writing: Teachers and children at work*. Portsmouth, NH: Heinemann.

Graves, D.H. (1985). All children can write. *Learning Disabilities Focus, 1*, 36-43.

Gregor, K. K. (1989). Facilitating word-finding skills of language-impaired children. *Journal of Speech & Hearing Disorders, 54*, 141-147.

Hall, T., & Strangman, N. (2002). *Graphic organizers: enhancements literature review*. Retrieved December 3, 2002, from: www.cast.org.ncac/index.cfm?=3015.

Hamman, T., & Griffin, K. (2002). The AlphaSmart Keyboard, versatility in the trenches. *Proceedings of the CSUN Technology and Persons with Disabilities Conference*.

Retrieved Dec.1,2002, from:www.csun.edu/cod/conf2002/proceedings/241.htm.

Hardin, S., & Miracola, F.. (2003). Writing more, more often and with better results. *Closing the Gap, 21*(5), 1, 10-11.

Harris, K. R., & Graham, S. (1996). Constructivism and students with special needs: Issues in the classroom. *Learning Disabilities Research and Practice, 11*(3), 134-37.

Harris, K. R., Graham, S., & Mason, L. (2002). POW plus TREE equals powerful opinion essays. *Teaching Exceptional Children, 34*, 74-77.

Harris, K., & Pressley, M. (1991). The nature of strategy instruction: Interactive strategy instruction. *Exceptional Children, 57*, 392-404.

Harris, K.R., Schmidt, T., & Graham, S. (1998). Every child can write: Strategies for composition and self-regulation. In K. Harris, D. Deshler, & M. Pressley (Eds.), *Learning in diverse schools and classrooms* (pp. 1-23). Cambridge, MA: Brookline Books.

Hayes, J. R., & Flower, L. (1987). On the structure of the writing process. *Topics in Language Disorders, 7*, 19-30.

Heinisch, B., & Hecht, J. (1993). Predictive word processors: A comparison of six programs. *TAM Newsletter, 8*, 4-5, 8-9.

Hogan, K., & Pressley, M. (Eds.) (1997). *Scaffolding student learning: Instructional approaches and issues.* Albany: State University of New York.

Hutchinson, A. (1983). The relationship between word-finding ability and reading with an emphasis on the language-learning-disabled child. *Special Education in Canada, 57*, 27-29; 31-32.

Johnson, D. (2002). Web watch: Writing resources. *Reading Online, 5*(7). Retrieved January 25, 2003, from: www.readingonline.org/electronic/elec_index.asp?HREF=web watch/writing/index.html.

Keller, B. (2002, October). *Phenomenal first drafts.* Paper presented at the 20th Annual Closing the Gap Conference, Minneapolis, MN.

Koester, H. H., & Levine, S. P. (1994a). Learning and performance of able-bodied individuals using scanning systems with and without word prediction. *Assistive Technology, 6*, 42-53.

Koester, H. H., & Levine, S. P. (1994b). Modeling the speed of text entry with a word prediction interface. *IEEE Transactions on Rehabilitation Engineering, 2*(3), 177-187.

Koorland, M. A., Edwards, B. J., & Doak, P. (1996). Evaluating a systematic keyboarding strategy for students with learning disabilities. *Computers in the Schools, 12*(3), 13-20.

Kumar, A. (2003) State revises FCAT rules for disabled. *St. Petersburg Times.* St. Petersburg, FL: January 22, p. 1B.

Kurtz, J. (2002, October). *Word prediction software.* Paper presented at the 20th Annual Closing the Gap Conference, Minneapolis, MN.

Laine, C. J. (2000, March). *Using a technology "toolkit" to cue written expression: Which features help? What are the effects?* Paper presented at California State University, Northridge, 15th Annual Conference: Technology and Persons with Disabilities, Los Angeles, CA.

Laine, C. J. (1999, July). *Word-prediction technology: Does it really help children's written expression?* Paper presented at the International Association for Special Education Conference, University of Sydney, Sydney, Australia.

Laine, C. J. (1998, July). *Using word-prediction technology to improve the writing of low-functioning children and adults.* Paper presented at the Australian Computers in Education Conference, Adelaide, Australia.

Laine, C. J., & Breen, M. B. (1994). Writing by talking to the computer: Experiences, ideas and questions. *Canadian Journal for Educational Communication, 23*, 89-101.

Laine, C. J., & Follansbee, R. (1994). Using word prediction technology to improve the writing of low-functioning hearing-impaired students. *Child Language Teaching and Therapy, 11*, 283-297.

Laine, C., J., & Sitko, M. C. (2001). Using computer assisted writing in inclusive settings. *Closing the Gap, 20*(1), 1, 12, 31.

Laine, C. J., Sitko, M.C., Colwell, J., & Spence, T.M. (2002, October). *Improving writing with assistive technology tools: Do they really help?* Paper presented at Closing The Gap Conference, Minneapolis. MN.

Laine, C. J., & Wilkinson, W. (1997). *Improving employment opportunities for persons with* disabilities through training: A case study using speech recognition systems. Unpublished internal report. London, ON: The University of Western Ontario.

Lauffer, K. A. (2000). Accommodating students with specific writing disabilities. *Journalism and Mass Communication Editor, 54*(4), 29-46.

Lavelle, E., Smith, J., & O'Ryan, L. (2002). The writing approaches of secondary students. *The British Journal of Educational Psychology, 72*(3), 399-412.

Lewis, R. B. (1998). *Enhancing the writing skills of students with learning disabilities through technology: An investigation of the effects of text entry tools, editing tools and speech synthesis. Final Report.* San Diego, CA: Dept. of Special Education, San Diego State University. (ERIC Document Reproduction Service No. ED432117)

Lewis, R. B. (2000). Musings on technology and learning disabilities on the occasion of the new millennium. *Journal of Special Education Technology, 15*(2), 5-12.

Lewis, R. B., Ashton, T. M., Haapa, B., Kieley, C. L., & Fielden, C. (1999). Improving the writing skills of students with learning disabilities: Are word processors with spelling and grammar checkers useful? *Learning Disabilities: A Multidisciplinary Journal, 9*(3), 87-98.

Lewis, R. B., Graves, A. W., Ashton, T. M., & Kieley, C. L. (1998). Word processing tools for students with learning disabilities: A comparison of strategies to increase text entry speed. *Learning Disabilities Research and Practice, 13*(2), 95-108.

Lie, K. G., O'Hare, A., & Denwood, S. (2000). Multidisciplinary support and the management of children with specific writing difficulties. *British Journal of Special Education, 27*(2), 93-99.

Lindsey, J. (Ed.). (2000). *Technology & exceptional individuals* (3rd ed.). Austin, TX: Pro-Ed.

MacArthur, C. A. (1996). Using technology to enhance the writing processes of students with learning disabilities. *Journal of Learning Disabilities, 29*(4), 344-354.

MacArthur, C. A. (1998a). Word processing with speech synthesis and word prediction: Effects on the dialogue journal writing of students with learning disabilities. *Learning Disability Quarterly, 21*(2), 151-66.

MacArthur, C. A. (1998b). From illegible to understandable: How word prediction and speech synthesis can help. *Teaching Exceptional Children, 30*(6), 66-71.

MacArthur, C. A. (1999). Word prediction for students with severe spelling problems. *Learning Disability Quarterly, 22*(3), 158-72.

MacArthur, C. A. (2000). New tools for writing: Assistive technology for students with writing difficulties. *Topics in Language Disorders, 20*(4), 85-100.

MacArthur, C. A., Ferretti, R. P., Okolo, C. M., & Cavalier, A. R. (2001). Technology applications for students with literacy problems: A critical review. *The Elementary School Journal, 101*(3), 273-299.

MacArthur, C. A., Graham, S., Haynes, J. A., & De La Paz, S. (1996). Spelling checkers and students with learning disabilities: Performance comparisons and impact on spelling. *Journal of Special Education, 30*(1), 35-57.

Male, M. (2003). *Technology for inclusion: Meeting the needs of all children* (4th ed.). Boston, MA: Allyn & Bacon.

Marfilius, S. (2002, October). *Mastering Microsoft Word.* Presentation at the Closing The Gap Conference, Minneapolis, MN.

Marfilius, S., & Fonner, K. (2003, March). *Sorting through word prediction programs.* Paper presented at California State University, Northridge, 18th Annual Conference: Technology and Persons with Disabilities, Los Angeles, CA.

McNaughton, D., Hughes, C., & Clark, K. (1997). The effect of five proofreading conditions on the spelling performance of college students with learning disabilities. *Journal of Learning Disabilities, 30*(6), 43-51.

McNaughton, D., Hughes, C., & Ofiesh, N. (1997). Proofreading for students with learning disabilities: Integrating computer use and strategy use. *Learning Disabilities Research and Practice, 12,* 16-28.

Mirenda, P., Wilk, D., & Carson, P. (2000). A retrospective analysis of technology use patterns of students with autism over a five-year period. *Journal of Special Education Technology, 15*(3), 5-16.

Montgomery, D.J., Karlan, G.R., & Couthino, M. (2001). The effectiveness of word processor spell checker programs to produce target words for misspellings generated by students with learning disabilities. *Journal of Special Education Technology, 16*(2), 27-42.

Morocco, C., & Neuman, S. (1986). Word processors and the acquisition of writing strategies. *Journal of Learning Disabilities, 19*, 243-247.

Olson, R. K., & Wise, B. W. (1992). Reading on the computer with orthographic and speech feedback: An overview of the Colorado Remediation Project. *Reading and Writing: An Interdisciplinary Journal, 4*(2),107-44.

Painter, D. D. (1994). *A study to determine the effectiveness of computer-based process writing with learning disabled students under two conditions of instruction: Peer collaborative process model and non-peer collaborative process model.* Unpublished doctoral dissertation, George Mason University.

Peake, P. (2002). Using Writing with Symbols 2000. *Proceedings of the CSUN Technology and Persons with Disabilities Conference.* Retrieved November 28, 2002, from: www.csun.edu/cod/conf2002/proceedings/215.htm.

Pisha, B. (1993). *Rates of development of keyboarding skills in elementary school aged children with and without identified learning disabilities.* unpublished doctoral dissertation, Harvard University. Retrieved February 3, 2003, from www.cast.org/udl/DevelopmentofKeyboardingSkills353.cfm.

Plotnick, E. (1997). Concept mapping: A graphical system for understanding the relationship between concepts. *ERIC Digest.* (Report No. EDO-IR-97-05). Syracuse, NY: ERIC Clearinghouse on Information and Technology (ERIC Document Reproduction Service No. ED407938)

Quenneville, J. (2001). Tech tools for students with learning disabilities: Infusion into inclusive classrooms. *Preventing School Failure, 45*(4), 167-170.

Raskind, M. H., & Higgins, E. (1995). Effects of speech synthesis on the proofreading efficiency of postsecondary students with learning disabilities. *Learning Disability Quarterly, 18*(2), 141-58.

Ray, L. (2002). Student authoring with IntelliPics Studio. *Proceedings of the CSUN Technology and Persons with Disabilities Conference.* Retrieved November 28, 2002, from: www.csun.edu/cod/conf2002/proceedings/73.htm.

Roth, F. P. (2000). Narrative writing: Development and teaching children with writing difficulties. *Topics in Language Disorders, 20*(4), 15-27.

Ruddell, R.B., & Boyle, O.F. (1989). A study of cognitive mapping as a means to improve comprehension of expository text. *Reading Research and Instruction, 29*(1), 12-22.

Schleef, L. (2003). Inclusive school communities: Accessible learning environments for all. *Closing The Gap, 22*(3), 1,14-15,28.

Schumaker, J.B., & Deshler, D.D. (1992). Validation of learning strategy interventions for students with LD: Results of a programmatic research effort. In B.Y.L. Wong (Ed.), *Contemporary intervention research in learning disabilities: An international perspective* (pp. 22-46). New York: Springer-Verlag.

Sitko, C.J., McBride, A., & Sitko, M.C. (1996).A computer-assisted writing process: Support for learning disabled adolescents and adults. In M.C. Sitko & C.J. Sitko (Eds.), *Exceptional solutions: Computers and students with special needs* (pp. 29-47). London, ON, Canada: The Althouse Press.

Sitko, C. J., Sitko, M. C., & McBride, A. (1992). Using technology to help learning disabled students access a process approach to functional writing skills. *Closing the Gap, 11*(3), 12-14, 36.

Sitko, M., & Sitko, C. (1995). Computer technology: Implications for students with special needs. In C. Crealock & D. Bachor (Eds.), *Instructional strategies for students with special needs* (2nd ed., pp. 385-443). Toronto, ON, Canada: Allyn and Bacon.

Sitko, M. C., & Sitko, C. J. (Eds.). (1996). *Exceptional solutions: Computers and students with pecial needs.* London, ON, Canada: The Althouse Press.

Sitko, M.C., & Sitko, C.J. (1999, November). *Empowering students with writing challenges: A computer-assisted writing process model.* Paper presented at the Special Education Technology for Today and Tomorrow (SETT)'99 Conference, Toronto, ON, Canada.

Smith, R.O. (2000). Measuring assistive technology outcomes in education. *Diagnostique, 25*, 273-290.

Spence, T. M. (2002). *Using speech synthesis technology to assist written composition by elementary students with learning disabilities.* Unpublished master's thesis, University of Western Ontario, London, ON, Canada.

Sturm, J., & Koppenhaver, D. A. (2000). Supporting writing development in adolescents with developmental disabilities. *Topics in Language Disorders, 20*(2) 73-92.

Sturm, J. M., & Rankin-Erickson, J. L. (2002). Effects of hand-drawn and computer-generated concept mapping on the expository writing of middle school students with learning disabilities. *Learning Disabilities Research & Practice, 17*(2), 124-139.

Tomkins, G. (2000). *Teaching writing: Balancing process and product* (3rd ed.). Upper Saddle River, NJ: Prentice Hall.

Treviranus, J., & Norris, L. (1987). Predictive programs: Writing tools for severely physically disabled students. *Proceedings of the 10th conference on Rehabilitiation Technology.* Washington, DC.

Troia, G., & Graham, S. (2002). The effectiveness of a highly explicit, teacher-directed strategy instruction routine: Changing the writing performance of students with learning disabilities. *Journal of Learning Disabilities, 35*(4), 290-305.

van Daal, V.H.P., & Reitsma, P. (1993). The use of speech feedback by normal and disabled readers in computer-based reading practice. *Reading and Writing: An Interdisciplinary Journal, 5*(3), 243-259.

Venkatagiri, H. S. (1994). Effect of window size on rate of communication in a lexical prediction AAC system. *Augmentative and Alternative Communication, 10,* 105-112.

Vygotsky, L. S. (1978). *Mind in society.* Cambridge, MA: Harvard University Press.

Wehmeyer, M.L., Lattin, D., & Agran, M. (2001). Achieving access to the general education curriculum for students with mental retardation. *Education and Training in Mental Retardation and Developmental Disabilities, 36,* 327-342.

Welch, A.B. (2000). Responding to student concerns about fairness. *Teaching Exceptional Children, 33*(2), 36-40.

Wiig, E. H., & Semmel, E. M. (1980). *Language assessment and intervention for the learning disabled.* Columbus, OH: Merrill.

Wing, C. S. (1990). A preliminary investigation of generalization to untrained words following two treatments of children's word-finding problems. *Language, Speech & Hearing Services in Schools, 21,* 151-156.

Wise, B.W., Olson, R.K., Ring, J., & Johnson, M. (1998). Interactive computer support for improving phonological skills. In J. L. Metsala & L. C. Ehrl (Eds.), *Word recognition in beginning literacy* (pp. 189-208). Mahwah, NJ: Erlbaum.

Wong, B.Y.L. (2001). Commentary: Pointers for literacy instruction from educational technology and research on writing instruction. *Elementary School Journal, 101*(3), 359-369.

Wong, B.Y.L., Butler, D.L., Ficzere, S.A., & Kuperis, S. (1997). Teaching adolescents with learning disabilities and low achievers to write, plan and revise compare-and-contrast essays. *Learning Disabilities Research & Practice, 12,* 2–15.

Zeijdel, C., & Fonner, K. (2002). Creating writing scaffolds in Clicker4. *Proceedings of the CSUN Technology and Persons with Disabilities Conference.* Retrieved November 28, 2002, from www.csun.edu/cod/conf2002/proceedings/293.htm.

Zhang, Y., Brooks, D. W., Frields, T., & Redelfs, M. (1995). Quality of writing by elementary students with learning disabilities. *Journal of Research on Computing in Education, 27*(4), 483-499.

Zipprich, M.A. (1995). Teaching web making as a guided planning tool to improve student narrative writing. *Remedial and Special Education, 16*(1), 3-15.

Sources of Hardware and Software

AlphaSmart, Inc., *AlphaSmart 3000, Dana.* www.alphasmart.com/

Brainium Technologies, Inc. (BTI) *DreamWriter.* Maple Ridge, BC, Canada. www. brainium.com/

Broderbund. *Kid Pix Deluxe, Mavis Beacon Teaches Typing.* Novato, CA. www.broderbund.com/

Claris. *Claris Works.* www.apple.com/products/claris/

Crick Software. *Clicker 4.* Moulton Park, Northampton,UK. www.cricksoft.com

Don Johnston Inc. *Co: Writer 4000, DraftBuilder, Write:OutLoud.* Volo, IL. www.donjohnston.com

Freedom Scientific's Learning Systems Group. *WYNN 3.1.* Palo Alto, CA. www.freedomscientific.com

IBM. *Via Voice.* Austin, TX. www.ibm.com/able

Information Services Inc. *WriteAway 2000.* St. John's, NF, Canada. www.is-inc.com

Inspiration Software. (1988-2002). *Inspiration, Kidspiration.* Portland, OR. www.inspiration.com

IntelliTools. *I Can Write Series.* Petaluma, CA: Author. www.intellitools.com

IntelliTools. *IntellilKeys, IntelliTalk II, Overlay Maker.* Petaluma, CA: Author. www.intellitools.com

Mayer-Johnson. *Writing with Symbols 2000.* Solana Beach, CA. www.mayer-johnson.com

Microsoft. *Microsoft Publisher, Microsoft Word, PowerPoint.* www.microsoft.com

Perfect Solutions Software. *Laser PC6.* West Palm Beach, FL. www.perfectsolutions.com

Quillsoft. *WordQ.* Toronto, ON, Canada. www.wordq.com

Scansoft. *Dragon Dictate, Dragon Naturally Speaking.* Peabody, MA. www.scansoft.com

Sunburst. *HyperStudio, Type to Learn.* Elgin, IL & Valhalla, NY. www.sunburst.com

textHelp! Systems. *textHELP! Read & Write.* Antrim, Northern Ireland. www.texthelp.com

30

Mathematics and Technology-Based Interventions

Paula Maccini and Joseph Calvin Gagnon

Eighth-and-ninth grade students in the United States scored significantly below their peers in other countries on several higher-level math tasks, including geometry, algebra concepts, measurement, and calculus (Beaton, Mullis, Martin, Gonzalez, Kelly, & Smith, 1996; Mullis, Martin, Beaton, Gonzalez, Kelly, & Smith, 1998). These international discrepancies in students' achievement on the Third International Mathematics and Science study may be due, in part, to the approaches taken to teaching mathematics in the various countries. In contrast to Japan, for example, in the United States, skills are broadly addressed and revisited year after year, with a focus on memorization and routine manipulation of numbers in formulas (Beaton et al., 1996; Mullis et al., 1998). Additionally, students in the United States engage in seatwork activities, which focus on routine procedures for 96% of their instructional time, compared to 41% for student in Japan (Berstein, 1997). Recommendations highlight the need for increased emphasis on math concepts and skills embedded in meaningful investigations and active student participation in learning.

One promising medium for enhancing math learning is technology-based instruction within the core curriculum. Technology-based instruction refers to use of a computer or other specialized systems as the mode of instruction (Vergason & Anderegg, 1997). Technology can support the movement away from a focus on memorization and routine manipulation of numbers in formulas and toward instruction and activities embedded in real-world

problems (Bottge & Hasselbring, 1993) and active student learning (Kelly, Gersten, & Carnine, 1990). Additionally, technology has been touted as a motivational and necessary tool for students, both at school and in future occupations. The motivational feature is particularly important for students with learning disabilities (LD), who are considerably at risk for school failure (Zigmond, 1990) and experience low motivation to succeed in the high school environment (Gregory, Shanahan, & Walberg, 1985). For example, use of technology may increase student motivation in school due to the stimulating, interactive nature of the medium (i.e., animation, hyperlinks, graphics) (Bender, 2001).

The use of technology, combined with the noted recommendations for change in both instructional focus and practice, may positively impact student achievement in the United States. This suggestion parallels current reform efforts proclaimed by both members of the mathematics education community and the federal government. For example, the National Council of Teachers of Mathematics Standards (NCTM, 1989; 2000) for teaching math were first published more than a decade ago to address dissatisfaction with U.S. student performance on international tests and the need to prepare students for the demands of an increasing technological society. Five overarching goals reflect the recommended practices and include the need to teach all students higher-level thinking and reasoning skills and mathematical problem-solving. Recently revised, the standards state the need to prepare all learners to: (a) value mathematics; (b) become confident in mathematics ability; (c) become mathematical problem solvers; (d) learn to communicate mathematically; and (e) reason mathematically (NCTM, 2000).

To achieve these goals, NCTM recognizes the importance of technology and strongly endorses integrating of instructional technological tools with the instruction and assessment of mathematics education for all learners. Specifically, the Council (NCTM, 1998) identified the need for: (a) accessibility to computers and related forms of technology for all teachers and learners; and (b) training and staff development experiences that promote technological exploration and selection of appropriate uses of technology to meet students' needs. Finally, NCTM (1998) noted the following recommendations:

- *Every student should have access to an appropriate calculator.*

- *Every mathematics teacher should have access to a computer with appropriate software and network connections for instructional and noninstructional tasks.*

- *Every mathematics classroom should have computers with Internet connections available at all times for demonstrations and students' use.*

- *Every school mathematics program should provide students and teachers access to computers and other appropriate technology for individual, small-group, and whole-class use, as needed, on a daily basis.* (p. 1)

In addition to the most recent revisions to the Standards by the NCTM (2000), current educational reform efforts include an emphasis on the use of and access to technology. The No Child Left Behind Act (NCLB) of 2001, "Amends Title II of the Higher Education Act of 1965 to authorize grants, contracts, and competitive agreements to consortia for carrying out programs that prepare prospective teachers to use technology to improve student learning, and programs that improve the ability of

institutions of higher education to carry out such programs" (U.S. Department of Education, 2003a, p. 1). Further, NCLB authorized continued funding for the Regional Technology in Education Consortia (R*TEC) program (U.S. Department of Education, 2003b). Program goals include, "assisting states, local educational agencies, teachers, school library and media personnel, administrators, and other education entities successfully integrate technologies into kindergarten through 12th grade (K-12) classrooms, library media centers, and other educational settings" (Regional Technology in Education Consortia, 2003, p. 1). These provisions highlight an emphasis on the use of technology in schools and the recognition that technology has the potential to profoundly impact instruction and student learning.

In addition to its general benefits, technology also has great potential for assisting youth with disabilities. Based on recent legislation (e.g., Individuals with Disabilities Education Act, 1997), students with disabilities are faced with increasing expectations as teachers work to provide access to the same challenging curricula as nonlabeled students. Additionally, teachers must prepare students with disabilities for rigorous local and state assessments.

Many students with LD perform poorly on assessments that are tied to state standards (Thurlow, Albus, Spicuzza, & Thompson, 1998). For example, Thurlow et al. determined that only 34% of students with LD passed a state test on basic math skills, versus 83% of their nondisabled peers. The results are consistent with respect to the research on common characteristics of students with LD in math. For example, Cawley, Baker-Kroczynski, and Urban (1992) noted that secondary-level students with LD function at around the fifth to sixth grade level in math and struggle on basic competency assessments. Specific areas of weakness in mathematics range from basic skills (Algozzine, O'Shea, Crews, & Stoddard, 1987), to algebraic reasoning (Maccini, McNaughton, & Ruhl, 1999) and problem-solving skills (Hutchinson, 1993; Montague, Bos, & Doucette, 1991). This is of serious concern given that students with disabilities are held to increasingly higher standards and will need higher-level math and reasoning skills to meet the demands of high school and beyond. In fact, in less than 20 years, one in every four jobs will require technical skills (Tarlin, 1997, as cited in Jarrett, 1998), and currently many careers require a strong basis in mathematics (NCTM, 2000).

Given the difficulties students with LD experience with mathematics and the promise of technology-based instruction as a tool to help these learners, the authors conducted a comprehensive review of the literature to determine effective technology-based practices for students with LD. The purpose of the current review of the literature is twofold: (a) to determine the nature and the effects of technology-based practices for secondary-level students with LD in math; and (b) to provide instructional implications and directions for future research.

Methodology

Criterion for Inclusion
To be included in our review, studies must have met the following criteria: (a) included secondary-level students (i.e., grades 6 through 12) with LD; (b) targeted mathematics performance as at least one dependent variable; (c) incorporated some form of technology-based intervention as the independent variable; and (d) be published in refereed journals between 1985 and 2002.

Search Procedures
The following search procedures were followed to locate relevant research studies: (a) an electronic search through the ERIC, ECER, and PsychINFO systems; (b) a hand search in the following refereed journals: *Learning Disability Quarterly; Learning Disabilities Research & Practice; Behavioral Disorders; Exceptional Children; Remedial and Special Education; Education and Treatment of Children; Teaching Exceptional Children; Technology and Special Education; Journal of Special Education*; and (c) an ancestral search through the studies obtained.

The following key descriptors were used to locate the articles: *special education; mild disabilities; learning disabilities; learning handicapped; mildly handicapped; mathematics; technology; computers; calculators; videodisc; hypermedia; hyperstudio; Internet; virtual reality.*

Seventeen articles were obtained from the initial search procedures. However, upon closer examination, six of them were excluded because they did not meet the following criteria: (a) math was not the dependent variable (Lieber & Semmel, 1989; Okolo, Rieth, & Bahr, 1989; Pease & Kitchen, 1987); or (b) the population did not target secondary-level students (O'Callaghan, 1998) or did not include students with LD (Pugalee, 2001; Szetela & Super, 1987). Thus, the final search included 11 articles that met all inclusion criteria (see Appendix A starting on page 618).

Results

The following variables related to technology-based interventions for secondary-level students with LD were analyzed: (a) nature of the sample (i.e., population, setting characteristics and study duration); and (b) nature of intervention used (i.e., computer-assisted adaptations and videodisc). In addition, researchers calculated the magnitude of the treatment effect(s) for each of the studies via the Cohen's d ($d = M_1 - M_2 / s_{pooled}$, where M is the mean of group 1 or 2 and s_{pooled} equals the root mean squared of the two standard deviations) (Cohen, 1988).

Nature of the Sample
A total of 704 secondary-level students from grades 6th through 12th participated in the studies targeted in the current review, with 149 of these students labeled LD (see Appendix A). The majority of participants were male ($n = 166$); 110 were female. Five studies did not report gender information (Bottge & Hasselbring, 1993; Christle, Hess, & Hasselbring, 2001; Kelly, Carnine, Gersten, & Grossen, 1986; Moore & Carnine, 1989; Woodward & Gersten, 1992). The mean number of instructional sessions was 11.5 (range of 5 to 18), and the mean duration of the instructional sessions was 41 minutes (range of 10 to 90 minutes) (see Appendix A).

Nature of Intervention
The nature of the technology-based intervention categories included computer-assisted instruction and videodisc-based instruction. Of the 11 articles obtained, three studies (27%) involved computer-assisted instruction (CAI)

interventions in either game (Bahr & Rieth, 1991) or tutorial (Gleason, Carnine, & Boriero, 1990; Woodward & Gersten, 1992) computer formats. The majority of interventions ($\underline{n}$ = 8; 73%) involved videodisc-based instruction with the following features: (a) contextualized math word problems (Bottge, 1999; Bottge & Hasselbring, 1993; Bottge, Heinrichs, Chan, & Serlin, 2001; Bottge, Heinrichs, Mehta, & Hung, 2002); (b) instructional design variables (Kelly et al., 1986; Kelly et al., 1990; Moore & Carnine, 1989); and (c) Web-based instruction within a universally designed environment (Christle et al., 2001).

Computer-Assisted Instruction

In the current review, computer-assisted instruction (CAI) refers to instruction delivered via computer-based software programs (Mercer, 1997). Three studies included CAI in either game (Bahr & Rieth, 1991) or tutorial (Gleason et al., 1990; Woodward & Gersten, 1992) computer formats.

Games

CAI that includes game software is designed to help motivate students while reviewing basic facts and/or problem-solving strategies (Mercer, 1997). In the first CAI study, Bahr and Rieth (1991) examined the effects of four goal structures on student achievement through CAI math tasks: cooperative, competitive, individualistic, and no goal structure. Additionally, the effects of the goal structures and time of test (i.e., pre-, mid-, posttest) were assessed for math achievement. Twenty-three pairs of mildly handicapped (i.e., LD, educable mentally retarded, emotionally disturbed) seventh-and eighth-grade students were selected via a six-step process: (a) two junior high schools were selected and one special education teacher from each school volunteered to participate; (b) students were assessed to ensure familiarity with at least one computational operation (i.e., multiplication, division, addition, subtraction); (c) students were assessed to eliminate students who were fluent in the basic facts of all operations; (d) the operations in which students most needed practice were identified; (e) based on an assessment, students were assigned to either single-digit subtraction or multiplication fact problems; and (f) students were ranked and paired based on same class enrollment, same gender, and same math deficits.

The 23 pairs of students were randomly assigned to one of the four goal structures, and for 12 days, each participated in a daily 10-minute computer-based drill and practice session. Within these sessions, each student worked for 5 minutes. Prior to the computer-based sessions, students received training in keyboarding, the software used, and record keeping. Each group used Zenith 158 microcomputers and either Minus Mission or Meteor Multiplication computer games. Students recorded correct and incorrect answers on a daily basis. Students in all conditions were able to exchange points earned during the sessions for tangible reinforcers.

As noted, students participated in one of the four goal structures as they completed the computer-based drill and practice math games. The cooperation condition required students to record individual correct responses and then calculate, record, and graph the daily mean for the pair. Students received 10 points when the average number of daily correct answers for the pair exceeded 50% more than the average number during baseline. If a pair did not achieve this goal, they earned 5 points. In the competitive condition, the student in each pair who answered the greater number of correct answers daily received 10 points, whereas the other student earned 5 points. Students in the individualistic condition received points based on individual correct answers. If a student's daily number of correct answers exceeded his/her baseline, he/she was awarded 10 points. Otherwise, the student received 5 points. Lastly, in the no goal condition, each student recorded the number of correct answers, receiving 10 points regardless of performance.

To assess the effects of goal structure and time of testing on student achievement, three dependent measures were included. Students completed the Sterling Informal Math Inventory (Sterling, 1976) as a pre-and postpencil-and-paper assessment. Additionally, an informal one-minute computation test focusing on software specific content was administered. The latter informal assessment was given as a pre-, mid-, and posttest. Also, students used the assigned software to complete 5-minute pre- and posttest trials.

Results indicated that, for all three dependent measures, students improved rates of correct responses. No significant effects were noted for any goal condition on achievement gains for pre- and posttest, and pre-, mid-, and posttest measures. Across goal structures (i.e., cooperative, competitive, individualistic, and no goal), the results of pretest and posttest effect sizes for the correct digits per minute (CDM) for each measure were: (a) the Sterling on overall math computation (range of $d = .1$ to .3); (b) content test (range of $d = .1$ to .9); (c) computer trials (range of $d = .9$ to 1.6); and (d) the Sterling on the specific math skills targeted in the intervention (range of $d = .2$ to .5). With one exception, error rates remained consistent over time and goal condition. On the Sterling probe, student error rates increased from pre- to posttest. However, rates increased only for the sections students did not practice in the software program. Error rates did not increase for the problems focused on the specific skills taught. The results of pre-posttest effect sizes for the error digits per minute (EDM) for each measure were: (a) the Sterling on overall math computation (range of $d = .1$ to .7); (b) content test (range of $d = -.7$ to .3); (c) computer trials (range of $d = -.8$ to .2); and (d) the Sterling on the specific math skills targeted in the intervention (range of $d = -.2$ to .5).

The researchers identified several limitations to the study. Due to the lack of a non-computer control group, it is not possible to identify if increased correct responses were specifically a result of computer use. Other factors may have influenced results, such as students assisting partners, spontaneous competition, and use of a reward program. Further, the decontextualized computation and lack of generalization and maintenance affect social validity.

Tutorials

Tutorial software programs are designed to help students: (a) review skills or concepts within a step-by-step computerized format; and (b) branch to enrichment and remedial segments or levels (Mercer, 1997). In addition to game-like CAI formats, two studies involved tutorial computerized programs (Gleason et al., 1990; Woodward & Gersten, 1992). For example, Gleason et al. (1990) developed a pretest-posttest design with random assignment of students to either a computer-assisted story problems (CASP) or a teacher-directed story problems (TDSP) condition. The purpose of the study was to determine if the computer-based program was as effective as the teacher-based program when teaching multiplication and division word problems using empirically validated teaching procedures. Nineteen middle school students with mild handicaps (MH), who were performing on a fourth-grade level, participated in the study. Both the CASP and TDSP conditions incorporated the following theory-of-instruction (Engelmann & Carnine, 1982) variables: (a) explicit strategy instruction for translating story problems into equations and solving for the solution; (b) teacher- or computer-based modeling; (c) teacher- or computer-based prompting or guided practice of the mathematical procedures; (d) fading of teacher- or computer-based prompts; (e) assessing student understanding; and (f) immediate correction of student errors. The medium of instructional delivery (i.e., computer or teacher-based) was the only difference in the two treatment conditions. Further, students in the CASP group could either write their answers on a worksheet and/or use the computer, whereas students in the TDSP condition could state the answer orally to the teacher or write it on the worksheet.

Students received 18 days of instruction covering one to two lessons per day. In the CASP condition, students were first provided two lessons of computer training on how to read and respond to the computer-based directions and prompts. It was determined that there was a significant difference between pretest and posttest for both the CASP and TDSP conditions ($d = 3.1, 2.3$, respectively). However, for the CASP and TDSP conditions, no significant differences were determined on the following: (a) pretest to picture posttest ($d = .2, .4$, respectively); (b) pretest to transfer test ($d = -.3, -.5$, respectively); and (c) pretest to oral transfer test ($d = -.3, .1$, respectively). Further, no significant differences were determined across treatment groups (CASP versus TDSP) on the following measures: (a) posttest ($d = -.2$); and (b) picture posttest ($d = .3$) and transfer test ($d = -.2$). A substantial difference was determined on the oral transfer test ($d = .7$).

Woodward and Gersten (1992) studied the implementation and effects of a videodisc program (Systems Impact, 1986) for 7 teachers and their 57 students with LD from a large school district. The researchers focused on (a) teacher implementation of the program; (b) teacher and student perceptions of the program; (c) teacher use of effective teaching behaviors (e.g., number of problems modeled, number of guided practice problems, number of product and process questions, number of logistical questions, number of probing questions during correction, success rate on independent work, amount of praise, and amount of criticism) following the program; and (d) effects of the videodisc program on student achievement.

Prior to the videodisc intervention, teachers participated in two one-hour training sessions emphasizing guided practice, monitoring student work, and teaching to mastery. Teachers were also instructed in use of remediation strategies. Participating teachers used the Mastering Fractions (Systems Impact, 1986) videodisc program for six weeks with students in their resource room. They were encouraged to use at least 45 minutes of each class period for lesson presentation and student practice.

Data were obtained via observation, interviews, and a criterion-referenced test used both a pre- and posttest. Salient findings based on observations included teacher use of guided practice 100% of designated times. However, teachers used the program for the entire 45 minutes only 66.6% of the time. Using observation, teachers were also rated on several behaviors using a 3-point scale (1 = never and 3 = always). Of importance were the high ratings on teacher circulation to monitor students ($X =$ 2.86), implementation of sufficient time for students to work and check answers ($X = 2.83$), and provision of specific remediation activities at designated points ($X = 2.66$). Teachers also commonly provided explanation of fractions concepts consistent with the videodisc program and engaged in few criticisms of

students. Also, teachers showed significant increases in the frequency of modeling strategies ($t = 2.13$, $df = 6$) ($d = 1.2$) and use of guided practice ($t = 4.27$, $df = 6$) ($d = 1.8$).

Teacher interviews revealed that (a) teachers found the program easy to use; (b) most felt the use of remediation and guided practice assisted student mastery of the material; (c) most felt that students participated more with the videodisc instruction; and (d) all teachers identified the graphics and special effects as the best features of the program. Particularly interesting was the finding that all teachers thought that the program had excellent potential for future use in both general and special education classes for math and science. However, they did point to the excessive amount of paperwork associated with the program (e.g., daily checks of independent seatwork, correcting daily quizzes).

Several results of student interviews and criterion referenced pre- and posttests are noteworthy. When interviewed, students identified positive feelings about the program, and 90% felt more confident as a result of having participated in the program. This was consistent with student gains on the criterion-reference test. The mean pretest score was 29.4 (SD = 9.38) whereas the mean posttest score was 79.0 ($SD = 10.08$) ($d = 5.1$). On the posttest, 64% of students met or exceeded the 80% score indicating they had met an acceptable level of mastery.

Videodisc-Based Adaptations

Seven studies in the present review focused on videodisc-based adaptations and involved the following: (a) instructional design variables (Kelly et al., 1986; Kelly et al., 1990; Moore & Carnine, 1989); (b) contextualized math problems (Bottge, 1999; Bottge & Hasselbring, 1993; Bottge et al., 2001; Bottge et al., 2002); and (c) Web-based instruction within an universally designed environment (Christle et al., 2001).

Instructional Design Variables

Kelly et al. (1986) compared the effectiveness of a videodisc curriculum and a traditional basal program to teach basic fraction skills. The main focus was the instructional design features of each program. Specifically, the Mastering Fractions program (Systems Impact, 1986) integrates components consistent with Engelmann and Carnine's (1982) instructional design theory into the videodisc program. For example, the program provides review each class period. In contrast, in the basal program concepts are not reviewed until after several sessions have been completed. Table 1 shows a summary of instructional design features of the two programs.

Students with LD and nonlabeled students were selected from a remedial and a general high school math class and randomly assigned to Mastering Fractions (Systems Impact, 1986) or basal conditions. Three types of data were collected to assess students in three areas: (a) pre-, post-, and maintenance criterion-referenced tests assessed skill acquisition; (b) formal observation provided data on student academic engagement and work completion; and (c) responses to a student questionnaire supplied information on student attitudes toward the math programs.

Based on this information, several salient results were noted. For the videodisc intervention, there was a significant difference found between pretest and posttest ($d = 1.1$), as well as pretest and maintenance scores ($d = 2.1$). Both interventions had an on-task rate above 80%. Additionally, the videodisc intervention had a statistically significant higher student on-task rate than the basal intervention. Independent classwork success rates for both interventions exceeded 90%. Lastly, error analysis revealed differences, including fewer errors in identifying diagrams representing fractions for those students participating in the videodisc intervention.

Kelly et al. (1990) also used the Mastering Fractions program (Systems Impact, 1986). These researchers investigated the effects of the instructional design principles with high school students in remedial and general math classes. To identify the sample, researchers administered an initial screening test focusing on prerequisite computational skills. Students scoring at least 80% were subsequently given a test to identify who already knew the fractions content. Students scoring above 50% on the second measure were excluded. The 28 final participants included 17 students with LD. Students were randomly assigned to the treatment condition, which involved curriculum design variables, or to the basal math instruction control group. The three curriculum design variables implemented within the intervention were (a) systematic practice in discriminating among related problems; (b) separating confusing elements and terminology; and (c) using of a wide range of examples. Other aspects of instruction were kept constant between intervention and control conditions.

The primary dependent measure was a curriculum-referenced test. Additionally, the researchers used observation to identify active student engagement during instruction. Although the mean performance improved for both groups, students in the treatment group scored significantly higher than the comparison group (96% versus 82%, $d = 1.27$). Students in the treatment group also made fewer errors, such as not confusing terms ($d = .55$), being able to discriminate between algorithms ($d = 1.17$), and solving a range of examples ($d = 2.12$). Students in both the instructional design and control (i.e., basal) conditions maintained high levels of active engagement. For example, students in the instructional design condition were on task 96% and students in the basal condition were on task 84% during the observation periods.

Moore and Carnine (1989) also studied the effects of a videodisc program that incorporated curriculum design variables (e.g., explicit strategy instruction, wide range of examples, cumulative review) versus a traditional basal approach to teach ratio and proportions. Following screening procedures, 29 high school students, including 6 students with special needs in math, were randomly assigned to either the treatment condition, active teaching with empirically validated curriculum design (ATCD), or the control condition, active teaching with basals (ATB). Both conditions incorporated variables of effective instruction, which included (a) lesson review; (b) teacher modeling with examples; (c) incorporating product questions (one-word response answers to "who," "what", etc.) and process questions (e.g., how and why) into instruction; (d) mastery learning set at 80% or higher; (e) guided practice and daily independent practice with teacher monitoring; and (f) immediate feedback. Both conditions included the same effec-

Table 1. Mastering Fractions Versus Basal Programs

Instructional Design Feature	Mastering Fractions	Basal
Review	Review each lesson. Review incorporated into more complex skills or reviewed cumulatively	Up to three sessions before review
Discrimination	Skills are introduced, practiced, and mixed with other types of problems. Specific instruction and remediation provide for discrimination	No practice provided across units (e.g., adding fractions, subtracting fractions)
Range of Examples	Students introduced to fractions less than one, improper fractions, and provided strategies for reading and writing both	All fractions examples have values less than one. Improper fractions not introduced until following academic year
Easily Confused Labels	Confusing terms (e.g., numerator, denominator) addressed in same lesson	Confusing terms (e.g., numerator, denominator) addressed in same lesson
Explicit Strategy Teaching	Students provided explicit problem-solving strategies	Students not always provided the strategy

tive teaching practices, but the control condition, ATB, was taught by the classroom teacher and included information from basal math texts, whereas, the treatment condition was delivered via a videodisc program (Systems Impact, 1987). The latter incorporated principles of instructional design such as: (a) explicit strategy instruction (i.e., teaching one strategy generalizable to many problem types); (b) teaching the procedure in steps and requiring mastery prior to advancement to the next step; and (c) discrimination practice (i.e., distinguishing when to use a particular strategy with a given problem type) and incorporating a range of examples.

Following treatment, it was determined that the mean performance for all students in the experimental condition was significantly higher than that for students in the control condition on a criterion-referenced posttest (82% versus 66%, d =1.1). The mean performance of the six students with special needs in math was 71%, which was similar to the performance of their nondisabled peers. Further, no significant differences were found two weeks after termination of the study on the maintenance probe between conditions (74% versus 67%, d = .3).

Contextualized Math Word Problems

Bottge and Hasselbring (1993) also used the Mastering Fractions (Systems Impact, 1985) videodisc program. These researchers completed a two-part study to identify the program's effectiveness for learning adding and subtracting fractions and generalizing skills to contextualized word problems. The study included 36 students within two ninth-grade remedial math classes. Approximately half of the students received special education services, were recently referred, or had recently terminated special education services; the remaining students were labeled at risk for failure in mathematics. The researchers assessed the efficacy of video-based math instruction versus teacher-directed instruction that included basal text. In Part 1 of the intervention, specific chapters (i.e., renaming and simplifying fractions) within the videodisc program were chosen based on an error analysis of student pretest scores. The pre-and posttest measures were given to all students in the school in general and pre-algebra classes. The measures included a fraction computation test, a word problem test, and a problem-solving test that was based on information embedded in an 8-minute video.

During the five-day intervention in Part 1, students viewed the videodisc, responded to questions based on the video orally or in writing, and completed workbook pages. Students in the intervention made significant gains on calculation problems and obtained scores similar to those of students in the comparison group of nonlabeled pre-algebra students. However, on the word problem test, the comparison group scored significantly higher than students identified as remedial.

Part 2 of the study followed the initial five-day intervention. Participants were paired based on scores from the fractions computation test and randomly selected to participate in contextualized or word problem groups. Students in the contextualized problem-solving group participated in a five-step process during the intervention: (a) view a video several times; (b) identify the central problem and subproblems; (c) complete worksheets; (d) discuss approaches to solving the problem; and (e) consider alternative approaches when the teacher altered the problem. During the word problem intervention, a consistent lesson routine was followed. First, a participant read the problem as it was displayed on an overhead projection and the students identified the relevant and extraneous information. Next, students identified the operation needed and computed the answer. Third, students completed independent practice worksheets. Students in the contextualized problem-solving condition scored significantly higher than those in the word problem condition ($d = 1.1$) on the video test. Students in both conditions scored significantly better on the word problem test following intervention ($d = .1$). Students in the contextualized problem-solving condition also scored significantly higher than those in the word problem condition on a maintenance video problem ($d = 1.1$).

In another study that involved anchored instruction, Bottge (1999) studied the effects videodisc-based instruction with 66 eighth-grade students from remedial and pre-algebra

classes. Based on their pretest scores on a computation test, students in one remedial math class were randomly assigned to either the experimental contextualized problem condition (CP) or the word problem (WP) condition. Further, two pre-algebra classes were randomly assigned to either the CP or WP condition. The treatment in both conditions included the following: (a) problem-solving and linear measurement skills; (b) variables of effective instruction (i.e., review of previous work, introduction of new material, guided practice, feedback, independent practice, and cumulative review); and (c) a cognitive problem-solving strategy. However, the method of delivery was different, as the CP condition incorporated videodisc-based instruction whereas the WP condition involved standard text-based word problems with teacher-directed instruction. Further, instruction within the CP condition included a modified, five-step version of a cognitive problem-solving strategy (Montague, 1997) whereas instruction in the WP condition included the original seven-step procedure. Specifically, the CP condition involved introduction to anchored instruction and videodisc-based technology via the program The 8th Caller. The math problem posed in the video requires students to determine if they have enough money to send out for pizza or if they need to purchase frozen pizza for their party. Following introduction to videodisc-based problems, students analyzed and solved embedded math problems presented in Bart's Pet Project, the video program examined in an earlier study (Bottge & Hasselbring, 1993). Instruction also incorporated a five-step problem-solving strategy: paraphrase, hypothesize, estimate, compute, and check. During the intervention, students were encouraged to work in groups and discuss their solutions with the support and facilitation of the classroom teacher.

Instruction in the WP condition involved direct instruction of standard word problems from basal math texts. In addition, the teacher introduced the cognitive problem-solving strategy for solving text-based problem: read, paraphrase, visualize, hypothesize, estimate, compute, and check. Finally, students were encouraged to share varying processes and results, as well as to develop their own problems and solutions.

Three measures were used to assess treatment effects: (a) fractions computation pre- and- posttest; (b) word problem pre- and posttest; (c) contextualized pre - and posttest; and (d) transfer test given two weeks after posttests. No significant differences were found across conditions on the following measures: (a) computation posttest for students in the remedial group ($d = -.5$) and pre-algebra group ($d = -.2$); and (b) word problem posttest for students in the remedial group ($d = .3$) and pre-algebra group ($d = -.4$). However, significant differences were obtained across contextualized posttest scores for CP participants in the remedial ($d = 1.7$) and pre-algebra condition ($d = 1.2$); and transfer problem for CP participants in the remedial ($d = 2.5$) and pre-algebra condition ($d = .9$). Though encouraging, these results should be interpreted with some caution as the mean scores were below a commonly accepted criterion of mastery of 80% or greater. Further, individual test results were not reported for the seven students with special needs included in the experimental conditions. Future research should disaggregate results to assess the validity of the treatment.

Bottge et al. (2001) compared the effects of a video-based intervention targeting pre-algebra skills to traditional problem-solving instruction with eighth-grade students in remedial math and pre-algebra classes. Seventy-five students participated in the study, which included 14 students from a remedial math class and the remaining students from three pre-algebra classes. Students in the remedial math class and one pre-algebra class were assigned to the video-based condition, enhanced anchored instruction (EAI). Included in this condition were 10 students with LD and 1 student with ED. The remaining two pre-algebra classes were assigned to the traditional problem instruction (TPI). Six students with LD, one student with ED, and one student with other health impairment (OHI) participated in the TPI condition.

Instruction in both the EAI and the TPI conditions included variables of direct instruction (Rosenshine & Stevens, 1986): (a) review of previously learned skills; (b) delivery of new information; (c) guided practice of the target skills; (d) independent practice; and (e) feedback and review. However, students in the EAI treatment were provided with a video-based problem, whereas the TPI condition included teacher-directed instruction using basal text material. Specifically, students in the EAI treatment were provided with a video-based problem Kim's Komet (Learning Technology Center at Vanderbilt University, 1996). The video-based program embedded algebraic skills (e.g., slope, linear functions, variables, making predications with distance, rate, time, measurement and reliability) in a real-world or contextualized problem. In the video-based problem, Kim is interested in competing in a soapbox model car derby and needs help predicting where she should let her car go on the ramp to successfully complete a loop, a banked curve, and a long jump at the end of the run. The students' charge is to construct a graph to help Kim with these predictions. Students were asked to answer two related problems posed in the video: (a) determine the three top qualifiers from three U.S. regions by calculating and comparing each car's speed relative to the times and distance across regions; and (b) graphically predict the rate of Kim's car at the end of the run as a function of the location of the release point along the ramp. Students then applied their predictions using hand-made wooden cars and a model car ramp that was built and constructed in a technology education classroom. The students measured the time it took the cars to travel to the end of the run relative to various release points on the ramp. Finally, graphs were constructed to predict where the cars should be released from and the speed needed to maneuver the different stunts.

In the TPI condition, students received teacher-directed instruction in standard word problems from basal texts that addressed the same algebraic content as the EAI treatment. The TPI condition also included pictorial displays of problems similar to the video-based problem. In addition to the text problems, during the second half of each instructional period, students applied their skills to a real-world task that involved planning a two-week road trip. Students used maps and Web-based information to help plan their trip. Teacher instruction included the following procedures: (a) providing a rationale for introducing the topics of distance, rate, and time; (b) modeling the problems using the formulas; (c) providing guided practice until students were able to perform the task independently; and (d) providing independent student practice. Students were also taught to cross out unnecessary information embedded in word problems.

Participants in both conditions were pretested and posttested on their computation (WRAT-III) and problem-solving skills. The problem-solving measure was developed by the authors and included word problems involving rate, time, distance, reading and interpreting graphs/charts, making predictions, whole number and decimal operations. Ten days after the intervention, participants took an EAI test and a TPI test that matched the instructional design and problem types addressed in both intervention conditions. Students in all conditions substantially improved from pretest to posttest on the problem-solving measure. For example, remedial math students in the EAI condition increased 36 percentage points ($d = 3.8$), pre-algebra students in the EAI condition increased 22 percentage points ($d = 1.4$), and pre-algebra students in the TPI condition increased 37 ($d = 2.2$) and 35 ($d = 2.4$) percentage points, respectively. However, students in all conditions did not reach a common criterion for mastery of 80% or greater. Posttest scores ranged from 63% to 74%.

On the arithmetic subtest (WRAT-III), students in the four classes either maintained or decreased performance from pretest to posttest. Specifically, the remedial students in the EAI class experienced a decrease of 6.65 percentage points ($d = -.5$), pre-algebra students in the EAI condition increased .45 percentage points ($d = .04$), and pre-algebra students in the TPI classes decreased 1.33 ($d = -.1$) and 1.16 ($d = -.1$) percentage points, respectively.

The highest posttest scores were obtained on the EAI and TPI maintenance measures, where most of the mean scores approached an 80% criterion level. For example, on the EAI maintenance test, remedial math students in the EAI condition increased 52 percentage points, pre-algebra students in the EAI condition increased 40 percentage points, and

pre-algebra students in the TPI condition increased 32 and 36 percentage points, respectively. On the TPI maintenance measure, remedial math students in EAI condition increased 45 percentage points, pre-algebra students in the EAI condition increased 35 percentage points, and pre-algebra students in the TPI condition increased 49 and 54 percentage points, respectively.

Bottge et al. (2002) further examined the effects of anchored instruction with 42 seventh-grade students from general education math classes. The sample included eight students with disabilities, six students with LD, one student with ED, and one student with LD and ED. An alternate ranking method was used to randomly assign participants from each of two general education math classes. Each class was then assigned to one of two conditions: enhanced anchored instruction (EAI) condition or the traditional problem instruction (TPI) condition. Finally, a special education teacher and general education were randomly assigned to one EAI and TPI class.

The math teacher first reviewed fractions with students in all conditions the first four days. Similar to previous research (Bottge, 1999), the method of delivery was different across conditions. The EAI condition incorporated videodisc-based instruction and the TPI condition involved standard text-based word problems with teacher-directed instruction. Further, instruction within the TPI condition included a seven-step problem-solving procedure. The EAI condition involved introduction to anchored instruction and videodisc-based technology via the program Fraction of a Cost. The math problem posed in the video required students to determine if they had enough money and materials to build a skateboard ramp and how they would build it with the available resources. Following introduction, students worked on a similar applied task in the technology education classroom and built wooden benches.

Instruction in the TPI condition involved direct instruction of standard word problems from basal math texts. The problems were similar to those in the EAI condition (e.g., application of measurement to a real-world problem) and included money and measurement skills.

The teacher also introduced the cognitive problem-solving strategy for solving text-based problems: read, paraphrase, visualize, hypothesize, estimate, compute, and check. Students were also taught a first-letter mnemonic strategy for remembering the cognitive strategy.

Three measures were used to assess treatment effects: (a) fractions computation pre- and posttest; (b) word problem pre- and posttest; (c) contextualized pre- and posttest; and (d) transfer test given 17 days following posttests. The total mean scores for students with disabilities (SP) were compared to the total mean scores of participants without disabilities (NSP) across pretest-posttest measures. No significant differences were found for SP and NSP, respectively, on the following measures: (a) computation test EAI condition ($d = -.3, -.1$) and TPI condition ($d = .1, .2$); and (b) computation test EAI condition ($d = .3, .2$) and TPI condition ($d = .2, .1$). In the EAI condition, significant differences were obtained from pretest to posttest on the contextualized test for SP and NSP participants ($d = 1.8, d = 2.0$, respectively). Moderate differences were obtained for participants in the TPI condition from pretest to posttest on the contextualized test for SP and NSP participants ($d = .4, d = .5$, respectively).

Further, across conditions (i.e., EAI versus TPI), no significant differences were determined for SP and NSP respectively on the following measures: (a) computation posttest ($d = -1.0., d = -.3$); and (b) word problem posttest ($d = -.2, d = .1$). However, across conditions, moderate to significant differences were determined for SP and NSP, respectively, on the contextualized test ($d = 1.1, d = 1.7$) and transfer task ($d = .7, d = 1.1$). The researchers noted that although students in the EAI condition overall performed higher than students in the TPI condition on the contextualized and transfer test, the scores for students with disabilities were equivocal. Bottge et al. (2002) hypothesized that several factors could have impacted treatment effects, including (a) the students were younger in the study than in past research focusing on anchored instruction (i.e., 7th grade instead of 8th and 9th grade as in previous studies); (b) the higher-performing students in each group may have taken responsibility for most of the group work; and (c) the lack of individualized attention by the teacher (i.e., the special and general education did not collaboratively teach each group).

Web-based Instruction (WBI) within a Universally Designed Environment

Christle et al. (2001) conducted a pilot study that involved video-based instruction with four middle school students with special needs. The project was part of the Technology Research in Practice (TRIP), which incorporates six integral principles: (a) anchored instruction (i.e., embedding math within real-world situations and having students solve problems that are meaningful and functional to enhance generalization); (c) generative learning (i.e., having students construct their own meaning of the mathematical concepts to promote retention); (d) collaborative problem-solving (i.e., having students work together to solve problems); (e) universal design (i.e., accommodating student needs within the learning environment and accessibility to the curriculum via several approaches and strategies); and (f) Web-based instruction (i.e., incorporating information from the Web into hypermedia programs for meaningful and supportive learning environments).

Incorporating these principles, Christle et al. (2001) created the TRIP web site with the lesson "The Jefferson Mall Lunch Bunch" (p. 26). The Web site includes a five-minute vignette of three middle school students who go to the mall and plan their lunch. The Web page also incorporates both teacher online support and lessons centered on the vignette (e.g., manual and materials of resources, suggestions, background activities, skills, student worksheets, analogous problems, evaluation suggestions and summative evaluation, extension activities) and accompanying student materials (e.g., anchor/story, student support, money and time challenge problems, feedback).

The pilot study was a single-subject multiple-baseline design across four middle school students, including two with LD, from a resource class. During baseline, the participants were assessed on their problem-solving rates to determine their current level of functioning. A student from a general education class was also assessed to determine the target criterion for students in the sample. Once stability was determined, the first student was introduced to the intervention (i.e., the Web site with the challenge problems and analogous problems). When the first student reached the target rate after seven intervention sessions, he took scheduled maintenance probe while the second student was presented with the treatment. This process continued until all subjects had been exposed to the treatment and assessed. The assessment measures addressed generalization of the target skills to real-world situations. As a result of the treatment, all four students successfully met the target criterion within 3 to 7 instructional sessions, and three participants maintained and generalized the skills up to 11 sessions after termination of intervention. Further, students mentioned that they enjoyed the project and thought the problems were more meaningful to their lives than standard text problems.

Discussion

A comprehensive review of the literature was conducted to determine effective technology-based practices for teaching mathematics to secondary level students with LD. The focus of the review was twofold: (a) to determine the nature and the effects of technology-based practices for secondary-level students with LD in math; and (b) to derive instructional implications and directions for future research. Eleven articles met the criteria for inclusion in the review and were summarized and analyzed with respect to the type of technology-based practice under investigation. The authors determined that the 73% ($n = 8$) of the interventions incorporated videodisc-based instruction, with the remainder of the studies ($n = 3$, 27%) using computer-assisted instruction (CAI) within game or tutorial formats. With the exponential growth in technological advancements, it is not surprising that the majority of studies reviewed incorporated features beyond traditional software programs. By comparison, less than a decade ago, Hughes and Maccini (1997) determined from a comprehensive review of the literature that only 19% ($n = 4$) of interventions included videodisc-based formats for students with LD.

In terms of overall effectiveness, technology-based practices show equivocal, but promising results for assisting students with LD in mathematics. Specifically, the effect sizes were mixed across the following categories: (a) CAI game formats (range of $d = -.8$ to 1.6) and (b) CAI tutorial formats (range of $d = -.5$ to 5.1). The most prominent (50%, $n = 4$) type of the videodisc-based intervention included contextualized math word problems that addressed a myriad age-appropriate and motivating storylines for secondary-level students, such as building a skate board ramp, competing in a soap-box derby, planning a party, and building benches for the remodeling of a high school. Overall, effect sizes (ES) were low on computation measures: (a) pretest to posttest ($d = -.5$ to .04); and (b) across conditions ($d = -1.0$ to -.3). However, they were mixed on word problem measures: (a) pretest to posttest ($d = -.4$ to 3.8); and (b) across conditions ($d = -.2$ to .1). On generalization tasks, overall ESs were significant on contextualized measures: (a) pretest to posttest ($d = 1.8$, $d = 2.0$); and (b) across conditions ($d = 1.1$ to 1.7). Further, overall ESs were significant on the transfer measure across conditions ($d = .7$ to 2.5). Significant ESs were obtained on a maintenance video problem ($d = 1.1$). The highest posttest scores were evident on the EAI and TPI maintenance measures, where most of the mean scores came close to meeting an 80% criterion level (Bottge et al., 2001).

The second most frequent ($n = 3$, 38%) type of videodisc-based instruction incorporated instructional design variables (e.g., discrimination, explicit strategy instruction, range of examples, and cumulative review) for helping students learn fractions, ratios and proportions, and related problem-solving skills. Overall, the studies reported moderate to significant improvements for students in the computer-based, versus noncomputer-based interventions. Specifically, ES were significant on the following: (a) pretest and posttest ($d = 1.1$) for teaching fractions (Kelly et al., 1986); and (b) across conditions (range of $d = 1.1$ to 1.27) for teaching fractions (Kelly et al., 1990) and ratio and proportions (Moore & Carnine, 1989). Further, ESs were moderate to significant on maintenance measures (range of $d = .3$ to 2.1).

Finally, one type of videodisc intervention utilized Web-based instruction within a universally designed environment (Christle et al., 2001). The multicomponent treatment was designed to support students' learning environment with the integration of anchored instruction, Web-based learning, collaborative problem-solving, and universal design features. The combination proved effective in the pilot study as all students met criterion and the majority of participants maintained and generalized the target skills.

Overall, the results of technology-based interventions are promising. However, four limitations must be considered when interpreting the results: (a) small sample size; (b) low skill levels for some student with disabilities; (c) lack of programming for maintenance and generalization; and (d) the date limitation of the literature review. As this review was limited to 11 published articles that met all criteria, generalization of the findings should be viewed with caution. Also, although 73% (n = 8) of the studies determined significant treatment effects, three of the studies noted that the proficiency levels of students with disabilities fell below the established criterion for learning of 80%. For example, Moore and Carnine (1989) determined that students with special needs achieved similarly to their nondisabled peers; however, the proficiency rate was 71%. Further, of the articles that obtained significant findings, only 45% (n = 5) of the interventions directly programmed for maintenance and 55% (n = 6) programmed for generalization. Future research needs to include these methodological considerations to strengthen the validity of treatment effects. Also, the date limitation of the present review extends from 1985 to 2002. However the conclusions are not based on a historical comprehensive analysis but rather a review of the recent literature. That is, the generalizability of the findings may be of concern when new technologies are utilized (i.e., the migration of video from videotape, videodisc, CDROM, to DVD and streaming video).

Despite the noted limitations, a number of practices emerged from the review of the literature demonstrating that the technology is a powerful, versatile tool that is conducive to mathematics learning for secondary-level students with LD. Specifically, technology-based instruction was found to be just as effective as teacher-directed instruction (Gleason et al., 1990) when both incorporate variables of effective instruction (e.g., explicit strategy instruction, modeling, guided practice, fading of prompts, assessment of student understanding, and immediate correction procedures). Finally, videodisc-based instruction with instructional design variables was found to be more effective than teacher-directed approaches involving standard instruction for reducing student errors (Kelly et al., 1986), and for discriminating between algorithms and solving a range of examples (Kelly et al., 1990). Further, videodisc-based programs that involved anchored instruction and problem-solving strategies helped students to generalize their performance to contextualized situations (Bottge, 1999; Bottge & Hasselbring, 1993; Bottge et al., 2002).

Educational Implications

Based on the summary and analysis of the studies included in the present review, educational recommendations that appear promising for helping secondary-level students with mathematics include the following:

1. Continue to incorporate effective teaching variables within (e.g., model, guided practice, review, feedback) within technology-based interventions for students labeled LD in secondary general education settings.
2. Incorporate effective instructional design variables within technology-based instruction to reduce student confusion and mathematical errors. For example, computer software should incorporate a wide range of examples and nonexamples into instruction for discrimination practice and generalization and pictorial representations to enhance concept development (Kelly et al., 1986; Kelly et al., 1990).
3. Incorporate videodisc-based interventions that embed interesting and age-appropriate problem-solving situations to promote maintenance and generalization (Bottge, 1999; Bottge & Hasselbring, 1993; Bottge et al., 2001; Bottge et al., 2002). As Bottge et al. (2001) noted, "Rather than capitalizing on

the insights and motivation that students bring to the classroom, schools may actually be wasting valuable time by withholding more authentic and motivating problems until 'prerequisite' skills are acquired" (p. 312). However, middle school students with special needs who are educated within inclusionary settings may need additional support to fully benefit from enhanced anchored instruction, including additional review of the videodisc within the resource room and cooperative learning strategies (Bottge et al., 2002).

4. Include Web-based learning environments (Christle et al., 2001) to enhance student learning and collaboration. A promising approach is the TRIP project (Christle et al., 2001), which extends the principles of anchored instruction, contextualized learning, and generative learning (Cognition and Technology Group at Vanderbilt, 1990) to include Web-based instruction (WBI) within a universally designed environment where students work collaboratively. As the authors point out, new research is needed to fully realize the effects of WBI, but the future appears promising.

5. Incorporate technology-based tutorial programs that embed basic math skills within problem-solving situations to help students practice remedial skills within context. For example, it is recommended that computers be available to students with LD in the general education classroom for students with LD who need tutorial assistance. Recommended programs include the *Hot Dog Stand* and *Geommetric SuperSupposer* (both programs are available from Sunburst Communications at www.sunburst.com/index/html).

Technological Advances and Future Research

Although most of the interventions in the present review included different forms of technology-based instruction, none of the articles examined the effect of graphing calculators on students' math achievement. This is of great concern given the recommendation by the NCTM (1998) that, "Every student should have

access to an appropriate calculator" (p. 1). Further, Milou (1999) determined that the majority of studies that focused on the effects of graphing calculators on student achievement and mathematical understanding had positive results for learners and that the tool was motivational for students.

In addition to the motivational features, it is recommended that teachers incorporate the use of graphing calculators into instruction for secondary-level students with LD to address concept development and error detections and other comparisons (Jarrett, 1998). For example, to enhance concept development, multiple representations (i.e., graphical, numerical) of a single math concept can be represented and analyzed via the graphing tool. Students can zoom in or out on a single data point or region on a graphic display for further analysis. Further, students can simultaneously compare their entered keying sequences and answers on the screen to examine patterns, relationships, and possible errors in data entry. For example, students can represent and analyze patterns of change that result when entering varying values using the "replay" function to determine the cost of an item relative to the annual inflation rate (Jarrett, 1998).

However, Milou (1999) also determined that although participating Algebra I and II teachers stated that the tool was motivational for their students, significantly fewer Algebra I teachers indicated using graphing calculators than Algebra II teachers. This is an important implication for students with LD, given that more teachers indicated teaching Algebra I to students with mild disabilities (LD, ED) than Algebra II (Maccini & Gagnon, in press) and that success in algebra is a common requirement for most school districts. Thus, it is important to help teachers to implement the use of the tool within their math classes via school inservices, and/or peer training (e.g., Algebra II teachers training other teachers).

Use of the Internet is also highly recommended for students with LD as both a tool for communication and a source of information (Bender, 2001). According to Bender (2001), the Internet refers to, "a worldwide network of interlocking and interactive computers, which provides a store of information for the user"

(p. 419). However, no studies currently exist that examine the efficacy of the tool and its extensive applications for students with LD. It would be interesting to explore applications of the World Wide Web for students with LD as a vehicle for communication (i.e., collaborating on projects with other students from around the world) and as a mechanism for sharing work (e.g., electronic bulletin boards, school Web site). The Internet also serves as a powerful research tool for helping students access a plethora of information and data via search engines. For example, students can juxtapose use of graphing calculators with the Internet to explore the application of math concepts across content areas. Drier, Dawson, and Garofalo (1999) describe an interactive lesson in which students download data from the Internet to their graphing calculators for data analysis and interpretation. For example, students can download data on the number of new AIDS cases from the Centers for Disease Control and Prevention Web site (www.cdc.gov) and analyze trends relative to the number of cases across years. The information can be graphically displayed and the scales altered to display certain trends in the appearance of the data (i.e., how scales changes can change the appearance of a slope or trend). The information can then be generalized across content areas as students learn how to critically examine graphical representations of data displayed in the media, newspapers, magazines, and so on.

Also, most of the studies reviewed involve development of innovative curricula. Noticeable by its absence, are studies involving commercially available math software (e.g., *Algebra Stars* by Sunburst), as well as adaptive math software (e.g., *IntelliMathic 3*). Consequently, we know little about the instructional value of many commercially-available products.

A final general consideration relates to the possible effects of economic constraints on the use of technology in schools. For example, the National Assessment of Educational Progress (Educational Testing Service, 1999) found that the mathematics achievement for eighth-grade students was positively correlated with the "higher-level" application of computer use and with teacher proficiency. However, it was determined that several disparities exist: (a)

students from minority, poor, and urban backgrounds had less exposure to the application of computers with higher-level concepts; and (b) students from poor and urban backgrounds were more likely to have math teachers with less professional development and training on the appropriate use of computers. It is encouraging that The No Child Left Behind Act of 2001 provides technological support for teachers and schools in low-income areas via grants to support access to information technology and related training (U.S. Department of Education, 2003c). Additionally, support exists to increase the number of qualified teachers. However, it is unclear how these provisions will specifically support teacher training in low-SES areas and the impact on student learning of mathematics. To address these inequities, it is important to provide intensive professional development opportunities for teachers in poor, rural, and urban settings (ETS, 1999).

Conclusions

This chapter summarized the efficacy of studies presently available on technology-based instruction for teaching mathematics to secondary-level students with LD, as well as the implications for practice and future research. A number of sophisticated programs exist that extend beyond traditional drill-and-practice software programs to include Web-based instruction and videodisc programs. The research in the present review demonstrates that technology-based interventions can significantly impact student learning and motivation to learn higher-level math concepts embedded within real-world problem-solving tasks. Critical components of effective interventions include extensive teacher involvement as facilitator and discussion leader, as well as components of effective instruction to guide student learning. Although complex programs are emerging, several areas deserve attention for teaching math to secondary-level students with LD, including the efficacy of standard and graphing calculators, Internet use, and multimedia systems. The powerfulness and versatility of these tools hold promise for helping students access a plethora of information, and may serve as a mechanism for exploration, concept modeling, and data analysis. However, NCTM (2000) cautions, "Technology is not a panacea. As with any teaching tool, it can be used well or poorly. Teachers should use technology to enhance their students' learning opportunities by selecting or creating mathematical tasks that take advantage of what technology can do efficiently and well-graphing, visualizing, and computing" (pp. 25-26).

References

Algozzine, B., O'Shea, D. J., Crews, W. B., & Stoddard, K. (1987). Analysis of mathematics competence of learning disabled adolescents. *Journal of Special Education, 21*, 97-107.

Bahr, C. M., & Rieth, H. J. (1991). Effects of cooperative, competitive, and individualistic goals on student achievement using computer-based drill-and-practice. *Journal of Special Education Technology, 11*(1), 33-48.

Beaton, A., Mullis, I., Martin, M., Gonzalez, E., Kelly, D., & Smith, T. (1996). *Mathematics achievement in the middle school years: IEA's third international mathematics and science study.* Boston, MA: Boston College, Center for the Study of Testing, Evaluation, and Educational Policy.

Bender, W. N. (2001). *Learning disabilities: Characteristics, identification, and teaching strategies* (4th ed.). Needham Heights, MA: Allyn and Bacon.

Berstein, B. (1997). Message and meaning: The third international math and science study. *Educational Horizons, 76*(1), 23-27.

Bottge, B. A. (1999). Effects of contextualized math instruction on problem-solving of average and below-average achieving students. *The Journal of Special Education, 33*(2), 81-92.

Bottge, B., & Hasselbring, T. S. (1993). A comparison of two approaches for teaching complex, authentic mathematics problems to adolescents in remedial math classes. *Exceptional Children, 59*, 556-566.

Bottge, B. A., Heinrichs, M., Chan, S., & Serlin, R. C. (2001). Anchoring adolescents' understanding of math concepts in rich problem-solving environments. *Remedial and Special Education, 22*, 299-314.

Bottge, B. A., Heinrichs. M., Mehta, Z. D., & Hung, Y. (2002). Weighing the benefits of anchored math instruction for student with disabilities in general education classes. *The Journal of Special Education, 35*, 186-200.

Cawley, J. F., Baker-Kroczynski, S., & Urban, A. (1992). Seeking excellence in mathematics education for students with mild disabilities. *Teaching Exceptional Children, 24*(2), 40-43.

Christle, C. A., Hess, J. M., & Hasselbring, T. S. (2001). Technology research in practice: Taking a virtual trip to the mall to learn math. *Special Education Technology Practice, 3*(2), 23-31.

Cognition and Technology Group at Vanderbilt. (1990). Anchored instruction and its relationship to situated cognition, *Educational Researcher, 19*(5), 2-10.

Cohen, J. (1988). *Statistical power analysis for the behavioral sciences* (2nd ed.). Hillsdale, NJ: Earlbaum.

Drier, H. S., Dawson, K., & Garofalo, J. (1999). Not your typical math class. *Educational Leadership, 56*(5), 21-25.

Engelmann, S., & Carnine, D. (1982). *Theory of instruction: Principles and applications.* New York: Irvington Press.

Educational Testing Service. (1999). *Does it compute? The relationship between educational technology and student achievement in mathematics.* Princeton, NJ: Author. Retrieved June, 24, 2003, from: www.ets.org/research/pic/pir.html.

Gleason, M., Carnine, D., & Boriero, D. (1990). Improving CAI effectiveness with attention to instructional design in teaching story problems to mildly handicapped students. *Journal of Special Education Technology, 10*(3), 129-136.

Gregory, J. F., Shanahan, T., & Walberg, H. (1985). Learning disabled 10th graders in mainstreamed settings. *Remedial and Special Education, 6*(4), 25-33.

Hughes, C. A., & Maccini, P. (1997). Computer-assisted mathematics instruction for students with learning disabilities: A research review. *Learning Disabilities: A Multidisciplinary Journal, 8*(3), 155-166.

Hutchinson, N.L. (1993). Students with disabilities and mathematics education reform-let the dialogue begin. *Remedial and Special Education, 14*(6), 20-27.

Individuals with Disabilities Education Act (IDEA) of 1997, P. L. No. 105-17. U.S. Department of Education, Washington DC. (ERIC Document Reproduction Service No. ED430325)

Jarrett, D. (1998). *Integrating technology into middle school mathematics: It's just good teaching*. Portland, OR: Northwest Regional Educational Laboratory.

Kelly, B., Carnine, D., Gersten, R., & Grossen, B. (1986). The effectiveness of videodisc instruction in teaching fractions to learning-disabled and remedial high school students. *Journal of Special Education Technology, 8,* 5-17.

Kelly, B., Gersten, R., & Carnine, D. (1990). Student error patterns as a function of curriculum design: Teaching fractions to remedial high school students and high school students with learning disabilities. *Journal of Learning Disabilities, 23,* 23-29.

Learning Technology Center at Vanderbilt University. (1996). *The new adventures of Jasper Woodbury* [Videodisc]. Mahwah, NJ: Erlbaum.

Lieber, J., & Semmel, M. I. (1989). The relationship of group configuration to the interactions of students using microcomputers. *Journal of Special Education Technology, 10*(2), 14-23.

Maccini, P., & Gagnon, J. C. (in press). Mathematics instructional practices and assessment accommodations by secondary special and general educators. *Exceptional Children*.

Maccini, P., McNaughton, D. B., & Ruhl, K. (1999). Algebra instruction for students with learning disabilities: Implications from a research review. *Learning Disability Quarterly, 22,* 113-126.

Mercer, C. D. (1997). *Students with learning disabilities* (5th ed.). Upper Saddle River, NJ: Prentice-Hall.

Milou, E. (1999). The graphing calculator: A survey of classroom usage. *School Science and Mathematics, 99*(3), 133-140.

Montague, M. (1997). Cognitive strategy instruction in mathematics for students with learning disabilities. *Journal of Learning Disabilities, 30,* 164-177.

Montague, M., Bos, C. S., & Doucette, M. (1991). Affective, cognitive, and metacognitive attributes of eighth-grade mathematical problem solvers. *Learning Disabilities Research & Practice, 6,* 145-151.

Moore, L. J., & Carnine, D. (1989). Evaluating curriculum design in the context of active teaching. *Remedial and Special Education, 10*(4), 28-37.

Mullis, I., Martin, M., Beaton, A., Gonzalez, E., Kelly D., & Smith, T. (1998). *Mathematics and science achievement in the final year of secondary school: IEAs third international mathematics and science study*. Boston: Boston College, Center for the Study of Testing, Evaluation, and Educational Policy.

National Council of Teachers of Mathematics (NCTM). (1989). *Curriculum and evaluation standards for school mathematics*. Reston, VA: NCTM.

National Council of Teachers of Mathematics. (1998). *The use of technology in the learning and teaching of mathematics* [position statement], Retrieved June 22, 2003, from: www.nctm.org/about/use_of_technology. htm.

National Council of Teachers of Mathematics, (NCTM). (2000). *Principles and standards for school mathematics*. Reston, VA: Author.

O'Callaghan, B. (1998). Computer-intensive algebra and students' conceptual knowledge of functions. *Journal for Research in Mathematics Education, 29*(1), 21-40.

Okolo, C. M., Rieth, H. J., & Bahr, C. M. (1989). Microcomputer implementation in secondary special education programs: A study of special educators' mildly handicapped adolescents' and administrators' perspectives. *The Journal of Special Education, 23*(1), 107-117.

Pease, P. S., & Kitchen, L. (1987). *Meeting the needs of rural special education in the information age: Using TI-IN network's interactive satellite based educational network*. Paper presented at the meeting of the Annual National Conference of the American Council on Rural Special Education, Webster, TX. (ERIC Document Reproduction Service No. EC 202 587)

Pugalee, D. K. (2001). Algebra for all: The role of technology and constructivism in an algebra course for at-risk students. *Preventing School Failure, 45*(4), 171-176.

Regional Technology in Education Consortia. (2003). *Mission-Improving student achievement with technology*. Retrieved June 22, 2003, from www.rtec.org/

Rosenshine, B., & Stevens, R. (1986). Teaching

functions. In M. C. Witrock (Ed.), *Handbook of research on teaching* (3rd ed., pp. 376-391). New York: Macmillan.

Sterling. (1976). D. A. (1976). *Sterling Informal Math Inventory*.

Systems Impact, Inc. (1985). *Mastering fractions*. Washington, DC: Author.

Systems Impact, Inc. (1986). *Mastering fractions*. Washington, DC: Author.

Systems Impact, Inc. (1987). *Core concepts in math and science: Mastering ratios*. Washington, DC: Author.

Szetela, W., & Super, D. (1987). Calculators and instruction in problem-solving in grade 7. *Journal for Research in Mathematics Education, 18*(3), 215-229.

Tarlin, E. (1997). Computers in the classroom: Where are all the girls? In E. Miller (Ed.), *Technology and schools, HEL focus series no. 3* (pp. 20-21). Cambridge, MA: Harvard Education Letter.

Thurlow, M., Albus, D., Spicuzza, R., & Thompson, S. (1998). *Participation and performance of students with disabilities: Minnesota's 1996 Basic Standards Tests in reading and math* (Minnesota Report 16). Minneapolis: University of Minnesota, National Center on Educational Outcomes.

U.S. Department of Education. (2003a). *The No Child Left Behind Act of 2001, Preliminary overview of programs and changes, preparing tomorrow's teachers to use technology (Title X, Part E, Amendments to Title II of the Higher Education Act of 1965)*. Retrieved June 22, 2003, from: www.ed.gov/offices/OESE/esea/progsum/teachers.html#top.

U.S. Department of Education (2003b). *The No Child Left Behind Act of 2001, Preliminary overview of programs and changes, Regional technology in education consortia (Title X, Parts B and G - Amendments to the Educational Research, Development, Dissemination, and Improvement Act of 1994, Parts J and N)*. Retrieved June 22, 2003, from: www.ed.gov/offices/OESE/esea/progsum/technology.html#top.

U.S. Department of Education. (2003c). *The No Child Left Behind Act of 2001Preliminary Overview of Programs and Changes FIE: Community technology centers (Title V, Part D, Subpart 11)*. Retrieved June 25, 2003, from: www.ed.gov/offices/OESE/esea/progsum/title5d.html#community.

Vergason, G. A., & Anderegg, M. L. (1997). *Dictionary of special education and rehabilitation* (4th ed.). Denver, CO: Love Publishing.

Woodward, J., & Gersten, R. (1992). Innovative technology for secondary-level students with learning disabilities. *Exceptional Children, 58*(5), 407-421.

Zigmond, N. (1990). Rethinking secondary school programs for students with learning disabilities. *Focus on Exceptional Children, 23*(1), 1-24.

Mathematics and Technology-Based Interventions for Secondary-Level Students with Mild Disabilities

Study	N/D/G/A/GR	Setting	Research Design and Intervention	DV	Results	Maintenance/ Generalization
Bahr & Rieth, 1991	(46) 32 LD, 13 EMR, 1 SED; gr 7 & 8; 14.1; 30M, 16F	Math classroom, self-contained classroom; 12 sessions, 10 min	Two-factor mixed design incorporating one between-subjects factor and one within-subjects factor; between-subjects factor incorporated cooperative, competitive, individualistic, and no goal control; computer d & p working to criterion.	Paper-and-pencil math computation test (pre- and posttest), paper-and-pencil computation test (pre-, mid-, and posttest); computer trial (pre- and posttest)	Students improved rate of responding regardless of goal structures (cooperative, competitive, individualistic, and no goal control).	--; --
Bottge, 1999	(66) 2 LD, 1 LD / SpL, 1 SpL, 1 ED, 1 OHI; gr 8; --; 37M, 29F	Math classes, technology education; 8 weeks, --	Pretest-posttest design (remedial groups), quasi-experimental, nonequivalent control pre-posttest design (pre-algebra groups); CP students solved contextualized problems on videodisc; WP students solved series of standard problems.	Fractions computation pre- and posttest; word problem pre- posttest; contextualized pre- and posttest; and transfer test given two weeks following posttests	Fractions computation posttest: no significant differences across conditions. Word problem posttest: no significant differences across conditions. CP group did significantly better on contextualized posttest and the video transfer task.	M; G
Bottge & Hasselbring, 1993	(36) 17 referred to, recently exited, or labeled sped; gr 9; --; --	Math classes; 5 sessions, 40 min	Two-group design study; Part 1: Videodisc computation intervention Part 2: Students assigned to contextualized problems on videodisc (CP) or instructed with series of standard word problems (WP).	Fractions computation and word problem test (pre- and posttest). Transfer tasks: a video-based contextualized problem and a text-based word problem	Fractions computation test: Intervention participants significantly increased scores. CP versus WP: Both groups significantly improved performance on word problem posttests. CP group did significantly better than WP on the contextualized posttest and the video transfer task.	M; G

(continued next page)

Appendix A.

Mathematics and Technology-Based Interventions for Secondary-Level Students with Mild Disabilities (continued)

Study	N/D/G/A/GR	Setting and Duration	Research Design and Intervention	DV	Results	Maintenance/ Generalization
Bottge, Heinrichs, Chan, & Serlin, 2001	(75) 16 LD, 2 ED, 1 OHI; gr 8; 13.6; 45M, 30F	Math classroom, technology education classroom; 12 sessions, 90 min	Four-group design study; EAI or TPI instruction in remedial math and pre-algebra classes; EAI students solved math problems on videodisc and applied knowledge in technology project; TPI students solved text-based word problems.	WRAT-III arithmetic subtest (pre- and posttest), math problem-solving test (maintenance), TPI or EAI math problem-solving test (maintenance)	Arithmetic test: Participants in both conditions either maintained or decreased scores from pre- to posttest. Word problem test: participants in all conditions substantially increased scores. EAI/TPI maintenance: mean scores in all conditions came close to 80% or above.	M; --
Bottge, Heinrichs, Mehta, & Hung, 2002	(42) 6 LD, 1 ED, 1 LD/ED; gr 7; 12.5; 20M, 22F	Math classroom, technology education classroom; 12 sessions, --	Four-group design study; EAI or TPI instruction in general education math classes; EAI students solved math problems on videodisc and applied knowledge in technology project; TPI students solved text-based math word problems.	Fractions computation, word problem test, and video-based contextualized problem test (pre- and posttest). Transfer tasks: performance-based assessment (kite frame)	Fractions computation and word problem test: no significant differences from pre- to posttest or across conditions. Contextualized test: Significant differences were obtained from pre- to posttest for EAI condition. Moderate to significant differences on the contextualized test and transfer task.	--; G
Christle, Hess, & Hasselbring, 2001	(4) 2 LD; gr middle school; --; --;	Resource room; --	Multiple-baseline design; measured rate of solving word problems on paper and on computer.	Math problems	All students met the target criterion within 3 to 7 instructional sessions, 3 students maintained and generalized the skills up to 11 sessions after termination of intervention.	M; G

(continued next page)

Mathematics and Technology-Based Interventions for Secondary-Level Students with Mild Disabilities (continued)

Study	N/D/G/A/GR	Setting and Duration	Research Design and Intervention	DV	Results	Maintenance/Generalization
Gleason, Carnine, & Boriero, 1990	(19) 19 MH; gr 6, 7, 8; --; 11M, 8F	Classroom; 18 sessions, 30 min	Two-group design; teacher-directed instruction and computer-assisted instruction both started with instruction in a new skill and in problem-solving; criterion-referenced tests measured skill acquisition.	Criterion-referenced story problem and computation test (pretest), criterion-referenced story problem test (posttest), story problem written and oral test (transfer)	No significant differences on posttest measures between conditions; however, students in both conditions improved their mean performance from pretest to posttest and obtained high mean percent scores on the picture posttest and oral transfer test. Students had difficulty transferring knowledge to more difficult problem that included more than one operation and irrelevant information.	--; G
Kelly, Carnine, Gersten, & Grossen, 1986	(28) 17 LD (Number of students with LD in final sample is undefined); gr 9–12; --;--	Math classes; --, 30 min	Two-group design; 30-minute videodisc lessons. Brief quiz (covering skills from previous lesson), lesson presentation, and a worksheet completed independently. Thirty-minute basal text lessons (i.e., introduction, teacher demonstration & discussion, followup activities and a worksheet completed indepen-	Screening tests, criterion-referenced (pretest, posttest, maintenance test), observation, independent seatwork, attitude questionnaire	Students receiving the videodisc curriculum scored significantly higher on both the posttest and maintenance test. For both interventions, on-task behavior was above 80% and independent classwork was above 90%.	M; --

(continued next page)

Appendix A.

Mathematics and Technology-Based Interventions for Secondary-Level Students with Mild Disabilities (continued)

Study	N/D/G/A/GR	Setting and Duration	Research Design and Intervention	DV	Results	Maintenance/ Generalization
Kelly, Gersten, & Carnine, 1990	(28) 17 LD; gr. 9-11; --; 23M, 5F	Math classes; 10 sessions, 45 min	Two-group design. Instructional design curriculum: Each 45-minute lesson began w/ a brief quiz covering skills from previous lesson, lesson presentation, and 15 minutes for independent completion a worksheet. A test was given every fifth lesson. Basal curriculum: Introduction, instruction, guided practice, followup activities, and independent completion of a worksheet. Review tests were given twice in the 10-day teaching unit.	Screening tests, criterion-referenced (pretest, posttest), observation, independent seatwork	Mean performance improved for both groups following intervention. Videodisc group scored significantly higher than the comparison group on the posttest (96% versus 82%).	--; --
Moore & Carnine, 1989	(29) --; gr 9-11; --; --	Math classes	Two-group design; math taught with basals giving objective, explanation and modeling; math taught with videodisc started with quiz, explanation and modeling, and	Math test (pretest), criterion-referenced test (posttest & maintenance)	Students in the videodisc condition performed significantly better than students in the basal condition on the posttest measure. No significant differ-	M; G

(continued next page)

Mathematics and Technology-Based Interventions for Secondary-Level Students with Mild Disabilities (continued)

Study	N/D/G/A/GR	Setting and Duration	Research Design and Intervention	DV	Results	Maintenance/ Generalization
Woodward & Gersten, 1992	(57) 57 LD; --; --; --	Math classes; 6 weeks	Single-subject research design; teacher training on effective use of video-disc technology, guided practice, monitoring students' work, and teaching to mastery; teachers implemented programs in classroom for 6 weeks.	Curriculum-referenced test (pre- and posttest)	Students identified positive feelings about the program and 90% felt more confident in their ability to complete fractions problems. This was consistent with student gains on the criterion-reference test. On the posttest, 64% of students met or exceeded the 80% score indicating they had met an acceptable level of mastery.	--;--

Note. Dashes represent data that were not reported.
N/D/G/A/GR = Number of participants, disability, grade, age, gender

gr = grade level
MS = middle school
HS = high school
Duration = number of sessions, time per session
min = minutes
DV = dependent variable
LD = learning disabilities
EMR = educable mentally retarded
SED = seriously emotionally disturbed
sped = special education
SpL = speech and language
ED = emotional disabilities
OHI = other health impaired
WRAT-III = Wide Range Achievement Test, Third Edition
TPI = traditional problem instruction

EAI = enhanced anchored instruction
MMH = mildly mentally handicapped
BD = behavior disorder
CP = computerized problems
WP = word problems
GO = graphic organizer
AO = advance organizer
WISC-III =Wechsler Intelligence Scale for Children – (Third Ed.)
WAIS-R = Wechsler Adult Intelligence Scale – Revised
WRMT-R = Woodcock Reading Mastery Tests – Revised
DATA-2 = Diagnostic Achievement Tests for Adolescents (2nd Ed.)
LASSI-HS = Learning and Study Strategies Inventory (high school version)

D & P = drill and practice
Exp = experiment
M = maintenance
G = generalization

31

Interactive Technologies and Social Studies Instruction for Students with Mild Disabilities

Cynthia M. Okolo

In some ways, this was an easy chapter to write, for research about using technology in social studies instruction for students with mild disabilities is extremely slim. This is not surprising. Compared to literacy, mathematics, and science, social studies has been a low-priority subject in today's schools. For example, the recent No Child Left Behind Act does not mandate regular assessment in social studies, as it does in other subject areas. The national debate about the content of social studies, which reached a peak in the mid 1990s, was rancorous (e.g., Nash, Crabtree, & Dunn, 1997; Gitlin, 1995; Wineburg, 2001). Disagreements still reverberate about what to teach, and the relative emphasis to be placed on process versus content (e.g., Blanco & Rosa, 1997; Brophy & Alleman, 2002; Wineburg, 2001).

Furthermore, students with disabilities traditionally have been exempted from social studies instruction (Curtis, 1991; Patton, Polloway, & Cronin, 1987). And, when they are included, evidence suggests that teachers rarely make the adaptations or accommodations that are needed for successful inclusion (Passe & Beattie, 1994; Schumaker et al., 2002). In our own research in urban, inclusive, middle-grade classrooms (e.g., MacArthur, Ferretti, & Okolo, 2001; Okolo, Ferretti, & MacArthur, 2002), we have found that social studies and science tend to compete for the same time slot in the school schedule, often at the end of the school day. Finally, social studies is the subject that is most likely to be sacrificed for other school events

such as assemblies and program such as drug education or foreign language lessons.

This neglect of social studies instruction for students with disabilities is unfortunate. The social studies offer rich opportunities for students not only to learn important content, but also to develop problem-solving and literacy skills (e.g., Ferretti & Okolo, 1996). Social studies is a multifaceted domain that encompasses the disciplines of history, economics, geography, and civics, and also draws from sociology, anthropology, political science, and psychology. The social studies requires students to read and interpret a variety of information from narrative and informational texts. Students also work with maps, graphs, images, and, increasingly, information that is available on the Web. Because history, in particular, requires investigation and interpretation (e.g., VanSledright, 2002), students have multiple occasions to practice and apply literacy and communication skills through reading, writing, presentation, and debate. Furthermore, because social studies problems are typically ill structured, students must reason and draw conclusions about the types of problems that they are most likely to encounter in everyday life (Ferretti & Okolo, 1996).

Social Studies and Students with Mild Disabilities

One factor that accounts for the low priority assigned to social studies instruction for students with disabilities may be the manner in which it is most often taught. Traditionally, elementary and secondary school social studies instruction has focused on memorization of places, people, events, and dates (Stearns, Seixas, & Wineburg, 2000), and is rooted in the textbook, the limitations of which have been well documented (e.g., Bean, 1994; Beck & McKeown, 1991; Brophy, 1990; Paxton, 1999).

Briefly, social studies textbooks are often ill structured and inconsiderate (Armbruster & Anderson, 1984) of the cognitive, metacognitive, and motivational needs of school-age readers (Allington, 2002; Cibrowski, 2003). Crammed with factual information that can overwhelm students and depress their interest in history and other social studies topics, textbooks are rarely organized in ways that help students see the big ideas or the connections among different periods of time and events, and especially, ways that might enrich their understanding of the contexts in which people lived, their multiple viewpoints, and the relationship between the social and historical contexts of yesterday and today. Further, information is often presented in an authoritative, one-sided manner that misrepresents the rich interpretative process and frequent contentions that are at the heart of historical inquiry (Wineburg, 2001).

Equally problematic, textbooks make assumptions about the reading abilities and background knowledge of their readers that are particularly unwarranted for students with reading and learning problems. Such readers require explicit instruction in reading skills and strategies that might help them identify the big ideas, as well as tools for gathering and recording evidence from multiple sources, analyzing multiple points of view, and constructing and communicating their interpretations. This is particularly unfortunate as extant data show that general educators-the teachers most likely to teach social studies to students with disabilities in inclusive classrooms-are uncertain about how to make accommodations in texts and instruction to meet the needs of these learners (e.g., Passe & Beattie, 1994; Schumaker et al., 2002).

History is a core subject in the K-12 social studies curriculum, and researchers have found that historical understanding demands a great deal of cognitive and literary sophistication, and the cognitive tools, experiential backgrounds, and literacy skills available to middle-grade learners pose challenges to its development (Okolo, Ferretti, & MacArthur, 2002). Students' concepts of time and distance and knowledge of geography develop with age and experience (e.g., Barton & Levstik, 1996; Brophy, 1990; Lee & Ashby, 2000; Wineburg, 1991). Historical empathy (Wineburg, 2000), or taking the perspective of others who lived in different circumstances and times, is constrained by students' level of cognitive development and by the knowledge they can bring to bear upon the lives of others. In order to draw conclusions about history, students must absorb and critique evidence from a wide range of conflicting sources and coordinate often conflicting points of view (Lowenthal, 2000). They must be sensitive to and able to detect bias in evidence, and be prepared to take bias into account when constructing complete and representative conclusions (Ferretti, MacArthur, & Okolo 2001). Although often in narrative form, historical evidence also is comprised of expository text and may be written in unfamiliar language because of its age. Given these demands, it is no wonder that even cognitively mature adults are challenged by history, and perhaps not so surprising that literacy, mathematics, and science instruction have been more successful in capturing the interest of special educators.

Technology and Social Studies Instruction

Technology offers several advantages for improving the teaching of social studies, for helping students understand complex concepts, and for enabling them to develop the problem-solving and decision-making skills that can promote their participation as informed citizens of a democratic society. Furthermore, technology can add a much-needed motivational boost to a subject that rarely ranks at the top of students' list of favorites (Rosenzweig & Thelen, 1998). This chapter will address the following uses of technology in social studies instruction: (a) data analysis, presentation, and communication tools; (b) supported text; (c) information archives; (d) online projects; and (e) simulations and virtual worlds. Where possible, research on the use of these technology-based applications with students who have mild disabilities will be discussed, including the potential benefits and challenges of these applications of technology. The focus of this chapter will be on students with mild disabilities, including those with learning disabilities, mild cognitive disabilities, and emotional/behavioral disabilities.

As mentioned above, the research base on technology, social studies, and students with mild disabilities is very thin. Although studies indicate that social studies teachers do not make widespread use of technology in instruction (Ehman & Glenn, 1991; Schumaker et al., 2002), a growing body of research and anecdotal evidence suggests how technology may improve outcomes for students who are not disabled. Yet, it is difficult to locate even descriptive articles about how teachers have used technology to meet social studies goals for students who have mild disabilities. Therefore, much of the discussion to follow draws upon research with students who do not have disabilities. Also, where applicable, conclusions about the potential impact and challenges are extrapolated from studies of technology use in literacy and other content areas.

Data Analysis, Communication, and Presentation Tools

A variety of technology-based tools are available to support students' analysis, interpretation, organization, and communication of social studies topics and content. *General-purpose tools*, available as software packages and on the Web, are as important in the social studies as they are in other content areas. Thus, word processing and other writing software facilitates the construction of written documents, including essays, diaries, and letters to the editor. Similarly, the graphics capabilities of word-processing programs facilitate the construction of documents such as travel brochures to advertise a distant country that students have studied or newspapers that offer an alternative version of a historical event such as the 1957 desegregation of Little Rock Central High School.

Databases and spreadsheets are other general-purpose tools that facilitate social studies

instruction. Norton and Harvey (1995) discussed the use of a database to help students explore mortality and its causes among a group of settlers who participated in the mid-1800s westward expansion of the United States. Paul and Kaiser (1996) described a unit in which students used a spreadsheet of data from a South African graveyard to analyze gender differences in lifespan. Spreadsheets and databases extend students' data-analytic capabilities through functions such as sorting, searching, computing, and reporting data. Furthermore, the charting and graphing features that accompany many general-purpose software programs help students to display their findings in a variety of representations.

Rather than taking an end-of-the-chapter test, students can engage in more disciplinary-consistent activities to demonstrate their social studies knowledge. For example, authoring and presentation tools support the process of documenting and communicating to broad audiences what students have learned. Thus, the multimedia capabilities of these tools enable students to integrate pictures, sounds, movies, and music with text. Research has shown that the construction of multimedia projects offers unique benefits, including increased knowledge of a topic that is maintained over time, and enhanced interest, motivation, and engagement (Lehrer, Erickson, & Connell, 1998). In our research program, we have used a variety of authoring programs with middle-grade learners in inclusive classrooms, ranging from *Digital Chisel* (Pierian Spring Software) to *HyperStudio* (Roger Wagner) to *PowerPoint* (Microsoft). Our participants have been excited by the opportunity to express themselves through multimedia and students with disabilities often find more avenues for success in the group when their contributions are not limited to print. Furthermore, students are proud of their professional-looking finished products (Ferretti & Okolo, 1996).

Several *special-purpose technology tools* are designed to accomplish more specific functions or to support activities that are more germane to social studies instruction. For example, research by Lynne Anderson-Inman and colleagues has shown that the concept mapping and outlining tools in *Inspiration* (Inspiration Software) can assist students with disabilities in actively constructing an understanding of a domain and creating more effective notes and syntheses of information (Anderson-Inman, 1994; Anderson-Inman & Zeitz, 1994). In social studies instruction, individuals and groups of students can use concept maps as a tool for organizing the information they are collecting and analyzing during their inquiries, and as tools for organizing reports and presentations.

Like other students, students with disabilities often have background knowledge that they could bring to bear upon an event or issue about which they are reading or learning in history and other subjects. Tapping into that background knowledge enhances their understanding. However, without support, students with disabilities may fail to do so spontaneously (Bos & Vaughn, 2002; Wong, 1980). Techniques such as brainstorming and discussing what one knows, wants to know, and has learned (or K-W-L, Ogle, 1986) have been used to help students access their background knowledge about topics in history and social studies (Okolo, Ferretti, & MacArthur, 2002). Concept-mapping program such as *Inspiration* also facilitate the capture and display of ideas and questions generated in brainstorming sessions such as these. Equipped with a computer and a projection device, a teacher can construct a concept map of key points on the fly. Students' ideas or questions can be represented as independent nodes in initial brainstorming sessions, and then linked to one another in substantive and hierarchical ways in later discussions or lessons. Concept maps can be viewed as outlines and outlines as concept maps. Maps created in this manner can be printed for individual or class use and pasted into class and individual projects, including Web sites and presentations.

Kidspiration (a child-friendly version of Inspiration) is appropriate for a range of learners with mild disabilities, especially because it offers text-to-speech capabilities to assist with reading and editing text. Both programs can be downloaded for a 30-day free trial from the Inspiration website (www.inspiration.com).

Chronological sequencing is a standard of most state and district curricula. *Timeliner* (Tom Snyder Productions) constructs electronic timelines that students can easily create, modify, and graphically display. We have found time lining particularly useful when introducing a new topic in history classes. Students are often uncertain about the chronology of events leading up to the ones they will study, and how are these events related. We have used *Timeliner* to construct timelines of key historical events around which teachers can structure classroom discussion. Students' personal copies can be used throughout the unit's activities and a class timeline can be revised and extended as new events are examined. The Tom Snyder website (www.teachtsp.com), which offers a downloadable trial version of the software, has a rich collection of ideas for implementing Timeliner in social studies and other content areas.

The above discussion has covered a range of tools with implications for improving social studies instruction as students engage in tasks that include the analysis, interpretation, organization, communication, and presentation of information. The degree to which these tools will be beneficial depends, to a great degree, on the skill of the teacher in structuring and guiding their use. Students will need instruction in using the vocabulary and functions that accompany the use of these tools (e.g., cell, formula; record, field, search). Teachers also must consider how to teach students to use these tools in mindful ways (Perkins & Salomon, 1989). For example, studies have shown that mere use of multimedia authoring tools or presentation software does not guarantee that students will learn more or differently than students who do not have access to similar tools (e.g., Okolo & Ferretti, 1997; Saye & Brush, 2002).

More sophisticated and specific-purpose tools may be difficult to integrate into the curriculum. For example, Hawkins and Sheingold (1986) reported that social studies teachers found databases difficult to integrate into topic-oriented curricula. Okolo et al. (2002) found that, although middle-school learners with mild disabilities could learn to use and were motivated by non-linear authoring tools for developing presentations of the results of their historical inquiries, it was very difficult to find sufficient time to integrate them into the social studies classroom on a regular basis.

Supported Text

Supported text is one of the labels used to describe text that is displayed via a computer and augmented with resources to facilitate a reader's comprehension, engagement, and motivation. Electronic enhancements may include hearing text read aloud, accessing definitions of unfamiliar words, obtaining background information about confusing or unfamiliar concepts, or acquiring alternative representations of information (e.g., viewing text in English, Spanish or American Sign Language; viewing a written description or a film clip). Speech is one of the most obvious and easily implemented augmentations to print-based text. Many common word-processing programs will read text aloud. Screen reading programs, such as *E-Reader* (CAST) and *Jaws* (Henter-Joyce), will read information from the World Wide Web (WWW). Further, the *Kurzweil 3000* (Kurzweil Educational Systems) enables educators to create electronic versions of scanned text that can be read and augmented with decoding, study skills, and test-taking tools. In summary, technology affords opportunities to enhance social studies textbooks in ways that make them more accessible to learners with disabilities.

Many researchers have investigated the use of supported text with learners who have reading and other learning disabilities (e.g., Okolo, Cavalier, Ferretti, & MacArthur, 2000), but not much of this work has been conducted in the context of social studies classes. Higgins and colleagues (Higgins & Boone, 1990; Higgins, Boone, & Lovitt, 1996) developed electronic study guides that consisted of segments of a history textbook augmented by explanatory passages, synonyms or paraphrases of difficult words or phrases, and multiple-choice questions that required a correct response before students could advance in the text. Results suggested that students with learning disabilities and low achievers learned at least as much from the study guides as they did from teacher lectures. MacArthur and Haynes (1995) developed enhanced versions of a science textbook for high school students with learning disabilities and found that students who used the enhanced textbooks scored significantly higher on tests of chapter content than students who read the same text, without enhancements, on the computer.

Lynne Anderson-Inman and her colleagues (Anderson-Inman & Horney, 1993, 1998; Anderson-Inman, Horney, Chen, & Lewin, 1994; Horney & Anderson-Inman, 1994) have examined the use of supported text in language arts classes for students with learning disabilities and hearing impairments. Their studies have documented different patterns of supported text use, ranging from superficial to integrative. Students who systematically integrated text with other electronic resources experienced higher comprehension than readers who skimmed and scanned information or who clicked on information of interest in a more haphazard fashion.

Research about text that is "read aloud" by computer-based software and screen-reading programs suggests that viewing text and hearing it read aloud enhances the comprehension of some learners with disabilities (e.g., Elkind, Cohen, & Murray, 1993; Montali & Lewandowski, 1996). However, Elkind and his colleagues (Elkind, 1998a, 1998b; Elkind, Black, & Murray, 1996) found that technology applications that read text to students support comprehension only under certain conditions, such as when the reader has a poor reading rate, has a strong oral vocabulary, and can quickly integrate auditory and visual information.

Edyburn (2002; 2003a; 2003b) describes a systematic approach for making text more accessible to readers that makes use of a variety of technology-based applications including text-to-speech software, concept mapping, and electronic quizzes. He also discusses principles of cognitive rescaling, or ways to manipulate text that increase or decrease its cognitive demands. These principles offer comprehensive guidance to special and general educators in their attempts to make text more accessible to a variety of learners.

In conclusion, supported text is one option for making written social studies materials, particularly textbooks, more accessible to students with mild disabilities. Merely having text read to students by a screen reader or software program is unlikely to resolve the problems associated with understanding and learning from social studies texts, however. Furthermore, textbook-based curricula limit students' opportunities to engage in social studies in ways that are consistent with the social studies disciplines and with current social studies standards—that is, as active inquirers who investigate, analyze, and interpret multiple sources and perspectives; draw and defend reasonable conclusions; and communicate the results of their investigations. The real power of supported text for learners with disabilities and, indeed, for all learners, lies in the ability to link any text with a multiplicity of alternative presentations and perspectives on a topic, and to provide the type of scaffolding that supports learners' needs and characteristics. As discussed next, information archives, online projects, and virtual environments incorporate many of the features of supported text.

Information Archives

Technology, through the resources on the World Wide Web, offers a voluminous information archive of sources and materials that can inform and contribute to students' active engagement in and understanding of social studies. Lee (2002) estimated that tens of millions of historical documents have been placed on the Web. For example, many major historical museums, state and national parks, and universities offer Web sites that contain rich primary-and secondary-source documents about historical characters and events. The Library of Congress has a rich archive of historical materials, and commercial ventures such as PBS and History Channel also offer instructionally relevant materials in support of their televised programs and videos. Many of these sites contain lessons plans that assist teachers in using source materials to develop students' historical understanding. In fact, the burgeoning use of the Web in history instruction has spawned the new specialization of *digital history*, or the study of the past using electronically reproduced primary-source texts, images, and artifacts and historical narratives, accounts, or presentations that result from digital historical inquiry (Lee, 2002).

In addition to history-oriented Web sites, a voluminous number of sites contains maps and mapping programs such as *National Geographic Online*, *Mapquest*, and university library map collections. Information to support civics

and economics instruction is widely available on Web sites sponsored by local, state, national, and international governments, public and private foundations, and institutions of higher education. In fact, so much information is available on the Web that authors are writing books and articles to help us cope with information glut and data smog (e.g., Shenk, 1998).

The storehouse of information available on the Web makes information accessible to students and teachers in ways heretofore unimagined. The multimedia nature of the Web facilitates rapid access to and clear display of information in a variety of media, ranging from text to movies to music to speeches. The multiplicity of information from different media, sources, and authors facilitates students' access to multiple perspectives, a key goal of social studies education. In its digital form, information can be accessed and manipulated via electronic search tools that not only help students locate desired information but also help them examine patterns and discover new connections (Bass & Rosenzweig, 1991). And, information archives often provide tools, including email, bulletin boards, and forums, that facilitate the development of social networks in which students and teachers can correspond and collaborate with one another and with individuals who have expertise with a particular collection of information (Lee, 2002). These features of information archives enable students to become "the novice in the archive," engaging in active exploration, interpretation, and communication in ways that have previously been reserved for expert learners (Bass & Rosenzweig, 1991).

Just as mere access to tools does not guarantee that students will engage in more meaningful social studies activities or gain richer understandings, mere access to information does not ensure that students will benefit from the potential experiences available in information archives. As most readers of this chapter realize, many Web sites are written above the reading level that has been attained by students with mild disabilities and other learning challenges (Debashis, 1995). Screen-reading programs can offer aural presentation of text, but, as discussed above, listening to information does not assist all learners in making better sense of it. Thus, teachers must prescreen Web sites for their readability before assigning them to students and/or build in the time and support necessary to help students understand what they are reading.

Likewise, it would be naïve to assume that information presented in pictures, movies, and music would, by virtue of its non-print form, be more accessible to students with disabilities. For example, when analyzing photographs and other historical images, students often lack knowledge of the past and of the technologies used to create these images (which can affect the way a photograph or picture appears). Furthermore, students' interpretations are filtered through their present-day lives and experiences. To draw the full benefits from these resources, therefore, students will need explicit guidance and scaffolding in analyzing and drawing conclusions from documents, information, and other materials available on the Web (Saye & Brush, 2002). To that end, we have developed guide sheets with a series of questions that we ask students to discuss, in groups and as a class, to facilitate their understanding of historical documents and images (Okolo & Ferretti, 1996b). Hicks (2003) describes a series of questions that students can adopt to guide their analysis and interpretation of information.

It is beyond the scope of this chapter to provide a comprehensive list of information archives that can be used in social studies classes; however, Table 1 offers a partial list and description of some popular social studies information archives.

Technology-Supported Projects

To this point, we have discussed technology-based applications, including tools, supported text, and information archives, that have rich potential to improve social studies instruction for learners with mild disabilities and their normally achieving peers. Although the design and the features of these applications offer much promise, the way in which they are used will determine their impact on students' learning and motivation. In this section, we will extend the discussion to consider the types of projects, or goal-based activities, that technology can support.

Project- or problem-based learning is not a new idea (e.g., Dewey, 1916), but structuring learning around the production of a specific product or the solution of a specific problem is especially relevant to social studies instruction. Although typical social studies instruction focuses on preparing for tests and other school-based tasks (e.g., Schumaker et al., 2002), the ultimate goal of social studies is citizenship preparation. Engagement in more authentic problem-oriented activities, in which students are working collaboratively to investigate and produce solutions, is important preparation for the types of responsibilities and leadership we hope to bestow upon future generations (Brown, Bransford, & Cocking, 1999).

Okolo, Ferretti, and MacAthur (Okolo et al., 2002) have investigated an approach to history instruction, Strategy Supported Project-Based Learning (SSPBL), that combines project-based learning, cognitive strategy instruction, lessons in historical analysis and interpretation, and technology tools to support historical understanding. Using this approach, instruction is designed to be optimally accessible to students with mild disabilities. Units are organized into big ideas, students view video anchors to examine key ideas, classroom discussion is used to monitor, support, and extend students' understanding, and students complete inquiry projects about specific historical topics in heterogeneous cooperative groups. This research has been implemented in fifth- and sixth-grade urban classrooms serving students with and without disabilities. Results include the findings that students in SSPBL classrooms demonstrate increased knowledge and historical understanding and improved attitudes and self-efficacy (Ferretti & Okolo, 1996; Ferretti, MacArthur, & Okolo, 2001; MacArthur et al., 2002; Okolo & Ferretti, 1996a, 1996b, 2000).

Glaser, Rieth, Kinzer, Colburn, and Peter (1999) employed multimedia-anchored instruction in history units investigating issues and problems related to money, power, and human relationships in the 1930s and during World War II. Eighth-grade students with LD and their nondisabled peers in an integrated social studies classroom viewed video anchors, *To Kill a Mockingbird* or *Playing for Time*, and then engaged in a series of activities in which they retold and segmented the anchor, analyzed major characters, and researched issues related to the anchors. Compared to a baseline condition, the anchored-instruction condition elicited higher rates of active involvement, increased the frequency of higher-level questioning, and stimulated more instances of higher-level reasoning about social problems.

The Web offers a plethora of opportunities for students to engage in collaborative projects that are oriented toward social studies goals including the investigation of history, the study of places and cultures, participation in civic and political activities, and social activism. For example, students can become members of a virtual expedition by joining an actual team of experts as they excavate Mayan ruins or explore Central America in a sea kayak. Most virtual expeditions extend over weeks or months, and offer educators a Web site that houses information about the expedition; pages for teachers (including lesson plans) and student activities; collections of relevant images, audio, and text; updates about expedition progress; and opportunities for students to interact with experts through email or other communication tools (Green, 1991).

Virtual museums are other rich sources of information and goal-directed activities to augment social studies instruction. Students and teachers can take virtual field trips to a variety of sites online that range in variety from a 1920 Utah farmhouse to Stonehenge. For example, the University of California at Los Angeles' (UCLA) Cultural Virtual Reality lab has recreated 3-D interactive reconstruction of the heart of imperial Rome that includes 22 historically accurate temples, courts, and monuments. Users can take a simulated journey through the ancient city by walking around, inside, and above it. The UCLA project is a highly sophisticated example of many online environments that support historical investigation. The Virtual Library Museums Pages, maintained by the International Community of Museums, list 1,031 virtual museum pages in the United States alone, icom.museum/vlmp/usa.html, ranging from sites such as the Smithsonian National Museum of American History to China the Beautiful. Although many of these sites provide only information about the actual museum and its features, a growing number offer online exhibits and activities for school-age audiences.

Okolo and Englert (2001) are developing the Virtual History Museum, a Web-based history learning environment designed to promote the historical understanding of all students and to offer cognitive supports and mediational tools that will enable full participation and success for students with mild disabilities. The Virtual History Museum (VHM) enables a teacher or student, who serves as a curator, to develop an exhibit about a topic, event, or artifact. Exhibits include activities that help viewers in the VHM investigate the exhibit and then communicate to others the results of their investigation. The VHM includes features to support students with disabilities, including text-to-speech capabilities and instruction in specific strategies that can aid historical understanding. Readers can become a guest of the VHM by visiting www.vhm.msu.edu, clicking on the Register button, and filling in the requested information.

Table 1 offers a selective list of online project sites, virtual expeditions, and virtual museums that support social studies instruction.

Research on the impact of many of the technology-supported projects on the participation, motivation, and learning of students with mild disabilities in social studies is meager. But, the studies cited above (e.g., Ferretti et al., 2001; Glaser et al., 1999; MacArthur et al., 2002; Okolo & Ferretti, 1996a, 1996b) show positive effects of technology on students' understanding of complex topics and motivation. Many of the issues discussed above are equally relevant to the implementation of technology-supported projects in the social studies. Thus, Web sites often contain material that is difficult to read and/or comprehend. Because many projects require extended time and engagement, teachers must be able to make time and room for them in the curriculum. With increased expectations to cover content for high-stakes assessment, many educators find it difficult to integrate technology-supported projects into their instruction. Participants in our research studies have found it more

Table 1. Information Archives and Online Projects

Name	Description	ULR
National Archives and Records Administration	A collection that documents the rights of American citizens, the actions of federal officials, and the national experience. Includes documents, posters, records, photographs and helpful background information about them.	www.archives.gov/
Library of Congress, American Memory Collection	A gateway to primary-source materials related to the history and culture of the United States. Includes activities and lesson plans to accompany the site's resources.	memory.loc.gov
History Matters	Designed for high school and college history teachers, the site has annotated hundreds of history Web sites and includes links to lesson plans, activities, primary documents, and guides for analyzing historical evidence.	www.historymatters.gmu.edu
History Wired	An online tour of the Smithsonian American History Museum.	Historywired.si.edu/index.html
Electronic Texts for the Study of American Culture	A collection of texts about American history and culture, available in hypertext format.	xroads.virginia.edu/~HYPER/hypertex.html
Ancient Cultures	A collection of documents and images to support the study of ancient cultures, including the Near East, Greece, and Islam.	eawc.evansville.edu/
Holocaust Museum	Information about the Unite States Holocaust Museum and online exhibitions that extend its collections.	www.ushmm.org
Ellis Island	Includes a search function that accesses records of immigrants to Ellis Island and online exhibits about the immigrant experience.	www.ellisisland.org
Social Studies Sources	Contains links to a broad array of social studies Web sites and other helpful educational resources for K-12 teachers.	www.indiana.edu/~socialst
Yahooligans	Yahooligans offers an extensive directory of sites to support history instruction, including a World Factbook with country maps, flags, and more and a collection of sites about United States history	www.yahooligans.com/Around_the_World/Countries
Best of History Web Sites	A collection of links to K-12 history lesson plans, teacher guides, activities, games, and quizzes.	www.besthistorysites.net/

(continued next page)

Table 1. Information Archives and Online Projects (continued)

Name	Description	ULR
The History Lab	A collection of history lessons that focus on teaching history through primary sources and that engage students in inquiry, reflection, interpretation and constructing hypotheses.	hlab.tielab.org
Local History Archives	Students in participating schools read and collect historical documents, photograph and research historical sites, and contribute their findings to a shared database.	lhap.tielab.org
Sallie Bingham Center for Women's History and Culture	Contains images and texts related to African-American women, Civil War women, and the Women's Liberation Movement.	scriptorium.lib.duke.edu/women/digital.html
The Presidents	A collection of texts from all presidents through George W. Bush.	www.ipl.org/div/potus
Ben's Guide to the U. S. Government for Kids	Offers learning tools for K-12 students, parents, and teachers about how the U. S. government works, the use of the primary source materials of GPO Access, and how to use GPO Access to engage in civic responsibilities.	bensguide.gpo.gov
Kids Voting USA	Offers a series of activities and lesson plans to support Civics education.	www.kidsvotingusa.org
Web de Anza Project	Provides students and scholars with primary-source documents and multimedia resources covering Juan Bautista de Anza's two overland expeditions from the Sonoran Desert to northern California, leading to the colonization of San Francisco in 1776. A good example of supported text on a Web site.	anza.uoregon.edu
Eye Witness History: Through the Eyes of Those Who Lived It	Samples of eyewitness accounts of historical events from the ancient world through the 20th century.	www.eyewitnesstohistory.com/
Repositories of Primary Sources	A listing of over 4,700 Web sites describing holdings of manuscripts, archives, rare books, historical photographs, and other primary sources.	www.uidaho.edu/special-collections Other.Repositories.html
Public Broadcasting System	A collection of resources to accompany PBS history programming.	www.pbs.org/history
The History Channel	A collection of resources to accompany the History Channel programming.	www.thehistorychannel.com

(continued next page)

Table 1. Information Archives and Online Projects (continued)

Name	Description	ULR
ThinkQuest	Global network in which students work together in teams to research a topic in the social sciences and then publish their research as an educational Web site for peers and classrooms around the world.	www.thinkquest.org
Newspapers Online	A collection of state, national, and world newspapers.	www.newspapers.com
On This Day	A listing of historical events and other items of interest that happened on a particular day.	www.on-this-day.com
DMarie Time Capsule	Users can type in a date from the 20th century and view news, sports headlines, birthdays, songs, and a sampling of prices.	www.dmarie.com/asp/history.asp
Online maps	Two popular sites for locating places, determining distances, and obtaining driving distances are Mapquest and Rand MacNally.	www.mapquest.com www.randmcnally.com

feasible to use project-based learning when they have some flexibility in their schedules and when the projects address more than one curricular area (Okolo & Ferretti, 2001).

Because projects often entail group work, teachers must also consider how to prepare students and structure activities to ensure productive collaboration and equitable participation. For example, students may need instruction, explicit guidance, and monitoring in the use of social skills that facilitate group work (e.g., Nastasi & Clements, 1991). Furthermore, without clear guidance and teacher monitoring, small-group discussions often remain at a low cognitive level (e.g., Okolo & Ferretti, 1996b). Teachers can help engage groups in higher-level thinking and discussion by asking probing questions, pointing out inconsistencies, encouraging students consider alternatives, and helping students to view knowledge as tentative (Saye & Brush, 2002).

Simulations and Online Gaming

Simulations have a long history of use in educational settings. Some of the first and best-known computer-based simulations for K-12 learners have involved social studies. For example, in Oregon Trail (MECC), a student takes the role of a mid-1800s emigrant crossing the Oregon Trail in a wagon train. The student must make multiple decisions about purchases, travel, interactions, and day-to-day living on the trail, with the goal of getting his or her family safely to Oregon Territory. Other simulations that address social studies content are described in Table 2.

Simulations typically have some connection to realistic situations, placing students in roles that would otherwise be too advanced, dangerous, or logistically unrealistic. As in project-based learning, students are goal-directed and have the opportunity to make multiple decisions about how to solve problems. Students often find simulations motivating and eagerly interact with content (e.g., geography, economics) that they would otherwise find uninteresting or overwhelming (Teague & Teague, 1995). Simulations can be used as springboards for other activities, including data gathering, organizational, and research skills. Educators have also reported that they facilitate the development of cooperative skills and group problem solving (Carroll, Knight, & Hutchinson, 1995).

Technology-based games, particularly those available on the Web, place students in virtual worlds that have characteristics similar to simulations. In typical online games, users assume the role of a character who has to solve problems, such as locating magical items or battling demons, in pursuit of a larger goal, such as rescuing a princess or cleaning up a polluted island. In a new generation of online games, such as The Sims, individual characters also interact with other characters online to accomplish specific goals. For example, a Sims player customizes his/her Sims' personality and appearance and then moves into a neighborhood, where s/he makes friends and advances through personal and professional activities that simulate everyday life and career. Users pursue goals such as friendship, professional advancement, and personal satisfaction. Jayakanthan (2002) contended that the computer gaming industry has become bigger than the music and movie industries, noting that, "the influence of computer games over youth today is akin to that of the cultural influence of music, political movements, and even religion on youth culture of the past" (p. 98).

The virtual environments of video and online games have been deservedly criticized for the degree to which they promote violence and aggression and perpetuate gender-based stereotypes (e.g., Healy, 1998; Zirkel, 2003). However, divorced from the content of typical videogames, the game design principles employed in these interactive environment offer potential educational benefits. First, learners are placed in an active role in which they must apply their knowledge and skills as they engage in tasks and solve problems that will help them attain a higher-order goal. Second, because they are characters in a virtual world, they must act in ways that are consistent with that world, which include using the tools, ways of behaving and thinking, and discourse that are appropriate to that world. Third, virtual worlds can be structured to encourage cooperation among users, so that learners who work together to share information and accomplish specific tasks are more likely to succeed. Fourth, learners can exercise choice and control over their actions in these virtual environments. Fifth, anyone who has watched a young videogame aficionado knows that children can acquire a huge store of knowledge through extended interactions with these games and the peer communities that support them (e.g., Gee, 2003; Prensky, 2000).

Language educators have championed the value of online experiences in second-language acquisition. For example, Garcia-Carbonell, Rising, Montero, and Watts (2001) noted that goal-directed virtual environments facilitate important affective aspects of language acquisition, including immersion in an authentic environment of language use, lowered anxiety, and increased motivation and enjoyment.

The Education Arcade, www.educationarcade.org, is a consortium of international game designers, publishers, scholars, educators, and policymakers who are committed to developing online games that teach. One of their prototype games is Revolution, a multiplayer, online, role-playing game situated in 1773 Williamsburg, Virginia. Players choose a role to play from predefined characters and interact with other players in a series of historical circumstances that culminate in the outbreak of the American Revolutionary War.

Okolo and Englert (2003) are developing an online history game entitled Living History. The setting for this game is Philadelphia's Independence Hall and other significant sites around Philadelphia at the time of the American Revolutionary War. Students will acquire knowledge about this pivotal time in American history by exploring the virtual environment and engaging in a series of challenges in which they must obtain specific information and demonstrate their knowledge in virtual activities that are consistent with the times, such as writing a letter home to one's family about the fervor around separation, or polling characters in the local tavern to determine how many of them would be willing to go to war with Britain. Students will also interact with other characters in the Living History environment to accomplish specific group goals, such as preparing for and holding a debate before Congress about separation. Guides, or historical characters with special knowledge and expertise, will be available in the virtual environment to scaffold historical interactions and to check and challenge students' developing understanding of this period of history.

Table 2. Simulations and Other Software to Support Social Studies Instruction

Name	Description	Producer or Distributor
Amazon Trail African Trail Oregon Trail	Students journey on a learning mission in which they interact with historic and cultural figures while learning about geography, history, culture, and science.	Riverdeep, www.riverdeep.net
The Carmen Sandiego Series (Where in the World, Where in the US, Where in Time)	Carmen Sandiego and her gang of thieves have stolen a treasure. The player, in the role of a detective, must make use of clues and reference materials to track down the criminal.	Riverdeep, www.riverdeep.net
Sim City	Players manipulate a number of different factors in the development of a community.	EA Games, simcity.ea.com
The Decisions, Decisions Series	Consists of 15 separate titles that engage students in simulations and decision making about historical and social issues such as immigration and prejudice.	Tom Snyder Productions, www.tomsnyder.com
Geography Search	Students learn geography skills and history by participating in a simulated voyage to the new world.	Tom Snyder Productions, www.tomsnyder.com
How Would You Survive?	Interactive adventures from the Aztec, Egyptian, and Viking civilizations.	Tom Snyder Productions, www.tomsnyder.com
Inspirer Geography Series	Teams of students travel throughout an area of the world in search of resources, commodities, and characteristics of states or countries while learning geography and problem solving skills.	Tom Snyder Productions, www.tomsnyder.com
The Graph Club, Graph Master	Software tool for creating, exploring, interpreting, and printing graphs.	Tom Snyder Productions, www.tomsnyder.com
Timeliner	Software for creating, illustrating, and printing timelines.	Tom Snyder Productions, www.tomsnyder.com
Neighborhood Map Machine, Mapmaker's Tool Kit, Where are We, Mapping the World by Heart	Each of these titles supports geography instruction by providing tools for creating and a variety of maps.	Tom Snyder Productions, www.tomsnyder.com
Jean Fritz History Series	Four CD-ROM books that introduce students to key historical figures and events.	Tom Snyder Productions, www.tomsnyder.com

Despite the promise of simulations and online gaming to promote learning and motivation, research about their use in K-12 education is scant. Poorly designed simulations and games may have a negative impact; yet, there has been very little investigation of how games can be optimally designed to stimulate the cognitive processes of young learners (Gredler, 1996). Simulations and games may present an oversimplified sense of reality, given that the virtual world can rarely replicate the consequences associated with real-life decisions (Teague & Teague, 1995). Furthermore, even the most thoughtfully designed simulations and online games run the risk of reifying cultural stereotypes, given that students may not have the opportunity to experience issues and events from all perspectives (Caroll et al., 1995). Bigelow (1995) described the critical role of debriefing, a process in which teachers help students to reflect upon who created a simulation or online game and for what purpose, to consider the groups who were not fully represented or included in the experience, and to question what their perspectives and experiences might have been.

Conclusions

Despite the intellectually demanding and sophisticated cognitive processes involved in learning and understanding topics in the social studies, educators have offered clear and compelling demonstrations of effective and motivating ways to teach social studies content to diverse learners (e.g., Alleman & Brophy, 2003; Lee, 2002; Lehrer et al., 1998; Levstik & Barton, 1997; Okolo & Ferretti, 1998). Technology can play an important role in providing rich and accessible social studies instruction. These include (a) data analysis, presentation and communication tools; (b) supported text; (c) information archives; (d) technology-supported projects; and (e) simulations and virtual worlds. All offer additional avenues to help learners develop a deeper understanding of and interest in history.

Very few of the approaches and applications discussed in this chapter are "out of the box" methods that teachers can implement with minimal time and preparation. Rather, most of the approaches described above make substantial demands on teachers' time. Time is a precious commodity in the classroom and in teachers' lives, and voices from the reform and professional development literatures have reminded us that teachers must have protected time within school day in which they can engage in professional development and collaborate in the planning and development of instructional activities and materials (e.g., Hawley & Valli, 1999). Furthermore, given the span of disciplines covered in the social studies, effective teaching demands deep content knowledge. Few elementary and special educators, in particular, are likely to have the depth of knowledge required to fully evaluate the quality of information available on the Web and in other sources. Nor do most have the breadth of knowledge required to design instructional activities that can offer a multiplicity of nuanced perspectives on social and historical topics. It is unrealistic to think that teacher education programs can provide novice teachers with sufficient expertise in the array of disciplines and complexity of topics that comprise our schools' social studies curricula. Like all good educators, effective social studies teachers must be lifelong learners who continue to investigate issues in the social sciences, connect these issue with their own life experiences and those of their students, and develop an extensive repertoire of pedagogical content knowledge (e.g., Okolo & Ferretti, 1998). Once again, ongoing professional development plays a key role in supporting these outcomes for educators. Models such as lesson study (Stigler & Hiebert, 1999) in which teacher collaborate in the development and analysis of lessons about key topics, offer powerful models for professional development in the social studies. Online communities, such as Tapped In (ti2.sri.com/tappedin), offer another avenue for sharing ideas and developing expertise.

Although the research base about the use of technology to improve social studies education for learners with disabilities is expanding, many questions remain unanswered. Because textbooks are likely to remain a staple of social studies instruction for years to come, additional research is needed about ways to construct text that is interesting and comprehrehensible for a variety of students (e.g., Beck, McKeown, & Worthy, 1995). Similarly, the field would benefit from further investigations of ways to effectively and feasibly adapt text to meet the needs of diverse learners (e.g., Edyburn, 2002, 2003b).

The increasing availability and affordability of screen-reading and text-to-speech software will render print-only versions of text obsolete. But, as discussed above, more research is needed to determine the conditions under which students can learn best from audio versions of text and ways to best supplement audio and print text with resources that enhance learners' comprehension and motivation. This is especially true in the social studies, in which students are working with text that often contains unfamiliar and complex vocabulary and content. The research about cognitive strategy instruction is replete with approaches for improving students' literacy, but only a small segment of this literature addresses the social studies (e.g., Klingner, Vaughn, & Schumm, 1998; Mastropieri, Scruggs, & Whedon, 1997; Mastropieri, Scruggs, Spencer, & Fontana, 2003). If students are to engage in authentic social and historical inquiry, then they need to learn a variety of strategies that include probing an author's intentions and underlying motivations, investigating bias in evidence, and synthesizing multiple perspectives (e.g., Ferretti & Okolo, 1996).

To engage in authentic disciplinary learning, students of the social studies need to interact with a variety of primary- and secondary-sources, ranging from maps and graphs to songs and diaries. The Web offers a rich repository of such documents that are freely available to all. The burgeoning array of electronic information is a boon to social studies instruction, but also presents new challenges to students, who must now learn to search for, analyze, and judge the credibility of a variety of online texts that include print, images, movies, and music. Yet, research about strategies that students can use to become more digitally literate is in its infancy.

Another area that is ripe for further investigation is the role that immersive, interactive environments can play in bringing the social sciences to life for students. Despite educators' enthusiasm about their potential contributions to student learning and motivation, poorly designed simulations and games may have negative effects. We need to better understand the principles of game design that facilitate learning, while also considering our responsibilities as educators to construct learning environments that will reinforce pro-social and ethical behaviors (Gredler, 1996). Educators also crave research-based ideas about how to effectively integrate games and simulations into more traditional instructional practices. The lesson plans and communities of practice that have sprung up around simulations such as Oregon Trail and Carmen Sandiego offer good examples of the types of support that facilitates the use of these applications in the classroom.

In closing, technology offers rich opportunities for improving social studies instruction for all learners, but it also brings new challenges to special and general educators who teach these subjects. Social studies and special educators, and the students they teach, will benefit from future evolutions in technology, the continued growth of Web-based resources, and increased knowledge of how to build powerful technology-based learning environments.

References

Alleman, J., & Brophy, J. (2003). *Social studies excursions: K-3.* Portsmouth, NH: Heinemann.

Allington, R. L. (2002). You can't learn much from books you can't read. *Educational Leadership, 60*(3), 16-19.

Anderson-Inman, L. (1994, March). *Computer-based study strategies for academic success: Empowering students with electronic study tools.* Proceedings of the Ninth Annual Conference on Technology and Persons with Disabilities. Los Angeles.

Anderson-Inman, L., & Zeitz, L. (1994). Beyond notecards: Synthesizing information with electronic study tools. *The Computing Teacher, 21*(8), 21-25.

Anderson-Inman, L., & Horney, M. A. (1993, April*). Profiles of hypertext readers: Case studies from the ElectroText project.* Paper presented at the Annual Meeting of the

American Educational Research Association., Atlanta. GA.

Anderson-Iman, L., & Horney, M. A. (1998). *Transforming text for at-risk readers*. In D. Reinking, M. C. McKenna, L D. Labbo, & R. D. Kieffer (Eds.), *Handbook of literacy and technology* (pp. 15-44). Mahwah, NJ: Lawrence Erlbaum.

Anderson-Inman, L., Horney, M. A., Chen, D. T. & Lewin, L. (1994). Hypertext literacy: Observations from the ElectroText project. *Language Arts, 71*(4), 279-287.

Armbruster, B. B., & Anderson, T. H. (1984). Structures of explanations in history textbooks, or so what if Governor Stanford missed the spike and hit the rail? *Journal of Curriculum Studies, 16*, 247-274.

Barton, L. S., & Levstik, K. C. (1996). *Doing history: Investigating with children in elementary and middle schools*. Mahwah, NJ: Lawrence Erlbaum.

Bass, R., & Rosenzweig, R. (1991). *Rewiring the history and social studies classroom: Needs, frameworks, dangers, and proposals*. Department of Education Forum on Technology in K-12 education: Envisioning a new future. Washington, DC: United States Department of Education.

Bean, R. M. (1994). Adapted use of social studies textbooks in elementary classrooms: Views of classroom teachers. *Remedial and Special Education, 4*, 216-226.

Beck, I.L., & McKeown, M. (1991). Substantive and methodological considerations for productive textbook analysis. In J.P. Shaver (Ed.), *Handbook of research on social studies teaching and learning* (pp. 496-512). New York: MacMillan.

Beck, I. L., McKeown, M. G., & Worthy, J. (1995). Giving a text voice can improve students' understanding. *Reading Research Quarterly 30*(2), 220-238.

Bigelow, B. (1995). On the road to cultural bias. *Rethinking School, 2003*(1). Retrieved November 15, 2003, from: www.rethinking schools.org/archive/10_01/10_01.shtml.

Blanco, F., & Rosa, A. (1997). Dilthey's dream: Teaching history to understand the future. *International Journal of Educational Research, 3*, 187-200.

Bos, C., & Vaughn, S. (2002). *Teaching students with learning and behavioral problems* (5th ed.). New York: Allyn and Bacon.

Bransford, J.D., Brown, A.L., & Cocking, R.R. (1999). *How people learn: Brain, mind, experience, and school*. Washington, DC: National Academy Press.

Brophy, J. (1990). Teaching social studies for understanding and higher-order applications. *The Elementary School Journal, 90*, 353-417.

Brophy, J., & Alleman, J. (2002). Primary-grade students' knowledge and thinking about the economics of meeting families' shelter needs. *American Educational Research Journal 39*(2), 423-468.

Carroll, T., Knight, C., & Hutchinson, E. (1995). Carmen Sandiego: Crime can pay when it comes to learning. *Social Education, 53*, 165-169.

Cibrowski, J. (1993). *Textbooks and the students who can't read them*. Cambridge, MA: Brookline Books.

Curtis, C. K. (1991). Social studies for students at-risk and with disabilities. In J. P. Shaver (Ed.), *Handbook of research on social studies teaching and learning* (pp. 157-174). New York: Macmillan

Debashis, A. (1995). Adventures in cyberspace: Exploring the information content of World Wide Web pages on the Internet. *Dissertation Abstracts International, 56-09A*, 3358 (Dissertation Abstracts Online).

Dewey, J. (1916). *Democracy and education*. New York: The Free Press.

Edyburn, D. L. (2002). Cognitive rescaling strategies: Interventions that alter the cognitive accessibility of text. *Closing the Gap, 21*(1), 1-4.

Edyburn, D. L. (2003a). Learning from text. *Special Education Technology Practice, 4*(3), 16-27.

Edyburn, D. L. (2003b). Reading difficulties in the general education classroom: A taxonomy of text modification strategies. *Closing the Gap, 21*(6), 1, 10-13, 30-31.

Ehman, L., & Glenn, A. D. (1991). Interactive technology in the social studies. In J. P. Shaver (Ed.), *Handbook of research on social studies teaching and learning* (pp. 487-499). New York: Macmillan

Elkind, J. (1998a). Computer reading machines for poor readers. *Perspectives, 24*(2), 4-6.

Elkind, J. (1998b). *A study of the Kurzweil 3000 reading machine in enhancing poor reading performance.* Portola Valley, CA: Lexia Institute.

Elkind, J., Black, M., & Murray, C. (1996). Computer-based compensation of adult reading disabilities. *Annals of Dyslexia, 46,* 159-186.

Elkind, J., Cohen, K., & Murray, C. (1993). Using computer-based readers to improve reading comprehension of students with disabilities. *Annals of Dyslexia, 43,* 238-259.

Ferretti, R. P., MacArthur, C. D., & Okolo, C. M. (2002). Teaching effectively about historical things. *Teaching Exceptional Children, 34*(6), 66-69.

Ferretti, R. P., MacArthur, C. D., & Okolo, C. M. (2001). Teaching for historical understanding in inclusive classrooms. *Learning Disability Quarterly, 24* 59-71.

Ferretti, R. P., & Okolo, C. M. (1996). Authenticity in learning: Multimedia design projects in social studies for students with disabilities. *Journal of Learning Disabilities, 29,* 450-460.

Garcia-Carbonelli, A., Rising, B., Montero, B., & Watts, F. (2001). Simulation/gaming and the acquisition of competence in another language. *Simulation and Gaming, 32*(4), 481-491.

Gee, J. P. (2003). *What videogames have to teach us about learning and literacy.* New York: MacMillan.

Gitlin, T. (1995). *The twilight of common dreams: Why America is wracked by culture wars.* New York: Holt.

Glaser, C. W., Rieth, H. J., Kinzer, C. K., Colburn, L. K., & Peter, J. (1999). A description of the impact of multimedia anchored instruction on classroom interactions. *Journal of Special Education Technology, 14*(2), 27-43.

Gredler, M. E. (1996). Educational games and simulations: A technology in search of a (research) paradigm. In D. Jonassen (Ed.), *Handbook of research for educational communications and technology* (pp. 521-540). New York: Simon & Schuster Macmillan.

Green, T. (2001). Tech talk for social studies teacher: Virtual expeditions: Taking your students around the world without leaving the classroom. *The Social Studies, 92*(4), 177-179.

Hawkins, J., & Sheingold, K. (1986). The beginning of a story: Computers and the organization of learning in classrooms. In J. Culbertson & L. L. Cunningham (Eds.). *Microcomputers and education. 85th National Society for the Study of Education Yearbook* (Part 1, pp. 40-58). Chicago: Chicago University Press.

Hawley, W. D., & Valli, L. (1999). The essentials of effective professional development: A new consensus. In L. Darling-Hammond & G. Sykes (Eds.), *Teaching as the learning profession* (pp. 1237-150). San Francisco: Jossey-Bass.

Healy, J. (1998). *Failure to connect: How computer affect children's minds—for better or for worse.* New York: Simon & Schuster.

Hicks, D. (2003). *How can digital historical inquiry be facilitated in K-12 social studies and history classrooms?* Retrieved November 16, 2003, from: msit.gsu.edu/dhr.teaching/scim_theory.html.

Higgins, K., & Boone, R. (1990). Hypertext study guides and social studies achievement of students with learning disabilities, remedial students, and regular education students. *Journal of Learning Disabilities, 23*(9), 529-540.

Higgins, K., Boone, R., & Lovitt, T. C. (1996). Hypertext support for remedial students and students with learning disabilities. *Journal of Learning Disabilities, 29*(4), 402-412.

Horney, M. A., & Anderson-Inman, L. (1994). The Electro-text project: Hypertext reading patterns of middle school students. *Journal of Educational Multimedia and Hypermedia, 3*(1), 71-91.

Jayakanthan, R. (2002). Application of computer games in the field of education. *The Electronic Library, 20*(2), 98-102.

Klingner, J. K., Vaughn, S., & Schumm, J. S. (1998). Collaborative strategic reading during social studies in heterogeneous fourth grade classrooms. *The Elementary School Journal, 99*(1), 3-22.

Lee, J. K. (2002). Digital history in the history/social studies classroom. *The History Teacher, 35*(4). Retrieved November 3, 2003, from www.historycooperative.org/journals/ht35.4/lee.html.

Lee, P., & Ashby, R. (2000). Progression in historical understanding among students ages 7-14. In P. N. Stearns, Sexias, P., & Wineburg,

S. (Ed.), *Knowing, teaching, and learning history* (pp. 199-222). New York: New York University Press.

Lehrer, R., Erickson, J., & Connell, T. (1998). Learning by designing hypermedia documents. *Computers in the Schools, 10*(1-2), 227-254.

Lowenthal, D. (2000). Dilemmas and delights of learning history. In P. N. Stearns, P. Sexias, P., & S. Wineburg, S. (Eds.), *Knowing, teaching, and learning history* (pp. 63-82). New York: New York University Press.

MacArthur, C. D., Ferretti, R. P., & Okolo, C. M. (2002). On defending controversial viewpoints: Debates of sixth-graders about the desirability of early 20th century American immigration. *Learning Disabilities Research and Practice, 17*(3), 160-172.

MacArthur, C. A., & Haynes, J. B. (1995). Student Assistant for Learning from Text (SALT): A hypermedia reading aid. *Journal of Learning Disabilities, 28*(3), 150-159.

Mastropieri, M. A., Scruggs, T. E, & Whedon, C. (1997). Using mnemonic strategies to teach information about U. S. Presidents: A classroom-based investigation. *Learning Disability Quarterly, 20*(1), 13-21.

Mastropieri, M. A., Scruggs, T. E., Spencer, V., & Fontana, J. (2003). Promoting success in high school world history: Peer tutoring versus guided notes. *Learning Disabilities Research and Practice, 18*(1), 52-65.

Montali, J., & Lewandowski, L. (1996). Bimodal reading: Benefits of a talking computer for average and less skilled readers. *Journal of Learning Disabilities, 29*(3), 271-279.

Nash, G. B., Crabtree, C., & Dunn, R. (1997). *History on trial: The culture wars and the teaching of the past.* New York: Knopff.

Nastasi, B. K., & Clements, D. H. (1991). Research on cooperative learning: Implications for practice. *School Psychology Review, 20*(1), 110-131.

Norton, P., & Harvey, D. (1995). Information = knowledge: Using databases to explore the tragedy at Donner Pass. *Learning and Leading with Technology, 23*(1), 23-25.

Ogle, D. M. (1986). K-W-L: A teaching model that develops active learning of expository text. *The Rreading Teacher, 39,* 564-570.

Okolo, C. M., Cavalier, A. R., Ferretti, R. P., & MacArthur, C. A. (2000). Technology, literacy, and disabilities: A review of the research. In R. Gersten, E. P. Schiller, & S. Vaughn (Eds.), *Contemporary special education research: Syntheses of the knowledge base on critical instructional issues* (pp. 179-250). Mahwah, NJ: Erlbaum.

Okolo, C. M., & Englert, C. S. (2002). *The virtual history museum: Technology tools and environments to support the historical understanding of students with disabilities.* Grant Proposal funded by United States Department of Education, Office of Special Education Programs.

Okolo, C. M., & Englert, C. S. (2003). *Living History: Interactive history environments for students in inclusive classrooms.* Grant Proposal funded by the United States Department of Education, Office of Special Education Programs.

Okolo, C. M., & Ferretti, R. P. (1996a). Knowledge acquisition and multimedia design in the social studies for children with learning disabilities. *Journal of Special Education Technology, 13*(2), 91-103.

Okolo, C. M., & Ferretti, R. P. (1996b). The impact of multimedia design projects on the knowledge, attitudes, and collaboration of students in inclusive classrooms. *Journal of Computing in Childhood Education, 7,* 223-252.

Okolo, C.M., & Ferretti, R.P. (1997). Knowledge acquisition and technology-supported projects in the social studies for students with learning disabilities. *Journal of Special Education Technology, 13,* 91-103.

Okolo, C. M., & Ferretti, R. P. (1998). Multimedia design projects in an inclusive social studies classroom: "Sometimes people argue with words instead of fists." *Teaching Exceptional Children, 31*(1), 50-57.

Okolo, C. M., Ferretti, R. P., & MacArthur, C. D. (2002). Westward expansion and the the-year old mind: Teaching for historical understanding in a diverse classroom. In J. E. (Ed.), *Advances in research on teaching. Volume 9. Social constructivist teaching. Affordance and constraints* (pp. 120-136). New York: JAI Press.

Passe, J. B., & Beattie, J. (1994). Social studies instruction for students with mild disabilities:

A progress report. *Remedial and Special Education, 15*(4), 227-233.

Paxton, R. J. (1999). A deafening silence: History textbooks and the students who read them. *Review of Educational Research, 69*(3), 315-339.

Patton, J., Polloway, E., & Cronin, M. (1987). Social studies instruction for handicapped students: A review of current practices. *The Social Studies, 78,* 131135.

Paul, J. R., & Kaiser, C. (1996). Do women live longer than men: Investigating graveyard data with computers. *Learning and Leading with Technology, 23,* 13-15.

Perkins, D. N., & Salomon, G. (1989). Are cognitive skills context bound? *Educational Researcher, 18*(1), 16-25.

Prensky, M. (2000). *Digital game-based learning.* New York: McGraw Hill.

Rosenzweig, R., & Thelen, D. (1998). *The presence of the past: Popular uses of history in American life.* New York: Columbia University Press.

Saye, J. W., & Brush, T. (2002). Scaffolding critical reasoning about history and social issues in multimedia-supported learning environments. *Educational Technology Research and Development, 50*(3), 77-96.

Schumaker, J. B., Bulgren, J. A., Davis, B., Grossen, B., Marquis, J., Deshler, D. D., & Lenz, K. B. (2002). *The educational context and outcomes for high school students with disabilities: General education classes and the satisfaction of general education teachers.* Lawrence: University of Kansas, Institute for Academic Access.

Shenk, D. (1998). *Data smog. Surviving the information glut.* San Francisco: Harper.

Stearns, P. N., Sexias, P., & Wineburg, S. (2000). *Knowing, teaching, and learning history.* New York: New York University Press.

Stigler, J. W., & Hiebert, J. (1999). *The teaching gap.* New York: The Free Press.

Teague, M., & Teague, G. (1995). Planning with computers: A social studies simulation. *Learning and Loading with Technology, 23*(1), 20, 22.

VanSledright, B. (2002). Confronting history's interpretive paradox while teaching fifth graders to investigate the past. *American Educational Research Journal, 39*(4), 1089-1115.

Wineburg, S. (1991). Historical problem solving: A study of the cognitive processes used in the evaluation of documentary and pictorial evidence. *Journal of Educational Psychology, 83*(1), 73-87.

Wineburg, S. (2001). *Historical thinking and other unnatural acts.* Philadelphia: Temple University Press.

Wong, B. Y. L. (1980). Activating the inactive learner: Use of question/prompts to enhance comprehension and retention of implied information in learning disabled children. *Learning Disability Quarterly, 3*(1), 29-37.

Zirkel, P. A. (2003). Virtual liability? *Phi Delta Kappan, 84*(7), 556-557.

32

Science in Special Education: Emerging Technologies

Jennie I. Schaff, Marci Kinas Jerome, Michael M. Behrmann, and Debra Sprague

Traditionally science has been taught in regular and general education classrooms in ways similar to other class instruction methodologies (Kimmel, Deek, & Frazer, 2002), typically lectures supplemented with abundant text in textbook formats. In recent years, however, researchers in the fields of special education and science have identified a need for a shift in science instruction presentation to include more dynamic and multisensory methods that engage and motivate learners (Kimmel et al., 2002). Such changes are primarily due to the evolution in technology and a more thorough comprehension of learning styles regarding individual learners.

Technology is a widely accepted way to attain the goal of motivation combined with dynamic instruction in the science special education classroom. Additionally, many assistive technologies have been identified and utilized in the special education environment to help students with disabilities attain specific goals. Some of these technologies include materials presented in Braille for a student who has visual impairments, speech output lab equipment for students who are blind, captioned presentations for students with hearing impairments, and adjustable tables and chairs for individuals with physical disabilities. If deemed appropriate for an individual student, such assistive technology modifications are usually appropriate throughout the school environment regardless of which class the student is in. Therefore, this chapter, will focus on emerging technologies that can be used in the special education environment.

The chapter is divided into four sections. The first discusses virtual reality and its uses in special education and in the science classroom. Next, follows a discussion of the use of MOOS (Multi-user domain, Object Oriented) and MUDS (Multi User Domain) in special education. Using the Internet and various resources on the Internet is discussed in the third section; including virtual laboratories, virtual high schools, and virtual field trips, among others. Finally, the chapter concludes by addressing personal digital assistant (PDA) technologies that can be used in special education.

Virtual Reality

Definition of Virtual Reality

Imagine students being able to walk on Mars without a spacesuit, talk to Socrates or Galileo, explore the relationship between mass, force, and friction in a world without gravity, or become a test particle and experiment with electrical fields. Such opportunities could make history and literature come alive for students or enable them to understand scientific concepts in a way that was never possible before. With the help of an emerging technology called virtual reality, such opportunities are now possible.

The term *virtual reality* has been used to describe many different types of computer-generated, or "virtual"-interactions, from text-based interactions in chat rooms to video arcade games played through a two-dimensional screen. For the purpose of this chapter we are defining virtual reality (VR) as a three-dimensional, computer-generated synthetic environment that gives the user a sense of being immersed in a real world. This immersion is based on visual, audio, and haptic (touch) feedback. Instead of using standard keyboards and screens, users wear head-mounted displays, data gloves, and headphones (for explanations of this equipment, see Sprague & Behrmann, 2001). While computer controls what they hear, see, and feel, users, in turn, control the computer by manipulating the objects they see, feel and hear, interacting within the synthetic environment (Aukstakalnis & Blatner, 1992).

Characteristics of Virtual Reality

Although VR has been used mostly in the military and corporate world's various studies conducted on VR's potential in education have shown it to be a potentially engaging learning experience (Sprague, 1996). In particular, VR offers a number of characteristics that may prove beneficial for students with disabilities. While many of them have been used effectively in a variety of teaching strategies, VR provides unique and powerful ways of employing them (Powers & Darrow, 1996).

Multisensory

Virtual reality, like the real world it emulates, has the capability to present information through multiple senses. Thus, VR allows users to see, hear, and feel the world around them. Multisensory cues (sight, sound, and haptic) can enhance the quality of the student's learning and interactive experiences (Dede, Salzman, Loftin, & Sprague, 1999).

Experiential Learning Environment

Virtual reality can be characterized as an experiential learning environment. Students actively interact with the environment. Learning-by-doing combined with reflective inquiry can induce learning; through experience, students are able to extend and modify their understanding of science concepts (mental models) based on discontinuities between expected and actual behaviors of phenomena (Dede, Salzman, Loftin, & Ash, 1997).

VR allows users to ask "what if" questions by enabling them to test out hypotheses and immediately see the outcome. Thus, students can compare initial conditions and end results. Further, they can perform the same experiment over and over until they fully comprehend the results.

Abstract to Concrete

In order to understand the world and how it functions, students must comprehend abstract concepts far removed from their everyday experiences. Mastery of abstract science concepts often requires learners to incorporate invisible factors that represent intangible forces (diSessa, 1983). However, real life experiences often distort or contradict the concepts students need to understand. As a result, most learners have difficulty understanding these scientific concepts (Reif & Larkin, 1991).

Virtual reality allows users to explore alternative realities because, unlike the real world, the laws of nature or the laws of physics do not bind it. By turning off these conditions (gravity, friction, etc.), students are able to identify their misconceptions about the ways in which the world functions. Once identified, students begin to alter their misconceptions and develop new mental models that demonstrate their ability to comprehend these abstract scientific concepts.

Control of Extraneous Stimuli

Students often find it impossible to manage extraneous stimuli. That is, they are not always clear on what is important and what can be ignored. VR allows for the creation of worlds in which extraneous stimuli can be controlled. Thus, using a scaffolding process, students may initiate learning in a highly simplified environment. As proficiency increases, the environment can become increasingly complex until it resembles the real world. Such a progression of environments in which stimuli are increased would be difficult to achieve in a traditional classroom (Middleton, 1992).

Through the use of the head-mounted display and headphones, it is also possible to eliminate distractions from the real world. Without such distractions, the user is forced to attend to the stimuli presented in the VR environment. This could increase the amount of time on task and the amount of learning that will occur.

Frames of Reference

One of the unique features of virtual reality is the ability to look at an environment from multiple viewpoints; referred to as frames of reference. In virtual environments, students can become part of a phenomenon and experience it directly. Alternatively, they can step back from the phenomenon to allow a global view of what is happening (Salzman, Dede, Loftin, & Chen, 1999). Enabling students to experience phenomena from multiple perspectives or frames of references appears to facilitate the learning process (Dede et al., 1997).

Barriers to Virtual Reality

Despite the numerous potentials of virtual reality, its use in education does face barriers. One such barrier is the cost of the equipment needed for full-immersive VR. For example, the development of high-end virtual environments requires computer equipment costing over $100,000 (Castellani, 1999) whereas the cost of head-mounted displays range from $300 to $6,500 (Goldstein, 2002). However, the prices are coming down due to advances in the entertainment industry and new developments in the field are producing low-cost alternatives that can be just as effective as full-immersive VR.

Related to the cost is the need for high-end computers required to produce VR environments that look and sound real. Such computers must have faster processors and more memory than what is found in the standard computers used in schools today. The trade-offs for inexpensive systems are low resolution of graphics, problems with modeling complex scenes, and a lag between user motion and the response time of the system, which can lead to simulation sickness (Holloway, Fuchs, & Robinette, 1991).

Simulation sickness can result in feelings of disorientation, headaches, eyestrain, nausea, and vomiting. Simulation sickness is a concern when using VR, but it does not happen to everyone. In fact, it happens to a very small percent of the users. Being aware of the risks involved and taking some precautions can help eliminate or reduce simulation sickness. For example, people susceptible to other forms of motion sickness may want to avoid VR. In addition, those who have an ear infection, cold, or epilepsy should refrain from participating in VR. Finally, taking frequent breaks and checking on the status of one's health before, during, and after the VR experience can help to reduce simulation sickness.

Some parents and educators worry about the use of VR with special education students. In particular, they feel these students need more interaction with other children and adults in real-world settings, rather than interactions in a virtual environment. That could further isolate students with disabilities from mainstream life (Goldstein, 2002). However, as we will see in the following section, VR has the power to help students with disabilities. Often disabilities do not matter in a virtual reality program.

Virtual Reality and Disabilities

Researchers at the Oregon Research Institute developed a VR environment to teach children with cerebral palsy and other neurological disorders how to operate an electronic wheelchair. To move in the VR world, students used a joystick like the one on wheelchairs to navigate around obstacles in the virtual world in the same way they would in the real world. Studies have shown that the amount of time needed to learn how to navigate with the electronic wheelchair was reduced for those who participated in the VR training (Inman, Peaks, Loge, Chen, & Ferrington, 1994).

Researchers are also looking at ways to use VR to help blind people learn to navigate through the real world, especially how to cross a street safely. Relying on auditory cues, users must cross a virtual street. If they step out in front of a car, they are "hit" and the computer system crashes. Users must then wait for the system to reboot, allowing them time to reflect on what they did wrong (Goldstein, 2002).

Using VR to learn how to safely cross a street has also been tried with two children with mild to moderate autism (Strickland, Marcus, Mesibov, & Hogan, 1996). The children soon became adept in the environment and were able to take virtual walks and locate objects. The researchers reported that the children "responded similarly to three different street scenes, but more study needs to be done to determine if they were generalizing across different surroundings" (p. 658).

Another project, the Virtual Reality Applications Research Team (VIRART), involved the design of virtual reality environments for students with moderate to severe learning disabilities. Researchers created a Virtual House, Supermarket, City, and Skiing to see if students with severe learning disabilities could learn skills that would transfer to the real world. Twenty-three students between the ages of 15 and 19 participated. The results showed that the students in the experimental group who used the Virtual Supermarket performed faster and more accurately in the real supermarket than did students in the control group who were not exposed to the Virtual Supermarket (Brown, Standen, & Cobb, 1998).

VR is also being used to diagnose and treat children with attention deficit hyperactivity disorder. Here students are placed in a virtual classroom and told to stay focused on a computer image or a computer blackboard. Each time they see a certain sequence of letters appear on the board, they hit a response button. Several virtual distractions are built into the system. These distractions include a door opening, hallway conversations, something being thrown into their line of sight, slamming of lockers, and a bright red car, driving pass the window. If the students look toward the distraction or miss the response, the researchers take note of the attention lapse (Goldstein, 2002), thereby noting the number of times the child was "off task."

Virtual Reality and Science

Currently, few fully immersive VR environments are available for educational use in K-12, presumably due to high costs reduce (Powers & Darrow, 1996). However, there are a few projects that have been or are being developed, especially in the area of science.

Researchers at George Mason University and the University of Houston, through the sponsorship of the National Science Foundation and NASA, teamed up to create two VR Worlds (NewtonWorld and MaxwellWorld) in a project called ScienceSpace. The purpose was to assess VR's potential and limitations as a learning tool. Designed to help students master challenging scientific concepts, NewtonWorld allows students to explore Newton's laws of motion as well as kinetic energy and linear momentum, whereas MaxwellWorld allows students to examine the nature of electrostatic forces and fields and helps them understand the concept of electrical flux (Dede et al., 1997). To learn more about ScienceSpace, visit their Web site at (www.virtual.gmu.edu).

The Virtual Gorilla Exhibit Project

This joint venture by the Georgia Institute of Technology and Zoo Atlanta, is exploring the use of virtual reality to help people learn experientially what would otherwise be difficult to learn. Based upon actual data provided by Zoo Atlanta (gorilla behavior data as well as terrain data and building blueprints), the researchers are modeling a gorilla exhibit where children can "be a gorilla" and experience first hand what it is like to be a member of a gorilla family group. They can walk around and interact with the virtual gorillas. In addition, they can test behaviors and elicit appropriate responses from the gorillas based upon the children's behavior and assumed role in the hierarchy of the family structure (Allison and Hodges, 1999). To learn more about the Virtual Gorilla Exhibit Project visit their website (www.cc.gatech.edu/grads/a/Don.Allison/gorilla/).

Non-Immersive Uses of Virtual Reality

Virtual reality usually refers to a synthetic environment that provides full immersion. However, some projects are being developed that apply the principles of virtual reality without being fully immersive, referred to as "desktop VR." The level of interaction in these environments is lower than in a full-immersed VR world, but desktop VR is the most popular form of VR used in schools due to its ease of use and low cost. Users can exist and interact in the world through the use of a computer keyboard and mouse, much like they would a flight simulator or video game. These projects run on a standard computer or over the Web and do not need special equipment.

Materialworlds

This real-time simulation environment runs over personal computers (Windows 95/98/ 2000) and requires Internet Explorer 4 or higher. A materialworld plug-in needs to be installed, available on the materialworlds Web site (www.materialworlds.com/). Simulations portray the solar system, Newton's laws of motion, simple machines, and structures (such as swings and bridges). Instructions are available for modifying the simulations or creating new ones.

Zoning In on Physics

Developers at George Mason University, through a grant from the U.S. Department of Education, designed a software program that capitalized on the potential of VR. Designed to meet the needs of high school students with mild learning disabilities, Zoning in on Physics (ZIOP) consists of four modules or zones focusing on Newton's laws of motion. Several features are consistent within each of the four zones. There is a shuttle that students can move by applying force through the use of a force button. Students can also adjust the amount of friction the shuttle will encounter. Friction is determined by choosing the ground texture. Students can choose between outer space (no friction), ice (low friction), grass (medium friction), and bricks (high friction). Finally, students can choose the frame of reference for viewing the shuttle. That is, they may choose an exocentric (looking at the shuttle from the outside) or an egocentric (looking at the shuttle from within) point of view. In the exocentric frame of reference, students may view the shuttle from the side, front, back, or bird's eye (looking down from the sky). In the egocentric frame of reference, students have a forward and backward view. Throughout the four zones, students experiment with force and friction in order to determine the speed and distance the shuttle will travel (Sprague & Behrmann, 2001).

Zoning in on Physics including the four modules, the player that allow the modules to run on various Window platforms, lesson plan ideas, and student worksheets is available free of charge from the project website (it.gse.gmu.edu/projects/ziop).

Barriers – The Awareness Challenge

The Rehabilitation Science Virtual Reality Lab has created a desktop VR program to help people understand what it is like to navigate in a wheelchair (Goldstein, 2002). In the program, called *Barriers-The Awareness Challenge*, people navigate (in a virtual wheelchair) through a typical school thereby identifying barriers wheelchair users. Barriers are anything that stops a person from doing things everybody else can do or that causes a person to be treated differently because of a disability. The program includes 24 different barriers, some involving the building, others dealing with attitudes and behavior of other people. The program is available from the project Web site at (www.health.uottawa.ca/vrlab/barriers/ barriers.html).

MUDs and MOOs in Special Education

In this technological age, there is a wealth of educational material and support available to teachers via the Internet. One such technology tool is MOOs. As mentioned, MOO stands for "Multi-user domain, Object Oriented." A MOO is essentially an online virtual community in which individuals, can simultaneously interact, dialogue, and manipulate the virtual environment in real time. MOOs are only one type of virtual community available via the Internet. A MOO is a type of MUD, "Multi User Domain." As with a MOO, individuals actively explore and participate in virtual communities in a MUD. In general, a MOO differs from a MUD in that most MOOs allow individuals to manipulate and create new objects and rooms in the virtual community, whereas a MUD does not.

MOOs are generally text-based environments in which the virtual world is described in very descriptive text. "You are standing in a great hall with beautiful furnishings, mirrors on the wall, and a great chandelier overhanging above." The intent of such descriptive text is to help develop a sense of a physical community, making individuals believe they are actually physically part of this virtual world. The sense of community and belonging is the allure of this type of technology.

Although the majority of MOOs are text-based, some utilize a more user-friendly graphic interface; allowing users to "click" on the place they want to move or the object they want to manipulate. Furthermore, in some MOOs it is possible for users to hear their text conversations with other users read aloud.

Individuals who participate in MOOs and MUDs are identified as a particular player, character or avatar, and generally select their own names and descriptions. The selection of a persona is crucial in maintaining the richness and depth of the virtual world. The creation of characters in MOOs allows individuals to personify themselves or develop new personas. In graphic based MOOs, users may represent themselves with a graphic avatar, thus increasing the physical sense of the environment.

To use a MOO, you log on to the MOO server generally through either an Internet browser or directly through a telnet client. To participate in the MOO, you will need a username and a password. While some MOOs allow for guest access, guest users are usually restricted from certain activities. Although most MOOs use a similar set of commands, it is important to read the documentation or the help files for individual MOOs for directions how to navigate that particular world.

Educational MOOs

Although MUDs and MOOs were generally created as social environments, they are increasingly being used in education, as they can be very motivating and useful tools. An educational MOO as Turbee (1997) describes,

> has an academic theme and uses a variety of MOO communication tools such as internal email, newspapers, documents, blackboards, and classrooms to accommodate a variety of teaching styles. Teachers can use these tools in harmony with the goals for the class while exploring the nature of MOO as a student-centered learning environment. (p. 3)

A multitude of educational MOOs are available focusing on a variety of subject areas and age levels (see Table 1). Educational MOOs may vary in their level of complexity and richness of content. It is important when looking at MOOs to consider the sponsoring organization or MOO programmer. While many educational MOOs are developed and maintained by university grants programs and educational organizations, others may not be well maintained or monitored for membership or content. Furthermore, many MOOs and MUDS are developed for technology sake with few or no educational goals (Bruckman, 1999).

Although the use of MOOs may not yet be widespread in education, the technology has its benefits. Since most MOOs are text-driven, their greatest benefit would be to increase students' reading and writing skills. The incentive of using technology and the magnetism of the virtual world motivate students to want to continually participate in textual discussions and explorations. With the development of characters and objects, MOOs may also inspire students' creative selves. As if they were actors on stage, students in a MOO environment may take on a persona unlike themselves in which they must think, speak, and act as that character would. Furthermore, participation in MOOs increases students' technology skills, including keyboarding, and also spelling (Kort, 2002).

Along with more academic skills, MOOs increase students' social skills. Since MOOs enable users to talk to others in real time, it is possible for students to not only collaborate with their own classmates in explorations, activities, and discussion, but to collaborate with students around the world. Through both structured and unstructured activities, students are exposed to different cultural perspectives. Furthermore, since MOOs provide a wealth of social experiences, students are both motivated and encouraged to engage other characters in conversations, thus continually enhancing social skills (Kort, 2002).

With the intense focus on writing skills, two areas that have lent themselves to MOOs are writing lab sites such as the Virtual Writing Center and foreign language communities such as MOOFrancais and schMOOze University (see Table 1). These sites immerse students in real-world writing experiences that are designed to provide them with authentic writing experiences through both dialogue and exploration. MOOs are also popular as meeting/learning centers for both professionals, such as TAPPED IN for educators and BioMOO for

Table 1. Educational MOOs on the Web

Educational MOOs	URL
BioMOO A virtual meeting place for biologists to discuss relevant issues	bioinformatics.weizmann.ac.il/BioMOO
Grass Roots MOO A virtual reality community, where people come together for support, education, and fun. It's a prototype community working on the development of a classical "Global Village" idea	www.enabling.org/grassroots
MicroMUSE MUSEs are multi-user text-based virtual communities. They derive from popular text-based adventure games and support real-time interaction among participants who collaborate to build their own world	www.musenet.org
MOOFrancais A French virtual community created on the Internet	www.umsl.edu/~moosproj/moofrancais.html
MOOSE Crossing Designed for kids 13 and under to expand creative writing skills and learn to program at the same time. Kids can create objects ranging from magic carpets to virtual pets, and virtual rooms and cities	www.cc.gatech.edu/elc/moose-crossing
schMOOze University Designed for people studying English as a second or foreign language could practice English while sharing ideas and experiences with other learners of English	schmooze.hunter.cuny.edu:8888
TAPPED IN K-12 teachers, librarians, administrators, and professional development staff, as well as university faculty, students, and researchers gather here to learn, collaborate, share, and support one another	www.tappedin.org
Virtual Writing Center A place where writers can get together and learn about their writing and writing skills	bessie.englab.slcc.edu

science professionals, and for students from around the world such as MOOSE Crossing. Although there are some educational science MOOs such as MicroMUSE, the science of using MOOs may involve the programming capabilities of the virtual environment. As part of their MOO experience, students can build objects and rooms using programming language. In creating objects, students must plan, design, and test their functions. Students can also work collaboratively to build more complex objects.

Students with Disabilities and MOOs

Although there are relatively few MOOs and MUDs designed specifically for individuals with disabilities such as the Grass Roots MOO (see Table 1), the use of such technology may be especially rewarding for students with disabilities. As mentioned previously, MOOs are an excellent tool for fostering reading and writing skills. For many students with disabilities, these areas can be a great struggle and a very unpleasant experience. Using MOOs provides students with motivating and realistic opportunities for literacy. Since students are participating in real-time discussions and activities, they are motivated to type quickly to stay engaged in conversation, but also accurately because others peers are reading their words.

Trent Batson and Steve Lombardo from Gallaudet University used one of the first text-based virtual environments in 1985. This online course was designed as a means to provide students who were deaf more real-life opportunities to further enhance their English writing skills, an area of difficulty for many students who are deaf (Batson, 1993).

One of the greatest benefits of using MOOs is the anonymity of the individual characters. In MOOs, users can define their own traits and characteristics. Unless an individual describes himself/herself as having a disability, no one in the virtual world would know any different (Ingvarson, 1996). Removing the stigma of a having a disability may help students feel more confident in both their participation and their writing ability.

Special Considerations When Selecting to Use MOOs and MUDs

Although many students with disabilities benefit from using MOOs and MUDs, some important factors need to be considered when selecting such technology for students with disabilities (see Figure 1). Text-based environments may enhance students' literacy skills with motivating and real-world experiences, but participating in a text-only environment presents barriers to some students with disabilities. For example, students struggling with reading and writing may find it difficult to participate independently in online activities because of the reading level and pace of interaction. Also, students may be overwhelmed, confused, or turned off by the text-only environments. Furthermore, the same students may become frustrated or lost in the environment as they are required to remember a lengthy set of commands to do anything in the world.

For students who are blind or visually impaired, using MOOs and MUDs creates unique but challenging experiences. For these students, using the Internet is generally a text-based experience. Therefore, it would seem that participating in text-based virtual worlds would be a motivating and practical application. However, participation in such technology may be limited due to accessibility barriers in the MOO clients. For example, for MOOs with graphics that are not coded to be read by screen readers, the individual with visual impairments is unable to grasp the important details of other users with whom they may be communicating. Although some Internet browser-enabled MOOs and Telnet clients may be accessible for screen readers, several others are not. It is important when considering using such activities with students who are blind or visually impaired that teachers select a client that is fully accessible for their students.

Turbee (1997) identifies some of the difficulties both teachers and students may face when using MOO technology. Some teachers are uncomfortable using MOOs because they essentially lose control of student learning as students become more involved in the MOO. Therefore, it is important that teachers develop guidelines and meaningful tasks prior to using the MOO to provide structure and guidance for students as they interact in the virtual world. Turbee also notes that some students may have a very emotional response when using MOOs as they interact with other characters. Because

Figure 1. Guidelines for developing accessible synchronous communication and collaboration tools. (Adapted from Barstow & Rothberg, 2002).

In response to accessibility barriers people with disabilities face when using online learning applications, the National Center for Accessible Media in collaboration with the IMS Global Learning Consortium through the SALT Project have developed *IMS Guidelines for Developing Accessible Learning Applications*. Within the section of guidelines for developing accessible synchronous communication and collaboration tools, several barriers and recommendations are identified for MOO technology.

7.5 Multi-User Domain Object Oriented Environments (MOOs)

MOOs are multi-user virtual environments in which users often control "avatars" (computer-generated actors) that move through the virtual world, interacting and communicating via speech generated from user-typed instructions. Both the environment navigation system and the communicative exchanges between avatars must be accessible.

Common MOO accessibility problems include:

• visual information in the MOO, including the appearance of the physical environment and the other avatars, cannot be accessed by users who are blind.

• audio output is inaccessible to users who are deaf or who have profound hearing loss.

• some exclusively mouse-driven functions.

• complex spatial navigation of the MOO.

• fast pace of conversation may limit access by users who communicate slowly.

Learning system developers may enhance the accessibility of MOOs for all users by following these practices:

• Provide a mechanism for automated text description of the virtual world.

• Ensure a real-time text transcript can be made available to participants. This text transcript might be translated into Braille or even (from the listener's perspective only) signed by a speaking avatar.

• Ensure that all mouse actions can also be completed, effectively, from the keyboard.

• Include powerful navigation tools for accomplishing high-level navigational instructions (e.g., "take me to the library").

• Provide mechanisms that allow users who communicate slowly to participate effectively (e.g., speaker designation).

what other individuals participating may say or do is out of the teacher or student's control, the student may be subjected to information that he or she is not prepared to deal with. Therefore, Turbee recommends that teachers regularly schedule in-class discussions that focus on student reactions to the MOO experience.

Teachers interested in using MOOs in their classroom need to carefully plan for the integration of such technology into their curriculum. According to Turbee (1997), teachers should spend several days, if not weeks, becoming familiar with both the technology aspects of using MOOs, such as using the specific MOO commands for navigation, and the psychosocial experience of using the MOO before introducing it to students. "Using a MOO can be like going to a foreign country, and students need to count on their teacher to be a knowledgeable guide" (Turbee, 1997, p. 4). Turbee also recommends that teachers select a user-friendly Telnet client. Several MOO clients are available for all platforms via the Internet. Individual MOO sites may recommend particular clients that work best with their sites or teachers can conduct their own Web search.

Overall, MOOs are a motivating and engaging educational tool that teachers may use to promote both rich writing and programming experiences. Through the use of MOOs, students may collaborate, explore, and build virtual worlds that may focus on particular themes or content areas. Although not designed specifically for students with disabilities, teachers are encouraged to use MOO technology to provide students with motivating and exciting real-world writing and social experiences.

Internet Environments

Virtual High Schools

Think for a moment about the following: Students of any age, from around the world, attending classes at any time on nearly any topic of interest. Imagine students who work collaboratively on line with varying ethnicities, and of varying abilities. Welcome to the concept of the virtual high school.

A unique component of the virtual high school is that it provides access to school for students who at one time were likely unable to attend a local school of their own. These students are now able to take regular high school classes and get credit and can actually graduate with a high school diploma upon meeting the school's curricular requirements.

A number of virtual high schools available on the Internet (Table 2) Some of them are their own entities, others work in conjunction with various school systems, with each school offering a number of different courses for one Virtual High School.

In most accredited virtual high schools, teachers are required to enroll in graduate level courses on online instruction to learn how to effectively implement their curricula using these new instructional methodologies.

Each virtual high school has its own sets of policies and procedures relating to the school. Such policies typically have to do with policies that would be found at a conventional high school. For example, students are expected to attend their classes on a daily basis, assignments must be handed in on time, and courses must comply with curricular standards.

For students with varying disabilities, the possibility of attending a virtual high school is now a reality. While this may not be an ideal option for some students, for others it may be almost perfect. Consider, for example, the student with severe physical disabilities who spends the majority of his day being transported from classroom to classroom trying to overcome barriers found within the school environment. This individual is clearly and rightfully extremely frustrated, and views school as a place causing more anguish than education. For such a student, a virtual high school may be an ideal option. The student can remain at home in a comfortable and accessible environment and does not have to spend a good portion of his day being transported and missing parts of classes. Additionally, writing takes time and this student often misses what is being said because he is desperately trying to take notes. However, in a virtual high school, opportunities for repetition of information are unlimited.

Virtual Labs

For students with limited fine-motor skills that limit their abilities to adequately and in a timely

Table 2. Listing of a Few Virtual High Schools

Virtual High School URL	Description
www.choice2000.org/	Choice 2000 is a public 7th-12th grade school online; accredited.
www.mindquest.bloomington.k12.mn.us	Mindquest Learning is operated by the Bloomington (Minnesota) Public Schools. It is designed for adults and older teens who have dropped out of school.
CyberSchool.4j.lane.edu/	Cyber School is using a curriculum specifically designed for students who are motivated to work independently toward entrance to college.
ehs.uen.org	Electronic High School offers over 120 courses for students from all over the world.

Figure 2. Virtual high school screen shot. Reprinted with permission.

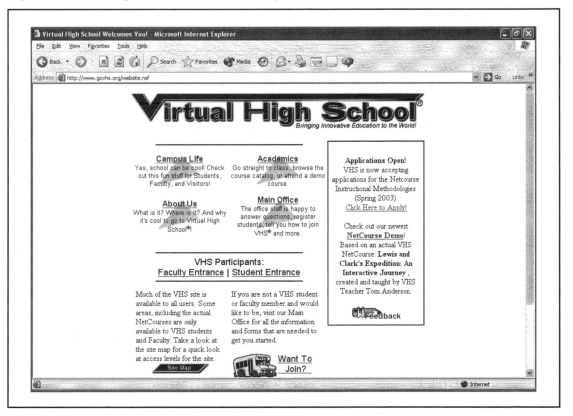

Table 3. Selected Virtual Lab Sites

Virtual Lab URL	Description
www.biologylab.awlonline.com	Biology Labs Online: offers a series of interactive simulations and exercises for high school and college biology classes.
www.froguts.com	Virtual Frog dissection with interactive movies.
www.quailhaven.com/academy/labs.htm	Science virtual labs including pig, frog and cat dissections.
www.riverdeep.net/science/science_highschool.html	Virtual labs and other online science products.

manner perform laboratory activities, a virtual lab is a possible option for learning. Virtual labs can be used for nearly any student with or without a disability. Basically, a virtual lab is exactly what its name implies: a lab that one experiences virtually.

There are a number of virtual lab sites on the Internet (see Table 3). While virtual labs were initially designed as supplements to a standard curriculum, they have evolved in their sophistication and are now used in virtual high schools and for different online courses.

The benefits of using a virtual lab for an individual with a disability is illustrated in the following two scenarios.

Scenario #1

Margot is a 15-year-old girl taking biology in high school. Margot is diagnosed with athetoid cerebral palsy and has limited fine-motor skills. Additionally, she has a visual impairment requiring her to frequently use a magnifier in order to make objects visible.

This week in Margot's biology lab, each student must dissect a frog using a dissecting kit that the school provides. The students are expected to precisely cut and identify different parts of the frog's body.

Without any accommodations, Margot must hold her magnifier over the dissecting kit in order to find the tools that she needs to use to make the incision and additional cuts. She must also hold the magnifier while setting the frog in an optimal position, referring to the directions sheet, holding her pencil to take notes, and when making the actual incision. As if this was not challenging enough, it is important to remember that Margot's vision is not as much of a challenge for her in doing these tasks as is holding a scalpel safely and without impulsivity or spasticity making the required cuts for dissection.

When science lab ends, Margot has yet to make the first incision into the frog, while her peers are well into the actual dissection at this very same point.

Scenario #2

Margot is a 15-year-old girl taking biology in high school. Margot is diagnosed with athetoid cerebral palsy and has limited fine-motor skills. Additionally, she has a visual impairment requiring her to frequently use a magnifier in order to make objects visible. This week in Margot's biology lab, each student must dissect a frog using a dissecting kit that the school provides. The students are expected to precisely cut and identify different parts of the frog's body.

During lab, Margot's teacher directs her to the computer lab. Margot uses the computer that has been set up for her ease of use with a screen enlarger, making whatever is on the screen appear larger. Her teacher tells her to visit www.froguts.com (see Figure 3), one of many virtual labs on the Internet that has a unit or lab on frog dissection. On this site, Margot is initially shown the various dissection tools and then watches a video clip of the set-up of a frog dissection. The virtual lab takes her through the steps of a frog

dissection while showing video clips of each main dissection step along the way. Because of her screen enlarger, Margot can see everything.

When performing a virtual lab, the user has the option to replay clips or sections of the lab as many times as desired. Additionally, if using a screen reader, the user has the option to slow down or speed up the rate of reading. This flexibility and opportunity for repetition is of great benefit to students like Margot, and also for students with learning disabilities and a variety of other disabilities.

At the end of the class period, Margot has accomplished as much as her peers. Since she lives near the local library, she has the opportunity to go on their computers and use the Internet over the weekend and on week nights after school if she is so inclined.

In looking at the two scenarios, it is clear that the latter is more optimal for a student with Margot's needs. Not only is it safer than having Margot utilize a scalpel, it is better for

Figure 3. Screen shot from Virtual Frog Dissection (www.froguts.com) Reprinted with permission.

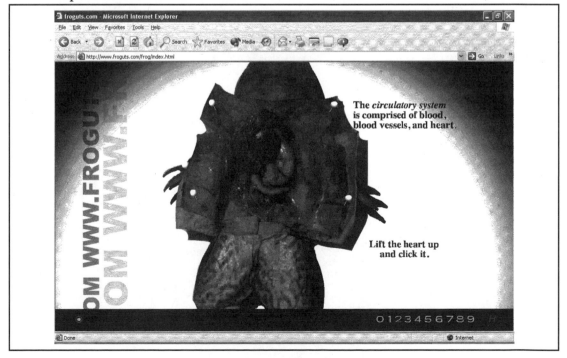

her self-confidence and independence and, of course, for her comprehension of the task at hand.

Virtual Field Trips

For students with disabilities, going on field trips can often be challenging. For example, for an individual with physical disabilities and for whom traveling and getting into and out of buildings is difficult and discouraging, the option of a virtual field trip is one that merits consideration. Also, for students with autism, for example, for whom external stimuli or change in routine are often very disruptive and disturbing, virtual field trips may be a good alternative to out-of-school field trips (see Figure 4). Finally, consider the student with learning disabilities who benefits from repetition and supplemental reinforcement of new ideas. For this student, virtual field trips may be a good method of supplementing the information learned on a previous school field trip.

Other benefits of virtual field trips include students not getting lost and little or no cost. The virtual field trips provide custom instructions that guide the individuals through the field trip (see Table 4). Typically, menu bars help with easy navigation. In addition, supplemental materials and links on the Web are often provided, again supplementing what the student has learned.

Handheld Devices

The recent introduction of low-cost handheld devices, commonly known as personal digital assistants (PDAs) has offered new options for engaging children and youth with disabilities in science learning activities. Due to rapidly decreasing prices, many PDAs can be purchased for under $100. Most use one of two operating systems, Microsoft's Pocket PC or Palm's OS. Higher-end PDAs, costing up to $500, often have more functionality, including removable memory, slots for additional hardware such as a GPS locator or an extra battery, color displays – some even have wireless connectivity and can be linked to wireless networks and access computers or browse the Internet. Pocket PC operating systems provide software that is compatible and capable of interacting with Microsoft Office applications (*Internet Explorer*, *Microsoft Word*, *PowerPoint*, *Outlook*, *Excel*). Software is also available for Palm products to provide similar interfaces. Database software is also available for PDAs, including *FoxPro*. Finally, Internet interfaces are available for collecting data using *Microsoft Access*.

PDAs and Students with Disabilities

PDAs are increasingly being found in special education classrooms where they can be used to help children with disabilities improve organizational abilities, obtain assistance in cognitive tasks requiring step-by-step directions, take notes and write reports, access reference material, and access educational or academic software applications (Behrmann & Kinas, 2002). There are even assistive technologies that incorporate PDA operating systems. *Dana* by AlphaSmart (www.alphasmart.com/) incorporates Palm's PDA functions with a full-size keyboard and a larger screen in a tough and durable portable laptop alternative that is commonly used as an assistive technology device for children with learning disabilities. PDAs, combined with specific devices to collect and analyze scientific data (i.e., sensors and probes) or data-collection and entry software applications, can be used to collect data experimentally and then synchronize those data with computer software, either wirelessly or through docking cradles, to analyze and visualize the effects of science experiments.

In a study of over 75 educational PDA applications projects nationwide, SRI International reports that about one-fifth of schools studied were using handhelds for special education.

Teachers are really looking to these devices to help special-needs students get organized. Overall, PDAs are used mostly in science classes, especially for environmental lessons. Kids attach probes to measure temperature and other environmental factors, then have the information automatically loaded into the device and analyzed. (p. 1)

For example, ImagiWorks (www.imagi works.com) produces PDA-compatible sensors to gauge distance and temperature and display

Figure 4. Panoramic view of the oval office on a White House virtual field trip (taken from www.whitehouse.gov/history/life/).

Table 4. Selected Virtual Field Trip Sites

Virtual Field Trip URL	Description
www.field-guides.com/	Over 30 free virtual field trips for grades K-12.
http://volcano.und.nodak.edu/vwdocs/ kids/vrtrips.html	Many different volcano virtual field trips.
www.uen.org/utahlink/tours/	Lots of fieldtrips broken down by topic area.
http://campus.fortunecity.com/newton/ 40/field.html	Virtual field trips from around the world.

the results through software on the PDA. The distance sensor can be used to conduct experiments in physics and mechanics whereas the temperature sensor can be used to detect changes in temperature over time. Their software is compatible with Palm OS PDAs and can also be used with sensors from Vernier (/www.vernier.com/probes/) which can measure such variables as light, acceleration, pH, color, air speed, sound levels, heart rate, voltage, and so on. The software enables a visual display on a PDA or a computer so students can see the effects of changing different variables in real time. They can also save the visual charts, which enable them to include them in reports and presentations.

PDA applications for both Palm and PocketPC systems are increasingly available. For example, there are downloadable maps and global positioning satellite (GPS) receiver hardware attachments that can be adapted to teach map and mobility skills. As a result, students can download accurate local street maps, set target locations, track their location and plot the path they have taken. They also get information on compass headings and can learn about points of interest in their community. Database applications are available in a broad range of topics from teaching nutrition and diet, to keeping track of exercise and weight and keeping a budget and entering expenses. Data can be entered on a regular schedule and displayed visually for analysis. Teachers can develop lesson plans and additional activities to provide structured learning experiences.

In addition to these general-use applications, new applications are being developed specifically for use with persons with disabilities. For example, *Pocket Coach* by AbleLink (www.ablelinktech.com/) combines customizable step-by-step audio and/or pictorial instructions to persons with memory or cognitive disabilities. Unnecessary buttons and controls can be deactivated to simplify the tasks required. Since many PDAs allow multiple programs to be open, it is possible to combine step-by-step directions to conduct a science experiment is possible, including incorporating pictures of the activity (e.g., putting the temperature probe into the water) along with audio instructions, which enables a student with a disability to systematically collect data. Other data-collection applications are available to collect frequency and duration data automatically.

Staff at the Kellar Institute for Human disAbilities at George Mason University have developed the Kellar Instructional Handheld data System (KIHdata System) for teachers to collect discrete trial data on student performance through a wireless connection with a PDA and an Internet server. This system may easily be adapted to enable students to collect data on scientific experiments, such as count the number of birds that go to the birdfeeder or determine how long they stay at the feeder. Using a camera attachment to the PDA, students could even take pictures of the birds they are observing. Then they could use the wireless browser and search out pictures of birds on the Internet to compare their observations and gather additional information that they could copy and paste into the PDA notepad for use in a report.

Just using the standard organizer functions of most PDAs can provide access to scientific learning. For example, students can use the calculator to solve math problems or use the stopwatch function to collect duration data. They can use the alarm function in the "Date Book" to remind them to take data during interval time sampling, and" To Do List" to check off step-by-step procedures similar to those described for the *Pocket Coach*. The "Memo Pad" can be used to collect anecdotal notes or to record data. Finally, with a little creativity, the "Address Book" feature can be converted to a database for collecting raw data.

Benefits of using PDAs in special education and science are numerous. First, their portability makes it easy to take the technology to the location where learning is occurring without the need for an electric outlet or a desk to put the device on. Flexibility is the second benefit, since many related software applications can be accessed easily and can be toggled between. Connectivity is the third major benefit, particularly with wireless PDAs, since students can instant message, access the Internet for email or information, and back up their data to computers or servers. Finally, the acceptability of the technology to users is a benefit. Students with disabilities often do not want technology that makes them seem different. PDAs are likely to be motivating to these students since they are essentially the same as those their parents and teachers use. Even adaptations such as attachable folding keyboards are seen as mainstream and are desirable to users.

Despite the many benefits, there are also limitations to PDA use in special education. Primary among these is the size of screen, which may limit font size or the detail of charts and graphs that are visually displayed. Therefore, devices may also not be accessible to individuals with vision impairments or those who need additional detail in order to understand the information on the PDA. Lack of color in low-cost PDAs can also limit the use of color to highlight visual displays and use pictures to illustrate activities. Cost may also be a limitation to providing access to enough children conducting science experiments and using the "personal" features of a PDA. Related to cost, even relatively low-cost PDAs may be lost or stolen. Finally, if a significant amount of textual information is required, the PDA's limited text-entry systems may also be a deterrent to use, unless a portable keyboard is used. Physical access to PDA hardware and software applications (i.e., assistive technology access) is another potential limitation that may necessitate utilization of a desktop computer. In cases where portability is a major issue, perhaps alternatives such as sub-notebook computers, touch screen or tablet computers, even though their costs may be 5 to 15 times that of a PDA, may be preferable. Xybernaut's (www.xybernaut.com) wearable computers use a touch-sensitive screen and a small, lightweight CPU designed for use by children with various disabilities. Microsoft has introduced its new *Windows XP Tablet PC Edition* operating system that works with hardware developed by several computer manufacturers. Finally, several sub-notebook computers are small weighing less than 3 pounds. For example, the Sony Picturebook is a full-function computer that also includes a video camera.

Conclusions

As technology continues to evolve, more sophisticated and new hardware and software continues to emerge. While historically emerging hardware and software applications have been developed with disability requirements as benchmarks (e.g., the *Kurzweil Reader* for persons who were visually impaired led to optical character recognition typically used in business and government), this has not been the case for curriculum development in education. Typically, the utilization of such technologies is introduced in the general education classroom before being introduced into the special education classroom. As a result, the applicability of such technologies within the special education environment is often overlooked. Frequently, it is lack of creativity and vision that limits access to these technologies rather than limitations of the hardware and software themselves.

The purpose of this chapter was to demonstrate the potential value of emerging technologies within the fields of science and special education. While research on the direct applicability of such technologies within this environment is lacking, this should not delay the use of these technologies in special education. Technology continues to grow as does its place within the field of education. Keeping this in mind, the benefits of technology are limitless. All that is needed are creative educators, with vision, who are willing to explore technological uses within the field of special education.

References

Allison, D., & Hodges, L. F. (1999, April). Virtual gorilla project. *AERA Symposium on Cross Project Research in Virtual Environments*, AERA 1999 Annual Meeting, Montreal, Canada.

Alphasmart website. (n.d.) Retrieved December 15, 2002, from: www.alphasmart.com.

Aukstakalnis, S., & Blatner, D. (1992). *Silicon mirage: The art and science of virtual reality*. Berkeley, CA: Peachpit Press, Inc.

Barstow, C., & Rothberg, M. (2002). *IMS guidelines for developing accessible learning applications: 7.5 multi-user domain object oriented environments (MOOs)*. Retrieved December 15, 2002, from: ncam.wgbh.org/salt/guidelines/sec7.html.

Batson, T. W. (1993). The origins of ENFI. In B. C. Bruce, J. K. Peyton, & T. W. Batson (Eds.),

Network-based classrooms: Promises and realities (pp. 87-112). New York: Cambridge University Press.

Behrmann, M., & Kinas, M. (2002). Assistive technology for students with mild disabilities Update 2002. *ERIC EC Digest #E623.*

Brown, D. J., Standen, P. J., & Cobb, S. V. (1998). Virtual environments special needs and evaluative methods. In G. Riva, B. K. Wiederhold, & E. Molinari (Eds.), *Virtual environments in clinical psychology and neuroscience* (pp. 91-102). Amsterdam, Netherlands: IOS Press.

Bruckman, A. (1999). The day after net day: Approaches to educational use of the Internet. *Convergence, 5*(1), 24-46.

Castellani, J. (1999). *Project DEVISE.* George Mason University Steppingstones Grant Proposal. www.virtual.gmu.edu/EDIT792/proposal.html.

Dede, C., Salzman, M., Loftin, B., & Ash, K. (1997). Using virtual reality technology to convey abstract scientific concepts. In M. J. Jacobson & R. B. Kozma (Eds.), *Learning the sciences of the 21st century: Research, design, and implementing advanced technology learning environments.* Hillsdale, NJ: Erlbaum.

Dede, C., Salzman, M., Loftin, R.B., & Sprague, D. (1999). Multisensory immersion as a modeling environment for learning complex scientific concepts. In N. Roberts, W. Fuerzeig, & B. Hunter. (Eds.). *Computer modeling and simulation in science education.* (pp. 282-319). Berlin: Springer-Verlag.

diSessa, A. (1983). Phenomenology and the evolution of intuition. In D. Gentner & A. Stevens (Eds.), *Mental models* (pp. 15-33). Hillsdale, NJ: Lawrence Earlbaum.

Goldstein, L. F. (2002, September 18). Virtual reality researchers target special ed.classes. *EducationWeekontheWeb*.www.edweek.org/ewewstory.cfm?slug=03virtual.h22.

Holloway, R., Fuchs, J., & Robinette, W. (1991, October). *Virtual-worlds research at the University of North Carolina at Chapel Hill.* Paper presented at the Conference on Computer Graphics, London, England.

Ingvarson D. (1996). Moving around the net: The educational potential of MOOs-a point of view. (ERIC Document Reproduction Service No. ED 417765)

Inman, D. P., Peaks, J., Loge, K., Chen, V., & Ferrington, G. (1994). Virtualreality training program for motorized wheelchair operation. *Proceedings from Technology and Persons with Disabilities Conference.* California State University, Northridge Center on Disabilities. Los Angeles.

Kimmel, H., Deek, F., & Frazer, L. (2002). *Science and mathematics to the special education population. Technology and hands-on strategies for teaching science.* Retrieved October 23, 2002, from: www.rit.edu/~easi/itd/itdv03n2/article3.html.

Kort, B. (2002). *The MUSE as an educational medium.* Retrieved December 15, 2002, from: www.musenet.org/~bkort/WCE/Muse.in.Education.html.

Middleton, T. (1992, September). *Matching the virtual reality solution to the special need.* Paper presented at the California State university at Northridge Technology and Persons with Special Needs Conference, Los Angeles, CA.

Powers, D. A., & Darrow, M. (1996). Special education and virtual reality: Challenges and possibilities. *Journal of Research on Computing in Education, 27*(1), 111-121.

Reif, F., & Larkin, J. (1991). Cognition in scientific and everyday domains: Comparison and learning implications. *Journal of Research in Science Teaching, 28,* 743-760.

Salzman, M.C., Dede, C., Loftin, R.B., & Chen. J. (1999). A model for understanding how virtual reality aids complex conceptual learning. *Presence:Teleoperators and Virtual Environments. 8*(3), 293-316.

Sprague, D. (1996, May). Virtual reality and precollege education: Where are we today? *Learning and Leading With Technology, 23*(8), 10-12.

Sprague, D., & Behrmann, M. (2001). Zoning in on physics: Creating virtual reality environments to aide students with learning disabilities" In M. Mastropieri & T. Scruggs (Eds.), *Advances in learning and behavioral disabilities: Technological applications* Vol. 15 (pp. 17-38). New York: JAI Press.

Strickland, D., Marcus, L., Mesibov, G., & Hogan, K. (1996). Brief report: Two case studies using virtual reality as a learning tool for autistic children. *Journal of Autism and Developmental Disorders, 26*(6), 651-659.

Thomas, K. (2002, February 6). Students gain computing power with PDAs. *USA Today*, p.1.

Turbee, L. (1997). Educational MOO: Text-based virtual reality for learning in community. *ERIC digest* (Report No. EDO-IR-97-01). Washington, DC: Office of Educational Research and Improvement. (ERIC Document Reproduction Service No. ED404987)

33

Using Technology to Facilitate and Enhance Curriculum-Based Measurement

Lynn S. Fuchs, Douglas Fuchs, and Carol L. Hamlett

A signature feature of effective special education practice is progress monitoring. With progress monitoring, the special educator initiates instruction using a validated instructional practice. However, given individual students' histories of academic failure, the teacher does not assume a this program shown to be effective with most other students will necessarily be successful for a specific child. Therefore, while implementing the program, the teacher assesses performance on a regular basis to gauge the child's responsiveness to instruction. Using this database, the teacher experiments with alternative instructional components, incorporating features that raise scores and discarding elements that do not. In this way, the teacher uses the ongoing assessment information to formatively develop an instructional program with demonstrated efficacy for the individual child.

At this time, curriculum-based measurement is the most conceptually sophisticated, well developed, and thoroughly researched progress-monitoring system. Curriculum-based measurement provides accurate and meaningful information about student standing and growth (cf. Fuchs & Fuchs, 1998) and, when special educators use it to inform their instructional decision making, they plan more successful programs that result in superior student growth (e.g., Fuchs, Deno, & Mirkin, 1984; Fuchs, Fuchs, Hamlett, & Ferguson, 1992; Fuchs, Fuchs, Hamlett, & Stecker, 1991; Jones & Krouse, 1988; Stecker & Fuchs, 2000; Wesson, 1991).

Yet, despite its demonstrated efficacy, as well as frequent calls for widespread use, curriculum-based measurement has failed to achieve status as a standard feature of special education practice. The reasons for this gap between research and practice are numerous, including problems with developing and sustaining expertise in an ever-changing pool of practitioners, an inadequate focus on research-based practices in school districts' professional development and teacher preparation programs, and the challenges that already-overworked teachers face in collecting, managing, and using data. The latter difficulty subsumes two problems. First, a large amount of time is required for teachers to conduct curriculum-based measurement on a regular basis (i.e., to prepare materials for testing, administer and score the tests, and graph and analyze the database). Second, teachers find it difficult to translate assessment information into meaningful instructional changes that can be feasibly implemented in programs serving large numbers of students.

In this chapter, we describe a research program we have conducted over the past 18 years to examine how technology can be used to surmount these challenges. The research program has focused on curriculum-based measurement in reading, spelling, and mathematics. This chapter is organized into two major sections that parallel the two major types of challenges faced by teachers: (a) how computers can be used to assume the mechanical measurement tasks, and (b) how computers can be used to help teachers translate the assessment information into instructional adaptations. We conclude by drawing implications for the fields of special education, technology, and assessment.

Technology Assuming the Mechanical Aspects of Measurement

Electronic Management of Data Collected by Hand

Early discussions (Hasselbring & Hamlett, 1985; Walton, 1986) about the potential for computers to solve ongoing assessment implementation problems focused on computerized data-management programs to store data, graph data, and analyze graphs. Specifically, these functions include graphing scores, drawing lines of best fit through scores, drawing goal lines, and formulating decisions about the need to modify programs to improve progress or to raise goals when actual progress exceeds anticipated progress.

In parallel fashion, the initial step of our research program consisted of developing and evaluating this type of data-management technology. Teachers collected and scored curriculum-based measurement by hand. They then entered their scores into a computer program that graphed the scores, drew lines from baseline performance to the desired year-end score to show the desired weekly rate of growth, drew regression lines through actual scores to show actual rates of improvement, and applied decision rules to advise teachers about whether to introduce an instructional improvement or to increase the goal. See Figure 1 for

Figure 1. CBM individual student graphs, top panel showing a "raise the goal" decision and bottom panel showing a "make a teaching change" decision.

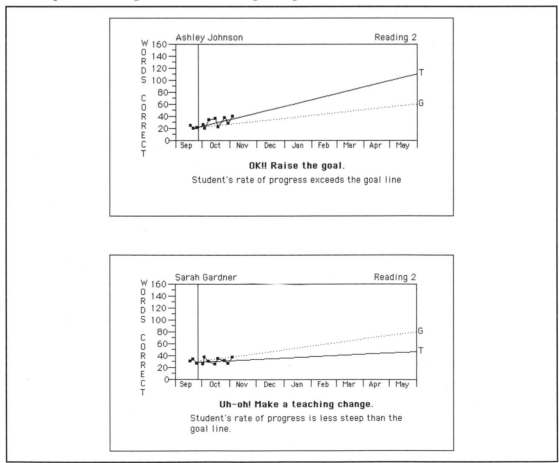

computer-generated decisions based on students' graphed scores.

We evaluated this data-management software with 20 special educators who conducted curriculum-based measurement, each with at least two pupils in reading, spelling, and math for 15 weeks. All teachers were required to prepare, administer, and score the tests by hand. Teachers were assigned randomly to a condition in which they used computerized data management or to one in which they managed their student performance data by hand.

Direct observations of the teachers showed that, despite speculation (see Hasselbring & Hamlett, 1985; Walton, 1986) that computerized data-management systems would improve efficiency, such software significantly increased the time needed to implement curriculum-based measurement. In fact, the data-management software required teachers to complete extra steps: After administering and scoring tests, teachers needed to get to a computer, identify pupils and academic areas to the computer, enter measurement dates and scores, save data, and view or print graphs. By contrast, the noncomputer teachers simply located their paper graphs and placed symbols at appropriate places on those graphs (Fuchs, Fuchs, Hasselbring et al, 1987).

Interestingly, however, although the use of data-management software required more time of teachers, they reported greater satisfaction with curriculum-based measurement in the computerized data-management condition (Fuchs, Fuchs, Hasselbring et al., 1987). Moreover, with the addition of a tutorial routine in the software that explained the rationale for the computer's program-changing and goal-raising decisions, teachers in the computerized data-management condition understood the data analysis better and subsequently complied better with curriculum-based measurement decisions (Fuchs, Fuchs, & Hamlett, 1988). In sum, although the data-management software failed to improve efficiency, it did result in greater satisfaction and greater understanding of and compliance with the data-utilization rules of curriculum-based measurement.

Automatic Data Collection

Our work with data-management software clearly indicated that, to decrease the time teachers spent implementing curriculum-based measurement, applications were required that more dramatically reduced the teacher's measurement burden. Toward that end, we (Fuchs, Hamlett, Fuchs, Stecker, & Ferguson, 1988) developed and evaluated software that automatically generated curriculum-based measurement tests, administered those tests to students at the computer, scored the tests, provided feedback to students, and saved the data for storage and analysis by the data-management software. We examined how this automatic data-collection and management software affected curriculum-based measurement efficiency with 20 special educators who implemented curriculum-based measurement, each with at least two pupils in reading, spelling, and math for 15 weeks. Half of the teachers collected data by hand and used the data-management software; the other half used the automatic data-collection software that saved the scores for the data-management program.

Direct observations of data-collection and evaluation activities indicated that teachers spent reliably and substantially less time in measurement and evaluation when computers automatically collected the data. In fact, most teachers spent no time administering or scoring student performance data. This was a dramatic improvement over teachers' data collection by hand. In addition, teacher satisfaction with curriculum-based measurement was greater with automatic data collection, and the ease with which teachers could be trained in curriculum-based measurement was greatly facilitated: We could introduce teachers relatively quickly to administration and scoring methods to ensure that they understood their students' assessment profiles, thereby yielding a high degree of accuracy and reliability in test administration and scoring. In subsequent work in the field, teachers have relied heavily on software that automatically collects and manages curriculum-based measurement.

More Recent Extensions

More recently, we have extended our efforts in computer-assisted data collection in two directions: one in reading and the other in math. In reading, we (Fuchs, Fuchs, Hosp, & Hamlett, 2003) developed software to assist teachers in collecting curriculum-based measurement oral reading data. A computer screen shows the teacher directions to read to the student. With a click, the screen advances to show an electronic copy of the curriculum-based measurement passage, which the student has in paper form before him/her. The computer also begins the 1-minute timing. As the student reads aloud, the teacher clicks on errors. At the end of 1 minute, the computer signals the teacher to end testing and to click on the last word read. Then, the computer calculates the score and shows a graph of performance over time for the teacher to share with the student. Teachers can use this software accurately with minimal training; besides, they like the software and find it feasible to use (Fuchs & Fuchs, 2003).

At the same time, we have extended our automatic data-collection work in mathematics from a focus on computation and concept/applications to an emphasis on problem solving. This extension is important because (a) schools increasingly have reoriented their curricular focus toward problem solving and (b) it takes teachers inordinate amounts of time to score a test of complex problem solving. We began by developing curriculum-based measurement assessments of extended, real-life mathematics problem solving, with six alternate assessments at each grade (grades 2-6). Then we developed software that performed the following functions: presents the assessment on the computer (a hard copy of the assessment is also available to the student); upon request, reads text (via a click on the word or paragraph requested); upon request, shows a video portrayal of the problem-solving situation; supports students in constructing responses onto the computer screen in ways that reduce reading and writing demands; scores the student's response; provides students with a score along with feedback to enhance subsequent performance; and summarizes for the teacher individual and classwide performance.

Elementary-age children with learning disabilities can be taught to use this software in a single 1-hour session. The time saved to the teacher in scoring a single administration for one child is approximately 30 minutes. And the problem-solving capacity of students with

learning disabilities increases when they use the software on a regular basis, with effect sizes exceeding half a standard deviation (Fuchs, Fuchs, Hamlett, & Appleton, 2002). See Figure 2 for sample screens.

Helping Teachers Translate the Assessment Information into Feasible Instructional Adaptations

As already noted, the combination of data-collection and data-management software greatly reduces the mechanical tasks required for curriculum-based measurement. Nevertheless, a second, persistent implementation problem involves difficulty in translating assessment information into meaningful instructional changes that can be implemented within the context of the large numbers of students found in today's special and general education classrooms. In our research program on computer applications to curriculum-based measurement, we have addressed this problem in three stages: through computerized skills analysis, through expert systems, and through classwide data analysis and instructional recommendations.

Skills Analysis

One major effort focused on using technology to enhance teachers' capacity to use assessment information for instructional decision making involved the use of computerized skills analysis. With curriculum-based measurement, the student's proficiency on all the skills embedded in the year's curriculum is sampled on every test (see Fuchs & Deno, 1991 for a related discussion). Consequently, in addition to the total test scores, which indicate the student's overall proficiency on the year's curriculum, the database contains information about the student's performance on each skill embedded in that curriculum. For example, in math, the student's total curriculum-based measurement test score may be 53 digits. However, one can analyze the student's performance on an item-by-item basis across several recent tests to determine which skills the student has mastered and with which skills he or she is having difficulty. Unfortunately, this type of item-by-item analysis is extremely time consuming for humans to

Figure 2. Sample screens showing automatic administration and data collection of CBM performance assessment in math.

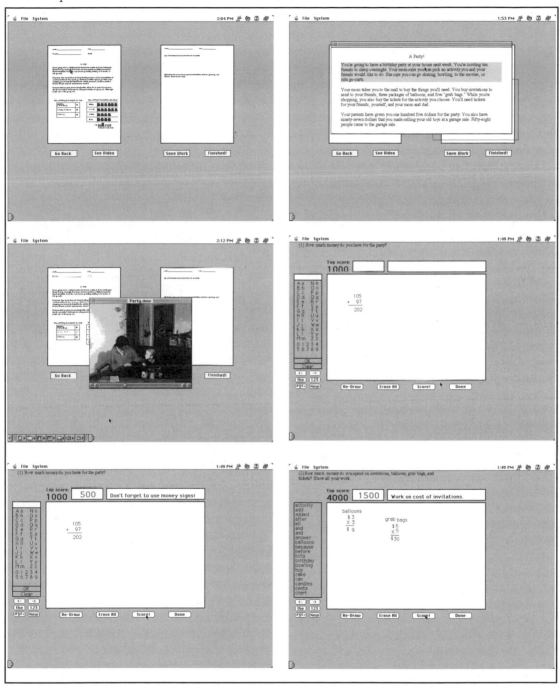

complete; and even given the necessary time, such analysis cannot be done by hand with adequate reliability. Fortunately, computers are ideal for completing this type of laborious, intricate analysis quickly and accurately.

We developed software that could complete item-by-item skills analyses in reading, spelling, and math. In math, for example, in addition to receiving a graph that shows a student's total scores over time, the teacher

Figure 3. CBM skills profiles in math computation and math concepts/applications.

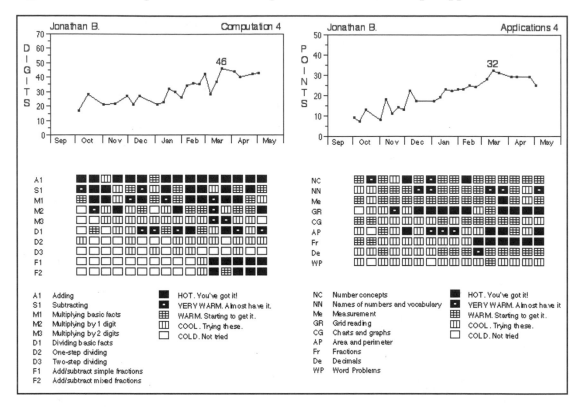

also receives a skills analysis (see Figure 3) describing the student's performance, for each current half-month interval denoted in the horizontal axis of the graph, on 10 clusters of skills represented in the annual curriculum. Each skill is placed in one of five categories: not attempted (white), not mastered (striped), partially mastered (checkered), probably mastered (black with a white dot), or mastered (black); thus, increasingly darkened boxes represent greater mastery. Students or teachers can look down a column to quickly identify mastery status on each skill in the curriculum at a particular point in time. They can also look across rows to determine how mastery has progressed over time for any particular skill.

The type and format of the skills analysis differed by academic area. In spelling, for example, (Fuchs, Fuchs, Hamlett, & Allinder, 1991b), the skills analysis lists the 50 words the student has spelled across most recently completed curriculum-based measurement tests. Those 50 words are listed from most correct to least correct in terms of the percentage of letter sequences within a word spelled correctly. For

each word, the computer identifies specific spelling errors. Then, on a second page, the computer identifies the percentage of errors committed within 27 different categories and recommends instruction on three error types, based on the frequency of the student's errors as well as the teachability of that particular skill (see Figure 4 for a sample skills analysis in spelling).

We ran three experiments (one in each academic area) in which special educators were assigned randomly to a control group or to one of two experimental groups: Curriculum-based measurement with computerized data collection and management (but no skills analysis) or curriculum-based measurement with computerized data collection, management, and skills analysis. Our findings were robust: Regardless of academic area, teachers who formulated instructional programs with the combination of graphed and skills analysis designed more specific program adjustments to assist students who were having difficulty and effected reliably greater achievement among their students (Fuchs, Fuchs, & Hamlett, 1989;

Figure 4. CBM skills profile in spelling.

Name: Angela Adams	Spelling 2	Date: 9/24	Page 1

Corrects (100% LS)	9 word(s)
Near Misses (60-99% LS)	24 word(s)
Moderate Misses (20-59% LS)	17 word(s)
Far Misses (0-19% LS)	0 word(2)

Type	Correct	Possible	Pct	Type	Correct	Possible	Pct
Sing cons	49	54	90	Final vow	2	5	40
Blend	6	7	85	Double	2	7	28
FSLZ	0	3	0	c/s	5	9	55
Single vow	26	32	81	c/ck	0	0	–
Digraph	5	6	83	-le	0	2	0
Vowel + N	3	8	37	ch/tch	1	1	100
Dual cons	13	21	61	-dge	0	1	0
Final e	1	8	12	Vowel team	0	11	0
igh/ign	0	0	–	Suffix	0	1	0
ild/old	0	0	–	tion/sion	0	0	–
a+l+cons	0	1	0	ance/ence	0	1	0
Vowel + R	6	12	50	sure/ture	0	0	–

KEY ERRORS

FSLZ	Vowel + N	Final e
across-acros	wonder-wunder	hope-hop
shall-shal	seven-sevn	kite-kit
pull-pul	lunch-luch	bake-bak
	second-seknd	rope-rop
	winter-wntr	same-sam

Name: Angela Adams	Spelling 2	Date: 9/24	Page 2

Corrects (100% LS)					
100	late	late			
100	job	job			
100	wash	wash			
100	hid	hid			
100	dig	dig			
100	arm	arm			
100	only	only			
100	milk	milk			
100	boy	boy			
Near Misses (60-99% LS)					
87	unhappy	unhapy	Double		
85	keeper	keper	Vowel team		
85	across	acros	FSLZ	Double	
83	sheep	shep	Vowel team		
83	shall	shal	FSLZ	Double	
80	seed	eed	Vowel team		
80	seed	sed	Vowel team		
80	pull	pul	FSLZ		
71	wonder	wunder	Vowel + N		
71	corner	corrr	Vowel + R		
66	puppy	puppie	Final vow		
66	earth	erth	Vowel team		
66	seven	sevn	Vowel + N		
66	lunch	luch	Vowel + N		
60	mark	mak	Vowel + R	Dual cons	
60	only	onlie	Final vow		
60	left	let	Dual cons		
60	hope	hop	Final e		
60	lamb	lam	Dual cons		
60	kite	kit	Final e		
60	bake	bak	Final e		
60	rope	rop	Final e		
60	same	sam	Final e		
60	felt	fet	Dual cons		Single vow
Moderate Misses (20-59% LS)					
57	circus	sercus	Vowel + R	c/s	
57	forest	fort	Suffix	Dual cons	Dual cons
57	keeper	kepr	Vowel team	Vowel + R	
57	chance	chans	ance/ence	c/s	
57	second	seknd	Vowel + N	Sing cons	
55	sidewalk	sidwalk	a+l+cons	Dual cons	Single vow
50	tractor	trater	Vowel + R	Dual cons	
50	twice	twis	Final e	c/s	
50	puppy	pupe	Final vow	Double	
44	mountain	montn	Vowel team	Vowel team	
42	bridge	brig	-dge		Sing cons
42	winter	wntr	Vowel + R	Vowel + N	Single vow
42	circus	sircs	c/s	Single vow	Single vow
40	breakfast	brekfus	Vowel team	Blend	Sing cons
40	telephone	telfon	Final e	Digraph	
37	trouble	trubel	-le	Vowel team	
33	apple	apul	-le	Double	

Fuchs, Fuchs, Hamlett, & Allinder, 1991b; Fuchs, Fuchs, Hamlett, & Stecker, 1990).

Expert Systems

Use of skills analysis helped teachers to plan more specific plans for modifying instructional programs to increase their probability of success. Most of the "specificity" in these plans involved clearer references to the skills teachers would remediate (i.e., a better description of what would be taught). Nevertheless, a persistent problem in the way teachers design instructional adaptations for students who are experiencing failure is developing a focus on *how* to teach that content not only on *what* to teach.

That is, when a student has failed to learn a skill, many teachers reteach the skill using the original instructional method (see Fuchs, Fuchs, Phillips, & Simmons; 1993; Putnam, 1987). Although recycling students through the same instructional procedure works in some cases, a higher level of adaptation occurs when teachers not only modify what they teach students, but also use a different strategy to try to provide an alternative route for the student's learning (see Corno & Snow, 1986). Unfortunately, teachers frequently have only one or two instructional methods to fall back on so, after a student has experienced failure with these few strategies, teachers often have difficulty identifying an alternative instructional method to address the same content.

In our work with expert systems, we addressed teachers' difficulty in identifying both *what* and *how* to teach students who were experiencing difficulty with content teachers already had taught. Thus, we developed expert systems in reading, spelling, and math that provided recommendations for what and how to teach students for whom curriculum-based measurement indicated that their academic progress was inadequate. Each participating teacher was assigned to a control group or a curriculum-based measurement experimental group. For each academic area, half of the curriculum-based measurement teachers used expert systems to help determine how to revise programs. The other half formulated instructional adjustments using their own judgment. In math, for example, the expert system

entered into dialogue with the teacher, requesting information about the student's graphed curriculum-based measurement performance, the students' curriculum-based measurement skills analysis, the student's work habits, the teacher's previous instructional program, and the teacher's curricular priorities. The expert system subsequently identified which skills should be taught, instructional strategies for acquisition of new content and for retention of already mastered material, and motivational strategies.

The extent to which these expert systems helped teachers plan better programs and effect greater achievement varied as a function of content area. In math (Fuchs, Fuchs, Hamlett, & Stecker, 1991), effects supporting the expert system were particularly impressive. Teachers who used the expert system designed better instructional programs that incorporated attention to a more diverse set of skills and that relied on a more varied set of instructional design features. Additionally, students in the expert system curriculum-based measurement experimental group achieved significantly and dramatically better than students in the nonexpert system curriculum-based measurement group and better than the control (i.e., noncurriculum-based measurement) group.

In reading (Fuchs, Fuchs, Hamlett, & Ferguson, 1992), effects differed for instructional planning and achievement. Teachers in the expert system curriculum-based measurement group planned instructional programs that incorporated more reading skills and that utilized more instructional methods. With respect to achievement, students in the expert system group achieved reliably better than nonexpert system curriculum-based measurement pupils and than control students on outcomes measures involving written retells-an outcome measure that mirrored expert system teachers' greater use of written story grammar instructional activities. On other reading outcome measures (i.e., oral reading fluency and maze), however, both curriculum-based measurement groups achieved comparably well and better than the control group.

Results in the area of spelling (Fuchs, Fuchs, Hamlett, & Allinder, 1991a) were least supportive of the expert system. That is, nonexpert and expert system teachers both effected reliably better achievement outcomes than the control teachers. However, the two curriculum-based measurement groups' achievement was not reliably different. Our analysis of teachers' instructional plans indicated that teachers in the expert system relied on practice routines recommended by the expert system to a great extent, but utilized the expert system's teacher-directed instruction recommendations less frequently. Consequently, the expert system advice did not substantially add to or improve the decisions teachers formulated on their own.

Although findings differed across the three subject areas, certain generalizations across content areas appear warranted. First, without the assistance of the expert systems, teachers found it difficult to generate important instructional adaptations that differed in meaningful ways from their standard instructional routines. Second, without the assistance of the expert systems, teachers tended to design instructional adaptations that mirrored the measurement system closely. For example, in reading, the nonexpert system teachers implemented a relatively large number of instructional changes that involved a cloze technique-when the curriculum-based measurement reading measurement task was a closely related maze technique (i.e., multiple-choice cloze). In spelling and math, teachers' instructional adjustments tended to involve reteaching problematic skills-as identified in the skills analysis-but using the same instructional strategy that previously had proven unsuccessful for the student.

In sum, across academic areas, expert systems tended to help teachers go beyond their standard instructional routines, to identify alternative teaching procedures that might assist students in learning content with which they were experiencing difficulty. Nevertheless, even with technology that helped teachers identify alternative, potentially effective instructional strategies, an important feasibility problem with meaningful use of curriculum-based measurement remained: Given curriculum-based measurement's focus on the individual learner, teachers might need to adjust different students' instructional programs, in different ways, at different times.

Given the large numbers of students with whom many special and general educators work, such an individual focus can be problematic. Therefore, the next step in our research program was to develop technology for helping teachers integrate curriculum-based measurement information and instructional recommendations across learners.

Group Analysis

In a series of research and development stages beginning in 1990, we developed group curriculum-based measurement analyses to enable teachers to examine performance for a whole classroom of students to identify patterns for instructional programming. As shown in the sample math class report in Figure 5, a group analysis covers one half-month interval and contains four types of summary descriptive information about the class performance. First, at the top of page 1 of the report, a classwide graph shows the overall progress of the students, with three paths of curriculum-based measurement scores over time: a path for the 25th percentile student in this teacher's class, a path for the 50th percentile student in the class, and one for the 75th percentile in the class. Below this graph, students who are performing below the class 25th percentile are listed, with advice that the teacher "watch" these students. The second type of descriptive information is shown on the middle of page 1, where the report identifies skills on which the class has improved, deteriorated, or stayed the same over the past month.

The third type of descriptive information appears on page 2, where a classwide skills analysis shows every student's mastery status on each skill cluster for the current half-month interval. The students are listed in the rows, and the skills are represented in the columns. The boxes are coded the same way as the individual student's skills analysis, with black boxes representing mastery, black boxes with dots representing probable mastery, checkered boxes representing partial mastery, striped boxes representing nonmastery, and empty boxes representing nonattempts. At a glance, the teacher can look across any row to determine how an individual student is doing on the multiple skills embedded in the year's

Figure 5. CBM class report in math.

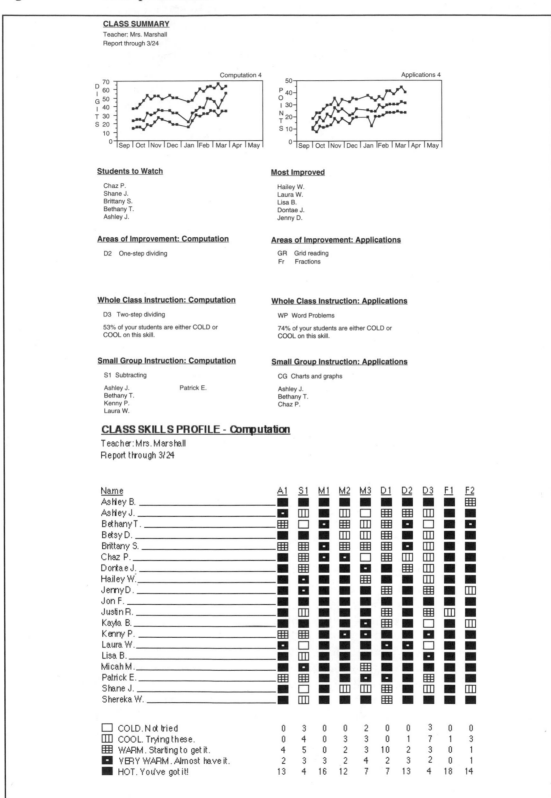

(continued next page)

Figure 5 CBM class report in math. (continued)

<u>CLASS SKILLS PROFILE - **Applications**</u>

Teacher: Mrs. Marshall

Report through 3/24

Name	NC	NN	Me	GR	CG	AP	Fr	De	WP
Ashley B.	■	■	▦	■	▦	▦	■	■	▦
Ashley J.	⬛	⬛	▦	▦	⬛	■	⬛	⬛	⬛
Bethany T.	▦	▦	▦	■	▦	▦	■	▦	☐
Betsy D.	▦	■	▦	■	▦	■	■	⬛	⬛
Brittany S.	▦	▦	▦	▦	▦	▦	▪	⬛	⬛
Chaz P.	▦	▦	▦	■	▦	■	▦	⬛	⬛
Dontae J.	■	▦	▦	■	▪	■	■	▪	☐
Halley W.	▦	▦	▦	▦	▦	▦	▦	▦	⬛
Jenny D.	■	▦	⬛	■	▪	■	■	▦	■
Jon F.	■	■	■	■	■	■	■	▦	▦
Justin R.	■	■	▦	■	▦	■	■	■	▦
Kayla B.	▦	▦	■	⬛	■	■	■	▦	⬛
Kenny P.	▦	■	■	■	■	■	■	■	☐
Laura W.	■	■	■	■	▦	■	■	▦	▦
Lisa B.	■	▦	▦	■	⬛	■	▦	⬛	⬛
Micah M.	▦	▦	⬛	■	⬛	■	■	⬛	⬛
Patrick E.	▦	■	▦	■	⬛	■	■	▦	☐
Shane J.	▦	⬛	⬛	▦	▦	■	⬛	⬛	⬛
Shereka W.	▦	⬛	▦	■	▦	■	■	▦	⬛

		NC	NN	Me	GR	CG	AP	Fr	De	WP
☐	COLD. Not tried	0	0	0	0	0	0	0	0	5
⬛	COOL. Trying these.	1	3	4	0	5	0	2	8	9
▦	WARM. Starting to get it.	12	10	12	4	11	2	1	8	4
▪	VERY WARM. Almost have it.	0	0	0	0	2	0	1	1	0
■	HOT. You've got it!	6	6	3	15	1	17	15	2	1

<u>RANKED SCORES - **Computation**</u>

Teacher: Mrs. Marshall

Report through 3/24

Name	Score	Growth
Shereka W.	61	+0.72
Jon F.	61	+0.85
Ashley B.	61	+1.31
Justin R.	58	+0.87
Lisa B.	57	+0.77
Jenny D.	57	+1.15
Micah M.	55	+1.06
Dontae J.	55	+0.85
Hailey W.	51	+0.88
Betsy D.	49	+0.95
Kayla B.	47	+0.87
Patrick E.	41	+0.65
Kenny P.	41	+0.93
Laura W.	40	+0.71
Chaz P.	38	+0.87
Shane J.	34	+0.86
Brittany S.	30	+0.53
Ashley J.	28	+0.43
Bethany T.	27	+0.59

(continued next page)

Figure 5 CBM class report in math. (continued)

PEER TUTORING ASSIGNMENTS
Teacher: Mrs. Marshall
Report through 3/24

Floater: Jon F.

M3 Multiplying by 2 digits	First Coach	Second Coach
	■ Justin R.	☐ Ashley J.
	■ Ashley B.	⊞ Bethany T.
	■ Jenny D.	⊞ Betsy D.
	⊞ Micah M.	☐ Chaz P.
	⊞ Hailey W.	⊞ Shane J.

De Decimals	First Coach	Second Coach
	⊞ Shereka W.	⊞ Kayla B.
	⊞ Patrick E.	⊞ Lisa B.
	■ Dontae J.	⊞ Kenny P.
	⊞ Laura W.	⊞ Brittany S.

CLASS STATISTICS: Computation+Applications
Teacher: Mrs. Marshall
Report through 3/24

Score

Average score	78.2
Standard deviation	17.7
Discrepancy criterion	60.5

Slope

Average slope	+1.41
Standard deviation	0.37
Discrepancy criterion	+1.04

Students identified with dual discrepancy criterion

	Score	Slope
Ashley J.	50.0	+0.73
Bethany T.	51.0	+1.01
Brittany S.	51.5	+1.01

curriculum, and can look down any column to determine how the class is doing on any one skill. At the bottom of each column, a frequency count is provided that shows the numbers of students in each mastery status.

The fourth type of descriptive information appears on page 5. This summary rank orders the students in the class from the highest to the lowest curriculum-based measurement median score over the past half month. It also provides a slope of improvement over time for each student, which indicates the average number of digits correct gain per week. Finally, it classifies students according to their benchmark status: already at grade-level benchmark, on track to achieve grade-level benchmark, or not predicted to achieve benchmark status.

Finally, the group analysis provides instructional recommendations. For example, at the bottom of page 1, the report identifies skills to teach in large- and small-group arrangements and, for small groups, which students should be included. On page 4, the computer reports peer-tutoring recommendations, listing skills for remediation. Under each skill, students who require remediation are listed as players (i.e., tutees); other students who have the requisite skills to serve as coaches (i.e., tutors) are also listed. The large-group, small-group, and peer-tutoring recommendations allow teachers to use the curriculum-based measurement information flexibly to adapt their instruction to meet individual needs, using routines that can be feasibly integrated into existing classroom structures. (We have also developed classwide peer tutoring methods that teachers can use to structure the process by which classwide peer tutoring occurs. For additional information on these classwide peer tutoring methods, see Fuchs, Fuchs, Hamlett, Bishop, & Bentz, 1994.)

During 1991-1992, we conducted an experiment to examine the efficacy of classwide curriculum-based measurement reports and instructional recommendations within general education classrooms with mainstreamed students with learning disabilities (Fuchs, Fuchs, Hamlett, Bishop, & Bentz, 1994). Results indicated that teachers who employed classwide curriculum-based measurement with instructional recommendations planned more responsively to individual student needs and effected substantially and significantly better math achievement than teachers who did not use curriculum-based measurement. These effects held across students with learning disabilities, as well as low-achieving nondisabled and average-achieving students. Additionally, and importantly, the general educators found the curriculum-based measurement process, which included both measurement and instructional decision making as deliberate emphases of the intervention, to be feasible to implement and enjoyable both for them and for their students.

Recent Developments

The computerized skills profiles in math and spelling, along with the class reports, offer a major advance in curriculum-based measurement – an advance made possible only via computer technology. In reading, however, early skills analysis was confined to reading comprehension on student retells. The major curriculum-based datum in reading is the number of words read aloud correctly in 1 minute; this score related well to other measures of reading competence and can be used to track students' overall reading development (Fuchs, Fuchs, Hosp, & Jenkins, 2001). Recently, we took on the challenge of developing a computer-facilitated diagnostic analysis for the standard curriculum-based measurement task where, as already described, competence is assessed via weekly 1-minute oral text reading and where graphed analysis of performance indicators signals teachers when a student's rate of development is inadequate and that alternative instruction is consequently required.

Our goal was to extend this framework in two ways (see Fuchs, Fuchs, Hosp, & Hamlett, in press for additional information). First, we sought to identify cut-points for the curriculum-based measurement scores (i.e., CBM scores below which with the need for instructional work in decoding, fluency, and comprehension is indicated). Second, we sought to develop brief follow-up assessments that would provide diagnostic analyses of decoding and comprehension strengths and weaknesses. Our notion was that the curriculum-based measurement performance indicator could be used efficiently to form instructional groups requiring decoding, fluency, or comprehension work; then, relatively brief follow-up assessment could be used to divide the decoding and comprehension groups further into clusters focusing on different skills matched to student needs.

Curriculum-based measurement cut-points for recommending decoding instruction were formulated using categorical and regression tree (CART) analysis. CART is an atheoretical tree-building technique for generating clinical decision rules. It comprises four steps, the first of which involves tree building via recursive splitting of nodes. Step 2 terminates tree building when a maximal tree (typically overfitting the data) is identified. The third step involves pruning, which results in a sequence of increasingly simpler trees and, in the final step, an optimal tree is selected to fit (without overfitting) the data. In addition to curriculum-based measurement, we entered into the CART analysis predictors that routinely are available to teachers: student demographics and teacher ratings. The predicted status was adequate versus inadequate decoding (*adequate decoding* was set at a standard score of 90 or higher on the Word Attack subtest of the Woodcock Reading Mastery Tests). Useful predictors incorporated within the decision tree were IEP reading status, teacher rating of reading competence (high, average, low), subsidized lunch status, grade, sex, teacher ratings of mathematics competence, and teacher ratings of classroom behavior problems (none, occasional, frequent). Curriculum-based measurement was used at six decision nodes, the first occurring at the second-level node (after reading IEP). The hit rate ([TP + TN]/n) was 87% (cross-validation: 84%); sensitivity (TP/[TP + FN]) was 98% (cross-validation: 86%); and specificity (TN/[TN + FP]) was 88% (cross-validation: 84%).

Continued work on larger sample sizes is warranted to explore appropriate CBM cutpoints for recommending decoding instruction. In our computerized decision-making framework, however, we have used this decision tree to identify students for decoding instruction. In addition, students are recommended for fluency practice if they are predicted to have adequate decoding status but their CBM scores place them lower than .5 standard deviations above the mean on a regional sample. The remaining set of students, who are predicted to achieve adequate decoding status and whose CBM scores place them more than .5 standard deviations above the mean, are identified for comprehension instruction.

Using the software we developed, teachers administer the standard curriculum-based measurement task with the assistance of a computer. As the student reads aloud from a printed copy of the passage, the teacher uses the cursor to mark errors on the screen. The computer terminates testing at 1 minute and calculates the number of words read correctly. Using the decision tree formulated via the CART analysis, the software considers the student's curriculum-based measurement score, demographics, and initial teacher ratings.

For students predicted to fall into the inadequate decoding group, the computer initiates administration of a Decoding Skills Battery we developed. We also designed software to support administration (and to ensure accurate identification of basals and ceilings) of this Decoding Skills Battery. The software prompts teachers where to begin testing, which page of items to administer next, and when to terminate testing. Administration takes 1-5 minutes. At the end of testing, the computer assigns each item a correct or incorrect code, determines mastery status for each skill, and identifies for instruction two skills (the next harder skills as introduced in the curriculum, which are nonmastered as indicated with the Decoding Skills Battery). Every three weeks, the computer generates individual student reports and a class report. See Figure 6 for a sample class report.

Directions and Implications

Directions

As we continue to develop technological applications for curriculum-based measurement and to conduct research on the efficacy of such applications, our work involves several related and new directions. First, we continue to explore strategies for optimizing the utility of curriculum-based measurement for instructional programming by developing diagnostic frameworks like the one just described. Second, we are also addressing more general issues in translating effective special education practices that move technological developments from model and typical practice. Work investigating the effects of contextual features to the efficacy of major technological innovation in our field is critical. We plan to study the effects of administrative support and staff involvement in planning and implementing technological innovations, specialized training and ongoing technical assistance, and the congruence between the innovation and salient dimensions of the curriculum.

Implications

Our research program on computer applications to curriculum-based measurement

Figure 6. CBM class report in reading.

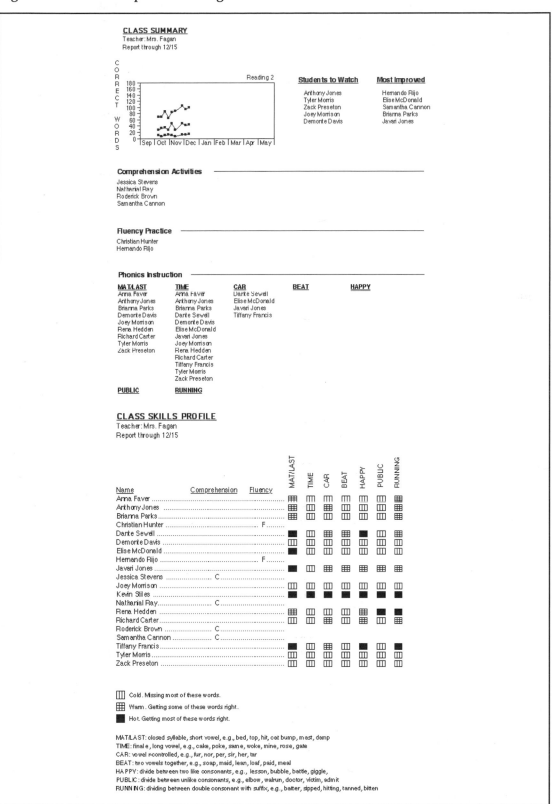

(continued next page)

Figure 6. CBM class report in reading. (continued)

CLASS SCORES
Teacher: Mrs. Fagan
Report through 12/15

Name	Score	Growth
Samantha Cannon	119	+5.11
Jessica Stevens	117	+3.92
Roderick Brown	96	+2.92
Nathanial Ray	93	+3.37
Christian Hunter	80	+4.22
Hernando Rijo	76	+5.91
Javari Jones	61	+2.35
Kevin Stiles	57	+0.31
Tiffany Francis	46	+1.48
Dante Sewell	44	+1.55
Brianna Parks	41	+2.49
Anna Faver	39	+1.55
Rena Hedden	33	+1.75
Elise McDonald	28	+2.10
Richard Carter	27	+0.14
Anthony Jones	26	+1.12
Tyler Morris	15	-0.25
Zack Preseton	13	+0.47
Joey Morrison	4	+0.01
Demonte Davis	4	+0.18

CLASS STATISTICS
Teacher: Mrs. Fagan
Report through 12/15

Score

Average score	51.2
Standard deviation	35.6
Discrepancy criterion	15.6

Slope

Average slope	+2.02
Standard deviation	1.76
Discrepancy criterion	+0.26

Students identified with dual discrepancy criterion

	Score	Slope
Demonte Davis	4.0	+0.18
Joey Morrison	4.0	+0.01
Tyler Morris	15.5	-0.25

permits several important conclusions about special education, technology, and assessment. First, technology can be used to reduce dramatically the need for teachers to conduct the mechanical tasks associated with measurement, such as test administration, test scoring, graphing, and data analysis. Although data-management software alone does not increase teacher efficiency in measurement, data-collection software (used in combination with data-management software) can eliminate most teachers' time in such tasks. Computers are ideally suited for completing such repetitive, routine work. Related applications for other types of assessment and instructional procedures should be developed to help reduce the need for teachers to engage in unchallenging work, thereby increasing their availability for critical instructional responsibilities.

Second, in addition to the mechanical aspects of measurement that teachers could complete (with expenditure of time), our research indicates that computers can also be used to complete work that human beings would not ordinarily be capable of (even with expenditure of time). For example, the computer-generated skills analysis provides a useful supplement to the traditional curriculum-based measurement indicator of overall proficiency. The skills analysis allows teachers to plan more specific instructional programs and to effect greater achievement for their students. Such skills analyses are not possible without the use of technology. Another example of information that computers can easily generate that teachers would not be capable of producing, is the group reports. These reports aggregate information about many students and automatically organize instructional recommendations. Again, our research indicates that these group reports increase teachers' capacity to plan responsive instructional programs, even in the context of large groups of students, and to effect better achievement outcomes. Researchers and developers should continue to consider how technology can be used not only to save teachers time, but also to enhance the quality and effects of their efforts by providing information and completing work that teachers would otherwise not be capable of producing.

Third, our work with expert systems and other instructional recommendation systems indicates that these and other related applications may help teachers plan sounder, more effective instruction. Nevertheless, our research also suggests that caution is in order: Use of our expert systems in different instructional areas produced differing results. Clearly, the availability of additional instructional recommendations alone is insufficient to increase teachers' capacity to plan better programs. The nature of the advice and the conditions under which such advice is offered are critical to efficacy. As electronic information and communication systems are developed to increase teachers' access to information, researchers and developers must consider carefully the quality and nature of the available information and the conditions under which such information is offered. In addition, the efficacy of such electronic information and communication systems must be evaluated rigorously before beneficial outcomes for students or teachers can be assumed.

Acknowledgment: Research described in this chapter was supported in part by Grant Nos. H023E90020, H003A10010, G008730087, and G008530198 from the U.S. Department of Education, Office of Special Education, to Vanderbilt University. Statements should not, however, be interpreted as official policy of the agencies.

References

Corno, L., & Snow, R.E. (1986). Adapting teaching to individual differences among learners. In M. Wittrock (Ed.), *Third handbook of research on teaching* (pp. 605-629). New York: Macmillan.

Fuchs, L.S., & Deno, S.L. (1991). Paradigmatic distinctions between instructionally relevant measurement models. *Exceptional Children, 57*, 488-501.

Fuchs, L.S., Deno, S.L., & Mirkin, P.K. (1984). The effects of frequent curriculum-based measurement and evaluation on pedagogy, student achievement, and student awareness of learning. *American Educational Research Journal, 21,* 449-460.

Fuchs, L.S., & Fuchs, D. (2003). Can diagnostic assessment enhance general educators' instructional differentiation and student learning? In B. Foorman (Ed.), *Preventing and remediating reading difficulties: Bringing science to scale* (pp. 325-351). Timonium, MD: York Press.

Fuchs, L.S., & Fuchs, D. (1998). Treatment validity: A unifying concept for reconceptualizing the identification of learning disabilities. *Learning Disabilities Research and Practice, 13,* 204-219.

Fuchs, L.S., Fuchs, D., & Hamlett, C.L (1988). Effects of computer-managed instruction on teachers' implementation of systematic monitoring programs and Student achievement. *Journal of Educational Research, 81,* 294-304.

Fuchs, L.S., Fuchs, D., & Hamlett, C.L (1989). Monitoring reading growth using student recalls: Effects of two teacher feedback systems. *Journal of Educational Research, 83,* 103-111.

Fuchs, L.S., Fuchs, D., Hamlett, C.L., & Allinder, R.M. (1991a). Effects of expert system advice within curriculum-based measurement on teacher planning and student achievement in spelling. *School Psychology Review, 20,* 49-66.

Fuchs, L.S., Fuchs, D., Hamlett, C.L., & Allinder, R.M. (1991b). The contribution. of skills analysis to curriculum-based measurement in spelling. *Exceptional Children, 57,* 443-452.

Fuchs, L.S., Fuchs, D., Hamlett, C.L., & Appleton, A.C. (2002). Explicitly teaching for transfer: Effects on the mathematical problem solving performance of students with disabilities. *Learning Disabilities Research and Practice, 17,* 90-106.

Fuchs, L.S., Fuchs, D., Hamlett, C.L., Bishop, N., & Bentz, J. (1994). Merging promising practices: Effects of curriculum-based measurement and peer tutoring on teacher planning and student achievement. *Exceptional Children, 60,* 518-551.

Fuchs, L.S., Fuchs, D., Hamlett, C.L., & Ferguson, C. (1992). Effects of expert system consultation within curriculum-based measurement using a reading maze task. *Exceptional Children, 58,* 436-450.

Fuchs, L.S., Fuchs, D., Hamlett, C.L., & Stecker,

P.M. (1990). The role of skills analysis in curriculum-based measurement in math. *School Psychology Review, 19,* 6-22.

Fuchs, L.S., Fuchs, D., Hamlett, C.L., & Stecker, P.M. (1991). Effects of curriculum-based measurement and consultation on teacher planning and student achievement in mathematics operations. *American Educational Research Journal, 28,* 617-641.

Fuchs, L.S., Hamlett, C., Fuchs, D., Stecker, P.M., & Ferguson, C. (1988). Conducting curriculum-based measurement with computerized data collection: Effects on efficiency and teacher satisfaction. *Journal of Special Education Technology, 9*(2), 73-86.

Fuchs, L.S., Fuchs, D., Hasselbring, T., & Hamlett, C.L. (1987). Using. computers with curriculum-based progress monitoring: Effects on teacher efficiency and satisfaction. *Journal of Special Education Technology, 8*(4), 14-27.

Fuchs, L.S., Fuchs, D., Hosp, M., & Hamlett, C.L. (2003). The potential for diagnostic analyses within curriculum-based measurement. *Assessment for Effective Intervention, 28*(3&4), 13-22.

Fuchs, L.S., Fuchs, D., Hosp, M., & Jenkins, J.R. (2001). Oral reading fluency as an indicator of reading competence: A theoretical, empirical, and historical analysis. *Scientific Studies of Reading, 5,* 239-256.

Fuchs, L.S., Fuchs, D., Phillips, N.B., & Simmons, D. (1993). Contextual variables affecting instructional adaptation. *School Psychology Review, 22,* 725-742.

Fuchs, L.S., Hamlett, C.L., Fuchs, D., Stecker, P.M., & Ferguson, C. (1987). Conducting curriculum-based measurement with computerized data collection: Effects on efficiency and teacher satisfaction. *Journal of Special Education Technology, 9*(2), 73-86.

Hasselbring, T.S., & Hamlett, C.L. (1985). Planning and managing instruction: Computer-based decision making. *Teaching Exceptional Children, 16,* 248-252.

Jones, E.D., & Krouse, J.P. (1988). The effectiveness of data-based instruction by student teachers in classrooms for pupils with mild handicaps. *Teacher Education and Special Education, 11*(1), 9-19.

Putnam, R. T. (1987). Structuring and adjusting

instructional planning content for students: A study of live and simulated tutoring of addition. *American Educational Research Journal, 24*, 13-48.

Stecker, P.M., & Fuchs, L.S. (2000). Effecting superior achievement using curriculum-based measurement: The importance of individual progress monitoring. *Learning Disabilities Research and Practice, 15*, 128-134.

Walton, W. T. (1986). Educators' response to methods of collecting, storing, and analyzing behavioral data. *Journal of Special Education Technology, 7*, 50-55.

Wesson, C.L. (1991). Curriculum-based measurement and two models of follow-up consultation. *Exceptional Children, 57*, 246-257.

34

Web-Based Resources and Instructional Considerations for Students with Mild Cognitive Disabilities

J. Emmett Gardner and Cheryl A. Wissick

The Expanding Influence and Challenge of the World Wide Web

According to recent estimates from the National Center for Education Statistics (NCES), 99 % of the public schools in the United States had connectivity to the Internet and the World Wide Web (Web) as of fall 2001 (Kleiner & Farris, 2002). Moreover, report between 1994 and 2001, access to the Web in instructional rooms rose from 3 to 87 %. Even considering that NCES defined instructional rooms to include classrooms and other rooms used for instruction (which encompass computer and other labs or library/media centers), the growth is phenomenal. In 1998, the ratio of students to instructional computers with Internet access was 12.1 to 1, whereas in 2001 it was 5.4 to 1 – more than a doubling in the availability of the Web to students (Kleiner & Farris, 2002).

Although the NCES did not differentiate between general or special education instructional settings or student-to-computer ratios for students with or without disabilities, it seems reasonable to conclude that by 2004, most special education teachers and students will have convenient and controllable access to the Web from within school and/or classroom. Intuitively, this access should be enough to ensure that teachers will have sufficient opportunity to use the Web as part of their instructional activities. Although most schools and classrooms now have access to the Web,

access does not guarantee that educators have successfully integrated the Web into their daily routines.

Acquiring and applying Web-based information in ways that affect student learning and teacher efficiency is a fundamental challenge to special educators (Wissick & Gardner, 1998). How this challenge is met procedurally depends on the type of outcomes that are being sought and the teacher's instructional and technological skills. Special education teachers' use of technology can generally be divided into two types of activities: those that support their personal versus their instructional productivity (Edyburn & Gardner, 2000). Personal productivity includes tasks that address individual responsibilities as teachers and professionals. In contrast, instructional productivity includes tasks that focus on how teachers design, organize, and deliver information to promote student learning. The same types of activities apply to use of the Web. For example, a special educator may want to locate information on the most recent IDEA regulations (e.g., www.ideapractices.org/) – professional responsibility- so she can properly advocate for a student with a behavior disorder at an upcoming meeting considering suspension. Similarly an instructional context, a high school teacher working with a student who has a learning disability in math may experiment with an interactive lesson on mean, median, and mode (www.shodor.org/interactivate/lessons/

sm1.html) that has the student measuring and observing how changing factors (such as the length of two out of 10 objects) can affect each of the statistics. This chapter will present a range of Web-based resources and considerations that benefits teachers' and students' personal as well as instructional productivity.

Presumptions

Some basic presumptions underlie this chapter with regard to the reader's understanding of the Web and how it relates to special education. First, while the terms *Internet* and the *World Wide Web* are often used synonymously, there is an important difference between the two. The *Internet* is often used to refer to the underlying *physical* structure of communication and connectivity that exists within the United States and other nations. Think if it as the backbone/spinal column that provides structure to the nerve cord that connects the nerves from different parts of our body to our brain. The term, *World Wide We*b, on the other hand, is often used to represent the *information* and *data* that are contained on Web sites and Web pages. Web sites are connected to one another all over the world via the Internet. For purposes of this chapter, our use of the term, *Web*, more closely resembles the World Wide Web as defined above.

A second presumption of this chapter is that the reader has a rudimentary working knowledge of the characteristics and features of the Web, and has experience performing many of the fundamental proficiencies associated with using the Web. These skills include browsing, creating bookmarks/favorites, and visiting Web directories or using search engines to find information. For the rare individual who has never used the World Wide Web or is just beginning to discover the effectiveness of browsing the Web for information and resources, Wissick and Gardner (1998) offered an introduction to using the Web in the context of special education resources and practices. For example, they discussed Web terminology, navigation between and within Web sites, and how to conduct a basic search on the Web and determine if the information returned is appropriate. More comprehensive overviews of the terms and concepts related to the Internet

and World Wide Web as they pertain to general education (but also apply to special educators) may be obtained through a variety of other sources, such as Ackerman and Hartman (2000), Robyler (2003b), or Male and Gotthoffer (1999).

Web sites, Web pages, and their content are dynamic and constantly changing. The third presumption of this chapter is that some of the Web-based content that has been cited here has undoubtedly been revised/updated, transformed, modified, or deleted by the time this book goes to press. An entire site may cease to exist. Web pages benefit from frequent updating to remain current. In an attempt to take advantage of the dynamic nature of the wed, readers should be able to access most of the themes and Web sites cited in this chapter by visiting *Web Toolboxes: QuickStarts for the Web* (Wissick, 2004a; www.ed.sc.edu/caw/tool box.html). One word of advice would be that although the links are available, the Toolboxes may be organized and presented using a different design than presented in this chapter.

A fourth presumption is that the reader will take advantage of the dynamic nature of the Web, and read and review this chapter concurrently with Web access. A picture *is* worth a 1000 words for a variety of the examples cited (especially when it comes to visualizing a WebQuest, or a TrackStar). Figures illustrating Web pages have been omitted in order to conserve space. It is presumed that the reader will access cited Web pages to experience in real-time the concepts and ideas being presented.

Finally, the chapter does not address how to design Web sites using HTML, Web authoring programs, and principles of universal design for learning. Rather, this chapter concentrates on how information and tools accessible on the Web apply to promoting instructional tasks that are more focused on students performing higher-order thinking skills in ways that make use of Web-based *information*. The Web remains an enormous source of information that contains content well beyond that found in a traditional school library. To use it wisely and efficiently, (a) teachers and students must be selective about *what* information will be used and for what *purpose*, and (b) teachers must be prepared to make specific decisions about *how* selected information will be *structured* to the best meet individual learning characteristics. A good source that conceptually illustrates how powerful information access and management via the web may be for teachers and students with mild cognitive disabilities, is the American Library Association's and Association for Educational Communications and Technology's (ALA/AECT) "Nine Information Literacy Standards for Student Learning" (American Library Association, 2003) at www.ala.org/aasl/ip_nine.html. According to ALA/AECT (1998, pp. 8-9), empowered information users are literate (i.e., able to appropriately access, evaluate, and use information), independent learners (i.e., able to independently pursue information to satisfy personal interests, creativity, and information seeking and knowledge generation) who are socially responsible in their use of information (i.e., they recognize the importance of having/using information accurately and ethically).

Applications of the Web in special education will vary depending on the purpose and nature of the task, the learning characteristics of those who benefit directly and indirectly, and the outcomes sought. It is this last perspective, consideration of the outcomes sought by special educators, that this discussion of the Web and Special Education will target. In this chapter we will examine how various principles, tasks, and responsibilities associated with what we do as special educators can be associated with components and features of the Web. These areas are: accessing special education information and resources, making learning meaningful, supporting student learning through instruction, promoting automaticity and fluency with interactivity, and accommodating student learning characteristics.

Accessing Special Education Information and Resources

It has been said that having "knowledge is power." Having easy and structured access to special education information and resources can empower teachers to make a variety of decisions related to personal, professional and instructional objectives. Irrelevant, inaccurate,

or outdated information, on the other hand, impedes a teacher's ability to acquire knowledge and make informed decisions. This section begins with a look at the importance of evaluating Web resources/information in terms of the validity and reliability of their content, including tips for more effective and efficient searching. Sources for valuable special education information and resources on the Web are also presented. Finally, large databases and/or warehouses of educational tools, lessons, and general information that are useful to all teachers are highlighted.

Determining the Validity and Reliability of Web Resources

Anyone can publish on the Web. As a result, there currently is little guarantee that information found on the Web is one hundred percent accurate or valid. When visiting a Web site, therefore, we must be critical consumers of the information presented. Grabe and Grabe (2000) stressed the importance of knowing how to identify specific indicators that Web-based information is reliable, accurate, verifiable, and objective. Numerous criteria for evaluating Web information have been offered. For example, Bull, Bull, Dawson, and Mason (2001) suggested that information users consider the authoritativeness of the information source and whether there is internal and external consistency. Authoritativeness can be established by being a well-known institution, such as *The New York Times*; or in the case of an individual by having a reputation in an information domain, such as Steven Hawkings in the area of theoretical physics. Internal and external consistency can be checked by asking two basic questions: (a) Are there places in the document that contradict themselves; and (b) does the information appear to be consistent and in agreement with other known sources?

Bakken and Aloia (1998) suggested that special educators can assess the quality of a Web site's information by examining the following areas:

- *Content (quality, accuracy, and scope);*

- *Completeness (adequacy of coverage, omissions);*

- *Clarity (ease of use, how well written is the content);*

- *Connections (number and quality of hyperlinks);*

- *Corroboration or credibility (documentation of sources, or inclusion of other sources to complement the information provided); and*

- *Currency (timeliness of information, up-to-date references). (p. 52)*

Finally, Marsh (2000) proposed a set of questions that teachers can ask to help decide whether Web-based information is accurate or not (see Table 1).

Using Search Engines Reliably

The ability to locate accurate resources with a simple search leads to efficient and effective use of the Web. Web searches frequently yield thousands of hits. Web search engines have improved in their ability to locate information on the topic. Therefore, one often does not have to look past the first few pages of links to find appropriate and surprisingly accurate information. In addition, as one becomes more practiced at searching the Web, more reliable hits occur more frequently. Many of the simple to use search engines, such as *Google* (google.com*), *Yahoo!* (yahoo.com*), or *AltaVista* (altavista.com) provide access to advanced search features and tutorials for more efficient searching. Most search engines also provide information in the form of a directory or lists of categories. Individuals who like to find information through browsing, can follow these links to different categories to evaluate the range and type of information available.

With practice, if you know the exact name of the topic (e.g., Asperger Syndrome) or want specific information in an area (e.g., learning strategies for students with AD/HD), using the same search engine consistently will yield effective results. A recent search for the topic *Asperger* in *Google* yielded 6 of the first 10 sources from education (.edu) or organization (.org) sites, and ones that fit the criteria for being authorities in the field. In comparison, a search for *Asperger Syndrome* yielded organizational, educational, and government (.gov) agencies in its first ten hits. Even though, the total hits for the topic topped 124,000, accurate and reliable sources occurred within the first 10 hits. Other tips for searching include rearranging the order of the words (such as *Syndrome Asperger*) or using quotes ("*Asperger Syndrome*"). When quotes are used around a topic, it forces the search engine to look for an exact match. Therefore, to search for *learning strategies for students with AD/HD*, a person might consider putting the whole phrase in quotes or using different terms such as ADD, ADHD. In addition search engines leave out frequently used words and prepositions. Consider how to rephrase a search without using them, such as *ADHD learning strategies*.

If the information needed to solve a problem is not found within the first two pages of "hits," changing the wording might help. It is probably more efficient to refine the search strategies and/or use different terms than spend excessive time reviewing extended pages of sites that can sometimes number in the hundreds. Often it a good strategy to consider the source of the site whether it is an organizational or an educational or governmental agency before even viewing the link. Most browsers reveal the URL of the link as part of the hit information. Finally, as a consumer of information and a professional responsible for your actions, evaluate and determine the accuracy and legitimacy of any Web-acquired information *before* its used in any official context.

As search engines become more efficient in locating links for requested information, determining what information is accurate and usable, versus inaccurate or not valid, continues to be a daunting task. As mentioned, a Web-based search can yield hundreds to hundred thousands of "hits." The knowledge and skills associated with searching for and evaluating Web-based information should not only be performed by special education professionals, but also modeled to and used by the students they teach. Additional discussion of how to conduct searches on the Web and/or how to teach students to use the Internet as a research tool may be found in Felt and Symans (2000), Grabe and Grabe, (2000), Kohut (2000), and Male (2003). The authoritative online source for search engine comparisons, reviews, and resources (e.g. search engine tutorials, search engine glossary, search engine technology, etc.) can be found at the Search Engine Watch Web Site (www.searchenginewatch.com*).

Table 1. Guide to Evaluating Web Sites and Other Online Sources

Factors Pertaining to How Information Is Represented on the Web	Key Questions
1. Your Knowledge	• How does the new information compare with what you already know about the subject from other sources and your personal knowledge? • Does it change what you know? • Does it make sense?
2. Authority	• Who is presenting the information? Who is the author? • Where did they get the information? • Do they provide evidence or examples to support their points? • Do they cite their sources? • Why do you think they are providing the information? • If it is a Web site, who is sponsoring the site? • If it is sponsored by a school, college, or university, is the information offered by students or teachers?
3. Age	• How old is the information? • Does it include recent information? • If it is a Web site, how long ago was it updated?
4. Depth	• How much information is given? • How broad is the coverage? • How in-depth is the information?
5. Form	• Is the information in a WWW or gopher document, a text file, a newsgroup posting, or an email message? • If it is a Web site, how sophisticated is the manner in which the information is being presented? Is it just text? Are there images and/or sounds?
6. Organization	• If it is a Web site, is the information clearly presented? • Is it well organized? • Is it easy to navigate?
7. Recommendations	• Have people whom you respect (friends/colleagues, teachers, librarians, parents, etc.) recommended this site as a good source of information? • Have print sources you trust (textbook, journal, local newspaper, or national magazine, etc.) featured this site or newsgroup?
8. Validity	• How true do you think the information is? • What makes you say so?
9. Importance	• Is this important information? • If so, why is it important?
10. Appeal	• If it is a Web site, does it appeal to you? In what ways? Why?

From: Marsh, M. M. (2000). *A student guide to misinformation on the web.* Houston, TX: Children's Software Press. Copyright 2000 by Children's Software Press. Adapted by permission.

Special Education Information and Resources

When a teacher accesses the Web for instructional purposes, it is probably to locate information needed to solve an educational problem. Possessing knowledge of and frequenting sites that are predominantly special education oriented in content and pedagogy is a logical starting point, considering that as of January 2003, over 171 million Web sites were estimated to exist on the Web (Network Wizards, 2003). To help cut down on the search options, a number of Web sites are specifically designed to organize information related to special education topics (see Table 2). These lists are by no means exhaustive of the information on special education available on the Web. Yet they provide a good example of the variety of sites that exist related to special education. In addition, a variety of compilations are available that have organized Web resources based on themes relevant to special educators (Edyburn, 2002; Lewis, 1998; Male & Gotthoffer, 1999; Wissick, 2004a).

There are pros and cons to using the sites found in Table 2 as gateways to finding special education resources. Obviously, individual sites set a particular tone upon entry into their home page. LDOnline.org, for example, focuses on collecting and authoring articles and resources that address factors related to the education of students with learning disabilities. However, much of the instructional content at LDOnline.org also applies well to students with milder forms of mental retardation, behavior disorders, and attention disorders. Another site, the IDEA Practices (www.ideapractices.org) contains the full text content of the Individuals with Disabilities Education Act, including, but not limited to, sources of information that help interpret and understand how the current version of IDEA applies to special education. The Assistive Technology Training Online Project's site (atto.buffalo.edu/) is primarily designed to provide training and tutorials on assistive technology devices and ways to use these technologies effectively. Thus these three sites, while different in focus, complement one another. All are "special education" sites, but each would be favored over the other depending on the primary type of information being sought (i.e.,

learning disabilities, special education policy, or assistive technology training).

In some instances, special educators have a good idea of the general type of information they are seeking (e.g., Asperger syndrome) but do not know whether a site specifically devoted to the topic exists. In this case, comprehensive sites like Disability Resources (www.disabilityresources.org/) or Internet Resources for Special Children (www.irsc.org) can act as topical directories. These sites do not emphasize writing their own content, but devote their efforts to searching the Web and updating and organizing special education links under broad but familiar categories, topics, or themes. Some of these topical directories also include their own internal search engine making it is easy to search for particular categories without knowing their unique directory systems.

General Education Instructional Information and Resources

A good portion of what special educators do today takes place in classroom and instructional settings that involve all students in both general and special education. Thus. in many respects, the instructional content and instructional strategies used by special educators are equally applicable to students regardless of whether they have a disability. Alternatively, an extensive body of general education Web sites that contain numerous resources on curriculum content and instructional methodologies can easily be applied to students with special needs. Table 3 lists a collection of excellent educational sites in alphabetical order. These sites provide a solid starting point for identifying instructional resources to enhance and supplement curriculum content, support standards and IEP objectives, create learning activities, or locating lesson plans and thematic units.

Accessing special education and general education information and resources on the Web is not difficult. Once you are aware of the various sites presented in Tables 2 and 3 and become comfortable with searching, you can begin determining whether information on a given site suits your needs. More important is understanding that even when a good set of

Table 2. Special Education Resources on the World Wide Web

Name of Web Page	URL/Address	Notes/Annotation
About.com (Special Education)	specialed.about.com/mbody.htm	The About.com resources for special education contains a myriad of links organized around special education subjects and includes a discussion forum.
Assistive Technology Training Online Project	atto.buffalo.edu/	AT project provides training, tutorials, and information on assistive technology.
Closing the Gap	www.closingthegap.com	A comprehensive Web site that features links to news articles, online forums, and the Solutions database for searching for specific assistive tchnology products.
ConnSENSE Bulletin	www.connsensebulletin.com/	Connecticut's Special Education Network to Software Evaluation, articles, and other information on assistive technology. Links to WAY COOL! Software reviews written by special education students.
Council for Exceptional Children	www.cec.sped.org/	The premier professional organization for special educators. Links to specific divisions of CEC to find resources on specific disabilities or subjects.
Disability Resources on the Internet	www.disabilityresources.org/	Nonprofit organization that monitors, reviews, and reports on resources related to disabilities. Identifies topics/subjects using the DRM WebWatcher, or search resources and information by states using the DRM regional resource directory.
IDEA Practices	www.ideapractices.org/	A comprehensive site that focuses entirely on IDEA.
Inclusion... Or Yours, Mine, Ours	rushservices.com/Inclusion/	Resources to help teachers and parents build support and confidence to include children in general education classrooms with success.
Internet Resources for Special Children	www.irsc.org	A listing of links for those who work with special children.
LD Online	www.ldonline.org/	A detailed and comprehensive set of resources and instructional strategies for the field of LD. There is information for parents, teachers and students with LD. A "must know" site for teachers working with students with mild disabilities.

(continued next page)

Table 2. Special Education Resources on the World Wide Web (continued)

Name of Web Page	URL/Address	Notes/Annotation
LD Resources	www.ldresources.com/	Richard Wandersman's site for resources and articles. Many great hints related to technology.
NCIPnet	www.edc.org/FSC/NCIP	National Center to Improve Practice promotes effective use of technology to enhance educational outcomes for students with disabilities.
Office of Special Education: University of Virginia	curry.edschool.virginia.edu/go/specialed/	Effectively organized hotlists of information on all disabilities and support information.
Special Education Resources on the Internet (SERI)	seriweb.com/	A collection of Internet-accessible information and resources of interest to those involved in the fields related to special education.
Wisconsin Assistive Technology Initiative	www.wati.org/	Includes many resources, articles, and downloads. See PDF files for downloadable versions of Yes I can and resource guides (www.wati.org/pdf Student_Handbook.pdf; www.wati.org/pdf/resourceguidegeneral.pdf).
Yahoo's Directory of Special Education Sites	dir.yahoo.com/education/special_education/	A directory of listing for special education.

From: Wissick, C. A. (2003b). *Web toolbox for educators: Special education resources.* Retrieved August 16, 2003, from:www.ed.sc.edu/caw/toolboxsped.html. Copyright 2003 by the University of South Carolina. Adapted by permission.

resources are identified, it is up to the teacher to determine *how* they are integrated into the special education curriculum and instructional activities. To accomplish this goal effectively, it is helpful to think of curriculum integration and the Web as a process. Begin by considering the type of educational problem you are facing, then locate possible solutions through Web-based sources (Gardner & Wissick, 2002; Wissick & Gardner, 1998). In the next section, we will discuss how to seek solutions that yield the most meaningful and interactive learning activities for your students.

Making Learning More Meaningful

The use of computer-based technologies within to the context of learning has yielded a variety of pedogological views regarding the best way to approach technology integration in education. For example, Robyler (2003a) remarked,

> In subsequent years, two trends have affected profoundly the course of education technology: (1) an increase in the number and type of technology resources available, and (2) dramatic shifts in beliefs about the fundamental goals and strategies of education itself.(p. 52)

These shifts in beliefs about the goals and strategies of integrating technology are nowhere more evident than in the International Society for Technology in Education's (ISTE) perspective on the type of learning environments technology should be cultivating. Based upon a review of ISTE's perspective (as well as the perspective of many others concerning the role of technology in education (e.g., Grabe & Grabe, 2000; Grabinger, 1996; Jonassen,

Table 3. Educational Resources on the Web

Title	URL Address	Notations
Educational Sites		
4 Teachers	www.4teachers.com/ 4teachframes.html	Site intended to provide teachers and educators with links to the many educational resources on the Web.
BBC Online: Education	www.bbc.co.uk/learning/	What is new in British education and the best resources online. Search for educational Web sites on a variety of topics.
Blue Web'N	www.filamentality.com/ wired/bluewebn/	A library of blue-ribbon learning sites, searchable and categorized in a matrix by content and activity type.
Busy Teacher's K-12 WebSite	www.ceismc.gatech.edu/ busyt/	Annotated hotlist of content area sites.
Discovery School	school.discovery.com	Resources for teachers and students related to Discovery Channel-sponsored activities.
Education Planet	www.educationplanet.com/	Searchable database of over 100,000 sites related to education.
Education World	www.education-world.com/	Searchable database of over 50,000 sites related to education curriculum ideas and hot picks of the week.
Educational Web Adventures	www.eduweb.com/	Interactive activities for a variety of topics to promote cooperative learning and problem solving.
Educator's Reference Desk	www.eduref.org	Includes searchable database for articles and lessons plans. Formerly AskEric.
Exploratorium	www.exploratorium.edu/	Includes the Learning Studio with 10 NEW cool sites each month. Searchable database of all past reviews.
Federal Resources for Educational Excellence	www.ed.gov/free/	Easy-to-find Internet-based education resources supported by agencies across the federal government.
Gateway to Educational Materials	www.thegateway.org	Searchable database by topic for lesson plans, Web sites, and published curriculum units.
Kathy Schrock's Guide for Educators	schooldiscovery.com/ schrockguide/	Classified list of sites found to be useful for enhancing curriculum and teacher professional growth, updated daily.
National Geographic Educational Materials	www.nationalgeographic.com/ education/	Searchable list of lessons and online adventures. Many resources for teachers.

(continued next page)

Table 3. Educational Resources on the Web (Continued)

Title	URL Address	Notations
Network of Regional Technology in Education Consortia	www.rtec.org	Links to the six regional technology education consortia. Be sure to visit HPRTEC and test out TrackStar. Each consortium has developed different tools to support instructional technology, visit them all.
National Network of Regional Educational Laboratories	www.nwrel.org/national/index.html	Ten educational research and development organizations supported by contracts with the U.S. Education Department, Office of Educational Research and Improvement (OERI). NCREL specializes in technology, and McREL specializes in curriculum and instruction.
Tramline Tours, Inc.	www.tramline.com/	Virtual fieldtrips and a blackboard with resources for teachers.
National Organizations' Standards		
The National Council of Teachers of Mathematics	www.nctm.org/standards/	National standards for mathematics.
National Council of Teachers of English	www.ncte.org/about/over/standards	National standards for English.
The National Council for the Social Studies	www.ncss.org/standards/toc.html	National standards for social studies.
National Science Education Standards	books.nap.edu/catalog/4962. html	National standards for science.
McREL	www.mcrel.org	National Content Standards and Benchmarks.
International Society for Technology in Education's (ISTE)	cnets.iste.org/students/	National Educational Technology Foundation Standards for All Students.

From: Wissick, C. A. (2004b). *Web toolbox for educators: Educational resources*. Retrieved January 31, 2004, from: www.ed.sc.edu/caw/toolboxsped.html. Copyright 2004 by the University of South Carolina. Adapted by permission.

Howland, Moore, & Marra, 2003; Robyler, 2003a), one of the most obvious and consistent ways of using technology in learning environments has involved having students participate in meaningful learning activities that are interactive rather than passive.

The concepts of meaningful learning and interactivity apply well to Web-based activities and instructional considerations in education. Grabe and Grabe (2000) viewed the Web as particularly capable of serving as a tool for communication, inquiry, and knowledge construction. This view is further elaborated in the five attributes of meaningful learning proposed by Jonassen, Howland, Moore, and Marra (2003). When these attributes and the characteristics of learning associated with them (see p. 6-9 of Jonassen et al., 2003, for further detail) are applied to contexts of Web-related learning, meaningful learning on the Web has the potential to be:

- *Active* (i.e., students will be engaged in meaningful learning when they are performing tasks that actively *manipulate* web-based information and *observe* the results of their actions);

- *Constructive* (i.e., students will be engaged in meaningful learning when they are asked to *articulate* and *reflect* on their Web-based activities to promote new understanding and the development of new mental models);

- *Intentional* (i.e., students will be engaged in meaningful learning when their web-related activities are tied to specific cognitive learning goals/objectives, where Web-related learning is *regulatory* (i.e., narrowly focused) and student must be *reflective* of how their actions on the Web are directed at achieving the goals/objectives;

- *Authentic* (i.e., students will be engaged in meaningful learning when their Web-related actions are clearly associated with more *complex* meaningful real-world tasks, or a *contextual* problem-based activity);

- *Cooperative* (i.e., students will be engaged in meaningful learning when their Web-related actions are *collaborative* and facilitate *conversations* that share and build knowledge as students work cooperatively to complete tasks and solve problems).

Gardner and Wissick (2002) have described how meaningful learning and interactivity apply to Web-related learning activities for students with mild disabilities. *Web toolboxes: QuickStarts for the Web* (Wissick, 2004a) offer links to a variety of interactive Web sites that provide activities for students to practice content-related knowledge and skills. The main toolbox links to content toolboxes for language arts, math, social studies, science and functional skills (www.ed.sc.edu/caw/tool box.html).

Especially for students in special education, an ultimate goal is to direct students towards higher-order thinking, problem solving, and/or the development of specific skills that authentically represent the knowledge and skills they will need to successfully perform as adults in community and vocationally based contexts. Through proper considerations and design of learning activities, teachers/educators have numerous opportunities to use the Web as a powerful tool to provide students meaningful, authentic, and interactive learning opportunities.

Supporting Student Learning Through Instruction

Using the Web to promote student learning through instruction essentially represents adopting the philosophy that integrating the Web into special education instruction is purposeful, systematically planned, and goal oriented. There are a number of ways this philosophy can be operationalized: (a) recognize that standards exist that identify what students should know about the Web and how to use it effectively; (b) understand that using the Web to promote learning is more effective when Web-based access/activities are tied to outcomes that differentiate the type of learning that is taking place; and (c) be knowledgeable of strategies and online tools that support Web-based learning.

The ISTE National Educational Technology Standards and the Web

In 2000, the International Society for Technology in Education (ISTE) published the *National Technology Standards for Students – Connecting Curriculum and Technology* (NETS) (ISTE, 2000). This landmark document, a result of the National Educational Technology Standards Project (2000), establishes the benchmark for what students should know and be able to do when it comes to using technology. The cornerstone of the NETS is a set of six categories of technology foundation standards (basic operations and concepts; social, ethical, and human issues; technology productivity tools;

technology communication tools; technology research tools; and technology problem-solving and decision-making tools), and accompanying performance indicators for four grade ranges (PreK-2, 3-5, 6-8, and 9-12) linked to the six categories. These standards and performance indicators are applicable to most students with mild disabilities and represent levels of performance that, with necessary supports and accommodations, should be aspired to. (The Council for Exceptional Children was a partner organization during the development of the NETS.) Note, in some places the NETS web-based standards and/or performance indicators are explicit, in other places they are implied which requires educators to discern appropriate Web-based knowledge, skills, and activities.

Learning Outcomes and the Web

There is nothing magical about promoting student learning in a Web-enhanced or Web-based environment. As with any other technology product or tool, it is the purposeful *application* of technology designed to correspond with local, state, and/or national curriculum standards and specifically identified student objectives that increases the likelihood of successful technology integration (Gardner & Edyburn, 2000).

A variety of perspectives can be used when considering ways to use integrate the Web into instruction. One such perspective is to consider the type of learning and thinking/intellectual skills that you want students to learn, and then identify activities and outcomes that require the application of representative knowledge and skills. For example, according to Guptill (2000), thinking in terms of Bloom's taxonomy of educational objectives (Bloom, Englehart, Furst, Hill, & Krathwohl, 1956) can yield a variety of Web-based activities that promote higher-level thinking skills. Table 4 presents Guptill's (2000) technology taxonomy for using the Web to improve student performance. Table 5 adds another perspective, illustrating how Web-based activities can be constructed in the context of Gagné's (1985) varieties of learning. Both sets of examples illustrate the importance of recognizing that many Web-based activities can be designed to address a broad range of learning outcomes (e.g., using thinking/intellectual skills and/or

learning declarative or procedural knowledge) that are relevant for different students with different needs.

Once the variety/type of learning outcomes have been identified, it is relatively easy to plug in state and local content area standards to create a Web-related learning activity that addresses those standards. From an alternative perspective, understanding that Web activities can address teaching/using intellectual skills in a variety of ways, teachers can begin with a state and local content area standard and creatively design a Web-based activity that addresses content area knowledge at different levels, such as in terms of a learning hierarchy (e.g., Bloom et al., 1956) or a variety of learning (e.g., Gagné, 1985).

Strategies and Online Tools That Support Web-Based Learning

Browsing and searching for information on the Web and identifying the type of Web-related performance that will be tied to learning outcomes is but one part of the larger picture that encompasses Web-based Instruction. A good portion of instruction involves the purposeful external organization of information by teachers into a lesson that includes consideration of how it will be delivered to students and what they will do with the information once they receive it. (See Gagné, 1985, and Gagné, Briggs, & Wager, 1992, for more elaborate discussions of the events and principles associated with instruction.) In the context of Web-based learning and special education, two areas should be considered: (a) how learning activities on the Web can be formatted; and (b) identifying supports and scaffolds for students with mild disabilities who traditionally need guidance in learning activities (Gardner & Wissick, 2001).

Formats of Web-based Learning Activities

According to March (1997), students either work with Web resources that have been assembled and organized for them by teachers (so students can used these resources to access and gather Web-based information more efficiently) or students are involved in activities that have been specifically designed to help them acquire and use web-based information to develop knowledge and/or comple-

Table 4. A Taxonomy of Web-Based Measures of Student Performance

Learning Hierarchy	Using Web-Based Applications and/or Using Web-Based Information To:
Knowledge	• Reinforce existing knowledge • Obtain new knowledge of major ideas • Obtain new knowledge of dates, events, places • Obtain new knowledge of technological and academic concepts
Comprehension	• Surf (and sift) through information on the Web, and read for understanding • Identify valuable Web sites, record sites • Group Web sites into categories • Interpret, compare, and contrast facts from different sites • Predict consequences-use interactive Web sites to develop understanding of concepts • Contact experts to clarify understanding of Web-based information • Interpret information from the web by connecting to multiple perspectives
Application	• Draw together associations between prior knowledge and a search of the Web • Individual or team collection of Web-acquired information • Classify Web-acquired information • Predict outcomes based on Web site search • Refine online searches, as needed • Download from the Web photographs, quotations, sound clips, virtual reality tours for use in a presentation • Create a Web-based presentation
Analysis	• Organization of Web-acquired information (text, graphics, sound clips) into conceptual categories • Sort and discern quality information from outdated or biased information acquired through the Web • Find solutions to questions using collaboration and investigations with peers and experts
Synthesis	• Combine information from different Web sites • Modify information from Web sites to meet assignment guidelines • Create and design Web sites, interactive projects, visual displays, and written text • Prepare essays, projects, visual displays, and/or interactive presentations • Compose meaningful text from information gathered from books, periodicals, and Web pages • Explain findings/synthesize findings in an oral report, information gathered from books, periodicals, and Web pages
Evaluation	• Assess value and quality of presentation • Compare and discriminate between information from different Web sites and make judgments regarding various elements • Verify the value of information from various Web sources • Recognize the difference between subjective vs. objective information presented at various Web sites • Support information with prior knowledge • Summarize evaluative findings in a written report or presentation

From: *Using the Internet to improve student performance*, by A.M. Guptill, 2002, *Teaching Exceptional Children*, 32(4), 16-20. Copyright 2000 by Council for Exceptional Children. Adapted by permission.

Table 5. Web-Based Activities in the Context of Gagné's (1985) Varieties of Learning

Gagné's Variety of Learning	Goal	Method/Description
Attitudes	The learner will develop an under-standing of the cultural differences between Native American and Hispanic people.	Working in small cooperative learning groups, the students will complete the WebQuest entitled *Dispelling the Myth: A Study of Cultures* (Lynch & Tennille, 2003) (coe.west.asu.edu/students/stennille/ST3/webquest.html)
Motor Skills	The learner will improve her/his operation of the mouse keys and mouse pad to browse the Web.	The student will begin using the mouse keys on an *IntelliKeys* alternative keyboard at the slowest response rate and cursor speed to browse the Web. As skillfulness improves using the keyboard to click on links while browsing, the response rate and cursor speed will be adjusted till an optimum level of controlling the cursor is achieved.
Cognitive Strategy	When deciding whether or not to use Web content in a report, the learner will apply a cognitive strategy.	Before using information obtained from Web-based content, the student will evaluate it using the strategy "IS it REAL": Information is the focus of my decision-Before using this information I have to evaluate it based on considering the: **S**ource of the information **R**eliability of the information **E**ven-sidedness of the information **A**uthor-authority behind the information **L**egitimacy of the information
Verbal Information	The learner will state five facts about Abraham Lincoln.	Students will browse a Web site devoted to Abraham Lincoln, and identify and select five facts. They will write these facts onto a worksheet provided by the teacher.
Intellectual Skill: Concrete Concept	The learner will identify common characteristics of dinosaurs.	Students will browse three dinosaur Web sites. They will look for flesh eaters or plant eaters; land-living or water-living; and very large or very small. Students will copy/paste pictures into two-column word processing templates that identify each column by characteristic, labeling each dinosaur accordingly.
Intellectual Skill: Defined Concept	The learner will describe domestic and international civil actions based on defined characteristics of their choice.	Students will use a search engine to identify and research five domestic and international civil actions. They will identify and define three or more defined concepts that can be applied to all five. For example: victims, heroes, underlying causes (e.g., racial, religious, or economic), length of action (e.g., short-days, medium-weeks, or long-years). They will given an oral report describing these actions based on their defined concepts.
Intellectual Skill: Problem Solving	The learner will make decisions based on applying a rule.	1. A hotlist is created that contains links to the community facts pages on Web sites for 15 towns in the state of Oklahoma. The student must visit each fact page and answer questions that contain a rule. For example, which towns have a public library and a public swimming pool?

(continued next page)

Table 5. Web-Based Activities in the Context of Gagné's (1985)Varieties of Learning (Continued)

Gagné's Variety of Learning	Goal	Method/Description
Intellectual Skill: Problem Solving	The learner will make decisions based on applying a rule.	2. Another and more advanced example of applying problem solving to Web activities would be teaching students with learning disabilities how to find information using Boolean operators (e.g. AND, NOT, or OR) in search engines. For example, finding information about musical instruments made out of wood that are not stringed instruments (e.g., instruments AND musical AND wood NOT stringed).

ment specific learning goals and outcomes (see Table 6).

One of the most elaborate and structured form of Web-based learning involves the WebQuest model (Dodge & March, 1995), which generally contains seven sequential elements, each serving to provide support to an inquiry-oriented assignment. The elements of a generic WebQuest consist of an *introduction*; a description of the *task*; a description of the *process* (methods and procedures); a description of *evaluation* criteria; a *conclusion* section that provides closure; a *credits and references* section that lists the sources of all information (images, music and text) including permissions; and a *teacher information page* (see Table 7 for further description regarding these elements). These elements are situated on a Web page that students link to and interact with during the course of completing the WebQuest. In addition, while these elements are often-cited as the characteristic features of a WebQuest, it is important to understand that a generic "one-size-fits-all" model is not the way WebQuests should be portrayed (B. Dodge, personal communication, March 2, 2004). Indeed, there exist a variety of WebQuest design patterns (see webquest.sdsu.edu/design patterns/all.htm) that can be coordinated with specific content areas and/or learning activities. These design patterns provide subtle but valuable differences in the organization of the introduction, task, process and evaluation sections.

WebQuests are designed with the specific intention to challenge students to arrive at conclusions through analyzing and synthesizing of Web-based information. In WebQuests students often work cooperatively, assume alternative roles and/or take different perspectives, and problem solve. Table 8 provides a "WebQuest" Toolbox containing a set of links that help summarize key concepts and information on how to obtain examples of WebQuests.

By their very nature, WebQuests are beneficial to student with mild disabilities. For example, the chunking of a WebQuest into elements that have distinctly separate but related functions helps guide and focus student attention towards the factors typically associated with each element (e.g., the process section contains the procedures involved in the Web-based activity, whereas the evaluation section clearly informs the students of the criteria that will be used). Further, challenging students to perform an authentic task and to actively use the Web fit the criteria of meaningful learning. The thrust to have students work together on WebQuests in small groups represents cooperative learning, an instructional methodology that has traditionally been viewed by the special education field as beneficial.

Despite these advantages, there are a number of caveats to using WebQuests with students with mild cognitive disabilities. By design, WebQuests are constructivist in nature. Learning is not presumed to come from a well-informed teacher imparting knowledge, but from the students' own experiences interacting and manipulating knowledge and information to construct their own unique representation of information (Roblyer, 2003a). WebQuests also focus strongly on problem solving and higher-order thinking, which means that some students with mild disabilities may find learning too unstructured and with too little direction. They may not possess

Table 6. Formats of Web-Based Activities

Web Activity	URL/Elaboration Reference	Description
Assembling Resources	www.filamentality.com/ wired/fil/formats.html	Activities that focus on accessing/using a pre-selected set of Web resources from which students can assemble information and resources with reduced effort.
Hotlists	www.filamentality.com/ wired/fil/ formats.html#Hotlist	A Web page or word-processed document that contains an active set of hyperlinks to a themed topic. For example, accessing www.ed.sc.edu/ caw/toolboxsped.html provides a hotlist containing the URLs of many of Table 2's theme: Special education resources on the Web. The intention is to direct students to reliable and valid Web sites to facilitate their development of initial understanding/knowledge of content, thereby reducing the potential for unsystematic searching of, and having to evaluate, Web content.
Scrapbooks	www.filamentality.com/ wired/fil/ formats.html#Scrapbok	A Web page or word-processed document that contains an active set of hyperlinks to Web sites that contain resources, often multimedia based (e.g., pictures/photographs, sounds, videos), but can be themed facts (e.g., links to different quotations about honesty, by famous authors).
Developing Knowledge and Complementing Learning Goals	www.filamentality.com/ wired/fil/formats.html	Goal-oriented, Web-based activities that provide compelling experiences that foster the attitudes, knowledge and skills of students.
Web Hunts	www.filamentality.com/ wired/fil/formats.html#Hunt	A sequence of specific Web pages (i.e., not the home pages of larger Web sites) essential to understanding a topic are hotlisted. Students must link to each page and answer a single question for each page. They are hunting for and discovering specific items of knowledge.
Subject Samplers	www.filamentality.com/ wired/fil/formats.html# Sampler	Students are given a small sample (~6) of Web sites organized around a main topic that provides alternative perspectives. Students are asked to reflect on the sample topic by making comparisons to experiences they have had, or to their personal interpretations of the sampled information. In contrast to a Web hunt, where obtaining the "correct" answer is central in subject samples more important that students perceive they have joined the community of learners surrounding the topic, and that their views on the topic are valued.

(continued next page)

Table 6. Formats of Web-Based Activities (continued)

Web Activity	URL/Elaboration Reference	Description
WebQuests	www.filamentality.com/wired/fil/formats.html#WebQuest	The most elaborate of Web-based activities, WebQuests are designed to promote higher-order thinking and problem solving. Students are posed a challenging task, a real-world scenario, or an authentic problem that may be controversial, disputable, or open to alternative opinions or perspectives. In order to arrive at a solution or conclusion, students must analyze and synthesize information, and often work in cooperative groups, performing alternative tasks in parallel to one another, and/or taking on different roles.

Adapted from: *Activity Formats,* by T. March, 1997, Retrieved July 16, 2003, from *www.kn.pacbell.com/wired/fil/formats.html.* Copyright 2003 by SBC Knowledge Network Explorer.

a sufficient repertoire of prerequisite skills, such as strategies to organize information, monitor their performance and progress, or create a sequence of smaller-scale problems and solutions as a means of reaching a larger conclusion that reflect a synthesis of all the gathered information. Further, at any given segment of a WebQuest, especially with respect to analysis and synthesis, any intellectual, cognitive, or emotional disabilities intrinsic to a student will come into play (see the subsequent section in this chapter on accommodating student learning characteristics for additional discussion on this topic). Therefore, when students with mild disabilities use WebQuests, teachers must consider providing instructional accommodations that restore some of the structure and direction to the learning process that student with mild disabilities often need.

Kelly (2002) noted that it is important to incorporate a variety of instructional supports when using WebQuests, especially in terms of the design of Web pages, readability, and curriculum adaptations to help simplifying directions for students with mild disabilities. According to Kelly, during the design phases of Web pages, teachers should represent knowledge in multiple formats by incorporating principles of universal design (see Center for Applied Special Education Technology's Universal Design for Learning Web pages, www.cast.org/udl/, for further discussion on this topic). They should also design WebQuests with state standards and classroom and IEP objectives in mind. With respect to readability, larger text size should be used, and teachers should write content considering the reading levels of their students. Finally, curriculum adaptations include providing support materials such as separate checklists and planning sheets for each of the section of the WebQuest. In addition to Kelly's recommendations, teachers should consider alternative Web browsers and text-to-speech screen readers (see Wissick, 2003c, for links to examples) that are relevant for students with mild disabilities. TeacherWebQuest (teacherweb.com/TWQuest.htm) offers online tools designed to help teachers create WebQuests without having to know how to program HTML.

Regardless of what model or perspective is used to format learning activities on the Web, the task also involves the traditional challenges of searching for or designing activities related to the content area of study. These types of activities may be found by conducting internal searches for content-related activities within the comprehensive education sites listed in Table 3, and performing searches using descriptors such as "fraction activities" and "Web sites." In addition, teachers can design many content area activities using any one of March or Dodge's Web-based activity formats, such as a hotlist of Web pages illustrating different real-world examples where calculating volume was important (math), or answering multiple-choice questions after performing a Web hunt acquiring information about the Vietnam War (history, and/or reading), or using a

Table 7. The Seven Elements of a Generic WebQuest

WebQuest Elements	Description
Introduction	At the beginning of a WebQuest, a student is linked to a paragraph that introduces the learning activity and/or lesson. This functions to provide an advance organizer and to capture/hook the student's attention and set the stage for the WebQuest task(s). This is also the section that communicates the Big Question (i.e., an essential question or a guiding question) that the whole WebQuest is centered around.
Task	The task section focuses learners on what they are going to do. Specifically, it provides a decisive and clear description of their culminating performance and what products and/or tools that will be involved in the WebQuest learning activities.
Process	The process section outlines the methods and procedures that will be performed to accomplish the task. Student are provided with clearly and concretely worded statements regarding: (a) what steps they will go through to accomplish the task; (b) what information and resources (printed materials/text, web page links/URLs, objects, worksheets/forms, audio visuals, etc.) they will be using, (c) what tools they will use to organize information; and (d) what scaffolding strategies and procedures they can use to organize information.
Evaluation	The evaluation section describes the evaluation criteria that must be achieved to demonstrate students have met performance and content standards. A central component of this section is the provision and use of assessment rubrics. These rubrics should align specific aspects/products of the culminating project and specific student behaviors with the task section of the WebQuest. Additional factors, such as whether individual and/or group efforts will be evaluated, should also be specified.
Conclusions	The conclusion section serves to bring closure and encourages reflection. A summary of what the learners have accomplished or learned is provided. Rhetorical questions or additional links can be included to encourage students to extend their thinking to other content outside the lesson.
Credits & References	This section cites the sources of all images, video, music, text/books, that was used as information in the WebQuest. If any of these are copyrighted, permissions need to be included. Links/URLs used in the process section need not be included. Dodge also respectfully requests that WebQuest Authors include a link to the WebQuest Page (webquest.sdsu.edu) and Design Patterns page (webquest.sdsu.edu/designpatterns). This allows newcomers access the most up to date information, template, and training materials.
Teacher Page	The teacher page section includes information to help other teachers implement the WebQuest. Information should include: a brief description of the target learner (e.g., 4th grade students with mild disabilities), the standards on which the WebQuest is based (e.g., district/state standards X, Y, & Z), notes for teaching the unit (e.g., a lesson plan) and, when appropriate, examples of student work.

Adapted from: *WebQuest*, by B. Dodge, 2004, Retrieved March 2, 2004, from *webquest.sdsu.edu/designpatterns/GENERIC/webquest.htm.*

Table 8. WebQuest ToolBox Introduction

WebQuests represent "… an inquiry-oriented activity in which some or all of the information that learners interact with comes from resources on the Internet" (Dodge, 1997). Use these links to learn more about Dodge's conceptualization of WebQuests (most of these links are accessible through the WebQuest Site *(webquest.sdsu.edu).* Begin with Link 1 as an overview and visit the remaining links (2-5) to develop a more in-depth understanding of the fundamental components of a WebQuest. At your convenience, use the resources and links at the end to acquire additional information about WebQuests.

Title/Focus Background	URL	Description Follow -5 to Learn about WebQuests
1. Some Thoughts About Web Quests	edweb.sdsu.edu/courses/ edtec596/ about_webquests.html	Begin by reading this to develop a sense of what a WebQuest is, and what the conceptual goals of a WebQuest are.
2. Building Blocks of a WebQuest (circa 1996).	projects.edtech.sandi.net/ staffdev/buildingblocks/p-index.htm	In Dodge's early model, WebQuests often consisted of six fundamental components.
3. Components of a more contemp-orary (circa 2004) WebQuest.	webquest.sdsu.edu/ designpatterns/GENERIC/ webquest.htm	Dodge is continuously developing/ expanding the conceptualization and components of a WebQuest. This version (March 2004) of the generic model has seven components. Excellent elaboration of component definitions.
4. The WebQuest Design Process	webquest.sdsu.edu/ designsteps/index.html	Lists the steps necessary to design a WebQuest with links to resources that embellish each step.
5. WebQuest Design Patterns	webquest.sdsu.edu/ designpatterns/all.htm	Variations in the design of WebQuests to account for content and instruction.
6. The Main Points of WebQuests	webquest.sdsu.edu/ necc98.htm	This handout developed by Dodge provides a summary of the main points of the readings you have completed on WebQuests.
Additional Resources		**Use These Resources to Acquire Additional Information About WebQuests**
The WebQuest Home Page	webquest.sdsu.edu/	This is the gateway to Dodge's compilation of information on WebQuests.
WebQuests and More	www.ozline.com/learning/	This is the gateway to March's compilation of information concerning WebQuests.
WebQuest Readings and Training Materials	webquest.sdsu.edu/ materials.htm	Use these links to acquire additional knowledge and skills to develop WebQuests.
Articles on WebQuests	www.webquestdirect.com.au/ whatis_articles1.asp teacherweb.com/	WebQuest Direct provides a searchable database of WebQuests.
The Teacher WebQuest Page	TWQuest.htm	This online tool/site helps teachers create WebQuests without needing to know HTML.

(continued next page)

Table 8. WebQuest ToolBox Introduction (continued)

Title/Focus Background	URL	Description Follow -5 to Learn about WebQuests
Search for WebQuests at the WebQuest Portal	www.webquest.org/ search/webquestquery2. php	Search Dodge's WebQuest site.
Search for WebQuests on Google.com.	google.com	Simply type in "WebQuest" and you will be presented with numerous web sites that have collected and organized links to WebQuests by topics, standards, etc.
Web Wizard Worksheet	wizard.hprtec.org	Use the Web Wizard Worksheet to create a WebQuest without needing to know HTML.

spreadsheet to adjust data obtained within a WebQuest, and having a pair of students give an oral report on the potential changes in pollution levels in the Hudson River if certain amounts of pollutants are curtailed (social studies, math, science).

There are times when a learning task is so broad that the learning activity(ies) cannot be boiled down or deconstructed into one or two unifying web-based activity formats. Table 9 provides an excellent illustration of how multiple features of the Web can be creatively applied to support student learning with the writing process (Smith, Boone, & Higgins, 1998). Table 10 illustrates how the Web supports interdisciplinary instruction by supporting reading, writing, science, and math-based activities associated with a thematic unit entitled "Simple Machines."

Finally, according to Harris (1998a, 1998b), teachers can assign certain types of short-duration projects that make use of Web/Internet-based activities, where students "telecollaborate" with one another to achieve learning outcomes tied to the curriculum. Harris organized these activity structures around three categories/classes of student actions: *interpersonal exchanges, information collection and analysis*, and *problem solving*. Table 11 presents these categories/classes and their associated Web/Internet-based activity structures. Additional elaboration and specific example of web

sites and URLs that correspond to each activity structures may be found in Harris (1998b).

Support, Accommodation, and Scaffolding Strategies and Tools

In this section we will examine a strategies and Web-based tools that are particularly helpful in providing supports, accommodations, and scaffolding strategies that might naturally accompany instruction delivered through these formats/structures. These strategies will vary with the content area being studied, the nature of the task and its context, and students' strengths and weaknesses. Learning scaffolds have been applied to technology and Web-based applications in the form of using technology and the Web to move students from one level of understanding to one that is more developed, and/or to provide support in areas where students still need assistance so that they can focus on successfully developing or performing other related tasks independently (Grabe & Grabe, 2000; Roblyer, 2003a).

The multimedia/hypermedia environment of the Web offers scaffolds serendipitously. That is the ability to see a name, place, or concept underlined and in bold on a Web page, and to click it as a link to additional forms of embellishment (e.g., pictures/figures, sounds, video, additional information) is a scaffold/support in and of itself. However, this very same feature can often

Table 9. The Internet-Expanded Writing Process

Writing Process Phases	Typical Writing Activities	Internet/Web-Based Activities
Prewriting	• Brainstorming • Outlining • Clustering • Collecting information	• Keyword searches • Browsing • Downloading information
Writing	• Series of drafts	
Revision	• Peer responses • Teacher responses • Editing • Revision	• Email drafts to other students for responses/feedback • Email drafts to experts for responses/feedback
Traditional (Print) Publishing	• Final drafts • Bound in a book • Can be read by others in class • Parents can read it	
Revision for Publishing on the Web		• Final draft reviewed for possible hyperlinks to other WWW sites • Additional searches made for possible links • Story is pasted into a WWW creation program (such as project poster at poster.hprtec.org/) • Hypertext links added
WWW Publishing		• Story file is transferred to a classroom WWW site on a networked computer • URL address is established • The story WWW page is registered with search page, *Yahooligans!*, for international access • The student author's uncle in Katmandu can read it online

From: "Expanding the Writing Process to the Web, " by S. Smith, R. Boone, & K. Higgins, 1998, *Teaching Exceptional Children, 30*(5), 22-26. Copyright 1998 by Council for Exceptional Children. Adapted by permission.

create confusion for students with mild disabilities as they navigate within and between Web sites and attempt to prioritize facts and information when their searches yield an overload of hits (Gardner & Wissick, 2002; Goldstein, 1998).

Instruction is a series of sequenced events that often involve different varieties of learning interacting with different learning characteristics and modalities (Gagné, 1985). Therefore, educators must have available a variety of strategies and technology tools to provide varying degree of support and learning scaffolds. For students with mild disabilities who are learning on the Web, the first strategy is to obtain proficiency in html and Web design, and apply this knowledge to create self-contained instructional activities on the web. Dodge (2003a) and March's (2003) conceptualization of WebQuests clearly depends on teachers' abilities to organize content and the sequence/events of the learning/instructional process, and to use hypermedia to navigate within (e.g., to different sections, to worksheets or supplemental print outs, to more detailed author written instructions/content/information) or outside (e.g., to Web sites, and Web pages, and other forms of media) the WebQuest. Coupled with additional teacher-created supports, such as worksheets, check sheets, journaling,

Table 10. Web Sites and Activities Across the Curriculum That Support a Thematic Unit on Simple Machines

Content/Skill	Website/URL	Web-Based Activity
Reading	How Stuff Works www.howstuffworks.com/	Students complete a search for a simple machine they use at home or school. They read the information on how it works and explain it to the class.
Writing	Inventors Workshop www.mos.org/sln/ LeonardoInventors Workshop.html	Students view a number of Leonardo's inventions and see if they can guess how they were to be used. Students create and/or illustrate stories about their own inventions. Students must explain how their invention is based on one of the simple machines.
Science	EdHeads Simple Machines www.edheads.org/activities/ simple-machines/index.htm	Students enter the house and identify the simple machines in one room. Students create a list of simple machines in their own house. Students play a game to identify the machines in each room and the type of simple machine. Students can print their results.
Math	EdHeads Simple Machines Glossary www.edheads.org/activities/ simple-machines/sm-glossary.htm	With the results from EdHeads game, students can track their progress in learning. Using a spreadsheet, students can count how many times they correctly identify each machine. Students can then calculate total correct identifications and percentages for each room, and simple machine totals. Combining individual scores students can calculate mean, median, and mode. This information can provide feedback for students on which simple machine they need to review using the glossary.
Social Studies	Simple Machines www.school-for-champions.com/ science/machines.htm	Students learn how the Ancient Egyptians and Romans used simple machines. Students can then devise their own catapult.

cooperative groupings, and so on, the WebQuest model offers teachers the greatest degree of control in terms of designing a self-contained instructional package that contains specific instructional scaffolds

One of the greatest challenges in designing WebQuests is whether or not the teacher possess the necessary html and web design skills, and whether or not the teacher has sufficient time to create the WebQuest. Although it is not extremely difficult to learn how to make a Web page and WebQuests are not all that complex to develop, it is unlikely that most special educators are html/web design proficient and/or in touch with sufficient resources or opportunities to be frequently publishing to the Web. Teachers can use a variety of alternative tools that do not require expertise in html/web

design, but can still provide a dramatic degree of instructional support. For example, online tools such as TeacherWebQuest (teacherweb.com/TWQuest.htm) help teachers plug in content to create a WebQuest.

The second strategy for providing Web-based accommodation/scaffolding involves taking advantage of a number of online tools that are designed specifically to organize Web-based information for the purpose of systematizing learning across multiple Web sites. These sites help student stay focused on content contained in specified Web sites germane to the learning activities, navigate between different Web sites without getting lost, and provide annotations and prompts. Equally important, these tools do not require that teachers are able to design a Web page or program in

Table 11. Examples of Harris' (1998a) Web/Internet-based Activity Structures

Activity Structure	Definition/Example
Interpersonal Exchanges	**Individuals or groups "talk" electronically with one another using electronic mail (email), asynchronous large-group discussions tools (such as Web conferences, bulletin boards, and newsgroups), or real-time text or audio and videoconference tools (Harris, 1998a, p. 7).**
• KeyPals	Students are paired with one another and use email to communicate regarding discussion topics. They are electronic penpals.
• Global Classrooms	Two classrooms in different locations work together to study a common topic A specific time frame is established, and students communicate and contribute information to each other.
• Electronic Appearances	A special guest, such as a subject-matter expert, communicates electronically with students for a one-time visit.
• Telementoring	A subject-matter expert or specialist in a particular occupation communicates in a more extensive and regular basis with students.
• Question-and-answer activities	Students contact a subject-matter expert or specialist to ask a question or two. Best when seeking information that cannot be found despite reasonable efforts, or additional information is needed to better understand information already found online.
• Impersonations	One or more members of the online group communicating with students, impersonate an individual associated with the topic of study. For example, for a unit on the Mississippi river circa 1870, students ask questions of a historian impersonating Mark Twain.
Information Collection and Analysis	**Student use the Web and its resources to collect, compile, and compare different types of information.**
• Information Exchanges	Students from any number of classes around the country or world exchange information related to common curriculum topics.
• Database Creation	Web-based information is collected and organized for study and analysis. Student collaborate to contribute information to online database, or gather information from the Web for the purpose of contributing to off-line databases used in curriculum-related activities.
• Electronic Publishing	Following data collection, students analyze the information thought the process of summarizing and writing a document (e.g., graphic, poem, essay, short story). This document is submitted for electronic publication to a student-oriented Web site or online publication.
• Telefieldtrips	Students in one location take an actual fieldtrip and share their information and experiences with another group of student electronically by variation students serve as online participants with adults who are researching a topic or historical site, with students taking on an active role with the researchers.
• Pooled Data Analysis	Pooled data analysis involves students at different locations combining comparable data from different locations and analyzing the data to discover patterns and similarities, and pose conclusions to more complex and interesting conclusions.

(continued next page)

Table 11. Examples of Harris' (1998a) Web/Internet-based Activity Structures (continued)

Activity Structure	Definition/Example
Problem Solving	**Students use the Web and its resources to support problem-based learning.**
• Information Searches	Students and/or teams are given clues and compete over an extended period of time (e.g., one or two weeks) by using the Web and/or traditional resources to answer questions. The questions require extensive and sophisticated research by, and communication among and between, students.
• Peer Feedback Activities	Students use the Web and/or email to disseminate ideas and expressions for the purpose of obtaining constructive responses and feedback from peers. Professionals may participate as telementors.
• Parallel Problem solving	Students at several different locations independently explore a problem. Subsequently they come together online to compare, contrast, and discuss their unique problem-solving methods.
• Sequential Creations	Students use the Web or email to collaborate in the creation of a product. This collaboration is sequential (e.g., Student A sends to Student B, who send to Student C). Thus the final product reflects a commonly owned but progressively fashioned product.
• Telepresent Problem solving	Students from different time zone or geographic locations come together asynchronously or in real time to contribute to problem-solving activities. They participate in a virtual meeting, where each participant may also be independently and simultaneously engaged in a similar task at different project sites.
• Simulations	Students solve problems in a simulated online experience. Students assume different roles and responsibilities and must problem solve as if they were doing these things in real life. Examples include trading stocks, or serving as delegates to forums like the United Nations.
• Social Action Projects	Students collaborate via the Web, email, or other electronic forms to solve an authentic global challenge. Telementors may be involved. Projects focus on solving social problems that have beneficial social, environmental, humanitarian and/or multicultural outcomes. Students go beyond simply learning about a problem by having the opportunity to take action(s) and observe the consequence of these actions.

HTML. Two sites that are particularly useful in this respect are free online tools called TrackStar (trackstar.4teachers.org/), Web Worksheet Wizard (wizard.hprtec.org/). To obtain a more robust understanding of these sites, it is highly recommended that you go online and review the capabilities of each tool.

The third strategy for providing accommodations and scaffolding Web-based learning is to incorporate indirect but sometimes equally valuable supports for guided or independent practice during or after the formal parts of instruction have taken pace. Although Web-based content and/or activities are considered integral to the instructional process, all of the supports and scaffolds do not have to be Web or technology-based. As reported by numerous sources in the areas of instruction, special needs, and technology (e.g., Gardner & Edyburn, 2000; Male, 2003; Okolo, 2000), teachers can employ a variety of external supports (worksheets, checklists, journaling, cooperative groupings, etc.) to accompany and complement computer and Web-based learning. Therefore, implicit within Web-based instruction is the concept that, when needed, teachers will provide students with the necessary social and "off-line" permanent products to increase the likelihood of success. According to Gardner and Wissick (2002), these can take the form of:

- Providing a worksheet or supplemental "how-to" handout that provides prompts, cues, or more elaborated directions regarding tasks to be performed at/with a particular Web site.

- Identifying activities that can involve students working together cooperatively to share information and reciprocally support each other during Web-based learning.

- Identifying specific learning strategies that students can be pretaught and/or prompted to apply at specific stages during Web-based learning.

- Predicting which students will find a particular Web site's content or activities difficult to process and providing increased teacher presence/feedback accordingly.

- Predicting when and where students might be lured into an online game or alternative activities not related to the task at hand and providing increased teacher presence to redirect them back on task.

- Making use of Web sites that provide teachers with free tools to create online versions of traditional learning support and activities, such as age- and content-level puzzles (e.g., online word search, crossword, and math square puzzles), vocabulary word glossaries, custom online quizzes (e.g., multiple choice, true/false, short-answer or essay questions), events calendars, and worksheets (e.g., lists of spelling/vocabulary words, step-by-step instructions on how to complete an activity/assignment, links to pictures/images, hotlists, and class announcements or newsletters).

Table 12 provides a list of online tools to help scaffold/support Web-based learning and online activities.

The fourth strategy is to provide support of Web tasks frequently performed by students through the use of simple but typical tools that require little effort on the part of the teacher to develop. These include:

- Bookmarking or creating a hotlist or Web toolbox of Web sites ahead to time that are used in forthcoming activities.

- Adding frequently used Web sites or search engines to the Toolbar (*Explorer*), Bookmark Bar (*Safari*), Bookmarks Personal Bar (*Opera*), or Personal Toolbar (*Netscape*) areas of browsers.

- Preparing a help sheet containing text-based directions and/or text with screen shots containing step-by-step instructions to perform common tasks, such as using particular search engines, how to create a bookmark/favorites folder of themed topics and so on.

Putting It All Together: Integrating Web Resources and Instruction

As we have seen, special educators have access to multiple Web-based tools and resources that can be used to meet a variety of responsibilities, in terms of both their personal/administrative obligations (e.g., knowledge of special education law, information to give to parents) and their instructional responsibilities (i.e., designing and delivering instruction to promote student learning). Gardner and Wissick (2002) described how knowledge of Web resources and Web-based instructional considerations can be synthesized and integrated to provide support for the design and delivery of thematic unit-based learning. Specifically, they identified 10 steps related to the design of thematic units and illustrated how the various steps may be supported by Web-based resources. The steps listed in Table 13 have been modified to include information cited in other areas of this chapter.

Table 12. Online Tools to Help Scaffold/Support Web-Based Learning and Online Activities for Students with Mild Disabilities

Title	URL Address	Notations
Discovery School Custom Classroom	school.discovery.com/teachingtools/teachingtools.html	Creating printable puzzles, glossary, and worksheets. Includes glossary builder and links to pictures.
e-Class	www.edgate.comeclass.html	Creating online courses, assigning homework, managing student grades, having discussions with students, and coordinating chat sessions
FunBrain Quiz Lab	www.quizlab.com	Integrating games and quizzes into lessons. Access to quizzes in eight subjects and ability to create quizzes with an easy-to-use authoring tool. Quiz results are graded automatically with scores emailed to the teacher.
Lesson Plan Builder	www.alfy.com/teachers/teach/lesson_builder/index.asp	Lessons considered for publication on the lesson plan page. Lessons can contain links to related Web sites. A handy tool to guide lesson planning.
Quia	www.quia.com	Tools to create learning activities, including a directory of thousands of online games and quizzes, templates for creating 13 different types of online games, including flashcards, matching, concentration, word search, Hangman, Challenge Board, quiz administration and reporting tools and teacher home pages.
QuizStar	quiz.4teachers.org/	A Web-based utility to create a custom quiz that others can take online.
RubiStar	rubistar.4teachers.org/	A Web-based utility to create custom rubrics for a variety of skills.
SchoolNotes	www.schoolnotes.com	Copernicus Education Gateway: Creating notes for homework and class information and posting them on the Web. Can also create flashcards for students to practice online.
Teacher Time Savers	www.teachertimesavers.com/	Commercial site selling thematic units developed by teachers. Teachers can submit and be paid for materials they have developed.
Teacher Web	www.teacherweb.com/	How-to create an online bulletin board to post class announcements, class calendar, and homework. Features tool for creating a WebQuest. Small fee involved for use.
TrackStar	trackstar.4teachers.org	TrackStar, a tool to create guided or scaffolded Web-based lessons.
Tramline Tours, Inc.	www.tramline.com/	Virtual field trips and a blackboard with resources for teachers.

(continued next page)

Table 12. Online Tools to Help Scaffold/Support Web-Based Learning and Online Activities for Students with Mild Disabilities (continued)

Title	URL Address	Notations
Web Worksheet Wizard	wizard.hprtec.org	A Web-based utility allowing you to create a lesson, worksheet, link to a TrackStar, quiz, or class page.
Web Toolbox	www.ed.sc.edu/caw toolboxhowto.html	Directions to create a MS Word-Based toolbox in order to organize and maintain links using your word processor.

From: Wissick, C. A. (2003a). *Web toolbox for educators: Create your own."* Retrieved August 16, 2003, from www.ed.sc.edu/caw/toolboxcreateyourown.html. Copyright 2003 by University of South Carolina. Adapted by permission.

Promoting Automaticity and Fluency with Interactivity

There are times when special education students need more direct instruction to rehearse and develop specific skills. A variety of students with mild disabilities are not particularly fluent when it comes to performing basic skills that underlie more complex math and reading activities. For some students it is important that they have or gain automaticity (sometimes characterized as the ability to perform a mental task with little effort and in a timely manner) in basic skills (e.g., math facts, phonemic awareness, decoding words, and spelling) or having sufficient declarative knowledge that can be easily retrieved (e.g., basic facts or relationships or understanding scientific terms or definitions) so that the mind is able to focus on processing the more complex and often multiple steps associated with higher-order thinking (e.g., math problem solving, reading for comprehension, writing for elaboration and story construction, and analysis/synthesis). A variety of Web sites offer activities that allow students with mild disabilities to practice and/or develop skills to become more automatic through online simulations, educational games, and skills practice. In all of these cases, the key to identifying and selecting activities is the degree of their interactivity.

Despite the plethora of educational Web sites, special educators face a challenge when attempting to locate sites that offer practice and improvement activities. According to Wissick (2000), traditional external search engines, such as Ask Jeeves, are not particularly effective in locating reliable activities when statements that one would intuitively think relevant such as "drill and practice programs for math facts" or "multiplication games" or word games" are used. Further, certain engines such as Google.com may reveal such a vast number of hits extensive effort will be required determine if they are relevant (e.g., some sites advertise multiplication games or are teaser sites that illustrate more elaborate software for purchase).

Wissick (2000) suggested that a more effective strategy begins by identifying a Web site that is known to include meaningful activities, interactive content, or links to other interactive sites. Often these are sites that employ titles with obvious education-related themes (such as those presented in Table 3), such as Ameritech Schoolhouse or EducationWorld.com, or represent a subject matter area, such as math, science, or language arts. Once you are inside, you use the site's internal search engine to query its database.

An alternative to searching within comprehensive or subject-matter education sites, is to adopt the pragmatic approach used by Wissick (2000, 2004a, 2004b), which is to maintain a Web toolbox that contains a collection of links to interactive activities organized by traditional academic content areas and grouped by elementary vs. secondary categories. Web toolboxes can be developed as charts for quick links to content-related activities.

Table 13. Steps and Considerations When Designing and Enhancing Thematic Units Using Web-Based Resources

Step	Strategy	Description/Examples
1	Identify a topic that thematically acknowledges the focus of the unit.	Select a topic or theme that clearly sets students' anticipation for learning. Topics should be reflective of the students' age and developmental level. For example, a thematic unit for third grade students could be: *Harriet Tubman and the Journey to Freedom*.
2	Identify and select goals, objectives, and standards for the unit.	Consider establishing goals that support blending and synthesizing cross-curriculum content and promote higher-order thinking skills. Technology-enhanced thematic units should involve students in activities that result in multiple learning outcomes in different content areas, and be tied to national, state, and local standards, as illustrated below. *Goals tied to technology*: Students will use technology tools to enhance learning, increase productivity, and promote creativity. *Goals tied to language arts standards*: (a) Students will present brief presentations, demonstrations, and oral reports to inform; (b) students will record information from print, Web-based, and non-print resources, and present findings in oral and written reports and other products; (c) students will plan and conduct investigations using available technology and present findings in written and oral forms. *Goals tied to social studies standards*: (a) Students will demonstrate an understanding of the way individuals, families and communities live and work together now and in the past; (b) students will compare and contrast the lives of European, African and Native American families in colonial times. *Examples of Web-based standards to consult*: (a) McREL's (2003) National Content Standards and Benchmarks (*www.mcrel.org/standards-benchmarks*); (b) The National Technology Standards for Students (ISTE, 2000) (*cnets.iste.org/students/*), (c) state standards, such as the Oklahoma Priority Academic Student Skills (PASS) (*www.sde.state.ok.us/home/ home01_test.html?http://sde.state.ok.us/publ/pass.html*).
3	Identify and collect a practical set of Web resources.	Assemble a group of informative and interactive Web sites that will anchor the instructional activities of the unit. Access Web sites specifically tailored to the educational content targeted. See Tables 3 and 4 in this chapter. Consult Wissick's (2004) Web Toolboxes (*www.ed.sc.edu/caw/ toolbox.html*). See Step 7 below for examples of specific sites identified and selected as the result of Step 3.
4	Consider how you want to format the learning activities.	Evaluate the range, variation, and interactivity of identified Web resources. Apply Web-based activity formats and resources when and where appropriate. Consult March's (1996) Filamentality Web site (*www.kn.pacbell.com/ wired/fil/formats.html*); and Harris' (2003) Virtual Architecture web site (*virtual-architecture.wm.edu/Foundation/index.html*).
5	Identify and collect additional resources to support content and activities.	Consider technology-enhanced units from a broadened perspective that includes essential software and productivity tools. Guest presenters, books, physical fieldtrips, and additional audiovisual materials such as videotapes should also be considered.

(continued next page)

recommended that teachers consider the cognitive strengths and weakness of their students and how each student's learning abilities interact with specific characteristics of multimedia as they select programs and activities. Some students may never be able to use the Web without a peer tutor or guide to help them focus on the activity at hand. Other students may simply need specific interventions or accommodations to successfully use the Web independently. Table 14 identifies some common learning patterns exhibited by students with mild disabilities, relates them to the Web, and matches them with intervention and accommodation strategies.

Another factor to consider when planning Web-based learning for students with mild disabilities is cognitive load. According to Sweller, van Merrienboer, and Paas (1998), cognitive load represents "the load that performing a particular task imposes on the cognitive system. It can be conceptualized as a task-based dimension (i.e., mental load) and a learner-based dimension (i.e., mental effort), both of which affect performance " (p. 265). Factors that influence how or when a person experiences cognitive load vary depending on his/her cognitive abilities, the complexity of the task, and the presence of environmental distracters (Kirschner, 2002). Web-based learning by its current nature consists of multimedia-based learning. Mayer and Moreno (2002, 2003) posited three assumptions the way the mind works during multimedia learning that apply to cognitive load: (a) we simultaneously process information through two separate channels, one for verbal/auditory information and the other for visual information; (b) learning involves substantial cognitive processing of information received via these two channels; and (c) individuals have a limited amount of working memory capacity available to actively process information received through either of these channels (p. 25). According to Mayer and Moreno (2003), when we experience a multimedia learning task that exceeds our cognitive system's capacity, we experience cognitive overload and are no longer able to effectively learn/process information.

Considering that many individuals with mild disabilities have attention and/or memory problems that influence short-term memory processing (Stanovich, 1986; Swanson & Cooney, 1996), it is easy to conclude that those individuals are at risk of experiencing cognitive overload during Web-based learning. Table 15 identifies some of Mayer and Moreno's (2003) factors that contribute to cognitive overload, which appear more readily under teacher control. Examples of strategies and solutions to reduce cognitive load during Web-based learning for students with mild disabilities are provided.

For student with mild disabilities, our attention should always be directed at understanding and accommodating the ways in which students' intrinsic difficulties in one or more basic cognitive and/or intellectual processes are will manifest themselves during web-related learning. Tables 14 and 15 illustrate this point.

In addition, educators must look beyond the existence of "basic" student attributes, and consider more complex ones that influence Web-based learning for student with mild disabilities. For example, Hartley and Bendixen (2001) contended that Web-based learning, by virtue of being hypermedia-based (e.g., links to information, that in turn may provide links to additional information, and so on), has created an information and learning environment that is different from traditional learning contexts. That is with the Web comes more and rapid access to information – both quantity and quality – than ever before. Learners now have to make particularly important decisions regarding what information to use and what not to use. Web-based learning has therefore become far more *discretionary*. In addition, learners are being exposed to models of learning that presume they already possess self-regulation skills (i.e., their ability to self-monitor and apply cognitive learning skills when deemed appropriate), increased cognitive flexibility to process information (i.e., their ability to process multiple perspectives and representations of knowledge, typically provided on the web though the use of multimedia and interactivity), and increased capacities for higher-order thinking skills (i.e., students are prepared and able to analyze and synthesize

Table 14. Intervention and Accommodation Strategies That Match the Learning Patterns of Students with Mild Disabilities Related to the Web

Student Learning Patterns Related to the Web	Intervention and Accommodation Strategies
Students have memory and attention difficulties; learning patterns are not consistent.	Provide advance organizers and activate prior knowledge before students access the Web.
Students do not take advantage of tutorials or other help features provided to increase learner control.	Choose Web sites that provide easy access to tutorials, references links, or help features. Review options for assistance and encourage use of those help features.
Students are impulsive in their navigation, clicking on any icon that catches their attention.	Provide students with lesson objectives before using the Web. Provide the context for exploration or allow students to state their own objectives for the exploration. Structure the activity using tools that allow you to build in scaffolds such as TrackStar or Xcursions.
Students use their cognitive processes to focus on the options for navigation such as the highlighted links and words instead of the content.	Provide concrete models for navigation that can be attached or placed near the computer. Challenge students to draw a map or diagram of the various paths in the program.
Students are not able to understand the visual metaphors used for navigation.	Review and discuss organization first, provide additional examples related to the navigation metaphor.
Students have problems forming relationships and seeing patterns between Web pages or between class instruction and the Web.	Provide closure activities to discuss patterns and relationships noticed by the students. Have students keep electronic journals of their observations.
Students do not have the metacognitive skills to be aware of what is needed to navigate a Web site.	Present options to students and have them suggest the best approach for their work. Have students review different aspects of the Web site and decide what assists their learning.
Students are passive learners, allowing others to tell them where to move and click.	Seek out Web sites that are engaging and focus on student interests as well as the curriculum objectives. Provide instructional scaffolds and direct activities to maintain involvement. Locate sites that provide experiments or animation to demonstrate concepts

information and arrive at conclusions by creating "new" representations of knowledge).

With the dramatically expanding prevalence of Web-based applications in classrooms, Hartley and Bendixen (2001) are concerned that for learners who traditionally have difficulties with self-regulation, cognitive flexibility, higher-order thinking, and demonstrate maladaptive perspectives concerning what knowledge should be known – such as students with mild disabilities – web-based learning may cause new challenges and roadblocks to learning.

Briefly, Hartley and Bendixen caution that providing access to information on the Web is not automatically advantageous for all students. For example, when using the open-ended environment of the Web, students, including

Table 15. Ways to Reduce Cognitive Load During Web-Based Learning for Students with Mild Disabilities That Are Directly Under Teacher Control

Mayer and Moreno's (2003) Cognitive Load Issues/Problems Applied to Web-Based Learning	Solution/Strategy for Web-Based Learning
Reducing the cognitive load placed on the student to process information visually. The cognitive processing demands of Web-based learning require students to attend primarily to text, plus pictures and/or animation on the Web. This sometimes creates too much information for the student to process at the same time and creates overload.	*Off-loading.* Move some of the essential visually processed information (e.g., text) to an auditory channel (e.g., audio). Information transfer can be more effective, and cognitive load can be reduced, when there is narration versus reading from on-screen text (Mayer and Moreno, 2003, p. 46). Possible solutions include -Using a screen reader -Pairing a student with a peer who reads screen information out loud
Reducing the cognitive load placed on the student to simultaneously process information visually and verbally. The cognitive processing demands of Web-based learning often require processing of visual and verbal information simultaneously (i.e., off-loading is not available as a solution). This can increase the cognitive load if a student has difficulty selectively controlling which information source to focus on.	*Segmenting.* Segment learning into smaller steps or chunks to allow students more time and/or control to process information at their own rate. Multichannel information (e.g., test, pictures, and/or animation) is more effectively processed when the student can focus on one chunk at a time (Mayer & Moreno, 2003, p. 47). Possible solutions include: - Allowing extended time between segments - Task analyzing/segmenting a Web-based activity into smaller steps and providing written check-sheets and other written support materials - Using scaffolding tools like TrackStar *(trackstar.4teachers.org)* *Pre-training.* Pre-train students to be familiar/experienced in central visual characteristics (Mayer & Moreno, 2003, p. 47) For example understand the layout of where/how information/links are represented, how to use a site's specific features, or where/how to enter information in Web sites or on Web page components. Possible solutions include: - Teaching students how to navigate and use specific features of specific Web sites as a prerequisite skill prior to any content-related learning activities using the site
Reducing the cognitive load placed on the student by extraneous or irrelevant information. Web pages often contain multiple sources of information (pictures, narrations, sounds/music) that is incidental/supplementary to the learning task at hand. This information may be interesting (such as pictures of Hawaiian flowers imbedded around text describing the history of Hawaii, or Hawaiian music/singing playing in the background) but not directly related and/or irrelevant to the focus of a particular task (e.g., learning about Hawaiian history). It becomes distracting.	*Weeding.* Eliminating interesting but incidental/extraneous information (Mayer & Moreno, 2003, p. 48). Possible solutions include - "Turning off" picture loading in the Web browser - "Turning off" background sounds, narration - "Turning off" frames - If a video is being played with narration that is technically essential but too embellishing, turning off sound and providing a more concise version. *Signaling.* Provide advance cues to help the learner to (a) identify what information should be selected over other information, and (b) organize the information as it is being gathered (Mayer & Moreno, 2003, p. 48). Possible solutions include - Using checklists/question & answer sheets - Providing prompts/cues using scaffolding tools like *TrackStar (trackstar.4teachers.org).*

those with mild cognitive disabilities, who believe that only knowing facts matters and/or that effort has little affect on learning, may not make much use of the Web's multiple and interactive links to sources of information. They may be less flexible, ill prepared to process large amounts of information, or indifferent to the sense of empowerment derived from gathering discretionary information. Moreover, if students possess knowledge of cognitive strategies that may be helpful during Web-based learning but are unable to monitor their learning so as to elicit or apply these strategies when needed, their lack of self-regulation skills will contribute to less effective Web-based learning.

For these reasons, aggressively touting the Web as an open-ended environment in special education that promotes higher-order thinking though online research projects, knowledge gathering, critical thinking, and authentic problem solving may be putting the cart before the horse. To quote Hartley and Bendixen (2001), "It might be more reasonable to argue that rather than *fostering* these skills, some uses of the Web for learning *require* these skills" (p. 24). Thus, despite all the benefits ascribed to the Web with respect to authentic, meaningful learning, problem solving, and construction of knowledge, if they are presented with Web-based learning tasks that require prior knowledge and the performance of skills that are *not* in students' cognitive repertoire, they will not succeed without some form of external supports provided by teachers or peers.

Final Thoughts

Numerous Web-based resources and instructional strategies are available to special education teachers for use with students with mild cognitive disabilities. Further, Web sites exist that provide both special education information and information pertaining to Web-related instructional practices that work for all students, not just those with mild disabilities. As a matter of practice, special educators should always consider ways to make Web-based learning more authentic and meaningful for students, and be prepared to apply a variety of Web-based tools and/or Web-related teaching strategies and support to enhance learning.

Integrating the capabilities of the web into special education does not an automatically guarantee that students will learn more information or learn more effectively. In the spirit of the special education model and in recognition of individual differences, the integration of Web-based learning into the curriculum should always include considerations that address the unique learning characteristics that all students, and especially those with mild cognitive disabilities, demonstrate.

References

Ackerman, E., & Hartman, K. (2000). *Searching and researching on the Internet and the world wide web*. Wilsonville, OR: Franklin, Beedle, & Associates.

American Library Association and Association for Educational Communications and Technology. (1998). *Information power: Building partnerships for learning*. Chicago, Il: Author.

American Library Association. (2003). ALA/The Nine Information Literacy Standards for Student Learning. Retrieved February 12, 2004, from: www.ala.org/aasl/ip_none.html.

Bakken, J.P., & Aloia, G.F. (1998). Evaluating the world wide web. *Teaching Exceptional Children, 30*(5), 48-53.

Bloom, B.S., Englehart, M.B., Furst, E.J., Hill, W.H., & Krathwohl, D.R. (1956). *Taxonomy of educational objectives. The classification of educational goals. Handbook I: Cognitive domain*. New York: Longmans Green.

Bull, G., Bull, G., Dawson, K., & Mason, C. (2001). Evaluating and using web-based resources. *Learning and Leading with Technology, 28*(7), 50-55.

Center for Applied Special Techology (2003). *Universal design for learning*. Retrieved August 16, 2003, from www.cast.org/udl/.

Descy, D. (1996). Evaluating internet resources. *TechTrends, 41*(4), 3-5.

Dodge, B. (1997). *Some thoughts about WebQuests*. Retrieved February 17, 2003, from: edweb.sdsu.edu/courses/edtec596/about_webquests.html.

Dodge, B. (2003a). *The WebQuest page*. Retrieved September 14, 2003, from: webquest.sdsu.edu/.

Dodge, B. (2004). *WebQuest*. March 2, 2004, from: webquest.sdsu.edu/design patterns/GENERIC/webquest.htm.

Edyburn, D.L. (2002). 99 essential web sites for special educators. *Special Education Technology Practice, 4*(3), 37-41.

Eisenberg, M. (2003). *The big 6 skills overview*. Retrieved November 30, 2003, from www.big6.com/showarticle.php?id=16.

Felt, E.C., & Symans, S.C. (2000). Teaching students to use the internet as a research tool. *Learning and Leading with Technology, 27*(6), 14-17.

Gagné, R. M. (1985). *The conditions of learning* (4th ed.). New York: Holt, Rinehart, and Winston.

Gagné, R. M., Briggs, L. J., & Wager, W. W. (1992). *Principles of instructional design* (4th ed.). Fort Worth, TX: Harcourt, Brace, & Jovanovich.

Gardner, J. E., & Edyburn, D. L. (2000). Integrating Technology to support effective instruction. In J.D. Lindsey (Ed.), *Technology and Exceptional Individuals* (pp. 191-240). Austin, TX: Pro-Ed.

Gardner, J.E., & Wissick, C.A. (2002). Enhancing thematic units using the world wide web: Tools and strategies for students with mild disabilities. *Journal of Special Education Technology, 17*(1), 27-38.

Goldstein, C. (1998). Learning at cybercamp. *Teaching Exceptional Children, 30*(5), 17-21.

Grabe, M., & Grabe, C. (2000). *Integrating technology for meaningful learning*. New York: Houghton Mifflin.

Grabinger, R. S. (1996). Rich environments for active learning. In D.H. Jonassen (Ed.), *Handbook of research for educational communications and technology* (pp. 665-692). New York: Macmillan.

Guptill, A. M. (2000). Using the Internet to improve student performance. *Teaching Exceptional Children, 32*(4), 16-20.

Harris, J. (1998a). Curriculum-based telecollaboration: Using activity structures to design student projects. *Learning and Leading with Technology, 26*(1), 6-15.

Harris, J. (1998b). *Virtual architecture—Designing and directing curriculum-based telecomputing*. Eugene, OR: International Society for Technology in Education (ISTE).

Hartley, K., & Bendixen, L.D. (2001). Educational research in the internet age: Examining the role of individual characteristics. *Educational Researcher, 30*(9), 22-26.

The International Society for Technology in Education (ISTE). (2000). *National technology standards for students connecting curriculum and technology*. Eugene, OR: Author.

Jonassen, D., Howland, J., Moore, J., & Marra, R. (2003). *Learning to solve problems with technology: A constructivist perspective*. Upper Saddle River, NJ: Prentice Hall.

Kelly, R. (2000). Working with webquests: Making the web accessible for students with disabilities. *Teaching Exceptional Children, 32*(6), 4-13.

Kirk, E. (1996). *Evaluating information found on the Internet*. Retrieved January 1999, from Milton.mse.jhu.edu:8001/research/education/net.html

Kirschner, P. A., (2002). Cognitive load theory: Implications of cognitive load theory on the design of learning. *Learning and Instruction, 12*(1), 1-10.

Kleiner, A., & Farris, E. (2002). *Internet access in U.S. public schools and classrooms: 1994-2001*. Washington, DC: National Center for Education Statistics. Retrieved June 19, 2003, from: nces.ed.gov/pubsearch/pubsinfo.asp?pubid=2002018.

Kohut, R. (2000). Metasearching the net. *Learning and Leading with Technology, 27*(6), 18-21.

Lewis, J.D. (1998). How the Internet expands educational options. *Teaching Exceptional Children, 30*(5), 43-41.

Lynch, H., & Tennille, S. (2003). *Dispelling the myth: A study of culture. A WebQuest on cultural diversity for fourth, fifth and sixth grade students*. Retrieved November 24, 2003, from: coe.west.asu.edu/students/stennille/ST3/webquest.html.

Male, M. (2003). *Technology for inclusion: Meeting the special needs of all students* (4th ed.). Needham Heights, MA: Allyn and Bacon.

Male, M., & Gotthoffer, D. (1999). *Quick guide to the Internet for special education*. Needham Heights, MA: Allyn and Bacon.

March, T. (1996). *Filamentality*. Retrieved July 16, 2003, from: www.kn.pacbell.com/wired/fil/

March, T. (1997). *Activity formats*. Retrieved

July 16, 2003, from: www.kn.pacbell.com/wired/fil/formats.html

March, T. (2001). *Working the Web for education: Theory and practice on integrating the Web for learning.* Retrieved November 16, 2003, from: www.ozline.com/learning/theory.html

Marsh, M.M. (2000). *A student guide to misinformation on the web.* Houston, TX: Children's Software Press.

Mayer, R.E., & Moreno, R. (2003). Nine ways to reduce cognitive load in multimedia learning. *Educational Psychologist, 38*(1), 43-52.

Mayer, R.E., & Moreno, R. (2002). Aids to computer-based multimedia learning. *Learning and Instruction, 12*(1), 107-119.

McREL. (2003). *McREL - Compendium of standards and benchmarks. Online standards database. Content knowledge.* Retrieved August 13, 2003, from: www.mcrel.org/standards-benchmarks/.

National Educational Technology Standards Project. (2000). Retrieved October 31, 2003, from: cnets.iste.org.

Network Wizzards. (2003). *Internet domain survey, January 2003.* Retrieved October 31, 2003, from: cnets.iste.org.

Okolo, C.M. (2000). Technology for individuals with mild disabilities. In J. Lindsey (Ed.), *Technology and exceptional individuals* (3rd ed.) (pp. 243-301). Austin, TX: Pro-Ed.

Peters-Walters, S. (1998). Accessible web site design. *Teaching Exceptional Children, 30*(5), 42-47.

Robyler, M.D. (2003a). *Integrating education technology into teaching.* Columbus, OH: Merrill Prentice Hall.

Robyler, M.D. (2003b). *Starting out on the Internet: A learning journal for teachers* (2nd ed.). Columbus, OH: Merrill Prentice Hall.

Rhyne (2001). *The journey to freedom: Harriet Tubman and the Underground Railroad.* Retrieved October 31, 2003, from: trackstar.4teachers.org/trackstar/ts/viewT rack.do?number=66283.

Smith, S., Boone, R., & Higgins, K. (1998). Expanding the writing process to the Web. *Teaching Exceptional Children, 30*(5), 22-26.

Stanovich, K. E. (1986). Cognitive processes and the reading problems of learning-disabled children: Evaluating the assumption of specificity. In J. K. Torgesen & B.Y.L. Wong (Eds.), *Psychological and education perspectives on learning disabilities* (pp. 87-131). New York: Academic Press.

Swanson, H.L., & Cooney, J. B. (1996). Learning disabilities and memory. In D.K. Reid, W.P. Hresko, & H. L. Swanson (Eds.), *Cognitive approaches to learning disabilities* (pp. 287-314). Austin, TX: Pro-Ed.

Sweller, J., van Merrienboer, J.J.G., & Paas, F.G.W.C. (1998). Cognitive architecture and instructional design. *Educational Psychology Review, 10*(3), 251-296.

TrackStar. (2003). *TrackStar.* Retrieved January 26, 2004, from: trackstar.4teachers.org.

Web Worksheet Wizard. (2003). *Web Worksheet Wizard.* Retrieved January 26, 2004, from: wizard.hprtec.org.

WebQuest Portal. (2003). *The WebQuest portal.* Retrieved November 24, 2003, from: www.webquest.org.

Wissick, C.A. (2000). Drill and practice: Web style. *Special Education Technology Practice, 2*(3), 37-39.

Wissick, C. A. (2003a). *Web toolbox for educators: Create your own web activities.* Retrieved August 16, 2003, from: www.ed.sc.edu/caw/toolboxcreateyourown.html.

Wissick, C. A. (2003b). *Web toolbox for educators: Special Education Resources.* Retrieved August 16, 2003, from:www.ed.sc.edu/caw/toolboxsped.html.

Wissick, C. A. (2003c). *Web toolbox for educators: Technology for mild disabilities.* Retrieved August 16, 2003, from: www.ed.sc.edu/caw/toolboxvendors.html.

Wissick, C.A. (2004a). *Web toolboxes for educators: QuickStarts for the Web.* Retrieved January 22, 2004, from: www.ed.sc.edu/caw/toolbox.html.

Wissick, C. A. (2004b). *Web toolbox for educators: Educational resources.* Retrieved August 16, 2003, from: www.ed.sc.edu/caw/toolbox sped.html.

Wissick, C.A., & Gardner, J.E. (1998). A special educator's learner's permit to the world wide web. *Teaching Exceptional Children, 30*(5), 8-15.

Section 7

Professional Development

35

Improving Practice Using Assistive Technology Knowledge and Skills

Elizabeth A. Lahm

Integrity without knowledge is weak and useless, and knowledge without integrity is dangerous and dreadful. Samuel Johnson (1709-1784)

The Individuals with Disabilities Education Act of 1990 (PL 101-476) recognized that technology advances increase the potential for including children with disabilities into general education programs as well as other settings. Specifically, the regulations required each school district to ensure that assistive technology (AT) devices or services, or both, be made available to a student with a disability to help ensure he or she receive a free and appropriate public education (FAPE). AT had to be provided as part of the student's special education, related services, or supplementary aids and services as described in the Individualized Education Program (IEP).

The current legislation governing special education programs, the 1997 Amendments to the Individuals with Disabilities Education Act (IDEA) (PL 105-17), goes a step further by mandating that AT be considered for each child receiving special education services and creates the need for professionals to develop adequate competencies for providing effective services to those requiring AT. The IEP team, consisting of individuals from differing disciplines familiar with the unique needs of a student, makes the first determination of the need for AT at the IEP meeting. This determination is often referred to as "consideration." The IEP team identifies functional areas for

which AT can be used to meet the functional demands of participating in their educational program. Thus, inferred in this legislation is the responsibility on the part of the professional to maintain an adequate level of knowledge and skills relative to AT in order to make informed "consideration" of assistive technologies for their students.

The consequences of limited knowledge about AT are costly! A frequent scenario is the IEP team member who has heard about a specific device that relates to the needs of a student and convinces the rest of the team that the device is appropriate. Shortly after purchase and implementation, the device is seldom used because it is not a good match for the student and is eventually abandoned, demonstrating to many that AT falls short of its proclaimed benefits. Precious resources of money and time have been lost, as well as potential student learning. In short, this limited knowledge about a limited set of AT devices has been costly.

The second type of scenario occurs when the IEP team members, none of whom has adequate AT knowledge, "consider" all they know about AT and report that the student does not need AT. As a result, the student who truly could benefit from AT continues to perform at much lower levels than his or her real potential. A year goes by and statewide tests now demonstrate low achievement and the school achieves less than desired on their overall achievement profile. The student's time has been wasted and the probability of graduation and meaningful employment has slipped a little further away. In addition, the teacher's self-esteem has been lowered because low achievement reflects on her ability to teach. Both losses are costly.

Today over 800 institutions of higher education provide training in special education, yet only 17 offer degree or certification programs for assistive technology specialists. This is hardly an adequate number to train ample specialists to meet the needs of school districts (National Clearinghouse for Professions in Special Education, 2003). Bair and Bair (1998) surveyed graduate programs in special education to determine the top 10 programs in the nation. None of these programs offers training for AT specialists, and when their Web sites are searched, only seven appear to include AT and/or instructional technology in their regular degree coursework (see Table 1).

The lack of special education training programs that address technology and assistive technology services perpetuates the state of assistive technology implementation today. For example, Bauder (1999) reported that only 26% of the students in Kentucky using AT had it written into their IEP, leaving AT implementation up to chance because neither the need for nor the record of its use would be passed from year to year. Another study in Kentucky found that only half of the special education teachers had AT training in their coursework and for those that did, a large part was general AT information provided in courses other that AT courses (Abner & Lahm, 2002).

Abner and Lahm (2002) found that 96% of surveyed vision teachers in Kentucky had access to a computer at home, most having Internet access with email and most using word processing on a regular basis. This high level of home use and self-directed learning is reported by others as well (Moffett, 1999). Similarly, many special educators and other related service providers are self-taught assistive technology specialists, but only 51% of teachers thought they were competent enough to teach their students to use the AT (Abner & Lahm, 2002). The lack of institutionalization of AT training within teacher training programs is cause for concerned about future adherence to the federal mandate for assistive technology to be considered for each student with an IEP.

The remainder of this chapter will explore the changing expectations of teachers in light of educational reform and current trends in special education, examine existing sets of assistive technology competencies from related disciplines, demonstrate how competencies can be used to improve practice, and discuss the need for more research in the area of assistive technology competency development.

Changing Expectations for Both Students and Teachers

The use of technology for instruction is seen as inevitable across all of education (Bushweller, 2002). Prominent organizations studying the trend note the value of technology use as well as the increasing prevalence of technology in schools. What is consistently of note however, is the lack of readiness of today's teachers for using the technology tools (Smith & Jones, 1999). In the remainder of this chapter, we will look at how steps are being taken on several fronts to change this deplorable situation.

Standards-Based Education

At the same time, as mandated by the No Child Left Behind Act (NCLB) (2001), states are developing higher teacher and student standards. Incorporating standards set by lead professional organizations of specific content areas (e.g., National Council for Teachers of Mathematics), state standards have become robust and extensive. Many states have a specific strand for technology (e.g., Kentucky, Illinois, Virginia) that closely follows the standards set by the International Society of Technology in Education (ISTE). Kentucky and Illinois also include specific standards for assistive technology that are to be met by general and special education teachers (more on these later). These new state standards increase the expectations of teachers and the students they teach.

It is estimated that over two million new teachers will be hired within the next decade to fill the vacancies created by retiring teachers and to meet the needs of increasing student enrollment (CEO Forum, 1999). The CEO Forum's first recommendation is for Schools of

Table 1. Ten Top-Ranked Institutions of Higher Education with Special Education Programs and the Inclusion of Technology Content in Coursework

Institution of Higher Education	Coursework That Includes Technology
University of Kansas	• Introduction to Educational Computing • Introduction to Computing in Education
Vanderbilt University – Peabody College	• Augmentative and Alternative Communication
University of Minnesota	• Computer Technology in Special Education • Aural and Speech Programming for Persons Who Are Deaf/Hard of Hearing • Models of Instructional Programming with Deaf and Hard of Hearing Students • Reading and Writing for Children with Visual Disabilities
University of Oregon	None noted
University of Virginia	• Positioning, Handling, and Self-Care Skills • Introduction to Classroom Computing • Seminar in Instructional Computing
University of Washington	None noted
University of Illinois – Urbanna	• Assistive Technology and Physical Disabilities • Augmentative Communication
University of North Carolina	None noted
University of Wisconsin - Madison	• Instructional Computing In Schools
Syracuse University	• Adult Learners with Special Needs

Education to prepare teachers according to new standards set by national accrediting institutions. To do that, Schools of Education must provide incentives for faculty to retool so they are able to train their students on the uses of technology for instruction (Office of Technology Assessment, 1995; Smith & Jones, 1999). States are demanding these new standards in new teachers through licensure. At the same time, teacher education faculty also must meet the demand.

The CEO Forum (1999) estimated that over 20% of today's teachers do not feel adequately trained to integrate technology into their instruction. Similarly, Moffett (1999) found that 56% of teachers surveyed in Kentucky rated themselves with limited or some awareness of basic computer operations and concepts with few or no skills. Sixty-four percent reported the

same level of awareness and skills in technology applications in instruction. A study of University of Kentucky undergraduate education students and recent education graduates currently teaching was conducted to determine their readiness to use technology for instruction (Lahm, 2002). The undergraduate students rated themselves with a 3.4 (aware but need skills) out of 5.0 (proficient) whereas first-year teachers rated themselves at 3.7. The undergraduates indicated more than just "awareness" on only 40% of the 45 competency items. By comparison, the graduates found themselves above the "awareness" level on 67% of 49 items. Thus neither group was ready to use technology in the classroom for instruction, a level one would hope for today, considering the emphasis technology has received in recent years.

Outcomes-Based Education

In addition to the emphasis on standards-based training, new emphasis, driven by the current political agenda through the NCLB, has been placed on outcomes-based education. This legislation requires accountability for all students' learning as measured against the state's standards and, thus, is moving the field forward in methods for measuring student outcomes. However, with NCLB, the focus of education has moved away from the methods and contents of teaching to a primary focus on demonstrating results ("Education Week on the Web," 2001).

Though measurable outcomes are not new to special education, inclusion of special education students in the general curriculum and statewide assessments is relatively new. Measuring the outcomes of a student included in the general curriculum is a new demand on special education teachers. The challenge comes in measuring outcomes when others control the instruction of a given student. Similarly, statewide testing is a formal process that does not lend itself to the customization and variability of testing previously used by most special educators. These and other changes in emphasis in education, along with the advances in technology for education, have changed the expectations placed on teachers and are driving the new standards by which teachers will be measured.

Existing Assistive Technology Competencies

There is strong support for AT training to be included in basic special education training programs. For example, in a statewide study conducted in Kentucky, Bauder (1999) found that 82% of survey participants thought AT should be a required area of study. While the development of technology competencies began as early as 1981, they were not necessarily required in teacher education programs. Berry and colleagues (1981) developed a core set of competencies for training professionals. Their goals were: (a) to provide experienced developers with a professional growth self-assessment tool, (b) to improve communication among instructional/training developers and other professional groups through the use of a common set of concepts and vocabulary, (c) to provide academic and professional preparation programs for developers with the information for program development, (d) to provide a basis for potential professional certification, (e) to aid employers in identifying qualified practitioners, and (f) to provide a basis for defining the emerging field of instructional development.

The National Council for Accreditation of Teacher Education (NCATE), the primary accrediting institution for teacher education programs, has been developing and collecting sets of competencies for teachers since 1954 (National Council for Accreditation of Teacher Education, 2003). They now include instructional technology competencies in their general set, requiring all Schools of Education seeking accreditation to demonstrate that their graduates can meet these competencies. Based on work done by ISTE, these competencies were first used by NCATE in 1998 (Ley, 1997). (The complete set of ISTE's [NETS Project, 2002] instructional technology competencies can be found online at cnets.iste.org/teachers/t_overview.html.)

Beyond general technology skills is the need for special educators to have assistive technology skills. Just as students without disabilities need to graduate with a host of technology skills, so do students with disabilities. The need for technology skills is imperative in today's technological society to participate in the work world. For students with disabilities, assistive technology skills can mean the difference between independence and dependence in non-work areas of life, and provide a quality of life not previously possible. As the cost of living increases and resources dwindle, it becomes even more important to train individuals with disabilities to achieve the highest level of independence possible, and thus reduce the fiscal responsibility of society to support them.

For the sake of the students with disabilities, their families, and society in general, it is critical that special educators attain a level of expertise in assistive technology that allows them to assist their students in achieving their best. To that end, as illustrated below, several professional organizations have established assistive technology standards to guide educators and related service providers to that level of expertise.

RESNA

The first set of AT competencies was released in 1995 by RESNA (n.d.), the Rehabilitation Engineering and Assistive Technology Society of North America. Two sets of competencies were developed, one for AT Practitioners (ATP) and another for AT Suppliers (ATS) (Minkel, 1996), recognizing that the person selling assistive technologies needed a different set of knowledge than those responsible for implementing the AT. In 2002 additional competencies were added for Rehabilitation Technology Engineers (RESNA, n.d.). RESNA's purpose for developing competencies was to ensure consumer safeguards and to increase consumer satisfaction. These competencies are required for the RESNA certification, which not only assures the recipient of AT services that the service provider is qualified and knowledgeable, but the funding agency of the services as well.

RESNA's competencies are viewed more as an outline of knowledge areas (RESNA, 2000b) and are not performance-based like the competencies used by NCATE. The knowledge areas in RESNA's *Fundamentals in Assistive Technology*, a study guide for the certification examination, are organized into 12 modules:

- Technical fundamentals

- Clinical fundamentals

- Assistive technology provision: assessment

- Assistive technology provision: accessing the technology

- Professional conduct and public policy

- Technologies for people who are blind or who have low vision

- Technologies for people who are deaf or hard of hearing

- Seating and positioning technologies

- Mobility technologies

- Augmentative communication technologies

- Computer access technologies

- Environmental control technologies

More than five years after the initial certification examination was given, over 1,100 service providers are certified (RESNA, n.d.). However, the RESNA certifications have not been widely accepted in most educational settings to-date.

AOTA

Building on the RESNA competencies, the American Occupational Therapy Association (AOTA) developed competencies for occupational therapists at three levels of practice: entry/basic, intermediate, and advanced (Hammel & Angelo, 1996) and with primary areas of competency: evaluation, intervention, and resource coordination. Within the set, basic and complex technologies were differentiated as well as basic and complex service delivery. Forty-two competency statements were identified as minimum requirements for registered occupational therapists. To-date, occupational therapists working as AT specialists in schools are more likely to have RESNA certification than are educators. Since the certification can improve their credibility with third-party payors (e.g., insurance companies), it is beneficial even in education settings.

CEC

The Council for Exceptional Children (CEC), in collaboration with NCATE, published a set of professional standards to define the knowledge base for special education teacher preparation programs and to specify a common set of competencies to inform certification requirements for special educators in each area of specialization (Council for Exceptional Children, 2000). National standards are used to promote the consistency in training across personnel preparation programs as well as in licensing across state educational agencies to enhance the future delivery of school services to students with special needs (Lombardi & Ludlow, 1997).

In 1999, Lahm and Nickels published the first set of technology specialization knowledge and skills that were used as the basis for developing CEC knowledge and skills. The current set is used by NCATE to evaluate the quality of teacher preparation programs. These are available online at www.cec.sped.org/ps/

perf_based_stds/index.html and will be included in the fifth edition of *What Every Special Educator Should Know: The Standards for the Preparation and Licensure of Special Educators* (Council for Exceptional Children, 2003). These are the only validated technology standards developed specifically for special educators.

State Assistive Technology Standards

Several states have developed standards specific to assistive technology for inclusion in their technology standards sets. Two of Kentucky's 16 technology standards address assistive technology. They are: "10.8. Requests and uses appropriate assistive and adaptive devices for students with special needs," and "10.9. Designs lessons that use technology to address diverse student needs and learning styles" (Kentucky Department of Education, 2003, ¶11).

Illinois is another example of a state that has developed specific assistive technology standards. Its tenth technology competency reads, "The teacher candidate demonstrates the ability to use a range of assistive technology to work effectively and equitably with students with disabilities" (Instructional Technology Passport System [ITPS], n.d., ¶1). Illinois uses authentic performance tasks to evaluate a teacher candidate's readiness to teach. For assistive technology, these include knowledge and expertise in the following areas:

- *Assistive technology devices and services*
- *Issues, barriers, and benefits of assistive technology*
- *Federal legislation for identifying and using assistive technology*
- *High and low assistive technology devices*
- *Various input and output devices*
- *Ways to arrange the setting to facilitate the use of assistive technology*
- *Funding sources to support the use of assistive technology*
- *Professionals who can support the use of assistive technology*
- *Roles of teachers in the selection, implementation and evaluation of assistive technology for student with disabilities. (ITPS, n.d., ¶3)*

"Educators cannot be expected, however, to become experts on leveraging technology overnight". (CEO Forum, 1997, p. 30)

Use of Competencies to Improve Practice

Teacher standards have been established to improve the practice of teaching and ultimately, student outcomes. To achieve these goals, technology professional development must be embraced by institutions of higher education, school districts, and individual teachers alike. Validated sets of competencies can be used as guidelines or road maps to achieving personal and systemwide expertise.

Technology training programs need many supports to be effective. Some require strong fiscal support while others require more commitment than money. Grant (n.d.) identified the following training supports:

- Access to equipment
- Technology assistance
- Sustainability
- Pedagogical assistance
- Administrative and community backing
- Time for learning and collaborating

As educational research has demonstrated, the best learning occurs when learning is active. Teachers should learn about technology in the same way their students are expected to learn (Grant, n.d.). Hoffman (1997) poses that self-study is the best method for learning about technology but many individuals require additional support to be successful. Technology is a hands-on skill area that cannot be sufficiently learned without practice (Handler, 1993). Further, research in professional development tells us that training must be ongoing to be effective (Grant, n.d.; Smith, 2000; Smith & Jones, 1999).

Higher Education Programs

Traditional teacher training programs organize learning topically, creating separate courses for each topic. In a typical 15-week semester, assistive technology can be covered with fair breadth and depth. Table 2 shows topic areas covered in a graduate level AT course. Appendix A describes the eight assignments used in that class to provide structured practice and implementation planning.

The single-course approach allows little practice in natural environments over extended periods of time. Instead, by infusing assistive technology knowledge and skill training across all courses, allowing students to see it modeled across other content areas and instructors, students not only receive more instruction in assistive technology but have an opportunity to practice it and receive critical feedback on its use, both critical components of technology training (Smith, 2000; Smith & Jones, 1999), as just mentioned. Table 3 shows an example of a course on transdisciplinary services that infuses technology into several topic areas and one assignment. Assistive technology competencies addressed by each of these topics are indicated. Additional examples of specific topics and assignments that include assistive technology across several courses are found in Table 4. Finally, Appendix C, illustrates how assistive technology competencies can be included in existing courses across all special education courses in an undergraduate program. The next challenge is to infuse assistive technology knowledge into general education courses.

It is easy to conceptualize assistive technology training infused across a full teacher training program but, in reality, it is difficult to achieve. One major reason is that special education faculties are under-trained in assistive technology and, thus, are reluctant to include it in their coursework. Retooling higher education faculty will take time and support. Providing a course release or sabbatical for a knowledgeable faculty member to support others during infusion planning is a potential economical means of providing faculty support (Bryant, Erin, Lock, Allan, & Resta, 1998). Pairing a knowledgeable student as a mentor to a reluctant faculty member is another method used by others (Smith, 2000).

A second factor working against infusion of AT is the already bulging curriculum (Bryant et al, 1998). Prospective teachers are required to cover more and more content and demonstrate achievement of high state standards. These requirements, coupled with the need to keep the program courseload reasonable, make it difficult to find room in existing courses to squeeze in assistive technology content. To properly infuse assistive technology into special education training programs may necessitate a complete revamping of courses so all content is more integrated, ensuring there are ample opportunities for practical experiences.

District Professional Development

Long-term intensive professional development programs are necessary to achieve lasting change and improved practice (Bradley & West, 1994; Franke, Carpenter, Fennema, Ansell, & Behrend, 1998; Guskey, 1986; Malouf & Schiller, 1995). It also is well known that short inservice programs or workshops do not produce sustained change (Gibbons, Kimmel, & O'Shea, 1997; Guskey, 1986), yet Abner and Lahm (2002) found that 88% of teachers surveyed relied on these modes of professional development for AT. Planners of assistive technology professional development should consider recent conceptualizations of professional development that call for programs that are "site-based, rigorous, sustained, and designed and directed by teachers" (CEO Forum, 1999, p. 10). Such programs require substantial investments to continue over the long term if they are to impact student learning.

The CEO Forum (1997) cites three necessary elements for successful professional development in technology: (a) being integral to the mission of the school district, (b) having support from the highest levels of administration and community, and (c) being endorsed by the teachers for whom the program is designed. To guide the development of these programs, several principles are posited (CEO Forum, 1997; Daniels, n.d.; Hassel, 1999):

- Setting realistic goals based on needs assessments of teachers and students

- Basing activities on the curriculum and standards

- Incorporating formative and summative evaluation activities

- Modeling best practices in technology implementation

- Utilizing "learning by doing" strategies

Table 2. Topics of an Assistive Technology Graduate Level Course

Assistive Technology (AT) Course Topics	
AT Competencies	Mounting
What Is Assistive Technology?	Computer Access
Human Factors and AT	Alternate and Expanded Keyboards
Tools, Transparency, and AT	Output Devices
Legal Basis for AT	Communication
Categories of AT	Environmental Interaction
AT Services & Consumers	Education and Transition
Human Function Model	AT and Academic Performance
What Are Human Factors?	Body Support, Alignment, and Positioning
Human Factors and AT Goals	Sports, Fitness, and Recreation
Essential Human Factors in AT	Travel and Mobility
Considering AT	Assistive Technology Research
Existence & Daily Living	Online Resources
Adaptations of Existing Equipment	Quality Indicators of Assistive Technology
Switch Types & Applications	Why AT Fails: A Human Factors
Scanning	Perspective

- Providing needed resources, incentives, and ongoing support

Barriers to the establishment of quality technology professional development programs include: (a) limited staff time to participate, (b) limited blocks of time for longer professional development activities, and (c) too much professional development that has little impact on teaching (Hassel, 1999). Each of these stems from a missing principle in the professional development program design, policies and practices in place to support professional development. Resources and commitment from administration and the community to allow ample time for participation in professional development are critical. Further, recognition for participation provides incentives for continued participation.

Hassel (1999) suggests numerous ways to overcome these barriers that can be put in place even when fiscal resources are not available and the political agenda is not supportive of robust professional development in technology. A few examples include:

Limited staff time to participate:

- "Use student teachers, interns, and parent volunteers to cover classrooms for short PD [professional development] activities" (p. 55).

- "Allow teachers to cover for each other for short periods of time" (p. 55).

- "Change class scheduling to include a short PD period every day" (p. 55).

Limited blocks of time:

- "Schedule special PD activities on weekends. Make this practice more attractive by arranging group babysitting for staff children, offering credit toward degrees, making it voluntary but with very enticing topics, or providing food" (p. 55).

- "Offer course credit toward graduate degrees (in partnership with a college or university) or toward relicensure to encourage participation in weekend or after-hour activities" (p. 56).

- "Ask staff to voluntarily lengthen the school day by a short time (one school did 10 minutes per day); consolidate the "excess" time for activities requiring large time blocks (the same school got four days per year out of the 10 extra minutes per day) " (p. 56).

Too much low-impact professional development:

- "Negotiate use of paid district or state-required PD time (inservice days) to focus on

Table 3. Technology Infused into an Existing Course: Transdisciplinary Services for Students with Multiple Disabilities

Session	Topics
1	Course Overview Characteristics of the Population
2	Overview of Transdisciplinary Services (44) Components/Quality Indicators of Transdisciplinary Service Delivery Ongoing Transdisciplinary Teaming Considerations • team meetings • communication • role release
3	Functional Assessment (31)
4	Person-Centered Planning (19, 48)
5	Family Issues
6	Simulated Transdisciplinary Assessment
7	Consensus-Building Activity (in-class)
8	Program Implementation for Students with Severe/Multiple Disabilities and Deaf Blindness • activity-based programming • IEP development
9	Inclusion Issues
10	Physical Therapy • gross-motor development-normal/abnormal • physical management • adapted equipment (7, 11) • approaches to intervention (i.e., NDT)
11	Occupational Therapy • fine motor development-normal/abnormal • adapted equipment: orthotics (7, 11) • sensory integration
12	Oral Motor/Feeding Nursing Medical terminology Health Care Procedures
13	Communication: Receptive • identify and facilitate non-verbal communication actions • providing consistent input
14	Communication: Expressive • technology for communication (7, 13) • teaching within routines
15	Hearing • hearing impairments associated with MD population • embedding skills into routines • adaptations (7) Vision • visual impairments associated with MD population • embedding skills into routines • orientation and mobility • adaptations (7)
16	Putting It All together Transdisciplinary Teams From Rural and Urban Settings

(continued next page)

Table 3. Technology Infused into an Existing Course: Transdisciplinary Services for Students with Multiple Disabilities (continued)

Group Project Assignment

Students will identify a topic area related to the education of students with deaf-blindness or multiple disabilities and develop a project related to that area. In keeping with the philosophy of the course, students will be asked to complete this project either with a partner or a group of other students (4-5 to each team). A contract must be developed between the team and the instructor explaining: topic area, description of project, role of each team member in completing the project, and general outline. Equal distribution of effort among team members is an expectation of the completion of this project. Team members will be required to evaluate their own performance as well as the performance of other team members.

- Development of some type of adapted equipment
- Development of a communication board for a child
- Development of a calendar box for a child
- Other

Note. Numbers in parentheses are competency numbers from the Personal Planning Instrument. Printed with permission from Jennifer Grisham-Brown, Ed.D., and Meada Hall, M.S., University of Kentucky, course instructors

---

your school's highest priority PD efforts. Use this time in blocks or spread it throughout the year" (p. 56).

Professional development can be either formal or informal. Formal activities are characterized by specific plans that yield depth and focus, structured practice, consultation with experts, and scheduled followup and coaching (Grant, n.d.). Informal activities are often embedded in the current job to support and extend the formal learning. These are characterized by inquiry, observation, mentoring, teacher collaboration, and partnerships with universities and businesses (Grant, n.d.). To be effective, informal activities should be designed by the teachers themselves. (Appendix B, *the Personal Planning Instrument,* provides several types of activities in both the formal and informal categories.)

Several models for delivering inservice professional development are in use today. The most common takes place through the local school district. For example, the Los Angeles Unified School District provides training to special and general educators through a team of AT specialists (S. Purcell, personal communication, March 20, 2002). Both district- and school-level needs are addressed, coordinated by the district's assistive technology coordinator. Some districts team up with other districts to form consortia for providing AT inservice opportunities. An example is Texas, which is served by 20 regional education service centers, each carrying responsibilities for delivering AT professional development to multiple districts (D. Carl, personal communication, May 24, 2002). In several states, the coordination of AT professional development occurs at the state level. Wisconsin is one example. The director of the Wisconsin Assistive Technology Initiative (WATI) coordinates and supports the efforts of 13 WATI consultants and sponsors statewide conferences and training events (P. Reed, personal communication, March 21, 2003).

Self-Directed Learning

As noted earlier, Hoffman (1997) believes that self-directed learning is the best method for technology professional development. In a survey conducted by Abner and Lahm (2002), self-directed learning was commonly used by teachers. They found conferences were used by 68% of surveyed teachers as a source of assistive technology knowledge. Even more participants learned about assistive technology through networking with their colleagues. A

Table 4. Examples of Specific Class Topics and Assignments Related to Assistive Technology

Course	Specific Topics	Assignments
Legal Issues in Special Education	Rehabilitation Act of 1973: Sections 504 and 508 Technology-Related Assistance Act IDEA: Consideration of AT Americans with Disabilities Act	Trace technology for persons with disabilities in legislation from the 1800s to the present. Discuss trends noted and relate them to changes in society.
Behavior Management and Instruction	Implementation of a trial plan to determine feasibility for instruction Configuring instructional software to collect appropriate progress data	Write an implementation plan for using two instructional software programs to teach the same skill in different ways. Identify methods for collecting appropriate data to determine their effectiveness.
Characteristics of Persons with Disabilities	Areas of function that can be addressed with assistive technology Assistive technology resources on the Internet	Identify two areas of function frequently impacted by learning disabilities. Using the Internet, identify and describe one low-, medium-, and high-technology device that can assist with each function. Locate two articles available on the Internet that address the use of assistive technology for each function.

great number of online and face-to-face training opportunities are available that individuals can independently pursue. The developers of these training programs include universities, nonprofit organizations, for-profit companies, and vendors. Some examples are included in Table 5.

Successful implementation of assistive technology is significantly impacted by the knowledge base of all services providers as well as student and parents. *A Personal Planning Instrument for Updating Knowledge and Skills in Assistive Technology* is included at the end of this chapter to help guide self-directed learning for readers who want to advance their knowledge of assistive technology. The instrument is based on the knowledge and skill statements that were validated by the CEC for special education technology specialists (Council for Exceptional Children, 2003; Lahm, 2003).

The primary audience of the instrument is individual educators, but with some adaptation it may be used to identify areas of professional development that would meet the needs of a larger group, including the school or district level. Other groups that might use the instrument for planning include parents, paraeducators, and administrators. The knowledge level of each of these groups impacts the level of support available for ongoing professional development in assistive technology.

Conclusion

This chapter presented a set of knowledge and skill statements that are being used to guide teacher preparation programs and that may be used to guide assistive technology professional development and self-directed learning. Though validated, these competencies are new to the field. Many questions remain about the competencies themselves and the strategies that are most effective for updating current teachers to reach those standards. Key questions that remain include:

1. How much does the special education classroom teacher need to know to implement AT across school environments?
2. Which portion of the competencies should general educators know in order to

Table 5. Example Opportunities for Self-Directed Assistive Technology Professional Development

		Online	Formal Curriculum	National Coverage	Fee-based	Free
The **Assistive Technology Training Online Project (ATTO)** provides information on AT applications that help students with disabilities learn in elementary classrooms. The site includes several modules on AT basics and tutorials on specific hardware and software.	University of Buffalo atto.buffalo.edu/	•		•		•
The **Assistive Technology Applications Certificate Program (ATACP)** can provide professional credibility in the AT field, which is the main reason why practicing professionals, as well as novices to the field, are taking advantage of this program. The training is offered across the country with online, live, and project components.	California State University at Northridge, www.csun.edu/ codtraining/	•	•	•	•	
The **Research Institute for Assistive and Training Technologies (RIATT@NASDSE)** helps individuals learn about assistive technology. They offer online courses and on-site training in assistive technology. Through the training program, individuals can earn a graduate degree, CEUs, or competency certificates.	RIATT@NASDSE www.nasdse.com/	•	•	•	•	
The **Bluegrass Technology Center** is a non-profit organization providing assistive technology services to Central and Eastern Kentucky. Workshops on different assistive technology topics are scheduled several times a year. CEUs are available for speech language pathologists and licensed child care providers.	Bluegrass Technology Center www.bluegrass-tech.org/		•		•	•
Innovative Solutions Group, LLC, is a for-profit organization that offers customized assistive technology needs analysis and training.	Innovative Solutions Group, LLC www.innosolu.comat_ eval_and_training1.html				•	
Don Johnston Learning provides a continuum of products, support materials, and services that facilitate successful use of technology in literacy instruction for struggling students. Don Johnston Learning uses proven methods of adult learning to provide effective options for busy professionals.	Don Johnston Learning www.donjohnston. com/ djlearning/index.htm			•	•	

implement assistive technology in inclusive classrooms?

3. What is the most effective way to stay informed in a rapidly changing field?

4. Which knowledge and skills are practical to infuse into undergraduate training programs?

5. What are good ways of informing emergency certified teachers?

6. What additional competencies are needed to address the emerging focus on universally designed products and instruction?

These and other questions should guide research in the field of assistive technology training over the next few years. As the field becomes more expert at updating the competencies of preservice and inservice teachers, parents and students can be more assured that the assistive technology being considered at IEP meetings is based on a credible foundation of assistive technology knowledge.

References

Abner, G., & Lahm, E. A. (2002). Assistive technology implementation with students who are visually impaired: Teacher readiness. *Journal of Visual Impairment and Blindness, 96*, 98-105.

Bair, J. H., & Bair, R. K. (1998). Linkages among top-ranked graduate programs in special education: A brief report. *Mental Retardation, 36*(1), 52-54.

Bauder, D. K. (1999). *The use of assistive technology and the assistive technology training needs of special education teachers in Kentucky schools*. Unpublished doctoral dissertation, University of Kentucky, Lexington.

Berry, M., Coleman, M., Durzo, J., Foshay, R., Fowler, B., Shrock, S., Schwen, T., Silber, K., Stevens, D., Terrell, B., Wileman, R., & Bralton, B. (1981). Competencies for the instructional/training development professional. *Journal of Instructional Development, 5*(1), 14-15.

Bradley, D. F., & West, J. F. (1994). Staff training for the inclusion of students with disabilities: Visions from school-based education. *Teacher Education and Special Education, 17*, 117-128.

Bryant, D. P., Erin, J., Lock, R., Allan, J. M., &

Resta, P. E. (1998). Infusing a teacher preparation program in learning disabilities with assistive technology. *Journal of Learning Disabilities, 31*, 55-66.

Bushweller, K. (2002). Report says e-learning redefining K-12 education [Electronic version]. *Education Week, 21*(36), 10.

CEO Forum. (1997, October). *From pillars to progress* (Year 1 Report). Retrieved December 29, 2002, from www.ceoforum.org/downloads/report97.pdf.

CEO Forum. (1999, February). *Professional development: A link to better learning* (Year 2 Report). Retrieved December 29, 2002, from: www.ceoforum.org/reports.cfm?RID=2.

Council for Exceptional Children. (2000). *What every special educator should know: The standards for the preparation and licensure of special educators* (4th ed.). Reston, VA: Author.

Council for Exceptional Children. (2003). *What every special educator should know: The standards for the preparation and licensure of special educators* (5th ed.). Reston, VA: Author.

Daniels, H. A. (n.d.). *The missing link in school reform: Professional development*. Oak Brook, IL: North Central Regional Educational Laboratory. Retrieved January 14, 2003, from www.ncrel.org/mands/docs/7-10.htm.

Education Week on the Web. (2001). *Glossary*. Retrieved December 28, 2002, from www.edweek.org/context/glossary/glossterm.cfm?glossid=88.

Franke, M. L., Carpenter, T., Fennema, E., Ansell, E., & Behrend, J. (1998). Understanding teachers' self sustaining, generative change in the context of professional development. *Teaching and Teacher Education, 14*, 67-80.

Gibbons, S., Kimmel, H., & O'Shea, M. (1997). Changing teacher behavior through staff development: Implementing the teaching and content standards in science. *School Science and Mathematics, 97*, 302-309.

Grant, C. M. (n.d.). *Professional development in a technological age: New definitions, old challenges, new resources*. Retrieved January 18, 2003, from ra.terc.edu/publications/TERC_pubs/tech-infusion/prof_dev/prof_dev_intro.html

Guskey, T. R. (1986). Staff development and the process of teacher change. *Educational Researcher, 15*, 5-12.

Hammel, J., & Angelo, J. (1996). Technology competencies for occupational therapy practitioners. *Assistive Technology, 8*(1), 34-42.

Handler, M. G. (1993). Preparing new teachers to use computer technology: Perceptions and suggestions for teacher educators. *Computers and Education, 20*, 148-153.

Hassel, E. (1999). *Professional development: Learning from the best.* Oak Brook, IL: North Central Regional Educational Laboratory. Retrieved January 14, 2003, from: www.ncrel.org/pd/toolkit/lftb.pdf.

Hoffman, B. (1997, January). Integrating technology into school. *The Education Digest,* 51-55.

Individuals with Disabilities Education Act Amendments of 1997, 20 U.S.C. §1400 *et seq.*

Instructional Technology Passport System. (n.d.). *Competencies: Assistive technology.* Retrieved January 14, 2003, from: www.itps.ilstu.edu/competencies/assistive_technology.htm

Kentucky Department of Education. (2003). *Kentucky's teacher technology standards.* Retrieved May 25, 2003 from: www.kentuckyschools.net/KDE/Instructional +Resources/Technology/ Teacher+Resources /default.htm.

Lahm, E. A. (2002). [Teacher readiness to use technology for instruction]. Unpublished raw data.

Lahm, E. A. (2003). Considering assistive technology: Arming school districts with knowledge. *Remedial and Special Education, 24*(3), 141-153.

Lahm, E. A., & Nickels, B. L. (1999). What do you know? Assistive technology competencies for special educators. *Teaching Exceptional Children, 32*(1), 56-63.

Ley, K. (1997). Facing NCATE review or just looking for technology standards? *Techtrends, 42*(4), 41-42.

Lombardi, T. P., & Ludlow, B. L. (1997, March). *Special education in the 21st century.* Morgantown: West Virginia University. (ERIC Document Reproduction Service No. ED406086)

Malouf, D. B., & Schiller, E. P. (1995). Practice and research in special education. *Exceptional Children, 61*, 414-424.

Minkel, J. (1996, September-October). Credentialing in assistive technology: Myths and realities. *RESNA News,* 1-6.

Moffett, C. (1999). *The impact of the Kentucky Education Reform Act on the perceived readiness of teachers to use technology: A preliminary investigation.* Unpublished educational specialist's thesis, University of Kentucky, Lexington.

National Clearinghouse for Professions in Special Education. (2003). Retrieved December 25, 2002, from: www.special-ed-careers.org/ .National Council for Accreditation of Teacher Education. (2003). *Quick facts.* Retrieved May 8, 2003, from: www.ncate.org/ncate/fact_sheet.htm.

NETS Project. (2002). *National educational technology standards for teachers: Establishing performance-based standards and assessments for improving technology competence in preservice education.* Eugene, OR: International Society for Technology in Education.

No Child Left Behind Act, 20 U.S.C. § 6301(2001).

Office of Technology Assessment. (1995). *Teachers and technology making the connection.* Washington, DC: United States Congress, Office of Technology Assessment.

RESNA. (2000a). *ATP/ATS/RET directory.* Retrieved June 1, 2003, from www.resna.org/cert/index.html.

RESNA. (2000b) *Fundamentals of assistive technology* (3rd ed.). Arlington, VA: Author.

RESNA. (n.d.). *RESNA credentialing program.* Retrieved December 30, 2003, from www.resna.org/NewCertPract/Getting Certificate.php.

Smith, S. J. (2000). Graduate students mentors for technology success. *Teacher Education and Special Education, 23*, 167-182.

Smith, S. J., & Jones, E. D. (1999). The obligation to provide assistive technology: Enhancing general curriculum access. *Journal of Law & Education, 28*(2), 247-265.

Appendix A

Assignments of an Assistive Technology Graduate Level Course

Assignment Descriptions

Computer Access Software Overlay

Develop a computer access overlay for a 15-year-old child with severe physical disabilities that requires him to use a single switch or single finger to access the computer. The student's cognitive ability is inferred in the instructional task selected. Choose one of the following learning activities and design an onscreen keyboard or alternative keyboard overlay:

1. Write a poem using Write:OutLoud, IntelliTalk II, or Read & Write Gold talking word processors.
2. Use And a One, Two, Three to practice identifying the syllables of a word. Use one subprogram or level only.
3. Use an Excel or Microsoft Works spreadsheet to record data during a study of local weather.
4. Play solitaire on the computer during free time.

Update Anson's Examples

The Anson textbook is a bit outdated, as is often the case with technology books. The purpose of the assignment is to update the examples of available technologies for each of the access strategies discussed. If you were asked to rewrite this book, what would you include? For starters, all of the Apple IIe and DOS applications could be eliminated. There are very few of those systems in use any more. The primary systems in use today include Windows-based and Macintosh. For each chapter, you will update the table of examples that appears at the beginning of the chapter. You need to identify the latest products that fit each access strategy. Develop a table similar to those in the textbook showing currently available technologies. For part one of this assignment, include chapters 4-15. For part two, include chapters 16-29.

Part 1	Part 2
Key latches: Locking the modifier keys	Speech recognition
Adjust or defeat auto-repeat: Avoiding unintended characters	Eye-controlled input
Delayed acceptance: Avoiding accidental keystrokes	Mouse emulators
Bounce keys: Avoiding accidental keystrokes	Mouse-driven keyboard
Keyguard: Avoiding accidental keystrokes	Scanning input
Expanded keyboards	Macro programs
Mini-keyboards: Accommodating limited range of motion	Abbreviation expansion
Keypad: Assigning mouse movements to the keyboard	Word prediction
After-market mice	Changing system beep
Keyboard-emulating interfaces	Visual beep
Morse code	Screen enlargers
Three-switch morse code	Screen readers Tactile output

(continued next page)

Communication Board

Develop a communication board for a 6-year-old nonverbal child with near-normal intelligence needing to participate in one of the following learning activities:

1. Selecting from a menu and eating lunch in the cafeteria with students without disabilities. Make the communication board general enough to meet the child's needs during most lunch periods.
2. Describe the week's spelling worksheet assignments to the parents and a request to be drilled on the spelling words before Friday's text.
3. Work in a cooperative group with two peers on science activities. You can focus on one developmentally appropriate topic within science.
4. Describe their family to the class based on a photograph brought in from home.

Electronic Database Searches

Familiarize yourself with the ABLEDATA and Closing the Gap databases that are online. Using one of the provided descriptions of a fictitious person with a disability, describe what function(s) that person is unable to perform that is required in his/her current setting. Describe the barriers that prevent the person from performing the function. Search both databases for potential assistive devices that address the student's needs. Make a list of the search terms you used for each search and print out the results. If any of your searches results in more than 10 items, try to narrow the search using more/better search terms. If you cannot achieve 10 or fewer, select the 10 you think would be best for this individual and include only those in your printed report. Briefly reflect on what you learned from this assignment. Is one database better than the other for your student's needs? In what situations would the other one be more appropriate? Which was easier to use and why?

Research Paper

In order to become more conversant about the latest developments in technology access for persons with disabilities, you will develop a research paper focused on an implementation issue. A list of possible topics will be provided. Other topics must be approved by the instructor. The paper must include on overview of the issue, a synthesis of the research reviewed, a conclusion drawn from the research, and a reflection on the implications of the research on implementation of assistive technology in your setting. A minimum of 10 articles must be referenced in the synthesis section with a minimum of 5 of them being research (data-based) articles. All articles must be dated no earlier than 1998, and no more than three of the articles can be from an electronic source (e.g., the Internet). A reference list of all articles used must be included at the end of the paper. APA format must be used both in the text and on the reference list. The paper must be word processed and submitted both electronically and in hard copy.

Brochure and Web Site Evaluation

Each student will develop an information brochure to give to colleagues or parents as a resource for Web sites on an assistive technology topic. A minimum of 10 and a maximum of 20 sites should be included. Each site listed must include a 2-5 sentence original annotation that tells the reader what type of information will be found at a given site and reasons for visiting it. One of the sites must be evaluated for validity, reliability, and timeliness of the information using the provided evaluation form. The evaluation should be a separate product and not be incorporated into the brochure. The brochure must include three columns (two-fold), two pages printed front-to-back, and incorporate two or more graphics.

(continued next page)

Assistive Device/Software Presentation

Each student will select a programmable device or program from a list of approved technologies. If you don't have access to one of these, make arrangements to borrow one from your local school district or Assistive Technology Center. Learn how to use the device or program and become "expert" at it. Customize the device/software for a specific individual and instructional task. The product of this assignment will be a disk with a customized overlay or program settings, print-outs of your customized overlays, programs, or materials, a "cheat sheet" for operating the technology, and a PowerPoint or Web-based presentation of the technology to the class.

The presentation will be made during the last class session. It should highlight the features, advantages, and disadvantages of their device/software, using the customized product developed for the assignment. The operation, maintenance, and programming required by the device will be demonstrated.

Final Exam

About mid-semester, you will receive several AT implementation topics. You are to select one topic and develop expertise in that topic by reading the literature, interviewing others with expertise in the area, and "implementing" the topic to gain personal experience. On the last night of class you will be given two discussion items for your topic. You will choose one and respond to it in writing prior to the scheduled final exam night for this class.

Appendix B.

Appendix B

Personal Planning Instrument for Updating Knowledge & Skills in Assistive Technology
For Assistive Technology Specialists, Teacher Educators, Special Education
Service Providers, and General Educators
© 2003 Elizabeth A. Lahm

Complete the following survey rating your knowledge and skill level in each area. Not all items on the survey are intended for everyone. Complete the items that pertain to your role, as listed below:

- Assistive technology specialists   complete all items in column 'A'
- Teacher educators   complete items not shaded in column 'T'
- Special educators   complete items not shaded in column 'S'
- General educators   complete items not shaded in column 'G'

When finished, review your ratings and identify your top 5 priority areas of knowledge deficit. Using the table on the last page, write personal goals and strategies for updating your knowledge and skills in these five priority areas.

Please rate your level of expertise in each of the following areas. A rating of "1" indicates no expertise and "5" indicates that you are an expert in that area. (Note: K = knowledge and S = skill)

Principle I: Foundations	Expertise Least → Most	A	T	S	G
1. Concepts and issues related to the use of technology in education and other aspects of our society. (K)	1 2 3 4 5				
2. Articulate a personal philosophy and goals for using technology in special education. (S)	1 2 3 4 5				░
3. Use technology-related terminology in written and oral communication. (S)	1 2 3 4 5				░
4. Describe legislative mandates and governmental regulations and their implications for technology in special education. (S)	1 2 3 4 5			░	░

Principle II: Development and Characteristics of Learners	Expertise Least → Most	A	T	S	G
5. Impact of technology at all stages of development on individuals with exceptional learning needs. (K)	1 2 3 4 5			░	░

Principle III: Individual Learning Differences	Expertise Least → Most	A	T	S	G
6. Issues in diversity and the use of technology. (K)	1 2 3 4 5				

(continued next page)

Appendix B. (continued)

Name: _____   Date: _____

Principle IV: Instructional Strategies	Expertise Least → Most	A	T	S	G
7. Identify and operate instructional and assistive hardware, software, and peripherals. (S)	1 2 3 4 5				
8. Provide technology support to individuals with exceptional learning needs who are receiving instruction in the general education setting. (S)	1 2 3 4 5		▨		▨
9. Arrange for demonstrations and trial periods with potential assistive or instructional technologies prior to making purchase decisions. (S)	1 2 3 4 5				▨

Principle V: Learning Environments/Social Interactions	Expertise Least → Most	A	T	S	G
10. Procedures for the organization, management, and security of technology. (K)	1 2 3 4 5		▨	▨	▨
11. Ergonomic principles to facilitate the use of technology. (K)	1 2 3 4 5		▨		
12. Evaluate features of technology systems. (S)	1 2 3 4 5			▨	
13. Use technology to foster social acceptance in inclusive settings. (S)	1 2 3 4 5				▨
14. Identify the demands of technology on the individual with exceptional learning needs. (S)	1 2 3 4 5		▨		▨

Principle VI: Language	Expertise Least → Most	A	T	S	G
15. Use communication technologies to access information and resources electronically. (S)	1 2 3 4 5				▨

Principle VII: Instructional Planning	Expertise Least → Most	A	T	S	G
16. Procedures for evaluation of computer software and other technology materials for their potential application in special education. (K)	1 2 3 4 5				▨
17. Funding sources and processes of the acquisition of assistive technology devices and services. (K)	1 2 3 4 5		▨	▨	
18. National, state, or provincial PK-12 technology standards. (K)	1 2 3 4 5				
19. Assist the individual with exceptional learning needs in clarifying and prioritizing functional intervention goals regarding technology-based evaluation results. (S)	1 2 3 4 5		▨		▨
20. Identify elements of the curriculum for which technology applications are appropriate and ways they can be implemented. (S)	1 2 3 4 5				
21. Identify and operate software that meets educational objectives for individuals with exceptional learning needs in a variety of educational environments. (S)	1 2 3 4 5				
22. Design, fabricate, and install assistive technology materials and devices to meet the needs of individuals with exceptional learning needs. (S)	1 2 3 4 5		▨	▨	▨
23. Provide consistent, structured training to individuals with exceptional learning needs to operate instructional and adaptive equipment and software until they have achieved mastery. (S)	1 2 3 4 5				

Personal Planning Instrument; p. 2 of 5

(continued next page)

Appendix B. (continued)

Name: _____   Date: _____

Principle VII: Instructional Planning (continued)	Expertise Least → Most	A	T	S	G
24. Verify proper implementation of mechanical and electrical safety practices in the assembly and integration of the technology to meet the needs of individuals with exceptional learning needs. (S)	1 2 3 4 5		▨		
25. Develop and implement contingency plans in the event that assistive or instructional technology devices fail. (S)	1 2 3 4 5		▨		
26. Develop specifications and/or drawings necessary for technology acquisitions. (S)	1 2 3 4 5			▨	▨
27. Write proposals to obtain technology funds. (S)	1 2 3 4 5			▨	

Principle VIII: Assessment	Expertise Least → Most	A	T	S	G
28. Use of technology in the assessment, diagnosis, and evaluation of individuals with exceptional learning needs. (S)	1 2 3 4 5				▨
29. Match characteristics of individuals with exceptional learning needs with technology product or software features. (S)	1 2 3 4 5				
30. Use technology to collect, analyze, summarize and report student performance data to aid instructional decision-making. (S)	1 2 3 4 5		▨		
31. Identify functional needs, screen for functional limitations and identify if the need for a comprehensive assistive or instructional technology evaluation exists. (S)	1 2 3 4 5				
32. Monitor outcomes of technology-based interventions and reevaluate and adjust the system as needed. (S)	1 2 3 4 5				
33. Assist the individual with exceptional learning needs in clarifying and prioritizing functional intervention goals regarding technology-based evaluation results. (S)	1 2 3 4 5		▨		
34. Work with team members to identify assistive and instructional technologies that can help individuals meet the demands placed upon them in their environments. (S)	1 2 3 4 5	▨			▨
35. Identify placement of devices and positioning of the individual to optimize the use of assistive or instructional technology. (S)	1 2 3 4 5				
36. Examine alternative solutions prior to making assistive or instructional technology decisions. (S)	1 2 3 4 5				
37. Make technology decisions based on a continuum of options ranging from no technology to high technology. (S)	1 2 3 4 5				

Principle IX: Professional & Ethical Practice	Expertise Least → Most	A	T	S	G
38. Equity, ethical, legal, and human issues related to technology use in special education. (K)	1 2 3 4 5				
39. Organizations and publications relevant to the field of technology. (K)	1 2 3 4 5				▨
40. Maintain ongoing professional development to acquire knowledge and skills about new developments in technology. (S)	1 2 3 4 5				▨

Personal Planning Instrument; p. 3 of 5

Name: _____   Date: _____

Principle IX: Professional & Ethical Practice (continued)	Expertise Least → Most	A	T	S	G
41. Adhere to copyright laws about duplication and distribution of software and other copyrighted technology materials. (S)	1 2 3 4 5				
42. Advocate for assistive or instructional technology on individual and system change levels. (S)	1 2 3 4 5		▨		▨
43. Participate in activities of professional organizations relevant to the field of technology. (S)	1 2 3 4 5				▨

Principle X: Collaboration	Expertise Least → Most	A	T	S	G
44. Roles that related services personnel fulfill in providing technology services. (K)	1 2 3 4 5				
45. Guidelines for referring individuals with exceptional learning needs to another professional. (K)	1 2 3 4 5				▨
46. Conduct in-service training in applications of technology in special education. (S)	1 2 3 4 5		▨		
47. Refer team members and families to assistive and instructional technology resources. (S)	1 2 3 4 5		▨		▨
48. Collaborate with other team members in planning and implementing the use of assistive and adaptive devices. (S)	1 2 3 4 5		▨		▨
49. Instruct others in the operation of technology, maintenance, warranties, and trouble-shooting techniques. (S)	1 2 3 4 5		▨	▨	▨

When determining personal learning strategies in the table on the next page, you may want to consider some of the following. You may have to determine or create their availability in your local area.

Formal Learning Opportunities	Informal and Job-Embedded Learning Opportunities
Participate in hands-on workshops in schools or universities	Participate in open lab hours at schools and universities
Participate in AT workshops with CEU credit	Borrow devices and/or software from an AT loan library
Borrow equipment from AT libraries to use while taking a class to incorporate into course assignments	Collaborate with local universities and local schools to write an AT grant
Utilize available technical assistance for coursework or classroom applications	Initiate local school collaboratives for sharing equipment
Enroll in independent study or Web-based courses if AT courses are not available	Establish and participate in AT study or user groups
Help your school establish a partnership with a university to obtain guided support for AT implementation	Participate in AT action research
Request AT coursework to be included in a graduate program	Participate in mentor programs
Include hands-on and collaborative AT implementation strategies into your coursework assignments	Maintain an active role in local general and special education associations
Collaborate with general educators in course assignments	Attend an AT conference and/or technology fair
Participate in summer institutes in AT	Identify and use a phone or email help line

Personal Planning Instrument; p. 4 of 5

Appendix B. (continued)

Name: _____   Date: _____

Complete the following table for the five priority areas you identified for your self.

Item Number	Personal Goal	Strategies for Achieving Your Goal

Personal Planning Instrument; p. 5 of 5

Illustration of Assistive Technology Competencies Infused into Existing Undergraduate Courses

	Principle I: Foundations	1. Concepts and issues related to the use of technology	2. Articulate a personal philosophy and goals	3. Use technology-related terminology	Principle III: Individual Learning Differences	6. Issues in diversity and the use of technology	Principle IV: Instructional Strategies	7. Identify and operate hardware, software, and peripherals	8. Provide technology support to instruction in the general education setting	9. Arrange for demonstrations and trial periods prior to purchase
Student Teaching				•				•	•	
Methods of Teaching		•		•				•	•	•
Curriculum Design				•						
Collaboration and Inclusion				•		•			•	
Transdisciplinary Services				•						
Characteristics of Persons w/Disabilities		•		•		•				
Assistive Technology in SE		•	•	•		•		•	•	•
Behavior Management and Instruction				•						
Instructional Technology in SE		•	•	•		•		•	•	•
Legal Issues in Special Education		•		•						
Early Childhood Special Education		•		•		•				
Introduction to Exceptional Children		•		•						

(continued next page)

Illustration of Assistive Technology Competencies Infused into Existing Undergraduate Courses (continued)

	20. Identify elements of the curriculum for technology applications	21. Identify and operate software for a variety of educational environments	23. Provide consistent, structured training to operate instructional and adaptive equipment and software	24. Verify proper implementation of mechanical and electrical safety practices	25. Develop and implement contingency plans	Principle VIII: Assessment	28. Use of technology in the assessment, diagnosis, and evaluation	29. Match characteristics of individuals with technology features	30. Use technology to collect, analyze, summarize and report student performance data
Student Teaching		●	●	●	●		●	●	●
Methods of Teaching			●				●		●
Curriculum Design	●	●						●	
Collaboration and Inclusion					●				
Transdisciplinary Services							●		
Characteristics of Persons w/Disabilities	●	●					●	●	
Assistive Technology in SE	●	●		●	●		●	●	
Behavior Management and Instruction			●						●
Instructional Technology in SE	●	●		●				●	
Legal Issues in Special Education									
Early Childhood Special Education	●	●					●	●	
Introduction to Exceptional Children									

(continued next page)

Illustration of Assistive Technology Competencies Infused into Existing Undergraduate Courses (continued)

(continued next page)

	31. Identify need for a comprehensive technology evaluation	32. Monitor outcomes and reevaluate and adjust the system as needed	33. Assist in clarifying and prioritizing goals regarding evaluation results	34. Work with team members to identify assistive and instructional technologies	35. Identify placement of devices and positioning of the individual to optimize use	36. Examine alternative solutions	37. Make technology decisions based on a continuum of options	Principle IX: Professional & Ethical Practice	38. Equity, ethical, legal, and human issues related to technology use
Student Teaching		●	●	●			●		
Methods of Teaching		●	●			●			
Curriculum Design									
Collaboration and Inclusion				●					
Transdisciplinary Services	●			●	●				
Characteristics of Persons w/Disabilities					●	●			
Assistive Technology in SE	●	●	●	●	●	●	●		●
Behavior Management and Instruction		●	●						
Instructional Technology in SE					●	●			●
Legal Issues in Special Education									●
Early Childhood Special Education					●	●			
Introduction to Exceptional Children									●

Illustration of Assistive Technology Competencies Infused into Existing Undergraduate Courses (continued)

	39. Organizations and publications relevant to the field of technology	40. Maintain ongoing professional development in technology	41. Adhere to copyright laws	42. Advocate for technology on individual and system change levels	43. Participate in activities of professional organizations	Principle X: Collaboration	44. Roles that related services personnel fulfill in providing technology services.	45. Guidelines for referring individuals to another professional	47. Refer team members and families to technology resources	48. Collaborate with other team members in planning and implementing
Student Teaching		•			•				•	•
Methods of Teaching										
Curriculum Design										
Collaboration and Inclusion				•						•
Transdisciplinary Services							•	•	•	•
Characteristics of Persons w/Disabilities	•									
Assistive Technology in SE	•	•	•	•	•		•	•	•	•
Behavior Management and Instruction										
Instructional Technology in SE	•	•	•		•					
Legal Issues in Special Education			•	•						
Early Childhood Special Education	•									
Introduction to Exceptional Children										

Note. These competencies are shortened versions of those listed in the Personal Planning Instrument. Only competencies indicated as necessary for beginning teachers are listed. Each refers to assistive and instructional technology whether specifically stated or not.

36

Using Technology to Enhance Collaboration to Benefit All Students

Pam Campbell and Bob Algozzine

As learners with disabilities are included in general education classrooms in greater numbers and for longer periods of time, educators-expert and novice alike-are looking for ways to teach more effectively. "Teachers simply need access to powerful information about teaching effectively that is easily available to them and sustained over time" (personal communication, Larry Maheady, November 8, 1999). Such information needs to be compiled and organized in a useful efficient format. Further, teachers need a way to share both the information and their expertise with one another. Technology can support and facilitate this process.

In 1975, Public Law 94-142 was passed; it guaranteed a free, appropriate education to individuals with disabilities and was heralded as the first compulsory special education law (Ysseldyke & Algozzine, 1982). In the brief history of mandatory special education, some would note that the field has undergone dramatic changes. Others would review the events and trends of the past 28 years and argue that the field has not progressed sufficiently. Regardless of their perspectives on progress, however, professionals agree that the field of special education continues to be driven by federal and state mandates, economic and societal conditions, technological innovations, and professional responsibilities.

Mandates are driving curriculum and assessment for students in schools and teacher preparation programs. Consequently, the ways in which teachers teach, regardless of setting, are changing. Economic and social conditions are increasing the diversity of our student population-at a rate much greater than that of their teachers. Because "one size does not fit all," teaching practices that provide appropriate opportunities for learners with diverse needs are essential. With advances in technology increasing exponentially, innovations in hardware and software are changing the ways in which we talk to one another, manage information, and learn. Thus, the need for teachers to be lifelong learners has never been greater.

In the midst of these change forces, educators recognize their continued responsibility to their students, their profession, and themselves. At the same time, they must ask themselves if they have taken full advantage of the opportunities presented by each of these challenges, and, whether they have had the vision and capability to integrate these challenges in ways that ultimately result in better services for individuals with diverse learning needs.

The purpose of this chapter is to synthesize research and practice in three areas of concern for educators of students with disabilities: special education, collaboration, and technology. The discussion is organized into the following sections-foundation for systematic analysis, methodology for locating relevant literature, the current knowledge base, recent trends and continuing issues, current status, and a research agenda for the future.

Foundation for Systematic Analysis

Given the focus of this chapter, each term-special education, collaboration, and technology-needs to be defined before moving on to a discussion of its collective integration. Each term is considered in turn.

Special Education

Special education is instruction designed for students with special learning needs. Some of these students have difficulty learning in general classrooms; they need special education to function in school. Others do well in general classrooms; they need special education to support mastery of additional skills to reach their full potential in school. Special education is evidence of society's willingness to recognize and respond to the individual needs of students and the limits of regular school programs to accommodate those needs.

Special education is a sophisticated series of educational alternatives for students needing special assistance in school. In 1975, President Gerald Ford signed into law the Education for All Handicapped Children Act (1975), the first compulsory special education law (now known as the Individuals with Disabilities Education Act, IDEA). It guaranteed students with disabilities and their parents certain rights, and it placed specific responsibilities on people who organize and deliver special education services.

In brief, the law mandates the following:

- A free, appropriate public education for children with disabilities.

- Well-planned school programs tailored to meet students' unique learning needs.

- Protection of the rights of students with disabilities under the same legal provisions that protect the rights of students without disabilities (due process).

- The right of students with disabilities to have decisions made about them in an unbiased manner.

- Educational environments like those provided students without disabilities.

Students receiving special education receive direct, related, or indirect services. *Direct services* are provided by working with students themselves to correct or compensate for the conditions that have caused them to fall behind in school or to enrich or accelerate the progress they are making. Teaching a student who is deaf to use sign language, a student with learning disabilities to read using a special method of instruction, or a fourth grader who is gifted to do algebra are all examples of direct services provided by teachers. *Related services* are provided by specially trained personnel directly (to students) or indirectly (to those who work with exceptional students). Thus, related services include psychological testing and counseling, school social work, educational/occupational therapy, adapted physical education, school health services, and transportation. Finally, *Indirect or consultative services* are provided by working with classroom teachers and others who work with exceptional students over a period of time to help meet the needs of the students. Helping a teacher identify the best method for teaching a student with learning disabilities to read or showing a teacher how to reposition a student who has physical disabilities are examples of indirect services provided by teachers and other professionals.

Collaboration

Collaboration means working together to solve problems and provide services to students with disabilities. Because general education teachers rarely are prepared to work with students with disabilities, collaboration among general and special educators has become an important education goal. As trends in special education change, so do trends in general education. For example, the inclusion of more students with special needs in the general education classroom is becoming increasingly prevalent around the nation. Historically, students with disabilities spent most of their school day in separate classrooms, usually without any adaptation to the general education curriculum. Today, many students with disabilities spend the majority of their school day in the general education setting receiving assistance accessing the same curriculum as their natural neighbors and peers. Best practices reflect general and special education teachers collaborating to provide these services.

Technology

Technology is the application of science and engineering principles to the development of products, practices, and procedures that enhance or improve human conditions, or at least improve human efficiency in some respect. The pressure to incorporate new technology into all areas of life is powerful. In special education, in particular, many feel compelled to jump headfirst on the technology bandwagon, desperately hoping not to be left behind in a rapidly changing world. This impulse to incorporate technology into special education comes with costs, however. Technology can be expensive and in constant need of upgrades and the attention of a well-trained support staff. Nevertheless, while bringing technology into special education has not been cheap, it has proven to be a worthwhile investment.

Parameters/Beliefs

With common understandings about special education, collaboration, and technology, the following set of parameters and beliefs is provided to guide the analysis of collaboration in special education via technology. If the overall goal is to improve the quality of education for students with disabilities, the following deserve consideration.

- All teachers must be well prepared to plan, manage, deliver, and evaluate appropriate and effective instruction throughout their careers;
- Powerful legal and political initiatives must advocate for the inclusion (mainstreaming) of students with disabilities in general education classrooms to the maximum extent possible;
- Teacher preparation programs and professional development activities must provide continual "practice" in collaboration across areas of specialization, grade/age levels, years of experience;
- Collaboration must be broadened to engage not only general and special educators in the school setting, but other also partners and relationships—those responsible and involved in ensuring the quality of teaching and learning;
- Opportunities for continual conversations

about best practice must be part of all collaboration efforts;
- Recent developments in technology must have an impact on the quality of teachers and the delivery of services to students with disabilities; and,
- Technology must enhance, not inhibit collaboration.

The knowledge bases in special education, consultation, and technology are very broad. This chapter will focus on information representing the convergence of consultation and technology to improve special education services. This work represents the first systematic review of this body of knowledge and provides conclusions for broad implications for the improvement of services for all students, especially those with disabilities.

Methodology Used to Locate Relevant Literature

A wide variety of electronic and print resources were screened to identify literature (published or in press) for possible inclusion in this review, including ERIC, EBSCOHost, PSYCINFO, Dissertation Abstracts International, and the Council for Exceptional Children databases. Search terms (e.g., collaboration, technology, teacher preparation) were combined with the word disabilities to narrow the search. Recent issues of relevant journals were searched manually to identify references not yet included in electronic databases. The reference sections of included articles as well as position papers, chapters, and books on special education, collaboration, and technology were reviewed to identify potentially relevant research. In addition, conference proceedings from the Council for Exceptional Children (CEC), The Teacher Education Division (TED) of CEC, the Technology and Media Division (TAM) of CEC, the Society for Information Technology in Teacher Education (SITTE), and the annual technology conference at California State University Northridge (CSUN) were researched from 2000-2003 for related presentations/papers not yet in press. Internet resources were reviewed as well, if they met criteria for credibility, including an affiliation with a Specialized Professional Association (SPA) such as CEC, or other professional organization such as the National Network for School Renewal (NNER), and so on. Finally, researchers and practitioners widely recognized as active in the field of special education were asked to identify and submit sources.

Abstracts, methods, and results sections of potential articles were reviewed by two researchers knowledgeable in special education, collaboration, and technology research to ascertain appropriateness for further consideration and inclusion according to six criteria. First, the article had to be published or "in-press" in a peer-reviewed journal between 1975 and 2003. (The year 1975 was selected because this was the date of the earliest mandatory special education law.) Second, the subjects had to be individuals classified with one of the disabilities recognized by IDEA or nonspecified "developmental disabilities." Third, studies had to involve individuals from age 3 to adulthood. Fourth, the source did not have to demonstrate experimental control and could be a report of a teaching intervention or a qualitative study. Fifth, the source had to be one that addressed learning new skills or acquiring new opportunities. Sixth, the information had to focus on the use of collaboration or of technology to improve special education practices.

Current Knowledge Base: Special Education, Collaboration, and Technology

Special education is a relatively young field that has experienced many changes in recent years. Social, political, legal, and scientific forces have created controversy and fragmentation among professionals and parents of students with disabilities. The consistent controlling force has been, and will likely continue to be, the mandates and funding of the federal government. This has resulted in a system of beliefs and practices that supports parents and professionals collaborating to bring about the best educational experiences for children and youth with disabilities. The rise of technology may serve to support collaboration in special education.

Special Education

Early special education efforts focused on protecting individuals with disabilities, primarily through isolation and segregation. By contrast, contemporary special education initiatives have focused on providing individuals with disabilities opportunities that are as much like those provided to their neighbors and peers without disabilities (i.e., not segregating, but integrating and including). Highly qualified teachers are needed for inclusion to work. The knowledge base regarding inclusion and preparing effective teachers is encouraging.

Inclusion

Early special education programs were provided in separate classrooms, separate schools, and even separate systems (e.g., institutions for people with mental retardation). The move to abandon segregated special education grew in the late 1960s with a growing interest in "normalization," or the belief that if people with disabilities are treated in a normal manner in normative settings they will act more normally (Cronis & Ellis, 2000; Wolfensberger, 1972; Ysseldyke, Algozzine, & Thurlow, 2000). A period of court-ordered deinstitutionalization and mainstreaming (placing people with disabilities in normal environments) followed, culminating in the passage of the Education for All Handicapped Children Act (1975). Public Law 94-142 required that students with disabilities be educated in the least restrictive environment in which an individualized education program could be reasonably implemented.

Most of the early efforts to educate students with disabilities in the same classrooms as their neighbors and peers were met with resistance, often by special education professionals who argued that in abandoning their service delivery model they had also abandoned those strategies that had proven effective in segregated settings (Cronis & Ellis, 2000; Ysseldyke et al., 2000). However, during the decades that followed, professionals supported educational practices that promoted staffing, instruction, accommodation, and support for children with disabilities in inclusive settings.

The inclusion movement had an impact on subsequent amendments to the Education for

All Handicapped Children Act. For example, in 1990 it was renamed as the Individuals with Disabilities Education Act (IDEA), and its language was changed to emphasize person-first syntax (e.g., students with disabilities instead of handicapped students). The IDEA'97 Amendments retained the major provisions of earlier federal laws, including the assurance of having a free appropriate public education (FAPE) for all children with disabilities, in the least restrictive environment (LRE), and the guarantee of procedural safeguards and due-process procedures.

It also included modifications that affected special education practice nationwide, including:

• Participation of students with disabilities in state- and districtwide assessment (testing) programs, with appropriate accommodations where necessary. The law also includes the development of guidelines, as appropriate, for participation of children with disabilities in alternate assessments, for children who cannot participate in regular assessments with accommodations and modifications.

• Development and review of the Individualized Education Program (IEP), including increased emphasis on participation of children and youth with disabilities in the general curriculum and involvement of general education teachers in developing, reviewing and revising the students' IEPs.

• Enhanced parent participation in eligibility and placement decisions.

• Streamlined student evaluation and reevaluation requirements.

• Beginning at age 14, and updated annually, a statement of the transition service needs of the student focusing on the student's courses of study.

• The availability of mediation as a means of more easily resolving parent-school differences. At a minimum, mediation must be available whenever a due-process hearing is requested.

• Disciplinary procedures for students with disabilities, including placement of certain students with disabilities in appropriate interim alternative educational settings for up to 45 days.

• Allowing children ages 3-9 to be identified as developmentally delayed, with the upper age limit at the discretion of the state and the local educational agency. (Previously, the developmental delay category was restricted to ages 3-5.)

Interestingly, while funding from federal and state sources as well as teacher credentialing practices dictate a separate system of education for students with disabilities, inclusion efforts have created reasons for blending general education and special education. Thus, as the move to provide more and more services in general education classrooms grew, the need for upgrading teacher preparation programs and teacher competencies also increased.

Preparing Well-educated Teachers
It is well known that what teachers know and how well they teach makes the critical difference in student learning (National Commission on Teaching and America's Future, NCTAF, 1996). Their knowledge and skills as teachers are the product of their preparation, their years of experience as teachers, and their professional development over time. The "three R's" for teacher education (that is, the basics for new teachers) are (a) the ability to teach effectively to rigorous student learning standards, (b) the ability to organize the classroom environment and manage student behavior to optimize student learning, and (c) the willingness and ability to collaborate effectively with parents and fellow teachers (Pugach & Johnson, 2002). Preparing teachers with knowledge and skills to address these areas is widely recognized as an important, albeit an illusive, educational goal:

> *While I am confident that teacher educators and prospective teachers understand the importance of the first two, such is not always the case with the third. In my experience, many prospective teachers are not aware of the importance of collaboration in their chosen professions, and too often teacher education programs approach collaboration as a predilection*

or disposition, rather than a set of skills to be taught and nurtured. (Lilly, 2002, in Pugach & Johnson, 2002, p. x)

To address these needs, many researchers, authors, and practitioners have been examining ways in which to reform and restructure education. Some have focused primarily on the renewal of schools (Comer, 1993; Holmes Group, 1986, 1990; Sizer, 1985, 1992, 1996; Wasley, 1994), others on the revision of teacher preparation programs (Goodlad & Lovitt, 1993; Holmes Group, 1996; Schon, 1987). Still others have recognized the need for greater collaboration between universities and the public schools (Cochran-Smith & Lytle, 1993; Holmes Group, 1990). In fact, Goodlad (1990, 1994) and the work of the National Network for School Renewal (NNER) believe that this process of renewal is possible only if ongoing and conducted simultaneously in the public school and universities—in both the liberal arts and sciences and teacher preparation programs. In this model, educators at universities and in public schools share their expertise, their roles, and their responsibilities in a truly collaborative manner to provide well-educated teachers of all students.

Despite progress, continuing negative teacher beliefs and attitudes, insufficient preparation, support, or resources, and the types/severity of disabilities involved continue to contribute to problems in implementing inclusive practices (Baines, Baines, & Masterson, 1994; Cronis & Ellis, 2000; McGregor & Vogelsberg, 1998; Salend & Duhaney, 1999; Ysseldyke et al., 2000; Zigmond, Jenkins, & Fuchs, 1995). Most discussions of inclusion and collaboration focus on the delivery of services at the classroom level. A broader perspective of collaboration that parallels the simultaneous renewal initiatives is proposed. That is, to provide quality teachers to meet the needs of all students in public schools, both teacher candidates and practicing professionals must be willing and able to collaborate effectively in meeting the needs of all students.

Collaboration

Collaboration in schools has typically focused on resolving problems around student learning. The focus may be an individual or group of students, classroom or school-wide concerns, or connections with parents and community resources. Within the public schools, recent reform initiatives such as Accelerated Schools (Hopfenberg, Levin, Chase, & Christensen, 1993), which seek "powerful learning" for all students by accelerating instruction, the Coalition for Essential Schools (Sizer, 1996), which has restructured instruction in high schools through the use of interdisciplinary instruction, highly engaged students, and demonstrations of learning, and the Comer School Development Program (Comer, 1997), which has engaged parents and community resources in creating safe and effective schools, provide excellent models for fostering and supporting collaboration in efforts to educate all students. However, it is the work of Goodlad (1986, 1994) that has enabled us to reconceptualize and broaden our definition of "collaboration" in ways that engage all teachers. It is a strategy that holds great promise for special education practice.

A Broader Definition of Collaboration

A broader view of collaboration addresses the needs of all students by addressing the needs of all teachers-those in preparation programs as well as those engaged in practice. Goodlad's National Network for Educational Renewal (NNER) is an example of 21 exemplary partnerships that are grounded in the principle of "simultaneous renewal" of teacher preparation programs and public school: one cannot be renewed without the full engagement of the other. These initiatives rely on sustained partnerships with public schools that differ significantly from previous arrangements.

Historically, the links between the public-private-charter schools and teacher preparation programs have been weak, if not superficial. Basically, schools provided practicum experiences and student teaching placements for teacher candidates and research sites for individual university faculty. However, in the last decade, there has been a movement to change the university/public relationship through the creation of Professional Development Schools (PDSs) that "provide opportunities for educational theory and practice to be joined together in diverse student-centered environments designed to take into account how students learn" (Futrell, Gomez, & Bedden, 2003, p. 381). These types of programs also provide opportunities for teachers-in-training, teachers, and teacher educators to work together to determine validated teaching and learning practice. All those who work in a PDS are given opportunities to learn from one another, to develop a better understanding of expectations within the school and the community, and to refine their repertoire of teaching skills and strategies. These opportunities for collaboration enhance teaching and learning in the general and special education classrooms, as well as in teacher education programs (Clark, 1999; Darling-Hammond, 1994; Goodlad, 1994; NCATE, 2001; Norlander-Case, Reagan, & Case, 1999; Rose, 2002).

In other words, educators in the PDSs and the university engage in thoughtful work with the goal of preparing and sustaining educators. They redesign courses and clinical experiences; they team teach in the PDS and at the university; they supervise practica students, student teachers, interns, and doctoral students; and they conduct research to answer their questions regarding effective practice. That is, they share responsibilities and engage in a shared vision of schooling and best practice. The work of the NNER, the Holmes Partnership, and other such PDS initiatives provides a broader perspective of collaboration—one that encompasses a wide community of learners and a model for providing inclusive services to students with disabilities. Therefore, our discussion of collaboration includes both teacher preparation and current practice. However, first, collaboration is considered in the context of special education.

Collaboration Within Special Education

The need for collaboration about students with disabilities was the result of the progression of special education from isolation and institutionalization to integration and inclusion; that is, the perspective that teaching all students well in general education classrooms to the maximum extent possible (LRE) is a matter of civil rights and best practice. Therefore, their teachers must be prepared to educate increasing

numbers of students with diverse needs—a responsibility that is beyond the capabilities of even the best prepared and most experienced teachers (Dettmer, Thurston, & Dyck, 2002) . The collaboration process has taken many forms in recent years; the more well-known models are outlined in the next section.

Collaboration models. Initial efforts to support inclusion practices provided expert (special education) teachers who supported general education classroom teachers, thereby providing indirect services to students with disabilities. Recently, more eclectic models have evolved, in which the problem-solving tasks may be similar but the style of interactions differs. Overviews of well-known models are provided below:

- In the *Triadic model* (Idol, Paolucci-Whitcomb, & Nevin, 1995; Tharp, 1975; Tharp & Wetzel, 1969), an example of "collaborative consultation", services flow from the consultant (expert) to and through the consultee (typically a teacher) to the target (typically a student).

- In the *Stephens/systems models* (Heron & Harris, 1987; Stephens, 1977), the consultant and consultee follow a cyclical process of data collection, problem identification, planning, implementation, and evaluation , which affords ongoing modifications to an intervention plan.

- *The Vermont Consulting Teacher Model* (Heron & Harris, 1987; Knight, Meyers, Paolucci-Whitcomb, Hasazi, & Nevin,1981) involved a collaboration among the Vermont State Department of Education, local school districts, and consultants from the University of Vermont. The purpose was to provide services statewide to teachers of students with disabilities. Components included university coursework, workshops, consultation, and parent involvement.

- *The School Consultation Committee Model* (McGlothlin, 1981) utilizes an outside consultant on an as-needed basis for participation in a standing Consultation Committee is typically that also includes the building administrator, a general and a special education teacher, and other related services personnel. The purpose of the Committee is to screen referrals, make assessments, develop plans, monitor their implementation, and evaluate their effectiveness.

- *The Resource/Consulting Teacher Program* Model (Idol et al.,1986; Idol-Maestas, 1981, 1983) is based on the Triadic Model and is intended to support students with disabilities in general education classrooms. Special education teachers (consultants) provide both direct instructional services to students and indirect services through consultation with general education teachers.

- *The Collaborative Consultation Model* (Idol et al., 1995; Pugach & Johnson, 2002; Walther-Thomas, Korinek, McLaughlin, & Williams, 2000) relies on the collective expertise of all participants, who agree on a common goal and the need for new outcomes. The actual process of collaborative consultation can vary. Participants may follow a prescribed set of steps as detailed by Dettmer et al. (2002) or Walther-Thomas et al. (2000) or function in a less formal manner. Regardless of the process used, parity, responsibility, shared resources, and accountability are required elements.

Focus of collaboration. The intent of these models has been the success of learners with disabilities in inclusive settings. Thus, collaboration about the needs of students with disabilities occurs at any point in the special education decision-making process: prereferral, diagnosis, placement, (IEP) development and implementation, instructional arrangements and delivery, modifications and adaptations, program and progress monitoring and assessment (formal/informal). Thus, the focus of collaboration will determine the content. For example, the focus might be the sharing of information and resources about the special education process, child development (Greenspan, Weider, & Simons, 1998); effective instruction (Algozzine & Ysseldyke, 1992, 1997); multiple intelligences (Gardner, 2000); validated practices in special education (Miller, 2002); and specific disabilities (Hallahan & Kauffman, 2003). Other types of collaboration might center on planning a process for creating diverse learning communities in a classroom (Vaughn, Bos, & Shumm, 2003); co/team teaching (Friend & Bursuck, 2002); curriculum-based assessment (Shinn & Hubbard, 1992); and implementing the collaboration process over time (Walther-Thomas et al., 2000).

Consulting and collaborating teachers can be effective catalysts for learning by finding multiple resources in and beyond school facilities and matching them with students' interests and needs.

Resources for learning include people (experts, models, coaches, guides); places (sites, sources); and things (data, materials, artifacts, equipment, and technology systems and procedure). The possibilities are virtually unlimited--local colleges and universities; business, industry, and professions; special-interest groups in the community; city, county and state agencies; homes with talented parents and grandparents; local service organizations; foreign student exchange; museums, libraries; vocational and technical schools; media; recreation; county extension offices; senior-citizen centers; even classrooms where students help other students. This wealth of resources is a rich pool from which to draw for students' special learning needs. (Dettmer et al., 2002, p. 304)

Challenges. For collaboration to be successful, several challenges need to be addressed. These include scheduling time for problem solving and professional development, the day-to-day demands of "the work," which include feelings of isolation (Friend & Cook, 2002) and prior exerience with poorly implemented changes (Bunch, Lupart, & Brown, 1997; Karge, McClure, & Patton, 1995; Vaughn, Schumm, Klingner, & Saumell, 1996; Walther-Thomas, 1997a). To address issues of time and scheduling, teachers and administrators have scheduled:

- blocks of time for groups of teachers (upper/lower elementary) to collaborate;
- early closings to provide time for collaboration or professional development activities;
- special activities such as music, art, physical education simultaneously so that groups of teachers can meet; and
- blocks of time for special activities according to grade/age levels at the elementary level. (Agnew, Van Cleaf, Camblin, & Shaffer, 1994)

In addition, support teachers (special educators, speech/language clinicians, physical or occupational therapists, school psychologists, counselors, social workers, nurses, administrators, etc.) can arrange their schedules to work with multiage, interdisciplinary or departmental teams of teachers during specific blocks of time (Boudah, Schumacher, & Deshler, 1997; Wiedmeyer & Leyman, 1991).

Results of collaboration. The empirical research base for consultation/collaboration with regard to inclusive practice has demonstrated positive effects for all students, their teachers, and their schools. Both academic and social benefits for students with mild/moderate/severe disabilities (Klingner, Vaughn, Hughes, Schumm, & Elbaum, 1998; Rea, 1997; Sapon-Shevin, Dobbelaere, Corrigan, Goodman, & Mastin, 1998; Stevens & Slavin, 1995; Walther-Thomas, 1997a; Walther-Thomas et al., 2000). Thus, the benefits support inclusive settings.

Rea (1997) collected extant data on schools over time, comparing the academic performance of middle school students with learning disabilities in inclusive schools with similar students who were served for comparable periods in pullout programs. (The groups were comparable in age, gender, ethnicity, socioeconomic status, IQ, years of special education services, years of education in one model or the other, and mothers' educational levels.) Students in the inclusive classrooms outperformed those in pullout programs across a number of important school performance indicators: they earned higher grades, achieved higher scores on standardized tests, attended more school days, failed fewer classes, and were involved in no more behavioral infractions than students in more restrictive placements. Similarly, three meta-analyses of 74 studies of academic learning in inclusive settings confirm greater academic learning for students with disabilities (Baker, 1994; Carlberg & Kavale, 1980; Wang & Baker, 1986).

Further, students without disabilities are not hindered academically or socially in inclusive settings (Klingner et al., 1998; McDonnell, Torson, McQuivey, &Kiefer-O'Donnell, 1997; Sharpe, York, & Knight, 1994; Tapasak & Walther-Thomas, in press.). In fact, improve-ments in problem-solving skills and self-esteem have been demonstrated. Further, benefits have been documented for classroom peers who may be at risk academically or socially (Walther-Thomas, 1997b), as well as for high-achieving peers (Stevens & Slavin, 1995). These findings may be the result of the presence of additional specialists in the inclusive classroom, allowing problems to be targeted and specific interventions implemented immediately (Levin, 1997; Walther-Thomas, 1997b) as well as greater attention to life skills (Bunch & Valeo, 1997; NRC, 1997) and the development of social competence via carefully orchestrated interactive physical and instructional arrangements and the development of problem-solving skills (Campbell & Siperstein, 1994; Giangreco, Dennis, Cloninger, Edelman, & Schattman, 1993; National Association of State Boards of Education, 1992). In a replication of a multiyear of inclusive schools by Zigmond et al. (1995), Waldron and McLesky (1998) found that 48% of students with learning disabilities made gains comparable to those of their classmates without disabilities.

There are benefits for teachers as well as the system-level special education process. Thus, positive outcomes/changes in consultee skills and attitudes, referral patterns or other system-level indicators have been documented (Fuchs, Fuchs, Dulan, & Roberts, 1992; Sheridan, Welch, & Orme, 1996). Similarly, Pugach and Johnson (2002) noted that peer collaboration reduced referral rates, increased teacher confidence in handling classroom problems, and expanded teacher tolerance for cognitive and social differences (Walther-Thomas, 1997b). Further, general and special educators have reported professional growth and enhanced personal support as a consequence of opportunities for collaboration in inclusive settings (Bunch et al., 1997; Bunch & Valeo, 1997; Sapon-Shevin et al., 1998; Walther-Thomas, 1997a). Specifically, they cited increased knowledge sharing and skills development and overall professional development (Walther-Thomas, Bryant, & Land, 1996; Giangreco et al., 1993) as contributing to their improved attitudes about students with disabilities and inclusion (Giangreco et al., 1993). In sum. they found inclusive practices to be invigorating (Peterson & Hittie, 2003).

Successful inclusive schools have been documented in the literature both at the elementary (Giangreco et al., 1993; Henderson, 2000) and secondary level (Jorgensen, 1998; Nicklen, 1994). Frequently, such success is due to specific planning to address the problems noted above. Schools have accomplished this by involving faculty in change and collaborative initiatives, providing administrative support and resources in the classroom, and supporting the implementation of effective instructional practices (Fisher, Sax, Rodifier, & Pumpian, 1999; Phillips, Alfred, Brulli, & Shank, 1990; Rainworth, 1992; Villa, Thousand, Meyers, & Nevin, 1996; Werts, Wolery, Snyder, & Caldwell, 1996)

Creating a culture of collaboration is an evolutionary process, one that involves both skills and beliefs. Belief systems cannot be mandated (Friend & Cook, 2000); however, technology may enhance inclusive collaborative practice by providing preservice and practicing teachers with the scaffolding necessary to apply validated practices successfully.

Integration of Technology into Collaborative Practice

Previously, technology has been defined as "the application of science and engineering principles to the development of products, practices, and procedures that enhance or improve human conditions," or at least improve human efficiency in some respect. To be useful, technology must support our goal to improve the "human condition" of students with disabilities and their teachers in some way. Wright and Lauda (1993) extend our understanding by defining technology as "a body of knowledge and actions, used by people, to apply resources in designing, producing, and using products, structure, and systems to extend the human potential for controlling and modifying the natural and human-made environment" (p. 7). In other words, it is not simply the fact that technology exists that enhances collaborative practice; rather, educators have a responsibility to make wise decisions regarding its use.

This section addresses recent technology mandates and recent technology innovations and their application to collaborative practice, with a specific example of technology used to enhance collaboration, as broadly defined.

Technology Mandates in Special Education

Two federal mandates currently define the formal processes for integrating technology into services for individuals with disabilities. First, the Technology-Related Assistance for Individuals with Disabilities Act (1988) has enabled states to create systems for delivering assistive technology and technology services to individuals with disabilities, including students. These services include consultation and the delivery of appropriate instruction, as well as instruction in acquiring and using technology.

Second, Amendments to IDEA in 1997 (Individuals with Disabilities Education Act Amendments of 1997, 1997) require consideration of assistive technology in developing IEPs for students with disabilities. "'Assistive technology is defined as any item or piece of equipment, that helps the individual participate in the school activities" (Dettmer et al., 2002, p. 265). Currently, research is ongoing regarding these two mandates and their implementation and effectiveness among students with disabilities.

Technology Innovations and their Application to Collaborative Practice

This section first outlines recent advances in technology and then describes their application to educational settings, focusing on collaboration. The context for this section is grounded in the broad conceptualization of collaboration—one that includes both the preparation and ongoing professional development of all teachers.

In 1965, Gordon Moore predicted the exponentially increasing capabilities of technology. Moore's Law continues on course with an immense impact in our personal and professional lives (Brand, 1999). The field of education is no exception. Technology continues to provide opportunities to enhance instruction and measurement. With respect to instruction, only 10 years ago, Lewis (1993) noted:

Telecommunications and multimedia technologies such as interactive video bring the world into the classroom. Electronic communication devices allow students to speak and add their voices to those of their classmates.

Adapted computers provide access to instruction in myriad subject areas from learning to count to calculus. (p. 3)

Further, technological tools can enhance learning for all students, not just those with disabilities. For example, students use computers to create, edit, and produce written work, search the Internet for resources and material, and use email to communicate with others in the natural course of their educational experience.

In addition, systems and software are available to assess and evaluate the progress of individual children in educational settings (Greenwood & Rieth, 1996). Thus, computers, digital cameras, and other devices can administer, score, evaluate, and provide simulation activities and response analyses. Access to databases, Internet resources, and communication alternatives is only limited by a teacher's or student's access to the resources of a classroom, school, university, local library, or home computer.

Educators may find the proliferation and various iterations of tools such as the computer, fax, video/digital recorders/players, pagers, cell phones, Personal Digital Assistants (PDAs) never-ending. Further, the various ways in which these tools can be connected continue to challenge the knowledge base. The steep learning curve about Local Area Networks (LAN) or Wide Area Networks (WAN), the Internet, wireless connections, and so on, continues unabated.

Clearly, there are differences between our individual and collective knowledge and skills regarding technology and collaboration. Thus, the notion of using technology to enhance and facilitate the collaboration process might not seem appropriate. However, this is not the case.

Instead, Dettmer et al. (2002) have found that "technology is revolutionizing the processes of consultation, collaboration, and teamwork in school settings" (p. 203). Technology is enhancing the exchange of information among teachers throughout the school day, both in terms of location and time. Consequently, the use of technology actually "frees" teachers to focus on the important issues involved in collaborating effectively. In particular, the use of technology has improved teachers' efficiency in terms of communicating with one another (Dettmer, 2002, p. 203).

Specifically, collaborators are finding that LANs or WANs reduce costs via shared software and can facilitate interactions among collaborators. Further, they afford opportunities for real-time conferencing and electronic scheduling, as well as access to information services and Internet resources. In addition, collaborating teachers find that Fax machines, telephones, cell phones, and pagers facilitate ongoing communication with colleagues, students, parents, and administrators. Software packages are enhancing the maintenance and monitoring of student records, grades and attendance, IEPs, assessment and evaluation results, recording, and storing as well as methods for previewing validated practices.

In summary, collaborative educators are finding that technology can support their day-to-day practice by:

- reducing stress and burnout;
- creating supportive networks;
- changing the "environment";
- enabling them to assume greater control of their lives;
- improving their management of time;
- enabling them to focus their energy;
- facilitating meetings: preparation, implementation, evaluation, followup;
- simplifying record-keeping;
- enhancing their management of resources; and
- enabling educators to be innovators and creators of software through product planners and software authors (Hofstetter, 2001).

In summary, when collaborators use technology to support their work in schools, they find it easier to manage their responsibilities via a number of electronic means, such as electronic messaging, and easy access to stored databases. Lewis (1993) noted "technology can increase a teacher's professional productivity and reduce the amount of time that must be spent in non-instructional classroom duties" (p. 126). Similarly, Dettmer et al., (2002) note:

Telecommunications and electronic networks are possibly the most valuable elements of technology that can revolutionize the way consultants and collaborating teachers engage in collaborative activities. (p. 215)

Thus far, the authors' perspective and research-based evidence regarding the use of technology in the practice of inclusive collaborative practice in the broadest possible sense have been detailed. In addition, a rationale for and examples of substantiated inclusive collaboration that addresses both university and field-based practices, thus sustaining both teachers in preparation and teachers in practice, regardless of setting, years of experience, and/or specialization/certification areas have been provided. The next section describes an example of a project that encompasses all aspects of collaboration.

SITE: A case in point. Creating educative communities wherein differences are not only expected, but accepted, is most likely the greatest challenge teachers face as the diversity their students represent continues to increase (24th Annual Report to Congress on the Implementation of the Individuals with Disabilities Act, 2003). By the very nature of their work, teachers engage in a moral endeavor (Fenstermacher, 1990), as they play critical roles in determining whether students have access to knowledge; special programs and alternative services; and, most important, appropriate and effective instruction in their classrooms.

In order for teachers to be more effective with all students in the general education classroom, innovative practices must be explored and collaboration among general and special educators encouraged. At the preservice level, teacher candidates must be prepared to collaborate in identifying and using effective instructional techniques and strategies for supporting students in inclusive classrooms (Evans, Townsend, Duchnowski, & Hocutt, 1996; Kauffman & Hallahan, 1993). Pugach (1996) suggests that preparation programs that engage both general and special educators in sound collaborative work hold the greatest promise for preparing all future teachers well. More specifically, programs that integrate collaboration throughout coursework, integrated clinical practice, and reflective seminars prepare teachers who, upon entering the profession of teaching, are not only aware of the

issues but also experienced in collaborative experiences (Norlander, Case, Reagan, Campbell, & Strauch, 1997).

Sharing Ideas about Teaching Effectively (SITE) (Campbell & Wang, 2000) is an interactive computer program that can foster such collaborative practice. Teachers can use SITE to enter, review, and retrieve Tactics (validated practices) and related literature about teaching students with disabilities (see Figure 1). Tactics are the actions that teachers take to influence and ensure the learning and success of their students. However, SITE is much more than a database; it provides the unique opportunity to engage in sustained collaborative "conversations" with colleagues through Peer Reviews. Specifically, Peer Reviews enable teachers to support one another across levels of expertise (novice vs. expert); roles (university- vs. school-based); and areas of specialization (content, grade/age levels, and/or general vs. special education). Thus, SITE provides a venue for the learning communities or seminars that Norlander-Case and Case (2001) view as essential for successful teaching to occur.

SITE was developed and implemented within a teacher preparation program that integrated coursework, seminars, and clinical placements throughout a three-year upper-division program. SITE was also integrated into other graduate courses and Professional Development Schools. Students made contributions based on their observations of mentors and colleagues in their clinic placements where they worked with students with disabilities in both general and special education classrooms. They also made recommendations regarding their Tactic's potential use in content area/s, grade level/s, for specified categories of disabilities (such as learning disabilities, mental retardation, hearing impairments, etc.) or learning differences (such as short-term memory, fine-motor skills, receptive language, etc.), and placement within Algozzine and Ysseldyke's (1992) model of effective instruction (Algozzine &Ysseldyke, 1992, 1997; Algozzine, Ysseldyke, & Campbell, 1994; Campbell & Tierney, 1996). In addition, students contributed a piece of related literature that supported their Tactic, and reviewed other Tactics and entered their reactions and recommendations.

Figure 1. Sharing Ideas about Teaching Effectively (SITE) home page.

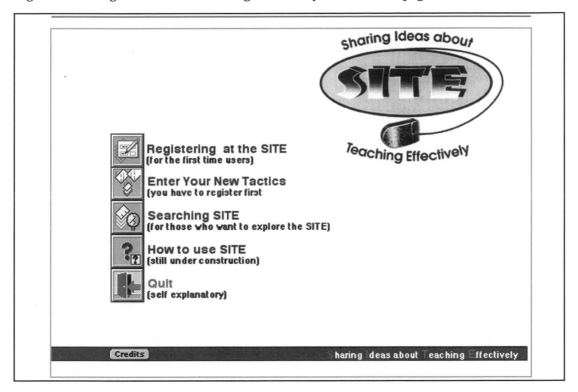

Users can search SITE in a number of ways—according to the Model of Effective Instruction, Category of Disability, Learning Difference/s, Grade Level/s, and/or Content Area/s (see Figure 2).

At the present time, SITE consists of 758 Tactics, 702 related Literature reviews, and 651 Peer Reviews. Preservice teachers entering Tactics organized their entries according to the Model of Effective Instruction as follows: Planning Instruction (9%), Managing Instruction (23%), Delivering Instruction (49%), and Evaluating Instruction (19%). Students were required to use the specific Classification of Disability of the student/s observed. While categories of disability are necessary for several reasons (accessing special education services, "organizing" research, facilitating dialogue within the profession, providing a voice for individuals with disabilities and their parents/advocates), they really do not provide the information that teachers need to address the very diverse needs of students with disabilities within and across categories of disability. Thus, SITE also organizes Tactics according to 23

"Learning Difference/s," and students had the option of selecting more than one Learning Difference.

The organization of their entries according to Classification of Disability and most frequently selected Learning Difference/s is presented in Table 1.

Entries could also be organized by grade level and content area. More than one grade level and content area could be selected for a Tactic (see Table 2).

Using SITE. If a teacher sought a validated practice or literature/research related to reading and a student with receptive language deficits at the elementary level, s/he would find 170 Tactics. The search could be narrowed further to just Elementary (140) or other criteria related to the model or Classification of Disability. The user could then scroll through, select, print the preferred selections, including the conversation (Peer Reviews) among other users. An example of a Tactic and Peer Review and Literature Review are presented in Figures 3 and 4. Examples of user printouts of the Tactic and Peer Reviews are provided in Figures 5 and 6.

Figure 2. Sharing Ideas about Teaching Effectively (SITE) search page.

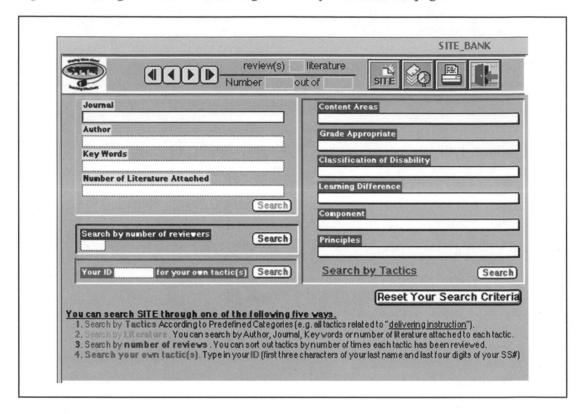

From this one example, it is clear to see that teachers were "talking" with one another about validated practices in their classrooms. As teacher candidates, it is reasonable that most of their entries focused on the Delivery of Instruction. However, they were not limited in their thinking or their recommendations to one another by certification area, grade level, or experience. They questioned one another and expanded the thinking of their colleagues to consider implementing a Tactic in other ways, content areas, grade levels, and with other types of learning differences.

Future plans. In addition to being incorporated into a teacher preparation program to fulfill the state-mandated special education requirement, SITE has been used in a number of other ways. For example, SITE has been integrated into other teacher preparation courses with specific disability-related issues as the focus (e.g., behavior management) and SITE has been used by students conducting literature reviews or inquiry projects. Professionals in the schools have used SITE as a tool for technology, content area, or special education team planning. Administrators have envisioned SITE as a sustaining professional development resource in general and special education classrooms, in media centers, and on LANs within their building and/or district. Finally, SITE and its prototypes have been disseminated nationally through articles in refereed journals (Aber, Bachman, Campbell, & O'Malley, 1994; Algozzine et al., 1994; Campbell & Olsen, 1994) and conference presentations (Campbell, 2002; Campbell, Adamson, & Norton, 2000) and workshops (Campbell & Norton, 2000.)

Currently, SITE exists on the Macintosh platform in two forms: a "writable" version that requires FileMaker Pro and a "read-only" stand-alone version that is not modifiable. The developers are working on a Web-based version of SITE that would not only expand its content and remove "platform" as a limitation, but also make it accessible to everyone, especially those in multiple complex settings, such as residential and hospital placements or remote locations.

Table 1. Organization of Tactic Entries: Classification of Disability and Learning Difference/s

Category of Disability	Percentage
Learning disability	38
Mental retardation	8
Severe emotional disturbance	12
Speech/language impairments	9
Remaining low-incidence categories	32

Learning Difference	Percentage
Attention	47
Receptive language/decoding (listening/reading	38
Expressive language/encoding (speaking/writing/spelling)	36
Social behavior	32
Self-control (behavior)	28
Self-confidence	

Table 2. Organization of Tactic Entries: Grade Levels and Content Area/s

Grade Level	Number	Percentage
Elementary	553	73
Middle school	428	56
High school	378	50

Content Area		Percentage
Reading		37
Writing		33
All areas		18
Social studies		18
Problem solving		18
Science		17
Calculation		14
Music		12
Physical education		3

In summary, SITE is a useful resource for teachers of students with disabilities and those who prepare future teachers, regardless of areas of expertise. SITE has demonstrated that collaboration among education can be facilitated and enhanced via technology.

- Technology can incorporate the essential components of collaboration (parity, accountability, responsibility, shared resources;

- Technology can be used to share common goals and problem-solve;

- Teachers can share effective practice across areas of specialization and years of experience;

- Teachers can find useful instructional resources outside their area of specialization and, conversely, teachers share their expertise with colleagues outside their area of "certification;

- Effective teaching tactics cross categories of disability, teaching specialization, and grade levels;

- Colleagues across areas of specialization, years of expertise, and grade levels can

Figure 3. Tactic cove.

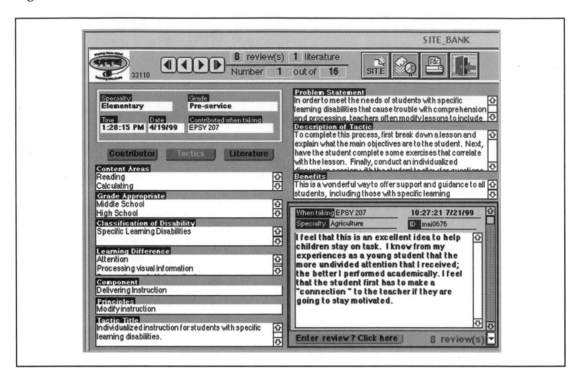

Figure 4. SITE literature page.

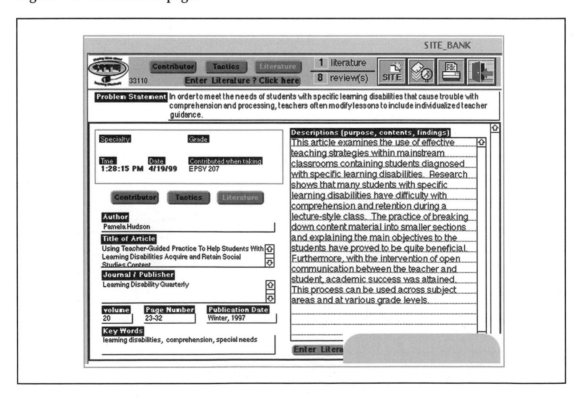

"speak a common language" with respect to effective teaching/instruction;

- Teachers provide supportive feedback to one another and also expand on one another's ideas;

- Teachers can utilize the literature and research outside their discipline to inform their daily practice; and

- Technology can facilitate the "conversation" needed to support instruction for individuals with diverse learning needs in general education classrooms.

SITE's focus is facilitating the inclusion of learners with disabilities in general education classrooms. Its success is dependent on the ongoing contributions (Tactic entry and review; supportive literature) and sustained "conversation" among all teachers through Peer Reviews.

Thus, SITE may serve as one way to enhance and, perhaps, redefine the role of the professional educator-one that relies on colleagues and informed conversation (Norlander-Case et al., 1999). The ultimate goal is improving instruction for all learners in general education classrooms where disabilities and learning differences are integrated and conversations about effective practice among all teachers are common. While projects such as SITE demonstrate that meaningful collaboration via technology is possible, using technology to facilitate collaboration remains a challenge. In the following section, recent trends and continuing issues are discussed.

Recent Trends and Continuing Issues

The overarching goal of collaboration is to improve the quality of education for students with disabilities. In this section, an overview of current trends that involve technology in the collaboration process is provided and issues that continue to challenge those trends are identified.

Recent Trends in Collaboration

In the following sections, examples of recent trends that engage potential collaborators in the collaboration process, enhance their

expertise, and expand the resources available to them are provided. Examples of the integration of technology are included for each.

Engaging Potential Collaborators in the Process

Collaboration proceeds in two ways, via specific models or structures for working together and the creation of truly collaborative cultures (Hargreaves & Dawe, 1990; Pugach & Johnson, 2002). These activities may occur in public school or university classrooms and may involve educators from within one setting or across settings. In elementary classrooms, general and special education teachers engaged in co-teaching have the advantage of the immediate demonstration of effective techniques with students with disabilities (Friend & Bursuck, 1999; Vargo, 1998). In secondary settings, team-teaching is often facilitated by assigning special educators to multiage or interdisciplinary teams of general education teachers or specific departments (Wiedmeyer & Leyman, 1991). Mentors and colleagues have served as critical friends (external partners) to plan and implement inclusive practices (Jorgensen, 1998). In university settings, inclusive seminars and courses for general and special education teacher candidates are often team-taught by faculty from different departments within the College of Education or educators from PDSs (Norlander-Case & Case, 2001; Norlander-Case et al., 1999).

Simply implementing a collaborative model does not guarantee collaborative cultures any more than the physical inclusion of students with disabilities in the general education classroom guarantees acceptance and achievement. Further collaborative structures, considered in isolation, can be construed as "contrived collegiality" (Hargreaves & Dawe, 1999, p. 230) where educators work together in a in a very specific manner. Thus, finding ways to communicate (i.e., identify problems, share resources and expertise, identify opportunities and solutions) is critical to the success of collaboration.

On the other hand, true collaborative cultures bring together the disparate infrastructures of individual classrooms, schools, and teacher preparation programs to support continual professional development via conver-

Figure 5. Tactic printout.

Elementary   Pre-service   This tactic has 8   review(s)   33110

1:28:15 PM 4/19/99   EPSY 207   1   literature attached

Content Areas
Reading
Calculating
Science
Social Studies
Reasoning/Problem Solving

Grade Appropriate
Middle School
High School

Classification of Disability
Specific Learning Disabilities

Learning Difference
Attention
Processing visual information
Processing verbal information'
Receptive language/decoding (listening, reading)
Expressive language/encoding (speaking, writing, spelling)

Component
Delivering Instruction

Principles
Modify instruction

Problem Statement
In order to meet the needs of students with specific learning disabilities that cause trouble with comprehension and processing, teachers often modify lessons to include individualized teacher guidance.

Tactic Title
Individualized instruction for students with specific learning disabilities.

Description of Tactic
To complete this process, first break down a lesson and explain what the main objectives are to the student. Next, have the student complete some exercises that correlate with the lesson. Finally, conduct an individualized discussion session with the student to allow for questions and answers

Benefits
This is a wonderful way to offer support and guidance to all students, including those with specific learning disabilities, and can be used across many subject areas.

sation, study, reflection, and inquiry (Norlander-Case et al., 1999). They are places where "critical dialogue" about teaching and learning can occur. While collaborative cultures often rely on specific collaborative structures (co-teaching, mentoring, etc.) for teachers to improve their skills, they provide opportunities for teachers to reflect on their practice together, focusing on a common goal, and with sustained opportunities for building trust among the participants. Creating collaborative cultures is an "evolutionary process, not one that can be mandated" (Pugach & Johnson, 2002, p. 19). The process takes time and requires partners who can withstand anxiety and view conflict and diversity as "friends" (Fullan, 1999, p. 18).

Norlander-Case and Case (2001) view learning communities in the form of inclusive seminars as essential components in the preparation of teachers. A seminar "provides an opportunity for students and teachers to explore together the many facets of [their] common interests" and "achieve scholarship beyond the usual," where "authority and responsibilities are shared among peers" (p. 18).

Study groups offer another model for creating collaborative communities that include teacher candidates, and university and school-based faculty (Edyburn & Gardner, 1999; O'Shea, Williams, & Sattler, 1999; Vargo, 1998). Within this arrangement, small groups "agree to come together to read, discuss, and share their mutual interests in order to extend the capacity of the organization" (Edyburn & Gardner, 1999, p. 6). Small groups of teachers meet to learn and reflect together and to determine current conditions and develop common understandings of processes underway (Luftman, 1996; Murphy, 1992; Sanacore, 1993).

Technology has been used to enhance both collaborative structures and collaborative communities. In addition to the systems and software described earlier, school and

Figure 6. Peer review printout.

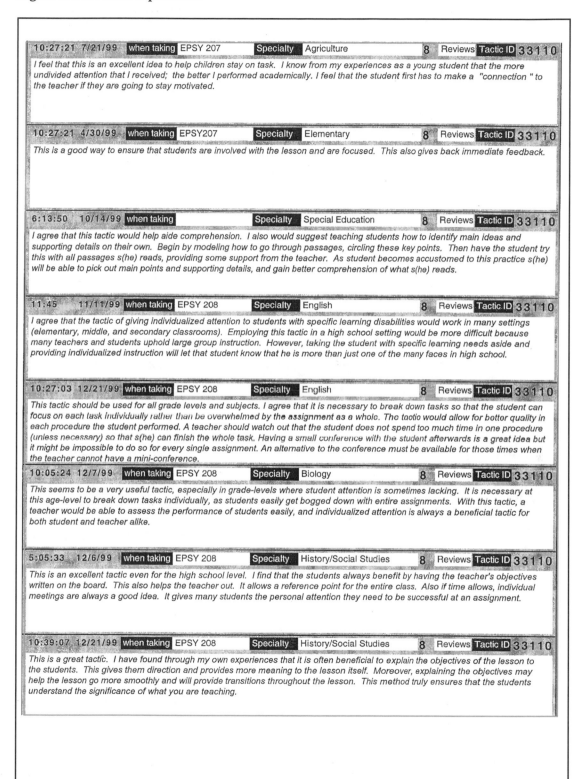

university-based faculty, together with parents, are using the Internet (chatrooms, listservs) to converse about questions or issues regarding best practice. For example, the Inclusion listserv at the University of Alberta *(www.quasar.ualberta.ca/ddc/include/intro.htm)* provides a forum for intense discussion among parents, teachers, and university faculty regarding strategies for inclusive teaching (Peterson & Hittie, 2003). At the University of Connecticut, the Dynacom system was used to provide direct video and audio links between university and PDS classrooms. Thus teacher candidates, university faculty, PDS teachers, and students in inclusive classrooms were able to engage in synchronous observations and conversations about best practice and shared readings (Campbell, 1995). In the following section, the ways in which technology has been used to enhance the expertise of collaborating team members are described.

Enhancing the Expertise of Team Members
During the past 15 years, there have been several reform and renewal movements designed to improve the teacher preparation and practice (Comer, 1997; Goodlad, 1994; Sizer, 1996). Most recently, there has been movement toward the implementation of standards, such as those provided by the National Council for Accreditation of Teacher Education (NCATE, 2000), the International Society of Technology (ISTE, 2003), the Interstate New Teacher Assessment and Support Consortium (CCSSO, 2003), the No Child Left Behind Act (2001), and the Council for Exceptional Children (CEC, 2003), to align teacher preparation and performance with student learning. Thus, there is an increased emphasis on "high quality" in the teaching force.

Given the restraints of time and location, technology is being used in a number of ways to enhance the expertise of educators involved in collaboration. For example, university courses are being delivered in whole or part via distance education. Software programs such as WebCT (2001) and Blackboard (Blackboard, 1997) enable teachers and students to engage in synchronous and asynchronous discussions, conduct and share group projects, and gain access to resources. Distance education is also being used to support and deliver new courses

and fieldwork experiences to prepare graduate students as assistive technology specialists at the University of New Mexico, George Mason University, the University of Kentucky, and the University of Nevada, Las Vegas (UNLV). The Ed.S Program at UNLV is in association with the Research Institute for Assistive and Training Technologies (RIATT) and the National Association of State Directors of Special Education (NASDSE). In the next section, the expanding technology resources that support collaboration are outlined.

Expanding Resources
In addition to having more opportunities for collaboration and improving their expertise, collaborators also have access to an increasing and exponentially expanding range of technology resources. Snapshots of the types of technology resources that are easily accessible via technology are provided below; many of them have been supported initially by federal and state grants.

- Publishing companies are providing a variety of technology resources for teachers and students: Web sites to support coursework, e-books, videotapes, and CDs are designed not only to teach content but to provide collaborative experiences among students and faculty.

- New alliances between educators and the private sector are supporting collaboration among teachers. Project ENHANCE at UNLV brings together teacher educators, public school personnel, and Teachscape, a private company, to deliver validated special education practice via online courses to practicing teachers. General and special educators and Teachscape experts are collaborating on this project.

- Regional support centers continue to "provide a range of service to schools-video and other media resources, consultants and inservice trainers on various topics, information regarding grants and collaborative opportunities, and professional development programs" (Peterson & Hittie, 2003, p. 151).

- Online resources provide information about specific disabilities (see the VRCBD and TPSS projects at: tiger.coe.missouri.edu/vrcbd/indexb.shtml), opportunities to engage in conversations with experts (Campbell & Tierney, 1996), and/or use cases as the basis for collaborative conversations among educators (see the Clearinghouse for Special Education Teaching Cases at: cases.coedu.usf. edu/).

- PT3 Grants (USDE: PT3, 2002) have been awarded to teacher preparation programs across the country to infuse technology into the preparation of teachers and their partners local school districts. At the University of Nevada Las Vegas, for example, Project THREAD has enabled faculty and graduate students to develop a series of digital materials for use in courses that highlight specific categories of disability from the perspectives of all members of the collaboration team (Higgins, Campbell, & Skylar, 2002).

These examples, as well as the opportunities for engaging in collaboration and enhancing skills, provide an overview of the current trends in the use of technology in collaboration. These trends may respond to Edyburn and Gardner's (1999) call for opportunities to determine common visions despite the "box" of systemic and individual limitations. Those limitations are examined in the following section.

Continuing Issues

The issues that challenge the integration of technology into the collaboration process are related to the inherent difficulties of systemic change, differences among the collaborators, and access to resources. Each is addressed in the following sections.

Difficulties in Changing Systems

Universities and public schools systems are rich in their individual traditional practice, which is often specific to their type, location, and mission. Further immense differences exist between public schools and universities in terms of their calendar and the roles and responsibilities of their faculty. Thus, while implementing systemic change within systems is difficult, it is even more challenging across systems (Fullan, 1999). Integrating technology in the service of collaboration is no exception.

First, in the university setting, technology is often viewed as an "add-on"—one more thing to do or teach rather than a component that is fully integrated into all aspects of a teacher candidate's program of study. The notion that a single course or module in technology is sufficient parallels the "one" special education course for general educators or single multicultural courses (Department of Education, 1996; Edyburn & Gardner, 1999; Knapp & Glenn, 1996; U.S. Congress, 1995). Willis adds the following additional barriers for teacher educators: the complexity of curricular integration, the difficulty of learning the process, the isolation of educators, lack of essential time to experiment, explore, and study innovations; projects that fail over time due to typical "top-down" implementation approaches that meet with resistance and resentment due to lack of ownership; failure of "bottom-up" projects; lack of critical consistent and adequate administrative support (Willis, in Edyburn, 1999, p. 6).

The systems of public schools present striking parallels: lack of school-wide knowledge and participation in the special education process, insufficient knowledge of team members regarding their responsibilities, and scheduling,. In addition, the lack of teacher time; access to hardware, software and support; sustained supportive leadership, a common vision or rationale for technology use; sustained professional development, coupled with the impact of current assessment practice compound the problem. (U.S. Congress, Office of Technology Assessment, quoted in Edyburn & Gardner, 1999).

Individual Differences

Systemic issues are also confounded by the lack of interest and/or expertise of individual collaborators. Unfortunately, "most efforts to implement technology in K-12 schools and colleges of education have been guided by the passion and insight of individuals... innovators and early adopters [who] represent only about 15% of the population" (Edyburn & Gardner, 1999, p. 6). In other words, for technology to be fully integrated into the collaborative process, educators need to move beyond individual pursuits "find opportunities for groups and entire organizations to discuss their ambitions and forge shared common visions" (Edyburn & Gardner, 1999, p. 6).

Access to Resources

Communication is fundamental to collaboration. If some essential partners (parents, students, teachers, schools, universities) have limited access to resources, issues of equity are raised. This becomes especially evident when technology is included among the resources, as. The issue of technology is still not accessible for many families and students.

Since the early 1980s, computer technology has been an integral part of the instructional and administrative functions of schools. As an increasing number of jobs demanded computer skills, students' access to educational technology in elementary and secondary school became essential. For example, in 1984 only 25% of jobs required technology skills, in 1993 the percentage had almost doubled to 47%, and by the end of the century, more than 60% of jobs in the nation required these skills. Unfortunately, this need created conditions of inequity that serve as obstacles for many of Americans.

Access to the latest technologies for wealthy communities is growing while access for poorer communities is holding constant at generally inadequate levels. This means that acquisition of computer skills used for information gathering and learning echoes a "digital divide" that is challenging most communities in the United States. People all over the country are faced with the possibilities of being left behind as society moves from the industrial revolution to the information revolution:

> As the Internet revolutionizes our economy, inner cities and rural America face an alarming new danger. They could lose jobs and investments they desperately need because affordable high-speed Internet services are passing them by. As small businesses realize they'll need that speed to survive, communities without it are being trapped across a digital divide. (Lieberman, 1999, B1)

Entire communities are being left out of the high capacity infrastructure improvements. Thus, rural America and the inner cities are being excluded as advanced technologies are delivered to affluent neighborhoods. While the children and youth in wealthy environments reap the continuing benefits of wealth, the achievement gap that separates them from their peers continues to grow.

For young Americans access to technology such as high-speed data access is important for learning in the twenty-first century; the employee in this new age will be required to use technologically advanced tools to solve problems. Professional educators must prepare students in the skills of gathering, organizing, and presenting information. The computer is a necessary tool for performing these tasks. Without access to technology in schools, the digital divide will become greater. Schools across America are in a position to deliver the training necessary for children to gain the skills they need to participate in the information revolution. The extent to which they do it will determine the ultimate benefits of collaboration.

Current Status

The current trends and ongoing issues discussed above are defining new roles for educators. For example, technology, in particular the Internet, can provide information and intra- and cross-site conversations about successful collaboration activities, thus reducing an individual teacher's sense of isolation. Technology can enhance personal productivity, reduce "administrivia", and increase time with colleagues, students, and parents-time to collaborate, problem-solve, and teach.

Friend and Cook (2000) view the advances in the use of technology that supports inclusive practice as a natural and logical component of collaboration among general and special educators. Similarly, Lipsky (1994) and Male (1997) believe that technology may make the full inclusion a reality. Finally, Dettmer et al., (2002) suggest that special educators should provide leadership in the use of technology to enhance collaboration.

> Consultants should provide leadership in schools to assure effective professional use of technology and to accommodate the needs of students with disabilities in general classrooms by participating in school-wide

planning groups, being a role model in the use of technology, and engaging in collaborative activities where technology is being used. Planning should include applications for professional collaboration as well as instructional use. (p. 215)

It is clear that educators are in the initial stages of understanding the potential for success as well as the pitfalls in integrating technology into the collaborative process. In the next section, areas for future investigation are suggested.

A Research Agenda for the Future

Thus far, this chapter has highlighted the current status of using technology to enhance the practice of collaboration that is focused on improving the educational lives of students with disabilities. Our search for research has been limited by the paucity of information about collaboration and technology. This point is made clearly in Edyburn's (2002) most recent synthesis of the special education literature, revealing only one article (Buss, 2001) that addressed collaboration using technology.

Meanwhile, Hasselbring (2001) urges professionals to be aware of the following:

Three broad technologies that will have a significant impact on the lives of students with high-incidence disabilities and the future of special education:

1. *devices increasing exponentially in speed and capacity while decreasing in size and cost;*
2. *delivery of information and materials anytime and anyplace as a result of advances in broadband and wireless technology; and*
3. *development of instructional materials and practices that are based on science-of-learning principles. (p. 15)*

Future Research Needs

Clearly, there is a gap between our currently published research base on the use of technology in collaboration and the demands, opportunities, and challenges that the technology of the future will present. The following topics/research questions and possible methodologies for closing the research-practice gap are suggested:

- Are there differences in the achievement of students with disabilities (as compared to themselves individually) when their teachers engage in collaborative practice that utilizes technology? (Waldron & McLesky, 1998)

- Is the practice of teacher candidates and/or practicing teachers improved through the use of technology in collaborative practice?

- Are there quantitative and/or qualitative differences in collaborative communities that utilize technology in collaborative practice and those that do not?

- Does technology incorporate the essential conditions of collaborative practice? For example, can technology be infused into Dettmer et al.'s (2002) Ten Step process for Consultation?

- Is there a relationship between the types of technology used and the effectiveness of individual collaborative models?

- Who is participating in collaborative practices (setting, specializations, grade levels) that utilize technology?

- Which forms of technology are best suited to specific collaboration goals, needs, limitations and/or models?

- What is the focus (content, teaching, evaluation, management) of collaborative "conversations" that utilize technology?

- What is the nature (supportive, supportive and corrective) of the collaborative conversations that utilize technology? (Benes, Gutkin, & Kramer, 1991)

- Does technology-based collaboration have an effect on individuals, collegial relationships, and/or organizational improvement? (Edyburn & Gardner, 1999)

- Does technology afford collaboration based on well-constructed collaboration models with sound theoretical bases? (Sheridan et al., 1996)

- How do technology-supported collaborative learning communities regarding students with disabilities fit within the components of Professional Development Schools?

- How might technology be used to enhance the involvement of families in the collaborative process?

These research questions are designed to start the conversation about information that is needed related to the use of technology in collaboration about special education. Methodological strategies are considered in the following sections.

Documenting Evidence-Based Practices

Currently, there is immense pressure to provide "evidence of research-based practice" in special education. Without such evidence, changes in special education law, policy, and funding priorities are pending. Special educators who are engaged in research are confronted by consumers of special education research who have a very limited view of methodologies that can document evidence of the achievement and competence of students with disabilities. Thus, it is essential that special education professionals continue to use appropriately, diverse methodologies, publish their findings, and educate multiple audiences.

Historically, special education researchers have selected both quantitative (group, single-subject, curriculum-based) and qualitative designs that enable them to answer research questions with the greatest reliability and validity. For example, Edyburn (2002b) describes three Web-based tools that are used for survey research. *Profiler* (profiler.hrptec.org), developed by the High Plains Regional Technology Consortium (HPRTEC) with support from the U.S. Department of Education is designed to "survey individuals and identify commonalities that support collaboration and mentorship among a learning community" (p. 55). Pryzwansky and Noblit (1990) encourage increased use of qualitative research methodology to extend research on school-based consultation.

In 1996, Rosenberg warned:

Although we have a powerful knowledge base for addressing the challenges, far too few profes-

sionals are applying what we, as a profession, know about effecting positive change in the lives of students. To put it another way, what we know about best practice-the years of informed research efforts-is not being put into practice! (p. 209)

Let us propose another perspective. It is quite likely that a great deal of "what we know about best practice" is being implemented and that the special education community could and should have been much more visible and vocal in communicating the validity of its practices and successes with students with disabilities. Assistive technology professionals talk about the "transparency of technology...when it is so much a part of our lives that we literally don't think about it" (Peterson & Hittie, 2003, p. 274). In the interim, when technology is "new," it needs to be learned, which can be a challenging process.

Similarly, special education is a relatively new field, and the need for educational professionals who know how to collaborate even "newer." Teacher preparation programs are implementing mandates to include special education information for all candidates. Practicing teachers are at a disadvantage as their preparation might not have included "special education" in the curriculum. Thus, educators share a collective responsibility for conducting and disseminating research regarding collaborative practice using technology.

If we believe in inclusion, we are supporting the belief in a society that is a community where everyone belongs . . . In order for inclusion to work teachers must be knowledgeable about the needs of their students. The special educators and the general classroom teachers need open lines of communication and need to learn from one another . . . I hope to become a teacher who can empower and educate all of her students no matter what their label . . . I want to encourage a classroom community that accepts differences and celebrates students' strengths. (personal communication, Preservice Music Educator: SITE Contributor, December, 1999)

References

Aber, M.E., Bachman, B., Campbell, P., & O'Malley, G. (1994). Improving instruction in elementary schools. *Teaching Exceptional Children, 26*(3), 42-50.

Agnew, J., Van Cleaf, D., Camblin, A., & Shaffer, M. (1994). Here's how: Successful scheduling for full inclusion. *Principal, 74*(2), 18-22.

Algozzine, B., & Ysseldyke, J. (1992). *Strategies and tactics for effective instruction.* Longmont, CO: Sopris West.

Algozzine, B., & Ysseldyke, J. (1997). *Strategies and tactics for effective instruction.* Longmont, CO: Sopris West.

Algozzine, B., & Ysseldyke, J., & Campbell, P. (1994). Strategies and tactics for effective instruction. *Teaching Exceptional Children, 26*(3), 34-36.

Baines, L., Baines, C., & Masterson, C. (1994). Mainstreaming: One school's reality. *Phi Delta Kappan, 76,* 39-40.

Baker, E. (1994). *Meta-analytic evidence for non-inclusive educational practices: Does educational research support current practice for special needs students?* Unpublished doctoral dissertation, Temple University, Philadelphia.

Benes, K.M., Gutkin, T.B., & Kramer, J.J. (1991). Micro-analysis of consultation and consultee verbal and nonverbal behaviors. *Journal of Educatonal and Psychological Consultation, 2*(2), 133-149.

Blackboard (1997). Retrieved March 11, 2004, from: www.blackboard.com.

Boudah, D., Schumacher, J., & Deshler, D. (1997). Collaborative instruction: Is it an effective option for inclusion in secondary classrooms? *Learning Disability Quarterly, 20,* 293-316.

Brand, S. (1999). *The clock of the long now: Time and responsibility.* New York: Basic Books.

Bunch, G., Lupart, J., & Brown, M. (1997). *Resistance and acceptance: Educator attitudes to inclusion of students with disabilities.* Toronto, Ontario, Canada: York University, Faculty of Education.

Bunch, G., & Valeo, A. (1997). *Inclusion: Recent research.* Toronto, Ontario, Canada: Inclusion Press.

Buss, A.R. (2001). A delphi study of educational telecollaborative projects: Identify critical elements and obstacles. *Journal of Education Computing Research, 24,* 235-248

Campbell, P. (1995). Technology and partner schools. *Center Correspondent, 8, 16-19.*

Campbell, P. (2002, September). *Integrating curriculum-based assessment (CBA) into teacher preparation through technology.* Invited speaker at the annual meeting of the International Council for Learning Disabilities, Denver, CO.

Campbell, P., Adamson, L., & Norton, A. (2000, February). *Expanding the conversation among teacher educators: Caring for diverse learners through technology.* Paper presented at the annual meeting of the American Association of Colleges for Teacher Education, Chicago.

Campbell, P., & Algozzine, B. (2003, July). Using technology to enhance collaboration. Workshop presented at the Summer Conference of the Teacher Education Division of the Council for Exceptional Children, Denver, CO.

Campbell, P. & Norton, A. (2000, January). *Sharing Ideas about Teaching Effectively (SITE) through technology.* Invited workshop at the annual meeting of the Technology and Media Division of the Council for Exceptional Children, Milwaukee, WI.

Campbell, P., & Olsen, G.R. (1994). Improving instruction in secondary schools. *Teaching Exceptional Children, 26*(3), 51-54.

Campbell, P., & Siperstein, G.N. (1994) *Improving social competence: A resource for elementary school teachers.* Boston: Allyn and Bacon.

Campbell, P., & Tierney, J. (1996). Using technology to improve instruction. *Teaching Exceptional Children, 28*(3), 8-12.

Campbell, P., & Wang, J.A. (2000). *Sharing ideas about teaching effectively (SITE)* [Computer Program]. Storrs: University of Connecticut.

Carlberg, C., & Kavale, K. (1980). The efficacy of special versus regular class placement for exceptional children: A meta-analysis. *The Journal of Special Education, 14,* 295-309.

Clark, R.W. (1999). *Effective professional development schools.* San Francisco: Jossey-Bass.

Cochran-Smith, M., & Lytle, S.L. (1993). *Inside outside: Teacher research and knowledge.* New York: Teachers College Press.

Comer, J. (1993). *School power: Implications of an intervention project.* New York: Free Press.

Comer, J. (1997). *Waiting for a miracle: Why schools can't solve our problems and how we can.* New York: Dutton.

Council for Exceptional Children. (2003). *NCATE approved programs.* Retrieved May 14, 2003, from: www.cec.sped.org/ps/perf_based_stds/index.html.

Council of Chief State School Officers (CCSSO). (2003). Interstate new teacher assessment and support consortium. Retrieved May 14, 2003, from: www.ccsso.org/intascst.html.

Cronis, T.G., & Ellis, D.N. (2000). Issues facing special education in the new millennium. *Education, 120,* 639-648.

Darling-Hammond, L. (Ed.). (1994). *Professional development schools.* New York: Teacher's College Press.

Department of Education. (1996). *Getting America's students ready for the 21st century.* Washington, DC: U.S. Government Printing Office.

Dettmer, P., Thurston, L., & Dyck, N. (2002). *Consultation, collaboration, and teamwork for students with special needs* (4th ed.). Boston: Allyn & Bacon.

Education for All Handicapped Children Act (EHA), § 20 U.S.C. 1400 (1975).

Edyburn, D.L. (2002a). 2001 in review: A synthesis of the special education technology literature. *Journal of Special Education Technology, 17*(2), 55-56.

Edyburn, D.L. (2002b). Web-based tools for designing, disseminating and analyzing surveys. *Journal of Special Education Technology, 17*(2), 55-56.

Edyburn, D.L., & Gardner, J.E. (1999). Integrating technology into special education teacher preparation programs: Creating shared visions. *Journal of Special Education Technology, 14*(2), 3-17.

Evans, D., Townsend, B.L., Duchnowski, A., & Hocutt, A. (1996). Addressing the challenges of inclusion of children with disabilities. *Teacher Education and Special Education, 19*(2), 180-191.

Fenstermacher, G.D. (1990). Some moral considerations on teaching as a profession. In J. I. Goodlad, R. Soder, & K. A. Sirotnik (Eds.). *The moral dimensions of teaching* (pp. 130-151). San Francisco: Jossey-Bass.

Fisher, M., Sax, C., Rodifier, K., & Pumpian, I. (1999). Teachers' perspectives of curriculum and climate changes: Benefits of inclusive education. *Journal for a Just and Caring Education, 5,* 256-268.

Friend, M., & Bursuck, W. D. (2002). *Including students with special needs: A practical guide for classroom teachers* (3rd ed.). Boston: Allyn and Bacon.

Friend, M., & Cook, L. (2000). *Interactions: Collaboration skills for school professionals* (3rd ed.). New York: Addison-Wesley Longman.

Fuchs, D., Fuchs, L.S., Dulan, J., & Roberts, H. (1992). Where is the research of consultation effectiveness? *Journal of Educational and Psychological Consultation, 3*(2), 151-174.

Fullan, M. (1999). *Change forces: The sequel.* Philadelphia: Falmer.

Futtrel, M. H., Gomez, J., & Bedden, D. (2003). Teaching the children of a new America: The challenge of diversity. *Phi Delta Kappan, 84,* 381-385.

Gardner, H. (2000). *Intelligence reframed: Multiple intelligences for the 21st century.* New York: Basic.

Giangreco, M., Dennis, R., Cloninger, C., Edelman, S., & Schattman, R. (1993). "I've counted Jon:" Transformational experiences of teachers educating students with disabilities. *Exceptional Children, 59,* 359-372.

Goodlad, J.I. (1986). *A place called school: Prospects for the future.* New York: McGraw-Hill.

Goodlad, J.I. (1990). *Teachers for our nation's schools.* San Francisco: Jossey-Bass.

Goodlad, J.I. (1994). *Educational renewal: Better teachers, better schools.* San Francisco: Jossey-Bass.

Goodlad, J.I., & Lovitt, T.C. (Eds.). (1993). *Integrating general and special education.* New York: Macmillan.

Greenspan, S.I., Weider, S., & Simons, R. (1998). *The child with special needs: Encouraging intellectual and emotional growth.* Cambridge, MA: Perseus.

Greenwood, C.R., & Reith, H.J. (1996). Current dimensions of technology-based assessment in special education. In E. L. Meyen, G.A. Vergason, & R.J. Whelan (Eds.). *Strategies for teaching exceptional children in inclusive settings* (pp. 279-291). Denver, CO: Love.

Hallahan, D.P., & Kauffman, J.M. (2003).

Exceptional learners: Introduction to special education. Boston: Allyn & Bacon.

Hargreaves, A., & Dawe, R. (1990). Paths of professional development: Contrived collegiality, collaborative. *Teacher Education, (6)*3, 227-241.

Hasselbring, T.S. (2001). A possible future of special education technology. *Journal of Special Education Technology, 16*(4), 15-21.

Henderson, W. (2000). *Inclusion: A catalyst for whole school reform* [Internet]. Boston, MA: Boston Public Schools. Retrieved May 15, 2003 from: *www.coe.wayne.edu/Community Building/ARTInclCatalyst.html.*

Heron, T.E., & Harris, K.C. (1987). *The educational consultant: Helping professionals, parents, and mainstreamed students.* Boston: Allyn and Bacon.

Higgins, K., Campbell, P., & Skylar, A. (2002). *Creating a digital scenario library for inclusion in the instruction of ESP 444: Special education techniques in regular classrooms.* Unpublished electronic media, University of Nevada, Las Vegas.

Hofstetter, F.T. (2001). The future's future: Implications of emerging technology for special education program planning. *Journal of Special Education Technology, 16*(2), 7-13.

Holmes Group. (1986). *Tomorrow's teachers.* East Lansing, MI: Author.

Holmes Group. (1990). *Tomorrow's schools.* East Lansing, MI: Author.

Holmes Group. (1996). *Tomorrow's schools of education.* East Lansing, MI: Author.

Hopfenberg, S.M., Levin, H., Chase, C., & Christensen, F.G. (1993). *The accelerated schools resource guide.* San Francisco: Jossey-Bass.

Idol, L., Paolucci-Whitcomb, P., & Nevin. A. (1986). *Collaborative consultation.* Austin, TX: Pro-Ed.

Idol, L., Paulucci-Whitcomb, P., & Nevin. A. (1995). The collaborative consultation model. *Journal of Educational and Psychological Consultation, 6*(4), 329-346.

Idol-Maestas, L. (1981). A teacher training model: The resource/consulting teacher. *Behavioral Disorders, 6*(2), 108-121.

Idol-Maestas, L. (1983). *Special educator's consultation handbook.* Rockville, MD: Aspen.

Individuals with Disabilities Education Act Amendments of 1997 (IDEA) 20 U.S.C. § 600 (1997).

International Society of Technology in Education (ISTE). (2003). *ISTE standards.* Retrieved May 14, 2003, from: www.iste.org/standards/.

Jorgensen, C. (1998). *Restructuring high schools for all students: Taking inclusion to the next level.* San Francisco: Jossey-Bass.

Karge, B.D., McClure, M., & Patton, P.L. (1995). The success of the collaboration resource programs for students with disabilities in grade 6 through 8. *Remedial and Special Education, 16*(2), 79-89.

Kauffman, J.M., & Hallahan, D.P. (1993). Toward a comprehensive delivery system for special education. In J.I. Goodlad & T.C. Lovitt (Eds.), *Integrating general and special education* (pp. 73-102). New York: Macmillan.

Klingner, J.K., Vaughn, S., Hughes, M.T., Schumm, J.S., & Elbaum, B. (1998). Outcomes for students with and without learning disabilities in inclusive classrooms. *Learning Disabilities Research and Practice, 13*(3), 153-161.

Knapp, L.R., & Glenn, A.D. (1996). *Restructuring schools with technology.* Boston: Allyn and Bacon.

Knight, M.F., Meyers, H.W., Paolucci-Whitcomb, P., Hasazi, S.E., & Nevins, A. (1981). A four-year evaluation of consulting teacher service. *Behavioral Disorders, 6,* 92-100.

Lewis, R.B. (1993). *Special education technology: Classroom applications.* Pacific Grove, CA: Brooks/Cole.

Levin, H.M. (1997). Doing what comes naturally, In D.K. Lipsky & A. Gartner, (Eds.), *Inclusion and school reform: Transforming America's classrooms* (pp. 389-400). Baltimore: Brookes.

Lieberman, D. (1999, October 11). On the wrong side of the wires. *USA Today*, B-1.

Lipsky, D.K. (1994). National survey gives insight into inclusive movement. *Inclusive Education Program, LRP Publications, 1,* 3, 4-7.

Luftman, J. N. (1996). *Competing in the information age: Strategic alignment in practice.* New York: Oxford University Press.

Male, M. (1997). *Technology for inclusion: Meeting the special needs of all students.* Boston: Allyn and Bacon.

McDonnell, J., Thorson, N., McQuivey, C., &

Kiefer-O'Donnell. R. (1997). Academic engaged time of students with low-incidence disabilities in general education classes. *Mental Retardation, 35*(1), 18-26.

McGlothin, J.W. (1981). The school consultation committee: An approach to implementing a teacher consultation model, *Behavioral Disorders, 6*(2), 101-107.

McGregor, G., & Vogelsberg, T. (1998). *Inclusive schooling practices: Pedagogical and research foundations: A synthesis of the literature that informs best practice.* Baltimore: Brookes.

Miller, S.P. (2002). *Validated practices for teaching students with diverse needs and abilities.* Boston: Allyn & Bacon.

Murphy, C. (1992). Study groups foster school-wide learning. *Educational Leadership, 50*(3), 71-74.

National Association of State Boards of Education. (1992, October). *Winners all: A call for inclusive schools.* Alexandria, VA: Author.

National Commission on Teaching & America's Future (NCTAF). (1996). *What matters most: Teaching for America's future.* New York: Teachers College Press.

National Council for the Accreditation of Teacher Education (NCATE). (2000). *Professional standards for the accreditation of schools, colleges, and departments of education.* Retrieved on May 14, 2003, from: www.ncate.org/standard/m_stds.htm.

National Council for the Accreditation of Teacher Education (NCATE). (2001). *Standards for professional development schools.* Retrieved on May 14, 2003, from: www.ncate.org/standard/m_stds.htm.

National Research Council. (1997). *Educating one and all: Students with disabilities and standards-based reform.* Washington, DC: National Academy Press.

Nicklen, J. L. (1994, January). A big boost for reform. *The Chronicle of Higher Education,* p. A42.

No Child Left Behind Act of 2001. (2001). Retrieved March 11, 2004 from: www.ed.gov/policy/elsec/leg/esea02/index. html.

Norlander-Case, K., & Case, C.W. (2001). *Well-educated teachers: The necessity of learning communities.* Seattle: University of Washington,

Institute for Educational Inquiry.

Norlander, K.A., Case, C.W., Reagan, T.G., Campbell, P., & Strauch, J.D. (1997). The power of integrated teacher preparation: The University of Connecticut. In L.P. Blanton, C.G. Griffin, J.A. Winn, & M.C. Pugach (Eds.), *Teacher education in transition: Collaborative programs to prepare general and special educators* (pp. 39-65). Denver, CO: Love.

Norlander-Case, K.A., Reagan, T.G., & Case, C.W. (1999). *The professional teacher: The preparation and nurturance of the reflective practitioner.* San Francisco: Jossey-Bass.

O'Shea, D.J., Williams, A.L., & Sattler, R.O. (1999). Collaboration across special education and general education: Preservice teachers' views. *Journal of Teacher Education, 50*(2), 147-157.

Peterson, J.M., & Hittie, M.M. (2003). *Inclusive teaching: Creating effective schools for all learners* (5th ed.). Boston: Pearson/Allyn and Bacon.

Phillips, W.C., Alfred, K., Brulli, A.R., & Shank, K.S. (1990). The regular education initiative: The will and skill of regular educators. *Teacher Education and Special Education, 13*(4), 182-186.

Pryzwansky, W.B., & Noblit, G.W. (1990). Understanding and improving consultation practice: The qualitative case study approach. *Journal of Educational and Psychological Consultation, 1*(4), 293-307.

Pugach, M.C. (1996). Reflections on current issues facing teacher education/special education. *Teacher Education and Special Education, 19*, 207-208.

Pugach, M.C., & Johnson, L.J. (2002). *Collaborative practitioners: Collaborative schools.* Denver, CO: Love.

Rainworth, B. (1992). *The effects of full inclusion on regular education teachers.* San Francisco: California Research Institute.

Rea, P.J. (1997). *Performance of students with learning disabilities in inclusive classrooms and in pull-out programs.* Unpublished doctoral dissertation, College of William and Mary, Williamsburg, VA.

Rose, E. (2002). A special issue on school-university partnerships in special education. *Remedial and Special Education, 23*(6), 322.

Rosenberg, M.S. (1996). Current issues facing

teacher education and special education. *Teacher Education and Special Education, 19*, 209-210.

Salend, S., & Duhaney, G. (1999). The impact of inclusion on students with and without disabilities and their educators. *Remedial and Special Education, 20*(2), 114-126.

Sanacore, J. (1993). Using study groups to create a professional community. *Journal of Reading, 37*(1), 62-66.

Sapon-Shevin, M., Dobbelaere, A., Corrigan, C., Goodman, K., & Mastin, M. (1998). Everyone here can play. *Educational Leadership, 56*(1), 42-45.

Schön, D.A. (1987). *Educating the reflective practitioner: Toward a new design for teaching and learning in the professions.* San Francisco: Jossey-Bass.

Sharpe, N.M., York, L.J., & Knight, J. (1994). Effects of inclusion on the academic performance of classmates withouth disabilities. *Remedial and Special Education, 15*(5), 281-287.

Sheridan, S.M., Welch, M., & Orme, S.F. (1996). Is consultation effective? A review of outcome research. *Remedial and Special Education, 17*, 341-354.

Shinn, M.R., & Hubbard, D.D. (1992). Curriculum-based measurement and problem-solving assessment: Basic procedures and outcomes. *Focus on Exceptional Children, 5*, 1-20.

Sizer, T. (1985). *Horace's compromise: The dilemma of the American high school.* Boston: Houghton Mifflin.

Sizer, T. (1992). *Horace's school: Redesigning the American high school.* Boston: Houghton Mifflin.

Sizer, T. (1996). *Horace's hope: What works for the American high school.* Boston: Houghton Mifflin.

Stephens, T.M. (1977). *Teaching skills to children with learning and behavioral disorders.* Columbus, OH: Merrill.

Stevens, R.J., & Slavin, R.E. (1995). The cooperative elementary school: Effects on students' achievement, attitudes, and social interactions. *American Educational Research Journal, 32*(2), 321-351.

Technology-Related Assistance for Individuals with Disabilities Act, 20 U.S.C. § 1401 (1988).

Tharp, R. (1975). The triadic model of consultation. In C. Parker (Ed.), *Psychological con-sultation in the schools: Helping teachers meet special needs* (pp. 135-151). Reston, VA: The Council for Exceptional Children.

Tharp, R., & Wetzel, R.J. (1969). *Behavior modi-fication in the natural environment.* New York: Academic Press.

U.S. Department of Education. (2002). *24th Annual report to Congress on the implementa-tion o the Individuals with Disabilities Educa-tion Act.* Retrieved March 11, 2004 from www.ed.gov/offices/OSERS/OSEP/OSEP2002AnlRpt/

U.S. Department of Education. (2002). *Preparing Tomorrow's Teachers to Use Technology (PT3) Program.* Retrieved May 13, 2003, from: www.pt3.org.

Vargo, S. (1998). Consulting: Teacher to teacher. *Teaching Exceptional Children, 30*(3), 54-55.

Vaughn, S., Bos, C.S., & Schumm, J.S. (2003). *Teaching exceptional, diverse, and at-risk students in the general education classroom.* Boston: Allyn & Bacon.

Vaughn, S., Shumm, J.S., Klingner, J., & Saumell, L. (1996). Teachers' views of instructional practices: Implications for inclusion. *Learning Disability Quarterly, 18*(3), 236-248.

Villa, R.A., Thousand, J.S., Meyers, H., & Nevin, A. (1996). *Restructuring for caring and effective education: An administrative guide to creating heterogeneous schools.* Baltimore: Brookes.

Waldron, N., & McLeskey, J. (1998). The effects of an inclusive school program on students with mild and severe learning disabilities. *Exceptional Children, 64*, 395-405.

Walther-Thomas, C.S. (1997a). Co-teaching: Benefits and problems that teachers and principals report over time. *Journal of Learning Disabilities, 30*, 395-407.

Walther-Thomas, C.S. (1997b). Inclusion and teaming: Including all students in the main-stream. In T.S. Dickinson & T.O. Erb (Eds.), *We gain more than we give: Teaming in middle schools* (pp. 487-522). Columbus, OH: National Middle School Association.

Walther-Thomas, C.S., Bryant, M., & Land, S. (1996). Planning for effective co-teaching: The key to successful inclusion. *Remedial and Special Education, 17*, 255-265.

Walther-Thomas, C., Korinek, L., McLaughlin, V.L., & Williams, B.T. (2000). *Collaboration for inclusive education: Developing successful programs.* Boston: Allyn & Bacon.

Wang, M.C., & Baker, E. (1986). Mainstreaming programs: Design features and effects. *Journal of Special Education, 19,* 503-521.

Wasley, P. (1994) *Stirring the chalkdust: Tales of teachers changing classroom practice.* New York: Teachers College Press.

WebCT (2001). Retrieved March 11, 2004, from: www.webct.com.

Werts, M.G., Wolery, M., Snyder, E.D., & Caldwell, N.K. (1996). Teacher perceptions of the supports critical to the success of inclusion programs. *Journal of the Association for Persons with Severe Handicaps, 21*(1), 9-21.

Wiedmeyer, D., & Leyman, J. (1991). The house plan: Approach to collaborative teaching and consultation. *Teaching Exceptional Children, 23*(2), 6-10.

Willis, J. (1993). What conditions encourage technology use? It depends on the context. *Computers in the Schools, 9*(4), 13-32.

Wolfensberger, W. (1972). *The principle of normalization in human services.* Toronto, Canada: National Institute on Mental Retardation.

Wright, T., & Lauda, D. (1993).Technology education: A position statement. *The Technology Teacher, 53,* 7.

Ysseldyke, J.E., & Algozzine, B. (1982). *Critical issues in special education.* Boston: Houghton Mifflin.

Ysseldyke, J. E., Algozzine, B., & Thurlow, M. (2000). *Critical issues in special education.* Boston: Houghton Mifflin.

Zigmond, N., Jenkins, J., & Fuchs, L. (1995). Special education and restructured schools: Findings from three multiyear studies. *Phi Delta Kappan, 76,* 531-540.

37

Technology and Inservice Professional Development: Integrating an Effective Medium to Bridge Research to Practice

Sean J. Smith and David Allsopp

Mrs. Nolan was confused as she retreated down the hall towards her office. She had just left her Special Education Parent Advisory Committee and was perplexed at what the parents had shared. Organized across themes, Mrs. Nolan always opened the meetings with a question and answer session followed by a substantial conversation concerning a specific topic. In this meeting, Mrs. Nolan wanted to hear from parents concerning the current use of assistive technology as well as technology in general in the lives of their children. Considering the recent investment the district had made in technology equipment for every classroom as well as the increased emphasis on every IEP team considering the use of assistive technology for the specific child, Mrs. Nolan expected to hear positive feedback. Instead, Mrs. Nolan has just spent the past two hours listening to parents discuss the limited use of technology, the ineffective application of technology when it was used, the inconsistent use from teacher to teacher, and an overall concern that technology was not being considered as one of the tools to help their child succeed.

When Mrs. Nolan arrived at her office, she sat down and reflected on the make-up of the advisory group. Were they parents of children with more specific needs that required the use of augmentative communication devices, mobility devices, modified equipment,
or similar adaptive technologies? Upon reflection, Mrs. Nolan realized that with the exception of two of the parents (who happened to be very quiet during the meeting), the majority were parents of children with learning and cognitive disabilities. Actually, many of these parents had children who spent at least half of their day in the general education classroom, with access to much of the software and hardware the district had recently invested in. Then why the negative feedback? Why were parents reporting that technology was not being used as an instructional tool to assist their child with a disability? Why were teachers not looking to technology as one of a variety of potential solutions? Why were IEP teams not identifying specific technologies to be used for the child with a disability?

Yes, Mrs. Nolan acknowledged that she had stressed moderation with teams when it came to listing specific technology software and hardware on a child's IEP. Technology cost money and the district, like many others in the area, was hesitant to state in writing specific hardware and software that it would need to purchase. However, she knew that many of the software and hardware applications that could benefit the majority of students with special needs the district served (students with learning disabilities and other high-incidence disabilities) were available to all students in the general education setting. Why then were parents reporting that they were not being used with their sons and daughters?

Use of Assistive Technology

Similar to Mrs. Nolan's experience, educators, parents, students, and lawmakers have realized that technology should be a primary tool available to all students with disabilities to assist in their overall growth and development. Since the passage of the Technology-Related Assistance for Individuals with Disabilities Act of 1988 (e.g., Tech Act) and the inclusion of assistive technology (AT) as an integral component of the Individuals with Disabilities Education Act of 1990 (IDEA), technology has been seen as an effective tool to assist individuals with disability in their overall growth and development. During the 1990s, it became obvious that technology could serve all students with disabilities and, for many, be a major catalyst in improving access to the general education curriculum (Edyburn, 2000). Acting on this fact, IDEA 1997 requires that AT be considered for every child receiving services under an Individualized Education Program (IEP). As a result, today every IEP must consider AT as a possible tool to further enhance a given child's education.

The challenge, similar to Mrs. Nolan's experience, is that schools, teachers, and parents are struggling with the integration of technology into the lives of individuals with disabilities. Regardless of the advances in and the access to technology, teachers and students continue to be challenged as they seek to effectively implement AT. This chapter overviews limitations to AT use, offers an understanding of current challenges as well as potential solutions as we seek to support students with disabilities to achieve in and out of the classroom. In addressing these issues, we will examine teacher staff development and its impact on altering the use of technology, the limitations of previous staff development efforts, critical features for successful training, and innovative ways to encompass these key features while meeting the demands of the classroom teacher.

Access to Technology

Since the early 1990s, there has been a steady, if not significant, improvement in general access to classroom-based and schoolwide technologies. These technologies have included multimedia computers capable of interacting with and benefiting from an increasingly connected public school building. Thus, combined student and teacher reports indicate a growth in the students-to-computers ratio. For example, the national student-to-computer ratio dropped from 125-to-1 in 1984 to just 3.8-to-1 in 2002 (Market Data Retrieval, 2002). What's more, in classrooms across the country, disparities in students' access to technology due to poverty appear to be diminishing. For example, according to data from the 2000 National Center for Educational Statistics (NCES), 83% of fourth graders eligible for the national free and reduced-price lunch program have access to a computer in their classrooms, compared with 87% of fourth graders who are not eligible for subsidized lunches. Meanwhile, the percent of schools with Internet access rose from 35% in 1994 to 95% in 2000. Similarly, teachers reported individual classroom connectivity at 72% during the 1999-2000 school year.

What does all this mean? For one thing, this combination of increased hardware and connected networks furthers a level of communication and collaboration that links students and teachers to vast reservoirs of information as well as diverse instruction. Further, improved hardware and increasing access to the Internet have opened an unprecedented level of information and links students and teachers to vast resources that are presented in a manner that often offers the accommodation and/or modification necessary for the individual with disability to achieve in the general education classroom. For students with special needs, this means that they are being educated in classrooms and school buildings that are becoming increasing technology-focused. While the growth may not have been in specialized equipment to meet the specific needs of a disability, the capabilities of the hardware in conjunction with the flexibility and accessibility of the Internet means an enhanced ability for students with disabilities to use technology in their learning and for teachers of these students to integrate the technology into their teaching to meet the diverse needs of all students.

Technology Use-Instructional

As we have learned in other chapters, technology can be an important instrument in furthering the development of a child with a disability by broadening access to the general education curriculum and community-based programs for all students. Thus, in both general and special education, research over the past decade has indicated that when used effectively, technology can have a positive effect on learning and achievement across all learning domains and all ages of learners. For example, based on analysis of 219 research studies, Sivin-Kachala (1998) found that:

• Students in technology-rich environments experienced positive effects on achievement in all major subject areas.

• Students in technology-rich environments showed increased achievement in preschool through higher education in both regular and special education environments.

• Students' attitudes toward learning and their self-concept improved consistently when computers were use for instruction.

Similarly, Kulik's (1994) meta-analysis of more than 500 individual research studies on computer-based instruction (both general and special education) found that:

• On average, students who used computer-based instruction scored at the 64th percentile on test achievement as compared to peers who did not use similar technology, who scored at the 50th percentile.

• Students often learn more in less time when they receive computer-based instruction.

• Students often respond that they like their classes more and appear more positive and motivated when their classes include computer-based instruction.

Taking into account national, state, and local curriculum standards that place further emphasis on high-order thinking skills, Wenglinsky (1998) assessed the effects of simulation and higher-order thinking technologies. Instead of reviewing previous literature, Wenglinsky involved a national sample of over 6,000 fourth graders and over 7,000 eighth graders. His research found:

• Students who used simulation and higher-order thinking software showed gains of up to 15 weeks above grade level.

• Students whose teachers received professional development on computers showed gains in math scores of up to 13 weeks above grade level.

• For both fourth and eighth graders, higher-order use of computers and teacher professional development on these applications were positively related to students' academic achievement in mathematics.

Technology Use-Assistive Technology
In special education, technology over the past two decades has been found to be a critical tool for meeting the learning needs of students with disabilities. In addition, advances in technology continue to illustrate how technology can be a primary tool in furthering access to the general education classroom for the student with a disability. For example, instructional applications via software and multimedia tools can provide individualized experiences critical for many students that require accommodations as well as (a) extra practice to promote mastery skills; (b) development of writing abilities to convey understanding in content-based curriculum; (c) simulations and problem-solving opportunities to assist in mastering national, state, and local curriculum standards; and (d) overall access to the general education curriculum.

The impact of technology on students with disabilities is illustrated in the following overview. Okolo, Bahr, and Rieth's (1993) review of literature on applications of computer-based instruction (CBI) with students with mild disabilities offers an understanding of the research undertaken from 1982 to 1992. That is, an initial focus on drill-and-practice applications has been replaced by the use of technology to promote effective learning in ways that emphasize students' learning of higher-order thinking skills. For example, the Cognition and Technology Group (1990, 1993a, 1993b) articulated through their work with anchored instruction how teachers could construct events that promote higher-order thinking skills, authentic learning, and creative problem solving. Woodward and Rieth (1997) extended as well as covered new ground not addressed in Okolo et al.'s review by summarizing the extensive observational and naturalistic studies, as well as research efforts in technology-based assessment. Most recent, Edyburn (2001, 2002, 2003) has begun to offer an annual synthesis of the special education technology literature to identify how widely technology is being used with individuals with disabilities and more important, to understand what we are continually learning about the potential uses of technology with students with disabilities.

We could continue this discussion of research that has been conducted on the uses and effectiveness of technology with individuals with disabilities, but that will be done in other chapters of this book. We share this overview of previous research only to illustrate that what we continue to learn about how technology can and should be used with students with disabilities.

Limited Use of Technology

With the access to computers, the growth in school connectivity, and the evidence to support technology as an effective tool, it is surprising that reports continue to indicate that technology is underused in most schools today. For example, the CEO Forum estimates that only 9% of all fourth graders use computers for schoolwork almost every day. When respondents were asked if they use the computers at least once or twice a week, the number rises to only 17%. Similarly, 55% of fourth graders surveyed "never" or "hardly ever" use the computer for schoolwork. Survey data from a 2001 *Education Week*/Market Data Retrieval/Harris Interactive (Education Week, 2001) poll of students found that only 29% of students said their teachers use a computer to help them understand in a different way. Similarly, teachers of a about a quarter of fourth graders, and just over half of eighth graders, reported not using computers in the class. Among teachers who did use computers, students reported that the most common uses were playing math games and engaging in drill-and-practice activities.

Tasks promoting higher-order thinking were reported to be much less frequently used

(CEO Forum). Surveys also indicate that when equitable access to technology is present, students may have unequal learning experiences. For example, when technology is used in lower socioeconomic environments it is used to reinforce basic skills, rather than to support higher-order thinking as found in higher socioeconomic environments (U.S. Department of Commerce, 2002).

Technology Use with Students with Disabilities

In special education, we continue to see limited application of technology tools in the general curriculum classroom (Edyburn, 2000). Instead, we see the limited use of what we refer to for this chapter as *traditional* assistive technology – technology used for individuals with specific disabilities (i.e., communication, physical). While this technology is critical, it often does not alter instruction in the general curriculum for the learner with a cognitive disability. Instead, it generally offers access to the learning and a medium in which to interact and further the learning process but without specific modification of the curriculum to improve learning. As a result, the learner with a disability often does not enhance his or her learning, and thus is no further included in the general curriculum classroom.

For example, Wehmeyer, Smith, and Davies (2005) explain that a wide array of assistive devices are available to students with intellectual disabilities; however, the percentage of students who could potentially benefit from assistive devices but did not currently have access to such devices was greater than the percentage of students who currently used such devices. That is, when asked about computer use:

> 68% of respondents indicated there was a computer in their home, and an additional 15% indicated that their son or daughter had access to o a computer in another environment, mostly in school programs. When asked to identify what the student with an intellectual disability did with the computer, most identified educational activities. For respondents whose family member did not use computers either at home or elsewhere,

78% indicated that they believed that their family member could benefit from a computer. (p. 310)

Thus, it appears we are increasing access but continue to be challenged with use and the application of the technology that is immediately available or potentially accessible with the appropriate support.

Technology Use-An Illustration

Before we continue, we believe it is necessary to address what determines use or successful integration of technology. Individuals have written articles, chapters, and books on this subject and a professional organization has actually created standards related to integration. Thus, we will not attempt to address this issue in detail. However, we want to discuss what determines a successful technology integration effort in order to offer a goal toward which professional development and related activities need to strive. Let's begin by agreeing on what technology integration is not. As numerous articles, chapter publications, and organizational reports have stated, technology integration in the preK-12 classroom is not simply access to specific hardware or software (Brand, 1998). Similarly, reserving classroom computer time for an individual student or computer lab time for a specific class does equate to technology integration, especially, in those circumstances where the classroom teacher does not accompany his or her class to the lab but look to the technology coordinator to facilitate the computer lab lesson. This is not effective technology integration, because although the teacher has made instructional time for computer use he or she has not developed an instructional program where the technology is addressing a specific learning goal integrated within the daily or unit lesson plan.

So, what does technology integration look like? Edyburn (2000) offers a model of the technology integration process. Unlike other integration models, Edyburn seeks to provide direction and information to the individual willing and interested in initiating technology integration. The process focuses on four phases: (a) selection, (b) acquisition, (c) implementation, and (d) integration.

The first phase, *selection*, focuses on planning, locating, reviewing, and deciding on technology that would meet the instructional and behavioral needs of the students. The second phase, *acquisition*, seeks to involve the teacher in previewing, evaluating and purchasing specific technology that would meet the needs of students. The thirds phase, *implementation*, advances teachers' attention from decisions on selection to concentrating on the organization and training (teacher and student) for successful use. Finally, the fourth phase, *integration*, focuses directly on using products in the classroom to enhance teaching and learning. This involves linking the technology to the curriculum, managing student access and use to the technology, assessing the use of the application and its related effectiveness, and extending learning to the tool to continue to incorporate the technology into student learning.

Technology Integration Standards

The International Society for Technology Education (ISTE) has established National Educational Technology Standards for both Students (2000) (NETS-S) and for Teachers (2000) (NETS-T). The standards identify major themes and related performance indicators, detailing what students and teachers should know about and be able to do with technology.

The NETS-S identify six major standards and related performance indicators that, if achieved would, improve student learning, communication, research, problem solving, and productivity. In addition to the standards, ISTE offers profiles listing performance expectations or what integration would look like for technology-literate students.

For teachers, the NETS-T offer benchmarks against which to measure whether successful teacher integration of technology has taken place. That is, the focus is on the teacher's ability to prepare students for the application of technology specific to the NETS-S. Like the NETS-S, the NETS-T provides standards and indicators in six major categories and offers performance indicators, benchmarks related to teacher preparation, assessment resources, and model lessons that integrate both subject area and technology standards. With these set of standards, ISTE offers a blueprint of what successful integration looks like for teachers and, thus, for their students. While these standards are not specific to the needs of the student with a disability, they are universal for general education teachers, who are increasingly the primary teacher for the student with a disability.

Reasons for Limited Technology Use

Why are teachers not using technology to support the learning of students with disabilities? Unfortunately, there is not a simple answer. Some have argued that it is either the bureaucracy of the public school system and/or the lack of planned, comprehensive, and systematic implementation for using the technologies to further student learning that has prevented most teachers from working with computers routinely (PCAST, 1997). Others have argued that organizational factors like competing goals (e.g., socialize students with community values and make them independent thinkers), powerful norms (e.g., teacher autonomy), and the school structure (e.g., the age-grade school) (Cuban, 1993). Further, Blackhurst (2001) suggests that the make up of the teaching profession challenge new adaptations like technology. For example, women and older teachers are often perceived as being resistant to integrating newer technologies than their male and younger counterparts. Below, we offer issues that have been presented in the literature as challenges to technology use. While there are a myriad reasons, we will concentrate on issues of staff development and the limitations cited by research.

School Culture
School cultures and the professional groups that interact in our educational system (e.g., teachers, administrators) often define and frame problems very differently from each other. Whether it is teachers who are gatekeepers or administrators, the wide range of beliefs and values represented can interfere with institutional change, especially as it applies to technology.

Cuban (2001) offers an alternative explanation to the limited technology adoption and use in the special and general education classroom, arguing that the cultural beliefs about how teaching should occur and the overall purpose of schooling are so wide-ranging, "that they shape the thinking of policymakers, practicioners, parents, and citizens concerning what ought to happen in schools between teachers and students" (p. 27). These cultural beliefs, Cuban contends, as well as the social institution and organizational structure of the school, have shaped what teachers do and, thus, what students learn. For example, school and classroom organization (e.g., 50-minute periods, age-grade schools, curriculum divided into chunks) hinders technology adoption in that it provides a structure where teachers often are limited in innovation. Thus, the nature of the cultural beliefs, competing purposes, school structures and the culture of teaching often prevent innovation (e.g., technology) in preference to stability and the norm of what is teaching practice.

Leadership Issues
Blackhurst (2001) reflects on over 33 years of personnel preparation and research in an attempt to clarify what is necessary for effective technology professional development. Founded on a curriculum development model that had been used extensively at the University of Kentucky, Blackhurst and his colleagues have worked closely with teachers and school districts to design effective inservice programs. Although they developed and implemented a proven instructional model, their efforts were not highly successful. They found that key administrators, starting with the superintendent, prevented effective use of assistive technologies in their decisions in how technology was to be made available (e.g., labs) and, thus, how it was to be used by teachers and students with disabilities. Similarly, Blackhurst and his colleagues found that lack of cohesion among team members and the inability to collaborate based on what they know and are willing to share impeded the use of technology. Based on these findings, Blackhurst's subsequent work has focused on training educational personnel to function as a collaborative team in order to facilitate the integration of technology.

Awareness Knowledge
Besides the limitation of knowledge of the

actual assistive technology device and its operation, the complexity of the selection process has been cited as an obstacle to integration. Again, this is primarily a training problem in that the various members of the IEP team are not knowledgeable enough to determine what technology would be appropriate for the child with a disability. As a result, when the team meets, they do not identify a technology or add a nebulous statement that subsequently leads to limited or no technology use.

Zebula and her colleagues (2000) found that while some states and local districts have issued technology guidelines to assist districts or their personnel in developing of assistive technology services, a significant majority have not. In the absence of either capacity-building professional development or state guidelines that IEP team could follow, Zebula and her colleagues have found that many districts have had to develop guidelines and services (that lead to integration) on their own. In many cases, IEP teams are mostly left with no training or guidelines to use when determining if a child with a disability would benefit from the use of assistive technology.

Selective Identification

Higgins and her colleagues (2000) argue that technology use by teachers for students with disabilities can be hampered by the nature of the specific technology and its related limitations. For example, educational software often forms the nucleus of the technology-based instruction being used in special and general education. Because of the variety of software, the constant updates, and the number of companies producing educational software, educators rely on the companies to produce quality educational software. Thus, the assumption is often made that software advertised and targeted for a specific academic need and student audience has been properly designed, developed, and evaluated for that targeted audience. Instead, Higgins and her colleagues found that software publishers provide little information about the development of their products instead, leaving it up to educators to evaluate and decide which software to integrate for a specific student with a disability.

To compound the challenge, summative technology survey instruments that could be used to identify effective software applications for students with disabilities are lacking. As a result, teachers often misuse software or become frustrated with software that does not meet the needs of his or her student. Likewise, training on software selection and identification is not at the forefront of many professional development agendas, further increasing the frustration of special education teachers.

Deficient Staff Development

Technology training, or the lack there of, has been a focus of many over the past decade. For example, in 1995, the Office of Technology Assessment (OTA) published the report, *Teachers and Technology: Making the Connection*. While subsequent reports by the CEO Forum, the Milliken Foundation and other entities have reinforced the initial findings, the OTA report offers a clear illustration of the challenges facing teachers as they attempt to integrate technology into their classroom instruction.

In brief, OTA's summative findings illustrate that a majority of teachers feel inadequately trained to use technology resources, particularly computer-based applications in the general and special education classroom. Interestingly, through OTA's national surveys and illustrative case studies, teachers reported a value in having students learn about and use technology. However, they also expressed the need for additional knowledge and concern over how to use the technology for instruction and additional time that would be required to be able to use a particular piece of hardware or software (OTA, 1995).

While districts have invested a tremendous amount of financial resources in software, hardware, and building connectivity, teacher training has received limited support in terms of dollars and overall attention (Cuban, 2001). Limited training opportunities are not simply tied to resources; but instead, an increasing barrier to technology training for teachers is the many competing priorities for limited staff development time (e.g., standard-based reform and training, local and state achievement test preparation). For example, a school district that dedicates a half day every week or every other week to professional development appears to offer multiple opportunities for technology training. Instead, the 30 odd days over a school year are often consumed by everything from improving test preparation skills to instruction on standards-based curriculum. Thus, increasingly, district professional development in special education has included topics like collaborative planning issues, furthering access to the general curriculum, effective use of paraprofessionals, and preparation for state and local assessments for students with disabilities.

Similarly, the "carrot" among State Departments of Education to require technology skill development among teachers is not there. For example, according to Education Week's *Technology Counts* (2002), only seven states require demonstrated technology competence, and only four states require technology training as a condition for recertification.

When technology professional development is offered, it often attempts to include too much information during a limited amount of time (Joyce & Calhoun, 1998). Instead of the previous how-to workshops that were found to be ineffective in terms of successful classroom integration, current efforts cram in everything from how to use the technology to developing lesson plans that integrate the technology application, leaving teachers them bewildered and no more prepared to implement the application then previous ineffective efforts (Guhlin, 2002).

Further, many are often limited to a one-shot approach whereby teachers are required to gather for a professional development day. During this daylong, or in some instances half-day workshop, teachers are briefly introduced to a software or hardware application which they are then expected to integrate into their classroom instruction. In other instances, trainings are organized across multiple training dates, but the content is often excessive and too much for the teacher to learn and subsequently apply to their classroom setting.

Effective Staff Development

If staff/professional development is to be a critical ingredient in integrating technology into the lives of students with disabilities,

professionals in charge of this process must be aware of the necessary components to ensure success. Previous efforts have shown us what doesn't work, current and future efforts must implement the type of instruction that creates an environment for technology change.

Expanding teacher learning and integrating new teaching approaches into the classroom is a challenging endeavor. Joyce and Showers (2002) argue that skill development of a new strategy is not enough to ensure transfer into classroom practice. Relatively few people who obtain a new skill in their approach to teaching will make that skill a part of their regular classroom practice unless additional instruction is received following the first workshop (Fullan, 2002; Joyce & Showers, 2002). Not until ongoing interactive demonstration and practice are added into the equation, and used effectively, will most teachers begin to transfer the new model into their active instructional repertoire (Joyce & Showers, 1999).

Recent research reports propose that effective teacher training must include five major components to elicit transfer of new skills to the classroom environment.

1. Theory must be presented to provide the conceptual basis for the new innovation. Presentation of theory can raise awareness for the participants; however, alone it is not powerful enough to achieve transfer of the skill to the classroom.
2. In conjunction with theory, modeling or demonstration of the teaching skill is key component in assisting participants in mastering a theory. Similarly, multiple illustrations including children and teachers appear to impact further mastery, especially when varied presentation mediums are employed including video and other media (Joyce, Calhoun, & Hopkins, 1999).
3. Demonstration should be followed by multiple opportunities to practice the new strategy within the workshop setting or under simulated conditions. Practice involves allowing participants to try out the new strategy or skill. Under the guidance of an instructor or within a simulated setting offering support parameters, practice is an efficient way of acquiring the skill or strategy

once awareness and modeling are in place.

4. The fourth component involves structured feedback. Whether self-administered or provided by a trainer, periodic critical feedback can result in considerable awareness of one's teaching behavior and knowledge about a new skill. Similarly, findings suggest structuring this component to provide a practice-feedback-practice sequence to ensure effective skill acquisition.

5. The final component for effective staff development involves the ongoing training. To avoid the one-shot failures, sustained coaching offers maximum support and ensures a change within classroom instruction. While ongoing support can be provided by the trainer, it can also be provided by colleagues, supervisors, professors, and related educational personnel.

Focusing the content of training is another crucial decision to make for district and building administrators (Joyce & Showers, 2002). To identify the agenda the needs and perceptions of the staff must first be identified. This way, the content can be developed with a direction and commitment by the staff, thus, ensuring participant buy in. Next, teachers need to be informed about current challenges or possible weaknesses related to the proposed changes. To that end, data must be examined to allow teachers to develop hypotheses about what is causing the specified problem. Identifying the cause would also allow participants to focus on one or two technology areas/skills for a given school year. In brief, classroom teachers need to be involved from the beginning in planning staff development so they can be certain their specific needs will be addressed. If planned with teacher input, a training program will:

• Identify needs and interests prior to the first training session;

• Develop and provide training targeted to these needs;

• Supplement current strengths, building upon what teachers can already do; and

• Promote varied instructional approaches to address teachers' needs and learning styles.

Training Purpose

According to McKenzie (2002), adult learning involves activities that match interests, needs, styles, and developmental readiness. Therefore, professional development should not be looked at as training, but as personal growth and discovery.

Training design involves exploring the types of outcomes desired, which in turn will determine the strategies used to present information. The authors identify four types of outcomes: *knowledge*, change in attitude, skill development, and transfer of training. If the outcome is knowledge of a new practice, curriculum, or educational theory, the training is considered successful when that new knowledge has been achieved. A *change in attitude* can involve positive change in self, students, content area, or in a particular group of students. Therefore, the training is considered a success when we have an understanding of our attitude, greater empathy toward a particular groups, and better understanding of curriculum areas. The *development of a skill* is the third type of outcome, which involves training performing a behavior or skill. This is completed when the individual can perform the skill successfully. Finally, *transfer of training* is the last outcome. This type of staff development is called "executive control," which means that the level of knowledge that generates consistent and appropriate use of new skills and strategies for classroom instruction. This is achieved when the individual uses the new knowledge and student learning is measured.

Types of Training

Once the outcome has been identified, the type of training can be identified. Bradshaw (2002) suggests that districts should offer a wide range of workshops and experiences for teachers. Many districts design "training of trainers" to assist in creating job coaches and technical support. Below, we mention two types of professional development that are gaining acceptance and are proving to have impact on creating sustainable change.

Peer coaching

The environment in which effective technological development of teachers occurs is built around collaborative learning. Because teachers vary in their level of expertise at the times of their training, the context that surrounds their technological professional development must provide a non-threatening environment that is sensitive to the individual teacher's level of expertise and experience. Also, according to Joyce and Showers (2002) teachers who take a proactive stance gain more from peer coaching than teachers who "submit" to it. McKenzie (2002) found that districts that invested in support systems that involve peer coaches had greater technology application results. Similarly, Bradshaw's (2002) examination of 27 school districts identified that a critical component of effective staff development involved coaches who assisted study groups and teams to share failures and successes as well as tricks and techniques that work. A number of collaborative approaches are available, but peer coaching and modeling has been the most effective in transforming workshop information to classroom application and practice (Brand, 1998).

Joyce and Showers (2002) identified five ways in which coaching contributes to transfer of training. First, coached teachers practice new strategies more frequently and develop greater skill than teachers who do not participate in coaching but have the same initial training. Second, coached teachers used their newly learned skills more appropriately when applying it to the classroom. Third, coached teachers showed long-term retention of the skill and increased the use of the skill over time. Thus, "six to nine months after training in several models of teaching, coached teacher had retained and, in several instances, increased their technical mastery of the teaching strategies." Fourth, teachers who are coached by a peer are more likely to explain the new expectations to students and ensure that they understand the behaviors that are expected of them. Finally, teachers who have been coached have a clear purpose and use of the new strategy.

Teacher Guided Professional Development

Another model for effective professional development is the Teacher Guided Professional Development (TGPD), a democratic approach for those interested in teacher-centered part-

nership-based approach to professional development, developed at the Center for Research on Learning at the University of Kansas. Not directly applied to technology integration, the model does include principles noted by previous research (Bradshaw, 2002; Joyce & Showers, 2002). The TGPD incorporates a number of process structures or procedures that groups can use to organize training and, thus, integrate the new instruction.

Similar to a needs assessment, TGPD integrates interviews and vignettes to help the leadership and the trainer understand their audience needs prior to a workshop. Interviews target teachers' and students' current reality, changes being experienced, current instructional practice, changes being sought, and overall perspectives or feelings about previous professional development. Next, TGPD organizes in short vignettes (one to three paragraphs) powerful narratives that summarize a theme repeated by teachers during interviews. The purpose is to identify Thinking Devices that can be incorporated into the training to encourage dialogue and interaction.

As the training progresses, TGPD integrates a process structure-dynamic planning-that can be used to help participants develop implementation plans as part of the training process. The goal of this step is to identify all the tasks that a group of teachers (or the individual) needs to complete for a technology application to be implemented. The process involves organizing task chronology, estimating the time it will take, naming of taskmasters who will ensure that tasks are completed, charting the tasks out, and identifying the measures of success.

Standards for Staff Development

Our discussion would not be complete if we did not include the National Staff Development Council's (NSDC) (2001) blueprint for what constitutes effective staff development. NSDC's Standards for Staff Development provide us standards grouped under three areas: context, process, and content. The underlying theme to the standards is a model of continuous improvement where teachers, school leaders, and the community work together to advance school and student improvement.

The standards have as their goal that staff development should improve the learning of all students and offer guidance for how to accomplish this task. For example, *context standards* focus staff development on improvement of student learning through collaborative learning communities. An effective learning community will have shared goals, equality to make decisions, and shared responsibility in ensuring effective outcomes. Likewise, context standards state the need for school and district leaders to provide guidance for continuous instructional improvement. Leadership is central in providing the climate and environment for learning communities to develop and evolve through the learning process. Leadership can also provide the resources necessary to support adult learning and allow for continuous collaboration.

Equally important to the success of staff development is the *process* necessary to improve the learning of all students. According to the NSDC, student data need to be used to determine priorities, monitor progress, and help sustain continuous improvement. Staff development that improves the learning of all students comes from multiple sources, and this must be considered in order to measure the true success of a training program. This is especially true for the integration of technology, which may have varied impact detectable through an assortment of evaluations. More important, the foundation of the adult instruction needs to apply research, contain an appropriate design, apply what we know about human learning and change, and infuse educators with the skills necessary to collaborate.

Finally, *content standards* specify that effective staff development is based on preparing educators to improve the learning of all students. As a result, training should deepen an educator's content knowledge, his or her ability to meet the needs of all learners, as well as appropriately assess whether students have achieved the desired understanding. If staff development has been successful, it has enhanced educators' ability to further involve families and stakeholders who have a vested interest in the growth and development of the student.

Implications of Staff Development

So what does this mean for technology and students with disabilities? It means that staff development for both special and general education teachers must consist of multiple layers and offer flexibility and consistency over a period of time in order to prove effective. Offering exposure and access to an application or hardware device is not enough if we seek integration. Similarly, the complexity of the selection process and the knowledge base required among educators (e.g., IEP team members) continue to challenge integration. Thus, quality training must be ongoing as technology continues to develop and alter what is possible for the individual with a disability.

Staff Development Solutions – Online Learning

Programs that feature the critical ingredients mentioned above are vital if we are going to succeed in further technology use. By contrast, staff development that continues to offer "one-shot" or limited exposure experiences to technology will continue to fail in the goal of the training. Indeed, as a type of quality-control measure, Joyce and Showers (2002) suggest that such training be prefaced with the statement "for awareness only."

Fortunately, the challenges set forth to implement new techniques, technologies, and reform efforts are coupled with a growing access to the Internet and the World Wide Web. In fact, one of the most beneficial components of technology-assisted professional development is in the ability of teachers to participate in direct instructional activities when it is convenient to them. Effective professional development offers an ongoing "24/7" feature that allows users to access when and where they desire based on their schedule, not that of a structured preplanned training day.

We are not presenting online instruction as a replacement for face-to-face instruction, but as an important option that can enhance efforts in technology training and further technology integration. By employing the Web as the instructional medium, we are further exposing teachers to technology applications that can benefit learners with a disability. According to

Killion (2002), online learning works best when coupled with on-site workshops. Thus, learners can access staff development during their plan time, before school, after school, or at home. Besides 24-hour-a-day admittance, access also involves access to information, experts, and groups of people. More important, online programs can be unscheduled, allowing for an indefinite access time.

Online courses wait until the learner is ready to move ahead. Adult learners are allowed to choose how much time they will spend on a given module or lesson, how many times they need to review the theory, watch the interactive demonstration and complete the practice activities. The emphasis of staff development to increase student learning and implementing new skills is met by allowing teachers the flexibility to learn, interact with resources, and apply this new knowledge.

No precedent in the history of pre- and inservice teacher education parallels the emergence of a new form of teaching-pedagogy as is occurring with online instruction (Ludlow, 2002). Changes in pedagogy have tended to be evolutionary. The seminar, didactic forms of instruction, mentoring, practica, and internships have all emerged over time. With the emergence of the Internet and the Web, however, we have seen unprecedented growth in the use of this pedagogy.

The merits of online instruction as an option in professional development go far beyond the obvious ones of flexibility in time and place and just-in-time delivery. While these advantages are important and made possible for the first time by the Internet and the Web, it is the potential quality of online instruction from a pedagogical perspective (i.e., employing NSDC standards) that makes it such a sound option. Thus, it is now possible to replicate in an electronic teaching/learning environment for adults many of the principles applied in face-to-face staff development instruction. More important, online experiences potentially offer what time and resource constraints preclude in today's educational environment. Examples include:

1. The flexibility in time and place of online instruction dramatically increases access to staff development.

2. Online instruction must be carefully designed prior to being delivered, which allows content specific to the stated needs of the teacher participants.

3. All content and communications between teachers and the instructor is open to review, thus providing opportunities for instructional accountability.

4. Participants are able to review instruction in its original form as often as they wish. This offers the user ongoing interaction with the content as well as with course participants and the instructor to ensure comfort with the technology as well as an understanding of how to apply it.

5. Modeling examples can be provided in reliable form and reviewed repeatedly with no variance. For example, in teaching teachers how to apply Inspiration to the writing process, interactive audio and visual illustrations can be provided to walk the learner through the process. More important, the illustration is available for repeated viewing to further support the participant understanding and hopefully later application of Inspiration.

6. Instruction and related feedback can be individualized so as to be personalized to each student.

7. Tracking student progress can be designed as an integral element of online instruction.

8. Controlled opportunities for repeated practice are available to the participants on a 24/7 basis.

9. Traditional geographic restrictions no longer limit information distribution.

10. Communication among students can be enhanced and diversified, offering various perspectives and frames of reference. Similarly, collaborative groups can be supported and reinforced through discussion forums, videoconferencing, chats and similar applications allowing for participants from a variety of buildings to continue to support each other as they strive to integrate the related technology.

Killion (2002) reports that colleges, universities, corporations, and professional associations are expanding the number of and diversity of online and Web-supported courses. For example, the University of Phoenix has over 40 campuses and has provided degrees and certification classes to over 400,000 working professionals (see www.uophx.edu). Community colleges have also been responsive to the opportunities offered by online instruction as have many regional universities that have strong commitments to outreach (e.g., www.kckcc.cc.ks.us/online). Even industry has entered the online instructional field. For example, for corporations like IBM, Southwestern Bell, Sprint, and Oracle, online training is the primary mode of adult professional development for thousands of employees (Prince & Beaver, 2002).

With the budget crisis that school districts face today as well as the poor funding staff development has received historically, online staff development is also appealing because of the potential reduction in costs. For example, Web-based staff development allows teachers to remain in their school while receiving training. Immediately, school districts save money on travel release days, substitutes, and staff developers. Theoretically, Web-based training and the initial investment are potentially no different for two teachers than they would be for 20,000 teachers.

Finally, when designed well, Web-based staff development increases the opportunities for participants to collaborate. While individualized instruction can be supported by group members with similar needs and knowledge levels, the online format allows for group interaction based on the specific individual needs of the learner. For example, *Profiler* (see hprtec.org), an online collaboration tool, was developed to further cooperation and collaboration among teachers to help them improve their skills around technology. The application works by seeking teacher profiles and specific needs in an area of technology. *Profiler* compiles this information and matches individuals in need of a specific technology skill with teachers who have this capability. Initially designed to connect teachers within a specific district, *Profiler* can develop collaborative groups across districts offering support in the online environment.

Regardless of the online tool used, learners can become members of community-based groups that share interests and knowledge level

via the online environment. By matching needs, the participant can maintain his or her individual learning experience while doing so with group support. Overall, developing training for the Web-based environment and conducting staff development via the Web offers a medium that can address the NSDC Standards and critical integration components in a flexible format.

Online Training Illustrations

Conducting staff development via an online format continues to gain support among school districts across the country. Many have begun to adopt Web-based software applications (i.e., Blackboard, WebCT) offering a usable template for all teacher enrichment activities. Other districts have invested in staff development products created by local and national organizations to deliver web-based training (Galland, 2002).

Assistive Technology Training Online

An example of a Web-based tutorial on assistive technology can be found at Assistive Technology Training Online Project (ATTO) (see atto.buffalo.edu/). Based out of the University of Buffalo, ATTO was developed to serve as an independent tutorial for novice and veteran teachers, parents, and related personnel interested in learning more about assistive technology. The site offers users information on AT applications for both the general and the special education classroom. For example, Tutorials is a section within the site that is designed to be used with products specific to the needs of children with disabilities (i.e., Jaws for Windows). Each tutorial offers users an overview of the application and its specific purpose. Next, it provides a downloadable tutorial created as a PDF document, Microsoft Word file, or as a Microsoft PowerPoint slide show. The tutorials are organized into different topic areas specific to the use of the application. For example, CoWriter 4000 (see atto.buffalo.edu/registered/Tutorials/cowriter/) provides tutorials on exploration of the application, directions and examples of collecting words, as well as a lesson on how to use the Topic Dictionary. For many of the tutorials, ATTO offers additional links to suggested lesson plans created by teachers and other users of the web.

For teachers interested in learning the basics of AT, ATTO offers a series of lessons on the *Foundations of AT, Curriculum Adaptations, Adapting Computers,* and general information on *Technology for Special Populations.* Each series of lessons are designed to be self-paced and users can pick and choose the content that meets their specific needs. For example, individualized education program teams working together to identify appropriate assistive technologies can use the *AT Decision Making Process l*esson to help teams identify AT and classroom strategies to put the puzzle pieces together for children to engage in learning.

Virtual Assistive Technology Courses

For individuals seeking certification in assistive technology, a variety of Web-based programs are also increasingly being developed. For example, the University of New Mexico (see star.nm.org/at/training) and California State University at Northridge (see www.csun.edu/codtraining) have offered courses and certification programs related to assistive technology since the 1990s. Recently, regional universities like Fort Hay State University in Ft. Hay, Kansas, and the University of Southern Maine in Portland, Maine, have also developed online certification programs. For example, the University of Southern Maine's program, the Virtual Assistive Technology University (see alltech-tsi.org/initiatives/vatu/), is a 21-graduate-credit hour or 31.5 continuing education unit program offered entirely online. Course titles include:

- Introduction to Learning Technology for Students with Disabilities

- Web Accessibility and Interactivity

- Universal Design in Education: Access to the General Education Curriculum

- Using Assistive Technology for Educating for Educating Students with Low-Incidence Disabilities

- Augmentative and Alternative Communication

- Assistive Technology Evaluation

- Seminar in Integrating Technology into Educational Programs

Like other online programs, the Virtual AT University offers teachers the opportunity to learn about and practice with technology applicable to the child with a disability. At this time, we do not know if these programs lead to direct integration of the technology into the classroom. However, we do know many of the staff development or university-based online programs infuse adult learning principles that, if followed, have the potential to lead to educational change and classroom integration.

Conclusions

Altering the use of technology among individuals with disabilities often begins with the abilities of the student's classroom teacher. If he or she is comfortable with a given application and capable of integrating into the educational process, the child will likely use the technology. However, if the teacher is not aware of the technology, is uncomfortable with technology in general, and does not look to technology as one of his or her many instructional tools, the chance of integration is unlikely for the student with a disability. The possibilities are almost limitless when technology is used effectively with students with disabilities. Thus, it is imperative that we enhance staff development of teachers specific to assistive technology integration.

Effective staff development plays a significant role in the successful and effective integration of technology into the classroom. Over the past decade, we have learned about the limitations of previous training efforts, gained an understanding of the critical features of effective professional development, and begun to apply these features to innovative mediums with the hope of enhancing their effectiveness. Regardless of the medium, the goal is to offer teachers flexible and ongoing training specific to their needs and the needs of their classroom. Trainings that integrate these features offer opportunities to learn an application, practice within the context of the classroom, and interact with peers as they struggle through similar experiences. While not always immediate in application, technology staff development, when conducted appropriately, can improve classroom use of technology. In so doing, teachers can integrate technology as one of their many tools in the instruction of students with disabilities.

References

Baker, E. L., and O'Neil, Jr. H.F. (Eds.). *Technology assessment in education and training* Hillsdale, NJ: Lawrence Erlbaum.

Bradshaw, L. K. (2002). Technology for teaching and learning: Strategies for staff development and follow-up support. *Journal of Technology and Teacher Education, 10*, 131-150.

Brand, G. A. (1998). What research says: Training teachers for using technology. *Journal of Staff Development, 19*, 10-13.

Cognition and Technology Group at Vanderbilt. (1990). Anchored instruction and its relationship to situated cognition. *Educational Researcher, 19*(6), 2-10.

Cognition and Technology Group at Vanderbilt. (1993a). Anchored instruction and its relationship to situated cognition revisited. *Educational Technology, 13*(3), 52-70.

Cognition and Technology Group at Vanderbilt. (1993b). Integrated media: Toward a theortical framework for utilizing potential. *Journal of Special Education Technology, 12*(2), 76-89.

Cuban, L. (1993). *How teachers taught.* New York: Teachers College Press.

Cuban, L. (2001). *Oversold and underused: Computers in the classroom,* Cambridge, MA: Harvard University Press.

Edyburn, D. (2000). 2000 Assistive technology and students with mild disabilities. literature. *Focus on Exceptional Children, 32*(9), 1-24.

Edyburn, D. (2001). 2000 in review: A synthesis of the special education technology literature. *Journal of Special Education Technology, 16*(2), 5-25.

Edyburn, D. (2002). 2001 in review: A synthesis of the special education technology literature.*Journal of Special Education Technology, 17*(2), 5-24.

Edyburn, D.L. (2003). 2002 in review: A synthesis of the special education technology literature. *Journal of Special Education Technology, 18*(3), 5-28.

Fullan, M. (2002). The change leader. *Educational Leadership, 59*(8), 16-20.

Galland, P. (2002). Techie teachers -Web-based staff development at your leisure. *TechTrends, 46*(3), 7-10.

Guhlin, M. (2002). Teachers must push technology's tidal wave: District technology initiatives must put the teacher in charge. *Journal of Staff Development, 23*, 40-41.

Higgins, K., Boone, R., & Williams, D. L. (2000). Technology trends. *Intervention in School and Clinic, 36*(2), 109-115.

Individuals with Disabilities Education Act of 1990, 20 U.S.C. § 1400 *et seq.*

International Society for Technology in Education. (2000). *National educational technology standards for students—connecting curriculum and technology.* Eugene, OR: Author.

International Society for Technology in Education. (2000). *National educational technology standards for teachers—connecting curriculum and technology.* Eugene, OR: Author.

Joyce, B., & Calhoun, E. (1998). *Learning to teach inductively.*Boston: Allyn & Bacon.

Joyce, B., & Showers, B. (2002). *Student achievement through staff development* (3rd ed.). Washington, DC: Association for Supervision & Curriculum Development.

Killion, J. (2002). Loading the e-learning shopping cart: first examine the product and service for student results. *Journal of Staff Development, 23*, 12-16.

Kulik, J.A. (1994). Meta-analytic studies of findings on computer-based instruction. In E. L. Baker & H. F. O'Neil (Eds.). *Technology assessment in education and training* (pp. 9-33). Hillsdale, NJ: Lawrence Erlbaum.

Lahm, E. A., Bausch, M. E., Hasselbring, T. S., & Blackhurst, A. E. (2001). National assistive technology research institute. *Journal of Special Education Technology, 16*(3), 19-26.

Ludlow, B. L. (2002). Web-based staff development for early intervention personnel. *Infants and Young Children, 14*(3), 54-64.

Market Data Retrieval. (2002). *Technology in education.* Washington, DC: Author.

National Center for Educational Statistics. (2002). *Internet access in U.S. public schools: 1994-2001.* Washington, DC: Author.

National Staff Development Council. (2001).

National staff development council's standards on staff development. Oxford, OH: Author.

Office of Technology Assessment (1995). *Teachers and technology making the connection*. Washington, DC: United States Congress, Office of Technology Assessment.

Okolo, C. M., Bahr, C. M., & Rieth, H. J. (1993). A retrospective view of computer-based instruction. *Journal of Special Education Technology, 12*(1), 1-27.

President's Committee of Advisors on Science and Technology. (1997). *Report to the president on the use of technology to strengthen K-12 education in the United States*. Washington, DC: Author.

Prince, C., & Beaver, G. (2002). Redefining the role of the corporate university: A UK perspective. *Industry & Higher Education, 16*, 213-221.

Sivin-Kachala, J. (1998). *Report on the effectiveness of technology in schools, 1990-1997*. Washington, DC: Software Publisher's Association.

Technology-Related Assistance for Individuals with Disabilities Act, 29 U.S.C. 2201 *et seq*

The CEO Forum. (2001). *Key building blocks for student achievement in the 21st century*. Eugene, Oregon: Author.

U.S. Department of Commerce (2002). *A nation online: How Americans are expanding their use of the Internet*. Washington, DC: Author.

Wehmeyer, M.L., Smith, S.J., & Davies, D.K. (2005). Technology use and students with intellectual disabilities: Universal design for all students. In D. Edyburn, K. Higgins, & R. Boone (Eds.). *Handbook of special education technology research and practice* (pp. 309-323). Whitefish Bay, WI: Knowledge by Design, Inc.

Wenglinsky, H. (1998). Does it compute? *The relationship between educational technology and student achievement in mathematics*. Washington, DC: Educational Testing Service Policy Information Center.

Woodward, J., & Rieth, H. J., (1997). A historical review of technology research in special education. *Review of Educational Research, 67*(4), 503-536.

Zabala, J., Blunt, M., Carl, D., Davis, S., Deterding, C., Foss, T., Hamman, T., Bowser, G., Hartsell, K., Korsten, J., Marfilius, S., McCloskey-Dale, S., Nettleton, S., & Reed, P. (2000). Quality indicators for assistive technology services in school settings. *Journal of Special Education Technology, 15*(4), 25-36.

38

Technology-Mediated Distance Education: Current Practice and Future Trends

Barbara L. Ludlow

Distance education is as old as the first correspondence course and as new as the most current efforts at online learning. The growth of telecommunications technologies at the end of the twentieth century spurred the rapid development of distance education applications at colleges and universities. Special education, a discipline faced with critical shortages of qualified personnel and a need to improve access to preservice and inservice training, was quick to embrace these new technologies to enhance personnel preparation and staff development efforts. Yet, the proliferation of distance education programs has far outstripped the research base that would serve as the foundation for policies and practices, both in higher education in general and in special education in particular.

This chapter will discuss current practices and future trends in technology-mediated distance education in special education based on a review of the professional literature, with special emphasis on research and evaluation efforts. First, it will offer a brief discussion of telecommunications technologies used for distance education followed by an overview of their applications in preparing special education personnel over the last two decades. Next, it will present a review of the literature between 1985 and 2002 and examine in detail data-based reports addressing the effects of various technologies used for preservice and inservice training. Finally, it will summarize the current state of the knowledge base about distance education and offer

suggestions for directions that this research should take in the years to come.

Overview of Technology-Mediated Distance Education in Special Education

Education at all levels has traditionally involved face-to-face teaching and learning, whether these interactions took place in homes, schools, or other public or private institutions. Distance education has a fairly short history, and technology-mediated distance education is an even more recent phenomenon. While special education as a discipline is a newcomer to the distance education scene, it is rapidly gaining national recognition for its innovative uses of different technologies for preparing personnel at the preservice and inservice levels.

History of Technology-Mediated Distance Education

Distance education, in which teacher and learner are separated by space and/or time, has evolved over three centuries in efforts to increase access to educational opportunities to various groups. Correspondence study, the earliest form of distance education, has served many purposes. It began with the need to train clergy and other professionals in the colonial system (Rowntree, 1986); it expanded as a way to provide public education to the masses in largely rural countries like Canada and Australia (Holmberg, 1990); soon it became a mechanism to serve nontraditional students who could not afford full-time study in the United

States and Europe (Keegan, 1996); and, now, it has enabled developing countries to provide public education without the expense associated with building schools and colleges (Tiffin & Rajasingham, 1995). Nevertheless, despite its widespread presence, correspondence study traditionally has been regarded as inferior to face-to-face teaching and generally has had little impact on conceptualizations of teaching and learning overall.

The rapid development of multiple forms of telecommunications technologies during the last century made possible distance education activities that more closely simulated many aspects of face-to-face teaching. Ludlow and Duff (2001) suggested that these technologies could be classified by their delivery mechanism (air waves versus land lines), the amount of time delay in interactions (real time or synchronous versus delayed time or asynchronous), and the direction of the signal (one-way or two-way communication). In technology-mediated distance education, the specific technologies used constrain the interactions between teachers and learners in different ways (Verduin & Clark, 1991). For example, synchronous two-way technologies, such as audio conferencing and video conferencing, allow real-time communication between teacher and learners that is quite similar to face-to-face teaching. Asynchronous technologies, whether one-way as in prepackaged videotapes or two-way as in online threaded discussions, are quite unlike face-to-face teaching because they do not allow for immediate feedback. Nevertheless, the potential for these technologies to support more natural interactions and to facilitate faster communication gave impetus to the distance education movement during the final decades of the last century.

Technology-mediated distance education first became possible in the1980s, when a number of rural states constructed statewide television systems. Much of this development was made possible through funding from the federally sponsored Star Schools Grants and through collaborative effort between the Annenberg Foundation and the Corporation for Public Broadcasting (Moore & Kearsley, 1996). These state systems were initially intended for use by public schools, especially to promote secondary programs in foreign languages and the sciences, but colleges and universities were quick to capitalize on them for reaching out to students and other adult learners at off-campus locations.

The growing availability of Internet access on campuses and in homes, and the ability of the World Wide Web to support multiple media, gave new impetus to the development of technology-mediated distance education. When the government-sponsored ARPANET was established in 1969, educators saw the potential for using this Internet to facilitate correspondence courses via email (Keating, 1999). The arrival of user-friendly Web browsers such as Netscape's Navigator and Microsoft's Internet Explorer, followed by Web course management systems like WebCT, Top Class, and Blackboard later promoted the development of online modules and courses (Kearsley, 2000). Instructors at colleges and universities as well as in state and local education agencies rapidly embraced Web-based distance education in recognition of its wider accessibility, lower cost, and potential for any-time, any-place learning.

History of Distance Education in Special Education

Special educators have made use of a wide variety of telecommunications technologies in distance education for both individual courses and complete programs. Promoted as a potential solution for addressing the critical shortages in special education and related services (Howard, Ault, Knowlton, & Swall, 1992), distance education programs have become common in preparing personnel for rural areas (Ludlow, 1998) and for low-incidence populations such as severe disabilities (Spooner, 1996), early intervention (Hains, Belland, Conceicao-Runlee, Santos, & Rothenberg, 2000), and vision and hearing impairments (DeMario & Heinze, 2001). The success of these efforts in curtailing personnel shortages was recently criticized for utilizing alternate routes of certification that could produce less-than-qualified personnel (Katsiyannis, Zhang, & Conroy, 2003). Nevertheless, as new technologies have become available, special educators have explored the potential of each technology alone and in combinations to deliver innovative preservice and inservice programs.

Television Broadcasts

Initial efforts at distance education in special education relied upon television technology, transmitting a one-way video/audio broadcast and using telephones for two-way interaction. The first reported use of technology-mediated distance education to train special education personnel was at the University of Utah, which began offering preservice program coursework via that state's microwave relay television system in 1983 (Egan, McCleary, Sebastian, & Lacy, 1989). Utah State University made the earliest use of television for inservice training in that rural state (Rule & Stowitschek, 1001). Soon after, the University of Kentucky used satellite broadcasts to offer first inservice workshops (Slaton & Lacefield, 1991) and later preservice courses (Collins, 1997). In 1990, West Virginia University launched the first graduate-level certification and degree program offered entirely at a distance using the state's satellite network (Ludlow, 1994). The University of Georgia became the first to harness the power of satellite for national distribution of an inservice program to disseminate information related to attention deficit disorders (McLaughlin, Bender, & Wood, 1997). Soon after, the Council for Exceptional Children (1997b) initiated a series of professional development sessions delivered by satellite. The use of satellite for distance education delivery has declined significantly in recent years, largely due to increasing transmission costs and wider availability of other technologies.

Telephone Conferencing

Some early programs also used the telephone, a readily available, low-cost, and familiar technology, to deliver distance education programming. Audio-conferencing was used at the University of Wyoming to deliver courses at off-campus locations (Shaeffer & Shaeffer, 1993), while Indiana University used an audiographics systems (voice plus faxed image) to deliver inservice training to teachers in rural areas (Knapczyk, 1993). Alaska continues to use some telephone conferencing for program delivery, since this is the only technology available in remote rural areas (Ryan, 1999).

Telephone conferencing was quickly superceded by television (satellite and interactive systems), although a few programs continue to use this format in combination with other technologies (to enable interaction during satellite broadcasts or to supplement online instruction).

Interactive television systems. When it became possible to transmit video and audio signal across high-speed telephone connections, a number of programs moved to use interactive television for distance education. For example, interactive television was first used at Murray State University in Kentucky for off-campus courses (Condon, Zimmerman, & Beane, 1989). The University of Kansas was one of the first institutions to make extensive use of this emerging technology, because two-way interactions facilitated training sign language training in their deaf education program (Luetke-Stahlman, 1995). The University of Kentucky incorporated interactive television into its satellite-based distance education program to reach additional field sites (Collins, 1997). Eventually, several universities in Kentucky joined forces to offer a collaborative program with faculty team teaching different courses (Grisham-Brown, Knoll, Collins, & Baird, 1998). At the same time, the University of North Carolina at Charlotte started a program that linked several campuses across that state (Jordan, Spooner, Calhoun, Beattie, Algozzine, & Galloway, 1999). The videoconferencing system at North Georgia College and State University also was used to facilitate supervision of student teachers placed in schools in remote locations in that state (Gruenhagen, McCracken, & True, 1999). Numerous other institutions of higher education and several state agencies and school districts have adopted and continue to consider the uses of interactive television for preservice and inservice training.

Online Instruction

Special educators have only recently begun to incorporate online instruction into distance education efforts. The earliest use of the Web for distance education in special education was a campus-based online graduate course reported by the University of Kentucky (Blackhurst, Hales, & Lahm, 1998). About the same time, a federally funded project at the University of Kansas developed a series of online modules in specific instruction and management strategies for use by preservice programs preparing special educators across the country (Meyen, Lian, & Tangen, 1997). Smith, with colleagues at the University of Florida, offered an online graduate course on attention deficit hyperactivity disorder to practicing educators in that state (Smith, Jordan, Corbett, & Dillon, 1999). Soon after, the University of Northern Colorado became the first to use the Web as the primary delivery mechanism to provide a low incidence disabilities personnel preparation program across a 14 state western region (Ferrell, Persichitte, Lowell, & Roberts, 2001). The Council for Exceptional Children began to use the Web for national inservice training of practicing special educators (Council for Exceptional Children, 1997a). West Virginia University initiated a series of summer courses offered entirely online as part of a regional inservice training initiative in 1999 (Ludlow, Foshay, Brannan, Duff, & Dennison, 2002). Today, educators across the country are rapidly exploring the applications of online instruction as a distance delivery mechanism for personnel preparation and staff development.

The latest developments in distance education involve Web-based applications that permit interactions in real time. A consortium of universities in the Northwest that included the University of Utah, Utah State University, the University of Montana, the University of Wyoming, and the University of Alaska designed the first preservice program delivered via desktop video-conferencing (Spooner, Agran, Spooner, & Keifer-O'Donnell, 2000). At Utah State University, special educators used desktop video-conferencing for supervision of practicum experiences (Menlove, Hansford, & Lignugaris-Kraft, 2000), while at Indiana University Southeast, it has been used for mentoring of practicing educators (Shea & Babione, 2001). Since Fall 2000, the satellite-based program at West Virginia University has added video streaming technology to offer live Web simulcasts to reach learners across the United States and in several international locations (Ludlow & Duff, 2002). As Web-based

video-conferencing (and audio-conferencing) improve and become more widely available, they are likely to see increased use (in combination with other online formats) in distance education programs in special education.

Trends in the literature.
In their review of the literature on distance education and special education, Ludlow and Brannan (1999) noted several key trends: distance education programs have been stable over time, but have adapted to each new technology as it emerged; distance education applications have focused on preparation of personnel in high-need areas, such as low-incidence disabilities and rural locations; distance education delivery systems rarely rely on a single technology, instead combining multiple formats to accomplish different goals; and, institutions of higher education and education agencies are beginning to engage in collaborative activities to reduce costs and enhance access to quality programs. The success of distance education programs in addressing preservice and inservice training needs suggests that these delivery systems have become an integral component of the personnel preparation enterprise and promise to continue to shape how teachers and therapists are trained for many years to come.

Review of Data-Based Studies in Distance Education and Special Education

To determine the state of the knowledge base on distance education in special education, an extensive search of the professional literature published between 1985 and 2002 was conducted for the purpose of identifying and analyzing data-based reports. Specifically, the goal was to examine the characteristics of these studies and their implications for practice, policy development, and future research related to distance education applications for personnel preparation and staff development in special education.

Search and Selection Process
The search involved the following activities: an online search of key databases; a hand search of journals that most frequently publish information on distance education and special

education or distance education research; and, a search for any additional references cited in reports located through the other searches.

The initial search was conducted in online databases including EBSCOHost, Wilson Omnifile, ERIC(CMS), PSYCHInfo, and Dissertation Abstracts, using the keywords *distance education* and *special education;* followup searches substituted the terms: *television teaching, telecourses, teleconferencing, satellite broadcasts, videotapes, video modules, video conferencing, interactive television, compressed video, online learning, electronic learning, e-learning, Web-based instruction, Web courses, Internet courses,* and *audio conferencing.*

A subsequent search involved reading the table of contents of every issue of four special education journals (*Journal of Special Education Technology, Teacher Education and Special Education, Rural Special Education Quarterly,* and *Remedial* and *Special Education*), as well as two distance education research journals (*The American Journal of Distance Education and Distance Education*). These journals are distinguished by the frequency with which they publish articles focused on distance education applications.

A final search required locating any additional references in the reports identified in the first two searches. These searches identified a total of 133 references, including articles in refereed journals, magazines, and conference proceedings as well as dissertations, several book chapters, and even one entire book. Nearly all of these materials were located in the original online search using the primary keywords *distance education and special education;* the additional keywords succeeded in finding fewer than 10 additional references, while the hand searches located only three more references.

The selection process involved reading all references to determine which ones represented studies with quantitative or qualitative data. This selection process identified 33 data-based reports: 23 published in refereed journals in special education, five in other education journals, three in conference proceedings, and another two available as dissertations.

The remaining literature could be characterized as mainly program descriptions with several reviews of the literature or position papers, all of which were eliminated from consideration for this review. Program descriptions were not included in this analysis, but many of them have been reviewed elsewhere (for example, Ludlow & Brannan, 1999).

Each report was then classified as a research study or an evaluation study, using criteria based on the classic text by Campbell and Stanley (1963). A report was considered to be a research study if it used either an experimental or quasi-experimental design with some attempt to control for internal or external threats to validity. A report was considered to be an evaluation study if it collected data on an intact group after implementation of a course or program. These criteria resulted in only two studies being classified as experimental research and two more as quasi-experimental research, with the remaining 29 studies classified as evaluation research. At this point, all of the data-based reports were reviewed to determine their design, findings, and conclusions in order to compare results and identify trends.

Limitations on the Review Process
Reviewing the professional literature on technology-mediated distance education in special education was a complicated task for a variety of reasons. Several problems that limit the interpretability of the findings and highlight the need for further study soon became evident; these problems are outlined below.

Access to Relevant Literature
The first problem is that not much literature is readily available. The number of articles published in professional journals has been relatively low and reports published in other outlets have been limited until the last several years. In addition, the majority of distance education efforts to-date have not been reported in retrievable form and, in fact, may never have been shared with the field in any forum. Consequently, any review of data-based studies (including this one) is limited to published reports that can be located by standard search strategies and, therefore, may miss some important studies and relevant findings.

Rapid eEvolution of Practice
A second problem is the fact that the practice of distance education has evolved rapidly as new technologies emerge, so programs are

changing constantly as they work to embrace new formats for teaching and learning. By the time an application is reported in the literature, the institution, program, or individual faculty member may already have moved on to implement a new model. Hence, any review may be outdated to some extent before it appears in print, and this review merely presents a snapshot of the research to-date.

Difficulty in Making Comparisons

Another problem is the disparity in research design and methodology used. Most reports describe individual courses, a few present partial programs, and fewer still discuss full programs offered entirely at a distance. This fact, combined with the wide variety of technologies in use and the many and varied measure used to assess outcomes, results in a mass of highly individualized activities that defy easy analysis. It can even be difficult to categorize a given report since programs and even courses frequently use multiple delivery systems. As a result of these trends, it can be problematic to make meaningful comparisons in any review.

Characteristics of the Literature

A final problem is the limitations inherent in the characteristics of the literature itself, in part due to the small number of studies, in part due to the wide variations in design components and outcome variables studied. There has been no systematic investigation in any study of the many dependent and independent variables in research investigations or even of the range of input and outcome variables in evaluation studies; consequently, it is difficult to draw more than preliminary conclusions at this point in time.

Summary of Data-Based Studies

The small number of data-based studies found in the literature justifies describing each study briefly to facilitate examination of key findings and overall trends as well as discussion of the problems inherent in investigating distance education. The studies are presented in this order: experimental research studies; quasi-experimental research studies; evaluation studies of individual courses or workshops; evaluation studies of complete programs. The studies

included in each category are then presented in chronological order from least to most recent.

Experimental Research Studies

Only two studies were located that could be considered experimental research in that they used random assignment of participants and inferential statistical testing of findings. Thus, these studies can be said to represent the field's best efforts at examining the phenomenon of distance education as it is applied in personnel preparation and staff development in special education.

Paulsen and her colleagues compared learner achievement and satisfaction in traditional instruction, instructional television and videotaped lectures (Paulsen, Higgins, Miller, Strawser, & Boone, 1998). They randomly assigned 67 learners in a preservice course in special education to one of three instructional methods; then they assessed performance on a 65-item pretest and posttest and a series of quizzes as well as determined satisfaction through a 26-item satisfaction survey and a 7-item instructor evaluation form. Results from the pretests and posttests, analyzed by means of ANOVAs and paired sample t-tests, indicated that learners achieved equally well on quizzes and tests across all methods. Satisfaction survey and instructor evaluation form data, also analyzed by ANOVAs and Scheffe' tests, showed that learners were generally satisfied with traditional instruction and interactive television but not with videotaped instruction, and they perceived the instructor as taking a less active role in the two technology-mediated formats. The authors concluded that technology formats do not produce differences in learning, but learners may have different perceptions of their effectiveness.

Smith, Smith, and Boone (2000) compared the academic performance of 58 learners in a traditional classroom versus an online learning environment in a course on technology integration in an undergraduate teacher education program. Learners enrolled in two sections of the course were randomly assigned to traditional or online groups for six activities administered in random order (two lecture interventions, two guided-instruction interventions, and two collaborative discussion activities). All learners completed six pretests and six posttests consisting of the same sets of multiple-choice questions covering course content in the lectures, guided instructional activities, and discussion readings. Data from the pretests and posttests were analyzed by means of 2 x 2 repeated-measures ANOVA. These analyses found no significant differences between traditional and online instruction for lecture interventions, guided-instruction interventions, or collaborative discussion activities. The authors concluded that selected methods of traditional instruction translate effectively into online learning.

Quasi-Experimental Research Studies

Two early studies were classified as quasi-experimental because they used learners as their own controls and applied inferential statistical tests. They may be seen as rudimentary efforts to apply more scientific methods to the study of distance education and may serve as exemplars of appropriate methodology where full control of conditions cannot be achieved.

Beare (1989) offered a preservice course on behavior and environment management to undergraduate and graduate students through a series of sessions available via live lecture, live lecture plus videotape backup, videotaped lecture, audiotaped lecture, and telelecture. He exposed 175 learners to each format, evaluating their performance on three exams and asking them to rate the formats on 21 items using a 5-point Likert scale. An analysis of variance revealed no differences between the formats on exam scores, while a Chi-square test showed no significant differences between the formats on any rated items. However, learners expressed a clear preference for live instruction in their written comments. Beare concluded that different distance delivery formats were capable of achieving similar outcomes.

McCleary and Egan (1989) compared the performance and perceptions of on- and off-campus students across three preservice special education courses delivered both live and via interactive television, with the instructor appearing live at the distant sites as well as on campus. They gave each group pre- and posttest exams based on textbook question pools and asked learners to rate aspects of the courses on and university course evaluation form using a 7-point as well as a media services survey using a 5-point Likert scale. An analysis of covariance on test scores showed no differences between live and televised instruction when adjusted for pretest differences. The ratings of instructor effectiveness were similar for all three courses (means = 5.16, 5.11, and 5.63), with paired t-tests showing with no differences between delivery formats. Learners also rated the level of difficulty about the same (means = 3.44, 3.85. 4.17), with no differences between formats, and they rated both formats about the same in comparison with convention instruction (means = 3.64, 3.29, and 3.42), again with no significant differences between formats. The authors concluded that distance delivery was equivalent to face-to-face instruction with respect to both learning outcomes and learner perceptions.

Program Evaluation Studies of Courses/ Workshops

Most of the studies (23 in all) in the existing literature represent investigations of a single course or workshop or several (2-4) courses or workshops that may or may not have been part of a complete program. Quantitative studies predominated, but two studies utilized qualitative methodology and one used a mixed-methods approach. These studies reported data from one or more intact groups, and all but one relied on descriptive statistics or content analyses. They are presented here grouped by technology, with the earliest studies investigating televised instruction and the more recent studies examining online instruction.

Egan and his colleagues compared learning outcomes and learner perceptions of 20 campus-based and 20 remote-site learners in a preservice course on methods in behavior disorders delivered via a two-way microwave television system (Egan et al., 1988). They assessed academic performance by means of an objective pretest and posttest with items randomly selected from a test bank. These data showed that neither group performed significantly better on the pretest or the posttest. All learners completed a course evaluation form that used a 7-point Likert scale to assess their perceptions on 10 items related to course quality. Remote-site learners also completed a media evaluation form that used a 5-point Likert scale to assess their reactions on 12 items related to technology-mediated instruction. On the course evaluation, all items were rated much higher by campus-based learners (means ranging from 5.94 to 6.38) than by remote-site learners (means ranging from 3.22 to 5.16), with the major problem identified as provision of feedback. On the media evaluation, remote-site learners rated all items as average (means ranging from 2.44 to 3.88), expressing concern about the provisions for discussion. The authors concluded that television was an effective delivery system but that more research was needed into specific variables related to successful instruction.

Savage (1991) reported the results of a course evaluation completed by eight learners enrolled in a preservice course for teachers of gifted students offered via satellite broadcasts. Learners were asked to submit written responses identifying strengths, weaknesses, and suggestions for change. All eight learners identified convenience as the main advantage of distance delivery, and several also cited the instructor's teaching style and content quality. They cited lack of instructor feedback on assignments as the major disadvantage of the delivery format, with seven learners recommending the addition of meetings on campus. The author concluded that the results were good enough to warrant continued efforts at distance education.

Slaton and Lacefield (1991) evaluated the reactions of 155 teachers to four inservice training sessions on learning disabilities delivered via satellite broadcasts with a keypad response system. Learners were asked to complete initial reaction forms after each session addressing ease of keypad use on a 5-point Likert scale. Ratings ranged from 4.13 to 4.43 across all four sessions. During each session, learners also responded to retention questions, video-based simulation questions, self-report and opinion questions, and activity-selection questions. Learners gave correct responses to 77% of retention questions across sessions and to 95.4% of one video-based simulation question and only 18.6% of the other question. Of 84 participants responding to an opinion question on their proficiency in content, 61% reported feeling somewhat prepared, 13% reported feeling well prepared, and 26% reported unprepared. Of 96 participants responding to an activity selection question, 76% reported they would like to see paperwork solutions and 24% would not. Learners also provided written evaluations of the series of sessions after they were completed. The authors concluded that this technology showed some promise for enhancing interactivity in distance delivery.

Egan and his colleagues compared learner perceptions of face-to-face teaching distance delivery formats (Egan, Welch, Page, & Sebastian, 1992). They asked 154 learners in face-to-face courses, 267 learners in prepackaged videotape courses, and 93 learners in interactive television courses to complete a media evaluation survey and conducted a series of ANOVAs on the ratings. Face-to-face teaching was rated significantly higher than videotape on 8 of 10 variables (not amount of material covered or level of difficulty) and higher than interactive television on half of the variables (clarity, organization, relevance to objectives, integration, visual materials, and text screens). Instructional television was rated higher than videotape on the single variable of text screens. The researchers concluded that their findings might reflect the greater intimacy associated with face-to-face teaching and that the similarity between interactive television and videotape may have been due to the use of live facilitators with both formats.

Lombardi and his colleagues studied two graduate courses in a post-baccalaureate certification program in mild disabilities offered collaboratively by faculty from three universities using satellite delivery (Lombardi, Bauer, Peters, & O'Keefe, 1992). They asked 209 learners to rate the course on an 11-item survey using a 10-point continuum scale ranging from excellent to poor. The learners rated all aspects of both courses in the excellent range, with item means ranging from highs of 9.27 and 8.33 for faculty knowledge of subject to lows of 7.25 and 7.43 for student involvement during class sessions. The authors concluded that satellite delivery was as effective as field-based courses in training practicing but uncertified special educators.

Welch and his colleagues (Welch, Gibb, & Egan, 1992) evaluated a staff development program on learning strategies delivered as a series of videotape presentations with study guides designed to be used by a school-based facilitator. They compared the knowledge and skills of 15 teachers on a pretest and posttests and asked participants to rate program effectiveness on a 10-item survey using a 6-point Likert scale. A two-sample *t*-test showed a significant gain in scores from pretest (combined mean = .14) to posttest (combined mean = .93). Participants also rated all items at 4 or above, with the lowest rating (mean = 4.43) for the usefulness of the tapes. They concluded that videotapes are an appropriate mechanism for inservice training, at least when supplemented with live facilitation.

Shaeffer and Shaeffer (1993) evaluated the success of a course on early childhood special education offered via audio-conferencing to six learners at a single remote site. Learners responded to a questionnaire with sentence completion items designed to assess what they liked best and least about the instructor's presentation, the use of audio-conferencing as a delivery system, and the overall learning experience. They identified threads in the written responses indicating (a) that learners felt that the instructor was able to personalize the course and encourage discussion but covered material too fast and spent excessive time in discussion; (b) that learners liked the convenience of audio-conferencing and the opportunity to interact with professionals in other areas, but disliked the lack of direct contact and the equipment problems; and (c) that they appreciated the convenience and networking possibilities of distance education but still preferred face-to-face instruction. The authors concluded that the positive aspects of distance delivery outweighed the negative aspects and facilitated offering courses in rural areas.

Luetke-Stahlman (1995) evaluated two courses taught via interactive television to graduate students at five sites in a distance education program in deaf education. Urban (on-campus) and rural (off-campus) learners completed a survey rating course components across 16 items using a 5-point Likert scale. Group means for both courses showed that all learners expressed satisfaction with most aspects of the course except that they felt it was harder to participate in discussion. Further, group means for each course showed that learners in the methods course were more satisfied with distance delivery than learners in the deaf studies course. Group means comparing urban and rural learners showed that they agreed on most items but rural learners expressed some concern with the technology. The data also showed that rural learners improved their attitude toward the technology over time. The author concluded that interactive television was effective and that learner satisfaction increases as learners become more comfortable with using new technologies.

Zentall and Javorsky (1997) evaluated a graduate course for inservice training in attention deficit hyperactivity disorder offered via satellite broadcasts. Learners were asked to complete an evaluation of course satisfaction with eight items using a 5-point Likert scale and open-ended questions. Descriptive data revealed that ratings on all items tended to be neutral or positive (means ranging from 3.6 to 4.1), and comments mostly addressed content rather than technology. The authors concluded that they would offer other courses using satellite transmission, but would make specific changes in the content and structure based on feedback.

Foegen and her colleagues conducted a case study to evaluate the effectiveness of using interactive television to deliver an inservice workshop on monitoring progress on Individualized Education Programs to 12 learners at a single remote site (Foegen, Howe, Deno, & Robinson, 1998). Learners used groupware technology at individual terminals to type responses to instructor questions; all responses were instantly transmitted via modem to the instructor, who could monitor participation by the whole class at any point in time. At the end of the workshop, learners were asked to compare distance delivery with and without groupware to face-to-face instruction on items using a 5-point Likert scale and to answer open-ended questions. The ratings data indicated that learners considered interactive television without groupware to be about as effective as face-to-face teaching across all items, but believed that distance delivery using groupware was more effective than traditional instruction across the same items. Two raters coded written responses as positive, negative, and neutral (mean level of agreement 88.5%) and sorted them into five categories (mean level of agreement: 84% for positive and 88% for negative statements). This content analysis of 74 responses identified 64 statements as positive perceptions and 17 statements as negative perceptions. The authors concluded that interactive television is an appropriate mechanism for inservice training and that interaction can be enhanced through the use of groupware response systems.

Blackhurst et al.(1998) used a Web course management system to deliver an online graduate course in telecommunications in special education and rehabilitation. Eight learners completed a survey with a series of Likert-scale ratings that addressed four factors: general reactions, format reactions, reactions to communications features, and reactions to examinations. For general reactions, 75% reported they liked online instruction a lot and 25% reported they liked it more than they anticipated. All (100%) found it easy or very easy to use and felt it had some or considerable effect on their technology skills. The authors concluded that the positive reactions of learners to Web-based coursework justify continued experimentation with use of this technology for instruction.

Grisham-Brown and her colleagues evaluated a multi-university course on transdisciplinary services offered by a team of instructors to 37 learners at six sites via interactive television (Grisham-Brown et al., 1998). Learners were asked to rate the course topics and format on17 items using a 5-point Likert scale and also answer some open-ended questions. Ratings across items and sites were clustered in the upper half of the scale, with over half in the upper quartile. However, the interactive television format was the lowest rated aspect of the course, with means from 3.0 to 4.5. The authors attributed this to technical difficulties and problems in conducting interactions across sites. They concluded that interactive television was a promising format for collaborative coursework but presented many challenges to be addressed in future efforts.

Spooner and his colleagues compared learner ratings of instruction on a standard evaluation of instruction form in two special education preservice courses offered on and off campus using interactive television (Spooner, Jordan, Algozzine, & Spooner, 1999). Surveys completed by 15 on-campus learners and 36 remote-site learners rated the course, instructor, organization, teaching, and communication using a 5-point Likert scale on an instrument with high reliability overall (r = .98) and for each cluster (range of r = .77 to .99). Statistical analyses using t-tests revealed no significant differences in overall ratings, with ratings for course, instructor, teaching, and communication similar for both groups across both courses, and ratings for organization differing only slightly between groups on one course. The authors concluded that interactive television is comparable to face-to-face instruction when the instructor and content are held constant.

Gallagher and McCormick (1999) assessed learner satisfaction with two courses in a graduate-level preservice program in early childhood special education offered twice via interactive television. They conducted structured telephone interviews with 103 learners asking them to rate the course on 23 items related to course satisfaction as agree or disagree and also to complete some open-ended questions. Their data across four sections, reported as percentages selecting agree, showed a mixed pattern but some clear trends. That is, learners were more likely to report they preferred on-site instruction in the first year (100% in one course and 74% in the other) than in the second year (62% in one course and 50% in the other). Further, they were also more likely to rate distance education instruction as good as typical instruction on campus in the second year (67% in one course and 80% in the other course) than in the first year (17% in one course and 33% in the other course. Respondent comments noted many advantages of distance education, including accessibility in remote areas, less time and expense in attending classes, and interaction with peers and experts on a statewide basis. Participants also cited disadvantages such as greater difficulty in interacting with others, technical problems, and less personal contact. The authors concluded that interactive television is an acceptable format for staff development.

Cramer (2000) conducted a pilot test comparing Web-based modules with interactive television delivery in a preservice course in special education. She asked 22 learners who chose to participate in the pilot study to respond to questions about online instruction by answering yes, no, or undecided. Her data showed that all of the learners (100%) were satisfied with instructor feedback, liked the efficient use of time, improved their technology skills, and would take another online course, only 85% felt that they did not miss face-to-face interactions. She concluded that experimentation with more online courses was warranted based on these results.

Cooke and deBettencourt (2001) collected course evaluation data in a case study of staff development using a special education course for general educators collaboratively designed and delivered by faculty at three universities. Their study compared synchronous and asynchronous delivery, with 41 learners at four sites participating via interactive television and 27 learners at two sites viewing videotapes of the sessions one week later. Learners rated the presentations, visuals, interactions, and group activities using a 4-point Likert scale on a form designed to evaluate tele-teaching strategies. Their results indicated that the percentage of respondents rating each course format as somewhat or extremely helpful was much higher for the interactive video group than for the videotape group for presentations (90% compared with 60%), for visuals (85% compared with 38%), and for interactions (88% compared with 0). However, both groups rated group activities, which were conducted outside the session, about the same, with 84% compared with 87% selecting somewhat or extremely helpful. Learners were also asked to rate as excellent, satisfactory or fair the organization, clarity, and relationship to competencies of the content across 14 sessions in three modules. Statistical analyses using t-tests showed that participants at interactive video sites rated content more favorably than those at videotape sites. The authors concluded that even when learners are successful in acquiring information from

videotaped presentations, they may still be dissatisfied with presentations that are not interactive.

Stenhoff and his colleagues (Stenhoff, Menlove, Davey, & Melina, 2001) investigated learners' reactions to four Web-based special education courses offered by five different instructors at the undergraduate and graduate level incorporating audio-conferencing with other online activities. Students rated the courses using a 4-point Likert scale on nine questions addressing student-teacher interactivity and student-technology interactivity. Their results (with 61 of 103 students responding) showed that the highest ratings were given to the instructor with the most distance education experience (62% for student interactivity and 69% for technology interactivity) and the lowest ratings to the one with the least experience (9% for both aspects). The authors concluded that instructor skill and comfort in using technology may be an important factor in learner satisfaction with distance education.

Lock (2001) evaluated four online graduate course using text materials, threaded discussion, and email contacts offered to practicing general and special educators in rural areas. They asked 41 learners to complete a survey rating presentation strategies, instructor effectiveness, and course content using a 4-point Likert scale. The courses were rated high by nearly all (99%) learners across all three areas. On individual items, the lowest ratings were for adequate university support (63%), adequate office hours (65%), and amount of time required (68%). The authors concluded the online instruction showed promise for inservice training, especially in rural areas.

Ludlow (2001b) evaluated learning outcomes and learner satisfaction in two staff development courses offered entirely online to 33 practicing professionals in early intervention and early childhood special education. She used three measures of learning outcomes: self-reported changes in knowledge about and attitudes toward technology on two 20-item Likert scales before and after the course; audit trails for hits and time online; and an eight-item email survey on how participants applied the information in their classrooms eight months later. She also used three measures of learner satisfaction: an 80-item survey using a 4-point Likert scale and open-ended questions in which participants rated all aspects of the online course; a 12-item survey similar in format in which they compared online and face-to-face instruction; and a focus group interview. The data showed that the first group of learners (with more technology experience) showed no change in knowledge or attitudes, but the second group (with limited experience) reported increased knowledge on many items (50% on the posttest) and improved attitudes on many items (50% to 90% across items). Learners made the most hits (mean = 102) and spent the most time (mean = 14 minutes, 24 seconds) viewing the assignments and made the fewest hits and spent the least time on the directions (mean = 35 hits, 7 minutes) or the policies and procedures (mean = 26 hits, 2 minutes). On the summary evaluation survey, participants identified as the most helpful components the interactive practice exercises, case studies, and chats (81% to 88%), and the least helpful as the group project (37% to 38%), the threaded discussions (55%), and media (57%). On the comparative evaluation survey, they felt the course had less interaction with other learners (100% and 41%) and they spent more time learning content (50% and 71%); 88% of the first group and 65% of the second group indicated they would take another online course. The focus group stated that they learned both content and technical skills, and they appreciated using the Internet for information and networking; however, they experienced stress when technical problems occurred and they had difficulty learning independently. Finally, of 18 respondents completing the followup survey, all but four reported that they used the information in the job setting. Ludlow concluded that Web-based instruction had promise for inservice training but that attention must be paid to technical support and interactivity.

Welch and Sheridan (2002) evaluated a technology-enhanced staff development program that used satellite broadcast sessions with audio conferencing plus videotape modules to train five elementary schools in collaborative partnerships. Learners were asked to respond to surveys after each session and module and again at the end of the project. The surveys required respondents to rate the helpfulness of project components on a 6-point Likert scale and also to answer open-ended questions on the strengths and limitations of each component and the project as a whole. The results showed that learners rated the helpfulness of the video modules as mostly helpful for strategies for partnerships (ratings of 4.9 to 5.5) and somewhat to very helpful for action planning (ratings of 4.0 to 5.0); results for the teleconferences were not reported. On the final survey, learners rated the production quality of the videos as good (5.47) and the quality of the support materials as very good (5.03); results for the teleconferences were not reported. Project staff also conducted individual interviews with 30 learners near the end of the project, asking them to comment on their perceptions of technology-mediated training. Most respondents felt the teleconferences were a viable means for interacting and sharing information, but found the structured discussion and time constraints to limit meaningful discussion across sites. Many respondents felt the video modules were appropriate in content and pacing, but some found them to be simplistic, slow, and redundant. Overall, the authors concluded that video-mediated training is a viable means of staff development, but does not replace the need for face-to-face contact between instructors and participants.

Beattie and his colleagues compared the course evaluation ratings of graduate students on and off campus in a distance education program that used interactive television to prepare preservice teachers in mild disabilities (Beattie, Spooner, Jordan, & Spooner, 2002). Their study involved 105 learners, with 24 taught in a traditional face-to-face section, 29 in a campus-based section of a distance education course, and 30,19, and 13, respectively, at three remote sites in that course. Learners rated the quality of the course, the instructor, and the overall learning experience across 23 items using a 5-point Likert scale on a standard evaluation of instruction form. Statistical analyses using t-tests found no significant differences between the groups.

The authors attributed these results to the close similarity between interactive television and face-to-face instruction.

Beard and Harper (2002) assessed perceptions of interactivity in 42 students in a Web-enhanced course on severe disabilities. They asked learners to complete a 10-item survey using a 5-point Likert scale to compare interactions in class and online and respond to open-ended questions. Learners gave high ratings to both delivery systems, but felt there was more interaction in class (mean = 4.68) than online (mean = 4.30). They also preferred traditional instruction (mean = 4.72) to Web-based instruction (mean = 4.28), although their written comments suggested they liked the flexibility offered by online learning.

Falconer and Lignugaris/Kraft (2002) conducted a qualitative inquiry into the use of desktop video-conferencing for practicum supervision in remote areas. They used participant observation and in-depth interview of five participants as data collection mechanisms and coding of field notes and interview transcripts followed by member checks for data analysis and interpretation. Their findings showed three categories of benefits for desktop video-conferencing (easier observation, enhanced communication, and greater collaboration) as well as two categories of limitations (technical problems and personal lack of familiarity with the system). They concluded that videoconferencing was an effective format for practicum supervision when appropriate training was provided to promote its use.

Program Evaluation Studies of Complete Programs

Only six studies attempted to collect data from learners about the effects of programs offered completely via distance education. Four studies used quantitative methods and two used qualitative methods to assess learner perceptions but not learner outcomes; one study was conducted during the program while the rest were conducted upon completion of each program.

Sebastian and her colleagues (Sebastian, Calmes, & Mayhew, 1997) contacted all of the graduates of a distance education program from 1988 to 1996 to study their perceptions of different delivery formats. Specifically, they asked learners to use a 5-point Likert scale to compare face-to-face teaching, interactive television, interactive television plus videotape, videotape with on-site facilitator, and videotape without facilitation. Face-to-face teaching received the highest rating (mean = 3.8) and videotape plus facilitator received the next highest rating (mean = 3.4), while videotape without facilitation received the lowest rating (mean = 2.47). They concluded that learners demonstrate a clear preference for some direct contact with an instructor.

Collins (1997) conducted an evaluation of a graduate-level distance education program in severe disabilities offered primarily via satellite with some use of interactive television to 13 sites. She mailed a survey to 115 former and current program participants asking them to rate program components using a 5-point Likert scale. Based on data from 46 completed and returned surveys showed that the mean ratings for modes of delivery were 4.5 for on-site, 3.4 for satellite, and 4.4 for interactive television, with library services identified as the least effective components across all modes. Learners also reported their preference for delivery modes, with 45% selecting satellite, 21% selecting interactive television, 21% selecting a combination approach, 15% selecting on-site, and 4% expressing no preference. On an open-ended question asking them to describe their experiences with the program, most learners offered positive comments about the quality of the content, the helpfulness and availability of the faculty, and the accessibility and effectiveness of the distance learning model. The author concluded that each delivery mode has advantages and disadvantages and that selection should be based on accessibility to learners and suitability to course content.

A dissertation completed by Gold (1997) used a three-part survey instrument to assess the perceptions of a small sample of learners regarding the extent to which a graduate-level distance education program in special education addressed their needs as adult learners. Their results showed 73% agreement that the program reflected principles of adult learning; 71% agreement that the program meet the needs of distance learners; and 75% agreement that the program represented a positive educational experience. Learner comments also identified program strengths as convenience, access, and instructor quality and program weaknesses as a need for more timely feedback, better communication, and special advising services. Gold concluded that distance education was successful in addressing many if not all learner concerns.

Hinds (2002) explored differences between traditional and distance learners in a special education program at a major university. He asked 22 distance learners and 39 campus-based learners to complete a demographic questionnaire. The data revealed major differences between the two groups: campus learners were younger (mean age = 22), unmarried (75%), and pursuing undergraduate degrees without full-time employment (100%), whereas distance learners were older (mean age = 43), married (89%), with children (75%), employed full-time (85%), and possessing a prior undergraduate or graduate degree (40%). He concluded that such differences complicate the findings of studies based on comparisons between these two groups.

A qualitative dissertation by Cooper (2000) used interviews with 12 teachers in Texas who received all or some of their certification coursework in several distance education programs in the area of vision impairments. The constant comparative approach used to analyze the data revealed several themes related to technology: participants preferred live to mediated instruction and interactive television to Web-based instruction; they cited numerous challenges related to distance education, such as learning to use the technologies and frustration with technical problems. The author concluded that teachers were satisfied overall with the distance education experience and felt they gained important skills needed for success in the classroom.

Day and Sebastian (2002) conducted a qualitative study of learners who participated in a graduate-level preservice program in the area of vision impairments delivered via interactive television and WebCT, a Web course management system. They used a phenomenological approach to explore the experiences and reactions of six participants (two on campus and four at remote sites) through interviews, focus groups, and review of artifacts such as email messages and bulletin board postings. The content analysis of data resulted in the emergence of three themes: perceptions of the technologies; opportunities to communicate and build relationships; and other issues and concerns. Five learners indicated they liked interactive video, with four appreciating its facilitation of cross-site interaction in real time; five learners believed the Web component was helpful, but three learners expressed mixed feelings about it, largely due to bandwidth problems in rural areas. Although five of the six learners reported that their communications had increased as a result of the technologies, only three felt that interactive television and Web-based instruction had enabled them to develop or strengthen relationships with the instructor and other learners. Other issues and concerns centered on access to the Internet and to its resources, which were appreciated by all participants although with some difficulty. The authors concluded that learners experience both successes and frustrations during technology-mediated distance education and that their own attitudes and skills related to specific technologies influence their perceptions to some degree.

Summary of Findings from the Review of Studies

This review searched the professional literature to identify, analyze, and discuss the implications of research reports that investigated various aspects of distance education in special education. An examination of these reports leads to the following general conclusions: special educators continue to experiment with a wide variety of technologies (singly and in combination) for distance delivery of personnel preparation and staff development programs; there have been few empirical studies and even fewer experimental investigations of distance education in special education; research/evaluation efforts have most often been focused on individual courses or workshops rather than full programs; and, technology-mediated instruction typically results in learning outcomes and learner satisfaction that is at least equivalent to those produced by live, face-to-face instruction.

Distance Education Delivery

The majority of the studies addressed distance education in special education in the context of preservice training (24 studies), rather than inservice training (9 studies). Nearly all of these preservice programs were at the graduate level (30 studies) rather than the undergraduate level (3 studies). More than half of the studies (21 studies) assessed the effectiveness of television delivery formats (15 studies of interactive television and 6 studies of satellite transmission). Only a handful of studies assessed online instruction (8 studies), tape presentations (6 studies), and telephone conferencing (2 studies). Most of the studies presented data from a single course, workshop or practicum experience (20 studies); a few studies addressed multiple courses (7 studies) or full programs (6 studies). As Ludlow and Brannan (1999) noted, the reports follow the evolution of distance delivery systems from early use of television formats to more recent use of Web-based models.

Findings such as these are typical of the distance education literature in general, which reveals studies representing a wide range of technologies and primarily focused on a single course offered at one point in time. A quick reading of tables of contents in all issues of *The American Journal of Distance Education* also shows initial emphasis on live and taped delivery via video followed by more current interest in delivery on the Internet and World Wide Web.

Research and Evaluation Methodology

The search produced only two experimental studies and two quasi-experimental studies. The small number of experimental studies is due in large part to the difficulty of using intact groups and the difficulty of achieving appropriate levels of control over internal and external variables in real-world situations. Most of the data-based reports found by the literature search conducted for this review fall into this category; consequently, nearly all of them (100 out of 133) were categorized as program descriptions. It is clear that educators involved in distance education in special education have been more willing and/or able share their personal experiences and reflections related to

instruction with emerging technologies than prepared to design and conduct investigations to demonstrate its effectiveness and document its outcomes.

Research designs have been the pre-posttest design (with randomization of learners) used by two studies and the multiple-treatments design (with learners as own controls) also used by two studies. All other studies did not report any controls. This finding is understandable, given the context in which most distance education programs have been implemented, primarily with intact groups in specific locations that limited the ability to employ randomized assignment to different conditions. Nearly all of the studies collected only quantitative data (29 studies), and only a handful collected only qualitative data (3 studies) or both quantitative and qualitative data (1 study). In general, the data analysis procedures used in the quantitative studies could be characterized as relatively unsophisticated, relying primarily on descriptive statistics such as frequencies, percentages, or means (30 studies). The statistical test most often used for data analysis was the t-test (7 studies), followed by ANOVA (4 studies), and Chi square (1 study). None of the studies reported effect size or other measures of practical significance. The data analysis procedures used in the qualitative studies were similarly simplistic, focusing on basic content analysis of themes without triangulation measures or matrix analysis procedures.

A number of reviews of the distance education literature in general have criticized the inadequacy of the research designs used in these studies, which are characterized by an overall lack of control and numerous flaws in method. For example, Berge and Mrozowski (2001), in a review of studies of distance education between 1990 and 1999, found that the majority failed to control key variables, used inadequate samples, employed outcome measures with limited validity and reliability, and reported only descriptive statistics. Some reviewers have concluded that the findings of such studies are uninterpretable due to the poor quality of the research (Institute for Higher Education Policy, 1999) as well as its atheoretical nature (Simonson, Schlosser, & Hanson, 1999).

The Institute for Higher Education Policy (2000) conducted case studies of six colleges and universities engaged extensively in distance education and recommended that both quantitative and qualitative data should be collected to insure meaningful program evaluation.

Measures of Effectiveness

The two primary measures selected to assess distance education courses and programs in special education have been learning outcomes and learner satisfaction.

Learning Outcomes

Learning outcomes typically have been assessed by means of quizzes specifically related to course content (7 studies) or by other performance assessments (6 studies). The special education research has consistently found no notable differences in learning outcomes between distance education and face-to-face instruction, whether for television delivery (23 studies), Web-based activities (8 studies), videotaped presentations (8 studies), or audio-conferencing (2 studies).

A series of reviews of the literature on distance education in general has examined outcomes of specific technologies and compared their effectiveness with face-to-face instruction, highlighting the lack of conclusive evidence supporting the superiority of any delivery system. Moore and Thompson (1997) found no differences in learning outcomes and only minimal differences in learner perceptions, with most learners appreciating the convenience of distance education but dissatisfied with the loss of personal contact. Phipps and Merisotis (1999) reached the same conclusion and argued that, despite the limitations of these studies, the repeated failure to find any differences confirmed the effectiveness of technology-mediated distance education. More recently, Shachar (2002), who conducted a meta-analysis of the effect sizes of 86 experimental and quasi-experimental studies, found that distance education students outperformed traditional students in two-thirds of these studies. To promote a better understanding of distance education, the Institute for Higher Education Policy (1999) has called for more studies addressing the outcomes of programs delivered entirely at a distance as well as for investiga-

tions into mechanisms through which the interaction between learner characteristics and technology features could impact learning outcomes.

Learner Satisfaction

Learner satisfaction usually is assessed through questionnaires, but may also be assessed in individual interviews or focus groups. The researcher in the studies reviewed here primarily employed Likert scales (30 studies) with some open-ended questions. A few studies relied on individual interviews (3 studies) or focus groups (2 studies). Overall, ratings data showed that learners expressed satisfaction with the various technologies used for distance education but frustration with technical problems and a desire for greater interactivity. Learner comments reflected the following themes: the more closely a technology resembled live instruction, the better they liked it; the more interaction they had with the instructor, the more satisfied they were across all technologies; and, learner attitudes toward technology-mediated instruction improved as their experience with instruction increased. It is important to remember that learner satisfaction, like all data based on self-report measures, must always be interpreted with caution.

The literature on learner satisfaction with distance education in general presents a similar picture, with reviewers generally concluding that findings suggest acceptance of most technologies but a clear preference for face-to-face instruction over any form of technology-mediated instruction. In their review, Moore and Thompson (1997) noted that most learners reported liking the convenience of distance delivery while still preferring the more personal contact of face-to-face instruction. Allen, Bourhis, Burrell and Mabry (2002) conducted a meta-analysis of learner satisfaction data across 25 studies that revealed slightly higher satisfaction for live instruction over all forms of distance education as well as a preference for television delivery over print or email materials. Fulford and Zhang (1993) argued that learner perception of interactivity, rather than live, face-to-face interaction, is the critical variable in satisfaction measures and that instructors can take steps to enhance those perceptions within each technology. Cobb (1997) asserted that different technologies do not produce different learning outcomes, but may differ in the amount of effort required, thereby influencing learner satisfaction. Moore and Kearsley (1996) believe that there may be an essential interactive dimension of teaching and learning (an immediacy effect) that is not well reproduced by technology-mediated instruction, particularly with some media and especially at a distance. However, Conrad (2002) feels that lower satisfaction ratings may be due to the general lack of familiarity with some technologies on the part of instructors and learners, asserting that such strong preferences may diminish over time with growing competence with new technologies.

Technology Comparisons

The literature on distance education in special education contains almost no research that attempts to assess the relative effectiveness of different technologies or to compare the costs of distance education with those of face-to-face instruction. Only a handful of studies (4 studies) compared technologies, which may be due to the fact that most programs use a single technology (which may be the only delivery system available at a given point in time). None of the studies reported any data about costs or cost comparisons between distance education and traditional education or across different technologies. This finding probably reflects the problems inherent in obtaining accurate and comparable cost data for different forms of instruction as well as the difficulties inherent in estimating the costs of technologies used at different points in time.

The general distance education literature contains numerous technology comparison studies. However, they have been criticized for conceptual errors as well as methodological flaws. Overall these studies, similar to those in special education, consistently have reported no differences between any technology and live instruction or between the different technologies, a finding that has been termed the "no significant difference phenomenon" (Russell,1999). A compilation of studies reported after the release of this book is available at two web sites: (teleeducation.nb.ca/ significantdifference) and (teleeducation.nb. ca/nosignificantdifference). Salomon (1994)

reasoned that comparison studies have found no differences primarily because they fail to adequately conceptualize the attributes of each technology that contribute to or constrain teaching and learning interactions. Smith and Dillon (1999) have since argued that such studies confound the technology with the method and that any differences may represent the instructional methods used rather than the delivery system; for example, comparing interactive video (verbal feedback) with audiotaped lectures (no feedback) may reveal differences due to the immediacy of feedback rather than media characteristics. Salomon (1997) believes that different technologies produce the same outcomes because they rely upon a traditional lecture-based model of instruction and fail to take advantage of the unique capabilities of each technology. Finally, Joy and Garcia (2001) suggested that comparison studies that consider a greater range of variables might be more likely to discover meaningful differences between the various technologies.

Reviews of the distance education literature have also noted the lack of cost comparisons that would provide a research base for estimating the cost effectiveness of various technologies prior to or after implementation of a distance education program. Until recently, educators have lacked coherent models for estimating costs and benefits in the realm of distance education, where many outcomes are difficult to measure and assign costs to. Whalen and Wright (1999) have developed a method of cost-benefit analysis of Web-based learning that calculates return on investment (ROI) after amortization of development costs. Further, Jewett (2000) has offered a computerized cost simulation model for comparing costs of distance and traditional education based on the assumption that consistent findings of no significant differences means that benefits of all technologies are the same.

Summary of Findings and Conclusions

This search of the professional literature for research-based reports of distance education applications in preservice and inservice programs that prepare special education personnel revealed that the research base is almost nonexistent. Although it is a small consolation, this state of affairs is consistent with the distance education literature in general. Unfortunately, most of the reported studies lacked rigorous controls to minimize internal and external threats to validity. Consequently, there is little reason to conclude that any differences found are reliable or that results are only attributable to technology-mediated instruction. In addition, study findings have limited generalizability due to small sample sizes, and the lack of information about participant characteristics and program components makes it difficult to determine to what other learners and contexts findings may legitimately be applied.

Nevertheless, this research does offer some insight into the outcomes and impact of technology-mediated distance education in special education, especially when interpreted in the light of similar findings in the distance education literature as a whole. Trinkle (1999) has declared that, even in the absence of carefully controlled studies, the repeated failure to find significant differences for distance education as a whole or for any particular technology does argue for accepting distance education as ("functionally equivalent") to face-to-face instruction. The same may be said for the special education literature, whose consistent findings across many programs, institutions, and learner groups, also establishes the comparability of technology-mediated and traditional instruction.

Perhaps it is not surprising that the professional literature on technology-mediated distance education in special education contains so few empirical studies. All of the reported research was conducted at major universities with research as part of their mission. Nevertheless, the amount of time and energy most faculty must spend to develop and deliver technology-based instruction and manage distance education courses and programs often leaves little time for scholarly activities. At some universities, a separate faculty may be assigned responsibility for distance education efforts using clinical rather than standard appointments that come with no expectation for scholarly productivity. In addition, institutions of higher education have traditionally downplayed and devalued studies of their own instructional practice in favor of laboratory and field-based research. Finally, faculty have not been encouraged to systematically collect data from their own innovations and share the results with others.

This lack of a research base to inform practice in distance education (in general, or specific to special education) has not slowed the rush to develop new applications and models of technology-mediated distance education. It is clear that economic (and to some extent political and social) forces rather than educational considerations are driving this rapid development. Some of these forces include pressure from consumers for more accessible preservice and inservice training, growing competition among institutions of higher education for enrollments, and shrinking budgets that increase the demand for cost control and revenue generation. These forces guarantee that programs and faculty will likely continue to make decisions about technology-mediated distance education based on clinical experience rather than empirical research for many years to come. Even so, carefully designed and well-controlled research and evaluation efforts still can and should play a role in informing future development and expansion of distance education.

Recommendations for Future Research

Deciding on the appropriate focus of research on technology-mediated distance education has generated considerable controversy over the last decade. On the one hand are those who argue against any more studies comparing different delivery systems on the grounds that the instructional strategy is the determining variable rather than the specific technology used (Clark, 1994). On the other hand are those who assert that comparison studies are needed that focus not on which technology is more effective but on the uses for which a specific technology is suited (Kozma, 1994). Finally, some believe that studies should address the intricate relationships between learner, technology, and outcomes in order to identify how to use whatever technology is selected to its best advantage (Schachter & Fagnano, 1999). Applications of distance education in special education no doubt will be informed by whatever studies are published in the literature on distance education in general; however, given the growing importance of distance education for preparing prospective and practicing personnel, special educators must also pursue their own research agenda in this area.

Here are some recommendations for research that is needed to establish a knowledge base for distance education in special education:

1. Investigations must be designed to examine the long-term outcomes and implications of distance education in comparison with traditional programs of personnel preparation in special education, asking questions such as the following: Do graduates of traditional and distance education programs achieve comparable scores on course grades, performance assessments, competency tests? Are personnel trained at a distance and/or with specific technologies as effective as traditionally trained personnel in meeting the needs of individuals with disabilities? How do employment opportunities, retention rates, and attrition patterns for these personnel compare with those from traditional programs?

2. Studies are needed that compare the effectiveness and efficiency of various technologies (television versus Web delivery, synchronous versus asynchronous formats) in accomplishing specific learning outcomes, addressing questions such as: Is live interaction superior to threaded discussions in developing skills for communication and collaboration? Are print documents, taped lectures, multimedia modules, or guided practice more efficient in developing knowledge, skills and dispositions for best practices (for example, reading instruction, behavior support, developmentally appropriate practice)?

3. Program evaluation studies should assess the results of distance education programs, such as: How do the outcomes for distance education programs compare with the outcomes for traditional preservice programs in terms of dropout rates? grade point averages? numbers certified or graduated? staff-student ratio? time to program completion? learner satisfaction? What impact does distance delivery have on addressing critical

personnel shortages in rural areas? on promoting recruitment and retention? on implementation of best practices in public schools and community agencies? and on learning outcomes for children and adults with disabilities?

4. Program evaluation studies can also provide in-depth data on program outcomes and participant perceptions about specific formats and practices used in technology-mediated distance education, posing questions such as the following: What type of threaded discussion questions elicit the most frequent and/or substantive interactions? What is the maximum number of sites or individuals that can be managed in an interactive television courses, in an online chat, in a desktop video-conference?

5. Cost-effectiveness analyses should address the extent to which each technology achieves a satisfactory balance between expenses and outcomes, such as: How do the costs for distance education programs compare with the costs of traditional programs (and with each other) in terms of costs per course? costs per student? costs per program? Can the extensive development costs for some technologies (especially Web-based instruction) be offset by the number of learners served of the duration of the program materials? Are some technologies more efficient for accomplishing specific desired outcomes?

6. Policy analysis studies are needed to determine the impact of distance education in addressing critical issues in personnel preparation in special education, including questions such as the following: What is the impact of distance education on the supply-demand imbalance in special education and disability services? Does it result in fewer unfilled positions or requests for permits or out-of-field authorizations? Does it result in lower attrition rates and better retention in positions?

Conclusion

Due to the small number of empirical investigations (and even fewer controlled studies) of technology-mediated distance education in special education, at present little can be said with confidence about its benefits, limitations, or appropriate uses. The difficulty of conducting experimental and even quasi-experimental research in this area and the limitations inherent in program evaluation efforts have produced only the weakest of databases to inform research, policy, and practice. Consequently, what little is known reflects the wisdom of practice garnered by colleagues who have experimented with distance education rather than the science of theory-grounded research accumulated from a series of well-designed studies.

The lack of research literature in general and the limitations of studies reported to date have been noted in other discussions of distance education in special education. For example, Ludlow (2001a) cited a need for more focused research to address questions related to the purpose for which each technology is used and to clarify how programs can make the best use of technology in personnel preparation. She urged researchers to move beyond simple comparisons of different technology formats into controlled investigations of technology-content-learner interactions. Kiefer-O'Donnell and Spooner (2002) likened distance education to an out-of-control locomotive as a practice being implemented without the research base that has distinguished special education as a profession over the years. They argued that the effectiveness question may never be answered until there is consensus on pedagogical principles and outcome measures for distance education. Meyen and his colleagues recently proposed a model for a programmatic research construct for electronic learning (Meyen et al., 2002). They defined a matrix of outcome variables, in situ variables, and independent variables that could be used to frame research questions for future studies of technology-mediated instruction at a distance.

These concerns are the same as those identified by reviewers of the general distance education literature. Thus, Sherry (1996) argued that existing research has been narrow in focus and has overlooked many critical variables that may impact distance delivery. As a result, he proposed that future studies focus on four key issues: learner characteristics and needs; interactions between technologies and instructional methods; access to programs; and the changing roles of teachers and learners. The Institute for Higher Education Policy Analysis (1999) criticized the existing research as "questionable" and its findings as "inconclusive." Their report identified gaps in research that need more investigation such as a conceptual framework for each technology, relevant differences in learner characteristics, and outcomes of total programs. Joy and Garcia (2000) have asserted that the no-significant-difference findings may be due to the simplistic nature of existing research. They recommended comparison studies that include more variables such as prior knowledge, learning styles, technical skills, instructional methods, instructor ability, and time on task.

In a democratic society and a capitalist economy, it may be inevitable that need and demand rather than data and evidence will drive policy and practice in distance education; perhaps the role of research is to rein in rather than drive innovation in education. In the real world of institutions of higher education and education agencies, the accumulation of program evaluation data across a wide range of contexts rather than the experimental investigation of theory-generated questions under well-controlled conditions may be a more realistic way to identify the most important outcomes of distance education. Special educators currently engaged in distance education in preservice or inservice preparation programs should be encouraged to control whatever factors can reasonably be controlled in each setting, to collect and analyze a range of quantitative and qualitative data, and to report their findings in the literature. In so doing they will not only obtain more accurate and meaningful information about the effectiveness of their own efforts at technology-mediated instruction, but they also will contribute to building a professional literature to support research-based practices in distance education in the field for years to come.

References

Allen, M., Bourhis, J. Burrell, N., & Mabry, E. (2002). Comparing student satisfaction with distance education to traditional classrooms in higher education: A meta-analysis. *The American Journal of Distance Education, 16*(2), 83-97.

Beard, L. A., & Harper, C. (2002). Student perceptions of online versus on campus instruction. *Education, 122*(4), 658-665.

Beare, P. L. (1989). The comparative effectiveness of videotape, audiotape, and telelecture in delivering continuing teacher education. *The American Journal of Distance Education, 3*(2), 57-66.

Beattie, J., Spooner, F., Jordan, L., Algozzine, B., & Spooner, M. (2002). Evaluating instruction in distance education classes. *Teacher Education and Special Education, 25*(2), 124-132.

Berge, Z. L., & Mrozowski, S. (2001). Review of research in distance education, 1990 to 1999. *The American Journal of Distance Education, 15*(3), 5-19.

Blackhurst, A. E., Hales, R. M., & Lahm, E. A. (1998). Using an education software system to deliver special education coursework via the World Wide Web. *Journal of Special Education Technology, 13*(4), 78-98.

Campbell, D. T., & Stanley, J. (1963). *Experimental and quasi-experimental designs for research.* Boston: Houghton-Mifflin.

Clarke, R. E. (1994). Media will never influence learning. *Technology Research and Development, 42*(2), 21-29.

Cobb, T. (1997). Cognitive efficiency: Toward a revised theory of media. *Educational Technology Research and Development, 45*(4), 21-35.

Collins, B. C. (1997). Training rural educators in Kentucky: A model with follow-up data. *Teacher Education and Special Education, 20*(3), 234-248.

Condon, M., Zimmerman, S., & Beane, A. (1989). Personnel preparation in special education: A synthesis of distance education and on-campus instruction. *Rural Special Education Quarterly, 9*(4), 16-19.

Conrad, D. L. (2002). Engagement, anxiety, and fear: Learners' experiences of starting an online course. *The American Journal of Distance Education, 16*(4), 205-226.

Cooke, N. L., & deBettencourt, L. (2001). Using distance education technology to train teachers: A case study. *Teacher Education and Special Education, 24*(3), 220-228.

Cooper, H. L. (2000). A study of participants in

distance education teacher programs in the field of vision impairment. (Doctoral Dissertation, Texas Women's University, 2000). *Dissertation Abstracts International, 61*, 11A.

Council for Exceptional Children. (1997a). CEC introduces electronic study group. *Teaching Exceptional Children, 29*(6), 11.

Council for Exceptional Children. (1997b). CEC's satellite broadcast – Highlights from focus on the IEP and assessment. *Teaching Exceptional Children, 30*(6), 86-87.

Cramer, M. M. (2000). Getting a "handle on distance education. In. Lemke, (Ed.)., *Capitalizing on leadership in rural special education: Making a difference for children and families. Annual National Conference Proceedings of the American Council on Rural Special Education, Alexandria, VA, March 16-18.* (ERIC Document Reproduction Services No. ED 439 886)

Day, J. N., & Sebastian, J. P. (2002). Preparing vision specialists at a distance: A qualitative study on computer-enhanced learning. *Journal of Visual Impairments and Blindness, 96*, 796-807.

DeMario, N. C., & Heinze, T. (2001). The status of distance education in personnel preparation in vision impairments. *Journal of Vision Impairments and Blindness, 95*, 525-532.

Egan, M. W., McCleary, I. D., Sebastian, J., & Lacy, H. (1989). Rural preservice teacher preparation using two-way interactive television. *Rural Special Education Quarterly, 9*(3), 27-33.

Egan, M. W., Welch, M., Page, B., & Sebastian, J. (1992). Learners' perceptions of instructional delivery systems: Conventional and television. *The American Journal of Distance Education, 6*(2), 47-55.

Falconer, K. B., & Lignugaris-Kraft, B. (2002). A qualitative analysis of the benefits and limitations of using two-way conferencing technology to supervise preservice teachers in remote locations. *Teacher Education and Special Education, 25*(4), 368-384.

Ferrell, K. A., Persichitte, K. A., Lowell, N., & Roberts, S. (2001). The evolution of a distance delivery system, that supports content, students, and pedagogy. *Journal of Vision Impairments and Blindness, 95*, 597-609.

Foegen, A., Howe, K. B., Deno, S. L., & Robinson, S. L. (1998). Enhancing the potential of distance education: A case study involving groupware. *Teacher Education and Special Education, 21*(2), 132-149.

Fulford, C., & Zhang, S. (1993). Perceptions of interaction: The critical predictor in distance education. *American Journal of Distance Education, 7*(3), 8-21.

Gallagher, P. A., & McCormick, K. (1999). Student satisfaction with two-way interactive distance leaning for delivery of early childhood special education coursework. *Journal of Special Education Technology, 14*(1), 32-47.

Gold, B. L. (1997). A formative evaluation of a distance learning program at CSUDH (California State University, Dominguez Hills, Graduate Education). (Doctoral Dissertation, Pepperdine University, 1997). *Dissertation Abstracts International, 58*, 11A.

Grisham-Brown, J., Knoll, J. A., Collins, B, C., & Baird, C. M. (1998). Multi-university collaboration via distance learning to train rural special education teachers. *Journal of Special Education Technology, 13*(4), 110-121.

Gruenhagen, K., McCracken, T., & True, J. (1999). Using distance education technologies for the supervision of student teachers in remote rural schools. *Rural Special Education Quarterly, 18*(3/4), 58-65.

Hains, A. H., Belland, J., Conceicao-Runlee, S., Santos, R. M., & Rothenberg, D. (2000). Instructional technology and personnel preparation. *Topics in Early Childhood Special Education, 20*(3), 132-144.

Hinds, J. (2002). Comparative evaluation of distance and on campus education: Is the deck stacked? In. Menlove, (Ed.)., *No Child Left Behind: The vital role of rural schools*. Annual National Conference Proceedings of the American Council on Rural Special Education, Reno, NV, March 17-19. (ERIC Document Reproduction Services No. ED 463 123)

Holmberg, B. (1990). *Foundations of distance education* (2nd ed.). New York: Routledge.

Howard, S. W., Ault, M. M., Knowlton, H. E., & Swall, R. A. (1992). Distance education: Promises and cautions for special education. *Teacher Education and Special Education, 15*(4), 275-283.

Institute for Higher Education Policy. (1999). *What's the difference? A review of contemporary research on the effectiveness of distance learning in higher education*. Washington, DC: Author.

Institute for Higher Education Policy. (2000). *Quality on the line: Benchmarks for success in Internet-based distance education*. Washington, DC: Author.

Jewett, F. I. (2000). BRIDGE: A model for comparing costs of using distance instruction and classroom instruction. *The American Journal of Distance Education, 14*(2), 37-47.

Jordan, L., Spooner, F., Calhoun, M. L., Beattie, J., Algozzine, B., & Gallaway, T. (1999). Beyond the large city: Distance education program in learning disabilities at the University of North Carolina at Charlotte. *Rural Special Education Quarterly, 18*(3/4), 44-57.

Joy, E., & Garcia, F. (2001). Measuring learning effectiveness: A new look at no-significant difference findings. *Journal of the Asynchronous Learning Network, 4*(1) [online] 15 May 2001. Available online at www.aln.org/alnweb/journal/Vol4_issue1/joygarcia.htm.

Katsiyannis, A., Zhang, D., & Conroy, M. (2003). Availability of special education teachers. *Remedial and Special Education, 24*(4), 246-254.

Kearsley, G. (2000). *Online education: Learning and teaching in cyberspace*. Belmont, CA: Wadsworth,

Keating, A. B. (1999). *The wired professor: A guide to incorporating the world wide web in college instruction*. New York: New York University Press.

Keegan, D. (1996). *Foundations of distance education* (3rd ed.). New York: Routledge.

Kiefer-O'Donnell, R., & Spooner, F. (2002). Effective pedagogy and e-learning. *Teacher Education and Special Education, 25*(2), 168-170.

Knapczyk, D. (1993). Use of distance education and audiographic technology in preparing teachers in rural communities. *Rural Special Education Quarterly, 12*(3), 23-27.

Kozma, R. B. (1994). Will media influence learning? Re-shaping the debate. *Technology Research and Development, 41*(2), 7-19.

Lock, R. H. (2001). Using Web-based information to facilitate inclusion practices in rural communities. *Rural Special Education Quarterly, 20*(4), 3-10.

Lombardi, T. P., Bauer, D., Peters, C., & O' Keefe, S. (1992). Satellite distance learning: Collaboration meets demands of special education teachers. *T. H. E. Journal, 20*(6), 59-62.

Ludlow, B. L. (1994). Using distance education to prepare early intervention personnel. *Infants and Young Children, 7*(1), 51-59.

Ludlow, B. L. (1998). Preparing special education personnel for rural schools. Journal of *Research in Rural Education, 14*(2), 57-75.

Ludlow, B. L. (2001a). Technology and teacher education in special education: Disaster or deliverance? *Teacher Education and Special Education, 24*(2), 143-163.

Ludlow, B. L. (2001b). Web-based staff development for early intervention personnel. *Infants and Young Children, 14*(2), 1-11.

Ludlow, B. L., & Brannan, S. A. (1999). Distance education programs preparing personnel for rural areas: Current practices, emerging trends, and future directions. *Rural Special Education Quarterly, 18*(3/4), 5-20.

Ludlow, B. L., & Duff, M. C. (2001). Guidelines for selecting telecommunications technologies for distance education. In B. L. Ludlow & F. Spooner (Eds.), *Distance education applications in teacher education in special education* (pp. 17-54). Arlington, VA: Teacher Education Division of the Council for Exceptional Children.

Ludlow, B. L., & Duff, M. C. (2002). Live broadcasting online: Interactive training for rural special educators. *Rural Special Education Quarterly, 21*(4), 26-30

Ludlow, B. L., Foshay, J. D., Brannan, S. A., Duff, M. C., & Dennison, K. E. (2002). Updating knowledge and skills of practitioners in rural areas: A Web-based model. *Rural Special Education Quarterly, 21*(1), 33-43.

Luetke-Stahlman, B. (1995). Deaf education in rural/remote areas: Using compressed/interactive television. *Rural Special Education Quarterly, 14*(4), 37-42.

McCleary, I. D., & Egan, M. W. (1989). Program design and evaluation: Two-way interactive television. *The American Journal of Distance Education, 3*(1), 50-60.

McLaughlin, P. J., Bender, W. N., & Wood, K. M. (1997). The Interactive Teaching Network: Distance learning applications for inservice and preservice teacher preparation

in attention deficit hyperactivity disorder. *Teacher Education and Special Education, 20*(2), 156-162.

Menlove, R., Hansford, D., & Lignugaris-Kraft, B. (2000). Creating a community of distant learners: Putting technology to work. In. Lemke, (Ed.)., *Capitalizing on leadership in rural special education: Making a difference for children and families.* Annual National Conference Proceedings of the American Council on Rural Special Education, Alexandria, VA, March 16-18. (ERIC Document Reproduction Services No. ED 439 890).

Meyen, E. L., Aust, R., Gauch, J. M., Hinton, H. S., Isaacson, R. E., Smith, S. J., & Tee, M. Y. (2002). e-Learning: A programmatic research construct for the future. *Journal of Special Education Technology, 17*(3), 37-46.

Meyen, E. L., Lian, C.H.T., & Tangen, P. (1997). Teaching on-line courses. *Focus on Autism and Other Developmental Disabilities, 12*(3), 166-174.

Moore, M. G., & Kearsley, G. (1996). *Distance education: A systems view.* Belmont, CA: Wadsworth.

Moore, M. G., & Thompson, M. M. (1997). *The effects of distance learning.* (ASCD Research Monograph No. 15). University Park: The Pennsylvania State University, American Center for the Study of Distance Education.

Paulsen, K. J., Higgins, K., Miller, S. P., Strawser, S., & Boone, R. (1998). Delivering instruction via interactive television and videotape: Student achievement and satisfaction. *Journal of Special Education Technology, 13*(4), 59-77.

Phipps, R., & Merisotis, J. (1999). *What's the difference? A review of contemporary research on the effectiveness of distance learning in higher education.* Washington, DC: The Institute for Higher Education Policy.

Rowntree, D. (1986). *The planning and management of distance education.* London: Croom Helm.

Rule, S., & Stowitschek, J. J. (1991). Use of telecommunications for inservice support of teachers of students with disabilities. *Journal of Special Education Technology, 11*(2), 57-63.

Russell, T. L. (1999). *The no significant difference phenomenon.* Raleigh: North Carolina State University, Office of Educational Telecommunications.

Ryan, S. (1999). Alaska's rural early intervention preservice training program. *Rural Special Education Quarterly, 18* (3/4), 21-29.

Salomon, G. (1994). *Interaction of media, cognition, and learning: An exploration of how symbolic forms cultivate mental skills and affect knowledge acquisition.* Hillsdale, NJ: Lawrence Erlbaum Associates.

Salomon, G. (1997). Of mind and media: How culture's symbolic forms affect learning and thinking. *Phi Delta Kappan, 78*(5), 375-380.

Savage, L. B. (1991). Satellite delivery of graduate courses for teachers of gifted students. *Rural Special Education Quarterly, 10*(4), 29-34.

Schachter, J., & Fagnano, C. (1999). Does computer technology improve student learning and achievement? How, when, and under what conditions? *Journal of Educational Computing Research, 20,* 329-343.

Sebastian, J. P., Calmes, L. J., & Mayhew, J. C. Jr. (1997). Distance learners talk back: Rural special educators evaluate their teacher preparation program. In. Montgomery, (Ed.)., *Promoting progress in times of change: Rural communities leading the way.* Annual National Conference Proceedings of the American Council on Rural Special Education, San Antonio, TX, March 26-29. (ERIC Document Reproduction Services No. ED 406107).

Shachar, M. (2002). Differences between traditional and distance learning outcomes: A meta analytic approach. (Doctoral Dissertation, Touro University International, 2002). *Dissertation Abstracts International 63,* 10A.

Shaeffer, M., & Shaeffer, B. (1993). Audio-teleconferencing: Creating a bridge between rural areas and the university in early childhood special education. *Rural Special Education Quarterly, 12*(1), 3-8.

Shea, C., & Babione, C. (2001). The Electronic Enhancement of Supervision Project (EESP). In. Mayhew, (Ed.). *Growing partnerships for rural special education.* Annual National Conference Proceedings of the American Council on Rural Special Education.San Diego, CA, March 29-31. (ERIC Document Reproduction Services No. ED 463 126)

Sherry, L. (1996). Issues in distance learning. *International Journal of Educational Telecommunications, 1*(4), 337-365.

Simonson, M., Schlosser, C., & Hanson, D. (1999). Theory and distance education: A new discussion. *The American Journal of Distance Education, 13*(1), 60-75.

Slaton, D. B., & Lacefield, W. E. (1991). Use of an interactive telecommunications network to deliver inservice education. *Rural Special Education Quarterly, 11*(2), 64-74.

Smith, P. L., & Dillon, C. L. (1999). Comparing distance learning and classroom learning: Conceptual considerations. *American Journal of Distance Education, 13*(2), 6-23.

Smith, S. J., Jordan, L., Corbett, N. L., & Dillon, A. S. (1999). Teachers learn about ADHD on the Web: An online graduate special education course. *Teaching Exceptional Children, 31*(6), 20-27.

Smith, S. B., Smith, S. J., & Boone, R. (2000). Increasing access to teacher preparation: The effectiveness of traditional instructional methods in an online learning environment. *Journal of Special Education Technology, 15*(2), 37-46.

Spooner, F. (1996). Personnel preparation: Where we have been and where we may be going in severe disabilities. *Teacher Education and Special Education, 19*(3), 213-215.

Spooner, F., Agran, M., Spooner, M., & Kiefer-O'Donnell, R. (2000). Preparing personnel with expertise in severe disabilities in the electronic age: Innovative programs and technologies. *Journal of the Association for Persons with Severe Handicaps, 25*(2), 92-103.

Spooner, F., Jordan, L., Algozzine, B., & Spooner, M. (1999). Student ratings of instruction in distance learning and on-campus classes. *Journal of Educational Research, 92*(3), 132-140.

Stenhoff, D. M., Menlove, R., Davey, B., & Melina, A. (2001). Preference of students' Responses and outcomes of distance education courses. In. Mayhew, (Ed.)., *Growing partnerships for rural special education. Annual National Conference Proceedings of the American Council on Rural Special Education, San Diego, CA, March 29-31.* (ERIC Document Reproduction Services No. ED 453 038).

Tiffin, J., & Rajasingham, L. (1995). *In search of the virtual class: Education in an information society.* New York: Routledge.

Trinkle, D. A. (1999, August 6). Distance education: A means to an end, no more, no less. *The Chronicle of Higher Education*, A 60.

Verduin, J. R., & Clark, T. A. (1991). *Distance education: The foundations of effective practice*. San Francisco: Jossey-Bass.

Welch, M., Gibb, G. S., & Egan, M. W. (1992). Empowering teachers with strategies for efficient learning and functioning through video-assisted staff development. *Rural Special Education Quarterly, 11*(3), 35-42.

Welch, M., & Sheridan, S. M. (2000). The Tele-Educational Consortium Project: Video mediated staff development for establishing educational partnerships. *Teacher Education and Special Education, 23*(3), 225-240.

Whalen, T., & Wright, D. (1999). Methodology for cost-benefit analysis of web-based tele teaching: Case study of the Bell Online Institute. *The American Journal of Distance Education, 13*(1), 24-44.

Zentall, S. S., & Javorsky, J. (1997). Attention deficit hyperactivity disorder research-to-practice through distance education. *Teacher Education and Special Education, 20*(2), 146-155.

Section 8

Trends and Issues

39

Using Learning Assessments to Design Effective Programs

Gerald Tindal and Lindy Crawford

In this chapter, we describe current applications of technology for effectively serving students with disabilities. Our focus is primarily on tools for teachers rather than stand-alone applications for students (tutorials). We frame these applications in the context of the Individuals with Disabilities Education Act and extend them to the development of universal designs. Specifically, we focus on teacher decision making for gaining access to the general education curriculum, having students participate in large-scale tests, and making accommodations decisions to provide valid inferences on outcomes. In this process, we use learning assessment systems to formatively evaluate student progress and provide different examples in both basic skills and secondary content. A technology base is emphasized for successful attainment of this process.

Using Learning Assessments to Design Effective Programs

Although the chapter is about the use of technology for serving students with disabilities, the central proposition is relatively technology free: Teachers need better data than they currently have to inform their development of instructional programs. This proposition is true both for students with and without disabilities. This need arises not just from a review of the literature or our particular bent on best practices; rather, the need is legislatively mandated. It is likely, however, that technology can serve as the primary medium to attain this outcome, primarily because of the tools currently available to teachers and researchers now and in the near future.

The purpose of this chapter is to describe the possibilities for using technology to support students with disabilities in the context of the current standards-based educational programs. First, a taxonomy is presented for organizing technological applications so that the nearly infinite varieties of educational exemplars can be considered from a functional perspective. Second, recent legislative mandates are considered, both as an impetus for many of the current directions as well as for constraints on future directions. In a relatively straightforward manner, legislation and policy are viewed as creating funding streams for both research and practice. In particular, the Individuals with Disabilities Education Act (IDEA, 1997) is considered with its emphasis on participation and accommodations where necessary. Third, principles of universal design are articulated and applied to outcomes assessment as a means to understand student needs and design instructional programs. An outcomes-based assessment program is described using goals and barriers to help distinguish between target and access skills.

In the end, the confluence of teaching and learning is described as residing in universally designed systems serving students and teachers. In this description of universal designs, we follow the lead taken by Fuchs and Fuchs (2001b) in their description of DATA whereby students are provided various accommodations while being formatively assessed to ascertain the effects of the accommodation. In this chapter, however, we provide an argument for specifically targeted instruction, not just appropriate accommodations, and for sensitive measures of progress, not just tests of performance.

Even though using computers to deliver programmed instruction has been shown to have positive effects on achievement (Fletcher-Flinn & Gravatt, 1995; Kulik & Kulik, 1991), the research addressed here is not about this application. First, software programs have a very short shelf life, given the rapid changes that occur bi-annually in both hardware and software. Second, this research generally has limited applications to students with disabilities as most of it has been conducted in general education environments. Finally, and most importantly, it is likely that more advances are to be made in technology tools for both teachers and students. This distinction is important between technology tutorials that are stand-alone and those that are tools (Lewis, 2000).

> *Tutorials direct the flow of interaction between the students and program, software tools do not. Learners who have difficulty attending to the important features in learning tasks may be unable to focus on the crucial aspects of hypermedia applications. Such students may also encounter problems in their attempts to negotiate in nonlinear instructional sequences and navigate from one part of the program to another. In addition, the mere existence of supports within software tools and hypermedia does not guarantee their usefulness.* (Lewis, 2000, p. 7)

And while tutorial programs have become less popular, the variety and importance of software tools have become more important, particularly in their use of hypermedia. Because of our emphasis on tools, and their complications of use with students, more is to be gained from teacher than student use. Therefore, the focus of this chapter is on technologies to support teachers.

Technology Applications for Teachers of Students with Disabilities

Three taxonomies are used to organize technological applications for teachers of students with disabilities. The first is a review of published literature in which the field is summarized in terms of content focus, medium, and applications. The second taxonomy is based on a recent review of Web-based applications available for both practitioners and researchers. The third organizational structure provides educators a nearly exhaustive way to deliver instructional programs with a technology backbone.

Content Focus of Published Literature

Edyburn (2000, 2001, 2002) has provided an annual review of technological applications for students with disabilities and reports on the following. In 2000, a total of 114 articles were reviewed from 26 journals (that had been published in 1999); in 2001, 197 articles were reviewed from 31 journals published the previous year (2000); in 2002, a total of 198 articles were reviewed from 31 journals published in 2001. This review process provides an excellent overview of the field, its target topics and outlet publications. Three findings are consistently reported: (a) a majority of publications appear in a relatively few journals, (b) the majority of publications address issues of practice not research, and (c) publications focus on topics which have application across disabilities not within any specific disability. Although the argument is made that the publication cycles of practice journals are more frequent than research journals, the list of journals also reflects many more practice than research journals.

Important for this review, however, is the range of topics addressed in these publications, which he addresses in both a curriculum focus and topical coverage. Clearly, primary attention is devoted to basic skills (education curriculum, functional curriculum, math, reading, and writing with all other areas represented by only one or two articles). In contrast, a total of 134 topics are addressed in these publications. While these topics are diverse, only seven have more than 10 publications represented: (a) accessibility, (b) assistive technology, (c) curriculum accommodations and modifications, (d) implementation, (e) instructional strategies, (f) technology integration, and (g) Web resources. These topics are so broad and the coverage so thin (with only about 12 articles per year) that it is unlikely any direction is systematically provided to the field. Rather, a smattering of issues appear and probably change considerably from year to year.

Medium Focus on Products and Services

Rather than focus on the published journals, Fetterman (2002) provides a description of tools currently available to practitioners and researchers alike, infusing in his presentation a series of examples from his work. While trying to be current, however, he also notes that "the irony in sharing information about current Web-based tools is that they remain current for about a nanosecond and thus the reason why discussions about technological tools or webs of meaning must be revisited" (p. 36). In his review of technologies, for example, he lists the use of Web surveys for collecting information in real time that provides virtual concurrent data reduction and analysis from anywhere by anyone, digital photography for expanding the type and variety of information documented and collected, voice recognition and transcription for transmitting information in different formats, file sharing and virtual offices for storing and accessing information, video-conferencing to ensure synchronous distance participation of individuals, chat rooms to extend participation to asynchronous participation of groups, and reporting and publishing via the Internet through journals, governmental agencies, and institutions both public and private. Given this incredible assortment of technologies and opportunities for helping educators serve students with disabilities, it is likely that most teachers have difficulty in staying knowledgeable, let alone functional in their use.

Classroom Focus on Learning

Finally, Jonassen (2000) recently published a comprehensive presentation of technological applications within the classroom and organized them into five categories of "mindtools" that he believes teachers can incorporate directly into their classroom. In his coverage, he provides broad instructional applications within which variations in software can occur:

Changes in operating systems or interfaces would not preclude their instructional use.

1. Semantic organization tools include databases and semantic networks. The emphasis is on student (and teacher) categorization of language to develop meaning.
2. Dynamic modeling tools include spreadsheets, expert systems, systems modeling, and microworlds. In this application, predictive and explanatory functions are highlighted with the use of data, both real and modeled.
3. Interpretation tools focus on either informational search procedures or visualization processes.
4. Hypermedia tools include knowledge construction in which nonlinear linkages are provided for students and teachers to navigate through content domains.
5. Conversation tools can be classified as either synchronous or asynchronous in which individuals interact in real time or delayed, respectively.

As Jonassen (2000) describes mindtools, they are "knowledge representation tools that use computer application programs...the process of using these tools as formalisms for representing the ideas being learned in personal knowledge bases represents an alternative approach to integrating computers in schools. Mindtools represent an effective and efficient way of integrating computers in schools" (p. 19). This description of technology tools is probably the richest and most practical application in the field. Nevertheless, noticeably absent in his applications is outcomes assessment of learning.

Summary of Technology Applications

Clearly, technological applications abound with no end in sight of the potential for use with teachers or students, whether or not the focus is on stand-alone programs or software tools. Furthermore, the field is likely to continue to spread in its literature base and its software applications. What is important is that teachers can place these tools in effective classroom practice.

Obviously, these applications apply to all students, though considerable concern exists over the differential application across various subgroups (those with disabilities, from economically poor backgrounds, from various ethnic groups, and with English as a second language). These groups are identified specifically for reporting outcomes in a disaggregated manner in the most recent legislation of No Child Left Behind (2001). And it is this context that looms most significantly in future applications of technology. Furthermore, as noted in this legislation, when schools are identified as needing improvement, the local educational agency must ensure the provision of technical assistance "in identifying and implementing professional development, instructional strategies and methods of instruction that are based on scientifically based research and that have proven effective in addressing the specific instructional issues that caused the school to be identified for school improvement" (Public Law 107-110, 115 STAT. 1482, Section 1116, (B), ii).

All educational programs, whether or not they are based on technological applications, must be implemented within the context of policy and legislative mandates. While four acts apply to students with disabilities (the American Disabilities Act, Section 504, Individuals with Disabilities Educational Act [IDEA, 1997], and No Child Left Behind [NCLB, 2000]), it is IDEA that has the most impact. In this next section, we present a summary of relevant research that has begun as a consequence of this special education legislation.

Research Related to Individuals with Disabilities Educational Act (1997)

Three critical requirements of this law are particularly critical in the use of technological applications for students with disabilities: (a) access to the general education curriculum, (b) participation in large scale testing, and (c) accommodations and modifications in testing programs. These three concepts are quite related: The general education curriculum becomes the driving force behind participation. However, to participate, students with disabilities may need accommodations; those accommodations should not be introduced only for testing but also be used within instructional programs to access the general education curriculum

(Ysseldyke, Thurlow, Bielinski, House, Moody, & Haigh, 2001). "Congress and the Department of Education are quite emphatic in insisting that the curriculum known as the general curriculum is the curriculum for all students. Only in cases where the IEP team can show that the general curriculum is inappropriate can the student's program veer away from the general curriculum" (Lashley, 2002, p. 12).

The key term, therefore, is *accommodations* introduced by IDEA and creating an entirely new line of research attempting to document, in both a logical and empirical manner, the differences between changes that simply explicate new conditions for understanding the same construct or result in new constructs. This term, however, links the decision to have students participate with access to the general education curriculum. And in this research, technology has become an integral facet.

Teacher Decision-Making on Participation and Accommodations

The literature on participation in large-scale testing is relatively new, with most of it presented in the form of program evaluation outcomes rather than results from carefully controlled studies. For example, the National Center on Educational Outcomes has regularly tracked the rates of participation reporting for various states and provided reports on their web site (www.nceo.edu). The research base behind teacher decision-making, nevertheless, remains quite scarce.

In a recent survey (Thompson & Thurlow, 2001), state directors of special education report that participation of students with disabilities is not only increasing but is more measurable. Nevertheless, considerable variation still exists in the percentages of participation largely as a function of different calculation formulae and because of the presence of "factors (such as high stakes for schools and lack of exposure of students with disabilities to test content) that continue to inhibit greater participation of students with disabilities in general assessment systems" (p. 7).

Crawford, Almond, Tindal, and Hollenbeck (2002) describe the results from their survey of teachers who participated in focus groups held across the state of Oregon.

In response to the purpose of statewide assessment, the vast majority of comments focused on the measurement of student achievement; other comments addressed increased accountability, higher expectation and standards for achievement, development of normative information, and finally improvement of instruction. Other issues that were raised in the focus group addressed teacher knowledge and attitudes, as well as test consequences and decision-making. "The majority of teachers expressed definite concerns about the inclusion of students with disabilities in this process" (p. 107) as well as "the use of assessment data to make high-stakes decisions, and the resulting pressure felt by teachers" (p. 109). What also was important, however, was the uniform lack of systematicity in decision-making (what, when, and how), which, though made by a team of individuals, lacked consistency and review. Although professional training was viewed as badly needed (see Tindal, 1999), it has not been forthcoming.

One of the few studies reported on training of teacher decision-making in participation is by DeStafano, Shriner, and Lloyd (2001). The central component in their model is the degree to which the general curriculum is the "determining factor in whether or not a student participated in an assessment of that curriculum" (p. 9). Their training program focused on aligning the Individualized Educational Program (IEP) with state standards and making accommodations decisions, with practice provided in decision-making. Using both an individual student survey and analysis of the IEP, they found that "After training, changes were seen in both participation and accommodation on the math and language arts assessment" (p. 17) and the relationship between instructional and testing accommodations was closer. The net effect was that decision-making was more differentiated with varying degrees of participation following training (partial participation, use of accommodations, and participation in the alternate assessment) rather than an "all-or-none" phenomenon.

As can be seen by this research "any consideration on participation necessarily bleeds into discussions about accommodations, alternate assessments, and the IEP decision-making process" (Thompson & Thurlow, 2001). And while this type of research is important, the findings beg the question about effects. To what degree do accommodations work, whether or not they are aligned with instruction?

Accommodations Research

The research on accommodations has focused primarily on non-technological applications but increasingly is beginning to include technology-based changes in testing (see the Tindal and Fuchs [1999] compilation of an extensive body of research that includes 106 studies conducted over two decades). Until that review, most of the research was conducted with little emphasis on decision-making in a standards-based educational environment or from any particular theoretical perspective. In an update on accommodations, Tindal, Helwig, and Hollenbeck (1999) further reported on an emerging body of research using Messick's (1989) different facets of validity: "The mark of distinction [for an accommodation] is the emphasis on construct validity. Improving performance is not the sole criterion for justifying an accommodation. Rather, the very construct of what is being measures is under scrutiny: (a) the task demands, (b) the scaling of behavior, and (c) the student being tested" (p. 13). Using the framework from Ysseldyke, Thurlow, McGrew, and Shriner (1994) (see Table 1), most of this research has begun to develop in a more articulate manner, focusing on the construct validity of the testing programs. Technology tools are becoming critical in this process.

Movement of Accommodations Research to Technology-Based Delivery

For example, in the area of mathematics testing, a number of studies have focused on the degree to which performance is influenced by access skills (like reading a multiple choice test) rather than the target skills. As these studies have unfolded, it is clear that (a) accommodations are typically bundled (more than one change is instituted) and (b) technology is becoming increasingly important in their delivery, even those not directly relying on it.

In a line of studies that began with a "read aloud" of math tests by the teacher compared to students silently reading the math test

Table 1. List of Test Changes

Timing/Scheduling	Setting
• Use flexible schedule • Allow frequent breaks during testing • Extend the time allotted to complete the test • Administer the test in several sessions, specify duration • Provide special lighting • Time of day • Administer test over several days, specify duration • Provide special acoustics	• Administer the test individually in a separate location • Administer the test to a small group in separate location • In a small group, study carrel • Provide adaptive or special furniture • Administer test in locations with minimal distractions

Presentation	Response
• Braille edition or large-type edition • Prompts available on tape • Increase spacing between items or reduce items/page-line margins • Increase size of answer bubbles • Reading passages with one complete sentence/line • Multi-choice, answers follow questions down bubbles to right • Omit questions which cannot be revised, prorate credit • Teacher helps student understand prompt • Computer reads paper to student • Word processor • Highlight key words/phrases in directions	• Increase spacing • Wider lines and/or wider margins • Graph paper • Paper in alternative format (word processed, Braille, etc.) • Allow student to mark responses in booklet instead of answer sheet

Test Directions	Assistive Devices/Supports
• Typewriter • Dictation to a proctor/scribe • Communication device • Signing directions to students • Read directions to student • Reread directions for each page of questions • Simplify language in directions or problems • Highlight verbs in instructions by underlining • Clarify directions • Provide cues on answer form	• Word processor • Student tapes response for later verbatim transcription • Calculator, arithmetic tables • Spelling dictionary or spell check • Alternative response such as oral, sign, typed, pointing • Brailler • Large diameter, special grip pencil • Copy assistance between drafts • Slantboard or wedge • Tape recorder • Abacus • Provide additional examples

Assistive Devices/Supports	
• Visual magnification devices • Templates to reduce visible print • Auditory amplification device, hearing aid or noise buffers • Audio taped administration of sections • Secure papers to work area with tape/magnets • Questions read aloud to student • Masks or markers to maintain place • Questions signed to pupil • Dark heavy or *raised* lines or pencil grips • Assistive devices speech synthesis • Amanuensis (scribe)	

themselves, Tindal, Heath, Hollenbeck, Almond, and Harniss (1998) reported significant effects in favor of the teacher read aloud; when the test was read to them, students with disabilities and an IEP in reading performed as well as students ranked low in reading proficiency by their teachers. In the self-reading condition, these groups were significantly different (in favor of low ranked nondisabled readers). This same finding was replicated in two other studies reported by Weston (1999) and Fuchs, Fuchs, Eaton, Hamlett, and Karns (2000).

This line of research quickly moved to a technology-based delivery, however, when logistics and standardization are considered as part of a realistic large-scale assessment program. For example, Tindal (2002) conducted nearly the same study using a video taped read aloud. This study was completed in 10 different states and therefore required greater attention to standardization of the treatment. Furthermore, assuming students with IEPs in reading need to have a math test read to them, it would be nearly impossible for a special education teacher with a case of 15-25 students to provide this accommodation for everyone who needed it. In this study, the interaction of the treatment (read aloud versus student read) and student classification (disabled with an IEP in reading versus low reading proficiency) was significant at the .07 level. Finally, in extending the technology applications to computers, Hollenback, Rozek-Tedesco, Tindal, and Glasgow (2000) studied the effects of a read aloud when it was delivered using a video tape (in a group administration) versus when it was delivered on a computer (in an individual administration). This study was framed in terms of pacing, as either the teacher or the student. The findings reflected superior performance when students with disabilities could control the delivery of problems, with an effect size of .34; this effect was greater for more skilled students (at or above the 50th percentile of their group).

Use of Technology to Better Understand Constructs

The research on accommodations has not only moved directly to a technology-based delivery

system but also has required more technology infrastructure in the development of treatments and analysis of populations. Currently, the studies to continue this work require extensive technology infrastructures to conduct the research. In next generation applications, however, these process tools are likely to be incorporated into classroom practice.

For example, in a study with 6th Grade students, Helwig, Rozek-Tedesco, Tindal, Heath, and Almond (1999) focused the analysis on subgroups of problems and students. They reported that the treatment of a read aloud was effective only for certain math problems (those with many words, multiple verbs, and unfamiliar words) and students who had otherwise intact math proficiency. Clearly, their analysis requires relatively sophisticated analysis of the treatment and its effects.

In another example where technology was instrumental in understanding the construct, Helwig, Rozek-Tedesco, and Tindal (2002) described a follow-up study in which a specific population of students was tested with specifically analyzed problem types in both a videotaped read aloud and a standard self-read administration. For elementary students with learning disabilities, performance was higher on difficult reading items when they were presented a videotaped read aloud than when students were required to read them; this finding did not hold for students in general education. In contrast, no such differences in performance were found for middle school age students with and without learning disabilities.

Summary of Research on Accommodation and Teacher Decision-Making

Research on accommodations has systematically moved toward an emphasis on construct validity in great part because of the technological advances incorporated into the research design and execution. This program of research has moved both directly in the use of technology to deliver accommodations as well as indirectly in the analysis of test items and populations with whom accommodations are applied. In the near future, these technology infrastructures are likely to be automated and systematized for teacher use in the classroom (see a description of the accommodation station later in this chapter).

While the field of research has moved steadily toward technology-supported infrastructures, the field of practice has remained relatively fixed in its emphasis on traditional decision-making with little analytic support through the use of technology. Teachers continue to collect classroom information in a relatively unstructured way and rarely render the information to provide useful rules for decision-making. While checklists have begun to appear, helping teachers codify their perceptions on a range of issues (see Schulte, Elliott, & Kratochwill, 2000, for a checklist to help teachers make accommodations decisions), it is unlikely that decision-making can be deemed effective. At best, teacher decision-making can only be compared to approved accommodations (see Hollenbeck, Tindal, & Almond, 1998; Thurlow & Weiner, 2001) which nevertheless lacks a standard of accuracy and begs the question of eventual effectiveness.

In the end, teacher decision-making on participation and accommodations often is inaccurate. For example, Fuchs and Fuchs (2001b) reported that teachers typically make more false positives in recommending accommodations for students who do not need (or benefit from) them. "Teachers awarded accommodations to a large percentage of students: 73% of students in reading, 65% in math computations, 93% in math applications, and 93% in math problem-solving. These figures contrast sharply with the percentages of students who, according to our data based rules, actually profited substantially (and differentially) from the accommodations: 41% in reading, 20% in math computations, 32% in math applications, and 42% in math problem solving" (p. 178). It therefore appears that the outcome on large-scale tests for students with disabilities may not be accurately reflected in the reports to the public. This outcome, however, has never been reported separately until very recently, and only with NCLB (2000) are these outcomes to be tracked over time.

Principles of Universal Design to Develop Technology-Based Solutions

Given the focus on legislative mandates and a scientifically based evidence within the context of standards-based assessments, the remainder of the chapter focuses on the opportunity for technology-based assessment applications to improve the access and inclusion of students with disabilities. An important component of these examples, however, is the need for principles of universal design. In the remainder of this chapter, a system is articulated for better understanding what students need. This system is outcomes based (see Reschley, Kicklighter, & McKee, 1988a, 1988b), in that student performance and progress is used to make decisions. Then, this information is used to articulate instructional programs, which may or may not be technology oriented. The outcomes-based data collection system itself, however, is inherently technology-based.

Universal Design

As the definitions of accommodations have become more articulated, the newest term to enter the field is *universal design for learning (UDL)*, which takes the argument of accommodations one step further. According to Rose (2000a), UDL changes the assumptions about teaching and learning: (a) children with disabilities are not qualitatively distinct but fall on a continuum with others; (b) all children require changes, not just those with disabilities; (c) the curriculum is varied and diverse, expanded beyond a textbook to include digital materials; and (d) focuses on "fixing" curricula rather than students. He believes it is important to be clear about the goals before changing materials, in which specific standards are reconsidered from a broader perspective than specific behavioral descriptions. In an example of UDL using the Center for Applied Special Technology (CAST) Web site, Rose (2000b) further articulates the importance of goals and describes essential barriers of information representation within the use of images, text, language, sound, moving video, and background knowledge; navigation barriers also are articulated with reference to physical and cognitive abilities; and finally, engagement barriers are considered with reference to blueprints for interaction.

While these descriptions serve well to justify the course of universal design, they fail to adequately define it. If we treat universal design as a concept, both attributes and examples and non-examples need to be explicated (Tindal, Nolet, & Blake, 1994). In this chapter, UDL is considered with three critical attributes.

1. Access skills are scaffolded, again as implied by Rose in "d" above (2000). A range of skill levels is assumed for students to understand any specific content.
2. Standard features that are designed before use and minimize post hoc changes are needed concurrent with use; post-hoc changes would represent accommodations and potentially modifications.
3. Multi-media are assumed, as implied by Rose in (2000). The medium perforce needs to provide multiple access venues for interaction.

While the field of architecture tends to be heavily referenced, more and better examples need to be articulated within education for the concept to take root. With these three attributes present, the following range of examples are likely to fit the definitions presented by Rose (2000a) and in this chapter. And in these examples, technological applications are likely to be the key in both their operationalization as well as efficient implementation.

Typical test administration relies on standardized procedures (Thissen & Wainer, 2001) to ensure comparability. For example, in most large-scale assessment programs, a paper-pencil test is administered with standard directions and minimum support given to students. In this way, all students have the same advantage for answering any item correctly. In contrast, a universally designed test would have an embedded filter to ascertain the unique needs of most students (to scaffold access skills). For example, based on surveys of preference and skill, students would be given only those items that fit within the skill ranges they possess (much like a computerized adaptive test but also including format of administration in addition to content). Furthermore, based on this scaffold, students would be allowed to select items that are embedded with standard features. Students could choose to have items presented in a variety of formats of structure (from standard to simplified in the use of language, with various tools available) requiring either selection or production responses. Finally, printed text as well as audio and video presentations would be possible for students.

To accomplish universally designed assessments, the first step is to decide on the goals of the assessment: What decisions need to be made? (see the Standards for Educational and Psychological Tests published by the American Educational Research Association, American Psychological Association, and National Council on Measurement in Education, 1999). This step is very similar to what Rose has delineated (2000a) and delimits the need for endless variation of format but focuses on only those relevant features, including the population for whom the tests and measures are to be used. The second step is to ascertain important background information (perspectives and skills) from all stakeholders, students, parents, and teachers to help develop a navigation system that is both physical (sensory) and cognitive. Finally, in the third step, measurement systems are developed that provide the most universal outcomes for learning and can be used to empirically base further individual adaptations: When learning fails to occur, two possibilities can be considered: (a) the measures are not sensitive and need to be tailored and/or (b) instruction is not effective. At no time in this process is the claim made that the student is not capable of learning at least something; the goal is to measure it appropriately, which may mean that adjustments are made in the type of measures employed or the formats and sampling plans used to create the measures. With this perspective, then teachers can proceed to measure learning and evaluate the effects of instruction.

Outcomes Assessment to Develop Universal Designs

For students with disabilities, participation in large-scale assessments has provided both an opportunity and a challenge. Generally, these tests are not flexibly formatted and as noted in the literature reviewed in the area of accommodations, considerable changes often need to be made so they can participate. And while technology continues to serve as a key element in operationalizing these changes, a more fundamental application of technology is likely to arise in the use of classroom assessments that are technology-based. Currently, four applications are available, allowing teachers to assess students formatively on their learning of basic skills or content knowledge and make predictions of eventual performance on large-scale tests.

Curriculum-Based Measurement (CBM) of Basic Skills

Presently, two applications can be used with minimum training and cost. The first application reported by Fuchs and Fuchs (2001a) is a system they developed over the past decade in reading and mathematics (see Fuchs, Hamlett, & Fuchs, 1998). They use core principles of CBM (alternate forms using brief tasks to formatively evaluate student progress and evaluate the effects of instruction) to ascertain students' improvement as follows.

1. In reading, a maze task (delivered on a personal computer) is used in which students select a word (from 4 options) to fill in a blank in a sentence, with approximately one word missing for every seven words presented. This measurement system has been validated as a technically adequate measure of comprehension (see Parker, Hasbrouck, & Tindal, 1992, for a review of the research supporting this measurement). Outcomes are analyzed according to the percentage correct and also for semantics and syntax; a progress graph also is available for individual and groups of students.
2. In mathematics, students are presented both computation and concept applications using paper and pencil and directed to solve the problem. After the test is done, either the teacher or the student enters the answers on a personal computer with each answer located to the specific problem. Outcomes are analyzed according to total percentage correct and specific algorithms. Again, both individual and group progress graphs are available.

Dynamic Indicators of Basic Essential Literacy Basic Skills (DIBELS)

Developed by Good and Kaminski (2002), this measurement system focuses on early reading skills (letter naming and sounding, phonemic awareness, onset, phonemic segmentation, and nonsense word blending). While the measurement system is administered in a relatively traditional manner (individually with scripted directions and student materials), the manner in which results are reported provides an interesting example of more futuristic technology applications. When the teacher has administered the test, the subscores are entered onto a database and integrated with a large sample of students from across the country. Individual graphs are immediately available, providing teachers with both criterion-referenced information about student mastery of specific skills as well as norm-referenced evaluations relative to the sampled database.

Easy Curriculum-Based Measures (EZCBM)

While the above software provides teachers a means for interpreting student performance in the basic skills, the tests are fixed by the stimulus materials presented in the test packet. In contrast, EZCBM is Internet based (see www.edprogress.com). Teachers can access a Web site to have alternate forms available randomly sampled from a larger universe of items. For example, if a teacher is interested in monitoring a student's learning of letter names, a random sample of upper-and lower-case letter names can be generated (depending upon the parameters specified ahead of time by the teacher: total number of letters to be sampled, sampling letters with and without replacement, ratio of upper to lower-case letters, etc.). Otherwise, in every other respect, the measurement system remains the same, including the potential for immediate analysis and graphic display of outcomes. This measurement system forms the basis for the alternate assessment program in Oregon with practice materials provided annually after the secure version of the test is made public (see brt.uoregon.edu).

Summary of Basic Skills Assessments

All three systems focus on alternate measurement forms, only the last of which is generated with a technology database using a specified sampling technique. All three however, provide teachers with graphic displays of both performance and progress on measures that have been linked to performance on large-scale tests (see Crawford, Tindal, & Stieber, 2001). The three measurement systems provide teachers specific information on skills that are foundational for learning to read, write, and compute and provide a means for teachers to evaluate the effects of instruction. Finally, all of them are based on measures that are sensitive to change over time.

Discourse for Problem-Solving

In this system, all students within the classroom are provided with a computer terminal that is linked to the teacher's main computer. Using Discourse GroupWare Classroom, teachers can either pre-program content or spontaneously deliver it. In either case, the software allows them to continuously monitor student performance. They also can provide feedback regarding response accuracy through light and sound delivered to the student's terminal. Students are provided questions and respond, "typing a response of varying length into that frame of the terminal. Then, the student can advance to the next frame or wait for another response demand from the teacher" (Shin, Deno, Robinson, & Marston, 2000, p. 56). Instruction can be delivered with students responding in either self-paced or teacher-led modes. In a recent study on the effects of this system with second-grade students, these authors report that the groupware helped students maintain more active responding which was highly related to achievement (even when differences in initial performance levels were removed). In their terms, universal responding was an important component of universal design.

Maze Curriculum-based Measurement of Content

In middle and high school, content becomes very important and subject-specific. Teachers now have content expertise and any supportive program for students with disabilities must be bridged within a larger context of collaboration or tutorial support. In taking the logic of the maze (sentences with missing words to be filled in from four options) and extending it into the content areas, McCoy, Ketterlin-Geller, Twyman, and Tindal (2003) have developed a concept maze that is internet-delivered. The following steps are used in developing this type of concept maze.

1. A curriculum is analyzed for knowledge forms (facts, concepts, and principles) as described by Tindal and Marston (1990).
2. With specific concepts and attributes identified within passages, examples are selected from the text and removed; four options (example words) are presented, one of which correctly completes the sentence.
3. The maze file is completed and the web site referenced. When this measure is given to the student, the web site is accessed and the student takes the test by selecting a word from a pop-up menu. When the student has completed all words in the passage, they submit their work. All items are directly transferred to a database, scored, and analyzed with the results sent to the teacher via an e-mail.
4. Teachers have the option of reviewing the results by student (percent correct and ranked from low to high) or concept (percentage of examples correctly associated with various attributes within concepts).

In the study by McCoy et al. (2003), students who completed the maze as one assignment in a unit on civilization provided better solutions to a problem solving prompt than did students who completed a traditional maze (brief description). The problem-solving prompt required students to create (a) a map used to locate a civilization on a remote island and (b) an essay explaining the various landmarks that they had established including why these landmarks were present and the function that they served in establishing a civilization. While students in the control condition (who completed traditional mazes) and students in the experimental condition both completed a fact test at equal levels of performance, the explanation essay was rated significantly better in terms of examples reflecting key attributes of civilizations.

Technology Applications for Students with Disabilities

In this chapter, we presented the argument that technology support for students with disabilities is likely to be through the use of teaching tools rather than through use of stand-alone student tutorials that students receive. Because the field of technology is so multifarious, however, any attempt to review its applications needs to be organized into some kind of structure or function. From three different analyses, we believe the published literature in journals is unlikely to affect any systemic incorporation in the classroom, primarily because of the "literature scatter" noted by Edyburn (2001): Too diverse and widespread to affect changes of note. However, as noted by Fetterman (2001), the tools available for teachers and researchers is nearly boundless and changing all the time. Therefore, using the taxonomy by Jonassen (2001) may be prudent. Even this taxonomy, however, lacks an empirical basis and individualized references, as required by the IEP.

Therefore, using the latest mandates of IDEA to help structure the needs for students with disabilities in the current context of standards-based assessments, the latest research findings were addressed in relation to access to the general curriculum, participation in large-scale tests, and accommodations to ensure valid decisions. We argued that teacher decision-making often is neither valid nor effective, though a technology infrastructure could well alleviate this problem for access as well as accommodations. This technology infrastructure would continue to stimulate the development of universal designs for learning. We finished the chapter with examples of how teachers could use technology built on universal design for learning in any of three basic skills assessment systems, a problem-solving system, or a content maze, to develop both performance and progress information on students. It is this combination of technology with teacher decision-making that can improve educational outcomes for all students.

References

American Educational Research Association, American Psychological Association, and National Council of Measurement in Education, (1999). *Standards for Educational and Psychological Testing*. Washington, D.C.: Author.

Crawford, L., Almond, P., Tindal, G., & Hollenbeck, K. (2002). Teacher perceptions on inclusion of students with disabilities in high-stakes assessments. *Special Services in the Schools, 18*(1/2), 95-118.

Crawford, L., Tindal, G., & Stieber, S. (2001). Using oral reading rate to predict student performance on statewide achievement tests. *Educational Assessment, 7*(4), 303-323.

Destefano, L., Shriner, J., & Lloyd, C. A. (2001). Teacher decision making in participation of students with disabilities in large-scale assessment. *Exceptional Children, 68*(1), 7-22.

Education Week: (2001). The digital divide.

Edyburn, D. L. (2000). 1999 in review: A synthesis of the special education technology literature. *Journal of Special Education Technology, 15*(1), 7-18.

Edyburn, D. L. (2001). 2000 in review: A synthesis of the special education technology literature. *Journal of Special Education Technology, 16*(2), 5-26.

Edyburn, D. L. (2002). 2001 in review: A synthesis of the special education technology literature. *Journal of Special Education Technology, 17*(2), 5-24.

Fetterman, D. (2002). Web surveys to digital movies: Technological tools of the trade. *Educational Researcher, 31*(6), 29-37.

Fletcher-Flinn, C. M., & Gravatt, B. (1995). The efficacy of computer-assisted instruction: A meta-analysis. *Journal of Educational Computing Research, 12*, 219-232.

Fuchs, L. S., & Fuchs, D. (2001a). Computer applications to curriculum-based measurement. *Special Services in the Schools, 17*(1/2), 1-14.

Fuchs, L. S., & Fuchs, D. (2001b). Helping teachers formulate sound test accommodation decisions for students with learning disabilities. *Learning Disabilities Research and Practice, 16*(3), 174-181.

Fuchs, L. S., Fuchs, D., Eaton, S. B., Hamlett, C., & Karns, K. (2000). Supplementing teacher judgments of mathematics test accommodations with objective data sources. *School Psychology Review, 29*, 65-85.

Fuchs, L.S., Hamlett, C., & Fuchs, D. (1998). *Monitoring Basic Skills Progress*. Austin, TX.

Good, R. H., & Kaminski, R. A. (2002). *Dynamic Indicators of Basic Early Literacy Skills*

(6th ed.) Eugene, OR: Institute for the Development of Educational Achievement.

Helwig, R., Rozek-Tedesco, M., Heath, B., Tindal, G., & Almond, P. (1999). Reading as an access to mathematics problem solving on multiple-choice tests for sixth grade students. *The Journal of Educational Research*, 93(2), 113-125.

Helwig, R., Rozek-Tedesco, M., & Tindal, G. (2002). An oral versus a standard administration of a large-scale mathematics test. *The Journal of Special Education*, 36(1), 39-47.

Hollenbeck, K., Tindal, G., & Almond, P. (1998). Teachers' knowledge of accommodations as a validity issue in high-stakes testing. *The Journal of Special Education*, 32(3),175-183.

Hollenbeck, K., Rozek-Tedesco, M.A., Tindal, G., & Glasgow, A. (2000). An exploratory study of student-paced versus teacher-paced accommodations for large-scale math tests. *Journal of Special Education Technology*, 15(2), 29-38.

Individuals with Disabilities Education Act Amendments of 1997, 20 U.S.C. ◊ 1400 et seq.

Jonassen, D. H. (2000). *Computers as mindtools for schools: Engaging critical thinking* (2nd ed.) Upper Saddle River, NJ: Merrill.

Kulik, C.C., & Kulik, J. A. (1991). Effectiveness of computer-based instruction: An updated analysis. *Computers in Human Behavior*, 7, 75-94.

Lashley, C. (2002). Participation of students with disabilities in statewide assessments and the general education curriculum: Implications for administrative practice. *Journal of Special Education Leadership*, 15(1), 10-16.

Lewis, R. B. (2000). Musings on technology and learning disabilities on the occasion of the new millennium. *Journal of Special Education Quarterly*, 15(2), 5-12.

McCoy, J., Ketterlin-Geller, L., Twyman, T., & Tindal, G. (2003). *Concept maze for developing critical thinking skills in students with disabilities*. Eugene, OR: Behavioral Research and Teaching Technical Report.

Messick, S. (1989). Validity. In R. L. Linn (Ed.), *Educational measurement* (pp. 13-103). New York: Macmillan Publishing.

Parker, R., Hasbrouck, J., & Tindal, G. (1992). The Maze as a classroom-based reading measure: Construction methods, reliability, and validity. *The Journal of Special Education*, 26(2), 195-218.

Public Law 107-100. (2001). No Child Left Behind Act of 2001.

Reschley, D. J., Kicklighter, R., & McKee, P. (1988a). Recent placement litigation, Part I, Regular education grouping: Comparison of Marshall (1984, 1985) and Hobson (1967, 1969). *School Psychology Review*, 17(1), 9-21.

Reschley, D. J., Kicklighter, R., & McKee, P. (1988b). Recent placement litigation, Part III, Analysis of differences in Larry P., Marshall, and S-1 and implications for future practices. *School Psychology Review*, 17(1), 39-50.

Rose, D. (2000a). Universal design for learning. *Journal of Special Education Technology*, 15(2), 56-60.

Rose, D. (2000b). Walking the walk: Universal design on the web. *Journal of Special Education Technology*, 15(3), 45-49.

Schulte, A.A.G., Elliott, S. N., & Kratochwill, T. R. (2000). Educators' perceptions and documentation of testing accommodations for students with disabilities. *Special Services in the Schools*, 16(1/2), 35-56.

Shin, J., Deno, S. L., Robinson, S. L., & Marston, D. (2000). Predicting classroom achievement from active responding on a computer-based groupware system. *Remedial and Special Education*, 21(1), 53-60.

Thissen, D., & Wainer, H. (2001). *Test scoring*. Mawah, NJ: Lawrence Erlbaum.

Thompson, S. J., & Thurlow, M. L. (2001). Participation of students with disabilities in state assessment systems. *Special Services in the Schools*, 26(2), 5-8.

Thurlow, M. L., & Weiner, D. J. (2001). Consideration in the use of nonapproved accommodations. *Special Services in the Schools*, 26(2), 29-37.

Tindal, G. (1999). [Oregon Education Association survey of membership.] Unpublished raw data.

Tindal, G. & Fuchs, L. (1999). *A summary of research on test changes: An empirical basis for defining accommodations*. Lexington, KY: Mid-South Regional Resource Center.

Tindal, G. (2002). *Accommodating mathematics testing using a videotaped read aloud administration*. Washington, D.C.: Council of Chief State School Officers.

Tindal, G., Heath, B., Hollenbeck, K., Almond, P., & Harniss, M. (1998). Accommodating students with disabilities on large-scale tests: An empirical study of student response and test administration demands. *Exceptional Children, 64*(4), 439-450.

Tindal, G., Helwig, R., & Hollenbeck, K. (1999). An update on test accommodations: Perspectives from practice to policy. *Journal of Special Education Leadership, 12*(2), 11-20.

Tindal, G., & Marston, D. (1990). *Classroom-based assessment: Evaluating instructional outcomes.* Columbus, OH: Charles Merrill.

Tindal, G., Nolet, V., & Blake, G. (1994). *Teaching and learning in content areas.* [Training Module 3]. Eugene: University of Oregon Research, Consultation, and Teaching Program.

Weston, T. (1999). *Investigating the validity of the accommodations of oral presentation in testing (learning disabilities, fourth grade)* (Doctoral dissertation, University of Colorado at Boulder, 1999). *Dissertation Abstracts International, 60,* 1083A.

Ysseldyke, J., Thurlow, M., Bielinski, J., House, A., Moody, M., & Haigh, J. (2001). The relationship between instructional and assessment accommodations in an inclusive state accountability system. *Special Services in the Schools, 34*(3), 212-220.

Ysseldyke, J.E., Thurlow, M.L., McGrew, K.S., & Shriner, J.G. (1994). *Recommendations for making decisions about participation of students with disabilities in statewide assessment programs* (Synthesis Report 15). Minneapolis: University of Minnesota National Center on Educational Outcomes.

40

Data-Mining Strategies for Researching the Effectiveness of Assistive and Instructional Technologies

John Castellani and Brian Castellani

Local education agencies are interpreting recent legislation (No Child Left Behind Act, 2002) and governmental requirements for student testing and data reporting as the impetus for re-thinking how data are used to enhance teaching and learning. Elementary and Secondary Education Act (ESEA) requirements that "leave no child behind" are encouraging the use of a yearly statewide achievement tests to measure student progress and hold schools accountable for adequate yearly progress (AYP) of all children (NCLB, 2002). While the federal government has set the current bar for accountability, according to an April 2003 Doyle Report, the methods schools are using to "account" are widely disputed.

In this era of educational reform, many educators are getting used to terms like evidenced-based instruction and data-driven decision making. However, this recent requirement, while urging the field of education to develop interventions that promote student progress, does little to foster communication about teaching and learning among educators and stakeholders. As a result, many opponents feel that the use of single tests does not appropriately measure AYP for many students (Postelwaite, 2003). With added changes in technology support from the federal government, national technology societies have encouraged connecting educational technology with rigorous assessment (Dickard, 2001). Educators invested in this match between student achievement and technology need to consider assessment models that can respond to the nuances of daily interactions between teacher, student, technology, and the broader educational system (Tsantis & Castellani, 2001).

While the field is just beginning to apply processes to respond to federal testing challenges, a small but growing group of educators are using data discovery methods for daily decision making about student achievement (Schoolnet, 2003). The efforts are intended to transform how data on technology and student achievement are collected, analyzed, and used for decision making. Rather than single-point-in-time test scores, responsive and real-time, data-driven processes are more useful accountability tools for making decisions about the influences of technology on student performance and function. Qualitative research models on the use of data discovery techniques for modeling complex quantitative data are beginning to emerge (Castellani & Castellani, 2003; Castellani, Castellani, & Spray, 2003) as well as the influence of data mining processes on special education data systems (Tsantis & Castellani, 2001; Carran, Tsantis, Castellani, & Baglin, 2002). Applying analytic strategies to these emerging electronic data systems has the potential to transform our ability to provide anticipatory guidance and predictive modeling to enhance teaching and learning.

Given the promise of using data mining for educational decision making, this chapter will examine how special education professionals can use data mining techniques to collect and analyze data for the purposes of predicting and reporting student achievement using assistive technology (AT). Specifically, this chapter will: (a) review current issues in special education, including the use of assistive technology to access the general education curriculum; (b) provide a framework for data collection and decision making; and (c) examine how data mining systems can be constructed based on methods for applying data discovery techniques.

Current Issues in Special Education

The requirement that children and youth with disabilities to participate in the general education curriculum is impacting the way administrators allocate resources. Finding and using technology resources to support children and youth with disabilities in classrooms is challenging. Further, when resources are available, it is sometimes difficult to decide where they need to be placed and ultimately assess how those technologies impact student performance. The amount of data available to make decisions is growing, however, the data are infrequently used in a consistent and systemic manner.

Data-driven decision-making remains one of the more challenging roles of every special education professional. This is partly due to the amount of data typically gathered over time to make instructional programming decisions for students. Data are typically available through traditional sources like attendance records, standard grading, and statewide testing, through students' IEP, as well as school and teacher demographics. As soon as children and youth begin receiving services, for some students, data will be available from birth through adulthood. However, communication of these data across early childhood and school and adult services is often non existent.

Initiatives such as the Schools Interoperability Network (IMS Global Learning Corporation, Inc., 2003) are making efforts to use and connect all available data on students for informed decision-making. This type of data connection and communication for the purposes of informed decision-making is a growing trend in education. These intercon-

nected data systems include historical data from birth through adulthood on all aspects of educational programming, from transportation to student achievement. The primary purpose of using interconnected data systems for students with disabilities is to match services to achievement. Specifically, aggregated data is used to (a) allocate resources and special education services at the state and district level; (b) ensure that students who are at risk do not "fall through the cracks;" (c) inform curriculum development and implementation in appropriate special and general education settings; d) inform parents, caregivers, and other stakeholders; and (e) to meet state and federal reporting requirements.

IEP requirements for considering assistive, instructional, and/or accessible technologies, promote the use of available data for making decisions about accommodations and adaptations for individual students or groups. As these students become integrated into general education classroom, systemic data becomes increasingly important. This is mainly due to the complex processes in assistive technology evaluation that are required for teachers to thoughtfully consider low and/or high tech strategies, which are requirements for student functioning.

While general education administrators and teachers work with IEP teams to develop individualized student programming, the decision-making process usually does not include real-time data based on student and teacher interactions in the classroom with the technology. More important, data on group or whole-school performance related to specific assistive or instructional technologies are often not available. Rather, decisions about students are made primarily on singular individual testing results, for example, speech/language, psychological/behavioral, and/or IQ scores, and do not consider the wider data available on students working actively with curriculum content and technology.

Given these issues, a general framework for data-driven decision-making is needed to improve not only the analysis of data, but also its organization and usefulness for guided and predictive decision making. The next section provides this framework.

Framework for Decision making

In *Data Analysis for Continuous Schoolwide Improvement*, Bernhardt (2003) lists seven questions to help focus the early stages of data-driven decision-making:

- What is the purpose of using data in the school or district?

- What do you expect students to know and be able to do by the time they leave school?

- What do you expect students to know and be able to do by the end of each year?

- How well will students be able to do what they want to do with the knowledge and skills they acquire by the time they leave school?

- Do you know why you are getting the results you get?

- What would your school and educational processes look like if your school were achieving its purpose, goals and expectations for student learning?

- How do you want to use the data you will gather?

In this perspective, data are seen as the vehicle to understanding larger systems issues, such as the influence of the whole-school environment on individual student achievement. Understanding these issues is critical for applying discovery techniques to available data. Knowing the overall context in which decisions are made directly influences the larger

picture of education. For example, if discovery methods are applied to only one component of a system, like technology, the larger context is lost since technology is not the sole predictor of student success.

Creating a spirit of discovery is integral to enacting change strategies across programs, services, and individuals. It is possible to build on the context for collaboration and "teaming" that is already established through federal requirements for constructing an IEP. Teams should consider how discovery processes influence student achievement and the effect on overall programs and services. By doing so, the IEP team can make more informed decisions based on the data that exist or needing to be collected while considering the impact of individual decisions on larger issues present in the school and/or districts. While the specific task of the IEP team is to construct an individualized education program for students, the resources allocated to the team and the classroom context necessary to support this education is the responsibility of a larger group of individuals (i.e., superintendents, special education directors, and principals). As a result, it is important to address the larger picture of education and the impact of applying discovery methods to one part of the system (see Figure 1).

Because every special education student has an IEP, the data-collection process has a relative structure. For example, teams can build upon goals, objectives, and accommodations regularly found in the IEP and set up further data collection requirements. This helps teams

Figure 1. Concept data structure.

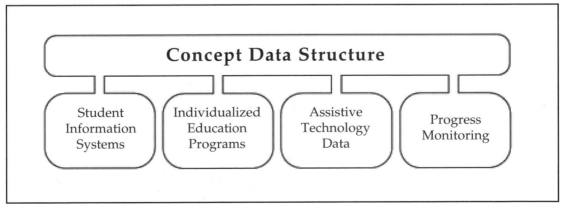

to measure student progress, leading up to, but not being restricted to end-of-term and state-wide testing. For students with disabilities, teams must consider more data than just one or even two end-of-term or mandated test scores. This is partly because the IEP is built to measure movement toward objectives, not just end-of-term or end-of-year mandated testing. At this point it is often too late to intervene, and as stated earlier, does not lead to anticipation about what teaching and learning strategies do and do not work in a timely and interactive process.

In order to establish best practices for individual students and the educators who work with them, educators must work in teams to build teaching and learning objectives through the use of available and potential data sources. This chapter will provide a framework that is useful for data-driven decision-making with a specific focus on the link between technology and student achievement. The steps required to implement this framework include: (a) analyzing the problem and building the data collection structure; (b) applying data discovery techniques and interpreting the results; (c) engaging in comparative analysis activities and making decisions about the results; (d) building decision-making models about teaching and learning profiles for the use of AT; and (e) applying these models against new data and noting changes in service delivery and student achievement.

Analyzing the Problem

Current models for AT evaluation require that the assessors of individual function consider specific matches to devices, adaptive and instructional software, and services. Some of these instructional technologies, such as electronic storybooks or even text readers, are widely used but are often not included as a requirement on the IEP. This is mainly due to: (a) the historical thinking and labeling of assistive technology as devices used only by individual with severe disabilities where connections between devices and function are very clear; (b) the broader nature of instructional technologies as instructional tools that all students can benefit from, which may not be seen as functional requirements; and (c) the use of low-tech strategies that may not even be labeled as an assistive technology because they are inherent within individual teaching styles (i.e., differentiated instruction).

This last item is the most important factor in determining whether AT should be included on the IEP. The changing nature of technology devices requires that individuals looking at inclusive education consider the broader requirements for curriculum and technology where students are consistently seen within their diagnosed disability and move toward a more holistic approach for delivering general education curriculum to them.

Data collection on instructional practices using technology becomes increasingly complex in broader and less "controlled" teaching and learning environments. This is especially true when students with disabilities begin accessing general education classrooms. Many general education teachers have never been involved in considering individualized instruction to the point of matching a technology to a student based on disability. Within these settings, developing the criteria for measuring if assistive technology is making a difference is particularly important. In these cases, data should be collected and analyzed "real time" so that the teachers can respond to unique differences in curriculum delivery for enhancing student outcomes.

Currently, data-driven decision-making systems are not in place to help teachers determine how technology is having an impact on individualized instruction. Educators should consider how to construct data systems that allow them to have real-time access to data that are important for making decisions about curriculum delivery. Systems that use data as a tool for decision-making have the potential to enhance the way data is visualized in real time and used to communicate with other teachers, parents, and administrators about student progress in the general education curriculum. For teachers (or others) working with general education curriculum in special education classes or at home, this same premise holds true.

Building the Data-Collection Structure

To realize a day when both general and special educators will have the tools to use data to make decisions about technology accommodations, it is necessary to plan for and build comprehensive data-collection and discovery systems that are more responsive to individual teaching strategies. The ultimate goal is to promote student performance on all periodic, end-of-term, and state required testing.

Such a discovery system should provide educators with the information necessary to make decisions about classrooms and students. A broader discourse on teaching and learning and an expansion of current "pockets of success" should include the greatest number of schools, teachers, students, and parents. By using data for making predictions about what works in classrooms, random acts of improvement can be transformed into schoolwide teaching and learning strategies.

Even a few years back, such thinking about large databases did not take place. Because data-mining techniques require large data sets, many educators may look at their current student information system and decide that it is not capable of even accessing – let alone apply data-mining techniques. However, many states are now creating data systems that are fed by local special education data managers.

One example is the state of Michigan, which has created a system of unique identifier codes (UICs) for every student in order to link student status data (e.g., UIC, grade level, teacher, school, date of birth, gender, age, race) and student performance data (e.g., UIC, results of statewide assessments, AP results, SAT results). Other linked data sets include professional staff data, financial data, higher education data and external data (e.g., census and US DOE data).

Other states have made similar progress, including Texas, Ohio, Florida, Mississippi, and Maryland. For example, the Texas Public Education Information Management System (PEIMS), through the establishment of a task force, started collecting some data sets on students in 1987-88 on students, adding others in subsequent years. It now contains 152 fields. Through this initiative, districts report data to the state electronically following established PEIMS data standards. This integrated database contains organization data; budget data; actual financial data; staff data; student demographic, program participation and prior year school leaver data; student attendance, course completion and discipline data (see www.tea.state.tx.us/peims/about.html).

The main purpose of this reporting system is to allow the states to anticipate and manage the impact of new and existing state and federal legislation on districts. Ohio, Florida and Missouri are also in the process of developing single student record systems in order to link data and build digital warehouses necessary for data analysis.

Similar efforts have been initiated to organize existing special education databases in order to report on and anticipate the needs of students with disabilities and those who work with them. In January 2002, the Maryland State Department of Education (MSDE) obtained a federal grant for the purpose of combining two existing special education databases (Individuals with Disabilities Education Act Part B and C data) into one seamless, integrated system. The impetus behind this endeavor was based on the need to track children with disabilities so that MSDE staff and local educational leaders could determine the effectiveness of early intervention and special education services over time and across programs. Collecting data for this type of iterative and interactive analysis, as is done in Texas, is intended to anticipate and manage the services delivered to special education students and to develop policies accordingly.

These types of initiatives indicate that systems are at least moving toward wide-scale common processes and definitions for determining individualized education. They also set the stage for using electronically captured data for decision-making about the accommodations and services delivered to individuals with disabilities and their families. The presence of such statewide systems should encourage special educators to begin thinking about more interactive possibilities for data collection, analysis, and decision-making. Even more importantly, educators should consider the use of discovery processes available through data mining processes in order to predict the outcomes of special education interventions on student access, participation, and progress in the general education curriculum (Carran,

Tsantis, Castellani, & Baglin, 2002). Once data systems are electronically linked in this fashion, it is possible to develop standards for adding new information (e.g., information on the use or non-use of AT) and use these data to make decisions about the appropriate use of assistive technology.

Building the Concept Data Structure

Once a data system is constructed and queries have been formulated, it is possible to begin looking at the systemic influences of the data on decision-making. Experts suggests that school reform is successful and sustainable when administrators, counselors, and teachers share a common vision, build a collaborative culture, and weave changes into the organization of the school (Fullan, 1991; Ruddick, 1991). For the purposes of establishing processes for collecting data, the decision-maker needs to consider the concept under study and the methods necessary to capture useful data.

Strategies used with special education students often include instructional and assistive technologies that have built-in features to collect data, such as Web-based assessment systems, augmentative communication devices with built-in data-collection features, and technology-based literacy materials that monitor how students are progressing through the software. When these technologies are linked to the IEP goal, the assessment system can be automatically monitoring students as they work in the classroom. Such periodic monitoring can take the shape of daily or weekly academic assessments, behavioral recording charts, and/or in our case, assistive technology trials. These trials are set up to determine when AT is used and similarly tracked to determine situations surrounding the abandonment of AT.

Currently, the information collected on students is assembled within the IEP, and most often it is difficult to match this information with classroom tests and quizzes, as well as classroom assignments and course content. As students work with educational content, it is necessary to link content to the goals and objectives set up by the IEP team. The IEP has as its goal to anticipate and guide a student's education. The more active and responsive the information in the IEP is, the better a teacher can predict the behaviors and teaching strategies necessary for ensuring student success. Within special education, there are many different places to look for this type of data, including school information systems, IEP's, assistive and instructional technology reports, and continuous and/or periodic progress monitoring reports (see Figure 2). Useful information exists within these systems for collecting data on assistive technology frameworks that advocate for assessments that consider the student, environment, task, and tools (Zabala, 2003).

In addition to the information available on children, demographic and teacher data can be combined with child-level data for decision making purposes. Educators considering such a wide variety of data points have a greater potential for discovering the patterns inherent in the delivery of services from a district level to teaching and learning supports needed in the classroom. Integrated thinking about where these data exist and how to drill through them so they are useful for the decision making process is key. Being able to collect real-time data on defined instances and attributes can greatly facilitate the consideration process, ranging from specific data used to support individual devices to classroom wide instructional technology tools. Systemic thinking about data-collection measures can provide a framework for solving common problems associated with assistive technology.

An outcome for using data mining in special education would be ongoing assessment and evaluation of current programs and their influence on model development, student performance reporting, and/or accountability. Data definitions and preparation include the development of concepts, concept descriptions, attributes, and instances. Data input "takes the form of concepts, instances, and attributes" with the "thing that is to be learned a concept description" (Witten & Frank, 2000). Instances and attributes surround a concept. The concept description we will use is: *the most applicable forms of assistive technology to promote student achievement.* It is necessary to make sure the data can reside in one single "clean" data set in order to be mined. Consider the data outlined in Table 1.

Here we have a data set on the use of instructional and assistive technologies that is

Figure 2. Development and evaluation of programs.

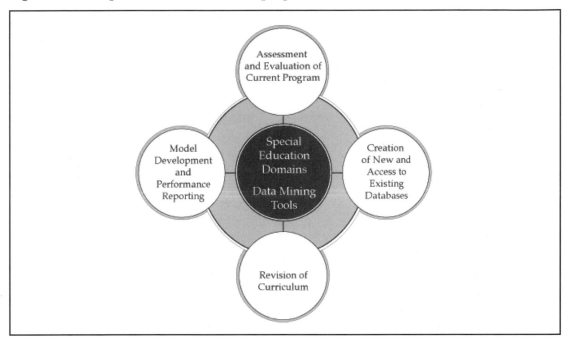

ready for analysis. The variables in the initial dataset are as follows:

1. Student Name
2. Class Size: High, Medium, Low Student/Teacher Ratio
3. Teacher: Ms. Amos and Ms. Smith
4. Type of Technology: Assistive versus Instructional
5. Type of Class: General versus Special Education
6. Class Grade

Now, given this set of data, "What do we want to know?" Part of what makes data mining different from typical database management is that researchers, as they are collecting and building the database, need to think about (a) why they are collecting these data, and (b) how these data and the inclusion of additional data will help answer the questions about which they are concerned. In other words, in data mining, database management is not only a prelude to analysis. It is part of the analysis itself. This is why these databases are called *intelligent*: they develop as the research takes place. To make this process of data collection and management clearer, let us consider a few examples.

Suppose, for example, we want to know which students are succeeding academically and what attributes are associated with their success. As with any database, the data can be arranged in any order. The variable of concern becomes the instance, and the variables examined to determine differences in instance are called *attributes*. As we put together our database, the first question we need to answer is, "What attributes best demonstrate student success?" In our database we already have a few attributes. Consider, Lynne, a successful student. The list of attributes for Lynne are: class size = low; teacher = Ms. Smith; technology = instructional; class type = general; and student achievement = A. But, is there anything else?

We might add other student variables. For example, based on previous work with Lynne, we might know that part of her success is due to the fact that she never misses a day of school, except when really sick, and that she is never referred for behavioral problems in class. Knowing that these variables might be important, we add them to our database.

Perhaps another important variable might be the experience of the teacher. In the case of the two teachers in our database, we know that both of them are new. Still, despite their lack of

Table 1. Data Comparison of Instructional Practice

Name	Class Size	Teacher	Technology	Class Type	Grade
Steve	High	Ms. Smith	Instructional	General	C
Amy	High	Ms. Smith	Instructional	General	C
John	Average	Ms. Amos	Assistive	Self-Contained	A
Gregg	Average	Ms. Amos	Assistive	Self-Contained	B
Jackie	Low	Ms. Smith	Instructional	Self-Contained	B
Elaine	Low	Ms. Smith	Instructional	Self-Contained	A
Bijul	Low	Ms. Smith	Instructional	Self-Contained	C
Al	Low	Ms. Smith	Instructional	General	A
Linda	High	Ms. Amos	Assistive	General	A
Dave	High	Ms. Amos	Assistive	General	A
Betsy	Low	Ms. Smith	Instructional	Self-Contained	F
Lynne	Low	Ms. Smith	Instructional	General	A
Vanessa	Average	Ms. Amos	Assistive	General	B
Kelly	Average	Ms. Amos	Assistive	General	B
Gail	Low	Ms. Amos	Assistive	Self-Contained	B

experience, both are well trained in using assistive technology and have already employed technology in their classrooms. Because "experience" and "expertise in assistive technology" are currently not in our database, we can add them. Another variable might be cost of technology. It might be that, while our two teachers are perfectly skilled in assistive technology, the school budget cannot afford the necessary technology. Again, knowing this type of information is important.

As illustrated in these examples, we could continue this process indefinitely. That is exactly the point. Over time, as questions change and analyses are completed, the purpose of data mining is to determine not just what results were found but also what data need to be added or removed or refined to better understand the phenomenon of study. For example, after a series of analyses we might refine our understanding of "technology used" because we realize that it is not enough to know if technology is being used. As such, we might add a variable that asks what type of technology was used and to what extent. Again, the process continues as long as the analysis does. It is for this reason that

the databases of data mining are referred to as intelligent and why data mining is an effective real-time approach to analysis. You can actually get your database to the point where you can keep track of information on a weekly or daily basis and know how your students are doing relative to key attributes and, equally important, whether changes in these attributes are affecting their success. A good example of this type of real time analysis is the stock market. In the case of education, data mining allows you to be an excellent education broker. You are important because you have the information everyone wants and needs.

Now that we understand how to manage our database, we will analyze the data. The next step in the process is the process of discovery.

Applying Data Discovery Techniques

Knowledge discovery in databases (or KDD) is the emerging science and industry of applying modern statistical and computational technologies to finding useful patterns hidden within large databases and across diverse data-collection points. The process of statistical analysis in these large data bases is called *data mining*, which combines techniques from machine learning, pattern recognition, and statistics to automatically extract concepts, concept interrelations and patterns of interest from large databases (Edelstein, 1996). As stated by Hand, Mannila, and Smythe (2001):

> Data mining is often set in the broader context of knowledge discovery in databases, or KDD. This term originated in the artificial intelligence (AI) research field. The KDD process involves several stages: selecting the target data, preprocessing the data, transforming them if necessary, performing data mining to extract patterns and relationships, and then interpreting and assessing the discovered structures, (Hand et al., 2001, p. 12)

As explained above, the goal of applying data mining techniques is to combine both machine and human learning to understand nonintuitive patterns in data. The example we used previously may be interpreted as intuitive because the pattern was established through "good practice" or from existing practice (i.e., we may already know that reduced class size leads to better student achievement when combined with a highly competent instructor). The patterns found through data-mining applications are useful for applying human understanding of phenomena and using such understanding to change the way interventions are developed and enacted. While many patterns may reveal themselves as intuitive, the strength of data mining lies in its ability to discover nonintuitive patterns and instances of an event. When these nonintuitive patterns are found, they are commonly referred to as "patterns of interestingness" (Tsantis & Castellani, 2001, p. 19) in that they signal a pattern in the data that is statistically significant and "mark" an instance. This type of "data marking," if you will, allows the human component to come in and take a look at what is happening in the data.

As stated by Streifer (2001), "The drill-down process starts with a global question or issue, which then is broken down into its component parts for analysis. Once the analysis is completed, all the data are considered from one's "helicopter view" to make a reasoned decision on next steps" (p. 12). Within the data-mining literature a variety of computational techniques

are used to "drill down" appropriately to find these patterns, including neural networking, genetic algorithms, and various data visualization techniques (Han & Kamber, 2001). The four most common approaches to dealing with initial sorting of data include classification learning, clustering, numeric prediction, and association learning (Witten & Frank, 2000). Of these techniques, the one we will discuss here is classification of data through decision tree analysis (e.g., Witten & Frank, 2000).

Decision Tree Analysis

Decision tree analysis (DTA) is part of the data-mining process that engages in data classification. DTA is considered a supervised data-driven technique that can handle a high level of complexity and nonlinearity. DTA is supervised because the class assignment for each person, object, or event is already known. In terms of concepts, attributes, and instances—as we discussed earlier—the person building the concept descriptions will already include how an assignment is made based on his or her experience working with the individual concept. In the case of assistive technology, an individual builds concept descriptions from federal, state, and/or local definitions of AT and collects data according to what needs to be known. As stated above, the human interaction with the database takes the form of concept definition and the assignment of attributes, thereby influencing the way variables in a data set can interact.

Take, for example, the idea of building a case for *disproportionality* and the use of *technology*. In order to inform data-collection instances based on the broad concept to be understood, we would look through our decision tree, after building the data set as described above, and run regression trees for patterns that we look through to understand the problem. If, for example, some unknown variable is the final indicator of a pattern (like the service transportation), we would want to go back and discover what it is about transportation that could possibly link to students being identified for special education. It may be that we find that there is a link between minority students and their reliance on school transportation. However, the regression analysis might yield the result that it is the strongest predictor for minorities in special education. However, we know that this link will do nothing to inform teaching and learning. In this sense, the link is disregarded and new trees are run in order to predict successful instances of teaching and learning only. In classification terms, these instances become *the case identities* through which we look for patterns associated with our assistive technology study. In other words, every instance that is defined may or may not lead to an answer to the original query. In this case, the sample is supervised and students are assigned to one of several cases, with the teaching and learning case being continually applied against new data.

Interpreting the Results

Through the use of specific techniques for decision tree analysis, the data mining process allows users to create profiles that provide more sophisticated understanding of the patterns and trends within the data. This is what makes data-mining a qualitative technique. While data-mining techniques may strike similar chords with individuals who have run multiple linear regression formulas, there is a difference in the approach one uses. The primary difference is the focus. That is, while traditional statistics search for aggregate trends, data-mining techniques such as DTA look for differences. In other words, while traditional statistics look for similarities across differences, DTA looks for differences across similarities. This does not make one better than the other, just different. It is for this reason that the goal of a DTA is to sort students and their attributes into groups.

In the cases we will discuss the different groups are based on learning profiles (e.g., we might know that reduced class size, use of assistive technology, and a highly qualified teacher are patterns that relate to student progress). This process of discovery is what makes these computational techniques qualitative in orientation (see Castellani et al., 2004; Castellani & Castellani, 2003). Rather than structuring the questions and applying data, the data and the questions are related. Once patterns in the data are found, the theory has the flexibility to be adapted to accommodate continuous theory development about specific instances that are verified.

It is for this reason that The National Center for Data Mining (NCDM) draws the distinction between traditional approaches to multiple linear regression research and data mining as follows. The NCDM suggests that formal statistical inference is assumption-driven, that is, a hypothesis is formed and then tested against the data. Data mining, in contrast, is discovery-driven in that the hypothesis is electronically extracted from the data through algorithms and in consequence is data driven rather than research-based or human driven (NCDM, 2000).

Because of this approach to data analysis, data-mining has been applied to large databases within business to improve services, retain clients, and increase revenues and within public health organizations to enhance treatment and reduce medial costs through preventative medicine. However, the purpose of engaging in data mining is the same: to look for new patterns in large amounts of data in an effort to turn new knowledge into actions. Depending on the agency conducting the process, these actions might include improved delivery of services, enhanced information about market trends, improved educational technology software products, or in the case of special education, influencing curriculum development, monitoring student growth and enhancing academic progress.

Consider the sample illustrated in Figure 3 and the ability to ascertain information about the type of pattern that leads to successful achievement in math. The subjects are all middle school students in a large urban school district. The data set (like the previous example) includes information about general vs. special education settings, student/teacher ratios in those settings, the use of instructional and assistive technology and student outcomes. The decision tree process yields that students who achieved a C or better in math were more likely to be in a general education classroom where the student-teacher ratio was low and where technology was applied to instruction. The percentages in this example relates to the number of individuals who represented the pattern as the pattern emerged.

In this example, division of general and special education classes determines the first

Figure 3. Example of data-mining exploration of key attributes impacting achievement.

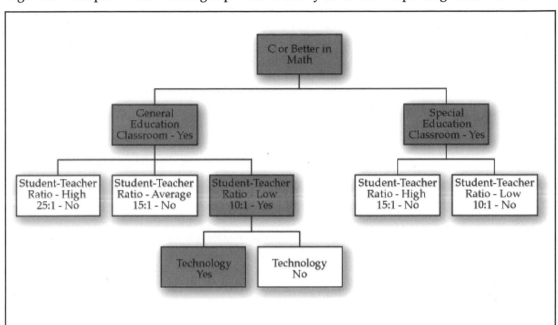

and second instance of our analysis. In the case of general education, the attributes included student performance against class size, type of setting, and the use of technology. The conclusions drawn from these instances might lead us to question how general education classrooms are structured in this district and explore why general education teachers' seem to have the ability to use technology more fluidly. This process leads us to comparative analysis.

Engaging in Comparative Analysis

Now that we have a basic understanding of what is in the data set, the next step is to engage in a comparative analysis. The goal of comparative analysis, as demonstrated in Figure 3, is to compare the decision trees to real life scenarios based on a human understanding of the concept being explored. The decision tree process is constantly looking for statistical significance of patterns being revealed in the data set. Not all patterns yield information useful for decision-making; some patterns may end with illogical conclusions.

We can apply this method to the example used earlier with respect to Ms. Amos and Ms. Smith. After examining the data from the teachers and students in the sample, you may come to the conclusion that, while you can make sense of the teaching and learning profiles for using assistive technology in Ms. Amos and Ms. Smith's classes, the application of instructional technology is not clear. This may occur if the data are not collected specifically for outcome measures (i.e., you label all technology as instructional and cannot drill down to specific tools or features of tools) or you simply did not add the data in at all (i.e., teachers are identified in the data set but demographic or education levels are not included). As a result, you may decide to discard this style, or wait to collect data on other teachers working with instructional technology to see if the original questions become clearer and a comparison can be made.

On the other hand, you might also find that, even though more students and teachers or respective data fields need to be added, you have the information necessary to intervene and the intervention is clearly defined. After having combed through the data, you might realize that after adding teacher demographic data to your data set, the following conceptual indicators are common: *class size* (successful classes are all small), *flexibility* (the teachers are both innovators with technology), *age* (the teachers are new to teaching and received recent training on the use of assistive technology and instructional technology), *teamwork* (the classes were actually team taught), *commitment* (they are both concerned equally with the progress of their students in the general education curriculum), and *student-centered* (they apply small group instructional strategies in order to manage classroom behavior). As such, tentatively, you decide to name the next model: *New School Teaching Styles*.

The use of data-discovery tools for this comparative analysis process can therefore be used for forecasting and model building. Educational forecasting at the classroom level could allow teachers and administrators to more accurately provide anticipatory guidance to anticipate student/teacher needs and to provide guidance toward successful teaching and learning. At the district and state level, forecasting could provide support for systemic reform for the use of technology. Such forecasting could be attained by using statewide data for applying district-level data mining models. This type of forecasting could assist states with policies for using assistive technology for assessment, allocating monies for schools to buy assistive technology devices, and disseminating information about the teaching and learning profiles to federal reporting offices.

Building Decision-Making Models

Program assessment that is linked to special education domains might result in the revision of curriculum based on trends in the data warehouse. For example, members of the IEP team could revise curriculum, alternate appropriate instructional strategies, and develop models for appropriate special education practice. Data mining becomes an iterative process of developing new models, or revising existing models, that are continually revised based on new trends found in the data, predictions made by the IEP team based on decision trees and online analytic processes, and the continual assessment of special education practice as programs are implemented in the school.

Applying the Model Against New Data
The final step in this process is to develop a data-mining model based on the discovery of

instances from running the decision tree analysis and applying the model against new data. This is one of the more important steps in the data-mining process and is used to determine the utility of your findings as new data and potential instances enter the data sets. If the instances hold true for your data, the model can remain the same. However, if the addition of new data demonstrates different or potentially a more in-depth understanding of the data set, the model needs to be amended. As the data grow, the reliability of your findings increases. Since we have only collected data on two sets of classes, the results examined in our faux study so far are limited. But following the logic of data mining and conceptual modeling, it is a start. So, the next task is to bring in more data, run the data mining model against this data, and review the output map, go back to the data to engage in the process of assessment, elaboration and refinement, and then start the process all over again until a level of saturation has been reached. Hopefully, in the end you have arrived at a useful typology of teaching and learning profiles.

Conclusion

As educational reformers have suggested, school reform is successful and sustainable when administrators, counselors, and teachers share a common vision, build a collaborative culture, and weave changes into the organization of the school (Fullan, 1991). While many educators have spent a good deal of time trying to work with systemic change, many of these efforts have not included anticipatory guidance strategies for using available data on the system they are trying to change. As noted earlier, when relying on single-point-in-time data, whether the data are statewide test scores or other static information, the potential to use that data for active decision making is questionable. When the data include interventions involving technology, it is important to use automated data collection, turn this information into knowledge, and apply this knowledge to the instructional strategies thereby setting up a process that monitors success and progress. This is particularly true for special and general educators who wish to make use of classroom data for inclusion of the assistive technology evaluation and monitoring process.

Although the available data on AT is growing (National Assistive Technology Research Institute, 2003), there is still a lack of research data to support the use of assistive and instructional technologies in the general education setting. Special education teachers are using technology to accommodate and adapt curriculum without the use of research or data-driven decision-making processes to guide practice. Data-mining processes hold one potential for building models from the "bottom up" as teachers and students interact with the technology in the classroom. In the near future, classroom teachers could have a data-driven decision-making system available on their desktop. This would allow them to retrieve information on students at any given time to predict what students need and monitor the patterns of their learning. Further, the administrators for the school or district can use this information to better communicate with other teachers and chairs in the school about student progress and systemic reform.

Many forms of data-based decision-making currently exist. It is the responsibility of those working with technology integration to develop systems using the technology that already has the ability to produce real-time decision-making through accessible data-based policies and practices to determine how this information can be transformed into daily strategies for improving the educational outcomes of student with disabilities. In order to ensure successful access for all children to access the general education curriculum, educators must explore the response of real-time data in decision-making, communicate this information to student, parents, and other teachers, and improve the ability of teachers to augment the research base of what is going on in the classroom on a daily basis.

While education research in itself is important for providing the educational community with evidence-based instruction about assistive technology, educational professionals should consider other advanced statistical measure for informing practice. For example, the development of data systems that promote greater communication between educators and stakeholders is critical to sustaining systems of instructional and assistive technology integration. Educators using available data for anticipatory guidance can enhance the definitions of intervention models and work toward greater understanding of assistive technology devices and services for accessing the general education curriculum. As these data systems progress, the use of one-point-in-time performance measure will be replaced by robust information available to inform all stakeholders about adequate yearly progress toward instructional goals and objectives.

Authors' Note: The authors would like to thank *imresourcing* for providing the figures and tables contained in this chapter.

References

Bernhardt, V. (2003). *Data analysis for continuous schoolwide improvement*. Chico, CA: Education for the Future.

Carran, D. T., Tsantis, L., Castellani, J., & Baglin, C. A. (2002). *Data-mining electronically linked part C-part B data sets to identify usage patterns and predict needs*. Paper presented at the Gatlinburg Conference on Research and Theory in Mental Retardation and Developmental Disabilities, San Diego, CA.

Castellani, B., Castellani, J., & Spray, L. (2004). Grounded neural networking: A new tool for studying social complexity. *Symbolic Interaction, 27*(4), 585-601.

Castellani, B., & Castellani, J. (2003). Data mining: Qualitative analysis with health informatics data. *Journal of Health Informatics Research, 13*(7), 1005-1018.

The Doyle Report. (2003). NCLB: A dramatic change for Title I testing, but too much so? *Spotlight*, 2.45, Retrieved November 5, 2002, from: www.thedoylereport.com.

Edelstein, H. (1996) Data mining: Exploring the hidden trends in your data. *DB2 Online Magazine*. Retrieved from www.db2mag.com.

Elementary and Secondary Education Act (EASE) as reauthorized by the No Child Left

Behind (NCLB) Act of 2002. Available at: www.ed.gov/legislation/ESEA02/

Fullan, M. G. (1991). *The new meaning of educational change* (2nd ed.). New York: Teachers College Press.

Han, J., & Kamber, M. (2001). *Data mining: Concepts & techniques.* New York; Aldine De Gruyter.

Hand D.J., Mannila H., and Smyth P. (2001). *Principles of data mining.* Cambridge: MIT Press.

IMS Global Learning Corporation, Inc. (2003). Schools interoperability framework. Available from: www.imsglobal.org/resources.cfm#specs.

National Assistive Technology Research Institute. (2003). Status of assistive technology services in schools. Available from: natri.uky.edu/natinfo/research/statmenu.html#schools.

Postlewaite, C. (2003). Federalizing education: States struggle with decreased autonomy and increased costs as they try to implement No Child Left Behind. *State Government News*, The Council of State Governments, April 2003. Available from: www.csg.org.

Schoolnet. (2003). *SchoolNet solutions.* Available from: www.schoolnet.com.

Streifer, P. (2001, April). The "drill down" process. *The School Administrator* [Web edition], American Association of School Administrators. Retrieved from www.aasa.org/publications/sa/2001_04/streifer_april%202001.htm.

Tsantis, L., & Castellani, J.D. (2001). Enhancing learning environments through solution based data mining tools: Forecasting for self-perpetuating systemic reform. *Journal of Special Education Technology, 16*(4), 39-52.

Witten, I.H., & Frank, E. (2000). *Data mining; Practical machine learning tools and techniques with java implementations.* San Fransisco: Academic Press.

Zabala, J. (2003). *The student, environment, task, and tools (SETT) assistive technology evaluation framework.* Available from: www.joyzabala.com.

41

Robotic Devices as Assistive and Educational Tools for Persons with Disabilities

Richard D. Howell

Progress, far from consisting of change, depends on retentiveness. Those who do not learn from the past are condemned to repeat it. – George Santayana (1905)

The idea of creating a robot that would replace or enhance the physical abilities of a person with severe physical disabilities is intuitively attractive to most people in today's technology-enabled society. Currently, there are approximately 4.5 million children with disabilities, ages 3-14 in the United States (U.S. Census, 2001). Of these, nearly 660,000 school children in the United States have impairments to the neuromuscular or skeletal system that impair their ability to fully engage in school or play with their nondisabled peers (Christoper & Gans, 1998). The lack of physical control by persons with physical disabilities constitutes a significant barrier to academic success, especially when coupled with other problems such as communication disorders and related medical problems. Accompanying the reality of diminished control are feelings of helplessness and frustration when having to rely on caretakers to make even the slightest changes to the environment.

In response to this situation, a variety of attempts have been made to develop robotic aids that would partially compensate for the lack of manipulative control and, in some cases, to find a useful niche as assistive devices in educational settings. Advances in autonomous robotic systems have been demonstrated in various sectors of society, ranging from the space program to the surgical rooms of hospitals. However, the promise of robots as assistive and educational tools remain tantalizingly elusive despite more than a decade of concerted research and development efforts across the world aimed at developing a functional assistive robotic system. The greatest successes in personal applications of robots have been seen in the medical and entertainment sectors, but unfortunately not in the educational sector. These past efforts have resulted in the development of better human-robot interfaces, engineering breakthroughs in the development of wheelchair-mounted robots, and a better idea of what types of curricular targets should be incorporated into robotically aided environments.

In this chapter, we will investigate the evolution of assistive and educational robots and the areas in which they have proven successful, as well as areas where they are still wanting. An emphasis will be placed upon the use of robotic devices in special education classrooms and settings. Finally, we will present an analysis of the issues that must be resolved in order to insure the development and use of a fully functional robotic tool for classroom and clinical use.

Historical Perspective

The robot first appeared as a conceptual entity in the early 1900s as a symbol of an increasingly technological and isolated "new world" in the movie *Metropolis* (1927) by director Fritz Lang. Over time the robot as a concept evolved into a anthropomorphic entity that mimicked real humans but lacked the capacity for emotions such as love or compassion. For several decades, robots were not seen as particularly beneficial or useful to people, and even became associated with the darker side of the industrial revolution as symbols of an uncaring, technocratic society ruled by faceless bureaucrats.

It was from these auspicious beginnings that robots came into being on the assembly-line floor as tireless, efficient tools in the production of cars, ships, and other large-scale production items. In this first meaningful task, robots proved to be highly efficient and a part of a changeover from complete human labor to a hybrid production environment in which robots work alongside humans. The performance of industrial robots demonstrated a quantifiable advantage over human workers on specified tasks, and spurred a new level of economic and industrial competition in the international community (Feigenbaum & McCorduck, 1983). A less obvious change in humans' perception of robots was simultaneously taking place among the general public whereby they were increasingly seen as "dumb machines" that were incapable of doing anything without human intervention. This evolving perception was much closer to reality than the hyperbolic visions of the 1950s and '60s that had them destroying or subjugating all humans in some mechanistic future controlled by machines.

An entire field of research and development has evolved that deals with solving the problems incumbent with these powerful, dumb machines – spanning a variety of fields including mechanical and electrical engineering, human factors, and cognitive psychology. The multidisciplinary research effort has significantly increased their reliability and capabilities and evolved new applications for robots. These new uses include prosthetic, medical, clinical, and even educational applications that bring robots into close proximity with human beings, thus the moniker "personal robot."

Robotic Applications for Persons with Disabilities

In the following section, we will look at robotic applications in the areas of prostheses, therapy, diagnosis, and special education.

Prosthetic Applications

The earliest work in which industrial robots were reengineered to become assistive robots was done by Larry Leifer and his colleagues (Leifer, 1983; Leifer, Van der Loos, & Michalowski, 1984) demonstrating that persons with high-level spinal cord injuries could use voice-activated robotic manipulators to do a variety of self-care tasks, such as brushing teeth or fixing meals. One of the most important contributions of this early work were specifications for personal robotic design parameters that included the following demands:

1. It (the robot) must be able to acquire data about the environment.
2. It must interpret the data in terms of an internal representation (or model) of the environment.
3. It should be able to plan and execute simple manipulative motions.
4. It must have a means of communicating with the user to present the results of data-taking, analysis, and planned motions.

This work evolved into efforts aimed at creating robots that would assist people in their ability to perform job-related tasks. Once again, an intuitively attractive application of robotic tools was embraced by the rehabilitation engineering community and spurred a number of initiatives worldwide. In particular, the European community initiated a number of related efforts, including France (MASTER system), Sweden (HADAR), and Britain (RAID). In general, these robotic workstations were built around low-cost, commercial robots (UMI-RTX) and control strategies that generally included both direct control (joystick) and programmable software using keyboard emulators (e.g., WIVIK). Eventually, these countries began collaborating under the auspices of European Community funding to create the Robot for Assisting the Integration of the Disabled (RAID) consortium consisting of industrial and academic partners from France,

Sweden, and Britain (Dallaway, Jackson, & Timmers, 1993). Other robotic research and development initiatives have targeted various types of activities of daily living, including kitchen activities (Casals, Merchan, Portell, Cufi, & Contijoch, 1999); home fetch-and-carry tasks (Schaeffer & May, 1999); eating, make-up, and grooming (Topping, 1994).

The Manus wheelchair-mounted robot (Kwee, 1986) is considered by most rehabilitation engineers as the first "true" rehabilitation robot. Its innovative mechatronic design has resulted in a highly capable and accurate manipulator that takes full advantage of the power wheelchair base. It was specifically designed to meet the needs of persons with disabilities for a mobile manipulator. Dallaway, Jackson, and Timmers (1993) refer to the Manus as a "...robotic system for use in an unstructured environment, clinical trials have shown that it provides a significant improvement in a user's ability to perform everyday functions more independently" (p. 39).

The most current versions of the robot have a reach of approximately 850 cm and can lift up to 2 kg at full extension. The robot is currently being marketed by Exact Dynamics, the Netherlands. The most significant problems experienced in this project which began in 1984 at the Institute for Rehabilitation Research, Netherlands have to do with the lack of an easy-to-use interface for direct control of the robot. This issue is not limited to the Manus, but is evident in almost every interface strategy used with assistive robotic tools. Miller (1998) reports that, "The control interface has been the major roadblock in the creation of a useful general purpose accessory arm for the wheelchair user. This problem has proven more daunting than the mass, power, and cost issues – which themselves are critical" (p. 135).

Users with disabilities anecdotally report greater independence through the use of Manus. One user states,

When I was born, I was diagnosed with an extremely rare disease called Arthrogryposis Multiplex Congenita Amyoplasia. Basically, I was born with certain muscles missing from my arms and legs. My left arm is in a flexed position, and my right arm is extended. My knees and hips are in permanent 90-degree positions, and I am confined to a wheelchair. Therefore, I have a very limited range of motion.

… The company in Holland that manufactures the MANUS donated an arm to me. The provision is that I use it and give feedback and a presentation about using a robotic arm. I am amazed by what it can do. It is the only device of its kind in the United States, and I was the first to get one. It made my life so much easier; I can do things by myself that I could not do before without assistance. For instance, I get myself a drink, get things that were normally out of my reach, and eat a sandwich on my own. In the short period of time that I have had the arm, it made a great impact on my lifestyle. I have had the arm for about a year now, and it has become integral part of my life, (Exact Dynamics, 2002, p. 2)

Perhaps one of the most surprising success stories related to the application of robots in activities of daily living is the Handy I Assistive Robot (Topping, 1994). This simple robot, initially developed in 1988, has been successfully marketed as an eating aid for persons lacking the control necessary to grasp and direct eating utensils. It has been enhanced to support a variety of daily tasks including, drinking, shaving, teeth cleaning, putting on make-up, grooming, painting and drawing, and playing games. Perhaps some of the initial design features that went into the Handy I are directly responsible for its high degree of utility and its success, including simplicity in design, importance of its primary function as an eating aid, relatively low cost, and the lack of engineering expertise in daily operation or troubleshooting. The company that markets the Handy I, Rehab Robotics Ltd., England reports sales of over 200 Handy I robots as of 2002, which supports the claim that it is the most successful assistive robotic device on the market today.

Therapeutic Applications

Currently, the focus of development and testing of therapeutic robotic tools is occurring in occupational and physical therapy. Specifically, contemporary research initiatives are seeking

Figure 1. The MANUS, also known "The ARM" (Assistive Robotic Manipulator) performs a functional task: serving beer. (Courtesy of Exact Dynamics, the Netherlands)

an answer to the question, "Can robotically aided rehabilitation technology be made viable for clinical and home use?" According to Reinkensmeyer et al. (2000), there is a clear economic incentive to increasing what is known as "therapeutic dosage" without requiring increased therapist time. Therapeutic dosage is the amount and intensity of intervention time by a trained therapist with a patient, typically in a clinical setting. In general, these therapeutic intervention efforts are characterized as being either diagnostic or treatment applications.

Diagnostic Applications

A diagnostic application is one in which the robotic device is used to evaluate several key motor impairments, including abnormal tone, lack of coordination, and general weakness. An interesting investigation was conducted by Reinkensmeyer et al. (2000) of the contribution of spasticity during reaching movement, rather than at the end of a movement as it has traditionally been the case. The diagnostic goal of their efforts was to provide an improved assessment tool for determining the degree of arm impairment after brain surgery. The various diagnostic measures that were possible through use of the arm and its control software included tone, spasticity, and a lack of coordination.

The first treatment application described by Reinkensmeyer (2000) involves their robotic tool the "Assisted Rehabilitation and Measurement Guide" (ARM) which provides a means to implement and evaluate active assist therapy for the human arm. Their clinical research has used ARM with three post-stroke subjects, all of whom received training with the robot prior to treatment sessions. Training consisted of three sessions per week over a two-month period or approximately 12 training sessions per subject, each session lasting one hour. According to the researchers,

Active assist therapy produced several quantifiable benefits. Tone was reduced in the two subjects in whom it was elevated at onset, and active range of motion, peak velocity, and the ability to initiate movement also improved. We hypothesize that these improvements are the results of repetitive stretching of soft tissues, coupled with repetitive practice in activating damaged motor pathways. (p. 8)

The second treatment application of therapeutic robotics was done by Lum, Burgar, and Van der Loos (1997), who report the results of a well-designed trial application of a robot (PUMA 260) for patient-initiated and therapist supervised movement therapy. Their preliminary results indicate that the MIME (Mirror-Image Motion Enabler) system can capture valuable quantitative data on patient performance within the therapy session and, "can show correlation with accepted clinical measures of functional outcomes" (p. 45). Later work by the Stanford Rehabilitation Robotics Design group conducted formal clinical efficacy trials using an improved robot (PUMA 560). The authors provided evidence that the robot-aided therapy had therapeutic benefits. Their findings indicated that, "The improved performance of the robot over conventional therapy was unanticipated. It is particularly encouraging that greatest improvements occurred in the shoulder and elbow measures, as these are the joints the robot therapy targeted. These results provide support for future studies of robot-assisted therapy in order to optimize functional interventions" (p. 53).

The third treatment application involves one of the strongest theoretically-grounded programs of research being carried out by researchers at MIT (Krebs, Volpe, Aisen, & Hogan, 2000). This work is in the area of robotically aided neurorehabilitation and recovery. The investigations are based in a neurosciences theory that activity-dependent plasticity underlies neuro-recovery. The robotic aid used in these studies was designed to assist and support clinicians in their work to facilitate functional recovery by persons with disabilities. This approach differs from mainstream rehabilitation robotics efforts by treating the robot as a tool for therapists as opposed to a tool for direct use by the persons with disabilities. The research team decided to focus on persons suffering from debilitating stroke, the leading cause of disability in the United States with approximately 700,000 new cases every year.

Another innovation employed in this line of research at MIT involves the development and use of a "back-driveable" robot, a low-impedance device capable of interacting safely and gently with humans called MIT-MANUS. It differs significantly from the typical industrial robot because of a configuration that permits safe, stable, and compliant operation when in close physical contact with humans. The clinical trials results are based on over five

years of research comprising 2,000 hours of robotically aided therapy with at least 76 patients. The results of the project are encouraging, with the authors reporting that, "Our results are in agreement with one of the prominent themes of current neuroscience research into the sequelae of brain injury or trauma, which posits that activity-dependent plasticity underlies neural recovery. In other words, there is good reason to believe that neurological changes that may underlie recovery are facilitated by the standard practice of providing targeted sensorimotor activity, and that this can be accomplished using robot technology" (p. 3). These findings lend support to the planned future research of this team, which will use the back-driveable robot to, "establish the practicality and economic feasibility of clinician-supervised, robot-administered therapy, including classroom therapy" (p. 4).

The fourth treatment application involves one of the most recent and promising therapeutic aids, the CosmoBot created by Dr. Corrina Lathan of AnthroTronix, Inc. This robot is described as, "an interactive robotic rehabilitation tool, disguised as a toy, which can be controlled via almost any part of the body or through voice activation" (p. 3) (Lathan, 2001; Lathan & Malley, 2002). In clinical trials with 30 therapists and 30 children, both able-bodied and with disabilities, the robot has shown definite promise as a tele-rehabilitation device. It has several unique command-and-control features including the multiple input options of voice, gesture, and touch. The ability to provide Internet-based monitoring and data access, and easy updating of the software control program is an advance over current robotic designs. Early design feedback from clinical trials have shown four areas of potential application for CosmoBot:

1. Education, therapy, and play can be combined when structuring both homework and therapy for students with chronic disabling conditions.
2. Literacy is advanced through pre-programmed, interactive "storytelling" routines that are activated by the child's voice.
3. A flexible, dynamic system is developed through multiple functionality: mimicking a child's movements, leading the child

verbally through exercises, and playing back previously recorded scenarios. The robot is easily programmed by a variety of users, including parents, therapists and the children themselves.

4. It facilitates social interaction through cooperative and group play. Small groups or individual children can operate the robot and the Web-enabled functions will eventually allow for online communities of children to play, develop, and share new information using the robot.

Special Education Applications

The future of robotic applications in special education remains much as it was in the early 1990s – ambiguous and unpredictable. Moore, Yin, and Lahm (1985) conducted an interview-based study of the ways in which artificial intelligence, robotics, and computer simulations might be applied to special education. The research methodology involved constructing several future scenarios that were rated by a panel of technology experts. The experts in the robotic area concluded that the robotic applications would require the most technical development before implementation could occur in special education. The panelists estimated that the earliest time for developing a functional "educational" robot might be nine years, with a predicted purchase cost of approximately $9,000. The authors concluded that,

> All robotic applications will face significant technical and cost barriers before they can be used with special education (for other than vocational purposes). The technical barriers primarily involve the development of adequate auxiliary control systems (e.g., vision and voice control), and the required degree of flexibility for use in everyday settings. (p. 76)

It will be only a small surprise to these authors if they were to learn that their predictions were not only correct, but that these same problems still persist albeit they have been better defined as a result of years of research and development.

Research Evidence of Effectiveness

The earliest documented work in educational robotics was conducted by Dr. Robin Jackson

and his students at the Cambridge University, England (Harwin, Ginige, & Jackson, 1986; Gosine, Harwin, & Jackson, 1989). The engineering and programming efforts of this research group concentrated on the development of a transportable robot control language, the Cambridge University Robot Language (CURL), and its application in a variety of simple educational tasks, including block play, painting, chemistry, and other problem-solving tasks. Dr. Jackson's initial efforts live on in the work of a number of his students who are now located in England, Canada, and the United States.

Robotics and Children with Developmental Disabilities

Hoseit, Liu, and Cook (1986) conducted one of the earliest applied research efforts in which robots were used with children having disabilities. This study investigated the ability of seven young children (chronological age < 36 months) with developmental disabilities to use switch-driven robotic manipulators. The goal was to design a computer-controlled, manipulative system that would increase the children's control options over objects and social events in their environments. Field-based performance data were collected using the frequency of switch closures, switch closure durations, and patterns of switch activations. Observational data were also collected, but no quantitative data were reported in the article. The authors concluded that, "the use of continuous switch activation to complete movements of the robotic arm proved to be valuable in determining if the child understood that the arm would eventually bring the desired object within his/her reach" (p. 243).

Robotic Aids in General Education Science Classes

Another line of research got underway at the Educational Robotics Laboratory at The Ohio State University (ERL/OSU) during the period 1989-1997. The goal of this project was to integrate robotic aids into a general classroom environment where they were used by cooperative teams of students with and without disabilities. The curricular goal was to teach the scientific method of inquiry within a manipulation-rich science education environment.

The conceptual framework underlying this initiative was based in the "vicarious learning" paradigm by Bandura and Walters (1965), who proposed that a type of social learning behavior called "modeling" allows an observer to learn a behavior in the absence of physically performing the behavior. Thus, it was postulated that using a robotic tool in an educational setting might be a powerful source of learning for individuals with severe physical disabilities who vicariously manipulated scientific materials using a robotic manipulator instead of their hands and arms (Howell, Damarin, Clarke, & Lawson, 1989).

Research and development efforts at ERL/OSU resulted in an easy-to-use switch-driven interface to the UMI-RTX industrial robot, which was placed in a general education classroom and used by cooperative teams in science education. The switch-activation routine employed a combination of the 5-slot guarded switch for students with disabilities and a standard keyboard for students without disabilities used to access robot control software, which provided axial, vector, and "on-the-fly" control over a tabletop environment (Howell & Hay, 1989). The robotic workstation became the focal point for a series of experiments in science education designed to teach students the scientific method via a sequenced series of "hands-on" experiments. The goal was to teach students to be scientists and how to approach the study of the physical world using a structured scientific inquiry method. Another dimension of the studies was the ability of cooperative teams of students with and without disabilities to work together in a scienc education setting.

The results of the studies indicated that both students and teachers saw benefits from using the robot as a tool. In general, the students said that they enjoyed working with the robot "very much;" however, teachers noted that they would need help integrating the robot into instruction and troubleshooting any problems that arose with the system. Based on these responses, the authors concluded that the future of personal robotics is far from assured. If several advances were to take place, we might see the emergence of robots in educational settings. These advances would include

a standard robot control software to enable the use of the same program across robotic systems, a well-defined set of criteria and procedures for insuring the safety of the users, robots that have been specifically developed for use by humans, and finally, cost-effective systems (Howell, Martz, & Stanger, 1996).

Other research and development efforts in science education have attempted to answer some of the design weaknesses in the robot manipulators that were experienced in previous work (R. Mahoney, personal communication, 1/28/2002). Noting the lack of a modular design, interchangeable tools, and preformatted activities, Mahoney developed a new tabletop robot called ROBOX. The intent is to create a manipulator platform that can increase students' proficiency in the use of a robotic tool in science education. Specifically, the goals are to create a simple, cost-effective (less than $1,000) tabletop robot with multiple uses. The research and development efforts of ROBOX are ongoing and may be the only K-12 educational robotics project taking place in the United States at this time.

Use of Robots as Vehicles for Play

Other educational applications have used robots as vehicles for play among young children. Play is considered to be a legitimate target because it is essential to a child's development. Play may also be an attractive goal for robotics researchers since it permits the development of both structured and unstructured games to be used by the actors.

Structured play has been used in a variety of settings by a number of researchers (Davies, 1995; Howell et al., 1996; Lathan & Malley, 2002). Other researchers have used robots within unstructured play settings (Dautenhahn & Billard, 2002; Wright-Ott, 1999). In every project, a different robotic device was used with children, including a mobile transport (GOBOT; Wright-Ott, 1999); a gestural sensing robot (JesterBot; Lathan & Malley, 2002); a tabletop system (Playing Robot; Davies, 1995); and an anthropomorphic, humanoid robot (Robota; Dautenhahn & Billard, 2002). Mahoney (2002) describes the development of a small, special-purpose, robot called "Picasso." This system uses a plotter with a paintbrush attachment and remote control wand. It embodies universal design principles that permit both children with disabilities and nondisabled children to access and use it.

Cook and Howery (1999) provided young children with disabilities, ages 4-7, a small robot to engage in three different forms of collaborative play. The goal of the research was to determine if the children would: (a) engage in play activities with the robot, (b) take appropriate turns in the activity, and/or (c) understand the sequence of steps necessary to complete their turn in the play.

The results indicated that the children were very motivated to engage in the play activity. Specifically, they appeared to be, "interested in the play and appeared to be excited by the activity. This is in marked contrast to observations of their play behaviors in other adapted play activities" (p.114). The authors also observed an increase in the children's turn-taking behaviors and their overall degree of cooperative play with the adults, concluding that, "Robot enhanced play for children with physical disabilities may allow a much wider breadth of play activities for children with disabilities thereby reducing their play deprivation and passivity in other tasks and situations" (p.117).

One of the more interesting approaches in this line of research is being carried out in Sweden, where a group of researchers are engaged in a collaborative research design activity called "evolutionary robotic design" (Lund, Pagliarini, Billard, & Ijspeert, 1998). In this play-based approach, children design and activate a range of simple robotic behaviors that permit Lego Dacta robots to engage in collision avoidance, linear planning, and games of chase. The project has successfully demonstrated proof of concept in initial clinical trials that are ongoing at this time.

Use of Robots by Children with Autism

Another intriguing area of current research is the use of robots with, and by, children with autism (Dautenhahn & Billard, 2002; Werry, Dautenhahn, Ogden, & Harwin, 2001; Werry & Dautenhahn, 1999; Cooper, Keating, Harwin, & Dautenhahn, 1999). The investigations to date have tended to marry play activities using robots as interactive partners with children exhibiting autistic behaviors. In providing a rationale for using robots as a therapeutic play aid, Werry and Dautenhahn (1999) asserted that, "They are able to produce consistent, repeatable, and reliable behaviors. This provides a stable environment for the user and builds a level of trust in the interactions present" (p. 267). The authors called this initiative AuRoRa (Autonomous Robotic platform as a Remedial tool for children with Autism). The initial set of clinical trials, performed with five children (one at a time), found that children with autism: (a) showed no fear of the robot, (b) all interacted with the robot in some form, (c) showed a visible interest in the robot, (d) performed "elements of active play and interaction," and (e) showed "a substantial amount of eye focusing and attention focusing" (p. 270). However, it is impossible to draw conclusions from this effort because of the relatively brief exposure the children had to the robots, ranging from 4 minutes to 14 minutes.

In a follow-up study of the interactive potential of the robot-child relationship, Werry; et al. (2001) described a situation in which, "the robot is in the role of a therapeutic teaching device, a tool that can be used to teach children with autism basic social interaction skills" (p. 58). A series of trials were run where the children with autism interacted with a mobile robot acting as a social mediator. The study population consisted of three pairs of children (total of six children), ages 8-12 years of age, the average length of the interactions for each pair was 9 minutes. The key features of the robotic architecture and software allowed it to be chased by the children and to produce brief utterances, the actions it was capable of included avoidance of obstacles – including people, following a heat source, and the generation of simple speech and phrases. The authors reported that, "When pairs of two children were playing with the robot, interesting interaction structures were observed, such as instruction, cooperation, possibly learning by imitation, and others" (p. 73).

The contention that the robot may have a new role, that of social agent, that could meet the cognitive and social needs of humans is an intriguing extension of the commonly held beliefs about robotic capabilities. This area of robotics research is still in its infancy and the results of clinical trials are far from convincing that interacting with robots have had any substantive or sustained effects on social skills, communication, or cooperative play in the children.

Social and Aesthetic Robots

The future development of robotic devices will draw much-needed support from two different lines of research in which robots engage in social interactions with humans in a dynamic fashion, and in which they begin to assume more human characteristics (see Figure 2). Cynthia Breazeal, a pioneer in the development of robots who learn and respond to social situations, asserts that "robots could engage in various forms of social learning (imitation, emulation, tutelage, etc.), so that one could teach the robot just as one would teach another person" (p. 5). She asserts that,

Social robots originated as a term to describe multi-agent robot systems that are inspired by swarm intelligence and collective behavior (e.g., bird flocking, ant colonies, termite mounds, fish schools). As a term, "social robots" is slowly being adapted to refer to what I coined as "sociable robotics" which focuses on human robot interaction of a style that is like human social interaction. Some might also apply it to

Figure 2. The KISMET robot was designed to engage social interaction. (Reproduced with permission of Cynthia Breazeal.)

include robots that are inspired by those social species where individuals are recognized and as is their place in the social hierarchy -- e.g. primates, dogs, etc. Sociable robotics, as I use it, specifically deals with robots that interact with humans in a human-like way. (Cynthia Breazel, personal communication, January 21, 2004)

In an interesting reversal of cognitive psychology principles, one of the goals of her research team is to use the robot to learn how to create a more open-ended learning system. In this manner, the robot/human interactions may lead to discoveries of how humans learn and build cognitive structures. The KISMET robot is in many ways a mechanical avatar for a human infant, who is engaged in an open learning situation with a human counterpart. It was designed to have specifically endearing features including big blue eyes and large ears with an expressive mouth. As such, it engages in dynamic interactions which increase its social responsiveness, and even makes demands upon the human for decreasing stimulation or input in order to maintain a state of "cognitive equilibrium."

The second line of research has variously been referred to as "evolutionary robotics" (Kaplan, 2002). The anthropomorphic potential and perspective is advocated by a number of contemporary roboticists who believe that robots will never become integrated as personal tools until they are a part of our daily lives. Their contention is that robots must be aesthetically compelling, socially aware and responsive, and even entertaining in order to gain a foothold in activities of daily living. In this respect, they should be aware of human presence, social conventions, and to show personality and emotionality.

Japanese robotics researchers have long held the notion that it is necessary to create an anthropomorphic shell around the robotic device – consistently increasing its "humanness" in terms of both looks and interaction style. Hiroaki Kitano (2000) asserts that, "The aesthetic element plays a pivotal role in establishing harmonious co-existence between the consumer and the product" (p. 1). He believes that the external design of robots influence human understanding of the internal mechanical functions and help create a bridge for psychological affiliation with the machine. Interestingly, some accommodations were made such as sizing their robot Pino around the height of a one-year old child (75 cm). Their belief was that an adult-size robot would be very threatening, leading to a sense of unease and discomfort by users. The general form was created through a study of children's folklore, specifically the Pinocchio character. They felt that this design would best reach their goal that, "Pino symbolically expresses not only our desire but humankind's frail, uncertain steps toward growth and the true meaning of the word human" (p. 4).

David Hanson, who refers to himself as a "sculptor-roboticist," has deviated from the norm in creating an almost human-like robot head called K-bot (Ferber, 2003). His goal is to create a "smart, sentient being" (p. 2). A research agenda has grown up around the project to include investigations into whether people might respond differentially to the three-dimensional face versus a computer-generated face, and to determine whether a face robot might permit a better understanding of human emotions by precisely defining and controlling these emotional states (see Figure 3). Asked about his ultimate goal, Hanson responded, "A compassionate robot, a peer, a friend. The goal is to let it loose" (p. 12).

Issues Facing Widespread Application of Educational Robotics

One of the most important perspectives regarding any innovative technology solution is whether they achieve their intended outcomes and justify their investments over time. Ehrmann (2002) asserts that the "problem lies more with the ways that we think about the process of using technology to improve outcomes" (p. 1). He goes on to say that,

> The single most important point [of this essay] is that educational outcomes take far longer to improve than the likely lifespan of a single generation of technology. Therefore, if an institution or a nation is to make educational and technological progress, its

> technological choices must to some degree be subordinated to some long-term educational priorities. (p. 2)

There are lessons to be learned in these words for researchers and advocates of educational and assistive robotics. The path of development is going to be much longer and more involved than anyone had imagined. It will take additional time, measured in years, to solve the significant engineering and interface issues that currently prevent the introduction of a reliable, easy-to-use, and cost-effective robotic manipulator for classroom use. This phenomenon has already been seen in educational robotics, where prototype after prototype has been developed and tested, sometimes lasting a decade. This has led to a related problem in that the prototype manipulator used in one study may not be the functional equivalent of one used in a subsequent study. Hence, the results of may not be comparable since the changes in capability may make previous results irrelevant.

This lack of substantive, consistent exposure to a stable robotic device has led to interventions that are called "clinical trials." These trials are usually too brief in duration and use too few subjects to be able to achieve any level of generalizability. The lack of substantive and convincing data would preclude any public school agency from spending scarce dollars on such unproven technologies.

Further, once this optimized robotic tool is in a commercially available form, it will take even more time to develop the educational activities, curriculum, and procedures necessary to ensure a positive educational outcome for students with disabilities. We only need to look at the development of software solutions for children with disabilities to approximate how long robotics may take to penetrate classroom practices. The first educational software designed specifically for students with disabilities was developed and marketed in the early 1980s, at a time when there were no special input devices at the time or specialized software. It has taken over 20 years for the use of specialized software for students with disabilities to reach acceptance and for specialized input devices and software solutions to become commercially viable.

Figure 3. K-Bot. (Courtesy of David Hanson)

One can posit that the challenges that faced software developers were less daunting than those facing the educational roboticists, who must not only develop a safe, reliable, and cost-effective hardware system, but also create the interfaces and educational activities that would make them able to be fully integrated into classroom practice.

The Future

Special education will probably have to wait a number of years depending on the progress made in other arenas, especially in medical and geriatrics research, to have available the highly capable, non intrusive, and reliable manipulators that are needed. It may be that the path of development will go through medical applications, then geriatrics applications, and finally educational use. Cooper et al. (1999) asserted that if the educational benefits of robots are to be fully realized, advances will have to take place that include:

(a) Raising awareness within the teaching profession of the potential of robot technology
(b) Making low-cost robots and associated software more widely available

(c) Developing a wide range of applications for a common robotic platform
(d) Producing, evaluating, and marketing teacher resources that integrate the robotic tools with curriculum materials

It will not be surprising to see truly functional assistive robotics arise from research and development conducted with geriatrics patients rather than from school-aged special education populations. The burgeoning numbers of "baby boomers" will undoubtedly experience a variety of disabling conditions that will be amenable to robotic applications. In addition, this population will have the expendable incomes, and the political clout, necessary to directly and indirectly create funding for research and development efforts. These applications will range from the need for personal assistants, to solutions for activities of daily living, including kitchen, bathroom, and recreational activities. The variety of applications will undoubtedly give rise to a number of solutions including mobile robots with fetch-and-carry capabilities, "seeing-eye" robots for navigation, inverted rail robots for home-bound activities of daily living, and lifting robots for getting in an out of beds and chairs.

According to Dallaway, Jackson, & Timmers (1993), "smart home concepts should mean that more mass-production standard domestic appliances will either be accessible to people with disabilities or, as in computer technology, hooks making them accessible via additional interface devices" (p. 43). The smart home of the future may not only have computer-controlled aspects, but include robotic assistive tools in the form of vacuum cleaners, lift-and-carry devices, and manipulative tools that travel throughout the house either on the ceiling or on the floors. In addition to a variety of hardware devices, commensurate breakthroughs in interface devices will allow persons with a range of disabling conditions to input and control the devices, including voice activation, gestures, touch panels, and eye-gaze control routines.

Special education may be the secondary beneficiary of these efforts in that many of the hardware and software advances can be applied to our populations with few modifications. The real effort of creating educational opportunities for persons with physical and manipulation disabilities could then begin in earnest.

REFERENCES

Bandura, A., & Walters, R. (1965). *Social learning and personality development.* New York: Holt, Rinehart, and Winston.

Breazeal, C. (2002). Learning social behaviors during human-robot play. Retrieved January 30, 2004, from www.ai.mit.edu/projects/sociable/ongoing-research.

Casals, A., Merchan, R., Portell, E., Cufi, X., & Contijoch, J. (1999). CAPDI: A roboticized kitchen for the disabled and elderly. In C. Buhler & H. Knops (Eds.), *Assistive technology on the threshold of a new millennium* (pp. 346-351). Amsterdam: The Netherlands. IOS Press.

Christoper, R.P. & Gans, B. (1998). Rehabilitation of the pediatric patient. In J.A. DeLisa & B. Gans (Eds.) *Rehabilitation medicine: Principles and practice* (3rd ed.) (pp. 1225-1257). Philadelphia, PA; Lippincott-Raven.

Cook, A., & Howery, K. (1999). Robot enhanced discovery and exploration for very young children with disabilities. *Proceedings of the Technology and Persons with Disabilities Conference.* Northridge, CA.

Cooper, M, Keating, D., Harwin, W., & Dautenhahn, K. (1999). Robots in the classroom – tools for accessible education. In C. Buhler & H. Knops (Eds.), *Assistive technology on the threshold of a new millenium* (pp. 1-852). Amsterdam, The Netherlands: IOS Press.

Dallaway, J., Jackson, R., & Timmers, P. (1993). Rehabilitation robotics in Europe. *IEEE Transactions on Rehabilitation Engineering,* 3, 35-45.

Dautenhahn, K., & Billard, A. (2002). Games children with autism can play with Robota, a humanoid robotic doll. Proceedings 1st Cambridge Workshop on Universal Access and Assistive Technology (CWUAAT). In S. Keats, P.J. Clarkson, P.M. Langdon, & P. Robinson (Eds.), *Universal access and assistive technology* (pp. 179-190). London: Springer-Verlag.

Davies, R.C. (1995). The playing robot: Helping children with disabilities to play. *Proceedings of the DARS '95, Human-Oriented Design of Advanced Robotic Systems Conference.* Vienna: Austria.

Ehrmann, S.C. (2002). *Technology changes quickly but education changes slowly.* The TLT Group. Washington, DC. Retrieved January 10, 2003, from www.tltgroup.org/resources/Visions/Outcomes.html.

Exact Dynamics. (2002). *Assistive robot manipulator.* Retrieved January 31, 2003, from exactdynamics.nl/.

Feigenbaum, E., & McCorduck, P. (1983). *The fifth generation: Artificial intelligence and Japan's computer challenge to the world.* Reading, MA: Addison-Wesley.

Ferber, D. (September, 2003). The man who mistook his girlfriend for a robot. *Popular Science.* www.popsci.com/popsci/science/article/0,12543,473054,00.html

Gosine, R.G., Harwin, W.S., & Jackson, R.D. (1989). Application of the CURL programming environment. *Proceedings of the 12th Annual Conference on Rehabilitation Technology,* 9, 192-194.

Gosine, R.G., Harwin, W.S., & Jackson, R.D. (1990). Vocational assessment and placement: An application for an interactive robot workstation. *Proceedings of the 13th Annual Conference on Rehabilitation Technology,* 10, 293-294.

Harwin, W.S., Ginige, A., & Jackson, R.D. (1986). A potential application in early education and a possible role for a vision system in a workstation based robotic aid for physically disabled. In R. Foulds (Ed.), *Interactive robotic aids. One option for independent living: An international perspective* (pp. 18-23). World Rehabilitation Fund.

Hoseit, K., Liu, N., & Cook, A. (1986). Development and use of a robotic arm system with very young, developmentally delayed children. *Proceedings of the Ninth Annual Conference on Rehabilitation Technology,.* Minneapolis, MN.

Howell, R.D., Damarin, S., Clarke, J., & Lawson, J. (1989). Design issues in the use of robots as cognitive enhancement aids for disabled individuals. In J. Mulick & R. Andorak (Eds.), *Transitions in mental retardation* (pp. 187-200). Norwood, NJ: Ablex Publishing Company.

Howell, R.D., & Hay, K.E. (1989). Software-based access and control of robotic manipulators for severely physically disabled students. *Journal of Artificial Intelligence in Education, 1,* 53-72.

Howell, R.D., Martz, S., & Stanger, C. (1996). Classroom applications of educational robots for inclusive teams of students with and without disabilities. *Technology and Disability, 5,* 139-150.

Kaplan, E.A. (2002). *IIAL on earth: Evolutionary robotics ER1.* Retrieved January 9, 2004, from www.laweekly.com/ink.printme_bola.php?eid=38785.

Kitano, H. (2000). PINO the humanoid robot. Retrieved January 9, 2004, from www.symbio.jst.jp~tmatsui/pinodesign.htm.

Krebs, H.I., Volpe, B.T., Aisen, M.L., & Hogan, N. (2000). Increasing productivity and quality of care: Robot-aided neuro-rehabilitiation. *Journal of Rehabilitation Research and Development, 37,* 6. Retrieved January 15, 2003 from www.vard.org/jour/00/37/6/krebs376.htm.

Kwee, H.H. (1986). Spartacus and Manus: Telethesis developments in France and the Netherlands. In R. Foulds (Ed.), *Interactive robotic aids. One option for independent living: An international perspective* (pp. 7-17). World Rehabilitation Fund.

Kwee, H.H., Duimel, J.J., Smits, J.J., Tuinhof de Moed, A.A., & van Woerden, J.A. (1989). The Manus wheelchair-borne manipulator: System review and first results. *Proceedings of the 2nd Workshop on Medical and Healthcare Robotics* (pp. 385-395). Cambridge, England.

Lathan, C. E. (2001). Development of a new robotic interface for telerehabilitation. *Proceedings of the 2001 EC/NSF workshop on Universal accessibility of ubiquitous computing: providing for the elderly.* Alcácer do Sal, Portugal.

Lathan, C.E., & Malley, S.M. (2002). *Telerehabilitation and robotics: Integrated systems for children with disabilities.* Presentation at the 2002 Conference on Disabilities; California State University Northridge, CA.

Leifer, L. (1983). *Robotics for the disabled.* Palo Alto, CA: Rehabilitation Research and Development Center.

Leifer, L., Van der Loos, H.F.M., & Michalowski, S.J. (1984) Design issues in the development of a robotic aid for human services. *Proceedings of the Second Annual International Robot Conference* (pp. 116-121). Long Beach CA.

Lum, P.S., Burgar, C.G., & Van der Loos, M. (1997). The use of a robot for post-stroke movement therapy. *Proceedings of the International Conference on Rehabilitation Robotics (ICORR '99).* Bath, UK.

Lund, H.H., Miglino, O., Pagliarini, L., Billard, A., & Ijspeert, A. (1998). Evolutionary robotics – a children's game. *Proceedings of IEEE 5th International Conference on Evolutionary Computation.* New Jersey: IEEE Press. *Metropolis.* (1927). Movie. Fritz Lang (Germany).

Miller, D.P. (1998). Assistive robotics: An overview. In V.O. Mittal, H.A. Yanco, J. Aronis, & R. Simpson (Eds), *Assistive technology and artificial intelligence* (pp. 126-136). New York: Springer-Verlag.

Moore, G., Yin, R., & Lahm, E. (1985). *Robotics, artificial intelligence, computer simulation: Future applications in special education.* Washington, DC: Cosmos Group.

Reinkensmeyer, D.J., Kahn, L.E., Averbuch, M., McKenna-Cole, A., Schmidt, B.D., & Rymer, W.Z. (2000). Understanding and treating arm movement impairment after chronic brain injury: Progress with the ARM guide. *Journal of Rehabilitation Research and Development, 37,* 6. Retrieved February 3, 2004 from: www.vard.org/jour/00/37/6/reink376.htm.

Santayana, G. (1905). *Life of reason, Reason in common sense.* New York: Scribner's Publishers.

Schaeffer, C., & May, T. (1999). Care-O-Bot: A system for assisting elderly or disabled persons in home environments. In C. Buhler & H. Knops (Eds.), *Assistive technology on the threshold of a new millenium* (pp. 340-345). Amsterdam, The Netherlands; IOS Press.

Topping, M. (1994). 'Handy I' a robotic aid to independence for severely disabled people. *Proceedings of the 3rd Cambridge Workshop on Rehabilitation Robotics,* 13-16.

U.S. Census Bureau. (2001). *1997 census bureau survey. Current population reports.*

Washington, DC: U.S. Government Printing Office.

Van der Loos, H.M.F., Michalkowski, S., & Leifer, L. (1987). Design of an omni-directional mobile robot as a manipulation aid for the severly disabled. *Proceedings of the Ninth Annual Conference on Rehabilitation Technology*, Minneapolis, MN.

Werry, I., & Dautenhahn, K. (1999). Applying robot technology to the rehabilitation of autistic children. *Proceedings SIRS99, 7th International Symposium on Intelligent Robotic Systems '99* (pp. 265-272).

Werry, I., Dautenhahn, K., Ogden, B., & Harwin, W. (2001). Can social interactions skills be taught by a social agent? The role of a robotic mediator in autism therapy. In M. Beynon, C.L. Nehaniv, & K. Dautenhahn (Eds.), *Cognitive technology: instruments of mind. Proceedings CT2001*, (pp. 57-74). London: Springer-Verlag.

Wright-Ott, C. (1999). *The GOBOT: A transitional powered mobility aid for young children physical disabilities*. Presentation at the International Conference on Rehabilitation Robotics (ICORR, '99), Stanford, CA.

Index

Index

A

Abstract thinking, 312
Academic content standards, 243, 526
Academic expectations, 440
Academic standards, 248
Access, 315
    and use of technology by individuals
        with disabilities, 109
    participation, and progress in the general
        education curriculum, 839
    to information, 483, 516, 628
    to learning, 483, 517, 628
    to text, 545
    to the general curriculum, 50, 313, 355,
        779, 824, 836, 847
    to the Internet, 683
Accessibility, 485, 515
    authoring tools, 160
    guidelines and standards, 157-158
    in the classroom, 374
    in the school, 373
    of color, 140, 144
    of forms, 140, 144-147
    of images, 140-143
    of multimedia, 140, 153-154
    of non-HTML content, 140, 154-155
    of PowerPoint, 156, 384
    of PDF, 154-155, 383
    of school environments, 355-377
    of tables, 140, 149-153
    on school grounds, 373
    on the school playground, 374
    resources, 158-160, 390-391
    standards, 138
    validation and repair tools, 159-160, 389
Accessible
    design, 94
    information technology, 379
    transportation, 372
Accommodations, 73, 138
    research, 827-829
Achievement gap, 261
Adapted
    keyboards, 583
    toys, 287
Adequate Yearly Progress (AYP), 835, 847

Administrative support, 191-192
Affect, 344-345
Age-appropriate use of technology, 277
Alerting and signaling devices, 395-396
Aligning instruction and assessment, 522,
    528-530
Alt tag, 387
Alternative
    financing, 38
    input, 429
    input devices, 380
    keyboards, 539, 576
American Sign Language (ASL), 535, 627
Americans with Disabilities Act (ADA), 12,
    824
Anchored instruction, 8, 318, 340, 486, 489,
    607, 612, 629
Annual goals, 65
Anorexia Nervosa, 345
Asperger Syndrome, 686
Assessment, 663-681, 821-834
    implementation problems, 664
    of assistive technology needs, 184-185
    of social needs, 435
Assistive technology, 9, 32, 81, 179, 229,
    273, 325, 355, 393, 507, 571, 643, 777
    Act, 31, 81
    and students with mild disabilities,
        239-269
    and the IEP, 61-77
    competencies, 234, 724-726
    consideration, 47, 62, 66-67, 180, 183-
        184, 211, 239, 244, 249-253, 275,
        280, 297-298, 400-401, 418, 778, 838
    decision-making, 96, 98, 257, 261, 299-
        302
    device defined, 12, 62, 229-230, 242,
        276, 756
    Device Framework, 285-287
    evaluation, 838
    implementation, 186-187
    in the inclusive classroom, 229-238
    knowledge and skills, 721-747
    lemon laws, 43-44
    outcomes, 187-188, 236, 239, 257-264,
        292-293, 302, 419, 840, 847, 858
    quality indicators, 179-207
    research designs, 258-259
    service defined, 12, 14, 63, 276
    Service Framework, 288-289
    services defined, 242

Mild cognitive disabilities, 683-718
Mild disabilities, 239-269, 623-641
Mindtools, 823
Mobility, 286, 367-369, 509, 645
Models
    of learning, 255
    of training, 234
    of writing, 572
    (*also see* Conceptual models)
Modifications, 73
Monitoring student progress, 525
Moore's Law, 756
Morse code, 429
Motivation, 636
Mouse, 583
Movement, 286
Multi User Domain (MUDs), 643, 647-648, 650
Multi-user Domain Object Oriented (MOOs), 128-129, 643, 647-652
Multimedia, 138, 318-319, 388, 486-487, 489, 532, 629, 635, 702, 756, 779
    texts, 552

N

National Educational Technology Standards (NETS-T) for Teachers, 234, 722, 781
National Educational Technology Standards (NETS-S) for Students, 781
National File Format (NFF), 513
National Instructional Materials Accessibility Standard (NIMAS), 485, 511-516
Natural environments, 278-280
No Child Left Behind (NCLB) Act, 47, 73, 243, 335, 522, 541, 600, 623, 722, 824, 835

O

Obtaining assistive technology for students, 39-40
Occupational therapists, 433
Occupational therapy, 363
Online
    assistive technology training, 789-791
    chat rooms, 345-346, 389, 469
    games, 633-634, 636
    instruction, 788, 795
    learning, 787-790
    learning projects, 631-633

Optical Character Recognition (OCR), 382, 532
Outcomes-based assessment, 821
Outlining, 359, 581, 625
Over-representation, 119

P

Paradox of assistive technology consideration, 252
Paraprofessionals, 433
Parent roles, 433-434
Part B Preschool Programs, 278
Part C Early Intervention Programs, 278
Participation in statewide assessments, 751, 824
PDF accessibility, 154-155, 383
Peer
    coaching, 785
    roles, 434
Performance
    over time, 666
    standards, 522
Personal Digital Assistants (PDAs), 358, 414, 656, 658-659
Personal perspectives, 24
    (*also see* Historical perspectives)
Personal
    privacy, 332
    productivity, 243, 683
Phonemic awareness, 546, 547, 548, 565
Phonics/word recognition, 548-552, 565
Physical
    access, 355-377
    access to literacy, 441-444
    disabilities, 355-377, 509, 849
    therapists, 433
    therapy, 363
Picture boards, 414
Play, 274, 277, 288, 290
Positioning, 286
PowerPoint accessibility, 156, 384
Preparing Tomorrow's Teachers to use Technology (PT3), 767
Presentation tools, 625
Preservice teacher preparation, 235
Principles of language education, 124
Print disabilities, 512
Problem solving, 312, 340
Process approach to writing, 573-574
Productivity tools, 10

Professional development, 189-190, 727
    in technology, 728, 730
    schools (PDS), 752-753, 758
Professional standards, 522
Program evaluation studies, 805
Progress monitoring, 663
Protection and advocacy systems, 37
Psychosocial aspects of assistive technology
    use, 85-86

Q

Quality Indicators of Assistive Technology
    (QIAT) self-evaluation matrices,
    192, 194, 197-207
Quality Indicators of Assistive Technology
    (QIAT) Services, 74, 75, 179
Quality of life, 6, 273

R

Race/ethnicity, 171
    and access, 107-109, 162
Rates of improvement, 664
Reading, 496, 545-569, 663, 670, 675
Recycling programs, 44
Reform, 459
Related services, 748
    defined, 363
Remediation vs. compensation, 245, 247-
    248, 364, 545
Research
    agenda, 321-322, 350-351, 418-419, 446,
        589-591, 613-614, 636-637, 731, 733,
        769, 810-811
    and innovation, 51
    on assistive technology, 53-55
    on computer-assisted language learning,
        125-130
Resistance to computers, 7
Retrospective studies, 49-50
Robot-assisted therapy, 853
Robotic devices, 849-862
Robots, 10, 25, 849
    diagnostic applications of, 852
    and play, 855-856
    prosthetic applications of, 850
    social and aesthetic robots, 857-858
    therapeutic applications of, 851

S

Scaffolding, 575
    strategies, 702, 703, 704
Scanner, 382-383
Sceen sharing, 469
School
    culture, 458-461, 782
    environments, 356
    reform, 521, 842
Science 361, 643-661, 854-855
    education standards, 523
Screen
    enlargement, 380
    magnification, 382
    reading software, 380
Search engines, 686
Second language acquisition, 634
Section 504, 138-139, 183, 512
Section 508, 12, 139, 155, 485
Self
    advocacy, 69, 455
    determination, 332, 455
    directed learning, 730-732
    help skills, 362
    regulation, 574
Semantic organization tools, 823
    (also see Concept maps and Graphic
        organizers)
Sign language interpreter, 539
Simulations, 125, 486, 633, 635-636
Single switch, 424
Social
    closeness, 435
    promotion, 523
    skills, 365, 367, 415
    studies, 623-641
Special Education Instructional Materials
    Centers, 15
Special factors, 249
Speech
    disorders, 431
    recognition, 360, 532, 545, 584, 585
    synthesis, 381, 586
    therapy, 363
Speech-language therapists, 433
Spell checking, 588
Spelling, 663, 669-671
    checkers, 328, 359, 585-586
Spreadsheets, 625, 825
    accessibility, 384